Principles of the Institu
International Organizations

This second edition of C. F. Amerasinghe's successful book, which covers the institutional aspects of the law of international organizations, has been revised to include, among other things, a new chapter on judicial organs of international organizations, as well as a considerably developed chapter on dispute settlement. There is a rigorous analysis of all the material alongside a functional examination of the law.

A brief history of international organizations is followed by chapters on, amongst others, interpretation, membership and representation, international and national personality, judicial organs, the doctrine of ultra vires, liability of members to third parties, employment relations, dissolution and succession, and amendment. Important principles are extracted and discussed, and the practice of different organizations examined.

CHITTHARANJAN FELIX AMERASINGHE was formerly Judge at the UN Tribunal in New York, and of the Commonwealth Secretariat Tribunal in London. He was also Professor of Law and later Honorary Professor of Law at the University of Ceylon, Colombo. He was Director of the Secretariat and Registrar at the World Bank Tribunal in Washington, and is currently a member of the Institut de Droit International. He has advised governments on international law and has written extensively on the subject. He is a Doctor of Law of the University of Cambridge. His publications include *State Responsibility for Injuries to Aliens* (1967), *Studies in International Law* (1969), *The Law of the International Civil Service* (two volumes, 2nd edition, 1994), *Documents on International Administrative Tribunals* (1989), *Case Law of The World Bank Administrative Tribunal* (three volumes, 1989, 1993 and 1997), *Local Remedies in International Law* (2nd edition, 2004), and a treatise entitled *Jurisdiction of International Tribunals* (2002).

CAMBRIDGE STUDIES IN INTERNATIONAL AND COMPARATIVE LAW

This series (established in 1946 by Professors Gutteridge, Hersch Lauterpacht and McNair) is a forum for studies of high quality in the fields of public and private international law and comparative law. Although these are distinct legal sub-disciplines, developments since 1946 confirm their interrelationship. Comparative law is increasingly used as a tool in the making of law at national, regional and international levels. Private international law is increasingly affected by international conventions, and the issues faced by classical conflicts rules are increasingly dealt with by substantive harmonization of law under international auspices. Mixed international arbitrations, especially those involving state economic activity, raise mixed questions of public and private international law. In many fields (such as the protection of human rights and democratic standards, investment guarantees, and international criminal law) international and national systems interact. National constitutional arrangements relating to 'foreign affairs' and to the implementation of international norms are a focus of attention.

Professor Sir Robert Jennings edited the series from 1981. Following his retirement as General Editor, an editorial board has been created and Cambridge University Press has recommitted itself to the series, affirming its broad scope.

The Board welcomes works of a theoretical or interdisciplinary character, and those focusing on new approaches to international or comparative law or conflicts of law. Studies of particular institutions or problems are equally welcome, as are translations of the best work published in other languages.

General Editors	James Crawford *Whewell Professor of International Law, University of Cambridge* David Johnston *Regius Professor of Civil Law, University of Cambridge*
Editorial Board	Professor Hilary Charlesworth *University of Adelaide* Mr John Collier *Trinity Hall, Cambridge* Professor Lori Damrosch *Columbia University Law School* Professor John Dugard *Director, Research Centre for International Law, University of Cambridge* Professor Mary-Ann Glendon *Harvard Law School* Professor Christopher Greenwood *London School of Economics* Professor Hein Kötz *Max-Planck-Institut, Hamburg* Dr Vaughan Lowe *Corpus Christi College, Cambridge* Professor D. M. McRae *University of Ottawa* Professor Onuma Yasuaki *University of Tokyo*
Advisory Committee	Professor D. W. Bowett QC Judge Rosalyn Higgins QC Professor Sir Robert Jennings QC Professor J. A. Jolowicz QC Professor Eli Lauterpacht QC Professor Kurt Lipstein Judge Stephen Schwebel

Principles of the institutional law of international organizations

Second Revised Edition

by

C. F. Amerasinghe, *PhD, LLD (Cantab.)*

CAMBRIDGE
UNIVERSITY PRESS

PUBLISHED BY THE PRESS SYNDICATE OF THE UNIVERSITY OF CAMBRIDGE
The Pitt Building, Trumpington Street, Cambridge, United Kingdom

CAMBRIDGE UNIVERSITY PRESS
The Edinburgh Building, Cambridge, CB2 2RU, UK
40 West 20th Street, New York, NY 10011–4211, USA
477 Williamstown Road, Port Melbourne, VIC 3207, Australia
Ruiz de Alarcón 13, 28014 Madrid, Spain
Dock House, The Waterfront, Cape Town 8001, South Africa

http://www.cambridge.org

First published 1996
Transferred to digital printing 1998
Second edition 2005

Printed in the United Kingdom at the University Press, Cambridge

Typeface Swift 10/13 pt.   *System* LᴬTEX 2$_\varepsilon$ [TB]

A catalogue record for this book is available from the British Library

ISBN 0 521 83714 6 hardback
ISBN 0 521 54557 9 paperback

Contents

Preface

This book was designed in 1996, at the time the first edition was published, to meet a perceived need for a work of both an academic and practical character, specifically on the *institutional*, as contrasted with the functional or operational, law of international organizations. While there was and is some literature on the subject, it did not and does not have an adequate academic orientation or was not or is not sufficiently specialized in the institutional field.

The first edition required updating, revision and addition of a much needed Chapter 8 on judicial organs *of* international organizations, consequent upon the attention being paid and emphasis being given in the life of international organizations to international administrative courts, particularly, and also to the two ad hoc international criminal tribunals as organs of organizations, in that they are established and financed by organizations.

The fact that the first edition sold out and is out of print was also a consideration for doing a second edition at this point in time. Some useful suggestions made by reviewers of the first edition have been taken into account for this second edition. Generally the book speaks for itself. One of the important characteristics of the book is that it identifies and discusses principles, where they exist, while acknowledging in other areas that practices could differ.

I was in no small measure encouraged to undertake this second edition by the positive reviews given to the original book, not to mention the fact that the first edition was well received and acclaimed in academia and among professional international lawyers and administrators. It should undoubtedly continue to be of use and interest alike to academics, practitioners and students both graduate and undergraduate.

XIII

I should like to express my gratitude to my friends, Laura and Emily Crow, who assiduously and with ardour typed the new chapter 8 and the expanded chapter 16.

C. F. Amerasinghe

Maryland
U.S.A.
November 2003

Abbreviations

AD	Annual Digest of Public International Law Cases (now ILR)
ADB	Asian Development Bank
ADBAT	Asian Development Bank Administrative Tribunal
Adelaide LR	Adelaide Law Review
ADF	African Development Fund
AFDB	African Development Bank
AFDI	Annuaire Français de droit international
AIDI	Annuaire de l'Institut de droit international
AJCL	American Journal of Comparative Law
AJIL	American Journal of International Law
AMF	Arab Monetary Fund
AOI	Arab Organization for Industrialization
ASDI	Annuaire Suisse de droite international
ASEAN	Association of South East Asian Nations
ASIL	American Society of International Law
BADEA	Arab Bank for Economic Development in Africa
BDARO	Basic Documents on African Regional Organizations (L. Sohn (ed.))
BIS	Bank for International Settlements
Brooklyn JIL	Brooklyn Journal of International Law
BYIL	British Yearbook of International Law
CACM	Central American Common Market
CAFRAD	African Training and Research Centre in Administration for Development

California Western ILJ	California Western International Law Journal
CARICOM	Caribbean Community
CDB	Caribbean Development Bank
CERN	European Organization for Nuclear Research
CGIAR	Consultative Group for International Agricultural Research
Chicago JIL	Chicago Journal of International Law
CIC	Caribbean Investment Corporation
CIEPS	International Center for Registration of Serials
CIPE	Centro Inter-Americano Promoción Exportaciones
CIPEC	Intergovernmental Council for Coffee Exporting Countries
CJEC	Court of Justice of the European Communities
CLJ	Cambridge Law Journal
CODAM	Committee on Executive Directors Administrative Matters (IBRD)
COE	Council of Europe
COEAB	Council of Europe Appeals Board
Col. JTL	Columbia Journal of Transnational Law
COMECON	Council for Mutual Economic Assistance
Commodity Fund	Common Fund for Commodities
Cornell ILJ	Cornell International Law Journal
CPR	Chinese People's Republic
CS	Commonwealth Secretariat
CSAT	Commonwealth Secretariat Administrative Tribunal
CYIL	Canadian Yearbook of International Law
EAC	East African Community
EADB	East African Development Bank
EBRD	European Bank for Reconstruction and Development
EC	European Communities
ECHR	European Commission on Human Rights
ECOSOC	Economic and Social Council

ECOWAS	Economic Community of Western African States
ECR	European Court Reports
ECSC	European Coal and Steel Community
ECtHR	European Court of Human Rights
EEC	European Economic Community
EFTA	European Free Trade Association
EIB	European Investment Bank
ELDO	European Space Vehicle Launcher Development Organization
EMBL	European Molecular Biology Laboratory
EPO	European Patent Organization
ERTA	European Road Transport Agreement
ESA	European Space Agency
ESAAB	ESA Appeals Board
ESO	European Southern Observatory
ESOC	European Space Operations Center
ESRO	European Space Research Organization
EU	European Union
Euratom	European Atomic Energy Community
Eurocontrol	European Organization for the Safety of Air Navigation
FAO	Food and Agricultural Organization
FCC	Federal Communications Commission
Fordham ILJ	Fordham International Law Journal
FRG	Federal Republic of Germany
GA	General Assembly (UN)
Ga. JCIL	Georgia Journal of Comparative and International Law
GAOR	Official Records of the General Assembly
GATT	General Agreement on Tariffs and Trade
GEF	Global Environmental Facility
GYIL	German Yearbook of International Law
Hague Recueil	Recueil de Cours of the Hague Academy of International Law
Harv. ILJ	Harvard International Law Journal
HLR	Harvard Law Review
Howard LJ	Howard Law Journal

IACHR	Inter-American Commission on Human Rights
IACtHR	Inter-American Court of Human Rights
IADB	Inter-American Development Bank
IADBAT	IADB Administrative Tribunal
IAEA	International Atomic Energy Agency
IAL	International Administrative Law
IAT	International Administrative Tribunal
IBE	International Bureau of Education
IBRD	International Bank for Reconstruction and Development
ICAN	International Commission for Air Navigation
ICAO	International Civil Aviation Organization
ICEM	Intergovernmental Committee for European Migration
ICJ	International Court of Justice
ICLQ	International and Comparative Law Quarterly
ICM	Intergovernmental Committee for Migration
ICO	International Cocoa Organization
ICRC	International Committee of the Red Cross
ICRISAT	International Crops Research Institute for the Semi-Arid Tropics
ICSID	International Centre for the Settlement of Investment Disputes
ICTR	International Criminal Tribunal for Rwanda
ICTY	International Criminal Tribunal for the former Yugoslavia
IDA	International Development Association
IDB	Inter-American Development Bank
IDBAT	IDB Administrative Tribunal
IFAD	International Fund for Agricultural Development
IFC	International Finance Corporation
IGO	Intergovernmental Organization
IIA	International Institute of Agriculture
IIC	Inter-American Investment Corporation
IIIC	International Institute of Intellectual Co-operation

IJIL	Indian Journal of International Law
ILC	International Law Commission
ILM	International Legal Materials
ILO	International Labor Organization
ILOAT	ILO Administrative Tribunal
ILR	International Law Reports
IMCO	Intergovernmental Maritime Consultative Organization
IMF	International Monetary Fund
IMFAT	IMF Administrative Tribunal
IMO	International Maritime Organization
INMARSAT	International Maritime Satellite Organization
INRO	International Natural Rubber Organization
Int. Org.	International Organization
INTELSAT	International Telecommunications Satellite Organization
Inter pol.	International Police Organization
IOM	International Organization for Migration
IPI	International Patent Institute
IPU	International Paleontological Union
IRO	International Refugee Organization
ISA	International Seabed Authority
ISO	International Organization for Standardization
ITA6	Sixth International Tin Agreement
ITC	International Tin Council
ITLOS	International Tribunal for the Law of the Sea
ITO	International Trade Organization
ITU	International Telecommunication Union
JCLIL	Journal of Comparative Legislation and International Law
JDI	Journal de droit international
JWTL	Journal of World Trade Law
LN	League of Nations
LNT	Administrative Tribunal of the League of Nations
LQR	Law Quarterly Review
Michigan JIL	Michigan Journal of International Law

MIGA	Multilateral Insurance Guaranty Agency
NATO	North Atlantic Treaty Organization
NATOAB	NATO Appeals Board
Nederlands TIR	Nederlands Tijdschrift voor International Recht
NGO	Non-governmental Organization
NILR	Netherlands International Law Review
Nordic JIL	Nordic Journal of International Law
NYUJIL	New York University Journal of International Law
NYUJILP	New York University Journal of International Law and Policy
OAPEC	Organization of Arab Petroleum Exporting Countries
OAS	Organization of American States
OASAT	OAS Administrative Tribunal
OAU	Organization of African Unity
OCAM	Organisation commune africaine et malagache
OCTI	Central Office for International Railway Transport
OECD	Organization for Economic Co-operation and Development
OEEC	European Organization of Economic Co-operation
OIHP	Office International d'Hygiène Publique
OJ Eur. Comm.	Official Journal of the European Communities
ONU	United Nations Organization
ONUC	United Nations Congo Operation
OPEC	Organization of Petroleum Exporting Countries
OZfR	Österreichische Zeitschrift für Recht
OZOR	Östèrreische Zeitschrift für Öffentliches Recht
PAHO	Pan-American Health Organization
PCA	Permanent Court of Arbitration
PCIJ	Permanent Court of International Justice
PLO	Palestine Liberation Organization
Polish YIL	Polish Yearbook of International Law

RBDI	Revue Belge de droit international
RDI	Rivista di diritto internazionale
RDIDC	Revue de droit international et droit comparé
RDILC	Revue de droit international et legislation comparée
REDI	Revista Española de Derecho Internacional
RGDIP	Revue générale de droit international public
RGSt	Reichgerichtentscheidungen im Strassachen
RHDI	Revue Hellénique de droit international
RI	Revue de droit international
Rs.	Resolution
SALJ	South African Law Journal
SAYBIL	South African Yearbook of International Law
SC	Security Council
SDR	Special Drawing Right
SG	Secretary-General (UN)
Soviet YBIL	Soviet Yearbook of International Law
StJIL	Stanford Journal of International Law
TC	Trusteeship Council
TEU	Treaty of European Union
TGS	Transactions of the Grotius Society
UAE	United Arab Emirates
UAR	United Arab Republic
UN	United Nations Organization
UNAT	UN Administrative Tribunal
UNCIO	United Nations Conference on International Organizations
UNCLOS	UN Convention on the Law of the Sea
UNCTAD	United Nations Conference on Trade and Development
UNDP	United Nations Development Programme
UNECLA	United Nations Economic Commission for Latin America
UNEF	United Nations Emergency Fund
UNEP	United Nations Environmental Programme
UNESCO	United Nations Educational, Scientific and Cultural Organization
UNFICYP	United Nations Forces in Cyprus

UNGA	UN General Assembly
UNGAOR	UNGA Official Records
UNHCR	United Nations High Commissioner for Refugees
UNICEF	United Nations International Children's Emergency Fund
UNIDO	United Nations International Development Organization
UNJY	United Nations Juridical Yearbook
UNRRA	United Nations Relief and Rehabilitation Agency
UNRWA	United Nations Relief and Works Agency
UNSC	UN Security Council
UNSG	United Nations Secretary General
UNTS	United Nations Treaty Series
UPU	Universal Postal Union
Vanderbilt JIL	Vanderbilt Journal of International Law
Vienna Convention	Vienna Convention on the Law of Treaties, 1969
VaJIL	VJIL
VJIL	Virginia Journal of International Law
WBAT	World Bank Administrative Tribunal
WEU	Western European Union
WEUAB	WEU Appeals Board
WHO	World Health Organization
WIPO	World Intellectual Property Organization
WMO	World Meteorological Organization
World Bank	IBRD
WTO	World Trade Organization
Yale LJ	Yale Law Journal
YBILC	Yearbook of the International Law Commission
ZAORV	Zeitschrift für Ausländisches Öffentliches Recht und Völkerrecht

Table of cases

1 Introduction

History of international organizations

Bilateral and even multilateral relations between states have a long history, but the establishment of public international organizations functioning as institutions is essentially a development of the late nineteenth century.[1] Consular relations designed to protect interests in commerce, and diplomatic relations concerned with representation of states, go far back in history: the former to the times of the ancient Greeks and Romans; the latter to a somewhat later period, taking its modern shape in the fifteenth century. It is in these institutions that the origins of the more complex institutions which started evolving in the early nineteenth century can be found. When bilateral relationships based on the existence of diplomatic embassies or missions were found to be inadequate to meet more complex situations arising from problems concerning not just two but many states, a means had to be found for

---

[1] For histories see, e.g., Leonard, *International Organisation* (1951), chapter 2; Mangone, *A Short History of International Organizations* (1954), particularly chapter 3; Eagleton, *International Government* (1956); Monaco, *Lezioni di Organnizzazione Internazionale* (1965), chapter 1; El-Erian, 'First Report to the ILC in Relations between States and Inter-Governmental Organizations', 2 YBILC (1963) at pp. 162*ff*.; Sands and Klein (eds.), *Bowett's Law of International Institutions* (2001) pp. 1*ff*. See also, on the rise of the UN and other organizations, Lachs, 'Quelques réflexions sur la communauté internationale', in Bardonnet, Combacau, Dupuy and Weil (eds.), *Le Droit international au service de la paix, de la justice et du développement: Mélanges Michel Virally* (1991) at pp. 352*ff*., Pescatore, 1 *Cours d'Institutions Internationales* (1978). Developments before the Second World War have been dealt with in Ghadbane, 'L'évolution historique, fonctionelle de l'organisation internationale et les institutions internationales à la lumière des idées idéales et réalistes jusqu'à la deuxième guerre', 31 *Revue Algérienne des Sciences Juridiques, Economiques et Politiques* (1993) pp. 287–342 (in Arabic). For the establishment of the LN and its significance in terms of the history of international organization, see Kennedy, 'The Move to Institutions', 8 *Cardozo Law Review* (1986–7) p. 841.

representation in the same forum of the interests of all the states concerned. This was the international conference. It was the *ad hoc* temporary conference convened for a specific purpose and terminating once agreement was reached on the subject matter and a treaty was adopted that evolved ultimately into permanent international organizations with organs that function on a permanent basis and meet periodically.

The Peace of Westphalia of 1648 was the result of such a conference as was the settlement in 1815 through the Congress of Vienna and the Treaty of Versailles in 1919. There were other conferences such as the Congress of Berlin of 1871 and the Hague Conferences of 1899 and 1907 which concerned other matters than peace. Conferences were convened to solve problems on a multilateral basis. The result of the conference would generally be a formal treaty or convention or, where such an agreement was not desirable or obtainable, a memorandum or minutes of the conference.

The system of *ad hoc* conferences was limited both in its reach and its quality.[2] The principal features of concern were that (i) for each new problem a conference had to be convened afresh (on the initiative of the state or states concerned), which generally meant delay and complexity in dealing with the problem; (ii) the conferences were used as platforms for rendering state policy rather than as fora for discussion and resolution, as, for example, are the organs of the UN now, and were the organs of the LN, with the result that flexibility was often lost, though sometimes negotiated deals were not absent; (iii) there was also no principle of state membership which involved responsibilities and obligations in addition to the important right to be represented, because the conferences were held on the invitation of a state or states which sponsored the conference; (iv) most importantly, the principle of equality was at the heart of the *ad hoc* conference system which meant that substantive decisions, especially, of whatever kind, were subject to the rule of unanimity and were not taken on the basis of some majority; (v) the *ad hoc* conference came to be associated with, and used as being appropriate for, political issues but not generally for legal questions; and (vi) in any event the conference proved inadequate for the solution of political problems. They were even more inadequate for the regulation of relations between the peoples of the different countries which were the result of their common interests. Thus, in the nineteenth century, there developed associations, international in character, among groups other

---

[2] See Sands and Klein (eds.), note 1 pp. 3*ff*.

than governments. There followed similar developments among governments which were, however, at that time rather in the administrative than in the political field.

In the western hemisphere, there were somewhat different but significant developments. The pan-American system resorted to conferences at a regional level, beginning in 1826, though they did not yield tangible results till the Washington Conference of 1885. These conferences had a periodic character after that and culminated in the formation of the OAS. They contributed to the techniques of international organizations in several ways:[3] (i) the conferences were not convened at the initiative of any one State, but the time and place of each were decided by the previous one; (ii) the agenda of each conference was prepared by the governing body of the standing administrative organ, the Pan-American Union (established in 1912); (iii) a greater possibility existed to undertake preparatory work before each conference than in the case of *ad hoc* conferences; and (iv) the periodic character of the conferences made possible the development of more elaborate and formal procedural arrangements.

By contrast the non-governmental unions or associations sprang from the realization by non-governmental bodies, consisting of both private individuals and corporate associations, that their interests had an international character which required that those interests be promoted in co-operation with similar bodies in other countries through permanent international associations. Perhaps the first conference of a private nature which led to the establishment of an association was the one which formulated the World Anti-Slavery Convention of 1840. Since then there have been a plethora of private associations or unions established, including the International Committee of the Red Cross (1863), the International Law Association (1873), the Inter-Parliamentary Union (1889) and the International Chamber of Commerce (1919), to mention only a few. Because of the proliferation of these private unions, in 1910 the Union of International Associations was formed to co-ordinate their activities, among other things. These private unions (which will not be the subject of this study, as will be seen) anticipated and antedated the development of the public unions. Their appearance suggests that the growth of the international organization was the result of a universal human need.

---

[3] See Venacke, *International Organization* (1934) p. 153.

The public international union which appeared also in the nineteenth century, especially in its second half, is more important for the development of the modern international organization. The public unions which sprang up at that time were international administrative unions – agencies which had a certain permanency and dealt with nonpolitical technical activities. These were also associations of governments or administrations as contrasted with private bodies. The Congress of Vienna had proclaimed the principle of freedom of navigation which led to the appearance of many river commissions.[4] A good example of these was the Rhine Commission which was invested with considerable powers, including both legislative and political powers. There were commissions for other rivers, such as the Danube, Elbe and Po. Numerous other administrative unions in many fields appeared pursuant to needs as they arose. The Universal Telegraphic Union was established in 1865 with an administration as its central organ. The Universal Postal Union was established in 1874. There were other unions which sprang up such as the International Union of Railway Freight Transportation (1890), the International Bureau of Industrial Property (1883), the International Bureau of Literary Property (1886) and the International Office of Public Health (1907).

Such unions generally had periodical conferences or meetings of the representatives of member states, decisions being taken usually by unanimous vote, and a permanent secretariat (bureau) which performed the administrative tasks. One of the principal contributions of the unions to the concept of the international organization was the institutional element which was secured through a standing organ, the bureau, and provided the stepping stone from the technique of the conference to that of the organization. In some cases, there were permanent deliberative or legislative organs as well (e.g., the UPU and the International Telegraphic Union). The trend towards the permanence of association was very marked.

There were departures from the unanimity rule which were an important phenomenon, particularly when linked with legislative powers, as in the case of the Rhine Commission. The distinction made between the convention, embodying general rules, and the *règlements*, which implemented those rules in a detailed manner, was important, particularly because the *règlements* could be amended by a much simpler process.

---

[4] See Chamberlain, *The Regime of International Rivers, Danube and Rhine* (1923).

Weighted voting and apportioning budgetary contributions enabled the solution of some of the most difficult problems to which an underlying principle of equality of states could not find appropriate answers. Moreover, interests other than those of states came to be represented, whether of dependent territories, private corporations or associations, and whether coupled with the right to vote or not, with the result that recognition was given to realities in a pragmatic way as never before and such recognition paved the way for future developments.[5] Such features, further, promoted in states the awareness 'of the potentialities of international organizations as a means of furthering an interest common to numerous states without detriment to that of any concerned'.[6]

It was in 1919 after the Treaty of Versailles, when the League of Nations was created, that an attempt was made to create a political organization of an open and universal character. Since then the public intergovernmental or inter-state organization has become firmly established in international relations, a development which culminated in the establishment of the United Nations and its specialized agencies.

The nineteenth century has been described as 'the era of *preparation for* international organization', this chronological period being between 1815 and 1914, while the years which have passed since the momentous events of 1914 must in a sense be regarded as 'the era of *establishment of* international organization, which, in these terms comes to be regarded as a phenomenon of the twentieth century'.[7] The institutionalization today of inter-state relations has led to international organizations influencing far more than in the past the shaping of international relations and the development of the international law intended for their regulation.[8] In an important sense great power diplomacy conducted at summit meetings has now given way increasingly to a new form of

---

[5] On these features see Sands and Klein (eds.), note 1, pp. 9–10.

[6] Hyde, *International Law* (1947) vol. I, p. 131.

[7] Claude, *Swords into Plowshares – The Problems and Progress of International Organization* (1971) p. 41. See also Kennedy, loc. cit. note 1 at pp. 844*ff.* and 987*ff.*, who portrays the 'institutionalization' of international life, specifically after 1918, as a progressive movement away from war and to preclude war.

[8] Anand, 'International Organizations and the Functioning of International Law', 24 IJIL (1984) at p. 53. Lukashuk notes the influence of international organizations on the functioning of international law and on the process of making and application of international legal norms: 'International Organizations and the Functioning of International Law', 24 IJIL (1984) at p. 68.

multilateralism achieved through international organizations such as the UN as negotiating arenas available to all states.[9]

Pervasiveness of international organizations

Public international organizations have grown exceedingly numerous,[10] especially since the Second World War. They are of diverse nature and of different sizes in terms of membership. They range from those that deal on a global basis with matters of general concern, such as peace (the UN) and development (the IBRD, the IFC and the IDA), to those that are concerned with the regimes of particular rivers (the river

[9] See McWhinney, 'The Evolution of United Nations Constitutionalism. The Emerging Constitutional Law of International Organization', 16 *Thesaurus-Acroasium* (1990) at p. 337.

[10] Some figures would give substance to this statement, shedding light on how common international organizations are in today's world. The *Yearbook of International Organizations 2002/2003* (2002, vol. 5, p. 3, Figure 0.1.1) records a grand total of 55282 'international organizations'. Of these, 48202 are definitely not public or inter-governmental but are private international organizations (non-governmental organizations), leaving 7080, as IGOs. It is not absolutely clear how many of these would fit the definition of public international organizations given later in this chapter. It would seem that some of them may not. A figure of 232 is given for what are termed 'conventional' bodies which are IGOs. These, it is assumed, must certainly be public international organizations. Of these, 35 are 'universal' (open) and 197 regional or intercontinental. One IGO (open) included in the figure 35 is a Federation of IGOs. A further 632 were found to be apparently inactive or dissolved. This leaves a total of 6116 organizations which may or may not be public international organizations, as such. It is unlikely that there are as many as 5131 extant public international organizations, as defined here, and which are the subject of this work (for the statistics see 5 *ibid.*, p. 35, Figure 1.1.1.). On the other hand, there could be more than 232 of them. It is difficult, it would seem, to give an exact or even approximate figure, in the circumstances, because there is no authentic record available. It may be possible, however, to conjecture that the figure for public international organizations as such is over 500 and probably under 700. Given that there are approximately 198 states or entities proximate to states (see The World Bureau LLC, *World Wide Government Directory 2003* (2003) pp. i–ii), this means that the proportion of organizations to states is over three to one. The following 32 organizations are definitely identifiable as 'universal' (open) IGOs, most of them being 'associated' in some way with the UN and many of them, though open, not having actual universal membership: UN, BIS, Common Fund for Commodities, FAO, IAEA, ICAO, Interpol, IFAD, ILO, IMO, INMARSAT, IMF, IOM, International Red Cross and Red Crescent Movement, INTELSAT, ITU, ISA, ITLOS, UNESCO, UNIDO, UPU, World Bank (IBRD), ICSID, IDA, IFC, MIGA, WEO, WHO, WIPO, WMO, WTO, World Tourism Organization. It must be noted that such organizations or agencies as the UNDP, UNRWA and the ICJ are not international organizations per se. They have no separate personality from the UN, as they now stand. For the leading regional organizations see *ibid.* pp. iii*ff*.

commissions) or control of whaling, on a much more limited scale. They have clearly had a significant impact on the lives of people in individual countries, while positively influencing relations between nations and creating an effective and friendly modality for the conduct of international intercourse. The lives of people all over the world have come to be touched by the work of international organizations, as is evidenced by the interest taken by them in the protection of human rights or development, for instance; and states, especially the less developed ones but not only they, have become accustomed to look to these organizations for assistance in the solution of problems. At the same time, it is clear that international organizations have come to be so common a feature of international life and accepted, as a response to the needs of international intercourse rather than as a fulfilment of a philosophical or ideological desire to achieve world government. What has evolved is a large number of international organizations, basically unconnected with each other, though such connections, especially in the UN system, may subsequently be established, and each endeavouring to operate and achieve objectives involving some order in a particular field within its membership which may be a large or small group of states.

Despite the fears and concerns of some governments that international organizations are increasing too fast and that they are a burden on their exchequers, they are still proliferating at a considerable rate. Generally, it is unusual for a new problem in international relations to be considered without at the same time some international organization being developed to deal with it. For instance, concern with the instability of commodities markets led to the establishment in the 1980s of the Common Fund for Commodities and the competition for the newly discovered wealth of the international seabed area resulted in the creation of the ISA under the Law of the Sea Convention of 1982, based on the concept of 'the common heritage of mankind'. More recently in the 1990s the problems of international trade, which was growing increasingly complex, led to the development of the WTO. International society has, in spite of the diversity of culture and political systems, been progressively drawn closer together and become more unified. People and their governments now look far beyond national frontiers and feel a common responsibility for the major problems of the world and for lesser problems that may subsist within smaller groups of states. Many of those problems have overflowed national boundaries, or called for attention beyond national limits, become international and demanded regulation and treatment in a wide sphere, with the consequence that governments have sought increasingly to deal with them through international organizations.[11]

International organizations, especially the global ones, have contributed much through their programmes. The contribution of the UN to the maintenance of international peace, particularly after the end of the Cold War, cannot be overestimated, while organizations like the FAO and the IBRD have done a great deal in the area of development and the promotion of better living conditions for the poor developing countries. International organizations have introduced a measure of peaceful coexistence and cooperative stability in international relations. The goals they have set and in large measure achieved and the values they have realized are of vital significance for all states and humanity as such. Clearly interdependence is increasingly being acknowledged and accepted as a practical reality,[12] which requires an organizational structure in international relations.

A very important premise for the growth of international organization and the increase in the number of IGOs is that states have accepted obligations and considerable limitations on their powers and liberties which were a consequence of their sovereign character.[13] On the other hand, the proliferation of IGOs, whether open or closed, raises some cause for concern, both because of overlapping jurisdictional authority and terms of reference[14] and because of the expense for states and taxpayers within states which must necessarily be incurred in order to

---

[11] For a doctrinal explanation of the growth of organization see Schiffer, *The Legal Community of Mankind* (1954) *passim*.

[12] See on some of these points Lachs, 'Legal Framework of an International Community', 6 *Emory International Law Review* (1992) at pp. 334–5.

[13] The relationship between membership of an IGO and restrictions on freedom of action flowing from state sovereignty and obligations is explored in Martin Martinez, *National Sovereignty and International Organizations* (1996). Such restrictions and obligations are a necessary corollary of membership in IGOs, though when states become parties to any kind of convention such limitations and obligations are accepted by states. The special feature of membership of an IGO is that such restrictions and obligations may be imposed in the future, i.e., after entry into force for the member state of the constitutive convention, by acts of the IGO, such as decisions, no subsequent special act such as becoming party to a convention or treaty being required.

[14] For discussion of some of the problems caused by proliferation of IGOs see Blokker, 'Proliferation of International Organizations: an Exploratory Introduction', in Blokker and Schermers (eds.), *Proliferation of International Organizations: Legal Issues* (2001) at pp. 14*ff*. There appear to be similar problems with the proliferation of international judicial bodies, standing or *ad hoc*, created by states. Such proliferation has been noted and sometimes criticized: see Guillaume, *ICJ Press Release 2000/36*; Romans, 'The Proliferation of International Judicial Bodies: The Pieces of the Puzzle', 31 NYUJILP (1999) at pp. 723*ff*.; Alford, 'The Proliferation of International Courts and Tribunals:

maintain IGOs. Consequently, there may be need for rationalization and even consolidation of functions which could result in a reduction in the number of IGOs, and in financial waste, while human resources will be more profitably, economically and sensibly utilized.

Classifications

The interest here is in the public international organization and not in the private international organization commonly known as the non-governmental organization (NGO). The public international organization is normally created by a treaty or convention to which states are parties and the members of the organization so created are generally states, though sometimes but rarely governments may constitute the membership.

International organizations may be classified in numerous ways, depending on the purpose for which the classification is being made. Four primary distinctions may be made as being relevant to the structure and functioning of international organizations: [15] (i) the distinction between public, governmental (or inter-state) organizations and private organizations; (ii) the distinction between universal (open) and closed organizations; (iii) the distinction between supra-national organizations and those that are not supra-national; (iv) the distinction between general organizations and functional or technical organizations. These are clearly useful distinctions. There are other distinctions that have been made[16] such as that between temporary and permanent organizations or that between judicial and non-judicial organizations, but these are not particularly helpful for the present purposes.

International organizations range from the inter-state body created by multilateral treaty or convention with potential and openings for universal membership and a very broad range of interests, such as the United Nations, to the specialized agencies of the UN with potential and openings for universal membership but with a narrow focus (e.g., the FAO, the IBRD and the UNESCO), to organizations with select or closed membership but relatively wide interests (e.g., the Council of Europe, the OAS and the OAU), to agencies which are restricted both as to membership

International Adjudication in Ascendance', ASIL, *Proceedings of the 94th Annual Meeting* (2000) at pp. 160*ff*.

[15] Schermers and Blokker, *International Institutional Law* (1995) pp. 31*ff*.

[16] See, e.g., Schwarzenberger, *A Manual of International Law* (1960) p. 227; Leonard, note 1 p. 41; El-Erian, loc. cit. note 1 at pp. 167*ff*.

and as to subject matter (e.g., the international river commissions), to organizations which are composed entirely of non-governmental entities (NGOs).[17]

The first distinction of relevance for the present purpose is that between public international organizations and private international organizations. A variety of definitions or identifications of the public international organization has been given.[18] A formal definition is not necessary for the present purpose. Suffice it to identify the basic characteristics which distinguish the public international organization from other organizations, particularly private international organizations. These are: (i) establishment by some kind of international agreement among states; (ii) possession of what may be called a constitution; (iii) possession of organs separate from its members; (iv) establishment under international law; and (v) generally but not always an exclusive membership of states or governments, but at any rate predominant membership of states or governments. Private international organizations do not have all these characteristics. Usually what is lacking is creation by international agreement, establishment under international law and an exclusive or predominant membership of states or governments. Sometimes one or the other of these may be lacking. For example, clearly NGOs are not established under international law, nor have exclusive or predominant state or governmental membership and are not public international organizations.[19]

Two further elements are sometimes mentioned in connection with public international organizations. These are: international personality (distinct from that of their member states) and treaty-making capacity.[20] Though these characteristics are generally shared by all public international organizations, it is doubtful whether they are intrinsic

---

[17] Kirgis, *International Organizations in Their Legal Setting* (1993) preface, p. v.

[18] See, e.g., Bastid, *Droit des Gens* (lectures – 1956–7) p. 329; Reuter, *Institutions Internationales* (1975) pp. 234*ff*.; Fitzmaurice, 'Report on the Law of Treaties', 2 YBILC (1956) at p. 108; El-Erian, loc. cit. note 1 at pp. 164*ff*. Schermers and Blokker, note 15 pp. 20*ff*.

[19] Most of these are established by individuals or associations of individuals, e.g., the International Student Service, the International Table Tennis Federation, l'Institut de droit international, the International Chamber of Commerce, and the International Planned Parenthood Federation. Membership may include governments and is not confined to non-governmental entities. NGOs are recognized by the ECOSOC of the UN: see UN ECOSOC Rs. 288 (X) at 1296 (XLIV), for the relationship with ECOSOC under Article 71 of the UN Charter. On NGOs generally see, e.g., Lador-Lederer, *International Non-Governmental Organizations* (1963); White, *International Non-Governmental Organizations: Their Purposes, Methods and Accomplishments* (1968).

[20] See, e.g., Fitzmaurice, loc. cit. note 18.

to the definition of a public international organization. Rather they are to be regarded as consequences of being a public international organization. This is not a problem for the present purpose, since, as will be seen, public international organizations generally have these characteristics, which private international organizations do not share.[21] The basic characteristics referred to above are sufficient to distinguish public international organizations from private international organizations.

The distinction between 'open' or 'universal' public international organizations and 'closed' organizations has also been made. In discussing the scope of membership of organizations a rapporteur of the ILC stated:

A universal organization is one which includes in its membership all the States of the world. This is not the case of any past or present international organization yet. Thus, it may be more accurate to use the terms 'universalist' suggested by Schwarzenberger or 'of potentially universal character' used in the treatise of Oppenheim. The French term 'à avocation universelle' conveys the same meaning as these two terms, which is that while the organization is not completely universal, it tends towards that direction. This was partially the case of the League of Nations and is, in a much broader sense, the case of the United Nations, especially after 1955, and the specialized agencies.[22]

The distinction to be made is between those public international organizations which are 'open' or 'universalist' in the sense that they contemplate, tend towards or are open to universal membership and those which have limited membership based on regionalism or some other criterion. The latter 'closed' organizations have been described as follows:

In contrast to universal organizations there are organizations which aim at membership from a closed group of States. No Members are admitted from outside the group. We shall denominate these organizations as 'closed' organizations, to emphasize their closed membership... There are three types of closed organizations: regional organizations, organizations of States with a common background, such as common language or common political system, and closed functional organizations.[23]

The fact that states may have to be admitted by election to an open organization or that there are certain conditions that have to be satisfied for admission (as in the case of even the UN) does not affect the 'openness'

---

[21] For a discussion of private international organizations see Schermers and Blokker, note 15 pp. 32ff.

[22] El-Erian, loc. cit. note 1 at p. 167.

[23] Schermers, *International Institutional Law* (1980) p. 23. In the later edition of this book, Schermers and Blokker, note 15 p. 37, the same idea is expressed in different words.

of the organization. What matters is that all states are eligible to be members. The UN family of international organizations is a good example of 'open' organizations. The IAEA and perhaps the Commodity Fund and the earlier Commodity Councils are examples of such organizations outside the UN family. As for 'closed' organizations, the ADB, the Council of Europe and the OAU are examples of regional organizations, the OECD and the Commonwealth Secretariat are examples of organizations of states with a common background, and OPEC and the International Bauxite Organization (consisting of bauxite producers) are examples of closed functional organizations.

The distinction between supra-national organizations, so called, and those that are not supra-national is relevant. In this work supra-national organizations, of which the EU (formerly the EC) is the only example, will not be studied as such. This supra-national organization has certain special characteristics which will not particularly be examined here. However, there are certain general principles which apply to it which also apply to other organizations and are the subject of this study.

The distinction sometimes made between judicial and non-judicial bodies needs to be addressed. There are international judicial bodies which cannot be regarded as separate organizations. The ICJ and IATs, for example, are organs, independent though they may be, belonging to other international institutions, and strictly do not have an existence of their own, although they may have their own statutes that created them. The Courts of Human Rights or the International Tribunal of the Law of the Sea are somewhat different, having been created under separate international conventions. They have a status of their own. The PCA is not a judicial international organization, although it may be regarded as a special kind of international organization which acts as an arbitration *centre*. None of the separate judicial organs or organizations will be specifically dealt with here except judicial organs which are organs *established by international organizations* (see Chapter 8). Judicial organs or organizations, which stand on their own as not being created *by* international organizations, generally have their special regimes and are not as such a suitable subject for a general work on international institutions which are largely of a political or technical nature. The reason IATs are included in the study is that they constitute an integral and important aspect of the treatment of employment relations in the law of international institutions and are organs established by IGOs. For the same reasons the ICTY and the ICTR will be discussed in this treatise. As will be seen in Chapter 3, the Iran-US Claims Tribunal, which is a judicial body with an independent status, has been recognized as having an international personality.

The BIS (Bank of International Settlements) appears to be a singular case, and to belong to a class by itself. It was created by an agreement among states, while at the same time, also with the consent of and on the initiative of the states parties to the agreement creating it, being given legal personality under the national law of a state. Switzerland, the state concerned, gave the BIS national legal personality under Swiss law. The BIS is incorporated as a legal person pursuant to Swiss law, clearly with the agreement and knowledge of Switzerland. The consequence of this is not necessarily to take away the international personality of the BIS, if it was the intention of the states creating it that it should have such personality and such personality was in keeping with and necessary for its functioning. Theoretically there is no reason which prevents the BIS from having this kind of dual personality, as long as it is clear that the states which created it did not expressly or by necessary intendment deprive the BIS of international personality which, as it appears, it was intended to have and which its functions require it to have. Suffice it to observe here that the BIS is in a special class because of the existence of the duality in respect of its legal personality. The implications of this feature will be discussed in Chapter 3.

The concept of international institutional law

The law governing the structure and general operations of public international organizations was described in 1962 by an author who used the language of private international law, as the 'personal' law of the organization.[24] It is the law governing its corporate life. That author further concluded:

If a body has the character of an international body corporate the law governing its corporate life must necessarily be international in character; it cannot be the territorial law of the headquarters of the body corporate or any other municipal legal system as such without destroying its international character. The law governing its corporate life will naturally cover such matters as the membership of the body, its competence, the composition and mutual relations of its various organs, their procedure, the rights and obligations of the body and its members in relation to each other, financial matters, the procedure of constitutional amendment, the rules governing the dissolution or winding up

---

[24] See Jenks, *The Proper Law of International Organisations* (1962) pp. 4ff.

of the body, and the disposal of its assets in such a contingency. It may also cover the mutual relations of the body, its members and its various organs in respect of matters involving third parties.[25]

Thus, the law governing the corporate aspects of international organizations is international in character from which it must be inferred that it is international law. The coverage of international institutional law described by that author is still generally viable, with some additions, perhaps.

While there are differences between open and closed organizations, by and large the institutional law of the two kinds of organizations is similar. Thus, the precedents and principles relating to both kinds of organizations may usefully be examined. For example, in the study of the liability of members of international organizations to third parties for the obligations of the organizations, to give but one instance, there is no material difference in the law governing the two kinds of institutions and the practice and precedents from both kinds of organizations may be studied conjunctively. To some extent the same may be said of the principles of interpretation of constitutional texts. There are clearly many other areas of similarity. Thus, in general, what applies to open organizations will also be applicable to closed organizations.

In the study of the law relating to public international organizations there is more than a single aspect that may be examined. The concern here is with the 'institutional' and related law of public international organizations, that is to say, those areas of the law relating to the institutional aspects of their operation and related aspects will be studied. These cover such subjects as the interpretation of texts, membership, budgeting, international personality and capacities, among others. It is primarily those areas which relate to the operation of organizations as international institutions that will be taken up here. There are the other functional aspects of organizational law which are also relevant to the law of international organizations. These include, for instance, the manner in which the UN exercises its powers of dispute settlement under Chapter VI of the Charter or peacekeeping by implementing enforcement measures under Chapter VII,[26] the exercise of the ILO's authority in the matter of labour conventions and the details of the exercise of

---

[25] *Ibid.* p. 3. See also *ibid.* p. 6: 'The personal law of an international body corporate consists of the international rules applicable to it and it therefore follows from this principle that its corporate life is not subject to any municipal law as such.'

[26] Sands and Klein (eds.), note 1 pp. 42–55.

power by the IBRD under its Articles of Agreement to make development loans. Functional aspects of the law as such will only be taken up insofar as they impinge on the institutional aspects of the law of international organization. The functional aspects of the law of international organization are important and interesting but a study of them would require a much larger canvas.[27] Probably each organization should be studied separately in terms of its functions and programmes.

At the same time, as has been pointed out,[28] it is difficult to make a clear demarcation between the institutional law of international organizations and other related fields of law, including the functional aspects of organizational law. Moreover, many aspects of international institutional law are closely related to public international law in general (e.g., the interpretation of constitutional texts). Thus, certain subjects of public international law in general which are also considered to be closely related to institutional law and of particular importance to it will be discussed here, including, for example, legal responsibility of and to organizations.

Since the work deals only with public international organizations, these will be referred to simply as international organizations throughout the work, unless it is necessary to distinguish private international organizations from them.

The nature of international institutional law

The law of international organizations can be described as special in kind. Indeed, it may be thought to be inherently a *lex specialis*, a law proper to each organization, lacking general implications. It was observed in 1962 that:

There are still no general rules or principles relating to international bodies corporate to which we can automatically turn when in search of their personal law. We have no recognized body of such rules or principles even as regards the existing types of international body corporate; as regards possible further types

---

[27] For studies of the work of particular organizations see, e.g., Marchisio and Di Blase, *The Food and Agricultural Organization* (1991); Valticos, *International Labour Law* (1979); Ghebali, *The International Labour Organization* (1989); Broms, *The United Nations* (1990); Szasz, *The Law and Practice of the International Atomic Energy Agency* (1970); Broches, 'International Legal Aspects of the Operations of the World Bank', 98 *Hague Recueil* (1959-III) p. 297; Gold, *Legal and Institutional Aspects of the International Monetary System* (1979); Lasok and Bridge, *Law and Institutions of the European Communities* (1998).

[28] See Schermers, note 23 p. 2.

of international body corporate we are entirely in the realm of speculation. For the existing types we have the constituent instrument of each of the bodies concerned, amplified somewhat by its constitutional practice, and calling for interpretation in accordance with the general principles of treaty interpretation recognized by international law. But we have no international equivalent for the common law relating to corporations or the modern statutory regulation of the various types of corporation.[29]

Another writer has consistently maintained that there is no 'law' of international organization but there are 'laws' of international organizations.[30] The implication is that, since the law governing each organization is to be found in or flows from its constitution and constitutions are individualized instruments, there can be no general law nor general principles of law applicable to all or several organizations.

There is evidence at this time that, though the individual constitutions and other legislative texts of each organization constitute in the last analysis the law governing its corporate structure and operations, there have come into existence in some areas certain general principles. First, there has been a cross-influencing among international organizations which not only is sensible but is to be desired. Many of the institutional problems both of a constitutional nature and otherwise, and also apart from problems in the area of functions, are comparable.[31] Thus, the solutions found by one organization in the institutional area can be of use to another, though in regard to functions there may be clear differences of need and of execution. Second, the comparative method, as applied to the structure and functioning of international organizations in the institutional area, could not only lead to mutual improvements but enhance results in functional fields. The object is not to establish stereotypes for all IGOs in respect of institutional legal matters. This would be a stultifying exercise. Rather the purpose is to enable in respect of each organization the fulfillment of specific

---

[29] Jenks, note 24 pp. 6–7.

[30] Reuter, 'Principes de droit international public', 103 *Hague Recueil* (1961-II) at pp. 525–6; Reuter, 'First Report on the Question of Treaties between States and International Organizations or between Two or More International Organizations', 2 YBILC (1972) at pp. 191, 197*ff.*; Reuter, note 17 pp. 252–3; Reuter, *Institutions et Relations Internationales* (1980) p. 285.

[31] In *de Merode*, WBAT Reports [1981], Decision No. 1 at p. 13, the WBAT drew attention to the fact that there were such general principles of law in the field of international administrative law which is part of the institutional law of IGOs.

needs in the institutional context and the best structure for functional purposes.[32]

While in general there exist the individuality and uniqueness of each organization in terms of its institutional operations and the law applicable to it, the manner in which the law has evolved shows that for certain purposes and in certain areas common principles of law are, indeed, applicable. Uniformity or similarities exist, for instance, in the general principles which apply (e.g., in interpretation), as a result of the application of conventional law (e.g., privileges and immunities), in customary international law which applies (e.g., responsibility of and to organizations), as a result of the application of general principles of law (e.g., *ultra vires* and employment relations), and because there are similarities in constitutional texts. On the one hand, similarities between constitutions in certain areas do exist and, on the other, much of the law applicable depends on interpretation. When reference is made to 'principles' (of the law of international institutions), these two features largely make such a reference conceivable. Particularly, because much of the institutional law applicable to organizations depends on interpretation of their constitutions, the principles which become relevant are not only general principles of interpretation of constitutional and other texts but general principles which have evolved through the interpretation of texts. These may be generally in the nature of *presumptions* of interpretation which apply in the absence of contrary indications in the relevant texts but have become broadly applicable. While there may be no general 'law' of international organization in a wider sense because there are patent differences in the constitutions of organizations, there certainly are, in the sense referred to above, principles applicable and deriving particularly from the interpretation of constitutional texts, which make it possible to discuss the general principles of the institutional law of international organizations. Such principles may flow particularly from relevant judicial decisions.

A constitutional or other text may, on the one hand, require obligatory action or inaction. The evolution of a practice in the interpretation of such a text in one organization may create law for that particular organization. Where there are similar texts in other organizations, two

---

[32] See Schermers, note 23 pp. 1–2, where a similar point is made but the writer also seems to say that there could be cross-influencing in the area of pure functional execution. This idea is more difficult. In any case it is not necessary for this analysis and exploration in the institutional field.

questions arise: first, does the similarity of texts create general principles; and, second, does the interpretative practice create general principles? The similarity of texts by themselves cannot be said to lead to a general principle, while the practice in interpretation could conceivably, if it is generally replicated in other organizations, lead to the establishment of a general principle in interpretation, depending on how far the practice has the elements of similarity and generality and is followed with consistency and, perhaps, a sense of obligation. On the other hand, a constitutional or other text may permit discretions and choices in the exercise of powers. Here again the practice of an organization in defining the extent of powers may create binding precedents for the organization itself, though the choices made or discretions exercised in the implementation of such powers would generally only give rise in any case to non-binding precedents within the organization. In this case also the similarity of texts would not create general principles as such, while the practice relating to the extent of powers may conceivably lead to a general principle in interpretation. The exercise of choices and discretion would not, of course, *a fortiori*, create general principles except insofar as they demonstrate the extent of powers. Always there is a difference between the similarity of texts and practices which reflect only a pattern and the consistency of practice which may create general principles applicable to more than one organization. In certain areas of membership and financing, for instance, what has been said above would hold true.

There are also some principles (in a broader sense) applicable to international organizations as such in certain areas of what falls within the ambit of institutional law, and its associated areas, which are to be traced to other sources of international law than constitutional texts and the surrounding law. Thus, in certain areas, such as privileges and immunities, there are rules which flow from conventional law, and are applicable generally. In areas, such as responsibility, customary international law engenders applicable principles, while in the field of employment relations,[33] for example, general principles of law in the classic sense are a source of applicable principles.

On the other hand, what is particular law for one organization may in fact not prevail as the law for another organization because of differences in constitutional texts, decisions of organs or practice. This eventuality does exist. Thus, there are situations in which general principles

---

[33] See my treatise, *The Law of the International Civil Service* (2 vols., 2nd edition, 1994).

may be elusive. What is left then is differing rules or practices or both. Strictly, in many areas each organization has its own law based on its constitution and other instruments. The same may be said of practices. In many respects the law applicable to or in an organization and its practices will be peculiar to it and its needs and does not depend on or create general principles. In these circumstances the law or practices of an organization are of interest only as examples of constitutional development and evolution. In some areas of the law, such as aspects of membership or financing, for instance, there are no general rules because organizations conduct themselves differently in terms of their constitutional powers and as a necessary result of variations in functions. What can be done in other areas is only to elucidate the manner in which constitutions are framed rather than to extract general principles of law applicable as such to all organizations. Similarities in these areas do not mean that binding general principles of law have been established. What emerges is that there are patterns that have been followed in the formulation of constitutions or texts or that there is a trend towards dealing with problems in similar ways. This is the case with certain aspects of such areas as amendment or the structure of, and voting in, organs of organizations.

In those areas where there are no general principles identifiable illustrations taken from the principal organization in terms of law and practices would show patterns or significant differences which would help to identify and clarify trends in international law, whether towards uniformity or diversity. Practices which are not initially law creating outside a particular organization are, thus, of importance, especially where they are common to more than one organization. In the long term these practices may lead to the creation of principles in the interpretation of constitutional texts, or, if they are significantly different, reflect an obstacle to the emergence of any uniform principles. Because all practice is not law creating, sometimes it is, so to speak, exponential. Such practice does, however, in the operation of organizations have some value as a precedent which may be relevant to the creation of a pattern of conduct, though mere consistent conduct does not *per se* create law.

It would have become evident that there are areas where it can be clearly discerned that there are general principles applicable to all organizations as such. In these areas stricter juridical analysis and exposition become possible, much easier and are invited. In other areas what is called for is description and comparison.

The organizational law which is examined and discussed here (and which is the institutional law) has the following specially significant and distinctive features:

(i)   the constitutional texts and law-creating practices of any organization will establish law for that particular organization, which law will not necessarily and as such be binding on other organizations (e.g., amendment and structure of organs);

(ii) where constitutional texts are similar, the interpretation or development by practice of those texts by one organization may, however, provide precedents or guidelines for another organization (e.g., membership);

(iii) in some areas customary international law as being generally applicable will govern (e.g., responsibility of and to organizations and interpretation of texts);

(iv) there are general principles of law which are applicable across the board in certain areas (e.g., the doctrine of *ultra vires*, and employment relations);

(v)   certain presumptions and implied principles (sometimes flowing from relevant judicial decisions) will apply as general law in the implementation and interpretation of organizational constitutional law (e.g., international personality, liability *vis-à-vis* third parties of members of an organization for its obligations); and

(vi) in some areas general conventional law will be relevant to the operation of all or most organizations (e.g., immunities and privileges).

The sources of the law

In general, the law relating to a particular organization will flow basically from conventional law, namely the constitution of that organization. The practice of organizations based on legal opinions of the legal advisers of the organizations and decisions taken by their organs will especially fill out or even expand constitutional texts, while customary international law and general principles of law may be relevant to the interpretation of texts. At the same time in certain areas such as employment relations the sources of law are peculiar to that area and more easily identifiable in terms of general application across the spectrum of international organizations.[34] Customary international law will also be relevant in areas such as the responsibility of and to organizations.

---

[34] For a discussion of sources in this area, see C. F. Amerasinghe, note 33 vol. I, Chapters 5–15.

The sources of the law being discussed vary with the subject matter and it may be necessary to draw on and examine numerous sources in a given context. Sources are not immutably the same for every conceivable situation.

The sources of the law relevant to the areas being examined may be listed as follows:

    (i)   the constitution of an organization and its interpretation;

   (ii)   legislative texts of an organization, such as statutes of administrative tribunals;

  (iii)   the law-creating practice of an organization;

  (iv)   general principles of law, such as are applied in international administrative law or in any relevant area;

   (v)   customary international law, such as applies to the interpretation of constitutions and legislative texts and to the responsibility of and to organizations;

  (vi)   conventional law, such as applies in the case of most open organizations to immunities and privileges;

 (vii)   judicial decisions, insofar as they apply general principles, for example, in the interpretation of texts.

While all these sources enjoy validity, it must be acknowledged, particularly at this point in history and time, that general principles of law are particularly important. Whether in the interpretation of relevant texts or otherwise in general, the impact of general principles of law cannot be underestimated. Indeed, as will be seen, there are several areas in which there are applicable *fundamental* general principles of law that are not only *inviolable* but also *invariable*: see on this point particularly Chapter 8 below and in a different context of international law, C. F. Amerasinghe, *Jurisdiction of International Tribunals* (2003) *passim*.

Methodology

The interest in this work is mainly in the analysis, elucidation and discussion of principles. Naturally principles would be found most often in case decisions of judicial (or quasi-judicial) organs. Thus, there would be in certain parts a concentration on jurisprudence. But principles may be established, where appropriate, in other ways too, e.g., by reference to general principles of law or reasoned inferences from established and recurrent practices where these practices are law creating.[35] There may

[35] See, e.g., Chapter 8 below on judicial organs and Chapter 9 on the law of employment relations.

be areas, however, where results are dependent more on provisions of individual constitutions. While similarity in constitutional provisions does not necessarily establish principles, it may be necessary, as in the areas of financing, dissolution and dispute settlement, to examine some constitutional texts more closely, even though there may be *fewer* relevant principles, the purpose being generally to establish a pattern or an absence of pattern. Thus, while principles will be the main concern, there will be parts of the study which will deal with constitutional provisions, their interpretation and the practice of organizations, because these areas are of basic importance to the institutional law of international organizations, even though there may not be clear general principles as such which can be discerned.

It is difficult to judge on the outside the conduct of an organization without knowing how a matter was played out or why decisions were taken. Thus, it would be useful to have access to the legal opinions of the legal advisers of institutions and other background material relating to decisions and practices of organizations.[36] These may well not be accessible to persons outside the organizations, may not be published or may not be for public consumption. Thus, often it is not possible to know the 'correct' explanation of phenomena. In these circumstances, a writer can only do the best he can with the material available to him and by making reasoned inferences.

There are certain organizations, especially closed organizations, material concerning which has been even less accessible. These include most of the organizations that were established in Eastern Europe such as COMECON, the International Investment Bank and the International Bank for Economic Co-operation. It is difficult, therefore, to assess whether a different law developed in regard to them. There is no reason, however, because of the problem, to question the general validity of the findings in this study.

There is also the fact of limited or absence of easy or ready access to many organizations which may be considered public international organizations that must be taken into account. Considering the large number of organizations, in general, the principal ones have been examined and studied. However, it may be assumed that what is said generally about them will apply to others also, *mutatis mutandis* and where appropriate.

---

[36] In this respect the publication of the records of meetings of the GA and SC and, in the UNJY, of some legal opinions of the UN Legal Counsel and of the Legal Advisers of specialized agencies of the UN is helpful.

It is not the object of this treatise to be an encyclopedia of practice, whether there are principles behind the practice or not, nor is it the intention not to take 'a practical approach' *per se* or to ignore technicalities of practice.[37] On the other hand, where there are identifiable principles, practice is used to illustrate them adequately, if necessary. For example, exhaustive illustration is avoided, where a clear principle has been laid down by judicial decision or otherwise. By the same token where an applicable general principle is not evident nor to be expected, as where practices differ, practice is used to demonstrate the diversity, and that without labouring the point with a conglomeration of varied practices. Moreover, where practices are technical because of operational requirements, they will be dealt with from the point of view of their institutional, and *not functional*, relevance.[38] These admittedly may be few and far between, though they do exist, e.g., in the financial and budgetary area. Enough has been said about objects and method to justify the particular technique adopted which is both rational and appropriate for the kind of book envisaged.[39] The treatise also keeps a steady balance between the analysis of jurisprudence and general principles of law, on the one hand, and the examination and rationalization of practice on the other, even though admittedly it is easier to extract principles from jurisprudence rather than from practice especially in certain institutional areas.[40]

---

[37] See minor and unjustified criticisms made in this connection of the first edition by Schreuer, 'Book Review', 91 AJIL (1997) at p. 760.

[38] Schreuer, *ibid.*, does not keep this distinction in mind in his review.

[39] It would not be appropriate in a treatise of this kind to give extensive accounts of the facts and decisions in cases discussed beyond what is necessary to illustrate the relevant principles and practices, as was suggested by Lyon, 'Book Review', 33 StJIL (1997) at pp. 164–5. The treatise is neither a case book nor an introductory work on the institutional law of international organizations.

[40] Some useful publications came to my attention too late for references to them to be included in this edition. Such are Schermers and Blokker, *International Institutional Law* (4th revised edition, 2003); Klabbers, *An Introduction to International Institutional Law* (2003); and Wellens, *Remedies against International Organizations* (2003). There are selected bibliographies on the institutional law of IGOs, both general and on particular organizations, in Schermers and Blokker, *op. cit.* above, pp. 1215*ff.*, and Klabbers, *op. cit.* above, pp. 345*ff.*

2　Interpretation of texts

The interpretation of constitutional texts of international organizations[1] and other texts connected with their functions is important for the law of international organization. There is something in common between the process of interpretation of constitutional texts and of resolutions and decisions of the organs of international organizations, such as the General Assembly of the UN, the Executive Directors of the IMF or the IBRD and the secretariat of the UN, or the administration of the IMF or the IBRD. Resolutions and decisions of deliberative or representative organs are made under powers assigned by the basic constitutional texts, while those of the executive organ may be made either under similar powers or under powers virtually intended to give the administration or management delegated authority from the deliberative or representative organs.

Two areas of interpretation will be considered in this chapter: the interpretation of constitutional texts and the interpretation of decisions of organs. The interpretation of constitutional texts is by far the most important aspect of textual interpretation. Constitutional texts are treaties or conventions and must be interpreted as treaties or conventions, though there may be special considerations which are relevant and they may have special characteristics. What is relevant in the case of decisions and resolutions of deliberative or representative organs which are generally interpreted in the same way as constitutional texts

---

[1] On the constitutional nature of these texts and the implication of this see, e.g., Monaco, 'Le caractère constitutionnel des actes institutifs d'organisations internationales', in *Mélanges à Ch. Rousseau: La Communauté Internationale* (1974) p. 153. See also Rosenne, 'Is the Constitution of an International Organization an International Treaty?', in *Communicazzioni e studi dell' Instituto di Diritto Internazionale dell' Universitá di Milano* (1966) p. 40.

is to identify certain, but few, important features which are special to their interpretation. There is a special case of delegated legislation which relates to employment within organizations. Because of its special nature, the special features of the interpretation of legislative texts relating to such employment will not as such be considered here. Certain aspects of the problem will be referred to in Chapter 9. Delegated legislation relating to employment may largely be by the administrative organ. Other forms of delegated legislation by the administrative organ, such as those that relate to finance, are treated in the same way as resolutions of the deliberative or representative organs.

Constitutional interpretation

Constitutional interpretation is a rather delicate area of the institutional law of international organizations. There are two basic questions that may be asked:

(i)   who may interpret constitutions of international organizations?; and
(ii) what are the main characteristics of the process of interpretation, including the principles applicable?

The answer to the first question is clearer than to the second.

Who may interpret

In performing their functions, the organs of international organizations in the first place, at least, interpret their constitutions. As the ICJ said:

In the legal systems of States, there is often some procedure for determining the validity of even a legislative or governmental act, but no analogous procedure is to be found in the structure of the United Nations. Proposals made during the drafting of the Charter to place the ultimate authority to interpret the Charter in the International Court of Justice were not accepted; the opinion which the Court is in course of rendering is an advisory opinion. As anticipated in 1945, therefore, each organ must, *in the first place at least*, determine its own jurisdiction.[2]

Though this statement was directed to the UN, it is true of all organizations that in the first place the organ concerned makes an interpretation of its constitution. The General Assembly (GA) has done this on

---

[2] The *Expenses Case*, 1962 ICJ Reports at p. 68 (italics added). See also [Pollux], 'Interpretation of the Charter', 23 BYIL (1946) at p. 58; Gordon, 'The World Court and the Interpretation of Constitutive Treaties', 59 AJIL (1965) at pp. 810–11.

several occasions, sometimes after considering a legal opinion given by the Legal Counsel.[3] The Security Council (SC) has also interpreted both the Charter and even the Statute of the ICJ itself in the course of its deliberations.[4] But this point is not confined to the principal political organs of the UN. The ILO Governing Body has to interpret the ILO Constitution – as, for example, when it interpreted Article 1(5) of the ILO Constitution on the withdrawal of members from the organization in 1977.[5] The Executive Directors of the IMF,[6] the IBRD, the IFC and the IDA[7] have frequently taken initial decisions expressly or impliedly interpreting the Articles of Agreement of these organizations. There may have been doubts about the interpretation initially but once the decision is taken it is acted upon. A dispute may arise thereafter between member states or member states and the organization as to the correctness of the interpretation which will have to be dealt with as a subsequent dispute.

In the event that a dispute arises about an interpretation of the constitutional instrument, it will depend on the provisions of the constitution itself how this dispute is to be settled. The provisions of the more important open organizations will be reviewed here. First, there is the situation where the constitution is silent about any particular mode of settlement. A prime example is the UN Charter. While Article 96(1) permits the GA and the SC to seek an advisory opinion on any legal question from the ICJ, it neither makes the advisory opinion binding on the organ

---

[3] See the legal opinions of the Legal Counsel given to the GA in the interpretation of its powers under the Charter, to be found in the UNJYs: e.g., the decision taken on the question what issues may be characterized as budgetary questions under Article 18(2) of the Charter: legal opinion of the Legal Counsel of 13 December 1972, in 1972 UNJY p. 160; the characterization of 'expenses' under Article 17(2) of the Charter, in regard to the expenses of the UN International School: legal opinion of the Legal Counsel of 30 November 1979, in 1979 UNJY p. 170.

[4] See, e.g., the action taken in 1982 on the implementation of Article 43 of the Charter: legal opinion of the Legal Counsel of 21 October 1982, in 1982 UNJY p. 183; the decision taken on the interpretation of Article 14 of the Statute of the ICJ: legal opinion of the Legal Counsel of 19 August 1981, in 1981 UNJY p. 145.

[5] See the Legal Adviser's opinion of 17 August 1977, in 1977 UNJY p. 248. The UNJYs contain many examples of legal opinions or reports relating to the interpretation of constitutions of UN specialized agencies given to various organs by the legal advisers of those specialized agencies. Similarly they contain similar opinions and reports given to various organs of the UN, other than the GA and the SC.

[6] See IMF, *Selected Decisions of the International Monetary Fund* (1993) *passim*.

[7] The decision taken in 1980 (and impliedly interpreting Article III, section 4(vii) of the Articles of Agreement) to make Structural Adjustment Loans which were not connected with specific projects was of this nature.

requesting it or on the UN, nor is the making of a request obligatory. Where an advisory opinion from the ICJ is sought and there is no prior or subsequent agreement among members of the organ or organization that the opinion will be treated as binding, a problem arises as to the effect of the opinion. Since it is not formally binding, in principle, the organ or organization can proceed to act upon its own interpretation of the constitutional instrument taken in the appropriate way. On the other hand, this would leave the advisory opinion in limbo, and seriously undermine the authority of the ICJ, a rather unsatisfactory result. The Article 96 procedure, which is a means of securing an opinion on the interpretation of the Charter by an organ of the UN, has been used on several occasions.[8] Although, after the advisory opinions were given, there may have been disagreement with it among certain member states, the UN organs concerned adopted them and acted upon them. It must be noted that there cannot be a contentious procedure before the ICJ between members and the organization because Article 34 of the Statute of the ICJ provides that only states may be parties to contentious cases before the Court, though arbitration between the organization and a state is possible.[9]

Because resort to an advisory opinion from the ICJ is not specified as the only method of settling a dispute about interpretation, a dispute on interpretation between members or between members and the organization could conceivably be submitted for settlement by any of the methods of settlement specified in Chapter VI of the Charter on the settlement of disputes which include conciliation or arbitration or reference to the ICJ either under the contentious procedure between states or under Article 96(1) of the Charter. Further, a dispute as to interpretation of the Charter may very well arise as only part of a larger dispute between member states. Such a dispute as to interpretation of the Charter could be disposed of by reference to arbitration or by reference to the ICJ under Article 36 of the Statute of the ICJ. The award or decision, however, would be binding only between the parties to the proceedings. Thus, while the dispute may be settled between the parties, the interpretation of the constitution given will not have a general effect and need not be accepted by other members of the organization.

---

[8] See, e.g., the *First Admissions Case*, 1947–8 ICJ Reports p. 57; the *Second Admissions Case*, 1950 ICJ Reports p. 4; the *Status of South West Africa Case*, 1950 ICJ Reports p. 128; the *Expenses Case*, 1962 ICJ Reports p. 151.

[9] The WIPO Constitution is another instrument that is silent on the matter of interpretation.

Before the ICJ, Article 63 of the Statute gives all the other member states of the organization the right of intervention, regardless of whether they are already signatories of the Statute and have accepted the jurisdiction of the Court.[10] This may create complications, particularly if all or a large number of members decide to exercise the right of intervention, which, however, has never happened. Would they be under an obligation to adopt the interpretation given by the ICJ in their dealings with the organization or any organ of the organization and what would the organization's responsibilities be in regard to the interpretation given? In any event, member states who were not parties to the case would not be bound by the interpretation, though the rulings of law may have some impact on them as well. Thus, orthodox settlement techniques are not really an effective method of securing interpretations of constitutions.

Second, some constitutions, such as those of the financial institutions, provide for binding determination by the supreme plenary organ as a body of last resort. The constitutions of the IMF, the IBRD, the IDA, the IFC, the MIGA and the IFAD prescribe that disputes relating to their interpretation between members and the organization or between members must first be referred to the Executive Directors, Executive Board, or Board of Directors as the case may be.[11] The decision given by this organ is final unless any member requires that the decision be referred to the Board of Governors or the Governing Council and the decision is then reversed.[12] Until then the organization may act, if it so wishes, on the basis of the decision. In the event the decision is reversed the decision of the Board of Governors or the Governing Council is final. There are

---

[10] For a discussion of the right of intervention pursuant to Article 63 and its implications generally see C. F. Amerasinghe, *Jurisdiction of International Tribunals* (2003) pp. 322*ff.*, Rosenne, *The Law and Practice of the International Court 1920–1996* (1997) pp. 1481*ff.*, Collier and Lowe, *The Settlement of Disputes in International Law* (1997) pp. 164*ff.*, Rosenne, *Intervention in the International Court of Justice* (1993) pp. 31*ff.* The discussion in these works of the ICJ Statute covers both Articles 62 and 63.

[11] See Article XXIX(a) of the IMF Articles of Agreement; Article IX(a) of the IBRD Articles of Agreement; Article X(a) of the IDA Articles of Agreement; Article VIII(a) of the IFC Articles of Agreement; Article 56(a) of the MIGA Convention; and Article II(i)(a) of the IFAD Agreement.

[12] See Article XXIX(b) of the IMF Articles of Agreement; Article IX(b) of the IBRD Articles of Agreement; Article X(b) of the IDA Articles of Agreement; Article VIII(b) of the IFC Articles of Agreement; Article 56(b) of the MIGA Convention; and Article II(i)(b) of the IFAD Agreement. On the issue whether the provisions of the IMF constitution violate the maxim *nemo judex in re sua* see Hexner, 'Interpretation by International Organizations of their Basic Instruments', 53 AJIL (1959) at pp. 367*ff.*

certain procedural safeguards prescribed. The Agreement establishing the Common Fund for Commodities has similar provisions on dispute settlement to those contained in the Articles of Agreement of the IBRD on which these provisions were modelled. However, in the event that a decision cannot be reached by the Fund's Governing Council, compulsory arbitration is prescribed.[13] Article IX(2) of the WTO constitution[14] vests the exclusive authority to interpret the constitution in the Ministerial Conference and the General Council. Presumably the decisions of the former would take precedence over those of the latter, in case of conflict.[15]

Third, some constitutions provide for binding final determination by the ICJ or by an arbitral tribunal as an alternative to the ICJ or by itself. The ILO Constitution provides in Article 37 that any question or dispute relating to its interpretation should be referred to the ICJ for decision. The UNESCO Constitution has a similar provision in Article XIV except that it also provides the alternative of reference to such arbitral

---

[13] See Articles 52 and 53 of the Agreement. Also see C. F. Amerasinghe, 'The Common Fund for Commodities', 7 *International Trade Law Journal* (1982–3) at p. 241. The commodity agreements generally vest the exclusive or final power of interpreting the agreements in the plenary organ: see, e.g., Article 62(1) of the International Cocoa Agreement 1986; Article 56(1) of the International Natural Rubber Agreement 1979; and Article 58(1) of the International Coffee Agreement 1983. The constitutions of the regional financial institutions generally follow the pattern of the IBRD Articles of Agreement: see Syz, *International Development Banks* (1974) pp. 84ff.

[14] See 33 ILM (1994) p. 15 at p. 19. The provisions of the GATT constitution are discussed in Bowett, *The Law of International Institutions* (1982) pp. 150–1. GATT, it will be recalled, preceded WTO.

[15] In the case of the IMF, the IBRD, the IFC and the IDA there is a special procedure where disputes arise between the organization and the members who have withdrawn or ceased to be members or between the organization and members during the liquidation or permanent suspension of the organization, as the case may be. These must be settled by a tribunal of three arbitrators. One is to be appointed by the organization, the second by the member, and an umpire is to be appointed by the President of the ICJ or such other authority as may have been prescribed by regulation adopted by the organization, unless the parties otherwise agree: see Article XXIX of the IMF Articles of Agreement; Article IX(c) of the IBRD Articles of Agreement; Article X(c) of the IDA Articles of Agreement; and Article VIII(c) of the IFC Articles of Agreement. Similar provisions appear generally in the constitutions of other financial institutions. The Agreement establishing the IFAD has substantially the same provision. In this case the third arbitrator (Chairman) is to be appointed by the two parties but failing such agreement he or she is to be appointed by the President of the ICJ or such other authority as may have been prescribed by regulations adopted by the Governing Council: see Article II(1)(c) of the IFAD Agreement. The Agreement establishing the Common Fund provides in Article 53 for arbitration in similar circumstances.

tribunal as the General Conference may determine.[16] Reference to the ICJ through the procedure for advisory opinions, because the constitution provides for this, would result in such opinions having a binding effect on the organization and members, unlike the case of the UN. In the case of the FAO[17] and the ICAO[18] the procedure prescribed is negotiation, failing which reference to the plenary organ or the Council respectively. Thereafter, an appeal lies to the ICJ, or alternatively in the case of the WHO to another body determined by the plenary organ; alternatively in the case of the ICAO to an *ad hoc* arbitral tribunal.[19] In the case of the FAO an advisory opinion of the ICJ, where such a procedure is chosen, would be binding on the parties and the organization. The prescription in the WHO Constitution[20] is similar to that of the FAO Constitution except that the alternative to the ICJ is another mode of settlement agreed upon by the parties. The provisions of the WMO Constitution[21] are similar to those of the FAO Constitution except that the appeal from the plenary organ is to an independent arbitrator appointed by the President of the ICJ unless the parties agree to another mode of settlement.

As between members, the constitutions of the ITU and the UPU establish certain binding procedures for settlement of disputes relating to their interpretation. Disputes between members must under Article 50 of the ITU Convention be settled either through diplomatic channels or according to procedures established by existing treaties between the members concerned or by any other method mutually agreed upon or failing these by arbitration. Such disputes must under Article 32 of the UPU Convention be settled by arbitration. On the other hand, no provision is made for settlement of disputes between the organization and its members in this regard. In the case of the ITU disputes between the organization and members may be referred to the ICJ under Article 96

---

[16] The latter technique has been used by the UNESCO: see the *UNESCO Constitution Case*, 16 AD (1949) p. 331.

[17] Article XVII(1).   [18] Article 84.

[19] Where the resort to the ICJ is not available and the parties cannot agree on the choice of the tribunal, Article 85 provides that each party to the dispute 'shall name a single arbitrator who shall name an umpire. If either contracting state party to the dispute fails to name an arbitrator within a period of three months from the date of the appeal, an arbitrator shall be named on behalf of that State by the President of the Council from a list of qualified and available persons maintained by the Council. If, within thirty days, the arbitrators cannot agree on an umpire, the President of the Council shall designate an umpire from the list previously referred to. The arbitrators and the umpire shall then jointly constitute an arbitral tribunal.'

[20] Article 75.   [21] Article 29.

of the Statute of the ICJ for advisory opinions which are not binding, because the GA of the UN has authorized this procedure for the ITU. But in the case of both the ITU and the UPU there is no restriction on the procedure adopted to settle disputes of this kind. Article 64 of the ICSID Convention requires that disputes between contracting states regarding the interpretation of the Convention which are not settled by negotiation be referred to the ICJ, unless another mode of settlement is agreed upon between the states concerned. The Convention is the Constitution of the ICSID. There is no specific provision for the settlement of disputes between the ICSID and contracting states, if such arise – which may be a lacuna. In this case the determination of the interpretation made initially by the ICSID or its relevant organ would continue to be valid, until a different interpretation is given under a mode of settlement agreed upon by the parties to the dispute and it is agreed that this mode is binding.

Fourth, some constitutions provide for non-binding opinions to be given, generally by the ICJ, but sometimes by another tribunal. Article 22(1) of the UNIDO Constitution prescribes in some detail the method of settlement of disputes between members concerning the interpretation of the constitution. Article 22(2) gives the organs of the organization power to request advisory opinions from the ICJ on any legal question arising within the scope of the organization's activities. These opinions would not be binding. Article 65 of the IMO Constitution requires that its interpretation be referred to the plenary organ for settlement or to another mode of settlement agreed upon by the parties. At the same time the article provides that nothing in it precludes any organ of the organization from settling any question of or dispute relating to interpretation of the Constitution that may arise during the exercise of its functions. Article 66 provides that any legal question that cannot be settled under the procedure of Article 65 should be referred to the ICJ for an advisory opinion. The opinion is advisory and, therefore, under the provisions of the ICJ Statute is not binding. Article XVII of the IAEA Statute prescribes as follows:

Any question or dispute concerning the interpretation or application of this statute which is not settled by negotiation shall be referred to the International Court of Justice in conformity with the statute of the court, unless the parties concerned agree on another mode of settlement.

Since an advisory opinion requested by the IAEA would have an effect in conformity with the Statute of the ICJ, it would not have binding effect as such. The Constitution of the ISA which is contained in Part V of the Law of the Sea Convention establishes an elaborate procedure for the settlement of disputes between members which could include disputes relating to the interpretation of the constitution of the ISA.[22] Article 191 of the Law of the Sea Convention, however, provides that on legal questions arising within the scope of activities of the Assembly or the Council of the ISA the Sea-Bed Disputes Chamber of the International Tribunal for the Law of the Sea shall give advisory opinions at their request. These opinions, given by an international tribunal other than the ICJ, are advisory and, therefore, not *per se* binding.

In general, advisory opinions by the ICJ may be sought by international organizations which are specialized agencies of the UN where the GA of the UN has authorized it under Article 96(2) of the Charter. The GA has given this authorization in the case of several specialized agencies, e.g., the UNESCO, the ILO and the WHO.

There are many regional and other closed organizations whose constitutional texts have not been examined here. Some of these organizations, namely the regional and other financial institutions, have in their constitutions provisions similar to those contained in the constitutional texts of some of the open financial organizations discussed here, while some closed organizations have very individualized provisions.

In certain disputes, those to which private individuals are parties or a private individual is one of the parties, national courts may be called upon to interpret the constitutions of international organizations in the course of settling such disputes.[23] In such situations the national courts concerned may give interpretations which are binding on the parties. This is not contrary to the provisions of constitutions where there are prescribed methods of settling disputes, because these provisions relate to disputes between members or between members and the organizations concerned regarding the interpretation of the constitutions. Because of immunities enjoyed by the various parties, it is unlikely that disputes between members or between members and the organizations

---

[22] See Articles 186*ff*. and Part XV of the Law of the Sea Convention. See also Adede, *The System for Settlement of Disputes under the United Nations Convention on the Law of the Sea* (1987) pp. 248*ff*.

[23] See, e.g., *J. H. Rayner Ltd. v. Department of Trade and Industry* [1989] 3 WLR 969, where the House of Lords (UK) interpreted the Sixth International Tin Agreement. For the IMF Articles of Agreement in the courts see Gold, *The Fund Agreement in the Courts* (vols. I–IV, 1962, 1982, 1986, 1989) *passim*.

will be litigated in national courts. However, in disputes to which a private individual or private individuals are parties, national courts are not precluded from adopting an interpretation given by a competent international organ or tribunal where such exists, and they may well choose to do this.

The process of interpretation

Difficulties with predictability

The interpretation of texts in international law is better described as an art and not as a science, although those who practice the art may often want to disguise the process of interpretation as a science. That is not to say that there are no rules or principles. Those there are, but when it comes to the choice of rules or principles to be applied in a particular set of circumstances, that choice is dependent on so many variables and imponderables that there can be serious disagreement and the answer to a problem of interpretation may appear subjective. Not only, for example, is there very often disagreement on whether the meaning of a text is clear or ambiguous, whether a particular meaning is the natural or plain meaning, what is the object and purpose of a document or what was the intention of the framers underlying the terms used, but interpreters may differ also, *inter alia*, on whether a textual interpretation should be adopted, whether a meaning should be given in the light of the object or purpose of a text to the exclusion of the plain and natural meaning or whether the intention of the parties to or framers of the instrument should be recognized at the expense of what may be regarded as the natural or plain meaning. Thus, much may be left to the preferences of the interpreter in terms of the goals sought to be achieved. More so than in other areas of the law, the end may determine the means adopted and the principle of interpretation chosen and its implementation may depend on the choice of the policy goal to be achieved. Nonetheless, it may be possible in the last analysis to identify a pattern in the choice of the principles applied by bodies whose decisions give authoritative interpretations and to this extent some guidance may be provided. The process and the difficulties referred to above in regard to interpretation of texts in international law is no different *in specie* from interpretation of texts in any system of law, particularly constitutional texts.

To illustrate the point that interpretation is not a science, some examples of the interpretation of constitutional texts may be examined.

Article II of the IBRD Articles of Agreement

In 1986 the Executive Directors of the IBRD were confronted with a problem relating to the interpretation of Article II of its Articles of Agreement caused by the introduction of the Special Drawing Right by the IMF and the Second Amendment of the Articles of Agreement of the Fund whereby the pre-existing basis for translating the term 'United States dollars of the weight and fineness in effect on July 1, 1944' into any currency was abolished. The issue of interpretation in this case was whether a text should be given its natural and ordinary meaning which seemed to be clear or whether a purely teleological interpretation should be adopted, perhaps on the basis that the text left a gap, because the situation that had arisen had not been contemplated at the time the Articles of Agreement were formulated. Article II, Section 2(a) of the Articles of Agreement of the IBRD defined its authorized capital 'in terms of United States dollars of the weight and fineness in effect on July 1, 1944'. The Executive Directors were called upon to interpret these words in the light of changed circumstances arising from the introduction by the IMF of the Special Drawing Right which was to replace the gold standard. Prefacing their discussion, among other things, with the statement that the General Counsel of the Bank had rendered a legal opinion[24] concluding in substance that, in the exercise of their statutory powers of interpretation, the Executive Directors may interpret references in the Articles to the 1944 dollar to mean either references to the last official value of the 1944 dollar in terms of current United States dollars (that is, $1.20635) or references to the Special Drawing Right established by the Fund, the Executive Directors, exercising their power of interpretation under Article IX of the Articles of Agreement, decided the issue

by reading the words 'United States dollars of the weight and fineness in effect on July 1, 1944' in Article II, Section 2(a), of the Articles of Agreement of the Bank to mean the Special Drawing Right (SDR) introduced by the Fund, as the SDR was valued in terms of United States dollars immediately before the introduction of the basket method of valuing the SDR on July 1, 1974, such value being 1.20635 United States dollars for one SDR.[25]

---

[24] This legal opinion is not available to the public but the conclusions of the opinion are substantially set out in Shihata, 'The "Gold Dollar" as a Measure of Capital Valuation after Termination of the Par Value System: The Case of IBRD Capital', 32 GYIL (1989) p. 55.

[25] World Bank, *Decisions of the Executive Directors under Article IX of the Articles of Agreement on Questions of Interpretation of the Articles of Agreement* (1991) p. 22 (Decision No. 13 of 14 October 1986).

It would seem that in regard to the changes in currency valuation that had occurred there was, apart from 'the 1944 gold dollar', another possible ordinary or natural meaning for the words of Article II, Section 2(a). The words could be taken as a reference to the current market price of 0.888671 grams of nine-tenths fine gold, expressed in US dollars or the current dollar equivalent of the 1944 dollar calculated by reference to the last established IMF par value for the US dollar (i.e., $1.20635).[26] However, this meaning would not have taken into account the Special Drawing Right (SDR), the creation of which and the abolition of the par value system had not been addressed at all by the framers of the IBRD constitution. Indeed, the IMF had to amend its constitution to permit the use of the SDR for various purposes. It was only by reference to a process of teleological interpretation, in other words by the application of the maxim *ut res magis valeat quam pereat*, that the meaning given to the words could be justified. In this case the solution adopted was intended to serve the objectives of the institution and its policies in the future in the light of developments that had taken place in the monetary sphere, rather than defeat or inhibit such objectives and policies. While the natural and ordinary meaning of the words interpreted was apparently not adopted and their purely literal sense was modified, a meaning was chosen which was more consistent with present day realities and fairer in its application to all the members of the institution. Nonetheless, what was done by the Executive Directors could be regarded as coming close to amendment of the constitution. Indeed, the possibility of future amendment was contemplated, with the interpretation adopted being regarded as valid till such amendment took place. In contrast to a literal or textual approach, a radical teleological approach to interpretation was taken, but the interpretation was by an authoritative body and has become binding and final. None could say that the result was not practical but this is surely an instance of the means serving the end.

First Admissions Case

In the *First Admissions Case*[27] the ICJ was called upon to interpret Article 4(1) of the Charter of the UN. The problem which arose here was whether the text was clear and what, in that case, was its ordinary and natural meaning, the issue resolving itself into what principles, both

---

[26] See Shihata, loc. cit. note 24 at p. 70 and p. 58.   [27] 1947–8 ICJ Reports p. 57.

main and subsidiary, should be applied to ascertaining meaning. This article provides that:

Membership in the United Nations is open to all other peace-loving States which accept the obligations contained in the present Charter and, in the judgment of the Organization, are able and willing to carry out these obligations.

Thus, five conditions are required for admission to membership of the UN, namely: (a) statehood; (b) being peace-loving; (c) acceptance of the obligations of the Charter; (d) ability to carry out these obligations; and (e) willingness to do so. The question raised was whether these conditions were exhaustive, in connection with the admission of certain states, some of the permanent members of the SC, particularly, concluding that they could make an assessment of whether it was politically desirable to admit them to membership. The majority of the Court came to the conclusion that

The natural meaning of the words used leads to the conclusion that these conditions constitute an exhaustive enumeration and are not merely stated by way of guidance or example. The provision would lose its significance and weight, if other conditions, unconnected with those laid down, could be demanded.[28]

Applying the maxim *expressio unius est exclusio alterius*, the Court decided that the meaning it gave was the natural and ordinary meaning of the words construed. A four-judge minority, however, found that 'the relevant provisions did not seem to be clear enough to provide a simple and unambiguous answer'[29] to the question raised. They applied the principle in these circumstances 'to the effect that no restriction upon this rule or principle (of freedom or liberty) can be presumed unless it can be clearly established, and in case of doubt it is the rule or principle of law which must prevail'.[30] Further, they used the *travaux préparatoires* to support their conclusion that other considerations than those listed could be taken into account by members of the organs concerned, though they had, among other things, to act in good faith. In this instance there was not only a disagreement as to whether the words being construed had a natural and plain meaning but the principles of interpretation applied by the nine judges in the majority and the six in the minority in order to give the text a meaning were different.

Article 14 of ICJ Statute
In the performance of their functions under Article 14 of the Statute of the ICJ concerning filling of vacancies on the Court the relevant organs

[28] *Ibid.* at p. 62.   [29] *Ibid.* at p. 83.   [30] *Ibid.* at p. 86.

of the UN had to make a decision on the interpretation of that article which stated that

[T]he Secretary-General shall within one month of the occurrence of the vacancy, proceed to issue the invitations provided for in Article 5.

The problem arose as a result of a vacancy occurring by death on the Court a few weeks before the term of office of the deceased judge and four other judges ended. The issue was whether the natural and ordinary meaning or a meaning intended to make the text of the article effective should be given. In a legal opinion provided by the Legal Counsel of the UN to the President of the Security Council the problem was stated as follows:

In the circumstances, a situation would result where a regular election to fill the seat concerned for a nine-year term of office, commencing on 6 February 1982, would in all probability be held before a casual election to fill the same seat for a brief period of a number of weeks ending on 5 February 1982. Because of the three-month time-limit between the dispatch of invitations for nomination of candidates and the election to fill the casual vacancy, as well as the preparation of the necessary documentation, that election could not take place at the earliest before the very end of November 1981 and a date in the middle of or late December would be more realistic. Regular elections are normally held in October of the year in which they take place.[31]

The language of the provision in the Statute seemed to be clear, but would have led, if taken literally, to an unreasonable result because of a lacuna. The advice given, which was followed, was:

Having in mind its responsibilities under Article 14 of the Statute of the Court to fix the date of an election to fill a casual vacancy, the Security Council may wish to consider whether that article necessarily applies in the circumstances described above. The legislative history of the article indicates that its purpose was to obviate extensive delays in the filling of casual vacancies and there is no indication it was meant to apply where only very brief periods are involved. In the present case no extensive delay would be occasioned by leaving the casual vacancy open, as the seat concerned would be filled during the regular elections for a term of office commencing on 6 February 1982. Having regard to the fact that periods of almost a year have in a number of cases elapsed between the occurrence of a casual vacancy and the election to fill it, the practice of the Security Council and of the General Assembly would also support a conclusion that, in the circumstances, the intention underlying Article 14 would equally

---

[31] 1981 UNJY at p. 146.

well be served by leaving the casual vacancy open and filling the seat at the regular election.[32]

Both legislative history and subsequent practice of the UN organ were cited to support an interpretation that was both practical and avoided an unreasonable result, though the language of the provision being construed seemed to be imperative. An exception to the provision was developed by finding a lacuna in the language and construing the text in the light of the *travaux préparatoires* and the practice of the organ. It would be difficult to dispute the wisdom of the solution but the case does show that natural and ordinary meanings are sometimes deliberately ignored in order to avoid inconvenient results.

Expenses Case

In the *Expenses Case*, four different approaches were taken to the problem of interpretation by the judges of the ICJ.[33] Three resulted in the same conclusion, one resulted in a different conclusion. The problem was what principle of interpretation should be applied in attributing meaning to the text, there being several different principles applied by the Court and different judges in the majority in reaching the same conclusion, while the judges in the minority reached a conclusion contrary to that of the majority though they applied the same principle as the Court. The issue was whether the term 'expenses' in Article 17 of the Charter was limited to 'regular' expenses or included expenditures incurred for the maintenance of international peace and security. Some member states had refused to finance the operations of the UNEF and the ONUC carried out pursuant to resolutions of the GA, particularly because they were operations not authorized by decisions of the SC under Chapter VII of the Charter. Article 17(2) provided that 'The expenses of the Organization shall be borne by the Members as apportioned by the General Assembly.' The majority on the Court had no doubt that, considering also the context of the Charter as a whole, the term 'expenses' had a plain and natural meaning, which included the expenditures in question. The majority only referred to the practice of the organization to support what it thought was the plain and natural

---

[32] *Ibid.*

[33] 1962 ICJ Reports p. 151. The application of principles of interpretation in this case was examined by me in 'The *United Nations Expenses Case* – A Contribution to the Law of International Organization', 4 IJIL (1964) p. 177.

meaning. Judges Winiarski and Koretsky,[34] dissenting, applied the same original principle applied by the majority, emphasizing the context of the Charter, but came to the opposite conclusion. Judge Spender arrived at the same conclusion as the majority but took a different route. He was of the opinion that the meaning of the text was not clear and unambiguous and, therefore, applied the principle of effectiveness, particularly because the Charter was a constitutional instrument. He was of the view that:

> It may with confidence be asserted that its provisions would received a broad and liberal interpretation unless the context of any particular provision requires, or there is to be found elsewhere in the Charter, something to compel a narrower and restricted interpretation . . . The stated purposes of the Charter should be the prime consideration in interpreting its texts.[35]

Judge Fitzmaurice, on the other hand, while finding, as Judge Spender did, that there were ambiguities, examined the *travaux préparatoires* and came to the same conclusion as the majority.[36] *Quot homines tot sententiae* – two sets of judges who took the same approach came to diametrically opposite conclusions and three sets of judges who took different approaches came to the same conclusion for different reasons.

What these examples show is that results of interpretation, particularly of constitutional texts, may be unpredictable and uncertain. They may depend on who is in a majority and to a large extent on a deliberate choice among several available policy goals which cannot sometimes be predicted with any certainty. But, as will be seen below, there may be more of a pattern than appears at first sight.

The Vienna Convention of 1969

Much has been written on the process and principles of interpretation of treaties in general.[37] The starting point is now the Vienna Convention

---

[34] 1962 ICJ Reports at pp. 230 and 284 respectively.
[35] *Ibid.* at p. 185.   [36] *Ibid.* at p. 209.
[37] See, e.g., Fitzmaurice, *The Law and Procedure of the International Court of Justice* (1986) pp. 42ff. and 337ff.; Rousseau, *Droit international public* (1971) vol. I, pp. 241ff.; de Visscher, *Problèmes d'interprétation judiciaire en droit international public* (1963); Sinclair, *The Vienna Convention on the Law of Treaties* (1984) pp. 114ff.; H. Lauterpacht, *The Development of International Law by the International Court* (1958) pp. 116ff.; McDougal, Lasswell and Miller, *The Interpretation of International Agreements and World Public Order* (1994); discussion in 43(1) AIDI (1950) pp. 366–460, 44(2) AIDI (1952) pp. 353–406, 46 AIDI (1956) pp. 317–49; Bos, 'Theory and Practice of Treaty Interpretation', 27 NILR (1980) p. 135; Yambrusic, *Treaty Interpretation* (1987).

on the Law of Treaties of 1969. Articles 31 and 32 state:

Article 31

General Rule of Interpretation

1 A treaty shall be interpreted in good faith in accordance with the ordinary meaning to be given to the terms of the treaty in their context and in the light of its object and purpose.
2 The context for the purpose of the interpretation of a treaty shall comprise in addition to the text, including its preamble and annexes:
   (a) any agreement relating to the treaty which was made between all the parties in connection with the conclusion of the treaty;
   (b) any instrument which was made by one or more parties in connection with the conclusion of the treaty and accepted by the other parties as an instrument related to the treaty.
3 There shall be taken into account, together with the context:
   (a) any subsequent agreement between the parties regarding the interpretation of the treaty or the application of its provisions;
   (b) any subsequent practice in the application of the treaty which establishes the agreement of the parties regarding its interpretation;
   (c) any relevant rules of international law applicable in the relations between the parties.
4 A special meaning shall be given to a term if it is established that the parties so intended.

Article 32

Supplementary means of interpretation

Recourse may be had to supplementary means of interpretation, including the preparatory work of the treaty and the circumstances of its conclusion, in order to confirm the meaning resulting from the application of article 21, or to determine the meaning when the interpretation according to article 31:
   (a) leaves the meaning ambiguous or obscure; or
   (b) leads to a result which is manifestly absurd or unreasonable.[38]

Apart from the requirement of good faith, which seems basic, in any case, interpretation is first to be: (i) according to the ordinary meaning of terms; but taking into account (ii) the context and (iii) the object and

---

[38] See 8 ILM (1969) p. 679 at pp. 691*ff*.

purpose of the treaty. Further, there are listed in paragraphs 2 and 3 six matters which either are included in the context or are to be considered together with the context, namely: (i) the preamble and annexes; (ii) an agreement made in connection with the conclusion of the treaty; (iii) an instrument made by one or more parties and accepted by the others as related to the treaty; (iv) a subsequent agreement regarding the interpretation of the treaty or its application; (v) subsequent practice; and (vi) rules of international law. This means that the primary rule of natural meaning is to be applied in the light of not only the context, but also the object and purposes of the treaty and the six other considerations referred to above. In other words an abstract natural meaning may be modified by any of the considerations referred to in the Convention. Preparatory work (not included among these matters) and the circumstances of the conclusion of the treaty, on the other hand, are no more than supplementary means of interpretation to be resorted to only secondarily and in certain circumstances.[39] The Convention thus gives the object and purpose of the treaty and the subsequent practice a place as part, so to speak, of the ordinary meaning. Thus, the principles of effectiveness and of subsequent practice are applicable as primary tools in the process of interpretation. The preparatory work, on the other hand, is secondary, thus reducing the importance of the true or actual intention of the parties, as such.[40]

Article 5 of the Vienna Convention makes it applicable to the constituent instruments of international organizations. However, although the Vienna Convention is in force and has been ratified by a plethora of states, there may be serious questions as to how it can bind international organizations which are not parties to the Convention and whether the ICJ is bound to apply it when giving an advisory opinion which is not a judgment pronounced in a contentious proceeding in respect of states who may be parties to the Convention. It must be recognized, on the other hand, that the argument may be made that the provisions on interpretation of the Convention reflect an established or emerging customary law, particularly by virtue of the Convention's being followed in this regard.[41]

---

[39] For an examination of how the practice of the ICJ and other tribunals conforms or not to the Vienna Convention on the Law of Treaties, see Sinclair, note 37 pp. 119ff.

[40] See also now on treaties in general, the *Qatar and Bahrain Case*, 1995 ICJ Reports at pp. 21ff.

[41] The Vienna Convention of 1986 on the Law of Treaties between States and International Organizations or between International Organizations, 25 ILM (1986)

The jurisprudence

An analysis of the precedents on constitutional interpretation will shed some light on how the task of interpretation has been approached by international judicial or quasi-judicial organs, which have been called upon to interpret the constitutions of international organizations.[42]

While the ordinary and natural meaning may have been emphasized in theory, there is often difficulty in ascertaining it. The PCIJ and ICJ have apparently adopted as their cardinal rule of interpretation, even in relation to constitutions, that words should be read, in their context, in their natural and ordinary sense, unless they are ambiguous or, so read, lead to an unreasonable result.[43] However, as was noted by Judge Spender, in a separate opinion in the *Expenses Case*:

p. 543, has similar provisions to those contained in the Vienna Convention on the Law of Treaties of 1969, but it does not apply to the constitutions of international organizations which are treaties between states. The latter convention made the rules incorporated in the former convention specifically applicable to international organizations to the extent they were incorporated in the latter convention: see, e.g., Isak and Loibl, 'United Nations Conference on the Law of Treaties between States and International Organizations or between International Organizations', 38 OZOR (1987/88) p. 49; Gaja, 'A "New" Vienna Convention on Treaties between States and International Organizations or between International Organizations: A Critical Commentary', 58 BYIL (1987) p. 267; Morgenstern, 'The Convention on the Law of Treaties between States and International Organizations or between International Organizations', in Dinstein and Tabori (eds.), *International Law at a Time of Perplexity: Essays in Honour of Shabtai Rosenne* (1989) p. 435.

[42] Earlier studies include: Gordon, 'The World Court and the Interpretation of Constitutive Treaties', 59 AJIL (1965) p. 794; E. Lauterpacht, 'The Development of the Law of International Organization by the Decisions of International Tribunals', 152 *Hague Recueil* (1976-IV) p. 387 at pp. 414ff. That the constitutive text of an international organization has a dual nature arising from the fact that it is a constitution in addition to being a multilateral convention has never been denied nor has it been gainsaid that because of this dual nature a somewhat special approach may be required in respect of interpreting certain aspects of the constitutive texts. See on this subject, e.g., C. de Visscher, *Problèmes d'interprètation judiciaire en droit international public* (1963) p. 143; Rideau, *Jurisdictions internationales et côntrole respect du des traités constitutifs des organisations internationales* (1969) pp. 4ff.; Quadri, *Diritto Internazionale Pubblico* (1974) pp. 527ff.; Bastid, *Les traités dans la vie internationale* (1985) pp. 127ff.; Reuter, *Introduction to the Law of Treaties* (1989) pp. 73ff.; Elias, *The Modern Law of Treaties* (1974) pp. 71ff.; Neri, *Sull' interpretazione dei traitati nel diritto internazionali* (1958) pp. 286ff.; McDougal and Gardner, 'The Veto and the Charter, an Interpretation for Survival', 60 *Yale LJ* (1951) p. 254; Focsaneau, 'Le droit interne de L'Organisation des Nations Unies', AFDI (1957) at pp. 326ff.; Tunkin, 'The Legal Character of the U.N.', 119 *Hague Recueil* (1966-III) at pp. 1ff.; Conforti, *Le Nazione Unite* (1986) pp. 10ff.; Martin Martinez, *National Sovereignty and International Organizations* (1996) pp. 75ff. and the other writers cited in the footnotes thereto.

[43] See, e.g., *Polish Postal Service in Danzig*, PCIJ Series B No. 11 at p. 39; *Second Admissions Case*, 1950 ICJ Reports at p. 8; *First Admissions Case*, 1947–8 ICJ Reports at p. 63.

This injunction is sometimes a counsel of perfection. The ordinary and natural sense of words may at times be a matter of considerable difficulty to determine. What is their ordinary and natural sense to one may not be so to another. The interpreter not uncommonly has, what has been described as, a personal feeling towards certain words and phrases. What makes sense to one may not make sense to another. Ambiguity may lie hidden in the plainest and most simple of words even in their natural and ordinary meaning. Nor is it always evident by what legal yardstick words read in their natural and ordinary sense may be judged to produce an unreasonable result.[44]

Judge Spender consequently placed emphasis on teleological canons of interpretation in conjunction with the meaning of the text in its context, particularly for constitutions such as the Charter of the UN, at the same time playing down the importance of actual intention and the relevance of the *travaux préparatoires*. This approach may seem to be in keeping with the provisions of the Vienna Convention on the Law of Treaties. On the other hand, perhaps in conflict with what is stated in the Vienna Convention on the Law of Treaties, he did not attach much significance to the subsequent practice of the organization. He stated:

Moreover the *intention* of the parties at the time when they entered into an engagement will not always – depending upon the nature and subject-matter of the engagement – have the same importance. In particular in the case of a multilateral treaty such as the Charter the intention of its original Members, except such as may be gathered from its terms alone, is beset with evident difficulties. Moreover, since from its inception it was contemplated that other States would be admitted to membership so that the Organization would, in the end, comprise 'all other peace-loving States which accept the obligations contained in the Charter' (Article 4), the intention of the framers of the Charter appears less important than intention in many other treaties where the parties are fixed and constant and where the nature and subject-matter of the treaty is different... The stated purposes of the Charter should be the prime consideration in interpreting its text... Despite current tendencies to the contrary the first task of the Court is to look, not at the *travaux préparatoires* or the practice which hitherto has been followed within the Organization, but at the terms of the Charter itself. What does it provide to carry out its purposes?[45]

---

[44] 1962 ICJ Reports at p. 184.

[45] *Ibid.* at pp. 184–5. Judge Spender repeated this view in the *South West Africa Cases (Preliminary Objections)*, 1962 ICJ Reports at p. 515, in a joint dissenting opinion (with Judge Fitzmaurice). The Court has also adverted to the requirement that in the interpretation of the Covenant of the LN too much importance must not be placed on *intention* (in contrast to the text): see the *Namibia Case*, 1971 ICJ Reports at p. 28.

Judge Spender gave its rightful place to the object and purpose of a constitution such as the Charter, placing it on the same threshold as the plain and ordinary meaning and also was correct in reducing the importance of the preparatory work. However, he may have erred in downplaying the role of subsequent practice.

The natural and ordinary meaning in context

As already stated, ascertainment of the natural and ordinary meaning in context has been accepted by the PCIJ and ICJ as its cardinal rule of interpretation. In the *Second Admissions Case* the ICJ stressed that the natural and ordinary meaning must be given to words 'in the context in which they occur' and not in the abstract.[46] Hence, it is not a narrow and quasi-literal interpretation of words, phrases or articles, taken in isolation, that is envisaged, but one related to the constitution as a whole. In both the *First Admissions Case* and the *Second Admissions Case* the Court applied the principle in interpreting the provisions of the Charter relating to admission of members. In the *IMCO Case*, where the Court had to interpret the term 'the largest shipowning nations' in the IMCO constitution, the fundamental principle that words must be read 'in their natural and ordinary meaning, in the sense which they would normally have in their context'[47] was clearly stated. There was no disagreement on the Court that this principle was applicable in the first place. The Court also made it clear that the rule meant that the whole of the text must be presumed to have some significance, so that an interpretation which would render part of it redundant was to be rejected.[48] However, it is not in cases where this principle can be successfully applied that differences of opinion usually arise. It is when other considerations are involved that the principle of the natural and ordinary meaning in context receives some qualification.

The object and purpose – teleology

It is not surprising that, even before the Vienna Convention on the Law of Treaties was drafted, the ICJ indicated that the principle underlying the text or the object and purpose of the treaty must be considered together with the context in giving the text 'a natural and ordinary

---

[46] 1950 ICJ Reports at p. 8. The same basic principle was affirmed in the *First Admissions Case*, 1974–8 ICJ Reports at p. 63.
[47] 1960 ICJ Reports at p. 195.   [48] *Ibid.* at p. 160.

meaning'.[49] For instance, the issue in the *IMCO Case* whether the term 'largest ship-owning nations' meant nations having the largest registered tonnage of beneficially owned ships or simply the largest registered tonnage regardless of beneficial ownership was decided in accordance with this prescription by focusing on the need to ensure maritime safety as the purpose of the provision concerned. Consequently the latter meaning was selected.

In the *IMCO Case* the term 'largest ship-owning nations' may have been ambiguous or unclear, thus triggering consideration of the object and purposes of the constitution. It has been said that objects and purposes may be considered only when the meaning of a text is ambiguous or where giving the text its natural and ordinary meaning would lead to an unreasonable result.[50] However, while in some cases of reference to objects and purposes as such to establish a meaning it may be possible to establish one of these conditions for the incidence of the exception, there may be circumstances where the interpreter goes more directly to the object and purposes because it is essential for the efficient functioning of the organization that a meaning established in this manner be adopted. This was apparently what was done in the case discussed above concerning the valuation of the IBRD's capital. This may also be the case where constitutional powers are implied. These are situations in which what appears to be the ordinary or natural meaning has been modified in the light of the objects and purposes of the constitution.

It has been said that the principle of effectiveness has two aspects.[51] The first embraces the rule that all provisions of a treaty must be supposed to have been intended to have significance and be necessary to convey the intended meaning so that an interpretation which reduces some part of the text to the status of a pleonasm or mere surplusage is *prima facie* not acceptable – 'la règle de l'effet utile'. The second covers

---

[49] *Ibid.* at pp. 160–1.

[50] See Fitzmaurice, note 37 p. 345. There are some other cases decided particularly by the PCIJ in which the objects and purposes of the constitution were used as a basis for interpreting it: see *Nomination of the Netherlands Workers' Delegate Case*, PCIJ Series B No. 1 at pp. 23, 25; *European Commission on the Danube Case*, PCIJ Series B No. 14 at p. 80; *Competence of the ILO to Regulate Conditions of Labour in Agriculture Case*, PCIJ Series B Nos. 2 and 3 at pp. 23 and 57; separate opinions in the *Second Admissions Case*, 1950 ICJ Reports at p. 18 *per* Judge Alvarez, at p. 23 *per* Judge Azevedo; and the *Namibia Case*, 1971 ICJ Reports at pp. 30, 50. See also the *Aerial Incident Case*, 1959 ICJ Reports at p. 139.

[51] See Berlia, 'Contribution à l'interprétation des traités', 114 *Hague Recueil* (1965-I) at pp. 306*ff.*; Thirlway. 'The Law and Procedure of the International Court of Justice 1960–1989', 62 BYIL (1991) at p. 44.

the rule that the instrument as a whole, and each of its provisions, must be taken to have been intended to achieve some end and that an interpretation which would make the text ineffective to achieve the object in view is *prima facie* suspect – 'la règle de l'efficacité'.

The first rule is really subsumed under the rule of the ordinary and natural meaning contextually derived. It is the second rule that pertains to effectiveness and involves giving the object and purpose an important place in the interpretative technique. The maxim *ut res magis valeat quam pereat* also accurately captures the spirit of the principle of effectiveness.

The doctrine of implied powers is a good example of the application of the teleological principle to the interpretation of constitutions, even where the contextual ordinary and natural meaning may lead to a different result which may not be unreasonable in the circumstances. What this doctrine tries to do is provide for a liberal and progressive approach to the powers of organizations even though constitutions may be silent on the particular powers concerned, in order to enable organizations effectively and purposefully to carry out their functions. Three examples of how powers have been implied may be given. In the *Reparation Case* the power of the UN to espouse claims on behalf of their staff members was in issue. The ICJ stated the general principle as follows:

Under international law, the Organization must be deemed to have those powers which, though not expressly provided in the Charter, are conferred upon it by necessary implication as being essential to the performance of its duties.[52]

In consequence it concluded:

Upon examination of the character of the functions entrusted to the Organization and of the nature of the missions of its agents, it becomes clear that the capacity of the Organization to exercise a measure of functional protection of its agents arises by necessary intendment out of the Charter.[53]

In the *Personal Work of Employers Case* the issue was whether the ILO had an implied power to regulate the work of employers. The PCIJ concluded that in the constitution of the ILO the framers

clearly intended to give the ILO a very broad power of co-operating with them in respect of measures to be taken in order to assure humane conditions of labour and the protection of workers. It is not conceivable that they intended to prevent the Organization from drawing up and proposing measures essential to the accomplishment of that end. The Organization, however, would be so

[52] 1949 ICJ Reports at p. 174.   [53] *Ibid.* at p. 182.

prevented if it were incompetent to propose for the protection of wage-earners a regulative measure to the efficacious working of which it was found to be essential to include to some extent work done by employers.[54]

In the *Effect of Awards Case* the ICJ had to decide, among other things, whether the UN had the implied power to establish an administrative tribunal to settle disputes between the organization and its staff. The Court held that

the power to establish a tribunal, to do justice as between the Organization and the staff members, was essential to ensure the efficient working of the Secretariat...Capacity to do this arises by necessary intendment out of the Charter.[55]

Indeed, though the issue of implied powers of organizations has been brought before the PCIJ and the ICJ on several occasions,[56] it is only in the *Competence of the ILO to Regulate Agricultural Production Case*[57] that the Court has refused to imply a power, that is, the power of the ILO

---

[54] PCIJ Series B No. 13 at p. 18.   [55] 1954 ICJ Reports at p. 57.

[56] See, e.g., apart from the cases discussed above, the *European Commission on the Danube Case*, PCIJ Series B No. 14 at p. 64; and the *Expenses Case*, 1962 ICJ Reports at pp. 159, 167–8. Implying powers is clearly a matter of interpretation. More will be said about implication of powers in Chapter 3. On implied powers of IGOs see Rouyer-Hameray, *Les Compétences implicites des organisations internationales* (1962); Makarczyk, 'The International Court of Justice on the Implied Powers of International Organizations', in *Essays in Honour of M. Lachs* (1984) pp. 500–18; Simon, *L'interprétation judiciaire des traités d'organisations internationales* (1981) pp. 391*ff.*; Chaumont, 'La signification du principe de spécialité des organisations internationales', in *Mélanges H. Rolin* (1964) pp. 55*ff.*; Martinez Sanseroni, 'Consentiemento del Estado y Organizaciones Internacionales', 37 REDI (1985) pp. 45–60; and sources cited in Chapter 3 below in the section entitled 'The consequences of international personality'.

[57] PCIJ Series B No. 3. A 'primary result or purpose' test was used but this has never been applied thereafter. The CJEC has also dealt with the implication of powers but in contrast with the decisions of the PCIJ and ICJ the implication of powers occupies a lesser place in its decisions. The reason is that the treaties setting up the three Communities permit the exercise of some powers in situations where they have not been expressly granted (ECSC Treaty, Article 95; EEC Treaty, Article 235; and Euratom Treaty, Article 203). Nonetheless, in a few instances the Court has had resort to the doctrine of implied powers. In *Fédération Charbonnière de Belgique* v. *The High Authority* (CJEC Case 8/55 [1954–56] ECR p. 245) the Court based certain powers of the ECSC on the objects of the constituent treaty. It did this, however, in a subsidiary way; express powers were the main basis of implication. In the *ERTA Case* (CJEC Case 22/70, 47 ILR p. 274) the Court emphasized the necessity of having 'regard to the whole scheme of the Treaty' establishing the EEC and invoked the 'objectives of the Treaty as regards transport'. The Court concluded that the organization possessed the power to enter into agreements relating to transport (at p. 304). That conclusion was also supported by an implication based on express powers (*ibid.*). In *Italian Government* v. *the High Authority* (CJEC Case 20/59 [1960] ECR p. 325) the Court was inclined to consider the

to regulate agricultural production. While courts and organs may not imply a power where it is denied by a constitution, when they do imply powers, they have not been concerned with the issue of the natural and ordinary meaning or whether such a meaning would lead to an unreasonable result. Rather they have directly invoked teleological principles of interpretation, without referring to an otherwise unreasonable result.

Both the PCIJ and the ICJ have stated that the power implied must bear some relationship to the functioning of the organization, the performance of its duties, or the achievement of its purposes. Thus, the doctrine of implied powers is not applied without some constraints. It cannot be used as a tool to give an organization power to act as it may want or to assume powers capriciously. The doctrine of effectiveness does not have an unlimited application. It has clearly not been used to give an organization powers which it obviously does not have. Also, though the IMF Board of Directors (a different organ from the PCIJ or the ICJ) could have on more than one occasion 'interpreted' its Articles of Agreement so as to give the IMF certain powers by improperly resorting to the principle of effectiveness, the IMF chose to have the Articles amended. The Articles have been amended three times.

Around the principle of effectiveness there appear to have been built certain negative presumptions of interpretation.[58] For instance, it has been judicially stated, though not by the ICJ, that there is no presumption that the sovereignty of states should not be restricted.[59] It

---

doctrine, but it found that in the specific situation the factors invoked ('general economic policy', 'the basic principle of the Treaty') did not permit any implication. The Court adopted the same attitude in *Netherlands Government v. The High Authority* (CJEC Case 25/59 [1960] ECR p. 355). The implication of powers by the CJEC, though based on the objects of the treaty, has been most often related to express powers. This could be a fairly limited approach to the application of the teleological principle. See also the *European Laying-up Fund Agreement Case*, 2 *Common Market Law Reports* (1977) at p. 295. On the CJEC's approach to the implication of powers see, e.g., Giardina, 'The Rule of Law and Implied Powers in the European Communities', 1 *Italian Yearbook of International Law* (1975) p. 99; Nicolaysen, 'Zur Theorie von den implied powers in den Europäischen Gemeinschaften', 1 *Europarecht* (1966) p. 129; Skubiszewski, 'Implied Powers of International Organizations', in Dinstein and Tabori (eds.), *Time of Perplexity* at pp. 865ff.

[58] See the discussion in E. Lauterpacht, loc. cit. note 42 at pp. 432ff.

[59] See the *Personal Work of Employers Case*, PCIJ Series B No. 13 at p. 22; the *European Commission on the Danube Case*, PCIJ Series B No. 14 at p. 36. *Contra* apparently the *UNESCO Constitution Case*, 16 AD (1949) at p. 336, which was a decision by a special arbitral tribunal established to interpret a provision of the UNESCO constitution and in which the reference to the restriction of sovereignty was made in a subsidiary

has also been implied in the decisions of the ICJ that the delegated nature of a power does not require that it be restrictively interpreted.[60] There may also be good grounds for limiting the relevance of the maxim *expressio unius est exclusio alterius*, especially in the sphere of implied powers.[61] On the other hand, there are situations in which the maxim has been invoked to restrict discretionary powers, among other things.[62]

Subsequent practice

The Vienna Convention on the Law of Treaties gives subsequent practice a substantive place in the ascertainment of the ordinary and natural meaning: subsequent practice may be taken into account in establishing such meaning. Subsequent practice may support what is the ordinary meaning of a text. It may also have an impact on what appears to be the ordinary meaning of a text, even though the text is not ambiguous. This subject is discussed in Chapter 14 as concerned with amendment. Where a text is ambiguous, subsequent practice could help to establish one of the several meanings all of which may be described as ordinary. The position may be the same where the ordinary meaning leads to an unreasonable result. On the other hand, where a text is silent and subsequent practice is used to fill in lacunae, the text is virtually altered when such practice is invoked in interpretation, but this seems to be a permissible use of practice.

In most of the decided cases subsequent practice has been resorted to in order to support a meaning already selected for other reasons. In

manner after the interpretation adopted had been arrived at for different reasons. See also the legal opinion given to the UN Secretariat on the interpretation of Article 19 of the Charter by the Legal Counsel of the UN where the statement was made after a teleological interpretation had already been given of the article that in case of doubt the provisions of the Charter 'should be interpreted so as to be as little burdensome' to the member states as possible: 1983 UNJY at p. 169.

[60] See, e.g., the *Reparation Case*; and the *Effect of Awards Case*. In both these cases the Court implicitly disagreed with Judge Hackworth who dissented on this ground: 1949 ICJ Reports at p. 198 and 1954 ICJ Reports at p. 80.

[61] See by implication the *Effect of Awards Case*, 1954 ICJ Reports p. 47; the *Expenses Case*, 1962 ICJ Reports p. 151; and the *Namibia Case*, 1971 ICJ Reports p. 16. In the former case Judge Hackworth, dissenting, stated that the maxim should apply in order to limit the powers of the GA of the UN, whereas the Court decided that such powers were not limited in the way indicated by Judge Hackworth.

[62] See the *First Admissions Case* 1947–8 ICJ Reports at pp. 57, 62–3; the *IMCO Case*, 1960 ICJ Reports at p. 150.

this situation the practice is of probative value. In the *Second Admissions Case* it was said that the organs responsible under the Charter for the admission of members 'have consistently interpreted the text in the sense that the General Assembly can decide to admit only on the basis of a recommendation of the Security Council'.[63] The evidence of practice of the GA and the SC was used to support an interpretation already adopted for other reasons.

However, in an opinion of the ICJ in the *Namibia Case* the Court used the practice of the Security Council and the General Assembly directly to give meaning to provisions of the Charter, where, it would appear, there were gaps in the language. Abstention by a permanent member of the SC was held not to constitute a bar to the adoption of resolutions under Article 27(3) of the Charter. This conclusion was supported by reference to presidential rulings and the positions taken by members of the SC, particularly the permanent members,[64] which constituted the practice. On the issue of whether the GA had competence in the sphere of mandates, it was held that the refusal of the GA to establish a temporary subsidiary organ to assist in the supervision of mandates did not mean that under the Charter it had no power to supervise mandates, because the refusal did not amount to a collective pronouncement that such power did not exist.[65] Clearly, the fact that the GA had continued to exercise supervisory functions over mandates supported such an interpretation. In this case the practice was constitutive of an interpretation.

In most of the decided cases it was possible to identify a recurrence or repetition of conduct on the part of the organ which constituted the practice to which reference was made. However, in the *European Commission on the Danube Case*[66] the practice relied upon occurred only on one occasion. In the *IMCO Case*[67] the practice had occurred once but this

---

[63] 1950 ICJ Reports at p. 9. See also, e.g., the *Competence of the ILO to Regulate Conditions of Labour in Agriculture Case*, PCIJ Series B Nos. 2 and 3 at pp. 38–41; the *Personal Work of Employers Case*, PCIJ Series B No. 13 at pp. 19–20; the *European Commission on the Danube Case*, PCIJ Series B No. 14 at pp. 57–8; the *First Admissions Case*, 1947–48 ICJ Reports at p. 63; the *UNESCO Constitution Case*, 16 AD (1949) at p. 335; the *IMCO Case*, 1960 ICJ Reports at pp. 167–8; and the *Expenses Case*, 1962 ICJ Reports at pp. 160*ff.*

[64] 1971 ICJ Reports at p. 22.

[65] *Ibid.* at p. 36. See also the case mentioned above of the interpretation of Article 14 of the Statute of the ICJ by the Security Council where practice was used to interpret a text: 1981 UNJY at p. 146.

[66] PCIJ Series B No. 14 at pp. 57–8.   [67] 1960 ICJ Reports at pp. 167–8.

was the only relevant occasion. In both these cases the practice was not relied on by itself to establish a meaning but was only used as evidence of a meaning clearly determined by other means. Yet, there is no clear indication in the jurisprudence whether practice must in essence consist of repeated conduct. By contrast in the *Namibia Case*, where practice was relied on to establish a meaning, the relevant practice had been repeated over a long period. It would seem that in general, where practice constitutes an interpretation, it must be repeated and consistent. Very rarely and for good reasons only something less than that may have an effect.

There is no mention further in the jurisprudence whether there should be a conviction that the practice pursued is obligatory,[68] as is required for the formation of customary international law. In the case of the practice of an international organization the conduct in issue is generally that of an organ of the organization which may or may not be determined by a sense of obligation. It would seem that in the absence of a jurisprudential analysis in the cases, the practice required to establish the meaning of a provision of a constitution would generally not be based on a sense of obligation but would arise from the exercise of discretionary power. What is important is that the conduct has been pursued by the organ in the belief that it was acting lawfully under the constitutive instrument. The *opinio juris* in this case is usually not a sense of obligation but a sense that the practice or conduct is lawful or not unlawful under the governing provisions of the constitution.

The practice is that of the organ concerned. However, there are problems connected with the issue of the measure of support for the practice. While the organ is generally composed of representatives of member states, one question is whether what is relevant is not the views of the members of the organ *per se* but the resulting conduct of the organ taken as an entity in itself, the size of the majority in favour of the practice not being relevant provided the conduct constitutes an act of the organ as a body and is attributable to the organ. Where a practice works as an amendment, the matter, as pointed out above, concerns amendment and will be discussed in Chapter 14 in that connection. There are three possibilities, where what may be legitimately regarded as a practice does

---

[68] But see the discussion by Judge Fitzmaurice in a separate opinion in the *Expenses Case*, 1962 ICJ Reports at p. 201.

not amend a text but fills in lacunae or gives meaning to a text when it is ambiguous or giving the natural and ordinary meaning would lead to an unreasonable result:

(i)   the practice may be unanimously supported by the membership of the organ;

(ii) the practice may be supported consistently by a large majority in the organ, falling short of unanimity; or

(iii) the practice may be supported only by a majority, there being a substantial minority against it.

In the case of (i), there seems to be no theoretical or practical problem. The practice would constitute an interpretation without difficulty because there is full agreement among members of the organ. Where there is a *large* majority in favour of the practice (situation (ii) above), it is arguable that a small obstinate minority, whether it is always the same minority or not, cannot obstruct an interpretation given by the membership of the organ. The reason for this will be discussed below in connection with the theoretical basis of practice as a source of interpretation. In the *Namibia Case* the practice, it would seem, had unanimous support (or, at any rate, was implicitly opposed by only a small minority) and, thus, had legal effect.

In the case of support only by a simple majority, as in (iii) above, the situation is more difficult. It may be argued that a divisive practice (i.e., one strongly opposed by a substantial minority) cannot have the same force as one generally accepted, even though the organ in question must act on the majority view. If this were not so, the rights of the minority would be determined by the majority. Acceptance of majority votes does not commit dissenters to the *principle* on which such a majority acts, although the organization necessarily acts in the given case or cases on the basis of that principle. The position may change with time and repetition, as members adjust themselves to a new practice but the mere fact of a majority vote, irrespective of its size, cannot be sufficient to establish a practice. This should be so whether such practice is used by courts or tribunals as a means of interpretation or by organs as a similar means in the course of their work, because in both cases an organ authorized to do so is interpreting the texts. The interpretation by the organ would in these circumstances not be an appropriate one. Although in theory it may be possible to find arguments against the position stated above, it makes good practical sense and can also be justified in theory.

As for the juridical basis of practice,[69] one explanation, perhaps the most attractive, is that practice as a means of interpretation of constitutions has an independent juridical basis. Practice becomes relevant and may be resorted to as a means of interpretation purely because it is the practice of the organization. This is the simplest and most convenient explanation and in cases where a practice has the substantial support of the member States, is a sufficient basis for the acceptance of practice as a source of interpretation.

Arguments may be made to base the use of subsequent practice in a broad sense in the interpretation of constitutions on agreement or consent, although this may have to be implied. It will be recalled that Article 31(3)(b) of the Vienna Convention of 1969 does associate practice as a source of interpretation with agreement. One argument is that, since the parties to the constitution, whether they are original parties or become parties subsequently, have agreed at the time of becoming parties to the constitution to the mechanisms of decision-making by the organization, they have also agreed to accept the decisions of the organization taken under the constitution, even though they have voted against or may disagree with such decisions, as reflecting *proper* conduct on the part of the organization. Hence, that a member state is in an opposing minority and does not immediately agree to or opposes a decision creating practice may be of no consequence, because ultimately the member concerned had agreed, by implication and at the time it became a party to the constitutive treaty, to accept the decision as reflecting the will of the organization, even though it disagreed with it at the time it was made. This argument would contradict what has been stated above concerning the protection of a substantial minority.

If practice is to be based on agreement or consent, there is a problem with this approach which must be addressed. While generally accepted practice may in any event be based on agreement or consensus in respect of the specific practice, there may be an argument against the use of a practice sponsored by a majority (not substantial), required as it may be by the constitution, as evidence for the interpretation of a constitutional text. Judge Fitzmaurice, among others, has made this point in the *Expenses Case*. The argument is that such a practice has in no way been agreed to by the minority which does not accept it, especially if it is a

---

[69] See the interesting discussion in E. Lauterpacht, loc. cit. note 42 at pp. 460*ff*. He is of the view that agreement, acquiescence and estoppel are not adequate bases for practice. See also the difficulties raised by Judges Spender and Fitzmaurice in the *Expenses Case*: 1962 ICJ Reports at pp. 191, 192, 201.

sizeable one, because, while those in the minority at the time of becoming parties to the constitutive treaty entered into commitments based on a treaty, they are not willing to see those changed simply because a majority of members so wish; in other words, they did not in fact agree, at the time of becoming parties to the constitutive instrument, to amendments to the treaty by the decision-making process of the organization involving only a majority vote but only to giving effect to or implementing the treaty by this method.

While a practice may not 'change' a constitutional provision in the sense of amending it, a substantial minority may be entitled to maintain that it did not implicitly agree to 'development' of the text against its will. The same argument may not be applied to a small minority. There is an element of implied agreement in the case of the latter, to the extent that it cannot obstruct the functioning of the organization. To this consequence which endows a practice with legality all the members may be presumed to have agreed at the time of becoming parties to the constitution, regardless of whether they disagreed as part of a small minority with the specific practice at the time the decision or decisions were taken to follow the practice.

It makes no difference that the practice has or has not been decided upon specifically and expressly as an interpretation of the constitution or that the issue has or has not been addressed. As the ICJ said in the *Expenses Case*, the relevant organ of the institution in the first place, at least, interprets its constitution and this interpretation, however it is done, would stand, unless overruled by a higher competent body, so that the adoption, whether by explicit or implicit interpretation, of practices by organs within the limits described above could be regarded as having been consented to by members at the time they became parties to the constitutive instrument.

The examples of practice used in interpretation, such as in the *Namibia Case*, it must be acknowledged, cannot really be said to have amounted to amendments of the constitution. As regards the practice of the GA referred to in that case, it did not necessarily contradict the language of the Charter of the UN but could be regarded as implementing, developing and filling in gaps in the Charter. As regards the voting in the SC, the position may be somewhat more difficult. Undoubtedly, if practice even with general agreement or consensus gives rise to an interpretation that contradicts and, therefore, amends the constitution of an institution, because it continues to be adopted as an appropriate interpretation, this is a question which pertains to amendment and not to interpretation as such. But it is not clear that practice that contradicted an express text was accepted as of interpretative value. Although the interpretative practice surrounding the voting provisions of Article 27(3) of the UN Charter, for instance, could be regarded as having given rise to an amendment, it has not been and need not be treated as such. A case may be made that the practice of treating an abstention as not giving rise to the absence of an affirmative vote in regard to the votes of the permanent members of the SC is not a contradiction amounting to an amendment of Article 27(3). Had the negative vote of a permanent member been disregarded in the tallying of votes, such a practice would have been in contradiction of the express terms of the Article and its adoption would have amounted to an amendment. The practice in fact adopted resulted in giving the meaning 'not negative' to the term 'affirmative' which is less removed and may be construed as development rather than amendment. Generally, it may be said that practice of interpretative value does not contradict or amend a text as such and thus can be regarded as being based on prior agreement where it is used to interpret a text.

Where the organ is not a plenary organ but of limited membership, practice relating to its functions developed with the necessary support in that organ would have interpretative value. It is not necessary that support for the practice be tested in relation to the full membership of the organization. This seems to have been the effect of the Namibia Case where the Court was satisfied that the properly supported practice of the SC in the SC, an organ of limited membership, was adequate to be effective as an interpretation of the UN Charter. It must be assumed that there was an implied agreement among all members to this position at the time the constitution was adopted, if the theory that implied consent is the basis of the interpretative value of practice is accepted.

That there may be development of and gap-filling in a constitutional text by resort to properly supported practice is not unreasonable. The principle of effectiveness employed in interpretation is also aimed at the same objective. If objection is raised to the use of practice in interpretation because it develops and fills gaps in a constitutional text, it may equally be argued that the principle of effectiveness which has the same aim should also be excluded. This would stultify the technique of interpretation, particularly of constitutional texts. Thus, the agreement which is being implied is not to something that is undesirable or unreasonable and can justifiably be implied. It is not necessary in any case to assimilate development and gap-filling to amendment.

Intention of the parties – travaux préparatoires

The actual intention of the parties at the time the constitution of an organization was formulated, as evidenced in the *travaux préparatoires*, has sometimes been sought in attempts to interpret constitutional texts. On the whole, however, subjective intention has not been regarded as important for the interpretation of such texts. The Vienna Convention on the Law of Treaties gives a subsidiary place to the ascertainment of intention as a means of interpretation. It is not to be used more or less unless all other means fail. Judge Spender made the point clearly in his separate opinion in the *Expenses Case* that intention was less important in the case of a constitution than of other treaties, particularly because the parties are not fixed and constant and because of the nature and subject-matter of the treaty.[70] Tribunals and other organs have in the course of interpreting constitutions referred only infrequently to the *travaux préparatoires* and the intentions of the parties. In most cases the preparatory work has been resorted to in a limited manner and generally to support an interpretation already arrived at by other means. In the *First Admissions Case* the ICJ did appear to give currency to the view that the task of interpretation was to ascertain the intention of the parties, when it said that Article 4(1) of the Charter 'clearly demonstrates the intention of its authors to establish a legal rule'.[71] But the Court applied the principle of the natural and ordinary meaning and did not rely primarily on the intention to establish the interpretation adopted. While establishing the meaning of a text may be described as ascertaining an 'intention', perhaps as reflected in the text, in the interpretation of constitutions particularly interpretation assumes a broader function.

In fact, resort to the *travaux préparatoires* by international courts in interpreting constitutions, when it has occurred, has generally been not to ascertain a meaning as such but to support a meaning already established. In the *First Admissions Case*[72] the ICJ did not resort to the preparatory work because it felt that the text was sufficiently clear, in spite of what it had said earlier about the significance of intention. In the *Reparation Case*[73] and the *Second Admissions Case* it was not resorted to at all, the Court stating in the latter case that, because the text was clear, reference to the preparatory work was not permissible.[74] In some of the cases

---

[70] 1962 ICJ Reports at p. 185.   [71] 1947–8 ICJ Reports at p. 62.   [72] *Ibid.* at p. 63.

[73] 1949 ICJ Reports at p. 174.

[74] 1950 ICJ Reports at p. 8. For cases in which the preparatory work was not referred to at all see, e.g., the *Competence of the ILO to Regulate Conditions of Labour in Agriculture*, PCIJ

where the preparatory work was not used as a tool of interpretation, the refusal of the court not to resort to it is underscored by the fact that judges who wrote separate or dissenting opinions may have done so.[75] In the *UNESCO Constitution Case* the tribunal, after denying the relevance of the preparatory work where the text was clear and the meaning of the text could otherwise be established, used the preparatory work only to support its interpretation of the text by finding that there was nothing therein to contradict that interpretation.[76] Similarly, in the *IMCO Case* the preparatory work was used to confirm an interpretation established by other means, though such work was referred to in detail.[77]

An 'agreed interpretation' of a text which is reflected in the *travaux préparatoires* stands on a different footing. There may be circumstances in which such interpretations are authoritative interpretations of the text, as was pointed out by the four-judge minority in the *First Admissions Case*[78] and dissenting Judge Alvarez in the *Second Admissions Case*.[79] The issue was

Series B Nos. 2 and 3 at p. 41; the *Effect of Awards Case*, 1954 ICJ Reports p. 47; the *Expenses Case*, 1962 ICJ Reports p. 151; and the *Reparation Case*, 1949 ICJ Reports p. 174.

[75] See, e.g., Judge Hackworth (dissenting) in the *Effect of Awards Case*, 1954 ICJ Reports at pp. 78*ff.*; Judges Fitzmaurice (separate), Winiarski (dissenting) and Moreno Quintana (dissenting) in the *Expenses Case*, 1962 ICJ Reports at pp. 209*ff.*, pp. 230*ff.* and pp. 247*ff.*, respectively; Judge Alvarez (dissenting) in the *First Admissions Case*, 1947–48 ICJ Reports at pp. 67*ff.*

[76] 16 AD (1949) at pp. 336*ff.*

[77] 1960 ICJ Reports at pp. 161*ff.* The practice of the IMF, in contrast to the tendency generally to de-emphasize the relevance of the preparatory work by the Vienna Convention of 1969, by Judge Spender and other judges and, perhaps, by the ICJ itself, has been at least seriously to refer to the *travaux préparatoires* in interpreting its constitution: 'The Fund has made abundant use of *travaux préparatoires*, although from time to time there has been discussion of the weight that should be attributed to them in general or in relation to a particular problem. It is probably safe to say that the degree of reliance on *travaux préparatoires* in the solution of a problem is proportional to their clarity. This working rule sometimes transfers the debate from the meaning of the text to the meaning of an earlier draft. Although uncertainty as to the inferences that can be drawn from *travaux préparatoires* sometimes tends to produce a general scepticism about their usefulness, when they have been clear they have made weighty or even decisive contributions to the solution of some problems of interpretation.' (Gold, *Interpretation by the Fund* (1968) p. 18). The IBRD and the IDA, among other financial institutions, have also followed the same practice, when they have found it necessary to consider interpretations of their constitution in the course of their operations. The legal opinions of the UN Legal Counsel to the GA have also made free use of the preparatory work at times: see the many examples in the UNJYs. It is a different question how useful or helpful such references to the preparatory work have been.

[78] 1947–8 ICJ Reports at p. 87.   [79] 1950 ICJ Reports at p. 30.

litigated in the *European Commission on the Danube Case*,[80] where, however, it was held that an interpretation to be found in the preparatory work did not have the status of an 'agreed interpretation'.

The approach taken by international courts and tribunals to preparatory work, which is to minimize its importance for interpretation, is in keeping with its relegation to the status of a subsidiary resource in the Vienna Convention on the Law of Treaties. It is also justified by good policy reasons. There is no better statement of the reasons for the reduced importance of the preparatory work in the interpretation of constitutions of international organizations than that of Judge Alvarez in the *Second Admissions Case*:

It will be necessary in future – unless in exceptional cases – when interpreting treaties, even those which are obscure, and especially those relating to international organizations, to exclude the consideration of the *travaux préparatoires*, which was formerly usual. The value of these documents has indeed progressively diminished, for different reasons: (a) they contain opinions of all kinds; moreover, States, and even committees, have at times put forward some idea and have later abandoned it in favor of another; (b) when States decide to sign a treaty, their decision is not influenced by the *travaux préparatoires*, with which, in many cases, they are unacquainted; (c) the increasing dynamism of international life makes it essential that the texts should continue to be in harmony with the new conditions of social life ... It is therefore necessary, when interpreting treaties – in particular, the Charter of the United Nations – to look ahead, that is, to have regard to the new conditions, and not to look back, or have recourse to *travaux préparatoires*. A treaty or a text that has once been established acquires a life of its own. Consequently, in interpreting it we must have regard to the exigencies of contemporary life, rather than to the intentions of those who framed it.[81]

The reason given that parties to constitutions may be unaware of what is stated in the preparatory work when they become parties to such constitutions may be questioned. They may be presumed to be aware of what is in the preparatory work at whatever time they become parties,

---

[80] PCIJ Series B No. 14 at pp. 33*ff*. On 'agreed interpretations' see the discussion in E. Lauterpacht, loc. cit. note 42 at pp. 444–5.

[81] 1950 ICJ Reports at p. 18. See also Judge Alvarez in the *First Admissions Case*, 1947–8 ICJ Reports at p. 68, where he stated: 'Moreover, the fact should be stressed that an institution, once established, acquires a life of its own, independent of the elements which have given birth to it, and it must develop, not in accordance with the views of those who created it, but in accordance with the requirements of international life.' In both cases Judge Alvarez dissented but his views on the use of the preparatory work were not in conflict with the Court's.

because of its relevance as background material. However, the other reasons given are valid.

Other considerations

It is clear that instruments such as those mentioned in the Vienna Convention on the Law of Treaties, agreed on before or after the conclusion of the constitutive treaty, are relevant to the interpretation of the treaty. In the same way the presumption that a constitution was not intended to be in conflict with general international law which is referred to in that convention is relevant to the interpretation of constitutional texts.[82]

Evaluation

The practice of international courts on interpreting constitutions has accepted the principles to be found in the Vienna Convention on the Law of Treaties but there may be identified a change in emphasis and in the pattern prescribed for the application of those principles in that instrument. What is significant for the interpretation of constitutional texts is that emphasis has been placed on the principle of effectiveness as a manifestation of the relevance of the object and purpose of an instrument and on subsequent practice as important elements in the identification of meaning, especially where there are lacunae, though in principle interpreting organs have generally deferred, as they should, to the principle of the ordinary meaning. At the same time, for good reason, the preparatory work has been down-played because the actual intention of the framers may be difficult to identify, even if there were complete agreement on a meaning, and such an intention may not be critically relevant for reasons clearly seen to be pertinent.

The natural and ordinary meaning may in certain circumstances be modified in the light of the principle of effectiveness, as happened in the case of the interpretation by the Executive Directors of Article II, Section 2 of the IBRD's Articles of Agreement. International organs acting judicially or quasi-judicially would seem to be ready to do this, even though the contextual natural and ordinary meaning enjoys some sanctity and it is conceivable that such organs may take that course of action *ut res magis valeat quam pereat*. In the case of constitutions which, so to speak, have a life of their own this is not to be discouraged, provided interpretation is not used as an excuse for amending a text, which has not occurred. In the case of constitutions there is more reason

---

[82] See, e.g., the *Namibia Case*, 1971 ICJ Reports at pp. 31, 41.

than in other cases to give effect to the principle of effectiveness, even where there is no ambiguity or possibility of an unreasonable result, because positive considerations of policy may require such an approach to be taken. There is every reason to treat constitutions as developing instruments.

Subsequent practice has been used in interpretation more selectively. It has sometimes happened that what appears to be an explicit text has been modified because of subsequent practice, as in the case of the interpretation of Article 14 of the ICJ Statute by the Security Council. But even in these cases it is evident that practice is used to fill in a gap or take care of an unforeseen situation rather than to contradict a text. Practice has generally been used to help a constitution to evolve where there is ambiguity, vagueness or a gap in the constitutional text, rather than to defy clear prescriptions. It is thus a mechanism for purposeful and agreed evolution.

The principles of effectiveness and subsequent practice have become forceful elements in constitutional interpretation in particular, because constitutions are regarded as organic instruments that have to be developed through interpretation. It may further be observed that: (i) there certainly are principles of interpretation applied in the case of constitutional texts; but (ii) the choice of the one to be applied is often dependent on the goal to be achieved which may in turn be a matter of judgment, a hierarchy of principles being less apparent; and consequently, (iii) it is sometimes difficult to predict what the result of interpretation is going to be.

Courts and organs do not ignore the natural and ordinary meaning of a text, where such meaning is the one they think is most appropriate, but at the same time in constitutional interpretation this is not always the meaning adopted. It may be argued that the principle of the natural and ordinary meaning still enjoys primacy even in the scheme of interpreting constitutional texts, because in those cases where other principles, such as those of effectiveness and subsequent practice, have been invoked and applied, there has been or could have been a finding that the result of applying the principle of the natural and ordinary meaning will have been 'unreasonable', which is technically when resort could be had to other principles. However, it is apparent from what has happened in judicial and quasi-judicial organs that this is not always the case, unless the concept of unreasonableness is twisted and the term is used to cover, willingly or not, any situation in which the principle of the natural and ordinary meaning is not applied. Apart from the fact that organs and courts do not always make a finding of unreasonableness of result before disregarding the principle of the natural and ordinary meaning, there may be serious and wide disagreement about whether a result is unreasonable or not. What decision-makers concerned try to do generally in constitutional interpretation is to establish the meaning that is most appropriate in terms of the functioning of the organization and in doing so they will not hesitate to give a meaning other than the textual one, even though they may pay attention to the latter meaning and be concerned about it. The goal sought to be achieved in these circumstances clearly goes beyond that of respecting the natural meaning of words in context.

Decisions of non-judicial organs

The decisions of deliberative, legislative and executive organs of organizations[83] may have to be interpreted either by the organs themselves, by other organs or by international or national tribunals. For example, the decisions of the GA or the SC relating to peacekeeping may fall into this category. The By-Laws of the IBRD are another example of such decisions. In 1982 a resolution of the GA relating to the UN Council for Namibia was the subject of interpretation before an organ of the UN. The Legal Counsel of the UN gave an opinion which was followed in which he advised that, because the resolution conferred a representative function on the Council, it had the power to conclude contracts on behalf of Namibia.[84] A special example of such decisions is the legislation relating to employment of staff members of international organizations which may have to be interpreted most frequently by international administrative tribunals.[85]

In the interpretation of the decisions of organs which are clearly of a delegated nature (excepting, for the moment, legislation relating to employment relations) the principles of interpretation used are generally similar to those used in the interpretation of constitutional texts, though there may be a change in emphasis and priorities. Consequently, it is sufficient to point out the general approach and more special factors.

---

[83] On these acts and also on their interpretation see, e.g., Bos, 'The Interpretation of Decisions of International Organizations', 28 NILR (1981) pp. 1–14; Skubiszewski, 'Enactment of Law by International Organizations', 41 BYIL (1965–66) pp. 188–274.

[84] See the opinion of the Legal Counsel of the UN of 14 April 1982: 1982 UNJY pp. 164–5.

[85] This subject will be discussed below in Chapter 9.

Wherever possible the rule of the ordinary and natural meaning in context is applied. In connection with the interpretation of Resolution 1(XX) of the Commission on Narcotic Drugs of 1965, which involved voting by correspondence in the Commission on Narcotic Drugs, the textual meaning was adopted.[86] In the interpretation of paragraph 5 of SC Resolution 253 of 1968, the natural and ordinary meaning was given, in concluding that holders of Southern Rhodesian passports could not be admitted to the territory of member states of the UN.[87] There have been occasions on which the textual meaning has been adopted, while support for that meaning has been sought in practice or in the *travaux préparatoires*, probably *ex abundanti cautela*. In considering Rule 27 of the GA Rules of Procedure relating to the issuance of credentials of members of the GA, the question that arose was what was the status of credentials issued by permanent representatives. The interpretation adopted was based on the textual meaning but support was also sought from the practice of the GA.[88] In 1982 a question arose as to the binding nature of the four criteria for the assessment of contributions reflected in paragraph 4(a) to 4(d) of GA Resolution 36/231 of 1981. The conclusion reached that the criteria were binding was based on the textual meaning for which support was found in the preparatory work.[89]

Practice has also been used in the interpretation of decisions of organs. In the interpretation of Rules 13 and 15 of the Rules of Procedure of the SC relating to the accreditation of representatives of members the practice of the SC in dealing with the problem was heavily relied on by the Legal Counsel of the UN in arriving at a conclusion which was adopted by the SC.[90] Similarly in the interpretation of Resolution 221(X)

---

[86] 1972 UNJY p. 171, where the opinion of the UN Legal Counsel takes this view.

[87] 1977 UNJY p. 192, opinion of the UN Legal Counsel. Other examples of the adoption of the textual meaning are the interpretation of GA Rs. 1798 (XVII) of 1962 regarding the travel expenses of members of Bureaux in UNDP (1978 UNJY p. 176); and the interpretation of Rules 75 and 88 of the Rules of Procedure of the GA regarding the closure of debate and conduct during voting in the GA (1983 UNJY p. 174).

[88] 1964 UNJY p. 225, opinion of the Legal Counsel of the UN.

[89] 1982 UNJY p. 182, opinion of the Legal Counsel of the UN. Other examples of the same procedure are to be found in the opinions of the Legal Counsel of the UN given in connection with the interpretation of paragraph 7 of GA Rs. 2063(XX) of 1965 (1966 UNJY p. 238); of the Statute of the International Institute for Education and Planning which was a resolution of the General Conference of the UNESCO (*ibid.* p. 266); and in the interpretation by the Legal Counsel of the UN for the GA of GA Rs. 2816 (XXVI) of 1971 relating to the collection of funds from private sources for disaster relief (1974 UNJY p. 162).

[90] 1983 UNJY p. 179.

of 1963 of the UN Economic Commission for Latin America the question of participation in seminars on foreign trade was resolved by reference to UN principles and practice.[91] There is, however, another principle which also operates which is in keeping with the position that practice cannot 'amend' the text of a resolution made under the constituent instrument. This is that a practice which is clearly contrary to a text cannot negate a text. This principle was applied to reject a practice in connection with the interpretation of Rule 90 of the Rules of Procedure of the GA concerning the explanation of his vote by a proposer of a motion.[92] So much for practice by itself as a tool of interpretation. It has also been used, as has been seen, to support a textual meaning, to support a meaning based on the principle of effectiveness, and to derive a meaning in conjunction with the preparatory work. While practice is an integral tool in the interpretation of decisions of organs, it is used with caution, since such decisions are of a delegated nature. It can certainly be used to fill in gaps and resolve ambiguities but its use could not be extended beyond this.

The principle of effectiveness (taking into account the context) has also been used to interpret decisions of organs in the absence of contrary indication. As has already been seen, it was applied in interpreting the GA resolution setting up the UN Council for Namibia to imply a power. It was applied also in interpreting paragraph 6 of the SC Resolution 1474 (ESIV) of 1961 both of which related to the import of arms and war materials into the Congo.[93] The principle was successfully applied in interpreting GA Resolution 2248 (S-V) of 1967 which concerned the powers of the UN Council for South West Africa, in order to give the Council power to issue travel documents to the inhabitants and citizens of South West Africa. There it was applied in conjunction with the practice of the Council.[94]

There are many instances of the preparatory work being resorted to in the interpretation of decisions of organs. In the case of decisions such as these it is arguable that there is reason legitimately to refer to them, because the intention of the framer may be more relevant. But this argument may lack cogency, if such decisions are regarded as objective

---

[91] 1963 UNJY p. 171, opinion of the Legal Counsel of the UN.
[92] 1966 UNJY p. 229, opinion of the UN Legal Counsel.
[93] See opinion of the UN Legal Counsel in 1962 UNJY p. 238.
[94] 1967 UNJY p. 309, opinion of the UN Legal Counsel. See also the opinion of the UN Legal Counsel interpreting GA Rs. 2659 (XXV) of 1970, where the principle of effectiveness was used in conjunction with the *travaux préparatoires*: 1971 UNJY p. 221.

texts that have an existence of their own, independent of their creators. Further, the relevant discussions may be unhelpful because they show inconclusiveness or a variety of opinions – more so than in the case of the preparatory work of constitutional texts. However, there are several examples of the preparatory work being used in the interpretation of such decisions. In the interpretation of paragraph 4 of the SC Resolution of 24 November 1961, relating to the detention of mercenaries by the UN in the Congo, the intention of the framers was sought in the *travaux préparatoires*.[95] In interpreting the phrase 'accredited staff of permanent missions' in GA Resolution 36/235 of 1981, since no definition could be found in the text, the intention of the framers was sought in the discussions in the Fifth Committee of the GA and a narrow definition given.[96] Apart from the use of the *travaux préparatoires* on their own, sometimes they are used, as has been seen, to support a textual meaning. They have also been invoked in conjunction with practice[97] and the principle of effectiveness[98] to establish a meaning. It would seem that more attention tends to be paid to the preparatory work than in the interpretation of constitutional texts, though such work may be judiciously used.

There may be certain presumptions which are applicable in the case of these decisions. It will be recalled that the Legal Counsel of the UN expressed the opinion to the Secretariat in relation to the interpretation of Article 19 of the Charter that in case of doubt Charter provisions should 'be interpreted so as to be as little burdensome to the State parties as possible'.[99] This presumption could apply *a fortiori* to decisions of organs. It will be noted that the presumption is applicable in case of doubt. Another presumption applicable is that decisions of organs must be interpreted so as to conform to the constituent instrument[100] and

---

[95] 1962 UNJY p. 241, opinion of the UN Legal Counsel.

[96] 1982 UNJY p. 204, opinion of the UN Legal Counsel. See also the interpretation by the UN Legal Counsel of GA Rs. 1808 (XVII) of 1962 (1963 UNJY p. 176); and of GA Rs. 1779 (XVII) of 1962 (1963 UNJY p. 183).

[97] Interpretation of Rule 62 of the GA Rules of Procedure, opinion of Legal Counsel: 1971 UNJY p. 195. There the preparatory work was found to be unhelpful and the practice was applied in the interpretation.

[98] In the interpretation of GA Rs. 2659 (XXV) of 1970 which dealt with the payment of administrative costs for a volunteers programme, the UN Legal Counsel applied the principle of effectiveness, while asserting that the *travaux préparatoires* did not contradict the meaning given: 1971 UNJY p. 221.

[99] 1983 UNJY pp. 167–9: opinion of 26 October 1983.

[100] See the interpretation of Rule 27 of the GA Rules of Procedure by the UN Legal Counsel in 1970, where it was concluded that effectively suspension of membership was not permitted by the rejection of credentials because the rule of procedure could

not to conflict with it. It goes without saying that, as in the case of the constituent instrument, subsidiary decisions must be construed in the light of general international law, particularly *ius cogens*. As already seen, there is a presumption that practice clearly contrary to a text cannot negate the text itself.

not be interpreted to have a result in conflict with the Charter of the UN: 1970 UNJY p. 169.

3 Legal personality

The status on the international and non-international plane of international organizations has for some time been fertile ground for text writers,[1] though there have been few international judicial decisions which have faced the subject directly or indirectly. The debate mainly concerns two issues:

(i)   Do international organizations have legal personality and when and how do they acquire it?

(ii) What are the consequences of the attribution of legal personality?

As noted in Chapter 1, international bodies created by treaty emerged at the beginning of the nineteenth century. The first international body created by states was perhaps the Administration général de l'octroi de navigation du Rhin which was established by the Treaty of 15 August

---

[1] See, e.g., some of the literature cited in Jenks, 'The Legal Personality of International Organizations', 22 BYIL (1945) at p. 267, footnote 1, Barberis, 'Nouvelle questions concernant la personalité juridique internationale', 179 *Hague Recueil* (1983), bibliography on international organizations at pp. 299*ff.*, and Jennings and Watts, *Oppenheim's International Law* (1992) vol. I, p. 18, footnote 15. See particularly, apart from the authors cited in this chapter, Schermers and Blokker, *International Institutional Law* (1995) pp. 975*ff.*; Schwarzenberger, *International Law* (1957) vol. I, pp. 137*ff.*; Seidl-Hohenveldern, *Das Recht der Internationalen Organisationen, einschliesslich der Supranationalen Gemeinschaften* (1979) *passim*; R. L. Bindschedler, 'Die Anerkennung imp Völkerrecht', 9 *Archiv des Volkerrechts* (1961–2) at pp. 387*ff.* The concept of international personality has come to be accepted by most authorities, including Soviet authorities who had rejected such personality earlier: see Osakwe, 'Contemporary Soviet Doctrine on the Juridical Nature of Universal International Organizations', 65 AJIL (1971) at pp. 502*ff.* More recently Sands and Klein (eds.), *Bowett's Law of International Institutions* (2001) pp. 469–512 also deal generally with the subject of the legal personality of IGOs, as does Bekker, *The Legal Position of Intergovernmental Organizations* (1994) pp. 37–85, though in a different and essentially theoretical manner. For more recent writings refer the writers cited in all the footnotes and in the headnotes on pp. 469, 470, 480 and 486 in Sands and Klein (eds.), op. cit. above in this footnote pp. 469–512.

1804 between France and the Holy Roman Empire, which was a closed organization. There were many more such closed organizations, but late in the nineteenth century a few organizations which were later to become open international organizations (e.g., the UPU (1874)) came into existence.[2] It was not until the creation after the First World War of the League of Nations and the International Labor Organization which were open organizations that the issue of the legal personality of international organizations came seriously to be discussed. Perhaps the earliest attempts to discuss the issue were by text writers, such as Anzilloti,[3] but these were rudimentary. There was much controversy on the issue in writings before the Second World War, the tendency being to concentrate on the personality of international organizations in national law and to concede that the League of Nations had a special status which gave it international personality[4] but to deny that other organizations whether open or closed had such personality. It was not until the issue of the capacity of the UN to make claims on behalf of its staff members against non-member states was raised that the question of the international personality of organizations was given systematic attention.[5] This problem led to the advisory opinion of the ICJ in the *Reparation Case*.[6] Interest in the subject was spurred not only by that opinion but by the increase in the number of international organizations, open and closed, since 1945. The matter is of importance, considering that the number of international organizations has greatly increased and they function in different ways and in diverse areas. It is not only personality on the international plane that matters but also personality on the non-international plane.

The rationale for personality

A question that arises *in limine* is whether it is necessary to have a concept of personality for international organizations or whether such

---

[2] See for the organizations of the nineteenth century, Barberis, loc. cit. note 1 at pp. 215–16.

[3] Anzilotti, 'Gli organi comuni nelle Societa di Stati', 8 RDI (1914), p. 156.

[4] See, e.g., Fischer Williams, 'The Status of the League of Nations in International Law', in Fischer Williams, *Chapters on Current International Law and the League of Nations* (1929) p. 477. There was also an attempt to distinguish between international persons and subjects of international law – a distinction which seems to be unimportant: see, e.g., Siotto-Pintor, 'Les sujets du droit international autres que les Etats', 41 *Hague Recueil* (1932-III) p. 251.

[5] Even Jenks in 1945, loc. cit. note 1, focused mainly on personality in municipal law.

[6] 1949 ICJ Reports p. 174.

organizations can function without having legal personality at all. The question has sometimes been raised[7] but hardly ever discussed in any detail. In the *Reparation Case* the ICJ assumed that it was unnecessary to answer this preliminary question, as had the PCIJ in the *Exchange of Greek and Turkish Population Case*.[8] In the former case the ICJ went directly to the question whether the UN had personality, while in the latter case the PCIJ simply assumed that the international body concerned had personality.

There are good reasons, mainly practical, why the concept of personality is useful for the law of international organizations. Conceptually, there is no problem with attributing legal personality to organizations. They would be additional artificial or legal persons, just as states are artificial or legal persons.

Without personality an organization would not be able to appear in its own right in legal proceedings, whether at the international or non-international level. There would also not be a single international person as such having the capacity in its own right to have rights, obligations and powers, whether implied or expressed, both at the international level and at the non-international level. Such rights, obligations and powers would be vested collectively in all the creating states, which may not have been the intention behind the creation of the organization, and also could create unnecessary practical problems, particularly in the area of responsibility, both active and passive. Contracts or treaties, for example, would be made between all the members and the other party and, in the case of treaties between the organization and a member state, would result in the state party to the treaty being also one of the other parties, insofar as it is a member of the organization. The question of implying powers to enable organizations to function effectively is a separate issue from personality. Whether powers are express or implied, what makes a difference is whether they are vested in the organization as a legal person or in the individual member states as a collectivity. Another separate issue, which concerns the effect of personality and is discussed in Chapter 13, is whether personality would presumptively shield the member states from liability, direct or secondary, for the obligations of the organization in the absence of their consent. The practical convenience of personality is what makes it theoretically justified. The

---

[7] See, e.g., E. Lauterpacht, 'The Development of the Law of International Organization by the Decisions of International Tribunals', 152 *Hague Recueil* (1976-IV) at p. 407.

[8] PCIJ Series B No. 10. See also, e.g., the *European Commission on the Danube Case*, PCIJ Series B No. 14 at p. 64.

choice is not between recognizing personality and chaos. Organizations can well function in the same way as unincorporated associations or partnerships in national law where the group has no legal personality as such. What is useful or even necessary is that states have the *option* of creating an organization which has personality and can function as a legal person rather than as an 'unincorporated' group because primarily it facilitates action and is deemed to be necessary for the functioning of the organization.

Personality at a non-international level

Legal personality and capacity at a non-international level is an issue in itself. National legal systems will have their own techniques and methods of determining whether an international organization has legal personality which is effective in those respective systems. These may or may not take into account the obligations at international law of states to give effect to such personality. There are several possibilities.

First, the situation may be considered where the constituent instrument specifically grants legal capacity to the organization in national law. This may be done expressly in one form or another or the grant may be inferred implicitly from the provisions of the constituent instrument. Thus, the constitution of the FAO provides in Article XV(1) that the organization 'shall have the capacity of a legal person to perform any legal act appropriate to its purpose which is not beyond the power granted to it by this Constitution'. The Articles of Agreement of the IMF and the IBRD more specifically provide that the Fund and the Bank respectively shall possess full juridical personality, and, in particular, the capacity:

- (i)   to contract;
- (ii) to acquire and dispose of immovable and movable property;
- (iii) to institute legal proceedings.[9]

The UN Charter in a different way in Article 104 states that the UN 'shall enjoy in the territory of each of its Members such legal capacity as may be necessary for the exercise of its functions and the fulfillment of its purposes'. There are many other constitutions of international organizations that have in effect provisions relating to legal capacity in national law.

---

[9] Article IX(2) and Article VII(2) respectively. See also Article 45 of the EBRD Agreement; Article VIII(2) of the IDA Articles of Agreement; Article VI(2) of the IFC Articles of Agreement; Article IX(2) of the IDB Agreement; Article 49 of the ADB Agreement; Article 51 of the AFDB Agreement; and Article 48(1) of the CDB Agreement.

In these cases member states are under an obligation to recognize the legal personality of the respective organizations in their legal systems.[10] How this is done may vary. Certain member states, such as the UK and most Commonwealth states, which require that treaties be implemented by legislation in order to become enforceable in their legal systems, would recognize the personality of the organizations by incorporating the constituent instruments in their law. Other member states, such as the USA, Germany and Austria, which automatically give effect in their national law to treaties to which they are parties, would recognize the legal personality of the organizations in their legal systems without incorporation. Non-member states would recognize the legal capacity of these organizations in their national systems on a different basis. Sometimes this may be the result of a special agreement, such as a head-quarters agreement, as in the case of the original relationship between the UN and Switzerland. But even in the absence of a special agreement there are other ways in which the legal personality of these organizations may be recognized in national law.[11] These are similar to the methods that may be adopted by member states, where the constituent instrument does not provide specifically for legal capacity in national law.

In the situations referred to above national courts could resort to the rules of their conflict of laws, resulting in the recognition of personality in national legal systems, because the international organization concerned has personality at an international level pursuant to its constitution. The technique is to apply the generally recognized rule of the conflict of laws that the legal status and capacity of a legal person is determined by its 'personal' law. The personal law in the case of an international organization is international law. Thus, if it can be established that at international law an organization has personality, then a national court would, by applying its conflict of law principles, recognize the legal personality of the organization.[12] This seems to be the most

---

[10] See the discussion of such provisions in Jenks, loc. cit. note 1 at pp. 269*ff*. For discussions of the legal capacity of international organizations in national law see also Sereni, 'International Economic Institutions and the Municipal Law of States', 96 *Hague Recueil* (1959-I) at pp. 168*ff*.; Seyersted, 'Applicable Law in Relations between Intergovernmental Organizations and Private Parties', 122 *Hague Recueil* (1967-III) at pp. 433*ff*.; Bridge, 'The United Nations and English Law', 18 ICLQ (1969) at pp. 694*ff*.; and Mann, 'International Corporations and National Law', 42 BYIL (1969) at pp. 153*ff*.

[11] See, e.g., *International Tin Council* v. *Amalgamet Inc.*, 524 NYS 2d (1988) p. 971; *Arab Monetary Fund* v. *Hashim and Others (No. 3)*, [1991] All ER p. 871 (HL).

[12] See the very relevant discussion in Mann, loc. cit. note 10 at pp. 153*ff*. See also Jenks, loc. cit. note 1 p. 267; Collier, 'The Status of an International Corporation', in Feuerstein and Parry (eds.), *Multum non Multa: Festschrift für Kurt Lipstein* (1980) p. 21.

rational method. This is how the New York courts in effect proceeded in *International Tin Council* v. *Amalgamet Inc.*[13] Though the USA was not a party to the International Tin Agreement which created the International Tin Council, because under that agreement the ITC had personality, the personality was recognized in national law, thus enabling the ITC to sue and be sued in the New York courts. There are many cases in which the personality of international organizations of which the USA is a member has been recognized in the course of granting them immunity from jurisdiction.[14] In these cases the constituent instruments would have been part of the law of the land, because they were treaties to which the USA was a party.

The practice of the courts of countries in Western Europe (and consequently of the courts of those countries which follow that practice) is also along the lines taken by the US courts. There are many examples of these courts admitting international organizations as claimants or respondents in suits filed before them on the basis that they had international personality, regardless of whether the state of the national court was party to the constitutive instrument of the organization or not. The Swiss Federal Court has admitted the UN (of which Switzerland was not a member, but with which Switzerland has an agreement regarding its headquarters) as a defendant without argument and recognized its immunity from jurisdiction in garnishment proceedings.[15] Similarly, in another case the Société européenne pour le financement de matériel ferroraire (Eurofima) which had been created by a treaty to which Switzerland was not a party was acknowledged to have personality in Swiss law by the Swiss Federal Court, because it was an international person, and given immunity from jurisdiction.[16] In UNRRA v.

---

[13] 524 NYS 2d (1988) p. 971.

[14] See, e.g., the *Broadbent Case*, 628 F. 2nd (1980) p. 27 (OAS); *Mendaro* v. *The World Bank*, [1983] US Court of Appeals No. 82-2247, CA 80-01204.

[15] *Re Poncet* [1948], 15 ILR p. 346.

[16] *Republique italienne, Ministère italien des transports et Chemins de fer de l'Etât italien* v. *Beta Holding SA et Autorité de sequestre de Bâle Ville* [1966], as discussed in Caflisch, 'La pratique suisse en matière de droit international public 1974', 31 ASDI (1975) at pp. 225–6. See also Caflisch, 'La pratique suisse en matière de droit international public 1977', 34 ASDI (1978) at pp. 61–2, where a case decided in 1978 by the Swiss Federal Tribunal in which it recognized the personality of the EEC is discussed. Switzerland was not a member of the EEC. More recently in the *Westland Helicopters Case* [1988] 28 ILM (1980) p, 867, decided by the Swiss Federal Tribunal, the court recognized the personality of the AOI of which Switzerland was not a member: see Dominicé, 'Le Tribunal fédéral face à la personalité juridique d'un organisme international', 108 *Zeitschrift für Schweizeritsches Recht* (1989) p. 517.

Daan,[17] decided by the Supreme Court of the Netherlands, the UNRRA's capacity to act as a legal person was questioned. The court held that the question of personality was one for international law and not of municipal law and, therefore, the UNRRA had personality and had capacity to act. In Italy NATO has been held to have legal personality, because it had international personality.[18] There are other cases decided in Western European countries in which the legal personality of international organizations, such as the UN and Eurocontrol, have been recognized.[19] In those cases decided in these countries in which the immunity of an organization is in question a precondition to considering such a claim of immunity would be the existence of its personality before the national court concerned.[20]

It will be seen below that international tribunals have international personality or are organs sharing in such personality attaching to an IGO (viz., the ICJ's position as a principal organ of the UN) and consequently can have personality in national legal systems. This feature came to light in connection with the Iran-US Claims Tribunal in *AS v. Iran-US Claims Tribunal*.[21] The discussion of the case below reveals that the tribunal had personality and could appear in the Dutch courts which is a characteristic of national law. The short point was that Dutch courts recognized

---

[17] [1950] 16 ILR p. 337.

[18] See *Branno v. Ministry of War* [1954] Italian Court of Cassation, 22 ILR p. 756; *Mazzanti v. HAFSE and Ministry of Defence* [1954] Tribunal of Florence, 22 ILR p. 758.

[19] See, e.g., *UN v. B.* [1952] Tribunal Civil of Brussels, Belgium, 19 ILR p. 490; *UN Works Agency v. Finanzlandesdirektion für Wien Niederösterreich und Burgenland* [1981] Austrian Administrative Court, 110 JDI (1983) p. 643; *Bavaria und Germanai v. Eurocontrol* [1977] Berber, Slg. (official collection) (1977) p. 1,524. There is a curious decision in which the German Landesarbeitsgericht recognized the immunity of NATO for the reason that its members enjoyed immunity: see Schröer, 'De l'Application de l'immunité juridictionelle des états étrangers aux organisations internationales', 75 RGDIP (1971) at pp. 722–3. The decision is equivocal insofar as it may be construed as denying NATO a legal personality of its own, though it is consistent with the contrary interpretation also. Where the country is a member of the international organization concerned, in Western European countries the position generally is that, since the state is a party to the constituent treaty, it would be enforceable in the courts of that country. Thus, legal personality would flow from the constitution, if the organization has international personality.

[20] As examples may be taken the numerous cases brought by staff members of organizations against organizations; see C. F. Amerasinghe, *The Law of the International Civil Service* (1994) vol. I, pp. 42*ff*., particularly footnotes 48*ff*. Most of these are US and European cases, though there are some decided by courts of Middle Eastern and North African countries.

[21] (1983), Local Court, The Hague, 15 NYIL p. 429 (English translation), 94 ILR p. 323 (English); (1984), District Court, The Hague, 16 NYIL p. 471.

the personality of the tribunal on the basis that it had international personality.

The practice of the UK courts and of other courts of states that follow the UK practice, however, is an example of rejection of the technique of giving effect to the personality of international organizations which has been discussed above. Where the UK is a party to the constitutive instrument of an organization, it is necessary that there be parliamentary action as a result of which the organization's personality is given effect to in national law, whether directly or through subsidiary action by the executive organ.[22] In *Rayner (JH) (Mincing Lane) Ltd* v. *Dept of Trade and Industry*[23] the House of Lords made certain observations explicitly rejecting in general the approach taken by the US and European continental courts. This rejection was intended to cover even cases where the UK was not a party to the constitution of an organization. The House of Lords made it clear that without a legislative act of the UK an international organization had no existence in UK law.[24]

As a result in *Arab Monetary Fund* v. *Hashim and Others (No. 3)*[25] an argument based on the latter approach was abandoned by counsel as being untenable in a case where the right of the AMF, an organization of which the UK was not a member, to file a suit as a legal person was questioned. In that case the House of Lords[26] consciously did not change its ruling

---

[22] See, e.g., *Rayner (JH) (Mincing Lane) Ltd* v. *Dept of Trade and Industry* [1990] 2 AC p. 418, decided by the House of Lords. The case has been reviewed in detail by Greenwood, in 60 BYIL (1989) p. 461 and CLJ (1990) p. 8. Marston, 'The Origin of the Personality of International Organizations in United Kingdom Law', 40 ICLQ (1991) p. 403, deals with the history of the legislation pertinent to the above case. The CS's legal personality for purposes of the national legal systems of the UK and of other members of the CS was required to be recognized, if necessary by legislation, according to the principal constitutive instrument which was an agreement among states (the Agreed Memorandum of 1965). The CS's legal personality in the national legal systems of member states of the CS is discussed in connection with immunities of the CS in Read, *Commonwealth Secretariat: its Legal Capacities, Immunities and Privileges* (1978).

[23] [1990] 2 AC p. 418.   [24] *Ibid.* at p. 510, *per* Lord Oliver.

[25] [1990] 1 All ER p. 685. See the comment by Hill, 'International Corporations in English Courts', 12 *Oxford Journal of Legal Studies* (1992) p. 135. See also Wengler, 'Die Rechtsfähigkeit des arabischen Währungsfonds in England', 37 *Recht der internationalen Wirtschaft* (1991) p. 391.

[26] [1990] 1 All ER at pp. 691–2. Lord Templeman in the House of Lords referred to the UAE, the host state, but also conceded that, if the organization enjoyed personality under the law of one or more members or the state where it had its seat, this would be adequate to give it legal personality in UK law: [1991] 2 AC at p. 167. See also for a discussion of the position of the court in the *Rayner (JH) (Mincing Lane) Ltd Case*, Bentil, 'Suing an International Organization for Debt Payment', 134 *Solicitor's Journal* (1990) pp. 475*ff.*

made in the *Rayner (JH) (Mincing Lane) Ltd Case* but extended it to cover even organizations such as the AMF of which the UK was not a member. It did not, however, as a consequence, refuse to recognize the personality of the AMF but found another way of giving effect to that personality in English law. It decided to support the solution proposed by the High Court when the case was heard by that court. The High Court had held that, where, because of an unequivocal statement of intent by the government of the UK, as was the case in respect of the AMF, there were clear indications that the UK government recognized or was ready to recognize the personality of the international organization in question, although it was not a member of that organization, this was sufficient to give the organization standing before a UK court. Further, the Court said that, because a foreign member state of the organization, namely UAE (referred to as Abu Dhabi), had accorded the AMF legal personality under its law so that the AMF was a *persona ficta* under that law, for the purpose of deciding whether the AMF had personality, the ordinary conflict rules would be applicable, whereby the law of UAE as the law of the place of incorporation could be chosen as the relevant law.[27] It follows from this approach that the foreign law which recognizes the legal personality of the international organization would, together with the rules of its conflict of laws, be the chosen law for questions relating to the organization. It is, only if the foreign law through its conflict of laws rules applied international law as the law governing the organization, which was the case here, that international law would be applicable in these circumstances. Otherwise the law applied would not be international law but a national law. Thus, this approach, while being circuitous, resulted in the personality of the organization being accepted in national law. The English Court of Appeal subsequently overruled the High Court and refused outright recognition of the personality of the Arab Monetary Fund. However, the House of Lords reversed the Court of Appeal, agreeing with the reasoning of the High Court (and Bingham LJ).[28]

---

[27] [1990] 1 All ER at pp. 691–2.

[28] [1990] 3 WLR p. 139 (Court of Appeal); [1991] 1 All ER p. 87 (HL). Bingham LJ dissented in the Court of Appeal, agreeing with the High Court. A consequence of the ruling of the House of Lords is that the personality of the organization in UK national law could depend on its having a personality in one of the foreign states concerned. If all these states decided to deprive the organization of personality in their states, it would lose its personality in UK law.

A reviewer of the first edition of the present treatise misunderstood my statement about what the UK House of Lords did and, consequently, misrepresented my

The status of an international organization in UK law would have the following features:[29]

(i) if the UK is a member and the required action is taken by the executive under the relevant legislation (the International Organizations Act 1968), the organization has personality; it is a corporation under the national law;

(ii) if the UK is not a member, but the organization is recognized by the executive organ, it will have personality under the UK law;

(iii) if the UK is not a member, but the organization has personality in one or more foreign countries that are members or the host state as a result of legislative measures in any of those countries or for other reasons, then it has personality in UK law;

(iv) if the UK is not a member and the UK has not taken the necessary executive action to recognize the personality of the international organization or any relevant foreign country has not taken action to recognize or does not recognize the personality of the organization, then the organization has no legal existence as such in the UK.

This situation would hold good *mutatis mutandis* for those countries that follow the UK system. Where the organization has personality under (iii) above there may be some question as to what law determines the consequences of personality, if the relevant law does not refer to international law as the 'personal' law of the organization through its conflict of laws principles or otherwise.

The singular case of the BIS has been referred to in Chapter 1. Switzerland, as the host state conceivably, gave the BIS the personality of a legal person under its national law. The consequence of this was not to take away an international personality that the BIS had as a result of the agreement of the states establishing it, but specifically to give it a legal personality under a national law of one of the parties to the agreement establishing it. This can be compared to any member of an IGO, e.g.,

explanation of the case discussed above: see Marston, 'Book Review', CLJ (1997) at p. 424. What I say in the text in this (second) edition is exactly the same as what was said in the earlier edition.

[29] Mann, 'International Organizations as National Corporations', 107 LQR (1991) at p. 361, summarizes the position but his summary does not appear to be complete. The UK law is influenced, among other things, by certain constitutional principles: (i) treaties must be implemented by a legislative act to be given effect in UK law; and (ii) the recognition of foreign public entities, such as states and international organizations, is within the prerogative of the Crown.

It is not entirely clear what the UK courts would do, where the UK is a member of an IGO but has not enacted the necessary legislation. The question is whether they may resort to the same techniques they have adopted for IGOs of which the UK is not a member.

the UN, giving the IGO the status of a legal person in its legal system by action taken under its legal system, regardless of whether the IGO would have had such personality without such action being taken.

Even where the constituent instrument of an organization does not expressly provide for legal personality in national law, member states are probably under an obligation to recognize such personality in their national legal systems. Such an obligation is an implied one, arising from the relationship between the members and the organization and from the principle of good faith. As for non-member states, there is probably no such obligation *per se* (even though, as will be seen, the international personality of organizations may be objective). The problem is that there is no legal nexus between the non-member states and the organization and it cannot be assumed that there is a general customary rule of international law requiring such recognition of personality in national legal systems. However, as has been seen in the *Arab Monetary Fund Case* referred to above, states may be more ready than not to try to recognize somehow the personality of organizations in their legal systems, where the personality is recognized elsewhere. Further, as *International Tin Council v. Amalgamet Inc.* demonstrates, possession of international personality could result directly in the acquisition of legal personality and capacity in national law.

At the same time, while it is for the courts of states to 'accept' or reject the personality of an organization at the national level and though personality would be ineffective at the national level without some form of acceptance, the requirement of such acceptance merely demonstrates the autonomy of legal systems of states. This kind of acceptance need not also be synonymous with recognition of international personality by the executive of a state. Indeed, the failure of courts in certain circumstances to accept the personality of an organization in their legal systems may even result in a breach of international legal obligations owed by states.[30]

The rights, obligations and powers flowing from the acknowledgment of personality at the non-international level would generally be determined both by reference to the constituent instrument of the organization and the relevant national law, though, as has been seen, some problems may arise by the approach of the UK courts to the personality of organizations where the UK is not a member of the organization. Once

---

[30] A reviewer of the first edition was rather confused on the issue of third states and acceptance of personality in national law and also does not reflect clearly what I said on this method which is the same as what I say in this edition: see Seidl-Hohenveldern, 'Book Review', 36 *Archiv des Völkerrechts* (1998) at p. 93.

personality is acknowledged, it may be concluded that it is at least full juridical personality to which a legal person in the legal system is generally entitled, to the extent possible, of course, whether the constituent instrument of the organization specifically describes the personality in this way or not. On the other hand, the specific rights, obligations and powers of the organization would also generally be defined and limited by the constituent instrument, where the national law refers to the constitution.

Attribution of international personality

Before the Second World War the PCIJ perhaps only hinted that international organizations had international personality. In the *European Commission on the Danube Case* it did state:

As the European Commission is not a State, but an international institution with a special purpose, it only has the functions bestowed upon it by the Definitive Statute with a view to the fulfillment of that purpose, but it has power to exercise these functions to their full extent, in so far as the Statute does not impose resrictions upon it.[31]

In comparing the Commission to a state and regarding it as being able to perform functions with international consequences, it is possible that the PCIJ had in mind that the Commission had some kind of international personality. The issues in the case concerned the powers of the Commission in a certain geographical area, the exercise of which would very well have required the Commission to be acting in its own right and as a legal person rather than as a collection of all the individual member states. But the issue of personality was neither argued nor discussed in the opinion. There were several other cases in which the PCIJ had to decide disputes about the powers of the ILO[32] but in none of these was the issue of personality directly raised or contested. In all but one case[33] the Court held that the exercise of the powers disputed was, under its constitution, within the competence of the ILO. The view may be taken, nevertheless, that it is difficult to see how the Court could

---

[31] PCIJ Series B No. 14 at p. 64. See also the *Exchange of Greek and Turkish Population Case*, PCIJ Series B No. 10.

[32] See particularly the *Employment of Women during the Night Case*, PCIJ Series A/B No. 50; the *Competence of the ILO to Regulate Conditions of Labour in Agriculture Case*, PCIJ Series B No. 2; the *Competence of the ILO to Regulate Agricultural Production Case*, PCIJ Series B No. 3; the *Personal Work of Employers Case*, PCIJ Series B No. 13.

[33] *The Competence of the ILO to Regulate Agricultural Production Case*, PCIJ Series B No. 3.

have been saying that in exercising the powers to regulate work (as all these powers were) it was not the ILO that was acting as a legal person in its own right but it was the members of the ILO exercising those powers in their individual capacities directly through the organization.

Having international personality for an international organization means possessing rights, duties, powers and liabilities etc. as distinct from its members or its creators on the international plane and in international law. What these rights, etc. are and how they are established is a subsequent question. International personality is very rarely dealt with explicitly or impliedly in the constitutions of international organizations. In a comment on the UN Charter by the Chairman of the US delegation to the San Francisco Conference is to be found the following statement:

This Article does not deal with what is called the 'international personality' of the Organization. The Committee which discussed this matter was anxious to avoid any implication that the United Nations will be in any sense a 'super-state'. So far as the power to enter into agreements with states is concerned, the answer is given by Article 43 which provides that the Security Council is to be a party to the agreements concerning the availability of armed forces. International practice, while limited, supports the idea of such a body being a party to agreements. No other issue of 'international personality' requires mention in the Charter. Practice will bring about the evolution of appropriate rules so far as necessary.[34]

As foreseen there, international personality of organizations has evolved, as necessary, rather than emanated from explicit statements in constitutions. The report of the Committee IV/2 of the San Francisco Conference made it clear that (a) Article 104 of the Charter was confined to a statement of the obligations incumbent upon each member state to act in such a way that the organization enjoyed in its territory a juridical status permitting it to exercise its function, and (b) as for international personality, in regard to which a proposal expressly to recognize in the Charter the international personality of the UN had been rejected at the conference, the Committee had considered it superfluous to have a text on the matter, because, in effect it would be determined implicitly from the provisions of the Charter taken as a whole.[35]

The relevance of the existence of the legal personality of an international organization in national law to the creation of its personality in

---

[34] Department of State Publication 2349, Conference Series 71 at pp. 157–8.
[35] UNCIO Doc. 933.

international law is questionable. The ICJ in the *Reparation Case*, when discussing the establishment of international personality for the UN, did say: 'It (the Charter) has defined the position of the Members in relation to the Organization...by giving the Organization legal capacity...in the territory of each of its Members.'[36] But it is not clear how much importance was attached to this fact as evidence of international personality, nor is it necessary that the enjoyment of legal personality in national law requires an organization to have international personality. There are other kinds of entities which have legal personality in national law but do not have such personality in international law.[37]

Before examining more closely the *Reparation Case* it would be useful to note the two main approaches to the problem of international personality. First, there are those who identify certain rights, duties and powers expressly conferred upon the organization and derive from these the international personality of the organization. This approach bases itself on the will of the member states, either expressed or implied in the constitution.[38] The second approach associates the international personality of organizations with certain criteria, the existence of which endows the organization with personality on the basis of general international law. The foundation of international personality is, it is said, not the will of the members but is to be identified in general international law.[39]

---

[36] 1949 ICJ Reports at p. 179.

[37] The case of the BIS is in point. The fact that it is incorporated by a special Charter under Swiss law and has legal personality thereby in Swiss law as a national law neither detracts from the BIS's having international legal personality nor does it entail as such the BIS's having such personality. National legal personality and international legal personality do not necessarily depend on each other, nor are they incompatible with each other or in contradiction to one another. What has happened in the case of the BIS, for example, is that, for practical reasons, when it was established by agreement among states, it was specifically given national legal personality under Swiss law. The latter act by itself did not *per se* derogate from international legal personality. For a brief description of the BIS and its functions see 1A *Yearbook of International Organizations (2003/2004)*, entry no. 03196.

[38] See, e.g., apparently Sands and Klein (eds.), op. cit. note 1 pp. 470*ff*. Balladore Pallieri, *Diritto internazionale publico* (1962) pp. 178*ff*.; Rouyer-Hameray, *Les Competences implicites des organisations internationales* (1962) pp. 68*ff*.

[39] See, e.g., Seyersted, 'International Personality of Intergovernmental Organizations', 4 IJIL (1964) at p. 53, who lays down the following criteria: international organs, (i) which are not all subject to the authority of any other organized community except that of participating communities acting jointly, and (ii) which are not authorized by all their acts to assume obligations (merely) on behalf of the several participating communities; Brownlie, *Principles of Public International Law* (1998) pp. 679*ff*., who summarizes the criteria required as follows: (i) a permanent association of states, with lawful objects, equipped with organs; (ii) a distinction, in terms of legal powers and

The approach taken by the ICJ in the *Reparation Case*, where the Court set out first to establish whether the UN had international personality as a precondition to answering the principal question put to it, was not quite in accord with the second approach referred to above. It did not specifically or solely refer to any of the objective criteria referred to by authors. What it did do was, first, look at several features of the organization which were reflected both in its constitution and in its practice and, second, come to a conclusion based on the 'intention' behind the constitution. It said, first:

The Charter has not been content to make the Organization created by it merely a centre 'for harmonizing the actions of nations in the attainment of these common ends' (Article I, para. 4). It has equipped that centre with organs, and has given it special tasks. It has defined the position of the Members in relation to the Organization by requiring them to give it every assistance in any action undertaken by it (Article 2, para. 5), and to accept and carry out the decisions of the Security Council; by authorizing the General Assembly to make recommendations to the Members; by giving the Organization legal capacity and privileges and immunities in the territory of each of its Members; and by providing for the conclusion of agreements between the Organization and its Members. Practice – in particular the conclusion of conventions to which the Organization is a party – has confirmed this character of the Organization ... It must be added that the Organization is a political body, charged with political tasks of an important character.[40]

Second, in its conclusion it said:

In the opinion of the Court, the Organization was intended to exercise and enjoy, and is in fact exercising and enjoying, functions and rights which can only be explained on the basis of the possession of a large measure of international personality and capacity to operate upon an international plane. It is at present

purposes, between the organization and its member states; and (iii) the existence of legal powers exercisable on the international plane and not solely within the national systems of one or more states. See also the literature cited in Brownlie, *ibid.* pp. 677*ff.* See also, e.g., Reuter, *The Law of International Institutions* (1958) pp. 214*ff.*; Sereni, *Diritto internazionale* (1960) vol. II, pp. 801*ff.*; Rama-Montaldo, 'International Legal Personality and Implied Powers of International Organizations', 44 BYIL (1970) at pp. 126, 144. The issue of personality has also been discussed in Llanos-Mansilla, 'Las organizaciones internationales como sujetos de Derecho internacional', 8 *Anuario Hispano-Luso-Americano de Derecho Internacional* (1987) p. 97; Schermers and Blokker, *International Institutional Law* pp. 975*ff.*; Schermers, 'International Organizations', in Bedjaoui (ed.), *International Law, Achievements and Prospects* (1991) at pp. 72*ff.* See also for both views literature cited in Sands and Klein (eds.), op. cit. note 1 pp. 469*ff.*
[40] 1949 ICJ Reports at pp. 178–9.

the supreme type of international organization, and it could not carry out the intentions of its founders if it was devoid of international personality. It must be acknowledged that its Members, by entrusting certain functions to it, with the attendant duties and responsibilities, have clothed it with the competence required to enable those functions to be effectively discharged...Accordingly, the Court has come to the conclusion that the Organization is an international person.[41]

The Court examined (i) several factors surrounding the establishment of the UN, (ii) provisions of its constitution and (iii) even the subsequent practice of the international community in relation to the UN, in coming to the conclusion that the UN had international personality. It did not hesitate to refer to the intention of the founders of the UN either. This leaves a very unclear picture of what, in its opinion, was necessary to establish international personality. Further, it made a pragmatic assessment of the basis of international personality when it stated:

Throughout its history, the development of international law has been influenced by the requirements of international life, and the progressive increase in the collective activities of States has already given rise to instances of action upon the international plane by certain entities which are not States. This development culminated in the establishment in June 1945 of an international organization whose purposes and principles are specified in the Charter of the United Nations. But to achieve these ends the attribution of international personality is indispensable.[42]

Thus, the establishment of international personality for an international organization does not appear to be as simple an exercise as identifying certain objective criteria which confer personality in general international law. The Court's view was that essentially (i) the achievement of the ends (purposes) of the organization must require as indispensable the attribution of international personality; (ii) the organization must be intended to exercise and enjoy functions and rights which can only be explained on the basis of the possession of international personality. To establish these elements an examination of the circumstances of the creation of and the constitution of the organization had to be undertaken. These elements did not refer entirely to the requirements for international personality, though they indicated ends to be fulfilled. Insofar as 'intention' was mentioned, it would seem that the Court was not referring to some subjective intention in the minds of the founders

[41] *Ibid.* at p. 179.   [42] *Ibid.* at p. 178.

but to an objective that was to be found in the circumstances of creation and the constitution, although this did not necessarily preclude reference to the *travaux préparatoires*. While subsequent practice was also referred to by the Court in evaluating whether international personality was present, it is probable that the Court was using it as supporting evidence rather than as a critical factor affecting the evaluation. It may also be noted that the Court did say that it found the attribution of international personality indispensable, if the UN was to achieve the ends designed for it. Indispensability must be regarded as a matter of logic flowing from the fulfilment of criteria to be established from the circumstances of the creation of an organization.

While there may be certain objective criteria, the fulfilment of which in a given case may entail the conclusion that the organization has international personality, the Court did not articulate these clearly. To some extent, they must be inferred. There may be factors which show that the organization does not have such personality. One of these factors, to take an extreme example, may be the existence of a clear denial of international personality in the constituent instrument. This would be in keeping with the search for 'intention' as objectively expressed in the creation of the organization. Similarly, there may be other relevant factors on the negative side, which lead to the conclusion that the organization has no international personality. These would depend on the circumstances of each case. But then it would also be clear perhaps that the required criteria, whatever they are, had not been fully satisfied. The point is that the total picture must be examined.[43]

As for what objective criteria are basic to the concept of international personality for international organizations, the Court did not commit itself on this subject, though some authorities have tried to identify these. The following may be suggested:

(i)   an association of states or international organizations or both (a) with lawful objects and (b) with one or more organs which are not subject to the authority of any other organized communities than, if at all, the participants in those organs acting jointly;

(ii) the existence of a distinction between the organization and its members in respect of legal rights, duties, power and liabilities, etc.

---

[43] Rama-Montaldo, loc. cit. note 39 at p. 126, states that the Court proceeded in an 'objective' manner. While the requirements for personality may be objective, this must not be allowed to hide the fact that the Court did examine many features and came to its conclusion inductively. See also the discussion of the cases of the PCIJ and the ICJ in E. Lauterpacht, loc. cit. note 7 at pp. 403*ff.*

(in the Hohfeldian sense) on the international plane as contrasted with the national or transnational plane, it being clear that the organization was 'intended' to have such rights, duties, power and liabilities.[44]

Although the Court did not refer to these criteria specifically, most of what is contained in them may be regarded as covered by what it said.

The real difficulty arises not in regard to the extraction of the above criteria from the Court's statement but in ascertaining whether the Court purported to require more than these criteria in order to establish international personality for international organizations. As already noted: (i) the fulfilment of these criteria is to be tested in relation to the 'intention' behind the establishment of the organization as reflected in the objective circumstances of such establishment including the constitution of the organization (which is what was done by the Court when it referred to such matters as several articles of the Charter); and (ii) any negative elements in those circumstances, including the constitution, must be taken into account in determining whether international personality does not exist. Beyond this, it may be concluded, the Court did not intend to go. By referring to several features of the Charter and other phenomena, the Court must be taken not to have been adding to the criteria required for the establishment of international personality but to have been satisfying itself that the criteria set out above had been fulfilled in the case of the UN.[45]

According to the criteria referred to above, there would be no difficulty in ascribing to all the open international organizations international personality. There is ample evidence in the circumstances of their creation, including their constitutions, that they were 'intended' to have international personality without which they could not function properly. Whether it is the UNESCO, the FAO, the IMF, or the IBRD, for instance, which is being considered, it is easy to see that it must have international personality because the two criteria referred to above are clearly satisfied. It is significant that during the crisis in the International Tin Council (an open but small organization), after which it ceased

---

[44] The identification of these criteria is a matter of pragmatic good sense. For example, Brownlie and Seyersted have in essence noted all or some of these criteria. Further, the identification attempts to keep within the confines of what the ICJ did and said in the *Reparation Case*. See also Rama-Montaldo, loc. cit. note 39 at p. 144.

[45] In *A-G* v. *Nissan* [1969] 1 All ER at p. 647, Lord Pearce pointed out that the UN was not a super-state, or even a sovereign state but was a unique *legal person* based on the sovereignty of its respective members.

to exist, the international personality of the Council was considered to have been established.[46] There is no reason why closed organizations should not in principle have international legal personality for the sole reason that they are closed.

The question of real universality or near-universality may also be raised, since the ICJ did advert to it. However, it was not in the context of the incidence of personality that this factor was referred to, when the ICJ said that the 'vast majority' of States in the international community enjoyed membership in the UN,[47] but in the context of the opposability of this personality to non-member States. The size of the membership of an organization, open or closed as it may be, therefore, has no bearing on the incidence of international personality. It is not one of the criteria required for international personality. The case of the ITC which had a comparatively small membership is very much in point here.

Although no open international organization has been found whose constitution expressly attributes international personality to it, there are several closed organizations where this has occurred.[48] In the light of the ICJ's references to the 'intentions' of the framers and its reliance on the Charter of the UN in establishing the international personality of the UN, it may be asked what importance is to be attached to such an explicit attribution of personality. The matter was not discussed by the Court but it may be suggested that such a grant of personality has validity insofar as it is evidence that the criteria for personality are regarded as having been satisfied. While such a grant of personality has validity, in any case, as among the creating states, there may be circumstances in which it has no effect *vis-à-vis* third states. Where, for

---

[46] See J. H. *Rayner Ltd* v. *Department of Trade and Industry* [1989] 3 WLR p. 969 (HL). See also *International Tin Council* v. *Amalgamet Inc.*, 524 NYS 2d [1988] p. 971, where the New York Courts recognized the ITC's international personality, and *Award in Westland Helicopters Arbitration* [1989] 28 ILM (1989) at p. 691, where the Swiss Federal Courts also recognized it.

[47] 1949 ICJ Reports at p. 185.

[48] See, e.g., ECSC Treaty, Article 6; EEC Treaty, Article 210; African Development Bank Articles of Agreement, Article 10; OPEC Fund Agreement, Article 1. Whether NGOs can have international personality and what it entails is outside the scope of this work. It may be of interest that in 1993 by agreement with the ICRC, a leading NGO, the Swiss government, among other things, recognized the 'international personality' of the ICRC. This case raises a number of interesting questions, such as, among others, what are the consequences of such recognition and what is the nature of the personality so recognized. The whole question of the international personality of NGOs is new. For a discussion of the question in relation to the Swiss agreement with the ICRC see Dominicé, 'L'accord de siège conclu par le Comité International de la Croix-Rouge avec la Suisse', 99 RGDIP (1995) p. 5.

example, it is obvious that in spite of this expressed attribution the organization does not have independent functioning capacity or organs (as required by the criteria) and that the attribution is a subterfuge for the creating states to avoid their direct responsibilities the attribution may legitimately be ignored by third states.

It is significant that towards the end of the twentieth century, ostensibly because international tribunals, whether arbitral tribunals or standing courts, had become a common feature in the life of the international community, but also because, it may be suggested, such international tribunals were an important and core aspect of international relations in the context of the preservation of peace and the securing of international justice, the issue of the international as well as national law personality of international tribunals came into the limelight. The matter had not been discussed by text writers but it was not only adverted to but faced head-on in the Dutch case, *AS v. Iran-United States Claims Tribunal*, a case which went up to the Supreme Court of the Netherlands.[49]

In *AS v. Iran-United States Claims Tribunal* the local court held that the defendant tribunal was an international organization with a legal personality derived from international law and that as a consequence of that and the applicable law derived from international law and Dutch legislation the tribunal was entitled to the relevant immunity from jurisdiction enjoyed by international organizations. The Dutch court said about personality.

The parties have not contested, and can thus be deemed to have accepted, that the defendant, the Tribunal, was instituted by the Claims Settlement Agreement between the Islamic Republic of Iran and the United States of America. This Agreement is embodied in the Declaration of the Algerian Government of 19 January 1981 concerning the settlement of claims by the Government of the United States and the Government of the Islamic Republic of Iran (*Trb.* 1981 No. 155). The parties have also accepted that the Tribunal is a joint institution of the two States concerned, with a legal personality derived from international law.[50]

The court referred to the fact that the parties had not contested the legal personality before the court of the tribunal. This, however, does not affect the holdings of the court. The matter related to jurisdiction

---

[49] (1983), Local Court, The Hague, 15 NYIL p. 429 (English translation), 94 ILR p. 323 (English); (1984), District Court, The Hague, 16 NYIL p. 471 (English translation), 94 ILR p. 326 (English); (1985), Supreme Court, 18 NYIL (1987) p. 357 (English translation), 94 ILR p. 327 (English).

[50] (1983), 94 ILR at pp. 323–4.

and could have been examined by the court as jurisdictional issues, if the view of the law as agreed was unsound. The District Court and the Supreme Court agreed with the lower court on the law on the points mentioned above.[51]

It is important that the personality was primarily *international* personality deriving from the international acts of two states in reaching an international agreement to create the tribunal with certain powers and functions which were essentially judicial but also entailed administrative acts. This case would, therefore, support the position that international tribunals, whether arbitral tribunals or standing courts, created by the agreement of states enjoy international personality because their functions, being essentially judicial, are similar in nature to those entrusted to the Iran-US Claims Tribunal. Where the court is constituted under the aegis of a wider treaty creating an international organization, such as the UN Charter, it would share in the international personality of the international organization or be endowed with a personality of its own, as the case may be, on the basis of the constitutive treaty or instrument. Thus, the ICJ and the ICTY and ICTR fall into this category as do IATs. Tribunals or courts such as the ITLOS, the human rights courts and the CJEC also depend on wider treaties for their personality. ICSID tribunals would benefit from the coverage of the ICSID Convention *but each tribunal created* under it would have personality.[52]

Objective personality

A consequential question is whether such organizations as have international personality according to the criteria discussed above, have 'objective' personality in the sense that their personality is opposable to non-member states without recognition. The ICJ in the *Reparation Case* dealt with this issue in relation to the UN by concluding:

Accordingly the question is whether the Organization has capacity to bring a claim against the defendant State to recover reparation in respect of that damage or whether, on the contrary, the defendant State, not being a member, is justified in raising the objection that the Organization lacks the capacity to bring an international claim. On this point, the Court opinion is that fifty States, representing the vast majority of the members of the international community, had the power, in conformity with international law, to bring into being

---

[51] 94 ILR at p. 326, 94 ILR at p. 327 respectively.
[52] See also C. F. Amerasinghe, *Jurisdiction of International Tribunals* (2003) p. 43.

an entity possessing objective international personality, and not merely personality recognized by them alone, together with capacity to bring international claims.[53]

It is important to note that what the Court did say was that fifty states representing the vast majority of the international community (at the time) had the power to create an entity possessing objective international personality. It did not say that there always had to be a vast majority of states creating an entity in order that the international personality of that entity be objective and effective vis-à-vis third states. If it had meant what it did not say, it would mean that the objective legal personality of the majority of international organizations which happen not to be universal or near universal (even though open) would be excluded.[54] However, the issue of how many member states at a minimum are required to endow an organization with objective personality was not an issue before the Court and was not decided by it.

In the light of this uncertainty and certain current trends in the practice relating to international organizations, the view could be taken that the number of states creating an entity is irrelevant for the purposes of objective legal personality. No recent instances are known of a non-member state refusing to acknowledge the personality of an organization on the ground that it was not a member state and had not given the organization specific recognition. It is possible to interpret the Court's opinion as having left open the question whether objective legal personality would only be extended in exceptional circumstances or whether objective legal personality was a general idea pertaining to the personality of international organizations. However, it would seem that subsequent practice, particularly at the international level, has led to the extension of the personality of international organizations quite generally, provided only that certain minimal criteria related more or less to the existence of personality exist. The result is that there has not been a separate *practice* of recognition or non-recognition such as continues to trouble the area of statehood. As will be seen, recognition is probably not relevant to the issue of the international personality of international organizations. It is arguable then that the Court's opinion has been 'interpreted' in subsequent practice to support a view of

---

[53] 1949 ICJ Reports at p. 185.

[54] Among open organizations the status of the IMF, the IBRD, the IFC and the IDA before Russia and the Eastern European countries became members, and of the present Common Fund for Commodities and ISA, would have been or would be in doubt.

objective personality whatever view of objective personality the Court intended to propound.

There are cases where an organization has without encountering difficulty successfully entered into legal relations with a non-member state which had not as such recognized the organization, and where the argument has not been used that such legal relations could not validly be created. In *International Tin Council* v. *Amalgamet Inc.*[55] the courts of New York accepted the international personality of the ITC (an open organization) which at the time had twenty-four members, though in that case the issue was not contested. The USA was not a member of the ITC nor had it expressly or implicitly done anything to recognize the ITC. The Swiss courts have also given effect to the personality of organizations of which Switzerland is not a member. But there may be difficulties related to the recognition of objective international personality by the UK courts, for instance, because of the special rules applicable in the UK national legal system. These require generally recognition or membership by the UK government of the organization and incorporation of the constituent treaty in the law of the UK or incorporation of the organization in a foreign state so as to enable the application of the constituent treaty and international law by reference to the rules of private international law.[56] These special rules, however, merely affect the manner in which the UK courts will give effect to international personality at a national level. They do not affect the issue of objective international personality which must be decided on the plane of international law.

The authorities are divided on the issue. There are those who are of the opinion that, like states, organizations must be recognized in order that they may have legal status, mainly on the ground that those states which are not parties to the constituent treaty are not bound by it.[57]

---

[55] 524 NYS 2d [1988] p. 971.

[56] See *Arab Monetary Fund* v. *Hashim and Others* [1990] 1 All ER p. 690. For the House of Lords' decision which upheld the High Court's see [1991] 1 All ER p. 871. There may be entities that do not obviously have the appropriate 'birth certificate', namely creation by an agreement among states or by appropriate international action. They may then have difficulty in establishing their separate international personality: e.g., the Agriculture Research Center set up under the auspices of the FAO. But such cases involve primarily the question whether the organization has international personality at all and not so much the question of recognition. Of course, recognition by the state in question would in practice settle the matter, as far as that state was concerned.

[57] See Schwarzenberger, *International Law* vol. I, pp. 128–30; R. Bindschedler, loc. cit. note 1 at pp. 387–8; and others cited in Seyersted, 'Is the International Personality of Intergovernmental Organizations Valid *vis-à-vis* Non-Members?', 4 IJIL (1964) at p. 234, footnote 250.

But most of these authorities would also not take full account of the ruling of the ICJ that the UN had objective legal personality, while *a fortiori* requiring that non-universal organizations and even organizations with a membership similar to the UN be recognized by non-member states. A variation of this view is that. except for the UN, which is a special case, it is necessary that non-member states recognize the personality of organizations for such personality to be effective in relation to them.[58] There are others who hold, pursuant to their interpretation of the opinion of the ICJ, that only universal or near-universal organizations do have objective personality (in the absence of recognition).[59] On the other hand, there are some who are of the view that once an organization is created with international legal personality by whatever number of states that personality is objective and is effective *vis-à-vis* non-member states as well.[60]

If the view of the ICJ in the *Reparation Case* is closely analyzed, it emerges that the Court approved the conclusion that in the case of at least one organization the constitutive effect of recognition was not operative. In so far as the Court rejected the constitutive effect of recognition in this case, it lent its imprimatur to the view that in the case of international organizations, at any rate, there *could* be circumstances in which recognition of personality was immaterial for the creation of legal status. Once that is conceded, the question may be asked why should such recognition be relevant at all to the creation of legal status for

---

[58] See, e.g., Seidl-Hohenveldern, 'Die völkerrechtliche Haftung für Handlungen internationaler Organisationen im Verhältnis zu Nichtmitgliedstaaten', 11 OZOR (1961) at pp. 497–507. This is the commonly held view. Seidl-Hohenveldern believed that treaties, including constitutive instruments, cannot bind third states and that, therefore, apparently recognition by third states is necessary for an IGO to have international personality *vis-à-vis* such states, the UN being excepted as a special case: see Seidl-Hohenveldern, loc. cit. note 30 at p. 93.

[59] Schermers and Blokker, *International Institutional Law* at p. 980: 'The International Court of Justice, considered furthermore, whether the international personality of the UN would also exist in its relations with non-member states. This question was also answered in the affirmative, on the ground that the vast majority of states had the power, in conformity with international law, to bring into being an entity possessing international personality also *vis-à-vis* non-member states, and not merely personality recognized by the member states above . . . In addition, other international organizations of a universal character could claim international personality *vis-à-vis* non-member states on the grounds cited by the International Court; closed international organizations could not.'

[60] Seyersted, loc. cit. note 39 at p. 240: 'Once an Organization or a State has been established, no matter how, it is *ipso facto* a general subject of international law. All that is required is that it possesses objective characteristics of a State or Organization.'

an international organization and, assuming it is in some cases, what are the circumstances in which such recognition should be relevant. As already pointed out, the Court, though referring to the near-universality of the UN, did not categorically make it a condition for the incidence of objective personality. The reference to universality was probably motivated by the desire to leave open the more general issue which it was not necessary to settle in the case and which had not been argued in specific terms. Thus, it is possible to argue that universality, near-universality or a large number of member states is not necessarily an essential element for objectivity of personality of international organizations.

Whatever the position was earlier, there may be a modern trend towards acknowledging that what is relevant to the issue should not be the actual number of member states. In theory whether a small number of states or a larger number establish an organization, non-member states will be in the same position vis-à-vis the organization in that they would not have taken part in, acquiesced in or expressly recognized the establishment of the organization by the fact of its establishment. Thus, it is some other factor or factors than numbers that should primarily detract from the objective personality of the organization. These, it is submitted, relate to such matters as fraud and absence of legitimate or proper purpose, though there is no example of an organization being refused recognition of personality for these reasons. In principle an organization should have objective personality, unless for some reason it is proved that there is such a vitiating factor. In theory also it would be easier to prove absence of proper or legitimate purpose where the number of member states is small.

As regards the requirement of recognition, some help in and support for interpreting its relevance in the context of the personality of international organizations is perhaps to be had from the position with regard to the recognition of states. An examination of the subject[61] resulted in the conclusion that recognition is not a prerequisite for the legal existence of a state vis-à-vis the recognizing or non-recognizing state once the criteria for statehood had been objectively found to exist. The absence of recognition is not really a legally relevant consideration in normal circumstances. In principle the denial of recognition to an entity which otherwise qualifies as a state cannot entitle the non-recognizing states to act as if the entity in question was not a state. The categorical constitutive position, which implies the contrary view, is suspect. On the

---

[61] Crawford, *The Creation of States in International Law* (1979) pp. 23–4.

other hand, it cannot be denied that, in practice, in regard to states recognition does have important legal and political effects. For example, where an entity is widely recognized as a state, especially where such recognition has been accorded on non-political grounds, that is strong evidence of the statehood of that entity, though it may not be conclusive. This may result in recognition rendering opposable a situation otherwise not opposable. But generally the conclusion reached is that the international status of a state 'subject to international law' is, in principle, independent of recognition.

Just as recognition is not in principle relevant to the objective determination of the legal status of statehood, though it continues to be in practice, and while it may sometimes have what may be described by and large as an estopping effect, in the case of the personality of international organizations it is also an acceptable position that recognition by non-member states is not necessary for the legal effectiveness of that personality *vis-à-vis* those states, unless as in the case of states, there are exceptional or ambiguous circumstances. Though the analogy between the two situations is not complete, the fact that in both cases what is at stake is the legal status of an entity warrants the disregard of the need for recognition in the one (international organizations), because it has come to be de-emphasized in the other (states). A consequence of that position is that organizations will *prima facie* have objective personality irrespective of the actual universality of their membership. Thus, non-member states (and nationals of such states) may not regard such organizations as lacking international personality in their dealings with them. This means that (objective) personality does not depend on recognition but on a legal status flowing from the existence of certain facts associated with the creation of the organization which implies a declaratory view of recognition, if it takes place at all, recognition not being necessary for the existence of personality.[62]

---

[62] The position in national law, as has been seen, may be different. In some legal systems, courts still rely to some extent and *prima facie* on recognition in order that international organizations may have personality *vis-à-vis* them. This seems to be the attitude of the UK, as was seen in *Arab Monetary Fund* v. *Hashim and Others (No. 3)*, where a statement made by the government of the UK was cited. The statement was to the effect that assuming the entity concerned 'enjoys, under its constitutive instrument or instruments and under the law of one or more member states or the state wherein it has its seat or permanent location, legal personality and capacity to engage in transactions of the type concerned governed by the law of a non-member state, the Foreign and Commonwealth Office, as the branch of the Executive responsible for the conduct of foreign relations, would be willing officially to acknowledge that the entity

The consequences of international personality

In the *Reparation Case* the ICJ made two important preliminary statements regarding the consequences of having international personality for international organizations. First, it made quite clear that in its opinion in the international legal system, as in any other legal system, different subjects could have different rights:

> The subjects of law in any legal system are not necessarily identical in nature or in the extent of their rights, and their nature depends upon the needs of the community.[63]

Second, it made a distinction between a state, a super-state and an international organization, when it said that attributing international personality to the UN

> is not the same thing as saying that it is a State, which it certainly is not, or that its legal personality and rights and duties are the same as those of a State. Still less is it the same thing as saying that it is 'a super-State', whatever that expression may mean. It does not even imply that all its rights and duties must be upon the international plane, any more than all the rights and duties of a State must be upon that plane. What it does mean is that it is a subject of international law and capable of possessing international rights and duties.[64]

There can be no doubt that the Court was of the view that acknowledging that an international organization has international personality does not mean recognizing (i) that it is a super-state; (ii) that it is a state; and (iii) that it has the same rights, duties, capacities, etc. as a state. These negative assertions were based on the assumption that legal persons, in the international legal system, are not the same, that their

---

concerned enjoys such legal personality and capacity and to state this.' ([1990] 1 All ER at p. 690). That statement was clearly based on the view that some form of acknowledgment of personality was necessary for the Arab Monetary Fund to have personality in the UK. This view is less acceptable at the present time than it might have been in the past. At the same time it must be recognized that, as seen in the same case, the English courts have found a way of circumventing the consequences of this constitutive view of recognition by reference to the principles of private international law, where an organization has been incorporated in another national legal system.

[63] 1949 ICJ Reports at p. 178.

[64] *Ibid.* at p. 179. See also the *WHO Agreement Case*, 1980 ICJ Reports at p. 89, where the Court reiterated that international organizations were not super-states. On this case, see Gray, 'The International Court's Advisory Opinion on the WHO–Egypt Agreement of 1951', 32 ICLQ (1983) p. 534.

legal nature depends on the needs of the international community and that they are not identical 'in the extent of their rights'.[65]

The comparison with statehood cannot be ignored, if value is to be given to the reasoning of the Court. It has to be acknowledged that, even if the Court believed that the acceptance of the international personality of organizations resulted in the vesting of inherent rights, duties and capacities in organizations somewhat independently of their constitutions as opposed to those that were only implied, these rights, duties and capacities were not the same in extent or content as those of states. Since there was a denial of super-statehood to international organizations, it would seem to be a logical conclusion that the Court's view was that the inherent rights, duties and capacities of organizations, if any, did not have to be as numerous or extensive as those of states, while not being identical.

That having been said, there are important questions which arise both from the Court's opinions and as a result of theories that have been propounded.[66] These are: (i) whether inherent rights, duties, capacities, etc. flow from the international personality of international organizations and what, if any, these are; or (ii) whether they have only powers implied in their constitutions or the circumstances of their creation; (iii) on what principles, rights, duties, capacities, etc. may be implied; and (iv) what is the effect of express or implicit prohibitions in the constitutional instruments.[67]

The views taken by theorists may be classified as follows:

(i)   those that assert broadly that international personality results in the same inherent capacities for States and international organizations,

---

[65] There are and have been other entities than states and international organizations in international law which have or have had international personality, e.g., protectorates, the Holy See, even individuals, etc. It is clear that the Court took the view that they did not have the same 'inherent' rights, duties, capacities, etc. as states, which seems to be the case, irrespective of whether they can be given or acquire such rights, duties, capacities, etc., as a result of agreements between states or other international acts.

[66] See the extensive discussion of some of the problems particularly in Seyersted, loc. cit. note 39 at pp. 1–40; Rama-Montaldo, loc. cit. note 39; Carroz and Probst, *Personalité juridique internationale et capacité de conclure des traités de L'ONU et des institutions specialisées* (1953); Sereni, *Diritto internazionale* vol. II, pp. 847ff.; Balladore Pallieri, *Diritto internazionale* pp. 178ff.; Rouyer-Hameray, note 38 pp. 69ff.; Kasmé, *La Capacité de L'ONU de conclure des traités* (1960) pp. 32ff.; Chiu, *The Capacity of International Organisations to Conclude Treaties* (1966); Geiser, *Les effets des accords conclus par des organisations internationales* (1977); Sonnenfeld, 'International Organisations as Parties to Treaties', Polish YIL (1981–2) pp. 177–200.

[67] Rights, duties, etc. will be referred to as 'capacities' for convenience.

the only limitations being (a) those that arise from express prohibitions in the constituent instrument and (b) those that are factual (see, e.g., Seyersted);

(ii) those that have concluded that while there are inherent capacities resulting from international personality, only those functions may be exercised which flow from the constitution expressly or by implication (see, e.g., Rama-Montaldo);

(iii) those that rest all the capacities of international organizations with international personality on expression or implication of powers in the constitution (see, e.g., apparently Rouyer-Hameray).[68]

An examination of what the ICJ has said and done reveals that it is not possible to give a categorical answer to the question of the legal consequences of personality for international organizations. The issues are complicated but it is useful first to look at what exactly the Court said and did in those cases in which the question came up in one way or another: namely, the *Reparation Case*, the *Effect of Awards Case*[69] and the *Expenses Case*[70] and a separate opinion in the *WHO Agreement Case*.[71]

In the *Reparation Case*, where the issue of the consequences of personality confronted the Court directly, the Court decided that: (i) the UN had the capacity, as a subject of international law, to maintain its rights by bringing international claims which involved the presentation and settlement of claims by resorting to protest, request for an enquiry, negotiation and request for submission to judicial settlement;[72] (ii) this capacity included the right to bring an international claim against a member (or a non-member) which has caused injury to it by a breach of its international obligations towards the UN;[73] and (iii) it also included the capacity to include in the claim for reparation damage caused to its agent or to persons entitled through him, as an assertion of its own right and not in a representative capacity.[74]

In regard to (i) personality meant that the UN was a subject of international law and capable of possessing international rights and duties and that it had capacity to maintain its rights by bringing international claims.[75] A state possessed the totality of international rights and duties recognized by international law but the rights and duties of an entity such as the UN depended upon its purposes and functions as specified or implied in its constituent documents and developed in practice.

---

[68] See also apparently E. Lauterpacht, loc. cit. note 7.
[69] 1954 ICJ Reports p. 47.   [70] 1962 ICJ Reports p. 151.   [71] 1980 ICJ Reports p. 73.
[72] 1949 ICJ Reports at pp. 179, 177.   [73] *Ibid.* at pp. 180, 185.   [74] *Ibid.* at p. 184.
[75] *Ibid.* at p. 179.

Because the functions of the organization were of such a character that they could not be effectively discharged if they involved the concurrent action, on the international plane, of fifty-eight or more Foreign Offices, member states had endowed the organization with capacity to bring international claims when necessitated by the discharge of its functions.[76] In regard to (ii) the damage in respect of which such a claim could be brought is limited exclusively to damage caused to the interests of the organization itself, to its administrative machine, to its property and assets and to the interests of which it is the guardian.[77] In regard to (iii) the Court conceded that the Charter did not expressly confer upon the organization the capacity to include in its claim for reparation damage caused to the victim or to persons entitled through him. Consequently, the Court considered whether the provisions of the Charter of the UN concerning its functions and the part played by its agents in the performance of those functions implied for the organization power to afford its agents the limited protection that would consist in the bringing of a claim on their behalf for reparation for damage suffered in such circumstances, a power which could only be deemed to exist if it could be necessarily implied as being essential to the performance of its duties.[78] It concluded:

Upon examination of the character of the functions entrusted to the Organization and of the nature of the missions of its agents, it becomes clear that the capacity of the Organization to exercise a measure of functional protection of its agents arises by necessary intendment out of the Charter.[79]

Points (i) and (ii) are closely connected. If the organization possessed the capacity referred to in (i), it would no doubt have the capacity referred to in (ii), because that is probably the principal example of the capacity to bring a claim at international law. Indeed, the Court seems to have inferred (ii) from (i) directly. The statements made are not clear as regards (i). In the first instance, it looked as if the Court intended to say that the capacity to bring an international claim was synonymous with international personality and was, therefore, inherent in it. But in the second quotation it relates it to the purposes and functions of the organization and makes it depend on being necessitated by the discharge of its functions. As regards (iii) the capacity to bring a claim was based fairly and squarely on 'necessary intendment' or on 'necessary implication' as being essential 'to the performance of duties'.

[76] *Ibid.* at p. 180.   [77] *Ibid.*   [78] *Ibid.* at p. 182   [79] *Ibid.* at p. 184.

In the *Effect of Awards Case*, the Court first found that the Secretary-General of the UN could settle disputes between the staff and the organization in the absence of other machinery without explaining the basis on which it came to this conclusion except for references to practice and then decided in regard to the power to establish an administrative tribunal, in the absence of an express authorization to do so in the Charter:

In these circumstances, the Court finds that the power to establish a tribunal, to do justice as between the Organization and the staff members, was essential to ensure the efficient working of the Secretariat. and to give effect to the paramount consideration of securing the highest standards of efficiency, competence and integrity. Capacity to do this arises by necessary intendment out of the Charter.[80]

The ideas of <u>essentiality and necessary intendment</u> were clearly mentioned.

In the *Expenses Case*, the approach taken to the issue of the lawfulness of activities for which the UN had incurred expenses was slightly different. The Court said:

[T]he Court agrees that such expenditures must be tested by their relationship to the purposes of the United Nations in the sense that if an expenditure were made for a purpose which is not one of the purposes of the United Nations, it would not be considered an 'expense of the Organization'[81] ... But when the Organization takes action which warrants the assertion that it was appropriate for the fulfillment of one of the stated purposes of the United Nations, the presumption is that such action is not *ultra vires* the Organization.[82]

The reference was to '<u>fulfillment of purposes</u>' as a criterion of capacity.

In the *WHO Agreement Case* the Court did not advert again to the source of powers as such, although it did refer to obligations which are binding upon organizations under general rules of international law, under their constitutions and under international agreements to which they are parties,[83] and asserted that the WHO had *prima facie* the power to choose the location of its headquarters or regional offices.[84] However, Judge Gros in a separate opinion stated, without disagreeing with the Court:

In the absence of a 'super-State', each international organization has only the competence which has been conferred on it by the States which founded it, and its powers are strictly limited to whatever is necessary to perform the functions which its constitutive charter has defined. This is thus a *competence d'attribution*,

---

[80] 1954 ICJ Reports at p. 57.   [81] 1962 ICJ Reports at p. 167.   [82] *Ibid.* at p. 168.
[83] 1980 ICJ Reports at p. 90.   [84] *Ibid.* at p. 89.

i.e., only such competence as States have 'attributed' to the organization. It is a misuse of terminology to speak of the sovereignty of the WHO or the sovereignty of the World Health Assembly; States are sovereign in the sense that their powers are not dependent on any other authority, but specialized agencies have no more than a special competence, that which they have received from those who constituted them, their member States, for the purpose of a well-defined task. Anything outside that competence and not calculated to further the performance of the task assigned lies outside the powers of the organization, and would be an act *ultra vires*, which must be regarded as without legal effect.[85]

Reference is made to what is necessary for the performance of functions assigned by the constitution.

Apart from the doubt whether the capacity to bring an international claim as such was regarded as inherent in international personality by the Court and if so what exactly was regarded as inherent, there is to be seen in the approach of the Court three distinct formulations:

(i) Organizations have those capacities and powers which arise by *necessary implication* out of their constitutions as being *essential* to the performance of their *duties (necessary intendment)*;

(ii) Organizations have those capacities and powers which are *necessitated* by the discharge of their *functions*;[86] and

(iii) Organizations have those powers and capacities which are *appropriate* for the fulfillment of their *stated purposes*.

There are not only differences in these formulations but subtle nuances. For example, it may be asked whether there is a difference between what is *essential* for the performance of *duties* and what is *necessary* for the performance of *functions*. Surely, there should be a difference between what is necessary and what is essential (what is necessary may not always be also essential) and between duties and functions (all functions may not be duties). What is more, what is appropriate for the fulfilment of stated purposes may or may not be what is necessary for the performance of functions or what is essential for the performance of duties. Thus, it would seem that capacities, according to the Court's view, could arise in three ways, it being necessary only that one of the tests be satisfied. The

---

[85] *Ibid.* at p. 103.

[86] This is the formulation referred to by Judge Gros and by the Court at one point in the *Reparation Case* (in relation to the general right to bring a claim). Judge Fitzmaurice in his separate opinion in the *Expenses Case* used the term 'as a matter of inherent necessity' (1962 ICJ Reports at p. 208) in describing the obligation that arose to finance the organization but this did not involve a reference to an inherent power as opposed to one which was 'necessitated by discharge of functions' or 'appropriate for the fulfillment of stated purposes', as described by the Court.

three tests are slightly different from each other, though there may be in the circumstances of a given case some overlap. They are not mutually exclusive and their application is cumulative.

All these tests are, however, both positive and based on implication.[87] They clearly apply where powers are not expressly prohibited by the constitution and require that capacities and powers be derived by the interpretation of constitutions.[88] It cannot be said, for instance, that the third test requires that a presumption be applied that all capacities and powers are enjoyed by organizations unless they are prohibited by their constitutions.[89] On the other hand, express grants or express prohibitions of powers and capacities must be recognized. It is not practical to predetermine in the abstract for all cases and in relation to all organizations what powers may be implied. To some extent much depends on the circumstances of the case. Some generally implied powers are discussed below. In implying powers what are of importance are the particular principles of interpretation. These have been described here and the general principle of interpretation which is relevant to the issue has been discussed also in Chapter 2 above.

What remains to be discussed is whether the Court left room for the recognition of inherent capacities and powers in addition to implied ones. It has been contended that there are capacities, such as the treaty-making power, the active and passive power of legation and the capacity to bring international claims, which inhere to their fullest extent in an organization, unless they are expressly prohibited in an organization's constitution, and regardless of the organization's purposes, functions,

---

[87] There are other cases decided by the PCIJ in which disputed powers were held to exist on the basis of implication (rather than inherence): see, e.g., the *Personal Work of Employers Case*, PCIJ Series B No. 13; the *European Commission of the Danube Case*, PCIJ Series B No. 14.

[88] While the two Vienna Conventions on treaty law are non-committal – the second convention of 1986 merely stating that the capacity of organizations to conclude treaties is governed by the 'rules' of the organization (Article 6: see 25 ILM (1986) at p. 549) – the ILC seemed to have been of the opinion that capacity depended on the constitutions of the organizations. See also the discussion in Seyersted, loc. cit. note 39 at pp. 56*ff.*

[89] Seyersted's conclusion is that such a presumption does arise as a result of this test: *ibid.* at pp. 54*ff.* Powers which are exercised as a result of being developed in the subsequent practice of the organization (see, e.g., the action taken by the GA of the UN under the 'Declaration Regarding Non-Self-Governing Territories' – Articles 73 and 74 of the Charter – to decide to which territories the Declaration applied and then to supervise their self-determination) cannot be described as 'inherent' powers. They also are implied powers. They are based on practice but their legal pedigree lies in their being implied.

etc.[90] This does not emerge, however, from the ICJ's jurisprudence. What may be possible is that there are inherent capacities and powers which are skeletal in their incidence, their content and extent being subject to implication or express grant.[91] It is not clear whether the Court intended to take this position in regard to the capacity to bring international claims, in view of what it said in the *Reparation Case*. Even if it did take this view, it is certain that much of the actual content and extent of capacities must be left to implication; for that is what the Court said in the same case and accepted in finding that the capacity to bring the two kinds of claims which were the subject of the request for an advisory opinion existed. That the Court believed that the implication of capacities was a valid and necessary exercise cannot be denied. Thus, the existence of inherent skeletal capacities would not eliminate the need to imply the content of capacities and powers in regard to the exercise of powers, functions and duties.

In the case of organizations in general, it is not difficult to imply the capacities and powers that are claimed also to be inherent, such as the treaty-making power and the power of legation. However, it is important to recognize that, whereas recognition of inherent capacities may result in organizations having an unlimited treaty-making power, for instance, the application of the doctrine of implied powers may result in the imposition of restrictions in the exercise of this power as a result of taking into account their functions, duties and purposes. Further, there may be differences between organizations in respect of powers and capacities.

The doctrine of inherent capacities, it must be recognized, cannot render nugatory the distinction made by the Court between international organizations and states in terms of international personality. The Court distinctly took the view that, while states were international persons *par excellence* with the fullest range of capacities and powers, international organizations were lesser entities. This is not surprising. For whether capacities are based on implication or inherence, it is unlikely that international organizations would have *per se* such capacities as those of administering territories and of owning a flag for ships on the high seas or exercising some of the other powers that states may exercise. This consideration may also give more credibility to the Court's

---

[90] See Seyersted, loc. cit. note 39 pp. 1*ff*.
[91] See Rama-Montaldo, loc. cit. note 39, particularly at pp. 126*ff*.

concentration on the implication of powers than to the doctrine of inherent capacity.[92]

Particular powers

Powers, rights and obligations (capacities) of international organizations derive in the last analysis, as has been pointed out above, from the constituent instruments. Where a power is expressly granted by the constitution, no problem arises in recognizing it. However, there are numerous powers, apart from those expressly granted, which organizations may have by implication.

At the non-international level an organization that has personality will generally, either by express grant or by implication, have the capacity to institute legal proceedings and be sued, to contract and to acquire, own and dispose of movable and immovable property.[93] An IGO may also claim the relevant immunities and privileges. This was the view taken of the principle of law in the Dutch *AS case* discussed earlier. But personality at the national level may embrace more than this. There is no reason why there should not be a presumption that international organizations would qualify to have some general powers, rights and even obligations that legal persons in any legal system have. They would have more to the extent that such capacities may be legitimately implied in their constitutions and less to the extent that the constituent instrument either expressly or impliedly so requires or capacities are inconsistent with

---

[92] The theory of implied powers has been discussed also in Kock, 'Die implied powers der Europäischen Gemeinschaften als Anwendungsfall der implied powers internationaler Organisationen überhaupt', in Bocksteigel *et al.* (eds.), *Law of Nations, Law of International Organizations, World's Economic Law: Festschrift für Ignaz Seidl-Hohenveldern* (1988) p. 279; Skubiszewski, 'Implied Powers of International Organizations', in Dinstein and Tabori (eds.), *International Law at a Time of Perplexity: Essays in Honour of Shabtai Rosenne* (1989) p. 855. There is much discussion in these sources of the position in the EU. Skubiszewski demonstrates that powers may be implied both in connection with express powers and in general by the application of principles. See also Rouyer-Hameray, *Les compétences implicites des organisations internationales* (1962); Chaumont, 'La signification du principe de specialité des organisation internationales', in *Melanges H. Rollin* (1964) pp. 55ff.; Simon, *L' interprétation judiciaire des traités d' organisations internationales* (1981) pp. 391ff.; Makarczyk, 'The International Court of Justice on the Implied Powers of International Organizations', in *Essays in Honour of M. Lachs* (1984) pp. 500–18; Martinez Sanseroni, 'Consentimiento del Estado y Organizaciones Internacionales', 37 REDI (1985) pp. 45–60.

[93] In the case of, e.g., the IMF and the IBRD, as has been seen, these powers, etc. are expressly granted. In the case of the UN, Article 104 of the Charter also makes an express grant of such and wider powers, etc.

their nature.[94] Further, some capacities attaching to national legal persons may, because they are special to such persons, not attach to international organizations. The governing principle is probably best stated explicitly in Article 104 of the UN Charter. This is that the implication of capacities is related to necessity for the exercise of the organization's functions and the fulfilment of its purposes. Both the extent and limits of capacities will be determined by this principle which has been explained in the previous section of this Chapter.

At the international level, capacities may also be expressly granted or implied, as has been seen. The interpretation of individual constitutions becomes important in this connection. However, there may be presumptions in regard to certain capacities.[95] Thus, international organizations exercise exclusive jurisdiction over their organs, have the capacity generally to conclude treaties and international agreements,[96] exercise a certain jurisdiction over matters arising on and within their premises and concerned with the functions of the organizations and the official duties of staff, have an active and passive *ius legationis*, have power to convoke and participate in international conferences, may become members of other international organizations, may be the subjects of active and passive responsibility, may bring claims, whether in respect of injuries to their staff or otherwise, and have claims brought against them and may engage in the settlement of their disputes by peaceful means. There may be others that are generally capable of implication if not expressly granted. However, in all cases, the extent of the power, right or obligation will be controlled by the express provisions of the constituent instruments or by implication by reference to the principles outlined in a previous section relevant to the implication of capacities. Thus, it is conceivable that a treaty on a certain subject-matter or for a certain purpose may be *ultra vires* a particular organization, while the exercise of certain kinds of jurisdiction (e.g., to incarcerate) may also not be permitted.

The point is best illustrated by reference to the treaty-making powers. In the *Reparation Case* itself the ICJ affirmed the treaty-making powers of

---

[94] On the powers of organizations in national law see also Colin and Sinkondo, 'Les relations contractuelles des organisations internationales avec les personnes privées', 69 RDIDC (1992) p. 7.

[95] There is a good discussion of these in Seyersted, loc. cit. note 39 at pp. 6ff. Seyersted regards these as 'inherent'. I prefer to describe them as implied.

[96] See on the evolution of the treaty-making power, Dobbert, 'Evolution of the Treaty-making Capacity of International Organizations', in Roche (ed.), *The Law and the Sea: Essays in Memory of Jean Carroz* (1987) p. 21.

the UN. While such powers must depend on the constitutions of organizations in that, though they need not be expressly given,[97] they must be conferred at least by reasonable implication as capacities required to enable the organizations to discharge their functions effectively,[98] there is a strong presumption in the absence of contrary indication that such powers are enjoyed by international organizations *qua* international persons, because they are necessary for the discharge of their functions and the fulfilment of their purposes. In the case of the UN and some of the other specialized agencies, e.g., the IMF, the IBRD and the IDA, the constituent instruments make it quite clear that the organizations have the capacity to enter into treaties. In the case of the Council of Europe, Article 40 of its Statute refers to agreements relating to privileges and immunities. In the case of the EU, the constituent instruments also expressly envisage the making of treaties by the organization. These express grants of power do not, though, limit the treaty-making capacity to what is expressly granted. On the other hand, as in the case of constituent instruments which do not specifically refer to a treaty-making capacity at all, in these cases also the capacity to make treaties is limited by the principle of necessary implication. In the case of the IBRD and the IDA, for example, the power to enter into developmental loan and credit agreements, among others, is expressly envisaged. But there are other international agreements which these organizations may enter into, e.g., relating to privileges and immunities, though they are not expressly mentioned in the constituent instruments. This does not mean that these organizations have an unlimited capacity to enter into treaties and international agreements. For example, they would not have the power to enter into trusteeship agreements, as the UN has. Thus, in all cases, the question whether an organization has power to make a particular treaty will have to be answered by the application of the interpretative principles of express authorization and necessary implication.[99] While there may be a presumption in the absence of contrary indication that organizations *qua* organizations have a general capacity to make treaties,

---

[97] Kelsen, among others, seems to think that these must be expressly granted: Kelsen, *Law of the United Nations* (1950) p. 330. See also Lukashuk, 'An International Organization as a Party to International Treaties', *Soviet YBIL* (1960) vol. I, p. 144.

[98] See, e.g., Weissberg. *The International Status of the United Nations* (1961) p. 37; E. Lauterpacht, loc. cit. note 7 at pp. 403*ff*. Bowett discusses the application of these principles: *The Law of International Institutions* (1982) pp. 341*ff*.

[99] *Pace* apparently Seyersted, loc. cit. note 39 at pp. 8*ff*., who thinks that organizations presumptively have the power to enter into any kind of treaty unless there is a prohibition in the constitution.

the particular kind of treaty they may make is determined on the basis of an express grant of power or by necessary implication from the constituent instrument, there being no reverse presumption that the power to make treaties is unlimited in the absence of specific prohibitions.

There may also be other powers which certain organizations may exercise, whether on the basis of an express grant or by implication, but which others do not have the capacity to exercise at all. Thus, in the case of the UN and the LN, the power of exercising territorial jurisdiction by administering territory in certain circumstances seems to have been implied.[100] This is special to such organizations and not a general power that may be implied in the case of all organizations. The specific powers envisaged in Article 81 of the Charter in respect of the trusteeship system of the UN included the power to administer territory. By implication, the power to exercise territorial jurisdiction was contemplated as being available in the solutions proposed for the Trieste and Jerusalem problems.[101] The LN exercised full powers of government in the Saar territory and limited powers in respect of Danzig.[102] It is certain that organizations such as the IMF, the IBRD, the FAO and the UNESCO would not enjoy such powers.

Similarly, the UN has power expressly given to it to conduct or organize military operations, control armed forces and even maintain armed forces.[103] These have been developed to some extent by implication. However, the limitations of the constituent instrument on these powers are to be observed and where they are extended by implication such implication may only take place by the application of the principles relevant to the implication of powers and to the extent permitted by such principles. There are, indeed, circumstances in which the conduct of military operations or the use of armed force by the UN is not permitted, though there may be a general power to exercise such powers. Such powers are not enjoyed by implication or otherwise by organizations in general, however.[104]

---

[100] See Seyersted, *ibid.* at pp. 10*ff*.

[101] See discussion of these cases in Seyersted, *ibid.*, and references therein. Instances of the exercise of the power to administer territory are to be found in footnote 24 in Chapter 6.

[102] See Seyersted, *ibid.* and references therein.

[103] See, e.g., the UNEF, the ONUC, etc.

[104] NATO and the OAS, for instance, are organizations which may have similar limited powers. Certain powers of organs of an organization may have to be implied, just as powers of the organization *vis-à-vis* third parties are implied: see, e.g., Caminos, 'L'exercice de pouvoirs implicites par le Secrétaire général de l'Organisation des États

The quasi-legislative power of the EU[105] which has some impact on the national legal systems of member states should also be noted. This is a power expressly granted by the constituent instruments (and developed to some extent by implication). This power is strictly a special power and is construed with a measure of caution. It is not the kind of capacity that other organizations generally have, whether by express grant or by implication.[106]

américains dans le cadre de l'établissement de la paix en Amérique centrale', 35 AFDI (1989) p. 189; and Caminos and Lavalle, 'New Departures in the Exercise of Inherent Powers by the UN and OAS Secretaries-General', 83 AJIL (1989) p. 395. See also *Howrani and Four Others*, UNAT Judgment No. 4 [1951], JUNAT Nos. 1–70, at p. 17, for the view that powers of an *organ* may have to be implied.

[105] See Lasok and Bridge, *Law and Institutions of the European Communities* (1991) p. 82.

[106] The powers of the SC of the UN to make binding decisions under Charter VII of the Charter are somewhat different.

4   Membership and representation

Matters concerning membership depend primarily on the provisions of the constitutions of international organizations and on the practice of each organization. Whether the area concerned is admission to membership, suspension from privileges, termination of membership or the related issue of representation of members, it is not easy to identify general principles relevant to the interpretation of all constituent documents. On the other hand, there may be consistent practices across many organizations in implementing provisions of constitutions that could be usefully studied.

Membership

Admission to membership

In some organizations, such as the UN and most of its specialized agencies, membership is 'universal' in the sense that (a) the organization is open or has 'universal vocation' and (b) most, though not quite all, states and state-like entities are members. In others, such as the regional organizations, political and technical – the OAS, the OAU, the ADB, the EU, the IDB, the Council of Europe and the Arab League, for example – membership is limited in various ways. Generally, whether membership is 'universal' or limited, the original signatories who formulated the constitution become members automatically, without the need for admission, upon signature and ratification of the constitution. But thereafter states eligible must generally be admitted by decision of one or more organs of the organization even in universal (or open) organizations.[1]

---

[1] There are some organizations which make membership available to all states by adherence, for example: see Codding, *The Universal Postal Union* (1964) p. 80 (the UPU

This applies also to original members who ceased to be members of the organization and want to become members once again. This is what happened to the USA when it withdrew from the ILO and sought membership again later, and to the UK and Germany in the UNESCO. Sometimes, as in the case of some of the specialized agencies of the UN, membership in the UN gives the state a right to membership in the specialized agency.[2] In the case of the IBRD membership of the IMF is a condition precedent to membership, while to become a member of the IDA or the IFC a state must be a member of the IBRD.[3] In either case membership of the one organization does not, however, give the state a *right* to membership in the other organization. It merely makes it eligible for membership.

In the case of the UN Article 4(1) requires, in addition to statehood, that states be peace-loving, accept the obligations of the UN Charter and, in the judgment of the UN, be both able and willing to carry out those obligations.[4] In the *First Admissions*

---

between 1848 and 1947); and Koers, 'Visserij Organisaties', in Van Themaat (ed.), *Studies over Internationaal Economisch Recht* (1977) vol. I, p. 25. The suggestion has been made that, where no provision is made in the constitution for admission of new members, this may be done by amendment of the constitution, and that constitutions may have to be amended in order to accommodate certain new members in organs, etc.: see Schermers and Blokker, *International Institutional Law* (1995) pp. 62*ff*. The admission of members is discussed in, e.g., Mosler, 'Die Aufname in Internationale Organizationen', 19 ZAORV (1958) p. 275; Higgins, *The Development of International Law through the Political Organs of the United Nations* (1963) pp. 14*ff*.; and Broms, *The United Nations* (1990) pp. 68*ff*.

[2] See, e.g., Article II(1) of the UNESCO constitution, and Article 6 of the IMO constitution.

[3] See Article II(1)(b) of the IBRD Articles of Agreement; Article II(1) of the IFC Articles of Agreement; and Article II(1) of the IDA Articles of Agreement.

[4] On the criteria for statehood see Higgins, note 1 pp. 17*ff*.; Crawford, *The Creation of States in International Law* (1979) chapter 4; and Dugard, *Recognition and the United Nations* (1987) pp. 127*ff*. Some questions have been raised about the membership of mini-states (also called micro-states and diminutive states) in the UN and other open organizations. In the UN there are some mini-states that have been accepted as members, such as The Maldives, Bhutan, Qatar, Andorra, San Marino, Monaco, Iceland and Bahrein. The problem identified is that the ability to carry out the obligations of the Charter relating to collective security is in doubt (the claim to statehood cannot be questioned). It may well be argued that, since such obligations arise from resolutions of the SC or the GA, these organs can tailor their resolutions in such a way as to exempt mini-states from obligations they cannot fulfill. The practice of the UN thus far has been to accept mini-states as members, if they apply for membership. Other open organizations have had no difficulty with the membership of mini-states. In technical organizations, the size of a state is not an issue, as it is not in financial institutions. The issue of mini-states has been discussed by several authors: e.g., Gunter, 'The Problems of Mini-State Membership in the United Nations System: Recent Attempts Towards a Solution', 12 Col. JTL (1973) p. 464; Gunter, 'What Happened to the United Nations

Case[5] the ICJ addressed several issues connected with the implementation of this article and in the course of its advisory opinion enunciated what could be general principles. While the Court did not deny that admission depended on the judgment of the organization, which meant that it could not be said that such a state had an unquestionable right to admission, it did take the view in effect that it was illegal to refuse admission to states considered to fulfil these requirements. On the other hand, it would not be appropriate to speak of a legal obligation to admit an applicant that fulfils the necessary conditions, since the applicant cannot be said to fulfil the conditions until the members have decided that it does, and some of the conditions are subjective, depending on the judgment of the organization. If the organization through any of its relevant organs rejected the application, there would be a presumption that, in the judgment of the organization, the requisite conditions had not been fulfilled. Negatively, the Court held that a member state could not juridically make its consent to admission dependent on conditions not expressly provided for in Article 4(1) and in particular, where a member state recognized the conditions set forth in that provision to be fulfilled, on the additional condition that other states be admitted to membership together with the state concerned.[6] The Court made it quite clear that in the case of the UN Charter it could not be argued

that the conditions enumerated represent only an indispensable minimum, in the sense that political considerations could be superimposed upon them, and prevent the admission of the applicant which fulfills them.[7]

This, it said, could confer upon member states 'an indefinite and practically unlimited power of discretion in the imposition of new

Mini-State Problem', 71 AJIL (1977) p. 110; Harris, 'Micro-States in the United Nations: a Broader Purpose', 9 Col. JTL (1970) p. 23; Mendelson, 'Diminutive States in the United Nations', 21 ICLQ (1972) p. 609; Schwebel, 'Mini-States and a More Efficient United Nations', 67 AJIL (1973) p. 108; Seyersted, 'Federated and Other Partly Self-governing States and Mini-States in Foreign Affairs and in International Organizations', 57 Nordic JIL (1988) at pp. 373*ff*.; and Omerogbe, 'Functionalism in the UPU and ITU', 27 IJIL (1987) p. 50.

Problems have also arisen in regard to the criteria for statehood, whether in connection with federated states or other entities: see the discussion in, e.g., Seyersted, loc. cit. above in this footnote at pp. 369*ff*.; Kirgis, 'Admission of Palestine as a Member of a Specialized Agency and Withholding the Payment of Assessment in Response', 84 AJIL (1990) p. 218; Osieke, 'Admission to Membership in International Organizations: The Case of Namibia', 51 BYIL (1990) p. 189; and (Note), 'Legal Aspects of Membership in the Organization of African Unity: The Case of the Western Sahara', 17 *Case Western Reserve Journal of International Law* (1985) p. 123.

[5] 1947–48 ICJ Reports p. 57.   [6] *Ibid.* at p. 65.   [7] *Ibid.* at pp. 62–3.

conditions'.[8] The Court concluded that 'the spirit as well as the terms of the paragraph precluded the idea that considerations extraneous to these principles and obligations (of the Charter) can prevent the admission of a State which complies with them'.[9] The Court applied the rule of effectiveness in the interpretation of the Charter – *ut magis valeat quam pereat* – in deciding in effect that where conditions are enumerated they must be deemed to be exhaustive, if not to do so would result in destroying their significance and weight. No doubt where in other constitutions conditions for admission are similarly enumerated the same principle could be applied.

The *First Admissions Case* arose as a result of the first applications for membership to the UN in 1946. Three applications, those of Afghanistan, Iceland and Sudan, were accepted without difficulty but in respect of the others, namely those of Albania, Ireland, Mongolian People's Republic, Portugal and Transjordan, conditions were mentioned which were not referred to in Article 4(1). These applications, thus, ran into difficulty. In 1947 the applications were debated again and because of the stalemate reference was made to the ICJ for an advisory opinion. The stalemate continued after the opinion. Another opinion was sought on a different point.[10] However, the deadlock in regard to the 1946 applications continued until 1955 when, on a 'package' basis, sixteen states were admitted to membership.[11]

In connection with membership of the UN the question was raised in 1955, when Austria became a member, whether a state committed to permanent neutrality can be a member. The issue concerns the ability of or willingness of such a state to carry out the obligations of the

---

[8] *Ibid.*

[9] *Ibid.* at p. 63. There was a strong dissenting minority (six) in this case. Four judges gave a considered joint opinion: *ibid.* at pp. 82*ff.* Article 4 of the Statute of the Council of Europe (i) limits membership to European states and (ii) makes admission conditional upon fulfilment of some provisions of Article 3. The same principle would apply in this case as outlined in the *First Admissions Case.* There are other constitutions, such as those of the ICAO and the OAS, which make admission conditional: see Scheman, 'Admission of States to the Organization of American States', 58 AJIL (1964) p. 968; and Kutzner, *Die Organisation der Amerikanischen Staaten (OAS)* (1970) pp. 161*ff.*

[10] The *Second Admissions Case*, 1950 ICJ Reports p. 10.

[11] See the account of this episode and its ramifications in Broms, note 1 pp. 86*ff.* The 'package' basis could not have been proper. The view taken by the ICJ in the *First Admissions Case* was not in effect accepted by the Soviet Union and later even by the USA (when it vetoed the admission of the two Vietnams in 1975): see Jacobs and Poirier. 'The Right to Veto United Nations Membership Applications: The United States Veto of the Viet-Nams', 17 Harv. ILJ (1976) p. 581.

Charter relating to collective security and peacekeeping. In fact Austria was admitted as a member when it applied, though it is committed to permanent neutrality. Further, during the UN operations in Cyprus and thereafter Austria has sent armed forces to assist the UN. Further, when Switzerland held a plebiscite to enable it to join the UN, no doubts were expressed about its eligibility for membership. It is arguable that, firstly, Charter obligations take precedence over any other international obligations, an analogy being drawn from Article 103 of the Charter which refers to treaty obligations, and, secondly, participation in collective security measures or peace-keeping under the UN Charter is not a violation of the obligations of permanent neutrality, because neutrality was not intended to extend to such measures.[12]

A question which was also discussed in the *First Admissions Case* concerned good faith in the exercise of the vote on admission. The Court and the dissenting judges apparently agreed that there was no obligation upon member states to state the grounds on which their vote was based and that there was no way of rectifying a vote based on improper grounds.[13] However, if reasons were given, these must conform to any rules or limitations applicable to the vote (on admission), stated in or resulting from the Charter (constituent instrument).[14] At the same time member states were under an obligation to act in good faith in exercising their vote, so that it would be improper, for instance, ostensibly to give as the ground of their vote an admitted and legitimate contention, while in reality basing their vote on another and illegitimate contention.[15]

This duty to act in good faith in the matter of admission could be extended to other organizations than the UN, to the actions of the organization as a whole (and to matters other than admission). Thus, to take

---

[12] If treaty obligations must give way, *a fortiori* other international obligations, including customary obligations would have to give way. On permanent neutrality and the UN see, e.g., Verdross, 'Austria's Permanent Neutrality and the United Nations', 50 AJIL (1958) p. 61; Zemanek, 'Neutral Austria in the United Nations', 15 *International Organization* (1961) p. 408; Gunter, 'Switzerland and the United Nations', 30 *International Organization* (1976) p. 129; and Kock, 'A Permanently Neutral State in the Security Council', 6 Cornell ILJ (1973) p. 137. A similar issue may be raised in regard to countries, such as Germany and Japan, whose constitutions have limitations which could affect their ability to fulfill UN Charter obligations. The answer to be given is similar to that which applies in the case of permanent neutrality. The UN had no problem admitting these states to membership.

[13] See 1947–48 ICJ Reports at pp. 61*ff.* for the Court's opinion and pp. 82*ff.*, 80 for the dissents.

[14] See *ibid.* at pp. 80*ff. per* Judge Azevedo.   [15] See *ibid.* at pp. 60*ff. per* the Court.

an example relating to admission, the financial institutions in general have a provision that membership is open to states 'in accordance with such terms as may be prescribed'[16] by the institution or a provision similarly formulated.[17] In setting the terms of admission, e.g., relating to quotas or subscriptions, but also otherwise, the organization would be under an obligation not to impose terms which are unrealistic in the context of the applicant's economic or other status in relation to other members of the organization.[18]

A relevant question is whether there are any requirements for membership in an organization which may be implied in a constitution. If the answer were in the affirmative, where conditions were expressly mentioned in a constitution, such requirements would be additional. Clearly, where expressly enumerated conditions are intended to be exclusive, no others may be taken into account. It is arguable that, whether a constitution states as much, as the UN Charter does, or not, an organization may consider whether an applicant for membership is willing and able to fulfil the obligations imposed by its constitution. In the case of the admission to the IMF of the successor states created upon the dissolution in 1991 of Yugoslavia, the IMF adopted a proposal that membership should be dependent upon such a condition. It was stated that the IMF had implicit authority to assess whether a state was capable of carrying out its obligations to the IMF in deciding to admit it as a member.[19] The approach is warranted. Though the issue of conditionality was

---

[16] See, e.g., the IBRD Articles of Agreement, Article II(1)(b); the IMF Articles of Agreement, Article II(2); the ADB Agreement, Article 3(1); the IDB Agreement, Article II(1)(b); and the IDA Articles of Agreement, Article II(1).

[17] The resolution by which admission is effected under these constitutions is in fact the result of a negotiated agreement between the applicant and the organization, the resolution being based on 'consultation' with the representatives of the applicant and confirmation by the applicant. See the IDA resolution admitting the Azerbaijan Republic sent to the Board of Governors on 13 February 1995.

[18] For discussion of questions relating to lesser forms of membership than full membership and other such matters, see, e.g., Sands and Klein (eds.), *Bowett's Law of International Institutions* (2001) pp. 534ff. See also Broms, note 1 pp. 121ff.; and Schermers and Blokker, note 1 pp. 113ff. These authors also discuss questions relating to what entities other than states qualify for some kind of membership.

[19] IMF, *Issues of State Succession Concerning Yugoslavia in the Fund* (14 July 1992) p. 7. The question was complicated because of earlier decisions taken by the IMF. The IMF's approach was criticized by the IBRD: World Bank, *Effects of the Disintegration of the Socialist Federal Republic of Yogoslavia (SFRY)* (25 November 1992) p. 5. The matter is discussed in Williams, 'State Succession and the International Financial Institutions: Political Criteria v. Protection of Outstanding Financial Obligations', 43 ICLQ (1994) at pp. 800ff.

raised in connection with succession, the implied condition is applicable generally.

Continuity, Creation and Succession of States[20]

A special problem relating to admission of members arises when states become independent (as in the case of the colonies) or break up (as in the case of the Soviet Union or Yugoslavia). The issue relates to continuity and succession – is there a case for taking the view that states automatically 'continue' or 'succeed' to membership in such circumstances or do they have to apply for membership anew?

It is generally accepted practice that on decolonization new states had to apply for admission to membership in organizations.[21] It was not accepted that the principle applied that new states could elect to be bound by the constitution of an organization of which its colonial ruler was a member on the understanding that the constitution was a treaty. Thus, when countries such as Ceylon and Ghana became independent from the UK, they had to apply for membership in the international organizations, though the UK may already have been a member of those organizations.[22]

A more difficult question arises when states break up, as when in 1947 India was divided to form Pakistan and India, when in 1991 the Soviet Union disintegrated, when in 1992 the Czechoslovak Republic was dissolved or when in 1992 Yugoslavia broke up. While each case has been treated on its merits and each instistution must technically decide the issues itself to the extent that the solutions are not dependent on solutions in other organizations, the basic principle applied has been that, if a continuator state to the previous member can be identified, then that state continues the membership of the previous member.[23] The identification of a continuator could depend on the agreement or vote of the other members of the organization. Where there is no general

---

[20] See particularly in relation to the international financial institutions, Williams, *ibid*. On the question of continuity, creation and succession in general see, e.g., Crawford, note 4; Marek, *Identity and Continuity of States in Public International Law* (1968); O' Connell, *State Succession in Municipal Law and International Law* (1967).

[21] See 2 YBILC (1962) at pp. 124*ff*.

[22] See also Schermers, *International Institutional Law* (1980) at pp. 58*ff*.

[23] See Mullerson, 'The Continuity and Succession of States by Reference to the Former USSR and Yugoslavia', 42 ICLQ (1993) at pp. 477*ff*. He states that there can be no question of *succession* to membership of international organizations (*ibid*. at p. 478). This statement must now be qualified in the light of the practice of the IMF and the IBRD, among other things.

agreement, problems may arise as to which organs are responsible for taking the relevant decision and by what majority. So far, however, serious disagreements have been avoided so that there has been general agreement on the course of action to be taken by the organization. This still leaves open how (on what principles) the issues whether there has been continuation and what entity is the continuator are to be determined. It would seem that, while these questions may usually be decided by agreement among the involved states themselves, ultimately there are no obvious principles upon which the issues have been decided. There has always been some element of pragmatism in the solution reached. However, that the concept of continuity is relevant to the survival of membership, although the notion has clearly been manipulated in practice, is a fact which must be accepted.

In the case of India and Pakistan, it was generally accepted in all organizations that India was the sole continuator state and continued its membership, Pakistan being a new state and, thus, having to apply for admission pursuant to the applicable procedure.[24] When Egypt and Syria merged to form the United Arab Republic in 1958[25] and Tanganyika and Zanzibar merged into the United Republic of Tanzania in 1964, the new united states were recognized as successors of the previous states in the organizations of which the latter had been members – with continuing membership. In the case of the break-up of the USSR the Russian Federation was by agreement among all concerned regarded as the continuator of the USSR in the organizations of which the latter had been a member, it, thus, becoming necessary for the other republics to be admitted as new members. In the case of Yugoslavia, however, in the UN and many of the specialized agencies, no continuator state as such was identified and all the states formed out of the former Yugoslavia had to be admitted to membership.[26] In the case of Czechoslovakia also

---

[24] See Misra, 'Succession of States: Pakistan's Membership of the United Nations', 3 CYIL (1965) p. 281.

[25] See Cotran, 'Some Legal Aspects of the Formation of the United Arab Republic and the United Arab States', 8 ICLQ (1959) p. 346; and Buergenthal, *Law-Making in the International Civil Aviation Organization* (1969) pp. 31*ff*. For the 'succession' of Egypt upon the dissolution of the United Arab Republic in 1961, and the treatment of Syria as a result thereof, see Young, 'The State of Syria, Old or New?', 56 AJIL (1962) p. 482. For the treatment of Singapore upon its secession from Malaysia in 1965, see Jayakumar, 'Singapore and State Succession: International Relations and International Law', 19 ICLQ (1970) p. 398. Bangladesh had also to apply for membership in international organizations when it seceded from Pakistan in 1971.

[26] See, e.g., Record of the 3,196th meeting of the SC of 7 April 1991: UN Doc. S/PV 3196, and related resolutions of the GA and other documents. Mullerson, loc. cit. note 23,

no continuator state was identified and both the Czech Republic and the Slovak Republic were admitted to membership of the UN and most specialized agencies.[27]

In the financial institutions an even more pragmatic approach is taken with differing results particularly because of the existence of outstanding obligations on loans and credits. Thus, in the case of Yugoslavia, all five republics which arose out of the old state became 'successors to the assets and liabilities' of Yugoslavia, 'the assets and liabilities' of Yugoslavia being divided among them, while it was found that Yugoslavia had ceased to exist and had ceased to be a member of the IMF.[28] In the IBRD the concept of 'succession' of all five new republics prevailed, with the shares of Yugoslavia being divided (not equally) among the five republics and a settlement being reached on the service of outstanding loans.[29]

The practice of international institutions in general in regard to membership where states merge to form one state, e.g., the merger of Syria and Egypt to form the United Arab Republic or the union of Tanganyika and Zanzibar into the United Republic of Tanzania, and the practice of

discusses the cases of dissolution of the USSR and Yugoslavia. See also Mullerson, *International Law, Rights and Politics* (1994) pp. 137ff.

[27] See, e.g., Resolutions 800 and 801 (1993) of 8 January 1993 of the SC: UN Doc. S/Res/800 (1993) and UN Doc. S/Res/801 (1993). When the two Germanies were unified, the FRG, the unified state, was the member of the UN which assumed the relevant obligations and rights of both Germanies. No significant problems were encountered.

[28] See IMF Press Release No. 92/92, dated 15 December 1992. A similar decision was taken on the demise of Czechoslovakia: IMF Press Release No. 92/96, dated 31 December 1992.

[29] See IBRD News Release No. 93/S42. Similar treatment was given the two new republics when Czechoslovakia broke up: IBRD News Release 93/S37. See also the Annual Report of the IBRD for 1992/93. The treatment of Yugoslavia, when it broke up, by the IMF and the IBRD has been discussed in Williams, loc. cit. note 19 at pp. 778ff. and 784ff. For the IMF's approach to the problem being discussed, particularly in relation to Yugoslavia and the Czech Republic, see IMF, *Succession of Territories and Dissolution of Members in the Fund* (14 July 1992); IMF, *Issues of State Succession*; IMF, *Socialist Federal Republic of Yugoslavia Cessation of Membership, Allocation of Assets and Liabilities in the Fund, and Succession to Membership in the Fund* (7 December 1992); IMF, *Quota Calculations for the Successor Republics of Yugoslavia* (7 December 1992); and IMF, *Czech and Slovak Federal Republic Cessation of Membership, Allocation of Assets and Liabilities in the Fund, and Succession to Membership in the Fund* (21 December 1992). For the World Bank's approach see World Bank, *The Bank's Practice with Respect to State Succession* (25 November 1992); World Bank, 'Effects of Disintegration'; World Bank, *Bank Portfolio of Loans in the Former Yugoslav Republics* (25 November 1992); World Bank, *Comments on the 'Conditional Succession' Approach Envisaged in the Fund's Paper* (25 November 1992); World Bank, *Socialist Republic of Yugoslavia Cessation of Membership and Succession to Membership* (11 February 1993); and World Bank, *Czech Republic and Slovak Republic – Succession to Membership Status of the Czech and Slovak Federal Republic* (23 December 1992).

the financial institutions, particularly the IMF and the IBRD, in regard to the dissolution of states, e.g., Yugoslavia and Czechoslovakia, is evidence that in certain institutions and for practical reasons, perhaps, the succession of states to membership in international organizations is a reality.[30] On the other hand, there are situations, as in the case of decolonization and some cases of disintegration, where succession is not accepted but the new states must seek fresh membership. Continuity of membership, as in the case of Russia, when the USSR broke up, is also accepted.

Suspension

Suspension in the case of the UN Charter is from 'the exercise of the rights and privileges of membership', as Article 5 reflects. In the case of the IBRD and most of the financial institutions reference is made to 'suspension' or 'suspension from membership' but this is later explained as absence of entitlement 'to exercise any rights' under the constitution.[31] Not all international organizations have provisions on suspension.[32] The general object of suspension seems to be to secure compliance by a member state with some or all of its obligations. The circumstances in which powers of suspension may be exercised vary considerably. Suspension in general is a sanction for non-fulfilment of financial obligations. Article 19 of the UN Charter provides for suspension in the sense of deprivation of a vote in the GA when a member is in arrears with its budgetary contributions to an amount equal to the contributions due for the preceding two full years.[33] The ILO constitution has similarly

[30] *Pace* Mullerson, loc. cit. note 23 at p. 478.

[31] See, e.g., IBRD Articles of Agreement, Article VI(2); IFC Articles of Agreement, Article V(2); and ADB Agreement, Article 42.

[32] The ITU constitution has no provision for suspension, nor has the UNESCO any independent express power of suspension, because suspension is only the result of suspension from the UN (Article II(4) of the Constitution). In the EU, where the CJEC has compulsory jurisdiction over members in questions involving non-fulfilment of the treaty obligations, suspension has not been thought necessary.

[33] This sanction was applied by the UN to Haiti in 1963 and to the Dominican Republic in 1968 (see UN Doc. A/7146 and the 1671 and 1672 Plenary Meetings of the GA, 12 June 1968). It was not applied in 1965 over the arrears of peace-keeping contributions because of the particular constitutional conflict over this issue. To avoid a confrontation, the GA operated during the nineteenth session by consensus, avoiding any vote. The USA and USSR, the main protagonists over the constitutional issue, joined in opposing Albania's attempt to force a vote: see Padelford, 'Financing Peace-keeping: Politics and Crisis', 19 *International Organization* (1965) p. 444; also Broms, note 1 pp. 133*ff.* The procedure under Article 19 of the UN Charter has been used when appropriate.

adopted two years, whereas the IMO constitution in Article 52 allows only one year's grace, and the ICAO constitution refers in Article 62 to 'a reasonable period'. Other constitutions extend the category of defaults for which suspension is a sanction, so that in the case of the WHO it applies 'in other exceptional circumstances' (Article 7 of the constitution) and Article 31 of the WHO constitution refers to a member who 'otherwise fails in its obligations under the present Convention'. Under Article 5 of the Charter suspension will be a possible sanction against a member 'against which preventive or enforcement action has been taken'. The financial institutions generally have a power of suspension for breach of obligations towards the organization as such.[34] The Council of Europe can under Article 8 of its constitution suspend a member for having 'seriously violated' the article of the constitution enjoining acceptance of the rule of law and observance of human rights. The ILO amended its constitution in order to suspend states subject to suspension in the UN and to enable suspension of a state found to be flagrantly and persistently pursuing a policy of racial discrimination or apartheid from any further participation in the Conference.[35]

The effect of suspension varies considerably. In the UN suspension under Article 19 involves merely loss of vote in the GA, although suspension under Article 5 involves loss of the 'rights' and 'privileges of membership' generally, presumably depriving a member of both representation and voting rights in all organs. The ILO constitution confines the effect of suspension for arrears of financial contributions to loss of vote, but extends it to the Conference, the Governing Body, any committee or the elections of members of the Governing Body.[36] The WMO constitution in Article 31 confines the effect to suspension of rights and privileges 'as a member', and the COE constitution in Articles 8 and 9 clearly covers loss of representation which results also in the loss of vote. The UNESCO constitution in Article II(4) provides for the loss of membership rights and privileges. Those organizations which provide services or more tangible advantages have provisions which bring about the suspension of these services and advantages. The WMO constitution in Article 31 refers to loss of voting privileges 'and other services', and all

---

[34] See the provisions referred to in footnote 31 above; and IDB Agreement, Article IX(2), AFDB Agreement, Article 44(1); and CDB Agreement, Article 41(1).

[35] See ILO Constitution, Article 1(6). The object of this amendment was to enable the organization to assume greater powers against such members as South Africa.

[36] Article 13(4). Under Article 1(6) suspension is from the exercise of the rights and privileges of membership of the ILO.

the financial institutions have similar comprehensive sanctions. Under Article V(5) of its constitution the IMF may limit a member's right to use the general resources of the IMF[37] and under Article XIII(2) it has the power to suspend a member's right to use SDRs. The other financial institutions generally provide for the suspension automatically to result in expulsion unless the member is restored to good standing by the Board of Governors. In the case of the IMF a further decision of the IMF Board of Governors under Article XXVI is required for compulsory withdrawal to take effect.

Generally, suspension is not mandatory but permissive. It is the result of an exercise of discretion by a competent organ. In those cases where it may appear to be otherwise there is provision for waiver of the sanction when failure to pay is due to circumstances beyond the control of the member.[38]

The procedure for imposing a suspension also varies. The power is generally assigned to the main plenary organ, although under Article 5 of the Charter the recommendation of the SC is a prior condition. In the case of the COE, where the Assembly is not composed of state representatives, the decision is entrusted to the Committee of Ministers who are state representatives. The vote required varies, and, although normally a two-thirds majority is required, a simple majority suffices in the ICAO and the WHO, for example.[39] An express requirement of prior notice to the offending member with the possibility of due process is rarely found as an essential part of the procedure of suspension, except in the financial institutions. It may be argued that in principle such a requirement with the possibility of due process should be implied in provisions for suspension because suspension is such a serious matter. It is not clear, though, that practice has always recognized the principle.

---

[37] See also Article XXVI(2). In June 1994 the IMF suspended the voting rights of Zaire pursuant to this Article. Zaire had persistently failed to fulfil its obligations under the IMF Articles of Agreement: see IMF Press Release No. 94/39 of 3 June 1994.

[38] See, e.g., Article 19 of the UN Charter and Article 13(4) of the ILO Constitution.

[39] This is the result of the application of Chapter XIII of the constitution of the WHO and Article 48(c) of the ICAO Constitution. Attempts have been made to invoke suspension for reasons other than those specified in the constitutions of some organizations. This is particularly so in the case of South Africa (in the ILO, the WHO, the UNESCO, the ITU, the UPU, the WMO and the ICAO). In fact in 1975 the WMO did suspend South Africa because the practice of apartheid was not conducive to the fulfilment of WMO's objectives, which may have been a strange reason.

Suspension, it should be noted, only affects rights and privileges of one kind or another. It does not release the member state from its obligations under the constitution of the organization.

Suspension is fraught with such grave consequences that in theory it is doubtful whether the power may be implied in the absence of express provision, unless there is express provision for expulsion. The lesser 'evil' may then be implied because a greater 'evil' is permitted. There is no practice on implied suspension, however.

Termination of membership

Termination of membership[40] may clearly take place when an organization is dissolved. But, while the organization continues to exist, membership may be terminated by withdrawal (a voluntary act of the member state), by expulsion (a measure taken by the organization against the member state) and by the loss of membership upon failure to accept an amendment of the constitution of the organization. Another reason for termination not often mentioned is the disappearance of the member state or loss of its essential characteristics as a state.

Withdrawal

The right to withdraw is expressly referred to in the constitutions of most of the specialized agencies,[41] but not in the Charter of the UN. The conditions attached to the right of withdrawal vary. The World Bank Group allows withdrawal simply upon submission of written notice, and permits this withdrawal to take effect immediately.[42] Other organizations impose clear limitations on withdrawal. In some cases it is not permitted during an initial period, so as to allow the organization time to become established.[43] In some cases a period is prescribed between

---

[40] See particularly Singh, *Termination of Membership of International Organizations* (1958).

[41] The WHO Constitution has no such provision. The Constitution of the UNESCO did not have one until 1954 when Article II(6) was introduced. The USA withdrew from the UNESCO in 1983 under this provision.

[42] See, e.g., IBRD Articles of Agreement, Article VI(1); IFC Articles of Agreement, Article V(1); and IDA Articles of Agreement, Article VII(1). In 1950 Poland withdrew from the IBRD, in 1960 Cuba and the Dominican Republic and in 1965 Indonesia.

[43] See, e.g., the FAO constitution, Article 19 (four years); and the ECSC Treaty, Article 97 (fifty years). See also Article 16 of the EMBL Constitution (sixteen years); Article 24 of the ESA Constitution (six years); Article XVIIID of the IAEA Constitution (five years); Article 69 of the IMO Constitution (one year); Article II(6) of the UNESCO Constitution (one calendar year after the end of the year in which notice is given); Article 13 of the NATO Constitution (twenty years). In the case of the Council of Europe Article 7 of its Statute specifies that withdrawal becomes effective at the end of the financial year.

the giving of notice to withdraw and the coming into effect of withdrawal, a kind of 'cooling-off' period to allow for reconsideration and other possibilities.[44] There is a question whether a member state can suspend its notice, once given, as North Korea did in withdrawing from the IAEA in 1993. The answer should be that it cannot, unless the rest of the members agree.

Another condition sometimes attached to withdrawal is that outstanding obligations must be fulfilled before withdrawal is effective. In general the obligations specified are simply the financial obligations incurred as part of the budgetary commitment.[45] When an organization finances itself, as is the case with the financial organizations, the settlement of accounts with a withdrawing member is even more complicated. For example, in the case of the IBRD under Article VI(4) the member remains liable for direct obligations to the IBRD and for contingent liabilities so long as its loans or guarantees remain outstanding, while the member's shares are repurchased by the institution at their book value subject to the latter's right of set-off for amounts due under loans or guarantees.[46]

---

[44] See, e.g., IDB Agreement, Article IX(1); ADB Agreement, Article 41(1); AFDB Agreement, Article 43(1); CDB Agreement, Article 40(1); WMO Constitution, Article 30(a); and ILO constitution, Article 1(5). See also Articles 18 and 19 of the Constitution of the Arab League and Boutros-Ghali, 'La Ligue des Etâts Arabes', 137 *Hague Recueil* (1972-III) p. 37. See also generally, Jenks, 'Some Constitutional Problems of International Organizations', 22 BYIL (1945) p. 23. Article 56 of the Vienna Convention on the Law of Treaties requires one year's notice in the case of treaties where no other period is specified in cases where withdrawal is permitted.

[45] See, e.g., Article 9 of the FAO Constitution; Article 5 of the ILO Constitution; Article 9(3) of the League Covenant. These provisions suspend effectiveness of withdrawal until financial obligations have been fulfilled. The USA withdrew from the ILO in 1975 under Article 5 of the Constitution and rejoined subsequently in 1980 (for a discussion of the US withdrawal from the ILO see Alford, 'The Prospective Withdrawal of the United States from the International Labour Organization: Rationales and Implications', 17 Harvard ILJ (1976) p. 623; Joyner, 'The United States' Withdrawal from the ILO: International Politics in the Labour Arena', 12 *International Lawyer* (1978) p. 721; also 14 ILM (1972) p. 1,582). There are other examples of members effectively withdrawing from organizations. The USA withdrew from the UNESCO in 1984 (for the principal documents relating to the US withdrawal see Kirgis, *International Organizations in their Legal Setting* (1993) pp. 264ff.; for a discussion of the legal issues raised for the UNESCO by the US withdrawal see 'The Report by the Director-General on Consequences of the Withdrawal of a Member State', 1985 UNJY p. 156). South Africa withdrew from the UNESCO in 1956. At various times the UK, Germany and Portugal have withdrawn from the UNESCO.

[46] When states withdrew from the IMF, agreements were reached for the settlement of all accounts: Gold, *Membership and Nonmembership in the International Monetary Fund* (1974) p. 386. For Indonesia's withdrawal from and re-entry to the IMF, see Gold, *ibid.* pp. 212ff.

In some cases the fulfilment of obligations other than financial ones is required. This was true under Article 1(3) of the LN Covenant.[47] The constitution of the ILO is a special case in providing in Article 5 that withdrawal shall not affect the continued validity of obligations arising under any international labour convention to which the member withdrawing is a party. The constitutions of the specialized agencies, however, do not contain such provisions.[48] Clearly withdrawal could not in any event affect obligations already incurred, at least in the case of financial obligations. A state may be more ready to pay, if its effective withdrawal is made conditional upon settlement.[49]

The difficult question is what happens in the absence of a withdrawal clause. Some have argued that in such a situation member states have no right of unilateral withdrawal,[50] this view being sometimes expressed as a consequence of the applicability of Articles 54 to 56 of the Vienna Convention on the Law of Treaties to constitutions of international organizations as to any other treaty.[51] Even on the assumption that the principle contained in the latter convention is applicable, it would seem that the nature of constitutions raises a presumption that a state must be deemed to be free to withdraw from an organization, unless it has surrendered that right either expressly or impliedly,[52] provided it gives the twelve months' notice required by Article 56(2) of the Vienna Convention. Policy considerations favouring the view that withdrawal is permissible even in the absence of express provision have been based on the concepts of sovereignty and self-determination, equity, expediency

---

[47] The provision was rather ineffective, because withdrawing members usually settled their debts but did not generally make amends for breaches of obligations. On withdrawal from the LN see Magliveras, 'The Withdrawal from the League of Nations Revisited', 10 *Dickinson Journal of International Law* (1991) p. 25.

[48] See, e.g., the constitutions of the ICAO, the WMO and the UPU.

[49] Many other problems may arise when states withdraw from an organization: see, e.g., Stein and Carreau, 'Law and Peaceful Change in a Subsystem: "Withdrawal" of France from the North Atlantic Treaty Organization', 62 AJIL (1968) p. 577.

[50] See, e.g., Feinberg, 'Unilateral Withdrawal from an International Organization', 39 BYIL (1963) at p. 215. See also R. L. Bindschedler, *Rechtsfragen der Europäischen Einigung* (1954) pp. 40*ff*.; discussion in Schermers and Blokker, note 1 pp. 87*ff*.; Unni, 'Indonesia's withdrawal from the United Nations', 5 IJIL (1965) p. 128; and Alexandrowicz, *World Economic Agencies* (1962) pp. 129*ff*.

[51] For example, Syz, *International Development Banks* (1974) p. 13.

[52] See, e.g., Sands and Klein (eds.), note 18 p. 548. See also Kelsen, *Law of the United Nations* (1950) chapter 7; discussion in Schermers and Blokker, note 1 pp. 91*ff*.; Singh, note 40 pp. 79*ff*.; Hoyt, *The Unanimity Rule in the Revision of Treaties* (1959) p. 78.

and general principles of law.[53] The first two may equally be regarded as having been limited by participation in the constituent instrument, while equity is a double-edged sword. Expediency may be a somewhat more cogent argument – a reluctant member cannot be forced to participate. On the other hand, the analogy of private organizations, where in national law membership may be cancelled unilaterally, is not very strong since private associations are of a different character.[54] In each case the issue is what are the rights and obligations the parties to the constituent instrument 'intended' to assume in this regard.

In the case of the UN, which contains no withdrawal clause, evidently because of the desire of the parties to emphasize their aspirations to stability and permanence, it is nevertheless clear from the *travaux préparatoires* that the right to withdraw 'in exceptional circumstances' was conceded.[55] The decision of Indonesia to 'withdraw' from the UN (and also the specialized agencies) in January 1965 was eventually followed by a decision in September 1966 to 'resume full co-operation'. The GA concurred in the Secretary-General's view that Indonesia's absence was to be regarded as a cessation of co-operation, not withdrawal.[56] Again, in the absence of any provision, states have 'withdrawn' from the WHO and the UNESCO, although their subsequent re-entry makes it

---

[53] See Schermers and Blokker, note 1 pp. 91*ff*. Akehurst, 'Withdrawal from International Organizations', 32 *Current Legal Problems* (1979) p. 143, takes the view that the presumption is to the contrary.

[54] The maxim *exceptio non adimpleti contractus* may also be invoked in the appropriate circumstances. However, the principle may not always be relevant and where the constitution provides other remedies in a situation in which it might be invoked it would not apply: see Brinkhorst and Schermers, *Judicial Remedies in the European Communities* (1977) pp. 25*ff*.

[55] See the report of Committee I/2 of the San Francisco Conference: UNCIO, Doc. 1178, I/2/76(2) p. 5. For the UN see Singh, note 40 pp. 92*ff*; Goodrich, Hambro and Simons, *The Charter of the United Nations* (1969) pp. 74*ff*.; Ohse, *Austritt, Ausschluss und Suspension der Mitgliedschaft in den Vereinten Nationen, mit Rückblick auf die Zeit des Völkerbundes* (1973) pp. 1*ff*. On the Indonesian case in the UN see, e.g., Blum, 'Indonesia's Return to the United Nations', 17 ICLQ (1967) p. 522; Dehousse, 'Le Droit de Retrait aux Nations Unies', 1 RBDI (1965) p. 20; Feinberg, loc. cit. note 50 at p. 189; Livingstone, 'Withdrawal from the United Nations – Indonesia', 14 ICLQ (1965) p. 637; Nizard, 'Le Retrait de l'Indonesie des Nations Unies', 11 AFDI (1965) p. 498; Unni, loc. cit. note 50; Broms, note 1 pp. 145 *ff*.; Schwelb, 'Withdrawal from the United Nations, the Indonesian Intermezzo', 61 AJIL (1967) p. 661.

[56] The Secretary-General negotiated a financial settlement whereby Indonesia paid 10 per cent of its usual assessment for 1965 and 25 per cent for 1966: see particularly Livingstone, loc. cit. note 55; Blum, loc. cit. note 55. In the IMF and the IBRD, both having express withdrawal clauses in their constitutions, Indonesia withdrew in 1965 and was formally *re-admitted* in 1967.

possible to regard this as a temporary rather than permanent decision.[57] A clear provision that a treaty such as a military alliance, creating an organization, was to be of a fixed duration might also imply a surrender of the right to withdraw.[58]

While the presumption referred to above may exist in the absence of contrary indication, it is clearly rebuttable and each constitution must be considered in its own right, on the understanding that all the tools of interpretation may be used to determine the real 'intention' behind the constitution.

Expulsion

There are provisions in the constitutions of some organizations, particularly the financial institutions,[59] providing for expulsion of members, but this is not always the case.[60] Article 6 of the UN Charter contemplates expulsion for persistent violation of the principles of the Charter;[61] the Statute of the Council of Europe in Article 8 for a 'serious violation' of certain fundamental principles of the organization as set out in Article 3; and the UNESCO in Article 2(4) of its constitution and the IMO in Article 11 of its constitution link expulsion from those organizations with expulsion from the UN. The financial organizations contemplate expulsion in the sense that, in the IBRD, the IFC and the IDA, for instance, a suspension automatically ripens into expulsion after one year, unless the Governors decide to restore the member to good standing; and in the IMF a member who persists in its failure to observe

---

[57] The Soviet bloc 'withdrew' from the WHO between 1949 and 1957; Poland, Hungary and Czechoslovakia 'withdrew' from the UNESCO between 1954 and 1963. In both cases the organizations regarded these states simply as having temporarily ceased to participate and in fact a nominal budgetary contribution to cover their years of absence was exacted when they resumed participation.

[58] A provision similar to Article 13 of the NATO Constitution allowing denunciation after twenty years must be regarded as an express provision preventing withdrawal during that period. For withdrawal from the EU, see, e.g., Dagtoglou, 'Recht auf Rücktritt von den römischen Verträgen?', in Schnur (ed.), *Festschrift für Ernst Forsthoff* (1972) at pp. 77*ff.*; Weiler, 'Alternatives to Withdrawal from an International Organization: The Case of the European Community', 20 *Israel Law Review* (1985) p. 282; Akehurst, loc. cit. note 53 at pp. 150*ff.*

[59] See, e.g., IMF Articles of Agreement, Article XXVI(2); IBRD Articles of Agreement, Article VI(2); IFC Articles of Agreement, Article V(2); IDA Articles of Agreement, Article VII(2); IDB Agreement, Article IX(2); and ADB Agreement, Article 42(2).

[60] E.g., the FAO Constitution appears not to have such a provision.

[61] For expulsion from the UN see Broms, note 1 pp. 142*ff.*; Sohn, 'Expulsion or Forced Withdrawal from an International Organization', 77 HLR (1964) at p. 1,418. The LN expelled the Soviet Union in 1939 for aggression against Finland.

its obligations can be 'compelled to withdraw'.[62] Expulsion, where permitted, is discretionary in one way or another.

In the absence of provisions for expulsion, it is doubtful whether there is a general principle or a presumption of interpretation which permits expulsion.[63] In the case of non-ratification of an amendment that comes into force the position may be different, as will be seen. In open organizations it may be argued that the aim of universality should preclude a presumption permitting expulsion, though, on the other hand, even in such organizations the existence of conditions for admission to membership should warrant the expulsion of members who fail to continue to satisfy those conditions, even in the absence of express provision for expulsion.[64] In open organizations attempts have been made to expel members, often without success,[65] but in 1969 the UPU expelled South Africa,[66] though there was no provision for expulsion in its constitution.[67] The preponderant evidence emerging from practice, however, does not conclusively or cogently support the existence of a presumption, for open organizations at any rate, that expulsion is legal without express provision. Generally, expulsion, when discussed, has failed to materialize. On the other hand, pressure has been successfully brought on members, such as South Africa, to withdraw from certain open organizations.[68] But this again supports rather than denies a

---

[62] See the provision cited in note 59. The IMF expelled Czechoslovakia in 1954 for failure to give information as required by its obligations: see IMF, *Summary Proceedings of Annual Meetings* (1954) pp. 135*ff*. Gold, *Voting and Decisions in the International Monetary Fund* (1972) p. 158; Gold, *Membership and Nonmembership* pp. 345*ff*. The IBRD expelled Czechoslovakia in 1954 for non-payment of its shares of capital: Resolution of the Board of Governors of September 1953.

[63] For views on the problem supporting this position see particularly, Singh, note 40 p. 80; Schermers and Blokker, note 1 pp. 100*ff*. On the other hand, it has been argued that expulsion, in order to protect the organization, is an implied power of any organization: see Khan, *Implied Powers of the United Nations* (1970) p. 124; Schermers and Blokker, note 1 p. 104.

[64] See Schermers and Blokker, *ibid.* p. 81.

[65] An attempt to expel South Africa from the UN was vetoed in 1974. A similar attempt in the WIPO in 1979 was also defeated.

[66] See 1969 UNJY p. 118. Many members, particularly European, declared this step to be illegal and continued to treat South Africa as a member of the UPU.

[67] There were also decisions to exclude South Africa from various agencies in the ITU and the UPU and to exclude Israel in 1974 from the European group in the UNESCO. Doubts have been expressed over the legality of these measures. In the case of the UNESCO and Israel the USA and France reduced their contributions and in 1977 Israel was readmitted to the European Group.

[68] See Schermers and Blokker, note 1 pp. 100*ff*. On the withdrawal of South Africa in 1964 from the ILO see Osieke, *Constitutional Law and Practice in the International Labour*

presumption that expulsion is illegal without express provision, because, had expulsion been regarded as legal, resort could have been had to it in those cases where such pressure took time to have effect, as it did in the case of South Africa in the ILO. In this case an amendment of the constitution permitting expulsion was adopted without resort being had to expulsion, as a result of which South Africa withdrew from the organization even before the amendment entered into force.

For closed organizations the situation, it has been argued, may be different. While the same arguments would be applicable as in the case of open organizations or organizations in general, it has been said that:

[A] closed organization is not intended to unite all States, but is restricted to a particular group of States. The participants in such a group are not only determined by geographical, but also by political and economic factors. If a State were to place itself outside the political or economic sphere of the organization, it would then no longer satisfy the criteria on which the organization is based. It would no longer belong to the group as it is understood by the organization and it could therefore lose its membership, even without express provision for expulsion, as soon as the organization declares this incompatibility.[69]

In support of this argument is cited the decision in 1962 of the OAS to exclude Cuba from participation in the organization without specific authorization in the constitution.[70] Several abstaining members and Cuba expressed misgivings over the legality of the measure. But in any case, the measure was more like a suspension rather than an expulsion. Also, there was doubt about the legality of the measure. The case does not, therefore, really support the existence of a presumption that expulsion is possible in closed organizations at least without specific authorization in the constitution.

The most cogent argument in favour of the absence of a presumption that expulsion is permissible without express constitutional authorization is, perhaps, that expulsion simply removes the recalcitrant member from the very pressures of general opinion which, constantly in play within the organization, are perhaps the best means of securing a return

Organization (1985) pp. 31*ff.* In some organizations efforts to expel South Africa failed: see Ruzié, *Organisations internationales et sanctions internationales* (1971) pp. 41*ff.* On South Africa and the WIPO see Wassermann, 'WIPO: the Exclusion of South Africa?', 14 JWTL (1980) at pp. 79*ff.*

[69] See Schermers, note 22 pp. 81–2.

[70] For this episode see Sohn, loc. cit. note 61 at pp. 1,417*ff.*; Kutzner, note 9 pp. 171*ff.*; Thomas and Thomas, *The Organization of American States* (1963) pp. 58*ff.* The matter was also discussed during the Cuban missile crisis.

to fulfilment of obligations. As was said as early as 1942, with expulsion in mind:

International institutions are not clubs from which unpleasant and disagreeable members can be blackballed to the general advantage; they are an attempt to create machinery of government for a world where the unpleasant and the disagreeable cannot be assumed not to exist. Denationalization is not normally regarded as an appropriate remedy when an individual fails to pay his income tax, and expulsion from an international institution is no more appropriate as a remedy when a Government defaults upon a payment due to the international fisc.[71]

This statement, though restricted to breaches of budgetary obligations, is applicable to illegal conduct in general.

Non-ratification of an amendment to the constitution

A problem may arise, when a constitution has been amended and the amendment has come into force, as to the consequences for those members who do not accept or ratify the amendment. Is there a power to expel such a member or is the member at liberty to withdraw from the organization? These questions will be examined in Chapter 14 below. Clearly, where an amendment does not come into effect until all members have accepted or ratified it, as in the case of the EU, no problem arises.

Disappearance or loss of essential characteristics

When a member ceases to fulfil the requirements of statehood as an essential condition of membership, membership would naturally cease, though the disappearance of a state cannot easily be assumed.[72] There are several cases since the creation of the UN in which states which have ceased to exist (e.g., by merger) have ceased to be members of international organizations. Thus, in 1958 Syria and Egypt ceased to exist when they formed the United Arab Republic. They ceased to be members of the organizations in which they had membership, though they

---

[71] Jenks, 'Financing of International Institutions', 38 TGS (1943) at p. 111. See also Jenks, 'Expulsion from the League of Nations', 16 BYIL (1935) at pp. 155ff.; and Jenks, 'Due Process of Law in International Organizations', 19 *International Organization* (1965) at pp. 163ff.

[72] See GA Official Records, 2nd session, First Committee (1947): UN Docs. A/C.6/162 and A/C.1/212. See also examples prior to the Second World War given in Schermers and Blokker, note 1 pp. 105ff.; and Green, 'The Dissolution of States and Membership of the United Nations', in Holland and Schwarzenberger (eds.), *Law, Justice and Equity, Essays in Tribute to G. W. Keeton* (1967) at pp. 153ff.; Marek, note 20 pp. 398ff.

were replaced by the United Arab Republic. In 1964 the same happened when Tanganyika and Zanzibar were united into the United Republic of Tanzania.[73] Yugoslavia ceased to exist in 1991, when it broke up into several states, in spite of the contention of Serbia-Montenegro that it continued the personality of Yugoslavia. In the organizations of which Yugoslavia had been a member, including the financial institutions, the membership of Yugoslavia was treated as having terminated and the successor states had to apply for membership. When Czechoslovakia was dissolved in 1993 into the Czech Republic and the Slovak Republic, the results were similar in those organizations of which Czechoslovakia had been a member.

In the case of Kuwait, when Iraq invaded the country in 1990, it is clear that organizations did not regard its membership as having come to end on the ground that it had been annexed and the state had disappeared or lost its essential characteristics. This is to be explained by the fact that Iraq was in occupation as an enemy power and, though Kuwait had evidently lost its independence and effective government, this was the result of an aggression in violation of the UN Charter which could not bring about the termination of the statehood of Kuwait, and in any event the annexation was not a *fait accompli* as long as the UN was taking collective action to reverse the consequences of the aggression. That Kuwait may have been unable effectively to exercise for a short time the privileges of its membership in organizations was not a factor affecting the reality of its membership.

The express provisions in the constitutions of such organizations as the IDA and the IFC, by which loss of membership in the IBRD results in the automatic cessation of membership in those organizations,[74] are also examples of termination of membership by loss of essential characteristics.

Representation

Representation of a member state in an organization concerns the question of which persons are to be recognized as entitled to represent that state in the organs of the organization. Issues of representation are not issues concerning admission to membership. Representation

---

[73] See also the dissolution of the Federation of Mali in 1960: Cohen (Higgins), 'Legal Problems Arising from the Dissolution of the Mali Federation', 36 BYIL (1960) at pp. 375*ff.*; and some examples discussed in Schermers and Blokker, note 1 pp. 105*ff.*
[74] See IDA Articles of Agreement, Article VII(3), and IFC Articles of Agreement, Article V(3).

presupposes admission. The question arises, for example, when there is a change of government in a member state by revolution or as a result of a *coup d'état*. Generally when there is a simple change of government, the issue, though technically posed, does not create problems, as there is no competition for representation. However, there have been occasions when the issue of representation has been raised even in such a situation.[75]

In principle it may be asserted that what is relevant is whether the governmental authority concerned is exercising effective authority in the state concerned or at least in most of it, so that a purely nominal authority, even though recognized or continuing to be recognized by a member – even a majority of the members – of the organization should not be entitled to represent the state. While this principle may be accepted in theory and has often been followed, sometimes political factors have occasioned departures from it.

The case of the competing claims of the Nationalist government and the government of the Chinese People's Republic (CPR) to represent China within the UN and the specialized agencies after 1949 is an example of how politics and voting strength can influence the question of representation.[76] The question of representation is not generally dealt

---

[75] Giving a governmental entity representation in an organization must be distinguished from recognition of that government by member states of the organization. Granting of representation by an organization (i.e., its organs) does not necessarily bind the member states of the organization to recognition of the government concerned, whatever view is taken of the function of recognition. On the other hand, an affirmative vote on representation by a member state may be an indication that it recognizes the government concerned: see on this point, Jennings and Watts, *Oppenheim's International Law* (1992), vol. I, pp. 178ff. and the literature there cited; Memorandum prepared by the UN Secretariat in 1950, UN Doc. S/1466; Higgins, *Development of International Law* pp. 130ff.; Dugard, note 4.

[76] See on the question of Chinese representation, e.g., Wright, 'The Chinese Recognition Problem', 49 AJIL (1955) p. 320; Steiner, 'Communist China in the World Community', 533 *International Conciliation* (1961); Broms, note 1 p. 121ff.; Lenefsky, 'The People's Republic of China and the Security Council – Deprived or Debatable?', 9 Col. JIL (1970) p. 54; Oraison, 'La representation de la Chine aux Nations Unies', 49 RDI (1971) p. 181; Green, 'Representation versus Membership: The Chinese Precedent in the United Nations', 10 CYIL (1972) p. 102; Bello, 'Chinese Representation in the United Nations', 50 RDI (1972) p. 44; Virally, *L'Organisation Mondiale* (1972) pp. 269ff. For discussions of the Chinese representation issue before the action taken by the UN in 1971, see, e.g., Briggs, 'Chinese Representation in the United Nations', 6 *International Organization* (1952) p. 192; Liang, 'Recognition by the United Nations of the Representation of a Member State: Criteria and Procedure', 45 AJIL (1951) p. 689; McDougal and Goodman, 'Chinese Participation in the United Nations: The Legal Imperative of a Negotiated Solution', 60 AJIL (1966) p. 671; and Bloomfield, 'China, the United States

with in constituent instruments, including the UN Charter. In practice the question is one for the rules of procedure in each organ of each organization. Within the SC representation is treated as a matter of credentials and under SC Rule 17 a representative to whom objection has been made continues to sit until the SC, by a simple majority vote, decides to expel him. As a result the Nationalist Chinese representative continued to sit until nine members were prepared to oppose him. Within the GA the vote on Chinese representation was initially regarded as procedural, but in 1962 was resolved to be an 'important question' requiring a two-thirds majority for any change. At different times attempts were made to discuss the substantive issues which lay behind this question, which was treated as procedural. Opposition to CPR representation was led by the USA but support for its position dissipated until, finally, on 25 October 1971 the GA recognized the representatives of the CPR as 'the only legitimate representative of China' and that the CPR was 'one of the five permanent members of the Security Council'.[77] The GA, thus, rejected any idea of Taiwan being given separate representation. The GA's own decision was quickly accepted and followed in the SC and the various specialized agencies.[78]

The Chinese case is not the only one concerning representation. Similar problems arose over the representation of Hungary in 1957 when a *coup d'état* took place.[79] Beginning in September 1979 for several years the question of which government (the Khmer Rouge or that of the People's Republic of Kampuchea) should represent Kampuchea (Cambodia) was taken up by the GA and its Credentials Committee after

---

and the United Nations', 20 *International Organization* (1966) pp. 653, 677. See also, for action taken in the specialized agencies of the UN, 'The Report on Representation of China within the United Nations System', 11 ILM (1972) p. 561; and 'United Nations: Addendum to Report on the People's Republic of China within the Organizations of the United Nations System', 12 ILM (1973) p. 1,526. The specialized agencies rapidly accepted the CPR government as the representative of China in their organizations.

[77] GA Rs. 2758 (XXVII).

[78] See *UN Yearbook* (1971) pp. 126*ff.* For consequential action taken in some specialized agencies which was not always immediate, see 11 ILM (1972) pp. 561*ff.* and 12 ILM (1973) pp. 1,526*ff.* In the case of the IMF, the IBRD and other financial institutions the arrangements for the change of representation came much later: see 20 ILM (1981) pp. 774*ff.* This was partly because of the issue of how the outstanding obligations on loans etc. of China were to be treated.

[79] See Sands and Klein (eds.), note 18 pp. 554–6. For the case of the Hungarian government representatives in the ILO see Osieke, note 68 pp. 62*ff.*

the Khmer Rouge was forcibly replaced by a government headed by Heng Sammin.[80]

A more unusual resort to representation is the use of a decision on it in order to exclude a government from participating in the work of the organization. This has happened both in the UN and other organizations. The South African government representatives were successfully prevented from representing that country in the GA of the UN in 1974 and 1981 by a majority in the GA rejecting their credentials. In 1970 the GA decided for the first time to reject the credentials of a delegation, namely the South African delegation. However, the President of the GA, Edvard Hambro, allowed the delegates of the Republic of South Africa, whose credentials had been rejected, to continue to participate in the meetings of the GA. The decision on the rejection of credentials was thus not regarded as tantamount to the application of Article 5 of the UN Charter on suspension. The practice of rejecting the credentials of the South African delegation, though with the same results as in 1970, continued until the President of the GA, Abdelaziz Bouteflika, made a new interpretation of the situation on 30 September 1974. His interpretation was that in a case where the credentials of a particular delegation had been rejected, this led necessarily to the conclusion that the delegation was not entitled to participate in the work of that session of the GA. He added that the state concerned did not cease to be a member of the organization and that the effects of the rejection were also limited to the question of the status of the South African delegation and to its position in the GA, all in accordance with the Rules of Procedure of this organ.

Bouteflika's decision to interpret the rejection of credentials in this matter was not unanimously supported. The USA was the foremost opponent of his interpretation, but the interpretation was confirmed by the GA by a vote of 91 to 22 with 19 abstentions. When the South African delegation arrived once more in 1981 to participate in the session of the GA, its credentials were again rejected by an even greater majority than two-thirds: 112 to 22 with 6 abstentions,[81] and the delegation was not allowed to participate in the work of the GA.

[80] See the discussion in Warbrick, 'Kampuchea: Representation and Recognition', 30 ICLQ (1981) p. 234; Kirgis, note 45 pp. 181*ff.* There have been other cases of acceptance of credentials: see, e.g., Bryant *et al.*, 'Recognition of Guinea (Bissau)', 15 Harvard ILJ (1974) p. 483; Schermers and Blokker, note 1 pp. 180*ff.* Recently the case of Afghanistan required a change in representation which has taken place.

[81] Now the South African delegation's credentials are accepted by all organizations. On the South African question see, e.g., Broms, note 1 pp. 129*ff.*; Abbot *et al.*, 'The General

The credentials of the delegation of Israel have also been challenged repeatedly. The Credentials Committee regularly, however, accepted the credentials of the delegation of Israel. In 1982 a new situation arose after this committee had again accepted Israel's credentials at the 37th Session of the GA. On 22 October 1982, forty-two member states challenged the decision of the committee. When the matter came up in the GA, the Finnish representative, in the name of the Nordic states, moved that the amendment to the decision of the committee which would have rejected the credentials of Israel be not voted upon. This proposal was adopted by 74 to 9, with 32 abstentions. Since 1982 the procedural debate has been a constant feature of the sessions of the General Assembly. A large group of states has repeatedly tried to challenge the credentials of Israel. The USA has taken a very strong attitude defending the credentials of Israel each time when the question has been debated. Usually the procedure followed has been similar to the one followed in 1982. A representative of the Nordic states makes a proposal that the motion to amend the Report of the Credentials Committee be not voted upon and until now the outcome has been the same.[82]

Views on the rejection of South Africa's credentials have remained divided. Bouteflika's interpretation has been defended.[83] On the other hand, there are those who suggest that the verification of credentials should not be used as a political tool against some delegations, because that would be exceeding the powers of the GA under the Charter of the

Assembly, 29th Session: The Decredentialization of South Africa', 16 Harvard ILJ (1975) p. 576; Muller, 'Discussions and Resolutions on South Africa in the United Nations in 1979', 5 South African YBIL (1979) p. 164; Ciobanu, 'Credentials of Delegations and Representation of Member States at the United Nations', 25 ICLQ (1976) p. 351; Tavernièr, 'L'année des Nations Unies, questions juridiques', 20 AFDI (1974) at pp. 488ff.; McWhinney, 'Credentials of State Delegations to the UN General Assembly: A New Approach to Effectuation of Self-Determination in Southern Africa', 3 Hastings Constitutional Law Quarterly (1976) p. 19; and (Note), 'WIPO, The Exclusion of South Africa', 14 JWTL (1980) p. 78.

[82] On the Israeli question see, e.g., Broms, note 1 pp. 130ff.; Halberstam, 'Excluding Israel from the General Assembly by a Rejection of its Credentials', 78 AJIL (1984) p. 179.

[83] See., e.g., McWhinney, The World Court and the International Law Making Process (1979) pp. 142ff.; Erasmus, 'The Rejection of Credentials: A Proper Exercise of General Assembly Powers or Suspension by Stealth?', SAYBIL (1981) pp. 40ff. Leben, 'Article 5', in Cot and Pellet (eds.), La Charte des Nations Unies (1991) at pp. 190ff. presents the views of those who support Bouteflika. See also Flauss and Singer, 'La Vérification des pouvoirs à l'Assemblée Générale des Nations Unies', 31 AFDI (1985) at pp. 642ff., 649ff.; Jhabvala, 'Credentials Approach to Representation in the UN General Assembly', California Western International Law Journal (1977) at pp. 633ff.

UN.[84] The actual *raison d'être* behind the verification of credentials has been a situation in which doubts had arisen that the persons presenting their credentials were not those rightfully entitled to do so. Normally cases where credentials are challenged arise when there are two or several competing governments on the territory of a single state and they all have sent representatives to participate in the session of the GA with credentials given by their respective governments. In such cases the Credentials Committee would rightly decide which credentials should be accepted by the GA and the GA would then take a decision on the matter. This seems to have been the idea behind the particular provision in the Rules of Procedure of the GA. The South African and Israeli incidents, however, are examples of trying to use the rejection of credentials as a political means to create a situation where the state whose delegation's credentials are questioned would lose its right to participate in the work of the GA, not as a result of any doubts as to the authenticity of the credentials but because of a feeling that the conduct of the state giving the credentials has been unacceptable.

The consequences in actual practice of adopting the Bouteflika approach is the same as the consequence of a decision taken by the GA upon a recommendation of the SC in cases of suspension under Article 5 of the Charter. Further, in this case the SC cannot restore the rights and privileges of membership, as it alone has power to do under Article 5. In the case of rejection of credentials a majority in the GA can continue to reach the same decision as long as it wants. This happened in the case of South Africa. Moreover, in the case of a decision under Article 5 to suspend the rights and duties of a member, a similar stand in two organs, the SC and the GA, is required. It is difficult, therefore, to avoid the conclusion that use of the rejection of credentials based on the Rules of Procedure of the GA as a political tool to indicate disapproval of the policies of a particular state is not a proper exercise of power.[85]

---

[84] See, e.g., the argument of Leben, loc. cit. note 83 at pp. 193*ff.* and authorities there discussed; Broms, note 1 pp. 132*ff.*

[85] This was also the conclusion reached by the Legal Counsel of the UN in 1970, when he advised the President of the General Assembly. He said rejection of credentials in these circumstances would be contrary to the Charter because it would amount to a suspension, without resort to the procedures of Article 5, of the right to participate in meetings of the GA which was one of the important rights and privileges of membership: 1970 UNJY at pp. 170*ff.*

5   Non-Judicial organs of organizations

International organizations achieve their purposes and perform their functions primarily through organs. There is always at least one organ within an organization but generally there are many more than one. These organs are principal organs, such as the GA and the SC of the UN or the Board of Governors of the financial institutions, and subsidiary organs, such as committees, or the UNCTAD in the UN. They may be plenary, such as the GA of the UN or the Board of Governors of the financial institutions (e.g., the IBRD, the IMF, the ADB and the IDB), or of limited membership, such as the SC or the ECOSOC of the UN or the Executive Committee of the OECD. Some organs are administrative and executive, e.g., the secretariat of the UN, headed by the Secretary-General, or the secretariats of the specialized agencies of the UN, headed by the executive heads of the organizations (Director-Generals or Presidents, etc.), or the secretariat of the Council of Europe or the OECD. Generally, the organs of organizations belong to one of these categories.[1]

There are also judicial organs which are generally principal organs, such as the ICJ or the CJEC, in whatever manner they are established, or have a special status, e.g., the IATs. Judicial organs will not be discussed in this chapter. Judicial organs which are established as organs *by* international organizations will be considered in Chapter 8. Other judicial organs, i.e., those established as principal organs by the constitutive instrument of an organization (e.g., the ICJ and CJEC) or those established as judicial bodies by instruments separate from constitutive instruments of international organizations as such (e.g., the EctHR, the IActHR, the ITLOS or those which are described as arbitral bodies such

---

[1] The EU, it should be noted, has a more complicated structure than other organizations but the organs are, nevertheless, organs of an international organization.

as the Iran-US Claims Tribunal) will not be dealt with except in passing in this work. In any event, to deal with them from an institutional
standpoint in a treatise of this kind would be inappropriate.

The structure, powers and working of the organs and the voting
scheme in them, if any, are determined by the constitutions and purposes and functions of the organizations concerned and will differ not
only as between organs but from organization to organization. Some
organs are constitutionally established, whether they are principal (e.g.,
the GA and the SC of the UN) or subsidiary (e.g., the Military Staff Committee under Chapter VII of the UN Charter); others are created *by* an
organ of the organization and then are generally subsidiary (e.g., committees of the GA or of the executive boards of the financial institutions)
but are not necessarily so (e.g., the IATs set up by organizations, such as
the UNAT, the ILOAT, the WBAT and the COEAB).[2]

Plenary organs

International organizations are created to attain goals that are regarded
as shared goals by their members. Thus, in principle, an international
organization has at least one organ, namely the plenary assembly, in
which all members without exception have representation so that they
can be kept informed of developments in and affecting the organization
and of the organization's actions and exercise of powers and contribute
to giving content in a more detailed fashion to the goals of the organization, possibly in terms of its own interests compared with those of
other members. This is irrespective of the voting power of each member
in this organ.

Composition

The first international organizations, namely the administrative unions,
such as the UPU, or the river commissions, had plenary assemblies which
were composed of government representatives of each member state.
Plenary assemblies are today also generally composed at least of government representatives of all member states. Examples are the GA of the
UN, the Council of the OECD, the Congress of the UPU, the Committee

---

[2] On organs of international organizations generally, see particularly: Seidl-Hohenveldern,
'Les organes des organisations internationales', chapter 3, sections 1 to 3, in Dupuy
(ed.), *Manuel sur les organisations internationales* (1988) p. 81; Torres-Bernadez, 'Les organes
des organisations internationales', chapter 3, section 4, in Dupuy, *ibid.* p. 100;
Schermers and Blokker, *International Institutional Law* (1995) pp. 139–47.

of Ministers of the COE and the Board of Governors of the IBRD, the IMF or the IDB.

The constitution of an organization sometimes has special provisions on the composition of the assembly. For example, the representatives of member states to the Congress of the WMO must be the directors of their meteorological services.[3] Other organizations require their plenary organ to be composed of high-level members of the governments of member states, namely ministers who enjoy a larger degree of decision-making power than civil servants. The Statute of the COE provides that the Committee of Ministers must be composed of the Ministers of Foreign Affairs of member states.[4] In the EU each member state is represented on the Council by a representative of the member state at ministerial level, authorized to commit the government of that member state.[5]

Some organizations have constitutional provisions creating various plenary bodies, each composed of representatives at different hierarchical levels, and each one being entrusted with a level of powers matching the rank of those representatives. Thus, the OAS constitution provides for the General Assembly as the highest organ,[6] makes provision for Meetings of Consultation of Ministers of Foreign Affairs,[7] and entrusts matters of lesser importance to the Permanent Council which has representatives of lesser rank (ambassadors).[8] The OAU has assemblies: the Assembly of Heads of State and Government and the Council of Ministers.[9] In some organizations having a sole plenary assembly, its sessions may be held sometimes at the ministerial level and sometimes at senior civil servant level.[10]

A few plenary assemblies are quasi-parliamentary. The first organ of this kind created was the Parliamentary Assembly of the Council of Europe. In this organ a number of seats is assigned to each member state, roughly proportional to its population. Each national parliament distributes these seats by the proportional method, choosing incumbents from among its members.[11] Until 1979 the (joint) Assembly of the European Communities, renamed 'European Parliament', was also set up

---

[3] Article 7(2) of the WMO Constitution.   [4] Article 14.

[5] See Article 146 of the TEU.

[6] Article 51 of the OAS Constitution.   [7] Article 59 of the OAS Constitution.

[8] Article 78 of the OAS Constitution.

[9] Article VIII and Article XII of the OAU Charter. COMECON had four levels of plenary assemblies.

[10] Article 7 of the OECD Constitution.   [11] See Article 25(a) and 26 of the COE Statute.

according to this indirect method. Since then, its representatives have been elected directly by the people of the member states.[12]

The activity of certain organizations concerns the population of the member states not only as voters, but also as members of social interest groups. They benefit from the interests such groups demonstrate in their activities by consulting them on relevant issues and thereby ensuring their support. Some of these organizations have created organs where these interests can be developed within the framework of their own institutions. The ILO was the first to accord a place to these interests within its plenary assembly, the General Conference. The delegation of each member state is composed of two governmental delegates and two delegates representing employers and workers respectively. The latter are appointed by the government with the assent of their respective professional organizations. Each delegate may vote individually on all issues submitted to the General Conference for deliberation. In cases where one of the members has not appointed a non-governmental delegate, as is its right, the other non-governmental delegate may take part in the deliberations of the Conference, but will not have the right to vote.[13] In the European Coal and Steel Community, representation of the interests of producers, labourers, consumers and traders was under the original treaty ensured in a Consultative Committee, composed of an equal number of representatives from these three groups.[14] The Committee's representatives were named by the Council of the EU, chosen from lists submitted by professional organizations and assuring adequate representation of the national interests of the various member states. The Convention of 25 March 1957, governing certain common institutions of the European Communities, established a common economic and social committee for the EEC and the Euratom. A certain number of seats was accorded to each member state, in rough proportion to its population.

---

[12] See Decision 76/787/ECSC, EEC, Euratom of 20 September 1976. On elections to the European Parliament see Villani, 'Osservazioni sull'elettorato passivo al Parlamento europeo: la legge italiana n. 9 del 18 gennaio 1989', 28 *Diritto-Communitario-e-degli-Scambi-Internazionali* (1989) p. 349. Elections are still direct under the TEU (Maastricht and after), though there have been changes in details. See now Articles 137–144 of the TEU.

[13] See Articles 3 and 4 of the ILO Constitution. See also Beguin, 'ILO and the Tripartite System', 523 *International Conciliation* (1959); Landelius, *Workers, Employers and Governments* (1965) pp. 21*ff.*, 259*ff.*

[14] Article 18 of the ECSC Treaty. The original treaties of the European Communities have been replaced by the EU Treaty (Maastricht and thereafter). It is not intended to deal with the organs as they were re-established by the latter treaty as such. What has been said about the organs established under the earlier treaties is sufficient.

The Council of the EU appointed the members of this Committee based on lists submitted by member states.[15]

There are some subsidiary bodies which have a plenary nature. These will be referred to below.

The financial institutions have a second deliberative body which can take decisions generally of a legally binding nature. This body is strictly not of a limited nature, though the number of its members is much smaller than the number of member states of the institution. It is a principal organ and is plenary in the sense that all the member states are represented in it, though it is not the plenary assembly. While the number of members of the body, generally called the Board of Executive Directors or the Executive Directors, is limited and may be increased in certain circumstances,[16] all the member states are represented in the organ. A small number of the members are appointed, generally each of the largest shareholders in the organization, and represent only the member state which made the appointment, while the others, the majority, are elected, each member representing several member states.[17] Elections generally take place in accordance with provisions to be found in schedules in or annexes to the constitutions of the organizations.[18] The groupings of the member states concerned under each representative elected are generally determined by negotiation.[19]

Powers

The powers of plenary organs are derived from the constitution of the organization. These may be expressly stated or may be ascribed under the doctrine of implied powers. Because the constitutions of organizations differ from each other, the powers of each plenary organ will also differ from organization to organization.

There may, however, be some powers common to all organizations that are exercised by the chief plenary organ having government delegates. In

[15] See Article 5 of the Convention. Now the TEU (Maastricht (1991) and Amsterdam (1997)) governs these committees.

[16] See, e.g., Article V(4)(b) of the IBRD Constitution; Article XII(3)(b) of the IMF Constitution; Article VIII(3)(b) of the IDB Constitution; Article 30(1)(i) of the ADB Constitution; Article 29(1) of the CDB Constitution; and Article IV(4)(b) of the IFC Constitution.

[17] In the case of the IFC and the IDA, for example, the Executive Directors who hold office are not elected independently of the IBRD elections.

[18] See, e.g., Schedule B of the IBRD Constitution and Annex B of the ADB Constitution.

[19] For a detailed description of the manner in which the body of Executive Directors in each development bank was constituted and elected see Syz, *International Development Banks* (1974) pp. 42*ff*. The arrangements are still the same.

principle, the right and duty of establishing the policy of an organization generally lies with this plenary assembly, as is the case with the GA of the UN. Also, generally the plenary assembly will have the power of requiring reports to be submitted to it from other organs on their activities. On the basis of these reports a debate usually takes place in the assembly. In the case of the financial institutions, the power of policy-making has generally been delegated to the second plenary organ consisting of the Executive Directors.[20]

Subsidiary plenary bodies, whether composed of government delegates or experts, may have work of a preparatory nature. This is the case with the seven standing committees of the GA of the UN. Some subordinate plenary bodies also assume executive functions. In the case of the EU the management committees, especially those set up to deal with agricultural problems, have been preparatory bodies but in practice possessed sufficient power to take decisions which were executive in nature. If such a committee accepted a proposal of the Commission of the EU, it would implement the proposal.[21] In the ITU the International Consulting Committee on Radio Communications, for example, has executive functions in a particular sector of the organization's activities.

Quasi-parliamentary assemblies have principally a consultative capacity. The Parliamentary Assembly of the Council of Europe formulates recommendations to the Committee of Ministers.[22] Under the original EEC and Euratom Treaties before the Commission of the EU submitted proposals to the Council it had to consult the European Parliament but the Parliament had powers of control, notably the power to ask questions of the Commission and Council of the EU, and including the right to adopt a motion of censure against the Commission (which had not been exercised to date).[23] The powers of the European Parliament were increased under successive treaties. Now the formal powers of the Parliament are broadly of three kinds: it participates in various ways, depending on the legal basis of the act in question, in the law-making

---

[20] See, e.g., IBRD Articles of Agreement, Article V(4)(a); IDB Agreement, Article VIII(3)(a); IFC Articles of Agreement, Article IV(4)(a); ADB Agreement, Article 31; and AFDB Agreement, Article 32.

[21] This was the position under the EEC Treaty, whatever the position now under the amended EU Treaty. The position is hardly different under the amended treaty for the EU – the Maastricht Treaty (1991) and the Amsterdam Treaty (1997).

[22] Article 22 of the Statute of the COE.

[23] On the advisory role of the Parliament, see EEC Treaty, Articles 43, 54, 56 and 87; and Euratom Treaty, Articles 31, 76, 85 and 90. For the other powers and rights see EEC Treaty Articles 140 and 144.

process of the Communities; together with the Council, it constitutes the budgetary authority of the Communities; and it exercises political super-vision over the performance by the Commission of its tasks.[24] Besides these formal powers, the European Parliament evidently considers that it is entitled, as the collective voice of the Community electorate, to express reactions to political events both within the Communities and in the wider world. It does not have an independent right of initiative but brings its influence to bear on the Commission and, so far as it is able, on the Council, to provoke any action by those institutions that it considers necessary. For that purpose, the position of the European Par-liament has been strengthened by the second paragraph of Article 192 (ex 138b) EC, an amendment introduced by the TEU, which provides that it may 'acting by a majority of its members, request the Commission to submit any appropriate proposal on matters on which it considers that a Community act is required for the purpose of implementing this Treaty.'

The powers of plenary assemblies, such as the ILO General Conference, where interest groups are also represented, are generally consultative. They may also have the power of assigning functions to the adminis-trative organ (secretariat) of the organization where the constitution provides for this, as does the constitution of the ILO in Article 10(3).

Organs of limited membership

Many organizations have bodies of limited membership which primarily reduce the workload of the plenary organs and enable activities of the organization to be continued during the periods between the sessions of the plenary organs. The relatively small number of members of these organs generally facilitates co-operative action and decision making, as in the ECOSOC, though sometimes controlled and limited membership, such as in the TC, had other purposes.

Composition

The composition of these bodies depends generally on the individual constitutions of the organizations to which they belong, where the con-stitutions deal with the issue. In turn the constitutions would address the needs of the organs having regard to their functions. For example,

---

[24] See Arnull *et al.* (eds.), *Wyatt and Dashwood's European Union Law* (2000) pp. 32*ff.* and Chapter 3, for an explanation of these three kinds of powers.

in the case of the TC of the UN, representation of special interests was necessary with the result that states particularly interested in the issue concerned were members of the organ.[25] In the case of the SC of the UN the five permanent members are designated by name in Article 23(1) of the Charter – they have a primary role in the maintenance of peace.

Sometimes, however, the composition of the organ is not fully dealt with in the constitution. For example, in the case of the ECOSOC, Article 61 of the Charter specifies only the number of members of the organ and the terms for which they are elected. The exact configuration of the membership has been decided by informal agreement in the GA.[26] In the case of the OECD, the constitution in Article 9 simply refers to an Executive Committee, the determination of how many members it will have and other matters being left to the Council of the OECD.

In other cases some elements of the membership may be specified in the constitution, while others may not. Thus, Article 23(1) of the Charter of the UN designates by name the five permanent members of the SC, while the other members are not described at all. Article 28 of the IMCO constitution originally required the eight states having the largest commercial fleets to be represented on the Maritime Safety Committee.[27] Article 7 of the ILO constitution has some provisions on the selection of members of the Governing Body.

Powers

Organs of limited membership such as the SC of the UN have their own powers and functions under the constitution of the organization. These powers and functions may be extensive, though sometimes confined to a particular field. The ECOSOC and the TC of the UN also have powers which are described in the Charter of the UN, apart from any implied powers.

In some cases the organ concerned has the power under the constitution to prepare the decisions that are taken by the plenary body, to execute them during the period between sessions and sometimes to

---

[25] See Article 86(1) of the UN Charter. Article 50 of the ICAO Constitution spells out in detail how many members the Council of ICAO will have and the composition of that body.

[26] See also Manno, 'Problems and Trends in the Composition of Non-plenary UN Organs', 19 *International Organization* (1965) p. 37.

[27] This gave rise to disputes which led to the advisory opinion of the ICJ in the *IMCO Constitution Case*, 1960 ICJ Reports p. 150. Now Article 28 of the IMO Constitution, as amended, requires all members of the IMO to be in the Maritime Safety Committee.

supervise their implementation by the administrative body. This seems to be the case to a large extent in the ILO.

Subsidiary organs

A distinction is made between principal and subsidiary organs in the discussion of organs of international organizations. Subsidiary organs as opposed to principal organs are referred to both in the Charter of the UN[28] and in other constituent instruments, such as the Constitution of the IMO,[29] the UNIDO Constitution[30] and the Charter of the OAS.[31]

Generally an organ which is not a principal organ would be a subsidiary organ. Principal organs are always created by constitutional provisions. Subsidiary organs may be created by the constituent instrument or under powers granted expressly or implicitly by the constitution. A subsidiary organ may be plenary in nature or of limited membership. Thus, a Committee of the Whole of a plenary organ, such as the Legal Committee (sixth) or Administrative and Budgetary Committee (fifth) of the GA or, indeed, any of its seven standing committees, is a subsidiary organ which is plenary in nature. However, many subsidiary organs are of limited membership. There are several committees of the Executive Directors of the IBRD, such as the Committee on Executive Directors, Administrative Matters (CODAM), which are of this nature. The Economic Commission for Africa of the UN is an example of a UN subsidiary organ of limited membership. A subsidiary organ may be composed of independent experts rather than representatives of states. Such is the International Law Commission or the Board of Auditors of the GA of the UN.

Before discussing the essential nature of subsidiary organs, which may be referred to in other terms in the constituent instruments – e.g., 'subordinate bodies',[32] 'commissions',[33] 'committees',[34] 'special organs'[35] – a

---

[28] See Articles 7, 8, 22 and 29.   [29] Article 2.   [30] Article 7.

[31] Articles 51, 74, 75, 83 and 91.

[32] See, e.g., Article 9 of the OECD Convention; and Article 9 of the NATO Constitution.

[33] See, e.g., Article 38 of the WHO Constitution; Article VI of the FAO Constitution; and Articles 17 and 24 of the COE Statute.

[34] See, e.g., the constituent instruments referred to in footnote 33.

[35] See, e.g., Article 41 of the OPEC Statute. In the *Effect of Awards Case* the ICJ also used the term 'secondary' in describing organs: 1954 ICJ Reports at p. 61. It would seem that this was not a term of art. There does not seem to be a need to distinguish between subsidiary and secondary bodies. On the other hand, the ICJ did refer to the UNAT as a 'subordinate' body: *ibid.* This characterization is inappropriate and will be discussed in Chapter 8.

preliminary issue that needs to be addressed is what authority does an organ or an organization need to establish subsidiary organs. Where the constituent instrument expressly grants an organ this power, no problem arises. However, under the doctrine of implied powers discussed in Chapter 3 above, even where no express power is granted by the constituent instrument, there is a general principle that organs have the power to establish the subsidiary organs required, because such a power is necessary for the discharge of the functions of the organization, or is essential for the performance its duties or appropriate for the fulfilment of the stated purposes of the organization. Nor does the specific mention of certain subsidiary organs in the constituent instrument or the express attribution to some organs only of the power to establish subsidiary organs necessarily limit this power to what is expressly granted. There is a presumption that all organs have vested in them the power to establish the necessary subsidiary organs over and above what may be expressly granted unless there is some indication to the contrary. Thus, both the GA and the executive bodies of the financial institutions have established many committees, among other things, as subsidiary bodies.

As to the nature and powers of subsidiary organs, general principle and practice have made possible a number of conclusions.[36] Subsidiary organs are organs established as subsidiary organs in constituent instruments of international organizations, or pursuant to that instrument by a principal organ of the organization as may be found necessary for the performance of the functions of the organ, or, more generally, of the organization in the exercise of express or implied powers. Sometimes subsidiary organs may be established by two or more principal organs of the organization. Through conventional arrangements or parallel actions they may likewise be set up by two or more principal organs of different organizations. Like any other organ, subsidiary organs are an integral part of the structure of the international organization concerned. They assist principal organs in the performance of their respective functions by facilitating the adoption and, sometimes the implementation, of decisions of principal organs. This kind of assistance is subordinate, though it may be material in character. The tasks or functions entrusted to a subsidiary organ are defined in the constituent instrument of the organization or in the decision or resolution of the principal organ which established the subsidiary organ concerned.

---

[36] See particularly Torres-Bernadez, loc. cit. note 2 at pp. 100ff., where the subject is discussed.

They may be supplemented subsequently through the adoption of constitutional amendments or further decisions or resolutions, as the case may be.

An important limitation, however, is that the functions entrusted to and performed by a subsidiary organ cannot go beyond the functions of the international organization concerned as defined in its constituent instrument, whatever may be the attribution of functions to it by a principal organ. Subsidiary organs, like any other organ of an organization, may, however, be the beneficiaries of a lawful enlargement of the functions of the organization resulting from a correct application of the theory of implied powers. A second limitation is that the functions of a subsidiary organ are dependent on the scope of powers of the related principal organ or organs. Principal organs may delegate some of their functions, or aspects of those functions, to subsidiary organs only when and to the extent that such a delegation would be allowable in the light of the objectives and balance of interests reflected in the constituent instrument of the organization concerned, including the division of competences and functions among major organs. In any case a principal organ cannot delegate more than it has. Further, in the performance of the tasks and functions entrusted to them subsidiary organs are under the supervision or control of the related principal organ or organs. The decisions adopted and conclusions reached by subsidiary organs are not binding for the related principal organ or organs.[37] Thus, the GA does not have to accept and sometimes has not accepted the decisions of some of its committees.

Termination or discontinuance of subsidiary organs established in constituent instruments is effected through the regular constitutional means. When set up by a principal organ, a subsidiary organ may be terminated or discontinued by an appropriate decision or resolution adopted by the principal organ concerned. The same principle applies in cases of revision or modification of the original terms of reference of the subsidiary organ.

These basic principles are subject to modification by the constituent instruments of the organizations concerned and to some extent by their internal law which includes their established practice.

---

[37] This is an important feature. As will be seen, where organs are created which can bind the organ creating them, e.g., IATs, they are not subsidiary organs. Torres-Bernadez is not in agreement with this view: see *ibid.* at pp. 141–2, where he described IATs as 'subsidiary organs'.

The organs referred to and discussed hitherto are both subsidiary and subordinate. However, there are organs which are neither subordinate, although they are not principal and are created by principal organs, nor subsidiary. As was made clear in the *Effect of Awards Case* by the ICJ,[38] IATs are of this kind. Thus, principal organs may create bodies which are not subsidiary, nor subordinate, and over which they have no functional control. These are usually judicial bodies. Such bodies can bind the principal organs, including the organs that created them, and the organizations.

Relationship *inter se* of principal organs

The relationship between subsidiary organs and the principal organs which create them has been seen to be one involving total control of the former by the latter and delegated authority. In the case of principal organs the relationship between them is on a different footing. The administrative organ (the secretariat) is also a principal organ but its relationship to the other organs will be dealt with below. Judicial organs will also be considered in Chapter 8 insofar as their place in the structure of organizations is concerned. Here consideration will be given to the relationship *inter se* of other organs, mainly 'deliberative' organs, such as the GA and the SC of the UN or the Executive Boards and Boards of Governors of financial institutions.

The basic principle is that, because principal organs are created by the constituent instrument, their relationship *inter se* will be determined by the provisions of that instrument, whether they are express or result from the correct application of the theory of implied powers. This relationship may be hierarchical or parallel or a mixture of both concepts.

It would seem from the Articles of Agreement of the IBRD that the Executive Directors of these institutions who constitute a principal organ derive their powers by delegation from the Board of Governors. Article V(2) of the IBRD constitution states that 'all the powers of the Bank shall be vested in the Board of Governors', and Article V(4) specifies that the Executive Directors 'shall exercise all the powers delegated to them by the Board of Governors'. However, there are a number of powers exercised by the Executive Directors which are specifically granted to them by the Articles of Agreement, such as the power to elect a President,[39]

---

[38] See 1954 ICJ Reports at p. 61. This point is discussed in C. F. Amerasinghe, *The Law of the International Civil Service* (1994) vol. I, p. 34*ff*.

[39] Article V(5)(a).

temporarily to suspend operations[40] and to convene the Board of Governors.[41] Thus, it is clear that the Executive Directors have powers which are not delegated to them as such, *pace* Article V(2) and (4), and it is doubtful whether the Board of Governors could either take away those powers or control their exercise. There are also certain powers that cannot be delegated by the Board of Governors,[42] while all those that are not specifically granted to the Executive Directors by the constitution are clearly delegated to the latter and can be exercised, controlled or taken back by the Board of Governors. The position in the other financial institutions is generally similar, though the original powers of the Executive Directors may differ from institution to institution.[43]

In the case of the UNIDO Article 8(4) of the constitution enumerates the powers that are non-delegable by the plenary organ to the body of limited membership, where there is a general power to delegate such powers. Thus, the right of taking decisions on the most important matters is reserved to the principal plenary organ.

In the case of the UN the relationship between the GA and the TC or the ECOSOC emerges from Chapters XII and X respectively of the Charter. While the GA may have had almost complete control over the TC as a result of Article 87,[44] the ECOSOC seems to have some independence from the GA depending on which of its powers is in issue, as is shown, for example, by Article 62 of the Charter, though the GA may have some control over it.

The relationship between the SC and the GA, on the other hand, is very different. In the *Second Admissions Case* the ICJ made it quite clear that both the SC and GA were principal organs of the UN and that the SC was not subordinate to the GA.[45] This was so, even though the GA was a plenary organ, while the SC was an organ with limited membership.

The relationship of the two organs in the areas of admission of members and peacekeeping has been examined by the ICJ. The *Second Admissions Case* concerned the relationship between the SC and the GA in the matter of the admission of members. Article 4(2) of the Charter provides

---

[40] Article VI(5)(a).   [41] Article V(2)(c).

[42] See Article V(1)(b) of the Articles of Agreement.

[43] The Articles of Agreement of the IMF are more clearly drafted, it would seem, insofar as Article XII(2)(a) of the Articles of Agreement recognizes that powers may be directly conferred by the Articles on the Board of Executive Directors. The EIB seems to be an exceptional case. For a discussion of the powers of the organs of financial institutions, including the EIB, in general see Syz, note 19 pp. 30*ff.* and 46*ff.*

[44] The trusteeship system has been defunct in practice since 1994.

[45] See 1950 ICJ Reports at pp. 8 and 10.

that admission will be effected by a decision of the General Assembly 'upon the recommendation of the Security Council'. The argument was advanced that, when the SC failed to decide in favour of an application for membership, it in effect recommended non-admission, and that this was, therefore, a 'recommendation' of the SC upon which the GA could decide to admit the applicant state, despite rejection by the SC. The Court rejected this view, concluding that the independent and separate consent of both the GA and the SC was necessary before a new member could be admitted. The actual admission was effected by the GA 'upon the recommendation of the Security Council'. Therefore, although the GA did not have to admit a state recommended for admission by the SC, it could not decide to admit one whose admission had not been recommended by the SC. The wording of Article 4(2) made it clear that the admission must be positively recommended by the SC as a precondition of admission by the GA. The Court said:

> To hold that the General Assembly has power to admit a State to membership in the absence of a recommendation of the Security Council would be to deprive the Security Council of an important power which has been entrusted to it by the Charter. It would almost nullify the role of the Security Council in the exercise of one of the essential functions of the Organization.[46]

A consequence of accepting the other view referred to by the Court would be that the role of the SC would in fact be reduced to one where it would merely study the case, present a report, give advice, and express an opinion – an advisory instead of an executive role. The argument that, when the SC rejected an application for admission, it in effect made a 'recommendation' against admission, upon which the GA could act and could decide to admit the applicant despite the adverse vote of the SC, was rejected by the Court when it said:

> Article 4, paragraph 2, envisages a favourable recommendation of the Security Council and that only. An unfavourable recommendation would not correspond to the provisions of Article 4, paragraph 2.[47]

It is clear that it was the Court's view that a so-called 'unfavourable recommendation' was not really a recommendation at all, but a refusal to recommend, and the requirements of Article 4(2) could not be met by treating the absence of a recommendation as equivalent to an 'unfavourable recommendation' upon which the GA could base a

---

[46] *Ibid.* at p. 9.   [47] *Ibid.*

decision to admit a state to membership.[48] The case is a good illustration of the general relationship between the two organs in areas where
their functions overlap, though the particular subject was the admission
of members.

In the *Expenses Case*[49] the Court was confronted with a different aspect
of the powers of these two organs. The case concerned the powers of the
two organs in respect of the maintenance of international peace and
security. The issue was how far did the powers of the SC in the field of
maintaining international peace and security detract from the powers
of the GA in the same field. First, the Court held that Article 24 of the
UN Charter gave the SC 'primary' and not 'exclusive' responsibility for
the maintenance of international peace and security.[50] This meant that
the GA was also concerned with the maintenance of international peace
and security and had certain functions in this field, as appeared from
the other parts of the Charter. As was explained by Judge Bustamante in
regard to the constitution of the UNEF, albeit in a dissenting opinion, the
impossibility acknowledged by the SC of carrying out its responsibilities
placed the organization in a dilemma and the GA acquired the right
to intervene, 'since the Organization was obliged to fulfil the principal
purposes of its existence under Article 1 of the Charter'.[51]

At the same time, the Court said, the second feature of the Charter
position was that the SC alone had power to require enforcement by
coercive action against an aggressor under Chapter VII.[52] This was true
even of action taken in connection with a state not found to be an aggressor, in which case under certain conditions action was available under
Chapter VII. Because primary responsibility was conferred on the SC 'in
order to ensure prompt and effective action' according to Article 24,
it was the SC that could impose an explicit obligation of compliance,
if, for instance, it issued an order or command to an aggressor under
Chapter VII. The SC alone could impose an obligation by a resolution in
connection with the maintenance of international peace and security
in regard to an aggressor. The Court did not limit the action taken to
coercive or enforcement action against an aggressor insofar as it said:

Articles of Chapter VII of the Charter speak of 'situations' as well as disputes,
and it must lie within the power of the Security Council to police a situation
even though it does not resort to enforcement action against a State.[53]

---

[48] *Ibid.* See the analysis of the Court's view on this issue by Fitzmaurice, *The Law and
Procedure of the International Court of Justice* (1986) vol. I, pp. 54–5.
[49] 1962 ICJ Reports p. 151.   [50] *Ibid.* at p. 163.   [51] *Ibid.* at p. 293.   [52] *Ibid.* at p. 163.
[53] *Ibid.* at p. 167.

Article 39 required a determination of 'the existence of any threat to the peace, breach of the peace or act of aggression' and merely stated that the SC may 'decide what measures shall be taken'. It was not laid down that action could be taken only against an aggressor.

The GA, however, said the Court, was also concerned with the maintenance of international peace and security but it had no power to require enforcement by coercive action, because Article 14 authorized it only to 'recommend measures for the peaceful adjustment of any situation, regardless of origin, which it deems likely to impair the general welfare or friendly relations among nations, including situations resulting from a violation of the provisions of the present Charter setting forth the purposes and principles of the United Nations'.[54] The distinction between decisions which the SC could make (which were binding) and recommendations (which were not) was understood to underlie the difference in powers. The GA had the power only to recommend measures in order to maintain peace.

The recommendation of measures under Article 14, continued the Court, was limited only by Article 12 and was not subject to the provisions of Article 11.[55] Article 12(1) reads: 'While the Security Council is exercising in respect of any dispute or situation the functions assigned to it in the present Charter, the General Assembly shall not make any recommendation with regard to that dispute or situation unless the Security Council so requests.' The Article referred to a circumstance in which the GA may not make recommendations under Article 14. The limitation in Article 11(2), that 'any question on which action is necessary shall be referred to the Security Council by the General Assembly either before or after discussion', did not affect Article 14. The Court was of opinion that, even if such 'action' under Article 11(2), which was enforcement action, was in fact necessary, the GA could proceed under Article 14 to recommend measures without reference to the SC, provided the requirements of Article 12(1) were satisfied, namely that the SC should not be exercising its functions in respect of the situation concerned.[56]

In the case of the EU, the European Parliament had under Article 137 of the EEC Treaty to be consulted by the European Commission before

---

[54] *Ibid.* at p. 163.   [55] *Ibid.* at p. 172.

[56] The peacekeeping powers of the SC and GA and the relationship between the GA and the SC explained in the *Expenses Case* are analysed in C. F. Amerasinghe, '*The United National Expenses Case* – A Contribution to the Law of International Organization', 4 IJIL (1964) at pp. 197*ff*.

it submitted proposals or measures to the European Council. However, the Commission was not obliged to follow the wishes of the Parliament, because it had to obtain the agreement of the Council. The Single European Act gave the Parliament's decision more significance. Whereas the Council took its decisions normally by majority vote, it had, however, to rule unanimously in order to ignore the Parliament's opinion.

The European Parliament has even now under the amended treaties (the TEU) a certain relationship to the Commission particularly, and to the Council, in the areas in which it has functions. In the legislative area it can even request the Commission to make a legislative proposal.

The supervisory powers of the Parliament in its relationship with the Commission and the Council have been strengthened. Under the TEU supervision by the Parliament and the activities of the Commission is made possible by the regular attendance of members of the Commission at part-sessions of the Parliament, and of Commissioners or their officials at meetings of Parliamentary Committees. The TEU expressly requires as an obligation that members of the Commission reply to written and oral questions and, following the first enlargement of the Communities in 1973, a question time was introduced. The TEU also requires the Commission to submit an annual general report to the Parliament. Further, by practice other reports on various subjects are published. These are significant sources of information.

Although the TEU does not require it, the Council replies to written questions from the Parliament, and, through the President or any other member of the Council, to oral questions. Council Presidents are invited to appear before Committees of the Parliament and they attend part-sessions to represent the views of the Council or to give an account of their management of Council business. Provision has been made for the Council to be represented in some way before Parliamentary Committees.

Now the supervisory powers of the European Parliament have been reinforced by the TEU in several ways. First, under Article 193 (ex 138c) the Parliament was given the right to establish temporary Committees of Inquiry to investigate 'alleged contraventions or maladministrations in the implementation of Community law', except where the matter is *sub judice*. Second, Article 194 (ex 138d) confirms by law an established practice by giving any citizen of the EU or any resident of a member state the right to petition the European Parliament on a matter within Community competence which affects him directly. Third, under Article 195 (ex 138e) the Parliament appoints an Ombudsman who has the power to receive complaints concerning maladministration in the activities of Community institutions or bodies (other than the CJEC or the Court of First Instance acting judicially). If the Ombudsman finds that there has been maladministration, there is a procedure established by which in the end he submits a report to the Parliament and the institution concerned. Fourth, Parliament's supervisory powers are given some teeth by Article 201 (ex 144) which enables the Parliament to pass a motion of censure by which it can force the resignation of the College of Commissioners.[57]

Many, indeed most, constituent instruments of international organizations deal with the relationship between principal organs in reasonably clear terms, especially where the relationship is more or less hierarchical, as do the Articles of Agreement of the IMF and the IBRD (and the constitutions of almost all other financial institutions). However, controversies are bound to arise particularly where relationships are complicated, for example, by concurrent or shared responsibilities. The ICJ has in the two cases in which it had to settle disputes as to the interpretation of the Charter of the UN in regard to such relationships taken a highly sophisticated approach. While in effect not denying that a constitution (of the UN, in those cases) must be interpreted so as to facilitate the achievement of the purposes of the organization rather than defeat them, the Court did take care as far as possible to protect the powers of each organ in its relations with other organs. But it is also apparent that it did this only insofar as was possible without destroying the effectiveness of the organization or crippling it. In some cases, as in the case of the peacekeeping powers of the SC and GA, this may virtually demand walking a tightrope in order to find a reasonable and pragmatic solution.

Voting

Distribution of votes in organs of international organizations is presumptively based on the principle that each member of the body has one vote,

---

[57] The motion of censure has been used as a sword of Damocles. The Commission presided over by Mr. J. Santer resigned *en banc* in 1999, following an adverse report by a Committee of Experts which had been appointed to investigate claims of fraud, mismanagement and nepotism. Evidently because it had become clear that a motion of censure would otherwise in all likelihood be adopted by the Parliament, the resignation took place.

On the aspect of the Parliament's supervisory powers see particularly Arnull *et al.* (eds.), note 24 pp. 36–38. The Parliament's participation in budgetary matters is dealt with in Chapter 11 below.

unless there is an indication to the contrary in the constitution or relevant basic instrument. This goes beyond the maxim 'one state, one vote', as it applies even when states as such are not members of an organ or are not the only members. Thus, in the GA of the UN, in the FAO Conference or in the Executive Committee of the COE each state represented has one vote. In the ILO General Conference each group representative has one vote. In the case of the GA Article 18(1) is explicit in that it states that each member has one vote. In the SC of the UN also each member has one vote, pursuant to Article 27(1), even though the votes of some members, as will be seen, exert more influence than those of others.

In the case of the financial institutions in general a system of weighted vote allocation in the principal organs has been explicitly adopted in their constitutions. The system is based on recognition of the importance of the contributing of capital by each member to the institution. The principle of equality of votes has been abandoned in lieu of distributing votes in direct proportion to financial contribution.

The type of arrangement for allocation of votes in these institutions is modelled on that implemented in the Articles of Agreement of the IMF and the IBRD. The relevant provisions assign 250 votes to each member plus one additional vote for each part of its quota equivalent to a certain value (IMF)[58] or for each share of capital stock (IBRD).[59] In the other agreements there is also a certain number of votes, which varies, allocated to each member irrespective of the number of shares held in the organization, the rest of the votes being assigned in direct proportion to the number of shares held.[60]

While in practice the method of securing a consensus may be resorted to by organs in the course of doing business,[61] generally now

---

[58] Article XII(5)(a).

[59] Article V(3)(a). On weighted voting in the IMF and the IBRD see Gianaris, 'Weighted Voting in the International Monetary Fund and the World Bank', 14 Fordham ILJ (1990–91) p. 910.

[60] See, e.g., IFC Articles of Agreement, Article IV(3)(a); IDA Articles of Agreement, Article VI(3)(a); IDB Agreement, Article VIII(4)(a); ADB Agreement, Article 33(1); AFDB Agreement, Article 35(1); and CDB Agreement, Article 32(5). See Syz, note 19 pp. 33*ff.* and 48*ff.*, for the system of voting in the international development banks. For other voting systems see Schermers and Blokker, note 2 pp. 529*ff.* A system of weighted voting has also been adopted in the Council of the EU, where the Council is required to act by a qualified majority: see Article 148 of the TEU.

[61] See literature cited in Schermers and Blokker, *ibid.* p. 506, note 131. The constitution of the League of Nations required unanimity for most decisions: Article 5 of the LN Covenant. There are still some constitutions which require unanimity, at least for certain decisions: see, e.g., Article 20 of the COE Statute; Articles 84, 99, 100, 235, 237

constitutions of organizations do not require consensus or unanimity for decisions to be taken. In the UN, with an exception for the SC, all UN decisions are taken by majority vote. The OAU, the OAS, the IAEA and the specialized agencies, for example, also take decisions by majority vote.

Majorities may vary. They may be simple (more than half the votes counted), qualified (e.g., two-thirds, three-fourths or three-fifths), relative (in the case of alternatives, larger by a number of votes than the number actually obtained for any other solution), or absolute (in the case of alternatives, greater than the number which can be obtained at the same time for any other solution). Sometimes a double majority may be required, as in the case of Article XXVIII of the IMF Articles of Agreement and Article VIII(a) of the IBRD Constitution, both relating to amendments. In the case of the SC the majority required for all decisions is now nine out of fifteen, with the five permanent members each having a power of veto in regard to nonprocedural matters.[62] Further, in general the majority required may in circumstances be of the membership[63] or of the total voting power[64] or of the members present and voting.[65] These are but a few examples of the variety of requirements that exist for majorities.

The approach taken to abstention from voting and absence has in general had a mitigating effect particularly on the severity of certain requirements in relation to majorities. This is apart from the impact of absences on quorum requirements after a session of an organ has begun.[66] At one time abstentions were apparently counted as negative votes, thus, among other things, preventing unanimity.[67] But now it would seem that, firstly, abstentions are not regarded as preventing

and 238 of the EEC Treaty; Article 6 of the OECD Constitution; and Article II(c) of the OPEC Constitution.

[62] Article 27(2) and (3). Under the Cartagena Agreement members of the Andean Common Market have a right of veto in relation to certain matters: Article II.

[63] See, e.g., Articles 108 and 109 of the UN Charter; Article 90 of the ICAO Constitution; and Article 3(c) and (e) of the WMO Constitution.

[64] The IMF Articles of Agreement has this requirement in over twenty cases: see Gold, *Voting and Decisions in the International Monetary Fund* (1972) pp. 120ff.

[65] See, e.g., Article 18(2) and (3) of the UN Charter. There is also the question of quorums for a meeting and for a valid vote to take place: see Schermers, 'The Quorum in Intergovernmental Organs', in Bockstiegel *et al.* (eds.), *Law of Nations, Law of International Organisation, World's Economic Law: Festschrift für Ignaz Seidl-Hohenveldern* (1988) p. 527. Qualified majorities (with weighted voting) have been adopted in the Council of the EU: see Article 148 of the TEU.

[66] See Schermers and Blokker, note 2 p. 540.

[67] See the case in the LN of the Japanese proposal relating to equality of treatment: Zimmern, *The League of Nations and the Rule of Law, 1918–1935* (1939) pp. 260ff.

unanimity, as is shown by the provisions of many constitutional instruments;[68] secondly, that abstinence is regarded as a failure to vote, which means that the abstainer is not regarded as 'present and voting';[69] and, thirdly, that in the SC when under Article 27(3) of the Charter the concurring votes of the permanent members are required for a decision, abstention on the part of a permanent member is not regarded as the absence of a concurring vote. The latter practice became established in the SC in the early days of the UN and was accepted as law-creating by the ICJ in the *Namibia Case*. There the Court held:

> The proceedings of the Security Council extending over a long period supply abundant evidence that presidential rulings and the positions taken by members of the Council, in particular its permanent members, have consistently and uniformly interpreted the practice of voluntary abstention by a permanent member as not constituting a bar to the adoption of resolutions. By abstaining, a member does not signify its objection to the approval of what is being proposed; in order to prevent the adoption of a resolution requiring unanimity of the permanent members, a permanent member has only to cast a negative vote. This procedure followed by the Security Council, which has continued unchanged after the amendment in 1965 of Article 27 of the Charter, has been generally accepted by members of the United Nations and evidences a general practice of that organization.[70]

However, in some cases, while abstention does not invalidate decisions which must be taken unanimously, the constituent instrument provides that such decisions are inapplicable to member states which abstained.[71]

The impact of absence on majorities or unanimity is also a matter of importance. The practice of the SC of the UN supports the view that absence is treated in the same way as an abstention, i.e., the absence of a permanent member is not regarded as a negative vote or a

---

[68] See, e.g., OECD Constitution, Article 6; COE Statute, Article 20(a); EEC Treaty, Article 148(3) and Euratom Treaty, Article 118(3), and now Article 148(3) of the TEU.

[69] See Rule 88 of the GA Rules of Procedure.

[70] 1971 ICJ Reports at p. 22. See on this issue Zacklin, *The Amendment of the Constitutive Instruments of the United Nations and Specialized Agencies* (1968) pp. 183ff.; Gross, 'Voting in the Security Council: Abstention in the Post-1965 Amendment Phase and its Impact on Article 25 of the Charter', 62 AJIL (1968) p. 315; Stavropoulos, 'Practice of Voluntary Abstention by Permanent Members of the Security Council under Article 27, Paragraph 3, of the Charter of the United Nations', 61 AJIL (1967) p. 737. For example, in 1965 the SC adopted a decision on Southern Rhodesia with seven votes (then the minimum needed) in favour and four permanent members abstaining (all except China): Resolution S 202.

[71] See, e.g., OECD constitution, Article 6(2); and COMECON Constitution, Article 4. The same provision exists for some cases in the IMF: see Gold, note 64 p. 113.

non-affirmative vote which would hinder the existence of a majority including the affirmative votes of the five permanent members.[72] In COMECON a problem arose when Albania ceased to participate in the organization, because, while unanimity strictly was not required, the consent of interested members was required for decisions. Even though Albania disagreed, the organization took the view that it could take valid decisions even in the fields in which Albania was interested, in spite of Albania's absence, such absence not being equivalent to opposition or failure to consent.[73] It would seem to be safe to conclude that in general absence would be treated in the same way as an abstention.

Problems may arise around the voting structure of an organization, in circumstances in which an organ performs functions outside the regular scope of its functions as explicitly envisaged in the constituent instrument of the organization. This situation prevailed in the *Voting Procedure Case*[74] which came before the ICJ. One of the subsidiary issues was whether it was possible for the GA to implement a procedure of voting requiring unanimity or qualified unanimity in connection with the administration of a mandate when the Charter of the UN, in Article 18, specifically referred to either a simple majority or a two-thirds majority as being required when the GA took its decisions. The Court was of the view that the GA could not do this without amendment of the Charter. The Court stated its conclusion as follows:

The constitution of an organ usually prescribes the method of voting by which the organ arrives at its decisions. The voting system is related to the composition and functions of the organ. It forms one of the characteristics of the constitution of the organ. Taking decisions by a two-thirds majority vote or by a simple majority vote is one of the distinguishing features of the General Assembly, while the unanimity rule was one of the distinguishing features of the Council of the League of Nations. These two systems are characteristic of different organs, and one system cannot be substituted for the other without constitutional amendment. To transplant upon the General Assembly the unanimity

[72] This was the position taken first in 1950 by the SC when the Soviet Union refused to participate in meetings of the SC, because it believed that China was allegedly represented by the wrong delegation.

[73] See Kaser, *COMECON* (1967) pp. 67, 245ff. In the case of the EEC France refused in 1965 to participate in the meetings of the Council. Unanimity, though required, could be obtained by the written procedure. The Council did not equate absence with abstention: see Schermers and Blokker, note 2 p. 540. This was a case where the constitution provided expressly that abstention could not prevent the existence of unanimity and also provided for an alternative procedure in the case of absence. Thus, it does not set a precedent for the treatment of absences in general.

[74] 1955 ICJ Reports p. 67.

rule of the Council of the League would not be simply the introduction of a procedure, but would amount to a disregard of one of the characteristics of the General Assembly. Consequently the question of conformity of the voting system of the General Assembly with that of the Council of the League of Nations presents insurmountable difficulties of a juridical nature.[75]

However, in the *Treaty of Lausanne Case* the PCIJ had in its advisory opinion stated that the Council of the LN which under the Covenant took non-procedural decisions by unanimity could 'undertake to give decisions by a majority in specific cases, if express provision is made for this power by treaty stipulations'.[76] In fact Article 9 of the Rules of Procedure of the Council made provisions for an exception to unanimity on these lines. There is, thus, an apparent conflict between the views of the PCIJ and the ICJ.

The ICJ was dealing with the unanimity rule in the *Voting Procedure Case,* which in effect it found repugnant to the spirit of the Charter provisions on voting in the GA. The mandate over South West Africa (Namibia) was inherited by 'succession' from the LN, the GA being placed in the position of having to implement the mandate over that territory resulting from the provisions of the LN Covenant and the mandate agreement. Thus, it is possible to take the view that the GA could not be compelled to administer the mandate with a voting system which was not at all envisaged by the Charter. In these circumstances the issue was not whether an intermediate system should have been implemented, because it is arguable that that was not a viable alternative. The GA had either to accept the voting system of the Covenant or reject it. If it rejected it, as it was really obligated to, it was left with no alternative but to use its own system of voting. The conclusion reached in the case by the ICJ appears correct. Further, the Court did point out that the acceptance of the unanimity principle would have created juridical difficulties. It could be inferred that this meant that it would have been possible for the GA to make decisions with a system of voting which was *not so different* from that required by the Charter for the GA and would not have been repugnant to the spirit of the Charter. There is no reason to conclude that the Court intended to preclude the adoption by the GA of a system of voting

---

[75] *Ibid.* at p. 75.

[76] PCIJ Series B No. 12 at p. 30. Judge Lauterpacht in the *Voting Procedure Case* issued this statement, to base his argument that departure from the GA's voting provisions of the Charter of the UN was possible in certain circumstances, provided that the procedure adopted was not 'entirely alien to the spirit of the Charter and as such inconsistent with it': 1955 ICJ Reports at pp. 110*ff.*

different from the one prescribed in the Charter, given the appropriate conditions.[77]

In the case of the provisions of the Treaty of Lausanne the voting rules could only have been less exacting than what the LN Council worked with under the Covenant. Thus, the issue of repugnancy or juridical difficulty did not arise and the system of voting under that treaty could legitimately have been implemented by the Council. In this case, unlike in the *Voting Procedure Case,* the alternative voting system was viable in terms of the requirements of the Covenant for the Council.

The two cases are reconcilable on the basis of the principle that an organ may depart from the voting system ordained by its constitution in order to act under other instruments than its constitution attributing to it the power to act, to the extent that, and only if, the voting systems required by those instruments are not repugnant to the spirit of its constitution with the result that they create juridical difficulties.

Administrative organs

In setting up the early international organizations the member states reserved for themselves the right of exclusive management by conferring this on the plenary organ composed of government representatives who had to approve every important decision unanimously. This body was not permanently in session. Thus, it was necessary to grant administrative power to another body, most often called the secretariat.

In executing the will of the organization, which is not necessarily the same as that of each of the member states, the secretariat had at least the right of requiring from member states submission and exchange of

---

[77] Crawford, *The Creation of States in International Law* (1979) pp. 352ff., believes that there was no real 'succession' by the UN in the case of South West Africa. He suggests that the exercise of supervisory functions was based on estoppel. The UN was competent by various provisions of the Charter, and South Africa accepted the competence by the combination of its membership of the UN and various other acts (including asking for permission to annex South West Africa). On this analysis there is less of a problem, because the GA was acting as such in respect of South West Africa, and not as a surrogate of the LN Council. But it is doubtful whether this was the view taken by the ICJ, because it did treat the case as one of compatibility between two different voting systems, which would not have been necessary had there been no 'succession'. Had there been no 'succession' but the situation was one based on competence and acceptance (a form of agreement), the acceptance being an important element, the Court could have based its finding on the fact that there was also implied *acceptance* of the GA voting system, the issue of unanimity and reconciling voting systems being irrelevant. The question of succession is discussed further in Chapter 15 below.

information useful for the functioning of the organization and also the right of verifying that each member state was truly in compliance with its obligations *vis-à-vis* the organization and other member states.

When the UPU, one of the earliest international organizations, was created, its secretariat, the International Bureau, was placed under the oversight of the Swiss government. Article 20 of the UPU Constitution now embodies this arrangement. In the case of the international organizations created later the member states decided to abandon this model and that, especially, in organizations having objectives other than strictly administrative ones, it was practically impossible to restrict the role of the secretariat to a purely administrative function. When the LN was established, the functions of the secretariat were not limited solely to the execution of orders received from the plenary or other body. The latter, and even policy-making bodies of limited membership, were not permanently in session. They could not anticipate all the situations which could confront the secretariat. This body had, therefore, to be endowed with a measure of discretionary power. Further, now the secretariat has considerable powers, based largely on the fact that it is the organ that is best informed on all documentation and practices of the organization. Secretariats make proposals, for example, for the agenda of a particular session or for the establishment of a budget, although the final decision on these matters may lie with a deliberative organ. The secretariat carries out many administrative functions, such as informing the public about the activities of the organization, producing the minutes of sessions, co-ordinating the activities of the various bodies within its own organization and even those of other organizations, and representing the organization in matters of international public law as well as in private law. There may be many other functions of an administrative or preparatory nature that secretariats perform. Particularly, in the financial institutions the administrative organ prepares projects for loans to be approved by the executive organs and even lays the groundwork for the formulation of lending policies. In certain cases the secretariat has been called upon to mediate or arbitrate.[78] Under loan agreements, financial institutions supervise projects extensively.

---

[78] In 1948 the UPU secretariat was called upon to arbitrate in litigation between two postal administrations, although the Constitution of UPU did not expressly provide for this. The arbitration was under a *compromis spécial* between the Postal Administration of Turkey and the Postal Administration of Syria: see 23 ILR (1960) p. 596. The SG of the UN mediated in the *Rainbow Warrior Incident*: see Ruling of the SG, 6 July 1986, 26 ILM (1987) p. 1,346.

Secretariats now have a significant influence over decisions taken by the policy-making and executive organs. Constitutions of most international organizations at this time take into account the 'political' importance of secretariats. The Charter of the UN, for instance, confers on the Secretary General the right of initiative *vis-à-vis* policy-making bodies. Article 99 of the Charter states:

> The Secretary General may bring to the attention of the Security Council any matter which in his opinion may threaten the maintenance of international peace and security.

The position is similar in the OECD under Article 10(2) of the Constitution and in the UNESCO, pursuant to Article VI(3) of the Constitution. In other organizations the Secretary-General chairs sessions of the plenary policy-making organ, which gives him an autonomous right of intervention. This is the case in NATO and the OECD, for instance. The right is not accorded the Secretary-General on an exclusively personal basis, but in his capacity as the most highly placed civil servant of the organization. Thus, ideas developed in the secretariat will ascend the hierarchical ladder and finally find their expression through the Secretary-General. In the financial institutions the head of the secretariat, i.e, the President or Managing Director, is generally also the chairman of the second plenary organ consisting of the Executive Directors where, while he cannot normally vote, he has the casting vote.[79] In the constitutions of these institutions it is generally provided in regard to the operational role of the head of the secretariat that he is the chief of the operating staff,[80] is the legal representative of the institution,[81] and shall conduct the ordinary business of the institution.[82] Final decisions on loans are, however, reserved for the Executive Directors.

The administrative organ may be decentralized, at least in relation to its subordinate units, sometimes geographically, as in the case of the WHO, or sometimes through the assignment to each of the different organs of the organization of its own secretariat, as in the case of the EEC.

---

[79] See, e.g., Article V(5)(a) of the IBRD Constitution; Article IV(5)(a) of the IFC Constitution; Article VIII(5)(a) of the IDB Agreement; and Article 34(5) of the ADB Agreement.

[80] See, e.g., Article V(5)(b) of the IBRD Articles of Agreement; Article IV(5)(b) of the IFC Articles of Agreement; Article 13(7) of the EIB Statute; Article VIII(5)(a) of the IDB Agreement; and Article 34(5) of the ADB Agreement.

[81] See, e.g., Article VIII(5)(a) of the IDB Agreement; Article 13(6) of the EIB Statute; and Article 34(3) of the ADB Statute.

[82] Article V(5)(b) of the IBRD Constitution; Article VIII(5)(a) of the IDB Agreement; Article 13(3) and (4) of the EIB Statute; and Article 34(5) of the ADB Agreement.

Exceptionally, some bodies which may be regarded as having a combination of secretariat features and those of a committee of member states' representatives have a power of autonomous decision-making. One of the few examples of this is the International Frequency Registration Board of the ITU, constituted under Article 10 of the ITU's Constitution. Each of its five members is appointed by a member state but enjoys an independence, *vis-à-vis* the appointing state, comparable to the independence of an international civil servant. Article 10(2) specifically states that the members do not represent their countries or a region but are custodians of an international public trust.

It is only on rare occasions that the administrative organs of international organizations are able to play a role other than that of assuring the effective internal administration of the organization concerned. This external role can sometimes go as far as the temporary administration of a territory awaiting a plebiscite. For instance, the LN administered the territory of the Saar from 1920 to 1935, the UN administered the territory of West Irian from 1962 to 1963, and the WEU administered the Saar in 1956. Among these external activities, those of the various UN peacekeeping forces are of a special nature. Although composed of contingents placed at the disposal of the UN by its member states, they are UN bodies, more like administrative bodies. Other external activities of the UN are undertaken on behalf of the Palestinian refugees. The needs of the developing world have led a large number of international organizations to lend their technical assistance to developing states by seconding qualified personnel from their own staffs.[83]

In the majority of organizations, the head of the secretariat is nominated by the plenary assembly. In the UN this is on the recommendation of the Security Council.[84] He holds office for a period of several years. In the case of some financial institutions the head is appointed by the second plenary body, the executive organ.[85]

As a general rule, the subordinate staff of the secretariat is appointed by the head of the secretariat of the organization. The rules concerning

---

[83] The Commission of the EU seems to have an ambiguous status: see Seidl-Hohenveldern, loc. cit. note 2 at pp. 18–19; Lasok and Bridge, *Law and Institutions of the European Communities* (1991) pp. 188ff.

[84] See Article 57 of the Charter.

[85] See, e.g., Article V(5)(a) of the IBRD Articles of Agreement; Article 36 of the AFDB Agreement; and Article XII(4)(a) of the IMF Articles of Agreement. In the IDB (Article VIII(5)(a) of the IDB Agreement), the ADB (Article 34(1) of the ADB Agreement), the CDB (Article 33(1) of the CDB Agreement) and the EIB (Article 13(1) of the EIB Statute), for instance, on the other hand, the final election is by the main plenary body.

the international civil service provide them with a certain job security, which is, however, less than that enjoyed by the members of the civil service in most states.[86] Almost all organizations now have the requirement that secretariat staff must possess the highest qualities in terms of performance, competence and integrity and the importance of recruiting on as wide a geographical basis as possible is often to be taken into consideration, mainly in the case of open organizations.[87] The secretariat would not be performing its functions independently and in the name of the organization, if it were to be influenced by the will of one or some member states rather than the interest of the organization. Hence, the constitutions of many international organizations have provisions prohibiting attempts by a member state to influence the members of the secretariat in the execution of their duties, and require absolute and exclusive loyalty on the part of the staff towards the organization.[88] This is also the *raison d'être* for the privileges and immunities granted to the organization and its personnel. Indeed, the relationship between the staff and the organization is such that they can expect protection from the organization. As the ICJ stated in the *Reparation Case*:

In order that the agent may perform his duties satisfactorily, he must feel that this protection is assured to him by the Organization, and that he may count on it. To ensure the independence of the agent, and, consequently, the independent action of the Organization itself, it is essential that in performing his duties he need not have to rely on any other protection than that of the Organization (save of course for the more direct and immediate protection due from the State in whose territory he may be). In particular, he should not have to rely on the protection of his own State. If he had to rely on that State, his independence might well be compromised, contrary to the principle applied by Article 100 of the Charter. And lastly, it is essential that – whether the agent belongs to a powerful or to a weak State; to one more affected or less affected by the complications of international life; to one in sympathy or not in sympathy with the mission of the agent – he should know that in the performance of his duties he is under the protection of the Organization. This assurance is even more necessary when the agent is state-less . . . Upon examination of the character of the functions entrusted to the Organization and of the nature of the missions

---

[86] See Ruzié, *Les fonctionnaires internationaux* (1970).

[87] See, e.g., Article 101(3) of the UN Charter; Article XII(4)(d) of the IMF Articles of Agreement; Article V(5)(d) of the IBRD Articles of Agreement; and Article 35 of the WHO Constitution.

[88] See, e.g., Article 100(1) and (2) of the UN Charter; Article XII(4)(c) of the IMF Articles of Agreement; Article V(5)(c) of the IBRD Articles of Agreement; Article VIII(2) of the FAO Constitution; and Article VI(5) of the UNESCO Constitution.

of its agents, it becomes clear that the capacity of the Organization to exercise a measure of functional protection of its agents arises by necessary intendment out of the Charter.[89]

In general, members of the secretariat identify very closely with the goals of the organization, transcending the partial identification of interests that employees normally have with their employers' interests. In fact, the work of international civil servants from the most diverse national backgrounds within the organization shows them on a daily basis that international co-operation is possible. That the loyalty to these ideals is strong is shown, for example, by the fact that the secretariat of the ITU once resorted to a 'political' strike to defend these ideals. In 1964, it refused its services to an administrative conference which adopted a resolution concerning its composition, and which – in the opinion of the secretariat – was incompatible with the Constitution of the ITU.

[89] 1949 ICJ Reports at pp. 183–4.

6   Acts of non-judicial organs: their legal effect

There are two important problems of legal principle relating to the acts of organizations. The first concerns the applicability, scope and effect of the doctrine of *ultra vires* in regard to these acts.[1] The second relates to the effects of acts performed by organs of organizations, such as the General Assembly of the UN, the Executive Directors of the IBRD, the deliberative assemblies of the FAO or the ILO and the secretariats of international organizations. The second matter will be discussed here, while the first problem will be dealt with in the next chapter.

The legal effect of the acts of organs of organizations, and consequently of organizations, is a matter which has exercised jurists for some time.[2] While most attention has been paid to the resolutions of

---

[1] This issue must be distinguished from that of acts or omissions which are violations of the law and lead to responsibility: see the discussion in E. Lauterpacht, 'The Legal Effect of Illegal Acts of International Organizations', in McNair, *Cambridge Essays in International Law* (1965) at pp. 88–9. The doctrine of *ultra vires* relates to the legal validity and invalidity of acts.

[2] There are some works which have dealt with international organizations in general: see, e.g., Detter Delupis, *Law Making by International Organizations* (1965); Detter Delupis, 'The Legal Value of Recommendations of International Organizations', in Butler (ed.), *International Law and the International System* (1987) p. 47; Skubiszewski, 'Non-Binding Resolutions and the Law-Making Process', 15 Polish YIL (1986) p. 135; Skubiszewski, 'Law-Making by International Organizations', 19 *Thesaurus Acroasium* (1992) p. 357; Economides, 'Les actes institutionels internationaux et les sources du droit international', 34 AFDI (1989) p. 131; Frowein, 'The Internal and External Effects of Resolutions of International Organizations', 49 ZAORV (1989) p. 778; Voitovich, 'Normative Acts of the Inter-Economic Organizations in International Law-making', 24 JWTL (1990) p. 21; Virally, 'La Valeur juridique des recommandations des organisations internationales', 2 AFDI (1956) p. 66; Virally, 'Sources of International Law: Unilateral Acts of International Organizations', in Bedjaoui (ed.), *International Law: Achievements and Prospects* (1991) p. 241; David, 'La portée juridique des actes institutionels', 19 *Thesaurus Acroasium* (1992) p. 223; and Yemin, *Legislative Powers in the*

the General Assembly of the UN, there has been work done on other organizations. It is not the purpose here to discuss in detail the legal or other effects of acts of the organs of all organizations but to identify any general principles which may apply to what may be described generally as resolutions (or decisions) of organs. Inevitably, the UN will be the basic model but any general principles would apply to other organizations.

A principle which seems to be basic is that the power to perform acts is derived from the constitution of an organization, whether such

United Nations and the Specialized Agencies (1969). Many of these authors, however, emphasize the UN. Most of the other specialized works on the subject concentrate mainly on the UN and in particular the GA: see, e.g., Sloan, *United Nations General Assembly Resolutions in our Changing World* (1991); Sloan, 'The Binding Force of a "Recommendation" of the General Assembly of the United Nations', 23 BYIL (1948) p. 1; Sloan, 'General Assembly Resolutions Revisited (Forty Years Later)', 56 BYIL (1987) p. 39; Basak, *Decisions of the United Nations Organs in the Judgments and Opinions of the International Court of Justice* (1969); Castañeda, *Legal Effects of United Nations Resolutions* (1969); Frowein, 'Der Beitrag der internationalen Organisationen zur Entwicklung des Völkerrechts', 36 ZAORV (1976) p. 147; Han, *International Legislation by the United Nations* (1971) pp. 58*ff*. and 68*ff*.; Higgins, *The Development of International Law through the Political Organs of the United Nations* (1963) particularly pp. 1–104; Higgins, 'The Role of Resolutions of International Organizations in the Process of Creating Norms in the International System', in Butler (ed.), *International Law* p. 21; Higgins, *Problems and Process: International Law and How we Use It* (1994) pp. 24*ff*.; Johnson, 'The Effect of Resolutions of the General Assembly of the United Nations', 32 BYIL (1955–56) p. 97; Joyner, 'United Nations General Assembly Resolutions and International Law: Rethinking the Contemporary Dynamics of Normcreation', 11 California Western ILJ (1981) p. 445; Khan, 'The Legal Status of the Resolutions of the United Nations General Assembly', 19 IJIL (1979) p. 552; Anand, 'International Organizations and the Functioning of International Law', 24 IJIL (1984) p. 51; E. Lauterpacht, 'The Development of the Law of International Organization by the Decisions of International Tribunals', 152 *Hague Recueil* (1976-IV) at pp. 447*ff*.; Lukashuk, 'Recommendations of International Organizations in the International Normative System', in Butler, *International Law* p. 31; Lukashuk, 'International Organizations and the Functions of International Law', 24 IJIL (1984) p. 68; Malintoppi, *Le Raccomandazioni Internazionali* (1958); Mendelson, 'The Legal Character of General Assembly Resolutions: Some Considerations of Principle', in Hossain (ed.), *Legal Aspects of the New International Economic Order* (1980) p. 95; Parry, *The Sources and Evidences of International Law* (1965) pp. 19*ff*.; Schachter, 'The Relation of Law, Politics and Action in the United Nations', 109 *Hague Recueil* (1963-II) at pp. 185*ff*.; Schachter, *International Law in Theory and Practice* (1991) pp. 84*ff*.; Schermers and Blokker, *International Institutional Law* (1995) pp. 741*ff*.; Schwebel (ed.), *The Effectiveness of International Decisions* (1971); Skubiszewski, 'The Elaboration of General Multilateral Conventions and of Non-contractual Instruments Having a Normative Function or Objective – Resolutions of the General Assembly of the United Nations – Provisional Report', 61, Part I, AIDI (1985) p. 85; Skubiszewski, 'Definitive Report and Draft Resolution', *ibid.* at p. 305; Skubiszewski, 'Revised Report', 61, Part II, AIDI (1985) p. 257 (see also 'Observations of Members of the Thirteenth Commission', 61, Part I, AIDI (1985) pp. 250–304 and 335–58); Tunkin, *Theory of International Law* (1974) pp. 161*ff*.; Tunkin, 'The Role of

power is explicit or implied. Consequently, the legal effect of these acts should depend on the constitutional provisions in question. For instance, an explicit effect is to be found stated in Article 25 of the UN Charter relating to 'decisions' of the SC of the UN in so far as it places upon members of the UN the duty to accept and carry them out in accordance with the Charter. A similar explicit effect is to be found in Article 9(a) of the constitution of the WMO which states that all members shall do their utmost to implement the 'decisions' of the Congress. Article 8(d), for example, gives the Congress power to make regulations on certain technical matters. While these regulations would be covered by Article 9(a), Article 9(b) gives members who find it 'impracticable to give effect to some requirement in a technical resolution' of the Congress the option of informing the Secretary-General of the organization whether its inability to give effect to it is provisional or final and to state its reasons. Another example is Article 22 of the WHO constitution which states that regulations adopted pursuant to Article 21 'come into force' for all members after due notice of their adoption except for those members who notify the Director-General of rejection or reservation within the period stated in the notice.[3] It is clear in such cases as these that the resolutions or acts are intended to have binding effects creating obligations and rights, even though there may be a possibility of opting out. They do, therefore, have binding effect. These all happen to be 'operational' acts as defined below.

Resolutions of International Organizations in Creating Norms of International Law', in Butler, *International Law* p. 5; and Vallat, 'The Competence of the United Nations General Assembly', 97 *Hague Recueil* (1959) p. 207. See also the extensive bibliography, mainly on General Assembly resolutions, in Sloan, *General Assembly Resolutions* pp. 567*ff.*; and the bibliography in Skubiszewski, 'Law-making', 19 *Thesaurus Acroasium* (1992), at pp. 384*ff*. There are judgments and opinions of the ICJ on the law relating to the UN which also touch on the issue: e.g., the *Expenses Case*, 1962 ICJ Reports p. 150; the *Namibia Case*, 1971 ICJ Reports p. 16; the *South West Africa Case (2nd Phase)*, 1966 ICJ Reports p. 6; the *Voting Procedure Case*, 1955 ICJ Reports p. 67; the *Corfu Channel Case (Preliminary Objection)*, 1948 ICJ Reports p. 15; the *Nicaragua Case (Merits)*, 1986 ICJ Reports p. 14; and the *Western Sahara Case*, 1975 ICJ Reports p. 16. I examined the opinion of the ICJ and the opinions of other judges on the resolutions of UN organs in the *Expenses Case* in 'The United Nations Expenses Case – A Contribution to the Law of International Organization', 4 IJIL (1964) at pp. 186, 193, 197*ff*. and 208*ff*. Some transnational arbitrations have also dealt with the subject: see, e.g., the *Texaco Arbitration* (1977) 53 ILR p. 389; the *LIAMCO Arbitration* (1977) 62 ILR p. 140; and the *Aminoil Arbitration* (1982) 66 ILR p. 518.

[3] See also the effect of the international standards referred to in Article 37 of the ICAO constitution which are described in Article 38 and Article 37. The indication is that they are binding unless the member takes certain action.

In most cases, however, reference is made either directly or indirectly to acts, such as recommendations or decisions, without further
explanation of their effect. In these cases the effect of the acts must
strictly be derived by implication and interpretation from the basic constitutional texts. This is so even if subsequent practice is invoked to
interpret constitutional provisions. Whether interpretation in a given
case is clear or otherwise, what is important is that in a given context
all the relevant provisions of, and circumstances surrounding, a constitution must be considered. There may also be a possibility of establishing
in the absence of contrary indications some presumptions in the case
of certain acts, such as 'decisions' and 'recommendations', of different
organizations or even of all organizations which have common features.

A second element to be considered is the intent behind the resolution
concerned. A resolution cannot in any case have a greater effect than
that which it was intended by the organ promulgating it to have. For
example, a resolution intended to be less than binding cannot have
a binding effect. On the other hand, the constitutional 'intention' is
hierarchically superior to the intent behind the resolution. No resolution
can have a greater effect than the constitution permits.

Whatever the terminology used to describe them, acts which are binding have the same effect, unless otherwise specified, in whatever organization they are performed. On the other hand, acts that are not binding
or do not share a binding effect, such as 'recommendations', may or may
not have the same legal effect, depending on the constitutional context
from which they derive. Another point of importance is that the use of
the term 'decision' to describe an act does not necessarily mean that the
act is binding, the legal effect of the act being dependent on the total
constitutional context. Thus, Article 18(2) and (3) of the Charter of the
UN refers to 'decisions' on important questions and on other questions
in the context of the majority needed to take them. It is clear from
other provisions of the Charter that not all these decisions are binding,
particularly among those that are important.

Institutional or organizational acts

There are certain acts performed by organs which by their very nature
have binding effect, because it is a reasonable interpretation of the
constitutional texts that they should have this effect. As a result these
acts are binding decisions which have the legal result of creating direct

obligations and rights for the organization, its organs, its members and even third parties. Most institutional or organizational acts[4] are of this nature. Such acts are to be distinguished from 'operational' acts which relate to the functions and achievement of aims of the organization. The difference between the two types of acts lies in the substance and function of such acts, there being no necessary difference as far as the addressee of an act is concerned. Both types of acts may be directed to anyone inside the organization (organs and staff members) or to the member states, other international organizations, and, whatever the legal effect may be, to non-member states and individuals. However, as a rule, institutional acts have their addressee within the organization (although certain financial decisions, administrative agreements and other decisions constitute important exceptions), whereas the bulk of operational acts are directed to states or to other international organizations.[5] The ICJ agreed in the *Expenses Case* that there were certain acts performed by the GA which had binding effects rather than being recommendations which were hortatory:

[T]he functions and powers conferred by the Charter on the General Assembly are not confined to discussion, consideration, the initiation of studies and the making of recommendations; they are not merely hortatory. Article 18 deals with 'decisions' of the General Assembly 'on important questions'. These 'decisions' do indeed include certain recommendations, but others have dispositive force and effect. Among these latter decisions, Article 18 includes suspension of rights and privileges of membership, expulsion of Members, 'and budgetary questions'.[6]

The examples given by the Court are of 'important' questions under Article 18 of the Charter which all happen to be institutional acts but it cannot be gainsaid that there are other institutional acts performed

---

[4] Detter Delupis, note 2 p. 42, prefers the term 'primary acts'. This term is not recommended because it establishes a hierarchy which does not really exist, implying that other acts which are not 'primary' acts, namely operational acts, are 'secondary'. The definition of the term given by Detter Delupis, however, is valid: see also Detter Delupis, loc. cit. note 2 at p. 47. It should be noted that the term used here is 'binding', to describe acts which have the effect of creating directly rights and obligations. The term 'dispositive' is reserved for cases where the acts have operative effect in the sense of determining an issue, by analogy with a disposition of property. Thus, an agreement is binding in that it creates right and obligations but may not be dispositive because it does not determine an issue, such as by setting up an organ.

[5] See Detter Delupis, note 2 pp. 42–3.

[6] 1962 ICJ Reports at p. 163. Vallat points out that more than 25 of the 111 articles of the UN Charter 'at least to some extent, confer powers of decision as distinct from recommendation upon the General Assembly': loc. cit. note 2 at p. 225.

by organizations than those included in Article 18 which have binding effect. In the *Namibia Case* the Court explained the position it had taken:

> For it would not be correct to assume that, because the General Assembly is in principle vested with recommendatory powers, it is debarred from adopting, in specific cases within the framework of its competence, resolutions which make determinations or have operative design.[7]

Institutional acts cover a broad range. They cover mainly the making of administrative rules such as rules of procedure for organs, rules creating subsidiary organs (including such organs as the UNEF and the ONUC) and the rules governing their operation, staff regulations and rules, rules and decisions relating to financial and budgetary arrangements (e.g., under Article 17 of the Charter of the UN, Article IV of the FAO constitution and Article 56 of the WHO constitution),[8] acts connected with the management of assets and investments, external administrative rules (e.g., UN regulations on the registration of treaties, regulations on non-governmental organizations, ICAO regulations on publication and information and language regulations) and administrative arrangements and implementing regulations (e.g., headquarters agreements and implementing rules, agreements on collaboration), establishment of administrative tribunals (which are not 'subsidiary' organs, but are established under the general power to regulate and deal with relations with staff, if not specifically established under the constitution),[9] the making of contractual and other arrangements to support the institutional aspects of the organization's operation (e.g., contracts for supplies and services connected with offices, building construction contracts and contracts for security services)[10] and the creation of special organs.[11] In these areas

---

[7] 1971 ICJ Reports at p. 50.

[8] It will be recalled that in the *Expenses Case*, while the Court did not regard the matter as within the scope of the request for the advisory opinion, both Judges Spender and Morelli did assert that where there was a legitimate expense of the UN, the apportionment, under Article 17(2), of the financial burden to meet this expense by the GA was final and binding and could not be questioned by the member States: 1962 ICJ Reports at pp. 183 and 218 respectively.

[9] See Chapter 8 below and the *Effects of Awards Case*, 1954 ICJ Reports at p. 61. The ICJ made it clear that the UNAT was not a 'subsidiary' organ established under Article 22 of the Charter.

[10] For a useful explanation of most of the so-called institutional acts see Detter Delupis, note 2 pp. 44–153.

[11] A good example of this is the creation of the Global Environmental Facility (GEF) by the World Bank. It was established by Resolution No. 91–5 of 14 March 1991, by the Executive Directors of the World Bank, albeit with related inter-agency arrangements

institutional acts are generally binding in their effect. They also cover, among other things, decisions on membership (e.g., under Article 4 of the UN Charter or Article II of the IBRD Articles of Agreement), including admission, suspension and expulsion of members.[12] In the case of such other decisions, the final decisions of the organization are generally binding, while there may be precedent decisions which have a some-what different effect, as will be seen below.

The institutional acts envisaged may or may not be explicitly pro-vided for in constitutions, while in many cases the power to perform them as acts with binding legal effect may have to be implied from the constitution. There may also be involved an element of delegation of power to perform some of these institutional acts but this will depend on constitutional interpretation. Clearly, where the matter is taken care of explicitly in the constitution, the relevant provisions will govern.[13]

It must be noted, however, that institutional acts may not always be decisively binding. Three examples of institutional acts of organs (all UN organs) which have been considered by the ICJ may be discussed in order to show how the legal effect of such acts may sometimes vary. First, the power of the Security Council to make recommendations under Article 4 of the Charter to the General Assembly in regard to the admission of members may be cited. While the Court said in the *Second Admissions Case* that the SC and the GA must co-operate in the matter and one is not subordinate to the other,[14] it also said that: (i) the recommendation of the SC was 'the foundation of the decision to admit'; and (ii) the General Assembly 'can only decide to admit upon the recommendation of the

---

for cooperation between the UNDP, the UNEP and the World Bank. The resolution came into effect on 28 October 1991. The structure and modalities of operation of the GEF were modified by Resolution No. 94–2 of 24 March 1994 of the Executive Directors of the World Bank. While the financing was to be based largely on the agreement of those participating in the GEF (see Annex B to Resolution No. 91–5), the World Bank set up this facility. Both the resolutions referred to were submitted to the Board of Governors of the World Bank. See also, perhaps, the Consultative Group on International Agricultural Research (CGIAR), created by the World Bank, and the World Bank Inspection Panel set up by IBRD Resolution No. 93–10 and IDA Resolution No. 93–6, both adopted by the Executive Directors of both institutions on 22 September 1993. The latter seems to be an internal organ of the IBRD and the IDA, before which affected parties in the territories of borrowing members who are not individuals have standing (para. 12).

[12] See, e.g., the *First Admissions Case*, 1948 ICJ Reports p. 57, and the *Second Admissions Case*, 1950 ICJ Reports p. 4.

[13] See, e.g., Article XII, Section 2 of the IMF Articles of Agreement and Article V(2) of the IBRD Articles of Agreement.

[14] 1950 ICJ Reports at pp. 8–9.

Security Council'.[15] The institutional act of the SC in this regard is not fully binding and dispositive in that it has a final effect but certainly it has a positive and negative effect in that: (i) it is a basis on which a binding and dispositive act of admission can be performed by the GA; (ii) the GA cannot act without it; and (iii) it must be a positive recommendation for the GA to take any action.[16] On the other hand, the GA could reject a positive recommendation of the SC, not being bound by it.[17]

Second, in the *Voting Procedure Case*[18] the ICJ dealt with the power of the GA to take certain decisions in connection with the continuing mandate over South West Africa, a matter that was not explicitly dealt with in the Charter. The GA had decided under Article 18(3) of the Charter that this was an important matter requiring a two-thirds majority in the GA. The question was whether it had authority to take this decision on the proper procedure with dispositive effect, binding both the GA and members of the UN. The Court held that by implication the GA had the power to take such a binding and dispositive decision under the Charter, although under the original mandates system decisions on the mandate had to be unanimous. The powers of the GA under the continuing mandates system were all directly or indirectly implied, including the power to take the procedural decision taken that was in issue in the case together with the effect it had.

Third, the effect of decisions to request advisory opinions of the ICJ under Article 96(2) has been the subject of consideration by the Court in many cases.[19] The Court's approach may be summarized as follows:[20] (i) the Court treats them as decisions addressed by one organ of the UN

---

[15] *Ibid.* at pp. 7–8.

[16] Judges Azevedo and Alvarez, dissenting, both apparently disagreed with the view of the Court: *ibid.* at pp. 27–9 and 34 and p. 20 respectively. United Nations, *Repertory of United Nations Practice, Supplement 2* (1964) vol. I, p. 191, states that the General Assembly would admit new members only on the basis of a positive recommendation of the Security Council.

[17] The four jointly dissenting judges (Basdevant, Winiarski, McNair and Read) in the *First Admissions Case*, 1948 ICJ Reports at p. 101, took the same view. Recommendations of the SC under Articles 5, 6 and 98, relating to suspension and expulsion of members and the appointment of the Secretary General, respectively, have the same effect as those made under Article 4.

[18] 1955 ICJ Reports p. 67. See also the separate opinions of Judges Lauterpacht and Klaestad: *ibid.* pp. 108*ff.* and pp. 86*ff.* respectively.

[19] See, e.g., the *Peace Treaties Case*, 1950 ICJ Reports p. 65, and the *Expenses Case*, 1962 ICJ Reports p. 150.

[20] See Basak, note 2 p. 36.

to another; (ii) the Court considers that these decisions (a) obligate it to issue an advisory opinion only when it considers that the circumstances of the case speak for such issuance, and (b) do not, on the other hand, obligate it in respect to the scope of the case as presented by the UN organ in the request; and (iii) the Court considers that the decisions of the GA in this matter have legal effects which no state can disregard; i.e., no state can prevent the Court from giving an advisory opinion if an appropriate decision of an authorized organ requesting an opinion has been taken. Hence in this indirect sense these decisions are binding in relation to member states. They have a certain dispositive effect, though their effect on the Court is different.

While institutional acts may by their nature be binding, and perhaps there is a presumption that they have this effect, ultimately it is the explicit or implicit provision of the constitution of an organization that will determine their effect. The specific intended effect of an act is also relevant, provided it does not exceed the effect authorized by the constitution.

Operational acts

Operational acts are those done in the course of the direct and substantive operations of organizations. Examples of these are decisions taken by the SC under Chapter VI or VII of the Charter in connection with peacekeeping, resolutions of the GA taken in the course of acting under provisions of the Charter empowering it to take action, resolutions of the WHO in the field of health authorized by its constitution, decisions taken by the IBRD in its developmental operations, particularly to make loans for development, and decisions of the IMF implementing the provisions of its Articles of Agreement, particularly in relation to the drawing of SDRs and to exchange rates. As in the case of institutional acts, but even more so, the legal effect of operational acts depends on the constitution of the organization. In some cases, as has already been seen, such as in the case of 'decisions' of the SC of the UN (taken specifically under Chapter VII of the Charter), the constitution makes it clear what is the particular legal effect of the act.[21] But in most cases the legal

---

[21] The ICJ made it clear that where the Security Council, acting under Chapter VII, took action which it intended to be binding upon members and to create legal obligations upon them to comply, generally by making 'decisions', this action had the effect intended by the Security Council and had dispositive effect: the *Expenses Case*, 1962 ICJ Reports at p. 163.

effect of such acts is not so expressly stated and must be gathered by implication from the constitutional provisions. Implication is not always easy and would have to be done by reference to the general principles of interpretation, particularly the principle of teleological or functional interpretation, while subsequent practice may also be relevant.

As already noted, the terminology used in the constitutional documents to describe an act is often not consistent and does not necessarily determine the legal effect of an act. What is important is to deduce the legal effect of acts from the authority given to the organization in the particular case or generally. The language used in a particular resolution may also only be indicative and not necessarily associated with the particular legal effects.

Some examples of acts of organs or organizations in the operational field may be given. The SC takes 'decisions' under Chapter VII of the Charter relating to enforcement action (these are binding). The SC may also take other action under Chapter VII of the Charter or under Chapter VI, relating to pacific settlement of disputes, the decision to take such action being couched in different verbal forms. Under Chapter VI the SC has taken action, 'deciding', 'calling upon', 'recommending', 'declaring', 'questioning', 'urging', 'demanding', 'condemning', etc. or finding that a situation exists.

Under this Chapter the SC has the authority to make binding decisions, it appears, only when, acting pursuant to Article 33(2), it 'calls upon' the parties to a dispute to settle the dispute by peaceful means in accordance with Article 33(1) or makes dispositive decisions of a preliminary nature. However, Article 24 gives the SC primary responsibility for maintaining international peace and security. This results in the SC being able to make decisions directly under Article 24, regardless of Chapter VI, such decisions being binding in accordance with Article 25 which gives the SC authority to make binding decisions. This is how the ICJ interpreted the UN Charter in the *Namibia Case*. In holding that Rs 276 (1970) of the SC had provisions in relation to Namibia which were legally binding on states, it said:

111. As to the effect to be attributed to the declaration contained in paragraph 2 of resolution 276 (1970), the Court considers that the qualification of a situation as illegal does not by itself put an end to it. It can only be the first, necessary step in an endeavour to bring the illegal situation to an end.

112. It would be an untenable interpretation to maintain that, once such a declaration had been made by the Security Council under Article 24 of the Charter, on behalf of all member States, those Members would be free to act in

disregard of such illegality or even to recognize violations of law resulting from it. When confronted with such an internationally unlawful situation, Members of the United Nations would be expected to act in consequence of the declaration made on their behalf. The question therefore arises as to the effect of this decision of the Security Council for States Members of the United Nations in accordance with Article 25 of the Charter.

113. It has been contended that Article 25 of the Charter applies only to enforcement measures adopted under Chapter VII of the Charter. It is not possible to find in the Charter any support for this view. Article 25 is not confined to decisions in regard to enforcement action but applies to 'the decisions of the Security Council' adopted in accordance with the Charter. Moreover, that Article is placed, not in Chapter VII, but immediately after Article 24 in that part of the Charter which deals with the functions and powers of the Security Council. If Article 25 had reference solely to decisions of the Security Council concerning enforcement action under Articles 41 and 42 of the Charter, that is to say, if it were only such decisions which had binding effect, then Article 25 would be superfluous, since this effect is secured by Articles 48 and 49 of the Charter.

114. It has also been contended that the relevant Security Council resolutions are couched in exhortatory rather than mandatory language and that, therefore, they do not purport to impose any legal duty on any State nor to affect legally any right of any State. The language of a resolution of the Security Council should be carefully analysed before a conclusion can be made as to its binding effect. In view of the nature of the powers under Article 25, the question whether they have been in fact exercised is to be determined in each case, having regard to the terms of the resolution to be interpreted, the discussions leading to it, the Charter provisions invoked and, in general, all circumstances that might assist in determining the legal consequences of the resolution of the Security Council.

115. Applying these tests, the Court recalls that in the preamble of resolution 269 (1969), the Security Council was '*Mindful* of its responsibility to take necessary action to secure strict compliance with the obligations entered into by States Members of the United Nations under the provisions of Article 25 of the Charter of the United Nations'. The Court has therefore reached the conclusion that the decisions made by the Security Council in paragraphs 2 and 5 of resolutions 276 (1970), as related to paragraph 3 of resolution 264 (1969) and paragraph 5 of resolution 269 (1969), were adopted in conformity with the purposes and principles of the Charter and in accordance with its Articles 24 and 25. The decisions are consequently binding on all States Members of the United Nations, which are thus under obligation to accept and carry them out.[22]

---

[22] 1971 ICJ Reports at pp. 52*ff*. In the *East Timor Case*, 1995 ICJ Reports paras. 31–2, the ICJ was confronted with resolutions on East Timor of both the SC and the GA. Much of what the Court said related to the interpretation of these resolutions. It left open the question whether any of the resolutions, including those of the SC (obviously made under Chapter VI of the Charter), were binding: 'Without prejudice to the question whether the resolutions under discussion could be binding...'

The GA may act under the general authority contained in Chapter IV of the Charter (particularly Articles 10 and 11), for example, in political, security and disarmament matters, in economic matters, in social, humanitarian and cultural matters, in legal matters and in regard to non-self-governing territories. Under Chapter IV the GA may make 'recommendations' but the language used in its resolutions varies. In the Charter there is a distinction made in general between 'decisions' and 'recommendations' but, as has been seen, Article 18 refers to 'decisions' of the GA, which term is intended to cover both its 'recommendations' and 'decisions' (the latter mainly but not always in the institutional field). The Charter makes it clear (in Article 25) that 'decisions' of the SC (under Chapter VII or under other provisions such as Article 24) are binding.[23] The power that the GA or the SC has under Chapter XII in relation to the trusteeship system which may entail the administration of territory[24] is a case where the organization can make binding decisions.

Another example of acts of organizations or their organs are those generally performed by non-financial organizations, such as the UNESCO, the ILO, the FAO and the Council of Europe, in the operational field. Where it is clear, from the express provisions of the constitutional documents, some instances of which have been given in the first part of this chapter, that these acts have binding effect, the situation is clear. Where this is not clear or it is not reasonably implicit in the constitutional provisions, the question remains what effect acts have. In general such institutions apparently do not have the power to make binding decisions in the operational field.

Financial organizations are the third example. Their situation is somewhat different. Their constitution may entitle them to make decisions which are in some sense binding in the area of loan and credit operations, though they may also have the power to act in such a way that they make decisions which are not binding.

A fourth example is the judicial or quasi-judicial power that organs may be given under their constitutions. The power of the ICAO Council

---

[23] See also the *Expenses Case* by implication: 1962 ICJ Reports at p. 163; and Judge Fitzmaurice in his separate opinion: *ibid.* at p. 210.

[24] Associated with these powers is the power under Article 81 to administer territory itself. The UN has, Article 81 aside, temporarily administered territories or exercised jurisdiction over them, with the result that to do so its organs made binding decisions. Examples of this capacity are Trieste and Jerusalem, Western New Guinea (1962–3), Cambodia (1992–3), Eastern Slovenia and Croatia (1996–8), Kosovo (since 1999), East Timor (1999–2002). The GA's establishment of the UN Council for Namibia by GA Rs 2248(S-V) of May 1967 was also implicitly based on its capacity to administer territory.

to settle disputes under Article 84 of its constitution[25] or the power that organs of financial institutions generally have under their constitutions to interpret their constitutions[26] may be mentioned in this connection.

Binding acts

These examples provide a framework in which to consider the legal effect of acts of organs, particularly those that are not binding. It may be stated, as a general principle, that unless there is specific and express provision in the constitutional instruments or an ineluctable implication arises from the provisions of such instruments, acts of organs do not have binding or similar effect in the operational field. The reason for this is that international organizations are created by the agreement of states and consent to be bound by their acts or to permit them to impose obligations and confer rights by their acts is not to be presumed. In the case, for example, of the SC and certain acts of the GA connected with the administration of territory, as will be seen, there is such express provision or necessary implication. It becomes always a question of establishing, whatever the language used in and the intent of the resolutions, whether the act, in the particular form it takes, was intended by the constitution to be binding. Again, while the resolution can only be binding if it was intended by its framers to be binding, it cannot have that effect unless the constitutional 'intent' permits it to have that effect. In the case of some other organizations, such as the WMO or the WHO, or as has been seen at the beginning of this chapter, certain acts may have, by express provision, the same effect. There are other examples of acts with binding effect performed by organizations which have been expressly authorized by their constitutions. The OEEC may be mentioned. Decisions taken by a majority vote in the Council of the OEEC were binding on the membership.[27]

---

[25] This is the power which was the subject of the *ICAO Council Case*, 1972 ICJ Reports p. 46, in which the ICJ pronounced on the propriety of the exercise of the power without having to consider the legal effect of the exercise of the power which, however, was obvious and not disputed.

[26] See, e.g., Article IX of the IBRD Constitution and Article XXIX of the IMF Constitution which give this power to the Executive Directors, with a possibility of appeal to the Board of Governors.

[27] See Elkin, 'The Organization for European Economic Cooperation (OEEC), its Structure and Powers', *Annuaire Européen* (1958) at p. 124. See also the River Commissions (Detter Delupis, note 2 p. 214), Article 15 of the International Coffee Agreement (1983) and other commodity agreements (Detter Delupis, *ibid.*). The EC (now the EU) has extensive

It may be appropriate to consider some of the examples given above, particularly those in which it appears that organs have the power to make binding decisions by necessary implication. The powers of the SC under Chapter VII, the powers of such organizations as the WHO and the WMO to make binding decisions, and the judicial and quasi-judicial power granted to organs of the financial institutions or to the ICAO Council, for instance, are clearly dependent on express constitutional provisions. It is the power such as that of the GA to administer territory which, however, is disputed, or the operational powers exercised by the Executive Boards of financial institutions that is based on necessary implication.

In the case of the financial institutions the situation is rather different. Their constitutions are usually very general, giving them the power to make loans and act in a like manner, though there are some detailed provisions or conditions governing their activity.[28] When the IMF Executive Board normally takes a decision to accept a request from a member to draw on its special drawing rights, the agreement becomes operative immediately upon the decision being taken. Thus, this decision creates rights and obligations for the organization and the member and is binding, even though it operates as consent to an agreement. Similarly, when the Executive Directors of the IBRD or the IDA decide to make a loan or a credit, this is done by taking a decision to approve a loan or credit to the member concerned.[29] This approval, unlike the decision of the IMF Board, does not in itself complete the loan or credit agreement. However, it is arguable that it creates a right in the member concerned to have the loan agreement completed and the loan made and imposes on the organization a corresponding obligation to make the loan, subject to such considerations as the intervention of *force majeure* or supervening conditions that may be applicable. There is, thus, an inchoate right to have the funds loaned and an inchoate obligation to loan funds. These are created by the decision of approval which is more than a mere agreement to agree. The decision is creative of rights in this sense. Further, financial institutions may have by agreement under their loan agreements or

power to make binding decisions with highly sophisticated effects. For this institution see, e.g., Lasok and Bridge, *Law and Institutions of the European Communities* (1991) *passim*, particularly pp. 218*ff*.

[28] See, e.g., Articles III and IV of the IBRD Articles of Agreement and Article V of the IMF Articles of Agreement.

[29] See, e.g., Resolution R94-170 of 17 August 1994 (IBRD loan to China); Resolution IDA R94-123 of 15 August 1994 (IDA credit to Albania).

credit agreements the power to make binding and dispositive decisions, e.g., to suspend the loan or credit.

In the case of the powers of the GA (and the SC) in relation to trusteeship agreements, necessary implication would seem to warrant the conclusion that resolutions approving trusteeship agreements and resolutions made in the exercise of functions under those agreements, including their termination and determinations concerning the future of the territories, had important legal effects which could be binding and dispositive. For example, in the *Northern Cameroon Case*[30] the ICJ noted the resolution of the GA terminating the trusteeship and considered the question before it moot, thus holding that the resolution had definitive legal effect. While in the trusteeship system generally the GA (or the SC) had power to make recommendations which were less than binding,[31] in cases where there was an agreement on the part of the administering authority that binding decisions could be taken by the GA (or the SC), such decisions would have had binding effect. Where the GA itself assumed functions under Article 81 of the Charter of administering trust territories, clearly it could take decisions in discharging its functions which were legally binding.[32] Moreover, the ICJ upheld the decision of the GA terminating South Africa's mandate over the mandated territory as being a formulation of a legal situation based on prior opinions of the Court. In the *Namibia Case* the ICJ, in dealing with the GA resolution terminating the mandate over South West Africa (Namibia) said:

General Assembly resolution 2145 (XXI), after declaring the termination of the Mandate, added in operative paragraph 4 'that South Africa has no other right to administer the Territory'. This part of the resolution has been objected to as deciding a transfer of territory. That in fact is not so. The pronouncement made by the General Assembly is made on a conclusion, referred to earlier, reached

---

[30] 1963 ICJ Reports p. 15, particularly at p. 32, where the Court states that 'the resolution had definitive legal effect'.

[31] See Judge Klaestad and Judge Lauterpacht in separate opinions in the *Voting Procedure Case:* 1955 ICJ Reports at p. 88 and pp. 116*ff.*, respectively.

[32] The UN has not administered territory under Article 81 of the Charter but did exercise a temporary administration in West Irian and was the *de iure*, though not *de facto*, administering authority for Namibia prior to its independence. As administrator of Namibia it (through its Council and Commissioner for Namibia – organs of the GA) passed a decree relating to natural resources and travel documents. The Netherlands' representative to the Fourth Committee stated in 1975 with respect to this decree that it had dispositive and binding effect and was not merely a recommendation that was hortatory: see UN Doc. A/C.4/SR 2151 at pp. 15–16.

by the Court in 1950...This was confirmed by the Court in its Judgment of 21 December 1962 in the *South West Africa* cases (*Ethiopia* v. *South Africa; Liberia* v. *South Africa*) (*ICJ Reports 1962*, p. 333). Relying on these decisions of the Court, the General Assembly declared that the Mandate having been terminated 'South Africa has no other right to administer the Territory'. This is not a finding on facts, but the formulation of a legal situation. For it would not be correct to assume that, because the General Assembly is in principle vested with recommendatory powers, it is debarred from adopting, in specific cases within the framework of its competence, resolutions which make determinations or have operative design.[33]

Thus was confirmed the powers of the GA to take binding (and dispositive) decisions in the area of the administration of mandates.

In regard to acts which are legally binding in that they create in particular legal obligations of obedience it is appropriate to conclude that (i) the constitution of the organization must first of all expressly or impliedly provide for legally binding acts in the circumstances and (ii) the resolution or act of the organ or organization concerned must reveal an intention to create legally binding obligations.

Recommendations

Where resolutions are not binding decisions or do not have their legal effects specified in the constitutional instrument or do not by implication have a particular legal effect that can be identified they are generally 'recommendations' and are not as such binding.[34] Consequently, first, the effect of acts which are less than binding has to be determined. Second, the issue arises what is the effect of the language used in such resolutions. The second question may be answered first and briefly. The language used may be relevant to determine the effect of the resolution, provided the effect intended does not go beyond the effect permitted by the constitutional context.

As for the answer to the first question, it must be noted that, on the one hand, the constitutional document may expressly state that what is described in a particular provision as a 'recommendation' in a given context has no binding effect[35] or, on the other hand, the constitutional

---

[33] 1971 ICJ Reports at p. 50. For discussions of the GA powers of administering territories and the ICJ opinions thereon, see Basak, note 2 pp. 107–28, 160–7; Crawford, *The Creation of States in International Law* (1979) pp. 335*ff.*

[34] Sloan, note 2 pp. 26*ff.*, has a comprehensive discussion of the legal effect of UN recommendations. See also Detter Delupis, note 2 pp. 207*ff.*, for a discussion of recommendations in general.

[35] See, e.g., Article 69 of the ICAO Constitution.

document may expressly state the opposite – namely, that a 'recommendation' in a given context has binding force.[36] There may also be express statements in constitutional texts of the specific effect, less than a binding effect, that a 'recommendation' may have. For example, Article 19(b) of the ILO constitution states that recommendations must be submitted by member states to their competent national authorities for consideration and report on the position of the law and practice with regard to matters dealt with therein.[37] Sometimes, by implication, what is called a recommendation may have a specific effect. As has been seen, positive recommendations of the SC made under Articles 4, 5, 6 and 98 are a precondition for binding (and dispositive) action of the GA, these acts being institutional. The question to be considered is what legal effect less than a binding effect do recommendations have, where the constituent instrument is not explicit. In the literature and jurisprudence it is GA and SC resolutions that have been principally discussed but what is said of them here would generally apply, *mutatis mutandis* for special circumstances arising from the context of constitutional instruments, to other organizations.

There is no special guidance for other uses of the term 'recommendation' in the UN Charter and the subject remains controversial. The effect of SC recommendations was considered in 1947 in the UN at the time of the *Corfu Channel Case*. In the discussions in the SC many members showed an inclination to consider that binding obligations could be created by SC recommendations. For example, the representative of Australia stated in discussing a draft resolution under Article 36 of the Charter: 'Any decision, any recommendation that we may make binds the United Kingdom and also binds Albania.'[38] The Chinese delegate supported this view.[39] The UK accepted this view and submitted the case to the ICJ by way of application, arguing that compulsory jurisdiction was established by the recommendation. The Court in its advisory opinion did not express a view on the matter because it found that Albania had accepted jurisdiction by responding to the application.[40] In a joint

---

[36] See, e.g., Article 14 of the ECSC Treaty and the comparable article in the Euratom Treaty; the North-East Atlantic Fisheries Convention; Usher, 'The Relationship between United Kingdom Law and European Community Law', in Butler (ed.), *International Law* pp. 103–6; and Articles 28–34 of the ILO Constitution which place the recommendations of a Commission of Inquiry on a par with decisions of the ICJ.

[37] See also Article 15 of the LN Covenant; Article IV(3) of the FAO Constitution; and Article IV(4) of the UNESCO Constitution. The constitutions of COMECON and the Caribbean Commission have comparable provisions.

[38] SC, official records, 2nd year, No. 34, at p. 723.   [39] *Ibid.* at p. 726.

[40] *Corfu Channel Case (Preliminary Objection)*, 1947–48 ICJ Reports at p. 26.

separate opinion, however, seven judges rejected the position of the UK.[41]

In regard to GA recommendations under Articles 10 to 14, 58 and 105, the Charter does not indicate what legal effects these recommendations may have.[42] Nor are the *travaux préparatoires* helpful. There are statements in the records that indicate that the word was understood by many delegations as conferring an extremely limited authority.[43] Some delegations, however, took a more liberal view of the GA's powers.[44] The Charter is silent on the matter, while current usage gives the term 'recommendation' many different meanings.[45] While 'recommendations' of the GA or the SC, as distinguished from 'decisions', are primarily hortatory, they may have certain legal effects and give rise to certain obligations. These effects may consist of (i) a duty to consider, (ii) a duty to cooperate, (iii) a duty to comply, (iv) a duty to 'assist', (v) providing an authorization for action, (vi) providing a basis for implementation or (vii) providing evidence for one of the formal sources of law. These possibilities will be considered in turn.

Duty to consider

The constitutions of some international organizations, as has been seen, impose a duty on member states to consider recommendations and to report on action taken. Other constitutions, such as the Charter of the United Nations, do not contain such provisions. Under the Charter, however, even in the absence of express provisions, the better view is that there is a duty on the part of member states to consider a recommendation in good faith and, if requested, to explain their action or inaction. This obligation arises implicitly from the fact of membership. Judge Lauterpacht in a separate opinion in the *Voting Procedure Case*, after noting that a resolution containing a recommendation cannot be simply disregarded, stated:

A Resolution recommending to an Administering State a specific course of action creates *some* legal obligation which, however rudimentary, elastic and imperfect, is nevertheless a legal obligation and constitutes a measure of supervision. The

---

[41] *Ibid.* at pp. 31–2.

[42] In the *East Timor Case*, 1995 ICJ Reports paras. 31–2, the ICJ left open the question of the binding nature of the GA resolutions which were the subject of the case: see footnote 22 above.

[43] See, e.g., Doc. 2 G/7(d) i, 3 UNCIO Docs. (1945) p. 220; Doc. 2 G/7(i), 3 *ibid.* p. 345; Doc. 719, II/8, 8 *ibid.* p. 33; Doc. 748, II/2/39, 9 *ibid.* pp. 128–9.

[44] See, e.g., Doc. 1151, II/17, 8 *ibid.* pp. 191, 196; Doc. 55, P/13, 1 Ibid. p. 446.

[45] See Sloan, loc. cit. note 2 (25 BYIL) at pp. 6–7.

State in question, while not bound to accept the recommendation, is bound to give it due consideration in good faith. If, having regard to its own ultimate responsibility for the good government of the territory, it decides to disregard it, it is bound to explain the reasons for its decision.[46]

Judge Klaestad expressed a similar view in his individual opinion in the same case.[47] This obligation is perhaps reinforced by Article 2(2) of the Charter which requires all members to fulfil in good faith their Charter obligations.

Duty to co-operate

The ICJ has indicated clearly that membership entails certain mutual obligations of co-operation and good faith on the part of member states and organizations. These obligations involve somewhat more than the duty to consider in good faith. Though the opinion was expressed in the context of a dispute between Egypt and the WHO concerning their Regional Office Agreement, the Court had no doubt that the obligation to co-operate in good faith is broadly based on the very fact of membership.[48] The Court said that it considered 'those obligations to be the very basis of the legal relations between the Organization and Egypt under the general international law, under the Constitution of the Organization and under the agreements in force between Egypt and the Organization',[49] and that 'the paramount consideration both for the Organization and the host State in every case must be their clear obligation to co-operate in good faith to promote the objectives and purposes of the Organization as expressed in its Constitution'.[50]

---

[46] 1955 ICJ Reports at pp. 118–19. Other authorities agree with this view: see, e.g., Mendelson, loc. cit. note 2 at p. 101; Bindschedler, 'La Délimitation des compétences des Nations Unies', 108 *Hague Recueil* (1963-I) at pp. 346–8; Asamoah, *The Legal Significance of the Declarations of the General Assembly of the United Nations* (1966) pp. 185, 190; Castles, 'Legal Status of UN Resolutions', 3 *Adelaide LR* (1967–70) at p. 76; Sohn, 'John A. Sibley Lecture: The Shaping of International Law', 8 Ga. JCIL (1978) at pp. 23–4; Pellet, 'A New International Legal Order: What Legal Tools for What Changes?', in Snyder and Slinn (eds.), *International Law of Development: Comparative Perspectives* (1987) p. 128; Skubiszewski, loc. cit. note 2 ('Elaboration . . . '), at pp. 170–1; Sloan, note 2 pp. 28–9.

[47] 1955 ICJ Reports at p. 88: 'As a member of the United Nations, the Union of South Africa is in duty bound to consider in good faith a recommendation by the GA under Article 10 of the Charter and to inform the GA with regard to the attitude which it has decided to take in respect of the matter referred to in the recommendation.'

[48] The *WHO Agreement Case*, 1980 ICJ Reports at p. 93, where the Court stated: 'The very fact of Egypt's membership in the Organization entails certain mutual obligations of co-operation and good faith incumbent upon Egypt and the Organization.'

[49] *Ibid.* at p. 95.   [50] *Ibid.* at p. 96.

A major purpose of establishing an international organization is to develop international co-operation and, consequently, a basic obligation of membership is to co-operate in achieving the objectives of the organization. Recommendations are a means for achieving purposes and objectives and, therefore, a duty of membership is to co-operate in promoting those obligations and purposes through such recommendations.[51] This co-operation should not be confused with co-operation in *carrying out* the recommendations which is not an obligation.

In regard to economic and social matters, Article 1(3) and (4), Chapters IX and X, particularly Articles 55, 56 and 60, and Article 13 of the Charter make it quite clear that members have pledged to 'co-operate' with the GA in these matters, thus reinforcing the view that a recommendation (which is what the GA can make in this connection) entails an obligation to co-operate. As noted, this obligation to co-operate applies not only in fields covered by Chapter IX of the Charter where the duty is express but, as an incident of membership, applies to all recommendations aimed at fulfilling the objectives and purposes of the UN or any organization, for that matter. While there may not be a general obligation to comply with a recommendation, an obligation to co-operate in good faith cannot leave a member state free simply to disregard the recommendation. It certainly involves the obligation to *consider* the recommendation in good faith which was considered earlier. But more may be involved. The ICJ in the *WHO Agreement Case* indicated that the obligation to co-operate included an obligation 'to consult together in good faith'.[52] If a member state, after considering a recommendation, concludes in good faith that it is unable to comply, it has a duty to consult with the organization on ways to achieve the organization's objectives and purposes, the fulfilment of which is the aim of the recommendation.

It may be suggested that, should there be repeated failures to accept recommendations of the organization and refusals to seek solutions through good faith consultation, the question of abuse of right will arise.[53]

---

[51] Writers generally agree with this view: see, e.g., Malintoppi, note 2 pp. 49ff; Virally, *L'Organisation mondiale* (1972) p. 87; Castañeda, note 2 p. 12; Tunkin, loc. cit. note 2 at pp. 7–9; Lukashuk, loc. cit. note 2 at p. 35; Sloan, loc. cit. note 2, "Recommendations . . . " pp. 29–31. It is not clear, whether the distinction between co-operation in achieving purposes and objectives and co-operation in actually carrying out the recommendations is made.

[52] 1980 ICJ Reports at pp. 95, 97.

[53] See Judge Lauterpacht in his separate opinion in the *Voting Procedure Case:* 1955 ICJ Reports at p. 120. Abuse of rights is discussed below.

Duty to comply

While there may be a duty to consider in good faith recommendations and a duty of co-operation, there generally is no duty to comply with recommendations as such.[54] Judge Lauterpacht, however, in the *Voting Procedure Case* did express in his separate opinion the view that, when the duty to co-operate in good faith is ignored to the point of becoming an abuse of right, this generates a breach of the obligation to act in good faith, so that at some stage compliance will be necessary in order to avoid an abuse of right. He said in regard to the mandates and trusteeship system:

> Although there is no automatic obligation to accept fully a particular recommendation or series of recommendations, there is a legal obligation to act in good faith. An administering State may not be acting illegally by declining to act upon a recommendation or a series of recommendations on the same subject. But in doing so it acts at its peril when a point is reached when the cumulative effect of the persistent disregard of the articulate opinion of the Organization is such as to foster the conviction that the State in question has become guilty of disloyalty to the Principles and Purposes of the Charter. Thus an Administering State which consistently sets itself above the solemnly and repeatedly expressed judgment of the Organization, in particular in proportion as that judgment approximates to unanimity, may find that it has overstepped the imperceptible line between impropriety and illegality, between discretion and arbitrariness, between the exercise of the legal right to disregard the recommendation and the abuse of that right, and that it has exposed itself to the consequences legitimately following as a legal sanction.[55]

It must be remembered that in that case the specific powers of the GA in regard to a mandated territory were in issue. However, the views of Judge Lauterpacht have more general application.

There is also the situation in which, where a hierarchial relationship exists, a recommendation in the operational field from a superior to a subordinate body may impliedly require compliance with the

---

[54] See Judges Lauterpacht and Klaestad in separate opinions in the *Voting Procedure Case*: 1955 ICJ Reports at pp. 118–19 and p. 88 respectively.

[55] *Ibid.* at p. 120. Tunkin has concluded that: 'Since recommendatory resolutions are one means for developing cooperation and achieving the objectives of the international organisation, a persistent disregard of such recommendations by a member State would constitute a violation of the organisation's Charter': loc. cit. note 2 at p. 9. See also, e.g., Basak, note 2 pp. 115, 117; Castañeda, note 2 p. 177; Conforti, 'Le Rôle de l'accord dans le système des Nations Unies', 142 *Hague Recueil* (1974-II) at pp. 266–7; Dugard, 'The Legal Effect of United Nations Resolutions on Apartheid', 83 SALJ (1966) at pp. 50–9; Malintoppi, note 2 pp. 49*ff*.

recommendation by the subordinate body. Thus, the GA, the ECOSOC and the TC may under Article 98 entrust functions to the SG of the UN. In such circumstances the latter must perform the functions entrusted to him, subject, of course, to the provisions of the Charter regarding his prerogatives. Likewise, subsidiary organs established by the GA are subject to its authority. A similar situation would prevail in other organizations. In this connection, the terminology used in the resolution becomes immaterial, provided it is clear that a directive is being given. There is, however, no general hierarchial relationship as such between an organization and its members.

A duty to comply may also arise as a result of the combination of elements extraneous to the recommendation. Here the obligation really inheres in another element than the intrinsic effect of the resolution. Where a state has accepted a recommendation or has otherwise agreed to be bound by it, it is the consent which is the source of the obligation to comply, but the resolution has an important effect as a catalyst. Agreements to be bound may be prior or subsequent to, or contemporaneous with the recommendation.[56] Further, the agreement may be reflected in a unilateral declaration as contrasted with a treaty and the declaration may cover one or more resolutions, be oral or written and be antecedent or subsequent to the resolutions.[57] That unilateral declarations can create binding obligations is well established in international law.[58] Acceptance or consent may also be implied from

[56] See, e.g., the Peace Treaty with Italy where the Four Powers agreed to accept as binding the recommendation of the GA relating to the future of certain Italian colonies in certain circumstances (49 UNTS at pp. 214–15), and the provisions in some trusteeship agreements where the administering authority undertook to apply in the trust territory certain recommendations of the UN and its specialized agencies (see agreements for Tanganyika, Togo and Swaziland, cited by Skubiszewski, loc. cit. note 2, 'Elaboration – Provisional Report' at p. 145; and see Sloan, loc. cit. note 2, 25 BYIL at pp. 16–17; Asamoah, note 46 p. 4; Castañeda, note 2 pp. 144–5, 147–9. The acceptance of the GA resolutions dealing with the Israeli–British–French invasion of Egypt is also a prominent example of acceptance by the states concerned: see GAOR, First Emergency Special Session, Supp. No. 1 (A/3354); Bowett, United Nations Forces, A Legal Study (1964) pp. 90ff. and 412ff.

[57] See the declaration made by the Comoros in applying for membership in the UN: 986 UNTS at p. 239.

[58] See, e.g., the Eastern Greenland Case [1193] PCIJ Series A/B No. 53; the Nuclear Tests Case (Australia v. France), 1974 ICJ Reports p. 253; and the Nuclear Tests Case (New Zealand v. France), 1974 ICJ Reports p. 457. See also Garner, 'The International Binding Force of Unilateral Oral Declarations', 27 AJIL (1933) at pp. 493ff.; Suy, Les Actes juridiques unilatéraux en droit international public (1962); Venturini. 'La Portée et les effects juridiques des attitudes et des actes unilatéraux des états', 12 Hague Recueil (1964-II) at

conduct.[59] In this connection the question may be raised whether acceptance or consent may be given by an affirmative vote or abstention on the resolution. In general, support for or absence of opposition to a resolution may be a political act depending on a number of factors and may not signify an intention to be bound.[60] Acceptance or consent is a question of intent which must be determined by all the circumstances of a particular case. If it is clear that a state intends to be bound by its vote, there is good reason to conclude that this is consent to be bound.[61] Estoppel or preclusion may also operate to create circumstances in which, because of actions before or after its vote or at the time of its vote, a state is bound to comply with a recommendation. If the conduct of a state gives rise to reasonable expectations on the part of other states and if other states have acted upon these expectations, a state may be precluded from not complying with the recommendation.[62]

Further, where there is an existing obligation and a recommendation relates to this obligation, there is a duty to comply, such duty deriving

---

pp. 363*ff.*; Rubin, 'The International Legal Effects of Unilateral Declarations', 71 AJIL (1977) p. 1; and P. de Visscher, 'Remarques sur l'évolution de la jurisprudence de la cour internationale de justice relative au fondement obligatoire de certains actes unilatéraux', in Makarczyk (ed.), *Essays in International Law in Honour of Judge Manfred Lachs* (1984) at pp. 461–5.

[59] See, e.g., Skubiszewski, loc. cit. note 2, 'Elaboration...', at pp. 170, 240.

[60] *Contra* Judge Winiarski, dissenting, and apparently Judge Fitzmaurice, in a separate opinion, in the *Expenses Case: 1962 ICJ Reports* at pp. 233*ff.* and p. 213, respectively. There is considerable disagreement on the significance of an affirmative vote or abstention: see for a discussion of this point, e.g., Basak, note 2 pp. 78*ff.*, 112, 127 and 195; Sinha, 'Identifying a Principle of International Law', 11 CYIL (1973) at pp. 116*ff.*; Virally, 'Panorama du droit international contemporain', 183 *Hague Recueil* (1983-V) at pp. 205*ff.*; P. de Visscher, 'Cours général de droit international public', 136 *Hague Recueil* (1972-II) at pp. 130*ff.*; R. Bindschedler, 'La Délimitation des compétences des Nations Unies', 108 *Hague Recueil* (1963-I) at pp. 345*ff.* The PCIJ in the *Railway Traffic between Lithuania and Poland Case*, PCIJ Series A/B No. 42 at p. 116, held that in certain circumstances an affirmative vote for a resolution constituted the acceptance of a resolution.

[61] See Sloan, note 2 pp. 34, 65 and particularly footnote 307. See also Article 11 of the 1969 Vienna Convention on the Law of Treaties (which may support this view); Judge Jessup (separate opinion) in the *South West Africa Cases (Preliminary Objections)*, 1962 ICJ Reports at pp. 41, 418 and 434; the *Railway Traffic between Lithuania and Poland Case*, PCIJ Series A/B No. 42 at p. 116.

[62] See Schachter, 'Alf Ross Memorial Lecture, The Crisis of Legitimation in the United Nations', 50 *Nordisk Tidskrift for International Ret: Acta Scandinavica juris gentium* (1981) at p. 16. See also for a discussion of estoppel in connection with GA resolutions, e.g., Schwarzenberger, *A Manual of International Law* (1976) pp. 233*ff.*; Skubiszewski, loc. cit. note 1, 'Elaboration...' at pp. 221*ff.*; and Asamoah, note 46 pp. 96*ff.* Examples of the operation of estoppel or preclusion are, however, not to be found.

from the original obligation, an extraneous element. It is clear that the duty to comply rests on the pre-existing obligation and not on the recommendation as such and that the particular language of the recommendation does not make a difference. The recommendation merely reinforces the pre-existing obligation.[63]

A slightly different situation arises, for example, under Article 105 of the UN Charter which provides for 'necessary' privileges and immunities for the organization, its representatives and officials. The same article authorizes the GA to 'make recommendations with a view to determine the details of the application' of the article or propose conventions for the same purpose. While the UN has proceeded generally in line with the latter alternative, were it to make recommendations determining the details of the Charter obligation, it is arguable that these would be binding.[64] The source of the obligation is the Charter but the recommendations would do more than merely confirm that obligation. They would implement it. By implication the Charter itself provides that the recommendations are binding.

Duty to assist

Where the constitution of an organization provides for a duty to assist in any action taken by the organization the question arises whether there is a duty to give assistance where the action flows from non-binding resolutions. A further question is whether there may be an implied duty to assist in these circumstances. This second question is more difficult to answer than the first. Tentatively, it may be suggested as an answer to it that a duty of the same content as exists where the constitution provides for such assistance is not inconsistent with the underlying purposes and objectives of international organizations and is to be recognized. As for the first question, it may be answered by considering the effect of Article 2(5) of the Charter of the UN which provides for a duty to give

---

[63] This is technically what happens when the GA calls upon a state to cease or refrain from the use of force in the enforcement of Article 2(4) of the Charter or demands that it abandon racial discrimination practices, though there may be controversies regarding application.

[64] In the Sixth Committee of the GA in 1967 the Legal Counsel of the UN pointed out that, whether or not states had acceded to the Convention on the Privileges and Immunities of the UN, they would have to recognize the privileges and immunities defined therein (see UN Doc. A/C.6/385). This flowed from Resolution 2323 (XXII) of 18 December 1967, adopted almost unanimously, which 'urged' states to do just this.

'every assistance' in any 'action' the UN takes in accordance with the Charter. The view has been expressed that:

There are at least two aspects to be considered. First, are recommendations themselves 'action'? And second, is action of a Member, taken in response to a recommendation, action of the Organization within the meaning of Article 2(5)? It is certainly possible, as a matter of legal interpretation, to give an affirmative answer to both of these questions. The adoption of a recommendation is an action in the broadest sense of the term and Article 2(5) puts no limiting qualification on the term 'any action'. It might also be considered that when a Member takes action, pursuant to a recommendation of the Organization, it is acting on behalf of, or at least in the interest of, the Organization. Nonetheless, it might seem anomalous if a duty to give assistance to the Organization in implementing a recommendation went beyond a duty to comply with that recommendation. A conservative answer would be that there is a duty to assist where other duties exist. In other words, there is a duty to assist where there is a duty to comply, and there is also a duty to assist with respect to the duty to consider and the duty to cooperate in the implementation of a recommendation. At the very least there is an obligation not to interfere with action being taken by other States in accordance with the recommendation.[65]

As stated here, the duty to assist is certainly a duty not to obstruct, aside from the other duties to consider and co-operate. State practice would seem to be in accord with this position. But there is a further duty at least to finance by way of assistance action by the organization pursuant to recommendations.[66]

Authorization for action

Recommendations may create legal authority for the action taken pursuant to them. As Judge Lauterpacht said in his separate opinion in the *Voting Procedure Case*, 'on proper occasions they [recommendations] provide a legal authorization for Members determined to act upon them individually or collectively'.[67] Recommendations of this kind which are not binding perform a legitimizing function both for the UN itself

---

[65] Sloan, note 2 p. 36. The peacekeeping force, the UNEF, and the operational agency, the UNEP, were established by decisions that were binding. Such decisions clearly bring Articles 2(5) and 2(2) into play. There was, therefore, a binding obligation to pay for the force as such since the duty of assistance extended to the financing of the force and beyond. See also particularly Judge Fitzmaurice in his separate opinion in the *Expenses Case*, 1962 ICJ Reports at p. 199. *Contra* dissenting Judges Winiarski, Moreno Quintana, Koretsky and Bustamante: *ibid.* at pp. 232, 250, 287 and 305, respectively.

[66] See the *Expenses Case*, 1962 ICJ Reports p. 151.

[67] 1955 ICJ Reports at p. 115.

and other states, and may also serve to delegitimize contrary action. Thus, a state implementing a recommendation would be protected from charges of illegality by other states, and the latter states may be under an obligation not to take action that would interfere with or obstruct the recommended action.[68]

Basis for implementation

Short of imposing a duty to comply, a recommendation may furnish the basis for implementation beyond authorizing action. This aspect of the effect of recommendations is particularly relevant to SC and GA resolutions in the peacekeeping area. Implementation may include sanctions applicable where there is a breach of a legal duty, and also other measures less than sanctions taken when there is no duty to comply with a recommendation.

Where the SC does not take action through binding decisions (under Chapter VII), it may act through the lesser recommendations. It also has a general residual power to act through recommendations under Article 24, particularly to support GA resolutions, as was pointed out by the ICJ in the *Namibia Case*, where it said:

Article 24 of the Charter vests in the Security Council the necessary authority to take action such as that taken in the present case. The reference in paragraph 2 of this Article to specific powers of the Security Council under certain chapters of the Charter does not exclude the existence of general powers to discharge the responsibilities conferred in paragraph 1. Reference may be made in this respect to the Secretary-General's Statement, presented to the Security Council on 10 January 1947, to the effect that 'the powers of the Council under Article 24 are restricted to the specific grants of authority contained in Chapters VI, VII, VIII, and XII...the Members of the United Nations have conferred upon the Security

---

[68] This view was originally promulgated in regard to the GA's resolution on the partition of Palestine: H. Lauterpacht, 'The United Nations General Assembly – Voting and Competence in the Palestine Question', in E. Lauterpacht (ed.), *International Law – Being the Collected Papers of Hersch Lauterpacht* (1977) vol. III, pp. 512–13. Then it was also relied on for action under the Uniting for Peace Resolution: see, e.g., Vallat, 'The General Assembly and the Security Council of the United Nations', 29 BYIL (1952) at pp. 74–5. The Collective Measures Committee established under that resolution considered that states should not be subject to legal liabilities under treaties as a consequence of carrying out collective measures recommended by the United Nations (GAOR, Sixth Session, see p. 33). This doctrine of authorization has supported the legitimizing of the use of force by liberation movements and of assistance to such movements. SC Rs. 678 relating to measures to be taken against Iraq for the liberation of Kuwait authorized the use of force. This resolution created legal authority for action taken pursuant to it by member states of the UN. There have been other SC resolutions of this nature.

Council powers commensurate with its responsibility for the maintenance of peace and security. The only limitations are the fundamental principles and purposes found in Chapter 1 of the Charter.'[69]

Apart from these powers of the SC, the GA also has certain powers to act through recommendations in the peacekeeping area, when the SC does not act. This view was implied in the judgment of the ICJ in the *Expenses Case*,[70] where it held that the expenses incurred by the UN under the Uniting for Peace Resolution for the UNEF and the ONUC were 'expenses of the organization' for the purposes of Article 17(2) insofar as they were based on acts of the GA which were *intra vires*.[71]

As a consequence of these powers of recommendation of the SC and GA, recommendations of both organs provide a basis for implementation in the absence of binding 'decisions', with the result that not only could those directly affected by the recommendations not complain, but there may be consequent obligations imposed on the membership following the action taken pursuant to such recommendations.

In relation to the authority to implement on the basis of recommendations it may be pointed out that the GA has in the past adopted at many sessions, and by large majorities, resolutions calling on states to apply economic measures similar to those provided in Article 41 of Chapter VII. It has also, in resolutions on Southern Rhodesia, called on the UK, as the administering authority, to take all necessary measures 'including in particular the use of force', which, in the view of the GA, however, the UK was authorized to do anyway.

Evidence for formation of law

Recommendations, particularly of the GA, may also be evidence, in certain circumstances, for the formation of law deriving from one of the recognized sources of law.[72] This is a specialized subject which pertains particularly to GA resolutions and may not have general application to

---

[69] 1971 ICJ Reports at p. 52.   [70] 1962 ICJ Reports p. 151.

[71] A consequence of the view expressed above is that members are all obligated financially to support recommended action: by implication the Court in the *Expenses Case* and more explicitly Judge Fitzmaurice in a separate opinion, 1962 ICJ Reports at p. 199. But see *contra* dissenting Judges Winiarski, Moreno Quintana, Koretzky and Bustamante: *ibid.* at pp. 232, 250, 287 and 305, respectively.

[72] Readers are referred particularly to the discussion in Sloan, note 2 pp. 41–2, 50 and 53–91. It should be noted that at the San Francisco Conference of the United Nations which formulated the Charter of the UN a proposal to empower the GA to enact rules of international law with the approval of the SC was rejected: 9 UNCIO Docs. at pp. 70, 316.

recommendations of all organizations. In any event, the kind of effect in issue is not a direct effect in the same category as the legal effects already discussed. To the extent that it can be discussed here, it may be said that recommendations may be evidence of practice of states and of organizations. This is particularly in relation to the creation of customary law, but it would appear that resolutions taking the form of recommendations may have relevance to other formal sources such as treaties and general principles of law.[73] Much depends in fact on what happens to the resolutions. Some of the discussion in the next section of this chapter is also relevant to the subject.

Other forms of resolutions

Organs, such as the GA of the UN, have adopted resolutions which are not in form recommendations but have a different content. Their content may constitute declarations, determinations, interpretations or agreements. The effect of these kinds of resolutions will be briefly considered here.

Declarations have been made by the GA of the UN. As was pointed out in 1981:

In the last few years, we have witnessed an increasing insistence on the authoritative character of General Assembly resolutions on intervention, self-determination, territorial occupation, human rights, sharing of resources and foreign investment. They purport to 'declare the law', either in general terms or as applied to a particular case. Neither in form nor intent are they recommendatory. Surprising as it may seem, the authority of the General Assembly to adopt such declaratory resolutions was accepted from the very beginning.[74]

Assertions in such resolutions do not appear to be recommendatory. They purport to reflect authoritative precepts dependent on the Charter or on established rules of international law adopted by the organs.[75] A difficulty is that the Charter has not expressly authorized a declaratory function for the GA.[76] However, practice over nearly fifty years may have enabled the GA to acquire the power to perform this function or, more

---

[73] Some writers have even discussed the relevance of recommendations to 'new' sources of law, see, e.g., Sloan, note 2 pp. 86ff. and authors there cited; Bedjaoui, *Pour un nouvel ordre économique international* (1979) pp. 140ff.; Elias, *Africa and the Development of International Law* (1972) pp. 71ff.; Skubiszewski, loc. cit. note 2, 15 Polish YIL p. 135.

[74] Schachter, loc. cit. note 62 at pp. 3–4.

[75] Schachter, note 2 pp. 85–6.

[76] See also Schermers and Blokker, *International Institutional Law* (1995) pp. 771ff.

likely, it may be an implied power inherent in the position of the GA. There have been no protests against the exercise of this power.

While the legal effect of declarations has been much discussed, their effect may be summarized as follows:

Declarations are a species of General Assembly resolutions based on inherent powers or established practice outside the express provisions of Chapter IV of the Charter. The practice of adopting declarations is consistent, universally accepted, and 'immemorial' in the sense that it goes back to the very beginning of the United Nations. While the effect of declarations remains controversial, they are not recommendations and are not to be evaluated as such. Where, however, there is an intent to declare law – whether customary, general principles, or instant, spontaneous or new law – and the resolution is adopted by a unanimous or nearly unanimous vote or by genuine consensus, there is a presumption that the rules and principles embodied in the declaration are law. This presumption could only be overcome by evidence of substantial conflicting practice supported by an *opinio juris* contrary to that stated or implied in the resolution.[77]

It is an open question whether other organizations have the power to make declarations of this kind in the field of their competence. Much will depend on how their constitutional instruments are interpreted and what the subsequent practice has been. For example, the Development Committee of the Boards of Governors of the IMF and the IBRD (a joint ministerial committee) in September 1992 reviewed and called to the attention of member countries the *Guidelines on the Treatment of Foreign Direct Investment* prepared by the World Bank Group. The Report to the Development Committee made earlier explained that the World Bank Group could not issue binding rules to govern the conduct of member States in any field. It is clear that these *Guidelines* were never intended to be, cannot be or are not dispositive, therefore. They do not seem to be in the nature of a declaration of the law either. They remain only guidelines[78] which the World Bank (and the IMF) suggest should be followed. As such, they are probably not even on a par with the recommendations considered above. A guideline is probably intended to have a lesser effect than a recommendation, though its effect may share some of the characteristics of the effects of a recommendation, such as imposing a duty to consider seriously before rejecting.

---

[77] Sloan, note 2 p. 47. Sloan has considered in detail the factors to be considered in detemining the effect of, *inter alia*, declarations of the GA: *ibid.* pp. 104*ff.*

[78] For the Guidelines and their history and an explanation of what they are intended to be, see *Legal Framework for the Treatment of Foreign Investment, Volume II: Guidelines* (1992) pp. 5–6.

Resolutions may satisfy the subjective element (*opinio juris*) of customary international law by expressing a belief in the existence of principles and rules of international law.[79] The ICJ in the *Nicaragua Case (Merits)*, in dealing with the question whether the obligation to refrain from the threat or use of force contained in Article 2(4) of the UN Charter was also a principle of customary international law, stated:

> The Court has however to be satisfied that there exists in customary international law an *opinio juris* as to the binding character of such abstention. This *opinio juris* may, though with all due caution, be deduced from, *inter alia*, the attitude of the Parties and the attitude of States towards certain General Assembly resolutions, in particular resolution 2625 (XXV) entitled 'Declaration on Principles of International Law concerning Friendly Relations and Co-operation among States in accordance with the Charter of the United Nations'. The effect of consent to the text of such resolutions cannot be understood as merely that of a 'reiteration or elucidation' of the treaty commitment undertaken in the Charter. On the contrary, it may be understood as an acceptance of the validity of the rule or set of rules declared by the resolution by themselves. The principle of non-use of force, for example, may thus be regarded as a principle of customary international law, not as such conditioned by the provisions relating to collective security, or to the facilities or armed contingents to be provided under Article 43 of the Charter. It would therefore seem apparent that the attitude referred to expresses an *opinio juris* respecting such rule (or set of rules), to be thenceforth treated separately from the provisions, especially those of an institutional kind, to which it is subject on the treaty-law plane of the Charter . . . As already observed, the adoption by States of this text affords an indication of their *opinio juris* as to customary international law on the question . . . This resolution demonstrates that the States represented in the General Assembly regard the exception to the prohibition of force constituted by the right of individual or collective self-defence as already a matter of customary international law . . . This description, contained in Article 3, paragraph (g), of the Definition of Aggression annexed to General Assembly Resolution 3314(XXXIX), may be taken to reflect customary international law.[80]

Again, with respect to the content of the principle of non-intervention, the Court refers to Resolution 2625(XXV).[81] The Court notes further that it must also enquire whether practice is sufficiently in conformity with the principle to make it a rule of customary international law, but it

---

[79] See, e.g., Mendelson, loc. cit. note 2 at pp. 39*ff*.; Tunkin, 'The Legal Nature of the United Nations', 119 *Hague Recueil* (1966-III) at p. 36; Mosler, *The International Society as a Legal Community* (1980) p. 90; Schachter, loc. cit. note 62 p. 7; Suy, in Cassese and Weiler (eds.), *Change and Stability in International Law-Making* (1988) at p. 85; Seidl-Hohenveldern, 'International Economic "Soft Law"', 163 *Hague Recueil* (1979–II) at p. 189.

[80] 1986 ICJ Reports at pp. 99*ff*., 101 and 103.   [81] *Ibid.* at pp. 106*ff*.

satisfies this requirement by determining that contrary practice is not supported by an *opinio juris*.[82]

In indicating an *opinio juris* on the part of the member states GA resolutions may supply the missing element in a line of existing state practice and thus convert usage into custom or they may inspire practice which will develop into law. But they may do something more. The same resolution may contain both the objective and subjective elements of custom – practice and *opinio juris*. Just as certainly a single act of a state may be practice accompanied by the belief that that practice is required by law, resolutions adopted in a particular case might also be practice accompanied by *opinio juris*, and there seems no logical reason why declaratory resolutions may not also combine the two elements. As has been stated:

> It could be on the theory that (1) a unanimous resolution constitutes the practice of 160 States and (2) a statement in the resolution that its contents are law constitutes *opinio juris*, that the idea of instant custom is based. The idea of instant custom has also rested on the view that an *opinio juris* expressed by the entire community of States will itself validate a rule of law.[83]

The ICJ in the *Nicaragua Case* took the view that certain GA resolutions not only indicated an *opinio juris* but in doing so reflected customary international law. Ordinarily *opinio juris* either accompanies practice, or appears at a later stage to convert it into law. It is possible, however, that an *opinio juris* expressed in a resolution of the GA will be itself sufficient, or may stimulate a practice which will eventually be consolidated into customary international law.[84]

Determinations consist generally of findings of fact and characterization. They may form part of decisions which are binding, recommendations which have a lesser legal effect or declarations. In general, they will have the legal weight of the resolution of which they are a part. Sometimes, however, they enjoy a weight of their own. The ICJ in the *Namibia Case* affirmed that the GA had authority to make determinations which have legal effect. Determinations in decisions which are binding will carry the weight of the binding decision. Thus, the decision under Article 4 of the UN Charter to admit a state to membership implied a

---

[82] *Ibid.* at pp. 108*ff.*   [83] Sloan, note 2 p. 75.

[84] See Abi-Saab, 'The Development of International Law by the United Nations', 24 *Revue Egyptienne de Droit International* (1968) at p. 100; P. de Visscher, *loc. cit.* note 60 at pp. 131*ff.* On the *opinio juris* required for customary international law and the resolutions of the GA see particularly the discussion in Sloan, note 2 pp. 73*ff.*

determination that the applicant is a state, is peace-loving, has accepted the obligations of the Charter and is able and willing to carry them out. Such a determination is binding for the purpose of admission which itself is the result of a binding decision.

Sometimes determinations found in recommendations, however, may have a greater or different effect than the recommendation. As has been said:

They may justify States in accepting and acting on the determinations in situations not covered by the recommendation and in expecting other States to respect their action. Resolutions concerning disputes and situations may contain, either expressly or implicitly, findings of fact in addition to recommendations. They may also characterize the facts or situations. Such findings and characterizations, as well as the recommendation, will affect the future course of the dispute or situation whether or not the parties or the States concerned accept any or all of the conclusions and recommendations. The conduct of third States toward the parties may well be influenced by the determinations, whether in the form of findings of fact or characterizations or both. These determinations will also have precedential effect for similar disputes and situations being considered.[85]

Thus, a finding that an armed attack has occurred and a characterization that it constitutes a breach of the peace or act of aggression, when made by the SC or the GA would be binding, being based on the application of a legal rule to a specific case and characterization of the legal rule, even though the finding and determination may result in a recommendation that is not binding.

Determinations may also appear in declarations confirming rules and principles as existing law. These would have special evidentiary weight. For example, Resolution 95(I) of 11 December 1946 of the GA, confirming the Nuremberg principles, reaffirmed the principles and removed doubts about their existence in customary international law.[86]

Interpretations of constitutional documents and sometimes of general international law or other treaties may be found in all categories of resolutions. Interpretations incorporated in binding decisions will be dispositive and binding for the particular case. In the case of other

---

[85] Sloan, *ibid.* p. 48.

[86] See *A-G of Israel* v. *Eichmann*, Supreme Court of Israel (1962), 36 ILR at pp. 296*ff.*; Higgins, 'The Development of International Law by the Political Organs of the United Nations', *ASIL Proceedings* (1965) at p. 119; Asamoah, note 46 p. 125; Castañeda, note 2 pp. 172*ff. Contra* Cheng, 'United Nations Resolutions on Outer Space: "Instant" International Customary Law?', 5 IJIL (1965) p. 40.

resolutions the legal effect of interpretations would depend, especially, on how far they are accepted generally and are not subjected to objections or protests.[87] It has been noted in Chapter 2 that, in the first place at least, organs have the authority to interpret their constitutions particularly in respect of their powers. But even apart from this authority, organs may have a residual power to give interpretations of international law, of course with varying effects, depending, *inter alia*, on the circumstances in which the interpretation is given and in what kind of resolution it appears.

As has been seen above, agreement or acceptance may be an extraneous element giving a recommendation a binding character. Declarations may also have their status confirmed by agreement. Further, agreement may be necessary to implement resolutions which have a legal effect of their own. Thus, while a subsidiary organ may be established by a binding and dispositive resolution, it will require the agreement of the state concerned to enable it to operate in that state's territory. Moreover, a prior agreement may give the organ authority to make a binding decision under it. But, apart from these situations, a resolution may be an instrument for recording an understanding or engagement, i.e., an 'agreement in simplified form'.[88] In these circumstances it may be a separate category deriving validity both from the resolution and the agreement.[89]

---

[87] Sloan has a good discussion of the relevant factors to be considered in this connection: see note 2 pp. 104*ff*.

[88] An example of this is the 'Declaration of Legal Principles Governing the Activities of States in the Exploration and Use of Outer Space' of 13 December 1963.

[89] Another issue that may be raised concerns how far resolutions may be 'soft law'. This relates to resolutions as a source of law which subject has been referred to above. The whole issue of 'soft law' is somewhat nebulous and unclear: see, e.g., Abi-Saab, in Cassese and Weiler (eds.), note 79, at p. 76; Seidl-Hohenveldern, loc. cit. note 79 at pp. 165*ff*.; Tammes, 'Soft Law', in T. M. C. Asser Instituut (ed.), *Essays on International and Comparative Law in Honour of Judge Erades* (1983) at pp. 187*ff*.; Tammes, 'A Hard Look at Soft Law' (Panel), *ASIL Proceedings* (1988) at pp. 371*ff*.; Mbaye, 'Le Droit au développement en droit international', in Makarczyk (ed.), *Essays in International Law in Honour of Judge Manfred Lachs* (1984) p. 173; and Weil, 'Towards Relative Normativity in International Law?', 77 AJIL (1983) at pp. 415*ff*.

7 Acts of non-judicial organs: the doctrine of *ultra vires*

In explaining the meaning of *ultra vires* in national law a leading law dictionary gives several possible meanings of the term depending on the context in which it is used and on the nature of the legal person in connection with whose acts the term is applied.[1] The principal general meaning ascribed is similar to that which was given in a case decided by a US court: an *ultra vires* act is one performed without any authority to act on the subject.[2] Text writers on national law do not generally attempt a comprehensive definition of the term. Writers on English administrative law refer to acts outside or 'beyond the scope' of the powers of bodies and then describe the elements which constitute acts *ultra vires*.[3] French administrative law commentators and lexicographers use the term 'excès de pouvoir' to cover the 'ensemble des violations ... du principe de légalité' but are more concerned about the misuse of authority or abuse of power.[4] In national law, particularly in

---

[1] *Black's Law Dictionary* (1950) p. 1,522. See also *Stroud's Judicial Dictionary* (1986) vol. V, pp. 2,706–7.

[2] *Haslund v. City of Seattle* [1976], 547 p. 2d at p. 1230.

[3] See, e.g., H. W. R. Wade, *Administrative Law* (1985) pp. 105*ff*. For US law see Schwarz, *An Introduction to American Administrative Law* (1958) pp. 72*ff*. For other works on the common law see Field, 'The Effect of an Unconstitutional Statute', *Indiana LJ* (1926) p. 1; Denner, 'Judicial Review in Modern Constitutional Systems', 46 *Administrative Political Science Review* (1932) p. 1,079; Allen, *Law and Orders* (1945) pp. 61*ff*.; Wynes, *Legislative, Executive and Judicial Powers in Australia* (1962) p. 39; H. W. R. Wade, 'Unlawful Administrative Action: Void or Voidable?', 83 LQR (1967) p. 499 and 84 LQR (1968) p. 97; Baxt, 'Is the Doctrine of Ultra Vires Dead?', 20 ICLQ (1971) p. 301; Griffith and Street, *Principles of Administrative Law* (1973) pp. 100*ff*.; de Smith, *Constitutional and Administrative Law* (1973) pp. 564*ff*.; and de Smith, *Judicial Review of Administrative Action* (1973) pp. 82*ff*.

[4] See Laferrière, *Traité de la juridiction administrative et des recours contentieux* (1989) vol. II, pp. 366*ff*.; Cornu, *Vocabulaire juridique* (1992) p. 332; de Laubedère, *Traité de droit administratif* (1984) vol. I, pp. 568*ff*.

common law jurisdictions, the term *ultra vires* is used in constitutional law, administrative law and corporate law but with differing emphasis. The doctrine, however, is accepted without question in national legal systems.

Before the definition of *ultra vires* in international institutional law is approached, it is useful to consider some of the basic questions which have been or may be raised in regard to the doctrine and in general the answers given to them.[5] The issue concerns the legal status and effects of acts and decisions of international organizations which are not in conformity with the provisions of their constitutional law or other governing law or with established rules and procedures. The questions asked are, for instance, whether such acts and decisions are unconstitutional and illegal, whether they give rise to binding legal obligations, how objections can be raised against them, who is competent to decide any such objections and what guarantees are available to members to protect their interests against such acts and decisions.

---

[5] Several writers have addressed directly or indirectly the issue of *ultra vires* in relation to international organizations: see particularly, e.g., Verzijl, 'La validité et la nullité des actes juridiques internationaux', 9 RDI (1935) p. 284; Hertz, 'Essai sur la problème de la nullité', RDILC (1939) p. 450; Wengler, Reports on 'Recours judiciaire à instituer contre les décisions d'organes internationaux', 44-I, 45-I, 47-I, II AIDI (1953, 1954, 1957, 1957) pp. 224, 265, 218, 225 respectively; Guggenheim, 'La validité et la nullité des actes juridiques internationaux', 74 *Hague Recueil* (1949-I) p. 195; Fawcett, '*Détournement de Pouvoir* by International Organizations', 33 BYIL (1957) p. 311; C. F. Amerasinghe, *Studies in International Law* (1969) p. 51 (a reprint of an article in 4 IJIL (1964) at pp. 210*ff.*); Baade, 'Nullity and Avoidance in Public International Law', *Indiana LJ* (1964) p. 497; Jennings, 'Nullity and Effectiveness in International Law', in *Cambridge Essays in International Law* (1965) p. 64; E. Lauterpacht, 'The Legal Effect of Illegal Acts of International Organizations', in *ibid.* at pp. 88*ff.*; Rideau, *Juridictions internationales et contrôle du respect des traités constitutifs des organisations internationales* (1969); Cahier, 'La nullité en droit international', 76 RGDIP (1972) p. 645; Osieke, 'Ultra Vires Acts in International Organizations – The Experience of the ILO', 48 BYIL (1976–7) p. 259; Osieke, 'Unconstitutional Acts in International Organizations – The Law and Practice of ICAO', 28 ICLQ (1979) p. 1; Osieke, 'The Legal Validity of Ultra Vires Decisions of International Organizations', 77 AJIL (1983) p. 239; Morgenstern, 'Legality in International Organizations', 48 BYIL (1976–7) p. 241; Ciobanu, *Preliminary Objections Related to the Jurisdiction of United Nations Political Organs* (1975) pp. 75–167; Schwarzenberger, *International Constitutional Law – International Law as Applied by Courts and Tribunals* (1967) pp. 53*ff.*; Brownlie, *Principles of International Law* (2003) pp. 665*ff.*; McWhinney, 'The Changing United Nations Constitutionalism. New Arenas and New Techniques for International Law-Making', 5 CYIL (1967) at pp. 68–73; Cahier, 'Les Caracteristiques de la nullité en droit international et tout particulièrement dans la convention de Vienne de 1969 sur le droit des traités', 76 RGDIP (1972) at pp. 659*ff.* Seidl-Hohenveldern, *Corporations in and under International Law* (1987) pp. 84*ff.*, discusses the matter and concludes, giving reasons, that the doctrine of *ultra vires* applies to international organizations.

The answers to such questions have had to be looked for outside the constitution of organizations with the result that conflicting views and opinions, influenced greatly by the situation in different national legal systems, have emerged. For instance, it has been variously maintained by legal writers and commentators that international organizations have the capacity to commit illegal acts; that member states have a right to raise objections concerning the legality of proposals before an organ of an international organization; that the organ whose competence and jurisdiction is questioned has the power to decide the matter; that acts and decisions adopted by international organizations in excess of their functions and powers are void; that such acts and decisions are only voidable; and that member states may refuse to implement acts and decisions of international organizations which they consider to be unconstitutional.[6] On the other hand, it has been asserted that the doctrine of *ultra vires* is not applicable to international organizations and that their acts and decisions are always legal and valid.

As has been said, 'questions of nullity and validity raise difficult and sophisticated problems even in highly developed systems of municipal law and it is therefore understandable if it is supposed that they are capable only of relatively crude application in the rough jurisprudence of nations'.[7] The proliferation of international organizations whose powers are basically derived from constitutions has given the problem a fresh momentum and the concept of *ultra vires* is now important in international law just as it is in national legal systems. The matter has received the attention of the ICJ in more than one case. Even though there is some disagreement on many matters concerning *ultra vires*, the better and more accepted view is that international organizations have the capacity to commit *ultra vires* acts and that their powers are not unbridled and uncontrolled. This view is a natural consequence of the fact that the functions and powers of organizations and their organs flow from constitutions and there are established procedures to be followed in the discharge of those functions and the exercise of powers. It is, therefore, possible that in the pursuit of their objects and purposes international organizations may engage in activities which are not authorized by their constitutions, and may adopt decisions in a manner which does not correspond entirely to the governing procedures. While

[6] See authors cited in footnote 5, and particularly the reference to these problems in Osieke, loc. cit. note 5, ICLQ at pp. 2–3.
[7] Jennings, loc. cit. note 5 at p. 64.

the absence of compulsory judicial review in general may create problems,[8] it does not entail the consequence that *ultra vires* acts cannot be
committed by international organizations or that there is no doctrine
of *ultra vires* applicable to their acts. The alternative to recognizing that
their acts may be *ultra vires* and are controlled by a doctrine of *ultra vires*
is the acceptance of a *carte blanche* for their acts and exercise of powers
which is unreasonable and contrary to the theory that their functions
and powers derive from and are limited by constitutions.[9]

In the institutional law of international organizations the meaning
of *ultra vires* in relation to the acts of international organizations has
not been defined with exactitude. While a definition in terms of action
taken outside or beyond the legally ascribed powers may be adequate,
there are certain attributes of the definition which it is necessary to
emphasize.

First, the subject matter of the doctrine consists of acts, generally 'decisions' or 'resolutions', of organs of organizations, whether these organs
are composed of a number of individuals or one individual. Thus, the
organ may be a plenary organ in which all members are represented
individually, such as the General Assembly of the UN, the Board of Governors of the IBRD or the IMF or the General Conference of the ILO,
or an organ of a more limited membership with decision-making powers, such as the Security Council, the Executive Directors of the IBRD
or the IMF, or the Governing Body of the ILO, or the executive organ of
the organization headed by the chief executive, such as the Secretary-
General of the UN, the President of the IBRD, the Managing Director of
the IMF or the Director-General of the ILO, who, however, may be represented for a particular purpose by a member of his or her staff. Second,
powers may be constitutional or derived from subsidiary legislation, as
the case may be. Third, they may also be explicitly granted or have to be
implied by interpretation, as was seen in Chapter 3. Fourth, an 'excess'
of power may result either from the disregard of substantive provisions

---

[8] See the discussion in the next section. In the *Namibia Case*, 1971 ICJ Reports at p. 45,
the ICJ did state that it had no powers of judicial review as such over the acts of organs
in the case before it, though incidentally it may have to determine the validity of such
acts, but this was not a denial of the possibility of acts being *ultra vires*. On the
contrary, there was an assumption that such acts could be *ultra vires*.

[9] As will be seen in the next section, the practice in organs of international
organizations also recognizes that *ultra vires* acts may be committed by organizations. It
may also be noted that it is a recognized ground for annulling arbitral awards that
tribunals have exceeded their powers: see E. Lauterpacht, loc. cit. note 5 at pp. 89*ff*.

or of procedural requirements provided these are legally established.[10] Fifth, what is in issue in the application of the doctrine of *ultra vires* is the legal validity of acts or the exercise of powers, not their legality or illegality in terms of breached obligations and the duty to make reparation. Sixth, the subject matter is the exercise of 'powers' which affects the rights and obligations of others than the organ or the organization itself.

The powers exercised through decision-making by organs of organizations have effect broadly in three areas. First, the exercise of power may affect the rights and obligations of persons in national (or transnational) law. Thus, a contract to provide supplies to an organization or to construct a building for it would be entered into generally with a legal person and would be governed by national (or transnational) law. Since the issue relates to the capacity to contract, in most national jurisdictions the exercise of the power to contract by the executive organ of the organization would, according to principles of the conflict of laws, be governed by the proper law of the organization which is international law, including the constitutional and internal law of the organization. Nevertheless, the issue of *ultra vires* in relation to capacity may have to be decided by a national court or a national arbitral tribunal or by a transnational arbitral tribunal. It is possible in such a case to have a definitive adjudication of the issue of *ultra vires* by a tribunal. The law applied would be the international law relating to the doctrine of *ultra vires*.[11]

Second, the impact of an exercise of power by an organ of the organization, particularly the executive organ, may be felt in the internal legal system of the organization. Thus, a decision by the executive organ (its representative) to downgrade a manager because he had disregarded the internal administrative or financial regulations of the organization

[10] A procedural issue was indirectly the subject of the *Namibia Case*, 1971 ICJ Reports p. 31, insofar as the case turned on whether a power could exist to supervise a former mandate when decisions on supervision were taken by a special majority vote rather than unanimously by a UN supervisory organ. See also, e.g., the *Admissibility of Hearings Case*, 1956 ICJ Reports p. 23; the *Voting Procedure Case*, 1955 ICJ Reports p. 67; and the *ICAO Council Case*, 1972 ICJ Reports p. 46.

[11] In the case of financial institutions, such as the IMF and the IBRD, if the question of *vires* has been decided by a binding interpretation by an organ of the institutions of the constitutions of those organizations (see Chapter 3 above), this decision would presumably be binding on national courts and tribunals and on transnational tribunals, e.g., in a case brought before the US FCC, namely *IBRD and IMF v. All American Cable and Radio Inc.* [1953] FCC, USA, 22 ILR p. 705, the FCC accepted the interpretation given of their constitutional provisions by the Executive Directors of the IBRD and the IMF as final and binding.

would have repercussions in the internal legal system of the organization. Questions that may arise would be, first, whether the organization (through its manager) acted *ultra vires* the internal regulations and, second, whether the decision of the executive organ to downgrade the manager was taken in a manner, both substantive and procedural, that did not result in an abuse of power or misuse of authority (which may be described as an *ultra vires* decision). There would also be a question as to whether the manager's performance was inadequate. All these questions would be decided by an IAT, if such exists for the organization concerned, as they relate to an exercise of power in the field of employment relations. The law applied to the first question would be international law – the constitution of the organization and its interpretation in this case – and the law applied to the second and third questions would be the internal law of the organization, including its written law (administrative and financial regulations, staff regulations and rules, etc.), and general principles of law. Thus, certain issues relating to *ultra vires* acts are to be decided by the application of international administrative law. IATs, their powers and the law they apply are discussed elsewhere in this work.[12]

Third, an exercise of power by an organ, particularly an organ such as the General Assembly or Security Council of the UN, the Governing Body of the ILO, or the Secretariat of the UN or of the IBRD, could have effects on states, members or not of the organization, or on other organizations. There may then be some question whether the exercise of the power was *ultra vires* in terms of the constitution and the subsidiary legislation of the organization. Such a question would clearly be a matter for international law and would normally have to be decided at an international level.

All these situations have one thing in common – the issue of *ultra vires* in regard to acts of the organization which are not directly connected with employment relations is one for general international law as such. Hence the need to examine the general principles of the law relating to the doctrine of *ultra vires* in institutional law. The law of employment relations (international administrative law), an area in which there is a plethora of judicial precedents, may or may not provide analogies.

---

[12] See Chapter 9 below. Also see for a reference to the powers of three particular IATs in this area, E. Lauterpacht, loc. cit. note 5 at pp. 97*ff*. The application of international administrative law to administrative decisions relating to staff will not be discussed here as such, as Chapter 9 purports to examine it generally. See also C. F. Amerasinghe, *The Law of the International Civil Service* (1994) vols. 1 and 2 *passim*.

The problem and relevance of final adjudication

In two of the three situations referred to above it is possible that the issue of *ultra vires* will be decided by a judicial body. In the case of the private law contract national courts may have to pronounce on it, barring a claim of immunity by the organization, where this is available. Alternatively, an arbitral tribunal may decide it. In the case of employment decisions an IAT would have the power to decide the issue of *ultra vires* as regards both the internal legal and the general international legal position. In both cases there is a mechanism for deciding in a binding and final manner the issue of *ultra vires*. In both situations the judicial bodies concerned may have to and may take into account the decisions of other international bodies. Thus, in the case of the IBRD and the IMF (and the financial institutions generally), since the Executive Directors and the Board of Governors are the final arbiters of constitutional interpretation,[13] their decisions on constitutional interpretation would be taken into account and applied by these judicial bodies. Similarly, an advisory opinion of the ICJ in the appropriate situation, though not binding on the organization, may be applied by an IAT. Further, if, upon the receipt of an advisory opinion on an issue of *ultra vires*, an organization has taken a decision, whether accepting, rejecting or adopting with modifications the opinion, the judicial body concerned may give weight to this decision, thought it is not clear whether every judicial body is bound to do so. IATs will probably apply all these decisions or opinions. As for other judicial bodies, perhaps much will depend on the approach of the particular legal system to the application of international law and decisions of international organizations.[14] The short point is that the national (or transnational) judicial bodies concerned or IATs will have the authority to decide in a binding manner the issue of *ultra vires* with the resources at their disposal and by whatever method their legal system indicates.

It cannot be said in any case that a doctrine analogous to the 'act of state' doctrine is applicable by national (or transnational) bodies nor is there evidence that such a doctrine has developed. Such a doctrine would result in the refusal of courts to examine the question whether an

---

[13] See, e.g., Article IX of the IBRD Articles of Agreement; and Article XXIX of the IMF Articles of Agreement. See also the discussion in Chapter 3 above.

[14] National courts have given effect to decisions of international organizations in many general circumstances where *ultra vires* was not in issue; see Schreuer, *Decisions of International Institutions before Domestic Courts* (1981) *passim*.

act is *ultra vires* because it is a matter solely within the jurisdiction of the foreign international person. The 'act of state' doctrine is to some extent the creation of particular national legal systems for their own constitutional or quasi-constitutional reasons. It may reflect some division of power between international and national levels, but in its articulation (especially in the US and more recently in the UK cases) it emerges as a rather obscure discretionary doctrine with no close relationship to any legal principles and with no predictable application. Its transposition to cases involving international organizations is unnecessary and not desirable. Where the court or tribunal itself decides the issue of *ultra vires* it is to be expected that it will apply the international law relating to *ultra vires*.

In both these situations the question may be asked whether the absence of a declaration of nullity or voidability by an international judicial body or other appropriate non-judicial organ precludes national, transnational or international administrative courts or tribunals from adopting any other conclusion than that the decision of the organization is valid, because there is such a presumption (*omnia rite esse praesumuntur*), in the absence of a finding to the contrary by an appropriate international judicial body or non-judicial organ. It is doubtful whether the absence of such a separate determination of the issue of *ultra vires* can be regarded as preclusive in this way.[15] Not only is there often no judicial body or non-judicial organ that has been presented with the issue in order that a decision may be made but any such decision may not be binding. Thus, if there is no other body that can make a final decision on the issue, there is certainly no reason to prevent the judicial body concerned from itself taking a decision on the issue. If, on the other hand, on the particular issue there does exist a body that can finally decide the issue,[16] in the event that it has not decided the issue or the

---

[15] There are cases in which national courts have examined the question whether an act of an international organization was *ultra vires* in the absence of any separate determination as referred to above: see, e.g., *Balfour, Guthri & Co. Ltd v. US* [1950] USA (California), 17 ILR (1956) p. 323; *Burns v. the King* [1951] Australia (New South Wales), 20 ILR (1953) p. 596; *UN v. Canada Asiatic Lines Ltd* [1952] Canada (Montreal), 26 ILR (1963) p. 622; *Keeney v. US* [1954] USA (District of Columbia), 20 ILR (1953) p. 382; *Studio-Karten GmbH v. Deutsches Komittee der UNICEF v. V.* [1976] (Germany), 1976 UNJY p. 247. Sometimes under the law it was necessary to consult the Foreign Office of the country. In the above cases it was found that the international decisions were not *ultra vires*.

[16] See the possible case of the members of the EU where the CJEC is such a body. See on this question particularly Zeeleeg, 'Fundamental Rights and the Law of the European Communities', 8 CML *Rev.* (1971) at p. 460.

issue has not been referred to it, it will depend on the prescription of the applicable law whether the judicial organ concerned should defer its judgment in the case till the relevant body has had an opportunity to decide. Unless the applicable law clearly indicates that there should be a deferral, there is no reason why the judicial organ should not proceed to decide the issue of *ultra vires* itself.[17] Indeed, there are precedents in which courts have proceeded to examine the issue of *ultra vires* without any mention of deferral, whether or not there was a possibility of a decision by an international body on the issue, and have found or tended to the view that the decision of the international organ was invalid.[18] The same applies, clearly, to the situation where the organ taking the decision or another organ of the organization that has the authority to do so has not taken a specific decision on the issue of *ultra vires* after being confronted with it.

The absence of methods of final adjudication on questions of *ultra vires* raises a separate set of issues as regards what happens when a decision of an international organ is questioned on this ground. If the matter is raised in an international adjudication between states or a court or tribunal is given jurisdiction over a dispute between states which concerns a decision of an organization, clearly the judicial body would have the power, as it has been suggested that other judicial bodies have, to examine and decide it. This was the situation in the *ICAO Council Case*,[19] where, under Article 84 of the Chicago Convention which allowed an appeal to

---

[17] The only situation to be found where courts or tribunals have not reviewed decisions on the ground that they were *ultra vires* are those involving the enforcement or recognition of international arbitral awards: see, e.g., *Freylinghuysen* v. *Key* [1884], US Supreme Ct. 110 US p. 63. See also for a discussion of these cases Schreuer, note 14 p. 137. These awards are different from decisions of international organizations. The nullity of international arbitral awards is also discussed in Reisman, *Systems of Control in International Adjudication and Arbitration* (1992) *passim*, particularly pp. 56–7, 69–71, 76–8, 81–6, 88–92 and 97–8. On the nullity of international judgments now, see C. F. Amerasinghe, *Jurisdiction of International Tribunals* (2003) pp. 491*ff*.

[18] See, e.g., the decision of the German Reichsgericht of 21 January 1930, reported in 63 RGSt. p. 395; *Ruiz Alicea* v. *US* [1950], US Court of Appeals, 17 ILR (1956) p. 42; the *Madzimbamuto Case* [1968] Rhodesia, 39 ILR (1970) at p. 338; *R.* v. *Ndhlovu and Others* [1968] Rhodesia, 53 ILR (1979) at pp. 86, 92; the *Inge Toft Case* [1960] Egypt, 31 ILR (1966) p. 517. Schreuer is of the view that in general, particularly because there are no internationalized review procedures, national courts should in any case decide issues of *ultra vires*: note 14 p. 137.

[19] 1972 ICJ Reports p. 46. Article 173 of the EEC Treaty, Article 33 of the ECSC Treaty and the corresponding provision of the Euratom Treaty conferred on the CJEC jurisdiction to supervise the legality of acts of the Council, Commission, High Authority, etc. There were also provisions governing annulment and the effects of such an order. Cahier, loc. cit. note 5 at pp. 650*ff*., discusses the position in the EC and concludes that the

the ICJ by a contracting state from a decision of the ICAO Council in a dispute between it and another state, India took Pakistan to court. One of the issues in the case was that the Council had no jurisdiction to deal with the matter submitted to it by Pakistan for various reasons and that the decision taken by the Council was, therefore, null and void. The ICJ held that it had competence to deal with the dispute but that the Council's decision was within its powers. However, where there is no possibility or likelihood that an impartial international judicial body can be seized of the issue, what is the position?

The consequences of this situation were discussed by the ICJ in the *Expenses Case*.[20] The Court made it clear, firstly, that each organ must determine, in the first place at least, the validity of its acts, there being a presumption, if and until a special decision on the matter is taken, that the acts are valid:

In the legal systems of States, there is often some procedure for determining the validity of even a legislative or governmental act, but no analogous procedure is to be found in the structure of the United Nations. Proposals made during the drafting of the Charter to place the ultimate authority to interpret the Charter in the International Court of Justice were not accepted; the opinion which the Court is in course of rendering is an *advisory* opinion. As anticipated in 1945, therefore, each organ must, in the first place at least, determine its own jurisdiction. If the Security Council, for example, adopts a resolution purportedly

doctrine of *ultra vires* is applied by the CJEC. Article 96 of the Havana Charter for the ITO which never came into force also gave the ICJ jurisdiction to give binding opinions on legal questions arising within the scope of the ITO's activities which would include questions concerning the legality of acts of organs: see E. Lauterpacht, loc. cit. note 5 at pp. 95–7. Clearly, where provision is made for judicial review in the constitution, there is a means of judicial determination of the validity of acts. There may be circumstances when the power of review is granted to a different organ, generally a judicial organ, in which the power of review may be expressly limited. This appears to be the case in regard to the powers of the Sea-Bed Disputes Chamber of the International Law of the Sea Tribunal under the Law of the Sea Convention (1982): see Article 109, and the discussion in Osieke, loc. cit. note 5 AJIL at pp. 247*ff*. Sometimes another non-judicial organ than the one exercising the power may have jurisdiction to review the validity of a decision of an organ: see the ILO Constitution. Further, the same organ may decide in the future that the exercise of power by the organ was not proper and take a different decision.

[20] 1962 ICJ Reports p. 151. What the Court and other judges said, though in relation to the UN, is applicable generally to other organizations. This case has been commented upon extensively, particularly insofar as it dealt with the question of *ultra vires*: e.g., Stoessinger, 'The World Court Advisory Opinion', in Waters (ed.), *The United Nations. International Organization and Administration* (1967) at pp. 242*ff*.; Verzijl, 'International Court of Justice, Certain Expenses of the United Nations (Article 17, paragraph 2, of the Charter)', 10 NILR (1963) p. 1; C. F. Amerasinghe, loc. cit. note 1 (IJIL).

for the maintenance of international peace and security and if, in accordance
with a mandate or authorization in such resolution, the Secretary-General incurs
financial obligations, these amounts must be presumed to constitute 'expenses
of the Organization'.[21]

As Judge Fitzmaurice explained in his separate opinion, what the organ
concerned was entitled to do was to determine the scope of its own
powers and the validity of their exercise.[22] The first important point
that emerges is that an act of an organ is presumed to be valid.[23] It may
be useful to recognize, though, as Judge Fitzmaurice did, that 'if the
invalidity of the expenditure was apparent on the face of the matter,
or too manifest to be open to reasonable doubt', such a presumption
would not arise.[24] The second point which may be deduced from the
absence of an adjudicating body with power to make final and binding
determinations is that:

It is no doubt true that any objection to a given exercise of powers, or to action
based on the presumed existence of certain powers, must be advanced in the
first instance in the organ concerned, and will be subject to a ruling by it, in
the form of a motion or resolution adopted by a majority vote.[25]

Clearly, members of an organ have the right to challenge the power
of the organ to make a decision because it is unconstitutional. It is then
that the organ will take the decision on the validity of its actions. There
have been several instances of such challenges in organs with consequent

---

[21] 1962 ICJ Reports at p. 168. In the Namibia Case Judge Fitzmaurice, dissenting, thought
that a non-judicial organ should not be empowered to take such a judicial decision:
1971 ICJ Reports at p. 298.

[22] 1962 ICJ Reports at p. 203. Judge Spender in his separate opinion confirmed the right
of an organ to determine its powers, in the first place, with the result that there may
be conflicts in interpretation between itself and other organs; and the right of an
organ to change the interpretation of its powers: ibid. at p. 197. There are many
examples of decisions in regard to the validity of the exercise of powers taken by the
organs exercising those powers, particularly in the ILO and the UN, discussed in
Osieke, loc. cit. note 5 BYIL p. 259, and Morgenstern, loc. cit. note 5. If such decisions
do not continue to be questioned, cadit quaestio.

[23] See also the Namibia Case, 1971 ICJ Reports at p. 22, where this position was affirmed.
Some doubt on this proposition was cast in the opinions of Judge Morelli, 1962 ICJ
Reports at p. 222 (separate), and Judge Winiarski, ibid. at p. 232 (dissenting), in the
Expenses Case. E. Lauterpacht agrees that there is a presumption of validity but that it
is a rebuttable one: loc. cit. note 5 at p. 117.

[24] 1962 ICJ Reports at pp. 204–5. This raises the question who decides this. It is suggested
that where there is a sizeable number of the members of the organization supporting
the validity of the decision there is no manifest clarity as to its invalidity.

[25] Ibid. at p. 203. Judge Bustamante, dissenting, agreed with this view: ibid. at pp. 296,
298 and 307.

decisions by the organs on the validity of their actions. Thus, in 1921 the French government raised in the International Labour Conference objections to the inclusion in the agenda of the Conference matters relating to agricultural labour and later to agricultural production. On both matters the conference decided that it was competent to deal with them. In 1949 the ICAO Council proposed to take certain action to fill vacancies on the Air Navigation Commission under Articles 54 and 56 of the Chicago Convention. The procedure proposed was objected to by some states, on the ground of legal propriety. After discussion a proposal was finally adopted by the vote of the Council. In 1971 the ICAO Assembly proposed to take a certain course of action to fill vacancies in the Council created by the amendment of Article 50(a) of the Chicago Convention. After considering a legal opinion some members still objected to the proposal on legal grounds. As a consequence an amended proposal was put to the Assembly.[26]

There are some consequences of the above position which, however, were not clearly drawn by the Court. Some of the judges who gave separate opinions drew these conclusions. It was said that a pronouncement by an organ that one of its acts was not *ultra vires* was not final and a disagreeing state may in the last resort not recognize the validity of the relevant act, though this right was explained as follows:

The problem is to determine what that right consists of and, more particularly, in what conditions it can be exercised. As indicated above, it can only be a right of last resort; for an unlimited right on the part of Member States to withhold contributions at will, on the basis of a mere claim that in their view the expenditures concerned had been improperly incurred, not only could speedily cause serious disruption, but would also give those Member States which, on the basis of the normal scales of apportionment, are major contributors, a degree of control and veto over the affairs of the United Nations which, equally, can never have been intended in the framing of the Charter to be exercised by these means, or Article 17, paragraph 2, would not be there.[27]

---

[26] Many examples, including the above, are discussed by Osieke, loc. cit. note 5 BYIL at pp. 262*ff.*, and loc. cit. note 5 ICLQ at pp. 5*ff.*

[27] 1962 ICJ Reports at p. 204. Judge Winiarski, dissenting, more or less agreed with this view when he said that a state could regard a resolution as a nullity only in an exceptional case: *ibid.* at p. 232. Judge Spender too admitted the right of a state to protest against an act which was *ultra vires*: *ibid.* at p. 196. Judge Bustamante, dissenting, also expressed the view that resolutions of organs of the United Nations were subject to review but did not refer to the right of last resort of states, although he did mention the usefulness of advisory opinions of the ICJ in determining whether an act was legal or not: *ibid.* at p. 304. Some states, e.g., the Soviet Union, continued

The right obviously arises after the objection to the relevant act has been raised and pronounced on by the organ concerned. But beyond this condition no clearer definition is given of the right of last resort. For instance, a question may arise as to whether it depends on the kind of majority by which the relevant organ decided that the objection was bad, apart from the fact that there may be difficulties in determining how meritorious are the legal arguments upon which the state in question founds its attitude. But the limitation is important; for it means that a state cannot lightly resolve to disregard a resolution of an organ which that organ has held to be valid after objections have been raised.

Judge Fitzmaurice gave an explanation for this right of last resort which, though not reflected in the Court's opinion, seems to be acceptable:

But the important practical point involved is how the validity or invalidity of any given expenditures can be determined, if controversy arises, seeing that as the Court points out, the Assembly is under no obligation to consult the Court, and, even if consulted, the Court can only render an opinion having a purely advisory character; and moreover, that there exists no other jurisdiction to which compulsory reference can be made and which can also render a binding decision.[28]

Judge Fitzmaurice did not attach any special importance to the role of advisory opinions as binding statements of the law in regard to the question of the legality of the acts of organs. The United Nations and other organizations with similar constitutions in this respect are not under an obligation to resort to advisory opinions of the International Court of Justice or other judicial bodies and, if they do, they are not under an obligation to accept them. It would seem then that Judge Bustamante was correct when he said, albeit in his dissenting opinion:

An advisory opinion, taking the place of judicial proceedings, is a method of voluntary recourse which, if only by way of elucidation, precedes the decision

---

not to contribute to the expenses of the UNEF and the ONUC even after the court's opinion was given and the conclusions were adopted by the GA, though they subsequently and recently have paid their dues. Many states in their presentations to the Court in the case took the view that they had a right of last resort not to recognize the validity of the relevant act: see Lauterpacht, loc. cit. note 5 at pp. 101ff.

[28] 1962 ICJ Reports at p. 202. The German Federal Constitutional Court in the *Maastricht Treaty Case* assumed that a right of last resort to reject an allegedly *ultra vires* decision existed: 33 ILM (1994) at p. 428.

which the Organization is called upon to give with regard to legal objections raised by Member States.[29]

Not all authorities agree that there is such a right of last resort.[30] The existence of the right was also questioned by Judge Morelli in his separate opinion in the *Expenses Case*.[31] The right has, however, been resorted to by some states in the past in international organizations.[32]

If there is a right of last resort, it is reasonable that it could be lost by acquiescence or by lapse of time.[33] Acquiescence is difficult to define. It may be too much to expect withdrawal from an organization as a means of objection but certainly an absence of protest would constitute acquiescence. Whether protest is sufficient is difficult to assert. Lapse of time may have an effect in two ways. It may preclude a party from objecting to the unlawfulness of the act or it may even, if rejected, operate to extend the powers of the organization to cover an initially *ultra vires* act.

The *IMCO Case*[34] and its sequel provide an interesting example of how the problem of *ultra vires* has been dealt with by an organization from the standpoint of adjudication and the action required of the organization as a result. The ICJ in its advisory opinion which was sought by IMCO merely decided that the action taken by the organization (through its Assembly) in electing its Maritime Safety Committee was *ultra vires* because it had misinterpreted the term 'largest ship-owning nations'. The ICJ for the first time held that an exercise of power by an organization was *ultra vires*.[35] The decision taken by the Assembly as a result of this opinion, which did not indicate what the consequences of the *ultra vires* act were, was that: (i) the Committee which was elected in 1959 should be dissolved; (ii) a new Committee should be constituted pursuant to the interpretation by the ICJ of the IMCO constitution; and (iii) the measures taken by the Committee during the period 1959 to 1961 were adopted and confirmed. There is here an acceptance of the ICJ's opinion as authoritative (though it is not binding) and an assumption

---

[29] 1962 ICJ Reports at p. 304.   [30] See Osieke, loc. cit. note 5 ICLQ at pp. 24–5.

[31] 1962 ICJ Reports at p. 225.   [32] See Ciobanu, op. cit. note 5 pp. 174–9.

[33] See Lauterpacht, loc. cit. note 5 at pp. 117*ff*. It would appear that some authorities do not fully agree that acquiescence is relevant: see Judge Nyholm in the *European Commission on the Danube Case*, PCIJ Series B No. 14 at p. 79 (separate opinion); Guggenheim, loc. cit. note 5 at p. 208.

[34] 1960 ICJ Reports p. 150. The case is discussed at length in Lauterpacht, loc. cit. note 5 at pp. 100–6.

[35] The PCIJ did this only in one case: the *Competence of the ILO to Regulate Agricultural Production Case*, PCIJ Series B No. 3.

that the result of the *ultra vires* act was to nullify the election, which required that the acts of the Committee be retroactively validated.[36] The solution adopted was not reached without some discussion and disagreement in the Assembly. There were questions as to the term of office of the Committee, whether and how there should be new elections for the whole or part of the Committee, and how the remaining six members who were not in the group composed by the largest ship-owning nations should be treated. However, in the outcome fresh elections for the whole Committee were held, the acts of the previous Committee were validated and the period of office of the new Committee was fixed at four years and not for the remainder of the period of office of the previous Committee.

First, there are certain inconsistencies[37] in the action taken by the IMCO Assembly but the solution must be regarded as pragmatic and as being more consistent with an understanding that the consequence of the misuse of power was nullity of the original act which made it void rather than voidable. Second, it is encouraging that the opinion of the ICJ was adopted and followed. Third, the manner in which the request for adjudication was framed and the resulting opinion left no alternative for the organization but, apart from adopting the opinion, to formulate some kind of plan of action as a solution.

The absence of compulsory judicial review, such as exists in the EU and generally in the internal international law of organizations relating to employment relations, creates a situation that is far from ideal.[38] In the result there is probably (i) a strong presumption of validity of acts of organs, (ii) a residual right of members or other states to protest in the face of this presumption, and (iii) what may be an impasse, if the organ itself or a supervisory organ that has jurisdiction refuses to annul the decision and the protesting states continue to contest the validity of the decision. As in the aftermath of the *Expenses Case*, in spite of a finding of legality by the ICJ and the acceptance of that decision by the GA, states

---

[36] E. Lauterpacht is not in complete agreement with the latter part of this interpretation of the effect of the resolution: loc. cit. note 5 at p. 105.

[37] A major inconsistency was that the statistics used for ascertaining the largest ship-owning nations were those applicable at the time of the election of the original Committee, while the Committee was given a tenure of a full four years.

[38] For reactions to this situation, see Lauterpacht, loc. cit. note 5 at pp. 115–17; Osieke, loc. cit. note 5 BYIL at pp. 279–80; Morgenstern, loc. cit. note 5 at pp. 253*ff*. The resolution of the Institut de droit international was rather imprecise and vague: 47-II AIDI (1957) at p. 488. See also the different conclusion of Wengler in his report: 45-I AIDI (1954) at p. 266.

which disagree with the finding of nullity may continue to protest and not accept the original decision of the organization, and there does not seem to be much that can be done about it.

The content of the doctrine of *ultra vires*

Just as there are problems created by the absence of a compulsory adjudicatory review system in the law of international institutions for the acts of organs outside the field of employment relations and possibly, in certain situations, in national legal relationships, there are also problems in defining the exact scope of the doctrine of *ultra vires*, particularly the consequences of an *ultra vires* act. It should be noted that in most cases where the decision or possible decisions of organs have been questioned (outside the field of employment relations and national law), it has been found, whether by the organ itself, a supervisory organ or an adjudicatory court or tribunal, that the act of the organization was not *ultra vires*.[39]

As far as vitiating elements go, there has been no dispute in the jurisprudence that they can be both substantive and procedural. They may relate to the constitutions of organizations or to subsidiary legislation. They may also arise from the violation of applicable general principles of law or other rules deriving from governing sources of law.[40]

IATs have developed a highly sophisticated and organized law relating to the validity and invalidity of acts of organizations in employment relations and the consequences of non-observance of the law.[41] Courts and

[39] See the decisions discussed in connection with interpretation of constitutions in Chapter 3 above; Osieke, loc. cit. note 5 at pp. 262ff., on the practice of the ILO; Morgenstern, loc. cit. note 5 *passim*. The two opinions of international courts in which acts have been found not to be *ultra vires* are the *Competence of the ILO to Regulate Agricultural Production Case*, PCIJ Series B No. 3, and the *IMCO Case*, 1960 ICJ Reports p. 150. It has been said that what constitutes an *ultra vires* act has never been incontrovertibly answered: Alvarez, 'Legal Remedies and the United Nations A La Carte Problem', 12 Michigan JIL (1991) at p. 260.

[40] See by implication the *ICAO Council Case*, 1972 ICJ Reports p. 46, where the alleged violation of general principles of due process in the taking of a quasi-judicial decision was one of the issues raised. See also for international administrative law: C. F. Amerasinghe, *The Law of the International Civil Service* (1994) vols. 1 and 2, *passim*.

[41] The law applied by IATs is too vast and complicated for detailed discussion here. In any case I have dealt with the subject in *The Law of the International Civil Service* to which readers are referred (particularly vol. 1). The law developed has been influenced to a great extent by French administrative law (as opposed to the common law which, however, is compatible in many areas with the international administrative law that has emerged). On remedies see particularly C. F. Amerasinghe, *ibid.* vol. 1 chapters 26–31. See also below Chapter 9.

tribunals have found that an abuse of power or misuse of authority may arise for substantive or procedural reasons and theoretically that any act of any organ could be pronounced on, if the statute of the IAT concerned gives it jurisdiction to do so or does not preclude it from doing so. The sources of the internal law are many, including the constitutions of organizations, other international law sources, written internal laws of the organization and general principles of law. In regard also to the effect of a decision tainted by irregularities, the IATs have, sometimes because of specific provisions in their statutes but more often as a result of interpretation and implied powers, resorted to granting many kinds of remedies, not limited to declaring the decision or decisions void or voidable. They have devised methods of even permitting decisions to stand while granting monetary compensation, on the basis that certain kinds of irregularities do not result in the nullity of the decision or that the situation is such that an otherwise invalid decision should not be declared null and void because of the circumstances of the case which make it impractical or undesirable that the decision be so declared.

National courts so far have tended to adopt the simple technique of regarding *ultra vires* decisions as invalid. In its judgment of 12 October 1993 in the *Maastricht Treaty Case*[42] the German Constitutional Court made it clear that the Treaty left room for jurisdictional conflicts without giving the EU exclusive competence to decide on the validity of the exercise of its powers. This was an acknowledgment that the EU could act *ultra vires* with the right being given to Germany as a member state to question the legal validity of its acts and the possibility that these acts could be invalid.[43] Though the court looked at the matter from a national constitutional perspective, it was nonetheless a recognition that *ultra vires* acts could be invalid. International law itself, on the other hand, does not seem to have a developed law relating to the content and effects of the doctrine of *ultra vires*. One reason for this is that in almost all cases international courts, like national courts and tribunals, have found the contested acts *intra vires*, and in the two cases in which the PCIJ and the ICJ have found the acts to be *ultra vires* the invalidity has been due to clear non-observance of substantive provisions of the constitutional law of the organizations concerned, the issues raised being as to the interpretation of that law. In those cases the Courts merely declared what the law required and did not pronounce on the consequences of the illegality. In the case decided by the PCIJ, as in the case decided

---

[42] 33 ILM (1994) p. 338.   [43] *Ibid.* at p. 428.

by the ICJ, the organization appears to have acted subsequently on the understanding that the acts were a nullity, there being no indication that voidability or other alternatives were accepted by the organizations as possible results.

It remains to be seen how far other international bodies than IATs will borrow the principles of international administrative law. There seems to be some justification in applying the principle, for instance, that some irregularities may not invalidate an act because they are not serious enough, while at the same time the possibility of awarding compensation in lieu of declaring an act null and void may not always be a feasible or desirable option. In any case, there are many aspects of international administrative law that may not be applied by analogy to other areas of international institutional law.

Where a constituent instrument deals with review and the effects of *ultra vires* acts, these provisions will govern. The treaties establishing the European Communities which, as has been seen, gave the CJEC jurisdiction to supervise the acts of the Council and the Commission state the grounds on which the jurisdiction may be invoked. These are very wide and cover lack of jurisdiction, substantial violations of basic procedural rules, infringements of the treaties or of any rule of law relating to effect being given to them or of misuse of powers.[44] But, generally, there are no conventional rules which apply to the legal validity of the acts of organs. Further, there is no clear indication generally in instruments which provide for supervision what is the effect, in terms of voidness or voidability, of invalidity.[45]

In the jurisprudence of international courts and tribunals other than IATs, there are certain principles relating to the legal consequences of *ultra vires* action (as contrasted with the establishment of an excess of power) to which reference has been made. One instance of this is the discussion of the problem of *ultra vires* acts in the *Expenses Case*. One of the rules that the ICJ stated in its reasoning was that an organization may be bound, as to third parties, by the *ultra vires* act of an organ (or agent of an organ or the organization) provided the act is not *ultra vires* the organization:

If it is agreed that the action in question is within the scope of the functions of the Organization but it is alleged that it has been initiated or carried out in

---

[44] See Article 173 of the EEC Treaty; Article 33 of the ECSC Treaty.
[45] See the discussion of the validity of alleged acts of the Council and Assembly of ICAO in Osieke, loc. cit. note 5 ICLQ at pp. 20*ff.* Lauterpacht, loc. cit. note 5 at pp. 96*ff.*, discusses the effects of illegal acts of the EC. See also Osieke, loc. cit. note 5 AJIL at pp. 244*ff.*

a manner not in conformity with the division of functions among the several organs which the Charter prescribes, one moves to the internal plane, to the internal structure of the Organization. If the action was taken by the wrong organ, it was irregular as a matter of that internal structure, but this would not necessarily mean that the expense incurred was not an expense of the Organization. Both national and international law contemplate cases in which the body corporate or politic may be bound, as to third parties, by an *ultra vires* act of an agent.[46]

This rule does not state the circumstances in which an organization would be bound in respect of third parties by an *ultra vires* act of an agent. But the Court demonstrated how the rule operated in relation to the expenses of the United Nations. It is clear also that there are circumstances in which an organization may not be bound by an *ultra vires* act of an agent *vis-à-vis* third parties. One of the circumstances is where the act is also *ultra vires* the organization.

There were some other principles, partly supplementary to the above rule, which could be culled, mainly from the separate opinion of Judge Morelli,[47] and which merit acceptance, although the Court did not adopt them. These were that: (i) an act of an agent or organ which conforms with all the conditions of the legal act is *intra vires* and is valid; (ii) an act of an agent or organ which does not conform with the conditions of the legal act so as to give rise to an *essential* defect alone is *ultra vires* and invalid; and (iii) an act of an agent or organ which does not conform with the conditions of the legal act but not so as to give rise to an essential defect is probably not *ultra vires* and invalid.

It would appear that there is a good explanation for these principles.[48] In any legal system the problem of the validity of legal acts consists of

---

[46] 1962 ICJ Reports at p. 168. Judge Winiarski disagreed with the Court on this issue: 'The Charter has set forth the purposes of the United Nations in very wide, and for that reason too indefinite, terms. But – apart from the resources, including the financial resources, of the Organization – it does not follow, far from it, that the Organization is entitled to seek to achieve those purposes by no matter what means. The fact that an organ of the United Nations is seeking to achieve one of those purposes does not suffice to render its action lawful': *ibid*. at p. 230. The aspects of the case discussed in the following pages were first addressed in C. F. Amerasinghe, loc. cit. note 5 IJIL at pp. 211*ff*.

[47] 1962 ICJ Reports at p. 221.

[48] See Judge Morelli: *ibid*. at pp. 221*ff*. It may be noted that Article 46 of the Vienna Convention on the Law of Treaties Between States and International Organizations or between International Organizations confirms that third parties are normally entitled to assume that treaties entered into with an international organization are valid and binding, notwithstanding *ultra vires* claims. Thus, an organization 'may not invoke the fact that its consent to be bound by a treaty has been expressed in violation of the rules of the organization regarding competence to conclude treaties as invalidating its

reconciling the requirement of *legality* with that of *certainty*. The former requirement means the denial of any value to an act not in conformity with the legal rule while the latter would be seriously jeopardized if the validity of a legal act were at all times open to challenge on the ground of its non-conformity with the legal rule. In certain national systems (especially of the European continent), in regard to the acts of public administrative authorities, there are a number of cases in which non-conformity with the legal rule constitutes a mere irregularity having no effect on the validity of the act while there are some more serious cases where such lack of conformity entails the invalidity of the act. Such invalidity might well constitute an *absolute nullity* operating *ipso iure* so that the act which it affects produces no legal effects. But these cases were of an exceptional character. In general invalidity of acts involve the voidability of those acts. This means that the act produces all its effects as long as it is not annulled by the competent organ. Thus the invalidity of the act depends on how effective recourse is to the competent organ. In the case of international organizations, however, there is nothing comparable to the remedies existing in national law in connection with administrative acts. Hence, the concept of voidability cannot be applied to the acts of international organizations. The act had to be either an *absolute nullity* or *fully valid*. The problem, then, is to determine in what cases such acts are an absolute nullity. This is a question of 'construction of the rules determining the conditions for a legal act which are of the nature of absolute requirements, that is to say where failure to satisfy the condition constitutes an essential defect involving the invalidity of the act'.[49] Since there is no such category as voidable acts, the same extension cannot be given to the invalidity of acts in international law as can be given under national law, by ignoring the distinction between acts that are voidable and absolutely null and regarding both categories as one under international law. This would lead to very serious consequences for the *certainty* of legal situations arising from the acts of organizations. For the effectiveness of such acts would be laid open to perpetual uncertainty because of the lack of means by which the need for certainty was satisfied in connection with administrative acts under national law. This means that there are a large number of cases where non-conformity with the legal rule has to be regarded as a mere irregularity not affecting the

---

consent unless that violation was manifest and concerned a rule of fundamental importance' (Article 46(2)).

[49] Judge Morelli: *ibid.* at p. 223.

validity of the act. It is only in specially serious cases that the act of an organization should be regarded as invalid such as where a resolution has not obtained the required majority or a resolution is vitiated by a manifest *excès de pouvoir* (e.g., in particular, a resolution the subject of which has nothing to do with the purposes of the organization). Where there has been a violation of the rules relating to competence, however, the defect is not so serious that absolute nullity is involved. In national law the result would have been voidability but in international law the irregularity does not affect the validity of the act at all.

This explanation which was proposed by Judge Morelli does not deal with the question what is an essential defect, though some examples of what he had in mind were given. It is, however, an elaborate discussion of some aspects of the problem of *ultra vires* in international institutional law and provides a basis for the deduction of the principles stated above. It is not clear whether the Court would have agreed with that deduction in its entirety.[50] What is clear is that these principles cannot be applied to render an act of an organ and the organization invalid, where such act is valid because it is *intra vires* the organization, though *ultra vires* the particular organ, as mentioned above. It is also clear, however, that there may be other situations of *ultra vires* action than this situation, where the act would not be invalid. The two salient features of the principles being discussed are that: (i) the theory of voidability is rejected in relation to international organizations (which seems to be in conformity with what the Assembly of the IMCO did after the decision of the ICJ in the *IMCO Case*);[51] and (ii) the concept of an 'essential defect' modifies an absolute

---

[50] The Court gave a somewhat different reason for finding that the acts of the UN in the case were not *ultra vires*. Judge Bustamante who dissented from the Court's opinion did not agree with the distinction between essential and non-essential defects because he was of the view that for a resolution to be valid there must be complete formal as well as substantive or intrinsic validity: *ibid.* at p. 290. Judge Fitzmaurice, it would seem, in his separate opinion did not agree that, in regard to 'expenses' of the organization, at any rate, there could be justifiable expenses unless they were made pursuant to a recommendation of the General Assembly that was in absolute conformity with the provisions of the Charter, while he did not elaborate a general theory of *ultra vires*, as Judge Morelli did: *ibid.* at p. 214.

[51] It is significant that Article 7(3) of the ILO Constitution states that an appeal against the declaration of the Governing Body as to which members of the ILO are of chief industrial importance 'shall not suspend the application of the declaration until such time as the Conference decides the appeal'. Thus, legal effect will be attributed to actions done on the basis of the declaration before the determination of invalidity by the Conference in a case where the declaration is determined to be invalid. Similar considerations apply to Article 86 of the Chicago Convention in regard to decisions of the ICAO Council.

theory of conformity with the conditions of a legal act, possibly to a greater extent than the narrow principle applied by the Court in the *Expenses Case*.[52]

The impact of *ius cogens* (peremptory norms of international law) on the powers of organizations is also of some importance. It is a well-established principle of treaty law that provisions of a treaty that contravene *ius cogens* are invalid.[53] Thus, agreement cannot override *ius cogens*. The principle would apply to provisions incorporated in the constitution of an international organization. Similarly, it would apply to decisions taken by virtue of or under the constitution by the organization. Apart from the limitations on powers which are written into the constitution of an organization or the limitations implicit in the express or implied grant of powers, it follows that an organization cannot exercise its powers so as to violate *ius cogens*, even though a constitution may permit or leave room for such an exercise. A good example is a resolution which discriminates in its content on the basis of race or religion. If such a resolution were to be adopted by an organization it would be *ultra vires* the organization because of substantive irregularity, regardless of how the terms of the constitution may be interpreted and whether there is or is not a prohibition against such conduct in the constitution.

The question of procedural defects requires some attention. These may arise, for example, where decisions are adopted by a method of voting other than that prescribed in the rules, as when secret ballots or a record vote are not used where they should be, when a committee is not appointed whose recommendation is required for a decision of a superior organ or when a decision is adopted by a smaller majority than that laid down in the governing rules. As was pointed out by Judge Morelli in the *Expenses Case*, irregularities must be essential in order to have an effect. In the *ICAO Council Case* the issue of the effect of procedural irregularities was specifically raised. The ICJ remarked that:

The Court however does not deem it necessary or even appropriate to go into this matter, particularly as the alleged irregularities do not prejudice in any fundamental way the requirements of a just procedure. The Court's task in the

[52] Essential requirements are not necessarily synonymous with substantive conditions, as non-essential requirements are not necessarily synonymous with procedural conditions. There may be some procedural conditions which are essential, as there may be some substantive conditions that are non-essential.

[53] See Article 53 of the 1969 Vienna Convention on the Law of Treaties.

present proceedings is to give a ruling as to whether the Council has jurisdiction in the case. This is an objective question of law, the answer to which cannot depend on what occurred before the Council. Since the Court holds that the Council did and does have jurisdiction, then if there were in fact procedural irregularities, the position would be that the Council would have reached the right conclusion in the wrong way. Nevertheless it would have reached the right conclusion. If, on the other hand, the Court had held that there was and is no jurisdiction, then even in the absence of any irregularities, the Council's decision to assume it would have stood reversed.[54]

Thus, generally procedural defects would not result in the invalidity of a decision, unless they result in the adoption of a wrong decision or a miscarriage of justice. As was said by Judge Dillard in his Separate Opinion in the *ICAO Council Case* in regard to adjudicatory decisions of the ICAO Council:

It is, of course, not impossible to contemplate a situation of gross abuse of procedural requirements leading to a miscarriage of justice. In such a situation the validity of the decision adopted may be legitimately challenged on appeal.[55]

What amounts to a wrong decision or a miscarriage of justice would depend on the specific circumstances of each case. An example of an essential procedural defect is when the rules require a two-thirds majority and a decision is adopted by a simple majority which violates the constitutional rights of the minority.

Finally, a word needs to be said about the doctrine of *ultra vires* in regard to the agreements, contracts and tortious acts of organizations. In this connection the law of state responsibility may provide some useful analogies. Thus, the validity of agreements and contracts would depend also on the scope of apparent authority of the organ, servant or agent concluding them, even though the actual exercise of power may be outside the actual authority granted. Moreover, tortious liability

---

[54] 1972 ICJ Reports at pp. 69–70. On procedural defects see, e.g., Fawcett, *'Détournement de Pouvoir* by International Organizations', 33 BYIL (1957) p. 311; Conforti, 'The Legal Effect of Non-Compliance with Rules of Procedure in the UN General Assembly and Security Council', 63 AJIL (1969) p. 479; Morgenstern, loc. cit. note 5; Osieke, loc. cit. note 5 BYIL; Osieke, 'The Exercise of the Judicial Function with Respect to the International Labour Organization', 47 BYIL (1974–5) p. 315; Osieke, loc. cit. note 5 ICLQ; Osieke loc. cit. note 5 AJIL.

[55] 1972 ICJ Reports at p. 100. See also the separate opinion of Judge Jiménez de Aréchaga: *ibid.* at p. 153.

of the organization in respect of acts of servants, agents and independent contractors would depend on the imputability or attribution of such acts, which could occur, even though they are outside the scope of actual authority, because they are within the scope of apparent authority.[56]

---

[56] See also Chapter 9 below on this point. For the law relating to imputability in the law of state responsibility see, e.g., Meron, 'International Responsibility of States for Unauthorized Acts of their Officials', 33 BYIL (1957) p. 85; C. F. Amerasinghe, *State Responsibility for Injuries to Aliens* (1967) pp. 51*ff.*; and now Chapter II (Arts. 4–11) of the ILC's Draft Articles on Responsibility of States for Internationally Wrongful Acts: *Report of the International Law Commission to the General Assembly 2001*, UN Doc. A/56/10, pp. 44*ff.*, and commentary, pp. 80*ff.*

8   Judicial organs

This chapter deals *briefly* with judicial institutions (organs or bodies) of the international legal system which are not national judicial bodies, concentrating on some of them, as described below. Only some of the more important aspects of relevant institutions will be discussed. This is not meant to be an exhaustive consideration of such institutions.[1] It must be remembered that, in respect of organs, the concern in this treatise, because of its subject matter, is with organs *of* international organizations, even though much, at least, of what is said may be true of all international judicial bodies and even national judicial bodies.

Forms of organs

Two forms of such judicial institutions of a strictly and essentially judicial character have evolved: (i) those which by and large have an entirely separate status, whether created by the constitution of an international organization or otherwise; and (ii) those which, though in principle independent, are created as organs proper *of* international organizations by the constitution of an international organization or by other organs of international organizations.

The first category includes:

(a) judicial institutions such as the PCIJ, created by a separate statute;
(b) judicial institutions such as the ECtHR and the IACtHR, created by human rights conventions but *connected* to, while not being described

---

[1] If a *full* examination of the subject of international judicial organs, which are more appropriately called 'institutions' as a genre, rather than organs, were to be made, it should be made in a separate work devoted to the subject.

in such conventions as, organs of the relevant organizations, namely the Council of Europe and the OAS, respectively;

(c) the International Tribunal for the Law of the Sea (ITLOS), created by the UN Law of the Sea Convention (UNCLOS) of 1982, and international arbitral tribunals, such as the Iran–US Claims Tribunal, established under an individual international agreement.

All these are not organs proper of international organizations, though they are in fact judicial institutions as such. They are also not described as organs of international organizations. Except for the PCIJ, they are characterized by the very limited jurisdiction which they enjoy.

To this first category also belong, as a fourth group, such judicial institutions as the *ICJ* and CJEC, set up respectively by the UN Charter and the Treaties Establishing the European Communities, which, while being courts of 'limited' jurisdiction (*juridiction d'attribution*), have a wide competence over matters of international law and the law respectively of the UN and of the EU. They are placed in a separate group because they may be distinguished from the institutions in groups (a) to (c) above on account of various characteristics, but principally because they were established by international agreements which primarily created public international organizations. They may or may not be *organs of* international organizations. The first is described in the relevant documents as such an organ, while the second is not. They are both equally judicial institutions, however.[2]

In spite of being an *organ of* the UN, the *ICJ* occupies a special position in relation to the other five principal organs of the UN, into whose hierarchical structure it is not integrated. This position resembles the legal status of the PCIJ, which was established outside the framework of the LN. The ICJ is an independent court, deciding cases in its own name, rather than in the name of the UN. In this respect it differs from the SC, whose decisions, also directly binding on states, are made on the basis of an express ascription of power under Article 24 of the Charter

---

[2] Two observations may be made here. First, the ICJ, in one sense, has a wider jurisdiction than the CJEC, although they are both courts of 'limited' jurisdiction as opposed to courts of 'general' jurisdiction (*juridiction de droit commun*), both terms being used in a technical sense. Secondly there arises the question, which is not discussed here, whether the ICJ, which is like the PCIJ, should at all be described in the UN Charter as a principal organ of the UN, though it may have been created by the UN Charter which established the UN. In addition, while the ICJ is described here as having a 'wider' jurisdiction, this is a relative description. The ICJ has, perhaps, in a sense the widest jurisdiction among tribunals in the international legal system.

and are, thus, those of the UN as a whole. The ICJ's capacity to act is limited to the fulfilment of its functions. It decides disputes between states parties to the Statute, pursuant to Article 35 of the Statute, but has jurisdiction to render advisory opinions, pursuant to Article 65, to the UN or any organization authorized to request such opinions.[3]

The basic provisions relating to the constitution of the *CJEC*[4] and the legal remedies it may dispense were contained in the three constituent treaties of the EU, in each of which a section devoted to the CJEC followed sections relating to the other main institutions. In the EEC Treaty, the relevant provisions were to be found in Articles 164–188. Detailed rules concerning the structure and functioning of the CJEC were embodied in three separate Protocols to the Statute of the CJEC annexed to each of the treaties. Apart from a few details, the provisions of these Protocols were identical. According to Article 4 of the EEC Treaty, the CJEC was one of the four main institutions of the Community, alongside the Assembly, the Council and the Commission, called upon to carry out in its own field 'the tasks entrusted to the Community'. According to these general provisions, the CJEC has considered its task to be not only that of settling disputes and implementing Community law proper, but also that of ensuring observance of the law in its broadest sense. Accordingly, the CJEC has taken an open approach to the question of the sources of the law governing its functions, deriving its inspiration broadly, i.e., not only from the constituent treaty and acts of so-called 'secondary Community legislation' (regulations, directives and decisions), but also from the common standards of the law of member states, namely general principles of law, and also international law, whenever external relations are involved.[5]

Judicial institutions of the kind in this first category are not considered here, as they are either not strictly organs *of* international

---

[3] On the ICJ, see particularly Amerasinghe, *Jurisdiction of International Tribunals* (2003) Chapters 12 and 13, for the ICJ's contentious and advisory jurisdiction respectively; Rosenne, *The Law and Practice of the International Court 1920–1996* (1997); Schwebel, 'Relations between the International Court of Justice and the United Nations', in Bardonnet, Combacau, Dupuy and Weil (eds.), *Le droit international au service de la paix, de la justice et du développement: Melanges Michel Virally* (1991) p. 431.

[4] For the CJEC, see particularly Brown and Kennedy, *Brown and Jacobs' The Court of Justice of the European Communities* (1994); and Lasok and Bridge, *Law and Institutions of the European Communities* (1998) pp. 281ff.

[5] The EU Treaty of 1997 (TEU) did not change the situation described above: see, *inter alia*, Amerasinghe, note 3 p. 811, for the effect of the EU Treaty on the earlier treaties and their protocols.

organizations or, if they are (this is the case with the ICJ, which is the only known example of this), are of a special kind.[6] The ICJ is characterized here as being of a special kind, simply because, though it is described as a 'principal organ of' the UN in the Charter, this is clearly not an appropriate description of it, considering, *inter alia*, its nature and characteristics as an international judicial institution.[7]

In the second category are judicial institutions or bodies which are *organs proper of* international organizations, whether they are created by constitutions of organizations or by decisions of other organs of international organizations. IATs, the ICTY and the ICTR are examples, and possibly the only current examples, of such judicial organs.

Most international organizations have either their own internal courts or use the internal courts of other organizations to settle employment disputes judicially. Almost all organizations are not expressly authorized by their constitutions to establish or use such tribunals (courts) but by implication constitutional texts have been interpreted to permit such an exercise of power by institutions. For example, the ICJ held that the GA had the power to establish the UNAT. Other organizations have established their own or use other IATs.[8] IATs are intended to be of a more or less permanent character and are generally so.

There are some important points, formal though they may be, to be noted. First, all IATs, being in essence and genuinely judicial organs, are *courts* in the true sense of the word,[9] and this is so, even though their constituent instruments may refer to them as tribunals rather than as courts.[10] The fact that they have been established by a decision taken

---

[6] The ICJ needs to be considered in a separate work: see at present, e.g., Rosenne, note 3; and Amerasinghe, note 3.

[7] The *Effect of Awards Case*, 1954 ICJ Reports at p. 57.

[8] See Amerasinghe, *The Law of the International Civil Service* (1994) vol. I, pp. 49ff.

[9] In the *Effect of Awards Case*, the ICJ made it quite clear that the UNAT was a *judicial* organ, which meant that it was a court: 1954 ICJ Reports, particularly at pp. 56–7 and 61. There has been no doubt that IATs are *judicial* organs. The LNT, the first IAT to be established on a permanent basis, was always acknowledged to be a *judicial* organ (court). On IATs as *judicial* organs *per se*, see Amerasinghe, note 8 vol. I, pp. 31–48; and Amerasinghe, 'The World Bank Administrative Tribunal', 31 ICLQ (1982) at pp. 748–53.

[10] In public international law, in practice the terms 'court' and 'tribunal' are used without essential difference in meaning. The reason why the point made here is being made is to avoid misunderstanding which may arise both as a result of the different nomenclature and as a result of the nature of the dispute settlement, indeed, in any legal system but especially in the public international legal system. This latter aspect is discussed here later.

by another organ of the international organization concerned does not make a difference. Indeed, if the ICTY and ICTR, created in the same manner, are courts, which is not the term used in their constituent instruments for them, there is no reason to differentiate between them and IATs as far as their nature is concerned, nor by the same token should there be reason to differentiate in respect of nomenclature, although this has been done generally.

The use of the term 'tribunal', it must be emphasized, does not negate the fact that the dispute settlement involved in both relates only to *disputes* which are *legal* and which therefore must as a rule be determined solely by the application of *norms* which are *legal*.[11]

If internal evidence, which in fact is not required, is sought of their judicial nature in the constituent instruments of the IATs – and this has never been really denied – there is such evidence. For example, the statutes of many IATs refer to their decisions as 'judgments',[12] which can only emanate from judicial organs. The use of such terms as 'jurisdiction' and 'competence' (*compétence*) or 'competent' (*compétent*) in IAT constituent instruments, when considered with other internal evidence,

---

[11] It is acknowledged that the term 'tribunal' and 'court' are synonymous in essence in public international law. A difference not of the essence may originally perhaps have been made between (i) the manner in which the bench was constituted (a tribunal being constituted by choice of the parties, and a court not by such choice but by some other designated means), and (ii) the *ad hoc* or permanent nature of the judicial organ. In any case, the difference is now not important in terms of essentials nor does usage conform to the postulated original usage. However, while the latter point remains true, it may be the case that, if a bench is constituted by choice of the parties, the judicial organ is always described as a tribunal and not as a court. Thus, arbitral bodies are always described as tribunals.

Arbitration, in public international law, as a method of dispute settlement, always essentially and without exception not only is concerned with *legal* disputes but must as a rule be based solely on the application of legal norms, as the text above states in regard to the relevant kind of dispute settlement. Conciliation and other methods of settlement are not required to be based on the application of legal norms. This is an important distinction which is of the essence.

Another point that needs to be noted is that, although as a rule dispute settlement, whether by tribunals or courts, is by the application of legal norms, an *ex aequo et bono* method of settlement may be used but this only in any case and at least with the agreement of the parties. This does not make a difference as far as what is said in the text above goes.

[12] See, e.g., the UNAT Statute, Articles 2(1) and 12(2)–(5), in UN Doc. A/C.6/55/L.18 at pp. 5–6; the ILOAT Statute, Article VI, in Amerasinghe (ed.), *Documents on International Administrative Tribunals* (1985) pp. 32–3; the WBAT Statute (1995), Articles II(1) and XI, in WBAT Doc. Rules/Rev.2 at p. 4; the IDBAT Statute, Article VIII(2)–(4), in Amerasinghe (ed.), *Documents* pp. 66–7; the OASAT Statute, Article VIII(2)–(4), in Amerasinghe (ed.), *ibid.* p. 87; and the LNT Statute, Article VI, in Amerasinghe (ed.), *ibid.* p. 179.

is also significant as an indication of their judicial nature.[13] The use of the term 'judges' to describe the members of an IAT bench is also significant.[14]

Secondly, IATs have been by implication in general regarded, traditionally, it seems, as 'internal' courts of international organizations, perhaps ever since the establishment in 1927 of the LNT, the earliest known IAT, and certainly in recent years.[15] However, they are also not only *international* courts but, as courts,[16] they are in essence no different from any other international court. The fact that their jurisdiction is over employment disputes between staff of one kind or another (and pensioners, perhaps) and organizations does not change their nature either as a *court* (of law) or an international one. They are simply courts of limited jurisdiction.

Thirdly, though the judges of IATs are called 'members' of the court or tribunal in many constituent instruments of IATs,[17] this has no significance for the determination of their nature as being judicial. It is clear that the functions of those on the bench of IATs are judicial, entirely because IATs are purely judicial organs or bodies, as has never been

---

[13] See, e.g., the UNAT Statute, Article 2(1), note 12 p. 2; the WBAT Statute, Article II(1), note 12 p. 1; the COE Statute, Article 4, in Amerasinghe (ed.), *ibid.* p. 122; the NATOAB Statute, Article 4.2, in Amerasinghe (ed.), *ibid.* p. 130; and the LNT Statute, Article II(2) and (4), in Amerasinghe (ed.), *ibid.* pp. 7 and 8.

[14] This usage is not universal. On the issue of 'judges', see below.

[15] This implication arises clearly, even when IATs may not expressly be referred to as internal courts, in circumstances in which references are made to the *internal* law of an international organization as being the applicable law. While there may be many sources of this international law (which is a part of public international law), it is correct to state that the internal law is the governing law. The logic, undoubtedly inescapable, is that because they apply internal law IATs are internal courts: see the extensive discussion in Amerasinghe, note 8 vol. I, pp. 9*ff.* and *passim*. In fact, and in spite of the above logic, the explicit description of IATs as internal courts is rarely found.

[16] This was categorically stated by the WBAT in *de Merode*, WBAT Reports [1981], Decision No. 1 at p. 19: 'The Tribunal, which is an *international* tribunal, considers that its task is to decide internal disputes between the Bank and its staff within the organized legal system of the World Bank and that it must apply the internal law of the Bank as the law governing the conditions of employment.' Emphasis added. The description '*International* Administrative Tribunal' is also significant in this regard.

[17] See, e.g., the constituent instruments of many IATs which are included in Amerasinghe (ed.), note 12; the current Statute of the WBAT, Article IV, WBAT Doc. Rules/Rev.2 at p. 2; and the current Statute of the UNAT, Article 3, UN Doc. A/C.6/55/L.18 at p. 3. Notable exceptions in which the judges are called 'judges' include the ILOAT Statute, Article III, in Amerasinghe (ed.), note 12 p. 32; and, earlier, the LNT Statute, Article III, in Amerasinghe (ed.), *ibid.* p. 178.

doubted and has been shown above in this chapter. The logical and rational deduction is that in truth those on the bench of IATs are judges in the real sense of the word, whatever the terminology used to describe them.[18]

The ICTY and the ICTR are international criminal courts with limited jurisdiction over certain international crimes described in the common usage as violations of international humanitarian law. These are *ad hoc* courts established to deal with specific situational disputes relating to international crimes committed in connection with particular situations (in broad terms, war situations) in the former Yugoslavia and Rwanda. The two courts, which are called tribunals in their constituent instruments, though they are in essence and genuinely courts, were established by resolutions of the SC[19] acting under Chapter VII of the UN Charter which gives the SC power to make resolutions which, as a result of the operation of Article 25 of the UN Charter, are decisions binding on the member states of the UN.[20]

It is judicial organs such as these three in the second category that are the subject of central discussion in this chapter. There is an obvious justification for this. The present work is concerned with the institutional law of international organizations. Thus, it is appropriate and necessary to discuss only judicial institutions which are also strictly organs *of* international organizations.

There is a third category, consisting of organs of international organizations which, though not judicial organs as such, perform functions which are described as 'quasi-judicial', for want of a better term. These functions share a judicial nature in a real sense. Such organs are the former ECHR and the IACHR. They are not the subject of consideration

---

[18] It should be noted that the CSAT Statute uses the term 'members' to describe those on the bench. It is clear from the Statute that the tribunal is intended to perform entirely judicial functions and is a purely judicial organ, even though it has jurisdiction over matters outside those connected with organizational employment. Hence, those on the bench are unquestionably judges. Because the CSAT is a truly judicial body, that it is named an 'arbitral tribunal' rather than an 'administrative tribunal' is irrelevant.

[19] SC Rs. 827 of 25 May 1993 (Yugoslavia) and SC Rs. 955 of 8 November 1994 (Rwanda). The judges of these courts are rightly called 'judges' in their Statutes. .

[20] There has been some writing on these tribunals: see, e.g., Amerasinghe, note 3 *passim*; O'Brien, 'The International Tribunal for Violations of International Humanitarian Law in the Former Yugoslavia', 87 AJIL (1993) at p. 639; Szasz, 'The Proposed War Crimes Tribunal for Yugoslavia', 25 NYUJIL (1993) at p. 405; Morris and Scharf, *An Insider's Guide to the International Criminal Tribunal for the Former Yugoslavia* (2 vols., 1995); and Alchavan, 'The International Criminal Tribunal for Rwanda: The Politics and Pragmatics of Punishment', 90 AJIL (1996) at p. 501.

here, as they are not *per se judicial* organs in the strict sense. This is clearly sufficient justification for their exclusion.

Much of what follows in this chapter about the judicial organs of the kind referred to in the second category above, which are the central subject of this chapter, is applicable in principle, *mutatis mutandis*, of course, to other international judicial institutions, strictly so-called, such as those referred to in the first category above. However, there is no need to elaborate here on this observation or matter. It is merely an observation which, in my opinion, has validity. Clearly, the subject of international judicial institutions and their special characteristics, as stated earlier in this chapter, should be considered in a separate work.[21]

Qualities of judicial organs flowing from the nature of the judicial power

The *essence* of the judicial power and function requires *independence* of the judicial organ in every sense.[22] The requirement of impartiality, for instance, as a quality is in reality only a corollary of the requirement of independence. It is unnecessary and unreal to regard impartiality as an unrelated concept distinct from independence in this context. Rather, impartiality should be regarded as an aspect, an important one at that, of independence in considering the judicial function or power, because the two qualities are inextricably involved in that context, whatever their abstract content may be and even if they may be considered separate for other purposes. Further, independence is of the *essence* because it is basically and in principle a guarantee of *justice* and, conversely, a safeguard against *injustice*. The feature of *essentialness* of independence cannot be over-emphasized.

While impartiality alone as a corollary has been referred to above, the concept of independence includes any less general quality, apart from impartiality, which is relevant to it. Such qualities include, for example, competence, absence of conflict of interest, and integrity. In fact, the qualities chosen later in this chapter for discussion are good examples

---

[21] For a current work on international tribunals in general, see Amerasinghe, note 3.

[22] The essentialness of independence as a quality of the judicial power and function in international law was, I believe, first raised by me as a matter of importance in Amerasinghe, note 8, vol I (1st ed., 1988) at pp. 68ff.; see also *ibid.* (2nd ed., 1994) at pp. 68ff. The ICJ has asserted that its *judicial character* must be preserved and the consequences thereof (see, e.g., the cases discussed in Amerasinghe, note 3 pp. 527ff.). Equally, the judicial character of any international tribunal must be preserved. Independence as an essential characteristic flows from judicial character.

of what is covered. Further, as will be explained, they are not the only ones.

These propositions are so obvious that they should not demand emphasis, or, indeed, even statement, but, because they may have been, and could be, ignored in practice, especially within the international legal system, it is necessary to restate them. It is for this reason primarily that they and their application are examined here.[23] Clearly, also for the present purposes the principle of independence which is in issue will be and needs to be discussed only in connection with the central subject matter of this chapter, as defined above, namely judicial *organs of* international institutions. However, this does not mean that the exposition is not relevant in general (*mutatis mutandis*, of course) to judicial institutions of the international legal system, as such.[24]

The basic principle that, because judicial organs as such must be *independent* (or by definition *essentially* independent), which includes their being impartial, their *independence* must be protected and ensured is clear and easy to state. However, it is apparent that the term 'independent' is jurisprudentially a vacuous or indeterminate term, i.e., of course, relatively (in fact). Hence, the logical process of application requires both what may be termed 'conceptual development' (concretization) and 'contextual factual application'.

When a fundamental principle, such as that of independence of a judicial organ, is developed (or concretized) conceptually, the original principle remains, while such development (or concretization) results technically in a narrower principle for the purpose of the specific

---

[23] The principle of independence of the judicial power (judiciary) and its ramifications have been examined and discussed by me in connection with the separation of the judiciary from the legislature and executive in certain important national systems of law: Amerasinghe, *The Doctrines of Sovereignty and Separation of Powers in the Law of Ceylon* (1970) pp. 185*ff*. (Chapters VII and VIII). The treatment of the principle there was confined to certain salient features of the application of the principle relevant particularly to the doctrine of the separation of powers in national constitutional law. It did not, therefore, cover *as such* the matters to be discussed below which are of a general nature and relevant to the independence of the judicial power *as such*, which is fundamental to all legal systems, including the international legal system, that qualify for the description 'civilized'. It is to be noted, on the one hand, that the aspects of the principle of independence of the judicial power examined and discussed below are those of particular relevance to the judicial power as an essential characteristic of the international legal system; on the other, that the treatment of the principle below is not exhaustive, for reasons both of space and of the requirements and limitations of the subject matter.

[24] This is obviously without prejudice to the relevance of the exposition and of the principle or principles involved to judicial institutions or organs outside the international legal system, i.e., in other legal systems than the international.

application, e.g., to qualifications of judges or the terms of their appointment in connection with the preservation of the independence of the judicial organ. Though the logical process may be identified, it is not always the case that the process results in a narrower principle which totally, or virtually in totality, eliminates vagueness or indeterminacy in the concept involved in the original fundamental principle. The level of indeterminacy may then only be reduced. However, this narrower principle certainly is of assistance and use in the process of applying the broader fundamental principle.

The contextual application is to specific fact situations and is in a way inextricably linked with the process of conceptual development (or concretization). The one generally informs and influences the other. What this entails in effect is that, while conceptual development (or concretization) may result in a certain narrowing in generality of the *concept* of judicial independence in terms of the specific application, the factual context may also result in a further redefinition of the concept in terms of that context.

As a result of this combined process of conceptual development (or concretization) and contextual application, the fundamental principle that judicial independence must be protected and ensured will acquire a specific application for the purpose in hand which practically reaches a conclusion relating to the effect of that fundamental principle. This conclusion, of course, may, broadly speaking, be positive or negative, as the case may be, in the light of what may be permitted without interfering with judicial independence or, conversely, obligatory in order to preserve and ensure such independence.

Further, conceptual development (or concretization) may depend to some extent on reference to other general principles of law, both of international law and of national law.[25] Some such relevant general principles may be implemented by express provisions in the relevant constitutive documents of tribunals in the case of the international legal system.[26]

It must be noted that only certain aspects of particular relevance to international tribunals of the kind which form the central subject matter of this chapter, and also of this part of this chapter, and with respect to which conceptual development (or concretization) must take place,

---

[25] See, e.g., Article 38(c) of the ICJ Statute (as of April 2003), which has been interpreted consistently to cover both kinds of general principles of law. The language of the article (both in English and in French) in fact implies this.

[26] For a special application of the two terms, 'conceptual development' and 'contextual application', see Amerasinghe, *Local Remedies in International Law* (2nd ed., 2003) pp. 431–5. The subject there is indicated in the title of that treatise.

will be examined here, albeit briefly. The choice of these aspects has been determined both by their perennial importance in relation to the tribunals, which form the central subject matter of this chapter and this part of this chapter, and because they have come into prominence in a modern context on account of developments in the international legal system relating to international organizations and to such tribunals. It is unnecessary to explore and describe in detail in all cases the content of this conceptual development by concretization. However, in the interest of clarity and better understanding, there may be in some cases a reference to and explanation of this content. The selection of aspects is neither exclusive nor comprehensive. Nevertheless, that does not mean that there are no other areas touching on the independence of the judicial power in the context particularly of the judicial organs being discussed, which may be examined and in which particular narrower, fundamental principles of law flowing derivatively from the basic principle relating to independence of the judicial power are applicable.

Therefore, for the purpose of this exposition, it is proposed briefly to consider later at an appropriate point in this chapter, such particular matters which concern judicial organs especially of international organizations, insofar as they are relevant specifically to the independence of such organs. The areas selected are not exclusive nor comprehensive in terms of what matters concern judicial independence. It must also be recognized that conceptual development (or concretization) may in certain cases not only be difficult and less extensive than in other cases but also be somewhat imprecise. The areas selected are the following:

   (i)   qualifications of judges and conditions for selection;
  (ii)   emoluments of judges;
 (iii)   reappointment of judges;
 (iv)   conflict of interest in relation to judges;
  (v)   the registry; and
 (vi)   legislative powers of the creating authority.

Before these areas are examined, it is necessary to consider, particularly in regard to the independence of judicial organs (or the judicial power), the concept of fundamental principles of law which is recognized in international law.

History of the concept of 'fundamental principles'

The concept of fundamental principles of law is a difficult one, both in general, as applied to law, and in particular, as relevant to the present subject of judicial independence. In international law the term *ius cogens* has been used to describe what may broadly be called 'fundamental principles' originally in relation to the law of treaties. This has apparently been a twentieth-century development, perhaps more emphatically after the Second World War. In general, the concept of fundamental principles, which, it seems, was practically for the first time applied in explicit terms to the law of treaties through the notion of *ius cogens*, was applied particularly and essentially in the law of treaties with a specific and defined connotation.[27]

It is not proposed here to discuss or establish when exactly recognition was given to the relevance of fundamental principles of law to the international legal system as such, nor in which area or areas the relevance of such principles was so recognized, nor what exactly the implications of the recognition of the relevance of such principles initially were. Suffice it to note for the present purposes that, first, it is, perhaps, only after the Second World War, i.e., in the early part of the second half of the twentieth century, that a truly responsible and informed awareness came into being of the relevance of fundamental principles of law to the international legal system at all, although some attention was paid to the matter; and, secondly, that such awareness revealed itself earliest in respect of the law of international agreements, including treaties. As a corollary of the above observations, it follows that before the early part of the second half of the twentieth century little, though some, attention was paid and value given to fundamental principles of law as applicable in any way as fundamental principles in the international

---

[27] *Ius cogens* in the law of treaties is discussed in, e.g., Sinclair, *The Vienna Convention on the Law of Treaties* (1984) pp. 17–18 and 203*ff.*, in the context usually of the 1969 Vienna Convention on the Law of Treaties. See also the books and articles on the law of treaties in general cited in the above work, in particular the monograph by Suy, *The Concept of Ius Cogens in International Law* (1967) and the articles by Virally, Marek, de Visscher and Gaja (referred to in Sinclair, *Vienna Convention* p. 238, n. 8). In addition, reference may be made to Scheuner, 'Conflict of Treaty Provisions with a Peremptory Norm of General International Law and Its Consequences', 27 ZAÖRV (1967) at p. 520; Zotiades, 'Stadtsautonomie und die Grenzen der Vertragsfreiheit im Völkerrecht', ÖZÖR (1967) at p. 90. It is surprising that O'Connell, *International Law* (1970) vol. I, in his examination of the law of treaties which includes reference to the 1969 Vienna Convention, does not discuss the subject of *ius cogens*. This work in two volumes is the best current treatise in English on public international law in general (as applied in time of peace, to which it is limited) in spite of its having been published in 1970. Virally's article was written before the 1969 Vienna Convention was signed, but, nevertheless, discusses *ius cogens* in relation to treaties as a phenomenon obviously in the pre-Vienna Convention era.

legal system, nor, *a fortiori*, was any thought given in anyway to the implications of the recognition of any principles of law as fundamental in the international legal system.[28]

For the purposes of the present discussion of the fundamental principle of independence of judicial organs of international organizations, it is not necessary to give detailed consideration to the history of the acceptance as an element of the international legal system of fundamental principles of law. But it may be useful to give a brief summary of such a history.[29]

Long before Grotius, it was generally accepted that above the positive law, based on the practice of states, there was another law rooted in human reason and deriving its force from the law of nature.[30] Grotius distinguished between the *ius gentium* (the customary law of nations) and the *ius naturae* (the natural law of nations). To the naturalists, in general, the law of nature was hierarchically superior to the *ius gentium*.

As a reaction to this approach, there began to develop, in the eighteenth century, a school of jurists, which included Bynkershoek, Moser and Martens, who encompassed custom and treaties as sources of positive international law. They did not wholly deny the role of natural law in filling gaps. Such jurists were described in general as positivists. In the late nineteenth and early twentieth centuries, the positivist school had considerable influence. The great contribution of the positivist school was to concentrate attention on state practice in the development of international law. However, the more extreme members of the positivist school were of the view that the will of states constituted the *only* valid source of international law. Logically, this view excluded the superiority of any general principles based on the notion of *ius cogens*.

It is possible that it was in the early part of the twentieth century that an awakening took place among text writers to the relevance of what

---

[28] An examination of the state practice, of the international judicial decisions (both of standing courts and *ad hoc* courts or tribunals) and of the literature on public international law prior to about 1945 reveals the above: for the pre-1945 literature, see, e.g., the general works listed in the 'Table of General Treatises on International Law' to be found in O'Connell, note 27 vol. II, pp. 1291*ff*.

[29] I have relied in the account that follows to some extent on Suy, note 27, and on Sinclair, note 27 pp. 203–14.

[30] See Pollock, 'The History of the Law of Nature', 2 *Journal of the Society of Comparative Legislation* (1900) at pp. 418*ff*. and 3 *Journal of the Society of Comparative Legislation* (1901) at pp. 24*ff*.

they saw as a *ius cogens*.[31] But it was really not until after the Second World War that both the rational and practical relevance of *ius cogens*, as it came regularly to be termed, began to be recognized. Such text writers as Von der Heydte, Verdross (writing again after the Second World War), Dahm, Berber, Guggenheim, Fauchille, Rousseau, Cavaré, Reuter, Suy, Virally, Marek, de Visscher, Gaja, Sinclair and Brownlie, among others, not only refer to and discuss *ius cogens* but accept positively the concept.[32] The *ius cogens*, connoting, as it did, 'peremptory norms' (English) or '*normes impératives*' (French), which was discussed by text writers, was, as it appears, associated only with treaties which resulted from the direct mutual consent of states.

At this point it is appropriate to consider some international and national judicial decisions in which reference has been made to the *ius cogens* principle.[33] There are a few cases decided by the ICJ in which individual judges or groups of judges in separate or dissenting opinions have made a variety of pronouncements on *ius cogens*, but only one in which the Court itself in its judgment could conceivably have recognized the principle as applicable, in that case, to the rule of inviolability of diplomatic premises.[34] This recognition was clearly *obiter*, because the question whether the rule of inviolability of diplomatic premises was *ius cogens* was not a material issue in the case. Individual judges of the ICJ have (i) referred to the *ius cogens* principle as relevant to the relationship between reservations and provisions of a treaty relating to the continental shelf,[35] (ii) referred to the principle of 'self-determination'

---

[31] See, e.g., Fauchille, *Traité de droit international public* (1926) vol. 1, p. 300, and later Verdross, 'Forbidden Treaties in International Law', 31 AJIL (1937) at pp. 571*ff*.

[32] For the above authors, see Suy, note 27, and Sinclair, note 27 pp. 207*ff*. Suy and Sinclair discuss the issue in their works. It must be noted also that there were some authors in the same era who acknowledged the existence of the concept but did not accept it as relevant particularly to the law of treaties which was the subject of their discussion: see, e.g., Schwarzenberger, cited in Sinclair, *ibid.* p. 208. It may also be mentioned that Fitzmaurice, a rapporteur during the early period of the ILC's work on the law of treaties, agreed that *ius cogens* was relevant to and operative in the law of treaties: see Sinclair, *ibid.* p. 209.

[33] These decisions are referred to in Sinclair, *ibid.* pp. 209*ff*. Only the cases in which the principle is clearly in issue, whether explicitly or implicitly, are discussed here.

[34] The *United States Diplomatic and Consular Staff in Tehran Case*, 1980 ICJ Reports at pp. 40 and 41. No comment is made on the validity of the *obiter dicta*.

[35] 1969 ICJ Reports at pp. 97–8 *per* Judge Padilla Nervo, at p. 182 *per* Judge Tanaka, and at p. 248 *per* Judge (*ad hoc*) Sorensen. All three judges agreed in effect that principles of international law which were *ius cogens* could not be subjected to unilateral reservations in a treaty.

as *ius cogens*,[36] and (iii) referred to principles relating to certain human rights which were in issue in the case as *ius cogens*.[37]

There are a few cases decided by national courts in which the concept of *ius cogens* in international law is mentioned. In a case decided in 1965 by the *Bundesverfassungsgericht* (Federal Constitutional Court) in the Federal Republic of Germany, the court referred in general to rules of customary international law 'which could not be stipulated away by treaty' as 'peremptory norms', describing such norms as 'legal rules which are firmly rooted in the legal conviction of the community of nations and are indispensable to the existence of the law of nations as an international legal order'.[38] In the *Flesche Case*, decided in 1949 by the Court of Cassation in the Netherlands, the court referred to *ius cogens* in connection with a rule in the international law of extradition concerning 'speciality'. The reference to *ius cogens* was made, in order to characterize that rule, so as not to permit the rule to be waived by agreement in a treaty, because it was an imperative norm of the international legal system.[39]

Finally, it is important that the 1969 Vienna Convention on the Law of Treaties in Article 53, which is the critical article, recognizes without question the notion of *ius cogens* (peremptory norm, *norme impérative*) in relation to treaties, as defined in the Convention, in that it states that: 'A treaty is void if, at the time of its conclusion, it conflicts with a peremptory norm of general international law.' Further, a peremptory norm is defined in that article as 'a norm accepted and recognized by the international community of States as a whole as a norm from which no derogation is permitted'.

It is evident that initially and until quite late in the twentieth century, although (i) recognition may have been given to the concept of *ius cogens* and (ii) it was generally agreed and not questioned that the concept meant that there were norms recognized by the international community of States from which 'no *derogation* was permitted', in the language of the 1969 Vienna Convention, the concept had been applied

---

[36] The *Barcelona Traction Co. Case*, 1970 ICJ Reports at p. 304 *per* Judge Ammoun in a dissenting opinion (the reference is to '*ius cogens*'), the *Namibia Case*, 1971 ICJ Reports at p. 75 (the reference is to 'imperative right').

[37] The *Namibia Case*, 1971 ICJ Reports at p. 75 *per* Judge Ammoun (the reference is to 'imperative character').

[38] *Assessment of Aliens for War Taxation Case* (1965), 43 ILR (1971) at p. 3. The court held there that the particular rule concerning alien treatment which was in issue in the case was not a 'peremptory norm'.

[39] 16 AD (1949) at p. 269.

exclusively in relation to treaties in order to identify terms of treaties which as a consequence of the existence of peremptory norms were void and to which effect could not be given. Further, while there was some concern about the contents of *ius cogens*, in the context of treaties, of course, no attempt was made to give even a broad definition of such contents, although, as has been seen, reference was made to isolated instances of what might be included in the concept of *ius cogens*.

It was not until 1988 that a step was taken to associate *ius cogens* in the essential sense of 'peremptory norms' or *normes impératives* with principles of law (i.e., in this case, public international law in its broadest sense), which were 'fundamental', with the consequence that, because they were fundamental, they were *hierarchically* superior to any other principles or norms which were not fundamental, whatever their source or form (e.g., whether written, based on custom or practice, or emanating from agreement or consent). This was done explicitly in the first edition of my treatise on *The Law of International Civil Service*, in dealing with general principles of law as a source of international administrative law.[40] There, after analysis of the existing cases, I concluded:

[T]here is considerable evidence that, at least in some cases, general principles of law are superior to the written sources of law. The reasonable conclusion seems to be that, *as regards the general principles of law of a fundamental nature, they are superior hierarchically to the written law in particular and could, indeed, be the supreme source of law relating to the international civil service.* On the other hand, clearly there are certain general principles which are not of such importance that they could not be modified or negated by the written law or by a rule emanating from another source. The rule against discrimination or equality of treatment and the principle that a staff member has a right to be heard before a disciplinary sanction is imposed on him are examples of general principles of a fundamental nature, as is the rule protecting acquired or essential rights.[41]

The conclusion was repeated in the same form after some updating of the case material, in the second edition, published in 1994, of the same treatise.[42] In discussing the same subject of hierarchy of sources

---

[40] (1st ed., 1988) vol. 1, pp. 155–7. It should be noted that in 1987 I had already drawn attention to the virtual 'primacy' of general principles of law as a source of international administrative law: Amerasinghe, 'Sources of International Administrative Law', in *International Law at the Time of Its Codification* (1987) vol. I, pp. 85ff. However, the concept of 'fundamental principles' in relation to some such general principles had not been expressly so characterized.

[41] Amerasinghe, note 8 vol. I (1988) at p. 156.

[42] *Ibid.* (1994) vol. I, pp. 156–7.

of international administrative law, I came to the same conclusion in the first edition of the present treatise, published in 1996.[43]

In relation to practice in particular as a source of international administrative law, while the generality of the conclusion reached above was sufficient to cover such practice, I concluded:

There is no authority on the relationship between practice and the general principles of law or on whether an administrative practice can override a general principle of law. There is good reason for believing that in the case of a fundamental general principle of law, such as the rule against discrimination, a practice cannot override it.[44]

The above conclusions confirming the hierarchical superiority as a source of law of *fundamental* general principles of law over all other sources of law were reached both on the basis of the case material available at the time from IATs and on the basis of logic and reason. The conclusions were clearly limited in the circumstances to international administrative law. But it was also pointed out in this context – and this is of critical importance – that international administrative law, though it may be of a special character as a system of law internal to international organizations, is, nevertheless, connected, as a *part of public international law*, with public international law, because it is obviously derived from and dependent on acts emanating from the treaty-making power of states.[45] There is a corollary which is logically to be drawn from

---

[43] *Principles of the Institutional Law of International Organizations* (1st ed., 1996) p. 350.

[44] Amerasinghe, note 8 (1st ed., 1988) at p. 167. The conclusion was repeated in the identical form in the second edition (1994) at p. 167.

[45] For this conclusion see *ibid.* at p. 25. The identical conclusion appears in the first edition of the same treatise, at p. 25. While the issue of the characterization of international civil service law was examined in both editions of the above treatise, for the present purpose the short discussion in another subsequent treatise by me – *Principles of the Institutional Law of International Organizations* (1st ed., 1996) p. 326 – is sufficient and accurate and essentially what I intended to write and did write. It contains the gist of what, obviously in an expanded form, should have been reflected in both editions of the earlier treatise on the law of the international civil service. Reference should, therefore, be made to the discussions in *Principles of the Institutional Law of International Organizations* (1st ed., 1996), i.e., the first edition of this work, on this point (at pp. 326*ff.*).

It is apparent that, if especially the sections on p. 22 of volumes 1 of both the second edition and the first edition of *The Law of the International Civil Service* (1994 and 1988, respectively) are read carefully, the conclusion reached on p. 25 of that work is blurred and not properly or effectively presented as not only the appropriate but the sole rational conclusion. The statement made above in the text of the present work (at this footnote, 45), which is similar to the one made in the first edition (1996) of this

the conclusion reached, in connection with international administrative law, that *fundamental* general principles of law are superior hierarchically to all other sources of law. This corollary is that the same conclusion is *a fortiori* applicable to the sources of public international law in general, it being noted, as already stated, that international civil service law is a part of public international law. In the absence of good reason, it is clear that this logical corollary cannot be rejected or qualified at all, on, for instance, grounds of policy. It is unnecessary to emphasize in this context that general principles of law are as such a principal source of law for public international law as a system of law.[46]

Finally, in my treatise on the *Jurisdiction of International Tribunals*, published in 2003, I concluded upon analysis that, in regard to the various aspects of the jurisdiction of *international* tribunals of whatever kind, there were applicable *fundamental principles of law* which not only imposed limitations on the exercise of such jurisdiction which could not be removed even by consent which is the usual basis of the jurisdiction of international tribunals, whether such consent is direct, indirect or derivative, but conversely also rendered it legally impossible to limit or take away even by mutual consent certain powers which were necessarily inherent in the exercise of such jurisdiction.[47]

Deductions

The jurisdictional powers of judicial organs referred to above, it must be noted, are part of and relevant to the judicial power as such in the international legal system. Logically, then, if there are fundamental principles of law which apply to the jurisdiction of international tribunals (or courts), there are fundamental principles of law which apply in

---

treatise, reflects the proper and rational formulation of the conclusion which should have been reflected in both editions of *The Law of the International Civil Service*, vol. I (1988 and 1994). As a consequence of the explanation given here, the whole of the last section of Chapter 1 of *The Law of the International Civil Service*, vol. I (pp. 22ff. of both editions), is not accurately presented. The discrepancies referred to here are drawn to the attention of the reader, because, whatever the reason for them, they are not in reality, even though this may sound strange, attributable to a failure or misfeasance on my part.

[46] Article 38(c) of the Statute of the ICJ refers to such general principles as a source of public international law. It is to be noted, however, that the *raison d'être* of the truth that such general principles of law are a principal source of public international law is not that that article of the ICJ Statute (or the corresponding article of the PCIJ Statute) stated it, but that the truth had already been fully recognized in public international law.

[47] Amerasinghe, note 3, *passim*, e.g., pp. 99–100 on consent in relation to jurisdictional powers in general.

appropriate situations and areas to the international judicial power in general, because jurisdictional powers are only an aspect of the powers which flow from the judicial power as such, in fact whether the judicial power in the international legal system or in any national system is in issue. The fact that there are fundamental principles of law which apply to jurisdiction signifies that it is possible, where appropriate, that fundamental principles of law apply to other aspects of the judicial power and, thus, to the judicial power in general. Moreover, not only is this *possible*, but, obviously, this *must* be so, although there is a separate issue as to what are the specific fundamental principles, whether in respect of the judicial power in general or, more particularly, in respect of the various aspects of such power.[48]

The deduction that there are fundamental principles of law relating to the judicial power (in general) is important for the present analysis and discussion which essentially concerns *judicial independence* (in respect of certain judicial organs of the international legal system) and, more particularly, some specific aspects relating to the judicial function which are of special significance insofar as they impact on judicial independence. It has been established that there are fundamental principles of law which apply to the judicial power in general and, consequently, to the various aspects, or, indeed, any appropriate aspect, of it. That *judicial independence* is an aspect, and a very important one, of the judicial power cannot be denied; this is self-evident. It follows logically, therefore, that there are fundamental principles of law of greater or lesser abstraction which apply in the area of judicial independence. Clearly, also as to the principles of law of lesser abstraction, not only must they be appropriate in themselves but the areas to which they apply must essentially relate to and be connected with judicial independence. In short, the latter principles of law which are, indeed, fundamental, must have for their purpose the preservation of judicial independence and must be directed at ensuring such independence, which, it cannot be gainsaid, is the basic fundamental principle of law and is of the highest abstraction.

As a consequence of the above, it is possible and, indeed, necessary to discuss and establish fundamental principles of law relating to the judicial power in general or to the particular aspect of the judicial power which is judicial independence. As pointed out earlier, though, in the

---

[48] This issue of specific fundamental principles will be addressed briefly below in regard also to *ius cogens* (peremptory norms, *normes impératives*, or fundamental principles of law) in public international law in general.

context of judicial independence only certain critical and selected areas relating to the judicial power have been selected for analysis and discussion here. Needless to say, they will be considered, again as implied earlier, to the extent that they impinge on judicial independence and also with the judicial organs of international organizations in mind, though much of what is said, if not everything, applies, *mutatis mutandis* perhaps, to international judicial institutions as such.

Implications of the fundamentality of certain general principles of law

General principles of law are applicable in public international law usually to the extent that they do not conflict with rules emanating expressly from consent or agreement and with rules based on customary practice, which also in a sense are based on consent. There are situations, however, in which general principles of law take precedence hierarchically over rules flowing from both the above sources. Then these principles are fundamental in that they are the supreme principles or rules of law applicable. In treaty law fundamental principles were in the past regularly described as *ius cogens*[49] without general or even particular use of the term 'fundamental principles of law'. In the 1969 Vienna Convention, as has been seen, the term used in the text itself, presumably to describe fundamental principles of law, is 'peremptory norms' (*normes impératives*), not *ius cogens*, though in the title to that article *ius cogens* is placed in parentheses also to describe peremptory norms.[50] Before the 1969 Vienna Convention, *ius cogens* as peremptory norms (*normes impératives*) was regarded as being relevant with respect almost exclusively to the law relating to international agreements in connection with which it had been freely discussed.[51] The general understanding of the term (or terms) in that context was that it (or they) referred to norms as rules which could not be opted out of by agreement. This approach culminated in the formulation of Article 53 of the 1969 Vienna Convention which referred, as has been seen, to conflict 'with a peremptory norm of general international law', peremptory norm being defined there as a norm of public international law from which no derogation was permitted.

---

[49] See, e.g., the literature cited in footnote 27 above.
[50] The same use of language appears in Article 64 of the 1969 Vienna Treaty Convention.
[51] See particularly Suy, note 27, pp. 18*ff.*, which treats the matter as connected with international agreements. See also the other literature cited in note 27 above.

While almost exclusive concern hitherto has been with peremptory norms being violated by agreement, there is no reason why such peremptory norms may not be violated in other ways than by agreement, such as by custom, which, however, may be regarded as being based on agreement in one form or another, or, indeed, by unilateral action which may be law-creating. Moreover, it must be recognized that peremptory norms may be relevant across the board to any area of public international law. As has already become apparent, what have been referred to as peremptory norms may more appropriately be described as 'fundamental principles of law', which is a term used in legal contexts in general. Further, and importantly, whatever other sources may give rise to such fundamental principles of law, it is clear that such principles may be and are usually general principles of law. In passing, it may be mentioned that an important consequence of this for public international law in general is that fundamental principles which are generally or basically general principles of law are hierarchically superior not only to rules in international agreements, including treaties, but even to customary rules or rules based on practice.

On the other hand, while emphasis must be placed on the above in a modern context, principles of law which are fundamental are superior hierarchically to other principles or rules of law from whatever source they may emanate. Clearly then, the principle of judicial independence, which has been referred to in the previous sections, is a fundamental principle of law applicable to public international law in general, as was evident, and, therefore, applies to international judicial organs, which are being discussed in this chapter, as a principle which is hierarchically superior to any other rule or principle. It is the hierarchical superiority, or even supremacy, of this principle which requires to be recognized as a result of the principle being fundamental.

It is also a consequence of this that, without being exclusive, particularly in interpreting international instruments, (i) by the application of the teleological principle of interpretation, what is omitted but is essential in terms of the fundamental general principle of independence will be implied, (ii) what is expressly stated will, in accordance with the same principle of interpretation, be interpreted so as to include and not exclude any relevant essential requirement, (iii) language which expressly limits a particular requirement so as not fully to reflect that essential requirement will be interpreted in such a way as to include what is essential by addition, even if express language has to be changed, and (iv) language which reflects excessive severity in terms of an express requirement will either be interpreted or be changed, so as to reflect the appropriate lesser requirement.

Particular matters relating to the principle of judicial independence

Six particular areas referred to earlier in this chapter were selected for discussion as being important in the context of the independence of the judicial organs which are the subject of this chapter. These are examined below.[52]

Qualifications of judges and conditions for selection

In accordance with the implications of the fundamental general principle of law that judicial organs must be independent, an appropriate derivative principle, for want of better words, is that *qualifications required of the judges must be such as to enable the independence of the specific judicial organs in issue not only to be ensured, respected and protected, but also not to be jeopardized and frustrated.* Consequently, qualifications must not only be relative to the nature of the judicial functions performed by each judicial organ, which is dependent primarily on its jurisdiction, but be appropriate for the proper and efficient discharge of those functions. On the other hand, the qualifications required must not be so excessive as to jeopardize the protection and ensuring of independence by being unnecessary and even irrelevant, so that the selection process becomes corrupted. It may be difficult always accurately and precisely to achieve the balance required, but as long as the qualifications selected do not reflect an abuse of discretion as being either inadequate or in excess, the principle relating to qualifications would not have been violated. Thus, as far as the three judicial organs of international organizations which are the specific subject of this study are concerned, the above principles will apply particularly with due consideration of their functions and jurisdictional sphere.[53]

---

[52] It has already been made clear that these six are not the only relevant matters. It must also be made clear that the discussion below will not be exhaustive. Not only is it not possible to anticipate or visualize all the conceptual and factual variations but an exhaustive consideration is not required, because the purpose of this chapter is principally to demonstrate how the concept of independence as an essential quality of the subject judicial organs and flowing from the nature of the judicial power may be developed and factually applied in practice.

[53] Incidentally it may be noted that the application of the principles to these judicial organs merely illustrates how the principles apply to specific examples of judicial organs. The principles, however, are of general application.

In regard to the ICTY and the ICTR, the jurisdiction of the judicial organs exists in both cases over serious violations of international humanitarian law.[54] Consequently, the qualifications required for judges and described in Article 13 of the ICTY Statute cannot, as it appears, be questioned as being inappropriate with the exception adverted to below. Article 13(1) reads:

The judges shall be persons of high moral character, impartiality and integrity who possess the qualifications required in their respective countries for appointment to the highest judicial offices. In the overall composition of the Chambers, due account shall be taken of the experience of the judges in criminal law, international law, including international humanitarian law and human rights law.[55]

It is to be deduced, though it is not properly stated, that only 'experience' and no more in criminal law and international law, including international humanitarian law and human rights law, is required as a basic *qualification*. Correctly, high moral character, impartiality and integrity are so required as primary characteristics. These required qualifications properly interpreted are clearly sufficient to enable the ensuring, respect for, and protection of, independence of the judicial organ concerned in the light of its functions and jurisdiction. The qualification which involves reference to 'highest judicial office' is *per se* too severe. More realistically and appropriately, suitable legal experience of any nature *per se* which warrants the reasonable conclusion that a candidate for appointment as a judge of the judicial organ concerned is competent efficiently and effectively to perform the judicial functions required of him is adequate for the purpose. Thus, to the extent that qualifications for the highest judicial offices are a requirement, the provision relating to qualifications is not in keeping with the fundamental principle and that specific requirement reflects an abuse of discretion. The effect of this deficiency is that, on the one hand, that express requirement alone must be struck down and, on the other, the requirement it should have reflected, namely that a candidate must have suitable legal experience to render him not only eligible but competent to perform the judicial

---

[54] See, e.g., Article 1 of the Statute of the ICTY, 32 ILM (1993) at pp. 1159 and 1203. A similar provision appears in Article 1 of the Statute of the ICTR, 33 ILM (1994) at p. 1602.

[55] 32 ILM (1993) at p. 1195. The ICTR Statute has a similar provision: see Article 12(1). Some implications of the provision in the ICTY Statute are discussed, *inter alia*, contextually in Morris and Scharf, note 20 p. 143.

functions in issue must be implied. As a consequence, though 'highest judicial offices' as a characteristic may be an *added* consideration, it may not be taken into account as an essential requirement. This is the only reasonable and logical interpretation of Article 13(1) of the ICTY Statute in the light of the fundamental principle of international law involved.[56]

The conceptual concretizations in relation to qualifications of judges of the fundamental principle of independence which were deduced above in relation to the ICTY (which apply also to the ICTR) results in slightly different applications in relation to IATs, obviously because of contextual differences. Basically, (i) whatever the formulation of the provisions in their statutes relating to the qualifications of judges, and (ii) even in the absence of specific provisions, as in the case of the pre-2000 Statute of the UNAT[57] and the ILOAT Statute,[58] the conceptual concretizations of principle described above in relation to the ICTY apply *mutatis mutandis*. In the case of the second alternative referred to above, they are implied in their totality. In the case of the first alternative they will be applied as fundamental principles, of course, and will, consequently, as the case may be, modify the express formulation to the extent that there is any conflict and even supplement it, where there are *lacunae*, to the extent of the *lacunae* concerned.

An example of a case in which there is an express formulation is the WBAT Statute as it existed in 2001. Article IV(1)[59] of that Statute stated that judges (i) must be of high moral character[60] and (ii) must possess the qualifications required for appointment to high judicial office or (iii) must be jurisconsults of recognized competence. Clearly, the requirement relating to high judicial office is irrelevant and, therefore, contains material which requires to be eliminated, as was the case in regard to the ICTY. As for the requirement relating to jurisconsults of recognized competence, this again is too broad in that being jurisconsults in *any*

---

[56] The provision in the ICTY Statute (Article 12) which provides that no two judges shall be of the same nationality does not deal with qualifications but a condition. See also Article 11 of the ICTR Statute.

[57] Amerasinghe (ed.), note 12 p. 6.   [58] *Ibid.* at p. 31.

[59] WBAT Doc. Rules/Rev.2 (1995) at p. 2. Dr Golsong, the then Deputy General Counsel of the World Bank, was primarily responsible for the drafting of the WBAT Statute.

[60] 'High moral character' clearly and on a reasonable interpretation covers, *inter alia*, impartiality, and cannot but cover 'integrity', which are characteristics specifically referred to in the ICTY and ICTR Statutes. Further, even if 'high moral character' did not cover *all* the basic qualifications required of a judge, what it did not cover would be implied as a consequence of the application of the basic fundamental principle of law.

branch or branches of law regardless of its or their relevance to the legal system of IATs is inadequate.

In fact, it is not easy to identify accurately, both exclusively and inclusively, and also completely, the requisite qualifications for judgeships in IATs, in any case. However, additionally, such identification has not in reality been accomplished,[61] partly because adequate attention has, for whatever reason, not been paid to IATs and their paramount importance in international relations and in the international legal system by both international organizations and states, as members of these organizations, whose nationals work there, and partly because, until recently, had such qualifications been properly and strictly stated as being inclusively necessary in the Statute or governing instrument, there would have been, purely for lack of minimum qualifications, an inadequate number of or no candidates from states, members of international organizations, belonging to some regions, whose representation on many of the major IATs is necessary or desirable. Now, provisions on qualifications of judges which expressly refer to them as requirements all miss the principal points. On the one hand, the above problems may have been impediments to requiring as *compulsory* the basic qualifications; on the other, it is undoubtedly possible rationally to address the issues involved, identify the required qualifications in terms of those issues and formulate them with accuracy. However, because of complexity and because it is not possible to anticipate and determine all the issues and factors surrounding the appropriate qualifications at any given point of time, the required qualifications may have to be stated in generalities and, in any case, there may have to be a certain amount of implication. Nevertheless, the fact cannot be gainsaid that in the practical application of statutes and constitutive instruments of IATs, the relevant qualifications can be identified in one way or another and, more importantly, be made the obligatory basis of selection.

In the light of the above, a few considerations and conclusions on the matter of qualifications of judges of IATs are offered here.

Being qualified for high judicial office in a national jurisdiction is not only irrelevant but by itself very detrimental in fact to the proper functioning of an IAT. The questions may be put in this way: would a lawyer who has years of experience as a judge in a French civil law jurisdiction

---

[61] See, e.g., all or, at least, most of the statutes of the fourteen IATs reproduced in Amerasinghe (ed.), note 12. The existing IATs whose statutes are reproduced there are now the leading ones.

(e.g., France) be appointed as a judge in a common law jurisdiction (e.g., England) on the basis purely that he has had judicial experience? A basic requirement is a knowledge of and experience in the law and legal system of the courts to which he is going to be appointed. In the case of the IATs there should strictly be, therefore, a requirement that the candidate have a knowledge of and experience in international administrative law.[62] This certainly would make judges for IATs hard to find, even today.

An attempt should, however, be made to come close to the ideal requirement and to have criteria which will make it possible for the candidate *substantively* (not formally) to adjust to and gain adequate knowledge of international administrative law, if he has not been exposed to it already. The point is that, for example, common law *judges* merely by being judges or qualified to be judges are totally ill-equipped to decide cases brought before IATs. There must be a requirement that makes the adjustment to international administrative law feasible on the basis of a like system or a system that is relevant, in the absence of a good knowledge of and adequate experience in international administrative law. The fact or formal requirement of being a judge or being qualified to be a judge is *per se* irrelevant.

In the light of these considerations, the following requirements are relevant, the point being that the candidate, if he does not have an exposure to international administrative law proper, should have a background of legal knowledge that would enable him to adjust to international administrative law, the latter system being now a well developed and distinctive system of law:

(i)   being a competent international administrative law jurist; or
(ii)   being a competent jurist with knowledge of civil service law in a civil law system; or
(iii) being a competent jurist with specialization in public international law in general (if possible, with knowledge of international organizational law).

[62] I was on both the UNAT (three years) and the CSAT (two and one half years) with some overlap but not entirely. I was, *inter alia*, a specialist in international administrative law. This, as stated, is unusual. None of the others on these two international courts during my tenure had such a qualification. I happened also to be a 'recognized jurist' with specialization in public international law as such and also in the law of international organizations, both as a practitioner and as an academic. Further, I had adequate knowledge of civil service law in the civil law systems. This combination of expertise is almost unique. That kind of qualification is idealistic, however desirable, and obviously cannot as such be made a requirement.

Requirement (ii) makes sense because international administrative law is clearly *based* on the general principles of French administrative law. There can be no doubt about that. It does not make sense to invoke comparative principles of administrative law, if, indeed, a corpus of relevant and useful principles can be found. The common law, for instance, does not have an administrative law that applies to the civil service, which is what matters. This remains true, though sometimes general principles of law as such applicable outside civil service law are applied. Requirement (iii) is recommended because (a) this is the principal way in which common lawyers could qualify (otherwise they would be excluded) and (b) public international lawyers have an exposure to the civil law – public international law has more in common with civil law, through Roman law – and they generally have some knowledge of the law of international organizations. Thus, they should be able to adjust to the law which is applied in international organizations. In fact, genuine public international jurists can make the adjustment – that is, those who have a broad exposure to public international law proper and to the law of international organizations. This does not include, for instance, international business lawyers *per se*.

The problem is that international administrative law is a very specialized field, particularly now, and it is necessary to require legal experience which will enable the candidate not merely to judge, which is a formal quality, but to do so with international administrative law as the substantive law to be applied. It should be emphasized that merely being a national judge, however eminent, is a totally irrelevant qualification as such. Equally, being an experienced labour lawyer, particularly in a common law system, is inadequate. Labour law has nothing in common with international administrative law, the latter being the administrative law which applies to a civil service. The principles are different. In effect it has been found that public international lawyers can adjust whereas labour lawyers are not really at an advantage because of their knowledge of labour law.

What is important is that the candidate have a background of legal knowledge which will enable him to decide international administrative law cases. The technique of judging is not important in itself. Even in national jurisdictions lawyers with no judicial experience are appointed to the highest court. The judicial technique comes with experience as a jurist. In any case, there is no use in being a brilliant judge if one knows nothing about the law that is applied in judging. It is no answer to say that the argument of the parties will demonstrate the law. That is not always the case. Both parties may get the law wrong. A pertinent question, then, is why legal experience in the legal system is an indispensable requirement for judicial appointment in national jurisdictions, and not judicial experience as such. The answer is that it is necessary to know or have easy access to the law being applied. It never happens that anyone but those who have acquired skill as lawyers and who know the relevant national law is appointed to the bench in national jurisdictions. There is no reason at all why the reasoning and principles behind this practice should not be applicable to appointments to IATs. On the contrary, there is every reason why it should. As a consequence of the underlying reasoning and principles, the only logical conclusion is that *judicial* experience *per se* is not a requirement for appointments to IATs.

Any requirements which are unlike or not of the same genre as those referred to above for qualifying as a judge of an IAT are not really qualifications. Provisions such as that no two judges on the same bench at any time should be nationals of the same state,[63] or that judges should be nationals of member states of the relevant international organization,[64] are only conditions. Clearly, they cannot be described as required qualifications. No mistake can be made about the difference between these or the like and true qualifications such as those discussed above. There is, however, a relationship between conditions such as these and the principle of independence. Stated simply, to the extent that they, no doubt as conditions rather than qualifications, interfere in any way with the maintenance of independence, including impartiality, of individual judges or the bench of the judicial organ, they subscribe to the violation of the fundamental principle of independence. It is not possible nor necessary to identify in what exact ways this violation takes place. Suffice it to say that the violation may be as a result, for example, of the interaction of circumstances arising from the implementation of the condition or conditions in respect of an appointment or appointments. It is also necessary to point out, in conclusion, that the violation may occur because the circumstances of the application of the condition or conditions results, for instance, simply in creating a situation which is likely (not certainly nor, possibly, perhaps) to result in interference, in the working of the judicial organ, with the dispensation of justice and

---

[63] See Article 3 of the UNAT Statute, note 12 p. 3; and Article IV(1) of the WBAT Statute, note 12 p. 2. See also Article 13(2) of the ICTY Statute, 32 ILM (1993) at pp. 1195–6, which contains similar and other conditions, and Article 12(3) of the ICTR Statute, 33 ILM (1994) at pp. 1606–7.

[64] Article IV(1) of the WBAT Statute, note 12 p. 2.

the rendering of just and fair judgments, on account, for instance, of the lack of required qualifications. It is to be noted that what matters is a likelihood of and not actual interference on the part of a judge or judges with justice, the latter being a post-appointment fact which cannot be established at the time of selection for appointment. In these cases, independence is characterized in terms of achieving justice and rendering fair and just judgments. This characterization is the result of conceptual development and also contextual application of the broad fundamental principle of law.

Emoluments of judges

In the case of all three judicial organs concerned here, there are no provisions in any of the constitutive documents relating to the emoluments of judges.[65] In any case and, therefore, in these circumstances, resort must be had to less abstract fundamental general principles of law which are applicable by conceptual development or concretization as flowing from the basic fundamental principle of independence which is of the essence of the judicial power. Consequently, in regard to emoluments, the less abstract fundamental principle developed is that all emoluments, of whatever nature, of judges must be dealt with in every respect and in such a way, whatever the *modus operandi*, that the independence of judges, which includes all the other qualities inherent in independence, is in broad terms not only safeguarded, preserved and promoted in all respects, but also not interfered with or diluted in any way. That general principle applies to all matters connected with judges' emoluments and extends to such matters which may be described as peripheral to emoluments. The identification of all those matters depends, clearly, to some extent on the circumstances of the case, though there are undoubtedly certain core matters which are also, in fact, common to all international judicial organs.

Based on the above considerations, the following analysis may be made, it being necessary to bear in mind that the subsidiary principles derived have as their objects the same purposes referred to above in connection with the basic fundamental principle. Of primary importance[66] are such matters as the fixing of salaries or fees, their reduction,

---

[65] The term 'emoluments' covers salaries, fees, honoraria and any other kind of reward for services rendered, just as 'remuneration' does.

[66] There are, obviously, areas other than those dealt with here that are of relevance to the subject of emoluments. The source of funds for payment of emoluments, for instance, is one of them.

and their increase. There may be other matters than these which are of concern, but the above are distinctly the most critical factors affecting independence.

The first derivative principle is that salaries or fees must be fixed clearly (a) at the beginning of a judge's tenure and (b) at such a level as is reasonable, taking into account all the relevant circumstances or factors, including the fact that the office is judicial and not of any other kind, which implies the recognition of qualities such as dignity and authority, and particularly the general level of salaries or fees of judges in the international legal system and, (c) most importantly, must be at such a level as is conducive to and preserves the independence of the judges and does not jeopardize it. Such independence, as already pointed out, includes all subsidiary qualities covered by that concept. These principles apply whether the appointees serve full time or part time. It follows quite logically from the above that there can be no judgeships in the three kinds of judicial organs being discussed that are not remunerated, or are honorary, or are inadequately remunerated (see (b) and (c) above), although in the case of many IATs this has been the case in the past, for example, the UNAT. In all cases, whatever the terminology used to describe the emoluments, (b) and (c) above must be satisfied.

Secondly, it is important that emoluments *not be reduced*, whether as a penalty or otherwise, during tenure of office. If this could happen, it would compromise the independence, including the impartiality, of judges. The problem of a reduction is a real one. It is known that emoluments (fees) of the judges of the UNAT were reduced in 2001 during their tenure of office. This is clearly a violation of the principle being examined and jeopardizes independence. In this connection, it may be of significance that the constitutional law of some states, as security against bias and partiality (towards the government as the appointing authority, generally, but even otherwise), specifically provides that the emoluments of the judges of their high court may not be reduced during tenure. It is to be noted that the practical effect in general of the prohibition of the reduction of remuneration during tenure is that not only can the remuneration of judges already appointed never be reduced but that of new appointees may not be below the level of that of the tenured judges. If it were, there would be a violation of another fundamental principle of law which does not permit discrimination. Clearly, in the interpretation of the constitutive instruments of the judicial organs being discussed, a term must be *implied* which prevents the reduction of remuneration of judges of such tribunals during tenure, because those instruments are silent on the matter. Such interpretation is undoubtedly, if an explanation were sought, on a teleological basis. But, even if there were to be express conditions in any constitutive instruments, which relate to emoluments, and contradict in any way the principle of non-reduction of remuneration as described and discussed above, they must be excluded, to the extent basically that the contradiction is eliminated. Further, it is also logical that a contradiction of the above nature cannot be necessarily implied in constitutive instruments, where there is no express provision reflecting the above contradictions.

Thirdly, though it may be thought that *increasing* judges' emoluments does not create problems at all with the principle of independence, at most this may be a general observation. There are circumstances in which increases of salaries may create such problems. Here too the conceptual development of the general principle relating to the independence of the judiciary has the same requirements *mutatis mutandis* as in the cases discussed in the previous paragraphs. Consequently, the question is whether an increase in emoluments can violate the derivative principle. Although it may be thought that increases can never be harmful to the principle, because, for instance, an increase inheres to the financial benefit of the recipient, there are circumstances in which an increase in emoluments could affect the required independence. A good example is a situation in which an increase may be exorbitant in the context, according to reasonable standards which are applicable. The point is that, even if the increase is applied to all judges which makes for equality of treatment and, thus, provides no basis for possible bias or prejudice resulting from inequality or discrimination, such an increase could very well be construed as a bribe given to the judges by the organization, which is in one way or another a party in the judicial proceedings, in order to secure a judgment favourable to it. Equally, if an increase of emoluments which is reasonable is made in advance of a particular case, such an action may also be construed as a bribe in like manner as in the previous case. In the final analysis, while the derivative principle may be clear, it is the total contextual situation to which it is applied that will determine the result of such application.

It should be noted that in the case of all the tribunals in issue the authority dealing with the remuneration of judges is an organ of an international organization which is always directly or constructively a party to the proceedings before each of those tribunals.[67] This fact is contextually relevant to the principles relating to independence.[68]

Reappointment of judges

The statutes of almost all IATs permit the reappointment of judges. The UNAT Statute now permits only one such renewal after a four-year term. There are other statutes that limit the number of renewals.[69] But most statutes have no limitations at all, and all permit renewals. As for the ICTY and the ICTR, their statutes provide for unlimited reappointments.

Renewals create a problem, regardless of whether the renewal is a single one. The problem was first adverted to in connection with IATs in the first edition of my treatise on *The Law of the International Civil Service*.[70] Subsequently, in an article entitled 'Judging with and Legal Advising in International Organizations' (which I was invited to contribute to the *Chicago Journal of International Law* (2001), vol. 2, p. 293), I adverted to the problem again. The problem is as follows. The organization is always the respondent in cases before the IAT. The organization also makes the appointments and the renewals. While an initial appointment by the organization may not interfere with impartiality and independence, because once an appointment is made there are no constraints on judges acting freely, the prospect of a renewal does create a conflict of interest. The possibility exists that the judge may favour the organization in the hope or expectation of his term being renewed. It is not whether he does or does not that matters but whether it is possible, or there is a temptation, for him to do so. That is where there is a conflict of interest. What is more, an analogy must be drawn with the maxim, 'justice

---

[67] The case of IATs needs no clarification or explanation. That the prosecutor in the case of the ICTY and the ICTR appears on behalf of the international community is a reasonable conclusion. It is clear in the circumstances that it is the UN that represents the international community. The GA, an organ of the UN, controls the remuneration of the judges of these tribunals.

[68] A slightly different view of principles relating to emoluments was taken earlier by me in Amerasinghe, note 8 (1st ed., 1988) vol. I, pp. 71*ff.* and (2nd ed., 1994) vol. I, pp. 71*ff.* After review, I have concluded that the view taken in the text above is correct.

[69] The UNAT Statute in Article 3.2 provides for only one reappointment. The WBAT Statute in Article IV.3 provides for unlimited reappointment. The IDBAT Statute in Article III.3 and the OASAT Statute in Article III.3 provide for reappointment for only one additional term. Some statutes such as the Statute of the Administrative Tribunal of the OECD are silent on the matter.

[70] Amerasinghe, note 8 (1st ed., 1988) vol. I, p. 71 (repeated in *ibid.* (2nd ed., 1994) vol. I, pp. 70–1).

must not only be done but must appear to be done'. The point does not need to be laboured.[71] As a consequence, an absolute prohibition of reappointment must be implied, if not expressly included, in the constitutive instruments of all the international tribunals being considered here. Moreover, it may be noted in this connection that the argument that judges are chosen generally from senior professionals who may not be particularly interested in reappointment, as they do not depend on their judgeships for a living, is not a relevant consideration. The background of candidates is clearly not a factor at all in this regard.[72] The solution is to have one non-renewable term.[73] Because there are several judges, continuity could be ensured by having the appointments start and terminate in different years, that is, appointments could be spaced out.[74]

What is said above in respect of IATs applies *mutatis mutandis* to the ICTY and the ICTR. It is to be noted that in the case of these tribunals, as already pointed out, the UN is, derivatively, at least, a party in the proceedings before the tribunals. Therefore, the derivative principle relating to reappointment growing from conceptual development of the basic fundamental principle relating to independence as applied to the three kinds of tribunals under discussion is that reappointment of judges of

---

[71] 2 Chicago JIL (2001) at p. 293.

[72] I want to point out that I was appointed to the UNAT in January 1998. My three-year term came to an end in December 2000. I did not seek re-election, although my government would have liked me to have been a candidate for reappointment, and it was quite clear that I would have been a shoe-in for the Asian seat. It was a matter of principle for me. I was a judge of the Commonwealth Secretariat Administrative Tribunal which adjudicates on staff employment cases as an IAT, principally, but among other things. I was appointed in November 1999 for three years. Always I had no intention of seeking or accepting reappointment and did not do so.

[73] As it may take time for a judge of any of the three kinds of tribunal to become accustomed to the nature of the judicial operations in them, it is advisable to give them a fairly long term, e.g. seven years.

[74] I should like to draw your attention to the fact that not only have I tested the problem on laymen, but I have mentioned it to counsel for staff members before tribunals, including UNAT and WBAT. They have all seen the point. Indeed, some of them thought that they should test the waters before national courts in 'enlightened' legal systems. They would argue that such courts must make an exception to the immunity of organizations and assume jurisdiction, because IATs with renewals of judges' terms (reappointments) are not impartial or independent on the face of it, and, therefore, are constituted in violation of fundamental principles of law; if staff members in these circumstances do not have access to national courts, they would have no recourse to a fair and impartial adjudicatory system. There would certainly be an inducement for national courts to regard the immunity of organizations as not applicable because of this.

these tribunals militates against their independence and is, therefore, prohibited.

Conflict of interest

A derivative principle (based on conceptual development) flowing from the fundamental general principle relating to *independence* (including and emphasizing impartiality) concerns conflict of interest in the case of a judge (or judges) or even judicial organs. Where there is a conflict of interest of any kind, the judge or judges or even the whole court or tribunal in respect of whom or which this conflict exists must not in effect take any part in the proceedings concerned. This is the basic principle. The principle is to be applied prospectively in a preventive manner at any time during the proceedings, with the result that the proceedings are terminated forthwith, or retrospectively in effect to nullify the proceedings. Conflict of interest is a general concept common, though perhaps with different names, in legal systems generally. In fact, the principle has apparently never been disputed in any system of law including public international law, though there have been difficulties in applying it. Difficulties in application to particular circumstances there may be, partly because the concept of conflict of interest must be left broad. The principle, however, is clear and accepted, and the concept unequivocally acknowledged. Further, that there is a possibility of conflict of interest which may be even serious cannot be doubted.

An example and a precedent related to an IAT which illustrates both the meaning of conflict of interest and the application of the principle is given here.[75] This will suffice to establish the importance and applicability of the principle, which, of course, *inter alia*, applies to the other two tribunals which are the subject of this chapter.

In brief, a tribunal composed of three judges appointed from the panel of five on the CSAT by the President of the CSAT, pursuant to the provisions of the Statute of the CSAT and including the President, was replaced by order of the President in mid-stream, that is, after the written proceedings had been completed and in the course of the oral proceedings, by a tribunal of one of the three judges, ostensibly in accordance with the Statute and the rules of the tribunal. The third judge[76] dissented from the order made by the President on the ground that

[75] On the case in question, see Amerasinghe, note 3 pp. 160*ff*. The case was the *Mohsin Case* (2001), CSAT Judgment No. 3.

[76] This was I. An account of what happened in the case is given in Amerasinghe, note 3 pp. 164*ff*.

it was illegal and invalid. The single judge tribunal which had been constituted proceeded subsequently to decide the case on the merits. Apparently, the issue of the jurisdiction of the tribunal was not raised by the parties, nor was it raised *proprio motu* by the single judge, so that it could be addressed by the parties. The judgment on the merits referred to the order of the President reconstituting the tribunal by replacement as a single judge tribunal.

The first issue in this case was whether the jurisdictional question was *res judicata*, even though it had not been raised. This question is not discussed here because it is not as such relevant to conflict of interest.[77] The second issue was whether the reconstituted tribunal of one judge could decide the question of its own jurisdiction arising from the circumstances of its constitution which resulted in its being unlawfully constituted. It will be noted in this connection that the single judge earlier supported as a judge of the earlier tribunal the President's order reconstituting the tribunal and the single judge was the judge appointed as a consequence of the order. It is unnecessary to discuss the merits of the issue of constitutionality. What is relevant is that the circumstances in which the single judge was appointed were open to question, raised an issue of the validity of the reconstitution of the tribunal, and the single judge was not only involved in the decision making the appointment and supported it but was the judge appointed. Clearly, in these circumstances, the single judge did not have the lawful authority to decide the question of the constitution of the tribunal on the answer to which rested the resolution of the issue of jurisdiction, because there was a clear conflict of interest. Whether the issue of jurisdiction, therefore, was raised or not, the judgment on the merits could be contested as being null and void by one or both of the parties because the tribunal's implied decision to assume jurisdiction was tainted as a result of conflict of interest. It is irrelevant that the one or both parties did not object to the tribunal's exercising jurisdiction. The existence of a conflict of interest would taint the exercise of jurisdiction in any case, whether there was an explicit decision on jurisdiction following argument by the parties or not, and whether there was tacit acquiescence on the part of one or both of the parties. An absence of jurisdiction cannot be cured by default.[78] The result was that the judgment on the merits had no validity and could have been annulled, basically because of a conflict of interest. The above explanation of the position and the

---

[77] On this issue in general, see *ibid.* at pp. 200*ff.*   [78] See *ibid.*

view taken above of the conflict of interest and its consequences are very important.[79]

In particular, the relevance of the principle of conflict of interest to decisions on *jurisdiction* (*compétence*) in general, in regard to which the issue of conflict of interest may legitimately be raised is a difficult one, even in the context of national legal systems. The idea that a tribunal has the authority both to determine whether it has jurisdiction to determine its own jurisdiction (of whatever kind) and to determine whether it has jurisdiction (of whatever kind) in a given case has within it a possibility that a conflict of interest may in principle exist. Because in both instances the tribunal, whether of one judge or more, may have an interest in preserving its own jurisdiction and makes the decision on the issue, it is possible to postulate an inherent conflict of interest. However, in spite of this reality, it has been the practice to recognize in the case of both national and international tribunals their legal authority to make these determinations, whether there is an appeal to a higher tribunal or not, though in general in national systems there is some control by a higher judicial authority. In the international system the authority has now in principle come never to be questioned to the extent that it may exist according to law in a given case.

The alternative to having the tribunal decide matters of jurisdiction is to have another independent tribunal determine it for the tribunal. But this would, *inter alia*, involve delays and be a very cumbersome procedure, whenever an objection to jurisdiction is raised. The fact, however, is that the possibility of a conflict of interest as such in the ordinary case *per se* has never been faced.[80]

---

[79] There are circumstances in national jurisdictions where the exercise of jurisdiction by a court has been declared null and void because of a conflict of interest in one of the judges of the court: see the *Pinochet Case*, 38 ILM (1999) at p. 432, a decision of the House of Lords of the UK in which a different bench of judges of the House set aside a judgment of the House in an earlier case on the same matter and between the same parties (*Pinochet Case*, 38 ILM (1999) at p. 581).

[80] In the *Betsey Case*, the two commissioners whose conclusion was subsequently accepted did refer to the possibility of another tribunal determining the issue of *la compétence de la compétence*: Moore, *History and Digest of International Arbitrations* (1898) vol. 3, p. 2282. However, this alternative was not mentioned in the context of a possible conflict of interest. The commissioners referred to two alternatives to recognizing *la compétence de la compétence*, one being reference to another tribunal, the other being the simple assumption that in any case the tribunal had jurisdiction. Reference back to the parties was not considered a viable alternative because this was said not to have been requested. Reference to another tribunal was regarded as not having been authorized

That having been said, the question that arises is whether, even *assuming* that the mere vesting in a tribunal of authority in relation to jurisdiction does not call for rejection as illegal because of a conflict of interest of the exercise of the authority to determine matters connected with its jurisdiction, the exercise of that authority could exceptionally be unlawful and invalid because of a conflict of interest. That there is a possibility of a serious conflict of interest in certain circumstances, as shown by the precedent described above, cannot be doubted. The particular question raised above, regardless of the answer to the more general question, must be answered in the affirmative.[81]

Mention may be made of a provision which appears in the statutes of some IATs, for example the IDBAT and the OASAT, to the effect that staff members or, in the case of the IDBAT, current or former staff members do not qualify for judgeships on the respective IATs.[82] This kind of disqualification is clearly based on the principle relating to conflict of interest. Further examples of similar disqualifications obviously and reasonably based on conflict of interest appear elsewhere in IAT statutes such as those to be found also in Article III(2) of the OASAT Statute.[83] Such disqualifications, correctly, are absolute and cannot be avoided. While these particular disqualifications are expressly included in those statutes, they are undoubtedly implied, if not expressed, in any IAT statute, because they are based on conflict of interest which militates against judicial independence. By the same token, if these disqualifications are expressly, or even conceivably by implication, excepted from IAT statutes, such an exception to disqualifications which is clearly based on a conflict of interest cannot be recognized and must be struck down. Undoubtedly, regardless of cases of circumstantial conflict of interest,[84]

---

by the treaty of submission and the alternative of assuming that the tribunal had jurisdiction in any case was said to be an unjust solution.

[81] It is emphasized, nevertheless, that the more general question needs further study. The question of conflict of interest and its impact on jurisdictional decisions was first raised and discussed by me in Amerasinghe, note 3 pp. 150*ff.* and pp. 201*ff.*

[82] Article III(1) of the IDBAT Statute, in Amerasinghe (ed.), note 12 p. 63; and Article III(2) of the OASAT Statute, in Amerasinghe (ed.), *ibid.* p. 85. See also Article I(1) of the COEAB Statute, in Amerasinghe (ed.), *ibid.* p. 121; and SR 34.2 of the ESAAB Statute, in Amerasinghe (ed.), *ibid.* p. 149.

[83] *Ibid.* at p. 85.

[84] The example taken from the experience of the CSAT discussed earlier would reflect what is referred to above as a circumstantial conflict of interest as contrasted with what is described as a non-circumstantial one.

there are other examples of absolute or other non-circumstantial disqualifications, based on conflict of interest, which are relevant to judgeships on IATs. These would be recognized and taken account of in the same manner as those specifically referred to above, again as referable to the fundamental principle of independence of judges of IATs.

The registry

The registry (sometimes called in English the 'secretariat' though this latter term is incorrect here because the three types of judicial organ (IATs, the ICTY and the ICTR) being discussed here, as already pointed out, are in essence and genuinely judicial organs and not organs of any other kind) needs to be considered in the context of the fundamental principle of law relating to *independence* of the judicial organ. While the registry is not part of the bench of judges of the judicial organ, it is part of the judicial organ (i.e., the relevant IAT, the ICTY or ICTR).

The fundamental principle of law is, as stated earlier, that the *independence* of the *judicial organ* be preserved, respected and ensured, not merely that of the *bench of judges*. But that having been said, when the broad basic fundamental principle is conceptually developed to apply to the registry as an integral and very important part of the judicial organ, namely the IAT or other tribunal, for a variety of reasons the narrower principle, though still fundamental, acquires a singular definition. One of the main reasons is that the registry is the administrative arm of the organ. A second is that the staff of the registry is a part of the international organization which established it, has administrative oversight over it and, most importantly, is always, as respondent, a party to cases brought before the tribunal. It is to be noted that, as far as emoluments (which in this case in reality include benefits and the like) of the registry staff are concerned, these are paid or provided by the organization which is also the case, it is acknowledged, with the emoluments of the judges. At the same time, as in the case of the judges, emoluments of registry staff are matters which are covered by the basic broad fundamental principle relating to independence and clearly must be considered in connection with any narrower principle relating to independence which may be developed.

What is said above points to a reality that is really self-evident in regard to developing conceptually the basic fundamental principle of independence, particularly in respect of the registries of all three types of judicial organ being discussed, namely that there are certain apparently unavoidable features of international organizations which would seem, according to reason, to militate against 'independence', even as conceptually developed. Examples, of which there are others, include the facts that (i) there is administrative oversight – of some kind, different perhaps in each case – of the registries by the international organization, and (ii) that the emoluments of registry staff must come from a source under the control of the international organization. The difficulty arises because the international organization concerned is involved in the cases that come before all these tribunals in a way which makes it either a party or similar to a party in those cases. In respect of IATs, the organization is always the respondent in cases; in respect of the ICTY and the ICTR, the prosecutor always acts in cases in the interest of the international community which is clearly represented by the UN as a, so to speak, 'corporate' legal person. Thus, the rhetorical question that may be asked is: if a party to the case controls or can control in some material way the registry as part of the tribunal concerned, is not this by itself an infringement of the tribunal's independence? The answer, as already stated, is self-evident, but in the international organizational system as it is now structured this feature cannot apparently be avoided. Even if it can be, it is necessary to deal with the feature as it stands. Thus, the only manner in which the principle of independence can be developed and applied to the registries of the relevant judicial organs is to min- imize the damage, so to speak. Therefore, all that the development of the narrower principle can do is to accept and take into account as a premise such features as have been adverted to above which basically, as is apparent, militate against independence.

That having been said, on the one hand, there is no reason at all to ignore as inapplicable the principle of independence, which must be applied, as a matter of essence, to the registry as part of the tribunal, and, on the other, because the broad fundamental principle is accepted as being applicable, it is unnecessary to pay special attention to develop- ing it conceptually in detail with reference to specific areas of relevance, such as the budget or discipline of staff. In the circumstances, it is suffi- cient to apply the broad general principle as conceptually developed only with a specific reference to the registry as part of the tribunal to which the principle is applicable. What may also be pointed out in passing, so to speak, is that the developed principle applicable to the registry must be directed especially, but not only, to ensuring the *impartiality*, as an important aspect of independence, of the registry and its staff, especially in dealing with and processing cases brought before the tri- bunal, but also in dealing with both the staff of the organization, both in particular and in general, and the administration of the organization, both potential parties or sources of parties to cases brought before the tribunal.

It follows that it suffices to deal with one important example of a contextual situation, it being recognized that without question the fundamental general principle of independence is applicable to it, reference being made where possible and appropriate to relevant instruments and practices. This example concerns the registrar or director (inaptly sometimes called the 'executive secretary') of the secretariat of an IAT. The fundamental principle of independence requires that the registrar's independence from the organization's administration be preserved to the greatest extent possible, not only in fact but also in appearance, in keeping, by analogy, with the maxim 'justice must not merely be done but be seen to be done'. As it is, it must also be noted, the principle referred to here is in any case an implied *fundamental* provision, with all the consequences of its having such a character, even if it is not mentioned in the constitutive documents of tribunals. While some statutes, such as that of the WBAT, make it quite clear that the registrar in the execution of his duties is responsible solely to the tribunal,[85] there is more to it than that. For example, he must not be requested by the administration to do anything outside his territory and involving the administration of the organization, nor must his performance reviews be handled in such a way that he is beholden to the administration of the organization for his performance assessments. The point is so obvious that it does not need to be laboured. Two examples of actual practice which interfere or interfered with the independence of the registrar are here given.

First, in one organization the Registrar was a part-time officer within the organization who worked for another department and whose performance reviews were done entirely by the head in the latter department. The question is not whether the President of the Tribunal or the Tribunal had input into, but whether the President or the Tribunal had sole responsibility for, the review with *no material input* from anyone else. The requirement creates some difficulties, but there are viable solutions to the problem.

Secondly, in another organization the Executive Secretary (as the registrar was known) was (sometimes as chairman) on

---

[85] WBAT Doc. Rules/Rev.2 (1995) at p. 2.

administration committees dealing with dispute settlement procedures in the organization. Not only should he not have been on such committees but he should not as such have been on any administration committees at all. It was important for his independence and impartiality that he not be seen as participating in activities outside his office which pertained in this case to the administration of the organization.

These two examples contain clear violations of the fundamental principle being discussed as conceptually developed and contextually applied to the registry of any of the tribunals under discussion.

The object is to keep the registrar as independent as possible, even though he may be a regular staff member. First, a guarantee of non-interference and non-influence in any way by the administration with the registrar must be written into the constitutive documents of all the tribunals being discussed. This is, however, merely a formal beginning. There must be a balance, needless to say, in the interpretation of the basic principle and its contextual application between, for instance, *needed* (and not complete) *supervision* by the administration of, for example, the budget, and necessary insulation of the registrar from the administration. Equally, it is implied, again as a fundamental requirement, that in the application of the basic principle of independence, the independence of the registrar from the staff (including its representatives) be in practice actually ensured and preserved, because the staff or its representatives are potential parties before the tribunal.

Further, because it is the independence of the registry as a whole which is in issue, the same considerations apply, *mutatis mutandis*, to *all* staff of the registry. The developmental application of the relevant principle to *all the staff* of the registry is as important as its development and application to the registrar.

Legislative powers of the creating authority

The principal problems, which may arise in connection with the legislative powers of the creating authority, stem from two distinctive contextual features. These are (i) that the legislative authority (which may have one or more organs performing the function of legislating) is the international organization which is also a party to proceedings before all the judicial organs being considered, thus creating what is obviously a conflict of interest, and (ii) the fact that, though there generally are no express limitations on the legislative power of the organization which relate to the maintenance and preservation of the independence of the judicial organs, there must be implied limitations, where necessary, which will achieve the same purpose.

As for the first feature, it is probably something that cannot be avoided in modern society. It is, perhaps, paralleled by what happens in national political and legal systems where the state which legislates in effect may also be a party in proceedings brought before the national courts, though in this case the state is not a party in all such proceedings. However, in spite of this unavoidable conflict of interest, fundamental principles of law referred to in the second feature above prevent the conflict of interest, among other things, from having adverse effects on the independence of the judicial organs.

It is unnecessary to elaborate on how the fundamental principle relating to independence is implemented in respect of legislative authority. Suffice it to say that the broad fundamental principle that the independence of the judicial organ at all times must be preserved, maintained and not infringed must be applied in such a way to legislative powers as to ensure that legislation not only has positive effects in terms of independence but does not have negative effects. For example, to give a very obvious example, legislation cannot dispense with appropriate and necessary legal qualifications for judges which could result in improperly qualified judges being appointed, nor include as required qualifications additional to those which are appropriate and necessary with the result that it is possible that the proper emphasis is not given to the latter qualifications which could have the result of the best candidates not being selected. It is apparent that the fundamental principle would apply in other respects which cannot be elaborated upon here.[86]

Concluding observations

While the above discussion and analysis has focused mainly on IATs and on the ICTY and the ICTR, which are the only known examples of *judicial organs* of international organizations which constitute the subject matter of this chapter, the conclusions of principle, and sometimes others,

---

[86] It may also be noted that there are other fundamental principles of law which apply to the legislative activity of international organizations in respect of legislation concerning the judicial organ in issue. These have the effect of both imposing limitations and compelling positive action in respect of legislative activity of organizations. The fundamental principle, in whatever formulation it takes, that staff members of organizations cannot be deprived of their acquired rights is, for example, a principle that controls the legislation that IATs apply. Needless to say, there are many other such fundamental principles.

are generally applicable, *mutatis mutandis*, to any judicial organ of international organizations of the same kind. Furthermore, it is to be noted that those general principles and their development or 'concretization' which pertain to the essence of the judicial function or power – and these are easily identifiable from the discussion above – no doubt apply generally, *mutatis mutandis*, of course, to judicial bodies of the international legal system.[87]

There are some other observations of a general but very pertinent nature which must be made.

First, there is considerable difficulty, it would have been noted, in being specific in regard to both broad and narrow principles when the basic fundamental principle of law of the independence of judicial organs is conceptually developed. This is so essentially because both the concept of independence in the basic principle and the content of the narrower principles which emerge with conceptual development are of a very general nature and comparatively indeterminate (or vague). This is not a defect in the principles, but instead stems principally from the nature of the concepts involved in them, which by the very nature of the subject share that character. The lack of specificity is also a result of the fact that all circumstances in which the principles concerned must be applied cannot be envisaged in the abstract and anticipated. A consequence of this latter fact is that a certain flexibility in the application of the principles themselves is not only needed but is advantageous. It is clear also that the vagueness or indeterminacy in both the broad and narrow principles, though perhaps inconvenient and open to criticism from the point of view of foreseeability of the results of the application of the principles, are unavoidable as a matter of common sense and the inherent nature of the principles. This admittedly places a heavy but unavoidable and necessary responsibility on those who must in one way or another recognize and apply the principles, which clearly must be appropriately and honestly discharged.

Secondly, in developing narrower principles, that is, by conceptual development, there are certain important premises which must be accepted and cannot be disregarded, although in themselves they militate against the independence of judicial organs. These premises depend on the structure and circumstances of international political society, to

---

[87] There is no reason why the general principles, *inter alia*, which are of the essence of the judicial function or power as such should not apply, with modifications where necessary, to the judicial power in national legal systems. This is, however, not in issue here.

which the international legal system belongs, and particularly of its organization, partly through international organizations which appear to be a necessary phenomenon which has evolved, to the best of our knowledge, in the best interests of that society. Furthermore, some of these premises, such as the source of funds for the emoluments of judges, to mention one obvious example, are common to both the international political society and national political societies, which may signify that, at least at present, they are inherent and unavoidable.

Thirdly, while some other issues have been addressed, this part of this chapter has concentrated on *independence* as an essential quality requiring the application, in the context mainly of the judicial organs which have been the subject of discussion and analysis, of a fundamental principle of law. Independence has been described in general as the *essence* of the judicial function as such. What this means in effect is that, when the fundamental principle of law relating to independence is in any way violated, because of the essential nature of that principle, the judicial organ in reality ceases, for all purposes, including practical purposes, to be exercising judicial functions. Stated in different terms, the judicial function, in this case, exercised by the judicial organ concerned requires by *definition* that the fundamental principle of law relating to independence, including any derivative principles of law resulting from the conceptual development of such basic principle, be respected, in order that the judicial organ remain a judicial body with power to perform judicial functions.

Independence of the judicial organ clearly is one of the most important qualities, if not the most important quality, to be respected and preserved. While, on the one hand, as pointed out earlier, only a limited but adequate conceptual development or concretization of the basic fundamental principle relating to independence has been attempted, on the other, there are other essential values than independence which are to be respected and preserved by fundamental general principles of law, if judicial organs, including those of the kind discussed, are to retain their character as judicial organs. There are fundamental principles of law which are applicable and relate to jurisdictional powers or judicial organs. These principles, or the more important ones among them, have been discussed by me in my treatise on *Jurisdiction of International Tribunals*.[88] There are also fundamental principles which ensure that certain inherent powers, essential to judicial organs and relating

---

[88] Amerasinghe, note 3, *passim*.

to remedies, cannot be taken away, whether absolutely, in a limited manner or relatively, from judicial organs.[89] Similarly, there are fundamental principles of law relating to evidence and procedure which must be respected.[90] These are but examples of areas in which fundamental principles of law are applicable.

What emerges as a result of the analysis and discussion here is that there are certain fundamental principles of law which certainly apply to judicial organs of the kind discussed in this chapter.[91] The effect of their being violated, whether, for instance, by legislation or by direct agreement of the parties to litigation, will depend on the principle violated and other factors.[92] In the case of the principle relating to independence, the result of violation is generally that the organ ceases to be a judicial organ acting judicially and, therefore, its acts and judgments are null and void.[93]

The status of judicial organs

The purpose of this part of the chapter is to discuss the status of judicial institutions which, first, are judicial organs, properly so called; secondly, are not organs of international organizations which, though not judicial organs as such, perform functions that are 'quasi-judicial' in nature (examples of which have been given at pp. 223–4 above); and, thirdly, are judicial organs *of* international organizations, such as those described at pp. 220–3 above. Thus, though the ICJ is described as a principal organ

---

[89] *Ibid.* pp. 385*ff.*

[90] The examples given here are neither exhaustive nor exclusive.

[91] The same fundamental principles should apply, *mutatis mutandis*, to other judicial organs, whether international or national.

[92] The effects, for example, may be nullity of acts and judgments of the organ (whether or not the organ has ceased to be a judicial organ), or may merely render the offending provision totally inapplicable and without effect, or may render the offending provision only partially inapplicable and without effect.

[93] It must also have become apparent, from the discussion and analysis, because of the nature both of the judicial function and of judicial organs that (i) there are fundamental principles of law applicable to international judicial organs as such, however created or established, (ii) the violation of such fundamental principles may have the effect of depriving the so-called judicial organ of its judicial character with power to perform judicial functions, (iii) without prejudice to (ii) above, the effect of legal provisions and other acts or omissions which result in the violation of such fundamental principles may vary, and (iv) such fundamental principles apply equally, where contextually appropriate, and *mutatis mutandis*, to judicial organs as such in any system of law, including national systems. This is not the place to examine all these matters. It is sufficient to draw attention to them and their importance.

of the UN in Article 7(1) of the UN Charter, it is not the object of consideration here, because it belongs to the first category as discussed at pp. 218–20 above.[94]

The real issue, as far as status is concerned, is whether judicial organs, properly so called, and belonging to the second category discussed at pp. 220–3 above are 'subsidiary' or not, and perhaps whether they are 'subordinate', if there is a difference in meaning between the two terms. Further, the question arises how they should be described, if they are not subsidiary (or subordinate). It is to be noted that terms such as 'subordinate' and 'secondary', in addition to 'subsidiary', were used to describe some such organs (for example the UNAT). These three terms were used by the ICJ in the *Effect of Awards Case*[95] in connection with the description of the status of the UNAT which was created (or established) by the UNGA. In dealing with the characterization of the UNAT, the ICJ said:

This view assumes that, in adopting the Statute of the Administrative Tribunal, the General Assembly was establishing an organ which it deemed necessary for the performance of its own functions. But the Court cannot accept this basic assumption. The Charter does not confer judicial functions on the General Assembly and the relations between staff and Organization come within the scope of Chapter XV of the Charter . . . By establishing the Administrative Tribunal, the General Assembly was not delegating the performance of its own functions: it was exercising a power which it had under the Charter to regulate staff relations. In regard to the Secretariat the General Assembly is given by the Charter a power to make regulations, but not a power to adjudicate upon, or otherwise deal with, particular instances.

It has been argued that an authority exercising power to make regulations is inherently incapable of creating a subordinate body competent to make decisions binding its creator . . . There can be no doubt that the Administrative Tribunal is *subordinate* in the sense that the General Assembly can abolish the Tribunal by repealing the Statute, it can amend the Statute and provide for review of the future decisions of the Tribunal and that it can amend the Staff Regulations and make new ones. There is no lack of power to deal effectively with any problem that may arise. But the contention that the General Assembly is inherently incapable of creating a tribunal competent to make decisions binding on itself cannot be accepted. It cannot be justified by analogy to national laws, for it is common practice in national legislatures to create courts with the

---

[94] Clearly, the ICJ is not in any way a 'subsidiary' organ *of* any other organ of the UN, the critical fact being that it is described as an organ *of the UN*, and not as an organ of any other organ of the UN.

[95] 1954 ICJ Reports at p. 61.

capacity to render decisions legally binding on the legislatures which brought them into being.

The question cannot be determined on the basis of the description of the relationship between the General Assembly and the Tribunal, that is, by considering whether the Tribunal is to be regarded as a subsidiary, a subordinate, or a secondary organ, or on the basis of the fact that it was established by the General Assembly. It depends on the intention of the General Assembly in establishing the Tribunal, and on the nature of the functions conferred upon it by its Statute. An examination of the language of the Statute of the Administrative Tribunal has shown that the General Assembly intended to establish a judicial body; moreover, it has the legal capacity under the Charter to do so.[96]

In the above citation from the advisory opinion of the ICJ it is not clear, in the first place, whether the terms 'subsidiary', 'subordinate' and 'secondary' were being used with an identical meaning or not. It would appear that the linguistic usage in the citation indicates that the terms were being used in such a way that differences were being made without explicit distinctions. Secondly, it is to be noted that the term 'subordinate' is used earlier in the citation actually to describe the UNAT, solely because the UNGA had the power (i) to abolish the UNAT by repealing the Statute of the UNAT, (ii) to amend such Statute, (iii) to provide for the review of the UNAT's judgments and (iv) to amend the Staff Regulations and make new ones.

The opinion is confused and unclear both as regards why the term 'subordinate' is used with certainty in the characterization of the UNAT and in regard to the *reasons* given for such characterization. In fact, some of the considerations taken into account in making the particular characterization, such as making provision for the review of judgments of the UNAT and amending the Staff Regulations, as such, and making new Staff Regulations, as such, would appear to be patently irrelevant to such characterization.

It should be noted that particularly as a result of the above confusion, lack of clarity and apparent use of the three terms, 'subsidiary', 'subordinate' and 'secondary', virtually as synonyms, the opinion clearly cannot be regarded as settling the issue of characterization (or, indeed, helping to settle it) nor does the opinion really help to solve the issue of what term or terms should be used to describe the UNAT.

It is also not clear, indeed, what meaning, if any, the Court attributed to any or all of the three terms referred to above and ostensibly the subject of discussion in the opinion! Additionally, the discussion in

---

[96] *Ibid.* (emphasis added).

the citation does not adequately indicate what 'question' is being answered.[97]

However, there are several points made in the opinion (i.e., in the part of the opinion cited above) which are of interest in regard to the issue being considered here. Some of these appear to contradict each other, some are abstruse and appear in fact to have little logical connection with the issue being discussed, all of them are, for whatever reason, difficult to comprehend in terms of such issue, and the relevance of some, if not all, to the issue may even be questioned. The relationship between some issues is not clear. An attempt will be made to summarize, quoting, where necessary, from the opinion, the points referred to above, which are ten in number.

The points are:

(a) the GA 'can abolish' the UNAT 'by repealing the Statute' of the UNAT;
(b) the GA 'can amend' the Statute of the UNAT;
(c) the GA 'can provide for review of the future decisions' of the UNAT;
(d) the contention that 'the GA is inherently incapable of creating a tribunal competent to make decisions binding on itself cannot be accepted';
(e) the argument that 'an authority exercising power to make regulations is inherently capable of creating a subordinate body competent to make decisions binding on its creator cannot be accepted';
(f) in regard to the UN Secretariat, the GA 'is given by the Charter a power to make regulations, but not a power to adjudicate on, or otherwise deal with, particular instances';
(g) the UN Charter does not confer judicial functions on the GA;
(h) the assumption that, in adopting the Statute of the UNAT, the GA 'was establishing an organ which it deemed necessary for the performance of its own functions' could not be accepted;
(i) by establishing the UNAT the GA 'was not delegating the performance of its functions'; and
(j) the GA intended to establish 'a judicial body'.

Before considering the effect of the above points on the issue being discussed, taking into account the various criticisms made above, the additional observation may be made that in general the manner in which the points were made is not conducive to a clear understanding of how the issue being discussed should be examined and a solution reached, nor is it clear that the Court kept in mind throughout its exposition

---

[97] The opinion uses the term 'determined' rather than 'answered'.

the precise issue which it was discussing or that it was always considering the really relevant issue relating to the status of the UNAT which,
unfortunately, had been identified by the Court only rather confusingly
and elusively.

As a consequence of the position described above, what will be done
here is to consider *de novo* the really relevant and simple issue raised in
the opinion in connection with the status of the UNAT, namely whether
the UNAT was a 'subsidiary' organ of the GA which the GA had created
pursuant to Article 7(2) of the Charter. It is clear that, if the answer to
the question whether the UNAT is a 'subsidiary' organ of the GA under
Article 7(2) is that it is not a subsidiary organ, then logically it could not
be (i) a 'subordinate' or (ii) a 'secondary' organ of the GA (or UN) *under that
article*, assuming that such concepts are relevant in connection with that
article and assuming that each of these terms is for this purpose given
a meaning which is an accepted meaning in the English language. For
legal purposes, in connection with the status of judicial organs, however
created (established), there is no reason to suppose that the meaning of
each term is different from the accepted meaning in common English
usage. In fact, it is not at all clear that the issues of 'subordination'
or 'being secondary' are relevant in connection with the application of
that article, though the question of 'subordination' may be considered
separately.

In view of the above considerations, it is clearly not only unnecessary
to consider whether the UNAT was a 'subordinate' or 'secondary' organ of
the GA (or UN) under Article 7(2) but it is imperative that such concepts
be eliminated from the discussion of that article. On the other hand,
as noted above, irrespective of Article 7(2), the question of whether the
UNAT, a judicial organ (body), is 'subordinate' in any way to any other
organ of the UN or, indeed, to the UN itself may be considered separately.
Thus, for the purposes of the present exposition there are two questions
to be answered in connection with the status of the UNAT which the
Court conceded is a *judicial organ* which the GA intended to establish:

(a)   is the UNAT a *subsidiary* organ of the GA for the purposes of Article
      7(2) of the UN Charter?[98]
(b)   irrespective of Article 7(2), is the UNAT, a judicial organ, in any way
      subordinate to any other organ of the UN?

---

[98] It is to be noted that the ICJ in its opinion in relation to subsidiarity, referred to
Article 7(2). It is difficult to understand how the GA may create 'subsidiary' organs
except under Article 7(2).

Subsidiarity

As to the first question, it is clear that the GA's power to establish 'subsidiary' organs flows essentially from Article 7(2), which is the only place in the UN Charter where there is mention of the power to establish 'subsidiary' organs. As stated in regard to IATs in general in the first edition of this book published in 1996:

> It is important to note that these are not subsidiary organs of the organ of the organization establishing them or of any other organ. They are true judicial organs with independence and the capacity to give binding decisions like any court of justice – binding on the organization over which they exercise jurisdiction and even on the organs creating them.[99]

It follows from this that the UNAT, which the Court conceded was a judicial organ, could not be and was not established as a subsidiary organ under Article 7(2).

The Court in the *Effect of Awards Case* conceded that the UNAT was a judicial body and that the GA did not have judicial functions (which, therefore, obviously it could not delegate to a subsidiary organ, if judicial functions may be delegated at all, which is a separate question).[100] It also took the view that the GA, particularly as a body exercising authority to make regulations, i.e., exercising legislative powers, was not inherently incapable of creating a tribunal competent to make decisions binding on itself, that the GA intended to establish a judicial body, and that

---

[99] Amerasinghe, *Principles of the Institutional Law of International Organizations* (1st ed., 1996) p. 162. The statement made there is accurate. The reference is only to the 'subsidiarity' of IATs as organs of international organizations. It must be pointed out that it is unlikely that the statement made on p. 36 of vol. I of the first edition of my treatise on *The Law of the International Civil Service* (1988) in the context of a discussion of the status of the UNAT, in particular, and IATs in general, that 'they [IATs] may be "subordinate", but not "subsidiary"', is attributable to me, whatever the explanation. However, insofar as the statement describes IATs as *not* being 'subsidiary', it is correct. Insofar as it expressed a view on 'subordination' (which will be discussed later in this chapter), it is clear, as will appear, that it is incorrect. The identical statement is repeated in the second edition of the same treatise (1994), vol. 1, p. 36. This statement also is incorrect to the same extent as the earlier one. A different statement was made at p. 450 of the first edition of the present work: 'It [UNAT] may be a subsidiary organ but was not subordinate.' This statement contradicts the statement cited in the text above from p. 162 of the same work. Thus, within the same work, there are contradictory statements. Whatever the explanation, I doubt that I should take responsibility for such a contradiction! What is said in the text above at this footnote (99) reflects the correct position: IATs are never, nor can they be, subsidiary organs. The question of subordination is discussed later in this chapter.

[100] The proposition thus formulated flows from points (g), (h) and (i) made above as derived from the *Effect of Awards Case*.

the GA, in establishing the UNAT, was not delegating the performance of its functions.

These observations are accurate and logically lead to the conclusions that (i) the GA was not creating a body or organ with power to exercise functions which were delegated, which organ or body would consequently have had to be established pursuant to Article 7(2), and (ii) was establishing a judicial body with power to exercise judicial functions which were not functions delegated by the GA.

The Court did not in its discussion refer to Article 7(2) dealing with the establishment of subsidiary organs. Although it may have been useful and logically tidier to do so in order to make its reasoning clearer, this may not have been necessary, because its unequivocal conclusion was to be that the UNAT was not a subsidiary organ exercising delegated power. On the other hand, as a corollary, the Court's view implies that subsidiary organs necessarily in one way or another exercise delegated power which is an important general premise. It may be observed in passing that this premise is a necessary premise in the interpretation of Article 7(2).

Equally important are the conclusions which are implied that (a) *judicial* organs cannot be *subsidiary* organs in any sense, (b) *judicial* organs do not and may not exercise *delegated* functions, and (c) the GA had an implied power under the UN Charter to create *judicial* organs such as the UNAT. The source and nature of the latter power in relation to administrative tribunals, which the Court recognized, were discussed by the Court earlier in the opinion in the same case.[101] It is to be noted that the Court did not in its opinion advert to or recognize at all the implied conclusions referred to in (a) and (b) above which are necessary corollaries flowing from the nature of judicial organs exercising judicial functions.

Subordination

As to the second question, the Court stated in effect that the GA, as a legislative body, did have the power to create a 'subordinate' body competent to make decisions binding on the GA. This statement already has implications which are relevant to the attribution of powers to judicial organs and the content of such powers, but this is not a subject of discussion here. What is important is the characterization of a body

---

[101] 1954 ICJ Reports at p. 57. On this power, see Amerasinghe, note 8 vol. I (1994) pp. 34*ff*.

exercising judicial functions, i.e., a judicial organ, such as the UNAT, as a *subordinate* body.

In view of the earlier findings that the UNAT, as a judicial organ, could not be a *subsidiary* organ of the GA, it would appear to be a contradiction that the UNAT be characterized, nevertheless, as a *subordinate* organ of the GA. It is logical that an organ which is not subsidiary cannot be subordinate. Equally, it is logical in the present context that an organ which is subordinate must necessarily be subsidiary. The characterization by the ICJ of the UNAT as subordinate is, thus, patently wrong.

The Court also pointed out that the GA as a legislative body with power to make regulations could create a body competent to make decisions binding on the GA. Clearly, the body referred to was a judicial organ. It described such an organ as 'subordinate'. While the UNAT as a judicial body has the power to make judicial decisions binding on its creator, the GA, this feature does not make the UNAT a 'subordinate' body, because it is a judicial organ giving such judicial decisions and a judicial organ cannot be subordinate in the sense intended by the Court.

Furthermore, it does not follow that, because the GA has power to make regulations (laws), a power which is referred to by the Court and which includes the power in effect to alter or change what may be described as the law-creating impact of judicial decisions of the UNAT by subsequent legislation, the UNAT is an organ subordinate to the GA. Any appropriate legislative body, whether in the international or a national legal system, could enjoy such a power in relation to judicial organs but this does not make the latter subordinate to the former. This legislative power in relation to judicial organs is an inherent feature of legal systems in general. Judicial organs are never characterized as subordinate to appropriate legislative bodies as a result of this feature.

The Court further noted three features of the relationship between the GA and the UNAT: (i) that the GA could abolish the UNAT by repealing the Statute of the UNAT, (ii) that the GA could amend the Statute of the UNAT, and (iii) that the GA could provide for review of the future decisions of the UNAT. As pointed out in brief earlier, there are limitations on the powers reflected in (i) and (ii) above. Granting that, the powers listed in (i) to (iii) above do not affect the status of the UNAT as a judicial organ. The existence of such powers in any context, let alone in regard to the UNAT, does not alter in any way the conclusion reached above that the UNAT is not a subordinate body or organ. These are attributes of the relevant legislative authority, in relation to any judicial organ, subject to appropriate limitations which the Court does not discuss.

Conclusion

The above discussion of the status of the UNAT as a judicial organ of the UN which addresses issues of subsidiary and subordinate nature has been confined to the UNAT as a judicial organ of the UN which had been created by the GA pursuant to implied powers under the UN Charter. However, the specific conclusions reached in that connection are *mutatis mutandis* of general validity insofar as they may be extended so as to cover judicial organs created by organs, not only of the UN,[102] but of international organizations in general. This is not purely a matter of analogy. There is necessarily implied in those conclusions the broader general proposition that such judicial organs cannot be subsidiary (or subordinate)[103] organs of an organ of an international organization (or of an international organization itself in circumstances, if any, in which there could be subsidiary (or subordinate) organs of an international organization itself). The latter general proposition in turn flows from a general principle of law which is implicitly recognized in all legal systems, including the international legal system, i.e., that a judicial body (or organ) cannot be subsidiary or subordinate to another body or organ.[104]

The general principle of law, on the one hand, not evidently discussed or explicitly enunciated in the context of any legal system, perhaps because it is obvious, is not, on the other hand, denied or contested. Rather, it is implicitly recognized and applied in practice. This principle flows in fact from a broad general principle of law, again implicitly recognized and applied in practice, which basically concerns the fundamental nature of organs or bodies which are truly judicial; and in essence requires them to be independent.[105] The latter broad principle is, as has been seen, the basis also of many of the conclusions reached

---

[102] It should be noted that the conclusions apply naturally to the ICTY and the ICTR, which are judicial organs created by the UNSC.

[103] The use of other terms such as 'secondary' in this context does not make a difference. It is inappropriate to describe such organs as 'secondary'. On the other hand, such organs may not be 'principal' organs in the sense that the ICJ is a principal organ of the UN under the UN Charter. But it is not proper to describe a judicial organ which is not such a principal organ as a secondary organ.

[104] There may be qualifications of this rule in respect of judicial bodies (or organs), within a system of judicial bodies (or organs), in any legal system, national or international. This is, however, not the subject of consideration here. This issue has in fact never been raised.

[105] This is not the place to discuss the broad general principle of *independence* of *judicial bodies* or *organs* and its many ramifications. Reference is made to my treatise, *The Doctrines of Sovereignty and Separation of Powers in the Law of Ceylon* (1970) pp. 185*ff*.

earlier relating to qualities of the judicial organs being considered flowing from the fundamental or essential nature of the judicial power in any legal system.

It is clear that no judicial organ, whether created by an organ or organs of an international organization or established directly or indirectly under an international agreement can in any way be a 'subordinate' or 'subsidiary' organ, i.e., even in relation to other organs of international organizations or to international organizations themselves. If the contrary were possible, the organ would cease to be judicial. Such is the nature of organs which are judicial. Thus, the characterization of such judicial organs as are the subject of this chapter as 'subsidiary' or 'subordinate' is not only totally inaccurate but equally irrational. They are, and are intended to be, simply independent judicial organs exercising judicial functions, as they should be.

(Chapters VII and VIII), where the principle is examined in the context of its application in several national systems of law.

9 The internal law: employment relations

It was not till after the Second World War that the internal legal order of international organizations received special attention, particularly in terms of theory.[1] Prior to that international law was essentially perceived as intended to regulate relations between states. This is understandable because the international organizations prior to the Second World War, excluding perhaps the LN, possessed only limited powers and limited autonomy and did not have the importance in international life that they have since acquired. After the Second World War the situation changed with the establishment of the UN and several open international organizations.

The internal law

Principally, the problems arising from the existence of an international civil service have resulted in a practice of recognizing the existence of

[1] See now, for example, Cahier, 'L'Ordre juridique interne des organisations internationales', in Dupuy (ed.), *Manuel sur les organisations internationales* (1988) p. 237; Cahier, 'Le Droit interne des organisations internationales', 67 RGDIP (1963) p. 563; Morawiecki, 'Legal Regime of the International Organization', 15 Polish YIL (1986) p. 71; C. F. Amerasinghe, *Law of the International Civil Service* (1994) vol. I pp. 1*ff.*; Focsaneaunu, 'Le Droit interne de l'Organisation des Nations Unies', 3 AFDI (1957) p. 315; Durante, *L'ordinamento interno delle Nazioni Unite* (1984); Skubiszewski, 'Enactment of Law by International Organizations', 41 BYIL (1965) p. 198; Conforti, 'The Legal Effect of Non-Compliance with Rules of Procedure in the UN General Assembly and Security Council', 63 AJIL (1969) p. 479; Balladore Pallieri, 'Le Droit interne des organisations internationales', 127 *Hague Recueil* (1969-II) p. 1; Colasa, 'La notion de droit interne des organisations internationales', 3 Polish YIL (1970) p. 95; Bernhardt, 'The Nature and Field of Application of the Internal Law of International Organizations', 10 *Law and State* (1974) p. 7; Monaco, 'Les Principes régissant la structure et le fonctionnement des organisations internationales', 156 *Hague Recueil* (1977-III) p. 79; and Margiev, 'On Legal Nature of Internal Law of International Organizations', 15 Soviet YBIL (1980) p. 99 (summary in English).

an internal law of international organizations. They have also led many writers to accept the existence of such an internal law. If the national law of the member states applied to relations between the organization and its staff, the courts of states would probably be competent to hear disputes, apart from employment relations being subject to the laws of member states, a situation which would have had drawbacks for the organization. It would then find itself subject to the control of members. Soon after the creation of the UN the view was expressed that there was no valid reason why an organization should be subject to the law of the state in which its headquarters was located, especially since its staff was of widely different nationalities. It has been said that the LN was a subject of international law capable of creating its own internal law:

L'ensemble des normes établies par la Société des Nations et relatives à son organisation constitue la partie la plus importante de son droit interne... droit qui peut avoir avec les droits internes des Etâts des relations analogues à celles des droits étâtiques entre eux.[2]

In 1931 the Italian Court of Cassation, overruling two lower courts, took a similar view in regard to the International Institute of Agriculture, stating that:

The particular system of the Institute must be sufficient unto itself, both in regard to substantive rules and to rules governing the relations of its internal management such as those concerning employment.[3]

Thus, international organizations have as a characteristic that with respect to their internal organization and functioning they are outside the jurisdiction of national law. Their life is governed by a set of rules and principles which constitute their internal law. With this framework they are not subject to interference by states in regard to the legal system or the laws that apply.

An international organization functions in two different spheres – the internal and the external. Of this dichotomy it has been said:

The internal sphere of functioning covers activities which aim at ensuring indispensable, in a way 'a minimum' of, conditions of survival and the very existence

---

[2] Borsi, 'Il rapporto d'impiego nella Società delle Nazioni', RDI (1923) at p. 283. This passage may be rendered as follows in English: 'The aggregate of norms established by the League of Nations pertaining to its organization constitutes the most important part of its internal law... a law which could have relationships with the internal law of States which are analogous to those of the internal law of States with each other.'

[3] *International Institute of Agriculture v. Profili* (1931) 5 AD at p. 415.

of the system and the efficient functioning of the mechanisms of an international organization ... The external sphere of functioning covers activities which aim at exerting a direct influence by an international organization on its environment, that is, in the first place, on Member-States and their conduct in mutual relations.[4]

The internal sphere is governed by the internal law. It covers more than employment relations. It includes the indispensable requirements for the institutional functioning of the organization, such as: (i) establishing with their mandates and deciding upon the composition of subsidiary representative organs and of subsidiary administrative organs; (ii) the appointment of members to such organs; (iii) the facilitating of decision-making in organs, especially by formulating rules of procedure; (iv) the organization and regulation of administrative services, namely the staff, required for the efficient functioning of the organization and for facilitating decision-making; and (v) the provision of facilities and the technical means as well as the financial resources to cover their costs and those of the staff. In the case of the UN which maintains military forces, these require for their activities rules governing such matters as discipline. These rules constitute another aspect of the internal law of organizations.

In all these areas organizations take decisions, make rules and establish regulations and staff rules, which govern the functioning of the organization. These are in addition to applicable provisions of the constitutive instruments which are binding not only on member states but on the organs and staff of the organization and constitute the highest level of internal law. All these decisions and rules together form an autonomous system which is the internal law of the organization, whether they are general in form and intended to cover a variety or a considerable number of future situations or are determinations for individual cases.

The relationship of decisions and rules within the internal law will depend on whether the organs concerned are of equal rank or whether a hierarchy exists between them and will be determined by the relevant constitutional provisions. Subordinate organs, whether created by the constituent treaty or by an act of an organ, may also take decisions

---

[4] Morawiecki, loc. cit. note 1 at p. 75. The functions of the EU in the area of adopting rules of general scope, binding on member states and directly applicable within their legal order is in the external sphere, although Cahier regards them as belonging to the internal sphere of the organization: Cahier, loc. cit. note 1 at pp. 240ff.

and enact rules within their competences. These decisions and rules are subordinate to those of higher organs.

There is also a distinction between rules and decisions which are binding and those which are non-binding political or administrative guidelines. The nature of a particular act will depend upon the powers of the organ and its intentions in a given case. For example, the *Principles of Staff Employment* of the World Bank Group, while having some binding effect, are also only policy guidelines in certain respects and to the extent that they are not concretized in the Staff Rules, as the preamble to that instrument indicates.

The view has been expressed that the internal law of international organizations is not really law;[5] internal rules, whether they are binding or not under the constitution of the organization, do not fall within the definition of law. How they are to be characterized, however, remains unclear, particularly as the internal law is admitted to have legal effects. Another opinion characterizes internal law as law but not as international law.[6] Internal law forms a new and separate legal order alongside international law but is *sui generis*. However, the better view is that the internal law is a branch of and forms part of international law.[7] The conclusion is based on the fact that the basis of the internal law is the constituent treaty of the organization and the power to enact the internal law and its effect are derived from this treaty and its interpretation. The treaty itself is international law and, therefore, generates international law which is also the implied intention behind the treaty. Moreover, because member states act through and in the organs of the organization or ultimately give the organs the authority to act, they are the final source of this branch of the law which is, thus, international law created by states.

By far the most important aspect of the internal law is the law that governs employment relations. Pertinent to this subject are the facilities available for the settlement of employment disputes. The history of such disputes and the methods of their settlement will be discussed in Chapter 16. In other areas than employment relations the internal law applied will be the constitutions of the organizations and relevant written laws which will be interpreted according to the general canons of interpretation.

---

[5] See Balladore Palliari, loc. cit. note 1.
[6] See analysis in Margiev, loc. cit. note 1. Miehsler takes the above view.
[7] See, e.g., Bernhardt, loc. cit. note 1; C. F. Amerasinghe, note 1 vol. I pp. 22*ff.* (in relation to the law of employment relations in particular).

The law of employment relations

Development

An internal law governing employment has been found to be necessary because of the development, expansion and proliferation of international organizations. Before the LN was established, organizations were
small and their secretariats were small, performing routine functions.
It was customary to entrust such functions to the management of a
member state:

> The Secretariat might include officials seconded from other states or even for-
> eigners recruited independently, and the officials in charge of it were often given
> a fairly free hand by the host state; but in principle the official's legal position
> was that of civil servants of the host state, which ran the Secretariat as part of
> one of its Government departments – sometimes with financial assistance from
> other members. Some organizations, such as the International Whaling Com-
> mission and the International Wool Study Group, still conform to this pattern.[8]

In recent years the number of human agents working for international
organizations has vastly increased because of the diversity of organizations and the expansion of their activities.[9] In the LN there were no
more than a few hundred employees; in the United Nations there are
thousands. In some cases within the same organization there has been
a large increase in the number of employees. Thus, in the 1940s the
IBRD had several hundred regular employees, while in the 1990s there
were more than 6,000 and now many more. The international civil servant has become an increasingly ubiquitous and active figure on the
international stage.

A result of these developments is that employment relationships have
been created in international secretariats which require regulation and
control. There is a great deal of activity in the field of employment
relations. Appointments are made, whether by contract or otherwise,
salaries are assigned or changed, benefits are awarded, decisions are
taken regarding promotions and pensions and the like, so that generally
there is need for the total employment relationship to be subjected to
some system of legal regulation and control. The parties involved in the
employment relationship, both administrations and employees, require
a legal regime to determine their rights and obligations and to give them

---

[8] Akehurst, *The Law Governing Employment Relations in International Organization* (1967) p. 1.
[9] What follows on the evolution of the internal law is based on my work in C. F.
Amerasinghe, note 1 vol. I pp. 3*ff.*

protection where it is needed. The argument that organizations should have untrammelled freedom and be governed entirely by expediency in their relations with employees rather than by law is unacceptable. Generally, international organizations function outside the sphere of operation of any state's legal system. To establish order the existence of a legal system governing employment relations becomes a *sine qua non*. A legal order is necessary not only to establish authority but also to control authority and allocate and determine responsibility.

Today most secretariats are genuinely international in the sense that they are not run as government departments of member states and have an integrity of their own and independence from their member states. A legitimate question that may be asked is what law governs the relationship between an employee and the administration of an international organization of this kind, such as the UN, the WHO, the EU or the IBRD.

Most organizations, as will be seen, have contractual relations with their employees, there being only a very few that base their relationship with employees in general on status. In view of this, it is of some significance that in the *Serbian Loans Case* the PCIJ stated that '[a]ny contract which is not a contract between states in their capacity as subjects of international law is based on the municipal law of some country'.[10] This view, taken literally, could lead to the conclusion that the employment relationship in international organizations, particularly if based on contract, should be governed by some national law. But this view of the PCIJ cannot be taken at face value. Agreements between states and international organizations are admittedly not governed by national law and yet they are not contracts between states in their capacity as subjects of international law. Further, there is support for the view that some contracts between states and aliens may be governed not by national law as such but by a quasi-national system if not by international law itself.[11] Thus, it cannot be said that there is an established principle that contracts or relationships between employees and international

---

[10] PCIJ Reports Series A No. 20 at p. 4. See also the *Brazilian Loans Case*, PCIJ Reports Series A No. 21.

[11] See the arbitral award between *Petroleum Development (Trucial Coast) Ltd and the Sheikh of Abu Dhabi* [1952] 1 ICLQ (1952) at p. 251; *Aramco v. Saudi Arabia* [1958] 27 ILR p. 165; *Sapphire–NIOC Arbitration* (1963), 13 ICLQ (1964) p. 1,011; Jessup, *A Modern Law of Nations* (1956) p. 139; Lalive, 'Contracts between a State or State Agency and a Foreign Company', 13 ICLQ (1964) p. 991; C. F. Amerasinghe, *State Responsibility for Injuries to Aliens* (1967) pp. 105*ff*.

organizations must be governed by national law because these are not between states in their capacity as subjects of international law.

Need for an independent system of law

There are several practical reasons why there should be an independent system of law governing employment relations in international organizations, or, at least, why such system should not be *per se* the national law or conflicts law of any particular state. First, international officials are usually recruited from many nationalities and may be assigned to serve in a variety of countries. It is desirable that all staff should normally be subject to identical rules, irrespective of where they are recruited, from where they come, or where they work. The application of the national law of a particular state, such as the host state, or even the conflicts law of a particular state, to their relations with the organization for which they work would result in an arbitrary and artificial choice.

Secondly, it is necessary to preserve independence of the international official from national pressures, whether of his own national state or of any other. This principle is basic to the operation of international organizations. It is often reflected in the constituent treaty of the organization with the result that obligations are imposed on all officials, including the head of the secretariat, on the organization and on member states.[12] However, it is not state interference that must be prevented, because it is very unlikely that any state, including the host state, will be able to interfere with the independence of the secretariat of an international organization by manipulating its own law. The real need is to satisfy a psychological demand related to such independence, flowing from the special nature of the commitment and allegiance involved.[13] There have been occasions on which, contrary to the requirements of national laws, international officials have been protected against arbitrary action by the administrations of international organizations only because of the

---

[12] See, e.g., Article 100 of the UN Charter; Articles 9 and 40 of the ILO Constitution; and Articles 5 and 7 of the IBRD Articles of Agreement. See the other provisions listed in Jenks, *The Proper Law of International Organisations* (1963) pp. 30–1. On the independence of international civil servants see, e.g., Grabowska, 'Independence of International Civil Servants', 17 Polish YIL (1988) p. 61; Green, 'The International Civil Servant, his Employer and his State', 40 TGS (1954) p. 147; Jenks, 'Some Problems of an International Civil Service', 3 *Public Administration Review* (1945) p. 93; Meron, 'Status and Independence of the International Civil Service', 167 *Hague Recueil* (1980-II) p. 285.

[13] See also Akehurst, note 8 p. 6.

existence of a separate system of law governing their employment relations.[14] In a series of cases beginning with *Duberg*[15] the ILOAT held that failure on the part of the employee to comply with his national law, compliance with which might have involved a conflict with his independence as an international civil servant, could not be used as a ground for not renewing a fixed-term contract or terminating employment with the UNESCO. Similarly, in the UN, the UNAT held in favour of some applicants who were treated unfavourably by the organization without the proper reasons being given, when the true reason for the action taken was failure to act in conformity with the law of the host state which was also their national state.[16]

Apart from these reasons, because it would be inappropriate to implicate any system of national law as such in the employment relationship in an international organization, there must be some system of law governing such relationship because it is necessary to allocate rights and obligations and particularly to protect the employee from the uncontrolled exercise of authority within the secretariat of the organization for which he works. Various reasons have been given for this thesis, including the fact that, particularly in the case of a non-national of the host state of an organization, the organization is immune from the jurisdiction of the local courts.[17] It is not accurate to stress the immunity from the jurisdiction of national courts as a reason for having an independent legal system governing employment relationships in international organizations. Immunity from jurisdiction relates only to the absence of a judicial system for deciding disputes arising from such relationships and does not necessarily mean that the relationships are outside the pale of law. It is the special position of the international civil servant within international society that makes it important that he have some independent system of law to protect him. Even with a special system of courts to decide disputes relating to the employment relationship

---

[14] In the 1950s there was a crisis in the UN and the UNESCO because of the attempts of the US to have dismissed certain officials who were *persona non grata* to it: see Bedjaoui, *Fonction publique internationale et influences nationales* (1958) pp. 576–618; Lie, *In the Cause of Peace* (1954) pp. 386–405; and Cohen, 'The United Nations Secretariat: Some Constitutional and Administrative Developments', 49 AJIL (1955) p. 295.

[15] ILOAT Judgment No. 17 [1955]. See also ILOAT Judgments Nos. 18–24 [1955].

[16] See *Howrani and Four Others*, UNAT Judgment No. 4 [1951] JUNAT Nos. 1–70 p. 8; and *Keeney*, UNAT Judgment No. 6 [1951], JUNAT Nos. 1–70 p. 24.

[17] See a statement which sums up the difficult position of the international civil servant in Carlston, 'International Administrative Law: A Venture in Legal Theory', 8 *Journal of Public Law* (1959) at pp. 331–2.

in international organizations, it is possible to apply a national system of law to the relationship. It is the features of the international civil service that provide a reason for having an independent system of law to govern the employment relationship in international organizations.

The internal law as the governing law

It has come to be generally accepted now that it is the internal law of the organization that governs the employment relationship of international civil servants with the international organization for which they work. It is a special system of law which is both an individual and organizational necessity and aims at formulating those rules for conduct which will ensure that an international secretariat will be able to function efficiently. It places the relationship between administration and staff concerning the latter's assuming, occupancy and termination of position in the secretariat in the domain of law. In this sense, irrespective of whether there are courts to decide disputes relating to the employment relationship in the organization, it is a real system of law.

IATs have accepted the applicability of this system of law and have agreed in characterizing it as the 'internal law' of the organization. In its very first case the LNT conceded that it was 'bound to apply the internal law of the League of Nations'.[18] More recently the WBAT stated:

> The Tribunal, which is an international tribunal, considers that its task is to decide internal disputes between the Bank and its staff within the organised legal system of the World Bank and that it must apply the *internal law of the Bank* as the law governing the conditions of employment.[19]

Later the legal situation of the staff of the IBRD was characterized as having 'a dominantly objective nature'.[20] Thus, it was recognized that there was a true legal system. The UNAT and the ILOAT have also acknowledged the applicability of the internal law.[21]

---

[18] *di Palma Castiglione*, LNT Judgment No. 1 [1929] at p. 3. Subsequently, in its second and third judgments the LNT made similar statements: *Phelan*, LNT Judgment No. 2 [1929] at p. 3; and *Maurette*, LNT Judgment No. 3 [1929] at p. 3.

[19] See *de Merode*, WBAT Reports [1981], Decision No. 1 at pp. 12–13. Emphasis is mine.

[20] *Ibid.* at p. 15.

[21] See *Aglion*, Judgment No. 56 [1954], JUNAT Nos. 1–70 p. 283 at pp. 293–4; *Waghorn*, ILOAT Judgment No. 28 [1957] at p. 6.

In *de Merode* it was admitted by the respondent[22] that particular or general national labour laws did not as such constitute the internal law of the organization applicable to the employment relationship within the organization. Implicitly the tribunal accepted this view that particular labour law principles and rules of particular states were not *per se* part of the legal system applicable to the organization, in so far as it did not regard such principles and rules as *per se* sources of the internal law of the organization.[23]

The nature of the employment relationship

The answer to the question what is the basis of the relationship of staff members with the organization is relevant to several issues. On the answer may depend several consequences, among others, what sources of law are applicable in certain situations. It would seem that in a limited number of situations, sources applicable to contractual appointments are not relevant to statutory appointments.

In certain legal systems civil servants' appointments are statutory. The civil service is governed by rights and duties set out in a *règlement* which is drawn up by the administration and is a legislative act.[24] In other systems civil servants are employed on the basis of a contract.[25] In the case of international organizations, both situations obtain. In the European Union, for instance, permanent officials are now appointed by a unilateral act of authority and are subject to a status.[26] In the *Monod Case* the Committee of jurists stated that the employment relationship between the LN and its staff members was based on statute and therefore was a status.[27] The OECD is another organization in which the

---

[22] See the Bank's argument in *Joint Memorandum in Support of Respondent's Answers* in *de Merode* at pp. 39–40.

[23] The ILOAT has held that English law as the national law of the applicant was not as such applicable in his case: *Waghorn*, ILOAT judgment No. 28 [1957] at p. 6. Though rarely, statutes of administrative tribunals may provide that national law is *per se* not applicable. Article VI.2 of the IDBAT Statute, for example, makes this clear: see C. F. Amerasinghe (ed.), *Documents on International Administrative Tribunals* (1989) pp. 65–6.

[24] See for France, Inez and Debeyre, *Traité de droit administratif* (1952), sections 875*ff*.

[25] See, for example, the USA, the UK and almost all British Commonwealth countries.

[26] See, e.g., *Campolongo*, CJEC Case 27 and 39/59 [1960] ECR at p. 402; and *Degreef*, CJEC Case 80/63 [1964]. See also S. Bastid, 'Le statut juridique des fonctionnaires de l'ONU', in Nijhoff Publishers (eds.), *The United Nations: Ten Years' Legal Progress* (1956) at p. 151. Earlier, appointments were apparently made on the basis of a contract of employment, although this was *sui generis*: *Kergall*, CJEC Case 1/55 [1955] ECR at pp. 156–7.

[27] League of Nations Official Journal, October 1925, at p. 1,443. See also the discussion of the case in S. Basdevant (Bastid), *Les Fonctionnaires internationaux* (1931) pp. 79*ff*. In

bond between the organization and its staff members is statutory and not contractual.[28]

The two most important organizations which at the present time base their employment relationships on statute and not contract are the EU and the OECD. Almost all the other international organizations, without exception, base their relations with their staff members on a contractual nexus. In the case of the UN there is no clear mention in the existing Staff Regulations and Staff Rules of a contract of employment; but provision is made for a letter of appointment which must correspond to an offer and an acceptance.[29] Some other specialized agencies follow this pattern.[30] In the case of other organizations, reference is made in the staff regulations or staff rules to appointment and acceptance and a contract of employment.[31]

Several IATs and the ICJ have made the point that employment in the organizations with which the relevant cases were concerned was on the basis of a contract. In the *Effect of Awards Case* the ICJ made statements to the effect that employees of the UN had contracts of service with the UN.[32] In several cases the UNAT has assumed that employment in the UN is based on contract.[33] The ILOAT has also on several occasions referred to contracts of service as the source of rights and obligations in many cases.[34] The NATO Appeals Board has said that dismissal is governed by the 'contract' (of employment).[35] In *Uehling*, the OASAT referred to 'the general principle of contract' of good faith,[36] while in *Mattarino*,[37] it

---

Desplanque, LNT Judgment No. 19 [1938] at p. 4, the LNT adverted to the issue. The Assembly of the LN in 1946 refused to accept the total analogy of private law contract: League of Nations, Official Journal, Special Supplement No. 194, 1946, p. 262.

[28] *Archer*, Decision No. 27 [1964], Recueil des Décisions 1 à 62, at p. 104.

[29] See Annex II of the Staff Regulations, C. F. Amerasinghe (ed.), *Staff Regulations and Staff Rules of Selected International Organizations* (1983) vol. I, p. 20.

[30] See, e.g., IMCO Staff Regulations and Staff Rules, Article IV, Annex II, Amerasinghe (ed.), *ibid.* vol. III, p. 40; ICAO Staff Regulations, Regulation 416, Amerasinghe (ed.), *ibid.* vol. III, p. 169; and OAS Staff Rules, Rule 104.5(d), Amerasinghe (ed.), *ibid.* vol. III, p. 240.

[31] In most organizations there may be certain posts that are filled by nomination when the appointment is based on status, e.g., the post of SG of the UN and the judgeships on the ICJ.

[32] 1954 ICJ Reports at p. 53.

[33] See, e.g., *Kaplan*, UNAT Judgment No. 19 [1953]; *Wallach*, UNAT Judgment No. 28 [1953]; *Halpern*, UNAT Judgment No. 63 [1956]; *Khavkine*, UNAT Judgment No. 66 [1966]; and *Mortished*, UNAT Judgment No. 273 [1981] at p. 7.

[34] See, e.g., *Darricades*, ILOAT Judgment No. 67 [1962]; *Pelletier*, ILOAT Judgment No. 68 [1964]; and *Kennedy*, ILOAT Judgment No. 339 [1978].

[35] *Stievenart*, NATO Appeals Board Decision No. 24 [1971] at p. 2.

[36] OASAT Decision No. 8 [1974] at p. 10.   [37] OASAT Decision No. 69 [1981].

discussed at length the nature of staff members' contracts. In *de Merode*,[38] the WBAT considered the situation in the IBRD. The tribunal analyzed the situation and concluded that:

> [E]mployment by the Bank resulted from an offer followed by an acceptance, that is to say a contract, and not, as in the case with employment in the civil service of certain individual countries, as a result of a unilateral act of nomination by the administration.[39]

The view accepted now is that, while the employment relationship is based on contract, there are certain elements which are statutory, irrespective of the agreement of the parties, and further that it is not only analogies from the private law of contract that are relevant to the employment relationship but such analogies are in certain instances modified by public law concepts which exist in the law governing the civil service of many states.[40] The main difference in effect between this view (qualified contract) and the view that employment is totally governed by contract is that, where the employment relationship is partly contractual and partly statutory, statutory elements may govern the employment relationship even though they are not incorporated in the contract of employment. Further, the power to alter terms and conditions of employment may be different in the two cases. The principal differences between the possible statutory and contractual basis of employment relate to the legal manner in which the employment relationship is created and may be dissolved and the relevance of contractual terms to the employment relationship.

Sources of the law

IATs have seldom discussed, as such, the question of sources of the law they apply, though they have not hesitated to derive the law applied from a variety of such sources. However, in *de Merode*[41] the WBAT explained at some length the sources from which the relevant rights and duties of the employer and employee flow. Some writers have discussed the question of sources on the basis that it is relevant and important for a

---

[38] WBAT Reports [1981], Decision No. 1.

[39] WBAT Reports [1981], Decision No. 1 at pp. 8–9. Both parties agreed that contract was the basis of employment in the IBRD.

[40] See *Kaplan*, UNAT Judgment No. 19 [1953], JUNAT Nos. 1–70 at pp. 73*ff*.

[41] WBAT Reports [1981], Decision No. 1 at pp. 9*ff*. See also *di Palma Castiglione*, LNT Judgment No. 1 [1929] at p. 3; and *Phelan*, LNT Judgment No. 2 [1929] at p. 3.

clearer and proper understanding of how international administrative law works.[42]

In seeking the sources[43] of employment law (international administrative law) it would be too naive and simple to draw analogies from the sources of public international law. It is tempting to assume that the sources of international administrative law may easily be derived, at least by analogy, from the sources of public international law, because international administrative law is a part of public international law. Thus, reference may be made to Article 38(1) of the Statute of the ICJ which is generally believed accurately to reflect the sources of public international law. However, neither have IATs referred to Article 38(1) of the Statute of the ICJ in their decisions nor is it generally agreed that international administrative law is public international law pure and simple,[44] although it may be a branch of public international law. At best, some analogies may be drawn from the sources mentioned in Article 38(1) of the Statute of the ICJ – for example, that staff regulations and other such written legal sources correspond to treaties or that the practice of an organization corresponds to custom – but there the similarity ends.

The statutes of IATs are not very helpful, as they are generally silent on the subject though, as in the case of the CSAT statute, international administrative law may be mentioned as the ultimate source. In fact, there are numerous formal sources from which tribunals have in practice derived the rules which they apply. Such reference has not rested on any preconceived theory of formal sources of international administrative law. Rather, practical necessity and judicial wisdom have determined what formal sources should be invoked in deciding cases.

Agreements

The UNAT and the ILOAT have accepted the fact that the contract of appointment is a source of law. In *Kaplan*, the UNAT conceded that the contract was a source of law, though there were other sources.[45] The

---

[42] See C. F. Amerasinghe, 'Sources of International Administrative Law', in *International Law at the Time of Its Codification: Essays in Honour of Roberto Ago* (1987) p. 67; C. F. Amerasinghe, 'The Implications of the *de Merode Case* for International Administrative Law', 43 ZAORV (1983) p. 1; Akehurst, note 8 pp. 29*ff.*; Plantey, *The International Civil Service* (1981) pp. 50*ff.*

[43] For a discussion of the meaning of sources see C. F. Amerasinghe, note 1 vol. I pp. 104*ff.* What is meant here is a 'formal' source.

[44] C. F. Amerasinghe, *ibid.*, pp. 22*ff.*

[45] UNAT Judgment No. 19 [1953] at p. 73. See also *Mortished*, UNAT Judgment No. 273 [1981].

same approach was taken by the ILOAT in *Lindsey*.[46] It may be safely asserted that the contract of employment is a repository of law. By the same token, where appointments are statutory the instrument of appointment would be a relevant source of law, particularly as regards salary and grade and the nature of the appointment. On the other hand, the Committee of Jurists of the League which decided the *Monod Case* stated that the organization did not have the power to bind itself by subsidiary contracts when appointments were statutory in nature.[47] In the contractual situation there are many consequences that flow from the contract's being a source of law.[48]

As a corollary to the relevance of the contract and contractual documents, reference has been made in several cases to the specific circumstances of each contract as a source of law. In *de Merode*, the WBAT said:

The specific circumstances of each case may also have some bearing on the legal relationship between the Bank and an individual member of the staff, particularly the actual conditions in which the appointment has been made.[49]

The UNAT also has had occasion to advert to the circumstances surrounding employment as being relevant to determining the law that applies. In several cases it was said that the terms of employment may be expressed or implied and may be gathered from correspondence and surrounding facts and circumstances.[50] The position in regard to statutory appointments may be different. The basis of statutory appointments

---

[46] ILOAT Judgment No. 61 [1962] at p. 6. For other tribunals see, e.g., *de Merode*, WBAT Reports [1981], Decision No. 1 at p. 9; *Steivenart*, NATO Appeals Board, Decision No. 24 [1971]; and *Uehling*, OASAT Decision No. 8 [1974] at p. 10.

[47] League of Nations Official Journal, October 1925, at pp. 1,443, 1,444.

[48] For example, even in the absence of an appointment, there may well be an enforceable contract for employment or it may be that a promise made to offer an applicant a post, in preference to any other candidate at the appropriate time, is valid in law: *Bulsara*, UNAT Judgment No. 68 [1957]. For other consequences see, e.g., *Labarthe*, ILOAT Judgment No. 307 [1977]; *Kennedy*, ILOAT Judgment No. 339 [1978]; *Higgins*, UNAT Judgment No. 92 [1964]; *Campolongo*, CJEC Cases 27 and 39/59 [1960]; *Silenzi di Stagni*, ILOAT Judgment 71 [1964]; and *de Merode*, WBAT Reports [1981], Decision No. 1.

[49] WBAT Reports [1981], Decision No. 1 at p. 12. See also for an explanation of what this means, *ibid.* at pp. 14, 54 and 56.

[50] See, e.g., *Sikand*, UNAT Judgment No. 95 [1968] at p. 79; and *Belchamber*, UNAT Judgment No. 236 [1978] at p. 16. For consequences see, e.g., *Mr. A.*, UNAT Judgment No. 86 [1962]; *Bhattacharyya*, UNAT Judgment No. 142 [1971]; and *Kergall*, CJEC Case 1/55 [1955] at p. 156.

is not the consensus of the parties but the act of nomination. Hence, the circumstances of employment or of the employment relationship, as opposed to the explicit terms of the instrument of nomination, cannot be a relevant source of law.

While in the contractual situation the contractual documents and the circumstances of employment are a primary source of law, they are not the sole nor, indeed, the most important source of law. In *de Merode* the WBAT said that the fact that staff members of the Bank entered its service on the basis of an exchange of letters did not mean that those contractual instruments were the sole repository of all the rights and duties of the parties to the contract; the contract was the *sine qua non* of the relationship between the staff member and the Bank but it remained no more than one of a number of elements which collectively established the ensemble of conditions of employment operative between the Bank and its staff members.[51]

Constituent instruments

IATs have readily conceded that the constituent instrument of an international organization is a source of law in employment relations. It is not often that these tribunals have had to pronounce on this issue, but where they have done so, there has been little debate about the accuracy of this position. The earliest case in which the question was addressed was *Howrani*[52] where the UNAT stated clearly that the Charter of the UN was a source of the law it must apply. The ILOAT has also referred to constituent treaties of international organizations as applicable in the area of conditions of employment.[53] Tribunals do not agree with

---

[51] WBAT Reports [1981], Decision No. 1 at p. 9. See also *Kaplan*, UNAT Judgment No. 19 [1953] at pp. 73–4, where the tribunal said that the relations between staff members and the UN involved various elements and, consequently, were not solely contractual in nature, that notwithstanding the existence of contracts, legal regulations established by the GA governed the legal regime, and that there were contractual as well as statutory elements which determined the legal position of staff members. The same language was used in Judgments Nos. 20–7 [1953].

[52] UNAT Judgment No. 4 [1951] at p. 21. See also, e.g., *Mortished*, UNAT Judgment No. 273 [1981] at p. 8; and *Mullan*, UNAT Judgment No. 162 [1972].

[53] In *Duberg*, ILOAT Judgment No. 17 [1955] at pp. 255ff., the ILOAT cited the constitution of the UNESCO as prohibiting the Director-General of the UNESCO from associating himself with the execution of policy of any state member in regard to his treatment of a staff member. See also *Aicher*, OECD Appeals Board Decision No. 37 [1964]; *von Lachmüller*, CJEC Cases No. 43, 45 and 48/59 [1960] ECR p. 463; and *de Merode*, WBAT Reports [1981], Decision No. 1 at pp. 9–11.

the contrary view.[54] On hierarchical priorities the general approach of tribunals is to regard the constituent instrument of the organization as the basic statute (constitution) of the organization which is the highest written law governing employment. This is borne out particularly by the *de Merode* judgment of the WBAT.[55]

Staff regulations, staff rules and written sources

The decisions of the main legislative organs of international organizations are the next in line as a source of law after the constitutional instrument. In *de Merode*[56] the WBAT said that in the IBRD these were decisions taken in the exercise of the power accorded to the Board of Governors and Executive Directors by Article V(2)(f) principally, to adopt rules and regulations necessary for or appropriate to the conduct of the Bank's business. The most formal constituted the By-Laws. The individual decision of the Board of Governors establishing the WBAT was also law-creating as were decisions of the Executive Directors affecting staff rights and obligations which were taken regularly. In the case of the UN the Charter gives the GA the power to establish the regulations governing the staff.[57] In most other organizations too the basic staff regulations are established by the plenary organ, composed of representatives of all the member states.[58] In addition to the power to make staff regulations the plenary organ or the organ empowered to draw up the staff regulations has the power also to adopt resolutions which are a source of law.[59]

Staff rules or their equivalent may be established by the administration of an organization in the exercise of powers derived from the

---

[54] See Akehurst, note 8 p. 61, for this view. It is that the constituent treaty could not be assumed *a priori* to be applicable, because it could be argued that it only created rights and duties between the member states and had no effect on the staff, particularly as it was not mentioned as a source of law in letters of appointment or in the statute of an administrative tribunal.

[55] WBAT Reports [1981], Decision No. 1 at pp. 9–11.

[56] WBAT Reports [1981], Decision No. 1 at p. 11.

[57] Article 101(1) of the Charter. See also the *Application for Review of Judgment No. 273 of the United Nations Administrative Tribunal Case*, 1982 ICJ Reports at p. 362.

[58] There are exceptions to this: see, e.g., the IMCO Convention, Article 23 (Council).

[59] See. e.g., *Howrani*, UNAT Judgment No. 4 [1951]; and *Smith*, UNAT Judgment No. 249 [1979]. For resolutions of the GA see the *Application for Review of Judgment No. 273 of the United Nations Administrative Tribunal Case*, 1982 ICJ Reports, at p. 362. See also, e.g., *Lanner*, OEEC Appeals Board Decision No. 31 [1960]; *Pagani*, Council of Europe Appeals Board Decision No. 76/1981 [1982]; *Bonneman*, NATO Appeals Board Decision No. 8 [1968].

constitution of the organization or delegated by the legislative organ.[60] Similarly manuals, circulars and other statements issued by the administration have a law-creating character. Both the UNAT and the ILOAT have held that staff rules must conform to and not conflict with staff regulations.[61] The UNAT has also applied manuals and administrative circulars, generally on the basis that they interpret the regulations and rules.[62] IATs are called upon to apply all these written instruments in disputes between organizations and their staff members and may then have to interpret them.[63] The general approach to these instruments taken by IATs has been to implement a textual approach tempered with a teleological approach. Practice may sometimes be relevant. The ordinary meaning of words taken in context has most often been adopted.[64] Sometimes the purpose of the text has specifically been invoked in interpretation. Thus, in *Maugis*[65] where a text which referred to the taking of home leave every alternate year was in issue, the term 'every alternate year' was interpreted by reference to the purpose of the staff rule. The rule was interpreted to mean that home leave had to be taken in the second year, the fourth year and so on, leave not taken during the year of entitlement being forfeited. Maxims such as *expressio unius est exclusio alterius* have been applied in the interpretation of texts.[66] The basic approach taken has been similar to the technique of interpretation of constitutional texts. However, especially in the case of those rules which are formulated by the executive organ rather than by the deliberative organ, the intention of the framers of the rule reflected in

---

[60] See *de Merode*, WBAT Reports [1981], Decision No. 1 at p. 11.

[61] See *Wallach*, UNAT Judgment No. 53 [1954]; and *Poulain d'Andecy*, ILOAT Judgment No. 51 [1960]. See also *Decisions No. 24–6* [1957], OEEC Appeals Board.

[62] See, e.g., *Robinson*, UNAT Judgment No. 15 [1952]; *Harris*, UNAT Judgment No. 67 [1956]. For other tribunals see, e.g., *Duberg*, ILOAT Judgment No. 17 [1955]; *Fisher*, ILOAT Judgment No. 48 [1960]; *Huber*, CJEC Case No. 27/63 [1964]; *Garcia*, OASAT Decision No. 56 [1980] at p. 6.

[63] See, e.g., *Salle*, WBAT Reports [1983, Part I], Decision No. 10.

[64] See, e.g., *Repond*, ILOAT Judgment No. 790 [1986]; *Diallo*, ILOAT Judgment No. 962 [1989]; *Villella A.*, OASAT Judgment No. 82 [1985]; and *Decisions Nos. 174–80*, NATO Appeals Board [1985]. A general principle of textual interpretation that has been applied is that which 'requires that rules be interpreted in accordance with the plain meaning of the words, without twisting their specific sense, particularly when the sense agrees with the common usage and with the legal meaning used in the judicial system operating in the organization': *Chisman and Others*, OASAT Judgment No. 64 [1982] at p. 15.

[65] ILOAT Judgment No. 945 [1988]. See also, e.g., *Benze (No. 7)*, ILOAT Judgment No. 926 [1988].

[66] See, e.g., *Novak*, ILOAT Judgment No. 975 [1989].

the preparatory work may be relevant sometimes, particularly if a reference to the meaning in context and taking into account the object and purpose of the text is not fruitful. This is rare, however.[67]

General principles of law

General principles of law are a source of international administrative law. The LNT applied general principles of law in deciding its very first case as early as 1929.[68] In *de Merode* the WBAT stated: 'Another source of the rights and duties of the staff of the Bank consists of general principles of law.'[69] The UNAT,[70] the ILOAT[71] and other IATs[72] have also held that general principles of law are applicable.

Tribunals have established and applied general principles of law as and when necessary, though there has been much discussion of the methods of deriving general principles of law and on whether such general principles are principles of national law or international law. Tribunals have not been averse to finding support for their view of a particular general principle of law in the decisions of other international administrative tribunals. For example, in *de Merode* in establishing the

---

[67] The UNAT has used the *travaux préparatoires* to confirm the meaning given by the administration to a UNGA resolution, which was otherwise proper: *Smith*, UNAT Judgment No. 249 [1979], JUNAT Nos. 231–300 p. 202. The UNAT has applied the principles of interpretation that clauses of a contract must not be interpreted as solely placing upon one of the parties all the burden and obligations, even when, as in the case of a staff rule, the clause has been drafted by one of the parties alone: *Howrani and Four Others*, UNAT Judgment No. 4 [1951], JUNAT Nos. 1–70 at p. 13; and that the legal text must remain effective rather than ineffective (*ut res magis valeat quam pereat*): *ibid.* at p. 17. The same tribunal also applied the principle of interpretation that a distinction should not be made where the law does not make one (*lege non distinguente nec nobis est distinguere*): see *Sanchez*, UNAT Judgment No. 301 [1983]. The principle that an organ must have those powers which, though not expressly provided in the governing text, are conferred upon it by necessary implication as being essential to the performance of its duties was also applied in *Howrani and Four Others*, UNAT Judgment No. 4 [1951], JUNAT Nos. 1–70 at p. 17.

[68] *di Palma Castiglione* [1929], LNT Judgment No. 1.

[69] WBAT Reports [1981], Decision No. 1 at p. 12. The parties agreed on the relevance of general principles of law.

[70] See, e.g., *Howrani*, UNAT Judgment No. 4 [1951] and *Vassiliou*, UNAT Judgment No. 275 [1981].

[71] See, e.g., *Ferrechia*, ILOAT Judgment No. 203 [1973]; and *Gubin and Nemo*, ILOAT Judgment 429 [1980].

[72] See, e.g., *Pagani*, Council of Europe Appeals Board, Decision No. 76/1981 [1982]; *Warren*, NATO Appeals Board, Decision No. 57 [1974]; *Alaniz*, OASAT Decision No. 13 [1975]; *Angelopoulos*, OECD Appeals Board Decision No. 57 [1976]; and *Algera*, CJEC Case No. 7/56 [1957].

distinction between essential or fundamental elements in the conditions of employment of staff members and non-essential terms of employment, the WBAT stated: 'In various forms and with differing terminology this distinction is found in the jurisprudence of other international administrative tribunals.'[73]

Most of the general principles of law applied over a wide range of subject matter are those of administrative or civil service law found in civil law systems.[74] General principles of civil service law, such as the principle that requires that, other things being equal, the competitor for a post who is a member of the career service must be preferred to one who is not,[75] have been referred to, as has the general principle of civil service law that the dignity of employees must be respected.[76]

There are some general principles of law applicable in general and in various areas, such as contract or the conflict of laws, which have been invoked by tribunals. Thus, reference has been made in *Mayras*[77] by the LNT to the contractual principle of *force majeure*, although it was found to be inapplicable in the case, and by the CJEC[78] to the principle of good faith. The principle of unjust enrichment has been invoked, explained and applied with varying results by the ILOAT,[79] the OASAT[80] and the CJEC.[81] Both the UNAT[82] and the ILOAT[83] have referred to the principle of estoppel in a general sense as being potentially applicable.[84] There are

---

[73] WBAT Reports [1981], Decision No. 1 at p. 19. See also, e.g., *Crawford*, UNAT Judgment No. 18 [1953]; and *Warren*, ILOAT Judgment No. 28 [1957]. The relationship of general principles to other sources will be discussed later in this chapter.

[74] For a discussion of the source, general principles of law, see C. F. Amerasinghe, note 1 vol. I pp. 151*ff*.; Jenks, *The Proper Law of International Organizations* (1962) pp. 70*ff*.; Akehurst, note 8 pp. 72*ff*.

[75] See *Bauta*, OASAT Judgment No. 25 [1976] at p. 21 (this is a general principle imported from national laws).

[76] See *Angelopoulos*, Decision No. 71, OECD Appeals Board [1979], Recueil des décisions 63 à 82 (1980) p. 27. The principle that an illegal administrative decision may, with impunity, be withdrawn within a reasonable time was accepted in *Algera*, CJEC Cases 7/56 and 3 to 7/57 [1957] ECR p. 39.

[77] LNT Judgment No. 24 [1946] at p. 5.

[78] See *von Lachmüller*, CJEC Cases 43, 45 and 48 [1960] ECR at p. 475.

[79] *Wakley*, ILOAT Judgment No. 53 [1961].

[80] *Ogle*, OASAT Judgment No. 34 [1978]; and *Reeve*, OASAT Judgment No. 59 [1981].

[81] *Danvin*, CJEC Case 26/67 [1968] ECR p. 315.

[82] *Smith*, UNAT Judgment No. 249 [1979], JUNAT Nos. 231–300 p. 202.

[83] *Waghorn*, ILOAT Judgment No. 28 [1957] at p. 7.

[84] In *Hatt and Leuba*, ILOAT Judgment No. 382 [1979], the ILOAT invoked the general principles of *forum conveniens* and of comity in deciding to adopt and apply a decision of the UNAT on a matter within the latter's competence.

numerous other principles of a general nature which have been referred to and applied by tribunals in the course of their judgments.[85]

General principles of law may be used in interpreting written texts so as to supplement them and fill in gaps. This is a common situation in which general principles are applied by tribunals. General principles of law have been applied consistently in connection with controlling the exercise of administrative powers and discretions.[86]

Practice of the organization

Another source of law is the practice of the organization. In *de Merode* the WBAT said:

The practice of the organization may also in certain circumstances become part of the conditions of employment. Obviously, the organization would be discouraged from taking measures favorable to its employees on an *ad hoc* basis if each time it did so it had to take the risk of initiating a practice which might become legally binding upon it. The integration of practice into the conditions of employment must therefore be limited to that of which there is evidence that it is followed by the organization in the conviction that it reflects a legal obligation, as was recognized by the International Court of Justice in its Advisory Opinion on *Judgments of the Administrative Tribunal of the ILO* (ICJ Reports 1956, p. 91).[87]

---

[85] Such principles relate, e.g., to the interpretation of judgments: *Crawford and Others,* UNAT Judgment No. 61 [1955], JUNAT Nos. 1–70 p. 331; to the hierarchy of laws: *Chisman and Others,* OASAT Judgment No. 64 [1982]; to reduction in salaries: *Chisman and Others,* OASAT Judgment No. 64 [1982]; to the application of amendments to laws: *Mrs P.,* CJEC Case 40/79 [1981] ECR p. 361; and to the giving of notice: *de Bruyn,* CJEC Case 25/60 [1962] ECR p. 21. In *Bauta,* OASAT Judgment No. 25 [1976], the OASAT recognized the general principle that one may do anything that is not forbidden by law. Again, for example, the following principles have been recognized: (i) good faith: e.g., *Fernandez-Caballero,* ILOAT Judgment No. 946 [1988]; *Ausems and Others,* COEAB, Appeals Nos. 133–145 [1986]; (ii) equality: *Kahn,* ILOAT Judgment No. 740 [1986]; *Fuchs,* COEAB, Appeal No. 130 [1985]; *Vlachou,* CJEC Case 143/84 [1986] ECR p. 478; and *Decisions Nos. 218–27,* NATO Appeals Board [1987]; (iii) proportionality: *Aras et al.,* ILOAT Judgment No. 805 [1987]; (iv) the Noblemaire principle: *Beattie and Sheeran,* ILOAT Judgment No. 825 [1987]. For other principles see, e.g., *Delangue,* ILOAT Judgment No. 687 [1985]; *Renault,* ILOAT Judgment No. 856 [1987]; *Niesing, Peeters and Roussot,* ILOAT Judgment No. 963 [1989]; *Cabo,* IDBAT Judgment No. 16 [1987]; *Coin,* COEAB, Appeal No. 132 [1986]; *Brown,* COEAB, Appeal No. 150 [1987]; *Monge,* OASAT Judgment No. 92 [1985]; *Gomez Pulido,* OASAT Judgment No. 97 [1987]; *Advernier,* CJEC Case 211/80 [1984] ECR p. 144; *Williams,* CJEC Case 141/84 [1985] ECR p. 2,233; *Vlachou,* CJEC Case 162/84 [1986] ECR p. 491; and *Licata,* CJEC Case 270/84 [1986] ECR p. 2,318. Estoppel has also been referred to: see, e.g., *Repond,* ILOAT Judgment No. 790 [1986] at p. 7; *El-Balmany,* UNAT Judgment No. 353 [1985] at p. 13; and *Gamble,* WBAT Reports [1987, Part I], Decision No. 35 at p. 6.

[86] These will be discussed later in this chapter. For a fuller discussion see C. F. Amerasinghe, note 1 vol. I pp. 257–440, vol. II, *passim.*

[87] WBAT Reports [1981], Decision No. 1 at pp. 11–12.

There was a strict requirement that a practice be followed by the organization in the conviction that it reflected a legal obligation. Apart from a consistent repeated pattern of behaviour on the part of the organization (or, perhaps, usually a succession of identical administrative decisions in previous analogous cases),[88] there had to be an *opinio juris*.[89] On the material aspect of practice which created obligations and rights the WBAT cited the judgment of the ICJ in the *Asylum Case* which it applied by way of analogy. That judgment reasserted the requirement of constant and uniform usage as an element of law-creating custom. Thus, where the facts 'disclosed so much uncertainty and contradiction, so much fluctuation and discrepancy', the ICJ was of the view that it was not possible to discern any constant and uniform usage accepted as law.[90]

The WBAT concluded in *de Merode* that between 1968 and 1979 there had not existed any established and consistent practice in the IBRD of increasing salaries across the board to a degree at least equal to the increase in the Consumer Price Index. However, the conditions of employment contained rules regarding salary adjustment resulting from an established practice, namely of making periodic adjustments in the salary of staff members reflecting changes in the cost of living and other factors.[91]

Practice has been relied on by other international administrative tribunals as law-creating. Thus, in some cases limitations regarding procedures according to which a power may be exercised have been implied from administrative practice.[92] Practice has in some cases been regarded as spelling out in greater detail rules which had already been laid down by the provision conferring a power.[93] In *Schumann* the LNT interpreted a text relating to pension benefits by reference, among other things, to the acknowledged practice of the administrative board of the Pension Fund of the League of Nations of recognizing that some staff members who did

---

[88] See Akehurst, note 8 p. 95.

[89] The ICJ expressed the view that practice could alter the written law: 'The fact is that there has developed in this matter a body of practice to the effect that holders of fixed-term contracts...have often been treated as entitled to be considered for continued employment...in a manner transcending the strict wording of the contract' (*Effect of Awards Case*, 1954 ICJ Reports at p. 91).

[90] 1950 ICJ Reports at p. 277.   [91] WBAT Reports [1981], Decision No. 1 at pp. 53*ff*.

[92] See *Vanhove*, UNAT Judgment No. 14 [1952]; and *Garcin*, ILOAT Judgment No. 32 [1958].

[93] See *Carson*, UNAT Judgment No. 85 [1962]. For other cases of practice being recognized see, e.g., *Desgranges*, ILOAT Judgment No. 11 [1953]; *Bang-Jensen*, UNAT Judgment No. 74 [1958]; and *Decision No. 49*, OECD Appeals Board [1974].

not have more than three years' service could receive benefits.[94] There are even cases in which tribunals have held that administrative practices could be legitimized, even though they were to the disadvantage of staff or curtailed their rights which already existed. This, however, is less frequent and seems generally to have been confined to the UNAT thus far. In *Dupuy*[95] the UNAT recognized that there was a long-standing practice on the part of the administration of inferring an abandonment of post from unauthorized absences, while such an inference was permitted also by the implicit recognition of this method of termination of service by the Staff Regulations.

Both the UNAT and the ILOAT stated clearly that not all practice is a source of law. In *Fernandez-Lopez*[96] the UNAT held that a general rule of practice adopted through inter-organizational consultations had not become law. It was said that the practice could not become law at that early stage unless it was incorporated in the written law of the organization. In *Rosescu* the ILOAT referred to a practice relied on by the applicant as a general practice as not a binding rule, which did not confer a right on the applicant nor laid any obligation on the organization.[97]

Other sources

In some judgments tribunals have referred to equity in deciding the cases. Equitable principles could be applied by international administrative tribunals in so far as they form part of the general principles of law. This would be the case where, for instance, equity was applied in regard to the discovery of documents[98] or in the interpretation of provisions concerning time limits.[99] This is not a true derivation of rules from equity in any technical sense as a source of law. It is the application of general principles of law.

There are a few areas in which equity in a general sense has been freely referred to or decisions have been given *ex aequo et bono*. The first of these is the area of damages. Tribunals have in the award of damages sometimes stated that damages were being fixed or calculated *ex aequo et bono* or used language of this kind.[100] Equity is not used as a basis for establishing the right to recover damages or for listing the heads of damages

---

[94] LNT Judgment No. 13 [1934].   [95] UNAT Judgment No. 174 [1973].
[96] UNAT Judgment No. 254 [1980].   [97] ILOAT Judgment No. 431 [1980] at p. 7.
[98] *Bang-Jensen*, UNAT Judgment No. 74 [1958].
[99] See *Elz*, CJEC Case No. 34/59 [1960] ECR at p. 109 *per* the Advocate-General.
[100] See, e.g., *Garcin*, ILOAT Judgment No. 32 [1958]; and *Howrani*, UNAT Judgment No. 11 [1951].

but merely for assessing the amount of damages once the right to damages and the heads of damage have been laid down. This technique is no
more than an application of reasonable standards to the assessment of
compensation. As the ICJ pointed out, tribunals in these circumstances
fix a reasonable figure for compensation because the actual amount to
be awarded could not be based on any specific rule of law.[101] The second
area in which equity is referred to sometimes is jurisdiction and judicial
procedure. There have been cases in which tribunals have assumed jurisdiction by interpreting their statutes by reference to justice or equity.[102]
These cases deal with interpretation strictly and the references to equity
are no more than the application of reason to the interpretation of the
text before the tribunal. In spite of *obiter* references to application of
equity in the settlement of disputes brought before administrative tribunals,[103] no case has been decided in which a rule has been derived
from equity as such or the decision has been made *ex aequo et bono
per se*.

International law is another possible source of law for international
administrative tribunals. In general tribunals have not referred to international law as such as a source of the law they apply. In so far as
international law embodies general principles of law which tribunals
may apply there is no problem. Those principles are applied by tribunals *qua* general principles and not as international law as such.
Thus, discrimination has been regarded as contrary to law in some cases
because of the general principle against discrimination, although sometimes international instruments may be referred to in support of the
decision.[104]

International law may have to be applied by tribunals because it is
incorporated implicitly in the written law of an organization. Thus,
where the question of immunities was in issue it has been held that
the matter was governed among other things by an international agreement which gave the head of the organization complete discretion in
the matter.[105] Similarly, international law may be applied by reference
in interpreting the written law of an organization.[106]

---

[101] See, e.g., *Judgments of the ILO Administrative Tribunal Case*, 1956 ICJ Reports at p. 100.
[102] See, e.g., *Leff*, ILOAT Judgment No. 15 [1954]; and *Bernstein*, ILOAT Judgment No. 21
[1955].
[103] See *di Palma Castiglione*, LNT Judgment No. 1 [1929]; and *Tranter*, ILOAT Judgment No.
14 [1954].
[104] See *Artzet*, COEAB, Appeal No. 8 [1972] at p. 88.
[105] *Jurado*, ILOAT Judgment No. 70 [1964].
[106] See *Stepczynski*, UNAT Judgment No. 64 [1956].

Apart from the above limited situations where international law *per se* may be applied, tribunals have not recognized international law as a real source of law. For example, it has been held that understandings between international organizations cannot limit the rights of staff members unless they are incorporated in the written law of the organization. [107] Further, ILOAT has held that an amendment to staff regulations intended to give effect to an agreement between organizations cannot override the staff's acquired rights.[108]

National law may in certain circumstances be a source of law but generally not *per se*.[109] The commonest situation where national law becomes relevant is where it is specifically incorporated in the written law of the organization. Thus, staff regulations may subject officials to local laws on social security. Local law may also be applicable because the contract or staff regulations make them applicable to certain classes of officials. Another instance where national law becomes applicable is where the written law is interpreted in the light of national law, because it is implied that the concept used in the written law is a national law concept.[110] Thus, the existence of a 'marriage' is generally determined according to national law.

Clearly national law could give rise to general principles of law. Indeed, most general principles of law applied by international administrative tribunals are derived from national law, even though there may be no explicit mention of this fact. For example, the principle that money paid by mistake could be recovered, which was applied in *Wakley*,[111] is traceable to national law. However, in these cases national law is not applied *per se* as a source of law. General principles of law are the true source of the law applied.

The hierarchy of sources

The general principle is that the written law of the organization is the main source of the internal law governing employment relations. IATs are careful to observe this principle. As among written instruments, the constitution of the organization would be at the top of the list. Other

---

[107] *Champoury*, UNAT Judgment No. 76 [1959].   [108] *Lindsey*, ILOAT Judgment No. 61 [1962].
[109] See, e.g., *Zihler*, ILOAT Judgment No. 435 [1980]; *Breukmann (No. 2)*, ILOAT Judgment No. 322 [1977]; and *Gallianos*, UNAT Judgment No. 126 [1969]. On national law see also Bedjaoui, 'Application de la loi locale aux fonctionnaires internationaux', 86 JDI (1959) p. 216.
[110] See Morgenstern, 'The Law Applicable to International Officials', 18 ICLQ (1969) p. 739.
[111] ILOAT Judgment No. 53 [1961].

instruments would have priority in accordance with the constitution, e.g., UNGA resolutions or decisions of the Executive Directors of the IBRD or the IMF incorporated in the By-Laws or otherwise made would take precedence over regulations and rules promulgated by the administration of the organization; circulars and memoranda would be at an even lower level. There has generally been no problem with identifying the hierarchy among written instruments.[112]

It is with regard to general principles of law and practice that problems may arise. General principles of law are normally applied in order to supplement the written law or as being implied in the interpretation of the written law. Where the written law reflects a general principle of law, there is no problem.[113] However, it is possible that a conflict may arise with the written law, where, for example, a general principle of law requires the administrative authority not to take a certain course of action but the written law expressly permits the administrative authority to take that action, as where the written law expressly permits discriminatory treatment as between the sexes but general principles of law prohibit such discrimination. There is some authority on the point but there is an apparent conflict among the authorities. In a few cases the view taken has apparently been that the written law takes precedence over general principles of law.[114] In *Mullan*[115] the UNAT refused to apply the general principle of law against discrimination between sexes in the face of an explicit Staff Rule which permitted such discrimination, because the rule was consistent with the Staff Regulations adopted by the GA. The applicant claimed that existing Staff Rule 107.5(a) of the UN, because it permitted the payment of a husband's travel expenses on home leave only if he were dependent, while the same Staff Rule enabled payment of a wife's travel expenses, whether she were dependent or not, established a distinction on the basis of sex which was contrary to the principle of equal conditions of employment enunciated in the Charter of the UN and embodied in a fundamental principle of law. However, there is some authority for the view that general principles of law can

---

[112] Equity, international law and national law do not pose problems either, as would have emerged from the earlier discussion.

[113] *Bustos*, ILOAT Judgment No. 701 [1985]; and *de Padiac (No. 2)*, ILOAT Judgment No. 911 [1988].

[114] In *di Palma Castiglione*, LNT Judgment No. 1 [1929] at p. 3, the LNT stated that it was only in the absence of rules of positive law that the application of general principles of law could be considered. See also, e.g., *Vukmanovic*, ILOAT Judgment No. 896 [1988].

[115] UNAT Judgment No. 162 [1972], JUNAT Nos. 114–66 p. 387.

be superior hierarchically to the written law of an international organization. First, there are some general principles of law, such as the rule against an amendment which violates acquired or essential rights, which are in fact applied even in the face of written rules to the contrary.[116] Secondly, the ILOAT said in *Ferrechia* that the rule that a staff member must be given the right to be heard before a disciplinary sanction is imposed on him, deriving as it does from a general principle of law, must be respected 'even where contrary provisions exist'.[117] This approach was followed by the Appeals Board of ELDO in *Decision No. 6*,[118] where the tribunal held that an express term in the applicant's contract of employment which resulted in the violation of the principles against non-discrimination could not be enforced. Thirdly, it is clear from the jurisprudence of tribunals that they do try to interpret the written law so as to conform to general principles of law and to establish that the written law does not violate general principles of law.[119]

Considerable importance is attached to general principles of law in the hierarchy of sources of law, even if there are statements to the contrary. Apart from *Mullan*, no decision has actually disregarded a general principle of law in the face of a conflicting written law. The exercise of legislative power in *Mullan*, though delegated, was contrary to the principle of non-discrimination, as admitted by the tribunal. Hence, it was no defence that it was within the scope of the main legislative instrument under which the delegated power was exercised. Both instruments were contrary to law, if they were both discriminatory. In fact the main legislative instrument which did not itself discriminate should have been construed in such a way as not to permit discrimination based on sex. Thus, it was not the Staff Regulations that were at fault but the manner in which the delegated legislative power had been exercised. If the principle of non-discrimination applies to primary legislation, as it has

---

[116] See in particular *de Merode*, WBAT Reports [1981], Decision No. 1, and the discussion later in this chapter.

[117] ILOAT Judgment No. 203 [1973]. In some cases the ILOAT pointed out that the written law was not in conflict with a general principle of law and could, therefore, be enforced, thus supporting the position taken in cases like *Ferrechia*: see, e.g., *Verdrager*, ILOAT Judgment No. 325 [1977]; *Haas*, ILOAT Judgment No. 473 [1982].

[118] *Decision No. 6*, ELDO Appeals Board [1971].

[119] See, e.g., cases cited in note 117 above. See also *Decision No. 203(a)*, NATO Appeals Board [1985]; *Razzouk and Beydoun*, CJEC Cases 75 and 117/82 [1984] ECR p. 1,530; *Callewaert-Haezebrouck (No. 2)*, ILOAT Judgment No. 344 (1978); and *Artzet*, COEAB, Appeal No. 8 [1973], *Case Law Digest* (1985) p. 42. See discussion of the cases in Amerasinghe, note 1 vol. I pp. 319*ff*.

clearly been regarded as being capable of doing, *a fortiori* it would control the exercise of delegated legislative power.[120] *Pace Mullan*, there is considerable evidence that, at least in some cases, general principles of law are superior to the written sources of law. The fact particularly that tribunals tend to interpret written rules so as to conform to general principles of law and not conflict with them is proof that tribunals do regard such principles as of special importance even in relation to the written law. The reasonable conclusion seems to be that, as regards the general principles of law of a *fundamental* nature, they are superior hierarchically to any written law in particular and could, indeed, be the supreme source of law relating to the international civil service. There are certain general principles which are not of such importance that they could not be modified or negated by the written law or by a rule emanating from another source. The rule against discrimination or equality of treatment and the principle that a staff member has a right to be heard before a disciplinary sanction is imposed on him[121] are examples of general principles of a fundamental nature, as is the rule protecting acquired or essential rights.

As for practice, in certain instances tribunals have held that a practice could not as such modify the written law, as opposed to interpret it. In *Broemser*[122] the WBAT held that the practice of deviating from evaluation procedures required by a Personnel Manual Statement of the World Bank could not be recognized, because the Bank was bound to adhere to established procedures from which it could not deviate, unless the form of practice had been embodied in a Staff Rule or otherwise been made a matter of public record.[123] In *Léger*[124] the ILOAT took a similar view in regard to the practice of the administrative authority relating to the place of the applicant's residence. The tribunal said:

Such statements of practice often relate, as in this case, to the way in which the Director intends to administer a staff rule and thus clarify and amplify it. But just as a staff rule must not conflict with the staff regulation under which it is made, so a statement of practice must not conflict with the rule which it is elaborating. Staff Rule 460 mandates that the place determined at the time

---

[120] The staff rule implicated in *Mullan* reads differently now.
[121] Except in the case of summary dismissal, when this is permitted.
[122] WBAT Reports [1985], Decision No. 27.
[123] In *von Stauffenberg et al.*, WBAT Reports [1987, Part I], Decision No. 38, the WBAT recognized the practice of voting by consensus in the Boards of Governors and Executive Directors.
[124] ILOAT Judgment No. 486 [1982].

of appointment should be recognized throughout the service. This forbids the change of residence which the complainant is asking the Tribunal to order.[125]

On the other hand, both the ICJ[126] and the ILOAT[127] recognized that the practice in the UNESCO of treating fixed-term contract holders as being entitled to be considered for renewal of their contracts was a source of law, even though it was categorically in contradiction to the provisions both of the contracts themselves and the Staff Regulations which stated that upon expiry the contracts came to an end without prospect of renewal.[128]

These cases raise the very important question when administrative practice can modify the written law of the organization. No serious doubt has been raised about the proposition that such practice cannot override the constituent treaty of the organization.[129] However, in regard to staff regulations and staff rules or their equivalent (the contracts of employment or other written sources), the cases referred to above reveal some conflicting views. It is reasonable that practices which are to the disadvantage of staff, in that they take away rights given by the written law, cannot override the written law, because staff rights should be given adequate protection. As for practices which benefit the staff, the cases show no uniformity. The ICJ and the ILOAT have taken the view that in regard to the renewal of fixed-term contracts practice can override the written law, while in *Léger* the ILOAT thought that a practice which contradicted the written law on the determination of residence could not override the written law. The decisions are difficult to reconcile. Short of concluding that *Léger* was wrongly decided, because of the weight of authority particularly of the ICJ, it may be necessary, while accepting in general the view of the ICJ and the ILOAT in the other cases, to leave open the possibility that in exceptional situations the view taken in *Léger*

---

[125] *Ibid.* at p. 6. Proof that the practice had been followed in other cases does not affect the situation: *Léger (No. 2)*, ILOAT Judgment No. 554 [1983].

[126] *Judgments of the ILO Administrative Tribunal Case*, ICJ Reports [1956] at p. 91.

[127] *Duberg etc.*, ILOAT Judgments Nos. 17–19 and 21 [1955].

[128] For other cases in which the ILOAT has applied practices which may have the effect of modifying the written law, see, e.g., *Redfern*, ILOAT Judgment No. 679 [1985] at pp. 6–7; *Rosetti*, ILOAT Judgment No. 910 [1988] at pp. 6–7. On fixed-term contracts see C. F. Amerasinghe, note 1 vol. II pp. 92*ff.*; Akehurst, 'Renewal of Fixed-Term Contracts of Employment in International Organizations', 32 *Revue internationale des sciences administratives* (1965) p. 83.

[129] See Advocate-General Roemer in *von Lachmüller*, CJEC Cases 43, 45 and 48/59 [1960] ECR at p. 484.

will be applied. Basically, the view taken by the ICJ and the ILOAT in the earlier cases seems to be a reasonable one, on the understanding that it applies to practices which work to the benefit of staff members.[130] What works to the benefit of staff members should be encouraged but not what does not.

There is no authority on the relationship between practice and the general principles of law or on whether an administrative practice can override a general principle of law. There is good reason for believing that in the case of a fundamental general principle of law, such as the rule against discrimination, a practice cannot override it. There are conceivably circumstances, however, in which a general practice may override a general principle, particularly where the practice tends to place the staff member at an advantage in relation to his position under the general principle of law. Thus, if a practice is established whereby in regard to specific payments made by mistake to staff members the administrative authority upon becoming aware of the mistake clearly relinquishes its right under a general principle of law to reclaim the monies paid by mistake, it may be that staff members will be able to rely on this practice to protect themselves.

The nature of control over administrative powers

The exercise of administrative powers, particularly, in connection with employment relations is controlled by the application of international administrative law. The substantive law applied has evolved over time.[131]

Review of the exercise of powers

International organizations generally exercise their powers *vis-à-vis* their staff through administrative decisions. When a staff member disputes an act or omission of the administration of an international organization, he usually questions a decision taken by the administrative authority. As a result IATs exercise judicial control over decisions taken by organizations in the exercise of their powers.

While technically the failure to act on the part of an administrative authority could be a violation of the law attracting the judicial control

---

[130] On changes of practice see *Cachelin*, ILOAT Judgment No. 767 [1986] at p. 7. On misapplication of practice see *Novak*, ILOAT Judgment No. 975 [1989] at pp. 6–7.

[131] Jurisdictional limitations and inadmissibility affect the exercise of control by tribunals: see the discussion in C. F. Amerasinghe, note 1 vol. I pp. 201*ff*.

of an administrative tribunal, generally such failures are also reflected in decisions taken by the administrative authority, negative though they may be. For example, where a staff member complains that the administrative authority has failed to pay him an allowance to which he claims to be entitled, even though the complaint is against an omission of the administrative authority, there will usually be an administrative decision taken by the organization refusing to pay the staff member the allowance. It is this decision which will be attacked by the staff member.[132]

Where direct *obligations* of an organization towards a staff member are not fulfilled, there may be found to have been a breach of contract or non-observance of terms of appointment. It is where the organization exercises *powers* affecting staff members, such as the power to terminate employment, to promote or to increase salaries, that a more subtle approach to control is required.

The substantive law that has been developed in this area by IATs since the establishment of the LNT is quite complex.[133] Only a brief look at the principal aspects of the law applied is possible here.

In regard to quasi-judicial powers, such as disciplinary powers, control is more extensive than in the case of other powers. As was said in regard to disciplinary powers in *Carew* by the WBAT:

In such cases the Tribunal examines (i) the existence of the facts, (ii) whether they legally amount to misconduct, (iii) whether the sanction imposed is provided for in the law of the Bank, (iv) whether the sanction is not significantly disproportionate to the offence, and (v) whether the requirements of due process were observed. The Applicant is, therefore, correct in his assertion that the Tribunal, in reviewing decisions in disciplinary cases, is not limited to determining whether there has been an abuse of discretion.[134]

---

[132] Similarly, a staff member on probation may be deprived of his entitlement to training but this failure on the part of the administrative authority will generally be reflected in decisions refusing adequate training, almost certainly precipitated by the staff member's internal complaints that his rights were not being respected. While administrative decisions constituting an exercise of power are the rule, theoretically there is nothing to prevent a failure to exercise a power which is not reflected in an administrative decision from being a violation of rights which is contestable before an international administrative tribunal, where the tribunal's statute does not require a decision, see C. F. Amerasinghe, *ibid.* vol. I pp. 257*ff*.

[133] See C. F. Amerasinghe, *ibid.* vol. I pp. 277*ff*. See also de Vuyst, 'The Use of Discretionary Authority by International Organizations in their Relations with International Civil Servants', 12 *Denver Journal of International Law and Policy* (1983) p. 237.

[134] WBAT Reports [1995], Decision No. 142 at p. 13. See also *Planthara*, WBAT Reports [1995], Decision No. 143 at p. 8.

Other tribunals have supported this approach.[135] The decision of the administration is examined in full in order to establish virtually whether it was one which the tribunal would have itself taken, had it been called upon to take the initial decision taken by the administration. It could be acting rather as a court of appeal than as a court of review.

In other areas where discretionary powers are exercised tribunals treat the matter as reviewing the exercise of power in order to ascertain whether there has been an abuse of discretion. Cases may be based on such diverse causes of action as salary adjustment, downgrading, termination of employment, probationary appointments, fixed-term contracts, abolition of posts, reorganization, promotion, reassignment, classification, discrimination, sexual harassment, absence of due process, disciplinary measures, grandfathering of salaries, retirement and expatriate benefits. Where an abuse of discretion takes place the exercise of powers is illegal and the staff member affected is entitled to a remedy.

In exercising control over the exercise of discretionary power by administrative authorities, tribunals will not substitute their own assessments or judgments for those of administrative authorities. In a situation involving a decision to abolish posts the UNAT referred to the well-established jurisprudence that the tribunal cannot substitute its own judgment for that of the administrative authority in respect of the reorganization of posts or staff in the interests of economy and efficiency.[136]

On the other hand, it is generally accepted that '[d]iscretionary power must not . . . be confused with arbitrary power'[137] and that '[d]iscretionary power is not absolute power'.[138] Consequently, it is recognized that there are certain limitations on the exercise of discretionary power. This

---

[135] See, e.g., *Connolly-Battisti (No. 2)*, ILOAT Judgment No. 274 [1976]. See also C. F. Amerasinghe, note 1 vol. II pp. 190*ff.*, for a discussion of the basic approach.

[136] *van der Valk*, UNAT Judgment No. 117 [1968], JUNAT Nos. 114–66 at p. 40. In *Kersaudy*, ILOAT Judgment No. 152 [1970] at p. 5, the ILOAT stated, in relation to its power to review a decision not to confirm a staff member on probation, that the tribunal may not substitute its own judgment for that of the administrative authority concerning the work or conduct of the probationer or his qualifications for employment as an international official. See also, e.g., *Decision No. 141*, NATO Appeals Board [1981], Collection of the Decisions 135 to 171 (1984) at p. 2 (reorganization); *Angelopoulos*, Decision No. 57, OECD Appeals Board [1976], Recueil des décisions 1 à 62 (1979) at p. 159 (evaluation for post); *Saberi*, WBAT Reports [1982], Decision No. 5 at p. 8 (performance); and *Pagani*, COEAB Appeal No. 76 [1982], Case-Law Digest (1985) at p. 100 (transfer).

[137] *Ballo*, ILOAT Judgment No. 191 [1972] at p. 6.

[138] *de Merode*, WBAT Reports [1981], Decision No. 1 at p. 21.

recognition has often taken the form of an explicit statement that the discretionary power (such as a power of amendment) may be exercised subject only to certain limitations,[139] or that the discretionary power must be exercised lawfully.[140] The element of control has often been explained by the ILOAT. Thus, in *Ballo*, a case concerning a decision not to renew a fixed-term contract, which was regarded by the ILOAT as a discretionary decision, the tribunal said that it must determine:

> whether that decision was taken with authority, is in regular form, whether the correct procedure has been followed and, as regards its legality under the Organization's own rules, whether the Administration's decision was based on an error of law or fact, or whether essential facts have not been taken into consideration, or again, whether conclusions which are clearly false have been drawn from the documents in the dossier, or finally, whether there has been a misuse of authority.[141]

Several other tribunals have referred in different ways to similar elements of control.[142] The control is not as extensive as in the case of a purely obligatory power or a quasi-judicial power. It may broadly be defined in terms of the prevention of 'arbitrary' conduct on the part of administrative authorities. It is sufficiently substantial to protect the interests of staff members while not impeding unduly the execution of the administrative or management function by international organizations.

Whether tribunals have indulged in general expositions of the grounds for controlling the exercise of discretionary power or not, they have followed similar principles in carrying out the function of controlling the exercise of discretionary powers. The similarities are so marked and the differences so few that it is difficult to avoid the conclusion that the general principles underlying the application of controls to the exercise of discretionary powers are undisputed and generally accepted.

---

[139] *Ibid.*

[140] *Ballo*, ILOAT Judgment No. 191 [1972] at p. 6. See also, e.g. *Pagani*, COEAB, Appeal No. 76 [1982], Case-Law Digest (1985) at p. 101.

[141] ILOAT Judgment No. 191 [1972] at pp. 6–7. See also, e.g., *Vangeenberghe*, COEAB, Appeal No. 77 [1982], *ibid.* at p. 110.

[142] See, e.g., *Decision No. 139*, NATO Appeals Board [1981], Collection of the Decisions 135 to 171 (1984) at p. 3; *Reid*, UNAT Judgment No. 210 [1976], JUNAT Nos. 167–230 at p. 407; *Einthoven*, WBAT Reports [1985], Decision No. 23 at pp. 14; *de Merode*, WBAT Reports [1985], Decision No. 1 at pp. 21–2; *Mendez*, OASAT Judgment No. 21 [1976] at p. 5; and *Colussi*, CJEC Case 298/81 [1983] ECR at p. 1,142.

In effect, the control over discretionary functions by tribunals has been exercised broadly in relation to three categories of illegality. Thus, a discretion may be abused because it involved *détournement de pouvoir* or irregular motive (which covers discrimination and inequality of treatment), substantive irregularity or procedural irregularity. The limitations flowing from these three kinds of illegality may depend on the written or unwritten law. While discretion implies the freedom to act, the discretion may well be circumscribed by the explicit provisions of the written law which may be framed in terms of obligatory conduct, e.g., where a certain procedure of rebuttal and defence is prescribed for the valid exercise of the power of appraising performance, a discretionary element in the taking of the decision to terminate employment or to confirm a probationary appointment. These obligations are to be seen as limitations on the exercise of discretionary power rather than as obligations in the abstract. Similar obligations may arise from general principles of law, such as the duty to derive reasonable conclusions from facts in the course of making assessments.

In addition the power to amend terms and conditions of employment requires special treatment because of the special nature of this power, an aspect of which includes the discretionary power to make such amendments. In general the law relating to the control of exercise of discretionary power has been regarded as flowing from the general principles of law.

Discrimination and improper motive[143]

Discretionary powers are reviewed on the ground that they were exercised in a discriminatory manner or for an improper motive (that there was a *détournement de pouvoir*). The review may take place in regard to legislative power, including the power to change conditions of employment, or administrative powers.

Discrimination may take place on, for example, the basis of sex, nationality or religion. It covers any unjustifiable distinction. There is an improper motive or an abuse of purpose when a power is exercised for a purpose or with an objective for which it was not intended. Personal ill will or prejudice is only one example of abuse of purpose. It is not necessary that an irregular purpose be present or be proved for the exercise of the power to be invalid; it is sufficient that the proper

---

[143] See for detailed discussion, C. F. Amerasinghe, note 1 vol. I pp. 277*ff.* and 313*ff.*

purpose is absent. It is only purpose that is relevant to the principle and not result or consequence.

Substantive irregularity[144]

Substantive irregularity pertains to the substantive content of the decision taken, as contrasted with the motive for the decision or the procedure followed in the taking of the decision. Thus, for example, the facts on which a decision is based, the conclusions drawn from the facts established and the relationship of the elements of the decision or the acts upon which it rests to the governing laws are matters concerning the substance or content of the decision.

In some of the general statements made by tribunals there are often references to substantive defects as a possible reason for characterizing a decision as tainted. In general terms substantive defects could conceivably be included in such broad concepts as 'abuse of discretion', 'arbitrariness', 'misuse of power' or 'abuse of power', but these seem to be catch-all phrases or terms which cover a multitude of sins and may not specifically refer to defects of substance. However, some general statements have been made describing the kinds of substantive irregularities which could occur. Thus the ILOAT often, and the COEAB by citing the ILOAT, have mentioned absence of authority, mistake of law or fact, omission of essential facts and the drawing of clearly mistaken conclusions as being grounds for impugning discretionary decisions.[145] Enumerations, such as those made by the ILOAT, are not meant to be exhaustive but rather reflect what the tribunals in their experience have most frequently encountered. There may well be other substantive irregularities, such as, for example, the consideration of irrelevant facts, which could vitiate a discretionary decision. The cases decided by tribunals reveal that there are several kinds of substantive irregularity which could taint a decision taken by the administrative authority.

---

[144] See for detailed discussion, *ibid.* vol. I pp. 342*ff.*

[145] See, e.g., *Ballo*, ILOAT Judgment No. 191 [1972] at p. 6; *Peltre*, ILOAT Judgment No. 330 [1977] at p. 4; *Vangeenberghe*, COEAB, Appeal No. 77 [1982], *ibid.* at p. 110. In *Maier*, ILOAT Judgment No. 503 [1982] at p. 4, the ILOAT stated that the tribunal should verify whether a discretionary decision, such as the decision not to confirm a probationary appointment, was tainted with illegality or was based on incorrect facts, or whether the administrative authority, in taking such a decision, had failed to take account of essential facts or had drawn from the evidence conclusions that were clearly false or manifestly unfounded.

Procedural irregularities[146]

The need for a fair procedure to be followed in the taking of discretionary administrative decisions has been emphasized by IATs. The recognition of the right of staff members to a fair procedure in the taking of discretionary decisions is particularly important, because it is often difficult to prove the existence of irregular motives or *détournement de pouvoir* as a ground for judicial review of a discretionary decision. Thus, judicial review of procedural factors constitutes a significant means of checking arbitrary action on the part of administrative authorities.

The UNAT has stated in general terms:

It is also true that the exercise of broad powers without adequate procedural safeguards inevitably produces arbitrary limitation upon the exercise of any power. The maintenance of the authority of the Secretary General to deal effectively and decisively with the work and operation of the Secretariat in conditions of flexibility and adaptability depends, in its exercise, in large measure upon the observance of procedural safeguards. In a very real sense, the mode must be the measure of the power.[147]

While the requirement of procedural propriety cannot be disputed, the content of that requirement may vary with the kind of discretionary decision in issue. Apart from the fact that the prescriptions of the written law may be different in different circumstances, the requirements of the unwritten law (i.e., general principles of law) in regard to procedure may also vary with the kind of decision taken. Thus, the procedural safeguards accorded to staff members in the usual disciplinary case are, perhaps, the most extensive, while in other cases administrative authorities are evidently under less severe constraints in terms of the procedure to be followed. What all discretionary decisions have in common is that a 'fair' procedure or 'due process' be followed when they are taken. What holds good for decisions relating to termination of service

---

[146] See for detailed discussion, C. F. Amerasinghe, note 1 vol. I pp. 366*ff*. See also Jenks, 'Due Process of Law in International Organizations', *International Organization* (1965) p. 163.

[147] *Howrani and Four Others*, UNAT Judgment No. 4 [1951], JUNAT Nos. 1–70 at p. 10. In *Salle*, a case concerning the non-confirmation of a probationary appointment, the WBAT stated: 'The Tribunal deems it necessary to emphasize the importance of the requirements sometimes subsumed under the phrase "due process of law". The very discretion granted to the Respondent in reaching its decision at the end of probation makes it all the more imperative that the procedural guarantees insuring the staff member of fair treatment be respected. (WBAT Reports [1983, Part I], Decision No. 10 at p. 23.)

for unsatisfactory service may not necessarily or always be applicable to decisions relating to promotion.

Rules of fair procedure may be derived from general principles of law, where the written law is silent on the subject concerned, or they may be derived from the written law or by an interpretation of the written law in the light of general principles of law. There are many examples of the application of general principles of law in the derivation of rules relating to procedural requirements. For example, in reviewing decisions not to renew fixed-term contracts the ILOAT, which treats such decisions as discretionary, has generally resorted to procedural rules which are derived entirely from the general principles of law. In *Garcin*, it was held that, even though there was no written law on the matter, the administrative authority should have had the applicant's periodic reports completed before deciding that his fixed-term contract would not be converted into a permanent one, so that he would have had an opportunity of having the decision modified.[148] In the case of transfer the ILOAT seems in *Frank (Nos. 1 & 2)* implicitly to have recognized that under a general principle of law the staff member being transferred should be consulted before the transfer is made.[149] The selection of a general principle of law to be applied in a given situation and the decision whether the application of such a general principle of law is warranted will depend on the circumstances of the case.

Limitations on the power of amendment[150]

Organizations have the power to change or amend the rules which govern the employment relationship with the result that such amendments apply to staff members employed before their adoption. This power does not depend on whether the employment relationship is based on contract or status. Granted the power to make rules governing the

---

[148] ILOAT Judgment No. 32 [1958]. For other general principles applied in reference to fixed-term contracts see, e.g., *Kirkbir*, ILOAT Judgment No. 116 [1968]; *Byrne-Sutton*, ILOAT Judgment No. 592 [1983]; and *Freeman*, ILOAT Judgment No. 600 [1984]. The right of defence has also been recognized as a general principle of law, even in the absence of provisions in the written law: *Kissaun*, ILOAT Judgment No. 69 [1964] (probationary appointments).

[149] ILOAT Judgment No. 154 [1970]. *Contra, Mendez*, OASAT Judgment No. 21 [1976]; and *Arning*, CJEC Case 125/80 [1981] ECR p. 2,539.

[150] See for detailed discussion, C. F. Amerasinghe, note 1 vol. I pp. 402ff. See also Akehurst, 'Unilateral Amendment of Conditions of Employment in International Organizations', 41 BYIL (1964) p. 286; Lemoine, 'Le Contrôle judiciaire des modifications de conditions de service des fonctionnaires internationaux', 8 AFDI (1962) p. 407.

employment relationship, it has been said by the UNAT: 'this power to adopt general provisions implies in principle the right to amend the rules established'.[151] In this regard, it becomes necessary to strike a balance between the interests of staff in certainty and continuity and the interests of the organization in being able to adjust to changing needs and to correct mistakes. While tribunals have recognized that organizations must have some freedom to carry on their operations, they have increasingly made an effort to protect the interests of staff as well.

The staff regulations of many organizations explicitly subject the amendment of the regulations to certain limitations. Thus, Regulation 12.01 of the UN Staff Regulations provides: 'These Regulations may be supplemented or amended by the General Assembly, without prejudice to the acquired rights of staff members.' Tribunals have interpreted such regulations as imposing limitations on the power of amendment.[152] Thus, in *Poulain d'Andecy* the ILOAT stated that the text of a written law 'under the most restrictive interpretation has the same scope as the principle of the prohibition of retroactivity'.[153] The principle seems to be generally accepted that no unilateral amendment should be made

---

[151] *Puvrez*, UNAT Judgment No. 82 [1961], JUNAT Nos. 71–86 at p. 85. See also *de Merode*, Decision No. 1, WBAT Reports [1981] at p. 15; *Effect of Awards Case*, 1954 ICJ Reports at p. 61.

[152] See *Kaplan*, UNAT Judgment No. 19 [1953], JUNAT Nos. 1–70 at p. 71; and *Puvrez*, UNAT Judgment No. 82 [1961] (ICAO), JUNAT Nos. 71–86 at p. 78. Since the decision in *Kaplan*, UNAT Judgment No. 19 [1953], JUNAT Nos. 1–70 at p. 71, which is the earliest decision on the subject of the unilateral amendment of conditions of employment since the creation of the UN, many jurists have examined, analyzed, explained and sometimes criticized the jurisprudence of international tribunals on the subject: see, e.g., Lemoine, 'Le contrôle judiciaire des modifications de conditions de service des fonctionnaires internationaux', 8 AFDI (1962) p. 497; Weil, 'La nature du lien de fonction publique dans les organisations internationales', 67 RGDIP (1963) p. 273; Baade, 'The Acquired Rights of International Public Servants', 15 AJCL (1966–7) p. 251; Ruzié, 'La condition juridique des fonctionnaires internationaux', 105 JDI (1978) p. 868; Ruzié, 'Le pouvoir des organisations internationales de modifier unilatéralement la condition juridique des fonctionnaires internationaux. Droits acquis ou droits essentiels: à propos d'une jurisprudence du Tribunal Administratif de la Banque Mondiale', 109 JDI (1982) p. 421; C. F. Amerasinghe, 'The Implications of the *De Merode Case* for International Administrative Law', 43 ZAORV (1983) p. 1; Maupain, 'L'élargissement du contrôle judiciaire des modifications unilatérales des conditions d'emploi des fonctionnaires intenationaux et la notion des droits acquis', *Revue internationale des sciences administratives* (1985) p. 33; and Apprill, 'La Notion de "droit acquis" dans le droit de la fonction publique internationale', 100 JDI (1983) p. 316.

[153] ILOAT Judgment No. 51 [1960] at p. 5. See also, e.g., on retroactivity *Decision No. 77*, NATO Appeals Board [1977], Collection of Decisions 65(b), 74–99 [1979] at p. 3; and *de Merode*, WBAT Reports [1981], Decision No. 1 at p. 21.

which is retroactive, whether such limitation is expressly embodied in the written law or not. The principle does not prohibit retroactive amendments which are for the benefit of staff members or which are made with the consent of staff members.[154] As was said in *de Merode*, retroactivity is defined in terms of depriving staff members of rights which have accrued for services already rendered.[155]

Apart from non-retroactivity, control is exercised over powers of amendment by various means. The approach of IATs has been different. Three examples are examined here.

In *Kaplan*, in 1953, the UNAT made a distinction between contractual and statutory elements:

> In determining the legal position of staff members a distinction should be made between contractual elements and statutory elements:
>> All matters being contractual which affect the personal status of each member – e.g., nature of his contract, salary, grade;
>> All matters being statutory which affect in general the organization of the international civil service, and the need for its proper functioning – e.g., general rules that have no personal reference;
> While the contractual elements cannot be changed without the agreement of the two parties, the statutory elements on the other hand may always be changed at any time through regulations established by the General Assembly, and these changes are binding on staff members.[156]

The tribunal did not identify contractual provisions as necessarily being those which were stated in the contract, though it did not elaborate on how 'contractual' terms could be identified. Applying the distinction to the facts of the case, the UNAT held that grounds for termination of a contract of employment were statutory and not contractual in nature, and could be unilaterally amended. The UNAT has adhered to this distinction and applied it in many cases. In several other cases the UNAT found that the terms of employment which had been amended

---

[154] The Appeals Board of the OECD, where employment is statutory, held that consent of the staff would permit retroactivity: see *Merigo*, Decision No. 40, OECD Appeals Board [1966], Reports des décisions 1 à 62 (1979) at p. 113.

[155] WBAT Reports [1981], Decision No. 1 at p. 21. On this aspect see also *Puvrez*, UNAT Judgment No. 82 [1961], JUNAT Nos. 71–86 at p. 78; *Capio*, UNAT Judgments No. 266 [1980], JUNAT Nos. 231–300 at p. 340; *Sue-Ting-Len*, UNAT Judgment No. 259 (1982), *ibid.* at p. 596; *Sun*, UNAT Judgment No. 296 [1982], *ibid.* at p. 611; *Schurz*, UNAT Judgment No. 311 [1983]; *Paveskovic*, UNAT Judgment No. 341 [1984]; *Hebblethwaite and Others*, OASAT Judgment No. 30 [1977]; and *Ryan and Others*, OASAT Judgment No. 35 [1978].

[156] UNAT Judgment No. 19 [1953], JUNAT Nos. 1–70 at p. 74. The distinction was repeated in *Middleton etc.*, UNAT Judgments Nos. 20–27 [1953], *ibid.* at pp. 76, 80, 86, 91, 95, 101, 106 and 110, which deal with the same situation as prevailed in *Kaplan*.

were statutory in nature in the sense that they affected in general the organization of the civil service and the need for its proper functioning.[157] It is evident from the manner in which the law has been applied that contractual stipulations include some provisions of the 'statutory' law.

In 1962 the ILOAT propounded a different approach to the problem of the protection of staff members against amendments affecting them. In *Lindsey*[158] the tribunal stated that there were three kinds of stipulations governing employment: (i) those included expressly or by implication in the contract of employment;[159] (ii) those which appear in the staff regulations, staff rules, and like instruments and which appertain to the structure and functioning of the international civil service and to benefits of an impersonal nature; and (iii) those in the staff regulations, staff rules and like instruments which appertain to the individual terms and conditions of service of an official in consideration of which he accepted appointment. It is likely that the tribunal regarded the stipulations governing employment which fell into the first category as generally unalterable. In a case subsequent to *Lindsey* it was said that these should be such that the parties intended them to be inviolate, if they were to be regarded as unalterable.[160] Those that fell into the second category were to be alterable in the interests of the service (subject, of course, to the principle of non-retroactivity and to such limitations as were imposed upon itself by the organization). Those in the third category were assimilable to contractual stipulations and could only be modified unilaterally in so far as such modification did not adversely affect the balance of the contractual nexus or infringe the essential terms in consideration of which the staff member accepted employment in the organization. Two points of importance emerge. In respect of contractual rights in the first category the ILOAT regard them as unalterable to the extent that the parties regarded them as inviolate. In respect to statutory rights in the

---

[157] In *Wallach*, UNAT Judgment No. 53 [1954], *ibid.* at p. 260, for instance, the UNAT held that the introduction of summary dismissal for serious misconduct by an amendment to the provisions of the staff regulations relating to disciplinary procedures was permissible (see also *Julhiard*, UNAT Judgment No. 62 [1955], *ibid.* at p. 340). In *Mortished*, UNAT Judgment 273 [1991], JUNAT Nos. 231–300 at p. 426, on the other hand, which concerned a relocation allowance, the UNAT held that the conditions could not be amended because the right to the allowance was acquired.

[158] ILOAT Judgment No. 61 [1962] at pp. 6*ff.*

[159] See *Elsen and Elsen-Drouot*, ILOAT Judgment No. 368 [1979] at p. 6, where this is clearly stated.

[160] *Ibid.*

third category (i.e., those which are of an individual nature) a limitation on alterability arises if they are essential, in that they induced the staff member to accept employment in the organization. The tribunal determines whether the conditions have been met on the assumption that the party or parties were behaving reasonably.[161] In the application of the principles relating to the protection of 'acquired rights', as the tribunal called them, there are many other aspects which require appreciation by a tribunal. Thus, for example, the distinction between impersonal conditions and those of an individual nature involve judgment on the part of the tribunal.

The ILOAT in *Lindsey* dealt with the argument that a 'package deal' could affect the application of the principles outlined above. It was held that increases in salary resulting from a comparative assessment of reward for services rendered, such as resulted from the equation of the salaries of ITU staff to those of UN staff, could not be set off against any loss which the applicant might have suffered as a result of the new conditions of service. It was also held that the changes in the pension scheme in which the applicant was a participant which reduced the contributions made by the organization and the amount of the maximum pension to which he was entitled were an infringement of acquired rights, because the conditions of service altered were essential ones which induced the applicant to join the organization. Similarly, the changes made in the conditions attaching to termination of service in the case of abolition of post were held to be a serious infringement of the applicant's conditions of service, the implication being that the changes affected essential conditions which induced the applicant to join the organization. On the other hand, the abolition of the right of family allowances in three instances after employment had been terminated was held not to be an infringement of acquired rights, because it was done in a context where conditions for the grant of family allowances were altered within the framework of a family welfare policy which the organization was entitled to establish.[162]

---

[161] See, e.g., *Asp*, ILOAT Judgment No. 357 [1978] at p. 3.

[162] There are many other cases in which the issue of infringement of 'acquired rights' was litigated before the ILOAT. In most of them the applicants were not successful in showing that their rights had been violated. For cases decided by the ILOAT on 'acquired rights' see, e.g., *Pherai*, ILOAT Judgment No. 441 [1980]; *Lamadie (No. 2) and Kraanen*, ILOAT Judgment No. 365 [1978]; *Asp*, ILOAT Judgment No. 357 [1978]; *Connolly-Battisti (No. 3)*, ILOAT Judgment No. 293 [1977]; *Settino*, ILOAT Judgment No. 426 [1980]; *Gubin and Nemo*, ILOAT Judgment No. 429 [1980]; *Vyle*, ILOAT Judgment 462

In 1981 the WBAT took a third approach. The key issue in *de Merode*[163] concerned the power of the IBRD to amend or change the general rules establishing the rights and duties of the staff. Some applicants contested the power of the IBRD to alter, for instance, the tax reimbursement system as applicable to US nationals.

The tribunal held that, though the IBRD had the inherent power unilaterally to amend conditions of employment of the staff, at the same time there were significant limitations upon the exercise of such power. On the other hand, the power unilaterally to amend conditions of employment could not be limited to favourable amendments, as far as staff members already in employment were concerned. Positively, the tribunal drew a major distinction between certain elements in the contract of employment which were *fundamental* and *essential* in the balance of rights and duties of the staff member and those which were *less fundamental* and *less essential* in this balance. The former could not be changed without the consent of the staff member affected. The latter could be changed unilaterally by the Bank in the exercise of its inherent power but subject to certain limits and conditions. The tribunal made it clear that the distinction between essential or fundamental and less essential or less fundamental conditions of employment did not necessarily correspond with the distinction between contractual rights and statutory rights. Thus, some 'contractual' conditions would be unilaterally changeable, subject to certain conditions, while some 'statutory' conditions would be unilaterally unalterable. Furthermore, it did not express itself in favour of the concept of acquired rights as being relevant to the problem. As for drawing a firm line between fundamental or essential and non-fundamental or non-essential elements, the tribunal did not do this in abstract terms, because it was difficult to distinguish categorically between what was equitable and inequitable. The distinction turned upon the circumstances of the particular case.[164] Non-fundamental and

---

[1981]; *Chomentowski*, ILOAT Judgment No. 596 [1984]; *de los Cobos and Wenger*, ILOAT Judgment No. 391 [1980]; and *Alonson (No. 3)*, ILOAT Judgment No. 514 [1982].

[163] WBAT Reports [1980], Decision No. 1. This case has been analyzed in C. F. Amerasinghe, 'Sources of International Administrative Law', 43 ZAORV (1983) p. 1; and C. F. Amerasinghe, note 1 vol. I pp. 432*ff*.

[164] The tribunal illustrated the application of the distinction: 'Sometimes it will be the principle itself of a condition of employment which possesses an essential and fundamental character, while its implementation will possess a less fundamental and less essential character. In other cases, one or another element in the legal status of a staff member will belong entirely – both principle and implementation – to one or another of these categories. In some cases the distinction will rest upon a

non-essential elements of the conditions of employment were subject to unilateral amendment by the organization. Since this was a discretionary power, there were two significant consequences. On the one hand, the tribunal would not, in any case brought before it, substitute its judgment for that of the competent organs of the organization in exercising that power. On the other hand, the power, being discretionary, was not absolute and was, therefore, subject to certain limitations in its exercise. Amendment of non-fundamental elements of the conditions of employment of employees could not be exercised in an arbitrary or otherwise improper manner.[165]

In regard to the tax reimbursement system the tribunal came to four conclusions. First, the system, based on the standard deduction, was a part of the conditions of employment of staff members and not a mere procedure. Secondly, there were two basic principles underlying the tax reimbursement system: (i) all employees should receive a salary free of national taxes; (ii) staff members who were subject to tax had a right to be reimbursed by the organization for the taxes they were required to pay. The 'safety-net' mechanism in the Bank's new tax reimbursement arrangements recognized the basic nature of this principle. Consequently, the organization did not have the power unilaterally to abolish the tax reimbursement system or to repay a lesser amount than the taxes which a staff member was required to pay. Thirdly, the standard deduction system was a method of implementing the above second basic principle and was therefore a non-essential element of the conditions of employment which could be unilaterally amended by the organization. Fourthly, the exercise of the discretion to replace the standard deduction system by the average deduction system had not been abused in the circumstances. The non-retroactivity of the measure and the procedure followed in deciding on it, among other things, attested to this.

In regard to salary adjustment the tribunal held that there was neither consistent practice nor any underlying belief on the part of the organization that there was a legal obligation to increase salaries to meet the full increase in the cost of living. Hence a practice creating an essential condition of employment had not been established. A practice had, however, been established of making periodic adjustments in the

---

quantitative criterion; in others, it will rest on qualitative considerations. Sometimes it is the inclusion of a specific and well-defined undertaking in the letters of appointment and acceptance that may endow such an undertaking with the quality of being essential.' (WBAT Reports [1981], Decision No. 1 at p. 20.)

[165] *Ibid.* at p. 22, where the WBAT explained what was meant by 'arbitrary'.

salaries of staff members reflecting changes in the cost of living and other factors. This practice was a fundamental element in the conditions of employment of Bank staff which the Bank could not change unilaterally.

Tribunals generally regard legislative acts of international organizations, including those of the highest organs, as subject to the purview of the internal law.[166] It is, therefore, logical that the power to amend legislation, whether original or subsidiary, should also be controlled. While this is true, the approach to amendment has not been uniform.[167]

There are a variety of approaches to the issue of respect for 'acquired rights'. The WBAT preferred not to discuss the issue in terms of acquired rights but in terms of essential and non-essential conditions of employment. The differences are in some respects real and it is not possible to reconcile all the aspects of the different views. Nor is it possible to maintain that the results must always be the same, when the different views are applied to a given situation. Thus, for example, in theory the WBAT may find that an amendment of a condition of employment is not permissible, because the condition is essential, while the ILOAT may find on the same facts that the amendment is not unlawful, because the condition of employment is of an impersonal nature. Or what is statutory and freely changeable for the UNAT may be essential and unchangeable for the WBAT. On the other hand, it is possible that similar solutions may be reached by many tribunals in similar situations. The concepts used are sufficiently broad and involve an adequate element of judgment in their application to enable some tribunals at least to agree on the conclusions they reach with other tribunals.

What does emerge is that all tribunals have, in order to protect staff members, sought to enforce some controls on the power of administrative authorities to amend conditions of employment, often in the absence of express terms in the internal law of international organizations. This has not been totally at the expense of the interests of the administrative authorities of the organizations. The track record of all tribunals in determining where administrative authorities have exceeded their powers and where they have not seems in general to be reasonably balanced. In the process of dealing with the power of unilateral amendment all tribunals have imposed some absolute limitations

---

[166] This is subject to the tribunal having jurisdiction over the particular legislative act.

[167] The approach by other tribunals than the three discussed here is dealt with in C. F. Amerasinghe, note 1 vol. I pp. 411–15, 428–31. For conclusions about the state of the law see *ibid.* pp. 439–40.

which preclude unilateral amendment of conditions of employment in certain circumstances, while, where unilateral amendment of conditions of employment is permitted, most tribunals have given indications that they will consider implementing qualified controls over the exercise of the power to make amendments.

10 Privileges and immunities

Privileges and immunities have been accorded to states and their diplomatic personnel by other states as a result of the development of customary international law.[1] These were largely based on a theory of equality, supported by the principle of reciprocity, and historically reflected the respect states had for each other's sovereignty. Now the law of diplomatic privileges and immunities has been largely codified in the 1961 Vienna Convention on Diplomatic Relations.[2] Customary international law, however, had nothing originally to say on the privileges and immunities of international organizations and their personnel which are a recent phenomenon. These privileges and immunities have, consequently, been largely accorded through treaties and conventions.[3] It has come to be recognized that for the effective exercise of the functions of international

---

[1] For a discussion of state immunities see Badr, *State Immunity* (1984), and Jennings and Watts, *Oppenheim's International Law* (1992) vol. I, pp. 341*ff.* and literature cited therein, particularly p. 341, note 2, p. 346, note 20 and p. 357, note 8. On diplomatic privileges and immunities see particularly Mclanahan, *Diplomatic Immunity* (1989); Lewis, *State and Diplomatic Immunity* (1990); Jennings and Watts, *Oppenheim's International Law* (1992) vol. 1, pp. 1090*ff.* and literature there cited.

[2] 500 UNTS p. 95. The Convention entered into force on 24 April 1964. The Convention is referred to hereinafter as the Vienna Convention.

[3] For a brief history of privileges and immunities accorded to the personnel of international organizations, see Michaels, *International Privileges and Immunities* (1971) pp. 7*ff.* This work also surveys the main treaty law on the subject. The privileges and immunities of international organizations are hereinafter referred to as 'international privileges and immunities'. On international privileges and immunities generally, see, e.g., J.-F. Lalive, 'L'Immunité de juridiction et d'éxecution des organisations internationales', 84 *Hague Recueil* (1953-III) p. 205; Ahluwalia, *The Legal Status, Privileges and Immunities of the Specialized Agencies of the United Nations and Certain Other International Organizations* (1964); Dominicé, 'L'immunité de juridiction et d'éxecution des organisations internationales', 187 *Hague Recueil* (1984-IV) p. 209; Cully, 'Jurisdictional Immunities of Intergovernmental Organisations', 91 Yale LJ (1982) p. 1167; Duffar, *Contribution à l'étude des privilèges et immunités des organisations internationales* (1982); Jenks,

organizations it is required that states concede privileges and immunities to international organizations, their premises and their personnel, including the representatives of member states to these organizations. These privileges and immunities are not always analogous to those of states, but are comparable. The conventional law according these privileges and immunities is contained in the constitutions of organizations, bilateral agreements and multilateral conventions, such as the General Convention on the Privileges and Immunities of the UN of 1946.[4]

International organizations enjoy privileges and immunities entirely because they are necessary for the fulfilment of their purposes and functions. Because the basis of such privileges and immunities is functional, organizations are and can expect to be accorded only those privileges and immunities which are necessary for that purpose. An organization requires certain privileges in respect of, and immunities from the jurisdiction of, not only the state in which it is located but also all its member states, should there be potential of its acts or staff or property coming under their jurisdiction.

A feature of the law governing the privileges and immunities of organizations and their personnel is that the nationality of the individual usually has no bearing on whether the privilege or immunity accrues. A national of a state may enjoy the privileges or immunities accorded to international personnel *vis-à-vis* his own state and his national state may not be able to exercise jurisdiction over him because he is a member of an international organization. However, certain privileges and immunities are accorded only to international personnel who are not nationals of the states granting such privileges and immunities. This is the case

---

International Immunities (1961); Sands and Klein (eds.), *Bowett's Law of International Institutions* (2001) pp. 486ff.; Dominicé, 'Le Nature et l'étendue de l'immunité de juridiction des organisations internationales', in Bocksteigel *et al.* (eds.), *Law of Nations, Law of International Organizations, World's Economic Law, Festschrift Ignaz Seidl-Hohenveldern* (1988) p. 11; Dominicé, 'L'arbitrage et les immunités des organisations internationales', in Dominicé *et al.* (eds.), *Etudes de droit international en l'honneur de Pièrre Lalive* (1993) p. 483; Szaniawski and Forysinkski, 'Le problème d'application de la Convention sur le statut juridique les privilèges et les immunités des organisations économiques intrétatiques functionnant dans certain domaines de coopération', 15 Polish YIL (1986) p. 29; Schröer, 'De l'application de l'immunité juridictionnelle des étâts étrangers aux organisations internationales', 75 RGDIP (1971) p. 712; de Bellis, *L'immunità delle organizzazioni internazionali dalla giurisdizione* (1992); Bekker, *The Legal Position of Intergovernmental Organisations – A Functional Necessity Analysis of their Status and Immunities* (1994); Muller, *International Organisations and their Host States* (1995); Reinisch, *International Organizations before National Courts* (2000) pp. 127–229 and *passim*.

[4] 1 UNTS p. 15. As of 31 December 1992, 131 states were parties to the Convention. This Convention is hereinafter referred to as the UN Convention.

generally with exemption from taxation on salary income, for instance, or the privilege of securing a special work permit or visa for a domestic from a foreign state to enter the state where the official resides (a privilege which is generally granted unilaterally and not under any international convention). In the case of diplomatic personnel, by contrast, the nationality of the diplomat is relevant to determining whether privileges and immunities will be accorded in two respects. First, the national state of a diplomatic representative always has jurisdiction over him – no immunity from jurisdiction is recognized. Second, where nationals of a state become members of foreign diplomatic missions in that state, they are not accorded the same privileges and immunities as foreign diplomats in foreign missions enjoy. Their privileges and immunities are more limited.

While diplomatic privileges and immunities may be backed by the principle of reciprocity, there is no such *quid pro quo* which operates in the case of international privileges and immunities. The organizations do not extend privileges and immunities on a reciprocal basis: in effect states accord international privileges and immunities unilaterally, albeit under legal constraints. In the case of international privileges and immunities the inducement for states to recognize them is their interest in the efficient and independent functioning of organizations without the fear of interference. However, there is a reciprocity of a more subtle kind. States have an interest in other states showing the same restraint.

The conventional law

The UN Charter provides in Article 105 for the privileges and immunities of the organization and its personnel in a very general way. This article states:

1 The Organization shall enjoy in the territory of each of its Members such privileges and immunities as are necessary for the fulfillment of its purposes.
2 Representatives of the Members of the United Nations and officials of the Organization shall similarly enjoy such privileges and immunities as are necessary for the independent exercise of their functions in connection with the Organization.
3 The General Assembly may make recommendations with a view to determining the details of the application of paragraphs 1 and 2 of this Article or may propose conventions to the Members of the United Nations for this purpose.

The article, though general in nature, ties privileges and immunities to purposes and functions. Most open organizations have constitutions with provisions of a similar general nature,[5] while the constitutions of some open organizations refer to the Specialized Agencies Convention.[6] The financial institutions are different. Their constitutions generally have detailed provisions on the subject. As an example may be given the Articles of Agreement of the IBRD which deal *in extenso* in Article VII with the purpose of immunities and privileges, the position of the IBRD with regard to judicial process and seizure or attachment of, or execution on, its property and assets and the extent of its immunity in that regard, the immunity of its assets from seizure by executive or legislative action, the freedom of its assets from restrictions, the immunity of its archives, the privileges it enjoys for official communications, the immunities and privileges of its officers and employees and the immunities enjoyed by it and its officers and employees in respect of taxation.[7]

Some closed organizations have provisions in their constitutions which recognize privileges and immunities,[8] while others have no provisions.[9]

With this diversity it was to be expected that some implementing or developmental conventional law would come into existence. There has consequently been a tendency to make detailed agreements in many

[5] See, e.g., the ILO Constitution, Article 40; the UNESCO Constitution, Article XII; the WHO Constitution, Articles 67 and 68; the IAEA Constitution, Article XV. See also the FAO Constitution, Article XVI; and the ICAO Constitution, Article 60.

[6] See, e.g., the IMO Constitution, Article 60.

[7] See also, e.g., the IMF Articles of Agreement, Article IX; the IDA Articles of Agreement, Article VIII; the IFC Articles of Agreement, Article VI; the MIGA Convention, Articles 43 to 50; the ADB Constitution, Articles 50 to 58; the IDB Constitution, Article XI; and the EBRD Constitution, Articles 46 to 55. A detailed account of the practice of the UN, the Specialized Agencies and the IAEA and of states in relation to these organizations with regard to the status, privileges and immunities of the organizations, representatives of member states and personnel is to be found in a paper prepared by the UN Secretariat in 1967 for the ILC in connection with its work on 'Relations between States and intergovernmental organizations': UN Doc. A/CN. 4/L.188 and Add. 1and 2, 2 YBILC (1967) pp. 154*ff*. There are many instances in the practice of organizations where the law has been interpreted and applied: e.g., in regard to the inviolability of premises of the organization or in regard to the immunities and privileges of representatives. It is not possible in a work of the present kind to discuss or refer to all these. The UN document cited above contains a very thorough account and examination of these problems.

[8] Council of Europe Statute, Article 40; and the OAS Charter, Articles 39 to 42. See also the OAU Charter, Article XXXI.

[9] See, e.g., the NATO Constitution and the Warsaw Treaty Pact Organization Charter.

cases in order to establish particular privileges and immunities. Two multilateral conventions are particularly important.

In the case of the UN, the UN Convention of 1946 is applicable. This convention implements Article 105 of the Charter. In the case of the specialized agencies the Specialized Agencies Convention of 1947 is applicable. The latter convention contains variations from the general provisions determined by each specialized agency concerned and set out in separate annexes. The pattern of the main contents of these agreements was followed in multilateral agreements made by many organizations, including the OAS[10] and the COE.[11] The EU also has made agreements modelled to some extent on these conventions.[12] There are also agreements made between organizations and their host states, such as the Headquarters Agreement between the USA and the UN[13] and the agreement between the COE and France.[14] Special agreements may also be made to take care of individual situations which arise in the work of the organizations.[15]

In some states international agreements have been implemented by national legislation. The International Organizations Immunities Act of 1945 in the USA and the UK International Organization (Privileges and Immunities) Act of 1968, which replaced a similar statute of 1950, are examples of these. There is also similar legislation in many member states of the Commonwealth.[16] While it is true that the source of privileges and immunities is the international agreements and international laws, the legislation may vary from state to state as may the interpretation and application of the international obligations in regard to privileges and immunities.[17] Before national courts reliance may have to be

---

[10] 1 *Annals of the OAS*, No. 3 (1949) p. 271.   [11] 250 UNTS p. 12.

[12] 1 *European Yearbook* p. 429.   [13] 2 UNTS p. 11.   [14] 249 UNTS p. 207.

[15] See, e.g., the agreement between the UN and the Republic of the Congo: *Annual Report of the Secretary General* (1961), A 4800 p. 170: UN Doc. S5004; and the agreement of 1957 between the UN and Egypt relating to the UNEF: 260 UNTS p. 61.

[16] See *Legislative Texts and Treaty Provisions concerning the Legal Status, Privileges and Immunities of International Organizations*, UN.ST/LEG/SER. B/10 and 11, for national legislation.

[17] For consideration of the laws of some countries relating to the privileges and immunities of organizations see, e.g., [Note], 'Applying the Foreign Missions Act of 1982 to International Organizations: Reciprocity in the Multilateral Context', 18 *New York University Journal of International Law and Politics* (1985) p. 229 (USA); Nakamura, 'The Status, Privileges and Immunities of International Organizations in Japan: An Overview', 35 *Japanese Annual of International Law* (1992) p. 116 (Japan); Zuppinger, 'Die Privilegien der Diplomaten und Konsularischen Vertreter Sowie der Mitgliederder in der Schweiz niedergelassenen internationalen Organisationen bei den direkten Steuern', in Haller *et al.* (eds.), *Im Dienst ander Gemeinschaft: Festschrift für Dietrich Schindler*

placed entirely on the relevant legislation, though if the application of the legislation in a given case falls short of the applicable international law, the state concerned will be in breach of its international obligations owed to the international organization concerned.

In a work of this nature it is not possible to examine all the existing agreements or constitutional texts. What can be done is to survey the general contents of some conventional instruments in order to establish general trends in the recognition of privileges and immunities, with special attention being paid to the UN Convention and the Specialized Agencies Convention.[18]

Privileges and immunities of organizations

Four main privileges and immunities merit attention: (i) immunity from jurisdiction; (ii) inviolability of premises and archives; (iii) privileges relating to currency and fiscal matters; and (iv) freedom of communications. These are clearly privileges and immunities which have been accorded because the fulfilment of the purposes and functions of organizations demand them.

Immunity from jurisdiction

Section 2 of the UN Convention provides:

The United Nations, its property and assets wherever located and by whomsoever held, shall enjoy immunity from every form of legal process except insofar as in any particular case it has expressly waived its immunity. It is, however, understood that no waiver of immunity shall extend to any measure of execution.

A similar section (Section 4) is included in the Specialized Agencies Convention. Some of the headquarters agreements, e.g., with Switzerland and Italy, have a similar provision.[19] The jurisdictional immunities are very wide in these instruments.

The financial institutions led by the IBRD (but excluding the IMF, where there is a wide immunity) have in their constitutions a provision

---

zum 65 (1989) p. 179 (Switzerland); Bentil, 'Suing an International Organization for Debt Payment', 134 *Solicitor's Journal* (1990) p. 475 (UK); Wenskstern, 'Verfassungsrechtliche Fragen der Immunität – internationaler Organisationen', 40 *Neue-Juristische-Wochenschrift* (1987) p. 1,113 (FRG).

[18] 33 UNTS p. 261. As of June 2000, 106 states were parties to the Convention. Hereinafter this convention is referred to as the Specialized Agencies Convention.

[19] The position in the EU is somewhat different: see Sands and Klein (eds.), note 3 pp. 493ff.

whereby this general immunity is qualified.[20] Section 3 of Article VII of the IBRD constitution expressly permits actions to be brought against the Bank in a court of a member state in which the Bank has an office, has appointed an agent for the purpose of accepting service or notice of process, or has issued or guaranteed securities, though it then prohibits actions in such courts by 'member States or persons acting for or deriving claims from members'. This immunity would cover primarily suits originating in loan agreements with states to which the Bank is a party. Property and assets are, however, immune from seizure, attachment or execution before the delivery of final judgment. The immunity of the Bank is reversed – there is a presumption of absence of immunity which is recognized only in the circumstances mentioned. It is not only in regard to disputes arising out of securities obligations that there is no immunity. It is likely that these institutions may be sued with regard to matters other than those arising out of their borrowing powers. In the American case, *Lutcher SA e Papel Candor* v. *IDB*,[21] the plaintiff who was a borrower from the IDB sought to enjoin the IDB from making a loan to its main competitor. While the US Court of Appeals held that the complaint did not state a cause of action, it also held that the IDB (whose constitution has a provision similar to that in the IBRD constitution) was not entitled to immunity from suit in this situation. This case supports the view that the absence of immunity is general and not limited to suits by bondholders. In the case of the ADB, the AFDB and the CDB, however, the constitutions provide that the types of suits from which there is no immunity are more limited. Actions may only be brought in connection with the exercise of powers to borrow, guarantee securities or to buy or sell or underwrite the sale of securities.[22]

Where there is a general immunity such as under the UN Convention the question arises whether, as in the case of state immunity, courts are permitted to distinguish between acts *iure imperii* (in sovereign authority), where immunity exists, and acts *iure gestionis* (as a private person), where there is no immunity. There is no judicial precedent relating

---

[20] The EIB seems to be a special case in that the immunity is even more restricted than in the case of other financial institutions: see Syz, *International Development Banks* (1974) p. 59.

[21] (1967), 42 ILR p. 138.

[22] See Article 50(1) of the ADB Agreement; Article 52(1) of the AFDB Agreement; and Article 69(1) of the CDB Agreement. Article 44 of the MIGA constituent instrument (1985) specifically grants immunity in personnel matters from the jurisdiction of national courts.

to the interpretation of the UN or Specialized Agencies Convention or instruments with like provisions. But where immunity was available, apparently under customary international law, in the absence of conventional provisions, the Italian Court of Cassation in *Branno* v. *Ministry of War*[23] decided that, since the subject matter of the action was a private contract, NATO did not have immunity from jurisdiction because it was acting *iure gestionis* and not *iure imperii*. However, now Italy's highest court has virtually reversed the previous decisions by deciding in 1992 that the FAO was entitled to a complete immunity in national courts.[24] In *Dupree Associates Inc.* v. *OAS*[25] a US Federal Court held that the OAS did not have immunity in a case concerning a bidding construction contract because international organizations were only entitled to restrictive immunity as foreign sovereigns were and the case concerned acts *iure gestionis*. The two conventions do not expressly make the distinction, however, and it is doubtful, assuming that the interpretation of the law is correct, whether such a distinction can be imported into the interpretation of the conventions. Where the governing instrument is silent on the matter, there is no reason to import the distinction. There is some difficulty in attributing to an organization the power to act *iure imperii*. To assume that the distinction has relevance to organizations is to assimilate them to states which is inappropriate. Their basis of immunity is not the same as for states. The test is whether an immunity from jurisdiction is necessary for the fulfilment of the organization's functions and purposes. To answer that question a reference to whether the organization was, in respect of the subject matter of the litigation, acting *iure imperii or iure gestionis* is irrelevant. Clearly this reasoning applies both to the interpretation of the conventional law and in the customary area, assuming there is one.

In *Bank Bumiputra Malaysia Bhd.* v. *ITC*[26] the issue concerning the immunity of the ITC from the jurisdiction of the Malaysian courts arose, when the plaintiff sought to recover outstanding loans made to the ITC.

---

[23] (1955), 22 ILR p. 756; *INDPAI* v. *FAO* (1982), 87 ILR p. 5 (Italy); *Porru* v. *FAO* (1969), 71 ILR p. 240 (Italy). These 3 cases were decided by Italian Courts. Many authors support this approach: see, e.g., Cully, loc. cit. note 3 at pp. 1187*ff*.; Sadurska and Chinkin, 'The Collapse of the International Tin Council: A Case of State Responsibility', VaJIL (1990) p. 853; Singer, 'Jurisdictional Immunity of International Organisations: Human Rights and Functional Necessity Concerns', VaJIL (1995) at pp. 135*ff*; Reinisch, note 3 pp. 131*ff*.

[24] *FAO* v. *Colagrossi* (1992), Corte di Cassazione, 101 ILR p. 393.

[25] (1977), 63 ILR p. 92.

[26] 80 ILR p. 24, decided in 1987 by the Malaysian High Court.

There, however, the court refused immunity to ITC on the ground that the applicable treaties granted ITC immunity only vis-à-vis the English courts but added that, because the ITC entered into a commercial transaction, it could not claim immunity in any event. In this second holding which was *obiter* the court appears to have regarded the immunity of the IGO as being similar to that of foreign sovereigns which meant that the distinction between acts *iure imperii* and acts *iure gestionis* became relevant. Thus, some courts are moving in the direction of accepting for the immunity of IGOs from the jurisdiction of national courts the distinction made in regard to sovereign immunity, unless, of course, there is express provision otherwise.

The history of judicial precedent in many national legal systems is, on the other hand, weighted heavily in favour of recognizing the immunity of organizations in employment-related matters, even where, as in the case of the IBRD, immunity is not explicitly granted by the conventional law except in special cases. The French Conseil d'Etât recognized this immunity as early as 1928 in *Lamborot*[27] *and Antin*.[28] In the former case, the court held that because the plaintiff was in charge of an international organization, namely, the Inter-Allied Commission, there was lack of jurisdiction in the court to deal with the issues raised pertaining to payment of salary. An international organization was not a party in this case; nevertheless, the court recognized that the subject matter was outside its jurisdiction. French courts have subsequently in numerous cases reaffirmed the immunity from their jurisdiction in employment-related cases of international organizations.[29]

The first case in which an international organization was the defendant in an employment-related case was *International Institute of Agriculture v. Profili*.[30] The case was finally decided by the Italian Court of Cassation in 1931 in favour of the defendant organization. The plaintiff, who had been dismissed from the service of the defendant organization, claimed compensation. The Court held that, because the Institute was an autonomous union, free as regards its internal affairs from interference by the sovereign power of the states composing the union except

---

[27] Recueil de Arrêts du Conseil d'Etât (1928) p. 1,304. See also *Porru* v. *FAO* (1969), 71 ILR (1986) p. 240 (Italy).

[28] Recueil de Arrêts du Conseil d'Etât (1928) p. 764.

[29] See, e.g., *Weiss* v. *IIIC* (1953), 81 JDI (1954) p. 754; *Klarsfeld* v. *French–German Office for Youth* (1968), 14 AFDI (1968) p. 370; and *Bellaton* v. *ESA* (1978), 25 AFDI (1979) p. 893. Other French cases are cited in Vorkink and Hakuta, *Lawsuits Against International Organizations: Cases in National Courts Involving Staff and Employment* (1983) *passim*.

[30] (1931), 5 AD p. 413.

when it consented thereto, in the absence of such consent there was nothing which authorized the intervention of an external jurisdiction. There are other Italian cases in which the immunity from jurisdiction of international organizations has been recognized in situations involving employment relations.[31]

More recently, the US Court of Appeals has confirmed that, subject to waiver, international organizations enjoy immunity from jurisdiction in the USA in cases brought by staff members in regard to their employment. In the *Broadbent Case*[32] the plaintiffs, former staff members of the OAS, brought an action against the OAS claiming reinstatement. They had received indemnities under the terms of a judgment of the OASAT which gave the OAS that alternative instead of reinstating the plaintiffs. The US Court of Appeals recognized the immunity from jurisdiction of the OAS, noting that, even on an application of a restrictive, as opposed to an absolute, theory of immunity, the relationship of an international organization with its staff was non-commercial. Later, in *Mendaro v. The World Bank*,[33] the US Court of Appeals took the same stand in a case brought by a former staff member of the World Bank alleging discrimination and harassment.[34]

---

[31] See, e.g., *Viccelli v. International Refugee Organization* (1951), 36 *Rivista di diritto internazionale* (1953) p. 470; *Mazzanti v. HAFSE and Ministry of Defence* (1955), *Guistizia civile* (1955) p. 461; *ICEM v. Chiti* (1973), *10 Rivista di diritto internazionale privato e processuale* (1974) p. 579; and *Mininni v. The Bari Institute of the International Centre for Advanced Mediterranean Agronomic Studies* (1981), 78 ILR p. 112. See other cases referred to in Vorkink and Hakuta, note 29 *passim*.

[32] 628 F. 2nd p. 27 (1980).   [33] 717 F. 2nd p. 610 (1983).

[34] In particular the Court discussed the implications of Article VII.3 of the Bank's Articles of Agreement as a result of which the plaintiff contended that the Bank's immunity had been waived. Article VII.3 provides that: 'Actions may be brought against the Bank only in a court of competent jurisdiction in the territories of a member in which the Bank has an office, has appointed an agent for the purpose of accepting service or notice of process, or has issued or guaranteed securities. No actions shall, however, be brought by members or persons acting for or deriving claims from members. The property and assets of the Bank shall, wheresoever located and by whomsoever held, be immune from all forms of seizure, attachment or execution before the delivery of final judgment against the Bank.' In spite of this provision which the Court described as poorly drafted, the Court agreed with the position of the World Bank that it did not give national courts jurisdiction in actions by staff members claiming violation of rights relating to their employment. The position in the USA in the case of many international organizations is also determined by the International Organization Immunities Act 1945, as amended (59 Stat. 6679, 22 USC pp. 288*ff*.), which recognizes the immunity of international organizations. In *Kissi v. Jacques de Laroissière* (1982), CA No. 82–1267, the US Court held that the IMF was immune from its jurisdiction in an employment-related case. See

There are many other states whose courts have recognized the immunity from jurisdiction of international organizations in employment-related cases. In several recent cases decided in the German courts the plaintiffs, staff members of the international organizations, have failed because the courts have recognized that the defendant international organizations were immune from their jurisdiction.[35] Some other states in which the immunity from national court jurisdiction of international organizations in employment-related cases has been specifically recognized are Argentina,[36] Mexico,[37] Chile,[38] Colombia,[39] Syria,[40] Egypt,[41] India,[42] Luxembourg[43] and the Philippines.[44] In this connection the

also *Weidner* v. *Intelsat* (1978), DC App., 392A. 2d p. 508; *Tuck* v. *Pan American Health Organization* (1981), DC Circ. 668 F. 2d p. 547; *Chiriboga* v. *International Bank for Reconstruction and Development* (1985), DDC 616 F. Suppl. p. 963; *Novak* v. *World Bank* (1983), DDC No. 81–1329; *Boimah* v. *United Nations General Assembly* (1987), EDNY 664 F. Suppl. p. 69; *Morgan* v. *International Bank for Reconstruction and Development* (1990), US District Court for the District of Columbia CA 90–0929; *Mukoro* v. *EBRD* (1994), UK Employment Appeal Tribunal, Appeal No. EAT/813/92; the *Jasbez Case* (1977), 77 ILR p. 602 (Italian Court of Cassation); and *ICEM* v. *Di Banella Schirone* (1975), 77 ILR p. 572.

For an assessment of some of the US cases see [Note], 'International Organizations – International Organizations Immunity Act – Waiver of Immunity for the World Bank Denied, *Mendaro* v. *The World Bank*, 717 F. 2d 610', 8 *Suffolk Transnational Law Journal* (1984) p. 412; [Note], 'How Much Immunity for International Organizations?: *Mendaro* v. *World Bank* (717 F. 2d 610)', 10 *North Carolina Journal of International Law and Commercial Regulation* (1985) p. 487; Griffith, 'Restricting the Immunity of International Organizations in Labor Disputes: Reforming an Obsolete Shibboleth', 25 Virginia JIL (1985) p. 1007; [Note], '*Boimah* v. *United Nations General Assembly* [664 F. Supp. 69]: International Organizations' Immunity is Absolutely not Restrictive', 15 Brooklyn JIL (1989) p. 497; Appril, 'Immunity of International Organizations in United States Courts: Absolute or Restrictive?', 24 Vanderbilt JIL (1991) p. 689; and Hammerschleg, '*Morgan* v. *International Bank for Reconstruction and Development* [752 F. Supp. 492 (1990)]', 16 *Maryland Journal of International Law and Trade* (1992) p. 279. Now see also Reinisch, note 3 pp. 192ff. and *passim*.

35 See *Groll* v. *Air Traffic Services Agency* (1979); *Strech* v. *Air Traffic Services Agency* (1979); *van Knijff* v. *European Space Agency* (1980); and *Heltzel* v. *Air Traffic Services Agency* (1981), all cited in Vorkink and Hakuta, note 29 pp. 36, 39 and 41.

36 See *Bergaveche* v. *UN Information Centre* (1958), and *Ezcurra de Mann* v. *IDB* (1979), *ibid.* pp. 16 and 35.

37 See *Diaz-Diaz* v. *UNECLA* (1954), *ibid.* p. 13.   38 See *A.* v. *UNECLA* (1969), *ibid.* p. 22.

39 See *Barreneche* v. *CIPE/General Secretariat of the OAS* (1971); and *Barrios* v. *CIPE/General Secretariat of the OAS* (1973), *ibid.* pp. 22 and 23.

40 See *WW* v. *UNRWA* (1955–56); and *XX* v. *UNRWA* (1955–56), *ibid.* p. 15.

41 See *Giurgis* v. *UNRWA* (1961), *ibid.* p. 18.   42 See *Matthew* v. *ICRISAT* (1982), *ibid.* p. 45.

43 See *De Bruyn* v. *European Parliamentary Assembly* (1960), *ibid.* p. 17.

44 See *Cohen* v. *Presiding Judge Pedro C. Navarro et al.* (1976), *ibid.* p. 27. In *Gupta* v. *IBRD and IDA* (1982), *ibid.* p. 43, the English High Court held that the plaintiff could not serve process for the purpose of English law on the defendant because the defendant did

subject matter is not regarded as coming within the concept of acts *iure gestionis*.[45]

However, there are a few cases in which national courts have assumed jurisdiction in actions relating to employment matters brought against international organizations. It is not clear whether these courts would exercise such jurisdiction in the case of all international organizations or whether the exercise of such jurisdiction was restricted only to specific organizations in specific cases. Some examples to be found of national courts exercising such jurisdiction are cases decided in the Middle East, particularly in Lebanon, Jordan, Syria, and Gaza, and that, too, in connection with actions against UNRWA.[46]

There also have been two cases in Italy and the Netherlands respectively in which jurisdiction has been exercised but these are special. In the Italian case, *Maida* v. *Administration for International Assistance*,[47] the Court of Cassation held that the administrative courts had jurisdiction in a case brought against an organ of the IRO, because Italian law had been adopted as the proper law of the contract of employment, but it did say that, if there had been an effective method of settling employment disputes in the IRO, this would have been sufficient to oust the jurisdiction of the Italian courts. In *Eckhardt* v. *Eurocontrol*[48] a Dutch court found that it had jurisdiction in an employment-related case brought against Eurocontrol because the constitution of Eurocontrol and other

---

not carry on business in the United Kingdom and, therefore, could not invoke the court's jurisdiction. The issue of immunity was avoided.

[45] See the *Jasbez Case* (1977), 77 ILR p. 602 (Italian Court of Cassation). Two recent cases in which the immunity from jurisdiction of an IGO was recognized are *Atkinson* v. *IADB* (1998), 38 ILM (1999) p. 91, decided by a US court, and *AS v Iran-US Claims Tribunal* (1985), 18 Netherlands YBIL (1987) p. 357, decided by the Dutch Supreme Court. In the former the court refused jurisdiction on the basis of immunity in an employment-related case, where garnishment of the salary of a staff member was sought by his ex-wife. There the subject matter was regarded as relating to the *ius imperii* of the IGO. In the latter case immunity was recognized in a case relating to employment brought by an employee of the defendant tribunal.

[46] Thus, in *W.* v. *UNRWA* (1952), *ibid.* p. 11, a labour tribunal in Lebanon assumed jurisdiction in the case, as it did in *X.* v. *UNRWA* (1953), *ibid.* p. 12. In both cases the Ministry of Foreign Affairs of Lebanon took objection to the exercise of jurisdiction and in the latter case execution of the judgment was refused. In *Y.* v. *UNRWA* (1954), *ibid.* p. 12, the Jordanian courts assumed jurisdiction in an employment-related case. The cases decided in Syria, *X.*, (1955–56), *ibid.* p. 15, and Gaza, *YY* v. *UNRWA* (1957), *ibid.* p. 16 and *ZZ* v. *UNRWA* (1957), *ibid.* p. 16, were similar. In the Syrian case, however, the Court of Cassation decided the case in favour of UNRWA, taking UNRWA's legal status into account.

[47] (1955), 23 ILR p. 510.   [48] (1976), 9 *Netherlands Yearbook of International Law* (1978) p. 276.

relevant instruments made provision for the assumption of jurisdiction by national courts.

Apart from these there are a few more cases in which immunity from suit in employment disputes was denied to IGOs. Two most important cases are *X v. International Centre for Superior Mediterranean Agricultural Studies*,[49] decided by a Greek court, and the *Margot Rendall Speranza Case*,[50] decided by a US court. In the former a national court decided that it had jurisdiction over an employment dispute with an IGO, even though absolute immunity had been expressly granted to the defendant organization. The reasoning related the case to labour relations which were not the result of the exercise of sovereignty but were concerned with the organization's private activity. The court noted that unqualified immunity had been granted but interpreted this grant of immunity as incorporating restrictive immunity on the model of the immunity from jurisdiction granted to states. In the other case the IFC was denied immunity from jurisdiction in a physical harm and harassment case brought by an employee. The basis for the denial was the absence of a policy judgment on the part of IFC in the acts of which the plaintiff was complaining. These two cases are very recent and are examples of a certain impatience on the part of national courts with the concept of immunity from jurisdiction and an inclination to find some way to circumvent the grant of immunity in employment-related cases.

Despite exceptional instances, some recognition is given to the immunity of IGOs from the jurisdiction of national courts in employment-related cases, whether there is an express grant of such immunity or not. On the other hand, it is difficult to deduce when and in what circumstances that immunity will not be granted. The decisions of national courts do not reflect a uniform approach. It is not even clear how influential a factor in the grant of immunity is the absence of an internal court of the IGO to adjudicate on employment disputes. This is especially so where there is in governing instruments no specific exclusion of the immunity in these cases and the organizations have provided independent internal courts to settle disputes in such cases.

Further, the Italian Court of Cassation[51] has recognized that an international organization has immunity in a case brought by trade unions concerning the violation of trade union rights. There was held to be no

---

[49] Court of Appeals of Crete, 1991: see Reinisch, note 3 p. 191.
[50] 942 F. Supp. p. 621 (DDC 1996) and 932 F. Supp. p. 19 (DDC 1996).
[51] See the *Camera Confederate del Lavoro Case* (1979), 78 ILR p. 86.

restriction in customary international law which required the exclusion of immunity in such a case. Immunity has also been recognized in an Italian case concerning execution.[52] The Italian court took the view that, since the assets were destined for the performance of the international aims of the organization, no issue of execution could be litigated. The implication that a distinction may have to be made in regard to execution which was similar to that made in the case of foreign sovereigns arose because of the nature of the agreement to which Italy was a party regarding the immunities of the organization. The UK courts have recognized the immunity of the ITC in winding-up proceedings.[53]

The more accepted approach taken by the courts in the employment-related area and in the other areas discussed above, which are more appropriately assimilated to acts *iure gestionis* than to acts *iure imperii*, would seem to confirm that the distinction is irrelevant to the immunities of international organizations.[54]

The immunity from jurisdiction that an organization has may be waived by the organization. The waiver may be express or implicit. In *ITC* v. *Amalgamet Inc.*[55] the New York Supreme Court held that the ITC had waived any immunity it may have had by entering into an arbitration agreement relating to the subject matter of the dispute. In *Standard Chartered Bank* v. *ITC and Others*[56] there was held to have been a waiver of immunity in the matter of a loan because of a condition agreed to in a facility letter that the loan was to be governed by English law and that the ITC would submit to the jurisdiction of the English courts in connection therewith.

Property, assets and currency

The UN Convention, the Specialized Agencies Convention and the provisions of the constitutions of almost all the financial institutions provide that the property and assets of the organizations shall be immune from all forms of judicial process. This is in addition to the property and assets being immune from execution. Further, these instruments afford a very broad protection for property and assets. Section 3 of the UN Convention provides that the property and assets of the UN shall be immune

---

[52] *Mininni* v. *The Bari Institute of the International Centre for Advanced Mediterranean Agronomic Studies* (1981), 78 ILR p. 112.

[53] [1988] (CA), 80 ILR p. 181. The immunity was granted by application of a UK statute.

[54] A private party who is sued cannot rely on the immunity of an IGO to exclude a national court's jurisdiction. See cases discussed by Reinisch, note 3 pp. 191ff.

[55] [1988], 80 ILR p. 31.   [56] [1987], 77 ILR p. 8 (UK).

from search, requisition, confiscation, expropriation and any other form of interference, whether by executive, administrative, judicial or legislative action. A comparable provision is to be found in the IBRD Articles of Agreement and with minor variation in the constitutions of other financial institutions.[57] The Specialized Agencies Convention also has a similar provision.[58]

Organizations dispose of or trade in considerable funds for the purposes of their operations. It has been found necessary to protect these. Thus, in regard to currency, the UN Convention provides:

Section 5. Without being restricted by financial controls, regulations or moratoria of any kind,

(a) the United Nations may hold funds, gold or currency of any kind and operate accounts in any currency;

(b) the United Nations shall be free to transfer its funds, gold or currency from one country to another or within any country and to convert any currency held by it into any other currency.

Section 6. In exercising its rights under Section 5 above, the United Nations shall pay due regard to any representations made by the Government of any Member insofar as it is considered that effect can be given to such representations without detriment to the interests of the United Nations.

The Specialized Agencies Convention has a provision similar to Section 5 of the UN Convention,[59] while Article VII(6) of the IBRD Articles of Agreement whose pattern is followed by the constitutions of most other financial institutions provides:

to the extent necessary to carry out the operations provided for in this Agreement, and subject to the provisions of this Agreement, all property and assets of the Bank shall be free from restrictions, regulations, controls and moratoria of any nature.[60]

---

[57] Article VII(4), IBRD Articles of Agreement; Article VI(4), IFC Articles of Agreement; Article VIII(4), IDA Articles of Agreement; Article XI(3), IDB Articles of Agreement; Article 50(3), ADB Agreement; Article 52(2), AFDB Agreement; Article 49(4), CDB Agreement; Article IX(4), IMF Articles of Agreement; Article 45(a), MIGA Convention; Article 28(2), EIB Statute; and Article 47, EBRD Agreement.

[58] Section 4. The property exclusion does not entitle an IOG not to submit to zoning regulations which apply to it: *PAHO* v. *Montgomery County, Maryland, County Council for Montgomery Council*, Court of Appeals of Maryland, 11 May 1995: see Reinisch, note 3 p. 204.

[59] Section 7.

[60] See also Article IX(6), IMF Articles of Agreement; Article VI(6), IFC Articles of Agreement; Article VIII(2), IDA Articles of Agreement; Article XI(6), IDB Articles of

Thus, member states have little control over the movement of these assets but in the case of the financial institutions their freedom is subject to the other provisions of their respective constitutions.

Premises and archives

The inviolability of premises and archives is provided for in all relevant agreements. The UN Convention expressly provides in Section 3 that the premises of the UN shall be inviolable, and in Section 4 that 'The archives of the United Nations, and in general all documents belonging to it or held by it, shall be inviolable wherever located.'[61] In the case of the financial institutions there is an express provision for the inviolability of archives[62] but the inviolability of premises is to be derived from the protection of property elsewhere in their constitutions.[63] Specifically, the freedom from search of property must imply that premises are inviolable while the reference to confiscation, sequestration and the like must also put the premises of the organizations outside the reach of states.

The inviolability of the premises means, as in the case of inviolability of diplomatic premises, that authorities of a state, particularly of the host state, may not enter the premises without the permission of the administrative head, even for the purpose of arresting or serving a writ on an individual. Moreover, the concept requires that inviolability be secured against all persons and not merely the authorities of the host state which implies that the host state must exercise due diligence in the protection of the premises. The principle of inviolability may raise some problems specific to international organizations. Organizations have no

Agreement; Article 53, ADB Agreement; Article 54, AFDB Agreement; Article 52, CDB Agreement; Article 45(b), MIGA Convention; and Article 49, EBRD Agreement. The EIB is an exception in this respect. It may be noted that the agreement between the UN and Egypt over the status of the UNEF did provide that the most favourable exchange rate should be available to the UN, though it is unlikely that organizations would be prejudiced in this respect, because of the obligation of member states to the IMF.

[61] See also Section 5 of the Specialized Agencies Convention.

[62] Article VII(5), IBRD Articles of Agreement; Article VI(5), IFC Articles of Agreement; Article VIII(5), IDA Articles of Agreement; Article IX(5), IMF Articles of Agreement; Article 46(a), MIGA Convention; Article 52, ADB Agreement; Article 53(2), AFDB Agreement; Article 52, CDB Agreement; Article XI(5), IDB Agreement; Article 2, EIB Protocol; and Article 48, EBRD Agreement. In the case of the ADB, the AFDB and the CDB, it is additionally provided that the inviolability shall extend to all documents held by the organizations.

[63] This is so whether or not there is an express provision made, as is done in most headquarters agreements. There are some examples of the breach of the principle of inviolability in the case of UNRWA during the 1967 conflict in the Middle East.

sovereign authority over the territory on which their premises are situated but merely have control and some jurisdiction in internal matters. Moreover, organizations possess no body of law to replace that of the host state in respect of civil or criminal offences committed within the premises. Admittedly, organizations may have power to lay down regulations operative within the headquarters district for the purpose of establishing therein conditions in all respects necessary for the full execution of their functions,[64] and such regulations will override any inconsistent local law, but the only effective sanction for their breach is expulsion from the premises, carried out either by a Headquarters Guard Force, such as the UN possesses, or by the local authorities who may be requested to enter for that purpose. It is important, therefore, that the territory should remain under the law and the jurisdiction of the host state, and the headquarters agreements generally so provide.[65] A crime committed on the premises will therefore normally be appropriately dealt with by the local courts.[66] Indeed, some of the agreements specifically provide that the organization is under a duty to prevent the headquarters district from becoming a refuge for persons avoiding arrest or the service of legal process.[67] The organizations may have a right to grant asylum in cases falling outside this particular duty, and some of the agreements specifically recognize such a right. It has been suggested that there is a right of the organization to afford asylum to its own officials against measures by the local authorities which are themselves a violation of the immunities of the organization and of the official.[68]

Archives, unlike other property (except premises) which is protected only from specific types of control, benefit from the principle of inviolability. The provisions of the ADB, the AFDB and the CDB agreements, as pointed out, go somewhat further. Their formulation extends the protection to all documents *held* by the institution, irrespective of who owns them. This would seem to ensure the confidentiality of operations of these institutions where decisions are reached with the help of diverse documents whose ownership may often be unclear.

Some problems were faced by the English courts in applying its statutory law incorporating an international agreement in the ITC litigation.

---

[64] The UN–USA Headquarters Agreement acknowledges this in Section 8.
[65] See, e.g., the UN–USA Headquarters Agreement, Section 7.
[66] E.g., in 1928 the Swiss courts arrested and tried an assailant within the Palais des Nations in Geneva.
[67] See Section 9(b) of the UN–USA Headquarters Agreement.
[68] See Jenks, *International Immunities* (1962) pp. 51–2.

In *Maclaine Watson & Co. Ltd* v. *ITC (No. 2)*[69] the Court of Appeal confirmed orders made by the High Court judge that full particulars of the nature, value and location of all the assets of the ITC wherever located be disclosed, for the purpose of enforcing an arbitration award in respect of which the ITC had no immunity. The argument was adduced that the order violated the official archives of the ITC. The Court of Appeal held that the order by itself did not do so and should be confirmed without qualification, even though the relevant law provided that the archives of the ITC were inviolable. The order related to the enforcement of an arbitral award from which there was no immunity and was part of the enforcement procedure. It was the view of the Court that if the ITC, having carefully considered the position in a responsible manner, should thereafter conclude that it could not properly comply with this order without infringing some immunity or inviolability which it should properly protect, then it should make the necessary application for that purpose. It may be concluded that inviolability could be claimed for the archives, although assets had to be declared.

In *Shearson Lehman Brothers Inc. and Another* v. *ITC (Intervener) (No. 2)*[70] the House of Lords made certain rulings about the inviolability of archives. The approach of the Court merits attention. It was found that under the law the ITC had the same immunity for its archives as did diplomatic missions. In consequence, where the issue was whether certain documents could be made use of in a court action, the rulings of the Court indicate how English law could construe the inviolability of archives. The Court came to a number of conclusions. First, the term 'archives' in the English law (which was presumably no different from international law) referred to all documents belonging to, or held by, the organization. Second, the purpose of the inviolability conferred by the law being to protect the privacy of diplomatic communications (which in this case included communications of the ITC), inviolability was not confined to protection against executive or judicial action by the host state but included the use in court by the parties to an action of documents accorded that inviolability. Third, once a document had been communicated by the organization to a member state or the representative of

---

[69] [1988], 80 ILR p. 211.
[70] [1987], 77 ILR p. 107. The House of Lords more or less overruled the Court of Appeal, while not agreeing entirely with the High Court which the Court of Appeal had overruled.

a member state, it ceased to belong to the organization and the protection of the law ceased to apply to it. This followed from the fact that the same law conferred inviolability upon the official papers and documents of representatives of member states to the organization and provided that that inviolability might be waived by the member state concerned. Fourth, accordingly, the organization could not claim the protection of the law in respect of documents which had been communicated to third parties by member states or their representatives, while the same was true of documents communicated by organizations with observer status at the organization. Fifth, because a letter normally belonged to the recipient once it was received, and not to the sender, it followed that a document communicated to a third party by an officer or servant of the organization, acting with actual or ostensible authority, was no longer a document belonging to the organization and thus was no longer inviolable. That was not the case if the document was communicated without any authority, actual or ostensible. However, the fact that an officer or employee of the organization was known to be acting in the course of his employment at the time when he communicated documents to a third party was strong *prima facie* evidence that he had ostensible authority to do so. Moreover, an officer or employee of the organization who was authorized to reassure a third party about the financial ability of the organization to conduct negotiations for a settlement was presumed to have ostensible authority to supply to the third party documents which might assist in promoting the authorized purposes. Sixth, the principle accepted in English law that a state which was indirectly impleaded in proceedings regarding property to which it claimed title had only to show that its claim was not manifestly illusory,[71] was not to be extended further than was strictly necessary. It did not, therefore, apply to prevent a court from receiving otherwise relevant and admissible evidence in proceedings to which a foreign sovereign or international organization was a party merely because that foreign sovereign or international organization could make out a *prima facie* case that the evidence in question was part of its inviolable documentary archives.

There had been a detailed analysis of the principles of inviolability also in the Court of Appeal.[72] However, much of what was said there was modified by the House of Lords. To that extent it does not reflect

---

[71] *Juan Ysmael and Co. Inc. v. Indonesia Government* [1954] 3 WLR p. 531.
[72] [1987], 77 ILR p. 124.

the law as accepted in the UK. However, there were some statements of principle that were not apparently overruled by the House of Lords and are still valid for English law. That Court was of the view that privileges and immunities of international organizations were an extension of traditional diplomatic privileges and immunities; so far as documents or archives were concerned, the purpose of these immunities was the preservation of confidentiality as well as the physical preservation of the documents. Accordingly, 'inviolability' in relation to the official archives of the organization meant not only that the documents were not to be seized or physically damaged, but also that they were to be protected from harm and from perusal and use without the organization's consent. These views must be interpreted, of course, in the light of what the House of Lords held.

Some comments are called for on the conclusions of the English courts. They assimilated the privilege of inviolability of archives enjoyed by organizations to that enjoyed by diplomatic missions. This in itself is inappropriate. The two privileges are comparable but not identical nor is the one based on the other. The purpose for which these privileges are granted may be different in each case.

There is then the question of the extent of the privilege of inviolability of archives. What documents constitute archives that receive the protection of inviolability? International organizations prepare papers for meetings which are sent to states members for their study and consideration, prior to deliberation of the organization. It would not be proper to say that these papers are received by the states members as third parties, in which case the papers would cease to be papers of the organization not covered by inviolability (even on the analogy of Article 24 of the 1961 Vienna Convention on Diplomatic Relations). Working documents are received by the states members in their capacity as official participants in the work of the organization and as the members of an organ. They retain their status as documents of the organization (and, therefore, could have the benefit of the protection of Article 24). To reach a different conclusion would lead to the result that as soon as the secretariat, which is one organ of an international organization, shares with the member states, who are members of another organ, confidential documents, those documents cease to have any protection from disclosure. On this view the papers of an international organization can only be protected if the organization is never in a position to use them for its work, because they must remain only within one organ, the secretariat. This, however, was in effect the position taken by the House of Lords, which held that documents issued by the ITC ceased to be the documents of the ITC once they had been sent to member states.[73]

Fiscal matters

The UN Convention provides in Section 7(a) that the organization, its assets, income and property shall be exempt from direct taxation, though it is not expected to claim exemption from taxes which are, in fact, no more than charges for public utility services. Direct taxes are those which ultimately fall upon the organization for payment, the characterization in the municipal law of a particular state being irrelevant.[74] Section 7(b) and (c) provides for the exemption from customs duties and import and export restrictions of articles required for official use and the publications of the UN. Section 8 provides that then the UN will not, as a rule, claim exemption from excise duties or sales taxes which are included in the price of property purchased but requires member states, whenever possible, to make appropriate arrangements for the remission or return of the amount of duty or tax. The Specialized Agencies Convention has similar provisions.[75] The constitutions of financial institutions have a provision generally whereby the institution, its assets, property, income and its operation and transactions authorized by the constitution shall be immune from all taxation and all customs duties and the institution is not liable for the collection or payment of any tax or levy.[76]

Communications

Sections 9 and 10 of the UN Convention establish the extent of the freedom of communication accorded to the UN. Broadly, the freedom covers the absence of censorship over official communications, the right to use codes, couriers and bags (like the diplomatic bag or pouch) and treatment for communications of the UN by national administrations as favourable as that accorded to any member states. The same principles

---

[73] Higgins, *Problems and Process: International Law and How We Use It* (1994) p. 93, takes the view reflected here.

[74] See 1964 UNJY pp. 220ff.

[75] Sections 9 and 10. The CDB Agreement follows this pattern in Article 55.

[76] Article VII(9)(a), IBRD Articles of Agreement; Article IX(9)(a), IMF Articles of Agreement; Article VIII(9)(a), IDA Articles of Agreement; Article VI(9)(a), IFC Articles of Agreement; Article 47(a), MIGA Convention; Article XI(9)(a), IDB Agreement; Article 56(i), ADB Agreement; and Article 57(i), AFDB Agreement. The EIB Protocol, Articles 3 and 4, is somewhat different. See also Article 53 of the EBRD Agreement which is more elaborate.

are found in the Specialized Agencies Convention.[77] The UN–USA Headquarters Agreement gives the UN the privilege of establishing and operating radio facilities and the UN has had the UN flag flying on its own aircraft and ships. In the case of the financial institutions the freedom given by their constitutions is less extensive. The only freedom mentioned is the third one referred to in the UN Convention, namely treatment for official communications as favourable as that accorded to member sates.[78]

The issue has arisen in the case of the IBRD and the IMF whether the treatment accorded to official communications included exemption from rates charged for communications services.[79] In 1949 the defendants, US cable companies, proposed to adopt revised tariffs of charges under which the IMF and the IBRD would be required to pay the same commercial rates for their official telecommunications messages as payable by private persons. Previously, the IMF and the IBRD had paid the same rates as applied to the messages of foreign governments sent from the US to their own countries, which rates were substantially lower than commercial rates. The IMF and the IBRD filed a complaint with the Federal Communications Commission (FCC) contending that the revised tariffs were unlawful on the ground that, so long as special government rates were in existence, the IMF and the IBRD were entitled to the same standard of treatment. They relied upon provisions in their constitutions and the interpretations of them under provisions enabling the institutions to interpret their constitutions. The interpretation given by the Executive Directors of both institutions under their constitutions was that they were entitled to the same treatment as governments.[80]

The FCC held that the question whether the word 'treatment' in the provisions of the constitutions of the IMF and the IBRD on official communications applied to rates was conclusively determined by the

---

[77] Sections 11 and 12. They are also found in several headquarters agreements. The ITU has objected to the grant of some of these freedoms to specialized agencies, though not to the UN: see Jenks, note 68 pp. 69*ff.*

[78] See Article VII(7), IBRD Articles of Agreement; Article IX(7), IMF Articles of Agreement; Article VIII(7), IDA Articles of Agreement; Article VI(7), IFC Articles of Agreement; Article 46(6), MIGA Convention; Article XI(7), IDB Agreement; Article 54, ADB Agreement; Article 55, AFDB Agreement; Article 54, CDB Agreement; Article 6, EIB Protocol; and Article 50, EBRD Agreement.

[79] *IBRD and IMF* v. *All America Cable and Radio, Inc.* (1953), Federal Communications Commission, USA, 22 ILR p. 705.

[80] IBRD, *Decisions of the Executive Directors under Article IX of the Articles of Agreement* (1991) p. 14; IMF, *Selected Decisions of the IMF* (1993) p. 397.

interpretations of the two institutions. They were thus entitled to the standard of treatment for which they had contended, but this involved certain conditions of reciprocity accorded the US government and US cable companies by other countries and their cable companies. The Commission ruled that the defendants must file revised tariffs based on governmental rates which would be effective where the conditions of reciprocity were satisfied.

The basic question in the proceedings was whether the term 'treatment', as used in the Articles of Agreement of the IBRD and the IMF, related to rate matters as contended by the complainants or was confined to other matters such as priorities and freedom from censorship as contended by the defendants. The application of the term 'treatment' in the Articles to rates had been conclusively determined by the Executive Directors' interpretation, by unanimous vote, to cover rates charged for official communications of the IBRD and the IMF. Under the terms of the Articles of Agreement, this interpretation was, in the view of the FCC, final. Thus, the US government was bound by the Executive Directors' interpretation of the term 'treatment' and was under an international obligation to act in conformity therewith. At the same time the language of the Articles of Agreement appeared in fact to be sufficiently broad and general to include rates, and nowhere was there any exclusion of rates, either expressed or implied, or any words of limitation. The FCC said that, while they were not persuaded that the payment of higher-than-government rates would impede the functions of these institutions, including their financial ability in exercising their functions, they could understand their interest in securing a standard of treatment equivalent to that of member governments, including rates for official communications.

Privileges and immunities of personnel

The principle which emerges from the many agreements is that the personnel of international organizations enjoy privileges and immunities, not for their personal benefit, but for the purpose of exercising their functions in relation to the organization. This is expressly stated, for example, in the UN Convention, both in relation to officials of the organization[81] and even to the representatives of members;[82] thus, in that convention waiver is a matter for the SG or the member state, as the case may be, whenever the immunity would impede the cause of justice

---

[81] Section 20.   [82] Section 14.

and can be waived without impeding the functions of, or the relations of, the organization. It is the fulfilment of the proposed functions of the organization that requires that these privileges and immunities be recognized.

Representatives of member states[83]

The immunities and privileges accorded to this category are generally very similar to those accorded to diplomatic agents but with rather greater emphasis on the functional basis of the privileges and immunities. There are differences between the two Conventions themselves and between those and the constitutions of the financial institutions.

Article 4 of the UN Convention and Section 15 of the UN–USA Headquarters Agreement are somewhat at variance, for whereas the latter accords diplomatic privileges and immunities, the UN Convention specifies immunity from legal process only in respect of words spoken or written and all acts done by representatives in their capacity as representatives, which is narrower than the general diplomatic immunity. There is also immunity from arrest, seizure of personal baggage, immigration restrictions or national service obligations, inviolability of papers and documents, the right of communication and exemptions from customs duties (but only in respect of personal baggage as opposed to all imports of personal use).[84]

The representatives are not accredited to the host state, but rather to the organization. However, under the UN–USA Headquarters Agreement, apart from the principal permanent representatives or permanent representatives with the rank of ambassador or minister plenipotentiary, the staff of any given mission have to be agreed upon between the host state, the SG and the sending state.[85] A further consequence of non-accreditation to the host states is the inapplicability of the remedy of declaring a representative *persona non grata*. It would also seem that a host state cannot apply reciprocity to the treatment of such representatives, as it may to persons accredited to it.[86] The Specialized Agencies Convention, unlike the UN Convention, does deal with this to the extent of allowing expulsion for activities outside the representatives' official functions.[87] Further, the representatives may be received from

[83] See also Sands and Klein (eds.), note 3 pp. 499*ff*. For an early discussion of the privileges and immunities of personnel in international organizations, see Jenks, note 68 pp. 85*ff*.

[84] UN Convention, Section 11.   [85] Section 15.

[86] See the opinion of the UN Secretariat reported in 2 YBILC (1967) at pp. 177–8.

[87] Section 25.

governments not recognized by the host state. In the Headquarters Agreement with the USA, privileges and immunities are granted to such persons only within the Headquarters district, or in transit between the district and residences or offices, or whilst at such residence or office, while other agreements tend to specify that immunities and privileges shall be granted irrespective of the relationship between sending state and host state.

Special problems arise in organizations in which a delegation from a state is not confined to governmental representatives. In the ILO the employers' and workers' delegates receive the same immunities and privileges as governmental representatives, save the right to use codes, couriers or sealed bags; waiver of immunities is a matter for the Governing Body. In the inter-parliamentary assemblies of the Council of Europe and the European Union the immunities are carefully defined and their functional basis is emphasized by their being modelled, not on diplomatic immunities, but more on parliamentary immunities in national law.[88]

In the case of the financial institutions the Governors or the equivalent are representatives of states to the organizations or their meetings. However, their immunities and privileges are in general included in those of the staff.[89]

There are some municipal court decisions on the immunity from jurisdiction of representatives of states in organizations[90] but these do not concern the application or interpretation of the UN or Specialized Agencies Convention or the constitutions of organizations such as the financial institutions. They are based on the application of national law or headquarters agreements. The first group of cases was decided in US courts. In *Friedberg* v. *Santa Cruz*,[91] an action against the wife of the Chilean Ambassador accredited to the UN in a negligent driving case, the decision of the lower court refusing the plea of immunity was quashed on the ground that the defendant being an ambassador's wife the matter was within the original and exclusive jurisdiction of the US Supreme Court. In *City of New Rochelle* v. *Page-Sharp*,[92] in which the Third Secretary of the Australian Mission to the UN pleaded immunity in reply to a

---

[88] See the COE Statute, Articles 13–15; and EEC Protocol, Articles 7–9.

[89] See, e.g., Article IX(8) of the IMF Articles of Agreement; Article VII(8) of the IBRD Articles of Agreement; Articles 47(b) and 48 of the MIGA Convention; Article 51 of the EBRD Agreement; Article XI(8) of the IDB Agreement; and Article 55 of the ADB Agreement.

[90] For the early cases see Crosswell, *Protection of International Persons Abroad* (1952) pp. 81ff.; Jenks, note 68 pp. 86ff.

[91] (1948), 15 AD p. 312.   [92] (1949), 16 AD p. 298.

summons for speeding, a New York Court in effect recognized the immunity. In *People* v. *Von Otter*[93] the same court upheld a plea of immunity in reply to a charge of unlawful parking by the wife of the Counsellor of the Swedish Delegation to the UN. In *Agostino* v. *de Antueno*,[94] a proceeding between landlord and tenant for the recovery of the possession of premises, a New York court held that the respondent, who was Third Secretary of the Permanent Delegation of Argentina to the UN, was not entitled to plead immunity. The decision appears to rest in part on the ground that the proceedings were basically *in rem* and not *in personam*. But it also involved the proposition that immunities, having been granted by federal action, are inapplicable to matters within state rather than federal jurisdiction. In *Tsiang* v. *Tsiang*[95] the defendant, who was accredited to the UN as Ambassador Plenipotentiary and Permanent Representative of the Republic of China, had been served with process in an action for separation brought by his alleged wife from whom he had secured in Mexico a divorce invalid by Chinese and New York State law; the service was set aside by the Supreme Court of New York State on the basis of a suggestion of immunity presented by the federal government. In *Pappas* v. *Francini*[96] a claim to full diplomatic immunity made by a member of the staff of the Italian Observer accredited to the UN prior to the admission of Italy to membership, denied by the Department of State, and not supported by the Chief of Protocol of the UN, was rejected by a New York court. In *Arcaya* v. *Paez*[97] a New York Court of Appeal granted immunity to the alternate representative to the UN of Venezuela in a libel case. The New York courts in the *Knockley Corporation Case*[98] recognized the immunity of the representative of Afghanistan to the UN in a tax deed case which involved title to property. In these US cases immunity was recognized without difficulty or, if not, the result turned on the technicalities of US law. The basic principle of immunity was admitted.

There have been some decisions by European courts. In the *Ali Ali Reza Case*[99] a French court of appeal in a case where eviction was requested in connection with the lease of a flat refused immunity to the Saudi Arabian delegate to the UN. The refusal turned on the interpretation of the French decree of 26 April 1947. The Italian Court of Cassation in

---

[93] (1952), 19 ILR p. 382.   [94] (1950), 17 ILR p. 285.   [95] (1949), 16 AD p. 298.
[96] (1953), 20 ILR p. 380.   [97] (1957), 23 ILR p. 436.   [98] (1957), 24 ILR p. 202.
[99] (1961), 47 ILR p. 275.

the *Pisani Balestra di Mottola Case*[100] applied the FAO–Italy Headquarters Agreement in recognizing the immunity of the son of the Costa Rican representative to the FAO in a case involving theft. It took the view that the pertinent immunity was the same as for diplomats.

These decided cases reflect the dependency on the national law of the results in claims of immunity from jurisdiction by representatives or those entitled through them, unless relevant international agreements are part of the national law whether automatically or by incorporation.

Officials

In general officials enjoy immunity from jurisdiction only in respect of their official acts.[101] In the case of the UN Convention[102] and the Specialized Agencies Convention[103] provision is made for high officials or the executive head respectively of the institution concerned to have full diplomatic immunity.

There are a few cases, not arising from the two conventions or headquarters agreements but relevant to other instruments in which these immunities have been an issue. In *Maclaine Watson & Co. Ltd* v. *ITC (No. 2)*[104] the UK Court of Appeal held that, under a UK statute which provided for immunity from legal process in respect of official acts virtually in the same way as the two conventions, an order requiring officers of the ITC to provide information relating to assets did not infringe their immunity. In a case decided by the Supreme Court of the Philippines it was held that under an agreement between the government and the WHO which granted full diplomatic immunity to officials of the WHO a warrant to search crates among the plaintiff's belongings could not be issued.[105] In the US the personal chauffeur of the UN SG was not

---

[100] (1969), 71 ILR p. 565. See also for the interpretation by a Swiss Court of the ILO–Swiss Headquarters Agreement of 1946 on the immunity from jurisdiction of members of the Governing Body of ILO, *Stahal* v. *Bastid* [1971], 75 ILR p. 76 (immunity in effect recognized).

[101] See Section 18(a), UN Convention; Section 19(a), Specialized Agencies Convention; IBRD Articles of Agreement, Article VII(8)(i); IMF Articles of Agreement, Article IX(8)(i); IFC Articles of Agreement, Article VI(8)(i); IDA Articles of Agreement, Article VIII(8)(i); IDB Agreement, Article XI(8)(a); ADB Agreement, Article 55(i); AFDB Agreement, Article 56(i)(i); EADB Agreement, Article 54(a); EIB Protocol, Article 12(a); EBRD Agreement, Article 51; and MIGA Convention, Article 48(i). Most headquarters agreements have the same provisions with the particular exception of the UN–USA Agreement.

[102] Section 19.   [103] Section 21.   [104] [1988], 80 ILR p. 211.

[105] *WHO and Verstuyft* v. *Aquino and Others* (1972), 52 ILR p. 389. See also *Zoernsch* v. *Waldock and Another* [1964], 41 ILR p. 438, where in the case of an official of the COE, under the UK legislation, his immunity in respect of official acts was held not to have

accorded immunity in a case involving a speeding charge while driving in the course of duty, because the act of driving in the circumstances could not be regarded as within the official activities of the organization.[106] This case was, perhaps, wrongly decided in principle. It also involved the application of a US statute which did not incorporate an international agreement. In the *Curran Case*[107] the New York courts correctly recognized the immunity of the SG of the UN under the US statute in a case involving grants of lands and easements.[108]

The UN Convention and the Specialized Agencies Convention both provide more or less in the same manner (with some slight differences) for other immunities for staff who are not entitled to full diplomatic immunity. For example, Section 18 of the UN Convention gives officials a number of immunities. They are to be exempt from taxation on the salaries and emoluments paid to them by the UN. They are to be immune from national service obligations and, together with their spouses and relatives dependent on them, from immigration restrictions and alien registration. They are to be accorded the same privileges in respect of exchange facilities as are accorded to the officials of comparable rank forming part of diplomatic missions to the government concerned. They are to be given, together with their spouses and relatives dependent on them, the same repatriation facilities in time of international crisis as diplomatic envoys. Finally, they are to have the right to import free of duty their furniture and effects at the time of first taking up their post in the country in question.[109] Both these conventions also

lapsed after he ceased to be a member of the staff of the COE; and the *ESOC Official Immunity Case* (1975), 73 ILR p. 683, where a court of the FRG held that an official of the European Space Operations Center (ESOC) was entitled to immunity from legal process in respect of statements made in his official capacity in regard to the plaintiff's employment, under an international agreement to which ESRO, a sister organization of ESOC, was a party. In the *Keeney Case* (1953), 20 ILR p. 382, the principle applied was apparently that immunity from legal process includes the privilege of non-disclosure of information acquired in an official capacity to a sub-committee of Congress, which privilege continues even after the official has ceased to be in the service of the organization.

[106] *Westchester County on Complaint of Donnely v. Ranollo* (1946), 13 AD p. 168.

[107] (1947), 14 AD p. 154.

[108] In the *Coplon and Gubitchev Case* (1949), 16 AD p. 293, the UN did not claim immunity in an espionage case. Espionage was not within official duties. For other cases in which the immunity of officials was not recognized because the acts concerned could not be regarded as having been performed in their official capacity see *Essayan v. Jouve* (1962), 1962 UNJY p. 290 (France); and *People of the State of New York v. Coumatos* (1962), 1962 UNJY p. 294 (New York).

[109] See also Sections 19 and 20 of the Specialized Agencies Convention.

provide,[110] however, that the privileges and immunities of officials are granted in the interests of the organization and not for the personal benefit of the individuals themselves. Thus, the organization may waive the immunity where it impedes the course of justice and can be waived without prejudice to the interest of the organization.

The financial institutions deal with the immunities and privileges of officials slightly differently. For example, the IBRD Articles of Agreement provide[111] that officials, not being local nationals, shall be accorded the same immunities from immigration restrictions, alien registration requirements and national service obligations and the same facilities as regards exchange restrictions as are accorded by members to the representatives, officials and employees of comparable rank of other members. They are to be granted the same treatment in respect of travelling facilities as is accorded by members to representatives, officials and employees of comparable rank of other members and are not to be taxed in respect of salaries or emoluments paid by the IBRD, provided they are not local citizens, local subjects or other local nationals.[112] Article VII of the UN Convention and Article VIII of the Specialized Agencies Convention deal with the privilege of transit for officials which the 'laissez-passer' is designed to secure.

Other persons

There are some special categories of persons or groups other than representatives or officials who also have certain immunities, that is, experts, judicial officers and UN and international armed forces. Their immunities and privileges are somewhat special and are based on particular provisions or special arrangements.[113]

---

[110] See Section 20, UN Convention; and Section 22, Specialized Agencies Convention.

[111] See Article VII(8)(ii) and (iii) and (9)(b).

[112] See for similar, though not identical, provisions, IMF Articles of Agreement, Article IX(8)(ii) and (iii) and (9)(b); IFC Articles of Agreement, Article VI(8)(ii) and (iii) and (9)(b); IDA Articles of Agreement, Article VIII(8)(ii) and (iii) and (9)(b); IDB Agreement, Article XI(8)(b) and (c) and (9)(b); ADB Agreement, Articles 53(ii) and (iii) and 56(2); AFDB Agreement, Articles 56(i), (ii) and (iii) and 57(i); CDB Agreement, Articles 54(b) and (c) and 55(5); EIB Protocol, Articles 12(b), (c), (d) and (e) and 13; EBRD Agreement, Articles 52, 53(6), 55 (waiver); and MIGA Convention, Articles 48(ii) and (iii), 47(b) and 50 (waiver). The restriction of the exemption of taxation to non-local nationals is found in many of the headquarters agreements.

[113] See especially Sands and Klein (eds.), note 3 pp. 508ff. and Jenks, note 68 pp. 93–110. For the privileges and immunities of experts see UN Doc. A/CN. 4/L.188, 2 YBILC (1967) at pp. 284ff. and 317ff.; UN Convention, Sections 22 and 23. In *Applicability of Article VI, Section 22, of the Convention on the Privileges and Immunities of the United Nations Case*, 1989

Customary law

A question that may be asked is whether there is now a customary international law governing international privileges and immunities. It is important to determine whether the immunities of an international organization are customary, and not based solely on conventional law, for several reasons. For example, *vis-à-vis* the host state there may exist no relevant headquarters agreement.[114] It may also be necessary to know whether the terms of a headquarters agreement or any of the applicable international agreements are exhaustive of the privileges and immunities that may be claimed, or whether in addition other immunites may be claimed which flow from customary international law. Further, in some states the courts will not give effect to the terms of a treaty unless that treaty has been incorporated in domestic law. If no such law has been enacted, or if its terms do not fully match those of the treaty,[115] the question may arise as to whether privileges and immunities should nonetheless be granted by virtue of the requirements of customary international law.

On the one hand, it has been argued that there was never any customary law in the area and that none has developed out of the conventional law or otherwise since the Second World War.[116] However, the argument

ICJ Reports p. 177, the ICJ gave an advisory opinion on whether Section 22 of the Convention was applicable *vis-à-vis* his national state to a person who had been appointed by a Sub-commission of the Commission of Human Rights to report on certain aspects of human rights and had also been a member of that sub-commission. Section 22 dealt with experts. The ICJ found that the section of the Convention was applicable, stating (at pp. 195–6) that:

> The Court takes the view that Section 22 of the General Convention is applicable to persons (other than United Nations officials) to whom a mission has been entrusted by the Organization and who are therefore entitled to enjoy the privileges and immunities provided for in this Section with a view to the independent exercise of their functions. During the whole period of such missions, experts enjoy these functional privileges and immunities whether or not they travel. They may be invoked against the State of nationality or of residence unless a reservation to Section 22 of the General Convention has been validly made by that State.

[114] For many years no headquarters agreement existed between the IMCO and the UK: see Higgins, *The Development of International Law through the Political Organs of the United Nations* (1963) p. 248, note 37.

[115] Compare, e.g., Article 8 of the ITC Headquarters Agreement with Article 6 of the relevant Order in Council of 1972.

[116] See, e.g., the view expressed by Liang, in 2 YBILC (1957) at p. 5.

may be made that particularly since the end of the Second World War the acceptance of the conventional law, especially the UN Convention and the Convention on the Privileges and Immunities of the Specialized Agencies, has given rise to practice which has resulted in the creation of customary international law. While it may be argued that this practice, among other things, may have resulted in at least an incipient customary law in certain areas, it must be acknowledged that: (i) *generally* international privileges and immunities have been accorded by states only under these conventions or other conventional law which have become part of their national law by incorporation or automatically; and (ii) there are hardly any examples of claims to or recognition of any of these privileges and immunities outside the orbit of conventional law. With the proliferation of international organizations, there may, on the other hand, be a growing tendency in the international community to recognize that at least certain international privileges and immunities are necessary for the efficient and independent functioning of international organizations, even in the absence of the applicable conventional law. This may be the case, for instance, particularly with organizational immunity from the jurisdiction of states. There are cases, some of them decided before the Second World War, in which courts have taken this position especially in regard to employment-related matters.[117]

---

[117] See, e.g., *Lamborot*, Recueil des Arrêts du Conseil d'Etat (1928) p. 1,304; *Antin, ibid.* p. 764; *Weiss* v. *IIIC*, 81 JDI (1954) p. 754; *Bellaton* v. *ESA* (1978), 25 AFDI (1979) p. 893; and *International Institute of Agriculture* v. *Profili* (1931), 5 AD p. 413. In *International Tin Council* v. *Amalgamet Inc.* (1988), 524 NYS 2d p. 971, a court in New York held that the ITC of which the USA was not a member nor with which the USA had an agreement governing privileges and immunities was not entitled to immunity from jurisdiction, because there had been a waiver of the immunity in the circumstances of the case, even if the ITC was entitled to claim immunity. The court, however, seems to have implied that in the absence of an agreement between the ITC and the USA or other agreement applicable to which the USA was a party the ITC could not claim immunity. The case was not a case involving employment relations but concerned a commercial relationship. See also *Branno* v. *Ministry of War* (1955), 22 ILR p. 756, where the Italian Court of Cassation did not deny that NATO could have immunity from jurisdiction, apparently under general international law; and the *ESOC Official Immunity Case* (1973), 73 ILR p. 683, where the issue was the immunity of officials and the Federal Labour Court of the FRG said that such immunity was generally recognized under international law. The view that there is a customary law of international privileges and immunities has been espoused for some time: see J.-F. Lalive, loc. cit. note 3 at pp. 304–5; now see for a modified view, Sands and Klein (eds.), note 3 pp. 489–90. Now see also the *AS Case* (1985), loc. cit. note 45. There is a discussion of custom as a source of law for international immunities and privileges in Reinisch, note 3 pp. 145–57. The various views are reflected there.

Assuming that there is at least an incipient customary law of international privileges and immunities, the question to be answered is what is covered by this customary law – does it extend to all matters included in the conventional law, which is principally the constitutions of organizations, multilateral agreements, such as the UN Convention, and international agreements, such as headquarters agreements? There is little authority on this subject by way of state practice or judicial decision. However, it will be recalled that there are some judicial decisions of national courts which recognized the immunity from jurisdiction of certain organizations principally in employment matters, even though there was no conventional law governing the situation. One may venture to suggest, therefore, that national courts will acknowledge that organizations are at least immune from their jurisdiction to the same extent as under the general conventional law, namely the UN and Specialized Agencies Conventions, even in the absence of a governing conventional law.

But there may be room for the recognition of some other privileges and immunities. The basis of the immunities and privileges of organizations even under the conventional law is generally acknowledged to be a functional one. Those privileges and immunities conceded in the two general conventions are intended to enable organizations to function independently in order that they may discharge their responsibilities efficiently. This being the *raison d'être* of the privileges and immunities recognized by conventional law, it is arguable that the basis of those privileges and immunities recognized at customary international law is the same. Hence, it is reasonable that customary law recognizes the same privileges and immunities as are basically granted under those two conventions unless for a functional reason a particular organization does not need to enjoy a particular privilege or immunity. In short, the international privileges and immunities recognized by customary law are those that each individual organization requires in order to discharge its responsibilities independently and without interference, there being a presumption that many of the privileges and immunities incorporated in the two general conventions are generally what are required for this purpose. It is difficult to identify exactly what these privileges and immunities might be. The inviolability of archives and the freedom of communication are perhaps two of them. The functional basis of international privileges and immunities in customary law could have the result not only that some organizations may have privileges and immunities that others do not but that an organization may not have in one state the privileges and immunities it enjoys in another, for instance, because the former state is not a member of the organization but also for other reasons. There is a stronger case for a customary law applicable between member states and organizations than between non-member states and organizations. Further, as pointed out earlier, the distinction between acts *iure imperii* and *iure gestionis* should strictly not be relevant for the jurisdictional immunity of international organizations, though it has been invoked and applied in some cases. The American *Third Restatement of the Law: The Foreign Relations of the United States* takes the view that international organizations are entitled, as a matter of customary law, to 'such privileges and immunities as are necessary for the fulfillment of the purposes of the organization, including immunity from legal process and from financial controls, taxes and duties'.[118]

There is also the question whether particularly organizations of limited membership, albeit with separate legal personality, receive immunities from the host state (and other member states) as a matter of customary international law.[119] In one case arising out of the ITC episode, it was said by the judge:

international organizations such as the ITC have never so far as I know been recognized at common law as entitled to sovereign status. They are accordingly entitled to no sovereign or diplomatic immunity in this country save where such immunity is granted by legislative instrument, and then only to the extent of such grant.[120]

The implication is that there is no customary law on the matter. But it is not the case that the ITC – or any international organization – is entitled to sovereign or diplomatic immunity. The issue is really quite different: it is whether international law requires that a different type of international person, an international organization, be accorded functional immunities. The basis for an affirmative answer lies in good faith (that is, provision of what is necessary for an organization to perform its functions) and not in respect for sovereignty or for its representation through diplomacy. There is no difference in principle between an organization of universal membership and one of limited membership. The issue is not, so far as the membership is concerned, one of 'recognition' of the personality of the organization. It is simply that

---

[118] *Third Restatement of the Law: The Foreign Relations of the United States* (1987) vol. I, section 467(i). The reporter's notes in support of this view all relate to universal organizations.
[119] See also Higgins, note 73 p. 91.
[120] Bingham J in *Standard Chartered Bank* v. *ITC and Others* [1987] 1 WLR at pp. 647–8.

members – and *a fortiori* the headquarters state – may not at one and the same time establish an organization and fail to provide it with those immunities that ensure its role as distinct from that of the host state (and other member states).[121] This point, a combination of good faith and functionalism, is clearly made for organizations in general in the Advisory Opinion of the ICJ in the *Applicability of Article VI, section 22 of the Convention on the Privileges and Immunities of the United Nations Case*.[122] The 'Fifth Report of the Special Rapporteur on Relations between States and International Organizations', however, is not clear on this point. On the matter of the inviolability of archives of organizations in general it cites certain treaties that provide for inviolability of archives,[123] but also concludes that 'doctrine and state practice' fully support the principle of the inviolability of archives.[124] It deduces this rule from the customary law relating to diplomatic missions, simply asserting that 'the principle is equally valid in the case of international organizations'.[125] The matter is treated by assimilation to diplomatic missions which is inappropriate.

As for non-member states, it has been implied by a court in the USA (New York) that an organization of which a state is not a member is not entitled to privileges and immunities in that state in the absence of a treaty commitment.[126] If this view were accepted, it would mean that a distinction would have to be made in the application of the customary law.

Claiming immunity and waiver

There are a variety of questions which may be asked in connection with international immunities, whether the questions are regarded as procedural or otherwise. Some of them are mentioned here. Does the immunity have to be claimed? Is there immunity, unless it is waived? Can immunity be impliedly waived? What amounts to waiver of immunity or acceptance of jurisdiction?

---

[121] Reuter, 'Le Droit au secret et les institutions internationales' 53 AFDI (1956) p. 60.
[122] 1989 ICJ Reports at pp. 192*ff*.
[123] A/CN.4/432 at p. 4 (1991): Agreement between the Government of Chile and the Economic Commission for Latin America, Article 1(i)(9), UN Leg. Ser. St/LEG/SER.B/10, p. 218.
[124] A/CN.4/432, para. 48 (1991).   [125] *Ibid.*, para. 46.
[126] *International Tin Council v. Amalgamet Inc.* (1988), 524 NYS 2d p. 971.

These questions pertain to immunities in general in so far as international law (and the national law concerned) recognize them. Moreover, the consequences of recognizing immunity apply to international immunities as much as to sovereign and diplomatic immunities. Hence, a detailed examination of them is not made here. Suffice it to address the question of international immunity in general from the jurisdiction of national courts.

In regard to the jurisdiction of courts generally reference is made to claiming or asserting immunity and waiving immunity. The mechanics of how exactly these immunities work has not usually been explored. In regard to a national court's jurisdiction, the mechanics are important, because the jurisdiction of a court may in one way or another not be pre-empted. The consequence is that, if a court has no jurisdiction to start with, then the failure of one or both parties, the court (*proprio motu*) and any other relevant entity to address the issue of jurisdiction cannot result in the court's having validly exercised jurisdiction and the court's decision will be null and void and may be questioned thereafter. In short, questions of jurisdiction must usually be raised before and addressed by the court, in whatever manner they come to the attention of the court. This is the position flowing from general principles of law relating to jurisdiction.[127]

International immunity (and sovereign and diplomatic immunity) appear to be of a special nature. It would seem that the position recognized in practice is not that the national court has no jurisdiction *per se*, whether it is *ratione personae, ratione materiae* or otherwise. It is that the person or legal entity entitled to claim the immunity claims it for the reason on which the immunity is based, so as to prevent the court from exercising jurisdiction. Thus, the presumption is that the court has jurisdiction, unless it is claimed, on whatever ground relating to international immunity, that the court is without jurisdiction. The governing principle is that immunity must be *claimed* by or on behalf of the party allegedly enjoying it. If it is not claimed, the court has jurisdiction. It makes no difference that the matter of immunity had neither been raised nor been addressed by the court.

The result is that, unless immunity is claimed, it is waived. As seen earlier in this chapter, an international organization (like a sovereign state) can, expressly or impliedly by its conduct, waive a relevant immunity. Clearly, then, failure by the party claiming it or a relevant entity to

---

[127] See C. F. Amerasinghe, *Jurisdiction of International Tribunals* (2003) pp. 201–2.

raise at the appropriate point in the proceedings the question of immunity results in waiver. This is the correct way, in terms of practice and custom, to explain immunity, strictly so-called, and waiver of immunity in the case, *inter alios*, of international organizations.

Abuse

In connection with diplomatic privileges and immunities the question has been raised whether certain instances of abuse of such privileges and immunities require a change in the law.[128] Equally, in the case of international privileges and immunities the possibility of abuse exists. One problem is to define abuse for this purpose. If, for example, immunity from jurisdiction in the case of an official of an international organization exists, obviously the immunity is meant to be claimed when a prosecution for a criminal offence is instituted against the official. It cannot be termed 'abuse' that immunity is asserted in each and every circumstance of prosecution or litigation. If this were the case, it would not make sense to accord immunity in the first place. The immunity is accorded with the expectation that it will be asserted. With this problem in mind it may be said that, for example, an official abuses customs privileges legally accorded to him by engaging in drug trafficking.

In case of abuse the UN Convention and the Specialized Agencies Convention both have provisions which require privileges and immunities to be waived by the organization or its representative, where representatives, official (or experts), as the case may be, are concerned.[129] The latter Convention goes further in Article 24 by providing for consultation, reference to the ICJ and, in the event that the ICJ finds the existence of abuse, withholding of the particular privilege or immunity from the specialized agency concerned. In the UN Convention there is no such provision, nor is there a provision dealing with abuse by the organization itself.

It would appear that the provisions of the Specialized Agencies Convention may be adequate to take care of abuse of all kinds and where immunities are not properly waived, though the procedure seems likely

---

[128] Higgins, 'The Abuse of Diplomatic Privileges and Immunities: Recent United Kingdom Experience', 79 AJIL (1985) at p. 641; Higgins, 'UK Foreign Affairs Committee Report on the Abuse of Diplomatic Privileges and Immunities: Government Response and Report', 80 AJIL (1986) p. 135.

[129] Articles 14, 20, 21 and 23 of the UN Convention and Articles 18, 22 and 23 of the Specialized Agencies Convention.

to be a long drawn-out one. On the other hand, the same cannot be said for the UN Convention. It may be suggested that a provision on the lines of Article 24 of the Specialized Agencies Convention should apply to the UN as well.

It is not clear whether the customary international law for which a case was made earlier in this chapter would provide for retaliatory action in the case of abuse. Given the provisions of Article 24 of the Specialized Agencies Convention it is unlikely that anything more than consultation, settlement by reference to third-party adjudication and withholding would be required. If such a rule does apply, it could be applied to the UN, in spite of the absence of provision in the UN Convention.

More generally, assuming that 'abuse' can occur, then the question which arises is whether there is a violation of international law, when, in circumstances where there is abuse, the immunity is claimed or the privilege is asserted by the organization, whether for itself or for personnel. It is possible that the assertion of privilege or claim to immunity in the case of such abuse amounts to, and may be characterized as, an *abus de droit* and, therefore, be a violation of international law. Then the law of reprisal, *inter alia*, would come into play. What better way of exercising this right is there than by not according the privilege or not recognizing the immunity, whether by administrative act or judicial decision?[130]

---

[130] The problem of abuse and identifying it once defined is a general one for all immunities and privileges whether international or state or diplomatic. It is not possible to address this problem here. The focus here is on the consequences of abuse, once it is established.

11   Financing

International organizations incur expenditures in the course of their activities and must find means of funding them. Financing is at the heart of the functioning of international organizations. Without adequate funds they could not achieve their purposes and functions. Expenditures of organizations have increased over the years, partly because of inflation, but also on account of expanding activity. Expenditures are provided for and financed through budgets. To illustrate the dimensions of budgetary expenditure and the increase in costs the UN may be taken as an example. In 1946 the budget appropriation of the UN was $19.3 million; in 1954 it was $47.8 million; in 1966, $121.6 million; for the two years 1980 and 1981, $1,339 million (i.e., about $669.5 million per year); and for the two years 1986 and 1987, $1,712 million (i.e., about $856 million per year).[1] For the years 1994 and 1995 the GA approved a budget of $2.6 billion (i.e., about $1.3 billion per year) and for the years 1996 and 1997 the budget was $2.5 billion (about $1.25 billion per year).[2] The reduction in these two years is the result of the agitation for reform and cost-cutting, principally among the larger contributors, particularly the USA. The biennial budget for 2002–2003 was $2.5 billion.[3]

Recent budgetary figures for the UN specialized agencies, excluding the World Bank Group and the IMF, are as follows:[4]

---

[1] See Galey, 'Reforming the Regime for Financing the United Nations', 31 Howard LJ (1988) at pp. 552–3.

[2] See the Programme Budget paper for 1996 to 1997, UN Doc. A/50/6 of 3 May 1995 at p. 3.

[3] GA Rs. 55/233.

[4] For the figures for the UN specialized agencies see Sands and Klein (eds.), *Bowett's Law of International Institutions* (2001) p. 566. For a consideration of financing see, e.g., Stoessinger, *Financing the United Nations System* (1964) *passim*.

Organisation	Budget
Food and Agriculture Organisation (FAO)	Biennial budget 1998–99 U.S. $650 million
United Nations Educational, Scientific and Cultural Organisation (UNESCO)	Biennial budget 1998–99 U.S. $544,367,000
International Civil Aviation Organisation (ICAO)	Budget for 1999 U.S. $51,126,000; 2000 $52,281,000; 2001 $53,657,000
World Intellectual Property Organisation (WIPO)	Biennial budget 1998–99 383 million Swiss Francs
International Labour Organisation (ILO)	Biennial budget 1998–99 U.S. $481,050,000
United Nations Industrial Development Organisation (UNIDO)	Biennial budget for 1998–99 U.S. $129.5 million
World Health Organisation (WHO)	Biennial budget for 1998–99 U.S. $842 million
International Telecommunications Union (ITU)	Biennial budget for 1998–99 302.6 million Swiss Francs
International Maritime Organisation (IMO)	Biennial budget for 1998–99 £36,612,000
World Meteorological Organisation (WMO)	Triennial budget for 1996–99 255 million Swiss Francs
Universal Postal Union (UPU)	Budget for 1999 35,451,300 Swiss Francs

The total administrative budget of the IMF for 2002–3 was $746 million and of the IBRD for fiscal 2002 was $1.5 billion.[5] As for the EU, its 1999 budget was about $104 billion (97 billion Euros) which is quite substantial. Other regional organizations have less substantial budgets. The programme budget of the OAS for the year 2000 was $88 million, while the current annual budget of the OAU is about $30 million.

In most international organizations most expenditures are for administrative purposes. In the UN it has been estimated that 85 per cent of the regular budget is administrative. Not taking into account the financial institutions, about 90 per cent of the expenditures of the specialized agencies of the UN and regional organizations are for administrative purposes. However, international organizations have to a greater extent begun to raise funds for operational activities, such as the peacekeeping

---

[5] For the IMF see the *IMF Annual Report 2002* p. 82. For the IBRD see the *IBRD Annual Report 2002* p. 113. In these institutions and others like them the operational budget is kept separate from the administrative budget and is generally very large.

activities of the UN or the aid to their member states. Because of the increase in activities entailing expenditures, member states have become interested not only in the general increase of the budgets but also in the purpose for which their contributions are used.[6] There has followed recently much controversy over accountability in international organizations. Particularly in the UN and its specialized agencies (excluding the financial institutions) there has been much concern among the major contributors of funds (the USA in particular) about the control that a majority which does not include them has over the contents of the budget and the size of the expenditures which are to be incurred.[7] At the present time disputes over funding of the UN (and other organizations) have arisen which have led to an ever-present risk of *de facto* bankruptcy of the UN. For these reasons the current state of the financing of international organizations has a crucial character.

While expenditures do not have to appear in the annual or other budget of an organization in order to qualify as expenses of an organization, most expenditures either appear in the regular budget or are approved by supplementary budgets. Most constitutions of organizations have provisions dealing with the approval of the budget,[8] but, even if they do not, as in the case of the constitutions of the IBRD and the IMF, it is the general practice in organizations to have a budget approved annually by the responsible organ. Where such organ is not specifically designated in the constitution, it would be the plenary organ or other organ to whom such powers have been delegated validly by the plenary organ.[9]

---

[6] See Kolasa, 'Financing', section 2 of chapter 4 in Dupuy (ed.), *Manuel sur les organisations internationales* (1988) p. 198.

[7] See particularly the discussion in Zoller, 'The "Corporate Will" of the United Nations and the Rights of the Minority', 81 AJIL (1987) p. 610; Nelson, 'International Law and the US Withholding of Payments to International Organizations', 80 AJIL (1986) p. 973; Alvarez, 'Legal Remedies and the United Nations à la Carte Problem', 12 Michigan JIL (1991) p. 229; and Galey, 'Reforming the Regime' p. 543. In 1986 the GA of the UN passed a resolution establishing decision making by consensus in respect of budgetary matters: UNGAOR, 41st Session. Supp. No. 53, at p. 57 (UN Doc. A/41/53 (1986)). Consequent upon that resolution the GA adopts the decisions of its Committe for Program and Coordination, which are reached by consensus.

[8] See, e.g., Article 17(1) of the UN Charter; Article 13 of the ILO constitution; Article XVIII(1) of the FAO Constitution; Article IX(2) of the UNESCO Constitution; Articles 55 and 56 of the WHO Constitution; Article 49(e) of the ICAO Constitution; and Article XIV of the IAEA Constitution. For the constitutions of financial institutions which are explicit, see, e.g., Article 31 of the ADB Constitution; and Article 27 of the EBRD constitution.

[9] In the case of the IBRD and the IMF there seems to have been a delegation of this function to the Executive Directors and the Executive Board respectively, though at

The budget includes both administrative and operational expenditures – i.e., expenditures arising from policy decisions that particular activities be undertaken.

The law relating to the financing of an international organization is fundamental to its existence and functioning. The financial policy of an organization must be built upon the substructure of this law. In this regard the particular provisions of the constitutions of the various organizations are of prime importance. On the other hand, the practices of the organizations in implementing their constitutions have complemented these provisions and something must be said about these.

The main matters to be considered in connection with financing are: (i) the budget process; (ii) the exercise of internal and external control over the use of funds provided in the budget; and (iii) how funds are raised. There are some other questions which also arise and will be discussed, such as what may be included in the expenses of an organization, the obligation to pay and its extent, and the nature of apportionment, where this technique is used, and approval of the budget.

The budget process

The adoption of the budget (together with supplementary budgets) is a binding legal act. The budget consists of estimates of income and expenditure generally on a yearly basis. With regard to expenditure each budget normally includes the administrative costs of running an organization (salaries of staff, costs of conferences, services, etc.) and costs which result from decisions of policy that particular activities be undertaken. The basic legal principle and, perhaps, the only significant principle is that the budget must be approved by the appropriate organ following the appropriate procedure. Both the organ and the regulatory procedure are normally reflected in the constitution, but the organ may, as in the case of the IBRD and the IMF, be a delegated organ.[10] The constitutions of organizations do not regulate financial matters in detail. The subject is

---

some stage the Board of Governors (i.e., composed of state representatives) gives its approval.

[10] See on the budget process of organizations, particularly, Jenks, 'Some Legal Aspects of the Financing of International Institutions', 28 TGS (1942) at pp. 93*ff.*; Singer, *Financing International Organizations: The UN Budget Process* (1961), especially pp. 30–121; Sands and Klein (eds.), note 4 pp. 567*ff*; Schermers and Blokker, *International Institution Law* (1995) pp. 678*ff.*; and Kolasa, loc. cit. note 6 at pp. 204*ff.* On the financing of organizations see also Hartwig, *Die Haftung der Mitgliedstaaten für Internationale Organisationen* (1993), chapter 13.

left to the internal law of organizations which generally has special sets of financial rules which have been enacted. The Financial Regulations and Financial Rules of the UN[11] establish the procedure for having the budget considered and approved by the GA. They also provide for the auditing of all budgetary expenditures and indicate the procedures to be followed by the competent organs of the UN for taking decisions involving expenditures. The Financial Regulations and Financial Rules of the UN are the model for similar instruments in other international organizations.

Generally, the budget estimates are prepared by the executive organ and then presented to the responsible organ. In the UN, for example, the SG is responsible for preparing the budget estimates. There are no general principles as such that apply to the preparation of the budget. Much depends on the law and practice of the organization concerned. As an example, the budget process of the UN may be examined.[12] In the UN the Financial Regulations provide that no organ 'shall take a decision involving expenditure unless it has before it a report from the SG on the administrative and financial implications of the proposal', and that, where the proposed expenditure cannot be made from existing funds, it shall not be incurred until the GA has made the necessary appropriation.[13] The budget estimates include the original estimates representing the costs of implementing decisions taken during the financial year to which the budget relates, revised budget estimates to cover new decisions, and supplementary estimates to cover 'unforseen or extraordinary expenses' arising after the budget has been voted. The estimates are reviewed successively by the Advisory Committee on Administrative and Budgetary Questions, the Fifth Committee of the GA and finally by the GA. It may appear that the Advisory Committee and the Fifth Committee duplicate each other's functions – the former has been called 'little more than a Fifth Committee in microcosm'.[14] However, the limited size of the former does enable it to spend more time on the budget problems than a plenary committee could do. A crucial question has always been how far the Advisory Committee and the Fifth Committee can, by reducing or eliminating an appropriation, interfere with or reverse a policy decision of another Main Committee or even the GA

[11] See UN Doc. 57/SGB Financial Rules/1/Rev. 2/1978.
[12] See Sands and Klein (eds.), note 4 pp. 567*ff*.
[13] See Financial Regulations 13.1 and 2.   [14] See Singer, note 10 p. 176.

itself; in principle they should have no such power, and in the last resort the GA would be free to overrule and reinstate any items so affected. Clearly, final approval of the budget is, under Article 17(1) of the Charter, a matter for the GA, acting by a two-thirds majority vote.

Within the specialized agencies and other organizations the preparation of the estimates is, similarly, a task entrusted to the administrative head of the organization. This is either expressly recognized or in practice the preparation of the initial proposals lies with the executive head. The actual approval or acceptance of the budget is generally a matter for the main plenary organ. In the UN Article 17(1) of the Charter vests the authority to consider and approve the budget in the GA. Where variation does occur is in the extent to which some organ of limited composition intervenes in the process. For example, whereas in the ILO and the FAO the Director-General submits directly to the plenary organ,[15] in the WHO[16] and the IMO[17] the executive head submits through the Executive Board and Council respectively.

Control over budgetary expenditure

The administration of the budget is in the hands of the executive branch of the organization, headed by the chief administrative officer, and is to a large extent governed by the financial regulations and rules (or their equivalent) of the organization, in the absence of constitutional provision. The control over budgetary expenditure is, however, generally entrusted to a special audit service which has an internal and external character.

Internal audit

In the UN the internal audit is carried out through a special audit service under the authority of the SG. Financial Regulation 10.2 requires that no obligation to spend funds may be incurred until appropriate authorization has been made in writing under the authority of the SG. The audit department, pursuant to Financial Regulation 10.1 and Financial Rule 11.12, reviews and makes comments and recommendations on the regularity of all transactions and the conformity of obligations and

[15] Article 13(2) and Article XVIII(1), respectively, of the ILO Constitution and the FAO Constitution.
[16] Article 55 of the WHO Constitution.   [17] Article 50 of the IMO Constitution.

expenditure with the appropriations and in general the economic use of the resources of the organization. In the IBRD, the IFC and other financial institutions it is generally an internal audit department that keeps a check on the regularity of expenditures.

External audit

In the UN the GA has established an external audit system to check whether funds appropriated in the budget have been spent in accordance with the provisions of the budget and of the Financial Regulations. The Board of Auditors consisting of three experts, each of them the Auditor-General or equivalent officer of a member state, has the primary responsibility, pursuant to Financial Regulation 12.01, for carrying out this function. The GA has set out in an Annex to the Financial Regulations the functions of, and principles governing the audit procedures to be followed by, this body.[18]

When the auditors have completed this task, the auditors are expected to make a report to the GA on the accounts which they have certified. The Annex to the Financial Regulations in paragraph 6(c) provides that the report should indicate, *inter alia*, expenditures not properly substantiated, cases of fraud and wasteful or improper expenditure, expenditure likely to commit the organization to further outlay on a large scale, expenditure in excess of appropriations and not in accordance with the intention of the GA and any defect in the general system governing financial control of receipts and disbursements or of supplies and equipment. The certified accounts and report of the SG, together with the report of the Board of Auditors, are transmitted by the Board to the GA which, as is to be implied from the UN Charter provisions, has the final responsibility in all financial matters. Thereafter, the normal procedure is for the GA to adopt a resolution, prepared by the Fifth Committee, by which it accepts the financial report and all accounts of the organization.[19] Most other international organizations have a basically similar external audit system.[20]

---

[18] See Kolasa, loc. cit. note 6 at p. 209, for these procedures.

[19] See United Nations, 1 *UN Repertory of Practice* pp. 526–7.

[20] Schermers and Blokker, note 10 pp. 697–701. In the IBRD and most other financial institutions the general practice is that a firm of independent accountants makes a report on the financial statements of the organization, based on their audits which are conducted in accordance with generally accepted auditing standards: see, e.g., the report of the auditors in *The World Bank Annual Report 1994* p. 194, *The World Bank Annual Report 2002* p. 37. See also *International Monetary Fund Annual Report 1996* p. 225,

The finding of resources

Funds to meet expenditures are raised by international organizations by a variety of methods: obligatory contributions of members, voluntary contributions, gifts, payments for services, taxes and, particularly in the case of the financial institutions, interest payments, income from investments and similar methods. Organizations, other than the financial institutions, depend principally on obligatory contributions made by members. The financial institutions are self-financing and do not require annual contributions from their members.[21]

Obligatory contributions

About 90 per cent of the total regular budget in most international organizations (with the exception of the financial institutions) is raised by obligatory annual contributions levied from member states. These contributions are determined on the basis generally of one of three principles: equal contributions, optional class of contributions and contributions based on a scale of assessment.

Only a few international organizations, among which are none of the more important organizations or the UN and its specialized agencies, have employed the principle of equal contributions. OPEC and the Central Commission for Navigation on the Rhine are two of them.

Two of the oldest open organizations, both now specialized agencies of the UN, use the technique of optional classes of contributions. They are the UPU and the ITU. The members of the ITU may choose their class of contributions for meeting the expenses of the organization.[22] The members of the UPU enter into agreements with the Swiss government on the class of contribution.[23] Only a few other organizations use this method of financing.

The scale of assessment principle is the most commonly used.[24] A certain percentage of the organization's expenditure is assessed to each member state on a scale. The competence to fix the scale of assessment

---

International Monetary Fund Annual Report 2002 p. 154, for reports by independent auditors.

[21] For early studies of the question of financing international organizations see Stoessinger, note 4; Singer, note 10. Raising funds for organisations by borrowing (loans) is a method that has been used: see Salmon, Le rôle des organisation internationales en matière de prêts et d'emprunts (1958).

[22] ITU Constitution, Article 16(4) and (5).

[23] 'Les Actes de l'UPU, révisés à Ottawa' (1957) p. xix.

[24] See Kolasa, loc. cit. note 6 at pp. 200ff.

is, as a rule, vested in the plenary organ. The UN Charter in Article 17(2) and UN Financial Regulation 5.1 expressly provide that the expenses of the organization shall be borne by the members 'according to the scale of assessments determined by the General Assembly'. The scale is periodically subject to review in order to take account of changes in the number of members and their relative prosperity. The GA has adopted a rule that 'the scale of assessments . . . shall not be subject to a general revision for at least three years unless it is clear that there have been substantial changes in relative capacity to pay'.[25] However, in practice the GA reviews annually the scale of assessments.[26]

In general, constitutions of international organizations do not deal with the criteria by which the contributions of members should be determined. The UN apportions its expenses among its members 'broadly according to capacity to pay'.[27] While the scale of assessments systems as applied by the UN took into account differences in size and economic power of individual member states, the problem remained how to measure the 'capacity to pay' of individual members.

The UN Committee on Contributions took the view that it would be difficult to measure capacity to pay merely by statistical means and that arriving at a definite formula would be impossible. However, it indicated that 'comparative estimates of national income would appear *prima facie* to be the fairest guide', but national income could not be the only criterion for capacity to pay. The other supplementary criteria were also relevant. Thus, in order to prevent anomalies in the assessments resulting from the use of comparative estimates of national income as the only criterion for capacity to pay, in 1946 the GA decided that three other factors should be also taken into account: (i) comparative income per head of population; (ii) temporary dislocation of national economies arising out of the Second World War; and (iii) ability of members to secure foreign currency.[28] In 1965 the GA decided to add one more factor to be taken into account, namely, in the case of developing countries, their special economic and financial difficulties.[29]

In 1981 the GA listed seven factors other than national and *per capita* income to be taken into account in measuring capacity to pay: particular consideration of least developed countries, economic disparities between

---

[25] GA Rules of Procedure, Rule 160.
[26] United Nations, *UN Repertory of Practice*, vol. I p. 537.
[27] GA Rs. 14A(I) and Rule 160 of the GA Rules of Procedure.
[28] United Nations, *UN Repertory of Practice*, vol. I p. 534.   [29] GA Rs. 2118 (XX).

developed and developing countries, conditions adversely affecting capacity to pay, heavy dependence on one or a few products, ability to secure foreign currency, accumulated national wealth and different methods of national accounting.[30]

The 'upper and lower limits on contributions' were introduced in 1972. Thus, as a matter of principle, the maximum contribution from any one member state to the ordinary expenses of the UN should not exceed 25 per cent of the total expenditure.[31] This provision was adopted in order to prevent the organization's becoming too dependent on one or a small group of its members. But, even so, a few states, namely the USA, Russia, Germany, the UK, France, Japan and China, pay a very high percentage of the total contributions.

At its third session the GA accepted the further principle that in normal times the *per capita* contribution of any member state should not exceed the *per capita* contribution of the member who bears the highest assessment (i.e., the USA).[32] In 1974 the *per capita* ceiling principle was abolished because it was found to be of doubtful value.[33]

In 1946 the GA determined that the minimum contribution was to be 0.04 per cent of the total contribution of all member states.[34] In 1972 this was lowered to 0.02 per cent to allow the adjustment necessary for the developing countries, in particular those with the lowest *per capita* incomes.[35] In 1980 the contribution of Saint Vincent, the smallest contributor, was set at 0.01 per cent.[36]

The assessment scale used by the UN is of particular importance because it is used as a model for many other international organizations. Several specialized agencies adopted financial regulations generally in line with those approved by the GA and apportioned their expenses according to the principles of the UN scale.[37] Some regional organizations, such as the OAS, the OAU and the EFTA, also follow the pattern introduced by the GA.[38]

---

[30] GA Rs. 36/231 A of 18 December 1981.   [31] GA Rs. 2961B(XXVII) of 13 December 1972.

[32] United Nations *UN Repertory of Practice*, vol. I pp. 536–7. For a discussion of this qualification and its limitations see Schermers and Blokker, note 10 pp. 610*ff*.; and 28 *UN Yearbook* (1974) pp. 910–11.

[33] GA Rs. 3228 (XXIX).

[34] GA Rs. 69(I). See also United Nations, *UN Repertory of Practice*, vol. I p. 537.

[35] GA Rs. 2961D (XXVII).   [36] 35 *UN Yearbook* (1981) p. 1,271.

[37] E.g., the ILO, the FAO, the UNESCO and the WHO. The IAEA also uses the same system.

[38] See Stoessinger, note. 4 pp. 217–46; Schermers and Blokker, note 10 pp. 612*ff*.

Limitations on apportionment

Where the obligation to contribute exists under the express or implied provisions of the constitution of an organization, any apportionment by the competent organ is binding. This emerges from the opinions of some judges in the *Expenses Case*,[39] although the Court regarded the issue as outside its terms of reference. Judge Morelli asserted that in the case before the Court characterization of the expenditures as 'expenses of the Organization' for the purposes of Article 17(2) meant that the GA was empowered to apportion those expenses among the member states.[40] Judge Spender maintained that once it was established that certain expenditures had the character of 'expenses of the Organization', any apportionment thereof made by the GA under Article 17(2) could not be legally challenged by any member state.[41] The views of these judges make sense and cannot be disputed, in principle. It is not only Article 17(2) of the UN Charter that gives an organ of the organization power to apportion expenses. There are many other constitutions that have similar provisions,[42] and in these cases the same principle would apply to apportionment as in the case of the UN. Clearly, what can be apportioned are the expenses of an organization, according to the definition accepted for such expenses.

There are some questions, however, that arise in this context. Does the principal deliberative organ or other organ entrusted with financial responsibilities have the power to apportion, even in the absence of explicit provision in the constituent instrument? Can the validity of an apportionment be questioned by a member state on the ground that it violates a fundamental principle of law (peremptory norm or *ius cogens*), such as non-discrimination or proportionality? Apart from apportionment, how much is a member state *liable* to contribute, as an obligation, to the expenses of an organization, i.e., for instance, is the liability of each member joint and several or is it shared or is there a different basis for liability?

There is a strong case for suggesting that even in the absence of provision for apportionment in the constitution of an organization, as in the case of the OAU Charter, for instance, the principal organ of the organization may apportion expenses with binding effect, which is what

---

[39] 1962 ICJ Reports p. 151.   [40] *Ibid.* at p. 219.   [41] *Ibid.* at p. 183.

[42] See, e.g., Article 13(c) of the ILO Constitution; Article XVIII(2) of the FAO Constitution; Article IX(2) of the UNESCO Constitution; Article 56 of the WHO Constitution; Article 38(b) of the COE Constitution; Article 20(2) of the OECD Constitution; and Article 53 of the OAS Charter.

happens in that organization. This would be an implied power of the organization *vis-à-vis* member states, because it is essential for the efficient performance of the organization's functions.

The second question is more difficult. Here the answer would depend on whether powers of organizations, particularly in the administrative field, are limited by certain general principles of law which may be regarded as fundamental and *ius cogens*, as in the case of powers exercised by organizations *vis-à-vis* their staff members. It is true that, for instance, the UN like many other organizations has evolved a system of apportionment that has become acceptable; that this is based on a variety of factors, including the capacity to pay, and has maximum and minimum limits and that this system is more or less equitable; but this does not mean that a system as applied to a particular member could not be questioned on the ground that it violates fundamental principles of law.

The third question needs an answer, if only to clarify the position of members, even though, in view of the acceptance of the systems of apportionment that have been implemented, it may be somewhat academic. The situation could arise, where some members default on their payments and are in arrears, perhaps but not only because they are too poor to pay. Does the organization have a claim for payment of its expenses from any other member who can pay? The answers to such questions are not readily forthcoming in the absence of jurisprudence and conclusive practice. In general in the case of arrears of some members[43] organizations have not made claims on other members necessarily or reapportioned. In some of these cases defaulting members have not clearly denied their obligation to pay, while in others they have. The practice would certainly indicate that, where apportionment has taken place, or is contemplated, organizations do not regard member states as jointly and severally liable, but liable only to the extent of the apportionment, whatever the position of some members on the obligation to pay or in the event of default by some members. In other circumstances the legal situation may depend on equitable considerations.[44] The answer is most probably that there is no joint and several liability. That there is no

---

[43] See, e.g., the arrears of the USA or the Soviet Union and France *vis-à-vis* the UN. The question here discussed is separate from whether states in arrears could be sanctioned under the constitution.

[44] The question raised here is different from and unconnected with the issue of liability of member states to third parties for the obligations of organizations which is discussed in Chapter 13.

joint and several liability is supported by the policy consideration that smaller and poorer states may be deterred from joining in the formation of many international organizations if they were fully liable to organizations for their expenses. The question of the proportion of liability is also possibly to be answered not on the basis of equal sharing but by the application of equitable considerations. It is arguable that there are some limitations on the liability to the organization of member states comparable to those which are applicable in the case of the relationship between shareholders and most national law corporations.[45]

Voluntary contributions and gifts

Many international organizations use a system of voluntary contributions and gifts. The UN also resorts to such a system. There are a number of programmes approved by the GA which have been funded in whole or in part by voluntary contributions from member states, non-member states and from other sources (e.g., the UNICEF, the UNHCR, the UNRWA, the UNIDO, the UNDP and UN peacekeeping operations). These voluntary contributions are not included in the regular budget of the UN. They have been designated as extra-budgetary funds. Special rules, organs and procedures were established for the raising and control of extra-budgetary funds.[46] The UNDP is perhaps the largest activity financed by voluntary contributions.

Self-financing

Many international organizations have some income of their own. There may be various sources of such self-support: income from services rendered to states, to individuals, to other organizations; income from investments and loans; royalties (in the case of the WIPO, for example); and income from staff assessment and levies or taxes.[47] In most international organizations the income from this kind of source is limited and plays a minor role in financing their activities. Only a few organizations have sources to satisfy all their financial needs. The financial institutions are the prime example of such organizations. They levy interest,

---

[45] There is little practice on this issue. In the ITC case the principle that there was no joint and several liability was endorsed, insofar as no one member was regarded as under an obligation fully to contribute to the debt of the ITC, but beyond that it would appear that it is not clear what obligation was accepted by the member states of ITC to contribute to its debt. The situation was further complicated by the settlement reached with creditors being based on an *ex gratia* payment: see Chapter 13.

[46] See United Nations, UN *Repertory of Practice*, vol. I pp. 527–9.

[47] See in general Singer, note 10 pp. 141–6.

commissions, service charges and handling charges. The ECSC was also made financially independent. Article 49 of the ECSC Treaty empowers the High Authority to procure the necessary funds by imposing levies on the production of coal and steel and by borrowing. The two other Communities did not follow this model. In 1970 it was, however, decided that the activities of the three Communities would be financed from their own sources of income, such as: (i) agricultural levies; (ii) customs duties; and (iii) a part of a maximum of 1 per cent of the value added tax. After a transitory period this new financial system definitively entered into force in 1979.

Expenses

There is a question as to what expenses could legitimately be regarded as expenses of an organization. The answer will determine, among other things, how much member states can legally be expected to be responsible for supplying to the organization.

The ICJ in its advisory opinion in the *Expenses Case*[48] was confronted with the interpretation of Article 17 of the UN Charter. The Court confined itself to deciding whether the particular expenditures relating to the peacekeeping operations of the UNEF and the ONUC were within the concept of 'expenses' for the purposes of Article 17(2) of the Charter. By nine votes to five it was held that these expenditures were such 'expenses'. The Court's opinion does not purport to give 'a more detailed definition of expenses'[49] (than was necessary for the purpose in hand) and, consequently, it did not consider the problem as fully as it might have done. Judge Fitzmaurice in a separate opinion, however, did go into considerable detail in considering this problem. There are also views expressed in some of the other separate opinions on this question. Separate opinions are of value insofar as they do not conflict with what the Court actually said or are reconcilable with the Court's view, particularly

---

[48] 1962 ICJ Reports p. 151. This case has been discussed extensively: see, e.g., C. F. Amerasinghe, 'The *United Nations Expenses Case* – A Contribution to the Law of International Organization', 4 IJIL (1964) p. 177; Gross, 'Expenses of the United Nations for Peace-Keeping Operations: The Advisory Opinion of the International Court of Justice', 17 *International Organization* (1963) p. 1; Jennings, 'International Court of Justice: Advisory Opinion of July 20, 1962: Certain Expenses of the United Nations', 11 ICLQ (1962) p. 1,169; Simmonds, 'The UN Assessments Advisory Opinion', 13 ICLQ (1964) p. 854; Verzijl, 'International Court of Justice: Certain Expenses of the United Nations', 10 NILR (1963) p. 1.

[49] 1962 ICJ Reports at p. 167.

as, in this case, the Court admitted that it was not giving a detailed definition of 'expenses'.

An analysis of the Court's judgment produces two kinds of propositions which may be broadly termed negative and positive. That is to say, propositions emerge which relate to what the term 'expenses' does not include or does not necessarily exclude, on the one hand, and propositions can be formulated as to what is actually included within the term, on the other. First, it may be useful to outline the various approaches taken in this case to the problem of expenses and the various views expressed.

The Court stated that the term 'expenses' in Article 17(2) could neither be limited to the normal administrative budget of the organization[50] nor excluded expenditures arising from operations undertaken for the maintenance of international peace and security.[51] It acknowledged that it did not purport to provide a more detailed definition but held that the expenditures incurred for the purpose of financing the activities of the UNEF and the ONUC under the relevant resolutions presented to it were 'expenses' for the purpose of Article 17(2). In doing so the Court did, however, offer certain general considerations:

It would be possible to begin with a general proposition to the effect that the 'expenses' of any organization are the amounts paid out to defray the costs of carrying out its purposes, in this case, the political, economic, social, humanitarian and other purposes of the United Nations ... Or, it might simply be said that the 'expenses' of an organization are those which are provided for in its budget.[52]

The Court offered a negative proposition when it agreed that for expenditures to be 'expenses' they must be tested by their relationship to the purposes of the UN, in the sense that if an expenditure were made for a purpose which is not one of the purposes of the UN it could not be considered an 'expense' of the organization.[53] Positively, the Court was not so specific. The Court did hold that provided the expenses were made in pursuance of an action which was within the scope of the functions of the organization, the fact that the action was initiated or carried out by an organ acting beyond the scope of its powers according to the Charter did not necessarily mean that the expenditure incurred was not an 'expense' of the organization:

If it is agreed that the action in question is within the scope of the functions of the Organization but it is alleged that it has been initiated or carried out in

---

[50] *Ibid.* at p. 159.   [51] *Ibid.* at p. 164.   [52] *Ibid.* at p. 158.   [53] *Ibid.* at p. 167.

a manner not in conformity with the division of functions among the several organs which the Charter prescribes, one moves to the internal plane, to the internal structure of the organization. If the action was taken by the wrong organ, it was irregular as a matter of that internal structure, but this would not necessarily mean that the expense incurred was not an expense of the Organization. Both national and international law contemplate cases in which the body corporate or politic may be bound, as to thirds parties, by an ultra vires act of an agent.[54]

Some authority for the principle was found in what the Court had already said in the *Effect of Awards Case*, namely that an award of the UNAT created an obligation of the organization which the GA had to honour.[55] In such a case an award redresses a breach of contract on the part of the organization, committed through the instrumentality of its agent, the SG, who has defaulted in the execution of the duties of the organization under a contract of service. It might be argued that such default by an organ in the exercise of functions assigned to it in accordance with the Charter is to be distinguished from the exercise by an organ of a function which some other organ should be exercising, which seems to have been the actual situation envisaged by the Court when it made the general statement of principle in the *Expenses Case*.

The absence of conformity with the provisions of the Charter relating to the division of functions among several organs alone was referred to and nothing was said about failure to conform to provisions relating to procedure such as voting or other kinds of excess of power. But more important is the fact that it was stated that such non-conformity with the Charter does not *necessarily* place the expenditures outside the pale of the expenses of the organization. Thus, it would seem that the Court contemplated certain circumstances in which non-conformity with provisions of the Charter would have the effect of disqualifying expenditures, while it was of the view that sometimes such non-conformity would not be an obstacle to expenditures qualifying as expenses. On the other hand, it cannot be asserted with certainty that the Court intended to lay down a principle that where there was conformity of a resolution with the purposes of the organization, and even though there was a violation of terms relating to the functions of an organ, expenditures incurred under such a resolution would *always* qualify as 'expenses of the organization' under Article 17(2). All that can be deduced from the Court's judgment is that expenditures incurred under such a resolution

---

[54] *Ibid.* at p. 168.   [55] 1954 ICJ Reports at p. 59.

may be 'expenses of the organization' for the purposes of Article 17(2) or would *probably* be such expenses. The limits of that principle were not discussed. It was established, on the other hand, that the particular expenditures incurred under the particular resolutions taken in connection with the UNEF and the ONUC – which were not only within the purposes of the Charter but in conformity with the various provisions of the Charter as well – were 'expenses of the organization' for the purposes of Article 17(2). As to the general principles involved and the general definition of such 'expenses', the Court did not give more than an indication of what the position might be.

Judge Spender took a somewhat different view. In his separate opinion he was categorical in stating the principle which governed the classification of expenditures made by the SG under resolutions made by the other organs of the UN. It was his view that whether such expenditures were to be classified as 'expenses of the organization' for the purposes of Article 17(2) depended only on whether the resolutions or the actions of the SG under which the expenditures were incurred were connected with the purposes of the organization. It was irrelevant whether the resolutions were taken in conformity with the other provisions of the Charter; and where the SG acted outside the scope of his authority, the expenditures would only be 'expenses of the organization' if he had acted within the scope of his apparent authority.[56] Judge Spender's view of the principles involved admitted of a special exception. Where the SG took action under a resolution which was in accord with the purposes of the organization, if he had acted outside the scope of his apparent authority, the resulting expenditure could not be regarded as an 'expense of the organization' for the purposes of Article 17(2). It was also said to be necessary that the GA should decide that the expenditures in question were 'expenses of the organization'.

Judge Morelli, in his separate opinion, propounded an equally broad test for determining the 'expenses of the organization' under Article 17(2). According to him any expenditure which was validly authorized by the GA under Article 17(1) as part of the budget was to be regarded as an 'expense of the organization' under Article 17(2), irrespective of the validity of the resolutions under which the expenses were incurred;[57] these expenses had to be actually authorized by the GA under Article 17(1), it being insufficient that they could possibly be so authorized by the GA,[58] and the circumstances in which an authorization

---

[56] 1962 ICJ Reports at p. 183.   [57] *Ibid.* at p. 224.   [58] *Ibid.* at p. 220.

would become invalid were extremely limited and that was when there was some essential defect.[59] Validity could only be defeated by an essential defect. The exact scope of 'essential defect' is not clearly stated. It will be recalled that the Court also left room for situations where the expenditure might not be covered by Article 17(2) both where the basic resolutions themselves were valid and where they were invalid according to the provisions of the Charter but within the purposes of the organization.

Judge Fitzmaurice recognized in his separate opinion that the opinion of the Court was *in fact* founded on the idea that Article 17(2) cannot be confined to administrative expenses, that at least those expenses incurred in the discharge of the essential functions of the UN such as its peacekeeping activities were covered by Article 17(2), that such activities as were undertaken by the GA in this field in connection with the UNEF and the ONUC operations were expressly provided for in the Charter and were in keeping with the conditions and limitations of the Charter and that, therefore, expenditures incurred under them were 'expenses of the organization' for the purposes of Article 17(2).[60] On the other hand, he thought that the Court's view that, even if the GA in carrying out its activities had not been acting in conformity with the division of functions established by the Charter, the resulting expenditures would still be 'expenses of the organization' for the purposes of Article 17(2), provided that they related to activities coming within the functions of the organization as a whole, should not be pressed too far.[61]

According to Judge Fitzmaurice, in order that an expenditure may be characterized as 'expenses of the organization' under Article 17(2), two conditions had generally to be satisfied. First, the expenditure must belong to the *genus* 'expense', that is to say, it must come within the class or category of expenditure normally regarded as having the basic nature of an 'expense' so called. Second, the expenditure must have been validly incurred, for a purpose which was itself valid and legitimate.

In explaining the first condition, Judge Fitzmaurice did not give a comprehensive definition but gave some examples of the considerations to be taken into account, in his view, in attributing expenditures to the *genus* 'expense'. One of the examples, at least, of limitations may seem to be questionable, even unacceptable. This is the limitation based on the obligatory functions of the UN, such as that relating to peacekeeping, as opposed to permissive functions of the organization. However,

---

[59] *Ibid.* at p. 223.   [60] *Ibid.* at p. 199.   [61] *Ibid.*

Judge Fitzmaurice gave a list of the types of expenditures which would fall within the *genus* 'expense': (i) all those expenditures, or categories of expenditures, which have normally formed part of the *regular* budget of the organization, so that a settled practice (*pratique constante*) of treating them as expenses of the organization has become established and is tacitly acquiesced in by all member states; (ii) insofar as not already covered by head (i): (a) administrative expenses; (b) expenditures arising in the course of, or out of, the performance by the organization of its functions under the Charter; and (c) any payments which the organization is legally responsible for making in relation to third parties or which it is otherwise, as an entity, under a legal obligation to make or is bound to make in order to meet its extraneous legal obligations.

The second requirement involved issues such as the powers of the authorizing organ, even if the object of the expenditures fell within the scope of the purposes of the organization, depending on the particular circumstances of the case and in regard to which no general solution was possible. But it meant that the resolutions authorizing the activities for which the expenditures were incurred had to be valid and in conformity with the Charter. The first requirement may be reconcilable with the Court's view of the law, insofar as the Court did leave room for expenditures incurred for the purposes of the organization not to be characterized as 'expenses of the organization'.

From the Court's opinion and the separate opinions an attempt may be made to deduce some principles, first as to the UN.

'Expenses' are not limited to expenditures under the 'administrative' budget of the UN

The Court pointed out that there was no such express limitation in Article 17(2) nor could such a limitation be implied by reference to Article 17(1) which referred to the approval of the budget by the GA. In view of this, such a qualification could only be read in, if it must necessarily be implied from the provisions of the Charter considered as a whole or from some particular provision thereof which made it unavoidable to do so in order to give effect to the Charter. The Court came to the conclusion that there was no room for such necessary implication for four reasons.[62] First, because in Article 17(3) the term 'administrative budget' is used in connection with the functions of the GA in regard to the specialized agencies, the distinction between the

---

[62] *Ibid.* at pp. 159–62.

administrative budget and the general budget of the UN was present to the framers of the Charter; hence, the absence of an explicit qualification in Article 17(1) or 17(2) means that such a qualification was not intended. Second, other parts of the Charter showed that a variety of expenses which were not administrative had to be included in the 'expenses of the Organization', e.g., Chapter IX and X and Article 98 which obligated the SG to perform functions entrusted to him by the other organs of the UN. Third, the GA did not in practice make such a distinction in its financial resolutions or in its budgeting; on the contrary, such operational matters as technical assistance had been included in the budgets. Fourth, it was consistent practice of the GA to include in the annual budgetary resolutions provisions relating to the maintenance of international peace and security; provision was also made for 'unforseen and extraordinary expenses' arising in that relation, and such measures had been adopted without dissent from 1947 to 1959 except in the years 1952, 1953 and 1954 when adverse votes were cast because UN Korean war decorations were included.

'Expenses' do not exclude expenditures resulting from operations for the maintenance of international peace and security
On this rule too the judges who gave separate opinions agreed with the Court. The argument that such expenditures were excluded was based on the premise that they fell exclusively to be dealt with by the SC and more especially through agreements negotiated in accordance with Article 43. The Court rejected this argument for the following reasons.[63] First, Article 18 included as decisions on important questions decisions on budgetary questions; these were decisions which had a binding effect and there was no indication that expenditures arising from the maintenance of international peace and security were excluded from the purview of the budget and from Article 17(2). Second, the responsibility of the SC for the maintenance of international peace and security was primary and not exclusive; although only the SC could require coercive action which was binding, the GA was also concerned with the maintenance of international peace and security. Third, the fact that the GA was not permitted to take any 'action' under Article 11(2) did not affect the position, as this referred only to 'enforcement action' under Chapter VII which was reserved for the SC; thus, expenses arising therefrom were not outside the purview of the GA. Fourth, it was not

---

[63] *Ibid.* at pp. 162–7.

imperative that measures for the maintenance of international peace and security should be financed through Article 43 and Article 43 alone, because the SC could act under some other article; for example, where the SC decided to police a 'situation' under Chapter VII it did not need to resort to Article 43.

Expenditures incurred pursuant to intra vires *acts of the organization which are in conformity with the Charter, whether they be decisions or recommendations of the SC or recommendations of the GA, are 'expenses of the organization'*
The Court and the judges giving separate opinions were agreed on this proposition.

Certain acts which are not in conformity with the Charter but are not ultra vires *would generate 'expenses of the organization'*
These acts were certain recommendations of the SC or GA which were within the scope of the functions of the organization and were in conformity with the Charter except that they did not conform to the provisions of the Charter relating to the division of functions among several organs and recommendations of the SC or the GA which were within the scope of the functions of the organization but were not in conformity with the provisions of the Charter in a non-essential particular (other than the division of functions between the organs). The principle emerges from the opinion of the Court and the opinions of Judges Morelli and Spender.

Expenditures incurred under acts that were ultra vires, *because they did not conform to the Charter in an essential particular or were not within the scope of the functions of the organization, are not 'expenses of the organization'*
This proposition is reconcilable with the opinion of the Court and the opinions of the Judges who gave Separate Opinions. According to Judge Spender such acts included acts done by the SG which were outside the scope of his apparent authority but not those which were within the scope of his apparent authority. Judge Spender's view is reasonable, though the Court did not deal with the issue.[64]

So much for what can be derived directly from the *Expenses Case* on the question of 'expenses of the organization'. Several problems which

---

[64] The Court merely said: 'Similarly, obligations of the Organization may be incurred by the Secretary-General, acting on the authority of the Security Council or of the General Assembly, and the General Assembly has no alternative but to honour these engagements' (*ibid.* at p. 169).

might arise in this field are not dealt with in the opinions in the case, which is to be explained perhaps by the limited nature of the question asked. One problem arises, for instance, in connection with tortious acts of servants or agents of the organization or for acts of servants which constitute a breach of contract. Clearly where the responsibility of the organization is to be engaged their tortious acts must be traced to the organization. This can be done where these acts rest directly or indirectly on the resolutions of either the SC or the GA or on the Charter itself in some other authorized way, their contract of service being important links in this relation. Hence, although the tortious acts themselves may not have been authorized by the Charter or by resolutions of the SC or GA or under the contracts of service, the liability of the organization and the characterization of the expenditures arising from such acts might rest on the notion of 'the scope of authority' of the agent or servant. In regard to breaches of contract the ICJ in the *Effect of Awards Case* dealt with the effect of an award of the UNAT for a breach of a contract of service. It was said that such an award created an obligation of the organization which the organization had to honour and that expenditures arising under such an award were within the compass of Article 17(2).[65] The Court in the *Expenses Case* cited this statement with approval.[66] An award of the UNAT establishes a breach of a contract of service attributable to the organization through the instrumentality of its agent, the SG or his delegate. The SG acts within the scope of his apparent authority in taking the decisions which lead to a breach of contract and this is the basis of the liability of the organization. It would not be difficult to apply the same notion by analogy to tortious acts of servants or agents. Judge Fitzmaurice does include this category of expenditure in his list of items covered by the *genus* 'expense' when he mentions 'any payments which the organization is legally responsible for making in relation to third parties; or which it is, otherwise, as an entity under a legal obligation to make; or is bound to make in order to meet its extraneous legal obligations'.[67] Like judicial or arbitral awards resulting from a tortious act or a breach of contract, settlements by the organization involving expenses could also be characterized as expenses of the organization in accordance with comparable principles.[68]

---

[65] 1954 ICJ Reports at p. 59.   [66] 1962 ICJ Reports at p. 169.   [67] *Ibid.* at p. 207.

[68] Judge Morelli thought that, in the case of all expenditures, in order to be an 'expense' they had to be included in the budget by the GA under Article 17(1) of the Charter: *ibid.* at p. 224. This is thought to be unnecessary.

It is not clear how far these principles applicable to the UN may be applied *mutatis mutandis* to the characterization of 'expenses' for organizations in general. The following propositions, transposed by analogy are, perhaps, true and in accord with the practice of organizations:

  (i)   Administrative expenses (those in the regular budget) are not the only expenditures for which an organization is responsible.
 (ii)   Expenses of an organization include expenditures resulting from the functional operations of an organization authorized by its constitution.
(iii)   Expenses incurred in accordance with resolutions of organs of an organization which are made in conformity with its constitution and are, therefore, not *ultra vires* are expenses of the organization.
 (iv)   Expenditures incurred pursuant to resolutions of organs which are within the scope of functions of an organization but are not in conformity with its constitution in a 'non-essential' particular are expenses of the organization.
  (v)   Expenditures incurred pursuant to resolutions of organs which are not within the scope of functions of an organization or are within the scope of functions of an organization but do not conform to the provisions of its constitution in an essential particular and are, therefore, *ultra vires* are not expenses of the organization.
 (vi)   Expenditures incurred by the executive organ of an organization pursuant to decisions of other organs, which are not *ultra vires*, or incurred directly pursuant to provisions of the constitution are not expenses of the organization if the act of the executive organ is outside the 'scope of its apparent authority', while they are such expenses if the act is within the 'scope of its apparent authority'.[69]
(vii)   The same principles apply to organizations in general as reflected above in regard to tortious acts of servants and agents, breaches of contract, judicial and arbitral awards and extrajudicial settlements. It may be concluded that all expenses incurred as a result of the responsibility of an organization are expenses of the organization.[70]

[69] This is a basic general principle which was adverted to by Judge Spender in the *Expenses Case* (1962 ICJ Reports at p. 183). It was not relevant in the context of the issues in that case. but it is applicable generally. For example, where the executive acts pursuant to a decision of a deliberative organ authorizing it to enter into a capital contract for construction of a building and in fact incurs expenditures in excess of the limits authorized, the expenditures would be expenses of the organization if the executive was acting within the scope of its apparent authority but not otherwise. Such a situation arose in connection with a building contract entered into by the World Bank. The World Bank did not dispute its obligation to pay the excess, presumably because of the 'apparent authority' of the executive. Apparent authority depends on the reasonable impression made on the third party.
[70] See discussion in Chapter 12 on responsibility.

THE OBLIGATION TO PAY   375

The proposition that is not so easily applicable to organizations in general relates to acts which do not conform to the provisions of the constitution relating to the division of functions among several organs. Under many constitutions this proposition would not be applicable because such acts would be *ultra vires* and would not generate expenses of the organization. However, it may be suggested that the proposition applies as a presumption where there is no contrary provision (express or implied) in the constitution. It must also be remembered that in many organizations the relationship between deliberative organs is hierarchical and not based on a sharing of concurrent powers or on co-existent jurisdictions, as in the UN, so that importance attaches to the scope of delegation.

The obligation to pay

Since the UNEF and the ONUC operations and the ensuing *Expenses Case*, there has been some controversy as to whether member states are under an unqualified obligation to pay what they have been assessed or whether there are circumstances in which a member state can legally withhold its contribution. The controversy has affected the funding of not only the UN but also other organizations, such as the UNESCO and the ILO. The Soviet Union and France particularly refused to pay their share of the expenses for the UNEF and the ONUC because they considered them to have been incurred under *ultra vires* decisions. They continued to refuse to pay even after the opinion in the *Expenses Case*[71] which was endorsed by the GA (but later agreed to pay). The USA which had supported the position that there was an obligation to pay has subsequently withheld funds unilaterally from the UN because it did not agree with certain expenditures of funds.[72] Writers generally favour the view that there is no right to withhold payment for any

---

[71] While the Court did not address the issue of the obligation to pay, Judges Fitzmaurice and Morelli in separate opinions, and Judge Spiropoulos in a declaration thought that all member states were under no obligation to contribute financially to the ONUC and the UNEF: 1962 ICJ Reports at pp. 199*ff.*, p. 224 and p. 180, respectively.

[72] The USA threatened to withhold funds in connection with the treatment of the PLO in the WHO: see Kirgis, 'Admission of Palestine as a Member of a Specialized Agency and Withholding the Payment of Assessments in Response', 84 AJIL (1990) p. 218, who thinks it would have been illegal. The USA withheld funds from the financing of the Law of the Sea Preparatory Commission: see Note, 'United Nations Financing of the Law of the Sea Preparatory Commission: May the United States Withhold Payment?', 6 Fordham ILJ (1982–3) p. 472.

reason,[73] let alone disagreement as a minority with decisions of the UN, though the opposite view has been expressed.[74] The better view is that decisions by the GA making assessments are in principle binding and create legal obligations, even though there may be a significant minority consisting of the larger contributors which disagrees with decisions to incur expenditures. There is no legal rationale for not basically recognizing this principle. Article 17 of the Charter gives the GA the power to make binding dispositions both as regards the budget (expenditures and income) and assessments. In practical terms, the absence of an obligation to pay would impede the organization in the performance of its functions and the achievement of its purposes.

Judge Fitzmaurice discussed the matter in general in his separate opinion in the *Expenses Case*[75] and qualified the general obligation to contribute which he conceded did exist. While beginning with the proposition that irrespective of Article 17(2) there was an obligation upon member states collectively to finance the organization, at least to the extent necessary to make the organization workable, he made a number of distinctions. The problems created were because of the differing legal effect of resolutions and the possible existence of a difference between essential and non-essential activities. As regards *decisions* of the SC, these were binding on all member states, no problem arose in connection with them and all member states were bound to bear expenses incurred under them, whether they agreed with the decisions or not and whether they were members of the SC or not. *Recommendations* of the SC or GA, however, were not binding *per se* and might cause problems. It could be argued that in certain circumstances a distinction should be made between those who voted in favour of such resolutions or abstained and those who voted against them, because the latter showed disapproval of the resolutions being carried out so that there could be some doubt sometimes about their obligation to contribute.[76] There were four categories of recommendations: (i) those made in the area of the essential activities of the UN, such as peacekeeping activities; (ii) those which prescribed action solely in the way of making a payment or financial contribution (e.g., for some purpose of aid or relief); (iii) those made in the area of more or less permissive or non-essential activities of the

[73] See particularly, Alvarez, loc. cit, note 7; Galey, loc. cit. note 1; Nelson, loc. cit. note 7.
[74] See Zoller, loc. cit. note 7, who is of the view that withholding of payments is justified, when in the view of the member it is compelled to do so to defend itself against the 'corporate will' or tyranny of the majority.
[75] 1962 ICJ Reports at pp. 210*ff.*   [76] *Ibid.* at pp. 213*ff.*

organization, such as its social or economic activities; and (iv) those made pursuant to permissive activities which were closely connected with essential activities. In the case of (i) and (iv) there was a duty to contribute, irrespective of how votes were cast. In the case of (ii) there was no obligation to contribute if a negative vote had been cast by the member state, because the making of the payment or contribution was not merely a means to an end but the end itself and it became apparent that, if even member states who voted against the recommendation were under an obligation to contribute, the recommendation itself would acquire a wholly obligatory character; and in any case the practice of the UN was to seek voluntary contributions in such a case. In the case of (iii) there was probably no obligation to contribute, if a negative vote had been cast, because there was no question of preventing or impeding the essential activities of the organization, in the event that dissenting member states did not contribute, and in practice, expenditures under such resolutions were financed by voluntary contributions.[77] However, Judge Fitzmaurice did point out that the line between essential and non-essential activities was not always easy to draw.

While the distinctions made by Judge Fitzmaurice relate to expenses incurred under non-binding resolutions, they are difficult to accept *in toto*. First, there is good reason to suppose that, where an expenditure is an expense of an organization, there is a strong presumption that all members must contribute to its defrayal. Second, the third class of expenditures which was singled out for different treatment is not materially or significantly different from those to which member states are under an obligation to contribute, because both kinds of expenditures flow from resolutions that theoretically have the same legal effect, even if the practice of the UN has been to finance the third class of expenditures by voluntary contributions. Third, the basis of the distinction made between that class of expenditures and other expenditures is rather tenuous, as Judge Fitzmaurice himself admits. On the other hand, one class of expenditures identified (the second) seems to be a different kind of expenditure for the reason given that, if member states were under an obligation to contribute, the legal effect of the resolution would be greater than it *de iure* had. But the incidence of an obligation to contribute will depend not only on the absence of opposition by the member state concerned to the resolution but, in the event a member state does oppose the resolution, on other considerations as well

[77] *Ibid.*

connected with the obligations of member states flowing from such resolutions as a result of their legal effect.[78]

Further, it must be recognized that the obligation to contribute will certainly arise not only in the case of decisions of the SC but also in the case of any resolution taken by the organization which legitimately has binding effect.

The better view as qualified by some of what Judge Fitzmaurice had to say may be clear. It is significant that the sanction provided in Article 19 of the Charter, whereby the delinquent member loses its vote in the GA if it is two years in arrears, has, indeed, though perhaps reluctantly, been applied. The USA was not in favour of its application in the case of the Soviet Union and France. The USA itself has been careful not to be two years in arrears. To argue from the reluctance on the part of members to apply Article 19 that there is a legal right to withhold payment subject, no doubt, to the power of the other members of the organization to apply the Article 19 sanction is illogical and unwarranted. The fact that there is a sanction which has, moreover, been applied is more consistent with the absence of a *right* to withhold payment rather than with a liberty to do so, even though there may be some restraint on the part of the organization in applying the sanction. The care with which the USA avoids being more than two years in arrears also may indicate that it is aware that the sanction could be applied as for a breach of obligation.

The issue has been prominent in connection with the UN. But the principle that generally there is an obligation to pay assessed contributions is applicable to other organizations as well, where the organization has the power constitutionally to make binding assessments. The practice in these organizations, particularly the attitude of members and of the organizations themselves, seems to point in this direction.

Where organizations are not self-financing, there may be other means than the obligatory contributions of member states of financing the expenses of organizations, such as voluntary contributions and self-supporting income. While such methods of financing may ease the burden of member states, they should not *de iure* affect the obligation of members to contribute, which still exists, although *de facto* this obligation may be reduced proportionately or fully in respect of an expense. Further a distinction made between 'ordinary' and

---

[78] See Chapter 6.

'extraordinary' expenses, as the ITU has sometimes made,[79] does not affect this obligation.[80]

Particularly where an organization is self-financing, there may be limitations imposed in the constituent instrument on the obligation to contribute. In the case of financial institutions, such as the IBRD, the IFC and the ADB, their constituent instruments generally limit the amount of the contributions members must make to the organization in any circumstances. Because these organizations generate their own income, they normally have sufficient funds to meet their expenses from their income. However, their constituent instruments generally have provisions such as are included in the Articles of Agreement of the IBRD which state that: (i) liability of members is limited to the unpaid portion of the issue price of shares;[81] and (ii) if the operations of the organization were terminated, members would be liable for uncalled subscriptions to capital stock and in respect of the depreciation of their own currencies until the claims of all creditors were discharged.[82] In these cases the obligation to contribute which is clear is limited in explicit terms.

The obligation to approve the budget

A question of some importance is what are the powers of the organ concerned in relation to the approval of the budget or expenses. This is different from what was the subject of the *Expenses Case*, namely whether an expense can be characterized as an expense of the organization and, the related question, to what expenses members must contribute.

Where in an organization there is a superior plenary organ which approves the budget and other organs have functions which are

---

[79] The ITU characterized as 'extraordinary expenses' those pertaining to plenipotentiary conferences, administrative conferences, meetings of the International Consultative Committee and special tasks entrusted to the Bureau.

[80] The constitutions of some organizations expressly provide that part of their budgets should be financed by voluntary contributions. For example, Article 25(3) of the ICM Constitution states that the 'operational' budget shall be met by such contributions, as does Article 13(2) of the UNIDO Constitution. Where such provision is made, members are under no obligation to contribute to the defrayal of these expenses as such. Those expenditures must be met entirely by voluntary contributions. This is the clear implication of such provisions, even if voluntary contributions are insufficient to meet such expenditures.

[81] Articles of Agreement, Article II(6).

[82] Articles of Agreement, Article IV(5). The constitutions of the financial institutions in general have similar provisions.

delegated or are supervised, budget approval does not create problems. The hierarchical structure obviates jurisdictional conflicts that cannot be resolved in legal terms. The plenary organ would control the operations and policies of the organization and could determine both what the organization should be doing and how much and how funds should be allocated for such activity. The question whether the plenary organ has an obligation to approve the budget or a discretion to do so becomes moot. In this situation, as in all situations, the plenary organ has in any event an obligation to approve, and no discretion to disapprove, expenditures on obligations already validly entered into by the organization through any of its organs or obligations incumbent upon it. This emerges from the *Effect of Awards Case*,[83] where the ICJ held that the GA had no option but to honour obligations of compensation awarded by the UNAT for injurious acts of the organization *vis-à-vis* staff members.

This is the regime that prevails in and applies to most international organizations. For example, in the financial institutions, such as the IBRD and the IFC, the Boards of Governors have overall control over the operations, including expenditures of the organization, even though a lesser organ (e.g., the Executive Directors) may be delegated the power to approve the budget. Ultimately it is the Board of Governors that controls what is spent and what is done by the organization. Thus, there can be no jurisdictional conflict arising from differences of opinion over programmes and the funds required for them.

In an organization such as the UN,[84] there are several principal organs which have authority to determine their own work programmes, e.g., the GA, the ECOSOC, the TC and even the Secretariat. Their relationship in respect of functions is not always hierarchical and vertical, unlike the relationship among organs in the financial institutions or most of the specialized agencies of the UN. However, Article 17(1) of the UN Charter provides that 'the General Assembly shall consider and approve the budget of the Organization'. Thus, while certain organs may have the power to determine their policies and programmes, it is the GA that holds the purse strings. The question is whether the power to approve the budget, particularly for the other principal organs, which is vested in the GA is discretionary and ministerial.[85]

---

[83] 1954 ICJ Reports p. 47.   [84] The EU may be another special case.

[85] The GA's powers and duties in this regard have been considered by Meron, 'Budget Approval by the General Assembly of the United Nations: Duty or Discretion?', 42 BYIL (1967) p. 91. See also Meron, 'Administrative and Budgetary Co-ordination by the

The language of Article 17(1) seems to indicate that the GA has a *discretion* to approve the budget. The *travaux préparatoires* of the Charter suggest that it was not intended to limit the discretion of the GA which was the principal organ with sole authority to consider and approve the budget.[86] But principles of construction of the constitutional texts of international organizations (particularly the principle of effectiveness) may conceivably point to a different answer and have been invoked. It has been said that the position taken in the *travaux préparatoires* would have a limiting effect:

> Such an interpretation would...impair the ability of the Organization to fulfil its functions and achieve its purposes as defined in the Charter. The Charter established several principal organs and gave each of them certain functions. When these organs, acting within their authority under the Charter, adopt decisions which require financial appropriations and which the General Assembly in the circumstances of the case cannot review, the General Assembly has a legal duty to provide the necessary financing, for it is under a legal duty to make the functioning of the various principal organs possible and may not hamper it. It has to honour the Organizations's *ex contractu, ex delicto* and other obligations incurred through the activities of the principal organs acting within the limits of their authority under the Charter... The General Assembly has the power not to approve the necessary appropriations but it has not the legal right to do so, and the responsibility of the Organization may be engaged as a result of such a refusal, whether in public or in private law (leaving aside any question of jurisdiction).[87]

While it is clear that obligations (*ex contractu, ex delicto* and otherwise) have to be honoured by the GA, it is not so clear that it does not have a legal right not to approve the appropriations necessary for the functioning of the organization, particularly of other principal organs. It is arguable that the GA has a duty to consider in good faith, bearing in mind particularly the need to fulfil the functions and purposes of the organization, the requests for finances of other organs; but beyond that it is difficult to assert that the GA has 'no legal right not to approve' appropriations which in its judgment, exercised in good faith, and after

---

General Assembly', in Mangone (ed.), *UN Administration of Economic and Social Programmes* (1966) p. 37.

[86] See particularly 8 UNCIO pp. 266, 418 and 534*ff.*; 17 UNCIO pp. 40, 322, 476 and 486; 18 UNCIO p. 391. The USA in the hearing in the *Effect of Awards Case* supported this view: *Effect of Awards Case, ICJ Pleadings* (1954) at p. 138.

[87] Meron, loc. cit. note 85 (BYIL) at pp. 120–1. The writer examines among other things, the Rules of Procedure of the GA and the Financial Regulations of the UN.

taking into account the need to fulfil the functions and purposes of the organization, it considers unnecessary or excessive.[88]

In September 1966 the SG requested approval of a supplementary estimate for the ICJ for 1965 of $72,500 in which was included $29,000 in connection with the *South West Africa Cases* heard and decided earlier in 1966. These expenditures had already been incurred. The Fifth Committee of the GA rejected, by a vote of 40 to 27 with 13 abstentions, the request for the additional appropriation. Though the SG was left to find the funds for these expenditures by budgetary transfers, the case shows that the GA does exercise a discretion, even where expenditures have already been incurred. The manner in which the discretion was exercised may be criticized in the circumstances, considering that it was the activity of the ICJ, another principal organ and the principal judicial organ of the UN, that was in issue. However, it is difficult for this reason to conclude that the GA does not have, in principle, the final discretion in approving the budget.

It is fortunate that the funding for the ICJ was found, because the ICJ is a judicial organ. As pointed out in Chapter 8, there is a fundamental general principle of law which may not be ignored or contravened, let alone be changed, namely that the independence of judicial organs must at all costs be respected and preserved. This principle has implications for financing the Court's work and continued functioning. In principle whatever funding is required by the Court or any judicial organ, for that matter, for functions it performs in the execution of its terms of reference as a judicial organ must be made available to it, as a matter of course, regardless of the manner in which this needs to be done. That the GA, for example, is the authority with power to approve the finances of the ICJ and provide it with funds does not give it power to oversee or control the Court's activities. If the GA assumes this power, it would be interfering with the independence of the judicial organ. It is independence that is in issue. If the ICJ, for instance, must satisfy the GA, an outside authority composed, moreover, of states which are potential parties to litigation before the Court, that its activities are worthy of being financially supported, surely its independence could be compromised. Thus, the approval of the financial requirements of the ICJ and, indeed, of any judicial organ created by the UN, e.g., the UNAT

---

[88] Among others, the Australian government took this view in its written statement to the ICJ in the *Expenses Case*: *Expenses Case, ICJ Pleadings* (1962) at p. 231. There were governments that took the opposite view in the same case: see, e.g., the Norwegian government statement, *ibid.* at pp. 367–8.

and the ICTY and ICTR, is for all practical purposes, obligatory, whether they are included in the original budget or come up for approval later, *via* supplementary budget requests.

The only possible circumstance in which a judicial organ's budget or financial requirements may not properly be approved by the responsible authority is where the judicial organ is abusing its functional authority or the funds are being misused or are intended for a purpose outside the terms of reference of the organ. The presumption, however, is that judicial organs are acting within their terms of reference. This is, moreover, a strong one. The presumption must be convincingly rebutted, if financial requests are to be denied.

In the case of the GA and the ICJ discussed above, the GA, it must be conceded, acted in such a way as to place upon the SG the obligation of finding the required funds by transfers from the funds allocated to the administrative budget of the UN as a whole. It did not in the course of the action it took characterize officially the work of the ICJ which was in issue as unnecessary or outside the terms of reference of the ICJ. Be that as it may, the fundamental principle of respect for the independence of judicial organs, as conceptually developed, requires that, first, the legitimate financial needs of judicial organs be met, second, prima facie what a judicial organ claims are its financial needs, both prospectively and retrospectively, be regarded as being its legitimate financial needs, and, third, the presumption of legitimacy be convincingly rebutted, if funds are in any manner to be refused.

The consequence of conceding that the GA has no legal duty to approve the budget but has a discretion to do so, subject to certain limitations, not only of good faith but of obligation to approve expenditures of a certain kind, is that the GA inevitably has a certain control over the functioning of the organization as a whole, even though there may be principal organs affected. But this seems to be in the nature of the organizational structure under the Charter and consistent with the attribution of financial control and responsibility to one plenary organ. It is clear also that the limitation of good faith also requires the GA not to obstruct the smooth functioning of the other principal organs or the achievement of the objectives and purposes of the organization by the arbitrary and irresponsible exercise of discretion in its exclusive area of financial control.

12 Responsibility to and of international organizations

A question of great importance for the law of international organizations relates to the responsibility *of* organizations and responsibility *to* organizations, *vis-à-vis* states and other international persons in particular. Where organizations have international personality, it may be asked whether they are responsible internationally for violations of the law, on what basis they are responsible and how this responsibility is enforced. The same questions may be posed in respect of international responsibility to organizations. In this chapter the issues surrounding the substantive law of responsibility will be discussed. Something must also be said first about the law that governs transactions to which international organizations are party, whether actively or passively.[1] However, only an outline of the issues and their resolution can be given here. The question of enforcement (settlement of disputes) is reserved for Chapter 16, where issues relating to the procedure for bringing claims will also be addressed.

There is not much international judicial precedent on the international responsibility of or to international organizations, though the practice that has been followed since the creation of the League of Nations and particularly after the Second World War has rested on certain assumptions. The principal, if not the only, international judicial case relating to the subject is the *Reparation Case*,[2] brought before

---

[1] A brief discussion will be included of the question of liability of and to organizations in national (and perhaps, transnational) law. Capacity in national law, which has been considered in Chapter 3, is not the only factor. What law is to be applied to transactions on the national (or transnational) level to which international organizations are party (actively or passively) is a question that arises.

[2] 1949 ICJ Reports p. 174.

384

the ICJ. The matter has also been discussed by text writers, but not extensively.[3]

It may be relevant to distinguish at the outset the issue of the international responsibility of organizations from the responsibility of organizations to their staff under their internal law. The latter is a species of responsibility under international law but does not involve the relations of organizations with states as such or between organizations. This subject has been dealt with elsewhere in this treatise.[4]

The concept of international responsibility has been the subject of a variety of interpretations.[5] For the present purpose, however, the

---

[3] The initial work on the subject is Eagleton, 'International Organization and the Law of Responsibility', 76 *Hague Recueil* (1950-I) p. 319, which appeared not long after the establishment of the UN and the decision in the *Reparation Case*. There were a few earlier writings, e.g., Q. Wright, 'Responsibility for Injuries to United Nations Officials', 43 AJIL (1949) p. 95, but none attempted a systematic exposé. There followed several other works which dealt with the subject mostly indirectly: see, e.g., Eustathiades, 'Les Sujets du droit international et la responsabilité internationale', 84 *Hague Recueil* (1953-III) p. 397; Parry, 'Some Considerations upon the Protection of Individuals in International Law', 90 *Hague Recueil* (1956-II) at pp. 714*ff*.; García Amador, 'State Responsibility: Some New Problems', 94 *Hague Recueil* (1958-II) at pp. 409*ff*.; P. de Visscher, 'La Protection diplomatique des personnes morales', 102 *Hague Recueil* (1961-I) at pp. 480*ff*.; Pescatore, 'Les Relations extérieures des Communautés Européenes', 103 *Hague Recueil* (1961-III) p. 1; El-Erian, 'Second Report on Relations between States and Inter-Governmental Organizations', 2 YBILC (1967) at pp. 218*ff*.; Ginther, *Die völkerrechtliche Verantwortlichkeit intenationaler Organisationen gegenüber Drittstaaten* (1969); Schermers and Blokker, *International Institutional Law* (1995) pp. 1,166*ff*.; and Sands and Klein (eds.), *Bowett's Law of International Institutions* (2001) pp. 456*ff*. See also Gonzalez, 'Les organisations internationales et le droit de la responsabilité', 92 RGDIP (1988) p. 63; and Krylov, 'International Organizations and New Aspects of International Responsibility', in Butler (ed.), *Perestroika and International Law* (1990) p. 221. Now see also Wellens, *Remedies against International Organizations* (2003).

[4] See Chapter 9. However, there is a sense in which the responsibility of an organization to a staff member may result in international responsibility to a state. This problem will be adverted to later in the appropriate place.

[5] A definition of responsibility has not been really broached or attempted, for example, in the Reports of Ago to the ILC, 2 YBILC (1969 to 1976) or in the earlier reports by García Amador, 2 YBILC (1956 to 1961) or in the later reports by Riphagen, 2 YBILC (1980 to 1986) and Arangio Ruiz, 2 YBILC (1989 onwards). Nor has a clear definition been given elsewhere. An approach is suggested which emphasizes international consequences in terms of the incidence of secondary remedial obligation. At this stage of the development of international law it may be useful to discuss and settle on an appropriate meaning for 'responsibility' in order to avoid obfuscation in the explanation of the law governing responsibility, whether it be of the state or international organizations. In the law of state responsibility a distinction between the concept of 'liability' and that of 'responsibility' has been made in more than one sense. This distinction was first made in a particular sense in the *Janes Claim* (USA v. *Mexico*) ((1926) 4 UNRIAA p. 82, particularly at p. 87), where it was said that a state is 'liable' to

important principles are that: (i) international organizations as legal persons are subjects of and subject to international law; and (ii) the breach of international law by an international person, whether by commission or omission, produces responsibility. Thus, international responsibility of or to international organizations depends on the violation of international law and the non-observance of international obligations.

It is necessary in this connection briefly to consider the question of the liability of organizations and to organizations in national (and perhaps, transnational) law. Capacity in national law is not the only factor – and this has been considered in Chapter 3. What law is to be applied to transactions at the national (or transnational) level to which international organizations are party (actively or passively) is a question that arises.

Law governing relations between international organizations and other parties

The law governing the relations between international organizations and states, whether as members or not, is generally international

punish a culprit in a murder, though at that point it was not 'responsible' internationally for the wrong done, but became responsible only if it failed to punish the culprit appropriately through its judicial system, for a non-performance of its judicial duty or a denial of justice (see also the *Putnam Claim* (1927) (*USA* v. *Mexico*), 4 UNRIAA at p. 151; *Kennedy's Claim* (1927) (*USA* v. *Mexico*) 4 UNRIAA at p. 94; and the discussion in C. F. Amerasinghe, *State Responsibility for Injuries to Aliens* (1967) pp. 51*ff.* and works there cited). It has also been suggested (see the discussion in C. F. Amerasinghe, *Local Remedies in International Law* (2003), chapter 4) that it may be possible to distinguish in a different sense between 'liability' and 'responsibility', where the rule of exhaustion of local remedies is applicable. The point is that while a state may be 'responsible' for a violation of international law and of its international obligations *vis-à-vis* another state in respect of the latter's nationals at the time of the injury it does not become 'liable' to make amends or litigate internationally in respect of that injury to the foreign state until local remedies have properly been exhausted. This distinction was made in the context of the denial of justice and the exhaustion of local remedies in the law of diplomatic protection. Obscurity that has arisen in connection with the use of the term 'responsibility' has been compounded by the distinctions made between liability and responsibility, without proper definition, in other areas of the law. Thus, in environmental law which is connected with the law of state responsibility, a different distinction has been made by certain authors between responsibility and liability based apparently on whether the substantive international obligation is strict or not. Similarly, there is a difference in the use of terms in the law relating to hazardous activities. There may be other areas in which the terms are used with different meanings. What is important in any context is that it be made clear in what sense terms are being used. Uniformity is not an end in itself but consistency is a virtue that cannot be overemphasized and, if possible, avoidance of variance in the same context is desirable in order that clarity may be achieved. On state responsibility now see the ILC's draft articles and commentary thereto: Crawford, *The International Law Commission's Articles on State Responsibility* (2002) pp. 61*ff.*

law. Thus, while in their relations with organizations as members the constituent instrument would basically be applicable as an international treaty, governed by international law, there may be relationships between states and organizations which involve separate agreements governed by international law, such as headquarters agreements and peacekeeping agreements.[6] However, there may also be direct relations between states and international organizations which are governed by a national law or national laws or by transnational law as the proper law. Thus the supply of gas or electricity by the state to an international organization will generally be governed by the national law of the state.[7] Tortious liability of states to international organizations may in the appropriate circumstances, as where armed forces or police damage the property of an organization, be governed by international law, and the converse situation of tortious responsibility of an organization to a state may also be governed by international law, as where an official of an organization in the performance of his functions damages state property. The ownership of immovable property and the rights and duties flowing therefrom are generally governed by national law of the state where the property is located (*lex situs*). Thus, the UN, the IMF and the IBRD, for example, have registered the ownership of the buildings they own in the USA in the appropriate registry. It is understood that the consequences of ownership in terms of rights *in rem* derive from the national law concerned, namely, the *lex situs*.[8]

---

[6] There may be situations where conventions to which international organizations are not party are law-creating (as international law) for international organizations, such as where the UN decided that it would apply the Geneva Convention of 1949 to govern its armed action in Korea and the UNEF operation, where the regulations governing the UNEF adopted several international conventions applicable to the conduct of military personnel (see UN Doc. ST/SGB/UNEF/1, section 44). The loan and credit agreements of the IBRD and the IDA respectively are governed by international law. This has been so for some time and is now made clear in a negative manner in section 10.01 of the General Conditions Applicable to Loan and Guarantee Agreements (1985) and in section 10.01 of the General Conditions Applicable to Development Credit Agreements (1985), if there was any doubt about the matter: see also Broches, 'International Legal Aspects of the Operations of the World Bank', 98 *Hague Recueil* (1959–III) at pp. 339*ff.*

[7] The principle *locus regit actum* may often be called in aid but this is not the only reason for the application of a national law. There are cases also where the agreement specifies that national law or a particular law should govern: see, e.g., the loan agreement of March–April 1957 between Switzerland and the ILO; and the agreement between FAO and Egypt of 17 August 1952. At one time the governing law of IBRD loan agreements was New York law.

[8] Specific references may sometimes be made to the local law: see the agreements made in 1960 among the WHO, the Swiss Confederation and the Republic and Canton of Geneva, whereby the WHO acquired a right *in rem* for the user of land for an indefinite

International organizations, however, also have diverse relations with entities other than states, such as natural persons and corporations. These relations are governed by national law or transnational law. Thus, there are many kinds of contracts which international organizations enter into, such as construction and maintenance contracts, contracts for the purchase of goods, contracts of service, insurance contracts, letters of credit and bond transactions, which are generally governed by some national law or laws.[9] The contracts of the IFC stipulated that New York law governed them, while those of the EIB referred to the local law of the borrower. The question of the governing law of contracts is a matter for the conflict of laws which tries to identify the proper law of the contract. Generally the intention of the parties, if expressed, is recognized, while in the absence of such express intention, an effort must be made to identify the implied intention of the parties (or the proper law) by examining all the circumstances of the case. As in the case of the national conflict of laws, different parts of a contract may be governed by different laws. It is also possible for the parties to choose transnational law as the governing law, that is, principles of international law or general principles of law or a mixture of both.[10] There is, in short, a wide latitude in the express choice of law of contracts or agreements, while, where no such express choice is made, principles of private international law will have to be applied in order to determine the proper law of the contract. A special problem arises with agreements between financial institutions (such as the IBRD) and non-state parties, which are made in association with and dependent upon agreements with states, e.g., loan agreements covered by a guarantee agreement with a state or a project agreement made in connection with a loan agreement with a state. It would seem to be the better view that because of provisions in the loan agreement or by implication resulting from

---

period, the deed providing for arbitration and specifying the Swiss law and residually general principles of law as applicable.

[9] See also Nurick, 'Choice of Law Clauses and International Contracts', 1960 *Proceedings of the ASIL* p. 61; Colin and Sinkondo, 'Les relations contractuelles des organisations internationales avec les personnes privées', 69 RDIDC (1992) p. 7. The relationship between an organization and its staff is, as a rule, governed by the internal law of the organization, as has been pointed out in Chapter 9.

[10] See Jessup, *Transnational Law* (1956), chapter 3; Mann, 'The Proper Law of Contracts Concluded by International Persons', 35 BYIL (1959) at pp. 34*ff.*; C. F. Amerasinghe, note 5, *State Responsibility*, pp. 114*ff.*; and J.-F. Lalive, 'Contracts between a State or State Agency and a Foreign Company', 13 ICLQ (1964) at p. 991, for the applicability of transnational law to contracts.

association, these agreements with non-state parties are governed by international law.[11]

Tortious liability may also exist between international organizations and persons that are not international persons. Here again, it is reasonable that the principle that the *lex loci delicti commissi* should govern. This would generally be the law of the jurisdiction in which the property of the international organization upon which the tort took place is located, if the tort took place on such property, because international organizations do not generally have law-making powers on property, though they may own such property.[12] The same principles would apply to the issue of tortious liability of organizations for damage caused as an occupier of immovable property because of defects in that property. Where an organization incurs tortious liability outside its premises to an individual other than a staff member because of some act or omission for which it is responsible, the law of the territorial state should govern as the *lex loci delicti commissi*. It is not desirable that the *lex fori* as such should have any relevance to the matter of tortious liability. In the case of what is now the EU, however, the law to be applied is the general principles common to the laws of member states.[13] Problems may arise where the UN has vessels or aircraft under its flag. The choice of the law applicable to torts committed upon them would then, perhaps, be based on convenience – pointing to the place of registration of the vessel or aircraft.[14]

---

[11] See Broches, loc. cit. note 6 at pp. 345*ff.*, where, however, the matter is not fully discussed. All these agreements are now registered with the UN Secretariat.

[12] Exceptionally an organization may have this power. In the case of the UN under the provisions of the UN–USA Headquarters Agreement, for instance, the UN has made regulations relating to liability in tort for acts of the organization in the headquarters district (see, e.g., Regulation No. 4 approved by the GA in December 1986). These regulations will govern tortious liability for damage caused on UN territory in the headquarters district: see Szasz, 'The United Nations Legislates to Limit its Liability', 81 AJIL (1987) p. 739; and Sloan, *United Nations General Assembly Resolutions in our Changing World* (1991) pp. 18–19.

[13] See originally Article 15 of the EEC Treaty; and Article 188 of the Euratom Treaty.

[14] Sands and Klein (eds.), note 3 pp. 465*ff.*, examine briefly the issues of applicable law in cases of contracts and tortious liability. They also examine the problem of criminal liability. While criminal liability is an issue whose solution may not be too difficult, it is not something that intrinsically concerns the responsibility of and to international organizations. In taking this view, I proceed on the basis that, firstly, at present there can be no criminal responsibility to international organizations, as such (they are not in the same position as states in this respect), and, secondly, international organizations are not at present regarded as capable of criminal responsibility (although this may be an issue for the future, as the UN, particularly, becomes involved in armed conflicts and the concept of criminal responsibility of states and

Responsibility to international organizations

Substantive rights in general

Whenever international personality is attributed to an international organization,[15] it is a legal person separate from and additional to its member states, and is not simply an aggregation of those states. It constitutes a distinct entity with functions, rights and duties of its own. While it has duties, there are counterpart obligations owing to it by, *inter alia*, member states, the performance of which the organization has a right to expect and, if necessary, to require. This principle was referred to by the ICJ in the *Reparation Case* when it stated that there was an

undeniable right of the Organization to demand that its Members shall fulfil the obligations entered into by them in the interest of the good working of the Organization.[16]

The Court emphasized that the effective working of the organization and the accomplishment of its task required that the undertakings of member states should be strictly observed. For that purpose the ICJ thought it

necessary that, when an infringement occurs, the Organization should be able to call upon the responsible state to remedy its default, and, in particular, to obtain from the State reparation for the damage that the default may have caused.[17]

The ICJ was called upon to consider the position *vis-à-vis* non-member states in the same case in connection with the capacity of the UN to bring a claim against a non-member state. The ICJ had found that capacity to bring an international claim depended on possession of international personality and rights and duties at international law which flowed from the elaboration of functions, powers, rights and duties in the Charter and related instruments. It found in effect that beyond that the international personality of the UN was a question of fact.[18] From this flowed rights of the organization *vis-à-vis* non-member states as well. However, the objective nature of the organization's personality did not mean that non-member states were in the same position towards it as member states, or had the same obligations towards it. The existence

---

other international persons becomes established). For another detailed study done some time ago of the issue of applicable law, see Seyersted, 'Applicable Law in Relations Between Intergovernmental Organizations and Private Parties', 122 *Hague Recueil* (1967-III) p. 427.

[15] There may be cases in which a group of states acting as one (an organization, in a sense) does not have personality, as was the case with the Administrating Authority in the *Certain Phosphate Lands in Nauru Case*: 1992 ICJ Reports p. 240.

[16] 1949 ICJ Reports at p. 184.   [17] *Ibid.* at p. 183.   [18] *Ibid.* at p. 185.

of international personality as an objective fact was, nevertheless, capable of producing consequences outside the confines of the organization, involving responsibility to the organization.[19]

That international organizations can possess rights under conventional law cannot be doubted. Thus, under the headquarters agreements or constitutions of organizations it was clearly envisaged that organizations would have rights *vis-à-vis* states. When organizations enter into treaties the same order would prevail. This was implicitly recognized in the *WHO Agreement Case*,[20] where the obligations of international organizations were specifically in issue and were affirmed. The rights of the UN under international agreements were recognized by the ICJ in the *PLO Observer Mission Case*.[21] But there are also undoubtedly obligations owed to international organizations by states primarily under customary international law, based on the analogy of the responsibility of states to each other. For example, states may have to conduct themselves actively or passively in such a way that they do not injure or damage the interests of international organizations, whether such obligations are based on risk, negligence or on absolute liability, as the case may be. The existence of obligations of international organizations at customary international law was referred to in the *WHO Agreement Case*[22] by the ICJ, it being reasonable to infer that conversely the organizations had rights as well. As an international person, an international organization may be expected to have such international rights.

The rights of organizations may cover an unlimited area depending on their capacity to enter into treaties and agreements and on the practical circumstances and situations in which they are placed and operate. It is not possible or necessary to identify all the rights that organizations may have. To some extent they may correspond to those that states have, but what is the source of these rights is a question. It is not clear whether they are generated by analogy from states (general principles of law) or by customary law. They certainly have the right to have loans repaid under and in accordance with loan agreements or aid agreements, for example, as is clearly the case with loans and credits made by the IBRD

---

[19] The ICJ's statements were made in the context of the UN's right to make claims for injuries to staff members but it is clear that the principles implied are applicable generally.

[20] 1980 ICJ Reports at p. 90. The case concerned the rights of the parties *vis-à-vis* each other under an international agreement relating to the location of an office of the WHO.

[21] 1988 ICJ Reports p. 12.   [22] 1980 ICJ Reports at p. 90.

and the IDA. They also have rights in respect to protection by states in which they have offices, whether under agreements or under general international law.[23] In the *Reparation Case* the ICJ thought that it could not be disputed that the UN had rights relating to damage to its property and other interests.[24]

However, attention has been paid particularly to the right of protection for their staff members that organizations have *vis-à-vis* states, since the advisory opinion of the ICJ in the *Reparation Case*. There the principal issue was whether the UN had the capacity to bring a claim against a state for injury caused to one of its staff members. In the opinion the ICJ, without discussing the matter in detail, took the view that states had obligations *vis-à-vis* the UN in regard to the protection from injury of its staff members in the course of performing their duties.[25] The exact content of the duty to protect or keep free from injury or damage was, however, not discussed, but it may be inferred that this was one owed under general international law and would correspond to that owed by states to other states in respect of the latter's officials.[26] On the other hand, there may be areas in which similarity between states and organizations does not exist because organizations do not operate or have powers in these areas.[27]

Establishing the substantive rights of organizations in general depends on identifying the particular circumstances of the case, and determining whether in those circumstances the obligation is based on risk, fault or absolute liability, with the help of any treaties or conventions that may be applicable or general international law which may often correspond or be analogous to the customary international law that applies between states.

A problem also may arise with obligations owed by non-member states. It must be recognized that the finding of the ICJ in the *Reparation Case*, on the topic of claims against non-member states, related solely to the capacity of the UN to make such a claim, and not to the basis on which such a claim could be brought. The Court did not purport to discuss

---

[23] Eagleton explores some of these rights in his work cited in note 3 above.

[24] 1949 ICJ Reports at p. 184. Other organizations, it may be inferred, have similar rights.

[25] *Ibid.* at pp. 181*ff.*

[26] This duty may be narrower than in the case of diplomats who are protected whether they are in the course of performing functions or not. The ICJ's findings in regard to the UN should probably be extended to cover other organizations.

[27] Organizations do not as such exercise rights of sovereignty, like states, which is a difference. They may, however, operate and own aircraft and ships, which would result in the law of the sea and air space being applicable to them.

the circumstances in which a non-member state could be said to be in breach of an obligation towards the organization such as would give rise to a claim. The non-member state does not owe specific duties to the organization under the law. Thus, there would be no foundation for claims under that law. However, a basis for claims may exist in particular cases. For instance, a non-member state may be a party to a treaty conferring rights on the organization from the breach of which a claim by the latter against the non-member state could well arise. Switzerland is a party to headquarters agreements, though it is not a member of some international organizations. Breaches of these agreements could give rise to claims by the organizations. Or again, a non-member state might have received an agent of the organization into its territory in circumstances implying agreement on its part to be bound, in the treatment of the agent, by the same obligations as are incumbent on member states. Moreover, there may be cases in which the rules of general international law may apply by analogy.

Rights in regard to staff

In regard particularly to the protection of staff, Article 100 of the UN Charter provides in effect that members of the staff of the UN are not to seek or receive instructions from governments or other authorities, that their responsibility is to the organization they serve, and that the member states are not to seek to influence them in the discharge of this responsibility. The constitutions of many other international organizations have similar provisions. Even if such provisions are not included in some constitutions, what is stated in them is implicit in the position of the staff of international organizations as international civil servants. In the *Reparation Case*, the ICJ declined to assimilate the legal bond resulting from the stipulations of the Charter between the UN, on the one hand, and the Secretary-General and the staff, on the other, to the bond of nationality existing between a state and its nationals. However, the Court derived certain consequences from the position of the international civil servant in his relationship with his organization:

In order that the agent may perform his duties satisfactorily, he must feel that this protection is assured to him by the Organization, and that he may count on it. To ensure the independence of the agent, and, consequently, the independent action of the Organization itself, it is essential that in performing his duties he need not have to rely on any other protection than that of the Organization... In particular, he should not have to rely on the protection of his own State. If he had to rely on that State, his independence might well be compromised, contrary to the principle applied by Article 100 of the Charter. And lastly, it is essential that – whether the agent belongs to a powerful or to a weak State; to one more affected or less affected by the complications of international life; to one in sympathy or not in sympathy with the mission of the agent – he should know that in the performance of his duties he is under the protection of the Organization.[28]

The Court had already concluded that the organization was a distinct international person as a consequence of which member states not only owed duties to it but were subject to being reminded, if need be, of certain obligations. Consequently, the independence of the organization became particularly important. However, the independence of the organization depended on the independence of the staff. For this reason the latter assumed special juridical significance. Thus, it was a logical conclusion that the organization's right *vis-à-vis* members, particularly, of the organization to protect and demand protection of its staff in the performance of duties, was implicit. It must be noted, nevertheless, that the Court's view also implied, first, that an international official does not cease to owe allegiance to his own country in his personal capacity; second, that in his official capacity and in the performance of his functions his first allegiance was to his organization; and, third, that in case of conflict[29] the latter allegiance must prevail.

The right to bring claims at international law

A related question concerns the right of organizations to assert their claims at international law, where their international rights have been infringed and responsibility to them has been incurred. In the *Reparation Case* the ICJ concluded that, as in the case of claims by states, the foundation of any international claim by an international organization must be a breach of an obligation owed to it on the international plane by the defendant state:

It cannot be doubted that the Organization has the capacity to bring an international claim against one of its Members which has caused injury to it by a breach of its international obligations towards it . . . As the claim is based on the breach of an international obligation on the part of the Member held responsible by the Organization, the Member cannot contend that this obligation is

---

[28] *Ibid.* at p. 182. It must be inferred that the ICJ's findings in relation to the UN as regards the problem presented to it may be extended to cover other organizations, indeed, any international organization.

[29] A conflict may arise when a staff member has to perform functions for the organization in his national state and these involve conduct which is not welcomed by his national state.

governed by municipal law, and the Organization is justified in giving its claim the character of an international claim.[30]

The Court stated that in the case of an international organization this capacity flowed from its purpose and functions, as specified or implied in its constituent documents and developed in practice.[31] In the case of the UN its functions were of such a character that they could not be effectively discharged, unless the organization were regarded as having been endowed with capacity to bring international claims when necessitated by the discharge of its functions.[32] The Court pointed out that:

> It cannot be supposed that . . . all the members of the Organization, save the defendant State, must combine to bring a claim against the defendant for the damage suffered by the Organization.[33]

The UN, as an organization, had the capacity to bring claims against states broadly in two categories of cases: (i) where, by reason of the wrongful act of the state in question, the organization itself had suffered direct loss or damage to its property, assets, finances or interests; and (ii) in respect of the personal loss or damage caused to or suffered by a servant or agent of the organization in the course of his duties, arising out of such an act, and additional to any damage caused to the organization itself by the same act. The Court referred to the inconvenience that would result if the organization were not endowed with a corporate capacity in the matter.

Capacity in the first type of case is easy to concede because it is really a necessary attribute of the corporate character of the organization and its possession of international personality. However, the position in regard to the second category is less obvious for two reasons: firstly, because the servant or agent of the organization would also be the national of some state which *prima facie* was entitled to claim on his behalf; and, secondly, because a claim by the organization on his behalf might seem at first sight to be at variance with the rule, normally applicable in the case of claims made by states in respect of persons, that only the state of which the injured party is a national can bring a claim on his behalf. The Court met these difficulties by invoking two basic principles. The first was a positive one, that the special relationship

---

[30] *Ibid.* at p. 180. On the right to bring claims there is a wealth of analysis of the ICJ judgment in Fitzmaurice, *The Law and Procedure of the International Court of Justice* (1986), vol. I pp. 86*ff.* (a reprint of his article in 29 BYIL (1952) p. 1).
[31] 1949 ICJ Reports at p. 180.   [32] *Ibid.*   [33] *Ibid.* at pp. 180–1.

between the organization and its servants required, for the effective discharge of the functions of the latter and through them the discharge of the organization's own functions, and for the effective preservation of the independence of both, that the organization should have the capacity to extend protection to its servant, and in case of need to bring a claim on his behalf. The second principle of relevance was that the rules concerning the nationality of claims applied only to those cases where the nationality of the injured person formed the sole basis for the legal wrong done to the claimant state, entitling it to make a claim, and that they did not preclude claims by entities of which the injured person was not a national where another basis justifying such a claim existed.

On the first of these points the Court introduced the problem by stating that the Charter did not expressly confer upon the UN the capacity to include, in its claim for reparation, damage caused to the victim or to persons entitled through him and that, therefore, an enquiry must first be made into whether the provisions of the Charter concerning the functions of the UN, and the part played by its agents in the performance of those functions, implied for the organization power to afford its agents the limited protection that would consist in the bringing of a claim on their behalf for reparation for damage suffered in such circumstances.[34] The work of the UN necessitated the dispatch of important missions to be performed in disturbed parts of the world, involving for the members of the mission unusual dangers to which ordinary persons were not exposed.[35] Further, the circumstances might also be such that a claim for any injury done to an agent of the organization in the performance of such a mission could not appropriately be brought by his national state or that the latter would not feel disposed to do so. Efficiency and independence of the staff required their protection.[36] The Court's conclusion was, therefore, that:

Upon examination of the character of the functions entrusted to the Organization and of the nature of the missions of its agents, it becomes clear that the

---

[34] Ibid. at p. 182.   [35] Ibid. at p. 183.

[36] Ibid. The GA had confirmed this in the preamble to its Resolution of 3 December 1948. This conclusion and the next one are now valid generally for other international organizations as well. The Court referred to disturbed parts of the world in its reasoning. But, ultimately, since there are missions undertaken to many parts of the world that are not disturbed, the disturbed nature of the locality of missions is not critical. All organizations, in any case, would probably send missions to disturbed parts of the world. Further, the degree of disturbance would not seem to matter. What is important is that, wherever in the world staff members go on mission or otherwise, they are in need of protection.

capacity of the Organization to exercise a measure of functional protection of its agents arises by necessary intendment out of the Charter.[37]

On the second issue of the absence of the nationality link, the Court explained why the special relationship between the organization and its servants or agents which did not depend on a nationality link made it possible for the organization to make a claim not merely for the loss or damage caused to itself, but in respect also of the personal loss or damage caused to the servant or agent himself.[38] The question was why, in bringing a claim in respect of a breach of an international obligation owed to itself, the organization should be able to do anything more than claim for the damage caused directly to itself, *qua* organization, and why it should be entitled also to make a claim on behalf of the agent personally. The national state of an injured alien could bring a claim on behalf of its national because it is regarded as having suffered injury in the person of its national in addition to having suffered a breach of an obligation owed to it. In the case of an international organization the international obligation was something other than the general international law obligation to afford certain treatment to aliens. The obligation arose from the nature, functions and requirements of an international organization which normally make it necessary that its agents be able to look to it, and not to any state, even their national state, for protection while carrying out their duties on behalf of the organization. There was a duty to afford protection to agents of the UN in the performance of their functions which arose as a general inference both from the Charter and from certain related instruments. Not only were these general undertakings of the members but Article 2(5) of the Charter required them to render the UN 'every assistance'.[39] Thus, the breach of an obligation owed to the organization gave the organization, like the national state of an injured party, its own right in making the claim, even though the claim was in respect of personal damage to the agent or his defendants.[40]

Having established that the tie of nationality was not crucial to the right of an organization to bring a claim on behalf of one of its servants, the Court, further, concluded, as a logical corollary, that the fact that the injured party was a national of the defendant state did not affect the right to claim. Because the action of the organization was in fact based not upon the nationality of the victim but upon his status as agent of

---

[37] *Ibid.* at p. 184.   [38] *Ibid.* at pp. 181–2.   [39] *Ibid.* at p. 183.   [40] *Ibid.* at p. 184.

the organization, it did not matter whether he was a national of the
state to which the claim was addressed. Thus, the fact of the possession
of the nationality of the defendant state by the agent did not constitute
any obstacle to a claim brought by the organization for a breach of
obligations towards it occurring in relation to the performance of his
mission by the agent.[41]

The conclusion of the Court is explicable by reference to the fact that
the reason why a claim cannot be brought by a state of which the injured
party is a national, when he is also a national of the defendant state, is
that, because the treatment accorded by the latter to the injured party
constitutes action on the domestic plane, as he is a national of the latter,
irrespective of any other nationality he may possess, there has been no
conduct on the international plane which could give rise to an international claim. There has been no violation of an international obligation
in these circumstances, because the injured party is not an alien *vis-à-vis*
the defendant state and the latter could not have committed a breach
of rules relating to the treatment of aliens which is what normally gives
rise to an international claim on behalf of an individual. The situation
may be contrasted with that in which the basis of the international claim
is not an obligation relating to the treatment of aliens as such but an
obligation designed to protect local nationals against certain kinds of
treatment at the hands of their own state, such as arises from human
rights or minorities provisions in treaties. In such cases the claim is not
based on the injury suffered by the claimant state in the person of its
national, arising out of a breach of the general international law obligation to treat aliens in a certain way. It is based on a separate right,
generally arising from a treaty, that exists independently of the issue of
nationality. A claim by an international organization for an injury done
to one of its agents in the performance of his functions is of a similar
kind. The claim does not arise from the breach of general international
law obligation to treat aliens in a certain way. But it is based on a breach
of certain obligations owed to the organization by member states arising
in consequence of the terms of its constitutive instrument and possibly
by analogy with general rules of international law.

The Court also dealt with the question of conflicting claims by an
international organization on behalf of its agent and by his national
state in connection with the same events. International tribunals were
already familiar with the problem of a claim in which two or more

---

[41] *Ibid.* at p. 186. The reasoning and conclusions of the Court are of general application
to all organizations. There is no reason why this should not be so.

national states were interested and knew how to protect the defendant state in such a case.[42] The general rule (to which there may be exceptions)[43] was that priority was not assigned to one or the other and that neither was compelled to refrain from bringing an international claim:

There is no rule of law which assigns priority to the one or to the other, or which compels either... to refrain from bringing an international claim.[44]

As regards the relationship with non-member states, the Court found that in principle the UN had capacity to bring an international claim against non-member states in respect of injuries done to its agents. Because the international personality of the organization, though in origin the creation of the Charter, existed as an independent objective fact, and therefore existed *vis-à-vis* non-members also together with the attributes and incidents deriving from the Charter and from the character and functions of the organization as thereby created, along with it went the capacity to bring international claims.[45]

Responsibility of international organizations

Once the existence of international personality for international organizations is conceded, it is not difficult to infer that, just as organizations can demand responsibility of other international persons because they have rights at international law, so they can also be held responsible to other international persons because they have obligations at international law. States have international responsibility generally because their duties flow from the control they have over territory, airspace, persons, etc. or from their relations with other international persons arising from treaties or otherwise. In the case of international organizations, they generally have no control over some of the elements over which states have control but they have a certain amount of control over persons and enter into treaties, agreements and other relations with other international persons which could give rise to international obligations generating responsibility in the appropriate circumstances.

[42] *Ibid.*   [43] See the *Nottebohm Case*, 1955 ICJ Reports p. 22.
[44] 1949 ICJ Reports at p. 185.
[45] *Ibid.* Here, again, the findings of the Court may be applied generally. It may be noted that there is authority supporting the position that recognition of the legal capacity of an organization in national law entails the freedom on its part to bring an action in a national court: see *International Refugee Organization* v. *Republic of SS Corporation et al.* [1951] 18 ILR p. 447; *International Tin Council* v. *Amalgamet Inc.* 524 NYS 2d [1988] p. 971; *Arab Monetary Fund* v. *Hashem and Others (No. 3)* [1990] 1 All ER p. 685.

Substantive obligations

International organizations are liable for breach of international agreements. For example, when the IBRD and the IDA enter into loan and credit agreements with states, which are international agreements governed by international law,[46] the failure on the part of the IBRD or the IDA respectively to carry out its obligations under such agreements would involve their international responsibility. There are international agreements entered into by other international organizations, such as the UN, the FAO and the ILO, even other than their own headquarters agreements, which could generate international responsibility in the event that the organizations failed to carry out their obligations under them. In the *WHO Agreement Case*,[47] for example, whether the WHO had violated its obligations under an agreement with Egypt was in issue before the ICJ, there being no question that the WHO could have been responsible to Egypt for the breach of its obligations under the agreement.

As in the case of responsibility to organizations, there can be no doubt that under customary international law, possibly on the analogy of the law governing relations between states, international organizations can also have international obligations towards other international persons arising from the particular circumstances in which they are placed or from particular relationships. In the *WHO Agreement Case* the ICJ specifically referred to the existence of obligations at customary international law for international organizations.[48] Clearly there are situations in which organizations would be responsible under customary international law for the acts of their servants or agents, when they are acting in the performance of their functions, or of persons or groups acting under the control of the organizations, such as armed forces in the case of the UN. Indeed, there have been claims arising from the Congo operations in the 1960s (ONUC) brought against the UN by states in respect of injury to their nationals which were based on violations of international law and which, however, were settled by negotiations between the UN and the states concerned.[49]

The content of the obligations of international organizations could easily be identified in the case of constitutive instruments, other treaties or other agreements, depending as it does on the interpretation and

---

[46] See Broches, loc. cit. note 6 at pp. 339*ff.*   [47] 1980 ICJ Reports p. 67.
[48] *Ibid.* at p. 90.
[49] See UN Docs. A/CN.4/195 and Add. 1, dated 7 April 1967, which are printed in 2 YBILC (1967) at pp. 218*ff.* The principal claimant was the Belgian government.

application of such instruments. In the case of customary international law, as in the case of obligations owed to organizations, the obligations will be based on fault, risk or absolute liability, as the case may be, depending on the obligation and the content of the applicable customary international law.

Generally, organizations have been found to be at fault in connection with damage resulting from conduct of their servants or agents or persons or groups under their control, such as armed forces. There may be delicate issues concerning who, among several international persons, is responsible in some cases where persons are under the control of more than one international person, such as where armed forces belonging to a state participate in an operation sponsored by the UN or pursuant to a decision of the UN. But in such cases the issue is one of attribution of responsibility on the basis of control. There is no reason why, where necessary, analogies should not be borrowed from the principles of imputability applied in the customary law of state responsibility, particularly, for injuries to aliens. Similarly, in the area of the general responsibility of international organizations for acts of servants or agents, analogies from the law of state responsibility may be relevant in appropriate situations in determining imputability.[50] The issue of imputability where acts of organs, servants, agents or independent contractors are concerned will, consequently, depend, particularly in the case of acts performed outside the actual authority granted, on whether the organ or individual concerned was acting within the scope of 'apparent authority'. Thus, though the act may in fact be done without authority, it may engage the responsibility of the organization, because it is within the scope of apparent authority.

Questions of responsibility have arisen particularly in the case of armed forces engaged in UN 'controlled' operations.[51] In such cases the UN has generally accepted responsibility for any illegal acts which may

---

[50] For these principles of imputability see, e.g., C. F. Amerasinghe, note 5 pp. 49*ff.*; Meron, 'International Responsibility of States for Unauthorized Acts of their Officials', 33 BYIL (1957) p. 85. The general question of the responsibility of organizations was discussed theoretically and embryonically by Eagleton, note 3 at pp. 385*ff.* He makes a useful distinction between indirect and direct responsibility which may have some resemblance to analogous distinctions made in the law of state responsibility for the treatment of aliens relating to responsibility for denials of justice and responsibility for an initial violation of international law: see also C. F. Amerasinghe, note 5, *State Responsibility* pp. 41*ff.*, for some discussion of these distinctions.

[51] See generally Seyersted, 'United Nations Forces: Some Legal Problems', 37 BYIL (1961) at pp. 406*ff.*; Amrallah, 'The International Responsibility of the United Nations for Activities Carried out by UN Peace-Keeping Forces', 23 *Revue Egyptienne de droit*

have been committed by armed forces (belonging to member states) acting under the UN aegis. The UN has acknowledged liability for activities carried out by both the UNEF and the ONUC, for instance.[52]

The principal issues that arise in these cases are (i) whether there has been an unlawful act or omission; and (ii) whether such act is imputable to the organization. In regard to the first issue, the UN has refused to bear responsibility for damages caused by its lawful military operations or arising from military necessity – these acts are not unlawful.[53] On the other hand, the UN has accepted responsibility for all damage not justified by military necessity.[54] The SG of the UN has stated in connection with the ONUC that the UN would not evade responsibility when its agents had clearly caused unjustifiable damage to innocent parties.[55] The UN has even compensated for damage caused by a shooting committed by a member of its force where no official function or superior order required him to shoot.[56] At the same time the UN has not accepted responsibility for acts committed in legitimate self-defence.[57] Sometimes, the UN has compensated not for unlawful acts but on the basis of equity and humanity.[58] In 1965 the SG of the UN summarized the general principles of responsibility for the acts of UN forces, which include but were not confined to legal principles:

It has always been the policy of the United Nations to compensate individuals who have suffered damages for which the Organization was legally liable. This policy is in keeping with generally recognized legal principles and with the Convention on Privileges and Immunities of the United Nations. In addition, in regard to the United Nations activities in the Congo, it is reinforced by the principles set forth in the international conventions concerning the protection of the life and property of civilian population during hostilities as well

---

international (1976) p. 57; Bowett, *United Nations Forces* (1964) pp. 149ff., 242ff.; Simmonds, *Legal Problems Arising from the United Nations Military Operations in the Congo* (1968) pp. 229ff.

[52] Seyersted, loc. cit. note 51 at pp. 420ff. The issues which arose in the case of the ONUC are discussed in Salmon, 'Les accords Spaak–U. Thant du 20 février 1965', AFDI (1965) p. 468.

[53] See Bowett, note 51 at p. 247, citing the agreement of 20 February 1965 between the Foreign Minister of Belgium and the UNSG; Simmonds, note 51 pp. 240–1, citing the letter, dated 6 August 1965, from the UNSG to the representative of the Soviet Union to the UN; Salmon, loc. cit. note 52 at pp. 480ff.

[54] E.g., as a result of destruction without necessity, murder, imprisonment, arbitrary expulsions and such acts: Salmon, *ibid.* at p. 481.

[55] UNSC Doc. S/6597, quoting the letter, dated 20 February 1965, to Mr Spaak.

[56] See Seyersted, loc. cit. note 51 at p. 420.   [57] See Salmon, loc. cit. note 52 at p. 482.

[58] See, e.g., the case of the three members of the Red Cross International Committee who were found killed in the Congo in 1961: Simmonds, note 51 pp. 190ff.

as the considerations of equity and humanity which the United Nations cannot ignore.[59]

Imputability of the acts of forces of the UN becomes possible where national contingents become organs of the UN by being placed under the authority of the UN or under a commander appointed by and taking orders from it and in circumstances where the states providing them have ceded their organic jurisdiction over them.[60] Where the contingents are organs of the national state and under the full organic jurisdiction of the national state, even if they were acting in execution of a UN decision, the UN cannot be held responsible for their acts, as was the case in Korea in 1950, for instance.[61] Further, the UN has not assumed responsibility in cases where acts have not been under its authority, as where they were committed by aircraft employed by states providing contingents for the purpose of supplying supplementary national supplies to their own contingents in the Congo.[62] Thus, also acts of Katangese mercenaries of the troops of the Congolese national army and of the Balubese, who were not members of the UN forces, were excluded from the scope of the UN's responsibility.[63]

In the case of the UNEF[64] compensation to the dependants of Egyptian nationals accidentally killed by members of the UNEF has always been paid by the UN and not by the government of the state providing the contingent concerned. In respect of awards by claims commissions established jointly by the UN and the host state under UNEF Regulation 15 and the Status Agreement with Egypt the UN appears to have undertaken a responsibility for obtaining satisfaction.[65]

The case of the Kuwait operation in 1990 is somewhat different, as was the Korean operation in 1950, where the UN did not regard forces as under its control and this was implicitly accepted by all parties

---

[59] Cited by Simmonds, *ibid.* p. 240.

[60] See Ritter, 'Le protection diplomatique à l'égard d'une organisation internationale', AFDI (1962) at p. 442 (citing Seyersted), and p. 444.

[61] See Seyersted, loc. cit. note 51 at pp. 362*ff.* and 421*ff.*   [62] Seyersted, *ibid.* at p. 421.

[63] See Salmon, loc. cit. note 52 at p. 482. The issues of illegality and imputability may to a large extent be settled by reference to the general principles of state responsibility.

[64] See Seyersted, loc. cit. note 51 at pp. 420*ff.*

[65] Paras. 12(i)(f) and 38(b)(i)(f) of the Status Agreement. In 1959 the total UNEF expenses for 'claims and adjustments' were $31,100. In subsequent budgets $20,000 were allocated for these purposes. See the Secretary-General's Summary Study, GAOR, 15th Session, Annexes A.i.27, at pp. 3 and 8; also Secretary-General's Summary Study, GAOR, 13th Session, Annexes A.i.65, at para. 120. On the UNEF see Seyersted, loc. cit. note 51 at pp. 420*ff.*

concerned.[66] During the Kuwait crisis the forces of national states apparently operated under a unified command pursuant to SC Resolution 678 (1990) of 29 November 1990[67] which 'authorizes Member States cooperating with the Government of Kuwait . . . to use all necessary means to uphold and implement' SC Resolution 660 (1990), dealing with the withdrawal of Iraqi forces from Kuwait. It is likely that here the forces were not under UN control.

As regards the UNFICYP, established in 1964 by the UN to help restore peace in Cyprus, it was contended in *Nissan* v. *Attorney-General*[68] that the British government was responsible for damage unlawfully caused by British troops. In the High Court and the Court of Appeal it was held that control of the British force lay in the UN and, therefore, the responsibility was not the government's.[69] The House of Lords held that the agreements between the government and the UN showed that the government was responsible.[70] The House of Lords did not deny that the UN was also responsible but did not deal with that question. What this case illustrates is that in such instances there may be concurrent responsibility because of dual control, so to speak. It may be that the UN does not have exclusive responsibility,[71] but this does not mean that the organization cannot be held responsible. On the other hand, concurrent responsibility will depend on the nature of the relationships within the forces and, as was pointed out by the House of Lords, the responsibility of the provider government will depend on the agreements (or the governing instrument).

In regard to outer space activities, the Space Treaty of 1967[72] in Articles VI and XIII provides for international organizations (e.g., the ESA and the INTELSAT) to be subject to obligations under the treaty, although

---

[66] For the Korean operation and the issues of responsibility which were the subject of some discussion, see Seyersted, *ibid.* at pp. 362*ff.* and 421*ff.*

[67] See Lauterpacht, Greenwood, Weller and Bethlehem (eds.), *The Kuwait Crisis: Basic Documents* (1991) p. 98.

[68] [1968] 1 QB p. 286 (QB); [1968] 1 QB p. 286 (CA); [1969] 1 All ER p. 629 (HL). The case is discussed by Brownlie, 'Decisions of British Courts during 1968 Involving Questions of International Law', 42 BYIL (1968–9) p. 217.

[69] See particularly Lord Denning [1968] 1 QB at p. 341.

[70] See particularly Lord Morris [1969] 1 All ER at pp. 646–7; Lord Pearce, *ibid.*, at pp. 647–8.

[71] See Brownlie, loc. cit. note 68 at p. 223.

[72] 6 ILM (1967) p. 386. The treaty was also in GA Rs. 222 (XXI), Annex. On the treaty see Ogunbanwo, *International Law and Outer Space Activities* (1975). For the position of international organizations in this connection see also Fitzgerald, 'The Participation of International Organizations in the Proposed International Agreement on Liability for Damage Caused by Objects Launched in Outer Space', 3 CYIL (1965) at pp. 268*ff.*

they may not be parties to the treaty. After twenty-eight years many of the principal obligations to be found in that treaty may have become part of customary international law. Whichever way the matter is looked at, international organizations could be responsible for breach of obligations incorporated in the treaty. The liability is based on negligence or fault or may, in certain circumstances, be absolute.[73] There are other conventions and instruments relating to space activities which may affect the responsibility of international organizations, such as the Liability Convention of 1972.[74] International organizations, particularly those of a technical-servicing nature, may incur responsibility for pollution and environmental damage, in the appropriate circumstances, under the provisions of international law which are relevant and govern liability in that area.[75]

A special problem may arise from the fact that there may be multiple jurisdictions involved in the regulation of activities on the premises of international organizations. International organizations do not have judicial or quasi-judicial powers over acts of individuals, who are not staff members, on their premises. These powers are usually exercised by

---

[73] See Ogunbanwo, note 72 pp. 154ff.

[74] 10 ILM (1971) p. 965. See on this Convention, e.g., Bueckling, 'Die Völkerrechtliche Haftung für Luftrecht und Weltraumgegenstände verursacht werden', 21 *Zeitschrift für Luftrecht und Weltraumrechtsftagen* (1972) p. 213; Foster, 'The Convention on International Liability for Damage Caused by Space Objects', 10 CYIL (1972) p. 137; Galicki, 'Liability of International Organizations for Space Activities', 5 Polish YIL (1972–3) p. 199; Diederiks-Verschoor, 'Pro and Contra Liability of International Organizations in Space Law', *Proceedings of the Seventh Colloquium on Outer Space* (1974) p. 186; Rajski, 'Convention on International Liability for Damage Caused by Space Objects, An Important Step in the Development of International Space law', *ibid.* p. 245; and Christol, 'International Liability for Damage Caused by Space Objects', 74 AJIL (1980) p. 345. Three conditions must be fulfilled before an international organization can become bound by the Convention: (i) the majority of its members must be parties to the Convention; (ii) the majority of its members must also be parties to the Space Treaty; and (iii) the organization itself must declare its acceptance of the rights and obligations under the Convention (Article XXII(1) of the Convention). The ESA accepted liability under the Convention by a declaration made on 23 September 1976. Another instrument in which the responsibility of international organizations is invoked is the 1980 Principles Governing the Use by States of Artificial Earth Satellites for Direct Television Broadcasting: UN Doc. A/AC. 105/271, Annex I, p. 8.

[75] See P.-M. Dupuy, *La responsabilité internationale des états pour les dommages d'origine technologique et industrielle* (1976) pp. 98ff., where the general law of responsibility for damage caused by the use of atomic energy, by pollution in the oceans and by ultra-hazardous activities is discussed; in connection with spacecraft the liability of international organizations is discussed at pp. 65ff.; see also Goldie, 'International Principles of Responsibility for Pollution', 9 Col. JTL (1970) at pp. 328ff.

the organs of the state in which the premises are located.[76] Thus, the question may arise, for example, how far and whether an organization is responsible as a result of an offence (such as assault or theft) committed by one individual against another on its premises over which the judicial organs of the state in which its premises are located have jurisdiction and in regard to which they have found that the offender was not guilty or liable, if there is good reason for concluding that the judicial decision of the courts of the state concerned constituted a denial of justice. If the scenario was solely on state territory without any involvement of the premises of an international organization, the law of state responsibility based on a denial of justice would be applicable in order to attribute responsibility to the state concerned. However, in the case being discussed, there are two authorities involved, and, while it may be possible to ascribe responsibility to the territorial state on the basis of state responsibility, if there have been denials of justice by the territorial state's judicial organs, the organization cannot be held responsible for a denial of justice as such or for the original offence. Responsibility, of course, could be ascribed to the international organization, as in the case of state responsibility, if there had been some element of negligence on the part of the international organization in allowing the offence to occur.[77]

The defendant

There is no question in view of the attribution of international personality to international organizations that they as persons, rather than the states members individually or in aggregate, can be the objects of international claims or suits.

---

[76] See Section 7 of the UN–USA Headquarters Agreement. Even without such a clause in a relevant agreement, the territorial state would have jurisdiction over such an offence as the one described.

[77] This is an original responsibility for negligence in the provision of security on its premises which resulted in the injury caused by the offence. It is not a direct responsibility for the offence itself by attribution. The legal position, it may be observed, is similar to that which prevails in the law of state responsibility for alien treatment. In the situation posed for the purposes of the responsibility of the international organization it is irrelevant that the victim is or is not a national of the territorial state. For a discussion of the general problems raised here, see Eagleton, loc. cit. note 3 at pp. 393ff.

13 The liability of member states *vis-à-vis* third parties

When states combine to form an organization, it has the power to perform certain functions which have legal consequences. In the course of performing these functions an inter-governmental organization may incur liabilities to third parties. These third parties may be states, other organizations, individuals or legal persons. The states may be member states of the organization itself or other states, while individuals and legal persons may be nationals of member states or not. The liabilities may arise from transactions, such as international agreements between states and the organization, which take place at an international level and are governed by international law, or from transactions which take place at a non-international level[1] and are governed by national law or transnational law, for example, whether they are between the

[1] Some examples of transactions which may be governed by national law are: (1) loans taken by the organization from states or state agencies where the intention is clear that the transaction should be at a national level (the International Bank for Reconstruction and Development (World Bank), for instance, among other institutions, used generally to make its borrowings from the central banks of states (i.e. state agencies representing the states themselves) expressly subject to some national law, but this practice has been changed); (2) loans taken by the organization from individuals or legal persons (most financial institutions, and particularly the World Bank, in general explicitly make their borrowings from such persons subject to a municipal law; sometimes the choice of law is not mentioned, as where a borrowing is made from a central bank on the assumption that it is highly unlikely that it would be assigned to a private person, natural or legal, by the Central Bank); (3) contracts, such as procurement or construction contracts, entered into between the organization and individuals or legal persons; and (4) delicts committed in the territory of a state against individuals or legal persons by the organization or by the organization's staff in the course of their duties. The last of these may also be international delicts.

organization and states, individuals or legal persons. Such liabilities may be contractual, quasi-contractual or delictual.

Whether the transactions are on the international plane or not, the question may be asked how far the member states of the organization are responsible for the liabilities of the organization and in what circumstances and to what extent the third party may have recourse to the member states for the purpose of having the liability discharged.[2] There is a further issue, that of the liability of member states to the organization, which has been discussed in connection with the financing of international organizations in Chapter 11. The first question is of considerable importance and will be discussed here.

The governing law and problems with the forum

In a transaction which is on the international plane and is primarily governed by international law, such as an international agreement, the question whether there is liability of member states to third parties would naturally be answered by reference to international law. On the other hand, even where the transaction is not on the international plane and is governed primarily by national or transnational law, it would appear that the same question should be answered by reference to international law because national legal systems characterize the issue of liability of member states under the rules of private international law as a matter to be governed by the proper law of the organization, which would be public international law.[3] It is also possible that in the interpretation of a national law which enacts a treaty or other body of

---

[2] The question has been considered by a commission of the Institut de droit international of which commission I was a member. The final report of the rapporteur to the commission is to be found in 66-I *Annuaire de l'institut de droit international* (1995) p. 461. This report examines the question in depth. My comments are to be found at pp. 348*ff.* and 434*ff.* of the same publication. See also C. F. Amerasinghe, 'Liability to Third Parties of Member States of International Organizations: Practice, Principle and Judicial Precedent', 85 AJIL (1991) p. 259. The most recent examination of the subject is by Hartwig, *Die Haftung der Mitgliedstaaten für Internationale Organisationen* (1993) pp. 335*ff.* (summary in English).

[3] See also Seidl-Hohenveldern, *Corporations in and under International Law* (1987) p. 104; Mann, 'International Corporations and National Law', 42 BYIL (1967) at p. 157; *Mazzanti v. HAFSE and Ministry of Defence* [1954] 22 ILR at p. 761 (Tribunal of Florence). The approach taken by most national legal systems need not be the only approach, however. Ultimately the matter of what law is applicable will depend on the national system which may generally or specifically take a different approach.

international law and, thus, makes it enforceable in the national legal system, reference is made to international organizational law.[4] In either case, therefore, it would appear that the issue should be settled according to the proper law of international organizations[5] which is international law. In general, the relevant law would not in these cases be national law as such.

However, that international law and not national law will be applied is only true as a general proposition. There may be circumstances where the national law will be applied, as where a state has a law prohibiting those responsible for the conduct of any trading association (not only 'companies', as defined by that state's law, and including, at least by implication, international organizations) to allow the association to trade while insolvent and creating a direct liability for a violation of the law. This law could be applied by that state's courts to member states responsible for an insolvent trading association. The liability of the member states would, of course, be a direct liability resulting from a law applicable to them specifically and not a secondary or concurrent liability for debts of the organization.

Further, as regards issues raised in national courts, problems may arise because of the attitude of courts to the application of international law. In the law of the United Kingdom, for example, the courts' attitude towards treaties complicates the choice of law governing the issue of liability of member states for debts of the organization. As was confirmed by the House of Lords in *J. H. Rayner Ltd.* v. *Department of Trade and Industry*, the courts of the UK cannot enforce rights granted or obligations imposed in respect of a treaty by international law without the intervention of the legislature.[6] Thus, in the law of the UK there cannot be a direct choice of international law as such as the law of the place of incorporation or as the national law of the organization, because

---

[4] See *Maclaine Watson & Co. Ltd.* v. *Department of Trade and Industry* [1988] 3 All ER at pp. 278, 295 *per* Kerr LJ, pp. 323, 334–5 *per* Nourse LJ, pp. 337, 342–3 per Ralph Gibson LJ (UK Court of Appeal).

[5] This is sometimes referred to as the 'national' law of the organization: see Mann, loc. cit. note 3; and Seidl-Hohenveldern, note 3.

[6] [1989] 3 WLR (HL) at pp. 980, 984, 985 *per* Lord Templeman and at pp. 1002, 1004, 1010 *per* Lord Oliver. The other three Law Lords agreed with Lords Templeman and Oliver. This case will be referred to as the *ITC Case (HL)*. It is the same case on appeal as *Maclaine Watson & Co. Ltd* v. *Department of Trade and Industry* [1988] 3 All ER (CA) p. 257, which was decided by the Court of Appeal and is referred to as the *ITC Case (CA)*. The two cases together may be referred to as the *ITC Case*.

it involves the application of a treaty, namely, the constitution of the organization. It is only if the constituent treaty is incorporated directly or indirectly that the doctrine of non-justiciability operative in English courts becomes inapplicable; at that point the treaty and international law may be referred to, *in the absence of any other contrary indication*, for the purpose of resolving issues such as the liability of member states for the debts of the organization.[7] In any event the legislation of the UK parliament is paramount and takes precedence over any principles of public and private international law that may be deemed to be applicable, so far as the UK courts are concerned. This problem of the choice of law in national courts is relevant, because in cases involving transactions which are not on the international plane member states will be sued in national courts, as happened in the cases arising from the demise of the International Tin Council (ITC).[8] Since a treaty and international

---

[7] See the *ITC Case (HL)* [1989] 3 WLR (HL) at pp. 1002 and 1004 *per* Lord Oliver.

[8] These cases involved an international organization with limited membership which could not be described as a universal international organization. But on the issue of liability of members to third parties the difference would seem to be immaterial. See for the salient facts of these cases *Maclaine Watson & Co. Ltd* v. *Department of Trade and Industry* [1988] 3 All ER p. 257 (CA). The ITC was an international organization established by treaty (the Sixth International Tin Agreement) concluded in 1982 between a number of sovereign states, including the UK and the EEC. The agreement provided that the ITC 'shall have legal personality' and that the executive chairman of the ITC was to be responsible for the administration and operation of the agreement in accordance with the decisions of the ITC. The principal functions of the ITC were to provide for adjustment between world production and consumption of tin, to alleviate surpluses or shortages of tin and to prevent fluctuations in the price of tin. The ITC had its headquarters in London and by the International Tin Council (Immunities and Privileges) Order 1972 the ITC was recognized as an organization of which the UK and other sovereign powers were members. Article 5 of the 1972 Order provided that the ITC was to have the 'legal capacities of a body corporate' and by Article 6 was given (subject to certain exceptions) immunity from 'suit and legal process'. In 1985 the ITC ran out of money and defaulted on a number of transactions it had entered into for the purchase of tin and on bank loans made to it. A series of actions were commenced by creditors of the ITC in which they sought: (i) to make the members of the ITC liable for the debts of the ITC (the direct actions); (ii) an order that the ITC was wound up under the Companies Act 1985 (the winding-up application); (iii) alternatively, that a receiver of the ITC's assets be appointed (the receivership application); and (iv) an order that the ITC disclose the extent and whereabouts of its assets for the purpose of the enforcement of an unpaid judgment debt arising out of an unsatisfied arbitration award obtained by one creditor against the ITC (the disclosure of assets application). It is noteworthy in this context that often it may be difficult for a third party who has suffered injury to initiate in an international forum by resort to diplomatic protection suit against the member states of an organization. As happened in the case of the ITC, the national state of the third party is more often than not one of the member states of the organization which would render diplomatic protection *vis-à-vis*

law reflected in the interpretation of a treaty cannot be applied by the courts of the UK because of the doctrine of non-justiciability, unless the treaty is incorporated by legislation, in general the courts of the UK will not be able to give effect to the constituent treaty of the organization or rights and obligations flowing from it, unless the legislature specifically incorporates the constituent instrument.[9]

When member states of an organization are sued in national courts, where such member states are foreign states, the question of sovereign immunity may also arise.[10] This will be an added impediment to the assertion of rights of third parties. Immunity or the lack of it may very well turn on the distinction between acts of a sovereign state performed *iure imperii* and *iure gestionis*. Non-justiciability may also be an impediment to a successful suit.[11] For other reasons, courts may not assume jurisdiction against their own states. But the problems that arise from such jurisdictional rules as those relating to sovereign or governmental immunity do not affect the importance or existence of the substantive law governing the liability of member states of organizations to third parties. For, apart from the intrinsic validity of the substantive law (where immunity is waived, for example), the substantive issue could be litigated in a national court. Another possibility is that arbitration, whether at a national or transnational level, by agreement between third parties and member states, may be resorted to as a means of settling a dispute. In such a case the substantive issue of international organizational law relating to the liability of member states of the organization to third parties may be decided by the arbitral tribunal in the course of settling the dispute.

that member state inapplicable. Further, it is unlikely that his national state would exercise diplomatic protection against the other member states with whom it would be jointly liable to its national. In the case of the ITC the third parties were mainly British and the UK was one of the member states of the organization. Thus, it was unlikely that the UK would have extended them diplomatic protection as a means of securing their rights.

[9] There may also be problems of recognition of international personality because of the rules of the national law concerned. This problem has been discussed in Chapter 3 above. See also *Arab Monetary Fund* v. *Hashim and Others (No. 3)* [1990] 1 All ER p. 685 (High Court); [1990] 3 WLR p. 139 (CA); [1991] 1 All ER p. 871 (HL) which case dealt with problems created by the approach taken by the UK courts. This case illustrates that national courts may find alternatives to refusing recognition of international personality.

[10] See *Maclaine Watson & Co. Ltd* v. *Department of Trade and Industry* [1988] 3 All ER (CA) at pp. 312*ff. per* Kerr LJ, at p. 336 *per* Nourse LJ, at pp. 348*ff. per* Ralph Gibson LJ.

[11] See also *MacLaine Watson & Co. Ltd* v. *Department of Trade and Industry* [1988] 3 All ER (CA) at pp. 291*ff. per* Kerr LJ, at pp. 335*ff. per* Nourse LJ.

The analysis above shows that as a general proposition international law as the proper law of the organization should be applicable at the national level to the issue of liability (direct or secondary) of member states for obligations of the organization. On the international plane the same issue would inevitably be governed by international law. Thus, the answer to the question whether there is such liability or not on the national level should be the same as the answer to the question of liability on the international plane and depend on the latter answer. The question would remain, however, whether there are circumstances in which individual states would nonetheless be responsible for their own conduct in relation to the organization under applicable national law. Even if the answer to this question is in the affirmative, the liability would not be a secondary or concurrent one but a direct one.

The importance of the organization's having personality

It is easy to see that, if an organization has no international personality its actions are no more than actions of all its member states, whoever acts ostensibly in the name of the organization being only an agent of some or all of the member states.[12] In such a situation there is no liability to a third party incurred by an international organization as such because there is no such entity. The liability incurred is a direct liability, probably joint and several, of all the states on behalf of whom the agent acts. Thus, in the old German Customs Union (Zollverein) all action taken at an international level was entrusted to one member (Prussia) which acted on behalf of the collective membership of the Union. Similarly, in the Belgo-Luxembourg Economic Union Belgium represents the Union in its international relations and acts on behalf of both members.[13] There

---

[12] That separate legal personality is crucial in order that the actions be no more than actions of all member states is implied in the *Certain Phosphate Lands in Nauru Case*, 1992 ICJ Reports p. 240. There was a tripartite administering power in the trusteeship arrangements in that case, but the Court implied that one of the states could be held responsible in its own right. In doing so it stressed that the administering authority was not a separate legal entity from the three states: see *ibid.* at p. 258, *per* the Court, and at p. 271, *per* Judge Shahabuddeen (separate opinion).

[13] See Schermers and Blokker, *International Institutional Law* (1995) p. 977. The assumption tentatively made above that liability would be joint and several may be controversial. The point was reserved in the *Certain Phosphate Lands in Nauru Case*, 1992 ICJ Reports at p. 258 (although the point was discussed in the pleadings extensively), and also *per* Judge Shahabuddeen in a separate opinion, *ibid.* at p. 271. The question has been discussed by Brownlie, *System of the Law of Nations: State Responsibility, Part I* (1983) pp. 189*ff.*, who thinks that liability is not joint and several in international law in the

is simply a relationship of principals and agent, the principals being primarily liable for the acts of the agent. One other issue that may arise in such a case is whether the principals can avoid liability because of an excess of authority by the agent. But this is not the issue here.

It is only if the international organization has personality that: (i) the organization *can* incur liabilities on its own behalf by entering into legal transactions in its own right; and (ii) the question can properly be posed whether in any circumstances the member states of the organization are also liable to third parties on account of such liabilities incurred by the organization. That the relevant factor is international personality cannot be doubted. These organizations are creatures of international agreement formed under international law and it is appropriate, therefore, that their personality be determined by international law.[14] What will be discussed here is the situation where an organization has international personality.

The liability of members

The issue then is whether, once it is established that international personality has been attributed by international law to a particular international organization, the member states (or member international entities) may be held liable either directly or indirectly for the obligations of the organization.

First, the problem may be considered as an incidence of international responsibility, concentrating on what happens where the action is confined to the international plane, as, for example, where an organization fails to honour obligations under a treaty into which it has entered with a state to make a loan or pay for services or the organization commits an international delict against a state. The question then, for example, in the case of a treaty, when the organization has not fulfilled its

---

absence of practice or other authority. Quigley, 'Complicity in International Law: A new Direction in the Law of State Responsibility', 57 BYIL (1986) at pp. 127*ff.*, also discusses the issue but with some new insights in the case of complicity.

[14] The question of international personality has been discussed in Chapter 3 above. It is possible that states may create an organization of states which, however, is not formed under international law but under a national law, e.g., the Bank of International Settlements. Because such an organization has personality at the national level, the same issue of liability of members to third parties would arise but under the law of incorporation. The organization is both a creature of international law and a creature of national law, however, which is what distinguishes the case from the one under discussion.

obligation, is whether the state party to the treaty can have recourse to the member states for payment or damages. In other words, what is the liability of member states to the state with which the organization entered into the treaty in respect of the organization's obligations to that state? As already noted, the liability of member states would clearly be a matter for international law. Second, a similar problem may arise in connection with non-international law obligations (i.e., under national or transnational law) to states, natural persons or juristic persons or even to other international organizations. The issue of the liability of member states to the third parties, though concerned with non-international law obligations of organizations, would in this case also, as already noted, be a matter for international law to decide, as the 'personal' or 'national' law of the organization. There is no reason to suppose or assume that the answer given to the question of liability of member states should be or is different in the two cases.

The approach taken by international law to the problem will first be considered in relation to the law of treaties and international delicts and then the solutions proposed or adopted for transactions on the non-international plane will be discussed.

Transactions on the international plane

The maxim *pacta tertiis nec nocent nec prosunt* which has always been applicable in treaty law would normally not permit the imposition of obligations, direct or indirect, upon member states of an organization without their consent by the conclusion of a treaty between the organizations and a state. Articles 34 and 35 of the Vienna Convention on the Law of Treaties have codified this principle.[15] Thus, this would mean that members of an international organization would normally not be liable

---

[15] The scope of the principle has been discussed generally by Chinkin, *Third Parties in International Law* (1993) pp. 52*ff.* (On the position in regard to treaties, and under the Vienna Convention on the Law of Treaties, see also Hartwig, note 2, Chapter 8. See also Articles 34 and 35 of the Vienna Convention on the Law of Treaties between States and International Organizations or between International Organizations (1986) which embody the same principles: 25 ILM (1986) p. 543. On this Convention see, e.g., Zemanek. 'Agreements Concluded by International Organizations and the Vienna Convention on the Law of Treaties', 3 *University of Toledo Law Review* (1971) at pp. 145*ff.*; Zemanek, 'The United Nations Conference on the Law of Treaties Between States and International Organizations or between International Organizations: The Unrecorded History of its "general agreement"', in Bocksteigel *et al.* (eds.), *Law of Nations, Law of International Organizations, World's Economic Law: Festschrift Ignaz Seidl-Hohenveldern* (1988) pp. 665*ff.*; and Reuter, 'Le droit des traités et les accords internationaux conclus par les organizations internationales', in Centre interuniversitaire de droit public et de

for the obligations of the organization without their consent, because they would not be responsible for breaches of treaties by the organization. There have been cases decided by the ICJ or other international tribunals in which third states have claimed rights under treaties[16] but none in which the issue raised has concerned obligations of third states or parties under treaties.

This general principle has been subject to exceptions; for example, where a treaty creates an objective regime.[17] It may also be pointed out that in the case of international organizations themselves which are created by states by a constituent treaty *inter se* and to which international organizations are not parties, international organizations as international persons in their own right have obligations imposed on them (and powers and rights attributed to them) without any requirement of consent on the part of the international organizations. These exceptions, however, do not militate against the argument that member states are not *per se* liable under treaties concluded by international organizations on account of the *pacta tertiis* principle because it is such a firm principle in international treaty law.

The liability of member states may also be in issue in connection with transactions other than treaties which take place on the international plane. Thus, the same questions may be asked in connection with international delicts, as might have occurred, for example, if internationally illegal acts were committed, when the US bombed North Korea during the Korean war, or national contingents during the UN Congo operation caused death or injury to nationals of other states or in the UN Cyprus operation caused damage to property. The question of the organization's responsibility in these circumstances has been discussed in Chapter 12. There may also be an overlap between liability in national law and liability at international law. In connection with the organization's liability, two questions would arise. One concerns the possible

l'Université Libre de Bruxelles (ed.), *Miscellanea W. J. Ganshof van de Meersh* (1972) vol. I at pp. 195*ff.*

[16] See, e.g., the *Certain German Interests in Upper Silesia Case*, PCIJ Series A No. 7. In the *Certain Phosphate Lands in Nauru Case*, 1992 ICJ Reports p. 240, one of the issues raised was whether a people, not party to the trusteeship agreement between Australia and the UN, could claim rights under the agreement. This case was subsequently withdrawn after the ICJ decided on the preliminary objections, following a settlement agreement concluded on 10 August 1993, between the parties. The Court removed the case from the list at the request of both parties by an Order dated 13 September 1993: 32 ILM (1993) pp. 1471–2.

[17] See the *SS Wimbledon Case*, PCIJ Series A No. 1. Article 38 of both Vienna Conventions on treaties leaves room for such exceptions as arise under customary international law.

joint liability of the particular states involved in the alleged delicts. The other is whether international law recognizes liability on the part of members of the organization.

As regards the first question, responsibility would be based on direct liability which is a possibility in international law. There would, in these circumstances, conceivably be joint and several liability attributable to the particular states involved in the alleged delicts, because they were co-perpetrators of those delicts. Liability would rest on the principles of delictual responsibility. It is doubtful that a state can in these circumstances plead, for instance, 'superior orders' of an international organization to exculpate itself.

In regard to the second question, while there could be liability for delicts of the organization attributable to states, the delict situation is different from the treaty situation. In the latter case the norm binding on the organization is not presumably, as such, binding on the state, notwithstanding that it is a member of the organization. The liability based on delictual responsibility is also different from any that may arise for the member states of the organization in general *qua* members of the organization. On the question whether members are liable *qua* members, there is no clear practice, unless it is presumed that the absence of admissions of liability on the part of members of the organization *qua* members in the above cases confirms that there is no such general rule of liability.[18] Here, as in the case of international agreements, the question concerns how and when the law would go behind the personality of the organization to pin liability on the member states. The crucial question is whether a state that supports a resolution authorizing an international organization to take action which results in a delict *vis-à-vis* another state is internationally responsible for that delict. Where the delict is specifically authorized, liability may be attributable to the state but this would be a direct liability as a tortfeasor or accomplice and not based on secondary or concurrent liability. Where the delict is not specifically authorized, any liability would be on the same basis, though the attribution of liability may depend on other factors, such as apparent

---

[18] See also *Nissan* v. *A-G* [1967] 3 WLR 1044 (CA), and [1969] 1 All ER p. 629 (HL). The House of Lords held, differing from the Court of Appeal, that the terms of the agreement between the UN and the government of Cyprus, concerning the legal status of the force, did not absolve the British government from liability for such acts. The responsibility was based on implied consent and did not arise by itself. Responsibility of the member state was that of a joint tortfeasor. It was not a genuine question of third party liability.

authority, inherent in the law of international responsibility. States that do not support such a resolution would presumably not be liable at all on the secondary or concurrent basis.

The position at the non-international level

The question of the liability of member states for the obligations of organizations *vis-à-vis* third parties is, it has been argued here, a question of international law, even though the transaction in regard to which the issue is raised may have taken place at the national or transnational level. Thus, whatever solution is adopted in regard to such transactions must also be good for transactions which take place at an international level. The question may be approached from more than one angle on the premise that a range of legal concepts or arguments may be invoked with a view to inflicting or denying such liability.

Primary and direct liability

One argument that member states are liable directly and jointly and severally for the obligations of the organization is based on the theory that, though the organization has international personality, conferred on it by its 'proper' law, namely international law, which is the relevant law for determining the issue of personality, nevertheless, the organization should in national law be regarded as an unincorporated body and as having acted through the name of the organization. This was one of the arguments advanced in the *ITC Case (CA)*.[19] The argument was rejected by the Court of Appeal. As Kerr LJ said:

> The purpose of the domestic legislation was to give recognition to the international organization as a legal entity in international law and to enable it to function as a legal entity, or as if it was a legal entity, within the framework of English Law.[20]

In the *ITC Case (CA)* the argument in favour of direct liability was made in the context of interpreting a national legislative instrument. It is clear that in the event legislation exists which covers an international

---

[19] [1988] 3 All ER p. 257 (CA). The argument was summarized by Kerr LJ: *ibid.* at p. 294. Another ground of direct liability is negligence on the part of the member states (some or all) in exercising control over the organization. This basis was invoked in the cases before the CJEC which were withdrawn: see footnote 66 below. See also particularly, Hartwig, note 2, Chapter 14; Sadurska and Chinkin, 'The Collapse of the International Tin Council: A Case of State Responsibility?', 30 VJIL (1990) at pp. 880*ff*.

[20] [1988] 3 All ER at p. 296.

organization and that legislation is supreme, as it is in the UK, that legislation must govern the situation regarding the legal personality of the organization for national law. However, as emerges from the *ITC Case (CA)*, there is a presumption that the legislation intended to incorporate a reference to international law as the personal (or 'proper') law of the organization, which reference might normally have been made by the common law in the course of applying principles of private international law. *A fortiori*, where the common law or general law is being applied, the private international law of the forum which would normally point to the personal or 'proper' law of the entity in order to determine the question of legal personality and its consequences should refer to international law as the proper law to determine the issue.

In the *ITC Case (HL)*, while the House of Lords did not develop its reasoning as fully as the Court of Appeal, it did agree with the result on the basis that the UK legislation gave the ITC a separate legal personality distinct from its members by virtue of bestowing on it the status of a body corporate in English law.[21] This avoided any need to refer to international law as the law governing the status of the organization. The reasoning of the Court of Appeal, however, remains a useful alternative where the situation was not as clear as in the case of the ITC.

On the other hand, there are circumstances where there may be direct liability, as where this is explicitly assumed as in a joint commitment. Liability based on a guarantee is also a form of direct liability, though it may be secondary as well.

Liability based on agency

Another argument that may be made and was made in the *ITC Case (CA)* is based on the idea of agency.[22] It proceeds on the basis that, while the international organization falls to be treated as a legal entity which is distinct from its members in the same way as a body corporate and, therefore, has a personality of its own, the organization which is normally liable in respect of the obligations it contracts may not be so liable when it contracts those obligations on behalf of its members as disclosed or undisclosed principals. The agency that, thus, arises would make the members directly liable and may be 'constitutional' or 'factual'.

---

[21] [1989] 3 WLR (HL) at p. 982 *per* Lord Templeman, at pp. 1004, 1005, 1008 *per* Lord Oliver.
[22] See the judgments of Kerr LJ: [1988] 3 All ER (CA) at pp. 307*ff*., and Ralph Gibson LJ: *ibid*. at pp. 356*ff*.

The issue of factual agency could arise in any situation. It does not hinge specifically on the nature of the personality of the organization nor does it flow from the constitutional relationship between the organization and its members, resting as it does on a factual situation. It is entirely possible that in a given factual situation the agency relationship between the organization and its members could be established, as where the organization is given a mandate by some or all of its members to enter into an agreement whereby the members would loan funds or for the purchase of capital goods to be delivered to members for which they would pay. In that case there would be a direct liability on the part of members for the obligations incurred. But then the organization itself would not be primarily liable, unless it has exceeded its power under the particular law of agency.[23]

'Constitutional' agency may arise when the constituent instrument by its terms, express or implicit, makes the organization an agent of the members who were undisclosed principals for a particular transaction or transactions. For this situation to obtain it must be shown that the structure set up by the constituent instrument was such that it was only consistent with the alleged agency and not with any other interpretation, it being inadequate to show that the way in which the organization *in fact* worked internally was, or may have been, consistent with the organization contracting on behalf of its members.[24]

To a large extent this is a matter of interpretation of the particular constituent instrument. Generally, it may be presumed that constitutional agency was not intended, the burden being to displace this presumption. While in a given case there may be constitutional agency, it is not easy to discover such agency in the case of the many international organizations that exist.

In the *ITC Case (CA)* itself the UK Court of Appeal held that there was no principal–agent relationship established by the constituent instrument between the members and the organization in respect of the transactions in issue. As Kerr LJ explained:

So what is there in the Sixth International Tin Agreement which demonstrates that in entering into buffer stock contracts or bank loans, or into any other transactions, the council must have been contracting as agent for the members as undisclosed principals? Counsel for the multi-brokers referred to many

---

[23] In the *ITC Case (CA)* the Court held that no factual agency had been established. See
Kerr LJ: *ibid.* at pp. 311–12 and Ralph Gibson LJ: *ibid.* at p. 357.
[24] See Kerr LJ: *ibid.* at p. 309.

provisions of the Sixth Agreement for this purpose. But in my view none of them suggest that in contracting in its own name the council was acting as agent for the members as undisclosed principals under contracts.[25]

The relationship between the member states and the ITC under the constituent instrument was found to be comparable to the situation under an instrument of incorporation. In the *ITC Case (HL)* the House of Lords took the view that under the UK legislation which gave the ITC the status of a body corporate there could be no constitutional agency, and further that the sixth International Tin Agreement (ITA 6) could not be used to contradict anything in the UK legislation but only to clarify any ambiguity in that legislation – and there was no ambiguity therein.[26] Thus, the issue was in fact decided on the basis of the English law and not international law. But Lord Oliver with whom the House agreed did say that, in the event the ITA 6 was relevant for the purpose, he supported the reasoning of Kerr LJ in the Court of Appeal.[27]

While constitutional or factual agency may theoretically be a proper basis for the direct liability of members of an international organization, it must be recognized that proof of such agency is not easy, there being a presumption in favour of the absence of such agency. Further, it is also clear that where such agency is proved to exist the liability of the members would not really be for the obligations of the organization but a direct liability for their own obligations which had been incurred by the organization acting as their agent on behalf of undisclosed principals.

Secondary or concurrent liability

Liability of members of an international organization to third parties may also be based on the theory that, while the organization has legal personality, under both international and national law, its members cannot claim limited liability which would absolve them from liability to third parties for the obligations of the organization as though they were shareholders in a national law corporation incorporated in such a way as to entitle them to claim limited liability. Just as in certain national systems of law, particularly the civil law systems, there are incorporated legal persons whose shareholders are liable concurrently

[25] *Ibid.*
[26] [1989] 3 WLR at p. 985 (HL) *per* Lord Templeman and at p. 1016 *per* Lord Oliver.
[27] [1989] 3 WLR at p. 1017 (HL).

or secondarily for the obligations of the corporation, so the theory goes, international organizations are legal persons whose members are liable concurrently or secondarily in the same way, provided there is no express limitation of liability so as to assimilate members to shareholders of limited companies.

The substance of the above theory rests on one of two bases. First, it seems to apply what purports to be a general principle of law derived from national law and applicable to legal entities where shareholders are liable concurrently or secondarily for the obligations of the legal entity itself. Second, in the alternative, it seeks to derive from the absence of express limitation in the constituent instrument of liability of members of an organization the concurrent or secondary liability of such members. It follows that the organization must be assimilated to a mixed legal entity in national law whose shareholders are concurrently or secondarily liable for the obligations of the entity.

Text writers

There are authorities which support both points of view or variations of them. Most authorities do not support secondary or concurrent liability. The leading authorities on both sides are discussed here.

The question seems first to have been faced in 1965. The author contrasted the position of members of an international organization with that of shareholders in a company in national law and took the view that, in the absence of a specific theory of limited liability in international law, members are liable for the obligations of their organizations.[28] This view is based on the theory that, whereas in national law there are rules of company or corporate law that produce effects *erga omnes*, there are no such rules of organizational law in international law; as a result, limited liability cannot be assumed to be a basic premise in regard to international organizations. However, Adam also raises the question – rather illogically, if the appropriate conclusion must be drawn from his premises – whether the liability of members must be conditioned on fault or negligence.

A second writer's position was similar to the one above. He stated that '[i]n general third States may disregard the existence of the organization as a person distinct from its members States'.[29] He cited some

---

[28] H. T. Adam, *Les Organismes Internationaux Spécialisés* (1965), vol. I p. 130.
[29] Seidl-Hohenveldern, note 3 p. 188.

questionable examples,[30] however, in support of this claim, examples that are not really in point. He later stated:

According to generally accepted principles of the conflict of laws the respective responsibilities of a corporate entity and of its members are determined by the national law of that entity. If the treaty establishing the enterprise does not contain any such rules, the member States will be jointly and severally responsible for its acts, as general international law does not contain any rules comparable to those which, in domestic law, limit responsibility of the members of a corporation for the latter's acts. Moreover, comparative law shows that in the domestic law of several States there exist corporate entities, whose members remain responsible for [the entities'] acts.[31]

In a subsequent article, commenting on the *ITC Case (CA)*, the same author reiterated his opinion that the members of an international state enterprise or organization 'have jointly and severally a concurrent liability for its debts'. He also cited the example of Eurochemic, which when wound up had run into debt well beyond its capital. Though the members initially wished to limit their liability to their respective shares of the capital, they finally gave satisfactory guarantees to Belgium, which took over the activities of Eurochemic, that they would respect the financial obligations resulting from their participation in its previous activities.[32]

---

[30] *Ibid.* at pp. 88–9. For the purpose of the present discussion it does not make a material difference that Seidl-Hohenveldern was discussing inter-state enterprises generally with limited membership. The examples cited were: (1) the liability of the host state for acts of the organization, which has no bearing on the liability of member states as such; (2) a case that did not involve the liability of members for the obligations of the organization to third parties (namely, the EEC's establishment in 1974 of the Centre for Professional Training in West Berlin); (3) a case where it was not at all clear that an international organization rather than a partnership had been established (an agreement between Chile and Peru in 1865); and (4) the specific exemption from liability of the host state for the acts of the International Atomic Energy Agency in its headquarters agreement with Austria, a question essentially of liability of the host state, which is in a special position *vis-à-vis* the organization, and not of the liability of members as such; however, the argument advanced is that such an exemption would not have been necessary had member states originally not been liable to third parties for the obligations of the organization.

[31] *Ibid.* at p. 199.

[32] Seidl-Hohenveldern, 'Piercing the Corporate Veil of International Organizations: The International Tin Council Case in the English Court of Appeals', 32 GYIL (1989) at p. 43 and pp. 51–2. That writer, has, however, now changed his earlier view to conclude that member states are not *per se* liable for an organization's debts. He is now in agreement with the views expressed by me: see Seidl-Hohenveldern, 66-I *Annuaire de l'Institut de droit International* (1995) at p. 433.

Another author also believed that the corporate personality of an international organization does not result in the exclusion of its members' liability for the obligations of the organization, although such liability may not be joint and several. He observed:

> Under national legal systems, companies can be created with restricted liability. An express provision thus enables natural persons to create, under specific conditions, a new legal person in such a way that they are no longer personally liable for the acts of the new person . . . In international law no such provisions exist. It is therefore impossible to create international legal persons in such a way as to limit the responsibility of the individual Members . . . When an international organization is unable to meet its liabilities, the Members are obliged to stand in, according to the amount by which each Member is assessed for contributions to the organization's budget.[33]

This view seems to assume that all organizations are financed only by contributions from members, whereas there are some, such as the financial institutions, that generate their own resources. Further, no explanation was given why the liability of members is not joint and several, rather than according to the amount contributed to the organization's budget.

A fourth writer, among others, agrees that there is no limited liability of members. He reasons as follows:

> Public international law (which includes, of course, the constituent treaty) also governs the international corporation's corporate status . . . This rule applies, in the first place, to the question whether the member States are in any way responsible for the corporation's liabilities and, if so, whether their liability is limited or unlimited. The existence of a body corporate does not necessarily relieve member States of such responsibility. The corporation may be the agent of its members. In France a partnership enjoys legal personality. In England an unlimited company is a body corporate. Yet in both cases members are, or may be, liable to the corporation's creditors.[34]

Here there is a combination of the ideas that an international organization may be acting as the agent of its members and that, in any case, members are presumptively liable for the debts of the organization, even though it may have personality in international law.

---

[33] Schermers, *International Institutional Law* (1980) p. 780. The view taken by me, that in principle member states are not liable for the debts of an organization, has now been adopted by Schermers: Schermers and Blokker, note 13 pp. 976*ff*.

[34] Mann, 'International Corporations and National Law', in his *Studies in International Law* (1973) p. 572, reprinted from 42 BYIL (1967) at pp. 160–1.

One writer, referring to the views described above, as well as others, suggested a different approach:

A question usually raised ... is whether the members of an international company can be held liable to third parties for its acts ... My point here is that we cannot conclude a rule of unlimited liability merely from the absence of a rule of limited liability in international law. All relevant provisions and circumstances must be studied to ascertain what was intended by the parties in this respect and the extent to which their intention was made known to third parties dealing with the enterprise. Present general rules of international law cannot, in my opinion, be quoted as basis of the unlimited liability of the parties to an international corporation for its acts or omissions, unless of course the corporation is considered, despite its independent personality, an organ of the states establishing it.[35]

He did not agree that there is a rule of unlimited liability, whether joint and several or joint and in proportion to the members' shares or assessed budgetary contributions, because there is no rule of limited liability in international law. The logic of this is *not* apparent. In any event it is to be questioned that there is no rule of limited liability in international law. It also does not make sense to state that there are no rules at all relating to liability of member states – neither establishing liability nor absence of liability. There must be one or the other, at least presumptively. As will be seen, there are basic principles. The logic, at least in terms of legal rights and duties is that, if there is no rule that requires a person to pay, he is entitled not to pay; that is to say, he is not liable to pay in law.

The better view[36] is that, firstly, a constituent instrument must be construed in the light of all the circumstances so as to determine the intention, express or implied, of the parties to it; and secondly, there is no presumption, when the constituent instrument does not indicate such an intention, that members of an international organization are concurrently or secondarily liable for its obligations. The presumption is to the contrary. However, policy reasons also suggested the need to limit this rule on the basis of estoppel: the presumption of non-liability

---

[35] Shihata, 'Role of Law in Economic Development: The Legal Problems of International Public Ventures', 25 *Revue Egyptienne de droit international* (1969) p. 125. Among others, Cahier agrees that there is no rule in international law that members are liable for the debts of the organization: 'The Strengths and Weaknesses of International Arbitration Involving a State as a Party', in Lew (ed.), *Contemporary Problems in International Arbitration* (1987) p. 244.

[36] C. F. Amerasinghe, 'Liability to Third Parties of Member States of International Organizations: Practice, Principle and Judicial Precedent', 85 AJIL (1991) at p. 280.

could be displaced by evidence that members (some or all of them) or the organization with the approval of members gave creditors reason to assume that members (some or all of them) would accept concurrent or secondary liability with or without an express or implied intention to that effect in the constituent instrument.[37] This is my view.

The rapporteur of the Institut de droit international more recently seems to have herself been of the view that the presumption in the absence of contrary indications was that there was no liability of member states.[38]

Practice

The solitary example given by Seidl-Hohenveldern (namely, that of Eurochemic) is inconclusive. The constituent instrument of Eurochemic was silent on the matter of members' liability for the debts of the organization. But there is no clear indication in or by reason of the agreement reached between the members and Belgium upon the winding up of the organization and the transfer of its functions to Belgium that the members took responsibility for the debts of Eurochemic because they were under a legal obligation to do so. The agreement could very well have been reached as an inducement to Belgium to take over the functions of Eurochemic in order to relieve Belgium, as the successor, of any responsibility for Eurochemic's debts. Assumption of responsibility for the debts of Eurochemic by the members may well have been the *quid pro quo* for the succession of Belgium to the functions of the organization. The facts are consistent with this interpretation. What might have happened if Eurochemic had been dissolved without any question of a successor is open to speculation. Thus, this instance is at best equivocal.

The dissolution of the LN does not support the secondary liability of member states for the debts of the organization. The surplus funds were distributed once liabilities of the organization had been discharged and nothing more.[39]

---

[37] For this qualification see now the decision in the *Westland Helicopters Ltd* v. *AOI (Partial Award)* arbitration which is referred to below.

[38] 66-I *Annuaire de l'Institut de droit international* (1995) p. 285 and *passim*. As the records show, there were conflicting views expressed in the Commission, a clear majority, however, being in favour of the rapporteur's view: *ibid.* p. 462 *passim*. See also for a similar view, Hartwig, note 2 *passim* and Chapter 19.

[39] See Annex A to Shihata's reply in 66-I *Annuaire de l'Institut de droit international* (1995) at pp. 316*ff*. Upon the dissolution of the East African Community liabilities as well as assets were distributed among the member states on the recommendation of a

What other practice there is of relevance is reflected in the constituent instruments of some organizations which are numerically by no means in the majority. These organizations are in general financial organizations or those that engage in some form of banking or commercial transactions in the discharge of their main functions. Some of these organizations are not universal organizations but the practice in relation to them may be studied as being relevant. In the constituent instruments of most of these there is a provision in which the liability of members is expressly limited in one way or another. A look at the earliest instrument which set up the IBRD, the prototype for all financial institutions, shows that there was: (i) an explicit limitation of the liability of members to the unpaid portion of the issue price of shares;[40] (ii) a requirement that every security issued or guaranteed by the organization should have on its face a conspicuous statement that it was not an obligation of any government unless expressly stated on the security;[41] (iii) a ratio at any given time of 1:1 for outstanding loans and guarantees in relation to the equity of the organization;[42] and (iv) a provision that in the event of termination of the operations of the organization members were liable for uncalled subscriptions to capital stock and in respect of the depreciation of their own currencies until the claims of all creditors were discharged.[43] It emerges from the manner in which these provisions are framed in the constituent instrument that it was clearly intended by the parties that members as such should not be liable for the obligations of the organization. That is to say, third parties could not under any circumstances have direct actions against members in respect of the debts of the organization, whether during the life of the organization or when the organization was being wound up or liquidated. On the other hand, members would be liable to the organization, like shareholders of a company on and only to the extent of their unpaid subscriptions, in the event that the organization was short of funds to meet its liabilities, whether during its life or at liquidation. There would be no liability to the organization on the part of members beyond their uncalled subscriptions. There is a 'gearing' ratio (the ratio between the IBRD's total

mediator and by agreement among these states. There was no assumption that member states were *per se* liable as a result of the treaty creating the organization or general principles of international law: see Annex B to Shihata's reply, *ibid.* at pp. 318*ff.* In the case of the LN it is significant that it was never seriously claimed that the members were liable for the debts of the organization to staff members who were discontinued, although such staff members remained unrequited.

[40] Article II(6).   [41] Article IV(9).   [42] Article III(3).   [43] Article VI(5).

amount of outstanding loans and guarantees and its subscribed capital) which has always to be 1:1. But this is not a debt–equity ratio and does not mean that the organization will always be solvent.[44] What is important is that the liability of members is limited, as in a limited liability corporation in national law, but in this case expressly.[45]

There are some constituent instruments in which the express formulation of the limitation on the liability of members is wider and more general, as where it is stated that 'No member shall be liable, by reason of its membership, for acts or obligations of the Fund.'[46] While this wording is not absolutely clear, it would be unreasonable to interpret it as excluding the liability to the organization on subscribed shares or for assessed contributions to the budget of members, though there can be no doubt that third parties can have no recourse against members as such. This is particularly so because the provisions on liquidation of the organization generally make it clear that members have such a liability on subscribed shares.[47] In a few cases there is added specific reference

---

[44] Debts arising from, e.g., administrative contracts, are apparently not included in the concept of debt for the purposes of the 'gearing' ratio.

[45] Other organizations in which there is a limitation of liability of members in a manner identical with or similar to that in the Articles of Agreement of the IBRD are, e.g., the IDB (Articles II(3)(d), IV(5), VII(2), X(3)), the AFDB (Articles 6(5), 21, 22, 25, 48, 49); and the MIGA (Articles 8(d), 22, 55). There are some differences in the 'gearing' or equivalent ratio in these instruments.

[46] Article 3(4) of the IFAD Agreement. For the same or similar wording see the constituent instruments of the IFC (Article II(4)), the IDA (Article II(3)), the African Development Fund (ADFD) (Article 10), the ADB (Article 5(7)), the Inter-American Investment Corporation (Article II(6)), the Caribbean Development Bank (CDB) (Article 6(8)), the Caribbean Investment Corporation (CIC) (Article 6(6)), the Common Fund for Commodities (Article 6), the International Seabed Authority (ISA) (Article 174(4) and Article 3 of the Statute of the Enterprise), the Arab Fund for Economic and Social Development (Article 8(1)), the Arab Monetary Fund (Article 48(a)), the Islamic Development Bank (Article 7(3)), the Inter-Arab Investment Guarantee Corporation (Article 7(4)), the BADEA (Article 5 (III)), the East African Development Bank (EADB) (Article 4(9)), the International Bank for Economic Cooperation (Article 2(3)) and the International Investment Bank (Article 3). Slightly different wording but with the same effect was used in the constituent instruments of the International Cocoa Organization (ICO) (1986) (Article 22(5)), the International Sugar Organization (ISO) (1987) (Article 29) and the International Natural Rubber Organization (INRO) (1987) (Article 48(4)). See also Article IV(4) of the Statute of the Fonds de Réetablissement of the Council of Europe: Adam, note 28 vol. I p. 275.

[47] See, e.g., the constituent instruments of the IFC (Article V(5)), the IDA (Article VII(5)), the ADF (Article 40), the ADB (Article 46), the IIC (Article VI(3)), the CDB (Article 45), the CIC (Articles 28 and 29), the Common Fund for Commodities (Articles 35–9), the Arab Fund for Economic and Social Development (Article 29), the Arab Monetary Fund (Article 21), the Islamic Development Bank (Article 48), the BADEA (Article 46) and the EADB (Article 41).

to the exclusion in securities of the liability of members to third parties.[48] But more importantly in many cases there is an express provision which makes it quite clear that members are liable to the organization for the unpaid portions of subscribed shares.[49] In all these cases, however, despite the differences in formulation and in the structure of the agreements, it is a fair conclusion that what was generally intended was the same result in regard to the liability of members to third parties for the obligations of the organization and to the obligations of members *vis-à-vis* the organization as obtained in the case of the IBRD.

In the case of the IMF, on the other hand, the constituent instrument is silent on the liability of members to third parties and to the organization for unpaid subscriptions, whether during the life of the organization or on liquidation.[50]

It may also be noted that generally organizations do not have to maintain a debt–equity ratio (which is different from a 'gearing' ratio) of 1:1, thus diluting any protection that third parties may have from such a requirement. In many cases there is no provision at all in the constituent instrument relating to this ratio.[51] In others the ratio is more than 1:1, leaving the possibility that debt may be well in excess of equity.[52]

The real difficulty is evaluating the practice of including in constituent instruments a clause excluding the liability to third parties of members of international organizations. Is the inclusion of such a clause in several constituent instruments to be regarded as recognition by the states concerned of a rule of international law that absence of a

---

[48] See the constituent instruments of the IFC (Article III(8)) and the ADB (Article 22).

[49] See the constituent instrument of the CDB (Article 6(7)), the CIC (Article 6(6)), the Arab Fund for Economic and Social Development (Article 8(2)), the Arab Monetary Fund (Article 48(b)), the Islamic Development Bank (Article 7(2)), the Inter-Arab Investment Guarantee Corporation (Article 7(4)), the BADEA (Article 5(III)), and the EADB (Article 4(8)).

[50] The agreement creating the OPEC Fund (an organization of limited membership) also does not provide expressly for the absence of liability of members to third parties but refers to the rights and obligations of the organization and of members *vis-à-vis* the organization when the organization is being liquidated: Article 11.02.

[51] See the constituent instruments of, e.g., the IBRD, the ADB, the AFDB, the IDB, the IMF, the MIGA, the CDB, the CIC, the ISA, the Arab Fund for Economic and Social Development, the Islamic Development Bank, the BADEA, the Inter-Arab Investment Guarantee Corporation, the International Bank for Economic Cooperation, the International Investment Bank, the ICO, the ISO and the INRO. In the case of the ADF, the IDA and the OPEC Fund, where there is no debt limitation provision, the institutions do not borrow.

[52] See the constituent instruments of the IFC (4:1) and the Arab Monetary Fund (2:1).

non-liability clause in a constituent instrument results in the members of the organization being liable to third parties for the obligations of the organization? A significant factor to be considered is that apart from the situation that arose in the case of the ITC there are no examples of member states either accepting or refusing to accept such liability to third parties where the constituent instrument is silent on the matter. In the only situation in which the issue arose, namely when the ITC collapsed, the members of the organization all denied that they were so liable. But it may be unwarranted to take this single incident as establishing definitively a law-creating practice even though the attitude of members was clear, just as much as the readiness of the members of Eurochemic to assume responsibility for the obligations of Eurochemic was at the most to be regarded as equivocal. In the absence of other evidence the practice of including a non-liability clause is ambiguous to the extent that it is as consistent with a belief that the absence of such a clause would entail the liability of members in the appropriate circumstances as with a desire to make absolutely clear *ex abundanti cautela* that members did not assume such liability, particularly because the issue had not been faced hitherto, with the result that it could be argued, as it was in the case of the ITC, that there was such liability.[53]

There are more than twice as many constituent instruments in which there is no reference to liability or non-liability of members to third parties as there are instruments in which some form of non-liability clause is included. On the basis of the conclusions reached above it cannot be inferred from the mere absence of non-liability clauses that the parties to the constituent instruments necessarily by that fact intended

---

[53] The view was expressed in the *ITC Case (CA)* by Ralph Gibson LJ that the express exclusion of liability in constituent instruments of numerous organizations did not imply that there was a rule that in the absence of such exclusion of liability members of international organizations assumed liability to third parties for the debts of the organization. He said: 'I am unable to accept that the practice shown in these treaties can fairly be regarded as recognition by the states concerned of a rule of international law that absence of a non-liability clause results in direct liability, whether primary or secondary, to creditors of the organization in contrast to the obligation to provide funds to the organization to meet its liabilities. Nothing is shown of any practice of states as to the acknowledgment or acceptance of direct liability by any states by reason of the absence of an exclusion clause.' [1988] 3 All ER (CA) at pp. 353–5. Both Kerr LJ, at p. 306 and Nourse LJ, at p. 330, agreed with Ralph Gibson LJ's views on this point, as did Lord Oliver and the other Lords in the *ITC Case (HL)*: [1989] 3 WLR at p. 1014 (HL). For an examination of the treaty practice see also Hartwig, note 2, Chapter 8.

to assume a concurrent or secondary liability to third parties for the obligations of the organizations because there is a general rule of international law that such liability exists. Further, in none of the constituent instruments in which non-liability clauses are absent is there any semblance of a provision whereby the members expressly assume a liability to third parties nor is there any indication that such an assumption of liability was intended by necessary implication. Conversely, there is no clear *practice* deriving from constituent instruments which would support the view that in the absence in the constituent instrument of an express or implied assumption of liability to third parties on the part of members for the obligations of the organization, the general law required that there be no such assumption of liability. It is a possible view that such practice as there is *conclusively* supports neither a general principle that, in the absence of an express or implied indication in the constituent instrument that liability to third parties was being assumed by members, such liability was to be considered not to have been assumed, nor a general principle that, in the absence of an express or implied indication in the constituent instrument that such liability was not being assumed by members, such liability was to be regarded as having been assumed.

In the ITC case, however, member states persisted in denying their liability and by this course of conduct gave a measure of support to the ruling of the English courts.[54] Thus, perhaps, it may also be inferred that there is a trend in practice towards the view that in the absence of an express or implied indication in the constituent instrument to the contrary there is a presumption that there is no concurrent or secondary liability of members to third parties for the debts of an organization. It would, therefore, be fair to conclude that there is an emerging practice which would support such a presumption, while the express or implied terms of the constituent instrument would primarily determine the issue. Further, the question may be asked whether it is not reasonable that, since one view entails the imposition of a liability, while the other does not, the view that does not involve the imposition of liability should presumptively prevail, because the burden, as Lord Oliver maintained in the House of Lords, is properly to show the incidence of such liability. The existence of the general practice

---

[54] See Mallory, 'Conduct Unbecoming: The Collapse of the International Tin Agreement' (1989), MPhil thesis for the University of Cambridge, at p. 33; [Anon.], 'Tin Creditors' £182.5m accord', *Financial Times*, 23 December 1989.

relating to transactions on the international plane would support such a presumption.

The case law

The decisions of the ICJ are not entirely helpful on this issue. The *Reparation Case*[55] established that an organization, such as the UN, did have international legal personality which resulted in the organization having the power to bear legal rights and obligations, but said nothing beyond that which could expressly illuminate the problem being discussed. It is significant, however, that the concept of international legal personality which was not fully defined further was regarded as giving the organization a status which was separate from the legal status of its members and enjoyed a certain independence. To some extent this may be regarded as implying the conclusion that the obligations of the organization and those of its members were separate but this conclusion in turn may require the implication of a particular concept of legal personality.

The other precedents concern organizations which were or could be regarded as less than universal. However, this consideration does not make a material difference to the issue being discussed because the principle applicable does not depend on the universality or non-universality of the organization. *Westland Helicopters Ltd.* v. *AOI*[56] was initially decided by an ICC arbitral tribunal. It found that, though the documents were

---

[55] 1949 ICJ Reports p. 174. The *Expenses Case*, 1962 ICJ Reports p. 151, which has been commented on extensively (see, e.g., C. F. Amerasinghe, 'The United Nations Expenses Case – A Contribution to the Law of International Organization', 4 IJIL (1964) p. 177; Gross, 'Expenses of the United Nations for Peace-Keeping Operations: The Advisory Opinion of the International Court of Justice', 17 Int. Org. (1963) p. 1; Jennings, 'International Court of Justice: Advisory Opinion of July 20, 1962: Certain Expenses of the United Nations', 11 ICLQ (1962) p. 1169; Simmonds, 'The UN Assessments Advisory Opinion', 13 ICLQ (1964) p. 854; Verzijl, 'International Court of Justice: Certain Expenses of the United Nations', 10 NILR (1963) p. 1), dealt with what constituted 'expenses of the organization' within the meaning of Article 17(2) of the Charter. It had nothing to say on the problem in hand. The *Namibia Case*, 1971 ICJ Reports p. 52, which dealt with the question whether a decision of the Security Council under Article 24 of the Charter is binding on the membership as a whole, also had no connection with the question of the liability of members to third parties. (This case has been discussed by Dugard, 'The Opinion on South-West Africa ("Namibia"): The Teleologists' Triumph', 88 SALJ (1971) p. 460; Higgins, 'The Advisory Opinion on Namibia: Which UN Resolutions are Binding under Article 25 of the Charter?', 21 ICLQ (1972) p. 270; Lissitzyn, 'International Law and the Advisory Opinion on Namibia', 11 Col. JTL (1972) p. 50.)

[56] [1984] 23 ILM (1984) p. 1071.

silent on the matter, the attribution of legal personality did not necessarily result in the exclusion of the liability of the four member states for the obligations of the AOI. The tribunal said of the liability of the members states:

> In the absence of any provision expressly or impliedly excluding the liability of the 4 states, this liability subsists since, as a general rule, those who engage in transactions of an economic nature are deemed liable for the obligations which flow therefrom. In default by the 4 states of formal exclusion of their liability, third parties which have contracted with the AOI could legitimately count on their liability.[57]

The tribunal's conclusion is based clearly on the premise that members of an organization are secondarily liable for the obligations of an organization, at least where it performs functions of an economic nature, unless there is an express exclusion of that liability. This view does not regard legal personality as by itself setting up a veil. It was founded on an analogy with co-operatives in certain civil law systems.

The view of the arbitral tribunal in the *Westland Helicopters* arbitration loses some of its force, however, because the arbitral award was challenged by one of the respondents in the Swiss courts where both the Court of Justice of Geneva and the Swiss Federal Tribunal annulled the award in respect of that respondent.[58] What is important is that both courts held that the AOI had total juridical independence from its members with the result that the member states were not also bound by the obligations undertaken by the AOI.[59] The Swiss courts clearly considered the conferment of juridical personality in the manner in which the constituent instrument intended to be a denial of the possibility that automatically the members were bound even secondarily by the obligations incurred by the organization. This view proceeds on the theory that ordinarily when a separate juridical or legal personality is given an entity created by states as a result of the constituent instrument, such personality necessarily precludes liability of the members for obligations of the organization, thus assimilating such personality to that of a limited liability corporation in national law.

In the *ITC Case (CA)* the majority of the UK Court of Appeal held that the members of the ITC were not concurrently or secondarily liable

---

[57] *Ibid.* at pp. 1083–4.   [58] [1988] 28 ILM (1989) p. 867.

[59] For the view of the Swiss Federal Tribunal see *ibid.* at p. 691 (Translation). The decision is discussed by Dominicé, 'Le Tribunal fédéral face à la personalité juridique d'un organisme international', 108 *Zeitschrift für Schweizerisches Recht* (1989) p. 517.

for the debts of the ITC, even though the constituent instrument did not expressly exclude such liability.[60] Most judges also placed emphasis on the constituent document and its interpretation. Nourse LJ further introduced the idea that it is important how far the intention behind the instrument was made known to third parties.[61] He then came to the conclusion that:

Throughout it must have been apparent to those states which were parties to successive international tin agreements that the orderly regulation of world production and consumption and the maintenance of a stable price were objectives for whose attainment vast quantities of tin would very likely have to be bought and sold. It must have been apparent that there could well be periods when production persistently exceeded consumption, so that the price would have to be maintained by correspondingly increased purchases. It must have been apparent that if the cost of those purchases could not be met out of funds in hand, third parties who gave credit to the ITC would have to look beyond those funds for satisfaction of their debts.[62]

Nourse LJ's conclusion seems to have been based on an interpretation of the constituent instrument by reference to surrounding circumstances and not on a denial of the presumption of the absence of liability. It

---

[60] Kerr LJ was not prepared to commit himself to any such principle at the level of international law but said that certainly in national law there could not be any such secondary or concurrent liability ([1988] 3 All ER at p. 307 (CA)). See also the *ITC Case (HL)* [1989] 3 WLR at p. 983 *per* Lord Templeman and at pp. 1008–9 *per* Lord Oliver. The other Law Lords agreed with them. Ralph Gibson LJ, on the other hand, was more certain that as a matter of international legal principle there was no such liability ([1988] 3 All ER at pp. 352–3 (CA)). While conceding that the constituent document and its interpretation were crucial, his view confirms that in the absence of a contrary indication the underlying principle is that a contract made as a separate entity by an international organization that has separate legal personality cannot impose a direct joint and several liability on the members simply by reason of their membership. Nourse LJ who dissented conceded, as did Ralph Gibson LJ, that the constituent instrument and its interpretation were paramount (*ibid.* at p. 330). For discussion of the ITC litigation and its sequel see, e.g., Sands, 'The Tin Council Litigation in the English Courts', 34 NILR (1987) p. 367; Herdegen, 'The Insolvency of International Organizations and the Legal Position of Creditors: Some Observations in the Light of the Tin Council Crisis', 35 NILR (1988) p. 135; Greenwood, 'Put Not Your Trust In Princes: The Tin Council Appeals', 48 CLJ (1989) p. 46; Mallory, loc. cit. note 54; Seidl-Hohenveldern, loc. cit. note 32; Sadurska and Chinkin, loc. cit. note 19 p. 845*ff.*; Ebenroth, 'Shareholders' Liability in International Organizations: the Settlement of the International Tin Council Case', 4 *Leiden Journal of International Law* (1991) p. 171; C. F. Amerasinghe, loc. cit. note 2; Higgins, loc. cit. note 38 above, *passim*; Hartwig, note 2 *passim* and Chapters 7 and 19 particularly.

[61] *Ibid.*   [62] *Ibid.* at p. 331.

was buttressed by a reference to both justice and propriety.[63] His interpretation of the constituent instrument clearly conflicted with that of
Kerr LJ and Ralph Gibson LJ and was, thus, a minority view of the situation, because both those judges did not reject the importance and
relevance of the constituent instrument and its interpretation. Thus,
this interpretation is less tenable from the point of view of judicial
precedent.

In the *ITC Case (HL)* the House of Lords was primarily concerned to
decide the case on the basis that, because the ITC had expressly been
given corporate status by legislation in English law there could be no
liability in contract for non-parties such as the members of the ITC, in
the absence of express parliamentary provision, no argument based on
ITA 6 as a result of any reference made by rules of private international
law being relevant, because ITA 6 had not been incorporated into English
law and particularly because it was clear that the legislation governed
the situation to the exclusion of the treaty.[64] But both Lord Templeman
and Lord Oliver[65] (with whom the other Lords agreed) did say that in any
case there was no clear evidence of a rule of international law requiring
that members of an organization be liable secondarily or concurrently
for the debts of the organization in the absence of a disclaimer of such
liability, it being clear that the burden was to prove the existence of
such a rule.

The Court of Justice of Geneva, the Swiss Federal Tribunal, the UK
Court of Appeal and the UK House of Lords accepted the principle that
the creation of a separate legal entity in the form of an international
organization does not raise a presumption that the members assumed
a concurrent and secondary liability for the obligations of the organization. Rather, a contrary presumption was created that the obligations
of the organization were separate from those of the members and created no such liability, albeit that the determination whether such a
liability existed depended primarily on the interpretation of the constituent instrument of the organization. The view taken by the arbitral
tribunal in the *Westland Helicopters* arbitration which reversed the presumption represents the minority view and one which was rejected in
the ultimate decisions taken in the cases concerned. Thus, the case law

---

[63] *Ibid.* at p. 334.
[64] [1989] 3 WLR (HL) at pp. 983, 984–5 *per* Lord Templeman and at pp. 1008–9, 1011, 1012,
1013 *per* Lord Oliver.
[65] [1989] 3 WLR (HL) at p. 983 and pp. 1014–15 respectively.

must be taken to favour the position taken by the Swiss and the UK courts.[66]

On the other hand, secondary liability would arise when it becomes apparent from all the circumstances of the case that the member states of an organization have implicitly undertaken to honour themselves the obligations of the organization in the event it failed to honour them. This is a case of an implied guarantee. In the *Westland Helicopters Ltd* v. *AOI (Partial Award)* arbitration[67] the tribunal took this view of the law in holding that the member states of the AOI were liable to the plaintiff. While conceding that there was no general rule of international law imposing liability on members of an international organization, the tribunal said that, taken with other indicators in the constituent elements, there was evidence that the member states had not intended to exclude their liability. Among these indicators were the size of the financial commitments, the speed with which all the share capital was

---

[66] Two cases were filed with the Court of Justice of the European Communities against the Council and Commission of the European Communities (EC), one by AMT (Tin Recoveries) Ltd. and Others and the other by Maclaine Watson & Co. Ltd. See Case 19/89, 32 OJ Eur. Comm. (No. C 62) (1989) p. 7; and Case 241/87, 30 *ibid.* (No. C 262) (1987) p. 5. Both cases arose out of the collapse of the ITC, of which the EC was a member. In Case 241/87 the application was based on the non-contractual liability of the EC, alleging, *inter alia*, negligence on the part of the community, because it knew that the ITC was insolvent and unable to meet its obligations (though it was continuing to trade) and had failed to warn third parties of the danger of trading with the ITC. This rationale for liability goes beyond, and is different from, that based on secondary or concurrent responsibility arising from the nature of international personality. In Case 19/89 the contentions were based, *inter alia*, on negligence (as in Case 241/87), breach of several provisions of the EEC Treaty, concurrent or secondary liability and direct liability. Both cases were withdrawn by the applicants and therefore removed from the list by the Court: 33 OJ Eur. Comm. (No. C 146) (1990) p. 12. The withdrawal of the cases was probably prompted by the agreement of the member states of the ITC to compensate the third parties concerned, although the former continued to deny liability. However, this is not recorded in the order of the Court. These cases do not shed any more light on the problem discussed here.
   Both applications to the Court were discussed by the EC Council and Commission, the political and executive organs of the organization, the main focus being the defences to be made. There was apparently no inclination to concede any of the applicants' arguments. The defendants in Case 241/87 had filed both an answer and a rejoinder, while in Case 19/89 the application was withdrawn before the defendants could take any action with regard to the pleadings (information supplied by courtesy of the Deputy Registrar of the Court). For an examination of the case law see also Hartwig, note 2, Chapter 11.

[67] The account of the case herein, including the award rendered on July 21, 1991, is taken from the final report of the rapporteur (R. Higgins) to the Commission of the Institut de droit international: 66-I *Annuaire de l'Institut de droit international* (1995) at pp. 393*ff*. The rapporteur was counsel in the arbitration.

to be paid, the provisions for increases in capital, together with the absence of a clause excluding member states' liability. This last factor was of itself legally neutral and did not raise a presumption of liability but, taken with everything else, invited the trust of third parties contracting with the organization in regard to its ability to cope with its commitments because of the constant support of the member states.[68] An express guarantee would clearly create secondary liability.

General principles of law

Since the practice is not absolutely clear, it is appropriate to examine the general principles of law, in order to see if there is any evidence of a general principle that may be applied. Some text writers[69] who support the principle of secondary or concurrent liability make much of the existence in most civil law systems, in addition to the limited liability company or corporation, of the company or corporation which is a mixed entity, such as the *société en nom collectif* of French law. In the case of such companies or corporations, while the entity has a separate juridical personality, shareholders are liable secondarily or concurrently for the obligations of the entity.[70] From the existence of this form of entity it is deduced that there is a general principle of law that, though the artificial person may have separate and distinct legal personality, their members or shareholders have a concurrent or secondary liability for the obligations of the entities.[71]

---

[68] See *ibid.*

[69] See e.g., Adam, note 28, vol. I p. 130; Seidl-Hohenveldern, note 3 pp. 88, 119–21, and Seidl-Hohenveldern, 'Piercing the Corporate Veil of International Organizations: The International Tin Council Case in the English Court Appeals', 32 GYIL (1989) at p. 52; Mann, 'International Corporations and National Law', in Mann, *Studies in International Law* (1973) p. 572, reprinted from 42 BYIL (1967) at pp. 160–1; Schermers, note 33 p. 780.

[70] For comparative information on this kind of entity see David, 'Rapport Général', in Bastid *et al.*, *La Personnalité morale et ses limites* (1960) pp. 12–13; Drobnig, 'Droit Allemand', in *ibid.* pp. 46–7. See also the discussion of the development in the nineteenth century of the limited liability company in English law with the resulting exclusion of the concept of the société en commandite (quasi-partnership) which was accepted in French law: Gower, *Gower's Principles of Modern Company Law* (1979) pp. 23*ff.*

[71] The argument was succinctly summarized by Kerr LJ in the *ITC Case (CA)*: 'If the ITC has legal personality or a degree of legal personality, then this is analogous to that of bodies in the nature of quasi-partnerships well known in the civil law systems, where both the entity and the members are liable to creditors, or the members are in any event secondarily liable for the debts of the entity. This concept is exemplified in the United Kingdom by a Scottish partnership, in France by a société en nom collectif and in Germany by a Kommanditgesellschaft auf Aktien.' [1988] 3 All ER at p. 274. General principles are examined also in Hartwig, note 2, Chapter 6.

While the existence in the civil law systems of the mixed legal entity such as is referred to above cannot be denied, it is equally clear that in the common law systems no such mixed entities exist. In common law systems incorporation which gives legal personality carries with it, whether one wants it or not, limited liability. Absence of incorporation manifests itself in such associations as partnerships and involves the direct liability of the partners. Thus, it is not possible to conclude that there is a general principle of law which requires that an entity with separate legal personality such as an international organization which is not explicitly set up with limited liability of its members must have the attributes of such a mixed entity. Moreover, in civil law systems the mixed entity exists side by side with the limited liability company, each one being established in a specific manner and form. In fact, if at all there is a presumption, it would seem that a limited liability company (the *société à responsabilité limitée*, the *société anonyme* or some other form of *société* with limited liability or their equivalents) is in these systems in case of doubt generally presumed to be created. It is generally understood that the mixed legal entity, on the other hand, must be clearly and specifically created. But it is also clear that the requirement of form is absent in international law (as is the requirement of legislative authority), so that it would not be possible to determine which sort of incorporation was intended and applicable in a given situation by reference to form, as it is in national legal systems. In any case it seems illogical to deduce a general principle of law requiring concurrent or secondary liability of members of international organizations in the absence of express contrary indications when the principle of limited liability exists only concomitantly with the principle of concurrent or secondary liability in some national law systems in which both principles coexist. There is no general situation in which the latter principle exists by itself to the exclusion of the former principle in regard to incorporated bodies.

On the contrary, as far as general principles are concerned, there is certainly a general principle of limited liability for incorporated entities which prevails in most systems of national law, including both the civil and common law systems, whereas the principle of concurrent or secondary liability in regard to such entities is not universal, but exists only in some (civil law) systems. Thus, if a general principle of law is to be regarded as existing, it is surely the principle of limited liability for incorporated bodies rather than that of concurrent or secondary liability in respect of such bodies. The difference between international law and those national law systems which permit incorporation only with limited liability is that in international law the creation of an organization with distinct juridical personality does not obligate the creators to limit their liability, if they truly intend the entity created to have a separate juridical personality, whereas in those national law systems the creation of an incorporated body would necessarily entail limited liability. In international law the creators of an organization are at liberty to create an entity with their liability limited or with their liability concurrent or secondary. In this connection the fact that an international organization is not created by legislation, while a legal person in national law traces its origin to legislation of some kind, does not have significance. Since in international law there is no legislative authority, other law-creating mechanisms take the place of legislation.

The problem to be solved is whether there is a presumption that the principle of limited liability applies in the absence of a contrary indication or whether the principle of concurrent or secondary liability presumptively applies. If general principles of law are invoked, since the principle of limited liability is more or less universal, while the other principle is not, should not the answer be that the principle of limited liability is presumptively applicable?

Deductions

While several text writers support the view that in the absence of contrary indications in the constituent instrument, members of organizations are concurrently or secondarily liable in some way for the obligations of the organization, it has become apparent that the practice does not necessarily support this view, the case law obviously contradicts it and general principles of law also would appear to support the opposite conclusion. However, there is general agreement among the textual and judicial authorities that what is primarily necessary is to ascertain the true intention of the framers of the constituent instrument of an organization in regard to the concurrent or secondary liability of members as manifested by all the circumstances of the formulation of the instrument. Since in international law, unlike in some national legal systems, there is no prohibition against the creation of organizations with similar personalities where such liability is not limited, states are free to choose whatever form of incorporation they would prefer. Further, since international law has no prescriptions as to form for the creation of one or the other kind of organization, no considerations of form are relevant. Consequently, it is logical and natural that emphasis should be given to the intentions of the framers as manifested in the constituent instrument. Thus, it is always first necessary to examine the constituent instrument and the circumstances of its formulation in order to determine what was intended by the framers and whether this intention was adequately communicated to third parties.

As has been seen, in less than one-third of the constituent instruments that exist the intention is made abundantly clear that no concurrent or secondary liability was assumed by the members. In one case at least express liability for the debts of the organization is assumed in the constituent instrument by members.[72] However, in the case of the remaining organizations, such as the UN, the FAO, the UNESCO, the IMF and the IMO,[73] there is no reference made either to the concurrent or secondary liability of members or to the exclusion of liability, nor is it clear from the provisions of the constituent instrument or the *travaux préparatoires* that concurrent or secondary liability was intended or excluded. Indeed, it is not at all clear from the evidence available whether the issue was addressed and, therefore, which of the alternatives was being chosen. However, it has been seen that practice tends towards supporting a presumption of an absence of concurrent or secondary liability.

The *Reparation Case*[74] established that an organization like the UN did have international legal personality, which resulted in its having the power to bear legal rights and obligations; but the decision said nothing beyond that which could expressly illuminate the problem discussed here. Significantly, however, the concept of international legal personality, which was not fully defined, was further regarded as giving the organization a status that was separate from the legal status of its members and that partook of a certain independence. To some extent, this may be regarded as implying that the obligations of the organization and those of its members were separate.

The Swiss Federal Tribunal, in particular, stressed that limited liability should be presumed because the intention of the framers of the constituent instrument in creating an organization with separate legal

---

[72] The Agence d'Appraisement of Euratom: See Adam, note 28, vol. I p. 276.

[73] The organizations are numerous. In addition to those mentioned the following are some that are in point: ASEAN, Arab League, CARICOM, Caribbean Meteorological Organization, CACM, Colombo Plan, The Commonwealth Secretariat, COMECON, Council for Arab Economic Unity, Council of Europe, ECOWAS, EC, EFTA, CERN, Eurocontrol, OCTI, CAFRAD, EMBL, EPO, ESO, CIPEC, CIEPS, WTO, UNIDO, WHO, ESA, GATT, ICSID, ICM, ILO, INMARSAT, INTELSAT, ITU, ITC, IPU, NATO, OPEC Fund, OAU, OAS, OAPEC, OCAM, OPEC, UPU, West African Economic Community, WEU, WIPO and WMO.

[74] 1949 ICJ Reports p. 174.

personality, rather than one similar to a partnership, is to give it 'total juridical independence' from the founding members. This independence necessarily implies that its rights and obligations are separate from those of the members, so that there is no justification for assuming that, in the absence of contrary indication, the members are concurrently or secondarily liable for its obligations. The view expressed by Lord Oliver in the ITC case also supports this conceptual position. He indicated that the effect of the creation of legal personality – irrespective of specific incorporation, particularly in accordance with the requirements of national law – is that the legal person contracts in its own name and there is thus no presumption that its creators are also liable.[75] This is more than saying that the absence of an exclusion of liability is 'legally neutral' which was apparently the view expressed in the *Westland Helicopters Ltd.* v. *AOI (Partial Award)* arbitration.

Furthermore, when the concept of legal personality emerged in national legal systems, it was generally associated with the limited liability of shareholders, rather than with their concurrent or secondary liability. Limited liability was the primary object of recognizing legal personality.[76] The modification of corporate personality so as to include shareholders' concurrent or secondary liability cannot therefore be regarded as having detracted from the hallmark of incorporation, which was limited liability. In consequence, it is not unreasonable conceptually to give primacy to limited liability in characterizing the international legal personality of organizations in respect of the liability of members to third parties.

The *pacta tertiis* rule applicable in the law of treaties and the apparent practice that has been established in regard to the international delicts of the UN also support a presumption that there is no concurrent or secondary liability as such *vis-à-vis* third parties of member states for obligations of international organizations.[77]

The rationale for the better view of the applicable principle

A further issue is whether the better view that there is a presumption of absence of liability is rooted in reason. The issue of whether third parties have adequate notice of the absence of liability of members may be

---

[75] [1989] 3 WLR at pp. 2008–9.

[76] For the growth and recognition of incorporation, as opposed to partnership, see Gower, *Gower's Principles of Modern Company Law* (1979) p. 23.

[77] Negligence as a basis of the liability of member states is concerned with direct liability.

settled conveniently from a formal point of view by reference to the essence of the concept of incorporation, whether in national or international law. Since it is not unreasonable to presume that 'incorporation' of an international organization normally and in the absence of contrary indications does not have as its consequence the secondary or concurrent liability of its members for the obligations of the organization, because this is a natural concomitant of incorporation, it would not be unreasonable to assume that the public should be aware of this principle of law. Thus, it is not the absence of liability that needs specifically to be brought to the attention of the public but the imposition of concurrent or secondary liability by the members upon themselves.

One qualification may be necessary by way of a *caveat*. In national law one of the principal objectives of incorporation is the creation of limited liability for shareholders, while in international law the purposes of creating an organization with international personality are manifold, the avoidance of liability for member states often not being an important consideration in the minds of its creators. As a consequence the presumption of limited liability which, it has been argued, exists for international organizations may in the appropriate case conceivably be displaced by other means than by an express or implied intention in the constituent instrument. It is possible that the presumption be rebutted on the basis of an estoppel to the extent that by their acts or conduct the member states hold themselves out as accepting concurrent or secondary liability or even to the extent that the organization with the express or implied approval of member states by its acts or conduct holds them out as accepting such liability. It is important that where it is the acts or conduct of the organization on which reliance is being placed then there must be some sort of approval by member states.

The position that has been found to be consistent with the sources must also be considered in the light of some of its consequences. It is arguable that third parties may be deterred from entering into legal relations involving liabilities on the part of organizations, if they are not assured that debts owed to them by the organizations will be fully discharged because the liability of members is limited. But the same argument may be used to discredit the concept of limited liability for shareholders in corporations even in national law. Experience has shown that limited liability has not affected the ability of such corporations to carry on their operations.

There may, however, be a difference between most international organizations and most national law corporations. The latter normally are

based on profit-making objectives, while most international organizations are not, being funded by budgetary contributions from members.
Thus, it may be argued, in the case of the national law corporation the
prospect of the corporation's making a profit and being solvent may be
regarded as a fair inducement for third parties to take the risk in their
dealings with it of the corporation's failing to honour its obligations or
going bankrupt, while in the case of the common type of international
organization, including the universal organization, the absence of such
prospect of profit would have the contrary effect and place an unjust
risk on third parties wishing to do business with it. But the logical consequence of the difference between the situations is to make a distinction
between those organizations which engage in financial or commercial
transactions and those that do not and not to jettison the principle of
limited liability in relation to all international organizations. However,
even in national law it is not clear that the concept of limited liability is
confined to profit-making corporations. While the origin of the concept
may be traced to the risks of profit-making as an objective, the applicability of the concept is certainly not coterminous with such an objective.
There are numerous non-profit-making corporate bodies which are limited liability corporations. Third parties do business with them as they
do with profit-making corporations. Thus, no real analogy can be drawn
from national law which would warrant the conclusion that non-profit-
making international organizations (such as the FAO and the UNESCO)
should from the point of view of the absence of liability of members
be treated any differently from profit-making or self-sustaining organizations (such as the IMF, the INRO, the ITC or the IBRD).

Further, against the value of protecting third parties from loss must
be set the possibility of undue interference from the member states in
the affairs of the independent organization. If member states are concurrently or secondarily liable as a matter of law, they may be inclined
to attempt to control the daily transactions of the organization in such a
way that its smooth operation as an independent entity with a separate
identity is jeopardized and becomes virtually impossible. In any event
resting the outcome of the issue of concurrent or secondary liability
on the theory that member states are responsible for decisions of the
organization in one way or another may not only involve sometimes a fic-
titious assumption of participation in decision-making but also raise the
question why the minority which is against a certain decision should
be held liable in the same way as the majority. It is significant that
in national laws shareholders of a limited liability corporation are not

held liable in the same way, though they must in other ways suffer the consequence of decisions taken by corporate bodies and exercise similar responsibility for the conduct of the corporation at least by delegation.

Another compelling consideration that favours the position that there is no concurrent or secondary liability on the part of member states is that the existence of such liability would deter most states, particularly the poorer ones, from becoming members of international organizations and participating in international co-operation. While it is not to be presumed that organizations would act irresponsibly or in such a way as unreasonably to incur obligations they cannot meet, it is a possibility that they would enter into obligations which cannot be fulfilled. In these circumstances states who become members are not likely to expect that in any case they would have to shoulder the liabilities of organizations on a concurrent or secondary basis.

Is it fair and just, then, that there should be a presumption in favour of the absence of liability, secondary or concurrent, of members rather than a presumption of such liability? In this connection there are the views of Nourse LJ in the UK Court of Appeal which reflect the argument in favour of concurrent or secondary liability.[78] One question then is why the same reasoning did not prompt the rejection of limited liability in national law. The best arguments against Nourse LJ's view are that: (i) it is in the nature of international corporate personality, as in national law, that basically the liability of members of an organization should be limited; (ii) the denial of this position could result in undue interference by members in the affairs of the organization; and (iii) third parties are by implication in fact put on notice of the limited nature of liability

---

[78] He said: 'Is it not both reasonable and just, and also *proper*, to impute to the members an intention that they should meet the bill for any amounts outstanding on the ITC's tin and loan contracts? We have heard much of the lofty motives which animated the founding states. When the gift of legal personality is explicable on grounds of expedience and practice, it is hardly respectful of such motives to hold that the members made it so as to escape liability for themselves. Why ever should they have wanted to do so? Are we to think that they put up this player, this poor player, to strut and fret its hour upon a municipal stage and then be heard no more, while all the time they were washing their hands of the enormous costs of the production? The obligations of hospitality are very great. When the benefits, too, are great, it is right that they should be. But is it not an insult to the dignity of sovereign states to credit them with the intentions of the guest, who, omitting to say that only his friend will pay, departs from the hostelry without meeting the bill? I would think better of international law than that. I could not say that so many good and learned men had toiled in that stannary these centuries past for us to find that they had won only lead. It cannot have been for nothing that Grotius taught us: "The law obliges us to do what is proper, not simply what is just."' [1988] 3 All ER at p. 334.

in the absence of contrary indication.[79] Further, policy considerations invoking justice and fair play are not ignored by the recognition of the absence of concurrent or secondary liability as a presumption and in ordinary circumstances, because it is a valued policy consideration that led to the recognition of the absence of such liability in cases of incorporation both in national and international law.[80]

The relationship between the organization and members

In spite of a presumption which operates in the absence of contrary indication and supports the general non-liability of members, there may be other legal principles which operate in favour of third parties and thus have a mitigating effect from their point of view. These relate to the relationship between the organization and its members in regard to funding and the rights and obligations of both *vis-à-vis* each other.[81]

Provision may be made in the constituent instrument for the members to bear 'the expenses of the Organization' or to contribute to discharging its obligations. This is the thrust of Article 17(2) of the UN Charter which states that such expenses 'shall be borne by the Members as apportioned by the General Assembly'. In such a case, where the organization incurs obligations to third parties, such parties are protected to the extent that there is an obligation incumbent upon the members to keep the organization in funds, though there is no liability to the third parties

---

[79] There are also, of course, alternatives to the assumption of risk by third parties, such as insurance and guarantees by the member states, which give added validity to the position taken. The practice of organizations in this regard is discussed in Hartwig, note 2, Chapter 9.

[80] There are some other considerations which may be referred to in passing in order to note their probable irrelevance. First, the question of *ultra vires* has really no bearing on the issue being discussed, because obligations incurred by acts that are *ultra vires*, if they are not attributable to the organization, are not obligations of the organization. Hence, there is no question of liability of members for the obligations of the organization. Where the obligations, though incurred as a result of *ultra vires* acts, still remain in law the obligations of the organization, the ordinary principles for absence of liability or liability of members will apply. Second, the law of state responsibility does not have any provisions that would make members of international organizations liable concurrently or secondarily for obligations of such bodies. There may be responsibility on the basis of a host state relationship or other concurrent or secondary liability: see Draft Article 12(1) on State Responsibility of the ILC, discussions in the ILC (1 YBILC (1975) at pp. 45, 46, 51, 53 and 59) and the 1975 ILC Report to the GA (2 YBILC (1975) at p. 87). See also Provisional Report of the rapporteur in 66-I *Annuaire de l'Institut de droit international* (1995) at pp. 406*ff.* and pp. 410*ff.*

[81] See also Hartwig, note 2, Chapter 13.

on the part of members. But this sort of obligation arises from the provisions of the constituent instrument.

By the same token, where a constituent instrument limits the responsibility of members to the organization, this limitation will be operative. For example, in the constituent instrument of most financial and commercial institutions, as has been seen, the liability of members to the organization is limited to the unpaid share capital. While members may be called upon at any time to pay this amount of their share capital in order that the organization may discharge its obligations, they cannot be subjected to a greater liability than that. It is also apparent that, where the organization is being liquidated, the same principles would apply in cases in which there are such limitations of liability to the organization, unless specific provision is made otherwise. In the case of most financial institutions it has been seen that the general rule is that liability of members to the organization at the time of liquidation is restricted to the payment of unpaid share capital.

Even where the 'gearing' or similar ratio is restricted to 1:1, as in the case of the IBRD, there may be debts at liquidation which the organization cannot meet fully. In such a case also the organization would not be solvent and could not have recourse to its members to meet its obligations. In any case, where the organization is not solvent, third parties would be governed by the rules established for the liquidation procedure. This is consonant with the nature of legal or corporate personality.

Conclusion

While there may be primary or direct liability of member states in the appropriate circumstances which are clearly identifiable and also liability based on agency attaching to member states for obligations of international organizations, whether on the international or non-international plane, it is secondary or concurrent liability that creates problems. There seems to be general agreement that the issue of the secondary or concurrent liability of members of an international organization for the latter's obligations must in the first place be decided by reference to the constituent instrument which is to be interpreted in the light of all the circumstances in order to determine the intention, express or implied, of the parties to it.

As to presumptions, while the views of textual authorities have differed, the judicial precedents, on the other hand, strongly support the view that there can be no presumption in international law that members are concurrently or secondarily liable for the obligations of the organization. Practice, which is not eminently clear, however, and a general principle of law, insofar as one can be identified, also tend in the same direction as judicial precedent. The view that is, thus, preferred is clearly supported by the principles of treaty law at the international level and seems to be the basis of practice in regard to delictual liability at the international level.

The logic inherent in the situation which derives from the recognition of international personality in the *Reparations Case* confirms the trends detected in judicial precedent, practice and general principles of law. In addition, there appear to be good policy reasons which justify the position derived from the sources.

On the basis of the evidence, the better view is that there is no presumption, in the absence of the indication of an intention in the constituent instrument, that members of an international organization are concurrently or secondarily liable for the obligations of the organization. The presumption is, thus, to the contrary. However, and there is some support for this in the sources, the presumption of non-liability could be displaced by evidence of some conduct on the part of members (some or all of them) or of the organization with the approval of members, or of an implied intention in the constitution which entitles creditors to assume that members (some or all of them) will accept concurrent or secondary liability. All this does not affect the incidence of primary or direct liability, liability based on factual or constitutional agency or liability based on guarantee or similar relationships.

The question of liability of members to the organization will normally be settled in accordance with the provisions of the constituent instrument. This subject has been dealt with more fully in Chapter 11.

14 Amendment of constitutions

Constitutions of international organizations, being organic instruments, may require change both in the light of experience in the organizations as well as in order to keep pace with developments in international society. Changing needs and circumstances may demand appropriate adaptations in the structure, functions and procedures of such organizations. The UN has amended its Charter several times. Articles 23, 27 and 61, relating to the composition of the SC and the ECOSOC, were amended in 1963 (the amendments entering into force in 1965). The membership of the SC was increased from eleven to fifteen and that of the ECOSOC from eighteen to twenty-seven. Again in 1971 the membership of the ECOSOC was increased from twenty-seven to fifty-four by an amendment of Article 61 (the amendment entering into force in 1973).[1] Article 109 of the UN Charter relating to the review conference was amended in 1965 (the amendment entering into force in 1968). Between 1945 and 1966 the thirteen specialized agencies of the UN and the IAEA adopted sixty-one amendments to their constitutions all of which have come into force.[2] The FAO had twenty-five, the UNESCO fourteen, the ICAO and the ILO five each, the WMO four, the IFC, the IMCO and the WHO two each, the IBRD and the IAEA one each and the IMF and the IDA none. Between 1966 and 1995 the IMF had adopted and brought into

---

[1] These two sets of amendments are discussed by Schwelb, 'Amendments to Articles 23, 27 and 61 of the Charter of the United Nations', 59 AJIL (1965) p. 834; Schwelb, 'The 1963/65 Amendments to the Charter of the United Nations: An Addendum', 60 AJIL (1966) p. 371; Schwelb, 'The 1971 Amendment to Article 61 of the United Nations Charter and Arrangements Accompanying It', 12 ICLQ (1972) p. 497; and Schwelb, 'Entry into Force of the Second Amendment to Article 61 of the United Nations Charter', 68 AJIL (1974) p. 300.
[2] Phillips, 'Constitutional Revision in the Specialized Agencies', 62 AJIL (1968) at pp. 657*ff.*

effect three amendments. Among the sixty-one amendments referred to above were twenty-six relating to the structure of the organization and the composition of its organs, nine pertaining to aspects of membership, nine granting new powers or modifying existing powers, seven making procedural changes and ten effecting drafting changes of an editorial nature.[3] The IMF amendments were all in the operational area. Thus, a wide range exists in the incidence of amendments. In 1965 the observation was made that there was some indication that proposals for amendment with a strongly political bias had a tendency to weaken rather than to sustain an organization.[4] Further, there is some evidence to support the conclusion that formal amendment is not the most productive method of adaptation and growth of a constitutional system.[5] Nonetheless, formal amendment of constitutions of international organizations is resorted to as a means of adapting to change and development in international society.

Express constitutional provision

Provision is made in most constitutions of international organizations for their amendment. Exceptionally, as in the case of the OECD, the ITU and the NATO constitutions, specific provision for amendment may not be made. Among the constitutions that make specific provisions for amendment, the UN Charter provides in Article 108:

Amendments to the present Charter shall come into force for all Members of the United Nations when they have been adopted by a vote of two thirds of the members of the General Assembly and ratified in accordance with their respective constitutional processes by two thirds of the Members of the United Nations, including all the permanent members of the Security Council.

Article 109 relating to the several review conferences, among other things, states:

> 2 Any alteration of the present Charter recommended by a two thirds vote of the conference shall take effect when ratified in accordance with their respective constitutional processes by two thirds of the Members of the United Nations including all the permanent members of the Security Council.

---

[3] Phillips, *ibid.* at p. 658.

[4] Jenks, 'Due Process of Law in International Organizations', 19 *International Organization* (1965) p. 176.

[5] See Luard (ed.), *The Evolution of International Organizations* (1966) pp. 9–24, who examines the process of change in international organizations.

Article VIII of the IBRD Articles of Agreement provides:

(a) Any proposal to introduce modifications in this Agreement, whether emanating from a member, a governor or the Executive Directors, shall be communicated to the Chairman of the Board of Governors who shall bring the proposal before the Board. If the proposed amendment is approved by the Board the Bank shall, by circular letter or telegram, ask all members whether they accept the proposed amendment. When three-fifths of the members, having four-fifths of the total voting power, have accepted the proposed amendments, the Bank shall certify the fact by formal communication addressed to all members.

(b) Notwithstanding (a) above, acceptance by all members is required by the case of any amendment modifying
  (i) the right to withdraw from the Bank provided in Article VI, Section 1;
  (ii) the right secured by Article II, Section 3(c);
  (iii) the limitation on liability provided in Article II, Section 6.

(c) Amendments shall enter into force for all members three months after the date of the formal communication unless a shorter period is specified in the circular letter or telegram.

The IMF Articles of Agreement (Article XXVIII), the IDA Articles of Agreement (Article IX), the AFDB Agreement (Article 60) and the CDB Agreement (Article 58) contain similar provisions. In the case of the IDB Agreement (Article IX), the IFC Articles of Agreement (Article V) and the ADB Agreement (Article 41) the amendment procedure is somewhat similar but, though members are bound when amendments take effect, they are also free to withdraw from the organization. Article 26 of the LN Convenant provided that amendments were to take effect when ratified by those members of the LN on the Council and by a majority of members of the LN in the Assembly, but they did not bind any member signifying dissent who, however, then ceased to be a member of the LN. Article 62 of the IMO Constitution provides:

Amendments shall be adopted by a two-thirds majority vote of the Assembly. Twelve months after its acceptance by two-thirds of the Members of the Organization, other than Associate Members, each amendment shall come into force for all Members except those which, before it comes into force, make a declaration that they do not accept the amendment. The Assembly may by a two-thirds majority vote determine at the time of its adoption that an amendment is of such a nature that any Member which has made such a declaration and which does not accept the amendment within a period of twelve months after the amendment comes into force shall, upon the expiration of this period, cease to be a party to the Convention.[6]

In the ILO Constitution Article 36 states that amendments (i) shall be adopted by a two-thirds majority of votes cast at the General Conference; and (ii) shall take effect when ratified or accepted by two-thirds of the members of the ILO including five of the ten members of chief industrial importance. Article XVIII of the IAEA constitution, among other things, provides:

> (C) Amendments shall come into force for all members when
>> (i) Approved by General Conference by a two-thirds majority of those present and voting after consideration of observations submitted by the Board of Governors on each proposed amendment, and
>> (ii) When accepted by two-thirds of all the members in accordance with their respective constitutional processes ...
> (D) At any time after five years from the date when this statute shall initially take effect ... or whenever a member is unwilling to accept an amendment to this statute, it may withdraw from the agency ...

The constituent treaties of the EC[7] required that amendments should be determined by common accord at a conference of member states after the Council had by a two-thirds majority decided to call such a conference to consider proposals made by any member state or the High Authority. These amendments came into force upon ratification by all member states. Now Article N of the TEU provides:

1. The government of any Member State or the Commission may submit to the Council proposals for the amendment of the Treaties on which the Union is founded.

If the Council, after consulting the European Parliament and, where appropriate, the Commission, delivers an opinion in favour of calling a conference of representatives of the governments of the Member States, the conference shall be convened by the President of the Council for the purpose of determining by common accord the amendments to be made to those Treaties. The European Central Bank shall also be consulted in the case of institutional changes in the monetary area.

The amendments shall enter into force after being ratified by all the Member States in accordance with their respective constitutional requirements.

---

[6] Compare Article 94 of the ICAO Constitution.
[7] Article 96 of the ECSC Treaty, Article 236 of the EEC Treaty and Article 204 of the Euratom Treaty.

As a final example of provision for amendment may be cited Article 41 of the COE Statute:

(a) Proposals for the amendment of this Statute may be made in the Committee of Ministers or, in the conditions provided for in Article 23, in the Consultative Assembly.

(b) The Committee shall recommend and cause to be embodied in a Protocol those amendments which it considers to be desirable.

(c) An amending Protocol shall come into force when it has been signed and ratified on behalf of two-thirds of the Members.

(d) Notwithstanding the provisions of the preceding paragraphs of this Article, amendments to Articles 23–35, 38 and 39 which have been approved by the Committee and by the Assembly, shall come into force on the date of the certificate of the Secretary-General, transmitted to the Governments of Members, certifying that they have been so approved.

Other constitutions have varying requirements relating to the adoption of amendments in terms of majorities, while they also specify when and how amendments enter into force and the effect of such entry into force on dissenting members.[8] These examples give an idea of the variety of amendment provisions that exist.

Principles in customary law

Where amendment provisions exist, these govern, though the customary law relating to multilateral treaties may be invoked to interpret such provisions, when there are lacunae. Where there are no amendment provisions, the customary law will apply. Article 40 of the 1969 Vienna Convention on the Law of Treaties which, pursuant to Article 5 of the Convention, is applicable to the constitutions of international organizations reads:

1 Unless the treaty otherwise provides, the amendment of multilateral treaties shall be governed by the following paragraphs.

2 Any proposal to amend a multilateral treaty as between all the parties must be notified to all the contracting States, each one of which shall have the right to take part in:

(a) the decision as to the action to be taken in regard to such proposal;

(b) the negotiation and conclusion of any agreement for the amendment of the treaty.

---

[8] See, e.g., Article XX of the FAO Constitution; Article XIII of the UNESCO Constitution; Article 73 of the WHO Constitution; and Articles 147 and 145 of the OAS Constitution.

3 Every State entitled to become a party to the treaty shall also be entitled to become a party to the treaty as amended.

4 The amending agreement does not bind any State already a party to the treaty which does not become a party to the amending agreement; article 30, paragraph 4(b), applies in relation to such State.

5 Any State which becomes a party to the treaty after entry into force of the amending agreement shall, failing an expression of a different intention by that State:

(a) be considered as a party to the treaty as amended; and

(b) be considered as a party to the unamended treaty in relation to any party not bound by the amending agreement.[9]

This reflects what is now the customary law.[10] At the time Article 40 was agreed upon in 1965, a rule of customary law had already emerged which was what became Article 40. Thus, it could not be said that there was a customary rule that all the parties to a multilateral treaty had to agree to and ratify an amendment before it could come into force and be effective. The rule of amendment as stated in Article 40, however, poses some rather difficult problems for certain multilateral treaties and particularly for constitutions of international organizations. For example, were the rule to be applied to an amendment of the provisions applicable to voting in the general congress of either the ITU or the OECD, how can the earlier voting provisions be applicable as between those members who do not agree to the amendment and those that do, while the amended provisions apply as between those members who accepted the amendment? In the case of a constitution of an international organization the constitution would be unworkable, if some amended provisions applied as between one group of members, while conflicting amended provisions applied as between another group of members or as between the two groups.[11] Some express constitutional provisions,

---

[9] The effect of Article 30(4)(b) referred to in this provision is to leave the unamended constitution in force between those who are not parties to the amendment themselves and between them and the other parties who subscribe to the amendment.

[10] See Sinclair, *The Vienna Convention on the Law of Treaties* (1984) p. 107; also 'Report of the International Law Commission on the Work of its Eighteenth Session', 2 YBILC (1966) at pp. 232*ff*.

[11] It will be noted in this connection that in the case of the restructuring of the OEEC which was, among other things, renamed the OECD by amendment of the OEEC constitution, all the members of the OEEC without exception agreed to the amendment so that no impasse was reached. It does not emerge, however, whether the members accepted that there was a need for universal agreement before the constitution could be changed or whether a majority could do this, regardless of the legal consequences.

such as those in the constitutions of the FAO and the OAS, also pose the same problems.

Could it be argued, therefore, that the customary practice that had grown up in regard to multilateral treaties should not or does not apply to the constitutions of international organizations, because they are a very special kind of multilateral treaty to which the practice had not been specifically applied?[12] Short of concluding that constitutions cannot be amended unless specific provision for their amendment has been made, it may be suggested either that amendment is only possible if all the members agree to the amendment – a principle conferring a veto on every single member – or that, while amendment may be possible by agreement among a simple or other majority, those members who refuse to agree to the amendment either cease to be members or must act as if bound by the amendment. The latter alternative seems to be out of accord with the consent principle. The Covenant of the LN explicitly provided in Article 26 that this was how the Covenant could be amended, only a special majority in ratifications being required for amendments to take effect. Article 26(2) provided that those who dissented from amendments once they came into effect ceased to be members of the LN. On the other hand, the former alternative would impede the orderly development of constitutions. However, this principle of absolute consent was incorporated, for example, in the treaties of the EC and in Article XXX of the GATT in regard to Part I (Articles I and II) and Article XXIX of the GATT.

There is no real guidance in practice on the solution to the problem, though the adoption of the absolute consent (unanimity) principle would seem to be in accord with the principle of the equality of states. On the other hand, there is no evidence of a custom that the principles incorporated in Article 40 of the 1969 Vienna Convention are not applicable to constitutions of international organizations. That Convention in other contexts, such as in Article 20(3), makes special provision for constitutions of international organizations and its failure to do so in Article 40 may well be significant. As already seen, the Convention is specifically made applicable to constitutions of international organizations.

---

[12] In the case of other multilateral treaties the *inter se* theory, as it is called, could also create the same kind of problem in certain circumstances. Article 40, nevertheless, clearly applies to them. There is no evidence in the reports or discussions of the ILC or in the *travaux préparatoires* of the 1969 Vienna Conference that a distinction was intended.

Analysis of special provisions

Perhaps, because of the difficulties demonstrated above, most constitutions have provisions relating to their amendment. Another possible
reason for the inclusion of special provisions on amendment is that the
framers of the constitution wanted to make it clear that amendment
required special treatment different from decisions taken in the implementation or interpretation of the constitution.[13] Where such special
amendment provisions are included, amendment can only be achieved
pursuant to these provisions. There is no possibility of circumventing
them and resorting to a customary law that may be applicable in the
absence of such provisions, whatever that law might be. Amendment by
practice, however, is a separate issue.

Some constitutions provide also for review conferences to deal with
proposals for amendment. This is additional to the normal procedure of amendment. Such provisions are to be found, for example, in
Article 109 of the UN Charter, Article XVIII(13) of the IAEA Constitution
and Article 236 of the EEC Treaty. But even where a review conference
decides on amendments the rest of the procedure for the entry into force
of amendments and the results of such entry into force is the same as
the normal procedure.

The procedure of amendment itself varies from organization to organization. There may be a 'one-step' or 'two-step' procedure and the procedure may be based on the 'consent' principle or the 'majority' principle.
In either case the result is that the amendment has effect and ends
up being legislative.[14] A 'one-step' procedure involves adoption of the
amendment by an organ of the institution, normally the plenary organ
(general congress), which adoption is sufficient to bring the amendment

---

[13] For discussion of amendment procedures in international organizations see, e.g.,
Schwelb, 'The Amending Procedure of Constitutions of International Organizations',
31 BYIL (1954) p. 49, and Schwelb, 'The 1963/65 Amendments to the Charter of the
United Nations: An Addendum', 60 AJIL (1966) p. 371; Zacklin, *The Amendment of the
Constitutive Instruments of the United Nations and Specialized Agencies* (1968); Phillips,
'Constitutional Revision in the Specialized Agencies', 62 AJIL (1968) p. 654; Gold, 'The
Amendment and Variation of their Charters by International Organizations', 1 RBDI
(1973) p. 50; Schermers and Blokker, *International Institutional Law* (1995) pp. 719*ff.* and
literature there cited; and Sands and Klein (eds.), *Bowett's Law of International Institutions*
(2001) pp. 451–4.

[14] The distinction between a 'legislative' principle and a 'consent' principle, often made
is, thus, not accurate. Bowett made this distinction: *ibid.* Any amendment, however it
is brought into effect, is in any case 'legislative' in that it binds the organization,
although it is not party to it.

into effect for all members, nothing further being required. The 'two-step' procedure, by contrast, requires, first, that action be taken within the institution by a vote of adoption of the amendment by an organ, generally the plenary or general congress, and, second, that the amendment be ratified or accepted by some or all of the member states, before the amendment comes into effect. Whether a one-step or two-step procedure is involved, the principle behind the entry into force of the amendment may be dependent on the majority principle. Where in the one-step procedure the adoption of the amendment requires unanimity, the principle involved is based on consent, while, where the adoption of the amendment requires less than unanimity the majority principle is the basis for the entry into force of the amendment. In the case of the two-step procedure whether the consent principle is involved will depend on whether the procedure at one of the two steps requires the approval of all member states. If at neither of the two steps unanimity is required, then the majority principle is involved. The consequences of the amendment for those not accepting or ratifying the amendments is a third and different question.

The consent principle

The consent principle seems to be involved in a one-step procedure in the case of the amendment of Part I and Article XXIX of the GATT. There are a few examples of the consent principle being applicable to a two-step procedure. True cases of the consent principle must be distinguished from instances of the majority principle where, however, the result of the amendment coming into effect on the basis of that principle is that it does not bind those who do not accept or ratify it which is really an ancillary consequence of that principle in those particular cases. Article 41 of the constitution of the COE provides that an amendment shall come into force when it has been signed and ratified by two-thirds of the members, provided the Committee of Ministers has approved it unanimously. Under the same Article amendments to Articles 23 to 25, 38 and 39 come into force once adopted by the Committee of Ministers and the Assembly upon the certification of the Secretary-General to that effect. The need for a unanimous vote in the Committee of Ministers ensures that there is consent on the part of all member states. In the case of the EEC Treaty Articles 235 and 236 ensured that amendments approved by a unanimous vote in the Council and adopted in a special conference by common accord only entered into force upon ratification by all members. Now the EU Treaty in Protocol N provides that amendments should be determined by common accord of the member states at a conference convened for the purpose of considering amendments upon an opinion delivered by the Council in favour of calling a conference of member states. The amendments come into force upon ratification by all member states.

The majority principle

Most constitutions, however, allow for amendment by a majority. As will be seen, a majority of members can bind a minority which has not agreed to the amendments at some stage. According to Article 108 of the UN Charter after adoption by a two-thirds vote in the GA, an amendment will come into effect for all member states when it is ratified by two-thirds of the member states including all the permanent members of the SC.[15] This is an example of a two-step procedure. Moreover, Article 7 of the WHO Constitution, Article 94 of the ICAO Constitution and Article 18 of the IAEA Constitution, for example, incorporate a two-step procedure as well which contains the majority principle. There is provision for adoption of the amendment by a special majority by the general congress which comes into effect upon ratification by at least two-thirds of the member states. The UNESCO Constitution has a general one-step procedure in Article XIII which requires adoption by the general congress by a two-thirds majority for the amendment to come into effect.

The two principles combined

There are examples of one-step amendment procedures where the majority principle predominates but there is included the consent principle for certain exceptional cases. Some financial institutions are good examples of this phenomenon. Thus, for example, Article VII of the IFC Constitution, Article XII of the IDB Constitution, Article 59 of the ADB Constitution and Article 58 of the CDB Constitution all provide that amendments enter into force upon approval by a certain number of member states in the general congress which exercise a certain proportion of the voting power, but that the affirmative vote of all members of the general congress is necessary for amendments of certain specific provisions to become effective.[16]

---

[15] For a comparable provision see Article 36 of the ILO Constitution.
[16] See also, e.g., Article XX of the FAO Constitution and Article 28 of the WMO Constitution where differentiation is made between provisions in regard to their amendments.

There are also several examples of such differentiation in the case of constitutions which adopt the two-step procedure. For example, Article VIII of the IBRD Constitution requires normally that a proposed amendment be approved by a weighted majority in the Executive Board and then be accepted by three-fifths of the member states having four-fifths of the voting power before it comes into effect, but exceptionally in the case of three provisions of the constitution requires that all member states agree.[17]

The consequences of an effective amendment

Regardless of the way in which an amendment comes into effect, it binds the organization. However, whether after the amendment comes into effect, members must accept the amendment for it to bind them,[18] or the amendment is binding on all members whether they accept it or not, by ratification or otherwise,[19] the problem may arise of members not wanting to accept or be bound by the amendment. In the case of the LN, according to Article 26 of the Covenant, such members were not bound by the amendment but ceased to be members of the LN. Alternatively, where this is provided for, dissenting states could withdraw form the organization.[20] But where withdrawal is not specifically provided for, the question is whether states may separate themselves from the organization by denouncing the constitution. In the ILC in 1964, when the amendment provisions of the draft convention on treaties (which became Article 40 of the 1969 Vienna Convention without any substantial changes) were considered, the rapporteur noted that the 'inter se

---

[17] See also, e.g., Article XXVIII of the IMF Constitution; Article IX of the IDA Constitution; Article 60 of the AFDB Constitution; and Article 52 of the EADB Constitution for similar provisions. A differentiation between provisions is also made in Articles 95 and 96 of the ECSC Treaty where, however, the normal rule for amendment is based on the consent principle and the exception is based on the majority principle.

[18] See Article 26 of the LN Covenant, perhaps.

[19] Most of the constitutions of organizations have provisions which give this effect to an amendment: see, e.g., Articles 108 and 109 of the UN Charter; Article 36 of the ILO Constitution; Article XX of the FAO Constitution; Article XIII of the UNESCO Constitution; Article VIII of the IBRD Constitution; Article XXVIII of the IMF Constitution; Article 59 of the ADB Constitution; and Article XII of the IDB Constitution.

[20] See, e.g., Article VI(i) of the IBRD Constitution; Article XXVI(i) of the IMF Constitution; Article V(i) of the IFC Constitution; Article 41 of the ADB Constitution; Article II of the UNESCO Constitution; and Article I(5) of the ILO Constitution.

technique[21] was quite common in the case of multilateral treaties, giving a number of examples.[22] He concluded that

> to admit a unilateral right of withdrawal in all cases might seriously detract from the usefulness in many fields of the present technique of progressive amendment of a multilateral treaty *inter se* without losing what was gained by acceptance of the original treaty.[23]

Amendment of constitutions of international organizations was not specifically addressed but it was not regarded as a special case or an exception to the rule which is now reflected in Article 40(4) of the 1969 Vienna Convention. The point was made earlier that, as the Convention makes specific exceptions for the constitutions of international organizations, where this was intended, [24] it is not possible to make an exception to the application of the Convention in this case. The fact that the Article provides for the case of the party to the treaty (a member state in this case) who does not become a party to the amended instrument would confirm that withdrawal was not envisaged as an alternative. *A fortiori* there would be no right of withdrawal as such where the member state does not want to be bound by an amendment which is binding on it.

A more difficult question is whether such states may be expelled from the organization. Where expulsion is provided for in the constitution,[25] expulsion may be effected under those provisions. Thus, under Article VI(2) of the IBRD Constitution, for instance, if a member state fails to fulfil any of its obligations to the organization as a result of its not accepting an amendment (which act in itself may be regarded as a failure to fulfil an obligation owed to the organization), it could be suspended from membership and automatically expelled after one year. Where there are no provisions dealing with expulsion by some procedure,[26] the issue of expulsion becomes more difficult. There is no reason why a member should be expelled for failure to agree to an amendment when its agreement is not required by the constitution. Particularly if there is a right of withdrawal, this would reinforce the conclusion that

---

[21] This means that states not parties to the amendment would continue to be bound by the unamended treaty in their relations with other parties to the treaty, while those states parties to the amendments would be bound in their relations with each other by the amended treaty.

[22] Waldock, 'Third Report on the Law of Treaties', 2 YBILC (1964) at p. 49.

[23] *Ibid.* at p. 52.   [24] See, e.g., Article 20(3) of the Convention.

[25] On expulsion see Chapter 4 above.

[26] See apparently, e.g., the original WHO Constitution.

there is no right of expulsion. If there is a failure to comply with obligations, the member may be dealt with accordingly. The recalcitrant member should be dealt with under the constitution while it remains a member of the organization. This may involve other penalties, such as suspension of rights. However, it is significant that, where constitutions of organizations have been amended, generally states have accepted the amendments, and not resisted them despite any earlier opposition to their content. Thus, for example, when Articles 23, 27 and 61 of the UN Charter were amended in 1963, the USA and UK had originally opposed the amendment. However, they later ratified the amendments[27] and have lived with them.

Variation

Occasionally, power is given by the constitution to an organ to apply a rule or principle different from the one established in the constitution. This is the case in regard to most of the financial institutions. Thus, these institutions have been granted the power to vary in certain respects their constitutions, which would otherwise have required an amendment, without going through the amendment process. The following areas, for example, may be identified: increase of capital stock or special funds,[28] issuing subsequent shares other than at par,[29] waiving of the maintenance-of-value provisions,[30] changing the rate of commission of loans or guarantees,[31] increasing the size of the executive body[32] and relaxing in certain circumstances the terms of loan agreements required by the constitution.[33] In these circumstances there is a departure from the constitution which is not strictly an amendment, because

---

[27] See Schwelb, loc. cit. note 1 (ICLQ) at p. 497.

[28] See, e.g., IBRD Constitution, Article II(2)(b); IFC Constitution, Article II(2)(i) and (ii); IDB Constitution, Articles II(2)(c), (d) and (e) and IV(3)(g); EIB Statute, Article 4(3); and ADB Constitution, Article 4(3).

[29] See, e.g., IBRD Constitution, Article II(4); IFC Constitution, Article II(3)(b); IDB Constitution, Article II(3)(c); ADB Constitution, Article 5(4); and AFDB Constitution, Article 6(4).

[30] See, e.g., IBRD Constitution, Article II(9)(c); EIB Statute, Article 7(4); IDB Constitution, Article V(3)(c); ADB Constitution, Article 25(3); and AFDB Constitution, Article 28(3).

[31] See, e.g., IBRD Constitution, Article II(4)(a) and (5)(a); IDB Constitution, Article III(12); ADB Constitution, Article 16(1); AFDB Constitution, Article 19(1); and CDB Constitution, Article 17(1).

[32] See, e.g., IBRD Constitution, Article V(4)(b)(ii); IDB Constitution, Article VII(3)(j); and CDB Constitution, Article 29(1)(b).

[33] See, e.g., IBRD Constitution, Article IV(4)(c); and ADB Constitution, Article 18(1).

the departure is permitted specifically and, therefore, there is no change of the text.

Interpretation and amendment

As was seen in Chapter 2, interpretation of constitutional texts may result in a departure from the natural and ordinary meaning of texts, particularly where the principle of effectiveness or of subsequent practice is applied in interpretation. There is a point at which developing a text may result in such change that it amounts to amendment rather than interpretation. The line between the two processes is a fine one.

Interpretation may legitimately fill in gaps and take care of situations which were not anticipated at the time the texts were formulated. However, where it changes a text radically, this is amendment. An example of such radical change would be where an interpretation purports to permit an organization to do what the constitutional text expressly prohibits. Or where a constitutional text clearly places an obligation on an entity, there being no question of gaps or lack of anticipation, an interpretation which permits the entity to avoid that obligation would amount to amendment of the text. As also seen in Chapter 2, an interpretation based on effectiveness such as that given to Article II(2)(a) of the Constitution of the IBRD in 1986 (the meaning of 'United States dollars of the weight and fineness in effect on July 1, 1944') may go quite far in the direction of change, even though it only fills a gap or takes care of a situation not anticipated. However, the principle cannot be denied that interpretation and amendment are two distinct processes and the former should not be used to circumvent the process appropriate for the latter. This is so certainly in the case of interpretations based on effectiveness. While each case must be considered on the basis of its own circumstances, the importance of not confusing the two processes remains. The fact that in many instances constitutions have been amended rather than reliance being placed on interpretation demonstrates that organizations and their members are conscious of not abusing the process of interpretation, where the change of the text would amount to amendment.[34]

---

[34] There were three amendments to the IMF Constitution, some of which have been extensive. On the third amendment, see International Monetary Fund, *Proposed Third Amendment of the Articles of Agreement of the International Monetary Fund: Report of the Executive Board to the Board of Governors* (1990).

The distinction between amendment and interpretation, however, becomes blurred, where practice changes the text of a constitution. The application of the principle of effectiveness cannot amend a text. This is clear. Similarly, resort to the *travaux préparatoires* cannot achieve that result. In the case of practice the situation is somewhat different.

Practice and amendment

The Draft Articles of the ILC on Treaties provided in Article 38 that 'a treaty may be modified by subsequent practice in the application of the treaty establishing the agreement of the parties to modify its provisions'.[35] The ILC relied for precedent upon the 1963 decision in the *Air Transport Services Agreement Arbitration*[36] between France and the United States regarding the interpretation of a bilateral 1946 agreement.[37] The tribunal spoke of a modification by practice at the outset of its consideration of the effect of the parties' actions on Pan American's right to serve Tehran. The tribunal, referring to the subsequent practice said:

This course of conduct may, in fact, be taken into account not merely as a means useful for interpreting the Agreement, but also as something more: that is, as a possible source of subsequent modification, arising out of certain actions or certain attitudes, having a bearing on the judicial situation of the Parties and on the rights that each of them could properly claim.[38]

The tribunal in fact found that the agreement had been modified in certain respects by the subsequent practice. The ILC concluded:

Although the line may sometimes be blurred between interpretation and amendment of a treaty through subsequent practice, legally the processes are distinct. Accordingly, the effect of subsequent practice in amending a treaty is dealt with in the present article as a case of modification of treaties.[39]

It then explained that the article provided that a treaty may be modified by subsequent practice in the application of the treaty establishing the agreement of the parties to modify its provisions and that in formulating the rule in this way the ILC intended to indicate that the subsequent practice, even if every party might not itself have actively participated in

---

[35] 'Reports of the Commission to the General Assembly', 2 YBILC (1966) at p. 182.
[36] (1963), 3 ILM p. 668.
[37] 'Reports of the Commission to the General Assembly', 2 YBILC (1966) at p. 236.
[38] (1963), 3 ILM at p. 713.
[39] 'Reports of the Commission to the General Assembly', 2 YBILC (1966) at p. 236.

the practice, must be such as to establish the agreement of the parties as a whole to the modification in question.[40]

In the *Temple of Préah Vihéar Case* the ICJ appears to have taken into consideration the conduct of the parties not only as a subsidiary means in case of doubt as to the interpretation to be given to the instrument under examination, but also as a possible source of a modification in the juridical situation, in the event that it had been sought to draw a different conclusion from the simple interpretation of the instrument in question. According to the Court:

> Both parties, by their conduct, recognized the line and therefore in effect agreed to regard it as being the frontier line.[41]

In both the *Air Transport Services Agreement Arbitration* and the *Temple of Préah Vihéar Case* subsequent practice was regarded as a possible source of *modification* of the treaties, which were both bilateral, and not merely of interpretation. There were other elements which contributed to the conclusions reached by the tribunal and the Court respectively but the subsequent practice was a material factor enabling those conclusions.

The proposal of the ILC, though based on two cases which concerned bilateral treaties, correctly did not distinguish between bilateral and multilateral treaties. The principle is the same for both kinds of treaties. Thus, the Article was applicable to the constitutions of international organizations as well.

The Article was, however, omitted at the 1969 Vienna Conference on the Law of Treaties, one of the grounds being that such a rule would create instability.[42] But Article 39 of the 1969 Vienna Convention provides that a treaty may be amended by agreement, whether this is formal or not in its expression. Article 40, dealing with multilateral treaties, must be understood to include this principle. Subsequent practice resulting in modification or amendment is a form of agreement. A consistent practice could clearly provide cogent evidence of common consent to a change. In any event, modification of this type occurs in practice: e.g., the inclusion in practice of fishing zones as a form of contiguous zone for the purposes of the 1958 Geneva Territorial Sea Convention.[43]

---

[40] *Ibid.*   [41] 1962 ICJ Reports at p. 33.

[42] *Official Records, First Session*, pp. 207ff. See Kearney and Dalton, 'The Treaty on Treaties', 64 AJIL (1970) at p. 525. The prevailing view was that it was also thought not to be properly included in a convention dealing only with treaties, rather than because it was thought to be impossible.

[43] It would seem that the original EC Treaties had been changed over time by a process of interpretation. The process was gradual but there were milestones, such as *Van Gend*

The practice required to modify or amend multilateral treaties, including the constitutions of international organizations, may involve somewhat more stringent requirements than in the case of bilateral treaties. What has to be proved is that the practice reflected an agreement among all the parties. This may be more difficult where there are several parties to an instrument rather than just two. Nonetheless, practice cannot for that reason be excluded as a means of modifying or amending constituent instruments of international organizations.

en Loos, CJEC Case 26/62 [1963] ECR p. 1. However, this process of interpretation is different from modification. The principle of effectiveness was applied by the CJEC in such cases to interpret constructively. It is doubtful whether there has been change or amendment to the treaty by the CJEC by this process.

15 Dissolution and succession

While it is to be expected that the existence of an international organization would come to an end when it has completed its task or when
another organization is established to perform the same or similar functions, this is not always the case. Effectively an organization could be
dissolved when its membership wishes to do so and the unwillingness of
most of the members to continue participation in an organization, for
whatever reason, could lead to dissolution. There are several instances of
dissolution of organizations, though not for the latter reasons, because
the assumption is that once an organization is established the functions
performed will continue to be required for international society. The LN
was dissolved by agreement of the members in 1946 but the UN virtually took its place. The ICAN was also dissolved in 1946, as was the IIA
by a decision of its Assembly, and the East African Common Services
Organization ceased to exist in 1967 under the terms of the Kampala
Treaty. But in these cases some other organization in effect continued
the functions of the dissolved organization. Organizations may cease to
exist by absorption (e.g., the IBE by the UNESCO in 1969 and the IPI by
the EPO in 1978), or by merger (e.g., the ESRO and the ELDO into the
ESA in 1975), there being also in effect a dissolution which took place in
these cases. An example of dissolution because the members considered
the organization *functus officio* is the dissolution of the EAC in 1976.

The main general issues that arise in regard to dissolution are (i)
how organizations may be dissolved and what happens upon such dissolution; and (ii) whether one organization may succeed to another
(succession) and how this takes place.[1] It may not be possible always

---

[1] Dissolution has been discussed generally in Sands and Klein (eds.), *Bowett's Law of
International Institutions* (2001) pp. 526*ff*; Schermers and Blokker, *International Institutional*

to keep the two matters distinct and separate. The IRO was dissolved in 1952 when it had almost completed its task but the reason for its dissolution was that the USA which funded it to the extent of about 60 per cent of its needs was unwilling to give it continued support.[2] While the IRO was dissolved, its activities were continued in part by the UNHCR and in part by the ICEM. In the case of the OEEC in 1960 the OECD took over its functions, its assets and its liabilities. This appears to be a case of dissolution and 'succession' but is properly regarded as a reconstitution of the same organization, with the addition of a few new members.[3] After the LN was dissolved the UN took its place in regard to overall functions[4] but there was no succession to property and obligations, their disposition being settled on the special basis of a liquidation, while the question has arisen whether actual succession to some of its functions by the UN took place.

Dissolution

There are some basic questions which may be asked about dissolution. First, there is the situation where the constitution of an organization provides for dissolution. In these cases further issues may arise as to whether there are any other methods of dissolution than those provided in the constitution and particularly whether there could be a departure from the provision relating to the discharge of liabilities and distribution of assets. Second, how does dissolution take place when no provision is made for it in the constitution of an organization? Third, what is the position as regards the discharge of liabilities and the distribution of assets in this situation? There may also be questions as to the effects of dissolution.

Law (1995) pp. 1015ff.; and Mackinnon Wood, 'Dissolution of the League of Nations', 13 BYIL (1946) p. 317. There is much that has been written on the succession of organizations: e.g., the works cited above; Chiu, 'Succession in International Organizations', 14 ICLQ (1965) p. 83; Hahn, 'Continuity in the Law of International Organization', 13 OZOR (1964) p. 167; D. P. Myers, 'Liquidation of the League of Nations', 42 AJIL (1948) p. 320; Tanzi, 'The Extinction of International Organizations: the case of IBI', *La Communità Internazionale* (1993) p. 731; P. R. Myers, *Succession between International Organizations* (1993) and the extensive works cited in the bibliography therein at pp. 161ff.; Kiss, 'Quelques aspects de la substitution d'une organisation à une autre', 7 AFDI (1961) p. 463; and Jenks, 'Some Constitutional Problems of International Organizations', 22 BYIL (1945) p. 11.

[2] See Holborn, *L'Organisation Internationale pour les Réfugiés* (1955) pp. 537ff.

[3] See Article 15 of the OECD Convention. There was continuity and identity. Hahn, loc. cit. note 1 at pp. 217ff., deals with this case.

[4] D. P. Myers, loc. cit. note 1 at pp. 321ff.; P. R. Myers, note 1 pp. 16ff.

The constitution of most organizations, including the UN and the majority of the specialized agencies of the UN, do not have provisions on dissolution, probably because they were intended to continue in existence indefinitely. The financial institutions, including those that are specialized agencies of the UN, without exception, have such provisions, probably not because they are intended to be dissolved at some time but because, if their operations must be terminated at a given time, they will have sizeable assets and certain liabilities which will have to be distributed or discharged. There are other organizations, particularly those that are intended to be temporary, as will be seen, which have dissolution provisions.

Express provisions on dissolution

Article VI(5) of the IBRD Articles of Agreement contains detailed provisions for dissolution by a vote of the majority of Governors (the highest representative body), exercising a majority of the total voting power. Liability to the organization for uncalled subscriptions is to remain until all claims by creditors and all contingent claims have been satisfied. Payment of creditors and claims takes priority over distribution of assets. Distribution of assets is in proportion to the shareholding of a member. Article XXVII of the Articles of Agreement of the IMF has provisions relating to liquidation and a special Schedule K deals with the same subject. The agreements setting up the ADB, the IDB and the EBRD require that two-thirds of the members and three-fourths of the total voting power must support a decision to liquidate and provide for the payment of claims and distribution of assets as in the case of the IBRD.[5] Some other constitutions expressly authorize the highest representative body to dissolve the organization, a qualified majority often being required.[6] There are some organizations, mainly closed regional organizations, that have some very special provisions for dissolution.[7] Temporary organizations generally have constitutions which provide for dissolution. The commodity organizations established for limited periods are examples of these.[8]

While it is to be expected that in the event of termination of operations the express provisions of constitutions will be applied, the question

---

[5] See Articles 45–7 of the ADB Agreement; Article X(2)-(4) of the IDB Agreement; and Articles 41–3 of the EBRD Agreement. The Agreement establishing the IFC, the IDA, the MIGA, the AFDB and the Common Fund for Commodities also have such provisions.

[6] See, e.g., the IFAD Agreement, Article 9.

[7] See, e.g., Article 25 of the ESA constitution; and Article 14 of the EMBL Constitution.

[8] See, e.g., the International Coffee Agreement, the Cocoa Agreement and the International Tin Agreement.

may be asked whether they can be departed from, changed or varied. There are two principal ways in which this could be done. First, it is possible that the provisions relating to amendment be invoked in order to negate the express dissolution provisions and substitute other methods of dissolution. New dissolution provisions can thus be introduced which may affect adversely the expectations of creditors particularly, or increase the burdens of members. However, this is a prerogative of the membership. Second, the membership as a whole may agree to dissolve the institution in any way it pleases, disregarding the express provisions of the constitutions. This is possible because treaties, including multilateral treaties, can be terminated or changed by agreement of all the parties. The fact that the instruments are constitutions would not seem to make a difference in international law. In this way too the provisions relating to liabilities and assets can be changed considerably. The agreement of all members would, however, be required.

There are other theoretical possibilities, such as withdrawal of all members but one (since an organization must be composed of at least two members), desuetude and denunciation, which could cause an institution to come to an end in a manner not provided for by, or in disregard of, the dissolution provisions. These are more appropriately discussed in connection with the situation where there are no provisions for dissolution, but it should be recognized that they are very unlikely to occur in the case of institutions that have dissolution provisions. In both cases the problems that will arise will be related not to the demise of the institution but to the treatment of liabilities and assets. In the case of the withdrawal of members the obligations owed by the withdrawing members and their rights would be determined by the withdrawal provisions which may not coincide with the dissolution provisions and may bring about different results. In these circumstances, it would not be clear what the position or the obligations of the last remaining member will be.

No express provisions on dissolution

The LN Covenant did not have any provisions for dissolution of the organization, as the UN Charter does not. The constitutions of the specialized agencies of the UN, excluding the IMF, the IDA, the IFC, the MIGA and the IBRD, do not have any such provisions either. Likewise, the constitutions of most closed organizations (e.g., the OECD and Council of Europe) and of some other organizations (e.g., the UNESCO, the WHO and the

FAO) do not have provisions on dissolution. The question to be answered is by what methods and how may these organizations be dissolved. Certain general principles apply.

The LN was dissolved by a decision taken by its Assembly, i.e., the general congress, without any formal convening of the Council. The decision was taken unanimously but only thirty-five of the forty-five members were present. However, none of the absent members later protested against the decision taken. There was a Board of Liquidation established for the sole purpose of liquidating the affairs of the organization. The physical assets, including buildings, equipment, archives, libraries, etc. were transferred to the UN which made payment for them. What was effected by the Board of Liquidation was more like a liquidation among shareholders in a private corporation. While the UN was not a successor of the LN as such, it took over some functions of the LN.

Some constitutions do expressly provide for the general congress to liquidate the organizations. However, as the example of the LN and other examples show, there is good evidence that there is a general principle of international institutional law that an organization may be dissolved by the decision of its highest representative body (the general congress), when there are no provisions governing dissolution.[9] This method has been used in several cases. For example, the UNRRA was dissolved and its functions transferred to other international organizations by its general congress.[10] The IRO was also dissolved by a resolution of its general congress, seventeen of the eighteen members being present.[11] ICAN was dissolved by a decision of its general congress after the ICAO constitution was adopted, the decision to take effect after 75 days, if no member objected.[12] In the case of both the IRO and ICAN none of the absent members protested against the decision to dissolve the organization. General congresses have usually taken the subsequent decisions relating to the winding up of tasks and machinery of the organizations.[13]

---

[9] See Schermers and Blokker, note 1 p. 1,024. *Contra* Kiss, loc. cit. note 1 at p. 469.

[10] See Woodbridge, *UNRRA, The History of the United Nations Relief and Rehabilitation Organization* (1950) vol. III, pp. 157*ff*.

[11] Holborn, note 2 pp. 748*ff*.

[12] There was also a decision that the Paris Convention under which the ICAN was established would come to an end upon 'denunciation' by the parties. This confused the issue: see P. R. Myers, note 1 pp. 20 and 44.

[13] See also the dissolution of the IIA. This was done by a Protocol which was approved by the Assembly (general congress) and came into effect twenty-two months later, after the thirty-fifth ratification, as required, was obtained: Cmd. 7413, 29 GBTS p. 3. It should be noted that there was no objection to the decision taken by the Assembly.

While the precedents confirm the general principle referred to above, they also show that in effect there was unanimity among, or no objection from, the membership in respect of the decisions to dissolve. Thus, it is not clear what the position would be, if only a majority or a qualified majority took the decisions. The presence of effective unanimity would be tantamount to agreement among all the parties to the treaty which would not create a problem. On the other hand, where there are no express provisions for dissolution, there is no reason why dissolution should not be treated like any other comparable matter under the constitution of the organization. For example, under the UN Charter it may be argued that a decision to dissolve should be treated as no more than an important matter under Article 18(3) requiring a two-thirds majority. The fact that the decision would have a dispositive effect is not an obstacle as there are other decisions with similar effect, such as budgetary and financial decisions, which are taken under the same provision. In fact, since the general congress of an organization can effectively bring the functioning of the organization to a halt by refusing to meet or have an agenda and by not voting a budget by the required majority, it is arguable that there is no reason why the general congress should not be permitted to dissolve the organization in the same way.

The constitutional amendment procedure may also be used to dissolve an organization, although dissolution is not the same as amendment. However, this has never been done. Desuetude or disuse is another possible method of dissolution,[14] which may not be of significance, however, for the more important and larger organizations. In this case the staff of the organization would cease to exist and the organization would no longer operate, thus resulting in its substantial disappearance. It has been argued that the doctrine of *rebus sic stantibus* may also operate to bring an organization's existence to an end in certain circumstances.[15] However, this doctrine does not operate to terminate legal relationships but operates to give one or more of the parties to a relationship the right to terminate it. The termination of the EAC is said to have been due to changed circumstances, both political and economic. But in that case

---

[14] Desuetude is mentioned by Schermers and Blokker, note 1 pp. 1,027*ff*. The *Yearbook of International Organizations* (1978/79) lists twenty-one public international organizations as dead or inactive. The International Commissions of the Elbe and Oder have now ceased to function after the withdrawal of Germany in 1936.

[15] See Schermers and Blokker, note 1 pp. 1,028*ff*. In 1948 the Soviet Union submitted that the existing Danube Commission had ceased to exist because of the *clausula rebus sic stantibus* but the Western powers did not accept this submission.

what happened was that, because the partner states could not agree on any mode of termination, no legal arrangements were made for the dissolution of the organization. Most activities and most personnel were taken over by the national governments. There was an implicit agreement that the Community would cease to exist by this method.

Withdrawal has already been mentioned as a possible method of dissolution. There is also the possibility of denunciation which is similar to withdrawal. There are some possible examples of this method being used. In the case of the OIHP, while it would have been possible to dissolve the organization by all the members notifying their intention to withdraw, the Permanent Committee decided to formulate a Protocol (1946) which provided that dissolution would take place when all the members had become parties to the Protocol or had denounced the Rome Agreement of 1907 which established the OIHP.[16] The principle of denunciation was accepted (apart from agreement) but there was a problem of obtaining denunciations or signatures to the Protocol from seven member states. Finally, the Permanent Committee decided that the OIHP should be *de facto*, if not *de iure*, dissolved by termination of the activities of the office (desuetude). The Permanent Committee entrusted the task of winding up to a Commission of Finance and Transfer[17] which worked with the Interim Commission of the WHO on the transfer of certain OIHP functions.

Actual agreement can be used to terminate the existence of an organization. Normally and in principle the parties to the agreement, whatever form it takes, should include all the members of the organization. Thus, the Kampala Treaty of 1967[18] which created the EAC brought to an end the existence of the East African Common Services Organization which was merged into the EAC. In this case, the members of the organization being dissolved were all parties to the later treaty. The former organization ceased to exist on the date the Kampala Treaty came into force. The dissolution of the ESRO and the ELDO and their merger in the ESA took place under the ESA Convention which came into effect on 30 October 1980, contained the ESA constitution and established the ESA. The parties to the ESRO, the ELDO and the ESA constitutions were the same states.[19]

[16] 9 UNTS p. 66.

[17] Resolution of 31 October 1946, *Procès-verbaux des séances du Comité permanent.* Session Ordinaire, October 1946, p. 140.

[18] 3 BDARO p. 1,145.

[19] See Chappez, 'La création de l'Agence spatiale européenne', 21 AFDI (1975) p. 801.

More difficult to explain on the basis of principle are agreements providing for the dissolution of one organization and the transfer of its functions to another organization. If the agreement is approved by the general congress of the organization being dissolved, it may be assumed to be an agreement to which all the members of that organization have expressly or impliedly agreed, but, if not, the agreement of all members could only be implied on the basis that the more restricted organ had the delegated power to act on behalf of the full membership. When the IIIC was replaced by the UNESCO in 1946, this was done by an agreement between the IIIC and the UNESCO which provided that the former organization would cease its activities and that the UNESCO would take over certain of its functions and assets.[20] The UNESCO accepted responsibility for the final liquidation of the IIIC's assets. The agreement dissolving the IIIC was approved by its governing body, the Administrative Council of the LN, but no other steps were taken. The absorption of the IBE by the UNESCO in 1969 was achieved by an agreement between the IBE and the UNESCO which also provided for its liquidation.[21] The IPI was absorbed by the EPO by an agreement between the two which was approved by the IPI Board of Administration in September 1977. The agreement provided for the dissolution of the EPO on 1 January 1978 and its liquidation.[22]

Consequences of dissolution

Sometimes the consequences of dissolution will depend on whether succession by one or more other organizations takes place. Succession which will depend on particular arrangements and agreements or, perhaps, on general principles will be discussed below. In any event, where the constitution of an organization provides for the liquidation of assets and liabilities, as in the case of the IBRD and other financial institutions, these provisions will apply. But apart from these provisions dissolution may have certain general effects. In the absence of such express provisions, the organization will have to decide on its liquidation procedure. This has been done in almost all the cases that have occurred.

---

[20] See UNESCO Doc. No. 1C/30, General Conference, First Session, p. 241: preamble, Articles 2 and 3.

[21] See Articles 2, 3 and 8: UNESCO Doc. No. 15/83 (1968), Annex II, pp. 2–3.

[22] See Doc. No. CI/Final 23/77 of the Interim Committee of the EPO. Mention may also be made of COMECON (1991), the Warsaw Pact (1991) and the Intergovernmental Bureau for Information (1991) as organizations which were dissolved. On this last organization see Tanzi, loc. cit. note 1 at pp. 731*ff.*

Agreements (including treaties), declarations and contracts (not made on the international plane) which are generally of a personal nature and to which the dissolved organization was a party will normally be terminated upon a dissolution.[23] This applies to agreements of employment with the organization. Creditors will have to depend on the terms of the liquidation to secure liabilities owed to them.[24] Agreements which have a 'real' nature and are more than personal have an objective nature and normally would survive the dissolution to the extent that they are objective. The survival of such agreements is not necessarily dependent on succession but on their objective nature. In the case of the LN mandates, they would have survived the demise of the LN, regardless of whether the supervision system was taken over by the UN, because they had an objective nature, as was held in the *Status of South West Africa Case*.[25] Thus, South Africa could not annex the mandated territory of South West Africa, because the mandate still continued and had not come to an end. On the other hand, the continuation of certain elements of the mandates system, such as the supervision mechanisms, may have depended on succession. Other objective dispositions made by a dissolved organization by treaty or agreement would survive the dissolution, even though the organization ceased to exist.

Decisions, recommendations and declarations of the dissolved organization which have been made before the dissolution need not cease to have effect, as such, as a result of the dissolution. Much will depend on the nature of the resolution. Succession of one organization to another may have other effects but the survival of legal effects of such resolutions does not necessarily depend on succession. On the other hand, upon the dissolution the internal rules of the dissolved organization would cease to have effect for the future. These rules would include the staff regulations and rules or their equivalent. It should also be noted that the staff of a dissolved organization have no *de iure* right to continue in their jobs. As already stated, their contracts which are personal come to an end on the dissolution of the organization.

---

[23] See the *Aerial Incident Case (Israel v. Bulgaria)*, 1959 ICJ Reports p. 127. See also for similar reasoning the *Temple of Préah Vihéar Case*, 1961 ICJ Reports p. 17.

[24] See the situation of discontinued staff members of the LN who, after the dissolution of the LN, had received judgments from the LNT in their favour flowing from their contracts of employment (*Mayras etc.*, LNT Judgments Nos. 24 to 36 [1946]). The LN refused to execute the judgments. The staff members had to be satisfied with the termination arrangements originally accorded to them.

[25] 1950 ICJ Reports p. 128.

Succession

When succession takes place between international organizations, there is a transfer of functions from one organization to another which is often accompanied by the transfer of ancillary rights and obligations.[26] Such succession has taken place generally by (i) replacement of one organization by another (e.g., the replacement of the LN by the UN and the ICAN by the ICAO); or (ii) absorption of one organization by another (e.g., the absorption of the IBE by the UNESCO); or (iii) by merger of organizations (e.g., the merger of the ELDO and the ESRO in the ESA); or (iv) by separation of one organ of an organization to form a new international organization (e.g., the separation of the UNIDO from the UN to form the UNIDO); or (v) by the transfer of specific functions from one organization to another (e.g., the transfer of the social and cultural functions of WEU to the COE). But, whatever the mode of succession, in the past succession has been by conventional methods. This means that the succession is effected by agreement, whether explicit or implied.

Where the membership of the organizations concerned is the same, the agreement has been recorded explicitly in constitutional provisions of the new organization, as in the case of the merger of the ESRO and the ELDO to form the ESA.[27] Sometimes the succession has been implicit in the formation of the new organization. This was apparently the case when the African and Malagasy states merged to form the African and Malagasy Common Organization in 1966.[28] While the constitution of the latter organization did not explicitly provide for the succession, the latter organization did take over the functions, liabilities and assets of its predecessors and no objections were raised.[29] This method of implicit succession may not be always possible for larger organizations.

Where the membership of the organization was different, the dissolution of the predecessor organization or organizations has taken place

---

[26] See P. R. Myers, note 1 p. 12 for a similar definition of succession between organizations.

[27] See Article XXI(2) of the Convention for the Establishment of the European Space Agency (1975). See also Articles III and IV of the Agreement for the Establishment of the Caribbean Organization (1960) which provided for the succession of the Caribbean Commission by the Caribbean Organization.

[28] See Ranjeva, *La Succession d'organisations en Afrique* (1978) p. 348. It will be recalled that the Vienna Convention on the Law of Treaties of 1969 in Article 59 provides for the tacit abrogation of a previous treaty by a subsequent treaty.

[29] See also the replacement of the International Committee for Co-ordination of Anti-Locust Activities in Central America and Mexico by the International Regional Organization of Animal and Plant Health in 1955.

separately by some of the methods discussed in the previous section and the transfer of functions and assets and liabilities, where envisaged, has taken place through some form of agreement, formal or informal, between the predecessors and successor organizations or through agreements between states on the transfer of functions under general conventions from one organization to another, whether these agreements appear in constitutional or special instruments. An example of an agreement between states is the protocol revising the existing international labour conventions endorsed by the ILO General Conference in 1946 by which certain functions under them were transferred from the Secretary-General of the LN to the ILO.[30]

Succession between international organizations has had effects on the transfer of functions, treaties, transfer of assets and liabilities, transfer of subsidiary institutions, and employees. The effects have depended on the succession agreements or action taken under them.[31] There are no general principles governing effects except that they are determined by agreement.

It is evident that some form of agreement, explicit or sometimes implicit, is the basis of succession between organizations, as far as the historical record shows. The question is, however, whether there can be 'automatic' succession of some kind. This does not concern the dissolution of the previous organization, which will, no doubt, be done according to the prescribed modes. While the question has not arisen frequently, it is necessary to consider it.

The idea of the possibility of 'automatic' succession was discussed by the ICJ in its advisory opinions in the *Status of South West Africa Case*[32] and the *Namibia Case*.[33] In the first case the Court held that (i) the obligation of South Africa under the mandate for South West Africa to administer the territory and to promote to the utmost the material and moral well-being of the inhabitants had survived the demise of the LN, because it was a 'real' obligation, this view being supported by the effect of Article 80(i) of the Charter which related to the new trusteeship system; and (ii) there was an obligation upon South Africa to submit to the General Assembly in respect of supervision and control over the administration of the territory. The second obligation involved a question of succession. The Court recognized that the supervisory functions

---

[30] Conventional methods of succession have been extensively discussed in P. R. Myers, note 1 pp. 40–59.

[31] See P. R. Myers, *ibid.* pp. 78–96.   [32] 1950 ICJ Reports p. 128.

[33] 1971 ICJ Reports p. 16.

of the LN had not been 'expressly transferred to the United Nations nor expressly assumed by that organization'.[34] But the Court gave several reasons for concluding that the UN was qualified to exercise the supervisory functions and indeed had the power to do so. The first reason was that the submission of reports and the acceptance of supervision was an important part of the mandates system which did not come to an end because the supervisory organ ceased to exist, when the UN had another international organ performing similar, though not identical, supervisory functions.[35] The second was that Article 80(i) of the Charter protected the rights of the inhabitants of mandated territories until trusteeship agreements were concluded, which protection could not be ensured without supervision.[36] The third was that the resolution of the LN concerning its dissolution had stated that mandataries would agree on other arrangements for the mandated territories with the UN and no other body, which assumed that supervisory functions exercised by the LN would be taken over by the UN.[37] The fourth reason was that the GA had under Article 10 of the Charter competence to discuss any matter within the scope of the Charter and to make recommendations to the members of the UN on such matters and there were several instances where the GA had in fact exercised the supervisory function.[38] For all these reasons the Court concluded that the GA was legally qualified to exercise the supervisory functions previously exercised by the LN with regard to the administration of the territory of South West Africa and that South Africa was under an obligation to submit to the supervision and control of the GA and to render annual reports to it.[39]

In the second case the Court reaffirmed this conclusion, noting that in 1950 South Africa had agreed to submit its administration of South West Africa to the scrutiny of the GA, which agreement had been manifested by many statements made by its representative before the Assembly of the LN and the GA of the UN. The Court was of the view that the transfer from the Council of the LN to the GA of the UN of the power to supervise the mandate was a corollary of the powers granted to the GA, as was the transfer of the obligation of South Africa to report.[40]

[34] 1950 ICJ Reports at p. 136.   [35] *Ibid.*   [36] *Ibid.* at p. 137.   [37] *Ibid.*   [38] *Ibid.*
[39] *Ibid.*
[40] 1971 ICJ Reports at p. 37. Judge Alvarez in his dissenting opinion in the *Status of South West Africa Case*, 1950 ICJ Reports at pp. 181*ff.*, and Judge Lauterpacht in his separate opinion in the *Hearing of Petitioners Case*, 1956 ICJ Reports at pp. 14*ff.*, supported the Court's view on this matter. See also Fitzmaurice's analysis of the Court's opinion in the earlier case: 'The Law and Procedure of the International Court of Justice: International Organizations and Tribunals', 29 BYIL (1952) at pp. 8*ff.*

There has been some criticism of the Court's reasoning and conclusions in these cases.[41] The principal ground is that there was no evidence of an agreement between the LN and the UN to the transfer of the supervisory functions accompanying a mandate, the evidence being to the contrary.

The Court's views in the two cases were based on the theory that (i) there was an identifiable intention on the part of the LN to transfer the supervisory functions for mandates, even though this may have had to be implied, and (ii) there was an implied power arising from the content of Articles 80(i) and 10 vested in the GA of the UN to perform these supervisory functions. These views would lead to the conclusion that the succession in this case was based on implication. There may have been other factors which influenced the judges in finding that these implications could be made, apart from the fact the mandate was an objective regime which survived the dissolution of the LN. The first was that the UN under the Charter had in any case powers in the same *functional field* as that in which the LN had operated in regard to mandated territories. That the functional field passed from the LN to the UN was a consideration of importance. The second was that the supervisory function was an *essential* element of the mandates system.

These features make it possible to attribute the succession to an implied conventional source in the case of the mandates system and other similar objective regimes, of which there are no known examples. It is unnecessary to describe the succession as 'automatic'.[42] While there must be community of interest in a functional field and essentiality in the elements to which there is succession, these by themselves do not generate the succession. There are also the elements of implied intention and implied power that have a place in the effectuation of

---

[41] There have been many judges of the ICJ who have dissented from and criticized in these and other cases the views and conclusions of the Court in these two cases: see Judges Read and McNair in separate opinions in the *Status of South West Africa Case*, 1950 ICJ Reports, respectively at pp. 164*ff.* and 154*ff.*; Judges Badawi, Basdevant, Hsu Mo, Armand-Ugon and Moreno Quintana in a dissenting opinion in the *Hearing of Petitioners Case*, 1956 ICJ Reports at pp. 65*ff.*; Judges Spencer and Fitzmaurice in a joint dissenting opinion in the *South West Africa Cases*, 1962 ICJ Reports at pp. 539*ff.*; Judge van Wyk in a dissenting opinion in the same case, *ibid.* at pp. 597*ff.*; and in a separate opinion in the *South West Africa Cases (Second Phase)*, 1962 ICJ Reports at pp. 108*ff.*; and Judge Fitzmaurice in a dissenting opinion in the *Namibia Case*, 1971 ICJ Reports at pp. 236*ff.* See also Hudson. 'The Twenty-Ninth Year of the World Court', 45 AJIL (1951) at pp. 14*ff.*

[42] P. R. Myers, note 1 pp. 59*ff.*, characterizes this as 'automatic' succession and discusses it in these terms.

the succession.[43] It is doubtful whether international law in principle acknowledges a broader concept of 'automatic' succession, where the implied intention and implied power could be dispensed with and the presence of a common functional field and essential elements would suffice for automatic succession, albeit in the case of an objective regime. Implied conventional succession is the most appropriate description of what took place in the case of the South West Africa mandate.

There could be some problems raised with the view taken by the ICJ and supported here that the UN 'succeeded' with respect to the mandates, the problem being with the notion of succession, not with the continuation of the mandates. The UN Charter did, after all, provide for voluntary placement under Chapter XII. Moreover, the Soviet Union was hostile to the LN by reason of its expulsion. Thus, it would have liked to ensure that there was no element of formal continuity. Hence, despite some unevenness in the reasoning, it would appear that the Court was concerned to point to some consensual basis for the assumption by the UN of responsibilities with respect to South West Africa. The continuation of the obligations in respect of the mandated territory arose from the fact that the territory had an 'objective' status, or involved at its heart an obligation assumed for the protection of an interest which survived, that is to say the interest of the people of the territory. South Africa's right to administer the territory or remain there as a matter of general international law was dependent upon a continuing acceptance of the sacred trust. These propositions were clearly acceptable. The question then remained as to what happened to the supervisory function which had been vested in the LN. There was no explicit intention on the part of the LN to transfer such functions. Therefore, the Court took the view apparently that in the circumstances the UN's assumption of power with respect to mandates had been or was impliedly accepted by the LN. The power of assumption by the UN was also based on implication (via Chapter XI). If South Africa's assent was needed, that also had been given by its conduct, but it is not clear that this was regarded as a requirement. Thus, what did exist was an implied conventional basis for the succession.

---

[43] P. R. Myers concedes that the ICJ did not in reality base its conclusions in the *Status of South West Africa Case* and the *Namibia Case* on an automatic succession in a broad sense: note 1 pp. 74ff. Sands and Klein (eds.), note 1 p. 531, take the view that there is *no* automatic succession.

It has been suggested[44] that it was unnecessary to base the UN's assumption of power in the case of the South West Africa mandate on succession as such (let alone 'automatic succession'), the situation being explicable on the basis of estoppel. The UN had the necessary power of supervision under Chapter XI of the Charter and South Africa by its acts accepted the exercise of this power with the result that it was precluded from objecting to such exercise. This view, however, leaves unanswered the question how the power of supervision in relation to a *mandate*, assumed by the UN, was relinquished and transferred by the LN. In any event this view was not shared by the Court.

[44] Crawford, *The Creation of States in International Law* (1979) pp. 351*ff.*

16 The settlement of disputes

Different kinds of disputes may arise which involve international organizations. First, there are those concerning the interpretation of the constitution of an organization. Disputes of this kind are generally between member states but may also be between the organization and member states or even between organs of an organization. The mechanisms for the settlement of such disputes have been discussed in Chapter 2.

Apart from this kind of dispute, there are other disputes in which organizations may be directly involved as parties, such as (i) those between them and states, their members or not, or other organizations, arising from conventional relationships or under general international law, (ii) those between them and their employees arising from the employment relationship and (iii) those between them and private parties or states or other organizations under relationships governed primarily by national law and within national or transnational systems of law. Such disputes are connected with the institutional sphere of an organization's life. Thus, the methods of settling such disputes will be examined in this Chapter.

There are also disputes between states in which the organization is interested for functional reasons, because those disputes arise from obligations within the functional framework of the organization as determined by its constituent instrument (e.g., disputes arising from the alleged violation of Article 2(4) of the UN Charter in the context of the functioning of the UN). These disputes are strictly not institutional. Nevertheless, a word will be said about them and their settlement, even though the examination of the subject will not be exhaustive.[1] Such disputes are being addressed here, because some disputes of this genre may be particularly significant and it is, so to speak, institutionally important for organizations that they be settled or solved. The dispute settling function of organizations is not as such a matter for discussion here. That is a functional aspect of the life of organizations which is not properly a subject to be addressed here.

(1) Disputes between states and organizations or between organizations

In regard to the settlement of disputes between states and organizations or between organizations, whether the organization is a respondent or a claimant, resolution will be under the established methods of pacific settlement of disputes which are referred to in Article 33 of the UN Charter, namely negotiation, enquiry, mediation, conciliation, arbitration, judicial settlement or other peaceful means of the parties' choice. The real issue is whether any of these methods of settlement is obligatory in a given case. This will depend on the conventional law which governs the situation, as there is no general obligation under customary international law to adopt a particular method, though there may now be a customary obligation to settle disputes peacefully. Thus, under the UN–USA Headquarters Agreement there is under Section 21 an obligation ultimately in the event of a dispute to submit to international arbitration by a tribunal of the arbitrators appointed in the specified manner. In the *UN Headquarters Agreement Case* the ICJ held that there could be no question that the Headquarters Agreement was a treaty in force 'binding the parties thereto', and that what was in issue was whether there was a dispute concerning the interpretation or application of the agreement or any supplemental agreement (which had not been settled by negotiation or other agreed mode of settlement as required by Article 21) to generate

---

[1] This subject touches on and is concerned to a great extent with the *functional* (and not institutional) aspects of the working organizations. These, as pointed out in Chapter 1, are outside the scope of this work. Only a brief examination of the subject will be given. See further, Malinverni, 'The Settlement of Disputes within International Organizations', in Bedjaoui (ed.), *International Law: Achievements and Prospects* (1991) p. 545; and D. Bindschedler, 'Le règlement des différends au statut d'un organisation international', 124 *Hague Recueil* (1968-II) p. 453. The contribution by Malinverni has been found to be particularly helpful.

the obligation to arbitrate.[2] The Court in its advisory opinion concluded that on the facts of the case the dispute had not been settled by negotiation, settlement by the US courts was not another agreed mode of settlement contemplated by the parties, and the USA was bound to respect the obligation to have recourse to arbitration under Section 21.[3] In loan agreements between the IBRD and member states and credit agreements between the IDA and member states it is provided that any controversy between the parties arising under the agreements 'which has not been settled by agreement of the parties shall be settled by arbitration by an Arbitral Tribunal' constituted as specified in the agreements.[4] In the UN–Switzerland agreement disputes are to be referred to a tribunal of three arbitrators appointed in a specified manner. In such cases as these the terms of the agreements providing for the settlement of disputes are binding and effective methods of settlement exist.[5] In the absence of provision for settlement made before disputes arise, the method of settlement will depend on subsequent agreement between the parties.

The Statute of the ICJ does not provide for international organizations to be parties to contentious cases before the Court (Article 34 restricts appearance as parties to states). They may, however, have resort to the mechanism of the advisory opinions of the ICJ for the settlement of disputes at international law. The availability of this recourse will depend on authorization pursuant to Article 65(1) of the ICJ's Statute or under

---

[2] 1988 ICJ Reports at pp. 14–15. The dispute arose from action taken by the USA in connection with the Permanent Observer Mission to the UN of the PLO in New York. On settlement of disputes between international organizations and states see Dominicé, 'Le règlement juridictionnel du contentieux externes des organisations internationales', in Bardonnet, Combacau, Dupuy and Weil (eds.), *Le Droit international au service de la paix, de la justice et du développement: Mélanges Michel Virally* (1991) p. 225.

[3] 1988 ICJ Reports at pp. 33ff. The Court made it clear also that it was a generally recognized principle of international law that provisions of national law could not prevail over those of a treaty (*ibid.* at p. 35).

[4] See Section 10.04 of the General Conditions Applicable to Loan and Guarantee Agreements, dated 1 January 1985; and Section 10.03 of the General Conditions Applicable to Development Credit Agreements, dated 1 January 1985. No dispute has gone to arbitration. Disputes that have arisen have been settled by negotiation and agreement.

[5] In the case of the three treaties of the EU the CJEC has under the treaties jurisdiction in disputes between the organization and states. This jurisdiction of the CJEC is too complex and specialized to be dealt with here. The Court has a varied jurisdictional competence: see Sands and Klein (eds.), *Bowett's Law of International Institutions* (2001) pp. 407ff. Both the organs of the three Communities and states members, *inter alia*, may be parties before the Court and must submit to the jurisdiction of the Court: see Lasok and Bridge, *Law and Institutions of the European Communities* (1991) pp. 258ff.

the other provisions of Article 65. Advisory opinions are not binding unless they are made so by consent or agreement. Sometimes they are made binding in agreements such as the UN Convention, the Specialized Agencies Convention and the IAEA Agreement on Privileges and Immunities. In the UN–USA Headquarters Agreement it is provided in Section 21(b) that an advisory opinion may be sought from the ICJ on a point of law during an arbitration. In the *WHO Agreement Case* the WHO requested from the ICJ an advisory opinion which was given concerning the obligations of the WHO under an agreement between the WHO and Egypt.[6] This opinion effectively resulted in the settlement of the dispute which had arisen between the parties.

The use of national courts for the settlement of disputes involving the responsibility of organizations is not precluded but likely to be thwarted by claims of immunity by the organizations, unless such immunity is expressly or impliedly waived. The immunity of the IBRD, the IDA and the IFC and other financial institutions, however, is usually restricted to claims brought by or claims deriving from member states and in connection with employment disputes.[7]

(a) The relevance of the rule of local remedies

Questions have been raised about the relevance of the rule of local remedies. The considerations are different depending on whether the organization or a state is the respondent.

Where the organization is the claimant, the rule clearly would not apply where a direct injury to the organization has been perpetrated.[8] It has been suggested that the rule of local remedies should be applied, apparently without qualification, to claims on behalf of staff members,

---

[6] 1980 ICJ Reports p. 67.   [7] See Chapter 10 above.

[8] See C. F. Amerasinghe, *Local Remedies in International Law* (2004) pp. 146*ff*. This is supported by the ruling in the advisory opinion in the *UN Headquarters Agreement Case* where the ICJ said:

> The Court must further point out that the alleged dispute relates solely to what the United Nations considers to be its rights under the Headquarters Agreement. The purpose of the arbitration procedure envisaged by that Agreement is precisely the settlement of such disputes as may arise between the Organization and the host country without any prior recourse to municipal courts, and it would be against both the letter and the spirit of the Agreement for the implementation of that procedure to be subjected to such prior recourse. It is evident that a provision of the nature of section 21 of the Headquarters Agreement cannot require the exhaustion of local remedies as a condition of its implementation.   (1988 ICJ Reports at p. 29)

because it would save the organization much trouble and give to the respondent state an opportunity to repair through its own means the injury caused by it.[9] This view is based on the idea that the reason for applying the rule of local remedies to the case of claims by international organizations against states is similar to that which underlies the rule which applies in the case of the relations between aliens and host states.

While in the proceedings before the ICJ in the *Reparation Case* counsel for the SG of the UN merely stated that, in the context of claims by the UN against states for injuries to its officials, there was 'room for consideration' whether the rule of local remedies was applicable,[10] in the memorandum of the SG to the GA of the UN, explaining what procedures should be taken pursuant to the case, no mention was made of the rule. Consequently no reference is made to the rule in the resolution of the GA dealing with the matter.[11] However, it has been suggested that, where a staff member of the organization has been threatened with a private nuisance, he should first have recourse to local remedies, no waiver of immunity being necessary because the acts are of a private character over which local courts would have jurisdiction in any case.[12] One author has suggested generally that after exhausting remedies a staff member of an international organization should be able to seek the protection of the organization which he serves rather than that of his national state, because of the primary allegiance which he owes to the organization.[13]

There are problems with the view that the rule of local remedies applies to claims by international organizations on behalf of their staff. In the *Reparation Case* what the ICJ acknowledged was that as a result of the according of international personality to international organizations such as the UN, such organizations had the right to bring claims on behalf of their staff members for injuries suffered in the performance

---

[9] See Eagleton, 'International Organization and the Law of Responsibility', 76 *Hague Recueil* (1950–1) at pp. 351*ff*. (in relation to the UN); Brownlie, *Principles of Public International Law* (2003) p. 481; and Cançado Trindade, 'Exhaustion of Local Remedies and the Law of the International Organizations', 57 RI (1979) at pp. 82–3.

[10] The *Reparation Case, ICJ Pleadings, Oral Arguments and Documents* (1949) at p. 89.

[11] See UN GA Resolution 365(IV) of 1 December 1949.

[12] Hardy, 'Claims by International Organizations in Respect of Injuries to their Agents', 37 BYIL (1961) at pp. 525*ff*. This is not a true application of the rule to a violation of international law, however. This is a case where international law would be violated only if there is a subsequent denial of justice by some defect in the administration of justice.

[13] Greig, *International Law* (1976) p. 823.

of their official functions.[14] The Court made a clear distinction between a staff member acting in his official capacity and treatment of such staff member in his personal capacity. Thus, where a staff member is injured while performing his official duties, the organization would have the right of protection, while where the injury takes place when he is in his private capacity or in his private life, his national state would have the right of protection. This is the better view, in the light of the *Reparation Case*, despite expressions of opinion to the contrary based on the premise that a staff member should not have to rely on his national state for protection in his private life, if he is to be able to maintain his independence in the performance of his official duties. Assuming that the correct position is that an international organization has a right of protection only where a staff member is acting in his official capacity, the question is whether the rule of local remedies is applicable where the organization is a claimant against a state. In the situation envisaged the ICJ made it clear that the organization was not subrogated to the rights of the staff member against the respondent state but was asserting its own right to have international law respected in respect of its staff members. The conclusion to be deduced is that the organization in protecting a staff member primarily asserts a right vested in itself to be able to achieve its objectives through its staff members. The protection of staff is incidental to the right to be able to achieve its objectives. This is different from the right a state asserts to have international law respected in the person of its nationals, which is a right of protection and no more. The right which an organization has is more akin to that which a state has of protecting its diplomats or officials. In both cases the claimant's right pertains to the achievement of some broad objective connected with its functions. The protection of the staff member, as with the protection of the diplomat or official, is incidental to the claim asserted on the basis of a direct interference with the rights of the international person. Thus, this is a situation which must be likened to the direct injury caused a state and involving also an injury to one of its nationals – a situation to which the rule of local remedies is inapplicable. On this basis, then, the rule of local remedies would not be relevant to claims by international organizations in which they seek, among other things, to protect their staff members.

If the view is taken that international organizations have the right to protect their staff members against injuries suffered outside their

---

[14] 1949 ICJ Reports at pp. 181–2.

official functions, the situation may be different. It may be argued that respect for the sovereignty of the respondent state warrants the exhaustion of local remedies, since the international organization is asserting what is, indeed, its right, but a right only to protect its staff member, which may legitimately be compared to the right of a state to protect its nationals from injury by the respondent state. Therefore, the same rationale based on respect for sovereignty should result in the application of the rule to a claim brought by an international organization as forms the basis for the application of the rule in a claim brought by a state.[15]

Where the organization is the respondent, the view has been expressed that diplomatic protection *vis-à-vis* an international organization is subject *mutatis mutandis* to the prior exhaustion of international or local remedies. Thus, the explanation has been given that, once the international personality of an international organization is recognized by a state, diplomatic action by the state in respect of a national allegedly wronged by the organization can only take place after the individual has exhausted the means of redress provided to him by the organization.[16] At the same time, it has been said that exhaustion of internal remedies is one of several possible alternative means of settlement before diplomatic protection is exercised.[17] Other writers recognize that it may be difficult for organizations to provide internal or local remedies for this purpose,[18] but they may offer other means of settling disputes between organizations and individuals, even though organizations may have procedural incapacity before international courts and tribunals.[19] Another writer rejected the argument based on the absence of reciprocity in

---

[15] The measure of damages which may be an issue in cases, particularly those involving staff members, has been discussed in Eagleton, loc. cit. note 9 at pp. 366–80, though there is almost nothing in the way of judicial precedent in the matter. Eagleton describes the discussion in the Sixth Committee on the matter and examines issues connected with damages to the individual, to the agent and to the UN. See also for damages paid in respect of claims on behalf of servants or agents of the UN, UN Docs. A/CN.4/195 and Add.1, dated 7 April 1967, which are printed in 2 YBILC (1967) at pp. 218*ff*.

[16] Ritter, 'La protection diplomatique à l'égard d'une organisation internationale', 8 AFDI (1962) at pp. 454*ff*. The position of staff members is special: see below.

[17] Ritter, *ibid.* at pp. 454–5; see also at pp. 427 and 456.

[18] See Brownlie, note 9 p. 481, note 166.

[19] See Jenks, 'Liability for Ultra-Hazardous Activities in International Law', 117 *Hague Recueil* (1966–I) at pp. 190*ff*. See also Fitzgerald, 'The Participation of International Organizations in the Proposed International Agreement on Liability for Damage Caused by Objects Launched in Outer Space', 3 CYIL (1965) at pp. 278*ff*.

relation to the local remedies rule as between an organization and a state, and also pointed out that it was impracticable, if not impossible, for an organization to provide local remedies.[20]

One of the basic requirements for the incidence of the rule of local remedies is the jurisdictional connection between the individual and the respondent state.[21] It has been suggested, on the basis of the evidence, that the connection is based on the right, according to accepted principles, of the respondent state to exercise jurisdiction over the individual, which is primarily dependent on a territorial link. An international organization, although it has international personality, lacks the capacity in ordinary circumstances to exercise such jurisdiction over an individual, whether he be a national of a state or not, when an injury is inflicted by it on that individual. While international organizations have international personality and the capacity to have rights and obligations at international law, they are not states, as was pointed out by the ICJ in the *Reparation Case*.[22] And in fact they do not have jurisdictional rights or powers over individuals in the same way that states have. Such organizations do not have developed judicial systems, apart from their own internal systems (which are international in nature) for settling disputes with their staff members. This supports the view that they do not have jurisdictional powers over individuals in general. It is, thus, questionable whether they can provide suitable internal remedies. Thus, it is difficult to see how the rule of local remedies would be applicable in the above circumstances.[23]

The view taken above that the local remedies rule does not apply where an individual is harmed by an international organization found support from the Institut de droit international, when it dealt with the question of injuries caused by UN forces. In its 1971 resolution the Institut made the duty to exhaust remedies dependent on the acceptance

[20] Eagleton, loc. cit. note 9 at pp. 351*ff*. I have discussed the problem of local remedies being considered here in C. F. Amerasinghe, *Local Remedies in International Law* (2004).

[21] See C. F. Amerasinghe, *ibid.* pp. 168*ff*. Extra-territorial acts of a state causing injury to aliens do not, for example, attract the rule of local remedies.

[22] 1949 ICJ Reports at p. 179.

[23] The creation of a War Crimes Tribunal by the UN (in the case of the Balkan war) in 1994 does not disprove the above argument. The War Crimes Tribunal is not an internal court. The point is that an organization does not have jurisdiction over individuals as such – the kind of jurisdiction that states have in their territories. Further, IATs are internal courts of a special kind, deriving from jurisdiction inherent in the employment relationship. In the case of injuries to nationals caused by the acts of UN-controlled armed forces in connection with UNEF and the Congo no mention was made of the rule of local remedies.

of the jurisdiction of the adjudicating body by the national state of the injured individual or on a binding decision of the UN.[24] Thus, there is an understanding that there is no general principle that the rule of local remedies is automatically applicable to the situation.[25]

(b) Diplomatic protection of staff members by national states

A special problem concerns the position of national states vis-à-vis international organizations in respect of wrongs done to staff members of organizations by the organization of which they are staff members. Clearly, the staff member must seek redress, first, through the internal channels of dispute settlement of the organization and, then, through international administrative tribunals having competence in the matter, if such exist. But, after such successful resort or in the absence of such mechanisms, the staff member may be unrequited. For example, an organization may refuse to execute a judgment of a tribunal. The question then is whether his national state can exercise diplomatic protection in respect of his grievance vis-à-vis the organization. National states have in different circumstance exercised the right of protecting their nationals against organizations, presumably on the basis that it is diplomatic protection.[26] It seems difficult to make a distinction in the case of a staff member in the above situation. The analogy based on the cases of dual nationality, one of which is the nationality of the defendant state in the law of state responsibility, where the exercise of diplomatic protection by the claimant state is precluded, may create a problem. This results

[24] Article 8: 54 AIDI (1971-II) at pp. 268ff.

[25] For the rapporteur's view which was the same see de Visscher, 'Les conditions d'application des lois de la guerre aux opérations militaires des Nations Unies', 54 AIDI (1971-I) at pp. 58–9. There were objections in the discussions at the Institut to reference to the rule at all, because it was not certain in any case that the rule of local remedies was applicable to the claims of individuals against international organizations: see Rosenne's statement 54 AIDI (1971-I) at pp. 58–9. Further, it was explained in answer to some problems raised that the rule would not in any case apply to direct injuries to the state by UN forces: see de Visscher, ibid., at pp. 219–20. In the result, however, it was clear that the incidence of the rule was based on the agreement of the national state of the individual, whether it had been given directly or indirectly. In the context of relationships between individual states and international organizations it may be mentioned in passing that in the EC (now EU) system the rule does not seem to be applicable, whether the action is brought by an individual against a state or by an individual against an organization: see Cançado Trindade, loc. cit. note 9 at pp. 98ff. This is also the case in the conventional system of the ILO: see, e.g., Cançado Trindade, ibid. at pp. 97–8.

[26] See UN Docs. A/CN.4/195 and Add. 1, reprinted in 2 YBILC (1967) at pp. 219ff.

from the relationship between the staff member and the organization in respect of the performance of his functions which is the foundation for the rights of the organization to protect him being regarded as in a sense an equivalent of a nationality and from the injury in respect of which the protection of his national state is sought being regarded as connected with the performance of his functions. However, the nexus which gives the organization the right to protect its staff member, as was pointed out by the ICJ in the *Reparation Case*, is not analogous to nationality but is based on special functional considerations. These considerations do not make that nexus comparable to nationality for the purpose of excluding claims against organizations and, thus, the fact that the organization may exercise protection in respect of the staff member should not be an obstacle to the espousal of a claim on his behalf by his national state.

(c) The institution of claims by organizations

The ICJ in the *Reparation Case* does not specifically deal with the issue of who could act on behalf of the organization in instituting claims. It may be inferred that, because of its separate juridical personality, distinct both from that of individual members and from the aggregate of them as a body, the UN as an entity may have to take action against any, some or all of its members (or even against non-members). This in turn would require that a specific organ be vested with the power to do so.[27] There is probably a residue of functions which are or may have to be exercised on behalf of the organization in its corporate capacity, which are not specifically vested in any of its organs and which by their nature are even unsuitable to be carried out by any organ consisting of an assemblage of states. What the Court said was that the functions of the organization were of such a character that they could not be effectively discharged, if they involved the concurrent action, on the international plane, of fifty-eight or more foreign offices, and concluded that the member states had endowed the organization with capacity to bring international claims when necessitated by the discharge of its functions.[28] The Secretariat, however, is clearly established in the Charter as one of the principal organs of the UN (Article 7). It is possible to deduce that in all those cases where the organization as an entity is required or entitled to take certain action, but where no specific organ of the organization is empowered to do so, either expressly or by necessary implication derived from

[27] On this point see Fitzmaurice, *The Law and Procedure of the International Court of Justice* (1986) vol. I pp. 81ff.
[28] 1949 ICJ Reports at p. 180.

its character or functions, or where its character and composition renders it unsuitable for the purpose, it is the Secretariat acting through the SG that has the residual capacity to take the action in question. Unless this interpretation is given to the Charter, the result would be that there are things which the organization is entitled or even bound to do but which it could not effectively do. Thus, in connection with legal proceedings and the making of claims, for instance, it seems sensible that the SG is the organ necessarily competent to represent and act for the organization. Further in the discharge of the organization's duty of reminding member states of certain obligations owed by them to the organization, it is reasonable that the SG be the appropriate, or even the only, authority that could act. Article 99 of the Charter, though strictly dealing with a special point, supports this view. In other organizations similarly, the chief executive officer would normally be, as a consequence of the interpretation of the constituent instrument, the competent organ vested with the authority to institute claims.

(2) Employment disputes[29]

(a) Settlement by administrative organs

Before IATs were established, internal disputes of international organizations relating to employment relations were usually settled finally, not by judicial means, but by the administrative decision of an executive organ with or without an appeal to the legislative or deliberative organ. Even after IATs have been set up the initial remedial decision after the dispute arises is usually taken by an executive organ. It is then left to the employee, if he is dissatisfied, to take the matter up in a judicial forum, if a judicial organ has jurisdiction in his case. The administrative decision is in this case a dispute-settlement procedure and is not the same as the decision which gave rise to the dispute, though the dispute may continue after the decision is taken. Thus, while the decision to terminate the employment of a staff member may be taken by the Director of Personnel of an organization after consultation or on the initiative of the administrative head of another department, the dispute to which that decision gives rise may have initially to be referred for settlement to a different officer in the organization who may even be the chief executive. Sometimes a deliberative organ of the organization may perform this function.

[29] See C. F. Amerasinghe, *The Law of the International Civil Service* (1994), vol. I pp. 26–81.

There is generally no constitutional provision authorizing such a person or organ to settle the dispute. Nevertheless, such administrative settlement has been the prevailing procedure in general, at least for preliminary purposes, in all international organizations. Its legality was supported by the ICJ in its advisory opinion in the *Effects of Awards Case*:

> In the absence of the establishment of an Administrative Tribunal, the function of resolving disputes between staff and Organization could be discharged by the Secretary General by virtue of the provisions of Articles 97 and 101. Accordingly, in the three years or more preceding the establishment of the Administrative Tribunal, the Secretary General coped with this problem by means of joint administrative machinery, leading to ultimate decision by himself.[30]

It has been suggested that the power of the SG of the UN, or, indeed, the executive head of any international organization, to decide internal disputes relating to employment matters exists irrespective of such express provisions as those cited by the Court, the point being that this power has been exercised by the administrative heads of all organizations even where the constitutions of those organizations do not contain any such provisions.[31] Indeed, the jurisdiction of the administrative head of an international organization to settle internal employment disputes has never been denied.

As pointed out by the ICJ in the *Effects of Awards Case*,[32] the SG of the UN dealt with the settlement of employment disputes by means of joint administrative machinery. Indeed, he continues to do so. In most organizations the administrative head of the institution sets up some kind of advisory board or committee to examine the dispute and advise him before he takes a decision in the process of settling a dispute. Thus, in the UN there is a Joint Appeals Board[33] and the World Bank established an Appeals Committee[34] (which was established in the late 1970s after much agitation by the staff) to which complainants could take their cases and which advise the administration after investigation. This kind of procedure is not ruled out, because an international organization has implied or inherent powers to settle internal employment-related disputes.

---

[30] 1954 ICJ Reports at p. 61.

[31] Seyersted, 'Settlement of Internal Disputes of Intergovernmental Organizations by Internal and External Courts', 24 ZAORV (1964) at pp. 8–9. See also Seyersted, 'United Nations Forces: Some Legal Problems', 37 BYIL (1961) at pp. 453*ff.*

[32] 1954 ICJ Reports at p. 61.   [33] See Staff Regulation XI.1 of the UN.

[34] See Statement 8.3 (August 1983) of the Personnel Manual of the World Bank and later Staff Rule 9.03 (1991).

There is nothing to prevent the administration from submitting the question in dispute to an internal or external legal organ for advice before the chief executive or deliberative organ to whom the dispute may be referred takes a decision. The Charter of the UN empowers the GA itself to seek and to authorize organs of the UN and the specialized agencies to seek advisory opinions from the ICJ.[35] Apart from the ICJ, other internal legal organs, such as a committee of jurists, may be used by an organization to give it legal advice before it takes an administrative decision in the process of settling an employment-related dispute. This may be done even where the constitution of the organization is silent on the matter. Thus, in determining the question whether it was liable to pay compensation to certain ex-officials of the Saar territory whom the Governing Commission had not brought within the scheme for the settlement of pensions which had been negotiated with Germany the League of Nations consulted a legal committee of the organization itself[36] which advised that there was no legal liability. In the UN the SG has had recourse to an *ad hoc* committee of jurists in order to seek advice on disputes arising from the principles of his personnel policy.[37] The SG's decision which was contained in a report took into account the opinion of this committee.[38] In regard to the GA of the UN the power to refer questions to other bodies or organs for legal advice was envisaged at the San Francisco preparatory conference.[39]

The mode of settlement discussed here is no more than through administrative decision. Even if advice is legal, the decision is made by the administrative or deliberative organ which referred the question, as an administrative decision. This applies even where an advisory opinion of the ICJ may be obtained. Rarely, the organization may be bound, because of a unilateral act, to accept the opinion of the organ or body consulted. Then, the mode of settlement becomes a judicial one. Generally administrative decisions in the field of employment relations do

---

[35] Article 96 of the Charter.

[36] See also the discussion in McKinnon Wood, 'Legal Relations between Individuals and a World Organization of States', 30 TGS (1945) at p. 144.

[37] See UN Doc. A/INF/SI of 5 December 1952.   [38] See UN Doc. A/2364 (1953).

[39] In Committee IV/1 it was stated: 'It would always be open to the General Assembly in appropriate circumstances, to ask the International Court of Justice for an advisory opinion concerning the meaning of a provision of the Charter. Should the General Assembly ... prefer another course, an *ad hoc* committee of jurists might be set up to examine the question and report its views ... It would appear neither necessary nor desirable to list or to describe in the Charter the various possible expedients' (12 UNCIO p. 170).

not have the same finality as judicial decisions, though they are final till they are questioned. On the other hand, if there is no judicial authority having compulsory jurisdiction in regard to the settlement of employment disputes, the organization cannot be prevented from or penalized for carrying out its own decisions. Thus, in effect, since execution in relation to internal decisions concerning employment rests with the organization itself, the decision does become binding, unless the organization voluntarily agrees to submit the dispute to a judicial organ for final settlement.

(b) Establishment of internal courts

(i) Authority

Since many international organizations have either their own internal courts or use the internal courts of other organizations to settle employment disputes judicially, the first question is whether they can have such internal courts, i.e., international administrative tribunals, judicially to settle such disputes. Few organizations have provisions in their constitutions expressly authorizing the establishment of such tribunals. The existence of such a power has depended on implication in the interpretation of constitutional texts.

In the view of the ICJ the GA of the UN had the power to establish an IAT. In the *Effect of Awards Case* the Court explained the reasons for its conclusion:

When the Secretariat was organized, a situation arose in which the relations between the staff members and the Organization were governed by a complex code of law ... It was inevitable that there would be disputes between the Organization and staff members as to their rights and duties. The Charter contains no provision which authorizes any of the principal organs of the United Nations to adjudicate upon these disputes and Article 105 secures for the United Nations jurisdictional immunities in national courts. It would, in the opinion of the Court, hardly be consistent with the expressed aim of the Charter to promote freedom and justice for individuals and with the constant preoccupation of the United Nations Organization to promote this aim that it should afford no judicial or arbitral remedy to its own staff for the settlement of any disputes which may arise between it and them.[40]

The Court based its conclusion on the principle that the organization must be deemed to have those powers which, though not expressly provided in the constituent instrument, were conferred upon it by necessary

---

[40] 1954 ICJ Reports at p. 57.

implication as being essential to the performance of its duties.[41] It referred to the necessity for giving effect to the paramount consideration of 'securing the highest standards of efficiency, competence and integrity', which is mentioned in Article 101 of the Charter. The ICJ in the *Effect of Awards Case* took the view that the UN had the authority to establish a true judicial organ with independence and the capacity to give binding decisions like any court of a national state. The IAT set up by the UN was not a subordinate organ of the GA exercising delegated powers and without power to bind the GA by its judgments.[42] The judicial organ created could decide disputes relating to employment and bind the organization, including the principal organ of the organization which created it, namely the GA.

The Court also said that the GA itself, in view of its composition and functions, could hardly act as a judicial organ – considering the arguments of the parties, appraising the evidence produced by them, establishing the facts and declaring the law applicable to them – and all the more so because one party to the disputes was the UN itself.[43] This confirms the position that the administrative tribunal was a judicial organ whose judgments could only be reviewed by another body of a judicial nature.

While the ICJ referred to Article 101 of the Charter, it did not take the view that the provisions of that Article were necessary to give the UN the authority to establish an administrative tribunal. What was basic to its reasoning was the notion of essentiality for the performance of its duties or functions. Though the LN and the IIA did not have provisions in their constitutions like Article 101 of the UN Charter, they both established

---

[41] *Ibid.* at p. 57 and p. 56, citing the *Reparation Case*, ICJ Reports 1949 at p. 182.

[42]   It has been argued that an authority exercising power to make regulations is inherently incapable of creating a subordinate body competent to make decisions binding its creator ... The contention that the General Assembly is inherently incapable of creating a tribunal competent to make decisions binding on itself cannot be accepted.

The question cannot be determined on the basis of the description of the relationship between the General Assembly and the Tribunal, that is, by considering whether the Tribunal is to be regarded as a subsidiary, a subordinate, or a secondary organ, or on the basis of the fact that it was established by the General Assembly. It depends on the intention of the General Assembly in establishing the Tribunal, and on the nature of the functions conferred upon it by its Statute. An examination of the language of the Statute of the Administrative Tribunal has shown that the General Assembly intended to establish a judicial body; moreover, it has the legal capacity under the Charter to do so.   (1954 ICJ Reports at p. 61)

[43] *Ibid.* at p. 56.

administrative tribunals without their authority to do so ever being questioned.

While some international organizations have specific provisions in their constituent instruments giving the organizations power to conduct their personnel relations, other organizations do not. In the case of the World Bank Group, for example, the Articles of Agreement of all the institutions give the President responsibility for the organization, appointment and dismissal of the staff, subject to the general control of the Executive Directors or Board of Directors.[44] It is implied in this responsibility and control given to the President and Executive Directors or Board of Directors that the setting up of a judicial entity to settle disputes in staff matters would be reasonable and functionally justifiable. The situation is comparable to that in the UN, where Chapter XV of the Charter is less explicit than the Articles of the World Bank Group on the functions of the SG and GA *vis-à-vis* the staff. In both cases, however, it is clear that functionally the chief executive and a legislative or quasi-legislative organ together have responsibility in staff matters. Thus, deriving a power vested in the organizations to set up an administrative tribunal is not difficult. On the other hand, the absence of express provisions dealing with the staff and personnel relations in the constituent instrument of an organization does not detract from such a power, because it is within the accepted purpose and function of all international organizations to employ staff and conduct smooth and effective personnel relations. Thus, an international organization would have the necessary authority to set up or submit to the jurisdiction of an administrative tribunal with the power to give, in the manner of a true judicial organ, decisions binding on the organization concerned, including its deliberative or legislative organ which decided to establish or submit to the jurisdiction of the tribunal.

(ii) Reasons

Even though international organizations may generally have the authority to establish IATs or to submit employment disputes to tribunals established by other organizations, the question remains whether it is indeed necessary to establish them. Judicial machinery is established because of its desirability for reasons[45] such as respect for human rights

---

[44] Article V(5)(g) of the IBRD's Articles of Agreement; Article IV(5)(b) of the IFC's Articles; and Article VI(5)(b) of the IDA's Articles. See also Article 33(a) of the MIGA Articles.

[45] See C. F. Amerasinghe, note 29, vol. I pp. 37*ff*.

and the need to eliminate the interference of national courts. Though some national courts have in the past exercised jurisdiction over international organizations in employment-related cases, in most cases in most states national courts have recognized the immunity of organizations from their jurisdiction.[46] Yet, the possibility exists that national courts may assume jurisdiction in employment-related actions brought against international organizations, particularly where there are no tribunals internal to the organizations to decide such disputes of the international organizations concerned.[47] One of the surest ways to avoid this eventuality is for international organizations to make provision for the reference of employment-related disputes to IATs.

Problems may also arise, if national courts exercised jurisdiction, from the possible multiplicity of fora for the settlement of disputes, in the event that each employee chooses his own national court for the settlement of disputes in which he is involved. This could lead to conflicting pronouncements on the law and not be conducive to consistency and the fair administration of justice. Further, the special nature of the law governing employment relations in international organizations, which is closely linked with delicate issues of administrative policy, makes national courts unsuited to deal with it.

(c) The structure of international administrative tribunals

Many international organizations have either set up their own, or accepted the jurisdiction of other, IATs to settle employment disputes. The first such tribunal to be established was that of the LN, the LNT.[48] The principal tribunals that now exist include the UNAT, the ILOAT, the WBAT, the IMFAT, the OASAT, the IDBAT, the ADBAT, the OECD Appeals Tribunal, the COEAB, the NATO Appeals Board, the ICM Appeals Board, the WEUAB and the ESA Appeals Board. The CJEC performs the function of an administrative tribunal now through its Court of First Instance. Other organizations than those that set up their own tribunals which refer disputes to IATs have accepted the jurisdiction of the UNAT or the ILOAT. The ICJ also has some powers in regard to employment disputes,

---

[46] See Chapter 10 above.

[47] The President of the World Bank made this point in his Memorandum to the Executive Directors, dated 14 January 1980: Docs. R80–8, IDA/R80–8 and IFC/R80–6, pp. 1–2.

[48] For an account of the establishment of the LNT and other tribunals, see C. F. Amerasinghe, note 29, vol. I pp. 49*ff*. There are many IATs whose decisions are not made available to the public.

both original (in cases arising in the Registry) and secondary. The judgments of all the above-mentioned IATs are published.

The statutes which set up these IATs are legislative acts of each organization and are separate instruments having an identity of their own. The structure of IATs does not depend on any general principles of law, the provisions relating to such structure in each statute being self-contained. The provisions may only be compared, sometimes with a view to identifying a pattern, but there may be no similarities. On the other hand, in interpreting them, general principles of law may be applicable. Moreover, as already seen in Chapter 8, certain fundamental general principles of law which cannot be violated apply to IATs and their structure.

Matters pertaining to the structure of IATs discussed in Chapter 8 in the context of the principle of independence (and impartiality) of tribunals will not be dealt with specially here. These matters are (i) qualifications of judges, and conditions for their selection, (ii) emoluments of judges, (iii) reappointment of judges, (iv) conflict of interest in relation to judges, (v) the registry and (vi) the legislative power of the creating authority in relation to IATs and their structure.

All that needs to be said here in regard to structure relates to the composition of IATs. In general no one IAT is composed in the same manner as any other. Three examples may be considered. The UNAT[49] is composed of seven judges, no two of whom may be nationals of the same state. However, only three judges try any particular case; other judges may sit without voting. Judges are appointed by the GA of the UN for four years and may be reappointed once.

The ILOAT[50] bench consists of three judges and three deputy judges, who must all be of different nationalities. The judges and deputy judges are to be appointed for periods of three years by the Conference of the ILO. A meeting of the tribunal must be composed of three members of whom at least one must be a judge. Generally deputy judges sit only when judges are not available, always provided that one of the members of the tribunal is a judge.

In the WBAT[51] the bench is composed of seven judges, all of whom must be nationals of member states of the IBRD, but no two of whom may be nationals of the same state. The judges are appointed by the Executive Directors of the IBRD from a list of candidates to be drawn

---

[49] See Article 3 of the UNAT Statute: C. F. Amerasinghe (ed.), *Documents on International Administrative Tribunals* (1989) p. 7.

[50] Article III of the ILOAT Statute: *ibid.* p. 32.

[51] Articles IV and V of the WBAT Statute: *ibid.* pp. 46–7.

up by the President of the IBRD after appropriate consultation. Judges are appointed for a period of three years and may be reappointed. A quorum of five is sufficient to constitute the tribunal, but a panel of not less than three judges may at any time be formed to deal with a particular case or group of cases. The alternative of a panel has been used by the WBAT.[52]

(d) Principal operational features of international administrative tribunals

The manner in which a tribunal operates will depend to a large extent on its statute and other written law. However, there are some general principles which may be adverted to and which are applied in their implementation.

(i) Jurisdiction in general

The jurisdiction of IATs is generally restricted to actions brought by staff members (or sometimes persons with derivative rights) against the organization, provided such cases concern their contracts or terms of employment.[53] While jurisdiction depends on the particular provisions of a tribunal's statute, there are certain general principles applicable in relation to them. First, the cases must arise from the contract of service or terms of employment. Secondly, they must be brought by staff members or by persons with derivative rights specified in the statute. Thirdly, the staff member is always the plaintiff and the organization is the defendant. Under the usual provision the tribunal would not be open, for example, to a claim by the organization against a staff member, or to disputes between staff members, or to disputes between such entities closely related to the organization, such as a staff union, staff association, or a staff enterprise, and an employee of that entity, or to

---

[52] See also, e.g., Article VII of the IMFAT Statute; Article III of the IDBAT Statute (ibid. pp. 63–5); Article III of the OASAT Statute (ibid. pp. 84–5); and Article I of the COEAB Statute (ibid. p. 121) for other provisions relating to the composition of tribunals. Reference is also made on the matter of structure of IATs to C. F. Amerasinghe, note 29, vol. I pp. 63ff. for a fuller examination. The emphasis here has been on the UNAT, the ILOAT and the WBAT which may be considered the most important IATs.

[53] See Article 2 of the UNAT Statute: C. F. Amerasinghe (ed.), note 49 p. 6; Article II of the ILOAT Statute: ibid. pp. 31–2; and Article II of the WBAT Statute: ibid. p. 45. The formulation in the IMFAT Statute is somewhat different: see Article II. See also Article II of the IDBAT Statute: ibid. pp. 62–3; Articles 59 and 60 of the Staff Regulations of the COE and Article 5 of the Statute of the COEAB: ibid. pp. 118–21; Article II of the OASAT Statute: ibid. pp. 83–4. There is a detailed discussion of jurisdiction and admissibility in C. F. Amerasinghe, note 29, vol. I pp. 201ff.

disputes between a staff representative organ, such as a staff association or union, and the organization. There are other problems of *locus standi* and also of jurisdiction *ratione materiae* and *ratione temporis* which have confronted tribunals.[54] Jurisdiction is clearly limited. There are a number of disputes, of an employment or non-employment nature, which may not be submitted to domestic courts because of the immunity from their jurisdiction of one or both of the parties but which still cannot be submitted to IATs.[55]

There are variations, however. For instance, the Statute of the ILOAT has a provision which gives it competence over any contractual dispute to which the ILO is a party as long as the contract so provides.[56] The ICJ in the past clearly had jurisdiction to decide cases brought by the Registrar of the ICJ against staff members in employment-related cases.[57] However, the power given to the Registrar to bring a claim against staff members appears to have been taken away under the new Staff Regulations adopted on 7 March 1979.[58]

The jurisdiction vested in IATs is over the organization as defendant and not over a special officer or the head of the organization, as the case may be, although sometimes the claims are nominally filed against the head of the organization, such as the SG of the UN.[59] Any distinction that may be made between the head of an organization and the organization as such in the nomenclature of the pleadings is not significant.

Claims by staff members in regard to their employment generally attack administrative decisions, though some statutes of IATs give them a wider jurisdiction. There is normally a period of limitation for the filing of the claims[60] which begins to run from the date of the final administrative decision contested. Most statutes of tribunals require the

---

[54] See C. F. Amerasinghe, *ibid.*

[55] See, e.g., temporary staff members may not be able to litigate before tribunals in employment-related matters. A contract for a sale of a car to the organization by a staff member will also generally be outside the jurisdiction of IATs.

[56] Article II.4: see C. F. Amerasinghe (ed.), note 49 p. 31.

[57] See Article 17 of the former Staff Regulations of the Registry: *ICJ Yearbook 1946–1947* p. 68.

[58] See Article II: *ICJ Yearbook 1978–1979* p. 130.

[59] See the *Effect of Awards Case*, 1954 ICJ Reports at p. 53.

[60] See Article 7.4 of the UNAT Statute: C. F. Amerasinghe (ed.), note 49 p. 9; Article VII.2 of the ILOAT Statute: *ibid.* p. 33; Article II.2 of the WBAT Statute: *ibid.* p. 45; Article V.2 of the IMFAT Statute; Article II.2 of the IDBAT Statute: *ibid.* p. 63; Article VI.2 of the OASAT Statute: *ibid.* pp. 85–6; Article 60.3 of the Staff Regulations of the COE: *ibid.* p. 120.

staff member to exhaust 'internal' remedies before coming to the tribunal.[61]

Statutes of IATs do not provide for such tribunals to give advisory opinions. Although giving an advisory opinion is not inconsistent with the judicial function, in the absence of express provision it is not likely that tribunals will assume the power to do so. They also cannot perform conciliatory functions nor mediate, particularly because there is no express provision empowering them to do so. In the absence of express provision, decisions must rest on a legal basis; they cannot be *ex aequo et bono*, even if the parties agree to such a basis.[62]

(ii) Procedure

Statutes of IATs usually provide that the tribunals should establish their own rules of procedure. There are hardly any rules of procedure about the admissibility of evidence.[63]

(iii) Nature of decisions

The judgments of IATs are final and binding.[64] That their decisions are final lays upon tribunals a heavy responsibility, since there is no other forum to which an appeal can be taken from their decisions.

In regard to the nature of the UNAT and its decisions the ICJ in the *Effect of Awards Case* stated:

This examination of the relevant provisions of the Statute shows that the Tribunal is established, not as an advisory organ or a mere subordinate committee of the General Assembly, but as an independent and truly judicial body

---

[61] See Article 7.1 of the UNAT Statute: *ibid*. p. 8. See also Article VII.1 of the Statute of the ILOAT: *ibid*. p. 33; Article II.2 of the WBAT Statute: *ibid*. pp. 45–6; Article V.1 of the IMFAT Statute (slightly different formulation); Article II.2 of the IDBAT Statute: *ibid*. p. 63; Article VI.1 of the OASAT Statute: *ibid*. p. 85; and Articles 59 and 60 of the Staff Regulations of the Council of Europe: *ibid*. pp. 118–21.

[62] Equity may also be applied to the extent that it gives rise to legal principles: see C. F. Amerasinghe, note 29, vol. I Chapter 14.

[63] For problems of evidence see C. F. Amerasinghe, 'Problems of Evidence before International Administrative Tribunals', in Lillich (ed.), *Fact-Finding before International Administrative Tribunals* (1992) pp. 205*ff*. The more important aspects of procedure are discussed in C. F. Amerasinghe, note 29, vol. I Chapter 33.

[64] See, e.g., the UNAT Statute, Article 10.2: C. F. Amerasinghe (ed.), note 49 p. 10; the ILOAT Statute, Article VI.1: *ibid*. p. 32; the WBAT Statute, Article XI.1: *ibid*. p. 48; Article XIII.2 of the IMFAT Statute; the IDBAT Statute, Article VIII.2: *ibid*. p. 66; the OASAT Statute, Article VIII.2: *ibid*. p. 87; and the COEAB Statute, Article 12.2: *ibid*. p. 124.

pronouncing final judgments without appeal within the limited field of its functions. According to a well-established and generally recognized principle of law, a judgment rendered by such a judicial body is *res judicata* and has binding force between the parties to the dispute... [T]he parties to this dispute before the Tribunal are the staff member concerned and the United Nations Organization represented by the Secretary General, and these parties will become bound by the judgment of the Tribunal. This judgment is, according to Article 10 of the Tribunal's Statute, final and without appeal. The Statute has provided for no kind of review. As this final judgment has binding force on the United Nations Organization as the juridical person responsible for the proper observance of the contract of service, that Organization becomes legally bound to carry out the judgment and to pay the compensation awarded to the staff member. It follows that the General Assembly, as an organ of the United Nations, must likewise be bound by the judgment.[65]

The ICJ also confirmed that this meant that the UN could not refuse on any grounds to execute the judgments of the UNAT.[66] What was said by the ICJ in regard to the binding and final nature of judgments of the UNAT is clearly applicable, *mutatis mutandis*, to the judgments of the other IATs.

In interpreting the phrase 'final and without appeal' in Article XI.1 of its Statute, the WBAT made it clear that there could be no appeal even to the same tribunal from its decisions:

Article XI lays down the general principle of the finality of all judgments of the Tribunal. It explicitly stipulates that judgments shall be 'final and without

---

[65] 1954 ICJ Reports at p. 53.

[66] 'The General Assembly has not the right on any grounds to refuse to give effect to an award of compensation made by the Administrative Tribunal of the United Nations in favor of a staff member of the United Nations whose contract of service has been terminated without his assent' (*ibid.* at p. 62). Some statutes explicitly state, in one way or another, that judgments of tribunals must be carried out by the organization: see, e.g., Article XII.2 of the WBAT Statute: C. F. Amerasinghe (ed.), note 49 p. 48. The view taken by the Assembly of the League of Nations was different from that taken by the ICJ. In adopting the conclusions of a report of a subcommittee of its Second Committee which were based more on 'what was politic and right' rather than on what was in accordance with strict law the Assembly decided that it was like a sovereign legislature, could retroactively annul judgments of the LNT by legislation and, therefore, was under no obligation to execute the judgments of the LNT. The Assembly of the League of Nations took this decision after the judgments in *Mayras etc.*, LNT Judgments Nos. 24 to 36 [1946], cases which were connected with the dissolution of the League of Nations. The episode is dealt with in Akehurst, *The Law Governing Employment Relations in International Organizations* (1967) pp. 210ff. The conclusion of the Assembly of the League of Nations cannot be regarded as reflecting the correct legal position, particularly in the light of the judgment of the ICJ in the *Effect of Awards Case*.

appeal.' No party to a dispute before the Tribunal may, therefore, bring his case back to the Tribunal for a second round of litigation, no matter how dissatisfied he may be with the pronouncement of the Tribunal or its considerations. The Tribunal's judgment is meant to be the last step along the path of settling disputes between the Bank and the members of its staff.[67]

(iv) Reasoning in decisions

Most statutes of IATs explicitly provide that the judgments of tribunals must state the reasons upon which they are based.[68] However, even if the requirement is not explicitly provided for in the statute of a tribunal, it is an implied requirement that decisions should be reasoned. The ICJ agreed with this view when it stated: 'Not only is it of the essence of judicial decision that they be reasoned...'[69]

There has been some discussion by the ICJ and the WBAT of what is meant by a reasoned judgment. The ICJ, while stating that failure to give a reasoned judgment could result in an error of procedure and that a statement of reasons is necessary for the validity of a judgment of an IAT, examined the question of what form and degree of reasoning will satisfy that requirement and concluded:

The applicant appears to assume that, for a judgment to be adequately reasoned, every particular plea has to be discussed and reasons given for upholding or rejecting each one. But neither practice nor principle warrants so rigorous an interpretation of the rule, which appears generally to be understood as simply requiring that a judgment shall be supported by a stated process of reasoning. This statement must indicate in a general way the reasoning upon which the judgment is based; but it need not enter meticulously into every claim and contention on either side. While a judicial organ is obliged to pass upon all the formal submissions made by a party, it is not obliged, in framing its judgment, to develop its reasoning in the form of a detailed examination of each of the various heads of claim submitted. Nor are there any obligatory forms or techniques for drawing up judgments; a tribunal may employ direct or indirect reasoning, and state specific or merely implied conclusions, provided that the reasons on which the judgment is based are apparent. The question whether a judgment is

---

[67] *van Gent*, WBAT Reports [1983, Part III], Decision No. 13 at p. 6.

[68] See, e.g., Article 10.3 of the Statute of the UNAT: C. F. Amerasinghe (ed.), note 49 p. 10; Article XI.2 of the WBAT Statute: *ibid.* p. 48; Article VI.2 of the ILOAT Statute: *ibid.* p. 33; Article VI of the Statute of the LNT: *ibid.* p. 179; Article VIII.3 of the IDBAT Statute: *ibid.* p. 66; and Article VIII.3 of the OASAT Statute: *ibid.* p. 87.

[69] *Application for Review of Judgment No. 158 of the United Nations Administrative Tribunal Case*, 1973 ICJ Reports at p. 210.

so deficient in reasoning as to amount to a denial of the right to a fair hearing and a failure of justice is therefore one which necessarily has to be appreciated in the light both of the particular case and of the judgment as a whole.[70]

In *van Gent* the WBAT cited the view of the ICJ and agreed with its general position 'which has rejected the contention that for a judgment to be adequately reasoned every particular plea has to be discussed and reasons given for upholding or rejecting each one'.[71] In that case the applicant argued that the tribunal had not examined all his pleas, although it had given him a remedy with which he was obviously not satisfied. The tribunal held in the case seeking review that its previous judgment in *van Gent*[72] had been adequately reasoned even though all the pleas had not been dealt with in detail. While all the claims or pleas of the applicant must be pronounced on, each claim or plea need not be examined in detail. It is sufficient that the reasoning be adequate in relation to the total case which is brought before the tribunal.

(v) Remedies

The remedies which an IAT may prescribe are generally referred to in the statute of the tribunal.[73] However, there may be a wider power of ordering redress than that specified in the tribunal's statute, which may be inherent in the judicial function.[74] The following remedies have generally been prescribed either individually or in combination: annulment, rescission, specific performance, compensation, damages and remand of a case.[75]

(vi) Interpretation, rectification and review

Tribunals clearly have the power inherent in the exercise of the judicial function, especially when there is no appeal from decisions given, of

---

[70] *Ibid.* at pp. 210–11.   [71] WBAT Reports [1983, Part III], Decision No. 13 at p. 9.

[72] WBAT Reports [1983, Part I], Decision No. 11.

[73] See, e.g., Article 9 of the UNAT Statute: C. F. Amerasinghe (ed.), note 49 pp. 9–10; Article XII of the WBAT Statute: *ibid.* p. 48; Article VIII of the ILOAT Statute: *ibid.* p. 33; and Article XV of the IMFAT Statute.

[74] See C. F. Amerasinghe, note 29, vol. I Chapter 26. Remedies in the various tribunals are discussed in *ibid.*, Chapters 27–32.

[75] Not all tribunals have prescribed or prescribe all these remedies. For example, the OECD Administrative Tribunal has not ordered specific performance and apparently does not consider that it has the power to do so. The Statute of the tribunal (Article 12(c)) does not expressly prohibit ordering of specific performance, so that the Statute like others of the same kind could be interpreted to permit the ordering of specific performance.

interpreting their previous judgments, even if no express provision is made for this function in their statutes.[76] In addition, rectifying clerical or mathematical errors would also be permitted, whether the statutes expressly permit this or not. Further, many statutes of tribunals generally provide for the review of judgments by the tribunal in the limited situation where new facts are discovered.[77] But the circumstances where the review may be granted are carefully circumscribed. Even where the statute of the tribunal is silent on the question of review in the case of the discovery of a new fact, the tribunal may, as the ILOAT has done in many cases, exercise this inherent power of review.

The Statutes of two tribunals, the UNAT and the ILOAT, provided for reference of decisions of these tribunals to the ICJ for a very special kind of review.[78] This reference to the ICJ was not by way of appeal. It afforded, by a special procedure, an opportunity to have the ICJ pronounce on certain specific matters and the scope of review is very limited.[79]

(vii) Enforcement of decisions

Apart from the finality and binding nature of judgments of tribunals, there is no procedure for enforcement of judgments within organizations. It would seem, thus, that all the cards are in the hands of the organizations. However, whether as a result of the advisory opinion of the ICJ in the *Effect of Awards Case* or not, there do not seem subsequently to have been any severe problems connected with the carrying out of judgments. There may occasionally be rumblings as a result of grave dissatisfaction on the part of an organization with a judgment of a tribunal, but by and large judgments of tribunals have been fully executed.[80]

---

[76] The IMFAT Statute, Article XVII, explicitly gives the IMFAT this power.

[77] See the UNAT Statute, Article 12: C. F. Amerasinghe (ed.), note 49 pp. 11–12; the WBAT Statute, Article XIII.1: *ibid.* pp. 48–9; the IMFAT Statute, Article XVI; the OASAT Statute, Article IX: *ibid.* p. 87; and Article VII.2 of the IDBAT statute: *ibid.* p. 66. See also C. F. Amerasinghe, note 29, vol. I Chapter 19.

[78] See Article 11 of the former UNAT Statute: C. F. Amerasinghe (ed.), note 49 pp. 10–11; and Article XII of the ILOAT Statute: *ibid.* p. 34. The power of review of UNAT judgments has now been removed.

[79] The power of review in general is discussed in C. F. Amerasinghe, note 29, vol. I Chapter 19.

[80] The LN, at its dissolution, refused to honour the judgments of the LNT in *Mayras* and other connected cases: LNT Judgments Nos. 24–36 [1946]. The OAS was unhappy with the decision in *Bucholtz and Others*, OASAT Judgment No. 37 [1978], and *Chisman and Others*, OASAT Judgment No. 64 [1982], but, nevertheless, executed them: see C. F. Amerasinghe, note 29, vol. I p. 80.

It would be unwarranted to focus too closely on the absence of means available to staff members to enforce judgments in favour of staff members, in the face of the existing record where judgments are honoured by international organizations. By the same token it would not be proper to question the efficacy of the system of administrative justice in international organizations on the ground that there is no effective enforcement machinery available to staff members. Indeed, the record in the administrative systems of international organizations seems to be even better than in the international legal system where there is some semblance of an enforcement machinery, rudimentary though it be. Perhaps the real sanction against refusal to execute judgments of IATs on the part of administrations lies in the psychological factor that lies behind the system of international administrative law, namely that, if organizations do not honour judgments given in favour of staff against them, they cannot expect full and undivided loyalty and dedication from a staff which would know that the safeguards of the system and the protection afforded by the system are not real and effective.

(3) Settlement of disputes involving private parties, states or organizations at the national level

There may be international courts which have jurisdiction over disputes involving international organizations and private parties but this is rare. As an example may be cited the CJEC.[81] In general private parties have no standing before international courts as opposed to transnational arbitral tribunals. But the ILOAT also has jurisdiction in the case of disputes arising from contracts to which the ILO is a party.[82]

While employment disputes between staff members and international organizations are subject to the jurisdiction of IATs, where these exist, reference to national courts would be possible for the settlement of other disputes between international organizations and private parties. The immunity from jurisdiction of organizations, to the extent that it is applicable, would be an obstacle to the use of such a forum, unless the organization concerned decides to waive the immunity. In the case of financial organizations their immunity is of a restricted kind, being

---

[81] For an explanation of the jurisdictional provisions of the EEC Treaty, the Euratom Treaty and the ECSC Treaty see Sands and Klein (eds.), note 5 pp. 407ff. See particularly, *inter alia*, the EEC Treaty, Article 164ff.; the Euratom Treaty, Article 134ff.; and the ECSC Treaty, Article 31ff.

[82] Article II(4) of the statute: C. F. Amerasinghe (ed.), note 49 p. 32.

generally limited to claims by member states or persons deriving claims from member states.[83] Further, where an organization is the plaintiff in a case any immunity it may have is waived.[84]

The existence of immunity from jurisdiction does not mean that liability does not exist. The UN Convention and the Specialized Agencies Convention both require that where there is immunity, appropriate modes of settlement should be provided,[85] thus recognizing that liability does not vanish because of immunity. Apart from negotiation and agreed settlement, arbitration is a possible method of settling these disputes. Arbitration would be directly under a national legal system, whether it is under national or transnational law. In both cases national courts would have control over the arbitration. In the event arbitration is selected, it is a necessary corollary that immunity has been waived after the arbitration has taken place.[86]

Where no mode of settlement is agreed upon between the parties or local courts have no jurisdiction, there is no reason why a private party should not seek a settlement by resorting to a request for diplomatic protection by his national state. The state would not be precluded from exercising such protection, in appropriate circumstances, of course.

Disputes of a similar nature to those discussed above may occur between organizations and states or other organizations. Such disputes are subject to settlement in the same way as those between organizations and private parties. The difference is that, unlike private parties, states and other organizations could plead immunity from the jurisdiction of national courts, where such immunity would be accorded them, thereby frustrating the resort to settlement by national courts. There would also be no element of diplomatic protection. However, ad hoc arbitration at a national or transnational level is available to the parties in any case, just as it is available to private parties for the solution

---

[83] See, e.g., Article VII(3) of the IBRD Articles of Agreement.

[84] The recognition of legal capacity in national law entails the freedom on the part of the organization to bring an action in a national court: see *International Refugee Organization* v. *Republic SS Corporation et al.* (1951) 18 ILR p. 447; *International Tin Council* v. *Amalgamet Inc.* 524 NYS 2d (1988) p. 971; and *Arab Monetary Fund* v. *Hashim and Others (No. 3)* [1990] 1 All ER p. 685.

[85] See, e.g., Section 29 of the UN Convention and Section 31 of the Specialized Agencies Convention.

[86] UN contracts generally have provided for arbitration according to the rules of the American Arbitration Association. The IBRD also provided for arbitration in its contracts with private parties, including private borrowers: see Broches, 'International Legal Aspects of the Operations of the World Bank', 98 *Hague Recueil* (1959–II) at p. 337.

of their disputes with organizations. Of course, any party entitled to immunity in national courts would thereby waive that immunity.

(4) Disputes between member states before international organizations

Disputes which concern and are dealt with by international organizations have a multilateral aspect to them, even if they are between two member states. An organization is not established on the basis of a mere series of bilateral legal relations between members but by multilateral treaty. Consequently, there exists among the members an intertwined network of reciprocal rights and duties based on the recognition of mutual interests. A balance is maintained by compliance with the constituent treaty by all member states. A dispute between two member states relating to rights and obligations flowing from the constituent instrument, thus, affects the organization as a whole. What appears to be a bilateral dispute assumes a multilateral character.

As between states, as a result of their sovereignty, at customary international law the peaceful settlement of disputes was based on the principle of voluntary settlement. A consequence of this principle was that a state party to a dispute could not effectively by unilateral reference invoke third-party settlement, because the other party was not under an obligation to appear before the third party. The agreement of the two states was required, in one form or another (e.g., by treaty, arbitration clause, etc.), for a third party, whether a judicial body or not, to settle the dispute. Nonetheless, there is now a general principle of international law that states must settle their disputes peacefully.[87]

The principle is historically linked to the existence of international organizations. For the first time, it was referred to in Articles 12*ff.* of the Covenant of the LN. In the case of the United Nations Article 2(3) of the Charter provides that 'All Members shall settle their international disputes by peaceful means in such a manner that international peace and security, and justice, are not endangered.'

What is of interest here is how an organization gets involved in the settlement of a dispute which is of concern to it, because the dispute is over the violation of an obligation flowing in one way or another from its constituent instrument or other relevant instruments and what this

---

[87] See also Article 33 (and Article 37) of the Charter, under which the parties to any dispute, the continuation of which is likely to endanger the maintenance of international peace and security, shall, first of all, seek a resolution by peaceful means.

involvement entails. As an example, the settlement procedure available to the UN, as a political organization, to settle disputes by peaceful and other means is briefly examined here. Chapters VI and VII of the UN Charter give the UN, acting through the relevant organ, authority to take action to settle or put to rest disputes between members in certain circumstances, especially those endangering peace. The role of political regional organizations, economic (e.g., WTO) and technical (e.g., WHO, ITU) organizations which also have dispute settlement mechanisms will not be discussed here. As stated at the beginning of this chapter, these disputes as such, or rather their genre, is not an appropriate subject for in-depth discussion in a work on institutional aspects of international organizations.

(a) Violations of Article 2(4) of the UN Charter

To take a hypothetical example involving alleged violations of obligations under the UN Charter, a case arising under Article 2(4) of the Charter may be considered. Although the Chapter VI and VII procedures do not strictly require a violation of Article 2(4), or a finding of such a violation, for measures to be taken pursuant to those Chapters, the UN may take the course of establishing whether there had been a breach of obligations under Article 2(4). The case may involve the use of force which the state concerned claims was used in reprisal or self defence. When the UN is seized of the case, it may need to interpret Article 2(4) of the Charter. In this event this will also involve invoking Article 1(1) and Article 51 of the Charter. In doing this the UN will be performing a judicial task, although it is a political body and may propose a non-judicial solution. The extent of its judicial function may be illustrated by referring briefly in the example given here to the interpretative function it must perform.

Read in context, Art. 2(4) of the UN Charter states that the threat or use of force against territorial integrity and political independence is prohibited, only if it is inconsistent with the purpose of the UN, as spelled out in Art. 1 of the Charter of the UN. The reasoning is as follows: Art. 1(1) states that the first purpose of the UN is 'to maintain international peace and security...' (maintenir la paix et la sécurité internationales...') and, while specific instances of how this end may be achieved are given, there is no explicit limitation to the purpose in terms of the means that may be used.[88] It is to be noted that it is equally a

---

[88] Article 1(1) reads in full: 'The Purposes of the United Nations are: 1) To maintain international peace and security, and to that end: to take effective collective measures

purpose that international *security* be maintained as well as international peace. Art. 2(4) then states:

> 2. The Organization and its Members, in pursuit of the Purposes stated in Article 1, shall act in accordance with the following Principles:
>
> ....
>
> (English) – 4. All Members shall refrain in their international relations from the threat or use of force against the territorial integrity or political independence of any State, or in any other manner inconsistent with the Purposes of the United Nations.
>
> (French) – 4. Les Membres de l'Organisation s'abstiennent, dans leurs relations internationales, de recourir à la menace ou à l'emploi de la force, soit contre l'intégrité territoriale ou l'indépendance politique de tout Etât, soit de toute autre maniere incompatible avec les buts des Nations Unies.
>
> ....

The French text is more appropriate for this exposition, although the English text does not obviously conflict with it. The words 'soit ... soit ...' are really the critical ones. Properly translated the relevant text means '*be it* against the territorial integrity or political independence of any State, (or) *be it* in any *other* manner inconsistent with the purposes of the United Nations'. Consequently, because of the particular formulation and especially because of the use of the word 'other' in the last phrase of the provision in relation to a 'manner inconsistent with the purposes' of the UN, it seems to be the only reasonable interpretation of the clause 'refrain from ... the threat or use of force against the territorial integrity or political independence of any State ...' that the threat or use of force which is prohibited against territorial integrity and political independence must be inconsistent (or not consistent) with the purposes of the UN. It must also be borne in mind that the chapeau of Article 2 states that the obligations which follow (including those in para. 4) are to be carried out 'in pursuit of the Purposes stated in Article 1'. What this entails is that force, or the threat of it, by any individual or collectivity of states against the territorial integrity and political independence of any state which is consistent (or not inconsistent) with the purposes of the UN is *permitted* (although not made *obligatory*).

for the prevention and removal of threats to the peace, and for the suppression of acts of aggression or other breaches of the peace, and to bring about by peaceful means, and in conformity with the principles of justice and international law, adjustment or settlement of international disputes or situations which might lead to a breach of the peace; ...'

Thus, because it is a purpose of the UN to maintain international *security*, in addition to, and not merely, international peace (Art. 1(1)), all the customary international law exceptions which permit the threat or use of force by one state against other states are preserved or survived. *This* is the provision which preserves the *totality* of the right of self-defence, the *totality* of the right of reprisal, and the *totality* of the right of humanitarian intervention, involving force, if any, and the *totality* of any other customary right to use force, all recognized by customary international law. It is not Art. 51[89] that *preserves* the right of self-defence or any part of it. Thus, there is a general right to use or threaten force in self-defence (including collective self-defence) whether it is *anticipatory* or in response to an actual armed attack. This is not the place to explain in detail the international law of self-defence. The right of self-defence remains *dehors* Article 51.

Then, one might ask, what is the effect of Art. 51? While it is not at all clear that the framers of the Charter knew or cared what exactly they were doing, the effect of that Article is to provide a certain specified procedure in the case *only* of an actual armed attack, where resort is had to self-defence. The reference to the right of self-defence is not really to preserve the customary law, which had already been done in Art. 2(4); it was referred to, because a certain procedure had to be followed in relation to the SC in the event of an actual armed attack.

The next question is — what happens when self-defence is resorted to in the absence of an actual armed attack? In these cases the SC must use Art. 39 and Art. 24 and act under them entirely. The Art. 51 procedure does not apply as such.

This interpretation, which has not yet been made hitherto is the only one that does not make nonsense of the Charter. Further, there is nothing in the *travaux préparatoires*, even if relevant, to contradict this interpretation which makes sense as the literal meaning given in context. Nor does subsequent practice, if it could affect the meaning given literally and contextually to Article 2(4), contradict this interpretation.

---

[89] Article 51 reads: 'Nothing in the present Charter shall impair the inherent right of individual or collective self-defence if an armed attack occurs against a Member of the United Nations, until the Security Council has taken the measures necessary to maintain international peace and security. Measures taken by Members in the exercise of this right of self-defence shall be immediately reported to the Security Council and shall not in any way affect the authority and responsibility of the Security Council under the present Charter to take at any time such action as it deems necessary in order to maintain or restore international peace and security.'

The same must be said of the right of reprisal (and, for that matter, the possible right of humanitarian intervention). There is nothing in the preparatory work or in subsequent practice, if either are relevant, to contradict the interpretation which requires both to survive under Art. 2(4) as legitimate uses of force against territorial integrity and political independence.[90]

(b) General powers of the UN under chapter VI of the Charter

As Article 33 in Chapter VI of the UN Charter indicates, disputes between states may be settled 'by negotiation, enquiry, mediation, conciliation, arbitration, judicial settlement, resort to regional agencies or arrangements, or other peaceful means of their own choice'. Reference to the organization is a possible alternative under this Article. There may also be circumstances, as under Articles 34 to 38 of the UN Charter, where an organ of an organization may intervene on its own motion for the purposes of settling a dispute.[91]

The peaceful settlement of disputes is among the purposes of the UN, as is reflected in Article 1(1) of the Charter. Under Article 2(3) specifically member states have an obligation to settle their disputes peacefully. They are free, however, under Article 33 to choose the means of settlement. Article 36(3) does by implication reflect a preference for legal disputes to be referred to the ICJ. Under the UN Charter disputes may be settled either by peaceful means by the intervention of the UN, particularly, under Chapter VI of the Charter, but also under Article 24 directly, or by

---

[90] There is an extraordinary amount of literature on the interpretation of Articles 1(1), 2(4) and 51 of the UN Charter: see the bibliographies in Simma *et al.* (eds.), *The Charter of the United Nations* (2002) p. 39 (Article 1), pp. 112–14 (Article 2(4)), pp. 788–9 (Article 51) and also the texts on these articles in the same work: *ibid.* pp. 39*ff.*, 114*ff.*, and 789*ff.*. None of the works, cited there, nor the text of the book on the UN Charter itself makes the points made above. The traditional manner of dealing with the use of force, as is shown by all the above works, is to regard Art. 2(4) as an absolute prohibition of the use of force, regardless of the earlier customary law, and to make an exception for a limited right of self-defence by reference to Art. 51. The result is that all other uses of force than the use of force in self-defence under Art. 51, i.e., as defined there, is outlawed. This approach makes illegal all the uses of force as permitted by customary international law except that which is in self-defence, as permitted and limited by Art. 51. Thus, writers and decision-makers have been hard put to it to justify the other uses of force permitted by the customary international law than the narrow instance of the use of force under Art. 51. The interpretation of the UN Charter provision given here by me avoids all the acrobatics that have become fashionable.

[91] For the manner in which organizations may become involved in the settlement of disputes see, e.g., Cassese, *Il Diritto internazionale nel mondo contemporaneo* (1984) p. 233; and Seidl-Hohenveldern, *Völkerrecht* (1994) pp. 391–3.

resort to force under Chapter VII of the Charter. Chapter VII goes beyond the settlement of disputes by peaceful means.

The peaceful settlement of disputes within the framework of the UN (the SC as well as the GA) is of an extensive nature. The UN may take a variety of measures in dealing with a dispute: for example, under Article 11(2) it may discuss a matter; under Article 33(2) it may call upon parties to settle their disputes by peaceful means; under Article 34 it may investigate; under Articles 37(2) and 38 it may recommend appropriate procedures or methods of adjustment or recommend terms of settlement. These measures are not necessarily exclusive, nor is the UN constricted by them when acting directly under Article 24. Generally, however, the UN tries, by making proposals, to facilitate the settlement of disputes by the states party to the disputes. The case of the Western Sahara is an example of the numerous measures that may be taken by the UN. It gave rise, *inter alia*, to resolutions by various organs of the UN, to different kinds of mediation and to an advisory opinion by the ICJ.[92] While the Charter refers specifically in certain parts of the Charter to serious disputes which are likely to endanger peace and security, the practice of the UN has rightly been to deal with any conflict, as is evidenced by the consideration in 1961 by the SC of the Eichmann Case between Argentina and Israel.[93] This it has been given the power to do under the Charter.[94]

[92] The *Western Sahara Case*, 1975 ICJ Reports p. 12.

[93] See, e.g., Escher, *Friedliche Erledigung von Streitigkeiten nach dem System Vereinten Nationen* (1985) p. 11; and Dinh, Dailler and Pellet, *Droit international public* (1987) p. 733.

[94] The ICJ has held that the existence of active negotiations between the parties does not prevent both the SC and the Court from exercising at the same time their separate functions: the *Nicaragua Case (Admissibility)*, 1984 ICJ Reports at p. 440.

Index

Standard Toolbar

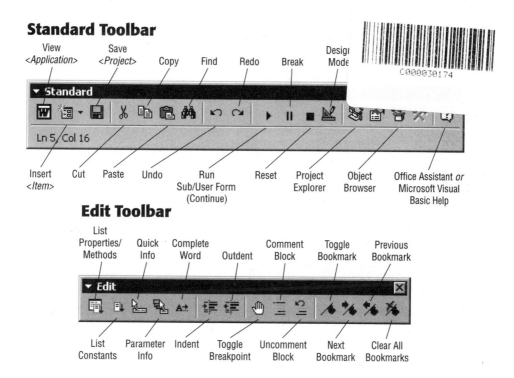

View
<Application>   Save
<Project>   Copy   Find   Redo   Break   Design Mode

Standard

Ln 5, Col 16

Insert
<Item>   Cut   Paste   Undo   Run
Sub/User Form
(Continue)   Reset   Project
Explorer   Object
Browser   Office Assistant *or*
Microsoft Visual
Basic Help

Edit Toolbar

List
Properties/
Methods   Quick
Info   Complete
Word   Outdent   Comment
Block   Toggle
Bookmark   Previous
Bookmark

Edit

List
Constants   Parameter
Info   Indent   Toggle
Breakpoint   Uncomment
Block   Next
Bookmark   Clear All
Bookmarks

Visual Basic Editor Keyboard Shortcuts

Keystroke	Action
Debugging and Running Operations	
F5	Run Procedure/Continue
Ctrl+F5	Break
F8	Step Into
Shift+F8	Step Over
Ctrl+Shift+F8	Step Out
Ctrl+F8	Run to Cursor
F9	Toggle Breakpoint
Ctrl+Shift+F9	Clear All Breakpoints
Shift+F9	Quick Watch
Ctrl+W	Edit Watch
Ctrl+F9	Set Next Statement
Displaying Visual Basic Editor Windows and Dialog Boxes	
F2	Object Browser
F4	Properties Window
Ctrl+L	Call Stack
Ctrl+R	Project Explorer
Ctrl+G	Immediate Window
Alt+F11	Application
F7	View Code
Shift+F7	View Object
Editing Operations	
Shift+F2	View Definition
Ctrl+Shift+F2	Last Position

Keystroke	Action
Editing Operations	
Ctrl+Z	Undo
Ctrl+Y	Repeat
Ctrl+X	Cut
Ctrl+C	Copy
Ctrl+V	Paste
Ctrl+A	Select All
Ctrl+F	Find
Ctrl+H	Replace
F3	Find Next Instance
Tab	Indent
Shift+Tab	Outdent (decrease indent)
Ctrl+J	List Properties/Methods
Ctrl+Shift+J	List Constants
Ctrl+I	Quick Info
Ctrl+Shift+I	Parameter Info
Ctrl+spacebar	Complete Word
File Operations	
Ctrl+S	Save File
Ctrl+P	Print
Ctrl+Q	Quit
Ctrl+M	Import File
Ctrl+E	Export File

MASTERING
VBA 6

MASTERING™
VBA 6

Guy Hart-Davis

SYBEX®

San Francisco • Paris • Düsseldorf • Soest • London

Associate Publisher: Harry Helms
Contracts and Licensing Manager: Kristine O'Callaghan
Acquisitions & Developmental Editor: Melanie Spiller
Editor: Linda Good
Technical Editor: Mike Gunderloy
Book Designers: Patrick Dintino, Catalin Dulfu,
          Franz Baumhackl
Graphic Illustrator: Tony Jonick
Electronic Publishing Specialist: Franz Baumhackl
Project Team Leader: Shannon Murphy
Proofreaders: Molly Glover, Dave Nash, Nancy Riddiough,
          Jennifer Campbell
Indexer: Ted Laux
Companion CD Coordinator: Kara Schwartz
Companion CD Technician: Keith McNeil
Companion CD Vocalist: Rhonda Holmes
Cover Designer: Design Site
Cover Illustrator/Photographer: Sergie Loobkoff

Library of Congress Card Number: 99-69349

ISBN: 0-7821-2636-7

Manufactured in the United States of America

10 9 8 7 6 5 4 3 2 1

SYBEX is a registered trademark of SYBEX Inc.

Mastering is a trademark of SYBEX Inc.

Screen reproductions produced with Collage Complete.
Collage Complete is a trademark of Inner Media Inc.

Microsoft material included in the book and on the CD:
Copyright © 1999 Microsoft Corporation, One Microsoft
Way, Redmond, Washington 98052-6399 U.S.A. All rights
reserved.

Internet screen shots using Microsoft Internet Explorer 5
reprinted by permission from Microsoft Corporation.

For Rhonda

The hourglass is shattered only by the magic of your touch;
And nothing really matters—no! Nothing matters very much!

—Peter Hammill,
The Siren Song

ACKNOWLEDGMENTS

Few three-pound cockroach-killing objects have received as much TLC as this book. Hold that thought for a moment, because I'd like to take a couple of pages to express my thanks to the brave people who worked on making this book *a)* happen, and *b)* readable:

- **Melanie Spiller**, Acquisitions and Developmental Editor, for persisting in using me as an author under heavy fire from assorted Sybex people I'd better not name here. Melanie—thanks again, and look, you can have my serving of *wasabi* as well if you really want it.

- **Mike Gunderloy**, VBA maniac deluxe and erstwhile Technical Editor, for excessive heroism in agreeing to perform the technical edit on this book after suffering through *Word 2000 Developer's Handbook*. Mike's known for being tough on authors but even tougher on the lint that spelunkers leave in his favorite caves… but I'll leave you to ask him about that.

- **Linda Good**, Editor, who made the mistake of returning to Sybex after a two-year escape just in time to be assigned this book. Linda kept the book on schedule, her temper wherever it resides, and most of the rules of grammar intact.

- **Harry Helms**, Associate Publisher, for taking over from Amy Romanoff as "the man at the helm, in command of the flight path" for this book. Harry put up with semi-weekly insults during the course of this book.

- **Franz Baumhackl**, Electronic Publishing Specialist, for typesetting this book and humoring such of my foibles as made it into print.

- **Shannon Murphy**, Project Team Leader, for coordinating the production of the book—in other words, for making sure that what should have got into the book, did.

- **Molly Glover**, **Dave Nash**, **Nancy Riddiough**, and **Jennifer Campbell**, Proofreaders, for proofreading the book and making sure the words were the right way up and around.

- **Ted Laux**, Indexer, for creating the index. Indexing is an under-appreciated art, somewhat akin to sewer-maintenance—people make a stink only when it doesn't work as it should. So every time you find a topic by using the index, I'd like you to give a quick mental cheer for Ted "Fiat Index" Laux—but I bet you'll forget.

- **Kara Schwartz**, **CD Coordinator**, and **Keith McNeil**, **CD Technician**, for organizing and producing the CD.
- **Rhonda Holmes**, for performing the vocals for the videos on the CD.

Assorted other thanks (I happen to have some left over) go to five other people who *didn't* work on this book:

- **Richard Mills**, for constant sarcasm—I mean, encouragement. (Don't ask.)
- **Jim Davies**, for being elsewhere but virtually around, and for having a wonderful wife. (Look, don't ask, okay?)
- **Peter Hammill**, for the excellent song from which the quote on the dedication page is taken. (No, don't ask.)
- **Gary Masters** and **Roger Stewart**, for not working on this book. (Don't ask. Really.)

That's a lot to ask you not to ask.

After reading all of this, are you still brave enough to read the book? Turn the page and find out.

CONTENTS AT A GLANCE

TABLE OF CONTENTS

INTRODUCTION

VBA—Visual Basic for Applications—is the most exciting thing that's happened to applications in the last decade.

Okay, so you could argue that point, producing examples such as *a)* mailmerge that actually works, *b)* presentation software that has turned the giving of presentations from something that sucked big-time into something approaching fun (for the presenter, not for their victims), and *c)* powerful drawing software such as AutoCAD and Visio. But VBA beats all of these into a cocked hat because it can manipulate all of them.

Remember the quote about "Give me a lever, and I will move the world"? These days, it's "Give me VBA, and I will automate the heck out of all the applications you use—and teach you to like it."

This book covers using VBA 6, giving examples that use Word 2000, Excel 2000, PowerPoint 2000, Project 2000, WordPerfect 2000, Visio 2000, and AutoCAD 2000. You can apply the principles you learn in this book to any of the other several hundred VBA-enabled applications as well, including those that use VBA 5 (such as Word 97, Excel 97, PowerPoint 97, Project 98, Visio Enterprise, and AutoCAD 14).

What Can I Do with VBA?

In a VBA-enabled application, you can use VBA to automate almost any action that you can perform interactively (manually, if you prefer) with the application. For example, in Word, you could create a document, add text to it, format it, and edit it; in Project, you could integrate tasks from multiple projects into one project; or in AutoCAD or Visio, you could quickly add custom objects to drawings (or yank custom objects out of drawings).

VBA performs actions faster, more accurately, more reliably, and far more cheaply than any human. The one thing VBA can't do (apart from drive a Viper or make a decent omelet) is make a fuzzy human decision, meaning that humans still aren't dispensable—but if you can define hard-and-fast conditions for making a decision, VBA will be more than happy to make it for you. By adding decision-making structures and loops (conditional repetitions) to your code, you can take it far beyond the range of actions that the human user can perform.

But wait—there's more. If you call in the next 20 minutes, VBA will also give you the tools to create interfaces for your code—message boxes, input boxes, and *user forms*, graphical objects that you can use to create forms and custom dialog boxes. Using VBA, you can essentially create a custom application that runs within the host application. For example, you could create within PowerPoint a custom application that automatically creates a presentation for you.

By using VBA, you can also access one application from another application. For example, when working with VBA from Word, you can use it to start a Visio session, create a drawing, and then plug it into a Word document. Similarly, when using VBA from Visio, you could cause Visio to fire up Word and borrow its spell checker for some problematic text.

Because VBA provides a standard set of tools that differ in capability according to the capabilities of the host application, once you've learned to use VBA in one application, you'll be able to apply that knowledge quickly to using VBA in another application. For example, you might start by learning VBA in order to manipulate Excel, then move on to using your VBA skills with Visio. You'll need to learn the components of the Visio application, because they're different from the Excel components, but you'll be able to transition the framework of your VBA knowledge without a problem.

This book takes a practical approach to speeding up and automating your work with VBA. Rather than starting with 300 pages of theory before showing you anything useful, I start you off with the easiest method of creating VBA code—using the Macro Recorder that some of the VBA-enabled Microsoft applications have. (Unfortunately, WordPerfect, AutoCAD, and Visio do not have the Macro Recorder—so if you're using one of those applications, you'll have a steeper learning curve.) From there, you'll move to editing recorded code before getting into the essentials of VBA syntax and some theory; then, you'll work your way into more complex topics.

What's in This Book?

This book teaches you how to use VBA to automate your work in VBA-enabled applications. For its examples, the book uses Word, Excel, PowerPoint, Project, WordPerfect, AutoCAD, and Visio to provide a sample range of VBA-enabled applications.

Here's what you'll find in the 20 chapters of the book:

- Chapter 1 provides a quick introduction to what VBA is, what it does, and why you should take advantage of it.

- Chapter 2 discusses how to record and edit a macro using the Macro Recorder in those applications that support it. You'll record macros in Word, Excel, Power-Point, and Project.

- Chapter 3 introduces you to the Visual Basic Editor, the application in which you create VBA code (either by editing recorded code or by writing code from scratch) and user forms. The second half of this chapter discusses how you can customize the Visual Basic Editor so that you can work in it more quickly and efficiently.

- Chapter 4 shows you how to edit recorded macros, using the macros you recorded in Chapter 2. You'll learn how to step through and test a macro in the Visual Basic Editor.

- Chapter 5 teaches you the essentials of VBA syntax, giving you a brief overview of the concepts you need to know, together with a little practice creating statements in the Visual Basic Editor.

- Chapter 6 shows you how to work with variables and constants, which you use to store information for your procedures to work on.

- Chapter 7 discusses how to use arrays. Arrays are like super-variables that can store multiple pieces of information at the same time.

- Chapter 8 teaches you how to find the objects you need to create your procedures. You'll learn how to use the Macro Recorder, the Object Browser, and the Help system to find objects, and how to use object variables to represent objects.

- Chapter 9 describes how to use VBA's built-in functions and how to create functions of your own to supplement them.

- Chapter 10 leads you through creating a straightforward procedure in each of the example applications.

- Chapter 11 shows you how to use message boxes to communicate with the users of your procedures and let them make simple decisions about how the procedures run, and how to use input boxes to allow them to supply the information the procedures need.

- Chapter 12 covers how you can use loops to repeat actions in your procedures: fixed-iteration loops for fixed numbers of repetitions, and indefinite loops that match their number of repetitions to conditions you specify.

- Chapter 13 shows you how to use conditional statements (such as If statements) to make decisions in your code. Conditional statements are key to making your code flexible.

- Chapter 14 discusses the theory and practice of object models, the logical structures in which VBA considers the applications to be organized. Because this book deals with seven applications, this chapter doesn't plumb any application's object model in any depth, but it shows you how to approach navigating the object model so that you can find the information you need.

- Chapter 15 discusses how to use VBA's user forms to create simple custom dialog boxes that enable the users to supply information, make choices, and direct the flow of your procedures.

- Chapter 16 discusses how to build more complex dialog boxes. These include dynamic dialog boxes that update themselves when the user clicks a button, dialog boxes with hidden depths that the user can reveal to access infrequently used options, dialog boxes with multiple pages of information, dialog boxes that you create or adapt programmatically, and dialog boxes with controls that respond to actions the user takes.

- Chapter 17 illustrates the benefits of building reusable modular code rather than monolithic procedures, then shows you how to build it. I daresay this topic sounds like it has all the appeal of amateur dentistry right now, but you'll love the time and effort modular code saves you.

- Chapter 18 explains the principles of debugging VBA code, examining the different kinds of errors you'll create and how to deal with them.

- Chapter 19 discusses how to build well-behaved code stable enough to withstand being run under the wrong circumstances and civilized enough to leave the user in the best possible state to continue their work after it finishes running.

- Chapter 20 discusses the security mechanism that VBA 6 provides for securing VBA code and ensuring that you or your users do not run malevolent code unintentionally. The chapter discusses digital certificates and digital signatures, how to choose an appropriate security setting for the application you're using, and how to make—and break—passwords. It includes a brief history of macro viruses to bring you up to speed on what's threatening to consume your precious data and bifurcate your hard drive.

- The Appendix contains a glossary of VBA-related terms.

How Should I Use This Book?

I've tried to organize the material in this book in a sensible and logical pattern. To avoid repeating information unnecessarily, the chapters build on each other, so the later chapters assume that you've read the earlier chapters.

Throughout the book, I've presented a variety of code samples in the seven applications this book covers. If you're lucky, a few of these you'll be able to apply directly to your work. But mostly you'll find them illustrative of the techniques and principles discussed, and you'll need to create code of your own that follows those techniques and principles.

Is This Book Suitable for Me?

Yes. Well, probably.

This book is for anyone who wants to learn to use VBA to automate their work in a VBA-enabled application. Automating your work could involve anything from creating a few simple procedures that would enable you to perform some complex and tedious operations in a single keystroke to building a custom application with a complete interface that looks nothing like the host application's regular interface.

My goal in this book is to get you doing useful things with VBA as quickly as possible. As a result, the approach of the book is not entirely linear; instead, I introduce early on the topics that you'll find most useful as you develop your own procedures with VBA.

For example, the Macro Recorder (in the Microsoft applications that have it) is a powerful tool for learning how to use VBA—and for finding the right objects, properties, methods, and arguments when you venture into unfamiliar territory. Some people regard it as a beginner tool that no serious developer would use. I start you off by using the Macro Recorder, and though you may have to endure the sneers of your peers who are doing things the hard way, you'll learn more quickly and make faster progress than they will as a result.

I mentioned earlier that I didn't want to bog you down with theory at the beginning of the book. Actually, there's plenty of theoretical material in this book, but I've tried to present each piece in as practical a context as possible. That means giving concrete (or at least graphical) examples of each piece of theory in action. For example, when you learn about loops, you'll get to execute short procedures that illustrate the use of each kind of loop, so that you can see them at work right away.

What Are These Odd Things in the Text?

This book uses a number of conventions to convey information succinctly:

- ➢ designates choosing a command from a menu. For example, "choose File ➢ Open" means that you should pull down the File menu and choose the Open command from it.

- + signs indicate key combinations. For example, "press Ctrl+Shift+F9" means that you should hold down the Ctrl and Shift keys, then press the F9 key. Some of these key combinations are confusing (for example, "Ctrl++" means that you hold down Ctrl and press the + key—in other words, hold down Ctrl and Shift together and press the = key), so you may need to read them carefully.

- Likewise, "Shift+click" means that you should hold down the Shift key as you click with the mouse, and "Ctrl+click" means you should hold down the Ctrl key as you click. "Ctrl+Shift+click" means…, okay, I see you've got it already.

- ←, →, ↑, and ↓ represent the arrow keys that should appear in some form on your keyboard. The important thing to note is that ← is not the Backspace key (which on many keyboards bears a similar arrow). The Backspace key is represented by "Backspace" or "the Backspace key."

- **Boldface** indicates items that you may want to type in letter for letter.

- program font indicates program items, or text derived from program lines. Complete program lines will be offset in separate paragraphs like the example below, while shorter expressions will appear as part of the main text.

```
Sub Sample_Listing()
    Lines of program code will look like this.
End Sub
```

- *Italics* usually indicate either new terms being introduced or variable information (such as a drive letter that will vary from computer to computer and that you'll need to establish on your own).

- ➡ (a continuation arrow) indicates that a single line of code has been broken onto a second or subsequent line in the book. Enter these lines of code as a single line when you use them. For example, the three lines below represent a single line of code:

```
MsgBox System.PrivateProfileString("",
➡"HKEY_CURRENT_USER\Software\Microsoft\
➡Office\9.0\Common\AutoCorrect", "Path")
```

You'll also see Notes, Tips, and Warnings throughout the book:

NOTE A Note provides additional information about (or related to) the current topic.

TIP A Tip provides useful information or a recommendation, usually related to the current topic.

WARNING A Warning alerts you to potential problems related to the current topic.

What's on the CD?

The CD contains the code listings and the key user forms that appear in the book, together with video walkthroughs of recording macros, navigating the Visual Basic Editor, and creating procedures in the Visual Basic Editor.

For a full listing of what's on the CD, look at the inside back cover of the book.

May I Start Reading the Book Now?

Yes.

Thank you for reading this book. I hope that you find it useful in your day-to-day work with VBA.

Turn the page.

CHAPTER 1

What Is VBA, and What Can You Do with It?

Welcome to the world of automating your work with Visual Basic for Applications (VBA).

This chapter discusses the basic concepts on which the rest of this book will build. I'll deal with the following questions:

- Why should you automate an application?
- What is VBA?
- Why is VBA important?
- Where does VBA fit into an application?
- When should you use VBA, and what can you do with it?

Reading that list, you'll notice that it's missing various key questions, such as, "How do you work with VBA?" I'm saving such questions for future chapters.

Why Automate an Application?

If you're browsing through this book, your first question is probably this: Why should you try to automate an application?

Each of the applications I'll discuss in this book (and I hope most, if not all, of the other applications you use) is designed for a particular purpose. For example:

- Word-processing applications such as Word and WordPerfect are designed for creating documents. These documents can be of various formats and types, from single-page items (such as a lost-cat plea or a Web page) all the way up to industrial-strength product manuals featuring photos, technical graphics, and thousands of cross-references.

- Drawing packages such as AutoCAD and Visio are designed for creating professional drawings. You can use them to design anything from an organization chart to a cathedral, placing lines and other objects with nanometrical precision.

- Excel is designed for manipulating, analyzing, and generally crunching numbers. As you'll know if you've used Excel, you can also create charts and data maps with it.

- PowerPoint is designed for creating presentations—anything from a looping presentation designed to run forever and a day at a kiosk or info-booth to a screaming spellbinder of a presentation delivered live by a professional.

- Project is designed for planning, evaluating, and managing projects. (A *project* in Project's sense is a related group of tasks that have a start date and finish date and lead to a goal.)

Beyond these applications—which I'll cover in some detail in this book, both in general examples and in application-specific examples—you're probably using a number of other applications, some of which support VBA. By using the principles and techniques described in this book, you can automate those VBA-enabled applications too.

Because most Windows applications are designed to be easy, you can start using them with relatively rudimentary computing skills. You need to be able to navigate the Windows GUI well enough to launch the application, and you need to be able to type or use some other form of text-input device—but that's about it. As a result, you can use the applications at a number of different levels, and (of course) with wildly varying degrees of knowledge and competence. If you want, or if you don't know any better, you can use Word or WordPerfect much the way you would use a typewriter, without even saving a document after you printed it out. Similarly, you could use AutoCAD or Visio as a hi-tech Etch-a-Sketch.

I don't know quite how you would abuse PowerPoint or Project in a similar way. I'll leave you to dwell on that puzzle if you wish—but if you're an old-timer with computers, you may remember the days when the ground-breaking VisiCalc spreadsheet software was sold as a complete computing solution. Buyers were proudly shown how they could use VisiCalc for word-processing … and many of them wound up doing so. (Happily enough, too, by many accounts.)

Nowadays (it's December 1999 as I write this), most people use a variety of applications that more or less fit their needs; they use them in more or less the ways their creators intended; and they use at least some of the features more or less correctly. Very few people use all the features of an application that would benefit them and save them time, and fewer still take the time to program the application even a little to save them and their colleagues even more time.

Did They *Deliberately* Make This So Difficult to Use?

I mentioned a moment ago that *most* Windows applications appear designed to be easy to use. Before you ask, there are a number of Windows applications that appear *not* to be designed to be easy to use. With a few, you've got to suspect incompetence rather than elitism or malice. But others are clearly designed with great thought, care, and skill, yet end up being difficult to use at first.

You probably have your own candidates for the incompetence (or elitism, or malice) category, so I doubt that I need to populate the list for you. On the other hand, you may have had the luck not to run into any applications that fit into the deliberately difficult category, so I should name at least one—Kai's Power Tools, which make few concessions to less-experienced users but offer great power to those determined enough to scale their precipitous learning curves.

With VBA, you can customize an application so extensively that you can create a finished document or perform a complex action with literally the click of a mouse button or a single keystroke. Unfortunately, programming the routine that would create the document (or perform the action) for you would usually take so long that the resulting savings of time paled into insignificance.

Most users settle for a modestly happy level of skill with each application they use regularly. They identify the features that are most useful to them in their daily work. They then essentially stop exploring the other features that the application offers unless some unusual and powerful stimulus goads them into learning more. If the application is easy to customize, and the user spends a fair amount of time using it, they may customize the user interface a little to bring their most-used commands to the fore.

And that's about as far as most people get.

Two areas that most people leave unexplored are macros and programming. These are really two facets of the same topic, with recorded macros typically providing a quick (and often somewhat dirty) entry into programming.

Back when PCs were truly difficult to use, macros rapidly acquired such a dreadful reputation that most people were unwilling to mess with them. These days, though, macros are easy to record and play back. With a little care, you can avoid any actions that might lose data or damage your computer system. If you never venture into macros and VBA code in applications that support VBA, you deny yourself the opportunity of further improving your work life by developing user forms (custom dialog boxes) to present information and choices to the user, gather information from the user, and put a graphical face on a custom procedure.

Before you embark on customizing an application with VBA, you'll want to make sure that you're aware of the full gamut of features that the application supports so that you won't spend time duplicating their functionality. For example, if you need to format a report quickly in Word, make sure that the AutoFormat feature won't do the trick before you build a custom solution. Similarly, because PowerPoint offers designs beyond the dreams of Nebuchadnezzar, you'll usually want to exhaust the built-in possibilities before creating a custom design. Again, before laboriously defining a custom shape of your own in Visio, make sure that none of the predefined shapes will fit the bill instead. (I'm not saying you need to know every detail of how every feature in the application works—just enough so that you're sure the functionality you want isn't built into the application.)

You know the old saw about those who don't study history being doomed to repeating its mistakes. Something similar happens with software—those who customize an application without bothering to learn what it can do are doomed to recreate its existing features (only usually in a more limited and more clumsy format).

Visual Basic for Applications

It's time for a few words of explanation about the main tool you'll be using for automating operations in the applications. Visual Basic for Applications is a programming language created by Microsoft that can be built into applications—mostly those that expose *Component Object Model (COM)* objects. Briefly, COM is Microsoft's standard for defining the interfaces that objects expose so that other objects can communicate with them.

You use VBA to automate operations in applications that support it. All the main Office applications—Word, Excel, PowerPoint, Outlook, FrontPage, and Access—support VBA, so you can automate operations through most Office applications. But Microsoft has been casting its net wider, aggressively licensing VBA to other software companies and to corporate developers. As a result, VBA is starting to show up in many applications as a lingua franca for extending applications to do your bidding in ways their creators never intended. (The count is about 200 at this writing, and it's growing apace; check http://www.msdn.microsoft.com/vba/ to see the latest information.)

VBA is based on Visual Basic, a programming language derived from BASIC. *BASIC* stands for Beginner's All-Purpose Symbolic Instruction Code. BASIC is supposedly user-friendly, because it uses recognizable English words (or quasi-recognizable permutations of them) rather than abstruse and incomprehensible programming terms. Visual Basic is visual in that it supports the Windows GUI and provides tools for drag-and-drop programming and working with shared graphical elements.

The Difference between Visual Basic and Visual Basic for Applications

Visual Basic for Applications consists of Visual Basic implementations that contain a common core of commands and application-specific objects. The set of objects available in each application is different, even (sometimes especially) in applications built by the same company.

For example, the set of VBA objects available in Word is different from the set of VBA objects available in Excel, because VBA implements features that Word has but Excel does not. However, because the commands and structure of VBA in Word and VBA in Excel are the same, you can quickly translate your knowledge of VBA in Word to VBA in Excel. For example, you'd use the Save method (a method is essentially a command) to save a file in Excel VBA, Word VBA, or PowerPoint VBA. In Excel VBA, the command would be `ActiveWorkbook.Save`, whereas in Word VBA, it would be `ActiveDocument.Save`, and in PowerPoint, it would be `ActivePresentation.Save`.

This difference probably seems small and unexciting—and indeed it is. In the first case, you're saving changes to the active workbook; in the second case, to the active document; and in the third case, to the active presentation—so you'd expect the objects involved (the workbook, the document, and the presentation) to be named differently. But as soon as you stray as far as the SaveAs command, which you can use to save a file under a different name than its current one, you encounter a sea of differences. Word has a number of SaveAs options that Excel doesn't have (and vice versa), and PowerPoint has yet others. AutoCAD has different options still. And when you get into manipulating parts of a document, presentation, drawing, or whatever, you're dealing with very different sets of objects.

Furthermore, the applications contain different sets of the VBA language to provide functionality for their various commands. For example, Word needs VBA commands for manipulating its Outline view, whereas Visio has a completely different concept of what an outline is. Likewise, Excel needs VBA commands for working with scenarios, a feature AutoCAD couldn't care less about. WordPerfect needs VBA commands for manipulating its PerfectScript scripting language, which applications such as Visio, AutoCAD, and Excel have no interest in. PowerPoint needs VBA commands for implementing slide shows, but Project cares only when the slide show task is due (and perhaps how complete it is at any given moment).

Essentially, VBA is a complete programming language for use with any application that it has been built into (or bolted onto). You use VBA to create macros and other subprocedures (I'll get into the distinctions in a bit), user forms, and modules. I'll discuss those in the next section.

One key point that you need to understand is that VBA always works with a host application (such as Word, Quattro Pro, or Visio). With the exception of some standalone projects that Microsoft Office 2000 Developer Edition enables, a host application always needs to be open for VBA to run. This means that you can't build standalone applications with VBA the way you can with Visual Basic. If necessary, you can hide the host application from the user so that all they see is the interface (typically user forms) that you give to your VBA procedures. By doing this, you can create the illusion of a standalone application; but I doubt you'll need to create this effect often, if at all. (If you do find yourself needing to do this frequently, consider programming in Visual Basic rather than VBA.)

Where Does VBA Fit into an Application?

So, where does VBA fit into an application? When you're working in a document, spreadsheet, presentation, or drawing, VBA is nowhere to be seen. Where is it hiding? *Is* it hiding?

VBA *is* hiding when the typical user is working in a VBA-enabled application—it isn't visible, and most applications don't even load it until you perform an action that requires VBA to be loaded. With some applications—for example, WordPerfect—you can choose not to include VBA support when you install the application. With others (notably the Microsoft Office applications), you'd have a hard time getting the application installed without including VBA.

When you perform an action that requires VBA, the application in question loads the VBA environment from your hard drive (or from whichever networked drive or removable medium you're running the application). It then stays loaded until you quit the application. The reason for delaying the loading of VBA until it is needed is to conserve memory (RAM). Most VBA-enabled applications are, in any case, big applications—for example, Word typically takes between 10MB and 20MB of memory (both RAM and virtual memory) even without VBA loaded. Loading VBA adds multiple megabytes to this total, and opening the Visual Basic Editor takes more—so it makes sense not to load VBA until it's actively needed.

Once loaded, the VBA environment shares the same memory space as the host application. So, if one crashes, the other usually goes down as well. (I've seen some exceptions to this rule, but you wouldn't want to bet even a day's coffee money on the likelihood of the host or VBA staying up when the other goes down.)

The user interface of VBA is the Visual Basic Editor. I'll introduce the Visual Basic Editor in Chapter 3 and then work with it throughout the rest of the book.

Where Is VBA Code Stored?

VBA code is stored in code modules, class modules, and user forms within a document or template. A *module* is essentially a storage container: A *code module* contains subprocedures, and a *class module* contains the definition of a class (a custom object). A *user form* is a custom dialog box—both the visual layout that the user sees on screen as the dialog box and the code that drives it.

A *procedure* is code that performs a particular task. There are two types of procedures: subprocedures and functions. A *subprocedure* (also called a *subroutine*) is a unit of code that begins with the declaration Sub and ends with the words End Sub. Within those boundaries, a subprocedure can perform a wide variety of tasks. A subprocedure does not return a result. A *function* is a unit of code that begins with the declaration Function, ends with End Function, and returns a result.

A *macro* is a type of subprocedure. Everybody's pretty much agreed on that; what they don't agree on is just what distinguishes a macro from other types of subprocedure. Some people claim a macro is limited to recorded code—code that a tool such as the Macro Recorder in the main Microsoft Office applications creates to record a series of actions you want to be able to repeat automatically—and that any subprocedure you write is not a macro. This view is elegant in the firm boundary that it sets, but it isn't widely held nowadays. If you consult Microsoft's Help files and publications, you'll get the impression that a macro is any subprocedure that doesn't take *arguments*—pieces of information that you pass to it. Most people, however, don't subscribe to this view.

All this confusion gives us something of a dilemma in this book: Should I use *macro* or *subprocedure* as a generic term for "unit of code that performs a task"? I'd like to slip between the two horns of this bull and use *macro* to mean a short procedure (usually recorded rather than created from scratch in the Visual Basic Editor), and the more general *procedure* to refer to a unit of written code, or several units of written code working together, that performs a particular task or tasks. Most of the "procedures" I refer to will be subprocedures (or subroutines, if you prefer).

Where Are the Modules and User Forms Stored?

The VBA code and user forms you create are mostly squirreled away in the files that you create with the host application. Depending on the application you're using and the files it creates, the code and user forms may be stashed in the documents or templates, in global templates, or in a global settings file. Here's how the applications I'll discuss in this book store code and user forms:

- Word defaults to saving VBA code and user forms in the Normal.dot global template, though you can choose to store your code and user forms in any open document or template if you prefer.

- Excel can store code and user forms either in the Personal.xls personal macro workbook or in a workbook or template of your choosing.

- PowerPoint can store code and user forms either in a presentation or a template, but it doesn't have any form of global template for general storage.

- AutoCAD can store code and user forms in external project files you create. You then load those project files manually as you need them for the drawing or drawings that you're working with. You can also embed a single VBA project in an AutoCAD drawing file to provide the project's procedures, user forms, and functionality in that file.

- Visio can store code and user forms in its drawings and in its global storage.

- WordPerfect can store code and user forms in either its global storage (Global-Macros, WordPerfect9.GMS) or in individual documents. WordPerfect cannot store code and user forms in templates.

- Project stores VBA code either in its global storage project (ProjectGlobal, Global.mpt) or in individual project files.

As you'll see later in the book, you can also export VBA code and user forms to separate files for storage and transfer. Doing so enables you to transfer code and user forms quickly from one project to another, either within the same application or from application to application.

Normally, when you're working in an application, you don't get to see VBA code. When you open a file that contains code, the application hides the code from you, much as it hides the information that the file uses to implement the visual information you see. For example, when you open a Word document, Word presents only the formatted document to you, hiding from you all the codes and formatting information that goes to implementing the formatting in the document. Likewise, that document can contain the code for procedures and user forms, but you won't see it in the document until you take an action that runs some of the code.

Before You Begin Creating Code...

Before you create any VBA code or user form, be sure that you need to do so, and that, as mentioned previously, a built-in feature of the application you're using can't perform the required task. It's all too easy to waste time building a complex and impressive VBA project that's completely unnecessary.

The best way to avoid this trap is (of course) to have a good idea of what the applications can do. If you're presenting yourself as a real expert in the application, you should at least have played with all its features and gained an impression of what they're designed to do. If you're in any doubt, spend a little time querying the Help files and any printed or online reference materials the vendor provides to make sure you understand what the application can do out of the box and what it cannot.

Here are a few examples of replicating a built-in feature:

- In Word or WordPerfect, recording and editing a long, involved macro that applies all sorts of formatting to a paragraph—exactly the sort of formatting you can incorporate in a style and apply in a second.

- In Excel, creating an elaborate mechanism for solving a worksheet scenario for a desired result rather than using the Goal Seek feature.

- In PowerPoint, laboriously writing code to create, position, and format a set of custom objects on a slide—a task that can be automated far more easily by manipulating the slide's master.

- In AutoCAD, creating a procedure or a Wizard to wrap up a project into a distribution file instead of using the Pack And Go feature

These are all significant wastes of time. But once you're sure that the application's built-in features don't provide the functionality you need, go right ahead and build yourself a custom solution using VBA.

What Can You Do with VBA in an Application?

In this part of the chapter, I'll briefly discuss the types of things you can do with VBA in order to provide a general context for the discussion in the rest of the book. Where appropriate, I'll give you some quick, general examples.

Because in this book I'll be dealing with significantly different applications, the range of tasks that you can accomplish with VBA in any one application tends to be very different from what you can do in another application. For example, the type of custom solution you might want to create with VBA to automate Word will typically perform a very different task than any custom solution you might want to create for AutoCAD or for Visio. But the general principles remain the same.

Generally speaking, in any application that provides a full-featured implementation of VBA, you can automate almost any operation that the application supports. For example, in Word, you can use VBA to automate operations that range from applying a straightforward but tedious piece of formatting on a word, to building a hosted application that will run at a certain time each day, access information from a variety of sources, prepare a report, and e-mail that report to a number of recipients it deems suitable. Likewise, in AutoCAD, you can create anything from a simple procedure that manipulates a single polyline in a given way, to a user-form–driven monster that allows you to change multiple aspects of a drawing all at once.

In this book, I'll discuss procedures that run the gamut from the extremely simple to the relatively complex. By starting with straightforward procedures, you'll learn the tools you need to create complex solutions of your own.

Automating Repetitive Tasks with VBA

The first thing you'll probably want to do with VBA is automate repetitive procedures or tasks in your work or your colleagues' work. Which procedures or tasks? Just about any, within reason, and depending on the amount of time you have at your disposal for working with VBA.

You'll find it instantly obvious that some tasks aren't suitable candidates for automation through VBA. For example, a one-shot task, no matter how complex, isn't a subject for a procedure—instead, just grit your teeth and do it. On the other hand, if you need to repeat a tedious task frequently or endlessly, consider creating a procedure to perform the grunt work for you. For example, you might need to add complex animation to every AutoShape in every PowerPoint presentation in a folder. You could slog through that by hand, but it's likely that you could save yourself a significant amount of time by creating VBA code that would do the work for you. Likewise, you might need to change some pieces of text in each of 50 AutoCAD drawings. For example, if the sponsor's name changed for the stadium you're designing, you might need to change the name shown on each of the drawings. Again, you could plow through them manually, but you could probably create a quick VBA procedure that would take the pain out of it for you. The code wouldn't need to be very sophisticated—just enough to get the job done. But the time that it saved you over performing the operation manually would be very real.

Automating Repeated Labor-Intensive Tasks

First, ask yourself this question: Does your everyday work include any labor-intensive task you find yourself performing repeatedly? Let's take WordPerfect as an example here. Such a task might be anything from a tiny but tedious editing or formatting task (such as transposing three words or applying complex formatting to a table), to a large-scale effort that involved linking multiple pieces of information from other applications into a document, formatting the whole thing, and printing it to a remote printer.

Beyond being more labor-intensive than you care to struggle through frequently, the task doesn't need to be complex. The questions to ask yourself are, how frequently do you need to perform the task, and are its details constant enough for you to be able to automate it.

Automating Files You Create Frequently

Next, evaluate the kinds of documents you create frequently in the applications you use. Let's take Excel as an example here. Do you often create invoices, expense reports, budget proposals, and other workbooks with distinct characteristics? If so, work out how much overlap there is among the documents that fall into each of these categories. For each category of workbook, create one or more templates. Then determine whether you can add code to the templates to add, lay out, format, or process the information more quickly.

Could you complete an invoice faster if you were able to use a custom dialog box to enter basic information that would then be entered automatically in relevant cells and ranges strewn throughout the workbook? What about adding custom commands to that dialog box that would allow you to quickly format or process parts of the individual worksheets? Could you create a procedure for feeding fresh information automatically into a sales-results worksheet as it became available, so that the sales managers could get a precise picture of how they were meeting or beating their targets without needing to harass their underlings to update the figures day after day?

Automating Tedious Tasks

When evaluating what you could do with VBA, consider even basic tasks that you don't think twice about performing. You don't need to automate a whole document or project—just automating one or two tedious tasks can make a difference.

Here are a couple of examples of small but tedious tasks that you could speed up significantly with a little VBA programming:

- In Visio, creating a callout for the currently selected item, entering default text in it, and formatting it to your standard specifications.

- In PowerPoint, applying background color and line color to an AutoShape, and choosing wrapping options for it.

- In Word, choosing File ➤ New and then drilling down through several levels of nested folders to find the template you need.

If you examine your working habits, you'll find any number of other small tasks that you could simplify or speed up by using VBA.

Creating Procedures That Others Can Use

Once you've established that you can create a procedure to perform a particular task, ask yourself who will use the procedure. If only you will use it, you must be sure it will actually save you time. On the other hand, if a whole department full of colleagues is ready to take advantage of your code, you'll find it much easier to justify the time and effort involved in creating the procedure. (The disadvantage of creating code for your colleagues is that you'll usually need to spend more time testing it, to make sure it works under the widest variety of circumstances you can imagine. I'll discuss how to give your code such flexibility and resilience in Chapter 18, "Debugging Your Code.")

If your responsibilities include developing procedures for a department, a location, or a whole company, you'll no doubt spend large chunks of your time establishing which tasks your colleagues perform most often, what help you can provide in performing those tasks, and how much effort is justified in automating one task versus another. You shouldn't need me to tell you to put the most effort most immediately where it will provide the greatest benefit to the greatest number of people.

Automating Complex One-Time Tasks

Somewhat different from the one-shot tasks I mentioned earlier are complex tasks that you need to perform only once per computer, but on many different computers. Consider creating a VBA procedure to take the strain out of such tasks. Let's use Word as an example here. If you're responsible for administering templates on a network, you might write a procedure to configure Word automatically (and perhaps to perform a few other tasks at the same time), rather than letting users confuse themselves by cavorting around the network drives in the Modify Location dialog box (and other dialog boxes). Similarly, if you've recommended a particular group of settings to Word users in your company, you might create a procedure to implement those settings on each new installation of Word.

When Is It Worth Creating a VBA Procedure?

Usually, the key to deciding whether automating a particular task is worth the effort of creating a VBA procedure is this: Will you—or your colleagues—save more time by using the procedure than it takes you to create it?

For a rough-and-ready procedure that you put together for a particular task and discard immediately afterward, the time savings is relatively easy to estimate. The task would take 30 minutes to perform manually; the procedure will take 5 to 10 minutes to write and another 5 to run, so you'll save 15 minutes. The only fly in the ointment is if you decide to create such a procedure and discover that doing so takes you three times as long as you estimated it would. (In that case, it's best to chalk it up as a learning experience.)

But if a procedure will save only a few minutes for each user whenever they need to, say, create a workbook or presentation of a particular type, you'll need to think harder to justify spending four or five hours of your time up front. Here, the question isn't what time savings you can expect in the long haul (because the time won't be your own), but whether creating such a procedure will make people's work life easier. If the workbook or presentation in question is one that people create frequently, it's probably a good bet to automate. With a little honest self-examination, you should be able to detect whether you're trying to fulfill a real need or just taking an opportunity to show off your imagination and your VBA skills.

The primary reason for creating a procedure that may not save much time is to avoid any difficulty the user may have performing an intricate process—choosing several setup or configuration options, for example. Such a procedure may result in a net saving of time if the user isn't competent to perform the task without intensive instruction. However, the main thrust behind creating the procedure is to get the process done correctly and with the minimum of fuss.

A secondary—but entirely valid—reason for creating a procedure that may not save time is the feel-good factor, both for the people who use the procedure and for the person who created it. A couple of clicks here and a few keystrokes there may not save users much effort, but they may appreciate customization and procedures that bring their most-needed commands to their fingertips. Even relatively modest VBA procedures and user forms can contribute greatly to the user-friendliness of an application—particularly if you design them as you should, focusing on the user's needs rather than the task's needs.

How Should You Approach Automating a Task?

Once you've established that you can and should automate a procedure, consider how to approach the automation. If the application you're using supports the Macro Recorder (discussed in Chapter 2, "Recording and Running Macros"), you can, of course, simply barrel ahead with the Macro Recorder. Alternatively, you can fire up the Visual Basic Editor and start lobbing assorted statements left and right. But usually the process of creating VBA code to solve a purpose will benefit from reflection up front.

The specifics of what you do will vary depending on the type and complexity of the procedure you're creating. But these are the general steps to take:

1. First, establish the goal of the procedure. If the procedure will consist of a set of subprocedures, set out what each of these will do.

2. Work out the basic steps of the procedure (or each component procedure), either in your head or in writing. When you're writing the code, one simple way of tracking the steps in a procedure is to enter them as comment lines in the procedure, and then fill in the code between them. (If the application supports the Macro Recorder, you can use the Macro Recorder to quickly hack in sections of recorded code.)

3. If you're creating a set of procedures, decide which steps will be performed by which procedure. Make your code as modular as possible so you'll be able to reuse it.

4. Establish roughly what any message boxes, input boxes, or dialog boxes in the procedure will do. Determine at what point you'll call them, which options they will contain, and which actions they will need to take.

5. Decide how sophisticated to make the procedure. If it's a simple macro that you're creating for your own use or for someone else's temporary use, you can probably get away with something pretty crude. If you'll be distributing the procedure across a production environment, you'll need to make it far more comprehensive and stable, if not completely bulletproof.

6. Decide how to create the code. If the application you're using supports the Macro Recorder, you may be able to record portions of it by using the Macro Recorder and then tweak that code. You may prefer to create all the code manually in the Visual Basic Editor; I'll discuss how to do this in Chapter 3. Alternatively, you can mix the two methods.

In the next chapter, I'll show you how to use the Macro Recorder (in those applications that support it) to create custom VBA code the easy way. You'll learn at how to record a macro, run a macro, and manage the macros you create. Turn the page.

CHAPTER **2**

Recording and Running Macros in the Microsoft Office Applications

FEATURING:

I n this chapter, you'll learn the easiest way to get started with Visual Basic for Applications (VBA): recording simple macros using the built-in Macro Recorder in the Office applications, and then running them to repeat the actions they contain. By recording macros, you can automate straightforward but tediously repetitive tasks and speed up your regular work. You can also use the Macro Recorder to create VBA code that performs the actions you need, then edit the code to add flexibility and power.

At this writing, only some VBA-enabled applications have VBA macro-recording capabilities, because Microsoft licenses the language but not the Macro Recorder. Most of the VBA-enabled Microsoft Office applications support the Macro Recorder, although FrontPage does not. Some other applications support macro recording in macro languages other than VBA. For example, WordPerfect has macro-recording capabilities, but only in the PerfectScript scripting language; any VBA code that you create from WordPerfect, you need to create from scratch. (You can also import code recorded or written for another application, and then modify it to work with Word-Perfect, but doing so will typically involve making extensive changes to the code.)

So in this chapter I'll show you examples using only the Microsoft applications discussed in this book: Word, Excel, PowerPoint, and Project. If you're hankering to work in WordPerfect, Visio, or AutoCAD, skip this chapter for the moment and proceed with the next chapter.

Macro Basics

A *macro* is essentially a sequence of commands you can repeat at will. You can repeat the actions by using a single command to run the macro. In some applications, you can also set a macro to run itself automatically. For instance, you might create a macro in Word to automate basic formatting tasks on a type of document you regularly receive in an inappropriate format. You could run the macro either manually or automatically upon opening a document of that type.

A macro is a type of *subprocedure*, and a subprocedure is sometimes also called a *subroutine*. Generally, people tend to use the terms *procedure* and *routine* rather than the two *sub* words when speaking more loosely. A macro is sometimes understood to consist of recorded code rather than written code, but many people use the word in a wider sense, so it can include written code as well. For example, if you record a macro and then edit it until it's a more compact and efficient shadow of its former self, or add actions to build it up from a 90-lb weakling into an incredible hulk, many people still consider it a macro. Don't sweat the difference.

In an application that supports the VBA Macro Recorder, you can create macros in two ways:

- Turn on the Macro Recorder and perform the sequence of actions you want the macro to perform.
- Open the Visual Basic Editor and type the VBA commands into it.

You can also compromise by recording the basic sequence of actions and then opening the macro and editing out any inappropriate actions. While editing the macro, you can add other actions; you can also add control structures and user-interface elements (such as message boxes and dialog boxes), so users of the macro (or procedure, or routine, as you prefer) can make decisions and choose options for how to run it.

Once you've created a macro, you can assign a way of running it. In most applications, you can assign a macro to a menu item, a key combination, or a toolbar button and run it at any time. In fact, you don't have to wait until you've created a macro to assign a way of running it—as you'll see in a moment.

Recording a Macro

In applications that support the Macro Recorder, recording a macro is by far the easiest way to create VBA code. You switch on the Macro Recorder, assign a method for running the macro (a toolbar button, a menu item, or a key combination), perform the actions you want in the macro, and then switch off the Macro Recorder. As you perform the actions, the Macro Recorder records them as instructions—*code*—in the VBA programming language. Once you finish recording the macro, you can view the code in the Visual Basic Editor and change it if necessary. If the code works perfectly as you recorded it, you never have to look at it—you can just run the macro at any time by choosing the assigned toolbar button, menu item, or key combination, or by running it directly from the Macros dialog box.

In the following sections, you'll look at the stages involved in recording a macro. As you'll see, the process is simple enough, but you need to be familiar with some background if you haven't recorded macros before. After the explanations and generalities, I'll present an example of recording a macro in each of the Office applications that this book covers. You'll examine and adapt those macros a little later in the book, after you learn how to use the Visual Basic Editor.

Starting the Macro Recorder

The first step in recording a macro is to start the Macro Recorder. But before you begin, think about what you're trying to do in the macro and set up the application so that everything's ready for the sequence of commands you want to record. For example, if you want to create an editing macro in Word, make sure you have a document open with suitable text or other contents, and then activate the window containing the document. (As you'll see shortly, in some applications you can pause the Macro Recorder when you need to take an action without recording it, but usually you'll get better results if you plan your macros beforehand.)

Then start the Macro Recorder by choosing Tools ➤ Macro ➤ Record New Macro (in Word, you can also double-click the REC indicator on the status bar if you have the status bar displayed). The Macro Recorder will display the Record Macro dialog box with a default macro name (Macro1, Macro2, and so on) and description that you can accept or change. Figure 2.1 shows the Record Macro dialog box for Word with a custom name and description entered.

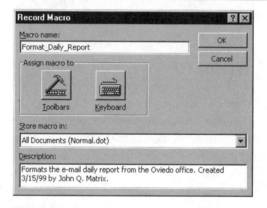

FIGURE 2.1

In the Record Macro dialog box, enter a name for the macro you're about to record; also, give the macro an illuminating write-up in the Description box.

The Record Macro dialog box looks a bit different in the various applications that use it because it needs to accommodate particular needs that each application has. In each case, you get to name the macro and add a description for it. In most cases, you also get to specify where to save the macro—for example, in a particular template, presentation, workbook, or project. Most versions of the Record Macro dialog box let you specify a way of running the macro, providing either a text box for entering a shortcut key combination, or a command button that takes you to a separate dialog box (such as the slimmed-down version of the Customize dialog box that Word uses).

Most of the Microsoft applications, and some other applications (such as WordPerfect), have a Visual Basic toolbar, from which you can take some actions with macros and the Visual Basic Editor. These Visual Basic toolbars also vary in the actions they support and, consequently, in the number of buttons they have. If the Visual Basic toolbar in the application you're using has a Record Macro button, you can click that button to display the Record Macro dialog box. Figure 2.2 shows Word's version of the Record Macro toolbar.

FIGURE 2.2

You can use the Visual Basic toolbar to work with macros.

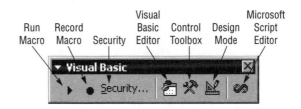

Here's the quick version of what the Visual Basic toolbar buttons do:

Run Macro button   Displays the Macros dialog box, in which you can choose the macro to run. (You can also use this dialog box to create a macro in the Visual Basic Editor, if you choose.)

Record Macro button   Displays the Record Macro dialog box. When you're recording a macro and the Visual Basic toolbar is on screen, the Record Macro button appears pushed in; you can click it to stop recording the macro.

Security button   Displays the Security dialog box, which you'll examine in Chapter 20. Briefly, this dialog box lets you choose which level of security Word should use; you can also specify trusted sources for macros.

Visual Basic Editor button   Starts or switches to the Visual Basic Editor, which I'll discuss in Chapter 3, "Using the Visual Basic Editor."

Control Toolbox button   Toggles the display of the Control Toolbox, which you use to add controls to documents. In some applications, you can also display the Control Toolbox from the context menu of toolbars or from the View ➤ Toolbars submenu.

Design Mode button   Switches the current document to Design mode, displays the Control Toolbox if it isn't already displayed, and displays the Exit Design Mode toolbar (which, as you might guess, you can use to exit Design mode). The Design Mode button is a toggle button. However, when you use it to exit Design mode, it doesn't hide the Control Toolbox—even if it displayed the Control Toolbox when you entered Design mode.

Microsoft Script Editor button   Displays the Microsoft Script Editor, which you use to create HTML and XML pages.

Naming the Macro

Next, enter a name for the new macro in the Macro Name text box in the Record Macro dialog box. The macro name can be up to 80 characters long and can contain both letters and numbers; but it must start with a letter. It can't contain spaces, punctuation, or special characters (such as ! or *), although underscores are allowed. See the sidebar for some suggestions on how to name your macros.

Strangely enough, the Microsoft applications don't prevent you from entering an invalid name in the Macro Name text box in the Record Macro dialog box. (Word 95, for instance, used to dim the OK button in its Record Macro dialog box, rendering it unavailable if you entered an invalid name so you couldn't proceed.) You still won't get very far beyond the dialog box, though. Figure 2.3 shows how Word, Excel, PowerPoint, and Project respond to an invalid macro name once it's entered. As you can see, Project's response is by far the most helpful, pointing out the problem and the macro-naming rules and restrictions.

FIGURE 2.3

If you enter an invalid macro name in the Record Macro dialog box, the application will let you know in its own way. Project is the most helpful, Word (at lower-right, masquerading as Visual Basic) the least.

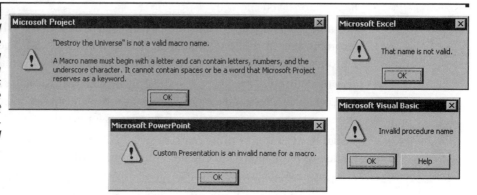

Enter a description for the macro in the Description text box. This description is to help you (and anyone you share the macro with) identify the macro and understand when to use it. If the macro will run successfully only under particular conditions, note them briefly in the Description text box. For example, if the user must make a selection in the document before running the macro in Word, note that requirement. If the macro will format the active presentation in PowerPoint, that's something the user needs to know too.

Choose where to store the macro. Your choices with the main Office applications are as follows:

- In Word, if you want to restrict availability of the macro to just the current template or document, choose that template or document from the Store Macro In drop-down list. If you want the macro to be available no matter which template you're working in, make sure the default setting—All Documents (Normal.dot)— appears in the Store Macro In combo box.

- In Excel, you can choose to store the macro in This Workbook (the active workbook), New Workbook, or Personal Macro Workbook. The Personal Macro Workbook is a special workbook named `PERSONAL.XLS` and stored in your `\Application Data\Microsoft\Excel\XLSTART\` folder. By keeping your macros and other customizations in the Personal Macro Workbook, you can make them available to any of your procedures—in that way, the Personal Macro Workbook is similar to Word's `Normal.dot`. If you choose New Workbook, Excel creates a new workbook for you and creates the macro in it.

- In PowerPoint, you can store the macro in the active presentation or in any other open presentation or template. PowerPoint does not provide a global macro storage container, although you can make your macros and code available to other presentations by using a presentation or template as global storage and determinedly keeping it open all the time.

- In Project, you can store the macro in the Global File or in This Project (the active project). The Global File is a special Project file stored in the `\Application Data\Microsoft\MS Project\1033\` folder (1033 is the Language ID for U.S. English; if you're using a different language, the folder will be different). Any macro stored in the Global File is available to all projects.

Each of the main Office applications automatically stores recorded macros in a default location in the specified file, template, or project:

- Word stores each recorded macro in a module named `NewMacros` in the selected template or document, so you'll always know where to find macros you've recorded. If the module doesn't exist, the Macro Recorder creates it. Because it receives each macro recorded into its document or template, a `NewMacros` module can grow to a significant size if you record a lot of macros. This growth applies in spades to the `NewMacros` module in the default global template, `Normal.dot`, which receives each and every macro you record unless you specify another document or template.

- Excel and PowerPoint store each recorded macro for any given session in a new module named `Module`*n*, where *n* is the lowest unused number in ascending sequence (`Module1`, `Module2`, and so on). Any macros you create in the next session go into a new module with the next available number. If you record macros frequently with Excel and PowerPoint, you'll most likely need to consolidate the macros you want to keep so that they're not scattered in many modules like this.

- Project stores each recorded macro in a new module named `Module`*n*, where *n* is the next unused number. You'll almost certainly want to consolidate the macros you record with Project.

Always Name and Describe Your Macros (Tedious Though It Is)

If you create many macros, it's vital to organize them so you know which to keep and which to toss. Recording macros lets you create code so quickly that it's easy to get confused about which macro does what.

You'll be tempted not to assign a macro description when you're in a hurry, or when you're playing with different ways to approach a problem and you're not sure which (if any) of your test macros you'll keep. Even so, make sure you enter a few notes for each macro that you record. Otherwise, it's easy to end up with a ton of recorded macros that have cryptic names and no descriptions. To figure out what each macro does and which ones you can safely discard, you'll have to plow through the code—and a recorded macro's code can be surprisingly long, even if the macro does nothing more than adjust a few options in a couple of dialog boxes.

Use a macro-naming convention to indicate which recorded macros you can kill without remorse. Start the name with a constant part, then add numeric values sequentially to keep track of the versions: For example, *Scratch* (Scratch01, Scratch02, and so on), *Kill* (Kill01, Kill02, and so on), or even *aaa* (which will keep the macros at the top of the list in the Macros dialog box). As a corollary, never use the default name that VBA assigns to a macro (Macro1, Macro2, and so on, using the next higher unused number tacked onto the word *Macro*), unless you choose to use the automatic name as the designator for a scratch macro; with names this vague, chances are you will never be able to identify your macros later.

Because VBA code increases the size of the file that contains it, it's a good idea to clear out unwanted macros frequently. Doing so will prevent your files from ballooning to absurd sizes.

Another Naming Consideration: How Will the ScreenTip Read?

When you create a toolbar button for a macro in an Office application, the application automatically assigns to the button a ScreenTip that consists of the macro's name. This default ScreenTip seems designed to encourage you to name your macros consistently, or at least comprehensibly—if you use a capital letter to indicate the start of each word, and perhaps use an underscore between words, the ScreenTip will be much easier to read than if you just use all lowercase letters or all uppercase letters.

Continued ▮▶

CONTINUED

The exception here is Word, which creates its ScreenTips in a more sophisticated way than the other Office applications, automatically adding a space before each capital letter that it judges to be the start of a new word. For example, if you name a macro `FormatDailyReport` and create a toolbar button for it, Word will give the button the ScreenTip *Format Daily Report*. But if the name of the macro contains a clump of capital letters, Word will break the macro name with a space before the first capital in the clump, but it won't divide the others. For example, if you create a macro named `FixTCPIPSettings`, Word will create the ScreenTip *Fix TCPIPSettings* rather than the *Fix TCPIP Settings* you might want. In this case, you'd do best to use an underscore in the macro name—`FixTCPIP_Settings`—to provide a readable division in the second half of the ScreenTip.

Assigning a Way to Run the Macro

At this point, you can choose a way to run the macro. If you're planning to use the macro in its recorded form (without altering it, or without using the code in the macro as the basis for another procedure) from its default location, this is a good time to assign the macro to a command-bar item or a keyboard shortcut. As I'll discuss later in the chapter, you can also assign a way of running the macro at a later point, just as you do with procedures you create in the Visual Basic Editor. So if you aren't sure you'll be using the macro in its recorded form—for example, if you think you might rename it—don't assign a way to run it yet.

The same goes if you plan to move it from the default module in which the application stores it to another module after creating it. (If you assign a way of running the macro when you record it, and then move the macro to a different module or file, the assigned way of running the macro will usually no longer work.) By moving your recorded macros into different modules, you can group related macros so you can compare the code, adjust them, or distribute them easily.

To assign a way to run the macro, follow the instructions in the next sections, which cover what you need to do in the various Office applications.

Assigning a Way to Run the Macro in Word

In Word, you use the Customize dialog box and the Customize Keyboard dialog box to assign a way of running a macro. I'll describe each method in turn.

To assign the macro to a toolbar button, a menu item, or a context menu item:

1. Click the Toolbars button in the Record Macro dialog box to display the Customize dialog box.

2. If it isn't already displayed, select the Commands tab to display the Commands page, shown in Figure 2.4. In the Categories list box, only the category *Macros* should be listed, and it should be selected.

3. Make sure Word has chosen the correct context in the Save In combo box at the bottom of the Customize dialog box. You can apply the customization to the default global template (`Normal.dot`), the active document, or the template attached to the active document. (If the active document is attached to `Normal.dot`, no other template will be available.)

4. If you're going to assign the macro to a toolbar button or a context menu item, make sure the toolbar or the Shortcut Menus toolbar is displayed. To display a toolbar or the Shortcut Menus toolbar, click the Toolbars tab of the Customize dialog box to display the Toolbars page, then select the check box for the toolbar or the Shortcut Menus toolbar to display it. Click the Commands tab to display the Commands page of the Customize dialog box again.

5. Click the macro's name in the Commands list box and drag the macro item to the toolbar, the context menu, or the menu, as appropriate, as shown in Figure 2.5.

FIGURE 2.5

To assign a macro to a context menu, select the Shortcut Menus check box on the Toolbars page of the Customize dialog box. Then drag the macro item from the Commands page to the relevant context menu.

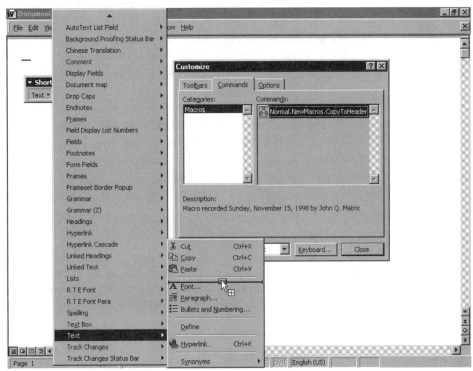

6. Word will add a button or menu item for the macro giving it the macro's full name, such as `Normal.NewMacros.CreateDailyReport`. This name consists of the name of the template or document in which the macro is stored, the name of the module that contains the macro, and the macro's name, respectively.

7. To rename the button or menu item, right-click it (or click the Modify Selection button in the Customize dialog box) and enter a more attractive and descriptive (and shorter) name in the Name text box on the context menu that appears.

 TIP Keep two points in mind. First, a macro's menu-item name or button name doesn't have to bear any relation to the macro's name. Second, you can also create new toolbars and new menus as you need them.

8. To assign an access key to an item, put an ampersand (&) before the character that you want to use as the access key, then press the Enter key.

- The access key doesn't have to be unique, but using it will be easiest if it is. If multiple menus or commands share the same access key, Word will select the first of them the first time you press the access key. You can then press the Enter key to display that menu or run that command, or you can press the access key again to access the next item associated with that key. For example, if you assign the access key **T** to the button for a macro named Transpose_ Word, Word will select the Tools menu (unless you've removed it) the first time you press Alt+T and the Transpose_Word button the second time you press Alt+T.

9. Click the Close button to close the Customize dialog box.

 NOTE As with the other ways of running a macro, you can assign a keyboard combination to run a macro either at the time you record the macro, or at any point after you finish recording it. If you intend to move the macro from the NewMacros module to another module, don't assign the keyboard combination until the macro has reached its ultimate destination.

To assign the macro to a keyboard combination:

1. Click the Keyboard button in the Record Macro dialog box to display the Customize Keyboard dialog box.

2. Click to place the insertion point in the Press New Shortcut Key box, and then press the key combination you want. Figure 2.6 shows the Customize Keyboard dialog box with a new shortcut key selected. A key combination can be any one of the following:

- Alt plus either a function key or a regular key not used as a menu access key
- Ctrl plus a function key or a regular key
- Shift plus a function key
- Ctrl+Alt, Ctrl+Shift, Alt+Shift, or even Ctrl+Alt+Shift plus a regular key or function key. Because pressing Ctrl+Alt+Shift and another key involves severe contortions of the hands for most people, it isn't a great idea for frequent use.

3. Check the Current Keys list box to make sure the key combination you've chosen isn't already in use. If it is, press the Backspace key to clear the current key combination (unless you want to reassign the key combination), and then press another combination.

FIGURE 2.6

Set a shortcut key combination for the macro in the Customize Keyboard dialog box.

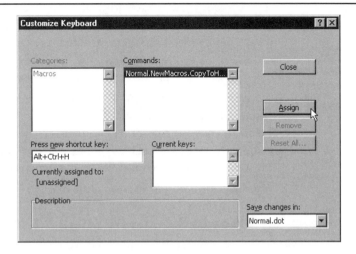

 TIP You can set up shortcut keys that have two steps—for example, Ctrl+Alt+F, 1 and Ctrl+Alt+F, 2—by pressing the second key (in this case, the 1 or the 2) after pressing the key combination. However, these shortcuts tend to be more trouble than they're worth, unless you're assigning literally hundreds of extra shortcut keys.

4. Click the Assign button to assign the key combination to the macro.

5. Click the Close button to close the Customize Keyboard dialog box.

Assigning a Way to Run the Macro in Excel

When you're recording a macro, Excel lets you do no more than assign a Ctrl shortcut key to run it. If you want to add a menu item or a toolbar button, you need to do so after recording the macro. Because you may well want to move the macro to a different module than the one VBA automatically stores it in, this may be no bad thing.

To assign a Ctrl shortcut key to run the macro you're recording:

1. Enter the key in the Shortcut Key text box.

2. In the Store Macro In drop-down list, specify where you want the Macro Recorder to store the macro. Your choices are as follows:

- This Workbook stores the macro in the active workbook. This option is useful for macros that belong to a particular workbook and will not need to be used elsewhere.

- New Workbook causes Excel to create a new workbook for you and store the macro in it. This option is useful for experimental macros that you'll need to edit before unleashing them on actual work.

- Personal Macro Workbook stores the macro in the Personal Macro Workbook, a special workbook named `PERSONAL.XLS` stored in your `\Application Data\Microsoft\Excel\XLSTART\` folder. By keeping your macros and other customizations in the Personal Macro Workbook, you can make them available to any of your procedures—in that way, the Personal Macro Workbook is similar to Word's `Normal.dot`. If the Personal Macro Workbook does not exist yet, the Macro Recorder creates it automatically.

   3. Click the OK button to start recording the macro.

Assigning a Way to Run the Macro in PowerPoint

PowerPoint does not let you assign a way to run a macro when you record it, though you can assign a way to run it afterwards, as discussed in the section, "Assigning a Way of Running the Macro," later in the chapter. You can choose to store the macro in any open presentation or template.

Assigning a Way to Run the Macro in Project

Like Excel, Project lets you specify a Ctrl shortcut key when you record a macro. Also like Excel, you can choose a storage location. Unlike Excel, you can choose relative or absolute references from the Record Macro dialog box.

Here's how to proceed:

1. Enter the key in the Shortcut Key text box.

2. In the Store Macro In drop-down list, specify where you want the Macro Recorder to store the macro.

3. In the Row References group box, choose between relative row references and absolute (ID) row references.

4. In the Column References group box, choose between absolute (field) column references (the default) and relative column references.

5. Click the OK button to start recording the macro.

Recording the Actions in the Macro

When you dismiss the Customize dialog box, the Customize Keyboard dialog box, or the Record Macro dialog box, the Macro Recorder will be ready to start recording the macro. For most applications, the Macro Recorder will display the Stop Recording toolbar (usually undocked in the upper-left corner of the screen); for Word, the Macro Recorder will also add a cassette-tape icon to the mouse pointer and will turn the REC indicator in the status bar black.

Now record the sequence of actions you want to immortalize. What exactly you can do varies from application to application, but in general, you can use the mouse to select items from menus and toolbars, to make choices in dialog boxes, and to select defined items (such as cells in spreadsheets or shapes in PowerPoint slides) in documents. You'll find a number of things that you can't do with the mouse, such as select items within a document window in Word. To select items in a document window, you have to use keyboard commands.

NOTE When you make choices in a dialog box and click the OK button, the Macro Recorder records the current settings for *all* the options on that page of the dialog box. So, for example, when you change the left indentation of a paragraph in the Paragraph dialog box in Word, the Macro Recorder records all the other settings on the Indents and Spacing page as well (Alignment, Before and After spacing, and so forth). You can edit out the code representing these settings later, if you don't want to use them.

In Word, if you need to perform any actions that you don't want recorded, pause the Macro Recorder by clicking the Pause Recording button on the Stop Recording toolbar. The Pause Recording button will take on a pushed-in look, and its ScreenTip will identify it as the Resume Recorder button. Click this button again to resume recording.

To stop recording, choose Tools ➢ Macro ➢ Stop Recording (or Stop Recorder, depending on the application), or click the Stop Recording button on the Stop Recording toolbar if it is displayed. In Word, you can also double-click the REC indicator on the status bar to stop recording.

The Macro Recorder has now recorded your macro and assigned it to the control you chose. If you didn't choose to assign a control (or if the application didn't let you assign one), be patient—I'll show you how to do so in just a moment, after discussing how to run a macro.

Running a Macro

To run a macro you've recorded, click the toolbar button, choose the menu item or context menu item, or press the key combination you assigned to it. The macro will run, performing the actions you recorded.

As you'd expect, the macro executes the commands you recorded in the sequence in which you recorded them. For example, suppose you create a macro in Excel that selects cell A2 in the current worksheet, boldfaces that cell, enters the text **Yearly Sales**, selects cell B2, and enters the number **100000** in it. The Macro Recorder will register five actions: selecting cell A2, applying the boldface, entering the text, selecting cell B2, and entering the second text. VBA will then perform all five actions each time you run the macro. Some applications (such as Word) will let you undo most actions executed via VBA after the macro stops running (by using the Edit ➤ Undo menu item or the Undo button on the Standard toolbar, undoing one command at a time as usual); other applications do not.

 NOTE If running the macro results in an error, chances are that the macro is trying to do something to a file or an object that isn't available. For example, if you record a macro in Excel that works on the active workbook, the macro will throw an error if you run it when no workbook is open. Likewise, if you record a macro in PowerPoint that works with the third shape on the active slide, that macro will fail if you run it on a slide that has no third shape. To get the macro to run properly, recreate the salient conditions under which you recorded it, and all should be well again.

If you chose not to assign the macro to a button, menu item, context menu item, or key combination (because the application prevented you, because you'll need to move the macro to a different module later, or because you simply have too many macros, as I do), you can run it by choosing Tools ➤ Macro ➤ Macros to display the Macros dialog box, selecting the macro from the Macro Name list, and clicking the Run button. You can also run a macro from within the Visual Basic Editor, as you'll see in Chapter 3, "Using the Visual Basic Editor," or from the Run Macro button on the Visual Basic toolbar.

 NOTE If you're using Office 2000's adaptive menus, the Macro item won't appear immediately on the Tools menu until you've used it at least once. So drop down the short menu, and either wait a second for Word to display the lesser-used items on the menu, or click the downward-arrow button at the foot of the menu to display them. (If you want to stop using adaptive menus, choose Tools ➤ Customize and clear the Menus Show Recently Used Commands First check box on the Options page. This setting works across all the Office applications.)

TIP To stop a running macro, press Ctrl+Break (Break is usually written on the front face of the Pause key on the keyboard). VBA will stop running the code and will display an angry dialog box telling you that *Code execution has been interrupted.* Click the End button to dismiss this dialog box.

Recording a Sample Word Macro

In this section, you'll record a sample macro in Word that you can work with later. This macro simply selects the current word, cuts it, moves the insertion point one word to the right, and pastes the word back in. This is a straightforward sequence of actions that you'll later view and edit in the Visual Basic Editor.

Follow these steps to record the macro:

1. If you don't have a new document open (or a document you don't care about), create a new document.

2. Double-click the REC indicator on the status bar or choose Tools ➤ Macro ➤ Record Macro. Either way, Word will display the Record Macro dialog box.

3. In the Macro Name text box, enter **Transpose_Word_Right**.

4. In the Store Macro In drop-down list, make sure All Documents (Normal.dot) is selected, unless you want to assign the macro to a different template. (In this example, I'll assume that the macro is in Normal.dot and that you'll take care of any consequences if you've put it elsewhere.)

5. In the Description box, enter a description for the macro. The Description box will contain something like *Macro recorded 4/1/2000 by Joanna Bermudez*, which is Word's best attempt to help you identify the macro later. Be more explicit and enter a description such as "Transposes the current word with the word to its right. Created 4/1/2000 by Joanna Bermudez".

 TIP You can change the description for a macro later, either in the Macros dialog box or in the Visual Basic Editor, but it's a good idea to start by entering an appropriate description when you record the macro. If you put off describing the macro until after you create it, you're apt to forget. As a result, you may end up with dozens of macros bearing names that were clear as the midday sun when you created them, but which now give little clue as to the macros' function.

6. Assign a method of running the macro, as described in the previous section, if you want to. Create a toolbar button, a menu item, or a context menu item, or assign a keyboard shortcut. (The method or methods you choose is strictly a matter of personal preference.) If you'll need to move the macro to a different module (or a different template or document) later, don't assign a method of running the macro at this point.

7. Click the Close button to dismiss the Customize dialog box or the Customize Keyboard dialog box (or click the OK button to dismiss the Record Macro dialog box if you chose not to assign a way of running the macro). Now you're ready to record the macro. The Stop Recording toolbar should appear on screen, and the mouse pointer should have a cassette-tape icon attached to it.

8. As a quick demonstration of how you can pause recording, click the Pause Recording button on the Stop Recording toolbar. The cassette-tape icon will disappear from the mouse pointer, and the Pause Recording button will change into a Resume Recorder button. Enter a line of text in the document: **The quick brown dog jumped over a lazy fox.** Position the insertion point anywhere in the word *quick*, then click the Resume Recorder button on the Stop Recording toolbar to reactivate the macro recorder.

9. Record the actions for the macro as follows:

    a. Use the Extend Selection feature to select the word *quick* by pressing the F8 key twice. The EXT indicator on the status bar will be darkened to show that Extend mode is active.

    b. Press the Escape key to cancel Extend mode. The EXT indicator on the status bar will dim again. (This step isn't absolutely necessary, but perform it anyway for good measure.)

    c. Press Shift+Delete or Ctrl+X to cut the selected word to the Clipboard. (You can also click the Cut button or choose Edit ➤ Cut, if you prefer.)

    d. The insertion point will now be at the beginning of the word *brown*. Press Ctrl+→ to move the insertion point right by one word so it's at the beginning of the word *dog*.

    e. Press Shift+Insert or Ctrl+V to paste in the cut word from the Clipboard. (Again, you could click the Paste button instead, or you could choose Edit ➤ Paste.)

    f. Press Ctrl+← to move the insertion point one word to the left. (This is an extra instruction that you'll use when you edit the macro.)

10. Click the Stop Recording button on the Stop Recording toolbar to stop recording the macro (or double-click the REC indicator on the status bar, or choose Tools ➤ Macros ➤ Stop Recording). Your sentence now reads, *The brown quick dog jumped over the lazy fox.*

That was pretty painless. But, as you might imagine, the problem with straightforward recorded macros is that they're limited in what they can do—for example, you can't display a message box or a dialog box. You can fix this limitation by editing the macro code in the Visual Basic Editor. You'll learn how to do that in the next chapter.

You can now run this macro by using the toolbar button, menu or context menu item, or keyboard shortcut that you assigned (if you chose to assign one). Alternatively, you can choose Tools ➤ Macro ➤ Macros and run the macro from the Macros dialog box. Try positioning the insertion point in the word *brown* and running the macro to restore the words in the sentence to their original order.

Recording a Sample Excel Macro

In this section, you'll record a sample Excel macro. This macro creates a new workbook, enters a sequence of months into it, and then saves it. Again, you'll work with this macro in the next chapter. Video_02.avi on the CD illustrates this procedure.

To create the macro, start Excel and follow these steps:

1. Choose Tools ➤ Macro ➤ Record New Macro to display the Record Macro dialog box, shown in Figure 2.7 with information entered.

FIGURE 2.7

Display the Record Macro dialog box for Excel and make your choices in it.

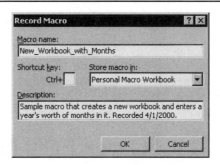

2. Enter the name for the macro in the Macro Name text box. For the example, I've used the name **New_Workbook_with_Months**.

3. In the Shortcut Key text box, enter a shortcut key if you want to. (You can change the shortcut key later, so there's no need to enter one at this point.)

4. In the Store Macro In drop-down list, choose whether to store the macro in the Personal Macro Workbook, in the active workbook, or in a new workbook. As discussed a little earlier, storing the macro in the Personal Macro Workbook gives you the most flexibility. For this example, don't store the macro in the active workbook, because you're going to delete the active workbook almost immediately.

5. Enter a description for the macro in the Description text box.

6. Click the OK button to dismiss the Record Macro dialog box and start recording the macro.

7. Choose File ➢ New to display the New dialog box.

8. Select the Workbook item on the General page of the dialog box, then choose the OK button. Excel will create a new workbook and will select the first sheet on it.

9. Click cell A1 to select it. (It'll probably be already selected; click it anyway, because you need to record the instruction.)

10. Enter **January 2000** and press the → key to select cell B1. Excel will automatically change the date to your default date format. That's fine.

11. Enter **February 2000** and press the ← key to select cell A1 again.

12. Drag from cell A1 to cell B1 so that the two cells are selected.

13. Drag the fill handle from cell B1 to cell L1, so that Excel's AutoFill feature enters the months March 2000 through December 2000 in the cells.

14. Click the Save button on the Standard toolbar (or choose File ➢ Save) to display the Save As dialog box. Save the workbook in a convenient folder under a name such as **Sample Workbook.xls**.

15. Click the Stop Recording button on the Stop Recording toolbar to stop the Macro Recorder. (Alternatively, choose Tools ➢ Macro ➢ Stop Recording.)

Close the sample workbook, and use Windows Explorer to navigate to it and delete it. Then run the macro and watch what happens. (If you don't delete the workbook, Excel will prompt you to decide whether to overwrite it when step 14 goes to save the new workbook.)

Recording a Sample PowerPoint Macro

In this section, you'll record a sample PowerPoint macro. This macro creates a new slide, moves and resizes one of the shapes on it, enters text in the shape, and formats the text. You'll examine the macro in Chapter 4. Video_03.avi on the CD illustrates this procedure.

To create the macro, start PowerPoint and follow these steps:

1. Open a new presentation based on any template you choose. (If PowerPoint has already opened a new presentation for you, feel free to use that presentation instead.) If the New Slide dialog box appears, dismiss it for the time being.

2. Choose Tools ➢ Macro ➢ Record New Macro to display the Record Macro dialog box, shown in Figure 2.8 with information filled in.

FIGURE 2.8

Display the Record Macro dialog box for PowerPoint and make your choices in it.

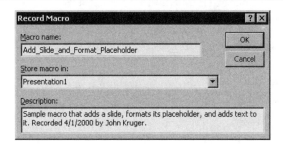

3. Enter the name for the macro in the Macro Name text box: **Add_Slide_and_Format_Placeholder**.

4. In the Store Macro In drop-down list, choose to store the macro in the active presentation rather than in another open presentation or template. The presentations in the Store Macro In drop-down list are identified by name rather than by a description such as *This Presentation* or *Active Presentation*. By default, PowerPoint selects the active presentation in the Store Macro In drop-down list, so you shouldn't need to change this setting.

5. In the Description text box, enter a description for the macro.

6. Click the OK button to dismiss the Record Macro dialog box and start recording the macro.

7. Choose Insert ➤ New Slide to display the New Slide dialog box.

8. Select the Title Slide layout and click the OK button. PowerPoint will close the New Slide dialog box and insert a new title slide in the presentation.

9. Click the first placeholder on the slide to select it.

10. Click in the selected border of the placeholder and drag it up towards the top of the slide to move the placeholder.

11. Click the sizing handle in the middle of the bottom side of the placeholder and drag it down toward the lower placeholder, deepening the placeholder.

12. Click in the placeholder (in the Click To Add Title area) and type the classic text: **The quick brown dog jumped over a lazy fox.**

13. Hold down Ctrl and Shift and press the Home key to select all the text in the placeholder.

14. Choose Format ➤ Font to display the Font dialog box.

15. Select font formatting, such as Impact font, Regular font style, and 54-point size. Click the Preview button to make sure that the result fits within the resized placeholder and looks legible.

16. Click the OK button to dismiss the Font dialog box.

17. Press the → key to deselect the selected text.

18. Click the Stop Recording button on the Stop Recording toolbar, or choose Tools ➢ Macro ➢ Stop Recording to stop recording the macro.

19. Save the presentation under a name such as **Sample Presentation.ppt**. (You'll need to save it so that you can work with the recorded macro later in the book.)

Now choose Tools ➢ Macro ➢ Macros to display the Macros dialog box, select the Macro, and click the Run button. VBA will run through the actions again, adding a new slide, moving and resizing the first placeholder on it, and entering and formatting the text.

Once you're satisfied that the macro is running as it should, close the presentation without saving changes. (One title slide containing details of the quick brown dog's exploits should be enough for any one presentation.)

Recording a Sample Project Macro

In this section, you'll record a sample Project macro that you'll examine later in the book. This macro will add a new task to a project and assign some information to the task. Video_04.avi on the CD illustrates this procedure.

To create the macro, start Project with a default new project and follow these steps:

1. Choose Tools ➢ Macro ➢ Record New Macro to display the Record Macro dialog box, shown in Figure 2.9 with information entered.

FIGURE 2.9

In the Record Macro dialog box, make your choices for the macro and click the OK button.

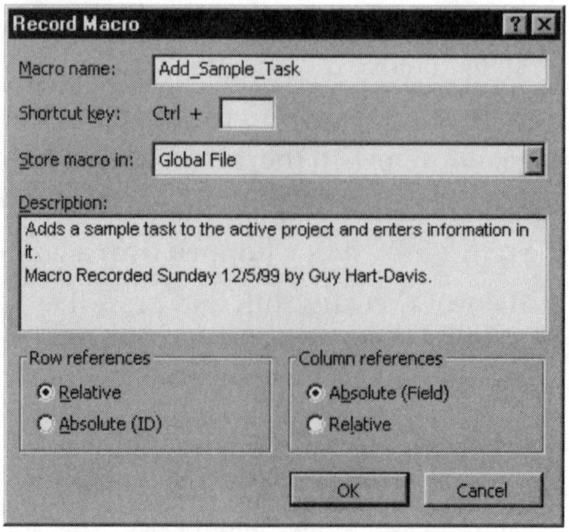

Record Macro dialog box with the following fields:
- Macro name: Add_Sample_Task
- Shortcut key: Ctrl +
- Store macro in: Global File
- Description: Adds a sample task to the active project and enters information in it. Macro Recorded Sunday 12/5/99 by Guy Hart-Davis.
- Row references: ● Relative ○ Absolute (ID)
- Column references: ● Absolute (Field) ○ Relative
- OK Cancel

2. In the Macro Name text box, enter a name for the macro. For this example, I'll use **Add_Sample_Task**.

3. In the Shortcut Key text box, you can enter any Ctrl shortcut key (for example, Ctrl+N) that you want to assign to the macro. Because this is a sample macro and you'll probably move it to a different module if you end up keeping it, I suggest not assigning a shortcut key for the moment.

4. In the Store Macro In drop-down list, make sure that Global File is selected so that the Macro Recorder stores the macro in the global macro storage. (The alternative is to store the macro in the active project, which doesn't suit this case so well, as you want to love and leave the active project rather than save it.)

5. In the Description text box, improve on Project's default description for the macro.

6. In the Row References group box, make sure that the Relative option button is selected.

7. In the Column References group box, make sure the Absolute (Field) option button is selected.

8. Click the OK button to dismiss the Record Macro dialog box and start recording the macro.

9. Choose Insert ➢ New Task to add a new task to the active project.

10. Click in the Task Name cell for the new task. (Do this even if the Task Name cell is already selected—I want you to record this command.)

11. Enter the name for the task. For the example, I'll use **Increase salary**.

12. Press Tab to move to the next cell, in the Duration column.

13. Set the duration to 14 days. (You need to give yourself some time for this task.)

14. Click in the Start column for the task and enter an appropriate starting date, such as the following Monday's date. Project will automatically enter the finish date in the finish column.

15. Choose Tools ➢ Macro ➢ Stop Recorder to stop recording the macro.

Now right-click in the row header for the row you just created and choose Delete Task from the context menu to delete the task. Choose Tools ➢ Macro ➢ Macros (or press Alt+F8) to display the Macros dialog box, then select the macro and click the Run button. Verify that you get the result you expected.

Assigning a Way of Running the Macro

If the application you're using didn't let you assign your preferred way of running it (or if you chose to wait until you'd moved the macro to a different module before assigning a way of running it), you can assign a way of running it as described in the following sections.

As you'll see, the procedures for assigning a macro to a toolbar button, a menu item, and a context menu item (in those applications that support customizing the context menus) are almost identical, so I'll go through them all together, noting variations as appropriate.

Assigning a Macro to a Toolbar Button or Menu Item

To assign a macro to a toolbar button, menu item, or a context menu item (in Word or PowerPoint), follow these steps (illustrated on Video_05.avi on the CD):

1. Right-click any displayed toolbar or the menu bar and choose Customize from the context menu to display the Customize dialog box. Alternatively, choose Tools ➤ Customize to display the dialog box; in Project, choose Tools ➤ Customize ➤ Toolbars.

2. If the Toolbars page of the Customize dialog box isn't displayed, click the Toolbars tab to display it. Figure 2.10 shows the Toolbars page of the Customize dialog box for Word. The Toolbars pages of the Customize dialog box for Excel, PowerPoint, and Project are similar but do not have the Keyboard button.

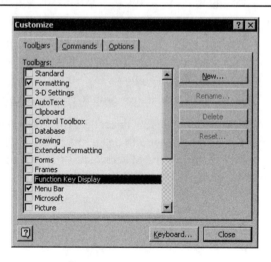

3. Make sure the toolbar to which you want to assign the macro is displayed.

- To display a toolbar, select its check box in the Toolbars list box.

- To hide a toolbar, clear its check box.

- To add an item to a context menu in Word or PowerPoint, select the Short-cut Menus check box. The application will display a toolbar with buttons that lead to drop-down lists for the different categories of toolbars. Figure 2.11 shows the Shortcut Menus toolbar for PowerPoint on the left, and the Shortcut Menus toolbar for Word on the right.

To add an item to a context menu in Word or PowerPoint, display the Shortcut Menus toolbar. Here you see Word's Shortcut Menus toolbar (on the left) and PowerPoint's (on the right).

- To create a new toolbar, click the New button to display the New Toolbar dialog box (shown in Figure 2.12 with a name entered), enter the name for the button in the Toolbar Name text box, and click the OK button.

If you need to, you can create a new toolbar to contain the button for your macro.

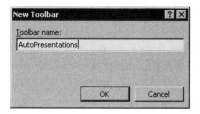

4. Click the Commands tab to display the Commands page. Figure 2.13 shows the Commands page of the Customize dialog box for Word, because again, Word's version of this dialog box is more complex than the other applications' versions: The other Office applications have neither the Save In drop-down list nor the Keyboard button.

FIGURE 2.13

*The Commands page
of the Customize
dialog box*

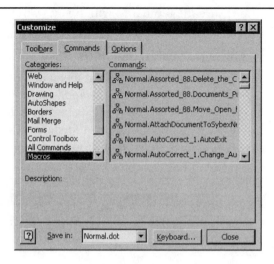

5. In Word, make sure that the Save In drop-down list is displaying the document
or template in which you want to save this customization. If it's not, select the
appropriate document or template from the drop-down list:

- If you save a customization in Normal.dot, the global template, it will be
available to all documents.

- If you save a customization in the template attached to the active document, the customization will be available to all documents to which that
template is attached. (If the active document has Normal.dot attached as its
template, the Save In drop-down list will not show another template.)

- If you save a customization in the active document, it will be available only
to that document.

6. In all the Office applications, scroll down and select the Macros item from the
Categories list box, as shown in the figure. (For Project, select the All Macros
item.) All the applications except Excel will display a list of the available macros.

- Word lists its macros by their fully qualified names, which consist of the
project (the template or document) and module that contain the macro
plus the macro's name. For example, a macro named Example_Macro stored
in the module named Demos in the Normal template will be listed as Normal
.Demos.Example_Macro.

7. Select the macro in the Commands list box and drag the macro to the toolbar,
menu, or submenu on which you want it to appear. Drop the button at the appropriate position; the application will create a button or menu item for the macro
and will give the button or menu item the macro's name. (Word gives the fully
qualified name, which produces awkwardly long buttons.)

TIP To create a new menu, select the New Menu category in the Categories list box and drag the New Menu item to the menu bar or a toolbar.

- In Excel, drag the Custom Button icon to a suitable position on the appropriate toolbar or the Custom Menu Item to the appropriate menu. Excel will create a custom button with the Be Happy face on it or a custom menu item with the text *Custom Menu Item*. At this point, the button or menu item has no connection with the macro. Right-click the button or menu item and choose Assign Macro from the context menu to display the Assign Macro dialog box (see Figure 2.14). Video_06.avi on the CD illustrates this technique.

FIGURE 2.14

In Excel, use the Assign Macro dialog box to assign the macro to the button or menu item you created.

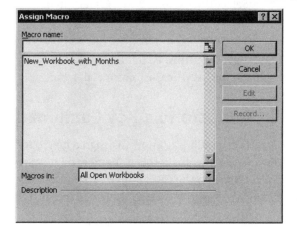

- To create a context menu item in Word and PowerPoint, drag the macro item to the button on the Shortcut Menus toolbar that represents the type of context menu to which you want to add the item. Then drag the item to the individual context menu to display the menu. Position the horizontal bar where you want the entry to appear, and then drop the entry. Video_07.avi on the CD demonstrates creating a context menu item.

8. Right-click the toolbar button, menu item, or context menu item you created to display the context menu. Then drag through the Name box to select its contents. Enter a suitable name for the new button or item. For a menu item or context menu item, put an ampersand (&) before the letter you want to use as an access key. Make sure this access key letter isn't already assigned to another menu item or context menu item—otherwise you'll have to press the access key twice to reach the second item, and you'll have to press the Enter key to execute the command.

9. Choose how you want the button or item to appear—as text, as an image, or as text with an image—by right-clicking the button or item and choosing Default Style, Text Only (Always), Text Only (In Menus), or Image And Text from the context menu. The default style for a toolbar button is an image; the default style for a menu item or a context menu item is text.

10. If you choose to use an image, you can manipulate it as follows:

    • Use the Copy Button Image item on the context menu to copy an image from another button, and the Paste Button Image item to paste the image onto your new button.

    • Choose the Edit Button Image item to display the Button Editor dialog box, in which you can draw a custom button pixel by pixel, then apply it to your button.

    • Select the Change Button Image item to display a pop-up panel of built-in button images that you can quickly apply. (You can then edit these as described in the previous bullet to customize them a bit.)

11. When you've finished adding toolbar buttons and menu items, click the Close button to close the Customize dialog box.

Assigning a Macro to a Key Combination

In this section, you'll learn how to assign a macro to a key combination.

I touched on how to do this in Word earlier in the chapter (for a refresher course, see Video_08.avi on the CD); and PowerPoint does not let you assign a macro to a key combination. As you'll see in a moment, Excel and Project use the same method as each other but differ from Word.

Assigning a Macro to a Key Combination in Word

To assign a macro to a keyboard combination in Word, choose Tools ➤ Customize to display the Customize dialog box, then click the Keyboard button to display the Customize Keyboard dialog box. Then proceed as discussed in the section, "Assigning a Way to Run the Macro in Word," earlier in this chapter.

Assigning a Macro to a Key Combination in Excel and Project

To assign a macro to a key combination in Excel or Project, follow these steps (illustrated in Video_05.avi on the CD):

1. Choose Tools ➤ Macro ➤ Macros to display the Macros dialog box.

2. Select the macro for which you want to assign a key combination.

3. Click the Options button to display the Macro Options dialog box. Figure 2.15 shows the Macro Options dialog box for Project; the Macro Options dialog box for Excel is laid out a little differently but offers the same features.

FIGURE 2.15

In Excel and Project, use the Macro Options dialog box to assign a macro to a key combination. This is the Macro Options dialog box for Project.

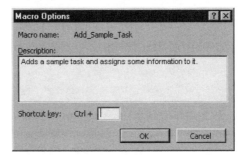

4. Enter the key combination in the Shortcut Key text box. As you can see in the figure, you can only use Ctrl key combinations (as opposed to, say, Ctrl+Alt key combinations).

 TIP You can also change the description of the macro in the Macro Options dialog box if you need to.

5. Click the OK button to close the Macro Options dialog box.

6. Click the Close button or the Cancel button to close the Macros dialog box.

Deleting a Macro

To delete a macro you no longer need, follow these steps (which are illustrated in Video_10.avi on the CD):

1. Choose Tools ➤ Macro ➤ Macros to display the Macros dialog box.

2. Choose the macro in the Macro Name list box.

3. Click the Delete button.

4. In the warning message box that appears, click the Yes button. Figure 2.16 shows Excel's variation of this warning message box.

FIGURE 2.16

When you delete a macro, the application checks to make sure you mean to do so.

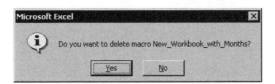

5. Click the Close button or the Cancel button to close the Macros dialog box.

In the next chapter, I'll show you how to use the Visual Basic Editor, which is the primary tool for working with VBA.

CHAPTER <u>3</u>

Using the Visual Basic Editor

In this chapter, I'll discuss how to use the Visual Basic Editor—the tool that Microsoft provides for working with VBA procedures and user forms. Unlike the Macro Recorder, which you'll remember from the previous chapter that Microsoft does not license to companies that license VBA, Microsoft does license the Visual Basic Editor with VBA. This means that when you're working with VBA, the environment looks much the same no matter which application you're using. As a result, you'll spend much of the rest of the book working in the Visual Basic Editor, so you need to know how it works and what you can do in it.

I'll start by showing you the basics of the Visual Basic Editor: its components, what they do, and how you use them. You'll then open the four macros you recorded in the previous chapter, examine their code, and make some minor changes to them. Once you've seen how the elements of the Visual Basic Editor work and examined some code, you'll be ready for a little theory. You'll get that theory in Chapter 5, "The Essentials of VBA Syntax," where I'll give you a brief introduction to the VBA language.

Before getting into VBA, however, I'll show you how to customize the Visual Basic Editor to make your work more comfortable. This customization doesn't take long, and you'll find the resulting ease of use more than worth the amount of time you invest.

Opening the Visual Basic Editor

You can open the Visual Basic Editor a couple of ways. (Video_11.avi on the CD illustrates opening the Visual Basic Editor and navigating to a macro.) To open it directly, choose Tools ➢ Macro ➢ Visual Basic Editor, and then navigate to the module containing the macro you want to work with. To open it indirectly, choose the macro to edit in the Macros dialog box; the application will open the Visual Basic Editor with that macro displayed. (If the Visual Basic Editor isn't already running, the application starts it and switches to it; if the Visual Basic Editor is running, the application simply switches to it.)

When you open the Visual Basic Editor directly, you use the Project Explorer window to navigate to your macro. The Project Explorer window works just like a standard Windows Explorer tree. Depending on the application you're using, you'll see different projects in the tree; I'll discuss the various projects later in the chapter.

To see how the Visual Basic Editor works, navigate to the Transpose_Word_Right macro that you created in Word in the previous chapter. To get there, open Word and follow these steps:

1. Choose Tools ➢ Macro ➢ Visual Basic Editor or press Alt+F11 to start the Visual Basic Editor. As you'll see in a moment, the Visual Basic Editor contains a number of different windows and can have a variety of configurations. Figure 3.1 shows the type of configuration you're likely to see when you open the Visual Basic Editor.

FIGURE 3.1

The Visual Basic Editor

Project Explorer

Code Window

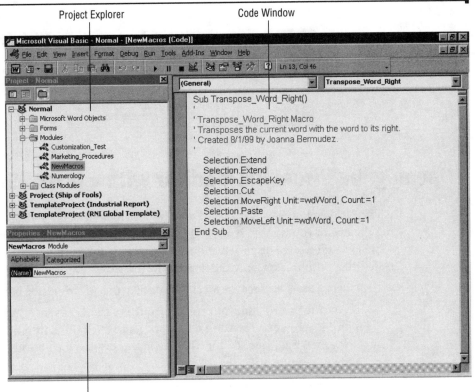

Properties Window

2. In the Project Explorer window in the upper-left corner of the Visual Basic Editor, expand the object for the current template (for example, the Normal object if you're working in the Normal.dot global template) by clicking the + sign to the left of its name.

3. Expand the Modules object and double-click the module that contains the macro. As I mentioned in the previous chapter, Word puts macros that you create into a module named NewMacros by default. The Visual Basic Editor displays the contents of the module in the Code window on the right side. In that window, select the macro you want to edit (in this case, Transpose_Word_Right) from the Procedure drop-down list, as shown in Figure 3.2. Alternatively, use the scroll bar to scroll to the macro you want to edit, which will be identified by the word *Sub*, the name you gave it, and a pair of parentheses—in this case, Sub Transpose_Word_Right().

That's one way to open a macro in the Visual Basic Editor. Now I'll show you an even easier way. Choose File ➢ Close And Return To Microsoft Word to close the Visual Basic Editor for the moment.

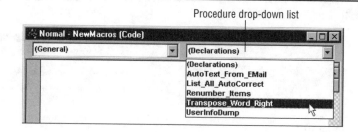

Opening the Visual Basic Editor with a Macro Selected

Instead of opening the Visual Basic Editor and then navigating to the module containing the macro you want to work with, you can open it with a specific macro you (or someone else) created displayed and ready to work on. Video_12.avi on the CD illustrates this technique. Open Word and follow these steps:

1. Choose Tools ➢ Macro ➢ Macros to display the Macros dialog box.

2. Select the macro you want to edit (in this case, Transpose_Word_Right, the Word macro you created in Chapter 2) and click the Edit button. Word will open the Visual Basic Editor with the macro displayed and ready for editing, as shown in Figure 3.3.

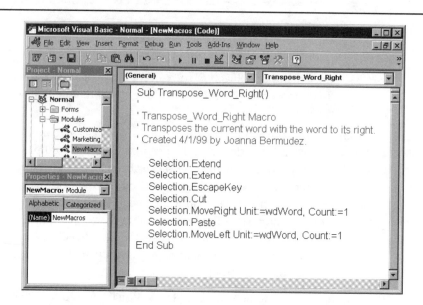

Now that you have the Transpose_Word_Right macro open in the Visual Basic Editor, let's look at the component pieces of the Visual Basic Editor and what they do.

Loading VBA Projects and Accessing Macros in AutoCAD

AutoCAD follows a different model than the other applications discussed in this book. As you saw earlier, you can not only embed a VBA project in an AutoCAD drawing, but you can also maintain separate VBA projects that you can load separately. This capability gives AutoCAD more flexibility than most of the other VBA-enabled applications.

To help you manage its VBA capabilities, AutoCAD provides a VBA Manager for loading and unloading VBA projects. Here's the brief version of how to use it (also see Video_13.avi on the CD):

1. From AutoCAD, choose Tools ➣ Macro ➣ VBA Manager to display the VBA Manager dialog box (shown below).

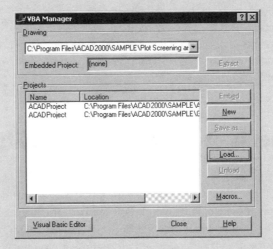

2. Click the Load button to display the Open VBA Project dialog box, shown below.

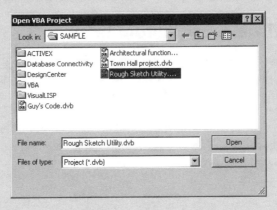

Continued ▮▶

CONTINUED

3. Select the project file you want to open and click the Open button. AutoCAD will load the VBA project and return you to the VBA Manager dialog box.

4. From the VBA Manager dialog box, you can also do the following:

- To unload a project, select it in the Projects list box and click the Unload button.
- Display the Visual Basic Editor by clicking the Visual Basic Editor button.
- Display the Macros dialog box by clicking the Macros button.
- Save a project file (not an embedded project) under another name by clicking the Save As button and specifying the name in the Save As dialog box.
- Embed a project file in the active drawing by clicking the Embed button.

5. When you're through managing VBA projects, click the Close button to close the VBA Manager dialog box.

You can also load a project quickly by choosing Tools ➤ Macro ➤ Load Project to display the Open VBA Project dialog box, selecting the project you want, and clicking the Open button. Video_14.avi on the CD illustrates this technique.

Components of the Visual Basic Editor

In this section, I'll discuss the components of the Visual Basic Editor: the menus, the toolbars, the Project Explorer, the Code window, and the Properties window. In looking at these elements, you'll visit many of the features that the Visual Basic Editor provides for working with code. Some of this discussion may seem intimidating at first, but it will make increasingly more sense as you begin working with actual code.

Video_15.avi on the CD illustrates the main features of the Visual Basic Editor.

The Visual Basic Editor Menus

Like most Windows applications, the Visual Basic Editor has a full complement of menus. In this section, I'll go through the key menus, providing a short description of each menu item. You'll see many of these menu items in action later in this chapter; you'll use others later in the book.

If the menus bore you stiff, skip this section for the time being. You can come back to it when you need to learn more about one of the menu items.

The File Menu

As you'd guess, the File menu provides commands for handling files: creating a new project, opening an existing project, importing and exporting code files, and closing the Visual Basic Editor. Here's a rundown of the standard items on the File menu (some applications, and enhanced packages such as Microsoft Office 2000 Developer, provide other items as well as these):

Save (Ctrl+S)   Saves the whole current project to disk. This item will appear as *Save* and the name of the project, so you can clearly tell from the menu which open project it will save. Usually, if a project has never been saved, choosing this menu item will cause the application to display the Save As dialog box, as if you'd issued a Save command in the application. Typically, you'll use this command to save a project that you've already named, so the Visual Basic Editor will save the project without displaying a Save As dialog box.

Import File (Ctrl+M)   Displays the Import File dialog box, which you can use to import a module, a user form, or a class into the current project.

Export File (Ctrl+E)   Displays the Export File dialog box, which you can use to export a module, a user form, or a class from the current project. This item is available only when you have an exportable item (a module, a class, or a user form) available in the Project Explorer. Use the Export File command to transfer code between projects on different computers or to make backups of your code.

Remove   Deletes the selected form, module, or class from the project. Before it does so, it displays a message box prompting you to export the item before removing it. If the item has any value and you haven't previously exported it, be sure to export it now—after you remove an item from a project, you won't be able to recover it. If no form, module, or class is selected in the Project Explorer, this menu item will be unavailable.

Print (Ctrl+P)   Displays the Print dialog box for printing a module or a user form. You can choose to print the current selection (if there is one), the current module, or the current project. If the selected object is a form, you can choose whether to print a picture of the form, or print its code, or both.

Close And Return To *<Application>* (Alt+Q)   Closes the Visual Basic Editor and returns the focus to the application.

The Edit Menu

The Edit menu provides commands for working in the Code window and in user forms. Some of these commands are standard to many mainstream Windows applications, and will be familiar; others are unique to the Visual Basic Editor. The Edit menu items are as follows:

Undo (Ctrl+Z) Undoes the previous action. The Visual Basic Editor supports multiple undo operations—just keep issuing the Undo command to undo further actions. If there's nothing that the Visual Basic Editor can undo, the menu item will display *Can't Undo*.

Redo Redoes the action last undone. The Visual Basic Editor supports multiple redo operations, up to the number of undo operations performed. If there's nothing the Visual Basic Editor can redo, the menu item will display *Can't Redo*.

Cut (Ctrl+X) Deletes the selected text or selected object from the module or form and copies it to the Windows Clipboard and (for Office applications) the Office Clipboard.

Copy (Ctrl+C) Copies the selected text or selected object from the module or form to the Windows Clipboard and (for Office applications) the Office Clipboard.

Paste (Ctrl+V) Pastes the text or object from the Windows Clipboard into the current window or onto the current user form.

Clear(Del) Deletes the selected text or selected object.

Select All (Ctrl+A) Selects all the code in the current module or all the objects on the current form.

Find (Ctrl+F) Displays the Find dialog box, shown in Figure 3.4, which you can use to locate strings of text in your code.

FIGURE 3.4

Use the Find dialog box to locate strings of text in your code.

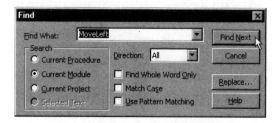

TIP The Find dialog box and Replace dialog box offer different search parameters (Current Procedure, Current Module, Current Project, or Selected Text), search directions, and options such as Find Whole Word Only, Match Case, and Use Pattern Matching (wildcards).

Find Next (F3)   Finds the next instance of the last text you searched for.

Replace (Ctrl+H)   Displays the Replace dialog box, shown in Figure 3.5, which you can use to replace one string of text with another string.

Indent (Tab)   Indents the current line of text or (if a selection spans multiple lines of code) all selected lines by one tab stop.

Outdent (Shift+Tab)   Removes one tab stop from the current line of code or (if a selection spans multiple lines of code) all selected lines. Any lines that have no indentation are unaffected.

List Properties/Methods (Ctrl+J)   Displays the list of properties and methods for the object whose name you entered in the Code window or the Immediate window.

List Constants (Ctrl+Shift+J)   Displays the list of constants for the property whose name you entered in the Code window or the Immediate window.

Quick Info (Ctrl+I)   Displays a ScreenTip showing the syntax for the current item.

Parameter Info (Ctrl+Shift+I)   Displays a ScreenTip showing arguments for a procedure or function.

Complete Word (Ctrl+Space)   Causes the Visual Basic Editor to complete automatically the word you've typed part of. If you haven't typed enough of the word for the Visual Basic Editor to identify it uniquely, the Visual Basic Editor will display a drop-down list of possible words from which you can choose the one you want.

Bookmarks   Displays a submenu for placing bookmarks, clearing bookmarks, and moving backward and forward through the bookmarks you've set.

The View Menu

The View menu provides the means for displaying and moving the various windows of the Visual Basic Editor. You can also display Word itself and information about the current selection. Here are the View menu items:

Code (F7) Displays the Code window for the item selected in the Project Explorer.

Object (Shift+F7) Displays the object selected in the Project Explorer.

Definition (Shift+F2) Displays the Object Browser showing the entry for the item selected in the Code window. When you issue this command for a procedure or function called in another procedure, it displays the code of the procedure or function.

Last Position (Ctrl+Shift+F2) Places the insertion point at the beginning of the last line of code edited.

Object Browser (F2) Displays the Object Browser.

Immediate Window (Ctrl+G) Displays the Immediate window, which you use for running one statement at a time.

Locals Window Displays the Locals window, which you use for tracking the value of variables in your code.

Watch Window Displays the Watch window, which you use for tracking the value of variables and expressions.

Call Stack (Ctrl+L) Displays the Call Stack dialog box, which you use for tracking which procedures and functions are currently active.

Project Explorer (Ctrl+R) Displays the Project Explorer, which you use for navigating among projects and their components.

Properties Window (F4) Displays the Properties window, which you use for setting and checking the value of objects' properties.

Toolbox Displays the Toolbox, which contains controls for building user forms. This item is available only when a user form is selected.

Tab Order Displays the Tab Order dialog box, which you use to rearrange the order of controls on user forms.

Toolbars Displays the submenu of toolbars available in the Visual Basic Editor—Debug, Edit, Standard, and UserForm—together with the Customize command.

***Application* (Alt+F11)** Switches to the active window in the host application, displaying it if it's minimized or hidden.

The Insert Menu

The Insert menu provides commands for adding items to your projects:

Procedure   Displays the Add Procedure dialog box for you to insert a new procedure into the current Code window.

UserForm   Creates a new user form in the currently selected project, naming it `UserForm`*n*, where *n* is the next higher unused number: `UserForm1`, `UserForm2`, and so on.

Module   Inserts a new module in the currently selected project, naming it `Module`*n*, where *n* is the next higher unused number: `Module1`, `Module2`, and so on.

Class Module   Inserts a new class module in the currently selected project, naming it `Class`*n*, where *n* is the next higher unused number: `Class1`, `Class2`, and so on.

File   Displays the Insert File dialog box for you to select a text file (`.TXT`), Basic file (`.BAS`), or class file (`.CLS`). A text file goes in the current Code window; a Basic file or a class file goes in the current project.

The Format Menu

The Format menu provides commands for laying out user forms (custom dialog boxes):

Align   Displays the Align submenu, which contains items for aligning objects horizontally (Lefts, Centers, Rights) and vertically (Tops, Middles, Bottoms). In addition, a To Grid option aligns objects to the grid that criss-crosses each user form.

Make Same Size   Displays the Make Same Size submenu, which contains items for making the selected objects the same width, the same height, or the same width and height.

Size To Fit   Resizes the height and width of an object so it fits its contents exactly.

Size To Grid   Resizes the height and width of an object so its boundaries run along the nearest grid lines on the user form.

Horizontal Spacing   Displays the Horizontal Spacing submenu, which you use to change the spacing of objects selected on the user form.

Vertical Spacing   Displays the Vertical Spacing submenu, which you use to change the vertical spacing of selected objects on the user form.

Center In Form   Displays the Center In Form submenu, which you use to center items horizontally and vertically on the form.

Arrange Buttons   Displays the Arrange Buttons submenu, which you use to arrange buttons evenly across the bottom of a user form or at the right side of a user form.

Group   Creates a group from the selected objects so you can manipulate them together.

Ungroup   Disbands a group of objects.

Order   Displays the Order submenu, which you use to rearrange the order in which objects are layered on the form.

The Debug Menu

The Debug menu provides commands for *debugging* your macros—testing them and getting the bugs (errors, glitches) out of them:

Compile   Identified on the menu with the name of the selected item (for example, *Compile VBAProject*). Compiles the code for the current project.

Step Into (F8)   Executes one statement of the current procedure.

Step Over (Shift+F8)   Executes a whole procedure at once. You use this command to execute one procedure *called* (invoked) from another after you've stepped into a procedure.

Step Out (Ctrl+Shift+F8)   Executes all the remaining statements in the current procedure. You'd typically use this command after stepping into a procedure and finding what you were looking for.

Run To Cursor (Ctrl+F8)   Executes all the statements up to the statement in which the insertion point currently resides.

Add Watch   Displays the Add Watch dialog box, which you use to add to the Watch list any variables and/or expressions you want to keep an eye on.

Edit Watch (Ctrl+W)   Displays the Edit Watch dialog box, which you use to edit the variables and expressions you've entered in the Watch list.

Quick Watch (Shift+F9)   Displays the Quick Watch dialog box, which displays the current value of the variable or expression selected in the Code window.

Breakpoint (F9)   Creates a breakpoint (a mark at which code execution enters Break mode) at the current line of code. If a selection spans multiple lines, this item creates a breakpoint in the last selected line. It's a toggle command, so if the line in question already has a breakpoint, the command clears it.

NOTE When code is running but execution is temporarily suspended, you're in Break mode. Break mode lets you step through your code one command or one procedure at a time (rather than running all the commands at once) when you debug or otherwise critique your code. A Breakpoint is a deliberately inserted stopping point. For more information about this feature, see the section "Setting Breakpoints" in Chapter 4.

Clear All Breakpoints (Ctrl+Shift+F9)   Clears all the breakpoints in the current code module.

Set Next Statement (Ctrl+F9)   Continues code execution at the statement in which the insertion point is currently positioned. (This item lets you quickly change execution to a different line of code.)

Show Next Statement   Highlights the next statement to be executed in the procedure. This item is useful when you've scrolled to a different part of the code and want to move quickly back to the code to be executed.

The Run Menu

The Run menu contains three items for running procedures and user forms, and one item for toggling Design mode on and off:

Run Sub/UserForm (F5)   Starts running the current procedure or user form. If no procedure or user form is selected (for example, if the insertion point is in the Declarations part of a code sheet), choosing this item displays the Macros dialog box, enabling you to select a macro (procedure) to run. When a procedure is running and the code is in Break mode, this item changes to Continue; select it to continue running the procedure without stepping through it.

Break (Ctrl+Break)   Stops the execution of the current procedure and places the code in Break mode.

Reset   Resets all module-level variables and clears the Call Stack.

Design Mode   Toggles Design mode on and off for the selected project.

The Tools Menu

The Tools menu provides commands for running procedures, adding references to other procedures you need, choosing options for how the Visual Basic Editor manifests itself, setting properties for the current project, and applying a digital signature to a project. Tools menu items are as follows:

References   Displays the References dialog box for the current project. You use the References dialog box to specify which object libraries and other VBA projects the current project should be able to access. For example, if the project requires Word to manipulate PowerPoint, you would add a reference to the PowerPoint object library in the References dialog box.

Additional Controls Displays the Additional Controls dialog box, which you use to add controls to the Toolbox.

Macros Displays the Macros dialog box, which provides quick access to the macros and procedures in all the available templates.

Options Displays the Options dialog box for the Visual Basic Editor. I'll discuss these options in the section "Customizing the Visual Basic Editor," later in this chapter.

Properties Identified by the name of the current project and the word *Properties*—for example, if the Normal.dot template is selected, this item will be Normal Properties. Displays the Project Properties dialog box, which you'll explore in the section, "Setting Properties for a Project" a little later in this chapter.

Digital Signature Displays the Digital Signature dialog box, which you use to apply a digital signature to a project.

NOTE The Digital Signature menu item does not appear in VBA 5 hosts such as Auto-CAD 2000 or Visio 5.

The Add-Ins Menu

The Add-Ins menu contains only one item by default: the Add-In Manager. This item displays the Add-In Manager dialog box, which you use to specify which add-ins to use for a project. For example, Microsoft Office 2000 Developer Edition includes a number of add-ins.

NOTE VBA 5 hosts such as AutoCAD 2000 and Visio 5 do not provide an Add-Ins menu in the Visual Basic Editor.

The Window Menu

The Window menu provides five commands familiar to users of Windows applications:

Split Splits the current Code window into two panes, so you can view two different parts of the code at the same time. To remove the split, choose Window ➢ Split again.

Tile Horizontally   Tiles all the non-minimized code and user form windows horizontally.

Tile Vertically   Tiles all the non-minimized code and user form windows vertically.

Cascade   Arranges all the non-minimized code and user form windows in an overlapping, "cascading" arrangement, so you can see the title bar of each window and quickly access the window you need.

Arrange Icons   Arranges all minimized code and user form windows into neat rows at the bottom of the Code window area in the Visual Basic Editor.

Below these commands is a list of the open code and user form windows. Choose a window from the list to activate it.

The Help Menu

The Help menu provides several items for help and information, depending on the host application. Typical items on the Help menu include the following:

Microsoft Visual Basic Help (F1)   Starts the Microsoft Visual Basic Help application, fronted by the Office Assistant (if you haven't explicitly dismissed it) in Office applications.

Contents And Index   Starts the Microsoft Visual Basic Help application and displays its Contents page.

MSDN On The Web   (Microsoft applications only.) Starts your Web browser and connects to the Microsoft Developer Network Web site.

About Microsoft Visual Basic   Displays the About Microsoft Visual Basic dialog box, which provides information about the version of Visual Basic you're using and also gives access to the System Information application.

The Visual Basic Editor Toolbars

The Visual Basic Editor provides four toolbars. You can display and hide the toolbars by right-clicking anywhere in the menu bar or in any displayed toolbar and choosing the name of the toolbar from the context menu. Alternatively, you can choose View ➢ Toolbars and make your selection from the Toolbars submenu.

The Standard Toolbar

The Standard toolbar, shown in Figure 3.6, provides commands for working with and running macros. I'll show you some of these commands in this chapter and others in coming chapters.

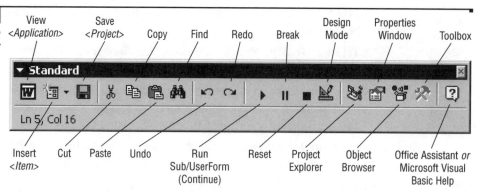

FIGURE 3.6

Use the buttons on the Standard toolbar for working with macros.

View *<Application>* Save *<Project>* Copy Find Redo Break Design Mode Properties Window Toolbox

Insert *<Item>* Cut Paste Undo Run Sub/UserForm (Continue) Reset Project Explorer Object Browser Office Assistant *or* Microsoft Visual Basic Help

View *<Application>*   Displays Word. This command is useful as a quick way to switch to the application window you were last working in; consider it an alternative to Alt+Tab or using the Taskbar.

Insert *<Item>*   Inserts the currently selected item—user form, module, class module, or procedure. You can click the drop-down button and select a different item from the resulting list.

Save *<Project>*   Saves the current project and all code in it. The current project is the one selected in the Project Explorer

Cut, Copy, and Paste   Cut, copy, and paste as usual.

Find   Displays the Find dialog box for finding and replacing text. The Visual Basic Editor's find-and-replace functionality is very weak compared to that in word processors such as Word or WordPerfect. For this reason, you may sometimes want to copy and paste the text of a code module into your word processor, run a complex find-and-replace sequence, and then drop it back into the Visual Basic Editor. Feel free to perform this sophisticated cheat: It works well, and can save you time and effort.

Undo and Redo   Work as usual, undoing and redoing your latest actions one by one.

Run Sub/UserForm   Starts (or restarts) running the current procedure or user form. The current procedure is the one in which the insertion point currently resides; the current user form is the one selected in the active window. If no procedure or user form is current, clicking this button displays the Macros dialog box for you to choose a macro to run. When a procedure or user form is running, the Run Sub/UserForm button changes into the Continue button.

Break   Pauses the currently executing procedure. (From the keyboard, you can press Ctrl+Break for the same effect.)

Reset   Stops the current procedure and clears all its variables.

Design Mode   Toggles Design mode on and off.

Project Explorer   Displays the Project Explorer window (if it isn't displayed) and activates it. This button doesn't toggle the Project Explorer off if it's displayed. To hide the Project Explorer, you need to click its close button or press Ctrl+F4 with the Project Explorer selected.

Properties Window   Displays the Properties window (if it isn't displayed) and activates it. This button too isn't a toggle: To hide the Properties window, click its close button or press Ctrl+F4 with the Properties window selected.

Object Browser   Displays the Object Browser (if it isn't displayed) and activates it. This button isn't a toggle either; use the close button or press Ctrl+F4 with the Object Browser selected to close the Object Browser.

Toolbox   Displays or hides the Toolbox when it's available.

Office Assistant or **Microsoft Visual Basic Help**   In Office applications, starts the Office Assistant. (If you've turned off the Office Assistant, clicking this button starts the Help system.) In non-Office applications, it launches the Microsoft Visual Basic Help application.

Line And Column Readout   Lists the current line number and column number of the insertion point in the active Code window. The column number is the number of characters (including spaces) between the left margin and the insertion point.

When Should You Run a Macro in the Visual Basic Editor?

As you saw in the previous chapter, you can run a macro from the host application in up to four ways: from the Macros dialog box, from a keyboard shortcut, from a toolbar button, or from a menu item or context menu item. You've just learned *how* to run a macro from the Visual Basic Editor. Now the question is, *when* should you run such a macro?

Running a macro from the Visual Basic Editor is useful not only for scrutinizing and debugging the macro (as you'll see shortly), but also for working with macros you create on the fly to deal with a specific problem. If you record such a macro, typically it will need looping or other tweaking in the Visual Basic Editor; and if you create such a macro from scratch, you'll be working in the Visual Basic Editor anyway. So, it often makes sense to arrange the Visual Basic Editor and the host application window in such a way that suitable areas of both are displayed. Then, run the macro from the Visual Basic Editor and watch the effects on the document or documents.

Continued

> **CONTINUED**
>
> For a macro with a short (or nonexistent) shelf life, there's no point in creating a keyboard shortcut, a toolbar button, or a menu item—and running it multiple times from the Visual Basic Editor is much easier than using the Macros dialog box. If you're still working in the Visual Basic Editor when the time comes to dispense with the macro's services, you can delete it in a couple of swift movements from the Code window.

The Edit Toolbar

The Edit toolbar, shown in Figure 3.7, provides more commands for running and editing macros. Here's a rundown of these commands:

FIGURE 3.7

Use the buttons on the Edit toolbar to run and edit macros.

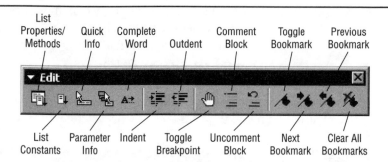

List Properties/Methods   Displays the pop-up List Properties/Methods list box when it's available.

List Constants   Displays the pop-up List Constants list box when it's available.

Quick Info   Displays information about the code where the insertion point is currently located.

Parameter Info   Displays pop-up information about the parameter where the insertion point is currently located.

Complete Word   Completes the word in which the insertion point is currently located.

Indent and Outdent   Indent and un-indent the current line of code or the currently selected lines. (You use indentation to indicate the relationship of one line of code to another, as you'll learn in the next chapter.)

Toggle Breakpoint   Toggles on and off a breakpoint at the current line.

Comment Block   "Comments out" the current line or selected lines by putting an apostrophe at the beginning of the line(s). (The apostrophe tells VBA that this line is a comment, which means that VBA won't try to execute it. VBA displays comment lines in a different color so you can readily identify them. For more information about this command, see the section "Commenting Out Lines" in Chapter 4.)

Uncomment Block   Removes commenting from the current line or selected lines.

Toggle Bookmark   Adds a bookmark to the current line (if it doesn't already have one) or removes a bookmark if the line already has one.

Next Bookmark   Moves the insertion point to the next bookmark.

Previous Bookmark   Moves the insertion point to the previous bookmark.

Clear All Bookmarks   Removes all bookmarks from the current project.

The Debug Toolbar

The Debug toolbar contains commands for running and debugging your macros. You'll take a closer look at this toolbar in Chapter 19.

The UserForm Toolbar

The UserForm toolbar contains buttons for working with user forms (such as dialog boxes). You'll start working with this toolbar in Chapter 13, "Making Decisions in Your Code."

The Project Explorer

The Project Explorer provides a way to navigate among the various components in the Visual Basic Editor. Figure 3.8 shows the Project Explorer for a Visual Basic Editor session with Word as the host application.

FIGURE 3.8

Use the Project Explorer to navigate to the module you want to work with.

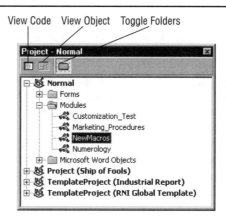

Depending on the host application and its capabilities, each project can contain some or all of the following elements:

- User forms (forms that make up part of the application's user interface, such as a custom dialog box).

- Modules containing macros, procedures, and functions.

- Class modules (modules that define objects, their properties, and their values).

- References to other projects or to library files (such as DLLs—Dynamic Link Libraries).

- Objects related to the application. For example, each AutoCAD project contains an AutoCAD Objects folder containing an object called ThisDrawing that you can use to work with the drawing's events (actions that the user can take). Each Word document and template contains a Microsoft Word Objects folder which holds a class object named ThisDocument. ThisDocument gives you access to the properties and events for the document or template.

For most host applications, each open document and template is considered a project and is displayed as a root in the project tree. The project tree also contains any global macro storage—such as the Normal.dot template in Word, the Personal Macro Workbook in Excel, the Global Macro Storage in WordPerfect, or the Global project in Auto-CAD—and any add-ins that are loaded.

As an example, in Figure 3.8, Normal.dot is identified as *Normal*, and the active document is identified as *Project (Ship of Fools)*. The template attached to the active document is identified as *TemplateProject(Industrial Report)*. A global template named TemplateProject(RNI Global Template) is also loaded; you can't tell it's a global template from the listing, but if you click its + sign to expand it, a message box will tell you the template is locked.

 TIP You can change the name of a project by using the Project Properties dialog box (which I'll discuss a little later in this chapter) or by selecting the project and entering a new name in the Properties window. Once you change the name, the project will be identified by that name in the Project Explorer, followed by the name of the document or template. For example, if you change the project name of the document Ship of Fools.doc to **Experiment**, the document project will be identified as Experiment(Ship of Fools) in the Project Explorer rather than Project(Ship of Fools).

You navigate the Project Explorer in the same way that you navigate the Windows Explorer tree: Click the boxed plus sign to the left of a project item to expand the view and display the items contained within the project, and click the resulting boxed minus sign to collapse the view and hide the items again. Double-click a module to display its code in the Code window; double-click a user form to display it.

You can display the Project Explorer by choosing View ➤ Project Explorer or by pressing Ctrl+R. To close the Project Explorer, click its close button. Because the Project Explorer provides fast and efficient navigation among the various elements of your VBA projects, it's usually easiest to keep it displayed unless you're short of screen space. You may also want to close it when you're working for long periods in the Code window and don't need to switch to other elements, or any time your need for screen acreage trumps your need for swift navigation. As you'll see later in this chapter, you can also undock the Project Explorer. This lets you push it aside when you need more room.

In Figure 3.8, three buttons appear on a toolbar at the top of the Project Explorer:

View Code   Displays the Code window for the selected object. For example, if you select a user form in the Project Explorer and click the View Code button, the Visual Basic Editor will display a Code window containing the code attached to the user form. If you select a module or a class module in the Project Explorer and click the View Code button, the Visual Basic Editor will display a Code window containing the code in the module. Usually, it's quicker to double-click the module or the class module you want to open than to select it and then click the View Code button.

View Object   Displays a window containing the selected object. The View Object button remains dimmed and unavailable until you select an object (such as a user form or a document) that can be displayed. If the selected object is a user form, clicking the View Object button will display the user form; if the selected object is a document, clicking the View Object button will display the Word document in the Word window.

Toggle Folders   Toggles the view of the objects in the Project Explorer between *folder view* (a view that shows the objects separated into their folders beneath the document projects or template projects that contain them) and *folder contents view* (which displays the objects within the projects that contain them). The left part of Figure 3.9 shows the Project Explorer for an application session sorted by folder view, and the right part shows the Project Explorer for the same situation in folder contents view. Whether you spend more time in folder view or folder contents view will depend on the size of your screen, the number of objects you put in any given project, and the way your mind works, not necessarily in that order. For many purposes, you'll want to toggle between folder view and folder contents view to locate objects most easily.

Folder view (left) displays the objects separated into folders beneath the projects that contain them. Folder contents view (right) displays the objects within the projects that contain them.

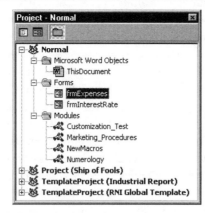

Apart from navigating to the items you need to work with, you can perform the following tasks with the Project Explorer:

- Add components to or remove them from a project. For example, you can use the Project Explorer to add a module or a user form to a project.

- Compare the components of one project to the components of another project. Such a comparison can be useful when you need to establish the differences between two or more projects quickly (for example, your reference copy of a company template and the copies users have been adding to).

- Move or copy items from one project to another. You can drag a code module, class module, or user form from one project to another in the Project Explorer to copy it, or from the Project Explorer in one session of the Visual Basic Editor to a project in the Project Explorer in another session. For example, you could drag a user form from a Visual Basic Editor session hosted by Visio to a Visual Basic Editor session hosted by AutoCAD to copy the user form.

- Import or export a code module or a user form to or from a project.

NOTE Many actions that you can perform through the Project Explorer you can also perform through the Visual Basic Editor's menu items, which is useful when the Project Explorer isn't displayed. In general, though, the Project Explorer provides the easiest way to navigate from module to module in the Visual Basic Editor, especially when you have several complex projects open at the same time. As you'd expect in a Windows application, right-clicking in the Project Explorer produces a context menu of commonly used commands.

The Object Browser

The Visual Basic Editor provides a full Object Browser for working with objects in VBA. You'll look at the Object Browser in detail in Chapter 8, and when you examine the object models for the various applications in Chapter 14, "Object Models." But, in the meantime, take a quick look at Figure 3.10, which shows the Object Browser for a Word VBA session. The Document object is selected in the left-hand panel, and its list of properties appears in the right-hand panel. You'll find that a number of these properties immediately make sense from your knowledge of Word documents. For example, the AttachedTemplate property tells you which template the document is currently attached to. Likewise, the Bookmarks property contains information on all the bookmarks in the document. The property information is displayed at the bottom of the Object Browser.

FIGURE 3.10

The Object Browser provides a quick way to look up objects and their properties. Here, you can see the properties contained in the Document object.

The Code Window

You'll do most of the actual work of creating and editing your macros in the Visual Basic Editor's Code window. The Visual Basic Editor provides a Code window for each open project, for each document section within the project that can contain code, and for each code module and user form in the project. Each Code window is identified by the project name, the name of the module within the project, and the word *Code* in parentheses. Figure 3.11 shows the Visual Basic Editor Code window with the `Transpose_Word_Right` macro open in it.

FIGURE 3.11

You create and edit macros in the Code window.

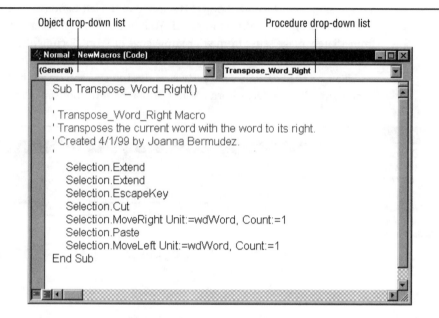

As you can see from the figure, two drop-down list boxes appear just below the title bar of the Code window:

- The Object drop-down list box at the upper-left corner of the Code window provides a quick way of navigating between different objects.

- The Procedure drop-down list box at the upper-right corner of the Code window lets you move quickly from procedure to procedure within the current module. Click the down-arrow button to display the drop-down list of procedures. You'll see that the first procedure is (Declarations), which takes you to the Declarations area of the current code sheet. In the Declarations area, as you'll see later in this chapter, you declare public variables and other VBA information that multiple procedures will need to know. Because the Declarations area is located at the beginning of the code sheet, choosing (Declarations) from the Procedure drop-down list box is an alternative way of moving the insertion point to the beginning of the code sheet. (Usually it's easier to use the scrollbar or a keyboard shortcut such as Ctrl+Home to move to the beginning of the code sheet.)

The Visual Basic Editor Code window provides a half-dozen features for helping you create code efficiently and accurately:

Complete Word   Completes the word you're typing, once you've typed enough letters to distinguish that word from any other. If you haven't typed enough letters to distinguish the word, the Visual Basic Editor gives you the closest possibilities. You can either type down through them or scroll through them to find the one you want. To activate Complete Word, press Ctrl+Spacebar or click the Complete Word button on the Edit toolbar.

Quick Info   Appears on the Edit toolbar. Displays syntax information on the current variable, function, method, statement, or procedure.

List Properties/Methods   Displays a pop-up list box containing properties and methods for the object you've just typed so that you can quickly complete the expression. List Properties/Methods is switched on by default and will automatically pop up the list box when you type a period within an expression. Select a property or method using either the mouse or the keyboard. Enter the property or method into the code either by double-clicking it, by pressing Tab (if you want to continue working on the same line after entering the property or method), or by pressing Enter (if you want to start a new line after entering the property or method).

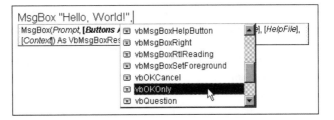

List Constants   Displays a pop-up list box containing constants for a property you've typed, so that you can quickly complete the expression. Again, you can use either the mouse or the keyboard to select the constant, and you can enter the constant by double-clicking it, by pressing Tab (to continue working on the same line), or by pressing Enter (to start a new line).

Data Tips Displays a ScreenTip containing the value of a variable the mouse pointer moves over when the Visual Basic Editor is in Break mode (a mode you use for testing and debugging macros).

```
Reply = MsgBox("Do you want to proceed?", vbYesNo)
Reply = 6
```

Margin Indicators Lets you quickly set a breakpoint, the next statement, or a bookmark by clicking in the margin of the Code window. You'll look at setting breakpoints, setting the next statement, and setting bookmarks later in this book.

Apart from these features, the Visual Basic Editor includes standard Office editing features such as copy and move, cut and paste, and drag and drop. Drag and drop is particularly useful, because you can drag code from one procedure or module to another.

Design à La Mode: What Time Is It Now?

As the Visual Basic Editor understands life, there are essentially three times or modes:

Design mode Also known as *design time*. Any time you're working in the Visual Basic Editor on your code, you're in Design mode. You don't have to be actively designing anything (although you often will be).

Run mode Also known as *runtime*. When code is running, you're in Run mode.

Break mode *Not* known as break time. When code is running, but execution is temporarily suspended, you're in Break mode. Break mode lets you step through your code one command or one procedure at a time (rather than running all the commands at once). You use it to debug or otherwise critique your code. You'll spend a lot of time in Break mode.

The Properties Window

The Visual Basic Editor provides a Properties window you can use to view and modify the properties of an object in VBA, such as a project, a module or class module, a user form, or a control (such as a button or check box in a dialog box). The drop-down list at the top of the Properties window lets you pick the object whose properties you want to view or modify. The Alphabetic page presents an alphabetical list of the properties in the item, and the Categorized page presents a list of the properties broken down into categories.

Figure 3.12 shows the properties for a relatively straightforward Excel workbook. For example, the HasRoutingSlip property is set to False, indicating that the workbook does not have an e-mail routing slip attached to it; and the Saved property is set to True, indicating that the workbook does not contain any unsaved changes.

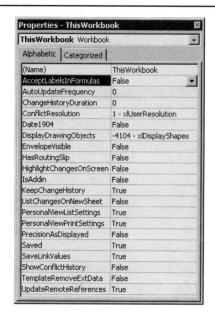

To display the Properties window, press F4 or choose View ➤ Properties Window. To change a property, click the cell containing the property name (if you want to select a different value for the property) or in the value cell (if you want to edit the value), and then change the value. You'll be able to choose different values depending on the type of property: For a True/False property, you'll be limited to those two choices in the drop-down list; for a text property such as Name, you can enter any valid VBA name.

You can resize the Properties window by dragging its borders or corners to display more properties, or to shrink the window so it takes up less space in the Visual Basic Editor. When the Properties window is docked below the Project Explorer (that is, in its default position), dragging the right border of either the Properties window or the Project Explorer resizes the other one of the pair as well.

The Immediate Window

As you'll have noticed from our scan through the menus and toolbars, the Visual Basic Editor includes a number of other windows that it doesn't display by default. Two of the key windows are the Object Browser and the Immediate window. You met the Object Browser a little earlier in this chapter; now, meet the Immediate window, which you'll use during the discussion of the VBA language in the next chapter. The Immediate window will help you see how VBA works, what the different parts of the VBA language are, and what those parts do.

The Immediate window, shown in Figure 3.13, is a small, unadorned window you can use as a virtual scratchpad to enter lines of code you want to test without entering them in the macro itself. When you type a line of code into the Immediate window and press the Enter key, the Visual Basic Editor executes that code.

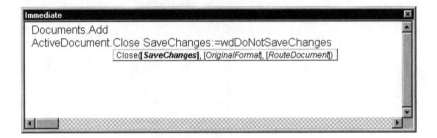

 NOTE You can also use the Immediate window to display information to help you check the values of variables and expressions while code is executing.

Setting Properties for a Project

While the thought of properties is fresh in your head, look quickly at the properties of each VBA project. You'll examine some of these properties right now, because it will be useful for you to know them. Others you'll revisit later in the book, when they become relevant.

To examine or set the properties for a project, right-click the project or one of its components in the Project Explorer and choose the Properties item from the context menu to display the Project Properties dialog box. Both the menu item and the resulting dialog box will be identified by the description of the project—for example, the properties dialog box for a template in Word will be identified as *TemplateProject–Project Properties*, and the properties dialog box for AutoCAD's Global project will be identified as *ACADProject–Project Properties*. Figure 3.14 shows the Project Properties dialog box for a Word document project.

FIGURE 3.14

Use the Project Properties dialog box to view and set the properties for a project, and to lock a project against change.

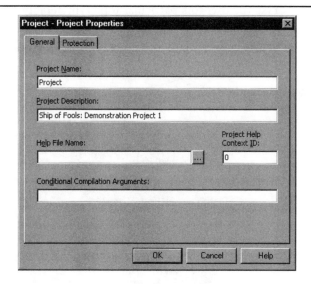

Here's what you can do on the General page of the Project Properties dialog box:

- Set the project name in the Project Name text box. This name identifies the project in the Object Browser (which you'll meet later in this chapter) and, when necessary, in the Windows Registry. Make sure the name is unique to avoid confusion with any other project. Technically, the project name is the name of the type library for the project (the *type library* describes the objects—such as modules and user forms—that the project contains); it is used to build the fully qualified class name of classes in the project (more on this later in the book).

- Enter a description of the project in the Project Description text box. This description will appear in the Description pane in the Object Browser to help the user understand what the project is. So be as concise, yet descriptive, as possible.

- Designate the Help file for the project by entering the name and path of the Help file in the Help File Name text box. Click the button marked with the ellipsis (…) to the right of the Help File Name text box to display the Help File dialog box. Then, select the file and click the Open button to enter the Help file name in the text box. (Alternatively, you can type the name and path.)

- Specify the Help context for the project in the Project Help Context ID text box. The Help context refers to a location in the Help file. The default Help context is 0, which causes the Help file to display the opening screen of the Help file (the same screen you'll see if you run the Help file from the Run dialog box or by double-clicking the file in Explorer). You can specify a different Help context to take the user to a particular topic—preferably, one relevant to the project on which they're seeking Help.

- Specify any conditional compilation arguments needed for the project.

Here's what you can do on the Protection page of the Project Properties dialog box, shown in Figure 3.15:

- Select the Lock Project For Viewing check box to prevent other people from opening the project, viewing it, and changing it without knowing the password.

- In the Password To View Project Properties group box, enter a password for the project in the Password text box, and enter the same password in the Confirm Password text box. Click the OK button and close the project. Now nobody will be able to open and view (let alone change) the project if they don't know the password.

TIP   If you enter a password in the Password text box and the Confirm Password text box, but you don't select the Lock Project For Viewing check box, the Visual Basic Editor will prompt you for the password the next time you try to display the Project Properties dialog box. However, you'll be able to open and view the project and its contents without supplying the password.

Customizing the Visual Basic Editor

Given how much time you're likely to spend in the Visual Basic Editor, you ought to customize it so you can work as quickly and comfortably as possible. For most people, this means the following:

- Choosing editor and view preference settings in the Visual Basic Editor to control how it interacts with you

- Choosing which windows to display in the Visual Basic Editor and laying them out to use your workspace as effectively as possible

- Customizing the toolbar and menus in the Visual Basic Editor so the commands you need are at hand (without cluttering up your workspace)

- Customizing the Toolbox so it contains the tools you need to build your user forms

In the upcoming sections, I'll offer some suggestions for optimizing the Visual Basic Editor. Check them against your version of reality and see how they match; choose the ones you like and try them out. If you choose not to implement any of the suggestions, that's fine—they should still give you some ideas for customizing the Visual Basic Editor.

Before you start, know that once you make a customization, it will apply across all hosts using that version of VBA. For example, if you change the font in the Visual Basic Editor session hosted by Excel 2000 to Complex (Cyrillic)—a fine if somewhat spare font—your subsequent Visual Basic Editor sessions hosted by VBA 6 hosts such as Word 2000 and PowerPoint 2000 will show all text in Code windows in Complex (Cyrillic).

Choosing Editor and View Preferences

Like any good Windows application, the Visual Basic Editor lets you customize its look and its actions. In this section, I'll discuss the options the Visual Basic Editor offers, from Editor settings to the way the component windows are docked in the main window. Along the way, I'll make a few recommendations on key settings. When I don't make a recommendation for a setting, I'll point out pros and cons you should know about when choosing settings for yourself.

To begin choosing editor and view preferences, choose Tools ➤ Options to open the Options dialog box. It contains four pages, as you can see in Figure 3.16. The first page is the Editor page, which is where you'll start.

FIGURE 3.16

*The Editor page of the
Options dialog box*

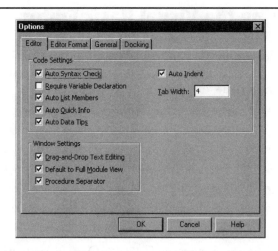

Editor Page Options

The Editor page of the Options dialog box includes the following settings:

Auto Syntax Check   Controls whether VBA displays warning message boxes when it discovers errors while automatically checking your syntax as you type expressions This feature is usually helpful because VBA can instantly point out errors that would otherwise remain unseen until you tried to run or debug your code. But, if your style is to flit from one unfinished line of code to another (and ultimately finish all the lines at your convenience), you may want to turn off this feature to prevent the Visual Basic Editor from bombarding you with message boxes for errors you're aware of but can't yet fix. Even if you turn Auto Syntax Check off, the Visual Basic Editor will still turn red the offending lines of code to draw your attention to them.

Require Variable Declaration   Governs whether you must declare variables explicitly. Declaring variables explicitly is a little more work than declaring them implicitly, but it's good practice and will save you time down the road—so make sure that this check box is selected.

Auto List Members   Controls whether the List Properties/Methods and List Constants features automatically suggest properties, methods, and constants as you work in the Code window. Most people find these features helpful, because they let you find the properties, methods, and constants you need to enter code quickly. When you've typed enough of the name of a property, method, or constant to identify it on the list, press Tab or another punctuation key to enter the rest of the name. Some experienced programmers turn these features off because they *know* all the properties, methods, and constants they need and prefer not to be distracted by a busy interface. Figure 3.17 shows the Auto List Members feature at work.

Use the Auto List Members feature to get maximum assistance from the Visual Basic Editor.

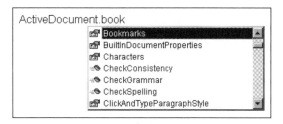

 NOTE Apart from the busy-ness of the interface, you may also want to turn off features such as Auto List Members, Auto Quick Info, and Auto Data Tips because they take up memory and processing power and may slow your computer. This small speed difference isn't likely to bother you unless your computer is ancient and slow (maybe a 486 with fewer megahertz than your age and less RAM than you have fingers and toes).

Auto Quick Info   Controls whether the Quick Info feature automatically displays information about functions and their parameters as you work with functions in the Code window. I recommend keeping this check box selected. Seeing a list of the required and optional parameters when working with a function can help you place your arguments correctly and avoid missing arguments that will trip up your code later. In addition, the list will remind you of optional arguments that can enhance the code you're trying to create. Figure 3.18 shows Auto Quick Info at work, displaying information about the SaveAs method of the ActiveDocument object.

Select the Auto Quick Info check box on the Editor page of the Options dialog box to make the Quick Info feature display information about the function you're working with.

ActiveDocument.SaveAs

SaveAs(**[FileName]**, [FileFormat], [LockComments], [Password], [AddToRecentFiles], [WritePassword], [ReadOnlyRecommended], [EmbedTrueTypeFonts], [SaveNativePictureFormat], [SaveFormsData], [SaveAsAOCELetter])

Auto Data Tips   Controls whether the Visual Basic Editor displays ScreenTips when you hover the mouse pointer over a variable or expression in Break mode. The ScreenTip displayed enables you to check the value of a variable or expression quickly without using a more space-expensive option such as the Locals window or the Watch window. Figure 3.19 shows an example of the information that Auto Data Tips displays when the mouse pointer is hovered over the variable TestWord.

FIGURE 3.19

Use the Auto Data Tips feature to quickly check the value of a variable or expression.

```
TestWord = Documents("Ship of Fools.doc").Paragraphs(7).Range.Words(1).Text
If TestWord = "Table" Then
TestWord = "Devastating"
```

Auto Indent   Controls whether the Visual Basic Editor automatically indents subsequent lines of code after you've indented a line. When Auto Indent is switched on, the Visual Basic Editor starts each new line of code indented to the same level (the same number of tabs or spaces, or the same combination of the two) as the previous line. When Auto Indent is switched off, the Visual Basic Editor starts each new line of code at the left margin of the Code window. Usually, automatic indentation is a timesaver, although it means that each time you need to decrease a new line's level of indentation, you must press Shift+Tab, click the Outdent button on the Edit toolbar, or delete the tabs or spaces.

Tab Width   Sets the number of spaces in a tab. You can adjust this setting from 1 to 32 spaces. The default setting is four spaces, which works well for the default font. If you choose to use a proportional font (such as Times or Arial) rather than a monospaced font (such as Courier) for your code, you may want to increase the number of spaces a tab represents in order to clarify the levels of indentation in your code.

Drag-And-Drop Text Editing   Controls whether the Visual Basic Editor supports drag-and-drop. Most people find this feature helpful. You can drag portions of your code around the Code window, or from one Code window to another. You can also drag code into the Immediate window (which will accept whole statements—indeed, whole procedures) and into the Watch window (which will choke on anything other than an expression it can deal with, and will issue an error message).

Default To Full Module View   Controls whether the Visual Basic Editor displays all the procedures in a module in one list (Full Module view) or displays them one at a time (Procedure view). If you're working with short procedures, you may find Full Module view useful; for most other purposes, the individual view provides a less cluttered and more workable effect. When working in Procedure view, you open the procedure you want to work with by choosing it from the Procedure drop-down list at the top of the Code window, as shown in Figure 3.20. Make your choice in the Options dialog box depending on whether you typically work with short or long procedures. You can easily toggle between Full Module view and Procedure view at will by clicking the Full Module view or Procedure view button in the lower-left corner of any Code window.

NOTE You can also use the Procedures drop-down list when working in Full Module view to quickly move to a procedure by name.

FIGURE 3.20

When working in Procedure view, use the Procedure drop-down list to move to a procedure.

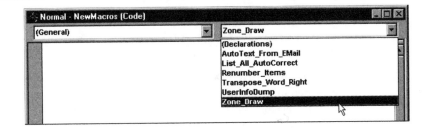

Procedure Separator Controls whether the Visual Basic Editor displays horizontal lines to separate the procedures within a module shown in Full Module view in the Code window. Usually these lines are helpful, providing a quick reference as to where one procedure ends and the next begins. (If you're using Procedure view, this check box isn't relevant.)

Editor Format Page Options

The Editor Format page of the Options dialog box, shown in Figure 3.21, controls how code appears in the Visual Basic Editor.

FIGURE 3.21

The Editor Format page of the Options dialog box

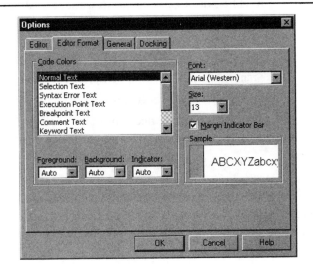

You can change the default colors for various types of text used in procedures by choosing them (one at a time) in the Code Colors list box and selecting colors from the Foreground, Background, and Indicator drop-down lists. Here's what the Code Colors choices mean:

Normal Text   Takes care of much of the text in a typical procedure. You'll probably want to make this a conventional color (such as black, the default).

Selection Text   Affects the color of selected (highlighted) text.

Syntax Error Text   Affects the color VBA uses for offending lines. (By default, this text is fire-engine red so that it jumps out at you.)

Execution Point Text   Affects the color VBA uses for the line currently being executed in Break mode. You'll usually want to make this a highlighter color (like the classic fluorescent yellow the Visual Basic Editor uses as the default) so you can immediately see the current line.

Breakpoint Text   Affects the color in which VBA displays breakpoints (points where execution of the procedure will stop).

Comment Text   Affects the color of comment lines. You may want to change this color to emphasize comments or to make them fade into the background. The default color for comments is dark green. When working with comments—for example, when cleaning up a project and documenting your code—you might temporarily apply a more striking color so your comments are easier to find.

Keyword Text   Affects the color of keywords (words recognized as part of the VBA language). Such text accounts for a sizable portion of each procedure. You should display keywords in a different color than normal text, because it's helpful to be able to distinguish keywords without needing to read the code. By default, keywords are displayed in dark blue, which is appropriately discreet but visibly different than the default black used for code.

Identifier Text   Affects the color VBA uses for identifiers. Identifiers include the names of variables, constants, and procedures you define.

Bookmark Text   Affects the color VBA uses for the bookmarks in your code.

Call Return Text   Affects the color VBA uses for calls to other procedures. By default, the Visual Basic Editor uses lime green for call return text.

You can change the font and size of all the text in the Code window by using the Font and Size drop-down lists on the Editor Format tab. You can also prevent the display of the margin indicator bar (in which items such as the Next Statement and Breakpoint icons appear) by clearing the Margin Indicator Bar check box. (Usually, these icons are helpful, but removing this bar can slightly increase your viewable-screen real estate.)

General Page Options

The General page of the Options dialog box, shown in Figure 3.22, contains several categories of settings. I'll discuss them in groups in the following sections.

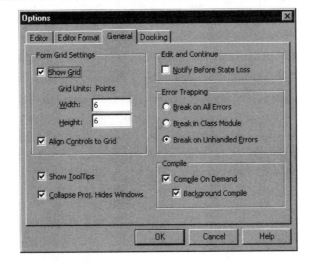

Form Grid Settings Group Box   The Form Grid Settings control how the Visual Basic Editor handles user forms:

- The Show Grid check box controls whether the Visual Basic Editor displays a grid pattern of dots on the user form in Design mode to help you place and align controls. Whether you leave this check box selected (as it is by default) or clear it is up to you. The grid pattern irritates me, and I turn it off except for those rare occasions when it can actively benefit me.

- The Width and Height text boxes set the spacing of the dots that make up the grid. You can set any value from 2 points to 60 points (the default setting is 6 points). If you display the grid on screen, you'll see the dots; if you don't display the grid, it still affects the Align Controls To Grid feature, discussed next. Experiment and find the coarseness of grid that you can most easily work with.

- The Align Controls To Grid check box governs whether the Visual Basic Editor automatically snaps the edges of controls you place or move to the nearest grid line. This option lets you place controls in approximately the right positions rapidly and easily, but it can be frustrating when you're trying to improve the layout of controls you've already placed on a user form. (If so, one option is to clear the Align Controls To Grid check box; another is to leave it selected but to temporarily decrease the size of the grid.)

The Edit And Continue Group Box   The Edit And Continue group box contains only one control—the Notify Before State Loss check box. This check box controls whether the Visual Basic Editor warns you, when you're running a project, if you try to take an action that will require VBA to reset the values of all variables in the module. You'll need to establish for yourself whether this warning saves you from missteps or merely slows you down when you know full well that you're about to reset a project.

Error Trapping Group Box   The Error Trapping group box contains three option buttons you use to specify how VBA handles errors that occur when you're running code:

Break On All Errors   Tells VBA to enter Break mode when it encounters any error, no matter whether an error handler (a section of code designed to handle errors) is active or whether the code is in a class module. Break On All Errors is useful for pinpointing where errors occur, which helps you track them down and remove them. If you've included an error handler in your code, you probably won't need this option.

Break In Class Module   Arguably the most useful option for general use. When VBA encounters an unhandled error in a class module (a module that defines a type of object), VBA enters Break mode at the offending line of code.

Break On Unhandled Errors   The default setting, this is useful when you've constructed an error handler to handle predictable errors in the current module. If there is an error handler, VBA allows the handler to trap the error and doesn't enter Break mode; but if there is no handler for the error generated, VBA enters Break mode on the offending line of code. An unhandled error in a class module, however, causes the project to enter Break mode on the line of code that invoked the offending procedure of the class, thus enabling you to identify (and alter) the line that caused the problem.

Compile Group Box   The Compile group box controls when VBA compiles the code for a project into executable code. Before any code can be executed, it needs to be compiled; but not all the code in a project must necessarily be compiled before the Visual Basic Editor can start executing the first parts of the code.

You can select the Compile On Demand check box if you want VBA to compile the code only as needed. VBA compiles the code in the procedure you're running before starting to execute that procedure, but it doesn't compile code in other procedures in the same module unless the procedure you're running calls them. As a result, execution of the procedure you run first in a module can begin as soon as VBA finishes compiling the code for that procedure. If the procedure then calls another procedure in the module, VBA compiles the code for the second procedure when the first procedure calls it, not when you begin running the first procedure.

Compile On Demand is usually a good option. It's especially useful when you're building a number of procedures in a module and have semi-completed code lying around in some of them. In contrast, if you clear the Compile On Demand check box, VBA will compile all the code in all the procedures in the module before starting to execute the procedure you want to run. This means that not only will the procedure start a little later (more code takes more time to compile), but any language error or compile error in any procedure in the module will prevent you from running the current procedure, even if the code in that procedure contains no errors.

Suppose you have a module named Compilation that contains two procedures, GoodCode and BadCode, which look like this:

```
Sub GoodCode()
    MsgBox "This code is working."
End Sub


Sub BadCode()
    Application.Destroy
End Sub
```

GoodCode simply displays a message box to indicate that it's working, whereas Bad-Code contains an invalid statement (there is, fortunately, no Destroy method for the Application object in any application I've seen). GoodCode will run without causing a problem, but BadCode will cause an error every time.

If you try to run GoodCode with Compile On Demand switched on, the procedure will run fine: VBA will compile the code in GoodCode, will find no errors, and will run it. But if you try to run GoodCode with Compile On Demand switched off, VBA will compile the code in BadCode as well before starting to run GoodCode—and it will stop with a compile error at the bogus Application.Destroy statement. This thorough checking before running any code is good for finished modules that work together, but it's the kiss of death when you're experimenting with code in a module.

On the other hand, you can see the advantage of compiling all the code in the module when GoodCode calls BadCode, as in the third line of this version of the procedure:

```
Sub GoodCode()
    MsgBox "This code is working."
    BadCode
End Sub
```

Here, compiling the code in BadCode before starting to run GoodCode is a good idea, because doing so prevents GoodCode from running if BadCode contains an error. If you run this version of GoodCode with Compile On Demand switched on, VBA will compile GoodCode and start to run it, displaying the message box in the second line. The BadCode call in the third line will then cause VBA to compile BadCode, at which point VBA will stop with the compile error. As you can imagine, you don't want this to happen in the middle of a complex procedure; in such a case, you'd want Compile On Demand switched off.

The Background Compile check box, which is available when the Compile On Demand check box is selected, controls whether the Visual Basic Editor uses idle CPU time to compile further code while it's running the code that it has already compiled. Keep Background Compile switched on unless you suspect that it's slowing the execution of your code.

Show ToolTips and Collapse Proj. Hides Windows   The final two options on the General page of the Options dialog box are Show ToolTips and Collapse Proj. Hides Windows. The Show ToolTips check box controls whether the Visual Basic Editor displays ToolTips (a.k.a. ScreenTips) for its toolbar buttons. While you're learning your way around the Visual Basic Editor, you'll probably want to display the ToolTips; after that, you may decide to switch them off and conserve the tiny amount of memory and processor cycles they consume.

The Collapse Proj. Hides Windows check box controls whether the Visual Basic Editor hides the Code window and other project windows that you collapse in the Project Explorer's tree. This check box is selected by default, and in general it's a useful feature. When you collapse a project in the Project Explorer, the Visual Basic Editor hides any Code windows or user form windows belonging to that project and removes them from the list that appears on the Window menu. When you expand the project again, the Visual Basic Editor displays the windows in their previous positions and restores them to the Window menu's list.

Docking Page Options

The Docking page of the Options dialog box, shown in Figure 3.23, controls whether the various windows in the Visual Basic Editor are dockable—that is, whether they attach automatically to a side of the window when you move them there. Keeping windows dockable usually makes for a more organized interface. However, you may want to make the windows undockable so you can drag them off the edge of the screen as necessary and arrange them as you like.

FIGURE 3.23

The Docking page of the Options dialog box

Choosing and Laying Out the Editor Windows

Next, you can choose how to lay out the windows in the Visual Basic Editor. Your layout depends largely on screen real estate and personal preference, but here are a couple of suggestions:

- Always maximize the Code window. If you write long lines of code and break them to a reasonable length only under duress once everything is working, you'll want to free as much space in the Visual Basic Editor window as possible. Much of the time that you're actively writing code, you can dispense with the Project Explorer, invoking it only when you need it. As a handy way of getting it back, put the Project Explorer command on the Code Window, Code Window Break, Watch Window, Immediate Window, and Locals Window context menus. (I'll discuss how to do this in the next section.)

- If you undock some of the windows, you can collapse them to icons at the bottom of the Visual Basic Editor window. I don't find this feature particularly useful (to tell the truth, I don't find it useful at all), but some people may.

- If you're using a multi-monitor arrangement, you'll wish you could drag the child windows outside the Visual Basic Editor parent window and onto the second monitor. Unfortunately, they won't go far beyond the boundaries of the parent window. But you can achieve a similar effect by expanding the Visual Basic Editor window from the right-hand monitor onto the left-hand monitor, and then docking the Properties window and the Project Explorer on the left-hand monitor. The appearance of the menu bar and toolbar will suffer, but you'll have more space for the Code window, and all three windows will be available. (Your optometrist will hate you, but hey, that's part of their job.)

Customizing the Toolbar and Menu Bar

As you might guess from the way it's constructed, the Visual Basic Editor supports the same toolbar and menu bar customizations as the Office applications. As a result, you can customize the interface of the Visual Basic Editor so that all the commands you need are right at hand.

To customize the Visual Basic Editor, choose View ➣ Toolbars ➣ Customize (or right-click one of the toolbars or the menu bar and choose Customize from the context menu) to display the Customize dialog box, shown in Figure 3.24.

FIGURE 3.24

Use the Customize dialog box to customize the Visual Basic Editor's menu bar, toolbar, and context menus.

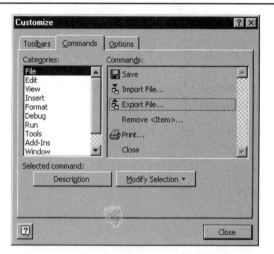

 NOTE Unlike the Office 2000 applications, the Visual Basic Editor doesn't let you create new menus or customize keyboard shortcuts—more's the pity.

You can now customize the toolbars, menus, and context menus to suit the way you work. Above all, if you use the context menus, be sure to customize them so they provide the commands you need. In particular, you may want to add two key commands to the context menus: Comment Block and Uncomment Block. As you saw earlier in the chapter, the Comment Block command adds a comment apostrophe (') to the beginning of each line of code in the selected block, making the line into a comment that VBA won't execute. The Uncomment Block command removes the first comment apostrophe from each command in the selected block, activating those lines that don't have further comment apostrophes. (Any line that's commented before you run the Comment Block command will remain commented after you run the Uncomment Block command. You can run the Uncomment Block command again to remove further commenting.) These commands are available from the Edit toolbar in the normal configuration of the Visual Basic Editor, but it's much easier to make them available at all times in the Code window from the context menu.

The Visual Basic Editor provides the context menus listed in Table 3.1. To customize a context menu, select the Shortcut Menus check box in the Toolbars list on the Toolbars page of the Customize dialog box, then drag the command you want from the Commands page of the dialog box onto your victim context menu.

TABLE 3.1: CONTEXT MENUS IN THE VISUAL BASIC EDITOR

Context Menu	Appears When You Right-Click In or On
MSForms	A user form
MSForms Control	A control on a user form
MSForms Control Group	A group of controls on a user form
MSForms MPC	A multipage control on a user form
Code Window	The Code window in Design mode
Code Window (Break)	The context menu in Break mode
Watch Window	The Watch window
Immediate Window	The Immediate window
Locals Window	The Locals window
Project Window	The Project window in Design mode
Project Window (Break)	The Project window in Break mode
Object Browser	The Object Browser
MSForms Palette	The clear space on a page in the Toolbox
MSForms Toolbox	The tab on a page in the Toolbox.
MSForms DragDrop	An item on a user form: drag it, and drop it elsewhere on the user form
Property Browser	A property in the Properties window
Docked Window	A docked window (for example, the Project Explorer)

Exactly how you customize the interface of the Visual Basic Editor is up to you—although I'll be happy to throw out a couple of suggestions to get you thinking about it:

- If you use the Locals window often to track the value of variables when stepping through your code, place a button for it on a toolbar that you always keep displayed (the standard button is on the Debug toolbar); or, place an item for it on the context menus for the Code window (both in Design mode and in Break mode), Watch window, and Immediate window.

- The same suggestion goes for the Watch window and the Immediate window. Put them on the context menus for the windows from which you'll invoke them.

- If you have a medium-sized monitor, you'll probably want to group all the toolbar buttons you use on one toolbar, so that you don't waste space by displaying multiple toolbars.

Customizing the Toolbox

Earlier in this chapter, you looked briefly at the Toolbox in the context of the Visual Basic Editor. Although a full discussion of creating and customizing user forms lies ahead of us, I'd like to talk about how you can customize the Toolbox. Such a discussion fits in with customizing the rest of the Visual Basic Editor to suit the way you work.

In this section, I'll show you how you can customize the Toolbox by adding controls, removing controls, and adding new Toolbox pages of your own. You'll typically do this to put your most-used controls on the Toolbox probably all on one page, to save yourself time. These controls will include customized variations on the regular Toolbox controls; by putting them on the Toolbox, you can avoid having to customize them again. For example, many dialog boxes you create will need an OK button that dismisses the dialog box, implements some code, and then continues execution of the procedure. Each OK button will need its `Name` property set to `cmdOK`, its `Caption` property set to `OK`, its `Default` property set to `True`, and its `Height` and `Width` properties set to something more sensible than the clunky dimensions the Visual Basic Editor assigns by default. Once you've made the effort to customize a command button, you can simply place a copy of the customized button on the Toolbox and reuse it for subsequent forms. (I'll show you how to do this in just a second.)

Another reason to customize the Toolbox is to add fancy controls that extend the things you can do with dialog boxes and user forms.

Adding Controls to the Toolbox

Let's start with adding controls to the Toolbox directly from a user form, because you'll probably want to do this first. For example, once you've created custom OK and Cancel buttons, you can copy them from the user form to the Toolbox so you can reuse them in any user forms you subsequently create.

To copy a control from a displayed user form to the Toolbox, just drag it and drop it, as shown in Figure 3.25.

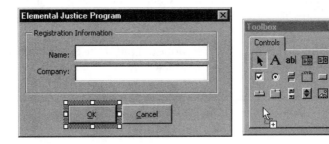

To add controls to the Toolbox, right-click in the page to which you want to add controls (I'll discuss how to add pages to the Toolbox in a moment), and choose Additional Controls from the context menu to display the Additional Controls dialog box shown in Figure 3.26. In the Available Controls list box, select the check boxes for the controls you want to add to the Toolbox, and then click the OK button. (To collapse the list to only the currently selected items, select the Selected Items Only check box in the Show group box.)

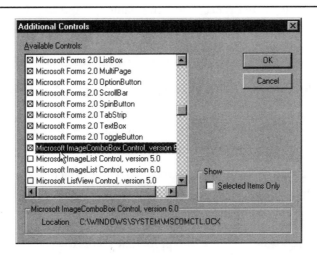

You can move a control from one page of the Toolbox to another by dragging it from the page it's on, moving the mouse pointer (still dragging) over the tab of the destination page to display that page. Then, move the mouse pointer down (again, still dragging) into the body of that page and drop the control.

Renaming a Toolbox Control

As you've seen, when you move the mouse pointer over a control in the Toolbox, a ScreenTip appears, showing the name of that control. To rename a control, right-click it in the Toolbox and choose the Customize item from the context menu to display the Customize Control dialog box, shown in Figure 3.27. (The menu item will be identified by the name of the control—for example, if the control is identified as New Label, the menu item will be Customize New Label.)

Enter the name for the control in the Tool Tip Text text box (delete or change the existing name as necessary); this name will appear as a ScreenTip when the user moves the mouse pointer over the control in the Toolbox. Then, if you wish, assign a different picture to the control's Toolbox icon, as described in the next section. Otherwise, click the OK button to close the Customize Control dialog box.

Assigning a Picture to a Control's Toolbox Icon

Each control in the Toolbox is identified by a picture. You can change the picture assigned to the control by using the Edit Picture button or the Load Picture button in the Customize Control dialog box.

Editing or Creating a Picture   To edit the picture assigned to the control, right-click the control, choose Customize from the context menu to display the Customize Control dialog box, and click the Edit Picture button to display the Edit Image dialog box shown in Figure 3.28. Here, you can adjust the picture pixel by pixel in the Picture edit box by choosing the appropriate color. You can also choose the Erase tool in the Colors group box and click the square you want to change. Use the Move buttons to move the entire image around the edit box (each direction button will be available only if the image doesn't touch that edge of the edit box); use the Clear button to erase the entire image and start from scratch. Use the Preview group box to see how the picture looks at the resolution it will appear in the Toolbox.

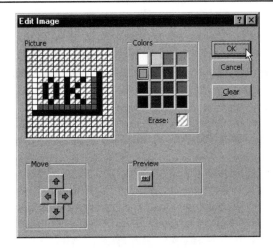

When you finish adjusting the image, click the OK button to return to the Customize Control dialog box. Click the OK button again to close that dialog box.

Loading a Picture   If you have existing pictures for controls (for example, images you or your colleagues created on another computer), you can load them to make the controls easy to identify.

To load an existing picture for a control, right-click the control, choose Customize from the context menu to display the Customize Control dialog box, and click the Load Picture button in the Customize Control dialog box to display the Load Picture dialog box. Select the picture and click the Open button to load it.

Removing Controls from the Toolbox

To remove a control from the Toolbox, right-click it and choose the Delete item from the context menu. The item will be identified by the name of the control—for example, if you right-click a control named Company Name Combo Box, the menu item will be named Delete Company Name Combo Box. If the item is a custom control, this action gets rid of the control, and you can't restore it (unless you have a copy elsewhere). If the item is one of the Microsoft-supplied controls that come with the Microsoft Forms 2.0 package (which is part of VBA), you can restore it from the Additional Controls dialog box by selecting the check box for the appropriate object (for example, Microsoft Forms 2.0 CommandButton).

You can also remove controls from the Toolbox by deleting the entire page they're on. I'll discuss how to do this in just a moment.

Adding Pages to the Toolbox

To add a page to the Toolbox, right-click the tab at the top of a page (or the label on the tab) and choose New Page from the context menu. The Visual Basic Editor will add a new page named New Page, to which it will add the Select Objects control. This control appears on every page in the Toolbox (so that it's always at hand), and you can't remove it.

You'll probably want to rename the new page immediately.

Renaming Pages in the Toolbox

To change the name of a Toolbox page, right-click its tab or label and choose Rename from the context menu to display the Rename dialog box. Enter the caption (that is, the label) in the Caption text box, enter any control tip text in the Control Tip Text text box, and click the OK button to close the dialog box.

Removing Pages from the Toolbox

To remove a page from the Toolbox, right-click its tab or label and choose Delete Page from the context menu. The Visual Basic Editor will remove the page from the Toolbox without any confirmation, regardless of whether the page contains controls.

Importing and Exporting Toolbox Pages

If you need to share Toolbox pages, you can save them as separate files and distribute them to your colleagues. Toolbox pages have a .PAG file extension.

To import a Toolbox page, right-click the tab or label on an existing page in the Toolbox and choose Import Page from the context menu to display the Import Page dialog box (an Open dialog box in disguise). Select the page you want to import and choose the Open button. The Visual Basic Editor will add the new page after the last page currently in the Toolbox, and will name it New Page. You can then rename the page as described earlier in this section.

Likewise, you can export a Toolbox page by right-clicking its tab or label and choosing Export Page from the context menu to display the Export Page dialog box (a disguised version of the Save As dialog box). Enter a name for the page (change folders if necessary) and click the Save button to save it. Now anyone can import the page as just described.

Moving Pages in the Toolbox

To move a page in the Toolbox, right-click its tab or label and choose Move from the context menu to display the Page Order dialog box. In the Page Order list box, select the page or pages you want to move (Shift+click to select multiple contiguous pages, Ctrl+click to select multiple pages individually) and use the Move Up and Move Down buttons to rearrange the pages as desired. Click the OK button to close the Page Order dialog box when you've finished.

Closing the Visual Basic Editor and Returning to the Host Application

When you finish an editing session in the Visual Basic Editor, you can either close the Visual Basic Editor or leave it running but switch to another window:

- To close the Visual Basic Editor, choose File ➤ Close And Return To *<Application>*, press Alt+Q, or click the close button on the Visual Basic Editor window.

- To leave the Visual Basic Editor running and work in another application, switch to the other application by using the Taskbar or pressing Alt+Tab.

In the next chapter, you'll put the Visual Basic Editor into action, editing the macros you recorded in Chapter 2. Turn the page.

CHAPTER 4

Editing Recorded Macros

FEATURING:

n this chapter, I'll show you how to use the Visual Basic Editor to edit a macro you've recorded. For the examples, I'll use the macros you recorded in Chapter 2 in Word, Excel, PowerPoint, and Project.

As you learned in Chapter 2, WordPerfect, Visio, and AutoCAD do not support the Macro Recorder; therefore, you cannot record VBA macros in these applications: You have to write VBA code from scratch, which you'll start doing in the next chapter. (WordPerfect has a macro recorder for recording macros in its own macro language, but it does not record in VBA.)

Even if you don't have an application that supports the Macro Recorder, you may still want to read through this chapter, because it shows you how to use some of the key editing features of the Visual Basic Editor.

There are three reasons for working with macros in the Visual Basic Editor:

- First, to fix any problems in the way a macro you recorded is executing. For example, if you made a misstep when recording the macro, the macro will keep performing that wrong instruction every time you run it, unless you remove or change the instruction.

- Second, to add further instructions to the macro to make it behave differently (as mentioned earlier). This is a great way to get started with VBA, because by making relatively simple changes to a recorded macro, you can greatly increase its power and flexibility.

- Third, to create new macros by writing them in the Visual Basic Editor instead of recording them. You can write a new macro from scratch or cull parts of an existing macro as appropriate.

The remainder of this book will be devoted largely to these topics. You'll begin by examining some quick methods of detecting problems in your macros, and then you'll edit the macros you recorded in Chapter 2.

Testing a Macro in the Visual Basic Editor

If a macro fails when you try to run it from the host application, the quickest way to find out what's going wrong is to open the macro in the Visual Basic Editor. (To open the macro in the Visual Basic Editor, choose Tools ➤ Macro ➤ Macros to display the Macro dialog box, select the macro, and click the Edit button.) Then run the macro by clicking the Run Sub/UserForm button on the Standard toolbar in the Visual Basic Editor. If the macro encounters an error and crashes, VBA will display an error message box on screen and will select the offending statement in the Code window. You can then use the editing tools described in the previous sections to change the statement.

WARNING Always test your macros on files (or copies of files) that you don't care about. There are many better ways to lose valuable work than to unleash untested macros on it.

Stepping through a Macro

For subtler problems—for example, if the macro is selecting almost, but not quite, the text you want, and you can't tell which command is superfluous (or plain wrong)—arrange the Visual Basic Editor window and the active application window so you can see them both. (For example, right-click in open space on the Windows Taskbar and choose Tile Windows Horizontally or Tile Windows Vertically from the context menu.) Position the insertion point in a suitable place in the application window and click the Visual Basic Editor window to activate it. Then position the insertion point in the macro you want to run and press F8 to step through the macro command by command. Each time you press F8, one line of your VBA code will be executed. (You can also choose Debug ➢ Step Into or click the Step Into button on the Debug toolbar, but usually the F8 key is easiest to use.) The Visual Basic Editor will highlight each command as it's executed, and you can watch the effect in the application window to catch errors. Figure 4.1 provides an example of stepping through a macro recorded in Word, and Video_16.avi on the CD demonstrates the process.

FIGURE 4.1

To catch what a macro is doing wrong, arrange the application window and the Visual Basic Editor window so that you can see them both. Then step through the macro by pressing the F8 key or using the Step Into command.

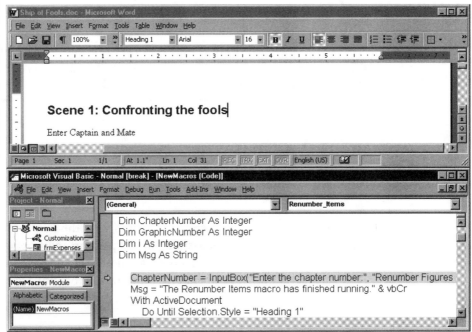

You'll learn about debugging macros in detail in Chapter 18, "Debugging Your Code." In the meantime, here are a couple of easy things you may want to try to resolve problems quickly in your macros: setting breakpoints and commenting out lines.

Setting Breakpoints

A breakpoint is a toggle switch you set on a line of code to tell VBA to stop executing the macro there. By using a breakpoint, you can run through functional parts of a macro at full speed, and then stop where you want to begin watching the code execute statement by statement.

To toggle a breakpoint on or off, right-click in a line of executable code (not a comment line) and choose Toggle ➤ Breakpoint from the context menu or click the Toggle Breakpoint button on the Edit toolbar. Alternatively, click in the margin indicator bar next to the line of code. A line on which you set a breakpoint is shaded brown by default. The breakpoint itself is designated by a brown circle in the margin indicator bar, as you can see in Figure 4.2. Video_17.avi on the CD demonstrates setting and removing breakpoints.

FIGURE 4.2

Use a breakpoint (the brown circle that appears in the margin indicator bar) to stop code execution at a line of your choice.

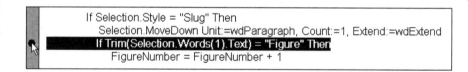

```
If Selection.Style = "Slug" Then
    Selection.MoveDown Unit:=wdParagraph, Count:=1, Extend:=wdExtend
    If Trim(Selection.Words(1).Text) = "Figure" Then
        FigureNumber = FigureNumber + 1
```

 NOTE Breakpoints are temporary in nature, and the Visual Basic Editor doesn't save them with your code. You must place them for each editing session.

Commenting Out Lines

By commenting out a line of a macro, you tell VBA not to execute it. Commenting can be a useful technique for removing suspect lines of code to see if their absence improves the macro.

To comment out the current line or selected lines, click the Comment Block button on the Edit toolbar. The Visual Basic Editor will place an apostrophe at the beginning of each line, which tells VBA to ignore that line. To uncomment the current line or selected lines, click the Uncomment Block button, and the Visual Basic Editor will remove the apostrophe from those lines. Unlike breakpoints, comments are stored when you save the code.

Video_18.avi on the CD demonstrates commenting.

 NOTE Three other points about commenting: First, you can also enter or delete comment apostrophes manually. Second, you can use comment lines at any point in the macro to annotate or explain what the code is doing (or what it's supposed to be doing). Third, the Comment Block command adds an apostrophe to the beginning of each line in the selected block, even for lines that are already commented off. Likewise, the Uncomment Block command removes apostrophes one at a time from each line in the selected block, rather than removing all apostrophes at once. This behavior helps preserve comment lines and enables you to use different levels of commenting.

Stepping Out of a Macro

Once you've identified and fixed the problem with a macro, you probably won't want to step through the rest of the macro command by command (unless the code has other problems, that is). To run the rest of the macro and the rest of any macro that called it (you'll read more about calling later), you can press the F5 key, click the Continue button on the Standard toolbar or the Debug toolbar, or choose Run ≻ Continue. If you just want to run the rest of this macro, and then return to stepping through the macro that called this one, use the Step Out command. The Step Out command finishes executing the current macro or procedure at full speed, but if the code then continues with another procedure, the Visual Basic Editor reverts to Break mode so you can examine that procedure's code.

To issue the Step Out command, press Ctrl+Shift+F8, click the Step Out button on the Debug toolbar, or choose Debug ≻ Step Out.

Video_19.avi on the CD demonstrates stepping out of a macro.

Editing the Word Macro

Now, let's edit the Transpose_Word_Right macro that you created in Word and use it to build another macro. To begin, open the macro in the Visual Basic Editor as described in the previous chapter: From Word, choose Tools ≻ Macro ≻ Macros to display the Macros dialog box, select the Transpose_Word_Right macro, and click the Edit button. In the Code window, you should see code something like that shown in Listing 4.1 (without the numbers, which I've added to help identify the lines of the macro).

Video_20.avi on the CD demonstrates editing the Word macro.

Listing 4.1

```
 1.  Sub Transpose_Word_Right()
 2.  '
 3.  ' Transpose_Word_Right Macro
 4.  ' Transposes the current word with the word to its right. _
 5.  ' Created 4/1/2000 by Joanna Bermudez.
 6.  '
 7.      Selection.Extend
 8.      Selection.Extend
 9.      Selection.EscapeKey
10.      Selection.Cut
11.      Selection.MoveRight Unit:=wdWord, Count:=1
12.      Selection.Paste
13.      Selection.MoveLeft Unit:=wdWord, Count:=1
14.  End Sub
```

Analysis

Here's what you've got in the Listing:

- Line 1 starts the macro with the Sub Transpose_Word_Right() statement, and line 14 ends the macro with the End Sub statement. The Sub and End Sub lines mark the beginning and end of the macro (as they do any subprocedure).

- Lines 2 and 6 are blank comment lines the Macro Recorder inserts to make your macro easier to read. You can use any number of blank lines or blank comment lines in a macro to help separate statements into groups. (A blank line doesn't have to be commented out—it can just be blank—but the Macro Recorder has added commenting to these blank lines to make it clear what they are.)

- Lines 3 through 5 are comment lines that contain the name of the macro and its description. The Macro Recorder entered these lines from the information in the Record Macro dialog box.

- Line 7 records the first keypress of the F8 key, which starts Extend mode.

- Line 8 records the second keypress of the F8 key, which continues Extend mode and selects the current word.

- Line 9 records the keypress of the Escape key, which cancels Extend mode.

- Line 10 records the Cut command, which cuts the selection (in this case, the selected word) to the Clipboard.

- Line 11 records the Ctrl+→ command, which moves the insertion point one word to the right.
- Line 12 records the Paste command, which pastes the selection into the document at the current position of the insertion point.
- Line 13 records the Ctrl+← command, which moves the insertion point one word to the left.

First, comment out line 13, which you recorded so you could build a `Transpose_Word_Left` macro from this one. Enter an apostrophe at the beginning of the line—anywhere before the start of the instruction is fine, but you may find it easiest to enter the apostrophe in the leftmost column, where it's clearly visible:

```
'   Selection.MoveLeft Unit:=wdWord, Count:=1
```

Alternatively, click anywhere in line 13 and click the Comment Block button to have the Visual Basic Editor enter the apostrophe for you.

When you move the insertion point out of line 13, VBA will check the line, identify it as a comment line, and change its color to the color currently set for comment text. When you run the macro, VBA will now ignore this line.

Stepping through the Transpose_Word_Right Macro

Try stepping through this macro in Break mode using the Step Into command. First, arrange your screen so you can see both the active Word window and the Visual Basic Editor window (for example, by right-clicking the Taskbar and choosing Tile Windows Horizontally or Tile Windows Vertically from the context menu). Then activate the Visual Basic Editor and click to place the insertion point in the `Transpose_Word_Right` macro in the Code window. Press the F8 key to step through the code one active line at a time (that is, skipping the blank lines and comment lines). VBA will highlight the current statement, and you'll see the actions taking place in the Word window.

The Visual Basic Editor will switch off Break mode when it reaches the end of the macro (in this case, when it executes the `End Sub` statement in line 14). You can also exit Break mode at any time by clicking the Reset button on the Standard toolbar or the Debug toolbar, or by choosing Run ➤ Reset.

Running the Transpose_Word_Right Macro

If the macro works fine when you step through it, you may also want to run it from the Visual Basic Editor by clicking the Run Sub/UserForm button on the Edit toolbar or the Debug toolbar. You can also click this button (which will then be identified as Continue) from Break mode to run a macro beginning from the current instruction.

Creating a Transpose_Word_Left Macro

Now, create a Transpose_Word_Left macro by making minor adjustments to the Transpose_Word_Right macro. Follow these steps, which are demonstrated on Video_21.avi on the CD:

1. In the Code window, select all the code for the Transpose_Word_Right macro, from the Sub Transpose_Word_Right() line to the End Sub line. As in most Windows applications, you can select using the mouse, the keyboard, or a combination of the two.

2. Copy the code by issuing a Copy command (for example, by right-clicking and choosing Copy from the context menu, or by pressing Ctrl+C or Ctrl+Insert).

3. Move the insertion point to the line below the End Sub statement for the Transpose_Word_Right macro in the Code window.

4. Paste the code by issuing a Paste command (for example, by right-clicking and choosing Paste from the context menu, or by pressing Ctrl+V or Shift+Insert). The Visual Basic Editor will automatically enter a horizontal line between the End Sub statement for the Transpose_Word_Right macro and the new macro you've pasted.

5. Change the name of the second Transpose_Word_Right macro to Transpose_Word_Left by editing the Sub line:

   ```
   Sub Transpose_Word_Left()
   ```

6. Edit the comment lines at the beginning of the macro accordingly:

   ```
   'Transpose_Word_Left Macro
   'Transposes the current word with the word to its left. _
   'Created 4/1/2000 by Joanna Bermudez.
   ```

7. Now all you need to do is replace the MoveRight method with the MoveLeft method to move the insertion point one word to the left instead of one word to the right. While you could do that by typing the correction or by using Cut and Paste to replace the Selection.MoveRight line with the commented-out Selection.MoveLeft line, try using the List Properties/Methods feature instead:

   • Click to place the insertion point in the MoveRight method.

   • Click the List Properties/Methods button on the Edit toolbar to display the list of properties and methods.

   • Double-click the MoveLeft method to paste it over the MoveRight method.

8. Now that you no longer need it even for reference, delete the commented Selection.MoveLeft line from the end of the macro.

You should end up with a macro that looks like the one in Listing 4.2.

Listing 4.2

```
Sub Transpose_Word_Left()
'
' Transpose_Word_Left Macro
' Transposes the current word with the word to its left. _
' Created 4/1/2000 by Joanna Bermudez.
'
    Selection.Extend
    Selection.Extend
    Selection.EscapeKey
    Selection.Cut
    Selection.MoveLeft Unit:=wdWord, Count:=1
    Selection.Paste
End Sub
```

Try stepping through this macro to make sure it works. If it does, you're ready to save it—and perhaps to create a toolbar button, menu item, context menu item, or keyboard shortcut for it in Word.

Save Your Work

When you finish working with this or any other macro, choose File ➢ Save to save the document or template that contains the macro and the changes you've made to it.

Editing the Excel Macro

In this section, you'll edit the Excel macro that you recorded in Chapter 2. This time, you won't create a new macro—instead, you'll add to the existing one.

Before you can edit the Excel macro, you'll need to unhide the Personal Macro Workbook if it's currently hidden. Choose Window ➢ Unhide to display the Unhide dialog box, select PERSONAL.XLS, and click the OK button. (To hide the Personal Macro Workbook again after editing the macro, choose Window ➢ Hide when the Personal Macro Workbook is active.) Video_22.avi on the CD demonstrates this process.

 NOTE If you stored the macro in another workbook rather than in the Personal Macro Workbook, open that workbook before trying to proceed.

Now take the following steps to open up the macro for viewing and editing:

1. Choose Tools ➤ Macro ➤ Macros (or press Alt+F8) to display the Macros dialog box.

2. Select the macro named New_Workbook_with_Months. (If you gave the macro a different name, select that name instead.)

3. Click the Edit button to display the macro for editing in the Visual Basic Editor. Listing 4.3 shows code similar to what you should be seeing.

Listing 4.3

```
1.  Sub New_Workbook_with_Months()
2.  '
3.  ' New_Workbook_with_Months Macro
4.  ' Sample Excel macro: Create a new workbook, use AutoFill, and save.
5.  '
6.  '
7.      Workbooks.Add
8.      Range("A1").Select
9.      ActiveCell.FormulaR1C1 = "Jan-2000"
10.     Range("B1").Select
11.     ActiveCell.FormulaR1C1 = "Feb-2000"
12.     Range("A1:B1").Select
13.     Selection.AutoFill Destination:=Range("A1:L1"), Type:=xlFillDefault
14.     Range("A1:L1").Select
15.     ActiveWorkbook.SaveAs Filename:= _
            "C:\\My Documents\Sample Workbook.xls", _
            FileFormat:=xlNormal, Password:="", WriteResPassword:="", _
            ReadOnlyRecommended:=False, CreateBackup:=False
16. End Sub
```

Analysis

Here's what happens in the macro in Listing 4.3:

- Line 1 starts the macro with the Sub New_Workbook_with_Months() statement, and line 16 ends the macro with the End Sub statement.

- Lines 2, 5, and 6 are comment lines that the Macro Recorder automatically adds. (The comment line in line 6 seems superfluous. It's there because Excel expects you to enter two lines in the Description text box in the Record Macro dialog box, and for this macro I entered only one line.)

- Line 3 is a comment line that gives the macro's name and describes it as a macro, and line 4 contains the description from the Record Macro dialog box.

- Line 7 creates a new blank workbook by using the Add method on the Workbooks collection object (a *collection object*, or more concisely a *collection*, is an object that contains objects of a given type).

- Line 8 selects the Range object A1, making cell A1 active.

- Line 9 enters Jan-2000 in the active cell. Notice that the Macro Recorder has stored the parsed date value rather than the text that you entered (**January 2000**). Also, keep in mind that the date displayed in the cell may be in a different format than MMM-YYYY.

- Line 10 selects the Range object B1, making cell B1 active, and line 11 enters Feb-2000 in that cell.

- Line 12 selects the range A1:B1.

- Line 13 performs a default AutoFill operation on the range A1:L1, and line 14 selects that range. Note how the Macro Recorder has recorded two separate actions, although in the Excel interface you performed only one action.

- Line 15 saves the workbook under the name and folder given. Note that the Macro Recorder has automatically broken this long statement onto four lines by using the continuation character, an underscore preceded by a space.

Now extend the macro by following these steps:

1. Select lines 8 through 13.

2. Issue a Copy command by pressing Ctrl+C, clicking the Copy button on the Standard toolbar, choosing Edit ➤ Copy, or by right-clicking in the selection and choosing Copy from the context menu.

3. Press the → key to collapse the selection and move the insertion point to after its end, so that the insertion point is at the beginning of line 14.

4. Issue a Paste command by pressing Ctrl+V, clicking the Paste button on the Standard toolbar, choosing Edit ➤ Paste, or right-clicking at the insertion point and choosing Paste from the context menu.

You should get a macro that looks like that in Listing 4.4.

Listing 4.4

```
1. Sub New_Workbook_with_Months()
2. '
3. ' New_Workbook_with_Months Macro
4. ' Sample Excel macro: Create a new workbook, use AutoFill, and save.
5. '
6. '
7.    Workbooks.Add
8.    Range("A1").Select
9.    ActiveCell.FormulaR1C1 = "Jan-2000"
10.   Range("B1").Select
11.   ActiveCell.FormulaR1C1 = "Feb-2000"
12.   Range("A1:B1").Select
13.   Selection.AutoFill Destination:=Range("A1:L1"), Type:=xlFillDefault
14.   Range("A1").Select
15.   ActiveCell.FormulaR1C1 = "Jan-2000"
16.   Range("B1").Select
17.   ActiveCell.FormulaR1C1 = "Feb-2000"
18.   Range("A1:B1").Select
19.   Selection.AutoFill Destination:=Range("A1:L1"), Type:=xlFillDefault
20.   Range("A1:L1").Select
21.   ActiveWorkbook.SaveAs Filename:= _
            "C:\My Documents\Sample Workbook.xls", _
            FileFormat:=xlNormal, Password:="", WriteResPassword:="", _
            ReadOnlyRecommended:=False, CreateBackup:=False
22. End Sub
```

Now, change the macro by taking the following steps:

1. Delete line 6. It's not doing any good, and it's taking up space in the Code window.

2. Delete line 20. It's not necessary for what the macro does—you don't need the macro to select the range, because the AutoFill instruction in line 13 is enough to perform the AutoFill operation without selecting the range.

3. Change line 14 to select cell A2 instead of cell A1:

```
Range("A2").Select
```

4. Change line 15 so that it enters the value 100 instead of Jan-2000:

```
ActiveCell.FormulaR1C1 = 100
```

5. Change line 16 to select cell B2 instead of cell B1:

```
Range("B2").Select
```

6. Change line 17 so that it enters the value 200 instead of Feb-2000:

```
ActiveCell.FormulaR1C1 = 200
```

7. Change line 18 so that it selects the range A2:B2:

```
Range("A2:B2").Select
```

8. Change line 19 so that it performs the AutoFill operation on the range A2:L2:

```
Selection.AutoFill Destination:=Range("A2:L2"), Type:=xlFillDefault
```

9. Break line 12 with a space, underscore, and carriage return before the Type argument, as shown below. Indent the second line by one tab.

```
Selection.AutoFill Destination:=Range("A1:L1"), _
    Type:=xlFillDefault
```

10. Similarly, break line 18 with a space, underscore, and carriage return before the Type argument.

11. Click the Save button or choose File ➤ Save to save the changes you made.

The macro should now read like the one in Listing 4.5.

Listing 4.5

```
1. Sub New_Workbook_with_Months()
2. '
3. ' New_Workbook_with_Months Macro
4. ' Sample Excel macro: Create a new workbook, use AutoFill, and save.
5. '
6.    Workbooks.Add
7.    Range("A1").Select
8.    ActiveCell.FormulaR1C1 = "Jan-2000"
9.    Range("B1").Select
10.    ActiveCell.FormulaR1C1 = "Feb-2000"
11.    Range("A1:B1").Select
12.    Selection.AutoFill Destination:=Range("A1:L1"), _
          Type:=xlFillDefault
13.    Range("A2").Select
14.    ActiveCell.FormulaR1C1 = 100
15.    Range("B2").Select
```

```
16.   ActiveCell.FormulaR1C1 = 200
17.   Range("A2:B2").Select
18.   Selection.AutoFill Destination:=Range("A2:L2"), Type:=xlFillDefault
19.   ActiveWorkbook.SaveAs Filename:= _
         "C:\My Documents\Sample Workbook.xls", _
         FileFormat:=xlNormal, Password:="", WriteResPassword:="", _
         ReadOnlyRecommended:=False, CreateBackup:=False
20. End Sub
```

Now step through the macro and watch what happens: It creates the new workbook as before and enters the months, but then it enters the values 100 through 1200 in the second row of cells. At the end, it saves the workbook as before, prompting you to overwrite the previous workbook (unless you've already deleted it).

Editing the PowerPoint Macro

In this section, you'll edit the PowerPoint macro that you recorded in Chapter 2. Video_23.avi on the CD demonstrates the editing. Start by opening up the macro as follows:

1. Open the PowerPoint presentation containing the macro.

2. Choose Tools ➤ Macro ➤ Macros to display the Macros dialog box.

3. Select the Add_Slide_and_Format_Placeholder macro.

4. Click the Edit button.

Listing 4.6 shows the macro almost exactly as it was recorded. I've broken some of the lines of code with the underscore continuation character.

Listing 4.6

```
1.  Sub Add_Slide_and_Format_Placeholder()
2.  '
3.  ' Sample macro that adds a slide, formats its placeholder, and _
       adds text to it. Recorded 4/1/2000 by John Kruger.
4.  '
5.     ActiveWindow.View.GotoSlide Index:= _
          ActivePresentation.Slides.Add(Index:=1, _
          Layout:=ppLayoutTitle).SlideIndex
```

```
6.      ActiveWindow.Selection.SlideRange.Shapes("Rectangle 2").Select
7.      ActiveWindow.Selection.ShapeRange.IncrementTop -144#
8.      ActiveWindow.Selection.ShapeRange.ScaleHeight 2.67, _
            msoFalse, msoScaleFromTopLeft
9.      ActiveWindow.Selection.SlideRange.Shapes("Rectangle 2").Select
10.     ActiveWindow.Selection.ShapeRange.TextFrame.TextRange.Select
11.     ActiveWindow.Selection.ShapeRange.TextFrame. _
            TextRange.Characters(Start:=1, Length:=0).Select
12.     With ActiveWindow.Selection.TextRange
13.         .Text = "The quick brown dog jumped over a lazy fox"
14.         With .Font
15.             .Name = "Times New Roman"
16.             .Size = 44
17.             .Bold = msoFalse
18.             .Italic = msoFalse
19.             .Underline = msoFalse
20.             .Shadow = msoFalse
21.             .Emboss = msoFalse
22.             .BaselineOffset = 0
23.             .AutoRotateNumbers = msoFalse
24.             .Color.SchemeColor = ppTitle
25.         End With
26.     End With
27.     ActiveWindow.Selection.ShapeRange.TextFrame.TextRange. _
            Characters(Start:=1, Length:=42).Select
28.     With ActiveWindow.Selection.TextRange.Font
29.         .Name = "Impact"
30.         .Size = 54
31.         .Bold = msoFalse
32.         .Italic = msoFalse
33.         .Underline = msoFalse
34.         .Shadow = msoFalse
35.         .Emboss = msoFalse
36.         .BaselineOffset = 0
37.         .AutoRotateNumbers = msoFalse
38.         .Color.SchemeColor = ppTitle
39.     End With
40. End Sub
```

Analysis

The macro in Listing 4.6 is initially a little daunting to look at, because PowerPoint's Macro Recorder is much more prolix than it needs to be. Here's what happens in the macro:

- Line 1 starts the macro, and line 40 ends it.

- Lines 2 and 4 are blank comment lines used to set off the description of the macro, which appears in line 3.

- Line 5 adds the slide to the presentation. This statement is a little complicated, but don't worry about it too closely just yet. For now, simply note two things: First, the statement uses the Add method with the Slides collection object to add a slide to the collection (i.e., to create a new slide), just as the Excel macro used the Add method to add a workbook to the Workbooks collection. (You can see a pattern emerging here.) Second, the layout of the slide is ppLayoutTitle, the VBA constant for the Title slide layout that you chose when recording the macro. (If you chose a different slide layout, you'll see a different constant listed here.)

- Line 6 selects the shape named Rectangle 2 in the Shapes collection on the active slide. (For the moment, don't worry about how you get to the active slide.)

- Line 7 uses the IncrementTop method with a negative value to change the vertical position of the selected shape (Rectangle 2), moving it up the slide. Line 8 then uses the ScaleHeight method to change the depth of the shape, deepening it.

- Line 9 selects the shape named Rectangle 2, and line 10 selects the TextRange object in the TextFrame object in the shape. When you're working interactively, PowerPoint makes this selection process relatively seamless: You click in a shape displaying the legend *Click to add title* (or whatever), and PowerPoint selects the text range in the text frame in the shape—but all you see is that the text in the shape becomes selected. As you can see from the VBA statements, you have to go through a couple of unseen layers in the object model before getting to the text.

- When you select the placeholder text, PowerPoint gets rid of it. The same thing happens when you select the placeholder text via VBA. So line 11 makes a new selection at the beginning of the first character in the text range.

- Line 12 starts a With statement that continues until line 26. A With statement is a way of simplifying object references, and everything between the With statement and the End With statement refers to the objects that the With statement mentions. In this case, the With ActiveWindow.Selection.TextRange statement in line 12 lets line 13 reference the Text property of the TextRange object in the Selection object in the ActiveWindow object much more simply (instead of ActiveWindow.Selection.TextRange.Text); and it lets line 14 reference the

Font property of the TextRange object in the Selection object in the ActiveWindow object easily (instead of ActiveWindow.Selection.TextRange.Font).

- Line 13 sets the Text property of the ActiveWindow.Selection.TextRange object to the text I typed.

- Line 14 then begins an unnecessary With statement that sets the properties of the Font object for the TextRange object. This code was recorded automatically when I typed the text. Line 15 sets the Name property of the Font object to Times New Roman; line 16 sets the Size property of the Font object to 44; line 17 sets the Bold property of the Font object to msoFalse, the Microsoft Office (mso) constant for False; and so on.

- Line 27 uses the Select method to select characters 1 through 42 in the text range. This is the result of pressing the Ctrl+Shift+Home key combination. Because this statement specifies the characters to select, you'll need to change it if you change the text that the macro inserts. (If you run the statement on a text range that has fewer than 42 characters, it will return an error. If you run it on a text range that has more than 42 characters, it will select only the first 42 characters in the text range—not what you want.)

- Line 28 begins another With statement that works with the Font object of the TextRange object—but this With statement records the actions you took in the Font dialog box, so you want to keep it.

- Line 39 ends the With statement, and line 40 ends the macro.

You'll edit this macro by slimming it down a little and changing the text it inserts. Edit the macro as follows:

1. Delete the unnecessary With statement in lines 14 through 25.

2. Delete line 26.

3. Change lines 12 and 13 into a single statement without With:

4. Now change the text that the new line 12 inserts. Enter text of your choice between the double quotation marks.

5. Change line 27 to use the Select method on the text range rather than specifying which characters to select. Delete Characters(Start:=1, Length:=42) to leave this statement:

    ActiveWindow.Selection.ShapeRange.TextFrame.TextRange.Select

6. Click the Save button on the Standard toolbar or choose File ➤ Save to save the changes you've made to the presentation.

You should now have code that reads like Listing 4.7.

Listing 4.7

```
1.  Sub Add_Slide_and_Format_Placeholder()
2.  '
3.  ' Sample macro that adds a slide, formats its placeholder, and _
       adds text to it. Recorded 4/1/2000 by John Kruger.
4.  '
5.      ActiveWindow.View.GotoSlide _
            Index:=ActivePresentation.Slides.Add(Index:=1, _
            Layout:=ppLayoutTitle).SlideIndex
6.      ActiveWindow.Selection.SlideRange.Shapes("Rectangle 2").Select
7.      ActiveWindow.Selection.ShapeRange.IncrementTop -144#
8.      ActiveWindow.Selection.ShapeRange.ScaleHeight 2.67, _
            msoFalse, msoScaleFromTopLeft
9.      ActiveWindow.Selection.SlideRange.Shapes("Rectangle 2").Select
10.     ActiveWindow.Selection.ShapeRange.TextFrame.TextRange.Select
11.     ActiveWindow.Selection.ShapeRange.TextFrame. _
            TextRange.Characters(Start:=1, Length:=0).Select
12.     ActiveWindow.Selection.TextRange .Text = _
            "President Gas on everything but rollerskates"
13.     ActiveWindow.Selection.ShapeRange.TextFrame.TextRange..Select
14.     With ActiveWindow.Selection.TextRange.Font
15.         .Name = "Impact"
16.         .Size = 54
17.         .Bold = msoFalse
18.         .Italic = msoFalse
19.         .Underline = msoFalse
20.         .Shadow = msoFalse
21.         .Emboss = msoFalse
22.         .BaselineOffset = 0
23.         .AutoRotateNumbers = msoFalse
24.         .Color.SchemeColor = ppTitle
25.     End With
26. End Sub
```

Now step through the changed macro and make sure it works as you expect it to.

Editing the Project Macro

In this section, you'll edit the Project macro that you recorded in Chapter 2.

Start Project. If you recorded the macro into a project, open that project. (If you recorded the macro into the Global Template, you'll be able to access it from any project.) Then open the macro for editing in the Visual Basic Editor by following these steps (Video_24.avi on the CD demonstrates the editing):

1. Choose Tools ➤ Macro ➤ Macros (or press the F8 key) to display the Macros dialog box.

2. Make sure that All Open Projects is selected in the Macros In drop-down list. (Select it if it's not.)

3. Select the Add_Sample_Task macro in the Macro Name list box.

4. Click the Edit button to open the macro in the Visual Basic Editor.

Listing 4.8 shows the Project macro as it was recorded. Chances are that your date and author are different, but the rest of the code should look the same.

Listing 4.8

```
 1. Sub Add_Sample_Task()
 2. ' Adds a sample task to the active project and enters information in it.
 3. ' Macro Recorded Sunday 12/5/99 by Guy Hart-Davis.
 4.     RowInsert
 5.     SelectTaskField Row:=0, Column:="Name"
 6.     SetTaskField Field:="Name", Value:="Increase salary"
 7.     SelectTaskField Row:=0, Column:="Duration"
 8.     SetTaskField Field:="Duration", Value:="14 days"
 9.     SelectTaskField Row:=0, Column:="Start"
10.     SetTaskField Field:="Start", Value:="12/6/99"
11. End Sub
```

Analysis

Compared to the PowerPoint macro discussed in the previous section, this Project macro is admirably concise—although (as you'll remember from recording it) it does much less than the PowerPoint macro. Here's what happens:

- Line 1 starts the Add_Sample_Task macro, and line 11 ends it.

- Lines 2 and 3 are comment lines created from the description I entered in the Record Macro dialog box. Notice that the Macro Recorder for Project hasn't created blank lines around the comment lines the way it does for most of the Office applications.

- Line 4 uses the `RowInsert` method to insert a row—the new task—in the active project.

NOTE If you think the `RowInsert` statement here looks a little peculiar, you're right— the full statement would be `Application.RowInsert`, but naming the `Application` object is optional because it's the default object for the `RowInsert` method, and the Macro Recorder has chosen to omit the object. The same goes for the `SelectTaskField` method and the `SetTaskField` method that subsequent statements in the macro use.

- Line 5 uses the `SelectTaskField` method to select the cell in the Name column in the current row. (Row:=0 is an offset measurement—no offset from the current row—rather than indicating the number of the row involved.)

- Line 6 uses the `SetTaskField` method to set the Name field to `Increase Salary`.

- Line 7 uses the `SelectTaskField` method to select the cell in the Duration column in the current.

- Line 8 uses the `SetTaskField` method to set the Duration field to `14 days`.

- Line 9 uses the `SelectTaskField` method (do you see a pattern beginning to emerge here?) to select the cell in the Start column in the current row.

- Line 10 uses the `SetTaskField` method to set the Start field to the chosen date (in this case, 12/6/99).

Now create a new macro that creates a new task. Follow these steps:

1. Select the macro in the code window. To select it, you can use most of the standard selection methods from the Office applications:

   - Click and drag.

   - Place the insertion point at the beginning or end of the macro, then hold down the Shift key and click at the end or the beginning.

   - If you're using Procedure view, or if `Add_Sample_Task` is the only macro in the module you're working with in Full Module view, you can also choose Edit ➢ Select All (or press Ctrl+A) to select the macro.

2. Issue a Copy command—for instance, right-click in the selected code and choose Copy from the context menu.

3. Collapse the selection to the end of the macro by pressing the → key or clicking in the Code window below the end of the macro.

4. Issue a Paste command to paste in the code you copied. For example, choose Edit ➤ Paste.

5. Change the Sub line of the new macro to Add_Another_Sample_Task.

6. Change the beginning of the first comment line so that it reads 'Adds another sample task.

7. Change the beginning of the second comment line so that it reads 'Macro created.

8. Change each instance of Start to Finish. You could do this easily enough manually, but try using the Replace feature as follows for practice:

- Select the new macro.

- Choose Edit ➤ Replace (or press Ctrl+H) to display the Replace dialog box (shown in Figure 4.3 with choices made).

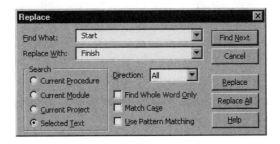

- In the Find What text box, enter **Start**.

- In the Replace With text box, enter **Finish**.

- In the Search group box, make sure the Selected Text option button is selected. (The Visual Basic Editor should select this option button by default when you display the Replace dialog box when you have text selected in the Code window.

- In the Direction drop-down list, make sure All is selected.

- Make sure that none of the three check boxes below the Direction drop-down list is selected.

- Click the Replace All button. The Visual Basic Editor will display the Microsoft Visual Basic dialog box shown in Figure 4.4 to tell you what results the search turned in.

FIGURE 4.4

When the Visual Basic Editor has finished searching your code, it displays the Microsoft Visual Basic dialog box shown here to tell you what luck it had.

- Click the OK button to dismiss the Microsoft Visual Basic dialog box, and then click the Cancel button to close the Replace dialog box.

9. Change the first `SetTaskField` statement so that it sets the task's Name field to `Improve job title`:

   `SetTaskField Field:="Name", Value:="Improve job title"`

10. Change the second `SetTaskField` statement so that it sets the task's Duration field to `28 days`:

    `SetTaskField Field:="Duration", Value:="28 days"`

11. Make sure the Replace operation has changed the third `SelectTaskField` statement so that it selects the cell in the Finish column:

    `SelectTaskField Row:=1, Column:="Finish"`

12. Change the third `SetTaskField` statement so that it enters a date a little over four weeks in the future in the Finish cell:

    `SetTaskField Field:="Finish", Value:="1/9/2000"`

Your new macro should look like the one in Listing 4.9 (again, your date and author will probably be different).

Listing 4.9

```
1.  Sub Add_Another_Sample_Task()
2.  ' Adds another sample task to the active project _
    and enters information in it.
3.  ' Macro created Sunday 12/5/99 by Guy Hart-Davis.
4.      RowInsert
5.      SelectTaskField Row:=0, Column:="Name"
6.      SetTaskField Field:="Name", Value:="Improve job title"
7.      SelectTaskField Row:=0, Column:="Duration"
8.      SetTaskField Field:="Duration", Value:="28 days"
```

```
 9.       SelectTaskField Row:=0, Column:="Finish"
10.       SetTaskField Field:="Finish", Value:="1/9/2000"
11.  End Sub
```

Now run the macro and make sure it works as it should.

When Should You Use the Macro Recorder?

As you've seen so far in this book, you can create VBA code either by using the Macro Recorder (in the applications that provide it) to record a series of actions when working interactively in the application, or by entering VBA statements into the Code window in the Visual Basic Editor. You're probably wondering when you should record a macro and when you should create code from scratch. After all, writing a procedure is more difficult (and therefore advanced) than recording a procedure—so why would anyone worth their salt record a procedure when they could write it instead?

As you'll see in the upcoming chapters, using the Macro Recorder has advantages and disadvantages. The advantages are:

- The Macro Recorder creates usable code every time (provided you run the macro under suitable conditions; more on this in a moment, when I get to the disadvantages).

- The Macro Recorder is quick and easy to use.

- The Macro Recorder can help you discover which VBA objects, methods, and properties correspond to which part of an application's interface.

The disadvantages of using the Macro Recorder are:

- Code created in the Macro Recorder may contain unnecessary statements, because the Macro Recorder records *everything* you do in the application —including all the options in every built-in dialog box you use when recording the macro. For example, if you start the Macro Recorder from Word, choose Tools ➤ Options to display the View page of the Options dialog box, click the Edit tab to display the Edit page, and change the Auto-Keyboard Switching setting, the Macro Recorder will record all the settings on the Edit page as well as all those on the View page. The result? About 40 lines of unnecessary code. (If you visit any other pages in the Options dialog box on the way to the Edit page, the Macro Recorder will record all the settings in those pages as well.) If you create the code manually in the Visual Basic Editor, you can achieve the same effect by using one statement.

- Code created by the Macro Recorder can work only in the active document rather than using other documents, because whichever document you're working with interactively becomes the active document. You'll learn in Chapter 14 how you can use objects in the applications' object models to work with documents other than the active document. For now, I'll just mention that there are several advantages to working with other documents. For example, you can hide the manipulations you're performing from the user (thus avoiding distressing them unnecessarily) and you can make your code run faster.

- The Macro Recorder can create VBA code for only *some* of the actions you perform in the host application. For example, if you want to display a dialog box or a user form in the course of a procedure, you need to write the appropriate statement manually—you can't record it. The subset of VBA actions available through the Macro Recorder is similar to the set of actions you can take in the host application when working interactively, so you can get a lot done with it. Still, you'll find it's limited compared to the full range of actions you can perform through VBA.

I suggest viewing the question this way. However good you become with VBA, you should still consider the Macro Recorder either a viable option for creating rough-and-ready macros, or as the basis of more complex procedures. You'll often find it makes sense to have the Macro Recorder handle as much of the strain of creating a procedure as possible. And there's no shame in using the Macro Recorder to quickly identify the VBA object or property that you need to reach.

The macro-editing you did in this chapter may have felt a little clumsy because you examined and changed the macros you recorded without really understanding the structure of the VBA language. In the next chapter, I'll set that straight by introducing you to the essentials of VBA syntax. The chapter is a little theoretical, so I'll keep it short—and after that, I'll get straight back into practical examples.

CHAPTER <u>5</u>

The Essentials of VBA Syntax

FEATURING:

n this chapter, you'll learn the essentials of VBA syntax, thereby laying the framework for the knowledge you'll build throughout the rest of the book. I'll define the key terms that you need to know about VBA to get going with it, and you'll practice using some of the elements in the Visual Basic Editor.

 NOTE You'll find lots of definitions for programming terms as you work your way through the chapter. If you come across something that doesn't yet make sense to you, skip ahead, and you'll most likely find it in the next few pages.

In the previous chapter, you examined the code of the macros you recorded in Chapter 2, looking at what each statement did (without worrying too much about the details) and making some minor changes just to prove that you could easily alter the code. Keep that macro code in mind as you read through the definitions in this chapter, and everything should begin to snap into place for you.

Getting Ready

To work through this section, get set up for working in the Visual Basic Editor with Word by following the steps shown below. I'm using Word because it's arguably the most widely distributed of the VBA-enabled applications. If you don't have it, read along anyway without performing the actions on the computer; the examples are easy to follow. (Much of this will work on any VBA host, though many of the commands I'll show you here are specific to Word.)

1. Start Word as usual.

2. Launch the Visual Basic Editor by choosing Tools ➤ Macro ➤ Visual Basic Editor or by pressing Alt+F11.

3. Arrange the Word window and the Visual Basic Editor window so that you can see both of them at once—for example, by right-clicking the Taskbar and choosing Tile Windows Horizontally or Tile Windows Vertically from the context menu.

   • If you're using a multi-monitor setup, you can dedicate one monitor to Word and another to the Visual Basic Editor.

4. Display the Immediate window in the Visual Basic Editor by choosing View ➤ Immediate Window or pressing Ctrl+G.

Procedures

A *procedure* in VBA is a named unit of code that contains a sequence of statements to be executed as a group. For example, VBA contains a function (a type of procedure) named Left, which returns the left portion of a text string that you specify. For example, hello is a string of text five characters long. The statement Left("hello", 4) returns (gives you) the leftmost four characters of the string: hell. (You could then display this four-character string in a message box, or use it in code.) The name assigned to the procedure simply gives you a way to refer to the procedure.

All executable code in VBA must be contained in a procedure—if it isn't, VBA can't execute it and throws an error. (The exception is statements you execute in the Immediate window which take place outside a procedure. However, the contents of the Immediate window exist only during the current VBA session.) Procedures are contained within modules, which in turn are contained within project files, templates, or other VBA host objects, such as user forms.

There are two types of procedures: functions and subprocedures. I'll give you some examples of creating subprocedures in Chapter 10.

Functions

A *function* in VBA is one of two types of procedures. A function is a type of complete procedure designed to perform a specific task. For example, the Left function I just mentioned returns the left part of a text string, and the Right function, its counterpart, returns the right part of a text string. Each function has a clear task that you use it for, and it doesn't do anything else. To take a ridiculous example, you can't use the Left function to print a document in Word or make characters boldface—for those tasks, you need to use the appropriate functions, methods, and properties.

VBA comes with a plethora of built-in functions, but you can also create your own. You'll create your own functions later in the book. They will begin with a Function statement and end with an End Function statement.

Statements

A *statement* is a unit of code that describes an action, defines an item, or gives the value of a variable. VBA usually has one statement per line of code, although you can put more than one statement on a line by separating them with colons. You can also break a line of code onto a second line to make it easier to read by using a line-continuation character: an underscore (_) preceded by a space (and followed by a carriage return).

You do so strictly for visual convenience; VBA still reads both lines as a single line of code. Note that you can't break a string enclosed in quotations by using a line-continuation character. If you need to break a line that involves a long string in quotes, your best alternative is to break the string into shorter strings and concatenate them using the & operator.

There's really no such thing as a typical VBA statement, because VBA statements can vary from a single word (such as Beep, which makes the computer beep, or Stop, which halts the execution of VBA code) to very long and complicated lines involving many components. That said, let's examine the make-up of several sample VBA statements in Word. Most of them use the ActiveDocument object, which represents the active document in the current session of Word; a couple use the Documents collection, which represents all open documents (including the active document); and one uses the Selection object, which represents the current selection. Don't worry if some of these statements aren't immediately comprehensible—you'll understand them soon enough.

Here are the example statements:

```
Documents.Open "c:\temp\Sample Document.doc"
MsgBox ActiveDocument.Name
ActiveDocument.Words(1).Text = "Industry"
ActiveDocument.Close SaveChanges:=wdDoNotSaveChanges
Documents.Add
Selection.TypeText "The quick brown fox jumped over the lazy dog."
ActiveDocument.Save
Documents.Close SaveChanges:=wdDoNotSaveChanges
Application.Quit
```

Let's look at each of these statements in turn.

```
Documents.Open "c:\temp\Sample Document.doc"
```

This statement uses the Open method on the Documents collection to open the specified document—in this case, Sample Document.doc. Enter this statement in the Immediate window, using a path and filename of a document that exists on your computer. Press the Enter key, and VBA will open the document in the Word window. As when you open a document while working interactively in Word, the document becomes the active document (the one whose document window is currently selected).

```
MsgBox ActiveDocument.Name
```

This statement uses the MsgBox function to display the Name property of the Active-Document object (in this example, Sample Document.doc). Enter this statement in the Immediate window and press the Enter key. VBA will display a message box over the Word window. Click the OK button to dismiss the message box.

```
ActiveDocument.Words(1).Text = "Industry"
```

This statement uses the *assignment operator* (the equal [=] sign) to assign the value *Industry* to the Text property of the first item in the Words collection in the ActiveDocument object. Enter this statement in the Immediate window and press the Enter key. You'll see Word enter **Industry** (in the current typeface, and probably without the boldface) at the beginning of the document you opened. Note that the insertion point is at the beginning of the word, rather than at the end of the word, where it would be if you'd typed the word. This happens because VBA manipulates the properties of the document rather than "typing" into it.

```
ActiveDocument.Close SaveChanges:=wdDoNotSaveChanges
```

This statement uses the Close method to close the ActiveDocument object. It uses one argument, SaveChanges, which controls whether Word saves the document that's being closed (assuming the document contains unsaved changes). In this case, the statement uses the constant wdDoNotSaveChanges to specify that Word shouldn't save changes when closing the document. Enter this statement in the Immediate window and press the Enter key, and you'll see VBA make Word close the document.

Now try these statements in the Immediate window:

```
Documents.Add
```

This statement uses the Add method on the Documents collection to add a new Document object to the Documents collection: In other words, it creates a new document. Because the statement doesn't specify which template to use, the new document is based on the default template (Normal.dot). Enter this statement in the Immediate window and press Enter, and Word will create a new document. As usual, this new document will become the active document.

```
Selection.TypeText "The quick brown fox jumped over the lazy dog."
```

This statement uses the TypeText method of the Selection object to type text into the active document at the position of the insertion point or current selection. (The Selection object represents the current selection, which can be an insertion point with nothing actually selected.) If text is selected in the active document, that selection will be overwritten as usual (unless you've cleared the Typing Replaces Selection check box on the Edit tab of the Options dialog box, in which case the selection will be collapsed to its beginning, and the new text will be inserted before the previously selected text). Because you just created a new document, nothing is selected. Enter this statement in the Immediate window and press the Enter key, and Word will enter the text. Note that this time the insertion point ends up after the text; the TypeText method of the Selection object is analogous to typing interactively.

```
ActiveDocument.Save
```

This statement uses the Save method (command) to save the ActiveDocument object. This statement is the VBA equivalent of choosing File ➤ Save while working interactively in Word. If you enter this statement into the Immediate window and press Enter, Word will display the Save As dialog box so you can save the document as usual. For now, however, click the Cancel button to dismiss the Save As dialog box. Word will display the Microsoft Visual Basic error message box. Click the OK button to dismiss it; you'll learn how to handle errors such as this in your code in Chapter 18, "Debugging Your Code."

```
Documents.Close SaveChanges:=wdDoNotSaveChanges
```

This statement is similar to the previous ActiveDocument.Close SaveChanges:=wdDoNotSaveChanges statement, except that it works on the Documents collection rather than the ActiveDocument object. The Documents collection, as you'll remember, represents all open documents in the current Word session. This statement closes all open documents without saving any unsaved changes in them. Enter this statement into the Immediate window and press Enter, and Word will close all the open documents.

```
Application.Quit
```

This statement uses the Quit method on the Application object to close the Word application. Enter the statement in the Immediate window and press the Enter key. Word will close itself, closing the Visual Basic Editor in the process, because Word is the host for the Visual Basic Editor.

Getting Help on Visual Basic for Applications

The Visual Basic Editor offers comprehensive help on the Visual Basic for Applications programming language. To view it, choose Help ➤ Microsoft Visual Basic Help from the Visual Basic Editor. Most of the statements and functions have examples, which can be particularly helpful when you're creating and troubleshooting code.

The Visual Basic Help files use a couple of conventions you should know about before you try to use them:

- Italics denote variables or values you'll need to change yourself.
- Brackets ([and]) denote optional arguments.

This book works with the same conventions, so you'll see them in use soon.

If your computer doesn't offer you any help on VBA, whoever installed the application in question may not have installed the relevant files (perhaps to save space). Install the files, and all should be well.

Keywords

A *keyword* is simply a word defined as part of the VBA language—for example, the name of a statement or of a function.

Expressions

An *expression* consists of keywords, operators, variables, and constants combined to produce a string, number, or object. For example, you could use an expression to run a calculation or to compare one variable against another.

Operators

An *operator* is an item you use to compare, combine, or otherwise work with values in an expression. VBA has four kinds of operators:

- *Arithmetic operators* (such as + and −) perform mathematical calculations.
- *Comparison operators* (such as < and >, less than and greater than, respectively) compare values.
- *Concatenation operators* (& and +) join two strings together.
- *Logical operators* (such as And, Not, and Or) build logical structures.

You'll look at the different kinds of operators and how they work in Chapter 6, "Working with Variables and Constants."

Variables

A *variable* is a location in memory set aside for storing a piece of information that can be changed while a procedure is running. (Think of it as a resizable compartment within the memory area.) For example, if you need the user to input their name via an input box or a dialog box, you'll typically store the name in a variable so you can work with it in the procedure.

VBA uses several types of variables, including these:

- *Strings* store text characters or groups of characters.
- *Integers* store whole numbers (numbers without fractions).
- *Objects* store objects.
- *Variants* can store any type of data. This is the default type of variable.

You can either let VBA create Variant variables in which to store your information, or you can specify which type any given variable can be. Specifying the types of variable has certain advantages that you'll learn about in due course.

For the moment, try quickly creating a variable in the Immediate window. Type the following line and press Enter:

```
myVariable = "Sample variable text"
```

Nothing visible happens, but VBA has created the myVariable variable. Now, type the following line and press Enter:

```
MsgBox myVariable
```

This time, you get a more gratifying result: A message box appears containing the text you entered in the variable.

You can declare variables either explicitly or implicitly. In the next few chapters, you'll use a few implicit variable declarations to keep things simple—you don't have to type anything for implicit variable declarations, because VBA will make them up when it needs them. After that, you'll start using explicit variable declarations to make your code faster and easier to read.

Constants

A *constant* is a named item that keeps a constant value while a program is executing. For example, you used the constant wdDoNotSaveChanges in the example statement ActiveDocument.Close SaveChanges:=wdDoNotSaveChanges. wdDoNotSaveChanges tells Word not to save changes when closing a document. Its meaning doesn't change at different times of program execution.

VBA uses two types of constant: *intrinsic constants*, which are built into an application such as Word; and *user-defined constants*, which you create. Each intrinsic constant is mapped to a numeric value in the group of constants in which it belongs. For example, wdDoNotSaveChanges is part of the WdSaveOptions group of constants and has a value of 2. You can use the value of the constant in your code instead of the name, but in most cases the names of the constants are easier to use and to read.

The names of built-in constants typically start with two letters indicating the application with which each constant is associated, as listed in Table 5.1. As you can see, names of individual constants are written in mixed case, with intercapitalization to make the names easier to read. The first two letters of individual constant names are lowercase, while the first letter of the name of a group of constants is uppercase (as in the WdSaveOptions group mentioned a moment ago).

TABLE 5.1: STARTING LETTERS OF BUILT-IN CONSTANTS

Start of Constant	Example	Application
ac	acCopy	Access
ac	ac180degrees	AutoCAD
ad	adLockReadOnly	ADO (ActiveX Data Objects)
db	dbAppendOnly	Data Access Object library
ol	olContactItem	Outlook
pj	pjActualCost	Project
pp	ppSaveAsPresentation	PowerPoint
vb	vbYes	Visual Basic/VBA
vis	visActionDisabled	Visio
wd	wdDoNotSaveChanges	Word
xl	xlDialogBorder	Excel

Arguments

An *argument* is a piece of information—supplied by a constant, a variable, or an expression—that you pass to a procedure, a function, or a method. Some arguments are required; others are optional. As you saw earlier, the following statement uses the optional argument SaveChanges to specify whether Word should save any unsaved changes while closing the active document:

```
ActiveDocument.Close SaveChanges:=wdDoNotSaveChanges
```

The Visual Basic Editor's helpful prompts and the Visual Basic Help file show the list of arguments for a function, a procedure, or a method in parentheses, with any optional arguments enclosed in brackets. If you're using the Auto Quick Info feature, the Visual Basic Editor will display the argument list for a function, procedure, or method after you type its name followed by a space. Figure 5.1 shows the argument list for the Open method. The FileName argument is required, so it isn't surrounded by brackets. All the other arguments (ConfirmConversions, ReadOnly, AddToRecentFiles, and so on) are optional, and so are surrounded by brackets. If you don't supply a value for an optional argument, VBA uses the default value for the argument. (To find out the default value for an argument, consult the VBA Help file.) The Visual Basic Editor uses boldface to indicate the current argument in the list; as you enter each argument, the next argument in the list becomes bold.

Documents.Open

Open(***FileName***, [*ConfirmConversions*], [*ReadOnly*], [*AddToRecentFiles*], [*PasswordDocument*], [*PasswordTemplate*], [*Revert*], [*WritePasswordDocument*], [*WritePasswordTemplate*], [*Format*], [*Encoding*], [*Visible*]) As Document

You can use arguments in either of two ways:

- Enter the name of the argument (for example, ConfirmConversions) followed by a colon and an equals sign (ConfirmConversions:=) and the constant or value you want to set for it (ConfirmConversions:=True). For example, the start of the statement might look like this:

```
Documents.Open FileName:="c:\temp\Example.doc", _
    ConfirmConversions:=True, ReadOnly:=False
```

- Enter the constant or value in the appropriate position in the argument list for the method, without entering the name of the argument. The previous statement would look like this:

```
Documents.Open "c:\Temp\Example.doc", True, False
```

When you use the names of the arguments, you don't need to put them in order, because VBA uses the names to identify them. Both of the following statements are functionally equivalent:

```
Documents.Open ReadOnly:=False, FileName:="c:\temp\Example.doc", _
    ReadOnly:=False, ConfirmConversions:=True
```

```
Documents.Open FileName:="c:\temp\Example.doc", _
    ConfirmConversions:=True, ReadOnly:=False
```

You also don't need to indicate to VBA which arguments you're omitting. By contrast, when you omit the argument names and specify the arguments positionally, the arguments must be in the correct order for VBA to recognize them correctly. If you choose not to use an optional argument, but instead to use another optional argument that follows it, you need to enter a comma to denote the omitted argument. For example, the following statement omits the ConfirmConversions argument and uses a comma to denote that the False value refers to the ReadOnly argument rather than the ConfirmConversions argument:

```
Documents.Open "c:\temp\Example.doc",, False
```

When you type the comma in the Code window or the Immediate window, Auto Quick Info moves the boldface to the next argument in the argument list to indicate that it's next in line for your attention.

 NOTE Typically, required arguments are listed before optional arguments, so you don't have to specify the omission of optional arguments in order to enter the required arguments.

What About the Parentheses around the Argument List?

When you're assigning the result of a function to a variable or other object, you enclose the whole argument list in parentheses. For example, to assign to the variable objMy-Document the result of opening the document c:\temp\Example.doc, use the following statement.

```
objMyDocument = Documents.Open(FileName:="c:\temp\Example.doc", _
    ConfirmConversions:=True, ReadOnly:=False)
```

When you aren't assigning the result of an operation to a variable or an object, you don't use the parentheses around the argument list.

Objects

To VBA, each application consists of a series of *objects*. Here are a few examples using the applications this book covers:

- In Word, a document is an object (the Document object), as is a paragraph (the Paragraph object) or a table (the Table object). Even a single character is an object (the Character object).

- In Excel, a workbook is an object (the Workbook object), as are the worksheets (the Worksheet object) and charts (the Chart object).

- In PowerPoint, a presentation is an object (the Presentation object), as are its slides (the Slide object) and the shapes (the Shape object) they contain.

- In Project, a project is an object (the Project object), as are the resources (the Resource object) and tasks (the Task object) it contains.

- In WordPerfect, each document is an object (the Document object), and the PerfectScript object contains all the PerfectScript commands available to WordPerfect.

- In AutoCAD, each drawing is an object (the Document object). Within a Document object, each layer is represented by a Layer object, and the model space and paper space are represented by the ModelSpace object and PaperSpace object, respectively.

- In Visio, each drawing is an object (the Document object), as are the pages (the Page object) it contains and the connects (the Connect object) and shapes (the Shape object) they in turn contain.

Most of the actions you can take in VBA involve manipulating objects. For example, as you saw earlier, you can close the active document in an application such as Word, AutoCAD, or Visio by using the Close method on the ActiveDocument object:

```
ActiveDocument.Close
```

Collections

A *collection* is simply an object that contains several other objects. Collections provide a way to access all their members at the same time. For example, the Documents collection contains all the open documents, each of which is an object. Instead of closing Document objects one by one, you can close all open documents by using the Close method on the Documents collection:

```
Documents.Close
```

Likewise, you can use a collection to change the properties of all the members of a collection simultaneously.

Properties

Each object has a number of *properties*. For example, a document has properties such as its title, its subject, and its author. You can set these properties through the Properties dialog box (File ➤ Properties). Likewise, a single character has various properties, such as its font, font size, and various types of emphasis (bold, italic, strikethrough, and so on).

Methods

As you've seen already in this chapter, a *method* is an action you can perform with an object. Loosely speaking, a method is a command. Different objects have different methods associated with them—actions you can take with them or commands you can specify that they perform. For example, the following methods are associated with the Document object in Word (and with other objects such as the Workbook object in Excel and the Document object in AutoCAD):

Activate   Activates the document (the equivalent of selecting the document's window with the keyboard or mouse)

Close   Closes the document (the equivalent of choosing File ➢ Close)

Save   Saves the document (the equivalent of choosing File ➢ Save)

SaveAs   Saves the document under a specified name (the equivalent of choosing File ➢ Save As)

That concludes our brief introduction to the VBA vocabulary. Now let's return to the area in which you'll be working with all these mysterious pieces of code: the Visual Basic Editor.

CHAPTER <u>6</u>

Working with Variables and Constants

I n this chapter, I'll cover the basics of working with variables and constants. *Variables* provide a way of storing and manipulating information derived from a procedure, and include String variables for storing text, various numeric data types for storing numbers (for example, Integer variables for storing integer values), Date variables for storing dates and times, Boolean variables for storing True/False values, and Object variables for storing objects. A *constant* is a named item that keeps a constant value while a program is executing.

The one type of variable that I won't discuss in this chapter is the Array variable, which is used to store multiple pieces of information at the same time (keeping them separate). I'll show you arrays in the next chapter.

Working with Variables

The good news is that VBA makes variables as easy to work with as possible. The bad news is that there's a lot of information you'll probably want to know about variables, even if you don't need to learn all of it right away, so you're facing something of a learning curve.

What Is a Variable?

Technically, a variable is a named area in memory that you use for storing data while a procedure is running. For example, in Chapter 5, you created a variable that stored a simple string of text that you then displayed in a message box:

```
myVariable = "Sample variable text"
MsgBox myVariable
```

The first statement sets aside an area in memory, names it `myVariable`, and assigns the string `Sample variable text` to it. The second statement retrieves the contents of `myVariable` from memory and uses the `MsgBox` function to display it in a message box.

Choosing Names for Variables

VBA imposes a number of constraints on variable names, but all in all, they're not too burdensome. Here are the details:

- Variable names must start with a letter and can be up to 255 characters in length. Usually, you'll want to keep them much shorter than this so that you can easily type them into your code, and so that your lines of code don't rapidly reach absurd lengths.

TIP The Visual Basic Editor's AutoComplete feature helps make long variable names a little more manageable: Type enough of the variable's name to distinguish it from any keywords and other variable names, and press Ctrl+spacebar. If you've typed enough to uniquely identify the variable, the Visual Basic Editor will insert its name; if not, it will display the drop-down list of keywords and names starting with those letters.

- Variable names can't contain characters such as periods, exclamation points, mathematical operators (+, −, /, *), or comparison operators (=, <>, >, >=, <, <=); nor can they internally contain type-declaration characters (@, &, $, #). (You'll learn about the type-declaration characters later in this chapter.)
- Variable names can't contain spaces but can contain underscores, which you can use to make the variable names more readable.

In other words, you're pretty safe if you stick with straightforward alphanumerics enlivened with the occasional underscore.

For example, all of the following variable names are fine and upstanding, although the last is awkwardly long to use:

```
i
John
MyVariable
MissionParameters
The_String_That_the_User_Entered_in_the_Input_Box
```

On the other hand, these variable names are not usable:

My Variable	Contains a space
My!Variable	Contains an exclamation point
Time@Tide	Contains a type-declaration character (@) and looks like a botched e-mail address
1_String	Does not start with a letter

Each variable name must be unique within the scope in which it's operating (to prevent VBA from confusing it with any other variable). Typically, the scope within which a variable operates is a procedure, but if you declare the variable as public or module-level private (which I'll discuss later in the chapter), its scope will be wider.

The other constraint on variable names is that it's not a good idea to assign to a variable a name that VBA already uses as the name of a function, a statement, or a method. Doing so is called *shadowing* a VBA keyword. It doesn't necessarily cause problems, but it may prevent you from using that function, statement, or method without specifically identifying it to VBA by prefacing its name with **VBA.** For example, instead of Date, you'd have to use VBA.Date—no big deal, but worth avoiding in the first place.

You're probably thinking that this isn't much of a restriction, and that anyone who hasn't taken leave of their senses should be able to easily avoid shadowing a VBA function, statement, or method with a variable name. But in fact, given how many VBA keywords there are, it's surprisingly easy to shadow one of them—especially when you suddenly lack inspiration for naming, say, a date or a time. Use Date or Time in this case, and you've shadowed a VBA keyword. Go directly to jail, do not pass Go, do not collect your lottery ticket....

Declaring a Variable

VBA lets you declare variables either implicitly or explicitly. As I'll explain shortly, each method has pros and cons. At the risk of dampening your involvement in the plot of this chapter, I'll mention at this point that explicit declarations are almost always a good idea, and when you've been working with VBA for even a little while, I'm pretty sure you'll be using them religiously. Because of this, I recommend you declare your variables explicitly right from the beginning, so that you get into the habit—but I'll show you how to declare a variable implicitly so that you'll know your options.

Declaring a Variable Implicitly

Declaring a variable implicitly means you simply use it in your code without declaring it explicitly. When you declare a variable implicitly, VBA checks to make sure that there isn't already an existing variable with that name. It then automatically creates a variable with that name for you and assigns it the Variant data type, which can contain any type of data except a fixed-length string.

For example, in the previous chapter, you declared the variable myVariable by using the following implicit declaration:

```
myVariable = "Sample variable text"
```

Here, myVariable is implicitly declared as a variable. VBA assigns it the Variant data type. In this case, the variable will be a string because it contains text. VBA usually assigns the variable the value Empty (a special value used to indicate Variant variables that have never been used) when it creates it, but in this case the variable receives a value immediately (because the string of text is assigned to it).

The advantage of declaring a variable implicitly is that you don't have to code it ahead of time. If you want a variable, you can simply declare it on the spot. However, declaring a variable implicitly also has a couple of disadvantages:

- It's easier to make a mistake when re-entering the name of an implicitly declared variable later in the procedure. For example, suppose you implicitly declare the variable FilesToCreate and then later type FllesToCreate instead. VBA won't query the latter spelling with its typo, but will create another variable with that name, and the new variable won't have the same value as the old one. When you're working with a number of variables, it can be difficult and time-consuming to catch little mistakes like these, which can throw a sizable monkey wrench into your code.

- The Variant variable type takes up more memory than other types of variable, because it has to be able to store various types of data. This difference is negligible under most normal circumstances, particularly if you're using only a few variables or writing only short procedures; but if you're using many variables on a computer with limited memory, the extra memory used by Variant variables might slow down a procedure or even run it out of memory. What's more important on an underpowered computer is that manipulating Variants takes longer than manipulating the other data types. This is because VBA has to keep checking to see what sort of data is in the variable.

You can get around this second disadvantage in a couple of ways: by using a type-declaration character to specify the data type when you declare a variable implicitly, or, as you will see in the next section, by telling VBA to force you to declare variables explicitly.

A *type-declaration character* is a character that you add to the end of a variable's name in an implicit declaration to tell VBA which data type to use for the variable. Table 6.1 lists the type-declaration characters.

TABLE 6.1: TYPE-DECLARATION CHARACTERS

Character	Data Type of Variable	Example
%	Integer	Quantity%
&	Long	China&
@	Currency	Profits@
!	Single	temperature!
#	Double	Differential#
$	String (variable length)	myMessage$

So you could implicitly declare the String variable UserName with the following statement, which assigns the value Jane Magnolia to the variable:

```
UserName$ = "Jane Magnolia"
```

And you could implicitly declare the currency variable `Price` by using this statement:

```
Price@ = Cost * Margin
```

You use the type-declaration character only when declaring the variable. Thereafter, you can refer to the variable by its name—`UserName` and `Price` in the previous examples.

Declaring a Variable Explicitly

Declaring a variable explicitly means telling VBA that the variable exists before you use it. VBA then allocates memory space to that variable and registers it as a known quantity. You can also declare the variable type at the same time—a good idea, but not obligatory.

You can declare a variable explicitly at any point in code before you use it, but custom and good sense recommend declaring all your variables at the beginning of the procedure that uses them. Doing so makes them easy to find, which will help anyone reading the code.

Declaring variables explicitly offers the following advantages:

- Your code will be easier to read and to debug. When you write complex code, this is an important consideration.

- It will be more difficult for you to create new variables unintentionally by mistyping the names of existing variables. As a corollary to this, it will also be more difficult for you to wipe out the contents of an existing variable unintentionally when trying to create a new variable.

- VBA can catch some data-typing errors at design time or compile time that with implicit declarations wouldn't surface until runtime. (A *data-typing error* occurs when you assign the wrong type of information to a variable. For example, if you declare an Integer variable and then assign a string of text to it, VBA gets unhappy, because it can't store string information in an Integer variable.)

- Your code will run a fraction faster because VBA won't need to determine each variable's type while the code is running.

The main disadvantage of declaring variables explicitly is that doing so takes a little more time, effort, and thought. For most code, however, this disadvantage is far outweighed by the advantages.

To declare a variable explicitly, you use one of the following keywords: `Dim`, `Private`, `Public`, or `Static`.

For example, the following statement declares the variable `MyValue`:

```
Dim MyValue
```

`Dim` is the regular keyword to use for declaring a variable, and you'll probably want to use it for most of your variable declarations. You use the other keywords to specify a different scope, lifetime, and data type for the variable in the declaration. In the previous example, the MyValue variable receives the default scope and lifetime, and the Variant data type, which makes it suitable for general-purpose use.

 TIP As I mentioned earlier, it's usually a good idea to declare all variable names together at the beginning of a procedure. Doing so makes the names easy to find so that you can quickly refer back to make sure you've got the right name, instead of trudging through dozens of lines of code to find the relevant declaration. It also makes your code much simpler to read and debug.

You can also declare multiple variables on the same line by separating the variable statements with commas:

```
Dim Supervisor As String, ControllerCode As Long
```

Be warned that when you declare multiple variables on the same line, you need to specify the data type for each, as in the previous example. You might be tempted to try a little abbreviation, like this, hoping for a couple of String variables:

```
Dim strManager, strMinion As String
```

Bzzzt. This won't work the way you'd hope. Instead, you'll find that strMinion will be a String variable, but strManager will be a Variant, because the As String part of the code only applies to strMinion. VBA's too literal to understand apposition.

Requiring Explicit Declarations for Variables

You can set VBA to require you to declare variables explicitly, either globally (for all modules you work with) or on a module-by-module basis. Most people find this feature useful, because you can use it to prevent yourself from declaring any variables implicitly, intentionally or otherwise. It's as if your toothbrush could force you to floss (only less painful).

To require variable declarations globally, choose Tools ➣ Options in the Visual Basic Editor to display the Options dialog box; click the Editor tab to display the Editor page; select the Require Variable Declaration check box in the Code Settings area; then click the OK button. (The Require Variable Declaration check box is deselected by default, enabling you to declare variables implicitly, which is usually the easiest way to start working with variables.) The Visual Basic Editor will then add an Option Explicit statement to new modules that you create. This statement requires explicit variable declarations for the module it's in.

Continued

CONTINUED

When you select the Require Variable Declaration check box, the Visual Basic Editor won't add the `Option Explicit` statement to your existing modules—you'll need to do that manually if you want to force explicit declarations in them too.

To require variable declarations only for specified modules, put an `Option Explicit` statement at the beginning of each module for which you want to require declarations. It needs to go before the `Sub` or `Function` statement for the first procedure in the module—if you put it inside a procedure, or between procedures, VBA will throw an error when you try to run any of the code in the module.

If you've set `Option Explicit` either globally or for a module, VBA will test the procedure before running it. More precisely, VBA will complain when it tries to compile the code and discovers that you haven't declared one or more of the variables, and will warn you if a variable isn't explicitly declared, as shown here. The variable will also be highlighted in your code.

If you get this message box, you can solve the problem either by declaring the variable, or by turning off the requirement of variable declarations for the module. To turn off the requirement, remove the `Option Explicit` statement from the module by selecting and deleting the line that contains it, or by commenting out this line.

Choosing the Scope and Lifetime of a Variable

The *scope* of a variable is the area in VBA within which it can operate. Typically, you'll want to use a variable with its default scope—that is, within the procedure in which it's declared (implicitly or explicitly). For example, suppose you have a module named Financial_Procedures that contains the procedures Breakeven_Table and Profit_Analysis_Table, each of which uses a variable named Gross_Revenue and another named Expenses. The variables in each procedure will be distinct from the variables in the other procedure, and there will be no danger of VBA confusing the two. (For the human reader, though, using the same variable names in different procedures rapidly becomes confusing when debugging. In general, it's a good idea to use unique variable names, even at the default procedure level.)

The *lifetime* of a variable is the period during which VBA remembers the value of the variable. You'll need different lifetimes for your variables for different purposes. A variable's lifetime is tied to its scope.

Sometimes you'll need to access a variable from outside the procedure in which it's declared. In these cases, you'll need to declare a different scope for the variable.

A variable can have three types of scope:

- procedure
- private
- public

Let's look at each of these in turn.

Procedure Scope

A variable with *procedure scope* (also known as *procedure-level scope* or *local scope*) is available only to the procedure that contains it. As a result, the lifetime of a local variable is limited to the duration of the procedure that declares it: As soon as the procedure stops running, VBA removes all local variables from memory and reclaims the memory that held them.

Procedure scope is all you'll need for variables that operate only in the procedure in which they're declared. For example, say you implicitly declare a Variant variable named Supervisor like this:

```
Supervisor = "John Random Loser"
```

You can then use the Supervisor variable in the rest of that procedure—for example, retrieving the text stored in it, or changing that text. When the procedure stops running, VBA will kill the variable and reclaim the memory it occupied.

 NOTE When you declare a variable implicitly, it's automatically assigned procedure scope.

To explicitly declare a local variable, use the Dim keyword or the Static keyword and place the declaration inside the procedure like this:

```
Sub Create_Weekly_Report()
    Dim strSupervisor As String
    Dim lngController As Long
    Static intReportNumber As Integer

...
End Sub
```

Here, the second line declares the variable `strSupervisor` as the String data type, the third line declares the variable `lngController` as the Long data type, and the fourth line declares the variable `intReportNumber` as the Integer data type. (I'll go through the different data types in the section, "Specifying the Data Type for a Variable," in a few pages' time.)

On the other hand, if you needed to pass any of these variables to another procedure that you called from the current procedure, procedure scope wouldn't be sufficient—you'd need to use either private scope or public scope.

Private Scope

A variable with private scope is available to all procedures in the module that contains it, but not to procedures in other modules. Using private variables enables you to pass the value of a variable from one procedure to another. Unlike local variables, which retain their value only as long as the procedure that contains them is running, private variables retain their value as long as the project that contains them is open.

To declare a variable with private scope, you can use either the `Dim` keyword or the `Private` keyword at the beginning of a module, placing it before the Sub statement for the first procedure in the module:

```
Dim strSupervisor As String
Private blnConsultant As Boolean

Sub Assign_Personnel()
```

You'll notice that the `Dim` statement here uses exactly the same syntax as the earlier declaration for the local variable—the difference is that to declare a private variable, the statement is placed at the beginning of the module rather than within a procedure. Because the `Private` statement has the same effect as the `Dim` statement for declaring private variables and can't be used within a procedure, it's clearer to use the `Private` statement rather than the `Dim` statement for declaring private variables. Your code will also be clearer if you stick with `Private` rather than mixing `Private` statements with `Dim` statements as I've done in this example (although VBA will happily accept the mixture).

 WARNING After you edit a procedure in the Visual Basic Editor, private variables and public variables will be reset (their values will be erased) when the Visual Basic Editor recompiles the code. If you're testing a project that uses private or public variables, you'll need to reinitialize (reassign values to) them after each edit you make.

Public Scope

A variable with public scope is available to all procedures in all modules in the project that contains it.

To declare a public variable, you use the `Public` keyword in the Declarations section at the beginning of a module, before the Sub statement for the first procedure in the module:

```
Public intMyVar As Integer
```

This statement declares the variable `intMyVar` as the Integer type.

 NOTE The Declarations section appears at the beginning of each module that contains declarations. For example, if you choose to use explicit variable declarations (by selecting the Require Variable Declaration check box on the Editor page of the Options dialog box), the Visual Basic Editor will enter the `Option Explicit` declaration at the start of each new module you create. If not, the Declarations section is created when you first enter a statement there manually.

Like private variables, public variables retain their value as long as the project that contains them is open. For example, if you wanted to track the user's name through a series of operations in Word, you could create an `AutoExec` procedure that prompted the user to enter their name when they started Word. By storing the result of their input in a public variable, you could then retrieve the value for use later in the same Word session. Listing 6.1 shows an example of using a public variable with an `AutoExec` procedure like this.

Again, public variables are reset when the Visual Basic Editor recompiles code, so you'll need to reinitialize them after editing your code.

Listing 6.1

```
1.  Public strCurrentUser As String
2.
3.  Sub AutoExec()
4.      strCurrentUser = InputBox("Please enter your name.", _
            "Current User Identity")
5.  End Sub
6.
7.  Sub Identify_Current_User()
```

```
8.      MsgBox "The current user is " & strCurrentUser, _
            vbOKOnly + vbInformation, "Current User"
9.  End Sub
```

Analysis

This code consists of three different parts:

- Line 1 declares the public String variable strCurrentUser.

- Lines 3 through 5 contain the AutoExec procedure. This procedure will run each time the user starts Word. Line 4 displays an input box that prompts the user to enter their name and stores their response in the public variable strCurrentUser.

- Lines 7 through 9 contain the Identify_Current_User procedure, which simply displays a message box that gives the name of the user, along with lead-in text and an information icon and title bar for completeness.

You could step through the AutoExec and Identify_Current_User procedures in the Visual Basic Editor by using the F8 key, but to see their effect, create the procedures and then exit Word. When you restart Word, the AutoExec procedure will display the input box for you to enter your name. At any point thereafter (until you exit Word), you can run the Identify_Current_User procedure, and VBA will display a message box with the name you entered.

 WARNING Because public variables retain their value when no procedure is running, they continue to take up space in memory. If you grossly abuse public variables, you might run short of memory or cause increased swap-file use on a computer with limited quantities of memory available.

Using Static Variables

Beside Dim, Private, and Public, there's also the Static keyword, which you can use for declaring *static* variables—variables whose values you want to preserve between calls to the procedure in which they are declared. Static variables are similar to public variables in that their lifetime is not limited to the duration of the procedure that declares them; the difference is that static variables, once declared, are available only to the procedure that declared them, whereas public variables are available to all procedures once they've been declared.

Static variables are useful for maintaining information on a process that you need to run a number of times during a session of the application, either to maintain a running total (for example, a count of the times you performed a procedure), or to keep at hand a piece of information that may prove useful when you run a procedure a second or subsequent time.

The following statement declares the static String variable strSearchTerm1:

```
Static strSearchTerm1 As String
```

 NOTE Like public variables, static variables take up memory once you've created them, so don't use them unnecessarily.

Specifying the Data Type for a Variable

VBA supports the following *data types* for variables:

- Boolean
- Byte
- Currency
- Date
- Decimal
- Double
- Integer
- Long
- Object
- Single
- String
- Variant

Over the next few pages, you'll examine each of these data types in turn. First, though, I should mention that you don't have to specify data types if you don't want to. Almost always, you can use the default Variant data type (as you've done a couple of times so far) and let VBA figure out how to handle the niceties.

There are three disadvantages to using the Variant data type for everything including the kitchen sink:

- First, the Variant data type takes up more memory than any of the other data types (except long strings). In the next few sections, I'll mention how much memory each data type takes up; even if you don't care about this information now, you may want to refer back to it later on in your explorations of VBA.

- Second, using the Variant data type causes your code to run more slowly. With short procedures (or long procedures involving relatively few variables), memory and speed are rarely an issue—in fact, you probably won't notice any speed difference unless you're dangerously hyper or you're running VBA on a sorely underpowered computer (or both).

- Third—and more of a concern—your code will be harder for humans to read and to debug.

When you get to Chapter 19, "Building Well-Behaved Procedures," which discusses how to optimize your code, I'll discuss the pros and cons of specifying data types for your variables. Right now, let's take a look at what the different data types mean.

Boolean

A Boolean variable is a two-position variable: It can be set only to True or False. You can use the keywords True and False to set the value of a Boolean variable, as in the second line below (the first declares the Boolean variable blnProduct_Available):

```
Dim blnProduct_Available As Boolean
blnProduct_Available = True
```

You can then retrieve the result of the Boolean variable and take action accordingly:

```
If blnProduct_Available = True Then
    MsgBox "The product is available."
Else                'blnProduct_Available = False
    MsgBox "The product is not available."
End If
```

When you convert a Boolean variable to another data type (such as a numeric value), True returns −1 and False returns 0. When you convert a numeric value to a Boolean value, 0 returns False and all other numbers (whether positive or negative) return True.

Boolean variables are a good place to start declaring the data types of your variables, simply because they're so easy to use. Boolean variables take up two bytes each.

Byte

A Byte variable takes up the least memory of any data type (appropriately enough, just one byte) and can store a number from 0 to 255. Given this limitation, you probably won't want to use Byte variables very often.

Currency

The Currency data type is designed for use with money. It allows for positive and negative numbers with up to 15 digits to the left of the decimal point and 4 digits to the right of it. Unlike the Single and Double data types that you'll look at in a moment, the Currency data type is exact, not rounded.

To implicitly declare a currency variable, use the type-declaration character @. For example, you might indulge your curiosity by working out your weekly salary with a little simple math:

```
Sub Calculate_Weekly_Salary()
    Salary@ = InputBox("Enter your salary.", _
        "Calculate Weekly Salary")
    WeeklySalary@ = Salary / 52
    MsgBox WeeklySalary
End Sub
```

Currency variables take up eight bytes each.

Date

The Date data type is relatively complex. VBA works with dates and times as floating-point numbers (numbers in which the quantity is given by one number multiplied by a power of the number base), with the date displayed to the left of the decimal point and the time to the right. VBA can handle dates from 1 January 100 to 31 December 9999 and times from 0:00:00 to 23:59:59.

You can enter date variables as literal date values—such as **6/3/36** or **June 3, 1936**—by placing a # sign before and after the literal date value:

```
#June 3, 1936#
```

When you move the insertion point from the line in the code window in which you've entered a literal date value between # signs, VBA converts the data to a number and changes the display to the date format set in your computer. For example, if you enter **June 3, 1936**, VBA will probably display it as 6/3/36. Likewise, you can enter a literal time value (for example, #10:15PM#) and VBA will convert it to a number and display it according to the current time format (for example, 10:15:00 PM).

Whether you're at the turn of a millennium or not, it's a good idea to always specify which century you're dealing with when you specify a year. If you don't specify the century, VBA assigns any year from 1 through 29 to the twentieth century and any year from 30 through 00 to the twenty-first century (in which I'm including the year 2000). Why use 1929 as the cut-off? Well, because the Black Thursday crash of the stock market marked a watershed in the flow of time....

Date variables take up eight bytes each.

Decimal

The Decimal data type stores unsigned integers scaled by powers of 10. (*Unsigned* here means that the integers carry no plus or minus designation, not that your check's going to be returned by the electric company.)

 NOTE In the Word 97 and Word 2000 implementation of VBA, you can't declare a Decimal variable—you can only use the Decimal data type within a Variant data type (which we'll examine in detail later in this section).

Decimal variables take up 12 bytes each.

Double

The Double data type is for floating-point numbers and can handle negative values from -1.79769313486232^{308} to -4.94065645841247^{-324} and positive numbers from 4.94065645841247^{-324} to 1.79769313486232^{308}.

 NOTE *Double* here stands for double-precision floating point—the way in which the number is handled by the computer. *Single* (which you'll look at later in the list) stands for single-precision floating point, which works with fewer decimal places and is consequently less accurate.

You can use the # type-declaration character to declare a Double variable implicitly. Double variables take up eight bytes each.

Integer

The Integer data type is the most efficient way of handling numbers from –32,768 to 32,767, a range that makes it useful for many procedures. For example, if you wanted to repeat an action 300 times, you could use an Integer variable for the counter, as in the following lines:

```
Dim intMyVar As Integer
For intMyVar = 1 to 300
    'repeat actions
Next intMyVar
```

Integer variables take up two bytes each.

Long

The Long data type is for integer numeric values larger or smaller than those the Integer data type can handle: Long variables can handle numbers from –2,147,483,648 to 2,147,483,647. (For numbers even larger or smaller than these, use the Double data type, but beware of its rounding.)

Long variables use the type-declaration character & for implicit declarations and take up four bytes each.

Object

The Object data type is for storing addresses that reference objects (for example, objects in an application's object model), providing an easy way to refer to an object.

Object variables take up four bytes each.

Single

The Single data type, like the Double data type, is for working with floating-point numbers. Single can handle negative values from -3.402823^{38} to -1.401298^{-45} and positive values from 1.401298^{-45} to 3.402823^{38}. As noted earlier, these numbers use fewer decimal places than the Double data type provides.

Use the exclamation point type-declaration character to declare a Single variable implicitly (if you must use implicit declarations). Single variables take up four bytes each.

String

The String data type is for handling text:

- Variable-length strings can contain up to about two billion characters. They take up 10 bytes plus the storage required for the string.

- Fixed-length strings can contain from 1 to about 64,000 characters. They take up only the storage required for the string. If the data assigned to the string is shorter than the fixed length, VBA pads the data with trailing spaces to make up the full complement of characters. If the data assigned to the string is longer than the fixed length, VBA truncates the data after the relevant character. VBA counts the characters from the left end of the string: For example, if you assign the string Output to a fixed-length string that's four characters long, VBA will store Outp. If you're typical, you'll use variable-length strings far more frequently than fixed-length strings, have 2.17 kids, and eat less broccoli than chocolate.

- Strings can contain letters, numbers, spaces, and punctuation, not to mention special characters.

- You can use the $ type-declaration character to declare a string implicitly, but (as usual) you'll do best to declare your strings explicitly, along with all your other variables.

Variant

The Variant data type, as mentioned earlier in this chapter, is assigned by VBA to all variables whose data type isn't declared—so a declaration such as Dim myUntypedVariable will create a Variant. (You can also declare a Variant variable explicitly: Dim myVariant As Variant, for example.) Variants can handle most of the different types of data, but there are a couple characteristics of Variants to keep in mind:

- First, Variants can't contain fixed-length string data. If you need to use a fixed-length string, you need to specify a fixed-length string.

- Second, Variant variables can also contain four special values: Empty (which means the variable hasn't yet been initialized), Error (a special value used for tracking errors in a procedure), Nothing (a special value used for disassociating a variable from the object it was associated with), and Null (which you use to indicate that the variable deliberately contains no data).

Because of their extra capabilities, Variant variables take up more memory than other types. Variant variables that contain numbers take up 16 bytes, and Variant variables that contain characters take up 22 bytes plus the storage required for the characters.

Deciding among Types for Variables

If you found the details of the different types of variables confusing, relax. First, as already discussed, you can usually avoid the whole issue of choosing a variable type by declaring the variable either implicitly or explicitly and letting VBA assign the Variant data type. Second, if you do choose to specify data types for some of your variables, you can apply a few straightforward rules to direct your choices:

- If the variable will contain only the values True and False, declare it as the Boolean data type.

- If the variable will always contain an integer (if it will never contain a fraction), declare it as the Integer data type. (If the number may be too big for the Integer data type, declare it as the Long data type instead.)

- If the variable will be used for calculating money, or if you require no-rounding fractions, use the Currency data type.

- If the variable may sometimes contain a fraction, declare it as the Single or Double data type.

- If the variable will always contain a string (rather than a number), declare it as the String data type.

 TIP If you aren't sure what type of variable will best contain the information you're planning to use, start by declaring the variable as a Variant. Then step through the procedure in Break mode with the Locals window displayed (View ➤ Locals) and see what Variant subtype VBA assigns to the variable: You'll see a listing such as Variant/Double or Variant/String in the Type column. Test the procedure a couple more times to make sure this subtype is consistent, and then try declaring the variable as the data type indicated by the subtype. Run the code a few times to make sure that the new data type works. This little info-boost from VBA can be especially helpful if you're hazy on the differences between, say, numeric data types such as Double and Single.

Working with Constants

As I mentioned way back at the beginning of this chapter, a constant is a named item that keeps a constant value during execution of a program.

VBA provides a number of constants, but you can also declare your own constants to help you work smoothly with information that stays constant through a procedure.

Declaring Your Own Constants

To declare your own constants, use the Const statement. By declaring a constant, you can simplify your code when you need to reuse a set value a number of times in your procedures.

Syntax

The syntax for the Const statement is as follows:

```
[Public/Private] Const constant [As type] = expression
```

Here, Public and Private are optional keywords used for declaring public or private scope for a constant. We'll examine how they work in a moment. *constant* is the name of the constant, which follows the normal rules for naming variables. *type* is an optional argument that specifies the data type of the constant. *expression* is a literal (a value written into your code), another constant, or a combination of the two.

As with variables, you can declare multiple constants in the same line by separating the statements with a comma:

```
Const conPerformer As String = "Rikki Nadir", _
    conTicketPrice As String = "$34.99"
```

Example

As you can see from the syntax, declaring a constant in VBA works in a similar way to declaring a variable explicitly. The main difference is that you have to declare the value of the constant when you declare the constant (rather than at a later point of your choosing) and you can't change its value afterwards (hence the name *constant*).

As an example, take a look at the statements below:

```
Const conVenue As String = "Davies Hall"
Const conDate As Date = #December 31, 1999#
MsgBox "The concert is at " & conVenue & " on " _
    & conDate & "."
```

The first line declares the constant conVenue as a String data type and assigns it the data Davies Hall. The second line declares the constant conDate as a Date string type and assigns it the date December 31, 1999. (When you finish creating this line of code and move the insertion point to another line, VBA will change the date to the date format set in your computer's clock—#12/31/99#, for example.) The third line displays a message box containing a string concatenated from the three text items in double quotation marks, the conVenue string constant, and the conDate date constant.

Choosing the Scope and Lifetime for Your Constants

The default scope for a constant declared in a procedure is local—that is, its scope is the procedure that declares it. Consequently, its lifetime is the time for which the procedure runs. However, you can set a different scope and lifetime for your constants in much the same way that you set a different scope for a variable: by using the `Public` or `Private` keywords when you declare the constants:

- To declare a private constant, place the declaration at the beginning of the module in which you want the constant to be available. A private constant's lifetime isn't limited, but it's available only to procedures in the module in which it's declared:

```
Private Const conPerformer As String = "Rikki Nadir"
```

- To declare a public constant, place the declaration at the beginning of a module. A public constant's lifetime isn't limited, and it's available to all procedures in all modules in the project in which it's declared:

```
Public Const conTicketPrice As String = "$34.99"
```

In the next chapter, you'll learn how to use arrays—variables that can hold multiple pieces of data.

CHAPTER **7**

Using Arrays

In this chapter, you'll learn how to use array variables—variables that can each store multiple values at the same time.

You'll start by examining what arrays are and what you use them for. You'll then examine how to create them, populate them, and erase them. Along the way, you'll look at how to resize an array to make it contain more (or fewer) values, how to specify the scope for an array, and how to find out whether a variable is an array or a regular, single-value variable.

What Is an Array?

An *array* is a variable on steroids—a variable that can contain a number of values that have the same data type. (Before you ask—if the array's data type is Variant, multiple types of data can be stored within it.) VBA treats an array as a single variable that can store multiple values. You can refer to the array itself to work with all the values it contains, or you can refer to the individual values stored within the array by using their index numbers, which indicate their position within the array. If you're having difficulty visualizing what this means, try picturing an array as a list. Each item in the list is located in its own row and is identified by an index number, so you can access the value of the item by specifying the index number.

That's a simple array, one that has only one dimension. You can also declare multidimensional arrays, which I'll get to in a couple of minutes.

An array is delimited by a lower bound and an upper bound. By default, the lower bound is zero, so the first item in an array is indexed as zero. This can be confusing, because you're always working with an index number that's one lower than the item's position in the array. However, you can change the default index number of the first item in an array to 1 by using an `Option Base 1` statement at the beginning of the module that contains the array. If you do so, the index number for each item in the array is the same as the item's position in the array:

```
Option Base 1
```

Declaring an Array

An array is a kind of variable, so you would declare it by using the regular keywords: `Dim`, `Private`, `Public`, or `Static`. The key difference is that when declaring an array, you add a pair of parentheses after the array's name (to indicate that it's an array), and you can also declare the number of items in it by using what's called an *array subscript*. For example, you could declare an array named curMonthProfit as the Currency data type containing 12 items by using the following statement:

```
Dim curMonthProfit(11) As Currency
```

Figure 7.1 shows a simple representation of the single-dimensional array created.

FIGURE 7.1

The single-dimensional array created by the statement Dim cur-MonthProfit(11) As Currency *can be thought of as looking like this.*

Element #	Name	Contents
0	curMonthProfit(0)	—
1	curMonthProfit(1)	—
2	curMonthProfit(2)	—
3	curMonthProfit(3)	—
4	curMonthProfit(4)	—
5	curMonthProfit(5)	—
6	curMonthProfit(6)	—
7	curMonthProfit(7)	—
8	curMonthProfit(8)	—
9	curMonthProfit(9)	—
10	curMonthProfit(10)	—
11	curMonthProfit(11)	—

You could also create an array without a specified number of subscripts by using the following statement:

```
Dim myArray()
```

As I mentioned, index numbering for the array begins at 0, so 1 is the second item, 2 the third, and 11 the twelfth. If you used an Option Base statement at the beginning of the module, you'd declare the array like this:

```
Option Base 1    'at the beginning of the code sheet

Dim curMonthProfit(12) As Currency
```

Figure 7.2 shows a simple representation of how this array would look.

FIGURE 7.2

The single-dimensional array created by the statement Dim cur-MonthProfit(12) As Currency *with the* Option Base 1 *statement*

Element #	Name	Contents
1	curMonthProfit(1)	—
2	curMonthProfit(2)	—
3	curMonthProfit(3)	—
4	curMonthProfit(4)	—
5	curMonthProfit(5)	—
6	curMonthProfit(6)	—
7	curMonthProfit(7)	—
8	curMonthProfit(8)	—
9	curMonthProfit(9)	—
10	curMonthProfit(10)	—
11	curMonthProfit(11)	—
12	curMonthProfit(12)	—

In this example, the array is assigned the Currency data type, but you can omit the data type and have VBA automatically use the Variant data type, the way it does for any variable you create without specifying the data type. The price for this type is slightly increased memory usage, which could (under extreme circumstances) slow the performance of the computer: Because an array needs storage for each item it contains, a large array can consume a significant amount of memory. This is particularly true with multidimensional arrays.

You can also specify both bounds of an array explicitly:

```
Option Base 1   'at the beginning of the code sheet

Dim curMonthProfit(1 To 12) As Currency
```

NOTE Because working with arrays is much easier if you use an Option Base 1 statement, I'll use Option Base 1 statements through the rest of this chapter.

Storing Values in an Array

To assign a value to an item in an array, you use the index number to identify the item. For example, the following statements assign the values London, Hong Kong, and Taipei to the last three items in the array strLocations:

```
Option Base 1

Dim strLocations(6) As String
strLocations(1) = "London"
strLocations(2) = "Hong Kong"
strLocations(3) = "Taipei"
```

Figure 7.3 shows how this array can be envisioned.

FIGURE 7.3

A simple String array with three values assigned

Element #	Name	Contents
1	strLocations(1)	London
2	strLocations(2)	Hong Kong
3	strLocations(3)	Taipei
4	strLocations(4)	—
5	strLocations(5)	—
6	strLocations(6)	—

Multidimensional Arrays

The curMonthProfit example in the previous section is a one-dimensional array, which is the easiest kind of array to use. But VBA supports arrays with up to 60 dimensions—enough to tax the visualization skills of anyone without a Ph.D. in multidimensional modeling. You probably won't want to get this complicated with arrays—two, three, or four dimensions are enough for most purposes.

To declare a multidimensional array, you separate the dimensions with commas. For example, the following statements declare a two-dimensional array named MyArray with three items in each dimension:

```
Option Base 1
Dim MyArray(3, 3)
```

Figure 7.4 shows how you might represent the resulting array.

FIGURE 7.4

You can think of a two-dimensional array as consisting of rows and columns.

Column 1	Column 2	Column 3
1,1	2,1	3,1
1,2	2,2	3,2
1,3	2,3	3,3

Multidimensional arrays sound forbidding, but a two-dimensional array is quite straightforward if you think of it basically as a table that consists of rows and columns. Here, the first series of 10 elements would appear in the first column of the (imaginary) table, and the second series of 10 elements would appear in the second column. The information in any series doesn't need to be related to information in the other series, although it does need to be the same data type. For example, you could assign 10 folder names to the first dimension of a String variable array, 10 file names to the second dimension (more strings), the names of your 10 cats to the third, the list of assassinated or impeached U.S. presidents to the fourth, and so on. You could then access the information in the array by specifying the position of the item you want to access (as it were, the second item in the first column of the imaginary table). We'll look at how to do this in just a minute.

Similarly, you could picture a three-dimensional array as being something like a workbook of spreadsheets—rows and columns, with more of the same in the third dimension (down, or away from you, depending on your current relationship to the force of gravity). But that's about the range of easily pictureable arrays—four-dimensional and larger arrays start to tax the imagination.

Declaring a Dynamic Array

You can declare both *fixed-size* arrays and *dynamic* arrays. The examples we've looked at so far were fixed-size arrays; for instance, the size of the curMonthProfit array was specified as 12 items.

Dynamic arrays are useful when you need to store a variable number of items. For example, for a procedure that arranges two windows side by side, you might create an array to contain the name of each open window. Because you won't know how many windows will be open when you run the procedure, you may want to use a dynamic array to contain the information.

To declare a dynamic array, you use a declaration statement without specifying the number of items, by including the parentheses but leaving them empty. For example, the following statement declares the dynamic array `arrTestArray` and causes VBA to assign it the Variant data type:

```
Dim arrTestArray()
```

Redimensioning an Array

You can change the size of, or *redimension*, a dynamic array by using the ReDim statement. For example, to redimension the dynamic array `arrTestArray` declared in the previous example and assign it a size of five items, you could use the following statement:

```
ReDim arrTestArray(5)
```

When you use ReDim to redimension an array like this, you'll lose the values currently in the array. If so far you've only declared the array as a dynamic array, and it contains nothing, losing its (nonexistent) contents won't bother you; but at other times, you'll want to increase the size of an array without trashing its current contents. To preserve the existing values in an array when you raise its upper bound, use a ReDim Preserve statement instead of a straight ReDim statement:

```
ReDim Preserve arrTestArray(5)
```

If you use ReDim Preserve to lower the upper bound of the array, you lose the information stored in any subscripts not included in the redimensioned array. For example, if you have a five-subscript array with information in each slot, and you redimension it using ReDim Preserve so that it has only three subscripts, you'll lose the information in the fourth and fifth subscripts. (Okay, this isn't rocket science, but you need to understand what happens.)

 NOTE ReDim Preserve works only for the last dimension of the array (which isn't a problem for one-dimensional arrays).

Returning Information from an Array

To return information from an array, you use the index number to specify the position of the information you want to return. For example, the following statement returns the fourth item in the array named arrMyArray and displays it in a message box:

```
Option Base 1
MsgBox arrMyArray(4)
```

The following statement returns the fifth item in the second dimension of a two-dimensional array named arrMy2DArray and displays it in a message box:

```
Option Base 1

MsgBox arrMy2DArray(2,5)
```

 NOTE To return multiple items from an array, specify each item individually.

Erasing an Array

To erase the contents of an array, use the Erase statement with the name of the array. This statement reinitializes the items in a fixed-size array and frees the memory taken by items in dynamic arrays (completely erasing the array). For example, the following statement erases the contents of the fixed-size array named arrMyArray:

```
Erase arrMyArray
```

Finding Out Whether a Variable Is an Array

Because an array is a type of variable, you may occasionally need to check whether a particular variable name denotes an array or a *scalar variable* (a variable that isn't an array). To find out whether a variable is an array, use the IsArray function with the variable's name. For example, the following statements check the variable MyVariable and display the results in a message box:

```
If IsArray(MyVariable) = True Then
    Msg = "The variable is an array."
```

```
Else
    Msg = "The variable is not an array."
End If
MsgBox Msg, vbOKOnly + vbInformation, "Array Check 2000"
```

Finding the Bounds of an Array

To find the bounds of an array, use the LBound (for the lower bound, the index number of the first item) and UBound (for the upper bound, the index number of the last item) functions. They take the following syntax:

```
LBound(array [, dimension])
UBound(array [, dimension])
```

Here, *array* is a required argument specifying the name of the array, and *dimension* is an optional variant specifying the dimension whose bound you want to return—1 for the first dimension, 2 for the second, and so on. (If you omit the *dimension* argument, VBA assumes you mean the first dimension.)

For example, the following statement returns the upper bound of the second dimension in the array named arrMyArray and displays it in a message box:

```
MsgBox UBound(arrMyArray, 2)
```

Sorting an Array

Another activity you'll often want to perform with an array is sorting, especially when you load information into the array from an external source rather than assigning values one by one in your code.

Sorting is easy to understand conceptually: You simply put things into the desired order—for example, you could sort the strings in one array into alphabetical order or reverse alphabetical order, or the integers in another array into ascending order or descending order. But (as you'd probably imagine) executing sorting programmatically is much more difficult.

In this section, I'll show you a simple form of sorting—the bubble sort, so called because the items being sorted to the earlier positions in the array gradually bubble up to the top. The bubble sort consists of two loops that compare two items in the array; if the second item belongs further up the list than the first item, the sort reverses their positions, and the comparisons continue until the whole list is sorted into order.

NOTE You'll examine loops in detail in Chapter 12.

Before I get into this, I should mention that the bubble sort is far from the most efficient method of sorting items—but it's easy to understand, and it gets the job done. (And, these days, processor cycles are relatively cheap—at least, compared to the old days, when inefficient sorting such as this would have brought swift retribution down on your neck.)

Listing 7.1 contains the code for the bubble sort.

Listing 7.1

```
1.   Option Explicit
2.   Option Base 1
3.
4.   Sub Sort_an_Array()
5.
6.       'declare the array and other variables
7.       Dim strArray(12) As String
8.       Dim strTemp As String
9.       Dim strMsg As String
10.      Dim X As Integer, Y As Integer, i As Integer
11.
12.      'assign strings to the array
13.      strArray(1) = "nihilism"
14.      strArray(2) = "defeatism"
15.      strArray(3) = "hope"
16.      strArray(4) = "gloom"
17.      strArray(5) = "euphoria"
18.      strArray(6) = "despondency"
19.      strArray(7) = "optimism"
20.      strArray(8) = "pessimism"
21.      strArray(9) = "misery"
22.      strArray(10) = "happiness"
23.      strArray(11) = "bliss"
24.      strArray(12) = "mania"
25.
26.      strMsg = "Current items in array:" & vbCr & vbCr
```

```
27.        For i = 1 To UBound(strArray)
28.            strMsg = strMsg & i & ":" & vbTab & strArray(i) & vbCr
29.        Next i
30.        MsgBox strMsg, vbOKOnly + vbInformation, "Array Sorting: 1"
31.
32.        For X = LBound(strArray) To (UBound(strArray) - 1)
33.            For Y = (X + 1) To UBound(strArray)
34.                If strArray(X) > strArray(Y) Then
35.                    strTemp = strArray(X)
36.                    strArray(X) = strArray(Y)
37.                    strArray(Y) = strTemp
38.                    strTemp = ""
39.                End If
40.            Next Y
41.        Next X
42.
43.        strMsg = "Items in sorted array:" & vbCr & vbCr
44.        For i = 1 To UBound(strArray)
45.            strMsg = strMsg & i & ":" & vbTab & strArray(i) & vbCr
46.        Next i
47.        MsgBox strMsg, vbOKOnly + vbInformation, "Array Sorting: 2"
48.
49.  End Sub
```

Analysis

Here's what happens in Listing 7.1:

- Line 1 contains an Option Explicit statement to force explicit declarations of variables, and line 2 contains an Option Base 1 statement to make the numbering of arrays start at 1 rather than 0. These two statements appear in the declarations part of the code sheet, before any other procedure. Line 3 is a spacer—a blank line inserted to make the code easier to read.

- Line 4 begins the Sort_an_Array procedure. Line 5 is a spacer.

- Line 6 is a comment line prefacing the declaration of the array and the variables. Line 7 declares the String array strArray with 12 subscripts. Line 8 declares the String variable `strTemp`. Line 9 declares the String variable `strMsg`. And line 10 declares the Integer variables X, Y, and i. Line 11 is a spacer.

- Line 12 is a comment line explaining that the next 12 statements (lines 13 through 24) assign strings to the array. The strings used are single words loosely associated with moods. Line 25 is a spacer.

- Lines 26 through 30 build a string out of the strings assigned to the array and then display it in a message box. This section of code is included to help the user easily see what's going on if they run the procedure full-bore rather than stepping through it. Line 26 assigns introductory text and two carriage returns (two `vbCr` characters) to the String variable `strMsg`. Line 27 starts a For... Next loop that runs from i = 1 to i = UBound(strArray)—in other words, once for each item in the array. (I could also have run the loop to i = 12 because I knew what the upper bound of the array was—but often you'll need to use flexible code such as this rather than hard-coding values.) Line 28 adds to `strMsg` the value of the counter variable i, a colon, a tab (vbTab), the contents of the array item currently referenced (`strArray(i)`), and a carriage return. Line 29 concludes the loop, and line 30 displays a message box containing `strMsg`, as shown in Figure 7.5. Line 31 is a spacer.

FIGURE 7.5

The Sort_an_Array *procedure displays a message box of the unsorted terms so that the user can see what's going on.*

- The sorting part of the procedure takes place in lines 32–41. Here are the details:
  - Line 32 begins the outer For... Next loop, which ends in line 41. This loop runs from X = LBound(strArray) (in other words, X = 1) to X = (UBound(strArray) - 1) (in other words, X = 11—the upper bound of the array minus 1).

- Line 33 begins the inner (nested) For... Next loop, which runs from Y = (X + 1) to Y = UBound(strArray). Line 40 ends this loop.

- Line 34 compares strArray(X) to strArray(Y). If strArray(X) is greater than strArray(Y)—in other words, if strArray(X) should appear after strArray(Y) in the sorted array—line 35 assigns strArray(X) to strTemp, line 36 assigns strArray(Y) to strArray(X), and line 37 assigns strTemp to strArray(Y), thus switching the values. Line 38 restores strTemp to an empty string. Line 39 ends the If statement. Line 40 ends the inner loop; line 41 ends the outer loop; and line 42 is a spacer.

- Lines 43 through 47 essentially repeat lines 26 through 30, displaying a message box (shown in Figure 7.6) of the sorted array—again, so that the user can see that the sort has worked.

- Line 48 is a spacer, and line 49 ends the procedure.

Searching through an Array

Another action you'll often need to perform with an array is searching to find a particular value in it. In this section, you'll look at two methods of sorting—a linear search, which you can perform on either a sorted array or an unsorted array, and a binary search, which you can perform only on a sorted array.

Performing a Linear Search through an Array

A *linear* search is a very simple form of search: You start at the beginning of the array and continue until you find your target, or until you reach the end of the array.

Before starting the code, display the Immediate window by pressing Ctrl+G or choosing View ➤ Immediate Window. This procedure prints information to the Immediate window so that you can see what's going on—and whether the code is running as intended.

Listing 7.2 contains the code for a simple linear search through a one-dimensional array.

Listing 7.2

```
1.  Option Explicit
2.  Option Base 1
3.
4.  Sub Linear_Search_of_Array()
5.
6.      'declare the array and the variables
7.      Dim intArray(10) As Integer
8.      Dim i As Integer
9.      Dim varUserNumber As Variant
10.     Dim strMsg As String
11.
12.     'add random numbers between 0 and 10 to the array
13.     'and print them to the Immediate window for reference
14.     For i = 1 To 10
15.         intArray(i) = Int(Rnd * 10)
16.         Debug.Print intArray(i)
17.     Next i
18.
19. Loopback:
20.     varUserNumber = InputBox _
            ("Enter a number between 1 and 10 to search for:", _
            "Linear Search Demonstator")
21.     If varUserNumber = "" Then End
22.     If Not IsNumeric(varUserNumber) Then GoTo Loopback
23.     If varUserNumber < 0 Or varUserNumber > 10 Then GoTo Loopback
24.
```

```
25.     strMsg = "Your value, " & varUserNumber & _
            ", was not found in the array."
26.
27.     For i = 1 To UBound(intArray)
28.         If intArray(i) = varUserNumber Then
29.             strMsg = "Your value, " & varUserNumber & _
                    ", was found at position " & i & " in the array."
30.             Exit For
31.         End If
32.     Next i
33.
34.     MsgBox strMsg, vbOKOnly + vbInformation, "Linear Search Result"
35.
36. End Sub
```

Analysis

Here's what happens in Listing 7.2:

- As in the previous listing, line 1 contains an Option Explicit statement to force explicit declarations of variables, and line 2 contains an Option Base 1 statement to make the numbering of arrays start at 1 rather than 0. These two statements appear in the declarations part of the code sheet, before any other procedure. Line 3 is a spacer.

- Line 4 begins the Linear_Search_of_Array procedure. Line 5 is a spacer.

- Line 6 is a comment line prefacing the declaration of the array and the other variables that the code uses. Line 7 declares the Integer array intArray with ten subscripts. Line 8 declares the Integer variable i, the quintessential counter variable. Line 9 declares the Variant variable varUserNumber, which the code uses to store the user's input from an input box. (More on this in a moment.) Line 10 declares the String variable strMsg. Line 11 is a spacer.

 NOTE The procedure declares the variable varUserNumber as a Variant rather than an Integer so that Visual Basic will not automatically stop with an error if the user enters something other than an integer (for example, text) in the input box.

- Lines 12 and 13 contain an extended comment line on the code in lines 14 through 17. (These two lines could be combined into one logical line by adding a continuation character at the end of the first line and omitting the apostrophe at the beginning of the second line; but in this case, I felt it preferable to begin the second line with the comment character as well.)

- Line 14 begins a For... Next loop that runs from i = 1 to 1 = 10. Line 15 assigns to the current item in the intArray array the integer result of a random number multiplied by 10: intArray(i) = Int(Rnd * 10). (Briefly, the Rnd function generates a random number between 0 and 1 with a decent number of decimal places. So, we multiply that random number by 10 to get a number between 0 and 10, then take the integer portion of the number.) Line 16 then uses the Print method of the Debug object to print the current item in intArray to the Immediate window, producing an easy way of keeping track of the values that the array contains. Line 17 ends the loop with the Next i statement. Line 18 is a spacer.

- Line 19 contains a label, Loopback, used to return execution to this point in the code if the user does not meet required conditions.

- Line 20 assigns to the Variant variable varUserNumber the result of an input box (shown in Figure 7.7) prompting the user to enter a number between 0 and 10.

FIGURE 7.7

The Linear_Search_ of_Array *procedure displays an input box prompting the user to enter a number between 0 and 10.*

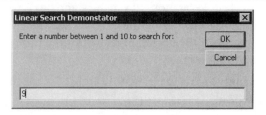

- Line 21 then compares the contents of varUserNumber to an empty string—the result you get if the user clicks the Cancel button in the input box or clicks the OK button without entering anything in the text box. If varUserNumber is an empty string, the End statement ends execution of the procedure.

- Line 22 uses the IsNumeric function to see whether the contents of varUser-Number are numeric. If they're not, the GoTo Loopback statement returns execution to the Loopback label, after which the input box is displayed again for the user to try their luck once more. Line 23 checks to see if varUserNumber is less than 0 or greater than 10; if either is the case, another GoTo Loopback statement returns execution to the Loopback label, and the input makes another appearance. Line 24 is a spacer.

 NOTE Note the flexibility of VBA here: The code solicits user input and makes sure that it's a number between 0 and 10 (inclusive). Though that number is still stored in a Variant rather than explicitly converted to an Integer, VBA still performs the comparison we need.

- Line 25 assigns to the String variable strMsg a preliminary message stating that the value (which it specifies) was not found in the array. (If the code finds the value in the array, it changes the message before it is displayed.) Line 26 is a spacer.

- Lines 27 through 32 contain the searching part of the procedure. Line 27 begins a For… Next loop that runs from i = 1 to i = UBound(intArray)—once for each subscript in the array. Line 28 compares intArray(i) to varUserNumber; if there's a match, line 28 assigns to strMsg a string telling the user at which position in the array the value was found, and line 29 uses an Exit For statement to exit the For… Next loop. (If line 28 does not match, the Next i statement in line 32 causes the code to loop.)

- Line 33 is a spacer. Line 34 displays a message box containing strMsg to convey to the user the result of the linear search operation. Figure 7.8 shows two examples of this message box—one successful, one not. Line 35 is a spacer, and line 26 ends the procedure.

FIGURE 7.8

Line 34 of Listing 7.2 displays a message box telling the user the result of the linear search operation.

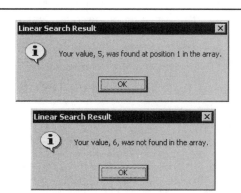

Performing a Binary Search through an Array

As you saw in the previous section, a linear search is easy to perform, but it's pretty dumb—it starts looking at the beginning of the array and then looks through everything else in turn. This single-minded and simple-minded approach works fine for small searches, such as the 10-subscript array you searched in the last example, but you wouldn't want to try it on anything the size of a phone book—even for a small town. For even moderately heavy-duty searching, you need a more sentient way of proceeding.

For conventional purposes, a *binary search* is a good way to approach searching a sorted array. A binary search formalizes the technique you probably use when searching for something that you expect to be in a given location—you focus down on the relevant area, and search it within an inch of its life.

The binary search determines the relevant area by dividing the sorted array in half, establishing which half will contain the search item, and then rinsing and repeating the divide-and-interrogate procedure until it either finds the search item or reaches the last subdivisible unit of the array without finding it. For example, say a binary search is searching for the value 789,789 in a million-subscript array that (conveniently) contains the numbers 1 through 1,000,000 in nicely sorted order. It divides the array into two halves, each of which contains a half million subscripts. It establishes whether the search item is in the first half or the second half, then narrows the search to the appropriate half and divides it into new halves. It establishes whether the search item is in the first of these halves or the second, then focuses on that half, dividing *it* into halves— and so on until it finds the term or has gotten down to a single subscript.

This is a simple example, but a million's still a hefty number. Listing 7.3 makes things even simpler by using an array of a thousand subscripts that contains the numbers 1 through 1000 in order: The first subscript contains the number 1, the second subscript contains the number 2, and so on up to 1000. The example is unrealistic, but it makes it easy to see what's happening in the code—which is the main point.

Listing 7.3

```
1.  Option Explicit
2.  Option Base 1
3.
4.  Sub Binary_Search_of_Array()
5.
6.      'declare the array and the variables
7.      Dim intThousand(1000) As Integer
8.      Dim i As Integer
```

```
9.      Dim intTop As Integer
10.     Dim intMiddle As Integer
11.     Dim intBottom As Integer
12.     Dim varUserNumber As Variant
13.     Dim strMsg As String
14.
15.     'populate the array with numbers 1 to 1000, in order
16.     For i = 1 To 1000
17.         intThousand(i) = i
18.     Next i
19.
20.     'prompt the user for the search item
21. Loopback:
22.     varUserNumber = InputBox _
            ("Enter a number between 1 and 1000 to search for:", _
            "Binary Search Demonstrator")
23.     If varUserNumber = "" Then End
24.     If Not IsNumeric(varUserNumber) Then GoTo Loopback
25.
26.     'search for the search item
27.     intTop = UBound(intThousand)
28.     intBottom = LBound(intThousand)
29.
30.     Do
31.         intMiddle = (intTop + intBottom) / 2
32.         If varUserNumber > intThousand(intMiddle) Then
33.             intBottom = intMiddle + 1
34.         Else
35.             intTop = intMiddle - 1
36.         End If
37.     Loop Until (varUserNumber = intThousand(intMiddle)) _
            Or (intBottom > intTop)
38.
39.     'establish whether the search discovered the search item _
            or not and add the appropriate information to strMsg
40.     If varUserNumber = intThousand(intMiddle) Then
41.         strMsg = "The search found the search item, " _
                & varUserNumber & ", at position " & intMiddle _
                & " in the array."
```

```
42.      Else
43.          strMsg = "The search did not find the search item, " _
                & varUserNumber & "."
44.      End If
45.
46.      MsgBox strMsg, vbOKOnly & vbInformation, "Binary Search Result"
47.
48.  End Sub
```

Analysis

Here's what happens in Listing 7.3:

- Yet again, line 1 contains an Option Explicit statement to force explicit declarations of variables, and line 2 contains an Option Base 1 statement to make the numbering of arrays start at 1 rather than 0. As usual, these two statements appear in the declarations part of the code sheet, before any other procedure.

- Line 3 is a spacer. Line 4 declares the Binary_Search_of_Array procedure, and line 5 is another spacer.

- Line 6 is a comment line prefacing the declaration of the array (the thousand-subscript Integer array intThousand, declared in line 7) and the other variables that the procedure uses: the Integer variables i (line 8), intTop (line 9), intMiddle (line 10), and intBottom (line 11); the Variant variable varUserNumber (line 12); and the String variable strMsg (line 13). Line 14 is yet another spacer.

- Line 15 is a comment line announcing that lines 16 through 18 populate the array with the numbers 1 to 1000 in order. To do so, these lines use a For… Next loop that runs from i = 1 to i = 1000, assigning the current value of i to the subscript in the array referenced by i—in other words, assigning to each subscript the number that corresponds to its position in the array. Line 19 is a spacer.

- Line 20 is a comment line introducing the section of code (lines 21 through 24) that uses an input box (shown in Figure 7.9) to prompt the user to enter a number to search for and makes sure they don't disregard the instructions too heinously. As in the previous listing, this section of code checks to make sure that the user didn't enter an empty string in the input box (line 23) and terminates execution of the procedure if they did. It also uses a label named Loopback (in line 21) to which the code returns if what the user entered in the input box (in line 22) turns out not to be numeric when line 24 checks. Because this time you know which numbers the array will contain, you won't need to check to make sure that the user enters a suitable value. If they want to enter a value that will not appear in the array, so be it.

FIGURE 7.9

The `Binary_Search_of_Array` procedure prompts the user to enter a number between 1 and 1000.

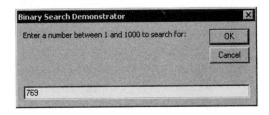

- Line 25 is a spacer, and line 26 is a comment that introduces the section of code that searches for the search item the user entered. Line 27 assigns to the `intTop` variable the upper bound of the array, and line 28 assigns to `intBottom` the lower bound. Line 29 is a spacer.

- Lines 30 through 37 contain a Do... Loop Until loop that performs the bulk of the binary searching. Here are the details:

  - Line 30 starts the Do... Loop Until loop with the Do keyword, and line 37 ends it with the Loop Until keywords and the condition ((varUserNumber = intThousand(intMiddle)) Or (intBottom > intTop)). You'll look at loops in detail in Chapter 12; for now, all you need to know is that a Do... Loop Until runs once, then evaluates the condition in the Loop Until statement to determine whether it should end or run again. The condition here specifies that the loop continue until either the value of the subscript in the array identified by intMiddle (intThousand(intMiddle)) matches the value in varUserNumber or the value of intBottom is greater than the value of intTop (intBottom > intTop).

  - Line 31 sets the value of the Integer variable intMiddle to the sum of intTop and intBottom divided by two: (intTop + IntBottom) / 2. Doing so gives us the midpoint for dividing the array. For example, in the thousand-subscript array, intTop has a value of 1000 on the first iteration of the loop, and intBottom has a value of 0, so intMiddle receives the value 500 (1000 divided by 2). I'll get to the second iteration in a moment.

- Line 32 tests whether varUserNumber is greater than the value stored in the subscript identified by intMiddle—intThousand(intMiddle), the midpoint of the current section of the array. If it is, the search needs to work on the top half of the array, so line 33 resets intBottom to intMiddle + 1. If it's not, the Else statement in line 34 kicks in, and line 35 resets intTop to int-Middle-1, so that the search will work on the lower half of the array.

- Line 36 ends the If statement, and line 37 tests the condition and continues or terminates the loop, as appropriate.

- Line 38 is a spacer. Line 39 contains a two-line comment introducing the code in lines 40 through 44, which establish whether the search found the search item and assign suitable information to the strMsg String variable. Line 40 compares varUserNumber to intThousand(intMiddle); if it matches, line 41 assigns to strMsg a string telling the user where the search item was found in the array. If it doesn't match, line 43 assigns a string telling the user that the search did not find the search item. Line 45 is a spacer, and line 46 displays a message box telling the user the result of the search. Figure 7.10 shows examples—one successful, one otherwise—of the message box.

- Line 47 is another spacer, and line 48 ends the procedure.

FIGURE 7.10

The Binary_Search_ of_Array *procedure tells the user whether the search was successful (top) or not (bottom).*

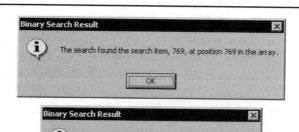

Let's look in a little more detail at what happens in the loop. Copy the code from the CD into the Visual Basic Editor (it'll work in any VBA-enabled application). Then open up the module and follow these steps:

1. Display the Locals window (View ➤ Locals) so that you can track the values of the variables intTop, intMiddle, and intBottom. Figure 7.11 shows the Locals window while the procedure is running.

FIGURE 7.11

Use the Locals window to track the values of the intTop*,* intMiddle*, and* intBottom *variables as the procedure runs.*

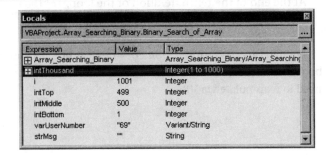

2. Set a breakpoint in the procedure on line 22 by clicking in the margin indicator bar next to the statement that begins varUserNumber = InputBox. (Because the statement is broken onto two lines, the Visual Basic Editor will display two brown dots in the margin indicator bar.)

3. Press the F5 key (or choose Run ➤ Run Sub/UserForm) to run the code up to the breakpoint. VBA will create and populate the array at full speed, then stop at line 22.

4. Press the F8 key to step through the next statements. The first press will display the input box. Enter the value **69** for this example and click the OK button.

5. As the code enters the Do loop and cycles through it, watch the values of the variables intTop, intMiddle, and intBottom in the Locals window. You'll see them change, as shown in the list below.

Iteration	intTop	intMiddle	intBottom
0	1000	–	1
1	499	500	1
2	249	250	1
3	124	125	1
4	124	62	63
5	93	94	63
6	77	78	63
7	69	70	63
8	69	66	67
9	69	68	69
10	68	69	69

At the end of the tenth iteration of the loop, `intThousand(intMiddle)` is equal to `varUserNumber`, so the loop ends.

Enough on arrays for the moment—but fear not, because they'll resurface later in the book. In the meantime, and in the next chapter, you'll learn how to find the objects you need to manipulate via VBA.

CHAPTER **8**

Finding the Objects You Need

FEATURING:

I n this chapter, you'll learn how to find the objects you need in the applications you're using. To learn the material in this chapter, you'll build on what you learned in the earlier chapters.

You'll start by examining the concepts involved: What objects and collections are, what properties are, and what methods are. You'll then learn how to find the objects, collections, properties, and methods you need to make your code work. To identify these items, you'll use a number of tools you've already read about, including the Object Browser (which you visited in Chapter 3) and the Help files for VBA.

Along the way, I'll discuss how to use object variables to represent objects in your code. Keep your wits about you, and read on.

What Is an Object?

As you learned in the early chapters of this book, VBA-enabled applications (like many other modern applications) consist of a number of discrete objects, each with its own characteristics and capabilities.

Generally speaking, building an application out of objects is called *object-oriented programming*. In theory, object-oriented programming has a number of benefits, including being easier to build and maintain, because you break down the code into objects of a manageable size.

Object-oriented programs should also be easier to understand than monolithic programs, because it's easier for most people to grasp the concept of individual objects with associated characteristics and actions than to remember a far longer list of capabilities for the application. It's also easier to get to the commands you need. For example, a table in Word is represented by a `Table` object, which is intuitive enough; and a column is represented by a `Column` object. The `Column` object has a `Width` property that sets and returns its width. It's easier to know this information when it's broken down into small and easy-to-understand pieces than to deal with some complex command such as `WordTableSetColumnWidth` or `WordTableGetColumnWidth`.

A third benefit of object-oriented programs is that they can be extensible: The user can build custom objects to implement functionality that the application doesn't contain. (That should come as no surprise: It's why you're reading this book.) For example, you can use VBA to build your own objects that do things that the applications themselves can't do.

Objects can—and frequently do—contain other objects. Typically, the objects in an object-oriented application are arranged into a logical hierarchy called the *object model* of the application. This hierarchy gives the logical relationship of the objects to each other through which you access them via VBA.

NOTE In this chapter, I'll discuss object models only a little, at the conceptual level: You need to know what an object model *is* in order to make sense of what you'll be learning in the following chapters, but you don't need to know the specifics of each object model to manipulate the objects used in the examples. Then in Chapter 14, " Object Models," you'll examine the object models of each of the applications covered in this book in some detail—enough detail to get you started on exploring the depths of each object model on your own, but not enough depth to fill up the rest of this book (which examining each object model in depth would do).

Most VBA host applications, including all the applications this books covers, have an Application object that represents the application as a whole. The Application object has properties and methods for things that apply to the application as a whole. For example, many applications have a Quit method that exits the application and a Visible property that controls whether the application is visible or hidden. (If you're drawing a blank on what objects, properties, and methods are, turn back to Chapter 5 and refresh your memory.)

In a typical object model, the Application object essentially contains all the other objects (and collections—groups—of objects) that go to make up the application. For example, Excel has an Application object that represents the Excel application, a Workbook object (grouped into the Workbooks collection) that represents a workbook, and a Worksheet object (grouped into the Sheets collection) that represents a worksheet. The Workbook object is contained within the Application object, because you need to have the Excel application open to work with an Excel workbook (under normal circumstances, anyway). In turn, the Worksheet object is contained within the Workbook object, because you need to have an Excel workbook open to work with a worksheet. Walking further down the object model, the Worksheet object contains assorted other objects, including Row objects that represent rows in the worksheet, Column objects that represent columns in the worksheet, and Range objects (which represent ranges of cells)—and these in turn contain further objects.

To get to an object, you typically walk down through the hierarchy of the object model until you reach the object. For example, to get to a Range object in Excel, you would go through the Application object to the Workbook object, through the Workbook object to the appropriate Sheet object, and then to the Range object. The following statement shows an example using the range A1 in the first worksheet in the first open workbook (more on this in a minute):

```
Application.Workbooks(1).Sheets(1).Range("A1").Select
```

Because you'd have to go through the `Application` object to get to pretty much anything in the application, most applications expose a number of creatable objects that you can access without referring explicitly to the `Application` object. As you'd expect, these creatable objects are usually the most-used objects for the application, and by going through them, you can access most of the other objects without ever referring to the `Application` object. For example, Excel exposes the `Workbooks` collection as a creatable object, so you can use the following statement, which doesn't use the `Application` object, instead of the previous statement:

```
Workbooks(1).Sheets(1).Range("A1").Select
```

You learned earlier in the book that any object could have properties and methods. In the next two sections, you'll learn about properties and methods a little more.

Properties

In VBA, a *property* is a characteristic of an object—an attribute of it, a way of describing an aspect of it. It follows that most objects have multiple properties that describe each relevant aspect of the object. Each property has a specific data type for the information it stores. For example, the objects that represent files (documents, workbooks, presentations, projects, drawings) in the assorted applications this book covers typically have a Boolean property named `Saved` that stores a value denoting whether all changes in the object have been saved (a value of `True`) or not (a value of `False`). These two values encompass the range of possibilities for the object: It can either contain unsaved changes or not contain unsaved changes, but there is no third way. (Don't get creative on this point, okay?)

Similarly, most objects that represent files have a `Name` property that contains the name of the file in question. The `Name` property is a String property because it needs to contain text, and that text can be set to just about anything (limited by the 255-character path that Windows can support, and certain naughty characters—such as colons and pipe characters—that it cannot).

To work with a property, you *return* (get) it to find out its current value or *set* it to a value of your choosing. Many properties are *read/write*, meaning that you can both return and set their values, but some properties are *read-only*, meaning that you can return their values but not set them.

The Saved property I just mentioned is read/write for most applications, so you can set it—which means that you can tell the application that a file contains unsaved changes when, in fact, it doesn't, or that it contains no unsaved changes when, in reality, it has some. (Changing the Saved property can be useful when you're manipulating a file without the user's explicit knowledge.) But the Name property of a file object is read-only—you'll typically set the name by issuing a Save As command, after which you cannot change the name from within the application while the file is open. So you can return the `Name` property but not set it.

When an object contains another object, or a collection, it typically has a property that you call to return the object or the collection. For example, among its many other properties, the Word `Document` object has a `PageSetup` property that returns the `Page-Setup` object for the document (the `PageSetup` object contains settings such as paper size, orientation, and margins for the document) and a `Tables` property that you call to return the `Tables` collection.

Each object of the same type has the same set of properties but stores its own values for them. For example, if you're running Visio and have three `Document` objects open, each can have a different `Name` property. The setting for a property in one object has nothing to do with the setting for that property in another object: Each object is independent of the other objects.

Methods

By contrast, a *method*—an action that an object can perform—is shared (so to speak) among the objects of that type. For example, the `Document` object in a number of applications has a `Save` method that saves the document. You can use the `Save` method on different `Document` objects—`Documents(1).Save` saves the first `Document` object in the `Documents` collection, and `Documents(2).Save` saves the second `Document` object—but it does the same thing in each case. An object can have one or more methods associated with it. Some objects have as many as several dozen methods to implement all the functionality they need.

As you'd imagine, what a method can do depends on the object involved. For example, objects in AutoCAD and Visio have many methods for drawing things, an endeavor in which Project's objects have little or no interest.

Some methods are associated with more than one object. For example, the `Delete` method is a relatively general method that is associated with many different objects. As its name suggests, the `Delete` method usually deletes the specified object. But other methods perform somewhat different actions depending on the object they're working with—so even if you're familiar with a method from using it with one object, you need to make sure that it'll have the effect you expect when you use it with another object.

Some methods take one or more arguments (some required, some optional); other methods take no arguments. When a method applies to multiple objects, it may have different syntax for different objects. Again, even if you're familiar with a method, you need to know exactly what it will do with the object for which you're planning to use it.

To use a method, you access it through the object involved. For example, to close the ActivePresentation object, which represents the active presentation in Power-Point, you use the Close method:

```
ActivePresentation.Close
```

Objectifying Objects, Methods, and Properties

If you have a hard time getting a grip on objects, methods, and properties (or if relating VBA's insubstantial objects to physical analogues entertains you), you can draw a somewhat strained comparison between logical objects, properties, and methods in VBA and physical objects, properties, and actions in the real world. The further you push this type of comparison (or analogy, if you're feeling strict), the more finely it gets strained; but in the grosser grain and the shorter term, it may give you a worthwhile boost of understanding.

Let's say you have a massive dog—a Pyrenean mountain dog, white, 200 lb, male, not, uh, *fixed*, 4 years old, named Max (after Max Frisch, of course).

Max performs all the usual dog actions—sleep, run, eat, bark, growl, chew things, various unmentionable actions that we'll skip over, etc.—and has a couple of unusual (for dogs) actions built in, such as slobbering on command, knocking down people, and intimidating bailiffs.

If Max were implemented in VBA, he'd be a Dog object in a Dogs collection. The Dog object for Max would have properties such as these:

Property	Property Type	Value
Name	Read-only String	Max
Sex	Read/write String	Male
Fixed	Read/write Boolean	False
Height	Read/write Long	36
Weight	Read/write Long	200
Age	Read/write Integer	4
Type	Read/write String	Pyrenean Mountain
Color	Read/write String	White

Continued

CONTINUED

Max would have methods such as `Slobber`, `Bark`, `KnockDown`, `Intimidate`, `Chew`, `Run`, and so on. Some of these methods would require arguments. The `Slobber` method would definitely need arguments like this:

```
Dogs("Max").Slobber OnWhat:="MyKnee", How:=dogSlobberDisgustingly
```

The `Dog` object would contain objects representing the many component pieces of the dog—ears, eyes, tongue, brain (probably), stomach, legs, tail, and so on. Each of these objects would have its own properties and methods as appropriate. For example, the `Tail` object would need a `Wag` method, which you would probably invoke something like this:

```
Dogs("Max").Tail.Wag Direction:=dogWagHorizontal, Frequency:=200
```

Working with Collections

When an object contains more than one object of the same type, the objects are grouped into a *collection*. For example, AutoCAD, Visio, and Word all use `Document` objects, which are grouped into the `Documents` collection; PowerPoint has a `Presentations` collection for `Presentation` objects, and Excel has the `Workbooks` collection I mentioned a moment ago.

As you might guess from these examples, the names of most collections are the plural of the object in question. There are a number of exceptions, such as the `Sheets` collection in Excel that contains the `Worksheet` objects; but by-and-large the names of most collections are easy to derive from the name of the objects they contain—and vice versa.

A collection is an object too and can have its own properties and methods. Most collections have fewer properties and methods than the objects. Most collections have an `Add` method for adding another object to the collection, and an `Item` property (the default property) for accessing an item within the collection. Some collections are read-only and do not have an `Add` method.

Most collections in VBA have the core group of properties listed in Table 8.1. (I've noted some of the exceptions.)

TABLE 8.1: CORE PROPERTIES FOR COLLECTIONS IN VBA	
Property	**Explanation**
Application	A read-only property that returns the application associated with the object or collection—the root of the hierarchy for the document. For example, the Application property for objects in Project returns Microsoft Project. (WordPerfect and AutoCAD use the Application property differently than this.)
Count	A read-only Long property that returns the number of items in the collection—for example, the number of Layer objects in the Layers collection in an AutoCAD drawing.
Creator	In Microsoft applications, a read-only Long property that returns a 32-bit integer indicating the application used to create the object or collection. In Visio, the Creator property returns the name of the user who created the object in question. WordPerfect and AutoCAD do not use this property.
Item	A read-only property that returns the specified member of the collection. Item is the default property of every collection, which means that you seldom need to specify it.
Parent	In Microsoft applications, a read-only String property that returns the parent object for the object or collection.

Working with an Object in a Collection

To work with an object in a collection, you identify the object within the collection either by its name or its position in the collection. For example, the following statement returns the first Document object in the Documents collection and displays its Name property in a message box:

```
MsgBox Documents(1).Name
```

 NOTE In most collections, numbering starts at 1, which makes it easy to identify the object you need. For example, Documents(1) gives you the first document, Workbooks(2) gives you the second workbook, and so on. But some collections (such as the Documents collection in AutoCAD) are *zero-based*—their numbering starts at 0 (zero) rather than 1. So in AutoCAD, you'd use Documents(0) to return the first Document object in the Documents collection.

As I mentioned a moment ago, you can use the Item property to return an object from the collection; but because Item is the default property of a collection, you don't need to use it. The following two statements have the same effect, and there's no advantage to using the Item method.

```
strName = Documents(1).Name
strName = Documents.Item(1).Name
```

Adding an Object to a Collection

To create a new object in a collection, you add an object to the collection. In many cases, you use the Add method to do so. For example, the following statement creates a new Document object in AutoCAD, Visio, or Word:

```
Documents.Add
```

Finding the Objects You Need

The Visual Basic Editor provides a number of tools for finding the objects you need:

- (Microsoft applications only) The Macro Recorder, which you used to record macros in the Microsoft Office applications in Chapter 2.
- The Object Browser, which I mentioned in Chapter 3
- The online Help system, which should provide detailed help on the objects in the application (though this depends on how much effort the software manufacturer put into the Help system)
- The List Properties/Methods feature

Using the Macro Recorder to Record the Objects You Need

If you're using a Microsoft application, chances are that the easiest way to find the objects you need is to use the Macro Recorder to record a quick macro using the objects you're interested in. As you saw in the early chapters of this book, by recording the actions you perform, the Macro Recorder creates code that you can then open in the Visual Basic Editor, examine, and modify to within a centimeter of its life.

 NOTE If you're not using a Microsoft application, you probably don't have this option open to you. Grin and bear the inconvenience. But if you *are* using a Microsoft application, the Macro Recorder provides a great way to access VBA objects.

Life in the Macro Recorder isn't a hundred percent rosy, though: There are a couple of problems with using the Macro Recorder to find your objects of desire:

- First, you can't record all the actions that you might want. Let's say you're working in Excel and want to create a statement that performs an action on a specified workbook in the Workbooks collection rather than on the active workbook. With the Macro Recorder, you can record only actions performed on the active workbook. (This is the case because the Macro Recorder can record only those actions you can perform interactively in Excel, and you can't work interactively with any workbook other than the active one.)

- Second, the Macro Recorder is apt to record statements that you don't strictly need, particularly when you're trying to record a setting in a dialog box.

As an example of the second point, crank up Word (if you have it) and try recording a quick macro to create an AutoCorrect entry. Start the Macro Recorder, choose Tools ➢ AutoCorrect to display the AutoCorrect dialog box, enter the text to be replaced in the Replace box and the replacement text in the With box, click the OK button to close the AutoCorrect dialog box, and stop the Macro Recorder. Then open the resulting macro in the Visual Basic Editor. You'll probably see code something like this:

```
Sub Add_Item_to_AutoCorrect()
'
' Add_Item_to_AutoCorrect Macro
' Macro recorded 4/4/00 by Rikki Nadir
'

    AutoCorrect.Entries.Add Name:="reffs",Value:="references"
    With AutoCorrect
        .CorrectInitialCaps = True
        .CorrectSentenceCaps = True
        .CorrectDays = True
        .CorrectCapsLock = True
        .ReplaceText = True
        .ReplaceTextFromSpellingChecker = True
        .CorrectKeyboardSetting = False
    End With
End Sub
```

Here, you get 13 lines of padding around the one line you need:

```
AutoCorrect.Entries.Add Name:="reffs", Value:="references"
```

This line shows you that to add an AutoCorrect entry, you need to work with the Entries collection object in the AutoCorrect object. You use the Add method on the Entries collection to add an AutoCorrect entry to the list.

By removing the nine lines containing the With... End With statement from this recorded macro, you can reduce it to just the line it needs to contain (together with the comment lines, which you could also remove if you wanted):

```
Sub Add_Item_to_AutoCorrect()
'
' Add_Item_to_AutoCorrect Macro
' Macro recorded 4/4/00 by Rikki Nadir
'
    AutoCorrect.Entries.Add Name:="reffs",Value:="references"
End Sub
```

In spite of its limitations, the Macro Recorder does provide quick access to the objects you need to work with, and you can always adjust the resulting code in the Visual Basic Editor.

Using the Object Browser

The primary tool for finding the objects you need is the Object Browser, which you met briefly in Chapter 3. In this section, you'll get to know the Object Browser better and learn to use it to find the information you need about objects.

Components of the Object Browser

The Object Browser provides the following information about both built-in objects and custom objects you create:

- Classes (formal definitions of objects)
- Properties (the attributes of objects or aspects of their behavior)
- Methods (actions you can perform on objects)
- Events (for example, the opening or closing of a document)
- Constants (named items that keep a constant value while a program is executing)

Figure 8.1 shows the components of the Object Browser.

FIGURE 8.1

*The Object Browser
provides information
on built-in objects and
custom objects. Here,
the application is
AutoCAD.*

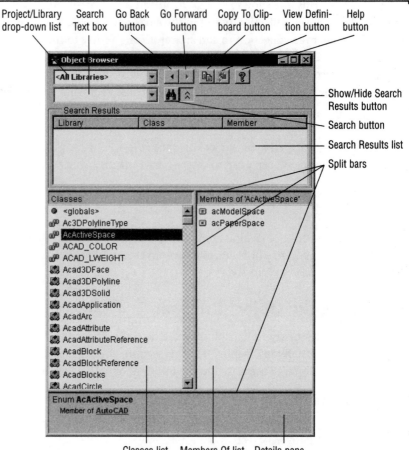

Here's what the different elements of the Object Browser do:

- The Project/Library drop-down list provides a list of object libraries available to the current project. (An *object library* is a reference file containing information on a collection of objects available to programs.) Use the drop-down list to choose the object libraries you want to view. For example, you might choose to view only objects in AutoCAD by choosing AutoCAD from the Project/Library drop-down list. Alternatively, you could stay with the default choice of <All Libraries>.

- In the Search Text box, enter the string you want to search for: Either type it in, or choose a previous string in the current project session from the drop-down list. Then, either press Enter, or click the Search button to find members containing the search string.

TIP To make your searches more specific, you can use wildcards such as **?** (representing any one character) and ***** (representing any group of characters). You can also choose to search for a whole word only (rather than matching your search string with part of another word) by right-clicking anywhere in the Object Browser (except in the Project/Library drop-down list or in the Search Text box) and choosing Find Whole Word Only from the context menu. The Find Whole Word Only choice will have a check mark next to it in the context menu when it's active; to deactivate it, choose Find Whole Word Only again on the context menu.

- Click the Go Back button to retrace one by one your previous selections in the Classes list and the Members Of list. Click the Go Forward button to go forward through your previous selections one by one. The Go Back button will become available when you go to a class or member in the Object Browser; the Go Forward button will become available only when you've used the Go Back button to go back to a previous selection.

- Click the Copy To Clipboard button to copy the selected item from the Search Results box, the Classes list, the Members Of list, or the Details pane to the Clipboard so that you can paste it into your code.

- Click the View Definition button to display a code window containing the code for the object selected in the Classes list or the Members Of list. The View Definition button will be available (undimmed) only for objects that contain code, such as procedures and user forms that you've created.

- Click the Help button to display any available Help for the currently selected item. (Alternatively, press the F1 key.)

- Click the Search button to search for the term entered in the Search Text box. If the Search Results pane isn't open, VBA will open it at this point.

- Click the Show/Hide Search Results button to toggle the display of the Search Results pane on and off.

- The Search Results list in the Search Results pane contains the results of the latest search you've conducted for a term entered in the Search Text box. If you've performed a search, the Object Browser will update the Search Results list when you use the Project/Library drop-down list to switch to a different library.

- The Classes list shows the available classes in the library or project specified in the Project/Library drop-down list.

- The Members Of list displays the available elements of the class selected in the Classes list. A method, constant, event, property, or procedure that has code written for it appears in boldface. The Members Of list can display the members either grouped into their different categories (methods, properties, events, and so on), or ungrouped as an alphabetical list of all the members available. To toggle between grouped and ungrouped, right-click in the Members Of list and choose Group Members from the context menu; click either to place a check mark (to group the members) or to remove the check mark (to ungroup the members).

- The Details pane displays the definition of the member selected in the Classes list or in the Members Of list. For example, if you select a procedure in the Members Of list, the Details pane will display its name, the name of the module and template or document in which it's stored, and any comment lines you inserted at the beginning of the procedure. The module name and project name will contain hyperlinks (jumps) so that you can quickly move to them. You can copy information from the Details pane to the Code window by using either Copy and Paste, or drag-and-drop.

- Drag the three split bars to resize the panes of the Object Browser to suit you. (You can also resize the Object Browser window to suit you.)

The Object Browser uses different icons to indicate the various types of object that it lists. Figure 8.1 shows three different icons; Table 8.2 shows the full gamut of icons and what they represent.

TABLE 8.2: OBJECT BROWSER ICONS

Icon	Meaning
	Property
	Method
	Constant
	Module
	Event
	Class
	User Defined Type

Continued ▶

TABLE 8.2 CONTINUED: OBJECT BROWSER ICONS	
	Global
	Library
	Project
	Built-in keyword or type
	Enum (enumeration)

A blue dot in the upper-left corner of a Property icon or a Method icon indicates that that property or method is the default.

Adding and Removing Object Libraries

You can add and remove object libraries by using the References dialog box (choose Tools ➤ References in the Visual Basic Editor). By adding object libraries, you can make available additional objects to work with; by removing object libraries that you don't need to view or use, you can reduce the number of object references that VBA needs to resolve when it is compiling the code in a project, thus allowing it to run faster.

When you start the Visual Basic Editor, it automatically loads the object libraries required for using VBA and user forms with the host application. You don't need to change this set of object libraries until you need to access objects contained in other libraries. For example, if you create a procedure in Visio that draws on Excel's functionality, you'll usually add to Visio a reference to Excel to make its objects available.

You can adjust the priority of different references by adjusting the order in which the references appear in the References dialog box. The priority of references matters when you use in your code an object whose name appears in more than one reference: VBA checks the References list to determine the order of the references that contain that object name and uses the first of them, unless specifically told to do otherwise by use of a disambiguated name.

To add or remove object libraries:

1. In the Object Browser window, right-click in the Project/Library drop-down list (or in the Classes window or the Members window) and choose References from the context menu; alternatively, choose Tools ➤ References in the Visual Basic Editor. Either action will display the References dialog box, shown in Figure 8.2.

As you'll guess from the title bar of the References dialog box and the Visio 5.0 Type Library entry in the list box, I displayed this dialog box from Visio.

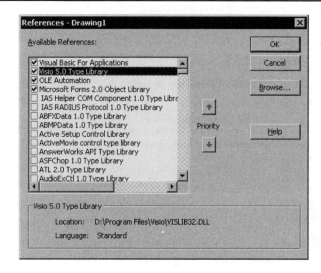

2. In the Available References list box, select the check boxes for the references you want to have available and clear the check boxes for the references you want to remove. You should find a reference for an object library for each application that supports Automation and is installed on your computer.

3. Adjust the priority of the references if necessary by selecting a reference and using the up- and down-arrow Priority buttons to move it up or down the list. Usually, you'll want to keep Visual Basic for Applications and the application's Object Library at the top of your list.

TIP You can add further reference libraries by clicking the Browse button to display the Add Reference dialog box, selecting the library file, and then clicking the Open button.

4. Choose the OK button to close the References dialog box and return to the Object Browser.

Navigating with the Object Browser

Now that you've seen the components of the Object Browser, let's look at how to use them to browse the objects available to a project:

1. First, activate a code module by double-clicking it in the Project Explorer.

2. Display the Object Browser by choosing View ➤ Object Browser, by pressing the F2 button, or by clicking the Object Browser button on the Standard toolbar. (If the Object Browser is already displayed, make it active by clicking it or by selecting it from the list at the bottom of the Window menu.)

3. In the Project/Library drop-down list, select the name of the project or the library that you want to view. The Object Browser will display the available classes in the Classes list.

4. In the Classes list, select the class you want to work with. For example, if you chose a project in step 3, select the module you want to work with in the Classes list.

5. If you want to work with a particular member of the class or project, select it in the Members Of list. For example, if you're working with a template project, you might want to choose a specific procedure or user form to work with.

Once you've selected the class, member, or project, you can perform the following actions on it:

- View information about it in the Details pane at the bottom of the Object Browser window.

- View the definition of an object by clicking the Show Definition button. Alternatively, right-click the object in the Members Of list and choose View Definition from the context menu. (Remember that the definition of a procedure is the code that it contains; the definition of a module is all the code in all the procedures that it contains; and the definition of a user form is the code in all the procedures attached to it.) As I mentioned before, the Show Definition button will be available (undimmed) only for objects that contain code, such as procedures and user forms that you've created.

- Copy the text for the selected class, project, or member to the Clipboard by clicking the Copy To Clipboard button, or by issuing a standard Copy command (such as Ctrl+C or Ctrl+Insert).

Using Help to Find the Object You Need

VBA's Help system provides another easy way to access the details of the objects you want to work with. The Help files provide you with a hyperlinked reference to all the objects, methods, and properties in VBA, including graphics that show how the objects are related to each other.

The quickest way to access VBA Help is to activate the Visual Basic Editor and then press the F1 key. VBA will respond by displaying the Microsoft Visual Basic Help window shown in Figure 8.3. If you're using an Office application and you've disabled the Office Assistant (as most people do to preserve their sanity and conserve processor cycles), you can also choose Help ➤ Microsoft Visual Basic Help; if you haven't disabled the Office Assistant, choosing Help ➤ Microsoft Visual Basic Help will display the Office Assistant.

TIP To get help on a specific item referenced in your code, place the insertion point somewhere in the appropriate word before pressing the F1 key. VBA will display the Help topics for that item.

FIGURE 8.3

*The Microsoft Visual
Basic Help window*

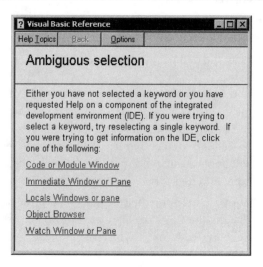

Once you've opened Help, you can search for help as you would in any other application. The Contents page provides an expandable list of topics; the Answer Wizard page (which only some applications provide) attempts to unearth all appropriate topics for the question you ask it; and the Index page provides an alphabetical list of keywords. Select the topic you want from the list to display it in the Help window. For example, if you display Help on the Document object in Word, you'll see a Help window like the one shown in Figure 8.4.

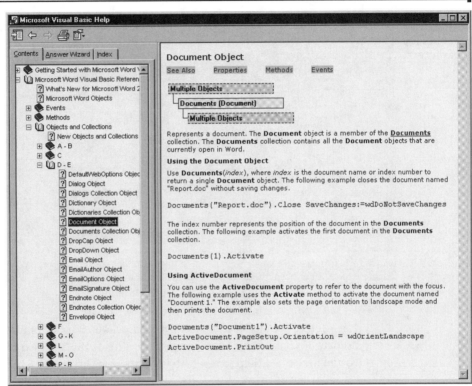

FIGURE 8.4

Here's what you'll get if you display Help on the Document object in Word.

Apart from the regular Help information you'll find in the Help window, a few items deserve comment here:

- The graphic at the top of the Help listing shows the relationship of the current object (in this case, Document) to the object (or objects) that contain it and to the objects it contains. You can click on either of these objects to display a Topics Found dialog box listing the relevant objects, as shown in Figure 8.5.

FIGURE 8.5

Click on one of the objects in the graphic to display the Topics Found dialog box listing the objects it contains. Here, you can see that the Document object contains a plethora of other objects, including Bookmarks and Characters.

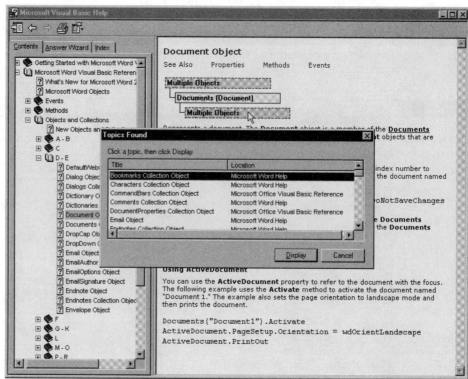

- If a See Also hyperlink appears at the top of the window, you can click it to display a Topics Found dialog box showing associated topics. For example, as you'd discover if you clicked on the hyperlink, one of the See Also topics from the Document Object Help screen is Help on the Template object.

- Click the Properties hyperlink at the top of the window to display a Topics Found dialog box listing the Help available for the properties of the object. You can then display one of the topics by selecting it in the list box and clicking the Display button (or by double-clicking it in the list box).

- Click the Methods hyperlink at the top of the window to display a Topics Found dialog box listing the Help available for those methods available for use on the object. Again, you can display one of these topics by selecting it in the list box and clicking the Display button, or by double-clicking it in the list box.

- Some objects also have one or more events associated with them. If the object has any events associated with it (as the Document object does here), you can access them by clicking the Events hyperlink at the top of the window. This will display a Topics Found dialog box.

 NOTE If only one topic is associated with a See Also, Properties, Methods, or Events hyperlink, Help will display that topic rather than the Topics Found dialog box.

Using the List Properties/Methods Feature

I showed you briefly the List Properties/Methods feature in Chapter 3. To recap, when you're entering a statement in the Visual Basic Editor and you type the period at the end of the current object, the List Properties/Methods feature displays a list of properties and methods appropriate to the statement you've entered so far.

The List Properties/Methods feature provides a quick way of entering statements, but you need to know the object from which to start. Sometimes using this feature is a bit like finding your way through a maze and being given eloquent but useless directions that end with the phrase, "But I wouldn't start from here if I were you."

Once you know the object from which to start, though, it's smooth sailing. For example, to put together the statement `Application.Documents(1).Close` to close the first document in the `Documents` collection in AutoCAD, Visio, or Word, you could work as follows:

1. Place the insertion point on a fresh line in an empty procedure (between the Sub and End Sub statements). Create a new procedure if necessary.

2. Type the word **Application**, or type **Appl** and press Ctrl+spacebar to have the Complete Word feature complete the word for you.

3. Type the period (**.**) after **Application**. The List Properties/Methods feature will display the list of properties and methods available to the `Application` object.

4. Choose the `Documents` item in the List Properties/Methods list. You can either scroll to it using the mouse and then double-click it to enter it in the code window, scroll to it by using the ↓ and ↑ keys and enter it by pressing Tab, or scroll to it by typing the first few letters of its name and then enter it by pressing Tab. The latter method is shown in Figure 8.6, which uses Word.

FIGURE 8.6

*Using the List
Properties/Methods
feature to enter code*

5. Type the **(1).** after **Documents**. When you type the period, the List Properties/ Methods feature will display the list of properties and methods available to the Documents collection.

6. Choose the Close method in the List Properties/Methods list by scrolling to it with the mouse or with the ↓ and ↑ keys. Because this is the end of the statement, press the Enter key to enter the method and start a new line, rather than pressing the Tab key (which would enter the method and continue the same line).

TIP For most people, the quickest way to enter statements in the Code window is to keep their hands on the keyboard. To help you do this, the Visual Basic Editor automatically selects the current item in the List Properties/Method list when you type a period or an opening parenthesis. In the previous example, you can type **Application.** to display the list, **Do** to select the Documents item, and **(** to enter the Documents item.

Using Object Variables to Represent Objects

As you learned earlier in the book, one of the data types available for variables in VBA is *Object*. You use an Object variable to represent an object in your code: Instead of referring to the object, you can refer to the Object variable to access or manipulate the object it represents.

Using Object variables makes it simpler to know which object a section of code is working with, especially when you're working with multiple objects in the same section of code. For example, say you create a procedure that manipulates the three open drawings in AutoCAD, copying a drawing element from one to the two others. If you have only those three drawings open, you'll be able to refer to them as Documents(0), Documents(1), and Documents(2), respectively, because they'll occupy the first (and only) three slots in the Documents collection. (Remember that the Documents collection in AutoCAD is zero-based, so numbering starts at zero rather than 1.) But if your procedure changes the order of the drawings, closes one or more drawings, or creates one or more new drawings, things will rapidly get confusing. If, however, you've created Object variables (named, say, adgDrawing1, adgDrawing2, and adgDrawing3) to refer to those drawings, it'll be much easier to keep them straight. This is because, no matter which document is first in the Documents collection, you'll be able to refer to the object represented by the Object variable adgDrawing1 and know that you'll be getting the drawing you intend.

To create an object variable, you declare it in almost exactly the same way as you declare any other variable, using a Dim, Private, or Public statement. For example, the following statement declares the object variable objMyObject:

```
Dim objMyObject As Object
```

As normal for the Dim statement, if you use this declaration within a procedure, it will create a variable with local scope. If you use it in the declarations section of a code sheet, it will create a variable with module-level private scope. Similarly, the Private and Public keywords create module-level private and public object variables, respectively.

Once you've declared the object variable, you're ready to assign an object to it. To do so, use a Set statement. The syntax for a Set statement is as follows:

```
Set objectvariable = {[New] expression|Nothing}
```

That syntax is a little unfriendly at first. Here's how it breaks down:

- *objectvariable* is the name of the object variable to which you're assigning the object.

- New is an optional keyword that you can use to implicitly create a new object of the specified class. Usually you'll do better to create objects explicitly and then assign them to object variables rather than using New to create them implicitly.

- *expression* is a required expression that specifies or returns the object you want to assign to the object variable.

- Nothing is an optional keyword that you assign to an existing object variable to obliterate its contents and release the memory they occupied.

For example, the following statements declare the object variable objMyObject and assign to it the active document (in AutoCAD, Visio, or Word):

```
Dim objMyObject As Object
Set objMyObject = ActiveDocument
```

The following statement uses the `Nothing` keyword to release the memory occupied by the `objMyObject` object variable:

```
Set objMyObject = Nothing
```

What's different about declaring an object variable versus declaring other types of variable is that not only can you declare the object variable as being of the type `Object`, but you can specify which type of object it is. For example, if an object variable will always represent an `AcadDocument` object, you can declare it as being of the `AcadDocument` data type. The following statement declares the object variable `docMyDocument` as being of the `Document` data type:

```
Dim docMyDocument As AcadDocument
```

Strongly associating a type with an object variable like this has a couple of advantages. First, once you've strongly typed the object variable, the Visual Basic Editor provides you with full assistance for the object variable, just as if you were dealing with the object directly. For example, once you've created that object variable `docMyDocument` of the `AcadDocument` object type, the Visual Basic Editor will display the List Properties/Methods drop-down list when you type the object variable's name followed by a period, as shown in Figure 8.7.

FIGURE 8.7

When you strongly type your object variables, you get the full benefit of the Visual Basic Editor's code-completion features for the object variables.

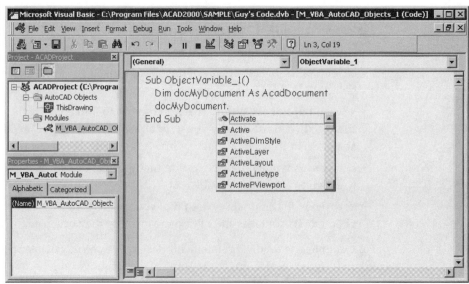

Second, when you strongly type an object variable, you make it a bit harder to get things wrong in your code. If you try to assign the wrong type of object to a strongly typed object variable, VBA will protest. For example, if you create a `Worksheet` object variable in Excel, as in the first of the following statements, and assign to it a `Workbook` object, as in the second statement, VBA will squawk with a Type Mismatch error—as well it should:

```
Dim wksSheet1 As Worksheet
Set wksSheet1 = ActiveWorkbook
```

Depending on how you look at things, you might consider this a disadvantage of strongly typing your variables—but finding out at this stage that you've created a problem is usually preferable to finding out later (for example, when you go to manipulate the `wksSheet1` object and discover it doesn't behave as you expect it to).

The main reason for *not* strongly typing an object variable is that you're not sure what kind of object it will store, or if the kind of object it will store may vary from one execution of the code to another. (If either is the case, your code will need to be flexible enough to accommodate objects of different types showing up for the object variable.) Usually, though, you'll want to go the extra mile and strongly type all your object variables.

If you're not sure which object type to use for an object variable, start by declaring the object variable as being of the `Object` data type. Then run through the code a couple of times with the Locals window (View ➤ Locals) displayed, and note the data type that VBA assigns to the object variable. For example, if you step through the following statements in a Visual Basic Editor session hosted by Excel, the readout in the Locals window will at first identify the object variable `wks` only as `Object` (as shown on the left in Figure 8.8), but then as `Object/Sheet1` (as shown on the right in Figure 8.8) when the second statement assigns the first sheet in the active workbook to it:

```
Dim wks As Object
Set wks = ActiveWorkbook.Sheets(1)
```

FIGURE 8.8

You can use the Locals window to help identify the object type that an object variable will contain.

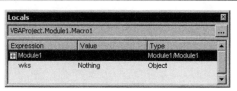 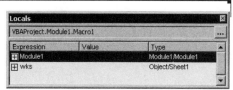

NOTE As you learned earlier in the book, you can be lazy and avoid specifying data types altogether. For example, the statement `Dim varMyVariant` will create a Variant variable because the statement does not specify a data type. Variant variables can contain objects as well as other data types—but as before, using Variants will require VBA doing a little more work each time it encounters the variable (because VBA has to determine what data type the variable currently is) and will deny you the benefits of strongly typing your variables.

In the next chapter, you'll learn how to create and use functions in VBA.

CHAPTER <u>9</u>

Using and Creating Functions

n this chapter, you'll learn about functions in VBA. VBA comes with a large number of built-in functions to perform commonly needed operations, but you can also create custom functions of your own to supplement VBA's functions. (You can also duplicate VBA's built-in functions if you're especially bored.)

There are essentially four things that you need to know about functions:

- What functions are, and what they do
- How to use functions
- What functions VBA has
- How to create functions of your own to supplement VBA's built-in functions

You'll learn all of the above in this chapter.

What Is a Function?

As you saw earlier in the book, a *function* is a type of procedure—a procedure that takes arguments (except in some rare cases) and returns a value (always). (By contrast, a subprocedure *can* take arguments—it doesn't have to, and many don't—but does not return a value.) Essentially, you feed information into the function, which processes it and spits out a value for you to use. (You can also call a function as a subprocedure and let the return go into never-never land, but you probably won't want to do so very often.)

Functions are so essential to VBA that we've already used several in this book before introducing them properly here. For example, in Chapter 7 you used the Rnd function to generate random numbers to fill an array named intArray and the Int function to turn the random numbers into integers:

```
intArray(i) = Int(Rnd * 10)
```

Rnd is one of the rare cases I mentioned—a function that does not have to take one or more arguments. (Rnd takes one optional argument, but the previous example doesn't use it.) Int, on the other hand, requires an argument—the number or expression that it's to turn into an integer—which here is supplied by the expression Rnd * 10. Here the Rnd function returns a value that the Int function uses; the Int function then returns a value to the procedure, which uses it to populate a subscript in the array.

As I mentioned earlier, an argument is a piece of information that VBA uses with a function, method, or command. You can tell when arguments are optional because they're enclosed within brackets. You can include or omit the arguments displayed in the brackets. For example, the syntax for the Rnd function looks like this:

```
Rnd([number]) As Single
```

The brackets indicate that the *number* argument is optional, and the As Single part of the syntax denotes that the value returned is of the Single data type. Different functions return different data types suited to their contents: Many functions return a Variant, but yes/no functions, such as the IsNumeric function used in Chapter 7, return a Boolean value. When necessary (and possible), VBA will convert the result of a function to a different data type needed by another function in the expression.

If any pair of brackets contains two arguments, you have to use both of them at once. For example, the syntax for the MsgBox function (which displays a message box) is as follows.

```
MsgBox(prompt[, buttons] [, title][, helpfile, context])
```

Here, *prompt* is the only required argument: *buttons*, *title*, *helpfile*, and *context* are all optional. But as you can see, *helpfile* and *context* are enclosed within a single set of brackets instead of each having its own pair. You need to use either both of these arguments or neither of them; you cannot use one without the other. (You'll visit with the MsgBox function at greater length in Chapter 11, "Using Message Boxes and Input Boxes.")

What Do Functions Do?

VBA's built-in functions perform a wide variety of tasks—everything from determining whether a file exists, to returning the current date, to converting data from one format to another. (For example, you can use a function to convert numeric data into a text string.)

In this chapter, I'll use something of a cross-section of VBA's functions, including functions for converting data from one data type to another, file-operation functions, date functions, and mathematical functions.

Using Functions

To use a function, you *call* it (or *invoke* it, if you're feeling sorcerous) from a subprocedure or from another function. To call a function, you use a Call statement, either with the Call keyword or just the name of the function.

 NOTE As you'll see later in the book, you call a procedure in the same way as you call a function.

The syntax for the Call statement is as follows:

```
[Call] name[, argumentlist]
```

Here, *name* is a required String argument giving the name of the function or procedure to call; and *argumentlist* is an optional argument providing a comma-delimited list of the variables, arrays, or expressions to pass to the function or procedure. When calling a function, you'll almost always need to pass arguments (except for those few functions that take no arguments); when calling a procedure, you use the *argumentlist* argument only for procedures that require arguments.

The brackets around the Call keyword indicate that it is optional. If you use this keyword, you need to enclose the *argumentlist* argument in parentheses. In most cases, it's clearer *not* to use the Call keyword when calling a function.

For example, the following statement calls the MsgBox function, supplying the required argument *prompt* (the string Hello, World!):

```
MsgBox "Hello, World!"
```

You could use the Call keyword (and enclose the argument list in parentheses) instead, as shown in the following statement, but there's little advantage in doing so:

```
Call MsgBox("Hello, World!")
```

 NOTE You can't run a function from the Visual Basic Editor unless you call it from a procedure—except by executing a function call from the Immediate window, which doesn't really count.

You can assign the result of a function to a variable. For example, consider the following code fragment. The first two of the following statements declare the String variables strExample and strLeft10. The third statement assigns a bland string of text to strExample. The fourth statement uses the Left function to return the left-most ten characters from strExample and assign them to strLeft10, which the fifth statement then displays in a message box.

```
Dim strExample As String
Dim strLeft10 As String
strExample = "Technology is interesting."
strLeft10 = Left(strExample, 10)
MsgBox strLeft10
```

Instead of assigning the result of a function to a variable, you can insert it directly in your code or pass it to another function. Take a look at the following statement:

```
MsgBox Right(Left("This is Booty and the Beast", 13), 5)
```

This statement uses three functions: the MsgBox function, the Left function, and the Right function. As you'd guess, the Right function is the conservative sibling of the

Left function and returns the specified number of characters from the right wing of the specified string.

When you have multiple sets of parentheses in a VBA statement, things happen from the inside, just as they did in those math classes that brightened your schooldays. So, in this example the Left function is evaluated first, returning the leftmost 13 characters from the string: This is Booty (the spaces are characters too). VBA passes this new string to the Right function, which in this case returns the rightmost five characters from it: Booty. VBA passes this second new string to the MsgBox function, which displays it in a message box.

 NOTE You can nest functions to absurd levels without giving VBA much trouble, but for most practical purposes, it's a good idea to limit nesting to only a few levels. That way, you (and others) will be able to read your code and troubleshoot it much more easily.

Passing Arguments to a Function

When a function takes more than one argument, you can pass the arguments to it in any of three ways:

- By supplying the arguments, without their names, positionally (in the order in which the function expects them).
- By supplying the arguments, with their names, in the order in which the function expects them.
- By supplying the arguments, with their names, in any order you choose.

The first method, supplying the arguments positionally without using their names, is usually the quickest way to proceed. The only disadvantage to doing so is that anyone reading your code may not know immediately which value corresponds to which argument—though they can look this up without trouble. To omit an optional argument, you place a comma where it would appear in the sequence of arguments.

Using argument names takes longer (and makes your code more verbose), but makes your code easier to read. When you omit an argument, you don't need to use the comma to indicate that you're skipping it.

There's no advantage to using named arguments out of order over using them in order unless you happen to find doing so easier or more amusing.

For example, the DateSerial function returns a Variant/Date containing the date for the given year, month, and day. The syntax for DateSerial is as follows:

```
DateSerial(year, month, day)
```

Here, *year* is a required Integer argument supplying the year; *month* is a required Integer argument supplying the month; and *day* is a required Integer argument supplying the day.

The following statement supplies the arguments positionally without their names:

```
MsgBox DateSerial(1999, 12, 31)
```

The following statement supplies the arguments positionally with their names:

```
MsgBox DateSerial(Year:=1999, Month:=12, Day:=31)
```

The following statement supplies the arguments, with their names, out of order:

```
MsgBox DateSerial(Day:=31, Year:=1999, Month:=12)
```

All three of these statements work fine. You'll only get a problem if you list out of order arguments that you're supplying without names (positionally) or if you name some arguments and don't name others.

Using Functions to Convert Data from One Type to Another

VBA provides a full set of functions for converting data from one data type to another. These functions fall into two distinct groups, so I'll show them to you separately, starting with the easier group.

Table 9.1 lists VBA's functions for simple data conversion.

TABLE 9.1: VBA'S FUNCTIONS FOR SIMPLE DATA CONVERSION

Function(Arguments)	Data Type Returned
CBool(*number*)	Boolean
CByte(*expression*)	Byte
CCur(*expression*)	Currency
CDate(*expression*)	Date
CDbl(*expression*)	Double
CInt(*expression*)	Integer
CLng(*expression*)	Long
CSng(*expression*)	Single
CStr(*expression*)	String
CVar(*expression*)	Variant

For example, the following statements declare the untyped variable `varMyInput` and the Integer variable `intMyVar`, then display an input box prompting the user to enter an integer. In the third statement, the user's input is assigned to `varMyInput`, which automatically becomes a Variant/String. The fourth statement uses the `CInt` function to convert `varMyInput` to an integer, assigning the result to `intMyVar`. The fifth statement compares `intMyVar` to 10, converts the result to Boolean by using the `CBool` function, and displays the result (`True` or `False`) in a message box.

```
Dim varMyInput
Dim intMyVar As Integer
varMyInput = InputBox("Enter an integer:", "Dial 10 For Truth")
intMyVar = CInt(varMyInput)
MsgBox CBool(intMyVar = 10)
```

Table 9.2 lists VBA's functions for more complex data conversion.

TABLE 9.2: VBA'S FUNCTIONS FOR COMPLEX DATA CONVERSION

Function(Arguments)	Returns
Asc(*string*)	ANSI character code for the first character in the string.
Chr(*number*)	The string for the specified character code (a number between 0 and 255).
Format(*expression, format*)	A variant containing *expression* formatted as specified by *format*. (Let that go for the moment. I'll explain how Format works later in the chapter.)
Hex(*number*)	A string containing the hexadecimal value of *number*.
Oct(*number*)	A string containing the octal value of *number*.
RGB(*number1, number2, number3*)	A Long integer representing the color value specified by *number1, number2,* and *number3*.
QBColor(*number*)	A Long containing the RGB value for the specified color.
Str(*number*)	A Variant/String containing a string representation of *number*.
Val(*string*)	The numeric portion of *string*; if *string* does not have a numeric portion, Val returns 0.

Using the *Asc* Function to Return a Character Code

The Asc function returns the character code for the first character of a string. (Asc stands for ASCII, but in fact the function returns the ANSI—American National Standards

Institute—number for a character.) *Character codes* are the numbers by which computers refer to letters. For example, the character code for a capital *A* is 65 and for a capital *B* is 66; a lowercase *a* is 97, and a lowercase *b* is 98.

The syntax for the Asc function is straightforward:

```
Asc(string)
```

Here, *string* is any string expression.

The following statements use the Asc function to return the character code for the first character of the current selection in the active document and display that code in a message box:

```
strThisCharacter = Asc(Selection.Text)
MsgBox strThisCharacter, vbOKOnly, "Character Code"
```

Using the *Val* Function to Extract a Number from the Start of a String

The Val function converts the numbers contained in a string into a numeric value. Val is a bit weird:

- It reads only numbers in a string.
- It starts at the beginning of the string and reads only as far as the string contains characters that it recognizes as numbers.
- It ignores tabs, line-feeds, and blank spaces.
- It recognizes the period as a decimal separator, but not the comma.

This means that if you feed Val a string consisting of tabbed columns of numbers, such as the second line below, it will read them as a single number (in this case, 445634.994711):

```
Item#   Price  Available   On Order  Ordered
4456    34.99      4           7        11
```

If, however, you feed it something containing a mix of numbers and letters, Val will read only the numbers and strings recognized as numeric expressions (for example, Val("4E5") returns 400000, because the expression is read as exponentiation). For example, if fed the address shown below, it returns 8661, ignoring the other numbers in the string (because it stops at the *L* of *Laurel*, the first character that isn't a number, a tab, a line-feed, or a space):

```
8661 Laurel Avenue Suite 3806, Oakland, CA 94610
```

The syntax for Val is straightforward:

```
Val(string)
```

Here, *string* is a required argument consisting of any string expression.

The following statement uses Val to return the numeric variable StreetNumber from the string Address1:

```
StreetNumber = Val(Address1)
```

Using the *Str* Function to Convert a Value to a String

Just as you can convert a string to a value, you can also convert a value to a string. You'll need to do this when you want to concatenate the information contained in a value with a string—if you try to do this simply by using the + operator, VBA will attempt to perform a mathematical operation rather than concatenation. For example, suppose you've declared a String variable named YourAge and a numeric variable named Age. You can't use a YourAge + Age statement to concatenate them, because they're different types; you first need to create a string from the Age variable and then concatenate that string with the YourAge string. (Alternatively, you can use the & operator to concatenate the two variables.)

To convert a value to a string, use the Str function. The syntax for the Str function is this:

```
Str(number)
```

Here, *number* is a variable containing a numeric expression (such as an Integer data type, a Long data type, or a Double data type).

The following short procedure provides an example of converting a value to a string:

```
Sub Age
    Dim intAge As Integer, strYourAge As String
    intAge = InputBox("Enter your age:", "Age")
    strYourAge = "Your age is" & Str(Age) & "."
    MsgBox YourAge, vbOKOnly + vbInformation, "Age"
End Sub
```

Using the *Format* Function to Format an Expression

The Format function is a powerful tool for whipping numbers, dates and times, and strings into the shape in which you need them.

The syntax for the Format function is as follows:

```
Format(expression[, format[, firstdayofweek[, firstweekofyear]]])
```

Here's what the components of the syntax are:

- *expression* is any valid expression.

- *format* is an optional argument specifying a named format expression or a user-defined format expression. More on this in a moment.

- *firstdayofweek* is an optional constant specifying the day that starts the week (for date information): The default setting is vbSunday (1), but you can also set vbMonday (2), vbTuesday (3), vbWednesday (4), vbThursday (5), vbFriday (6), vbSaturday (7), or vbUseSystem (0; uses the system setting).

- *firstweekofyear* is an optional constant specifying the week considered first in the year (again, for date information):

Constant	Value	Year Starts with Week
vbUseSystem	0	Use the system setting.
vbFirstJan1	1	The week in which January 1 falls (the default setting).
vbFirstFourDays	2	The first week with a minimum of four days in the year.
vbFirstFullWeek	3	The first full week (7 days) of the year.

You can define your own formats for the Format function as described in the following sections. First, though, I'll show you the predefined numeric formats that you can use without even thinking of cracking a sweat.

Using Predefined Numeric Formats

Table 9.3 lists the following predefined numeric formats that you can use with the Format function.

TABLE 9.3: PREDEFINED NUMERIC FORMATS

Format Name	Explanation	Example
General Number	The number is displayed with no thousand separator.	124589
Currency	The number is displayed with two decimal places, a thousand separator, and the currency symbol appropriate to the system locale.	$1,234.56
Fixed	The number is displayed with two decimal places and at least one integer place.	5.00
Standard	The number is displayed with two decimal places, at least one integer place, and a thousand separator (when needed).	1,225.00
Percent	The number is displayed multiplied by 100, with two decimal places, and with a percent sign.	78.00%

Continued ▶

TABLE 9.3 CONTINUED: PREDEFINED NUMERIC FORMATS

Format Name	Explanation	Example
Scientific	The number is displayed in scientific notation.	5.00E+00
Yes/No	A non-zero number is displayed as Yes; a zero number is displayed as No.	Yes
True/False	A non-zero number is displayed as True; a zero number is displayed as False.	False
On/Off	A non-zero number is displayed as On; a zero number is displayed as Off.	Off

For example, the following statement returns $123.45:

```
Format("12345", "Currency")
```

Creating a Numeric Format

If none of the predefined numeric formats suits your needs, you can create your own numeric formats by using your choice of combination of the characters listed in Table 9.4.

TABLE 9.4: CHARACTERS FOR CREATING YOUR OWN NUMBER FORMATS

Character	Explanation
[None]	Displays the number without any formatting. (You won't usually want to use this option.)
0	Placeholder for a digit. If there's no digit, VBA displays a zero. If the number has fewer digits than you use zeroes, VBA displays leading or trailing zeroes as appropriate.
#	Placeholder for a digit. If there's no digit, VBA displays nothing.
.	Placeholder for a decimal. Indicates where the decimal separator should fall. The decimal separator varies by locale (for example, a decimal point in the U.S., a comma in Germany).
%	Placeholder for a percent character. VBA inserts the percent character and multiplies the expression by 100.
,	Thousand separator (depending on locale, a comma or a period).
:	Time separator (typically a colon, but again this depends on the locale).
/	Date separator. (Again, what you'll see depends on the locale.)

Continued ▶

TABLE 9.4 CONTINUED: CHARACTERS FOR CREATING YOUR OWN NUMBER FORMATS

Character	Explanation
E- E+ e- e+	Scientific format: E- or e- places a minus sign next to negative exponents. E+ or e+ places a minus sign next to negative exponents, and places a plus sign next to positive exponents.
- + $ ( )	Displays a literal character.
\[character]	Displays the literal character.
"[string]"	Displays the literal character. Use Chr(34) (the character code for double quotation marks) to provide the double quotation marks.

For example, the following statement returns a currency formatted with four decimal places:

```
Format("123456", "$00.0000")
```

Creating a Date or Time Format

Similarly, you can create your own date and time formats by mixing and matching the characters listed in Table 9.5. As you can see, there are more options than you can confidently shake a stick at, but you'll find they're easy to use.

TABLE 9.5: CHARACTERS FOR CREATING YOUR OWN DATE AND TIME FORMATS

Character	Explanation
:	Time separator (typically a colon, but this depends on the locale).
/	Date separator (also locale-dependent).
c	Displays the date (if there is a date or an integer value) in the system's short date format and the time (if there is a date or a fractional value) in the system's default time format.
d	Displays the date (1 to 31) without a leading zero.
dd	Displays the date with a leading zero for single-digit numbers (01 to 31).
ddd	Displays the day as a three-letter abbreviation (Sun, Mon, Tue, Wed, Thu, Fri, Sat) with no period.
dddd	Displays the full name of the day.
ddddd	Displays the complete date (day, month, and year) in the system's short date format.

Continued ▶

TABLE 9.5 CONTINUED: CHARACTERS FOR CREATING YOUR OWN DATE AND TIME FORMATS

Character	Explanation
dddddd	Displays the complete date (day, month, and year) in the system's long date format.
ddddddd	Displays the date formatted as a logarithmic percentage of your computer's distance in light years from Alpha Centauri—whoa, belay that one. Doesn't exist.
aaaa	Displays the full, localized name of the day.
w	Displays an integer from 1 (Sunday) to 7 (Monday) containing the day of the week.
ww	Displays an integer from 1 to 54 giving the number of the week in the year (*sic* on that 54 because of partial weeks starting and ending the year).
m	Displays an integer from 1 to 12 giving the number of the month without a leading zero on single-digit months. When used after h, returns minutes instead of months.
mm	Displays a number from 01 to 12 giving the two-digit number of the month. When used after h, returns minutes instead of months.
mmm	Displays the month as a three-letter abbreviation (except for May) without a period.
mmmm	Displays the full name of the month.
oooo	Displays the full localized name of the month.
q	Displays a number from 1 to 4 giving the quarter of the year.
y	Displays an integer from 1 to 366 giving the day of the year.
yy	Displays a number from 00 to 99 giving the two-digit year.
yyyy	Displays a number from 0100 to 9999 giving the four-digit year.
h	Displays a number from 0 to 23 giving the hour.
Hh	Displays a number from 00 to 23 giving the two-digit hour.
N	Displays a number from 0 to 60 giving the minute.
Nn	Displays a number from 00 to 60 giving the two-digit minute.
S	Displays a number from 0 to 60 giving the second.
Ss	Displays a number from 00 to 60 giving the two-digit second.
ttttt	Displays the full time (hour, minute, and second) in the system's default time format.
AM/PM	Uses the 12-hour clock and displays AM or PM as appropriate.
am/pm	Uses the 12-hour clock and displays am or pm as appropriate.
A/P	Uses the 12-hour clock and displays A or P as appropriate.
a/p	Uses the 12-hour clock and displays a or p as appropriate.
AMPM	Uses the 12-hour clock and displays the AM or PM string literal defined for the system.

For example, the following statement returns Saturday, April 01, 2000:

```
Format(#4/1/2000#, "dddddd")
```

Creating a String Format

Not content only with letting you create custom numeric formats and date and time formats, Format also lets you create custom string formats. Your options with strings are a little more limited, as Table 9.6 shows.

TABLE 9.6: CHARACTERS FOR CREATING YOUR OWN STRING FORMATS

Character	Explanation
@	Placeholder for a character. Displays a character if there is one and a space if there is none.
&	Placeholder for a character. Displays a character if there is one and nothing if there is none.
<	Displays the string in lowercase.
>	Displays the string in uppercase.
!	Causes VBA to fill placeholders from left to right instead of from right to left (the default direction).

For example, the following statement assigns to strUser a string consisting of four spaces if there is no input in the input box:

```
strUser = Format(InputBox("Enter your name:"), "@@@@")
```

Using the *Chr* Function and Constants to Enter Special Characters in a String

To add special characters (such as a carriage return or a tab) to a string, you need to specify them by using a built-in constant (for those special characters that have built-in constants defined) or by entering the appropriate character code using the Chr function. The syntax for the Chr function is straightforward:

```
Chr(charactercode)
```

Here, *charactercode* is a number that identifies the character to add.

Table 9.7 lists the most useful character codes and character constants.

TABLE 9.7: VBA CHARACTER CODES AND CHARACTER CONSTANTS

Code	Built-in Character Constant	Character
Chr(9)	vbTab	Tab
Chr(10)	vbLf	Line-feed
Chr(11)	vbVerticalTab	Soft return (Shift+Enter)
Chr(12)	vbFormFeed	Page break
Chr(13)	vbCr	Carriage return
Chr(13) + Chr(10)	vbCrLf	Carriage return/line-feed combination
Chr(14)	–	Column break
Chr(34)	–	Double straight quotation marks (")
Chr(39)	–	Single straight quote mark/apostrophe (')
Chr(145)	–	Opening single smart quotation mark (')
Chr(146)	–	Closing single smart quotation mark/ apostrophe (')
Chr(147)	–	Opening double smart quotation mark (")
Chr(148)	–	Closing double smart quotation mark (")
Chr(149)	–	Bullet
Chr(150)	–	en dash
Chr(151)	–	em dash

NOTE The straight and smart quotes and apostrophes can sometimes be difficult to work with in Word because of Word's determination to help you make all your straight quotes smart. For example, during a Find and Replace operation, if you search for a single smart quote and replace it with another character, Word will assume that you want to affect the single straight quotes in your document as well. The solution is to specify the character number in the Find and Replace dialog box, or in a VBA Find and Replace operation, rather than using the character itself.

Say that you wanted to build a string containing a person's name and address from individual strings containing items of that information, and that you also wanted the individual items separated by tabs in the resulting string so that you could insert the string into a document and then convert it into a table. To do this, you could use a statement like the one below. Here, VBA uses a For... Next loop to repeat the action until the counter i reaches the number stored in the variable intNumRecords:

```
For i = 1 to intNumRecords
    AllInfo = FirstName & vbTab & MiddleInitial & vbTab _
    & LastName & vbTab & Address1 & vbTab & Address2 _
        & vbTab & City & vbTab & State & vbTab & Zip _
        & vbTab & BusinessPhone & vbTab & HomePhone & _
        & vbTab & BusinessEMail & vbTab & HomeEMail & vbCr
    Selection.TypeText AllInfo
Next i
```

The second line (split here over five physical lines) assigns data to the string AllInfo by concatenating the strings FirstName, MiddleInitial, LastName, and so on with tabs—vbTab characters—between them. The final character added to the string is vbCr (a carriage-return character), which creates a new paragraph.

The third line enters the AllInfo string into the current document, thus building a tab-delimited list containing the names and addresses. This list can then be easily converted into a table whose columns each contain one item of information (the first column contains the FirstName string, the second column the MiddleInitial string, and so on).

Using Functions to Manipulate Strings

String variables are among the most useful variables for working with Word in VBA. You can use them to store any quantity of text, from a character or two up to a large number of pages; you can also use them to store file names and folder names. Once you've stored the data in a string, you can manipulate it and change it according to your needs.

Table 9.8 lists VBA's built-in functions for manipulating strings. Because some of these functions are more complex than other functions you've seen in the chapter, and because they're frequently useful, you'll look at detailed examples after the table.

TABLE 9.8: VBA'S STRING-MANIPULATION FUNCTIONS

Function(Arguments)	Returns
InStr(*start*, *string1*, *string2*, *compare*)	A Variant/Long giving the position of the first instance of the search string (*string2*) inside the target string (*string1*), starting from the beginning of the target string.
InStrRev(*stringcheck*, *stringmatch*, *start*, *compare*)	A Variant/Long giving the position of the first instance of the search string (*stringmatch*) inside the target string (*stringcheck*), starting from the end of the target string.
LCase(*string*)	A String containing the lowercased *string*.
Left(*string*, *number*)	A Variant/String containing the specified number of characters from the left end of *string*.
Len(*string*)	A Long containing the number of characters in *string*.
LTrim(*string*)	A Variant/String containing *string* with any leading spaces trimmed off it.
Mid(*string*, *start*, *length*)	A Variant
Right(*string*, *number*)	A Variant/String containing the specified number of characters from the right end of *string*.
RTrim(*string*)	A Variant/String containing *string* with any trailing spaces trimmed off it.
Space(*number*)	A Variant/String containing *number* of spaces.
StrComp(*string1*, *string2*, *compare*)	A Variant/Integer containing the result of comparing *string1* and *string2*.
StrConv(*string*, *conversion*, *LCID*)	A Variant/String containing *string* converted as specified by *conversion* for the (optional) specified Locale ID (*LCID*).
String(*number*, *character*)	A Variant/String containing *number* of instances of *character*.
StrReverse(*expression*)	A String containing the characters of *expression* in reverse order.
Trim(*string*)	A Variant/String containing *string* with any leading spaces or trailing spaces trimmed off it.
UCase(*string*)	A String containing the uppercased *string*.

Using the *Left*, *Right*, and *Mid* Functions to Return Part of a String

Frequently, you'll need to use only part of a string in your procedures. For example, you might want to take only the first three characters of the name of a city to create the code for a location.

VBA provides several functions for returning from strings the characters you need:

- The Left function returns the specified number of characters from the left end of the string.

- The Right function returns the specified number of characters from the right end of the string.

- The Mid function returns the specified number of characters from the specified location inside a string.

 NOTE VBA provides two versions of a number of string functions, including the Left, Right, and Mid functions: the versions I show you here, which return String-type Variant values, and versions whose names end with $ (Left$, Right$, Mid$, and so on), which return String values. The functions that return the Strings supposedly run faster (though you're not likely to notice any difference with normal use) but will return an error if you use them on a Null value. The functions that return the String-type Variants can deal with Null values with no problem.

Using the *Left* Function

As already stated, the Left function returns a specified number of characters from the left end of a string. The syntax for the Left function is as follows:

```
Left(string, length)
```

Here, the *string* argument is any string expression—that is, any expression that returns a sequence of contiguous characters. Left returns Null if *string* contains no data. The *length* argument is a numeric expression specifying the number of characters to return. *length* can be a straightforward number (such as, 4, or 7, or 11) or an expression that results in a number. For example, if the length of a word were stored in the variable named LenWord, and you wanted to return two characters fewer than LenWord, you could specify LenWord – 2 as the *length* argument; to return three characters more than LenWord, you could specify LenWord + 3 as the *length* argument.

For example, you could use the Left function to separate the area code from a telephone number that was provided as an unseparated 10-digit chunk by your friendly local mainframe. In the following statements, the telephone number is stored in the String variable strPhone, which we'll assume was created earlier:

```
Dim strArea As String
strArea = Left(strPhone, 3)
```

This statement creates the variable Area and fills it with the leftmost three characters of the variable strPhone.

Using the *Right* Function

The Right function is the mirror image of the Left function and returns a specified number of characters from the right end of a string. The syntax for the Right function is as follows:

```
Right(string, length)
```

Again, the *string* argument is any string expression, and *length* is a numeric expression specifying the number of characters to return. Again, Right returns Null if *string* contains no data, and *length* can be a number or an expression that results in a number.

To continue the previous example, you could use the Right function to separate the last seven digits of the phone number stored in the string strPhone from the area code:

```
Dim strLocalNumber As String
strLocalNumber = Right(strPhone, 7)
```

This statement creates the variable strLocalNumber and fills it with the rightmost seven characters from the variable strPhone.

Using the *Mid* Function

The Mid function returns the specified number of characters from inside the given string. You specify a starting position in the string and the number of characters (to the right of the starting position) to return.

The syntax for the Mid function is as follows:

```
Mid(string, start[, length])
```

As in Left and Right, the *string* argument is any string expression. Mid returns Null if *string* contains no data.

start is a numeric value specifying the character position in *string* at which to start the *length* selection; if *start* is larger than the number of characters in *string*, VBA returns a zero-length string.

length is a numeric expression specifying the number of characters to return. If you omit *length* or use a *length* argument greater than the number of characters in *string*, VBA returns all characters from the *start* position to the end of *string*. Once more, *length* can be a straightforward number or an expression that results in a number.

Sticking determinedly with the phone-number example, you could use Mid to return the local exchange code from a 10-digit phone number (for instance, 555 from 5105551212). Here, the telephone number is stored in the variable strPhone:

```
Dim strLocalExchange As String
strLocalExchange = Mid(strPhone, 4, 3)
```

This statement creates the variable strLocalExchange and fills it with the three characters of the variable strPhone starting at the fourth character.

NOTE If the phone number were supplied in a different format, such as **(510) 555-1212** or **510-555-1212**, you'd need to adjust the *start* value to allow for the extra characters. For example, if the area code were in parentheses and followed by a space, as in the first instance here, you'd need a *start* value of 7; if the area code were divided from the rest of the phone number only by a hyphen, as in the second instance here, you'd need a *start* value of 5.

You can use Mid to find the location of a character within a string. In the following snippet, the Do Until… Loop walks backwards through the string strFilename (which contains the FullName property of the template attached to the active document) until it reaches the first backslash (\), storing the resulting character position in the Integer variable intLen. The message box then displays that part of strFilename to the right of the backslash (determined by subtracting intLen from the length of strFilename)—the name of the attached template without its path:

```
Dim strFilename As String, intLen As Integer
strFilename = ActiveDocument.AttachedTemplate.FullName
intLen = Len(strFilename)
Do Until Mid(strFilename, intLen, 1) = "\"
    intLen = intLen - 1
Loop
MsgBox Right(strFilename, Len(strFilename) - intLen)
```

This example is more illustrative than realistic for two reasons: First, you can get the name of the template more easily by using the Name property rather than the FullName property; and second, there's a function called InStrRev that returns the position of one string within another by walking backwards through it.

Using *InStr* and *InStrRev* to Find a String within Another String

The InStr function allows you to find one string within another string. For example, you could check a string derived from, say, the current paragraph to see if it contained a particular word. If it did, you could take action accordingly—for instance, replacing that word with another word, or selecting the paragraph for inclusion in another document.

The InStrRev function is the evil twin of the InStr function, working in a similar way but in the reverse direction.

The syntax for InStr is as follows:

```
InStr([start, ]string1, string2[, compare])
```

The arguments are as follows:

- *start* is an optional argument specifying the starting position in the first string, *string1*. If you omit *start*, VBA starts the search at the first character in *string1* (which is usually where you want to start). However, you do need to use *start* when you use the *compare* argument to specify the type of string comparison to perform.

- *string1* is a required argument specifying the string expression in which to search for *string2*.

- *string2* is a required argument specifying the string expression for which to search in *string1*.

- *compare* is an optional argument specifying the type of string comparison you want to perform: a *binary comparison*, which is case sensitive, or a *textual comparison*, which is non–case sensitive. The default is a binary comparison, which you can specify by using the constant vbBinaryCompare or the value 0 for compare; while specifying this value isn't necessary (because it's the default), you might want to use it to make your code ultra-clear. To specify a textual comparison, use the constant vbTextCompare or the value 1 for *compare*.

 TIP A textual comparison is a useful weapon when you're dealing with data that may arrive in a variety of cases. For example, if you wanted to search a selection for instances of a name, you'd probably want to find instances of the name in uppercase and lowercase as well as in title case—otherwise you'll find only title case (assuming you specified the name in title case).

You could use InStr to find the location of a certain string within another string so that you could then change that inner string. You might want to do this if you needed to move a file from its current position in a particular folder or subfolder to another folder that had a similar subfolder structure. For instance, suppose you work with documents stored in a variety of subfolders beneath a folder named In (such as f:\Documents\In\), and after you're done with them, you save them in corresponding subfolders beneath a folder named Out (f:\Documents\Out\). The short procedure shown in Listing 9.1 automatically saves the documents in the Out subfolder.

Listing 9.1

```
1.  Sub Save_in_Out_Folder()
2.      Dim strOName As String, strNName As String, _
            intToChange As Integer
3.      strOName = ActiveDocument.FullName
4.      intToChange = InStr(strOName, "\In\")
5.      strNName = Left(strOName, intToChange - 1) & "\Out\" _
            & Right(strOName, Len(strOName) - intToChange - 3)
6.      ActiveDocument.SaveAs strNName
7.  End Sub
```

Analysis

The code in Listing 9.1 works as follows:

- Line 1 begins the procedure, and line 7 ends it.

- Line 2 declares the String variable strOName (as in *original name*), the String variable strNName (as in *new name*), and the Integer variable intToChange. Line 3 then assigns strOName the FullName property of the ActiveDocument object: the full name of the active document, including the path to the document (for example, f:\Documents\In\Letters\My Letter.doc).

- Line 4 assigns to the variable intToChange the value of the InStr function that finds the string \In\ in the variable strOName. Using the example path from the previous paragraph, intToChange will be assigned the value 13, because the first character of the \In\ string is the thirteenth character in the strOName string.

- Line 5 assigns to the variable `strNName` the new filename created in the main part of the statement. This breaks down as follows:

  - `Left(strOName, intToChange - 1)` takes the left section of the `strOName` string, returning the number of characters specified by `intToChange - 1`—the number stored in `intToChange` minus one.

  - `& "\Out\"` adds to the partial string specified in the previous bullet (to continue the previous example, `f:\Documents`) the characters `\Out\`, which effectively replace the `\In\` characters, thus changing the directory name (`f:\Documents\Out\`).

  - `& Right(strOName, Len(strOName) - intToChange - 3)` completes the partial string by adding the right section of the `strOName` string, starting from after the `\In\` string (`Letters\My Letter.doc`), yielding `f:\Documents\Out\Letters\My Letter.doc`. The number of characters to take from the right section is determined by subtracting the value stored in `intToChange` from the length of `strOName` and then subtracting 3 from the result. Here, the value 3 comes from the length of the string `\In\`; because the `intToChange` value stores the character number of the first backslash, you need count only the *I*, the *n*, and the second backslash to reach its end.

- Line 6 saves the document using the name in the `strNName` variable.

The syntax for `InStrRev` is similar to that of `InStr`:

`InStrRev(stringcheck, stringmatch[, start[, compare]])`

Here's what the arguments are:

- *stringcheck* is a required String argument specifying the string in which to search for *stringmatch*.

- *stringmatch* is a required String argument specifying the string for which to search.

- *start* is an optional numeric argument specifying the starting position for the search. If you omit *start*, VBA starts at the last character of *stringcheck*.

- *compare* (as for `InStr`) is an optional argument specifying how to search: `vbTextCompare` for text, `vbBinaryCompare` for a binary comparison.

Using *LTrim*, *RTrim*, and *Trim* to Trim Spaces from a String

Often you'll need to trim strings before concatenating them to avoid ending up with extra spaces in inappropriate places, such as in the middle of eight-character file names.

As you saw in Table 9.8, VBA provides three functions specifically for trimming leading spaces and trailing spaces from strings:

- LTrim removes leading spaces from the specified string.
- RTrim removes trailing spaces from the specified string.
- Trim removes both leading and trailing spaces from the specified string.

 TIP In many cases, you can simply use Trim instead of figuring out whether LTrim or RTrim is appropriate for what you expect a variable to contain. At other times, you'll need to remove either leading or trailing spaces while retaining their counterparts, in which case you'll need either LTrim or RTrim. RTrim is especially useful for working with fixed-length String variables, which will contain trailing spaces if the data assigned to them is shorter than their fixed length.

The syntax for the LTrim, RTrim, and Trim functions is straightforward:

```
LTrim(string)
Rtrim(string)
Trim(string)
```

In each case, *string* is any string expression.

You could use the Trim function to remove both leading and trailing spaces from a string derived from the current selection in the active document in Word. The first line in the code below declares strUntrimmed and strTrimmed as String variables. The second line assigns the data in the current selection to the strUntrimmed string. The third line assigns the trimmed version of the strUntrimmed string to the strTrimmed string:

```
Dim strUntrimmed As String, strTrimmed As String
strUntrimmed = Selection.Text
strTrimmed = Trim(strUntrimmed)
```

Using *Len* to Check the Length of a String

To check how long a string is, use the Len function. The syntax for the Len function is straightforward:

```
Len(string)
```

Here, *string* is any valid string expression. (If *string* is Null, Len also returns Null.)

You can use Len to make sure that a user's entry in an input box or in a text box of a dialog box is of a suitable length. For example, the CheckPassword procedure shown in Listing 9.2 uses Len to make sure that the password the user enters is of a suitable length.

Listing 9.2

```
1.  Sub CheckPassword()
2.      Dim strPassword As String
3.  BadPassword:
4.      strPassword = InputBox _
            ("Enter the password to protect this item from changes:" _
            , "Enter Password")
5.      If Len(strPassword) = 0 Then
6.          End
7.      ElseIf Len(strPassword) < 6 Then
8.          MsgBox "The password you chose is too short." _
                & vbCr & vbCr & _
                "Choose a password between 6 and 15 " &
                "characters in length.", _
                 vbOKOnly + vbCritical, "Unsuitable Password"
9.          GoTo BadPassword
10      ElseIf Len(strPassword) > 15 Then
11.         MsgBox "The password you chose is too long." _
                & vbCr & vbCr & _
                "Choose a password between 6 and 15 " &
                "characters in length.", _
                 vbOKOnly + vbCritical, "Unsuitable Password"
12.         GoTo BadPassword
13.     End If
14. End Sub
```

Analysis

Listing 9.2 provides a relatively crude check of a password, making sure that it contains between 6 and 15 characters (inclusive). Here's how the code works:

- Line 2 declares a String variable named strPassword.

- Line 3 contains the label BadPassword, to which the GoTo statements in line 9 and line 12 redirect execution if the password fails either of the checks.

- Line 4 assigns to strPassword the result of an input box that invites the user to enter the password for the item.

- Lines 5 through 13 then use an If statement to check that the password is an appropriate length. First, line 5 checks strPassword for zero length, which would mean that the user either clicked the Cancel button or the close button on the input box, or clicked the OK button with no text entered in the input box. If the length of strPassword is zero, the End statement in line 6 terminates the procedure. If the password passes that test, line 7 checks to find out if its length is less than six characters; if so, the procedure displays a message box alerting the user to the problem, and then redirects execution to the BadPassword label. If the password is 6 or more characters long, line 10 checks to see if it's more than 15 characters long; if it is, the user gets another message box and another trip back to the BadPassword label.

Using *StrConv*, *LCase*, and *UCase* to Change the Case of a String

For changing the case of a string, VBA provides the StrConv (whose name comes from *string conversion*), LCase, and UCase functions. Of these, the easiest to use is StrConv, which can convert a string to a number of different formats varying from straightforward uppercase, lowercase, or *propercase* (as VBA refers to initial capitals) to the Japanese *hiragana* and *katakana* phonetic characters.

Using *StrConv*

The StrConv function has the following syntax:

```
StrConv(string, conversion)
```

Here, the *string* argument is any string expression, and the *conversion* argument is a constant or value specifying the type of conversion required. The most useful conversion constants and values are these:

Constant	Value	Effect
vbUpperCase	1	Converts the given string to uppercase characters.
vbLowerCase	2	Converts the given string to lowercase characters.
vbProperCase	3	Converts the given string to propercase (a.k.a. title case—the first letter of every word is capitalized).
vbUnicode	64	Converts the given string to Unicode using the system's default code page.
vbFromUnicode	128	Converts the given string from Unicode to the system's default code page.

For example, suppose you received from a database program a string called `str-CustomerName` containing a person's name. You could use `StrConv` to make sure that it was in title case by using a statement such as this:

```
strProperCustomerName = StrConv(strCustomerName, 3)
```

 NOTE `StrConv` doesn't care about the casing of the string you feed it—it simply returns the case you asked for. For example, you can feed `StrConv` uppercase and ask it to return uppercase, and it'll be perfectly happy.

Using *LCase* and *UCase*

If you don't feel like using `StrConv`, you can also use the `LCase` and `UCase` functions, which convert a string to lowercase and uppercase, respectively.

`LCase` and `UCase` have the following syntax:

```
LCase(string)
UCase(string)
```

Here, *string* is any string expression.

For example, the following statement lowercases the string `MyString` and assigns it to `MyLowerString`:

```
MyLowerString = LCase(MyString)
```

Using the *StrComp* Function to Compare Apples to Apples

As you've seen already, you can compare one item to another item by simply using the = operator:

```
If 1 = 1 Then MsgBox "One is one."
```

This straightforward comparison with the = operator also works with two strings, as shown in the second line below:

```
Pet = InputBox("What is your pet?", "Pet")
If Pet = "Dog" Then MsgBox "We do not accept dogs."
```

The problem with this code as written is that the strings need to match exactly in capitalization for VBA to consider them equal: If `Pet` is dog or DOG (not to mention dOG, doG, dOg, or DoG) rather than Dog, the condition isn't met.

To get around this, you can use the `Or` operator to hedge your bets:

```
If Pet = "Dog" Or Pet = "dog" Or Pet = "DOG" Or Pet = "dogs" _
    Or Pet = "Dogs" or Pet = "DOGS" Then MsgBox _
    "We do not accept dogs."
```

As you can see, such code rapidly becomes clumsy—and I still haven't covered dOG and its miscapitalized canines. You could change the case of one or both strings involved to make sure their case matched, but it's simpler to use the StrComp function, which is designed for this job. The syntax for StrComp is as follows:

```
StrComp(string1, string2 [, compare])
```

Here, *string1* and *string2* are required String arguments specifying the strings to compare, and *compare* is an optional argument specifying textual comparison (vbTextCompare) or binary comparison (vbBinaryCompare).

The following statement uses StrComp to settle the pet question once and for all:

```
If StrComp(Pet, "dog", vbTextCompare) = True Then _
    MsgBox "Get out!"
```

Using VBA's Mathematical Functions

VBA provides a solid suite of functions for standard mathematical operations. Table 9.9 lists these functions with examples.

TABLE 9.9: VBA'S MATHEMATICAL FUNCTIONS

Function(Argument)	Returns	Example
Abs(*number*)	The absolute value of *number*—the unsigned magnitude of the number.	Abs(-100) returns 100
Atn(*number*)	The arctangent of *number* in radians.	Atn(dblMyAngle)
Cos(*number*)	The cosine of angle *number*.	Cos(dblMyAngle)
Exp(*number*)	e, the base of natural logarithms, raised to the power of *number*.	Exp(5) returns 148.413159102577
Fix(*number*)	The integer portion of *number* (without rounding). If *number* is negative, returns the negative number greater than or equal to *number*.	Fix(3.14159) returns 3 Fix(-3.14159) returns -3
Int(*number*)	The integer portion of *number* (again, without rounding). If *number* is negative, returns the negative number less than or equal to *number*.	Int(3.14159) returns 3 Int(-3.14159) returns -4
Log(*number*)	The natural logarithm of *number*.	Log(dblMyAngle)
Rnd([*number*])	A random number.	Rnd(1) returns a random number

Continued ▶

TABLE 9.9 CONTINUED: VBA'S MATHEMATICAL FUNCTIONS

Function(Argument)	Returns	Example
Sgn(*number*)	−1 if *number* is negative, 0 if *number* is 0, 1 if *number* is positive.	Sgn(7) returns 1 Sgn(-7) returns −1 Sgn(0) returns 0
Sin(*number*)	The sine of the angle specified by *number* (measured in radians).	Sin(dblMyAngle)
Sqr(*number*)	The square root of *number*. If *number* is negative, VBA throws a runtime error.	Sqr(9) returns 3
Tan(*number*)	The tangent of the angle specified by *number* (measured in radians).	Tan(dblMyAngle)

Using VBA's Date and Time Functions

VBA provides a full complement of date and time functions, as listed in Table 9.10. The table provides some simple example of working with the functions. The sections after the table provide somewhat longer examples of working with the more exciting and complex functions.

TABLE 9.10: VBA'S DATE AND TIME FUNCTIONS

Function(Arguments)	Returns	Example
Date	A Variant/Date containing the current date according to your computer.	MsgBox Date might display 04/01/2000 (the format will depend on your Windows date settings).
DateAdd(*interval*, *number*, *date*)	A Variant/Date containing the date the specified interval after the specified date.	DateAdd("m", 1, "6/3/00") returns 7/3/2000.
DatePart(*interval*, *date*)	The part (specified by *interval*) of the specified date	See the example below in the next section.
DateSerial(*year*, *month*, *day*)	A Variant/Date containing the date for the specified year, month, and day	dteCompanyFounded = DateSerial(1997, 7, 4)
DateValue(*date*)	A Variant/Date containing the specified date)	dteDeath = "July 2, 1971"

Continued

TABLE 9.10 CONTINUED: VBA'S DATE AND TIME FUNCTIONS

Function(Arguments)	Returns	Example
Day(*date*)	A Variant/Integer between 1 and 31, inclusive, representing the day of the month for *date*.	`If Day(Date) = 1 And Month(Date) = 1 Then MsgBox "Happy new year!"`
Hour(*time*)	A Variant/Integer between 0 and 23, inclusive, representing the hour for *time*.	`dteHour = Hour(dteLoggedIn)`
Minute(*time*)	A Variant/Integer between 0 and 59, inclusive, representing the minute for *time*.	`dteMinute = Minute(dteLoggedIn)`
Month(*date*)	A Variant/Integer between 1 and 12, inclusive, representing the month for *date*.	`strThisDate = Month(Date) & "/" & Day(Date)`
MonthName(*month*)	A String containing the name of the month represented by *month*.	`MsgBox MonthName(Month(Date))` displays a message box containing the current month.
Now	A Variant/Date containing the current date and time according to your computer.	`MsgBox Now` might display 04/01/2000 9:25:15PM. (The format of date and time will depend on your Windows date settings.)
Second(*time*)	A Variant/Integer between 0 and 59, inclusive, representing the second for *time*.	`dteSecond = Second(dteLoggedIn)`
Time	A Variant/Date containing the current time according to your computer.	`MsgBox Time` might display 9:25:15PM. (The time format and time will depend on your Windows date settings.)
Timer	A Single giving the number of seconds that have elapsed since midnight.	`If Timer > 43200 Then MsgBox _` `    "This code only works in the morning.": End`
TimeSerial(*hour*, *minute*, *second*)	A Variant/Date containing the time for the specified hour, minute, and second.	`TimeSerial(11, 12, 13)` returns 11:12:13AM (the format will depend on your Windows date settings).
TimeValue(*time*)	A Variant/Date containing the time for *time*.	`TimeValue(Now)`
Weekday(*date*)	A Variant/Integer containing the day of the week represented by *date*.	See the next entry.

Continued

TABLE 9.10 CONTINUED: VBA'S DATE AND TIME FUNCTIONS		
Function(Arguments)	**Returns**	**Example**
WeekdayName (*weekday*)	A String containing the weekday denoted by *weekday*.	WeekdayName(Weekday (#4/1/2000#)) returns Saturday, the day of the week for April Fool's Day 2000.
Year(*date*)	A Variant/Integer containing the year represented by *date*.	dteThisYear = Year(Date)

Using the *DatePart* Function to Parse Dates

The DatePart function lets you take a date and dice it into its components. You can often achieve the same effect as DatePart by using other date functions, but DatePart is a great weapon to have in your VBA armory.

The syntax for DatePart is as follows:

DatePart(*interval*, *date*[,*firstdayofweek*[, *firstweekofyear*]])

The components of the syntax are as follows:

- *interval* is a required String expression giving the unit in which you want to measure the interval: yyyy for year, q for quarter, m for month, y for the day of the year, d for day, w for weekday, ww for week, h for hour, n for minute (because m is for month), and s for second.

- *date* is a required Variant/Date giving the date you want to dice.

- *firstdayofweek* is an optional constant specifying the day that starts the week (for date information): The default setting is vbSunday (1), but you can also set vbMonday (2), vbTuesday (3), vbWednesday (4), vbThursday (5), vbFriday (6), vbSaturday (7), or vbUseSystem (0; uses the system setting).

- *firstweekofyear* is an optional constant specifying the week considered first in the year:

Constant	Value	Year Starts with Week
vbUseSystem	0	Use the system setting.
vbFirstJan1	1	The week in which January 1 falls (the default setting).
vbFirstFourDays	2	The first week with a minimum of four days in the year.
vbFirstFullWeek	3	The first full week (7 days) of the year.

For example, the following statement assigns the current year to the variable dteThisYear:

```
dteThisYear = DatePart("yyyy", Date)
```

Using the *DateDiff* Function to Return an Interval

The DateDiff function returns the interval between two specified dates. The syntax for DateDiff is as follows:

```
DateDiff(interval, date1, date2[, firstdayofweek[, firstweekofyear]])
```

The components of the syntax are as follows:

- *interval* is a required String expression giving the unit in which you want to measure the interval: yyyy for year, q for quarter, m for month, y for the day of the year, d for day, w for weekday, ww for week, h for hour, n for minute (because m is for month), and s for second.

- *date1* and *date2* are the dates between which you're calculating the interval.

- *firstdayofweek* is an optional constant specifying the day that starts the week (for date information). The default setting is vbSunday (1), but you can also set vbMonday (2), vbTuesday (3), vbWednesday (4), vbThursday (5), vbFriday (6), vbSaturday (7), or vbUseSystem (0; uses the system setting).

- *firstweekofyear* is an optional constant specifying the week considered first in the year:

Constant	Value	Year Starts with Week
vbUseSystem	0	Use the system setting.
vbFirstJan1	1	The week in which January 1 falls (the default setting).
vbFirstFourDays	2	The first week with a minimum of four days in the year.
vbFirstFullWeek	3	The first full week (7 days) of the year.

For example, the following statement returns the number of weeks between June 3, 2000 and September 30, 2000:

```
MsgBox DateDiff("ww", "6/3/2000", "9/30/2000")
```

Using the *DateAdd* Function to Add to a Date

The DateAdd function lets you easily add an interval of time to, or subtract an interval of time from, a specified date, returning the resulting date. The syntax for DateAdd is as follows:

```
DateAdd(interval, number, date)
```

The components of the syntax are as follows:

- *interval* is a required String expression giving the unit of measurement for the interval: yyyy for year, q for quarter, m for month, y for the day of the year, d for day, w for weekday, ww for week, h for hour, n for minute, and s for second.

- *number* is a required numeric expression giving the number of intervals to add (a positive number) or to subtract (a negative number). If *number* isn't already of the data type Long, VBA rounds it to the nearest whole number before evaluating the function.

- *date* is a required Variant/Date or literal date giving the starting date.

For example, the following statement returns the date ten weeks from May 27, 2001:

```
DateAdd("ww", 10, #5/27/2001#)
```

Using File-Management Functions

In this section, I'll show you a couple of key file-management functions that VBA provides: the Dir function, which you use to find out whether a file exists, and the CurDir function, which returns the current path.

Using the *Dir* Function to Check Whether a File Exists

Before performing many file operations, you'll want to check whether a particular file exists. If you're about to save a new file automatically with a procedure, you may want to make sure that the save operation won't overwrite an existing file; and if you're going to open a file automatically, you may want to check that the file exists in its supposed location before you issue an Open method—otherwise, VBA will throw an error.

To test whether a file exists, you can use a straightforward procedure such as the one shown in Listing 9.3.

Listing 9.3

```
1.   Sub Does_File_Exist()
2.       Dim strTestFile As String, strNameToTest As String, _
             strMsg As String
3.       strNameToTest = InputBox("Enter the file name and path:")
4.       If strNameToTest = "" Then End
5.       strTestFile = Dir(strNameToTest)
6.       If Len(strTestFile) = 0 Then
7.           strMsg = "The file " & strNameToTest & _
                 " does not exist."
8.       Else
9.           strMsg = "The file " & strNameToTest & " exists."
10.      End If
11.      MsgBox strMsg, vbOKOnly + vbInformation, _
             "File-Existence Check"
12.  End Sub
```

Analysis

This procedure in Listing 9.3 uses the Dir function to check whether a file exists and displays a message box indicating whether it does or doesn't. This message box is for demonstration purposes only—in most cases, you'll use the result of the test to direct the flow of the procedure according to whether the file exists. Here's how the code works:

- Line 2 declares the string variables strTestFile, strNameToTest, and strMsg.

- Line 3 then displays an input box prompting the user to enter a filename and path; VBA assigns the result of the input box to strNameToTest.

- Line 4 compares strNameToTest to a blank string (which means the user clicked the Cancel button in the input box or clicked the OK button without entering any text in the text box) and uses an End statement to end the procedure if it gets a match.

- Line 5 assigns to strTestFile the result of running the Dir function on the strNameToTest string. If Dir finds a match for strNameToTest, strTestFile will contain the name of the matching file; otherwise, it will contain an empty string.

- Line 6 begins an If... Then statement by testing the length of the `strTestFile` string. If the length is 0, the statement in line 7 assigns to `strMsg` text saying that the file doesn't exist; otherwise, VBA branches to the `Else` statement in line 8 and runs the statement in line 9, assigning text to `strMsg` saying that the file does exist. Line 10 ends the `If` statement.

- Line 11 displays a message box containing `strMsg`. Line 12 ends the procedure.

 WARNING Time for a quick Warning here: The code shown in Listing 9.3 isn't bullet-proof, because `Dir` is designed to work with wildcards as well as regular characters. As long as you have a textual file name in `strNameToTest`, you'll be fine, because `Dir` will compare that text to the filenames, and the result will let you know whether you have a match. But if `strNameToTest` contains suitable wildcards (say it's `c:\temp\*.*`), `Dir` will tell you that the file exists—but of course there's no file by that name, just one or more files that match the wildcards. You can check on line 5 whether the name returned by `Dir` is exactly the same as the input name, but then you need to make sure you do a case-insensitive comparison. This literalness of `Dir` is a nice illustration of GIGO (garbage in, garbage out)—from the computer's (and VBA's) point of view, it's doing what you asked it to, but the result is far from what you intended.

Returning the Current Path

You can return the current path (the path to which the host application is currently set) on either the current drive or on a specified drive by using the `CurDir` function. Often, you'll need to change the current path to make sure the user is saving files in, or opening files from, a suitable location.

To return the current path, use `CurDir` without an argument:

```
CurDir
```

To return the current path for a specified drive, enter the drive letter as an argument. For example, to return the current path on drive D, use this statement:

```
CurDir("D")
```

Creating Your Own Functions

In this section, you'll learn how to create your own functions. You create a function just like you create a procedure, by working in the Code window for the module in which you want to store the function. (You can't record a function—you have to write it.)

To create a function, you use a Function statement. The syntax for the Function statement is as follows:

```
[Public | Private] [Static] Function function_name [(argument_list)] [As type]
    [statements]
    [function_name = expression]
    [Exit Function]
    [statements]
    [function_name = expression]
End Function
```

That probably looks a little unfriendly, particularly if you're looking at it before your second cup of coffee (or local equivalent). Here's how the syntax breaks down:

- Public is an optional keyword that you can use to make the function publicly accessible—accessible to all other procedures in all loaded modules. (This public availability can be overridden by putting an Option Private statement in the module that contains the function. Doing so limits the function's scope to the project that contains it.)

- Private is an optional keyword that you can use to make the function accessible to the other procedures in the module that contains it.

- Static is an optional keyword that you can use to make local variables in the function retain their value between calls to the function.

- function_name is a required argument supplying the name of the function. Functions follow the same naming rules as other VBA items: Alphanumerics and underscores are fine, but no spaces, symbols, or punctuation.

- argument_list is an optional argument supplying the list of variables that represent arguments passed to the function. argument_list takes the syntax shown below:

    ```
    [Optional] [ByRef | ByVal] [ParamArray] variable_name[( )] [As type]
        [= default_value]
    ```

    - Optional is an optional keyword that you can use to denote that an argument is optional (that it is not required). Once you've used Optional to declare an optional argument, all the other arguments in argument_list have to be optional. In other words, you have to put the required arguments before the optional arguments, just the same way VBA does.

- `ByRef` is an optional keyword that you can use to specify that an argument be passed *by reference*; `ByVal` is an optional keyword that you can use to specify that an argument be passed *by value*. Briefly, you can pass an argument either *by reference* or *by value*. When a procedure (a function or sub-procedure) passes an argument to another procedure by reference, the recipient procedure gets access to the memory location where the original variable is stored and can change the original variable. By contrast, when an argument is passed by value, the recipient procedure or function gets only a copy of the information in the variable and can't change the information in the original variable. By reference is the default way to pass an argument, but you can also use the `ByRef` keyword to state explicitly that you want to pass an argument by reference.

- `ParamArray` is an optional keyword you can use as the last argument in *argument_list* to denote an optional array of Variants. You can't use `ParamArray` with `ByVal`, `ByRef`, or `Optional`.

- *variable_name* is the name of the variable that represents the argument.

- *type* is an optional keyword giving the data type of the argument (Byte, Boolean, Currency, Date, Decimal, Double, Integer, Long, Object, Single, variable-length String, or Variant. For non-optional arguments, you can also specify an object type (for example, a `Worksheet` object) or a custom object (one you've created).

- *default_value* is an optional constant or constant expression that you use to specify a default value for optional parameters.

- *type* is an optional argument specifying the data type of value that the function returns: Byte, Boolean, Currency, Date, Decimal, Double, Integer, Long, Object, Single, variable-length String, Variant, or a custom type.

- *statements* represents the statement or statements in the function. In theory, *statements* is optional, but in practice, most functions will need one or more statements.

- *expression* represents the value the function returns. *expression* is also optional.

Now that the formalities are out of the way, I'll get down to business. The easiest way to start creating a function is to type **Function**, the name of the function, and the necessary arguments in parentheses, and then press Enter. VBA will enter a blank line and an `End Function` statement for you:

```
Function MyFunction(MaxTemp, MinTemp)

End Function
```

If you like to make the Visual Basic Editor work *for* you as much as possible, you can also start creating a new function by choosing Insert ➤ Procedure to display the Add Procedure dialog box. Enter the name for the procedure in the Name text box, select the Function option button in the Type group box, and select the Public option button or the Private option button in the Scope group box. If you want all local variables to be statics (which you usually won't), select the All Local Variables As Statics check box. Click the OK button to enter the stub for the function, and then enter its arguments in the parentheses manually.

The Function statement assigns to the given function name (in the example above, MyFunction) the value that the function returns. In parentheses, separated by a comma, are the arguments that will be passed to the Function statement: In our example, the function will work with an argument named MaxTemp and an argument named MinTemp to return its result. You can define the data type of the arguments if you want by including an As statement with the data type after the argument's name. For example, you could use the following statement to set the MaxTemp and MinTemp arguments to the Double data type:

```
Function MyFunction(MaxTemp As Double, MinTemp As Double)
```

Passing an argument by reference is useful when you want to manipulate the variable in the recipient procedure and then return the variable to the procedure from which it originated. Alternatively, passing an argument by value is useful when you want to use the information stored in the variable in the recipient procedure and at the same time ensure that the original information in the variable doesn't change.

As mentioned above, by reference is the default way of passing an argument, so both of the following statements pass the argument MyArg by reference:

```
Function PassByReference(MyArg)
Function PassByReference(ByRef MyArg)
```

To pass an argument by value, you must use the ByVal keyword. The following statement passes the ValArg argument by value:

```
Function PassByValue(ByVal ValArg)
```

If necessary, you can pass some arguments for a procedure by reference and others by value. The following statement passes the MyArg argument by reference and the ValArg argument by value:

```
Function PassBoth(ByRef MyArg, ByVal ValArg)
```

You can explicitly declare the data type of arguments you pass in order to take up less memory and ensure that your procedures are passing the type of information you intend them to. But when passing an argument by reference, you need to make sure that the data type of the argument you're passing matches the data type expected in the procedure. For example, if you declare a String and try to pass it as an argument when the receiving procedure is expecting a Variant, VBA will throw an error.

To declare the data type of an argument, include a data-type declaration in the argument list. The following statement declares MyArg as a string to be passed by reference, and ValArg as a variant to be passed by value:

```
Function PassBoth(ByRef MyArg As String, ByVal ValArg As Variant)
```

You can specify an optional argument by using the Optional keyword. Place the Optional keyword before the ByRef or ByVal keyword if you need to use ByRef or ByVal:

```
Function PassBoth(ByRef MyArg As String, ByVal ValArg As Variant, _
    Optional ByVal MyOptArg As Variant)
```

Like a procedure, a function can have private or public scope. Private scope makes the function available only to procedures in the module that contains it, and public scope makes the function available to all open modules. If you don't specify whether a function is private or public, VBA makes it public by default, so you don't need to specify the scope of a function unless you need it to have private scope. However, if you do use explicit Public declarations on those functions you intend to be public, your code will be somewhat easier to read than if you don't:

```
Private Function MyFunction(MaxTemp, MinTemp)
Public Function AnotherFunction(Industry, Average)
```

 TIP You can restrict all the functions and procedures in a module to private scope by using an Option Private Module statement in the Declarations area of the module.

Let's look at an example of how a function works. First, you declare it and its arguments. The following statement declares a function named NetProfit:

```
Function NetProfit(Gross As Double, Expenses As Double) As Double
```

NetProfit uses two arguments, Gross and Expenses, declaring each as the Double data type. Likewise, it explicitly types its return value as a Double. Explicitly typing the arguments and the return value can help you avoid unpleasant surprises in your code, because VBA will help you catch any attempt to pass the wrong data type to the function and will alert you should the function be prevailed upon to try to return a data type other than its declared type.

Armed with the arguments (and their type, if they're explicitly typed), you call NetProfit as you would a built-in function, by using its name and supplying the two arguments it needs:

```
MyProfit = NetProfit(44000, 34000)
```

Here, the variable MyProfit is assigned the value of the NetProfit function run with a Gross argument of 44000 and an Expenses argument of 34000.

Once you've created a function, the Visual Basic Editor will display its argument list when you type the name of the function in a procedure in the Code window, as shown in Figure 9.1.

FIGURE 9.1

The Visual Basic Editor displays a ScreenTip of Quick Info on functions you create, as well as on its built-in functions.

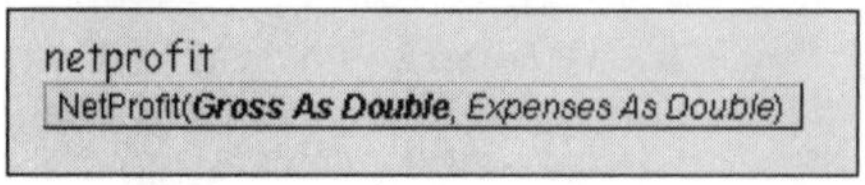

```
netprofit
  NetProfit(Gross As Double, Expenses As Double)
```

Listing 9.4 contains an example of calling a function: The ShowProfit procedure calls the NetProfit function and displays the result in a message box.

Listing 9.4

```
1.  Sub ShowProfit()
2.      MsgBox (NetProfit(44000, 34000)),, "Net Profit"
3.  End Sub
4.
5.  Function NetProfit(Gross As Double, Expenses As Double) As Double
6.      NetProfit = (Gross - Expenses) * 0.9
7.  End Function
```

Analysis

In Listing 9.4, lines 1 to 3 contain the ShowProfit procedure, which simply calls the NetProfit function in line 2, passes it the arguments 44000 for Gross and 34000 for Expenses, and displays the result in a message box titled Net Profit.

Lines 5 to 7 contain the NetProfit function. Line 5 declares the function as working with two Double arguments, Gross and Expenses, telling VBA what to do with the two arguments that line 2 has passed to the function. Line 6 sets NetProfit to be 90 percent (0.9) of the value of Gross minus Expenses. Line 7 ends the function, at which point the value of NetProfit is passed back to line 2, which displays the message box containing the result.

Listing 9.5 contains a function that returns a String argument.

Listing 9.5

```
1.  Sub TestForSmog2000()
2.      Dim intCYear As Integer, strThisCar As String
3.  BadValueLoop:
4.      On Error GoTo Bye
5.      intCYear = InputBox("Enter the year of your car.", _
            "Do I Need a Smog Check?")
6.      strThisCar = NeedsSmog(intCYear)
7.      If strThisCar = "Yes" Then
8.          MsgBox "Your car needs a smog check.", _
            vbOKOnly + vbExclamation, "Smog Check 2000"
9.      ElseIf strThisCar = "BadValue" Then
10.         MsgBox "The year you entered is in the future.", _
            vbOKOnly + vbCritical, "Smog Check 2000"
11.         GoTo BadValueLoop
12.     Else
13.         MsgBox "Your car does not need a smog check.", _
            vbOKOnly + vbInformation, "Smog Check 2000"
14.     End If
15.  Bye:
16.  End Sub
17.
18.  Function NeedsSmog(CarYear As Integer) As String
19.      If CarYear > Year(Now) Then
20.          NeedsSmog = "BadValue"
21.      ElseIf CarYear <= Year(Now) - 3 Then
22.          NeedsSmog = "Yes"
23.      Else
24.          NeedsSmog = "No"
25.      End If
26.  End Function
```

Analysis

Listing 9.5 contains the procedure TestForSmog2000 (lines 1 to 16) and the NeedsSmog function (lines 18 to 26). The TestForSmog2000 procedure calls the NeedsSmog function, which returns a value indicating whether the user's car needs a smog check. TestFor-Smog uses this value to display a message box informing the user whether or not their car needs a smog check. Here's how the code works:

- TestForSmog2000 starts by declaring the Integer variable intCYear and the String variable strThisCar in line 2.

- Line 3 contains the BadValueLoop label, to which execution returns from line 11 if the user has entered an unsuitable value for the year of their car.

- Line 4 contains an On Error statement to direct execution to the Bye label in line 15 if an error occurs. An error will occur if the user cancels the upcoming input box (or chooses its OK button with no value entered in its text box).

- Line 5 displays an input box prompting the user to enter the year of their car. This line assigns to the intCYear variable the value the user enters in the input box.

- Line 6 then sets the value of the String variable strThisCar to the result of the NeedsSmog function running on the intCYear integer variable.

- Execution now shifts to the NeedsSmog function (line 18), which evaluates int-CYear and returns the value for strThisCar. Line 18 declares the function, assigning its value to NeedsSmog. The function takes one argument, CarYear, which is declared as the Integer data type.

- Line 19 checks to see whether CarYear is greater than the value of the current year (Year(Now)). If so, line 20 sets the value of NeedsSmog to BadValue, which will be used to indicate that the user has entered a date in the future. If not, the ElseIf statement in line 21 runs, checking if the value of CarYear is less than or equal to Year(Now) - 3, the current year minus three. If so, line 22 sets the value of NeedsSmog to Yes; if not, the Else statement in line 23 runs, and line 24 sets the value of NeedsSmog to No. Line 25 ends the If statement, and line 26 ends the function.

- Execution then returns to the calling line (line 6) in the TestForSmog2000 procedure, to which the NeedsSmog function returns the value it has assigned to the strThisCar variable.

- The rest of the TestForSmog procedure then works with the strThisCar variable. Line 7 compares strThisCar to Yes; if it matches, line 8 displays a message box stating that the car needs a smog check. If strThisCar doesn't match Yes, line 9 compares ThisCar to BadValue. If it matches, line 10 displays an alert message box, and line 11 returns execution to the BadValueLoop label in line 3. If strThisCar doesn't match BadValue, the Else statement in line 12 runs, and line 13 displays a message box stating that the car doesn't need a smog check.

- Line 14 ends the If statement; line 15 contains the Bye label; and line 16 ends the procedure.

You don't have to use a function as simply as the examples I've been showing here: You can also include a function as part of a larger expression. For example, you could add the results of the functions NetProfit and CurrentBalance (which takes a single argument) by using a statement such as this:

```
CurrentEstimate = NetProfit(44000, 33000) + CurrentBalance(MainAccount)
```

Enough of functions for the moment. In the next chapter, you'll create some procedures in the seven applications this book discusses.

CHAPTER 10

Creating Procedures

I n this chapter, you'll practice creating procedures from scratch in the Visual Basic Editor. I'll start the chapter by making sure you have the Visual Basic Editor set up as I expect you to. After that, I'll walk you through an example of creating a procedure in each of the applications covered in this book.

In each example, I'll show you how to use the various types of help available to find the objects you need. As a result, parts of the chapter may seem exploratory—but I hope that showing you how to find the information you need, rather than simply force-feeding you canned chunks of information, will help you get started with creating your own procedures.

Setting Up the Visual Basic Editor for Creating the Procedures

In the following sections, I'll expect you to have set up the Visual Basic Editor as described below. Video_25.avi on the CD walks you through setting up the Visual Basic Editor.

- If the Project Explorer isn't displayed, choose View ➤ Project Explorer or press Ctrl+R to display it.

- If the Properties window isn't displayed, choose View ➤ Properties Window or press the F4 key to display it.

- Unless you really prefer things otherwise, dock the Project Explorer in its conventional position at the upper-left corner of the main Visual Basic Editor area. Dock the Properties window below the Project Explorer, again in its default position.

- Close any Code windows or user form windows that are open.

- Set the Visual Basic Editor up to require variables to be declared explicitly. Choose Tools ➤ Options to display the Options dialog box, select the Require Variable Declaration check box on the Editor page, and click the OK button. That way, the Visual Basic Editor will automatically enter the Option Explicit statement for all future modules and user forms you create.

Remember the key points from the previous chapters. In particular, think back to Chapter 8, where you learned that there are several ways of finding the objects: the Help system, the Object Browser, and the Macro Recorder. In the sections that follow, we'll use all three methods as appropriate.

 NOTE If you have the determination (and the applications) to work through all of the following sections, you'll notice some repetition. That's because I'm assuming that most readers will be interested in only some of the applications discussed: The repetition is to avoid their missing key information.

Creating a Procedure for Word

The procedure you'll create for Word is short but sweet. It causes the Track Changes feature to toggle the way deleted text is displayed between Strikethrough and Hidden. You'll be able to switch instantly between having the deleted text remain on screen with a line through it and having it, uh, *disappear*.

Follow these steps (which are illustrated in Video_26.avi on the CD) to create the procedure:

1. Start Word if it's not already running.

2. Record a quick macro to get at the object, property, and settings you need. (I know, this feels like you're cheating, but the Macro Recorder is truly a gift when it comes to finding objects.) Follow these sub-steps:

   - Choose Tools ➤ Macro ➤ Record New Macro to display the Record Macro dialog box.

   - Either accept the macro name that the Macro Recorder automatically assigns, or create a scratch name of your own that will remind you to delete the macro. I'll accept the default, which happens to be Macro4 on my system.

   - Leave the Store Macro In drop-down list set to All Documents (Normal .dot). Leave the description alone unless you're *really* planning to forget to delete the macro at the end of this section.

   - Click the OK button to start recording the macro.

   - Choose Tools ➤ Options to display the Options dialog box. Click the Track Changes tab to display the Track Changes page, select Strikethrough in the Mark drop-down list in the Deleted Text area, and then click the OK button to close the Options dialog box.

   - Again, choose Tools ➤ Options to display the Option button. This time, the Track Changes page should come up on top of the stack of pages. Now, select Hidden in the Mark drop-down list in the Deleted Text area, and again click the OK button to close the Options dialog box.

   - Double-click the REC indicator on the status bar, or click the Stop Recording button on the Stop Recording toolbar, or choose Tools ➤ Macro ➤ Stop Recording, to stop recording the macro.

3. Choose Tools ➤ Macros ➤ Macros to display the Macros dialog box. Select the macro you just recorded and click the Edit button to open it for editing in the Visual Basic Editor. You'll see something like this, depending on what you called

the macro, and depending on what your computer thinks you're called and what it thinks the date is.

```
Sub Macro4()
'
' Macro4 Macro
' Macro recorded 5/27/2000 by Guy Hart-Davis
'
    Application.DisplayStatusBar = True
    With ActiveWindow
        .DisplayHorizontalScrollBar = False
        .DisplayVerticalScrollBar = True
        .DisplayLeftScrollBar = False
        .StyleAreaWidth = InchesToPoints(0)
        .DisplayRightRuler = False
        .DisplayScreenTips = True
        With .View
            .ShowAnimation = True
            .Draft = False
            .WrapToWindow = True
            .ShowPicturePlaceHolders = False
            .ShowFieldCodes = False
            .ShowBookmarks = False
            .FieldShading = wdFieldShadingWhenSelected
            .ShowTabs = False
            .ShowSpaces = False
            .ShowParagraphs = False
            .ShowHyphens = False
            .ShowHiddenText = False
            .ShowAll = False
            .ShowDrawings = True
            .ShowObjectAnchors = False
            .ShowTextBoundaries = False
            .ShowHighlight = True
        End With
    End With
    With Options
        .Pagination = True
        .WPHelp = False
```

```
            .WPDocNavKeys = False
            .ShortMenuNames = False
            .RTFInClipboard = True
            .BlueScreen = False
            .EnableSound = False
            .ConfirmConversions = False
            .UpdateLinksAtOpen = False
            .SendMailAttach = False
            .MeasurementUnit = wdInches
            .AllowPixelUnits = False
            .AnimateScreenMovements = False
            .VirusProtection = False
            .ApplyFarEastFontsToAscii = False
            .InterpretHighAnsi = wdHighAnsiIsHighAnsi
        End With
        Application.DisplayRecentFiles = True
        RecentFiles.Maximum = 9
        With Options
            .InsertedTextMark = wdInsertedTextMarkDoubleUnderline
            .InsertedTextColor = wdByAuthor
            .DeletedTextMark = wdDeletedTextMarkStrikeThrough
            .DeletedTextColor = wdByAuthor
            .RevisedPropertiesMark = wdRevisedPropertiesMarkNone
            .RevisedPropertiesColor = wdAuto
            .RevisedLinesMark = wdRevisedLinesMarkOutsideBorder
            .RevisedLinesColor = wdAuto
        End With
        With Options
            .InsertedTextMark = wdInsertedTextMarkDoubleUnderline
            .InsertedTextColor = wdByAuthor
            .DeletedTextMark = wdDeletedTextMarkHidden
            .DeletedTextColor = wdByAuthor
            .RevisedPropertiesMark = wdRevisedPropertiesMarkNone
            .RevisedPropertiesColor = wdAuto
            .RevisedLinesMark = wdRevisedLinesMarkOutsideBorder
            .RevisedLinesColor = wdAuto
        End With
    End Sub
```

4. *Ouch.* Am I really sure this is the quickest way to the object you need? Yes, but be patient enough to scan the code. Down, down… see it? That's right—the first 50-odd lines of code in this recorded macro are a wasteland as far as you're concerned, but that `DeletedTextMark` property for the `Options` object looks pretty good. And in the last couple of sections of code, you've got the values you need for that property: `wdDeletedTextMarkStrikeThrough` and `wdDeleted-TextMarkHidden`. You're all set.

5. Select the whole of that macro, from `Sub` statement down to `End Sub` statement, and press the Delete key before you forget. (If your memory's poor, take out everything from the `With Options` section down to the `DeletedTextMark` sign before losing the macro.)

6. Make sure the Visual Basic Editor is set up as described in the section, "Setting Up the Visual Basic Editor for Creating the Procedures," earlier in this chapter.

7. In the Project Explorer window, right-click anywhere in the `Normal` item and choose Insert ≻ Module from the context menu. The Visual Basic Editor will insert a new module in the `Normal.dot` global template, will display a Code window for it, and will expand the `Normal` tree if it was collapsed.

8. Press the F4 key to activate the Properties window for the new module.

9. Enter the name for the new module in the Properties window. For the example, I'll use the name `Procedures_to_Keep_1`.

10. Click in the Code window to activate it.

11. If the Visual Basic Editor hasn't already entered an `Option Explicit` statement in the declarations area of the code sheet, enter the statement manually now.

12. Below the `Option Explicit` statement, enter the `Sub` statement for the procedure and press the Enter key. Name the procedure `Toggle_Track_Changes_between_Hidden_and_Strikethrough`:

```
Sub Toggle_Track_Changes_between_Hidden_and_Strikethrough
```

13. The Visual Basic Editor will enter for you the parentheses at the end of the Sub statement, a blank line, and the End Sub statement:

```
Sub Toggle_Track_Changes_between_Hidden_and_Strikethrough()


End Sub
```

14. Press the Tab key to indent the first line below the Sub statement.

15. Type **If Options.** to display the List Properties/Methods drop-down list.

16. Type down (**d-e-l**) or use the ↓ key or the mouse to select the `DeletedTextMark` entry.

17. Type **=** to display the List Properties/Methods list of constants for the `Deleted-TextMark` property, as shown in Figure 10.1.

FIGURE 10.1

The Visual Basic Editor's List Properties/Methods list provides the constants available for the `DeletedTextMark` property.

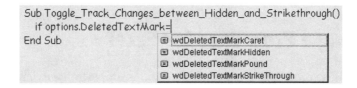

```
Sub Toggle_Track_Changes_between_Hidden_and_Strikethrough()
    if options.DeletedTextMark=
End Sub                          ☑ wdDeletedTextMarkCaret
                                 ☑ wdDeletedTextMarkHidden
                                 ☑ wdDeletedTextMarkPound
                                 ☑ wdDeletedTextMarkStrikeThrough
```

18. Select the `wdDeletedTextMarkHidden` item; then type **Then** and press the Enter key.

19. Enter **Options.DeletedTextMark=wdDeletedTextMarkStrikethrough** and press the Enter key.

20. Type the `ElseIf` statement and the rest of the procedure as follows:

```
ElseIf Options.DeletedTextMark = wdDeletedTextMarkStrikeThrough Then
    Options.DeletedTextMark = wdDeletedTextMarkHidden
End If
```

21. Make sure your procedure looks like this:

```
Sub Toggle_Track_Changes_between_Hidden_and_Strikethrough()
    If Options.DeletedTextMark = wdDeletedTextMarkHidden Then
        Options.DeletedTextMark = wdDeletedTextMarkStrikeThrough
    ElseIf Options.DeletedTextMark = wdDeletedTextMarkStrikeThrough Then
        Options.DeletedTextMark = wdDeletedTextMarkHidden
    End If
End Sub
```

22. Press Alt+F11 to switch to Word, and create a short document that uses Track Changes marks including deleted text.

23. Arrange the Word window and the Visual Basic Editor window side by side, and test the procedure by pressing the F5 key.

Note that you can also set this procedure up as a `With` statement using the `Options` object, so that it looks like this:

```
Sub Toggle_Track_Changes_between_Hidden_and_Strikethrough_2()
    With Options
        If .DeletedTextMark = wdDeletedTextMarkHidden Then
```

```
                    .DeletedTextMark = wdDeletedTextMarkStrikeThrough
                ElseIf .DeletedTextMark = wdDeletedTextMarkStrikeThrough Then
                    .DeletedTextMark = wdDeletedTextMarkHidden
                End If
            End With
        End Sub
```

Creating a Procedure for Excel

The procedure you'll create for Excel is simple in the extreme: When the user runs Excel, the procedure maximizes the Excel window and opens the last file worked on. While these actions are relatively banal, the procedure provides an example of working with events in Excel.

Create a Personal Macro Workbook If You Don't Have One Yet

If you haven't already created a Personal Macro Workbook in Excel, you'll need to create one before you can create this procedure. Follow these steps, which are illustrated in Video_27.avi on the CD:

1. Choose Tools ➢ Macro ➢ Record New Macro to display the Record Macro dialog box.
2. Accept the default name for the macro, because you'll be deleting it momentarily.
3. In the Store Macro In drop-down list, choose Personal Macro Workbook.
4. Click the OK button to dismiss the Record Macro dialog box and start recording the macro.
5. Type a single character in whichever cell is active, and press the Enter key.
6. Click the Stop Recording button on the Stop Recording toolbar to stop recording the macro.
7. Choose Window ➢ Unhide to display the Unhide dialog box. Select Personal.xls and click the OK button.
8. Choose Tools ➢ Macro ➢ Macros to display the Macros dialog box.
9. Select the macro you recorded and click the Delete button to delete it. Click the Yes button in the confirmation message box.

You'll now have a Personal Macro Workbook that you can use.

Follow these steps (illustrated in Video_28.avi on the CD) to create the procedure:

1. Start Excel if it's not already running.

2. If your Personal Macro Workbook is currently hidden, choose Window ➤ Unhide to display the Unhide dialog box, select PERSONAL.XLS in the Unhide Workbook list box, and click the OK button.

3. Choose Tools ➤ Macros ➤ Visual Basic Editor, or press Alt+F11, to open the Visual Basic Editor.

4. Make sure the Visual Basic Editor is set up as described in the section, "Setting Up the Visual Basic Editor for Creating Procedures," earlier in this chapter.

5. In the Project Explorer window, expand VBAProject (PERSONAL.XLS) if it's collapsed.

6. Expand the Microsoft Excel Objects folder.

7. Double-click the ThisWorkbook item to open its Code window. As its name implies, this object represents the workbook.

8. In the Object drop-down list at the upper-left corner of the Code window, select Workbook. The Visual Basic Editor will automatically create the stub of an Open event for the Workbook object:

```
Private Sub Workbook_Open()


End Sub
```

9. Both the actions you want to take with Excel—maximizing the application window and opening the application's most recently used file—are clearly related to the Application object, so you won't need to dig through the Object Browser or the Help file to find the objects you need. Type **Application.W** and look at the entries that refer to windows. You've got it—WindowState is the one you want. Select that entry and type an = sign to bring up the List Properties/Methods list of possible constants (see Figure 10.2).

FIGURE 10.2

Use the List Properties/ Methods list to see the options available to you.

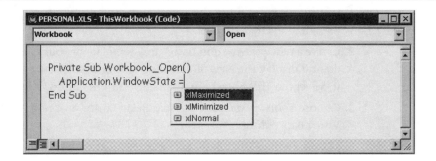

10. Select the `xlMaximized` item and press Enter to start a new statement.

11. Type **Application.** and select `RecentFiles` from the List Properties/Methods drop-down list. Then type **(1).** (to indicate the first item in the `RecentFiles` collection), and select the `Open` method from the List Properties/Methods list.

    ```
    Application.RecentFiles(1).Open
    ```

12. That's it. Your procedure should look like this:

    ```
    Private Sub Workbook_Open()
        Application.WindowState = xlMaximized
        Application.RecentFiles(1).Open
    End Sub
    ```

13. Press Alt+F11 to return to Excel.

14. Choose File ➢ Save to save the Personal Macro Workbook.

15. Choose Window ➢ Hide to hide the Personal Macro Workbook.

16. Open a sample document, make a change to it, save it, and close it.

17. Choose File ➢ Exit to exit Excel.

18. Restart Excel. The application window will maximize itself, and the most recently used file will open.

Creating a Procedure for PowerPoint

The procedure you'll create for PowerPoint is short and straightforward, but it saves the user enough effort over the long run to make it worthwhile. It adds a title slide to the active presentation, inserting a canned title that includes the current date and the company's name as the presenter.

Follow these steps (illustrated in Video_29.avi on the CD) to create the procedure:

1. Start PowerPoint if it's not already running. (If it's already running, close any presentations that are open.)

2. Create a new presentation based on a template of your choosing. If PowerPoint doesn't display the New Slide dialog box, choose Insert ➢ New Slide to display it. Select the Title Slide item; then click the OK button.

3. Choose Tools ➢ Macros ➢ Visual Basic Editor, or press Alt+F11, to open the Visual Basic Editor.

4. Make sure the Visual Basic Editor is set up as described in the section, "Setting Up the Visual Basic Editor for Creating the Procedures," earlier in this chapter.

5. In the Project Explorer window, right-click anywhere in the `VBAProject(Presentationn)` item (the *n* there denotes a number that will vary depending on

whether this is the first presentation you've created in this PowerPoint session) and choose Insert ➤ Module from the context menu. The Visual Basic Editor will insert a new module in the project, will display a Code window for it, and will expand the project tree if it was collapsed.

6. Press the F4 key to activate the Properties window for the new module.

7. Enter the name for the new module in the Properties window: General_ Procedures.

8. Click in the Code window to activate it.

9. If the Visual Basic Editor hasn't already entered an Option Explicit statement in the declarations of the code sheet, enter the statement manually now.

10. Below the Option Explicit statement, enter the Sub statement for the procedure and press the Enter key:

    Sub Add_Title_Slide

11. The Visual Basic Editor will enter the parentheses at the end of the Sub statement, a blank line, and the End Sub statement for you:

    Sub Sub Add_Title_Slide()

    End Sub

12. Press the Tab key to indent the first line below the Sub statement.

13. Now identify the objects you need by using the Help system. You'll be working with the active presentation, so type **activepresentation**, place the insertion point anywhere in the word, and press the F1 key to fire up Microsoft Visual Basic Help. It'll give you the ActivePresentation Property screen shown in Figure 10.3.

FIGURE 10.3

The ActivePresentation Property screen

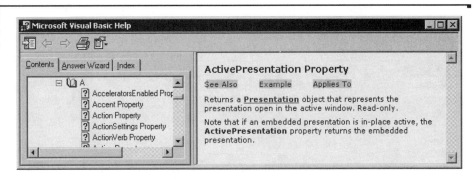

14. Click the link to the Presentation object on the ActivePresentation Property screen to display its Help screen (see Figure 10.4).

FIGURE 10.4

The Presentation Object screen

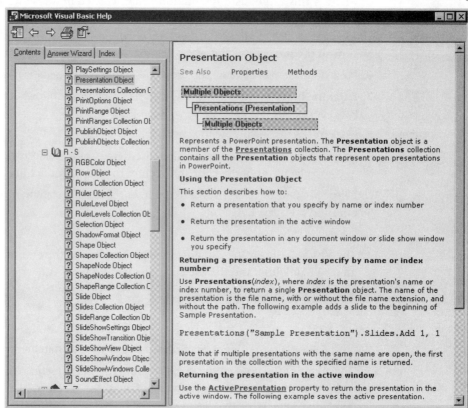

15. Click the lower Multiple Objects box in the partial object hierarchy towards the top of the Presentation Object Help screen. Microsoft Visual Basic Help will display the Topics Found dialog box (see Figure 10.5).

FIGURE 10.5

In the Topics Found dialog box, you can choose the object you're interested in and then select the Display button.

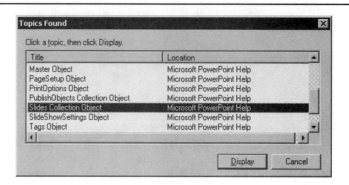

16. Select the Slides Collection Object entry and click the Display button to display it (see Figure 10.6).

FIGURE 10.6

The Slides Collection Object screen contains the information you need for creating a new slide.

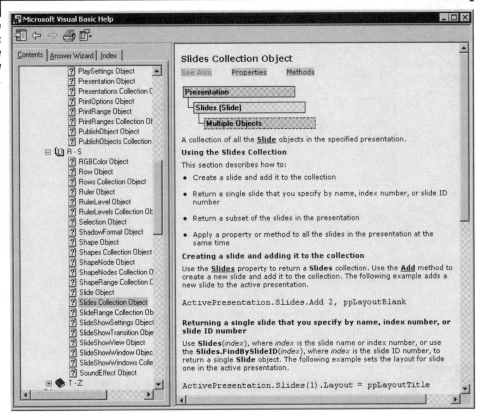

17. From this screen, take two pieces of information: First, that a slide is represented by a Slide object (organized into the Slides collection), and second, that you use the Add method to create a new slide.

18. Return to the Visual Basic Editor and delete that activepresentation you added.

19. Declare an object variable of the Slide object type to represent the slide the procedure will create:

```
Dim sldTitleSlide As Slide
```

20. Then use a Set statement to assign to the sldTitleSlide object a new slide you create by using the Add method:

```
Set sldTitleSlide = ActivePresentation.Slides.Add(
```

21. When you type the parenthesis, the Auto Quick Info feature displays for you the syntax for the Add method, as shown in Figure 10.7.

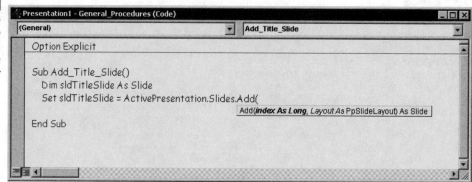

22. Type the **Index** argument and the value **1** (because the title slide is to be the first slide in the presentation):

```
Set sldTitleSlide = ActivePresentation.Slides.Add(Index:=1,
```

23. Break the statement to the next line with a line-continuation character (an underscore preceded by a space). Then type the **Layout** argument and pick the ppLayoutTitle constant from the List Properties/Methods drop-down list, as shown in Figure 10.8.

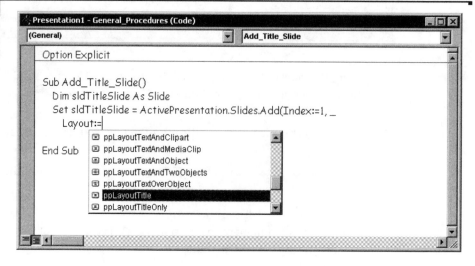

24. Type the parenthesis to end the statement:

```
Set sldTitleSlide = ActivePresentation.Slides.Add(Index:=1, _
    Layout:=ppLayoutTitle)
```

25. You'll be working with the `sldTitleSlide` from here on, so create a `With` statement using it:

```
With sldTitleSlide


End With
```

26. Next, you need to manipulate the two items on the slide. To do so, you need to know the objects that represent them. As usual, you could use the Macro Recorder to find out, but this time, try a more direct method: Place the insertion point on the line within the `With` statement and type . (a period) to display the List Properties/Methods drop-down list of available properties and methods for the `Slide` object.

27. Sometimes the List Properties/Methods drop-down list will be of little help, because you'll find so many possibly relevant properties and methods that you can't identify the property you need. But if you scan the list in this case, you'll see that the `Shapes` property (which returns the `Shapes` collection) is the only promising item.

28. Choose View ➢ Immediate or press Ctrl+G to display the Immediate window for a bit of testing.

28. Type the exploratory statement below into the Immediate window and press the Enter key. In the PowerPoint window, VBA will select the first `Shape` object on the slide.

```
ActivePresentation.Slides(1).Shapes(1).Select
```

29. So far, so good; but how do you add text to the shape? Go back to the Code window and try typing down through the object hierarchy from the first `Shape` object. `TextFrame`... that looks promising—and inside it, a `TextRange` object with a `Text` property. That's what you need. Assign to it the text **Pollution Update:** (with a space after it) and the date (supplied by the `Date` function):

```
Shapes(1).TextFrame.TextRange.Text = "Pollution Update: " & Date
```

30. Assign information to the second Shape in the same way:

```
.Shapes(2).TextFrame.TextRange.Text = "Rikki Nadir Industrials, Inc."
```

31. The whole procedure should look like this:

```
Sub Add_Title_Slide()
    Dim sldTitleSlide As Slide
    Set sldTitleSlide = ActivePresentation.Slides.Add(Index:=1, _
        Layout:=ppLayoutTitle)
```

```
            With sldTitleSlide
                .Shapes(1).TextFrame.TextRange.Text = _
                    "Pollution Update: " & Date
                .Shapes(2).TextFrame.TextRange.Text = _
                    "Rikki Nadir Industrials, Inc."
            End With
        End Sub
```

32. Test the procedure; then delete all slides from the presentation. Choose Tools ➤ Customize and add a toolbar button or menu item for the `Add_Title_Slide` procedure.

33. Save the presentation under a name such as `Procedures.ppt`.

34. Create a new presentation; then test the toolbar button or menu item for the procedure.

Creating a Procedure for Project

The procedure you'll create for Project ensures that a number of options settings are set to their company-approved defaults for each user session. By using a procedure to set these settings, you can not only avoid unsuitable settings, but also save the time it would take the user to dig through the nine pages of the Options dialog box to check and set the settings manually (or get them wrong).

The first group of settings that the procedure will set are grouped in the user interface on the Save page of the Options dialog box (Tools ➤ Options), as shown in Figure 10.9:

- Make sure the Save Microsoft Project Files As drop-down list on the Save page of the Options dialog box is set to `Project (*.mpp)`.

- Set the File Locations path to `f:\users\projects\` and the Workgroup Templates location to `f:\users\templates\`. (You'll need to adapt the path to point to a drive and folder you have.)

- Set the AutoSave feature to on, and set it to save all projects (as opposed to the default setting of only the active project) every ten minutes without prompting the user.

The second group of settings is on the View page of the Options dialog box, as shown in Figure 10.10:

- Make sure the status bar, scroll bars, and entry bars are displayed (for ease of use).

- Make sure that Project is set to display a Taskbar item for every project open rather than just one Taskbar item for the whole application. Having an item for each project lets the user switch between projects much more easily.

FIGURE 10.9

The save options that the Project procedure manipulates appear on the Save page of the Options dialog box.

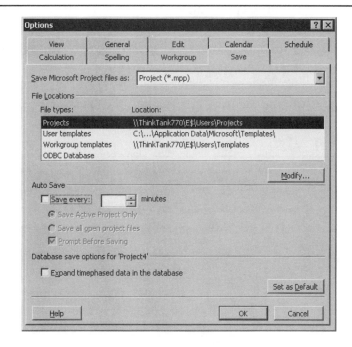

FIGURE 10.10

The view options that the Project procedure manipulates appear on the View page of the Options dialog box.

The third group (or rather a pair) of items is on the General page of the Options dialog box, as shown in Figure 10.11:

- The company wants the user name to be set to the company's name, Rikki Nadir Industries, Inc., rather than that of the individual perpetrators. (The figure shows a perp's name just waiting to be replaced.)

- To the company's savvy users, the PlanningWizard is more of a bane than a boon, so the procedure needs to nip it in the bud.

FIGURE 10.11

The general options that the Project procedure manipulates appear (not surprisingly) on the General page of the Options dialog box.

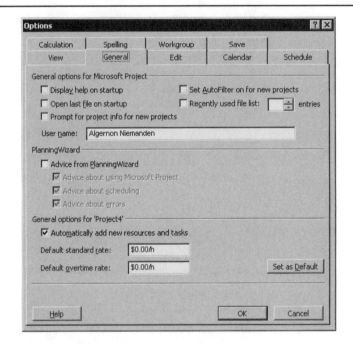

Follow these steps (illustrated in Video_30.avi on the CD) to create the procedure:

1. Start Project if it's not already running.

2. Choose Tools ➤ Macros ➤ Visual Basic Editor, or press Alt+F11, to open the Visual Basic Editor.

3. Make sure the Visual Basic Editor is set up as described in the section, "Setting Up the Visual Basic Editor for Creating the Procedures," earlier in this chapter.

4. In the Project Explorer window, right-click anywhere in the `ProjectGlobal` (`GLOBAL.MPT`) item and choose Insert ➤ Module from the context menu. The Visual Basic Editor will insert a new module in the global project, will display a Code window for it, and will expand the `ProjectGlobal` tree if it was collapsed.

5. Press the F4 key to activate the Properties window for the new module.

6. Enter the name for the new module in the Properties window. For the example, I'll use the name `RNI_Procedures_1`.

7. Click in the Code window to activate it.

8. If the Visual Basic Editor hasn't already entered an `Option Explicit` statement in the declarations area of the code sheet, enter the statement manually now.

9. Below the `Option Explicit` statement, enter the Sub statement for the procedure and press the Enter key. I'm going to call the procedure `Standardize_Settings`:

   ```
   Sub Standardize_Settings
   ```

10. The Visual Basic Editor will enter the parentheses at the end of the Sub statement, a blank line, and the End Sub statement for you:

    ```
    Sub Standardize_Settings()

    End Sub
    ```

11. Press the Tab key to indent the first line below the Sub statement.

12. Now you need to find out which objects to manipulate. This time, we'll use the one-two punch of the Object Browser and the Help system.

13. Choose View ➤ Object Browser, or press the F2 key, to display the Object Browser.

14. In the Project/Library drop-down list in the upper-left corner of the Object Browser, choose the `MSProject` item to restrict the search to Project items.

15. In the Search Text combo box, enter **options**.

16. Click the Search button to perform the search. Figure 10.12 shows an approximation of what you should be seeing: a list of the items in the MSProject library that contain the word *options*. (You'll notice that I've resized the Object Browser window so that it appears as a separate window rather than taking up the whole of the Code window area. That's just me—I happen not to like having the Object Browser sprawling all over the place.)

FIGURE 10.12

Use the Object Browser to find the Project items that contain the word options.

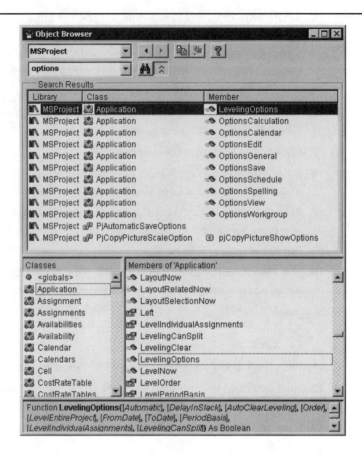

17. Scan the results. It looks like you've hit pay dirt. Now select the `OptionsSave` item in the Members column of the Search Results list box. The Object Browser will display the entry in the lower Members Of list box, showing its syntax in the Details pane at the bottom of the Object Browser window (see Figure 10.13).

18. Select the syntax in the Details pane, and then click the Copy To Clipboard button to copy it to the Clipboard for pasting into the Code window.

19. Minimize the Object Browser for the time being (don't close it—you'll want a few more of these search results in a moment).

Select the Options-Save *item to display its information in the Details pane.*

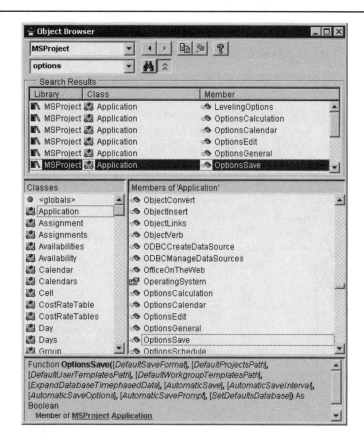

20. Restore the RNI_Procedures_1 Code window and issue a Paste command to paste the syntax into it:

```
Sub Standardize_Settings()
  Function OptionsSave([DefaultSaveFormat], [DefaultProjectsPath],
    [DefaultUserTemplatesPath], [DefaultWorkgroupTemplatesPath],
    [ExpandDatabaseTimephasedData], [AutomaticSave],
    [AutomaticSaveInterval], [AutomaticSaveOptions],
    [AutomaticSavePrompt], [SetDefaultsDatabase]) As Boolean
End Sub
```

21. Comment out that line for the moment; you can use it as a point of reference for creating code that sets the items you need.

22. Type the following partial statement:

```
OptionsSave DefaultSaveFormat:=
```

23. Here, you don't get a helpful List Properties/Methods list telling you what to fill in. Time to go to the other main source of help—the Help system. Click to place the insertion point in the word `OptionsSave` and press the F1 key. The Microsoft Visual Basic Help system will launch, and will display the information for the `OptionsSave` method (see Figure 10.14).

FIGURE 10.14

For help on the details of the `OptionsSave` *method, turn to the Microsoft Visual Basic Help application by selecting the method and pressing F1.*

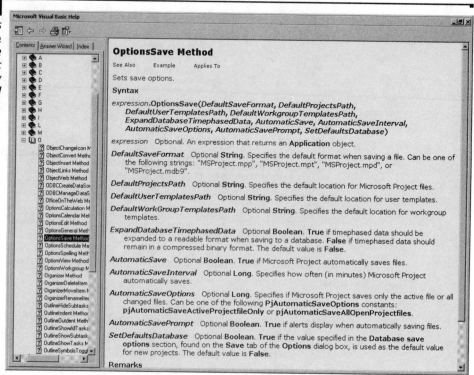

24. Now there's the information you need: The `DefaultSaveMethod` argument is a String, and it looks like the String you want is `MSProject.mpp`. Go ahead and type in "**MSProject.mpp**".

```
OptionsSave DefaultSaveFormat:="MSProject.mpp"
```

25. Next, you need to set the File Locations path. To do that, enter the `Default-ProjectsPath` argument after the obligatory comma of separation and a line-continuation character. You'd guess that the path must be a string, and a quick check of the Help file confirms this:

```
OptionsSave DefaultSaveFormat:="MSProject.mpp", _
    DefaultProjectsPath:="f:\users\projects\"
```

26. Add to the statement the argument for the Workgroup Templates location, `DefaultWorkgroupTemplatesPath`. Again, this is a String argument:

```
OptionsSave DefaultSaveFormat:="MSProject.mpp", _
    DefaultProjectsPath:="f:\users\projects\", _
    DefaultWorkgroupTemplatesPath:="f:\users\templates\"
```

27. Add the AutoSave information to the statement by using the `Automatic-Save` argument, the `AutomaticSaveInterval` argument, the `AutomaticSave-Options` argument, and the `AutomaticSavePrompt` argument. As you might imagine, `AutomaticSave` and `AutomaticSavePrompt` are Boolean arguments, while `AutomaticSaveOptions` and `AutomaticSaveInterval` are Long arguments:

```
OptionsSave DefaultSaveFormat:="MSProject.mpp", _
    DefaultProjectsPath:="f:\users\projects\", _
    DefaultWorkgroupTemplatesPath:="f:\users\templates\", _
    AutomaticSave:=True, AutomaticSaveInterval:=5, _
    AutomaticSaveOptions:=pjAutomaticSaveAllOpenProjectFiles, _
    AutomaticSavePrompt:=False
```

28. That's the first group of options taken care of. Now for the view options. Choose Window ➤ Object Browser to display the Object Browser again. See anything promising among those items containing *options*? Right—the `OptionsView` method is the one you need. But the syntax on this method is even worse than on the `OptionsSave` method.

29. Never mind: Crank up the Help file for `OptionsView` and work out what you need: the `DisplayStatusBar` argument, the `DisplayEntryBar` argument, the `DisplayScrollBars` argument, and the `DisplayWindowsInTaskbar` argument. Because these are all represented by check boxes in the user interface, you'd expect them to be Boolean—and they are. Here's the statement:

```
OptionsView DisplayStatusBar:=True, DisplayEntryBar:=True, _
    DisplayScrollBars:=True, DisplayWindowsInTaskbar:=True
```

30. Now take care of the general options. Given that you've just used the `Options-Save` method for the save options and the `OptionsView` method for the view options, it seems a safe bet that you'll need the OptionsGeneral method for the general options.

31. On the next line in the Code window, type **Options** and press Ctrl+spacebar to display the List Properties/Methods drop-down list. Sure enough, there's OptionsGeneral. Select it by typing down, by using the ↓ key, or by using the mouse, and press the spacebar to display the ScreenTip with the syntax, as shown in Figure 10.15.

FIGURE 10.15

Use the Auto Quick Info feature to learn the syntax for the OptionsGeneral *method.*

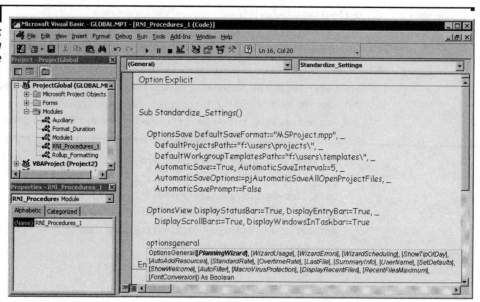

32. The arguments you need here are PlanningWizard, which the Help file reveals to be as Boolean as its UI check box would suggest, and UserName, which clearly must be a String. Here's the statement to enter:

```
OptionsGeneral PlanningWizard:=False, _
    UserName:="Rikki Nadir Industries, Inc."
```

33. Now finish up the procedure: Add a comment at the beginning to explain what the procedure is going to do, and add spacer lines as suits your taste in code density and logical separation.

34. Test the procedure by pressing the F5 key. Then press Alt+F11 to display the Project window, choose Tools ➢ Options, and make sure the settings are correct.

35. Choose File ➢ Save GLOBAL.MPT or press Ctrl+S to save your work.

Creating a Procedure for WordPerfect

The procedure you'll create for WordPerfect performs a mundane operation: It opens an existing document, copies a chunk of text (identified by a bookmark), closes the document, and pastes the chunk of text into the active document. For the sake of the example, we'll assume that the bookmark text is apt to vary, so you wouldn't want to commit it to the QuickWords feature built into WordPerfect.

As you'll see in a moment, WordPerfect has an interesting and somewhat unusual implementation of VBA: Instead of exposing WordPerfect's functionality as a hierarchy of Component Object Model (COM) components that VBA can parse, Corel has chosen to expose only a few objects, including the obligatory `Application` object, and a `PerfectScript` object that gives you access to the PerfectScript programming language that WordPerfect (and the other Corel applications) uses for its own macro-recording capabilities. This implementation is similar to the implementation of the older WordBasic macro language in VBA through the `WordBasic` property in Word.

As a result, the WordPerfect object model looks substantially different than the object models of most other applications... but more of this in Chapter 14, which is devoted to exploring the object models of the applications discussed in this book.

Apart from user forms, which are coordinated as usual by VBA's Microsoft Forms engine, you get to do almost everything with VBA by using the `PerfectScript` object to issue PerfectScript commands.

If you're familiar with PerfectScript, you'll make the transition to using Perfect-Script from VBA with little bother. As you'll see, you have to rearrange the syntax a little, but after that, most everything will work the way you're used to.

A quick way of getting started with using VBA with WordPerfect is to record a macro in PerfectScript and then port it to VBA—which is what you'll do in this section.

Follow these steps (illustrated in Video_31.avi on the CD) to create the procedure:

1. Start WordPerfect if it's not already running.

2. Create a document that contains the bookmark the procedure will use:

   - Start a new document.
   - Save it under the name `Boilerplate Text.wpd` in a convenient location. My document is in the folder `f:\users\common\text\`.
   - Enter a sentence—anything will do provided it's easily recognizable. Select the sentence.
   - Choose Tools ➤ Bookmark to display the Bookmark dialog box.

- Click the Create button to display the Create Bookmark dialog box.
- Enter **TextChunk** in the Bookmark Name text box, and click the OK button to close the Create Bookmark dialog box and the Bookmark dialog box.
- Save and close the document.

3. Create a new document.

4. Choose Tools ➤ Macro ➤ Record, or press F10, to display the Record Macro dialog box (see Figure 10.16).

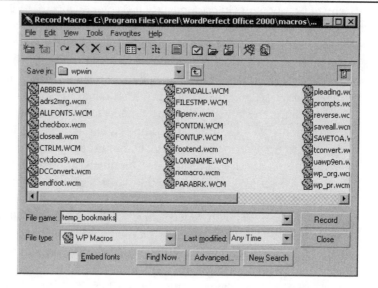

5. Enter a name, such as temp_bookmarks, in the File Name text box and click the Record button to start recording the macro.

6. Choose File ➤ Open to display the Open File dialog box. Navigate to and select your Boilerplate Text.wpd document, then click the Open button to open it.

7. Choose Tools ➤ Bookmark to display the Bookmark dialog box. In the Bookmarks list box, select the item for the TextChunk bookmark, then click the Go To & Select button. Issue a Copy command to copy the text.

8. Choose File ➤ Close to close Boilerplate Text.wpd. Then issue a Paste command to paste the text.

9. Choose Tools ➤ Macro ➤ Record to stop recording the macro.

10. Choose Tools ➤ Macro ➤ Edit to display the Open Macro dialog box (see Figure 10.17).

FIGURE 10.17

Use the Edit Macro dialog box to open the macro you recorded.

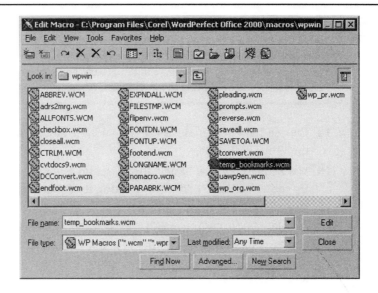

11. Select the macro you recorded and click the Edit button to open it. You should see a macro listing that looks similar to the one below. (The numbering is Word-Perfect's own, not an addition of mine.)

```
1 Application (WordPerfect; "WordPerfect"; Default!; "EN")
2 FileOpen (Filename: "f:\users\common\text\Boilerplate Text.wpd")
3 BookmarkBlock (Name: "TextChunk")
4 EditCopy ()
5 Close ()
6 EditPaste ()
7
```

12. As you can see, it's pretty straightforward: The first statement records the application used, the language, and so on. The second statement opens the document. The third statement selects the bookmark. The fourth statement copies the selection. The fifth statement closes the document. The sixth statement pastes the material into the active document. The seventh line is a stub—a number without a statement.

13. Copy the second through sixth lines to the Clipboard, then close the macro document.

NOTE You can't access the Visual Basic Editor directly from WordPerfect (by pressing Alt+F11 or choosing Tools ➤ Visual Basic ➤ Visual Basic Editor) when you have a macro window active, although you can activate the Visual Basic Editor as usual either by *cool-switching* (Alt+tabbing), or clicking the Visual Basic Editor's icon on the Taskbar. I think the idea is to keep you from trying to run VBA on a PerfectScript macro.

14. Choose Tools ➤ Visual Basic ➤ Visual Basic Editor, or press Alt+F11, to display the Visual Basic Editor.

15. Make sure the Visual Basic Editor is set up as described in the section, "Setting Up the Visual Basic Editor for Creating the Procedures," earlier in this chapter.

16. In the Project Explorer window, right-click anywhere in the GlobalMacros (WordPerfect9.GMS) item and choose Insert ➤ Module from the context menu. The Visual Basic Editor will insert a new module in the global macros project, will display a Code window for it, and will expand the GlobalMacros tree if it was collapsed.

17. Press the F4 key to activate the Properties window for the new module.

18. Enter the name for the new module in the Properties window. For the example, I'll use the name WP_Procedures.

19. Click in the Code window to activate it.

20. If the Visual Basic Editor hasn't already entered an Option Explicit statement in the declarations area of the code sheet, enter the statement manually now.

21. Below the Option Explicit statement, enter the Sub statement for the procedure and press the Enter key. I'm going to call the procedure Insert_Boilerplate:

```
Sub Insert_Boilerplate
```

22. The Visual Basic Editor will enter for you the parentheses at the end of the Sub statement, a blank line, and the End Sub statement:

```
Sub Insert_Boilerplate()

End Sub
```

23. Press the Tab key to indent the first line below the Sub statement.

24. Paste in the statements from the WordPerfect macro. The Visual Basic Editor will turn them red because they're not valid VBA statements. Don't worry about that, but comment them out so that they don't actively interfere with code execution.

25. Start a `With` statement with the `PerfectScript` object:

```
With PerfectScript

End With
```

26. Starting on the line within the `With` statement, create VBA statements that use the PerfectScript commands you recorded. Where a PerfectScript command uses parentheses, remove them. Also remove the named arguments for simplicity:

```
With PerfectScript
    .FileOpen "f:\users\common\text\Boilerplate Text.wpd"
    .BookmarkBlock "TextChunk"
    .EditCopy
    .Close
    .EditPaste
End With
```

27. Delete the commented-out lines of PerfectScript code.

28. Test the procedure to make sure it works, then choose File ➤ Save Word-Perfect9.GMS to save the global macro project.

Creating a Procedure for Visio

The procedure you'll create for Visio is simple in the extreme. It starts a new drawing based on the blank template, adds three shapes to the first page, saves the drawing, and closes it.

Most of the items that you'll be working with in this procedure are obvious, so you won't need to go delving into the Help file. As you learned earlier in the book, Visio uses the `Document` object to represent a drawing document. From working interactively, you know that any drawing can contain one or more pages, so it's no great leap to guess that these pages are represented by `Page` objects in a `Pages` collection. On the pages, you typically draw shapes, which in turn are represented by `Shape` objects ranged into a `Shapes` collection.

Follow these steps (which are illustrated in Video_32.avi on the CD) to create the procedure:

1. Start Visio if it's not already running.

2. If you have a Visio document that you're using as a code repository, open it now. Otherwise, open a blank document that you can use to store the code.

3. Choose Tools ➤ Macro ➤ Visual Basic Editor, or press Alt+F11, to display the Visual Basic Editor.

4. Make sure the Visual Basic Editor is set up as described in the section, "Setting Up the Visual Basic Editor for Creating the Procedures," earlier in this chapter.

5. In the Project Explorer window, right-click anywhere in the project for the document in which you want to create the procedure and choose Insert ➤ Module from the context menu. The Visual Basic Editor will insert a new module in the project, will display a Code window for it, and will expand the project's tree if it was collapsed.

6. Press the F4 key to activate the Properties window for the new module.

7. Enter the name for the new module in the Properties window. For the example, I'll use the name `Examples`.

8. Click in the Code window to activate it.

9. If the Visual Basic Editor hasn't already entered an `Option Explicit` statement in the declarations area of the code sheet, enter the statement manually now.

10. Below the `Option Explicit` statement, enter the Sub statement for the procedure and press the Enter key. I called the procedure `SimpleDoc`:

```
Sub SimpleDoc
```

11. The Visual Basic Editor will enter for you the parentheses at the end of the Sub statement, a blank line, and the End Sub statement:

```
Sub SimpleDoc()

End Sub
```

12. Press the Tab key to indent the first line below the Sub statement.

13. Declare three Shape object variables that will represent the three shapes the procedure draws:

```
Dim shpShape1 As Shape
Dim shpShape2 As Shape
Dim shpShape3 As Shape
```

14. Declare one `Document` object variable that will represent the document it creates:

```
Dim docThisDoc As Document
```

15. Use the `Add` method of the `Documents` collection to create a new document, using a Set statement to assign the document to the docThisDoc object variable.

```
Set docThisDoc = Documents.Add(
```

16. As you type the opening parenthesis in the statement, the Auto Quick Info feature will show you that the `Add` method for the `Documents` collection takes one argument, `FileName`. Clearly, `FileName` must be a String argument; but you need more information. To get this information, place the insertion point in the Add method and press the F1 key to display help on the Add method. Figure 10.18 shows the resulting Help screen. Toward the bottom of the screen, you can see the information for the Documents collection: You use an empty string to create a new drawing based on no template. Complete the statement:

```
Set docThisDoc = Documents.Add(FileName:="")
```

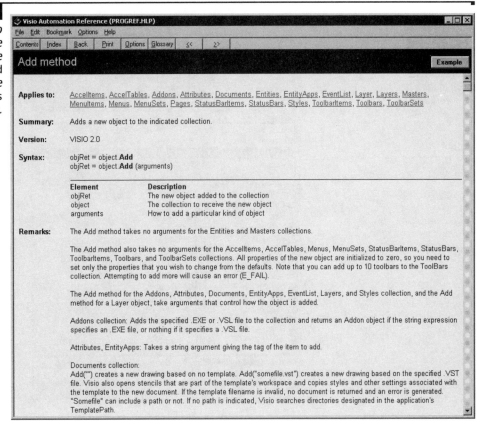

17. Start a With statement that works with the docThisDoc, placing inside it a nested With statement that works with the first Page object in docThisDoc:

```
With docThisDoc
    With .Pages(1)


    End With
End With
```

18. Find the methods you need to draw the shapes on the page:

- Press the F2 key to display the Object Browser.
- Select Visio in the Project/Library drop-down list.
- Enter **rectangle** in the Search text box.
- Click the Search button to execute the search. You should see something like Figure 10.19, which shows the `DrawRectangle` method applying to three objects, one of them the `Page` object.

FIGURE 10.19

Use the Object Browser to search for the method to draw a rectangle.

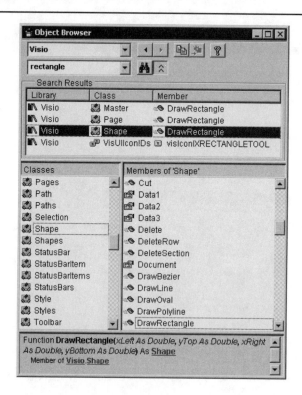

19. Use the `DrawRectangle` method to draw two rectangles of a size that amuses you. Use `Set` statements to assign the rectangles to the `shpShape1` and `shp-Shape2` object variables:

```
Set shpShape1 = .DrawRectangle(1, 8, 2, 7)
Set shpShape2 = .DrawRectangle(3, 8, 4, 7)
```

20. Start another `Set` statement on the next line. Type the period (**.**) to start the right-hand side of the statement, and find the method for drawing a line in the

List Properties/Methods drop-down list. The method is DrawLine—no great surprise. Now draw the line from one object to the other:

```
Set shpShape3 = .DrawLine(2, 7.5, 3, 7.5)
```

21. Use the Text property of the rectangular Shape objects to enter text in the shapes:

```
shpShape1.Text = "Left"
shpShape2.Text = "Right"
```

22. Move the insertion point to below the End With statement for the nested With statement, then use the SaveAs method to save docThisDoc. As you type the statement, the Auto Quick Info feature will show you that the SaveAs method takes a single String argument specifying the filename:

```
.SaveAs "c:\winnt\temp\test.vsd"
```

23. Use the Close method to close docThisDoc, as shown at the end of the full procedure below:

```
Sub SimpleDoc()

    Dim shpShape1 As Shape
    Dim shpShape2 As Shape
    Dim shpShape3 As Shape
    Dim docThisDoc As Document

    Set docThisDoc = Documents.Add(FileName:="")

    With docThisDoc
        With .Pages(1)
            Set shpShape1 = .DrawRectangle(1, 8, 2, 7)
            Set shpShape2 = .DrawRectangle(3, 8, 4, 7)
            Set shpShape3 = .DrawLine(2, 7.5, 3, 7.5)
            shpShape1.Text = "Left"
            shpShape2.Text = "Right"
        End With
        .SaveAs "c:\winnt\temp\test.vsd"
        .Close
    End With

End Sub
```

24. Arrange the Visio window and its Visual Basic Editor window side by side, then step through the procedure and watch the action unfold.

25. Save your code document.

Creating a Procedure for AutoCAD

The procedure you'll create for AutoCAD sets up the user's workspace for their regular work:

- It sets the AutoSave path and the Template path.

- It turns on the log file option.

- It turns on the option to create a backup copy of the file with each save.

- It turns on full-time CRC validation.

- It specifies a custom dictionary.

- It turns on the AutoSave option, specifying an interval of 5 minutes.

- It loads two non-embedded VBA projects automatically (stored in .DVB files), saving the user a little valuable time messing with the Open VBA Project dialog box and the VBA Manager dialog box. These VBA projects are custom projects, not ones that ship with AutoCAD.

Follow these steps (which are illustrated in Video_33.avi on the CD) to create the procedure:

1. Start AutoCAD if it's not already running.

2. If you have a VBA project you want to use, load it now: Choose Tools ≻ Macro ≻ Load Project to display the Open VBA Project dialog box, select the VBA project, and click the Open button.

3. Choose Tools ≻ Macro ≻ Visual Basic Editor, or press Alt+F11, to display the Visual Basic Editor.

4. Make sure the Visual Basic Editor is set up as described in the section, "Setting Up the Visual Basic Editor for the Creating Procedures," earlier in this chapter.

5. In the Project Explorer window, right-click anywhere in the project in which you want to create the procedure and choose Insert ≻ Module from the context menu. The Visual Basic Editor will insert a new module in the project, will display a Code window for it, and will expand the project's tree if it was collapsed.

6. Press the F4 key to activate the Properties window for the new module.

7. Enter the name for the new module in the Properties window. For the example, I'll use the name RNI_General.

8. Click in the Code window to activate it.

9. If the Visual Basic Editor hasn't already entered an Option Explicit statement in the declarations area of the code sheet, enter the statement manually now.

10. Below the `Option Explicit` statement, enter the Sub statement for the procedure and press the Enter key. I'm going to call the procedure `Set_Up_Workspace`:

```
Sub Set_Up_Workspace
```

11. The Visual Basic Editor will enter for you the parentheses at the end of the Sub statement, a blank line, and the End Sub statement:

```
Sub Set_Up_Workspace()

End Sub
```

12. Press the Tab key to indent the first line below the Sub statement.

13. Start by declaring a String variable named `strACDPath` to contain the common part of the various paths the procedure will use:

```
Dim strACDPath As String
```

14. Assign to the String variable the string—in this case, f:\users\common\autocad\(you'll need to change this path unless you happen to have this drive and folder structure):

```
strACDPath = "f:\users\common\autocad\"
```

15. That was the easy part. Now you need to find the objects the procedure will manipulate.

16. Try going the hard way. Type **Application.** into the procedure and scan the List Properties/Methods drop-down list. Most of the settings you need to manipulate appear in the Options dialog box, so look for an Options property. No good... but there's a `Preferences` property that will return a `Preferences` object. Try selecting that.

17. Again, type a period (**.**) to get the List Properties/Methods drop-down list. This time, the `Files` property looks promising. Select it.

18. Here you go. Select the `AutoSavePath` property and assign the string for it:

```
Application.Preferences.Files.AutoSavePath = strACDPath & "backups"
```

19. Now turn that into a `With` statement so that you can go digging through the properties and methods of the `Files` collection more easily:

```
With Application.Preferences.Files
    .AutoSavePath = strACDPath & "backups"

End With
```

20. Position the insertion point on the blank line and type another period (**.**) to display the List Properties/Methods drop-down list again. This time, choose the

CustomDictionary property and assign to it a string specifying where the custom dictionary is:

```
.CustomDictionary = strACDPath & "RNI AutoCAD Dictionary.cus"
```

21. On another line within the With statement, type another period (.) and scan further down the List Properties/Methods drop-down list. Select the TemplateDwg-Path property and assign to it a string specifying the template path to use:

```
.TemplateDwgPath = strACDPath & "Templates"
```

22. On yet another line, type a period (.) and scan through the list again. See anything else you need? No? Then delete the period and start another With statement:

```
With Application.Preferences.
```

23. Scan down the list for Save options. The OpenSave method looks promising. Type down through that, and then build a With statement that uses the AutoSaveInterval, CreateBackup, FullCRCValidation, LogFileOn, and SavePreviewThumbnail properties:

```
With Application.Preferences.OpenSave
    .SavePreviewThumbnail = True
    .CreateBackup = True
    .AutoSaveInterval = 5
    .FullCRCValidation = True
    .LogFileOn = True
End With
```

 NOTE The AutoSaveInterval property is a little unusual: You'd expect there to be a Boolean property named AutoSave or something similar, but in fact AutoCAD uses the AutoSaveInterval both to turn AutoSave on and off, and to specify the interval when it is on. So a zero value for AutoSaveInterval turns AutoSave off, and a value greater than zero (and less than 600) specifies the interval.

24. Now, create the statements to load the VBA project files. Again, start from the Application object and type down. Nothing under VBA... but just above that is an UnloadDVB method. Find the corresponding LoadDVB method, and you're home and dry. The LoadDVB method takes a string specifying the VBA project file to load (in this case, two custom project files; you'll need to create ones of your own, or change the names):

```
Application.LoadDVB strACDPath & "DVB\RNI_1.dvb"
Application.LoadDVB strACDPath & "DVB\RNI_2.dvb"
```

25. Tidy up the code. Note that Preferences is a creatable object, so you don't need to specify Application before it. Eliminate those Application references. Then integrate the two With statements into two nested With statements under a With Preferences statement, as shown in the full procedure below:

```
Sub Set_Up_Workspace()

    Dim strACDPath As String

    strACDPath = "f:\users\common\autocad\"

    With Preferences
        With .Files
            .AutoSavePath = strACDPath & "backups"
            .CustomDictionary = strACDPath & "RNI AutoCAD
Dictionary.cus"
            .TemplateDwgPath = strACDPath & "Templates"
        End With
        With .OpenSave
            .SavePreviewThumbnail = True
            .CreateBackup = True
            .AutoSaveInterval = 5
            .FullCRCValidation = True
            .LogFileOn = True
        End With
    End With
    Application.LoadDVB strACDPath & "DVB\RNI_1.dvb"
    Application.LoadDVB strACDPath & "DVB\RNI_2.dvb"

End Sub
```

26. Run the procedure to test it, and then save your work.

In the next chapter, you'll learn how to use message boxes and input boxes to increase the power and functionality of your procedures.

CHAPTER 11

Using Message Boxes and Input Boxes

FEATURING:

In this chapter, you'll start to see how you can add a user interface to recorded or written code in order to increase the code's power and functionality. I'll discuss the three easiest ways of communicating with the user of your code, the two easiest ways of enabling the user to make decisions in a procedure, and the easiest way of soliciting input from the user. Along the way, I'll go over how to decide what is the best way to communicate with the user in any given set of circumstances. This will set the scene for starting an examination of more complex interactions with the user via custom dialog boxes, later in the book.

In most applications, VBA offers up to four ways of communicating with the user of a procedure:

- Displaying messages on the status bar at the bottom of the window (if the application provides a status bar). As you'll see in the next section, this can be an effective way of communicating with the user—with a couple of medium-sized caveats.

- Displaying a message box (usually in the middle of the screen). Message boxes are useful both for communicating with the user, and for providing them with the means to make a single choice based on the information you give them. You'll spend the bulk of this chapter working with message boxes.

- Displaying an input box (again, usually in the middle of the screen). You can use input boxes to communicate with the user, but their primary purpose is to solicit one item of information. Input boxes also provide the user with the means of making a single choice to direct the flow of a procedure, although the mechanism for presenting this choice is much more limited than that in a message box. You'll look at input boxes toward the end of this chapter.

- Displaying a dialog box (once again, usually in the middle of a screen). You can use dialog boxes both to communicate with the user, and to let them make a number of choices. As you'll know from your own experience with Windows and Windows applications, dialog boxes are best reserved for those times when other forms of communication won't suffice; in other words, there's no point in using a dialog box when a simple message box or input box will do. You'll look at creating custom dialog boxes by using VBA user forms later in the book.

Getting Started

Before I get into adding ways of communicating with the user, you need to make sure you're all set for editing in the Code window in the Visual Basic Editor. Follow these steps:

1. Start the application for which you're creating code.

2. Fire up the Visual Basic Editor by pressing Alt+F11 or by choosing Tools ➤ Macro ➤ Visual Basic Editor. (If you're using WordPerfect, choose Tools ➤ Visual Basic ➤ Visual Basic Editor.)

3. Open a procedure for editing in the Code window: Use the Project Explorer to navigate to the module that holds the procedure, and then either scroll to the procedure in the Code window, or choose it from the Procedures drop-down list in the Code window.

 TIP Alternatively, choose Tools ➤ Macro ➤ Macros (Tools ➤ Visual Basic ➤ Macros in WordPerfect) to display the Macro dialog box, select a procedure you've created in the Macro Name list box, and click the Edit button to display the Visual Basic Editor with the procedure open in the Code window.

If you want to work in a new procedure rather than in an existing one—which is probably a good idea, because it'll help prevent you from doing any damage—you can create a new procedure by entering the Sub keyword and the procedure's name on a blank line in a module, and then pressing Enter. VBA will supply the parentheses and End Sub statement. For example, you could type the following and press the Enter key:

```
Sub Experimentation_Zone
```

VBA will add the parentheses and End Sub statement, together with a separator line to separate the procedure from any adjacent procedures in the Code window:

```
Sub Experimentation_Zone()


End Sub
```

Test the procedure as described in Chapter 3 by using the F8 key to step through it in Break mode, or by clicking the Run Sub/UserForm button to run it without highlighting each statement in turn. (You can also run it by typing the procedure's name into the Immediate window and pressing the Enter key.)

Now that you have a procedure ready to work on, let's begin by looking at how to add a status-bar message to a procedure, and the reasons for doing so.

Displaying Status Bar Messages in Word and Excel

In Word and Excel, which let you easily display information on the status bar, status-bar messages provide the best way to tell the user what's happening in a procedure without halting execution of the code. By including instructions for printing information to (displaying information on) the status bar at strategic points in a procedure, you can indicate to the user not only what the procedure is doing, but also that it's still running. (Sometimes a procedure may appear to the user to have stopped, while in fact it's working furiously but displaying no changes on-screen.)

The main disadvantage of displaying messages on the status bar is that the user may miss them if they're not paying attention or if they're not expecting to see messages there. If the application in question uses the status bar extensively to give the user information (as Word and Excel do), this shouldn't be a problem—but if there's any doubt, notify the user (perhaps via a message box) at the beginning of a procedure that information will be displayed on the status bar.

 NOTE Visio also lets you manipulate the status bar, but the process is relatively involved, and I won't discuss it here.

To display a message on the status bar in Word or Excel, set the StatusBar property of the Application object to an appropriate string of text. The following example displays the status bar information shown in Figure 11.1.

```
Application.StatusBar = _
    "Word is formatting the report. Please wait..."
```

FIGURE 11.1

In some applications, you can display information on the status bar.

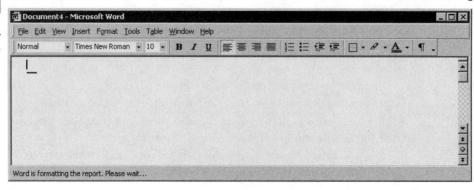

Typically, any information you display on the status bar will remain displayed there until you change it, or until the application displays a message there itself. For example, if you display a message on the status bar and then invoke the Copy command in Excel, Excel will display its normal Copy message, *Select destination and press*

ENTER or choose Paste, on the status bar, wiping out your message. Application messages trump user-created messages.

If you display a message on the status bar in the course of a procedure, you'll usually need to update it later in the procedure so as to avoid leaving a misleading message on the status bar after the procedure has finished running. For example, you might display another message saying that the procedure has finished, or clear the status bar by displaying a blank string on it.

To clear the status bar, assign an empty string to it, as in the following statement:

```
Application.StatusBar = ""
```

To see the effect of this statement, run it from the Visual Basic Editor with the Word or Excel window (or at least its status bar) visible. You'll see the effect best if you run a statement that displays information on the status bar (such as `Application.StatusBar = "Hello, World!"`) first so that the status bar has information for the `Application.StatusBar = ""` statement to clear:

```
Application.StatusBar = "Hello, World!"
Application.StatusBar = ""
```

Message Boxes

Your second tool for providing information to the user is the garden-variety message box, with which you'll be familiar from any number of Windows applications. As you'll see in this section, the humble message box can play an important role in almost any procedure or module. Displaying your first *Hello, World!* message box tends to be exhilarating, but after awhile you can grow blasé to the usefulness of the message box. This is a shame, because even a straightforward message box can significantly enhance the user-friendliness of the most complex procedure.

Classic uses of message boxes include:

- Telling the user what a procedure is about to do (and giving them the chance to cancel out of it if it isn't what they thought it was).

- Presenting the user with an explanation of what a procedure will do next and asking them to make a simple decision (usually, to let it proceed or to send it on a different course).

- Warning the user of an error that the procedure encountered and allowing them to take action on it.

- Informing the user that a procedure ran successfully and that it has finished. This message is particularly useful for procedures that turn off screen updating or otherwise hide from the user what they are doing, because such procedures may leave the user unsure whether the procedure is still running or has finished. You can also use the message box to report what the procedure has done—for example, that it changed particular items, or that it discovered problems in the document that require attention.

In this chapter, I'll show you how to create a message box suitable for each of these tasks. In later chapters, you'll create specific message boxes to enhance various procedures.

The Pros and Cons of Message Boxes

To any seasoned user of Windows, the advantages of using a message box are clear:

- The user can't miss seeing the message box. (If you want, you can even display a message box that the user can't escape by *coolswitching*—Alt+Tabbing—to another application. You'll look at this a little later in the chapter.)

- You can present the user with a simple choice among two or three options.

The limitations are also pretty clear:

- A message box can present only one, two, or three buttons, which means it can offer only a limited set of options to the user.

- The buttons in message boxes are predefined in sets—you can't put a custom button in a message box. (For that, you have to use a dialog box.)

- You can't use features such as text boxes, group boxes, or list boxes in message boxes.

Message Box Syntax

The basic syntax for message boxes is as follows:

```
MsgBox(prompt[, buttons] [, title][, helpfile, context])
```

Here's what the elements of this syntax mean:

MsgBox   The function that VBA uses to display a message box. You typically use it with a number of arguments enclosed in parentheses after it, as you'll see in a moment.

prompt   A required argument for the MsgBox function that controls the text displayed in the message box. *prompt* is a String argument, meaning you need to type in text of your choice; it can be up to 1023 characters long, although it's usually a good idea to be more concise than this. (Any *prompt* longer than 1023 characters is truncated to 1023 characters without warning.)

buttons   An optional argument that controls the type of message box that VBA displays by specifying which buttons it contains. For example, as you'll see in a couple of pages, you can display a message box with just an OK button; with OK and Cancel buttons; with Abort, Retry, and Ignore buttons; and so on. You can also add arguments to the *buttons* argument that control the icon in the message box and the modality of the message box. We'll also look at these options later in this chapter.

title   An optional argument that controls the title bar of the message box. This too is a string argument. If you don't specify *title*, VBA uses the application's title—`Microsoft Word` for Word, `Microsoft Project` for Project, `WordPerfect` for WordPerfect, `AutoCAD` for AutoCAD, and so on. Such a generic title helps the user not one whit, so you'll usually want to specify the title.

helpfile   An optional argument that controls which Help file VBA displays when the user presses F1 within the message box to get help.

context   An optional argument that controls which topic in the Help file VBA jumps to. If you specify the *helpfile* argument, you need to specify the *context* argument as well.

In the following sections, you'll look first at how you can build the simplest of message boxes, and then at how you can add the other arguments to it to make it more complex.

Displaying a Simple Message Box

You can display a straightforward message box by specifying only the `prompt` as a text string enclosed in double quotation marks:

```
MsgBox "This is a simple message box."
```

Run from Visio, this statement produces the simple message box shown in Figure 11.2. With *prompt* as the only argument supplied, VBA produces a message box with only an OK button, and with the application's name in the title bar. This message box does nothing except display information.

FIGURE 11.2

When you use only the prompt argument to display a simple message box, VBA uses the application's name as the title.

You can enter this `MsgBox` statement on any blank line within a procedure. After you type the `MsgBox` keyword, VBA's Auto List Members feature prompts you with the syntax of the function, as shown in Figure 11.3.

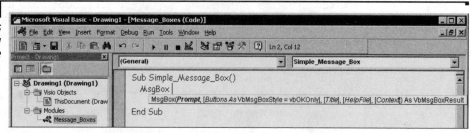

 NOTE If you look at the Help listing for the `MsgBox` function, you'll see that the syntax appears a little differently: The `helpfile` and `context` arguments share a bracket—`[, helpfile, context]`—rather than each having its own bracket. This is because you can use both of them or neither of them, but you can't use either on its own (more on this in a moment). The ScreenTip isn't able to convey this distinction. Because codependent optional arguments are relatively rare, this limitation of the ScreenTip seldom causes much of a problem; but if you find VBA balking at a statement that apparently carries the arguments shown in the ScreenTip, check the Help file.

Once you've entered the `MsgBox` statement with its required argument (*prompt*), you can display the message box by stepping through the code (by pressing the F8 key) or by running the procedure (by clicking the Run Sub/UserForm button, by choosing Run ➤ Run Sub/UserForm, or by pressing the F5 key).

Instead of entering a text string for the *prompt* argument, you can use a String variable. The following example uses a String variable named `strMsg`:

```
Dim strMsg As String
strMsg = "This is a simple message box."
MsgBox strMsg
```

This method can be useful when you're working with long strings, or when you need to display a string that has been defined earlier in the procedure or a string dynamically created by the procedure.

Displaying a Multi-line Message Box

By default, VBA displays short message strings as a single line in a message box and wraps longer strings onto two or more lines as necessary, up to the limit of 1024 characters (1KB of characters) in a string.

You can deliberately break a string over more than one line by including line-feed and carriage-return characters in the string as follows:

- Chr(13) or vbCr represents a carriage return.
- Chr(10) or vbLf represents a line-feed.
- Chr(10) + Chr(13) or vbCrLf represents a line-feed–carriage return combination.

In message boxes, these three characters all have the same effect. Your code will be easier to read if you use a constant (vbCr, vbLf, or vbCrLf) than the corresponding Chr() construction; it'll also be quicker to type. Usually, it's clearest to use the vbCr constant, specifically.

You can add a tab to a string by using Chr(9) or vbTab. Again, vbTab is easier to read and to type.

For example, the following code displays the WordPerfect message box illustrated in Figure 11.4. Note that each part of the text string is enclosed in double quotation marks (to tell VBA that they're part of the string). The Chr(149) characters are bullets, so the text after them starts with a couple of spaces to give the bullets some air:

```
Dim strMsg As String
strMsg = "WordPerfect has finished formatting the report you requested." _
    & vbCr & vbCr & "You can now run the following procedures:" & vbCr _
    & vbCr & Chr(149) & " Distribute_Report will e-mail the report to " _
    & "the head office." & vbCr & vbCr & Chr(149) & _
    " Store_Report will copy the report to the holding directory." _
    & vbCr & vbCr & Chr(149) & " Backup_Report will create a backup " _
    & "of the report on the file server."
MsgBox strMsg
```

FIGURE 11.4

You can display a multi-line message box by using line-feed and carriage-return characters within the prompt *string.*

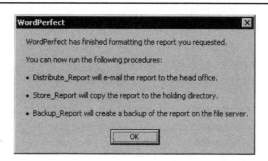

TIP You'll notice that in this example, a space appears on either side of each of the ampersands (&) and the equal sign. You can enter these spaces yourself or have VBA enter them for you when you move the insertion point to another line, which causes VBA to check the line you've just been working on.

Choosing Buttons for a Message Box

As you saw a little earlier, the *buttons* argument controls which buttons a message box contains. VBA offers the types of message boxes shown in Table 11.1, controlled by the *buttons* argument.

TABLE 11.1: MESSAGE BOX TYPES, CONTROLLED BY THE *BUTTONS* ARGUMENT

Value	Constant	Buttons
0	vbOKOnly	OK
1	vbOKCancel	OK, Cancel
2	vbAbortRetryIgnore	Abort, Retry, Ignore
3	vbYesNoCancel	Yes, No, Cancel
4	vbYesNo	Yes, No
5	vbRetryCancel	Retry, Cancel

You can refer to these message box types by using either the value or the constant. For example, you can specify either 1 or vbOKCancel to produce a message box with OK and Cancel buttons. The value is easier to type; the constant is easier to read. Either of the following statements produces the message box shown in Figure 11.5 when run from PowerPoint:

```
Dim lngR As Long
lngR = MsgBox("Apply standard formatting to the slide?", vbYesNo)
lngR = MsgBox("Apply standard formatting to the slide?", 4)
```

FIGURE 11.5

The vbYesNo *constant produces a message box with Yes and No buttons.*

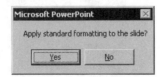

From VBA's point of view, it doesn't matter whether you use values or constants in the message boxes for your procedures. For the human, though, the constants are far preferable. Even if you're the only person who will ever see your code, it will be much easier to read if you use the constants. If other people may have to thrash their way through your procedures to debug them once you've distributed the procedures or moved on from your current position, this applies in spades.

Choosing an Icon for a Message Box

You can also add an icon to a message box by including the appropriate value or constant argument. Table 11.2 shows the options.

TABLE 11.2: ARGUMENTS FOR MESSAGE BOX ICONS

Value	Constant	Displays
16	vbCritical	Stop icon
32	vbQuestion	Question mark icon
48	vbExclamation	Exclamation point icon
64	vbInformation	Information icon

Again, you can refer to these icons by using either the value or the constant: either 48 or vbExclamation will produce an exclamation point icon. Again, I recommend using the constant for legibility.

To link the value or constant for the message box with the value or constant for the icon, use a plus sign (+). For example, to produce a message box containing Yes and No buttons together with a question mark icon (see Figure 11.6), you could enter **vbYesNo + vbQuestion** (or **4 + 32**, **vbYesNo + 32**, or **4 + vbQuestion**):

```
lngR = MsgBox("Apply standard formatting to the slide?", _
    vbYesNo + vbQuestion)
```

FIGURE 11.6

Adding an icon to a message box

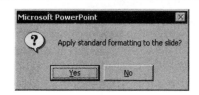

Setting a Default Button for a Message Box

You can set a default button for a message box by specifying the button in the MsgBox statement. This step is seldom necessary for every procedure (unless you happen to write dangerous procedures or you have colleagues prone to random behavior), but it can be a wise move when you distribute procedures that take drastic action. For example, consider a procedure that deletes the current document without having to close it and then switch to a file-management program (such as Windows Explorer) or dredge around in one of the common dialog boxes (such as the Open dialog box or the Save dialog box). Because this procedure can destroy someone's work if they run it inadvertently, you'd probably want to set a default button of No or Cancel in a confirmation message box so that the user has to actively choose to run the rest of the procedure.

As usual in the Windows interface, the default button in a message box is selected visually with a black border around its outside and a dotted line around its text area. You can move the selection to another button by using Tab or Shift+Tab or the →, ←, ↑, or ↓ keys.

 NOTE Because the user can choose the default button by simply pressing Enter, having the appropriate default button on a message box or dialog box can help the user deal with the message box or dialog box more quickly. Because the first button in a message box is set to be the default button by, uh, default, you must specify the default button only when you need it to be a button other than the first.

Table 11.3 lists the arguments for default buttons.

TABLE 11.3: ARGUMENTS FOR DEFAULT MESSAGE-BOX BUTTONS

Value	Constant	Effect
0	vbDefaultButton1	The first button is the default button.
256	vbDefaultButton2	The second button is the default button.
512	vbDefaultButton3	The third button is the default button.
768	vbDefaultButton4	The fourth button is the default button.

The vbDefaultButton4 item may have you scratching your head a bit: Don't all the message boxes I've mentioned have only one, two, or three buttons? That's right—but you can add a Help button to any of the message boxes, making for a fourth button on those boxes that already have three buttons (such as vbYesNoCancel). We'll look at how to do this in the section, "Adding a Help Button to a Message Box," a little further along in the chapter. (The information really belongs in this section, but because it's related to specifying a Help file and context for the message box, I'll leave it until you reach those topics.)

In VBA, unless you specify otherwise, the first button on each of the message boxes is automatically the default button: for example, the OK button in a vbOKCancel message box, the Abort button in a vbAbortRetryIgnore message box, the Yes button in a vbYesNoCancel message box, the Yes button in a vbYesNo message box, and the Retry button in a vbRetryCancel message box. VBA counts the buttons in the order they're presented in the constant for the type of message box (which in turn is the left-to-right order in which they appear in the message box on-screen). So in a vbYesNoCancel message box, Yes is the first button, No is the second button, and Cancel is the third button.

To set a different default button, specify the value or constant as part of the *buttons* argument. When run in Project, this statement produces the message box shown in Figure 11.7.

```
Dim lngQuery As Long
lngQuery = MsgBox("Do you want to delete this project?", _
    vbYesNo + vbCritical + vbDefaultButton2)
```

FIGURE 11.7

Specify a default button to steer the user toward a particular button in a message box.

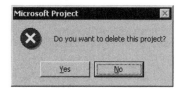

Controlling the Modality of a Message Box

VBA can display both *application-modal* message boxes and *system-modal* message boxes—in theory, anyway. The difference between the two is that application-modal message boxes stop you from doing anything in the current application until you dismiss them, whereas system-modal message boxes stop you from doing anything *on your computer* until you dismiss them. Most message boxes are application modal, allowing you to coolswitch (or switch via the Taskbar) to another application and work in it before you get rid of the message box, which gives you a reasonable amount of flexibility. In contrast, some installation message boxes are system modal, insisting that you concentrate your attention on them and them alone. As I'm sure you remember, General Protection Faults (GPFs) and Unexplained Application Errors (UAEs) in Windows 3.*x* were so system modal it was painful; and it's sad to see that Windows 95 and Windows 98 continue this tradition with their notorious "Blue Screen of Death" when something goes horribly wrong.

You probably know from your own experience how frustrating system-modal message boxes can be, and when designing procedures, you should use system-modal message boxes only when absolutely necessary. In practice, this means almost never. For most conventional purposes, application-modal message boxes will do everything you need them to—and won't confuse or vex users of your procedures.

In theory, you can control the modality of a message box by using the two *buttons* arguments shown in Table 11.4.

TABLE 11.4: ARGUMENTS FOR MESSAGE-BOX MODALITY

Value	Constant	Result
0	vbApplicationModal	The message box is application modal.
4096	vbSystemModal	The message box is system modal.

In practice, these arguments seem to have less than the intended effect: Even if you use the vbSystemModal argument, the user can switch to another application (provided that one is running) and continue working. However, the message box stays "on top," remaining displayed—enough to annoy the user, but not to stop them in their tracks.

By default, message boxes are application modal, so you need to specify modality only on those rare occasions when you're producing a system-modal message box. When you do, add the vbSystemModal constant or 4096 value to the *buttons* argument:

```
Response = MsgBox("Do you want to delete this document?", _
    vbYesNo + vbCritical + vbDefaultButton2 + vbSystemModal)
```

System-modal message boxes don't look any different from application-modal message boxes.

Specifying a Title for a Message Box

The next component of the message box is its title bar, which is controlled by the *title* argument. As I mentioned earlier in this chapter, the *title* argument is optional; VBA supplies the application's name as the title if you choose not to specify one yourself. This generic title bar is the perfect argument (that's *argument* in the conventional sense for once this chapter) for your specifying a title bar: Just about anything you care to put in the title bar of a message box will be more informative than the default, so you might as well go ahead and do so.

The *title* argument is a string expression and can be up to 1024 characters in length (longer strings are truncated with no warning or error message), but in practice, any title longer than about 75 characters gets truncated with an ellipsis. If you actually want people to read the title bars of your message boxes, 25 characters or so is a reasonable maximum.

 TIP The title bar is usually the first part of a message box that the user notices, so make your title bars as helpful as possible. Conventional etiquette is to put the name of the procedure in the title bar of a message box and then use the prompt to explain what choices the buttons in the message box will implement. In addition, if you expect to revise your procedures, you may find it helpful to include their version number in the title so that users can easily check which version of the procedure they're using (and update to a more current version as appropriate). For instance, the Delete Workbook procedure is identified as version 2000 in the message box shown in Figure 11.8.

Specify the *title* argument after the *buttons* argument like this:

```
lngQ = MsgBox("Do you want to delete this workbook?", vbYesNo _
    + vbCritical + vbDefaultButton2, "Delete Workbook 2000")
```

FIGURE 11.8

Usually, you'll want to specify the title *argument for your message boxes.*

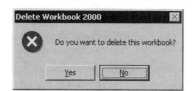

As with the *prompt* argument, you can use a string variable as the *title* argument, which can prove useful if you want to include in the title of the message box a string created or stored in the procedure. For example, in a procedure that offers to delete a document, you could retrieve the name of the document to be deleted and display it in the title bar of a message box, or (perhaps better) in the prompt so that the user couldn't misunderstand which document the procedure was referring to.

NOTE You *can* include line-feed and carriage-return characters in a *title* argument, but VBA will display them as square boxes in the title bar rather than doing anything inventive like creating a two-line title bar, so there's little point. The same goes for tabs—they don't work the way you would want them to.

Adding a Help Button to a Message Box

To add a Help button to a message box, use the vbMsgBoxHelpButton constant. You add this argument to whichever buttons you're specifying for the message box:

```
lngQ = MsgBox("Do you want to delete this workbook?", vbYesNo _
    + vbCritical + vbDefaultButton2 + vbMsgBoxHelpButton, _
    "Delete Workbook 2000")
```

Adding the vbMsgBoxHelpButton argument simply places the Help button in the message box—doing so doesn't make it do anything useful, such as displaying a Help file, until you specify which Help file and topic it should use. Figure 11.9 shows the message box that this statement produces.

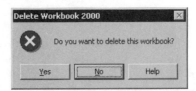

Specifying a Help File for a Message Box

The final arguments you can use for a message box are the *helpfile* and *context* arguments. The *helpfile* argument is a string argument specifying the name and location of the Help file that VBA will display when the user summons help from the message box. The *context* argument is a Help context number within the Help file. These arguments are primarily useful if you're writing your own Help files, because otherwise it's difficult to access the Help context numbers, which are buried in the

Help files. If you're writing your own Help files, the syntax for specifying the *help-file* and *context* arguments is simple:

```
Dim lngQ As Long
lngQ = MsgBox("Do you want to delete this workbook?", vbYesNo _
    + vbCritical + vbDefaultButton2 + vbMsgBoxHelpButton, _
    "Delete Workbook 2000", "c:\Windows\Help\My_Help.hlp", 1012)
```

In this case, the Help file is specified as My_Help.hlp in the \Windows\Help\ folder. VBA will display the help topic numbered 1012.

When the user clicks the Help button in the message box, VBA displays the pre-ordained topic in the Help file. The message box stays on screen, so that when the user has finished consulting the Help file, they can make their choice in the message box.

 TIP The Help context number for the opening screen of a Help file is 0. This number can be useful if you need to display a Help file for which you don't know the Help context numbers, although it means that the user will have to find the information they need on their own.

Three Unusual Constants for Special Effects

VBA provides three special constants for message boxes. You probably won't need to use these often, but if you do, they'll come in handy. Specify them in the *buttons* argument:

vbMsgBoxSetForeground   Tells VBA to make the message box the foreground window. You shouldn't need to use this constant often, because message boxes are displayed in the foreground by default (so that you can see them).

vbMsgBoxRight   Tells VBA to right-align the text in the message box.

vbMsgBoxRtlReading   Tells VBA to arrange the text from right to left on Hebrew and Arabic systems. It has no effect on non-BiDi systems.

Using Some Arguments without Others

As usual, you can either specify or omit optional arguments. If you want to specify later arguments for a function without specifying the ones before them, use a comma to indicate each unused optional argument. For example, if you wanted to display the message box we looked at in the previous example without specifying *buttons* and *title* arguments, you could use the following statement:

```
Response = MsgBox("Do you want to format the report?",,, _
    "c:\Windows\Help\Procedure Help.hlp", 1012
```

Here, the triple comma indicates that the *buttons* and *title* arguments are omitted (which will cause VBA to display a vbOKOnly message box with a title bar containing the application's name), preventing VBA from confusing the *helpfile* argument with the *buttons* argument. Alternatively, you could use named arguments, which makes for less concise but easier-to-read code:

```
Response = MsgBox("Do you want to format the report?", _
    HelpFile:="c:\Windows\Help\Procedure Help.hlp", Context:=1012)
```

 NOTE Because the commands in VBA are laid out with the required arguments first, followed by the optional arguments in approximate order of popularity, you may not need to use commas to indicate omitted arguments very often.

Retrieving a Value from a Message Box

So far in this chapter, you've examined the different items you can specify for a message box:

- The prompt to the user (the only compulsory item)
- The buttons the message box contains, and the default button if necessary
- The icon for the message box
- The modality of the message box
- The title of the message box
- A Help button
- The Help file and its context

Apart from the vbOKOnly message box, the other message boxes have little usefulness until you retrieve a value from them that tells you which button the user clicked. Once you've established which button they clicked, you can point the procedure in the appropriate direction.

To retrieve a value from a message box, declare a variable for it. You can do so quite simply by telling VBA that the variable name is equal to the message box (so to speak):

```
Response = MsgBox("Do you want to create the daily report?", _
    vbYesNo + vbQuestion, "Create Daily Report")
```

But typically you'll want to declare a variable of the appropriate type (a Long variable) to contain the user's choice, as we've been doing in the examples throughout this chapter. Here's another example:

```
Dim lngResponse As Long
lngResponse = MsgBox("Do you want to create the daily report?", _
    vbYesNo + vbQuestion, "Create Daily Report")
```

When you run the code, VBA stores the user's choice of button as a value. You can then check the value and take action accordingly. Table 11.5 shows the full list of buttons the user may choose; again, you can refer to them by either the constant or the value.

TABLE 11.5: CONSTANTS FOR SELECTED BUTTONS

Value	Constant	Button Selected
1	vbOK	OK
2	vbCancel	Cancel
3	vbAbort	Abort
4	vbRetry	Retry
5	vbIgnore	Ignore
6	vbYes	Yes
7	vbNo	No

For example, to check a vbYesNo message box to see which button the user chose, you can use a straightforward If statement:

```
Dim lngUserChoice As Long
lngUserChoice = MsgBox("Do you want to create the daily report?", _
    vbYesNo + vbQuestion, "Create Daily Report")
```

```
If lngUserChoice = vbYes Then
    Goto CreateDailyReport
Else
    Goto Bye
EndIf
```

Here, if the user chooses the Yes button, VBA goes to the line of code identified by the CreateDailyReport label and continues running the procedure from there; if not, it terminates the procedure by going to the Bye label at the end. The If condition checks the response generated by the choice the user made in the message box to see if it's a vbYes (generated by clicking the Yes button or pressing Enter with the Yes button selected). The Else statement runs if the response was not vbYes—that is, if the user chose the No button or pressed Escape, there being only the Yes button and the No button in this message box.

Enough of message boxes for the time being. Let's take a look at input boxes.

Input Boxes

When you want to retrieve one simple piece of information from the user, you can use an input box. You'll be familiar with input boxes by sight if not by name: They usually look something like the example shown in Figure 11.10.

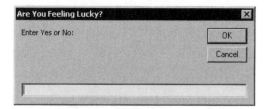

 TIP To retrieve two or more pieces of information from the user, you could use two or more input boxes in succession, but usually a custom dialog box is a better idea. You'll start looking at custom dialog boxes in Chapter 15.

Input Box Syntax

The syntax for displaying an input box is straightforward and similar to the syntax for a message box:

```
InputBox(prompt[, title] [, default] [, xpos] [, ypos] [, helpfile, context])
```

Here's what the arguments mean:

prompt   As with the `MsgBox` function, a string that specifies the prompt that appears in the input box; it's the only required argument. Again, as with `MsgBox`, *prompt* can be up to about 1024 characters long, and you can use line-feed and carriage-return characters to force separate lines. However, unlike the `MsgBox` prompt argument, the `InputBox` prompt doesn't automatically wrap, so you must use these characters to make it wrap if it's longer than about 35 characters.

title   A string that specifies the text in the title bar of the input box. Again, if you don't specify a *title* argument, VBA enters the application's name for you.

default   A string that you can use to specify default text in the text box. Entering a *default* argument can be a good idea both for cases when the default text is likely to be suitable and when you need to display sample text so that the user can understand what type of response you're looking for. Here's an example of default text being suitable: If you displayed an input box asking for the user's name, you could enter the Name value from the User Information tab of the Options dialog box as a suggestion.

xpos and **ypos**   Optional numeric values for specifying the on-screen position of the input box. *xpos* governs the horizontal position of the left edge of the input box from the left edge of the screen (not of the Word window), whereas *ypos* governs the vertical position of the top edge of the input box from the top of the screen. Each measurement is in *twips*, which are units of measurement not entirely unrelated to pixels. If you omit these two arguments, VBA will display your input boxes at the default position of halfway across the screen and one-third of the way down it.

 NOTE   The short version is that you don't really want to know what twips are. But a computer screen at 800x600 resolution is around 10,000 twips across and 8000 twips high. If you need to position your input boxes and dialog boxes precisely, experiment with twips at different screen resolutions until you achieve satisfactory results or until you give up in disgust.

helpfile and **context** Optional arguments for specifying the Help file and context in the Help file to jump to if the user summons help from the input box.

Again, you can omit any of the optional arguments. But if you want to use an optional argument later in the syntax sequence than one you've omitted, you need to indicate the omission with a comma or use named arguments.

Unlike message boxes, input boxes come with a predefined set of buttons—OK and Cancel, plus a Help button if you specify the *helpfile* and *context* parameters—so there's no argument for specifying the buttons for an input box. The following example declares the String variable strWhichOffice and assigns to it the result of the input box shown in Figure 11.11.

```
Dim strWhichOffice As String
strWhichOffice = InputBox( _
    "Enter the name of the office that you visited:",
    "Expense Assistant 2000", "Madrid", , , _
    "c:\Windows\Help\Procedure Help.hlp", 0)
```

FIGURE 11.11

The input box comes with a predefined set of buttons.

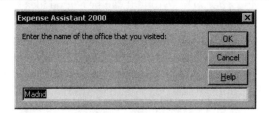

Retrieving Input from an Input Box

To retrieve input from an input box, you need to declare the numeric variable or String variable that will contain it. Here, the variable strWhichOffice will contain what the user enters in the input box:

```
Dim strWhichOffice
strWhichOffice = _
    InputBox("Enter the name of the office that you visited:", _
    "Expense Assistant 2000", "Madrid", , , _
    "c:\Windows\Help\Procedure Help.hlp", 0)
```

Once you've done that, and the user has entered a value or a string and chosen the OK button, you can use the value or string as usual in VBA. To make sure that the user has chosen the OK button, you can have VBA check to see that the input box hasn't returned a zero-length string (which it also returns if the user chooses the OK button with the text box empty) and take action accordingly:

```
strWhichOffice = InputBox _
    ("Enter the name of the office that you visited:", _
    "Expense Assistant 2000", "Madrid", , , _
    "c:\Windows\Help\Procedure Help.hlp", 0)
If strWhichOffice = "" Then End
```

When Message Boxes and Input Boxes Won't Suffice

As you've seen in this chapter, a strategically positioned message box can greatly enhance a procedure by enabling the user to make a choice at a turning point, or by presenting the user with important information. But once you've used message boxes for a while, you're apt to start noticing their limitations. You can present only a certain amount of information, and you're limited in the way you can display it (to whatever layout you can conjure up with new paragraphs, line breaks, tabs, and spaces). You can use only seven sets of buttons, which limit the possibilities of message boxes. While you *can* get creative and enter complex messages in message boxes to make the most use of the buttons they present, you'll usually do better to use a custom dialog box instead. As you'll see in Chapters 15 and 16, custom dialog boxes are relatively simple to create, and they give you far more power and flexibility than message boxes do. Figure 11.12 shows an instance where a dialog box would clearly be preferable to an overworked message box.

FIGURE 11.12

How to overuse a message box. If you're lucky, the user of the procedure will take enough time to figure out what you're trying to do with the message box, but you'd do better to use a dialog box instead.

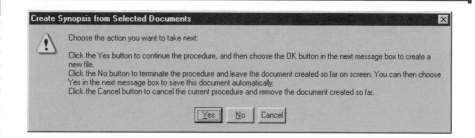

You'll generally want to avoid writing procedures that present the user with a number of choices via a sequence of message boxes. Consider the sequence of message boxes and input boxes shown in Figure 11.13. This sequence would be better combined into one dialog box.

This sequence of message boxes and input boxes could be combined into one dialog box.

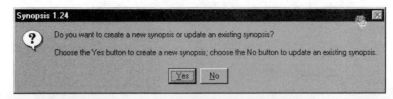

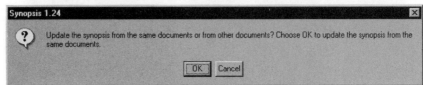

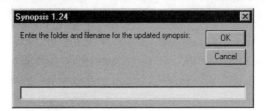

Similarly, input boxes are useful for retrieving a single piece of information from the user, but beyond that, their limitations quickly become apparent. If you find yourself planning to use two or more input boxes in immediate succession, that should raise a red flag to use a dialog box instead.

I'll show you how to create the simpler kinds of custom dialog boxes in Chapter 15 and the more complex kinds of dialog boxes in Chapter 16.

CHAPTER 12

Using Loops to Repeat Actions

As in life, so in VBA: At times, you may want to repeat an action to achieve a certain effect. Sometimes, you'll want to repeat an action a predetermined number of times: Break six eggs to make an omelet, or create six new documents based on a certain template. More often, you'll want to repeat an action until a certain condition is met: Buy two lottery tickets a week until you win more than $2,000 on the lottery, or repeat an action for every instance of a value that appears in an Excel spreadsheet. In these cases, you won't know when you'll triumph against the wretched odds of the lottery, and you won't know how many instances of the value will appear in the spreadsheet—you'll just carry on until the condition is met.

In VBA, you use *loops* to repeat actions. By using loops, you can transform a simple recorded macro into one that repeats itself as appropriate for the material it's working on. VBA provides a number of expressions for creating loops in your code. In this chapter, you'll learn about the different types of loops and typical uses for each.

When Should You Use a Loop?

To repeat an action or a series of actions in VBA, you can either record that repetition into a macro by using the Macro Recorder (if the application in question supports the Macro Recorder), or edit a procedure containing the relevant commands and use Copy and Paste to repeat them. For example, you could record a macro containing the code for creating a new presentation based on the default template, open the macro in the Visual Basic Editor, and then copy that statement to five other lines to create a procedure that created six new presentations. But almost invariably, it's much better to use a loop structure to repeat the commands as necessary.

Loops have several straightforward advantages over simple repetition of code:

- Your procedures will be shorter—they will contain less code and fewer instructions—and easier to maintain.

- Your procedures will be more flexible: Instead of hard-coding the number of repetitions, you'll be able to control the number as necessary. (*Hard-coding* means writing fixed code as opposed to variable code.)

- Your procedures will be easier to test and debug, particularly for people other than you.

That said, if you just need to repeat one or more actions two or three times in a procedure, and that procedure will always need to repeat the action the same number of times, there's nothing wrong with hard-coding the procedure by repeating the code. It'll work fine, it's easy to do, and you won't have to spend time with the logic of loops. The code will likely be longer and a tad harder to maintain, but that's no big deal as long as it works.

The Lowdown on Loops

In VBA, a loop is a structure that repeats a number of statements, looping back to the beginning of the structure once it has finished executing them. Each cycle of execution of a loop is called an *iteration*.

There are two basic categories of loops:

- *Fixed-iteration loops* repeat a set number of times.
- *Indefinite loops* repeat a flexible number of times.

The running of either type of loop is controlled by the *loop invariant*, also called the *loop determinant*. This can be either a numeric expression or a logical expression. Fixed-iteration loops typically use numeric expressions (for example, to run through five iterations of a loop), whereas indefinite loops typically use logical expressions (for example, to continue taking an action until the end of the document is reached).

VBA provides expressions for the following loops:

- Repeating an action or a sequence of actions a given number of times (For... Next)
- Repeating an action or a sequence of actions once for each object in a collection (For Each... Next)
- Performing an action or a sequence of actions if a condition is True and continuing to perform it until the condition becomes False (Do While... Loop or the mostly obsolete While... Wend loop); or vice versa, performing the action or sequence of actions while a condition is False until it becomes True (Do Until... Loop)
- Performing an action or a sequence of actions once, and then repeating it while a condition is True until it becomes False (Do... Loop While); or vice versa, performing the action or sequence of actions once and repeating it while a condition is False until it becomes True (Do... Loop Until)

Let's look first at the For... loops, which deal with a fixed number of repetitions.

Using *For...* Loops for Fixed Repetitions

For... loops execute for a fixed number of times. For... Next loops repeat for a number of times of your choosing, while For Each... Next loops execute once for each element in the specified collection.

For... Next Loops

For... Next loops provide you with a straightforward way to repeat an action or a sequence of actions a given number of times, specified by a counter variable. The counter variable can be hard-coded into the procedure, passed from an input box or dialog box, or even passed from a value generated by a different part of the procedure (or a different procedure).

Syntax

The syntax for For... Next loops is as follows:

```
For counter = start To end [Step stepsize]
    [statements]
[Exit For]
    [statements]
Next [counter]
```

The following list explains the components of the syntax. As we saw in earlier chapters, the brackets show optional items and the italics show placeholders.

counter A numeric variable or an expression that produces a number. By default, VBA increases the *counter* value by an increment of 1 with each iteration of the loop, but you can change this increment by using the optional Step keyword and *stepsize* argument. Note that *counter* is required in the For statement and is optional in the Next statement; however, it's a good idea to include *counter* in the Next statement to make your code clear, particularly when you're using multiple For... Next statements in the same procedure or nesting one For... Next statement within another.

start A numeric variable or numeric expression giving the starting value for *counter*.

end A numeric variable or numeric expression giving the ending value for *counter*.

stepsize A numeric variable or numeric expression specifying how much to increase the value of *counter*. To use *stepsize*, use the Step keyword and specify the *stepsize* variable. As I just mentioned, *stepsize* is 1 by default, but you can use any positive or negative value (depending on whether you want the value to increase or decrease).

Exit For A statement for exiting a For loop.

Next The keyword indicating the end of the loop. Again, you can specify the optional *counter* here to make your code clear.

Here's what happens in a For... Next loop:

1. When VBA enters the loop at the For statement, it assigns the *start* value to *counter*. It then executes the statements in the loop; when it reaches the Next statement, it increments *counter* by 1 or by the specified *stepsize*, and loops back to the For statement.

2. VBA then checks the *counter* variable against the *end* variable. When *stepsize* is positive, if *counter* is greater than *end*, VBA terminates the loop and continues execution of the procedure with the statement immediately after the Next statement (which could be any action, or the end of the procedure). If *counter* is less than or equal to *end*, VBA repeats the statements in the loop, increases *counter* by 1 or by *stepsize*, and loops back to the For statement again. (For a loop in which *stepsize* is negative, the loop continues while *counter* is greater than or equal to *end* and ends when *counter* is greater than *end*.)

3. The Exit For statement exits the For loop early. You'll look at how to use the Exit For statement later in this chapter.

I'll show you the different uses of For... Next loops a little farther on in the chapter as well.

Straightforward *For... Next* Loops

In a straightforward For... Next loop, you first specify a counter variable and the starting and ending values for it:

```
For i = 1 to 200
```

Here, i is the counter variable, 1 is the starting value, and 200 is the ending value. As mentioned earlier, by default VBA will increase the counter variable by an increment of 1 with each iteration of the loop. Here, it will be 1, 2, 3, and so on up to 200; a value of 201 (or greater—although in this example, it can't reach a greater value than 201 because the *stepsize* is 1) will terminate the loop. You can also use a Step keyword to specify a different increment, either positive or negative; more on this in the next section.

 NOTE i is the archetypal integer counter variable used in a For... Next loop. Use it for your loops if you want to; use something else if that makes you feel more comfortable.

Next, you specify the actions to perform in the loop, followed by the Next keyword to end the loop:

```
Application.StatusBar = _
    "Please wait while Excel checks for lunatic prices: " & i & "..."
Next i
```

This code will produce a status bar readout indicating Excel's progress in checking your spreadsheet for improbable values.

So far, so good. But how about something a little more practical? Say you need to check every paragraph in Word documents you receive from contributors to make sure they don't contain any unsuitable formatting. You could use a loop that runs from 1 to the number of paragraphs in the active document (which is stored in the Count property of the Paragraphs collection in the ActiveDocument object) to check each paragraph in turn and provide a reference point for the user in the status bar display:

```
Dim i As Integer
For i = 1 To ActiveDocument.Paragraphs.Count
    CheckParagraphForIllegalFormatting
    Application.StatusBar = _
        "Please wait while Word checks the formatting in " _
        & " this document: Paragraph " & i & " out of " _
        & ActiveDocument.Paragraphs.Count & "..."
    Selection.MoveDown Unit:=wdParagraph, _
        Count:=1, Extend:=wdMove
Next i
```

This code snippet should be started at the beginning of the document. It runs the CheckParagraphForIllegalFormatting procedure on the current paragraph, displays a message in the status bar indicating which paragraph out of the total number it's working on, and then moves down a paragraph. When VBA reaches the Next statement, it increases the i counter by 1 (because no *stepsize* variable is specified) and loops back to the For statement, where it compares the value of i to the value of ActiveDocument.Paragraphs.Count. The procedure will continue to loop until i has reached the value of ActiveDocument.Paragraphs.Count, which will be the final iteration of the loop.

Likewise, you could use a simple For... Next loop to quickly build the structure of a timesheet or work log in Excel. The following statements use a For... Next loop to insert the labels 1.00 through 24:00 in the current column in the active sheet of the active workbook:

```
Dim i As Integer
For i = 1 To 24
    ActiveCell.FormulaR1C1 = i & ":00"
    ActiveCell.Offset(RowOffset:=1, ColumnOffset:=0).Select
Next i
```

Here, the Selection.TypeText statement inserts the automatically increased string for the counter—i—together with a colon and two zeroes (to create a time format) and a vbCr carriage-return character to create a new paragraph after each. The loop runs from i = 1 to i = 24 and stops when the automatic increase takes i to 25.

For... Next Loops with Step Values

If increasing the counter variable by the default 1 doesn't suit your purpose, you can use the Step keyword to specify a different increment or decrement. For example, the following statement increases the counter variable by 20, so the sequence will be 0, 20, 40, 60, 80, 100:

```
For i = 0 to 100 Step 20
```

You can also use a decrement by specifying a negative Step value:

```
For i = 1000 to 0 Step -100
```

This statement produces the sequence 1000, 900, 800, and so on, down to 0.

Instead of the "x out of y" countdown example given in the previous section, you could produce a NASA-style countdown running from ActiveDocument.Paragraphs .Count to zero:

```
Dim i As Integer
For i = ActiveDocument.Paragraphs.Count To 0 Step -1
    CheckParagraphForIllegalFormatting
    Application.StatusBar = _
        "Please wait while Word checks the formatting in this document: " & i
    Selection.MoveDown Unit:=wdParagraph, Count:=1, Extend:=wdMove
Next i
```

Using an Input Box to Drive a *For... Next* Loop

Sometimes you'll be able to hard-code the number of iterations into a For... Next loop, as in the previous examples. Depending on the type of work you're involved in, this will probably be the exception rather than the rule. At other times, you'll take a number from another operation, such as the `ActiveDocument.Paragraphs.Count` property in the example above. But often you'll need to use input from the user to drive the loop. The easiest way of doing this is to have the user enter the value into an input box.

For example, Listing 12.1 contains a simple procedure named `CreateDocuments` that displays an input box prompting the user to enter the number of documents they want to create. It then uses a For... Next loop to create the documents in WordPerfect.

Listing 12.1

```
1.  Sub CreateDocuments()
2.      Dim intDocs As Integer
3.      Dim i As Integer
4.      intDocs = InputBox _
              ("Enter the number of documents to create:", _
              "Create Documents")
5.      For i = 1 To intDocs
6.          PerfectScript.FileNew
7.      Next i
8.  End Sub
```

Analysis

Here's what happens in the `CreateDocuments` procedure in Listing 12.1:

- Line 2 declares the Integer variable `intDocs`, and line 3 declares the Integer variable `i`.

- Line 4 displays an input box prompting the user to enter the number of documents they want to create.

- Lines 5 through 7 contain a For... Next loop that runs from `i = 1` to `i = intDocs` with the default increment of 1 per iteration. Each iteration of the loop executes the `PerfectScript.FileNew` statement in line 6, creating a new document based on the default project.

WARNING WordPerfect can handle a maximum of nine open documents at a time, so the highest number you can practically enter in the input box is nine minus the number of documents currently open. Entering a larger number in the input box will result in VBA's trying to create a new document when nine are already open, which will cause an error.

Using a Dialog Box Control to Drive a *For... Next* Loop

For those occasions when an input box won't suffice, you can easily use a value from a dialog box to drive a For... Next loop. I haven't yet demonstrated how to create dialog boxes, but in this section you'll get a sneak preview by looking at a `Create_Folders` procedure designed to reduce the tedium of creating multiple folders with predictable names, such as for the chapters of a book.

For the sake of argument, say that you're using a four-digit number to identify the book (perhaps part of the book's international standard book number, or ISBN), the letter *c* for *chapter*, and a two-digit number to identify the chapter. So you'd end up with folders named *1234c01*, *1234c02*, *1234c03*, and so on—simple enough to create manually, but very boring if you needed more than a dozen or so.

In its simplest form, this dialog box would provide a text box for the number of folders to be created (though you could also use a drop-down list for this, or even a spinner) and a text box for the ISBN of the book. It might look like the example shown in Figure 12.1.

FIGURE 12.1

When you need more information than an input box can supply, use a custom dialog box to drive a For... Next loop.

You display the dialog box by using the Show method, perhaps with a Load statement first, like this:

```
Load frmCreateFolders2000
frmCreateFolders2000.Show
```

I've named my dialog box frmCreateFolders2000; as before, any valid VBA name will work. The first text box—identified with the Number Of Folders To Create label—is named txtFolders; the second text box is named txtISBN.

The Cancel button here has an End statement attached to its Click event, so that if the user clicks it, VBA ends the procedure:

```
Private Sub cmdCancel_Click()
    End
End Sub
```

The OK button in the dialog box has the code shown in Listing 12.2 attached to its Click event.

Listing 12.2

```
1.    Private Sub cmdOK_Click()
2.
3.        Dim strMsg As String
4.        Dim strFolder As String
5.        Dim i As Integer
6.
7.        frmCreateFolders2000.Hide
8.        Unload frmCreateFolders2000
9.        strMsg = "The Create_Folders procedure has created " _
              & "the following folders: " & vbCr & vbCr
10.
11.       For i = 1 To txtFolders.Value
12.           strFolder = txtISBN.Value & "c" & Format(i, "0#")
13.           MkDir strFolder
14.           strMsg = strMsg & "    " & strFolder & vbCr
15.       Next i
16.
17.       MsgBox strMsg, vbOKOnly + vbInformation, _
              "Create Folders"
18.
19.   End Sub
```

Analysis

Here's the breakdown of the cmdOK_Click procedure in Listing 12.2, which runs when the user clicks the OK button in the dialog box:

- Line 2 is a spacer.
- Line 3 declares the String variable strMsg, which will contain a string to display in a message box at the end of the procedure.
- Line 4 declares the String variable strFolder, which will contain the name of the current folder to create in each iteration of the loop.
- Line 5 declares the Integer variable i, which will be the counter variable for the For... Next loop.
- Line 6 is a spacer.
- Line 7 hides frmCreateFolders2000.
- Line 8 unloads frmCreateFolders2000.
- Line 9 assigns some introductory text to strMsg, ending it with a colon and two vbCr carriage-return characters to make the start of a list.
- Line 10 is a spacer.
- Lines 11 through 15 contain the For... Next loop that creates the folders. Line 11 causes the loop to run from i = 1 to i = txtFolders.Value, the value supplied by the user in the Number Of Folders To Create text box. Line 12 assigns to the strFolder String variable the Value property of the txtISBN text box, the letter *c*, and the value of i formatted via the Format function to include a leading zero if it's a single digit (so that 1 will appear as 01 , and so on). Line 13 uses the MkDir command with strFolder to create a folder (that is, make a directory— the old DOS command mkdir lives on in VBA) of that name. Line 14 adds some spaces (for an indent), the contents of strFolder, and a vbCr character to strMsg. Line 15 then loops back to the For statement, incrementing the i counter. VBA then compares the i counter to txtFolders.Value and repeats the loop as necessary.

 NOTE This procedure creates the new folders in the current folder, without giving the user a choice of location. Chances are you won't want to do this in real-life situations. You might want to change a folder to a set location (so as to keep all the project files together); but more likely you'll want to let the user choose a suitable location (perhaps by displaying a common dialog box).

For Each... Next Loops

The For Each... Next loop, which is unique to Visual Basic, has the same basic premise as the For... Next loop—you're working with a known number of repetitions. In this case, though, the known number is the number of objects in a collection, such as the Slides collection in a presentation or the Documents collection of AutoCAD or Word documents. For example, you could choose to take an action for each Slide object in a presentation—you wouldn't need to know how many slides were in the collection, provided there were at least one. (If there were none, nothing would happen.)

Syntax

The syntax for the For Each... Next statement is straightforward:

```
For Each object In collection
    [statements]
    [Exit For]
    [statements]
Next [object]
```

VBA starts by evaluating the number of objects in the specified collection. It then executes the statements in the loop for the first of those objects. When it reaches the Next keyword, it loops back to the For Each line, reevaluates the number of objects, and performs further iterations as appropriate.

Here's an example: The Documents collection contains the open documents in Word. So you could create a straightforward procedure to close all the open documents by using a For Each... Next loop like this:

```
For Each Doc in Documents
    Doc.Close SaveChanges:=wdSaveChanges
Next
```

VBA closes each open document in turn by using the Close method. The statement uses the wdSaveChanges constant for the SaveChanges argument to specify that any unsaved changes in the document be saved when the document is closed. As long as there are open documents in the Documents collection, VBA repeats the loop, thus closing all open documents and then terminating the procedure.

 TIP This example provides a straightforward illustration of how a For Each... Next loop works, but you probably wouldn't want to use the example in practice; instead, you'd probably use the Close method with the Documents collection (which contains all the open documents) to close all the open documents more simply. However, you might use a For Each... Next loop to check each document for certain characteristics before closing it.

Using an *Exit For* Statement

As you saw earlier in this chapter when looking at the syntax for For statements, you can use one or more Exit For statements to exit a For loop if a certain condition is met. Exit For statements are optional and are seldom necessary; if you find yourself needing to use Exit For statements in all your procedures, there's probably something wrong with the loops you're constructing. Still, if they work for you, that's fine by me.

On those occasions when you do need Exit For statements to exit a loop early, you'll typically use them with straightforward conditions. For example, in Word, if you wanted to close open windows until you reached a certain document that you knew to be open, you could use an Exit For statement like this:

```
Dim Doc As Document
For Each Doc in Documents
    If Doc.Name = "Document1" Then Exit For
    Doc.Close
Next Doc
```

This For Each... Next statement checks the Name property of the document to see if it's Document1; if it is, the Exit For statement causes VBA to exit the loop. Otherwise, VBA closes the document and returns to the start of the loop.

You can also use multiple Exit For statements if you need to. For example, you might need to check two or more conditions during the actions performed in the loop.

Using *Do...* Loops for Variable Numbers of Repetitions

Do loops give you more flexibility than For loops in that you can test for conditions in them and direct the flow of the procedure accordingly. The various permutations of Do loops include the following:

- Do While... Loop
- Do... Loop While
- Do Until... Loop
- Do... Loop Until

These loops break down into two categories:

- Loops that test a condition before performing any action. Do While... Loop and Do Until... Loop loops fall into this category.
- Loops that perform an action before testing a condition. Do... Loop While and Do... Loop Until fall into this category.

The difference between the two types of loop in each category is that each `While` loop repeats itself *while* a condition is `True` (until the condition becomes `False`), whereas each `Until` loop repeats itself *until* a condition becomes `True` (while the condition is `False`). This means that you can get by to some extent using only the `While` loops or only the `Until` loops if you're feeling lazy—you'll just need to set up some of your conditions the other way around. For example, you could use a `Do While... Loop` loop with a condition of x < 100 or a `Do Until... Loop` loop with a condition of x = 100 to achieve the same effect.

In this discussion, I'll assume that you want to learn about all the different kinds of loops so that you can diligently use each when it's most appropriate. We'll start with the `Do While... Loop` loop, which I find to be the most useful of the four types.

Do While... Loop Loops

In a `Do While... Loop` loop, you specify a condition that has to be `True` for the actions in the loop to be executed; if the condition isn't `True`, the actions aren't executed and the loop ends. For example, you might want to search a document for an instance of a particular word or phrase and take action once you find it. Figure 12.2 shows a `Do While... Loop` loop.

FIGURE 12.2

A `Do While... Loop` loop tests for a condition before performing the actions contained in the loop.

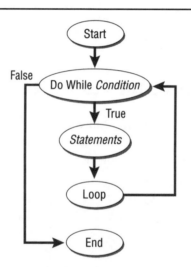

Syntax

The syntax for the `Do While... Loop` loop is straightforward:

```
Do While condition
    [statements]
```

```
        [Exit Do]
        [statements]
    Loop
```

While the *condition* is met (Do While), the statements in the loop are executed. The Loop keyword returns execution to the Do While line, which is then reevaluated. If the *condition* remains True, the loop continues; if the *condition* is False, execution continues with the statement on the line after the Loop keyword. You can use one or more Exit Do statements to break out of the loop as necessary.

Say you wanted to construct a glossary from a long Word document that used italics to explain main terms in the body text and list paragraphs (which both used Times New Roman font) without picking up italic variable names in code snippets. You could command Word to search for Times New Roman text with the italic attribute; if Word found instances of the text, it would take the appropriate actions, such as selecting the sentence containing the term, together with the next sentence (or the rest of the paragraph), and copying it to the end of another document. Then it would continue the search, performing the loop until it found no more instances of italic Times New Roman text.

Listing 12.3 shows an example of how such a procedure might be constructed with a Do While... Loop loop. This listing includes a number of commands that we haven't examined yet and that I'll just mention briefly here as an illustration of how the loop works.

Listing 12.3

```
1.    Sub GenerateGlossary()
2.
3.        Dim strSource As String
4.        Dim strDestination As String
5.        Dim strGlossaryName As String
6.
7.        strSource = ActiveWindow.Caption
8.        strGlossaryName = InputBox _
                ("Enter the name for the glossary document.", _
                "Create Glossary 2000")
9.        If strGlossaryName = "" Then End
10.
11.        Documents.Add
12.        ActiveDocument.SaveAs FileName:=strGlossaryName, _
                FileFormat:=wdFormatDocument
13.        strDestination = ActiveWindow.Caption
```

```
14.      Windows(strSource).Activate
15.
16.      Selection.HomeKey Unit:=wdStory
17.      Selection.Find.ClearFormatting
18.      Selection.Find.Font.Italic = True
19.      Selection.Find.Font.Name = "Times New Roman"
20.      Selection.Find.Text = ""
21.      Selection.Find.Execute
22.
23.      Do While Selection.Find.Found
24.          Selection.Copy
25.          Selection.MoveRight Unit:=wdCharacter, _
                 Count:=1, Extend:=wdMove
26.          Windows(strDestination).Activate
27.          Selection.EndKey Unit:=wdStory
28.          Selection.Paste
29.          Selection.TypeParagraph
30.          Windows(strSource).Activate
31.          Selection.Find.Execute
32.      Loop
33.
34.      Windows(strDestination).Activate
35.      ActiveDocument.Save
36.      ActiveDocument.Close
37.
38.  End Sub
```

Analysis

The GenerateGlossary procedure in Listing 12.3 pulls italic items in the Times New Roman font from the current document and inserts them in a new document that it creates and saves. Here's what happens:

- Line 1 begins the procedure, and line 2 is a spacer.

- Lines 3, 4, and 5 declare the String variables strSource, strDestination, and strGlossaryName, respectively. Line 6 is a spacer.

- Line 7 assigns to the String variable strSource the Caption property of the active window. It will use this variable to activate the document as necessary throughout the procedure.

- Line 8 displays an input box requesting the user to enter a name for the document that will contain the glossary entries pulled from the current document. It stores the string the user enters in the variable `strGlossaryName`.

- Line 9 then compares `GlossaryName` to an empty string (`""`) to make sure that the user hasn't clicked the Cancel button to cancel the procedure or clicked the OK button in the input box without entering a name in the text box. If `Glossary-Name` is an empty string, line 9 uses an `End` statement to terminate execution of the procedure.

- Provided line 9 hasn't stopped the procedure in its tracks, the procedure rolls on. Line 10 is a spacer. Line 11 then creates a new document based on the `Normal` `.dot` global template. This will become the glossary document.

- Line 12 saves the document with the name the user specified in the input box.

- Line 13 stores the `Caption` property of this document in the `strDestination` variable, again making it available to activate this document as necessary throughout the procedure. You now have the source document identified by the `strSource` variable and the destination document identified by the `strDestination` variable.)

- Line 14 uses the `Activate` method to activate the `strSource` window. Line 15 is a spacer.

- Line 16 uses the `HomeKey` method of the `Selection` object with the `wdStory` unit to move the insertion point to the beginning of the document, which is where the procedure needs to start working to catch all the italicized words in Times New Roman.

- Lines 17 through 20 detail the Find operation the procedure needs to perform: Line 17 removes any formatting applied to the current Find item; line 18 sets the Find feature to find italic formatting; line 19 sets Find to find Times New Roman text; and line 20 specifies the search string, which is an empty string (`""`) that causes Find to search only for the specified formatting.

- Line 21 then performs the Find operation by using the `Execute` method. Line 22 is a spacer.

- Lines 23 through 32 implement the `Do While... Loop` loop. Line 23 expresses the condition for the loop: `While Selection.Find.Found` (while the Find operation is able to find an instance of the italic Times New Roman text specified in the previous lines). While this condition is met (is `True`), the commands contained in the loop will execute.

- Line 24 copies the selection (the item found with italic Times New Roman formatting).

- Line 25 moves the insertion point one character to the right, effectively deselecting the selection and getting the procedure ready to search for the next instance in the document. You need to move the insertion point off the selection to the right so that the next Find operation doesn't find the same instance. (If the procedure were searching up through the document instead of down through it, you'd need to move the insertion point off the selection to the left instead by using a `Selection.MoveLeft` statement.)

- Line 26 activates the `strDestination` window, putting Word's focus in it.

- Line 27 then moves the insertion point to the end of the glossary document, and line 28 pastes the copied item in at the position of the insertion point. Moving to the end of the document isn't strictly necessary here, provided that the `Normal.dot` global template doesn't contain any text—if `Normal.dot` is empty, the new document created in line 11 will be empty too, and the start and end of the document will be in the same position. And after each paste operation, Word positions the insertion point after the pasted item. However, if `Normal.dot` contains text, this step is necessary, so I've included it here.

- Line 29 uses the `TypeParagraph` method of the `Selection` object to enter a paragraph after the text inserted by the paste operation.

- Line 30 activates the `strSource` document once more, and line 31 repeats the Find operation.

- The `Loop` statement in line 32 then loops execution of the procedure back to line 23, where the `Do While Selection.Find.Found` condition evaluates whether this latest Find operation was successful (`True`).

- If it was successful, the loop continues; if it wasn't, execution of the procedure continues at line 34, which activates the glossary document again. Line 35 saves the active document (the glossary document, because it was just activated), and line 26 closes it.

- Line 37 is a spacer, and line 38 ends the procedure.

Do... Loop While Loops

A Do... Loop While loop is similar to a Do While... Loop loop, except that in the Do... Loop While loop, the actions in the loop are run at least once, whether the condition is True or False. If the condition is True, the loop continues to run until the condition becomes False. Figure 12.3 shows a Do... Loop While loop.

In a Do... Loop While loop, the actions in the loop run once before the condition is tested.

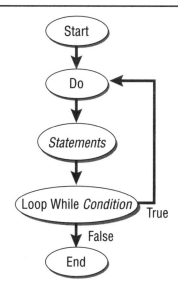

If Do While... Loop loops make immediate sense to you, Do... Loop While loops may well strike you as a little bizarre—you're going to take an action *before* checking a condition? The truth is, Do... Loop While loops can be very useful, but they lend themselves to different situations than Do While... Loop loops.

Consider the lottery example from the beginning of the chapter. In that situation, you execute the action before you check the condition that controls the loop: First, you buy a lottery ticket, and then you check to see if you've won. If you haven't won, or you've won only a paltry sum that doesn't meet your wealth cutoff point, you loop back and buy more tickets for the next lottery. (Actually, this is logically a Do... Loop Until loop rather than a Do... Loop While loop, because you continue the loop while the condition is False; when you win a suitably large amount, the condition becomes True.) Likewise, in a procedure, you may want to take an action and then check whether you need to repeat it. For example, you might want to apply special formatting to a paragraph, then check to see if other paragraphs needed the same treatment.

Syntax

The syntax for a Do... Loop While loop is as follows:

```
Do
    [statements]
    [Exit Do]
    [statements]
Loop While condition
```

VBA performs the statements included in the loop, after which the Loop While line evaluates the condition. If it's True, VBA returns execution to the Do line, and the loop continues to execute; if it's False, execution continues at the line after the Loop While line.

As an example of a Do... Loop While loop, consider this crude password checker that you could use to prevent someone from running a procedure without supplying the correct password:

```
Dim varPassword As Variant
Do
    varPassword = InputBox _
        ("Enter the password to start the procedure:", _
        "Check Password 1.0")
Loop While varPassword <> "CorrectPassword"
```

Here the Do... Loop While loop displays an input box for the user to enter the password. The Loop While line compares the value from the input box, stored in var-Password, against the correct password (here, CorrectPassword). If the two aren't equal (varPassword <> "CorrectPassword"), the loop continues, displaying the input box again.

This loop is just an example—you wouldn't want to use it as it is in real life. Here's why: Choosing the Cancel button in the input box causes it to return a blank string, which also doesn't match the correct password, causing the loop to run again. The security is perfect; the problem is that the only way to end the loop is for the user to supply the correct password. If they're unable to do so, they will see the input box ad infinitum. If you wanted to build a password-checking procedure along these lines, you might specify a number of incorrect passwords that the user could enter (perhaps three) before the procedure terminated itself, or you could simply use an End statement to terminate the procedure if the user entered a blank string:

```
Do
    varPassword = InputBox _
        ("Enter the password to start the procedure:", _
        "Check Password 1.0")
    If varPassword = "" Then End
Loop While varPassword <> "CorrectPassword"
```

Do Until... Loop Loops

A Do Until... Loop loop is similar to a Do While... Loop loop, except that in a Do Until... Loop loop, the loop runs while the condition is False and stops running when it's True. Figure 12.4 shows a Do Until... Loop loop.

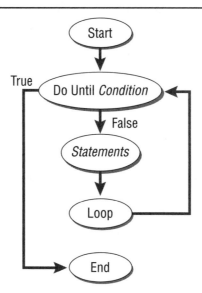

A Do Until... Loop *loop runs while the condition is* False *and stops running when the condition becomes* True.

NOTE Do Until... Loop loops are useful if you're not of a negative mindset and you need a condition to run when it's False. Otherwise, you can achieve the same effects using Do While... Loop loops and inverting the relative condition.

Syntax

The syntax for Do Until... Loop loops is as follows:

```
Do Until condition
    statements
    [Exit Do]
    [statements]
Loop
```

When VBA enters the loop, it checks the *condition*. If the *condition* is False, VBA executes the statements in the loop, encounters the Loop keyword, and loops back to the beginning of the loop, reevaluating the *condition* as it goes. If the *condition* is True, VBA terminates the loop and continues execution at the statement after the Loop line.

For example, consider our lottery experience redefined as a procedure in Listing 12.4.

Listing 12.4

```
1.   Sub Lottery_1()
2.       Dim sngWin As Single
3.       Do Until sngWin > 2000
4.           sngWin = Rnd * 2100
5.           MsgBox sngWin, , "Lottery"
6.       Loop
7.   End Sub
```

Analysis

The procedure in Listing 12.4 is as straightforward as it is frivolous:

- Line 2 declares the Single variable sngWin. Line 3 then starts a Do Until loop with the condition that sngWin > 2000—the value of sngWin variable must be larger than 2000 for the loop to end; until then, the loop will continue to run.

- Line 4 assigns to sngWin the result of 2100 multiplied a random number produced by the Rnd function, which generates random numbers between 0 and 1. (So the loop needs to receive a random number of a little more than .95 to end—a chance of a little less than one in 20, or considerably better than any lottery on which I've been foolish enough to waste my money so far.)

- Line 5 displays a simple message box containing the current value of the Win variable so that you can see how lucky you are.

- Line 6 contains the Loop keyword that completes the loop.

- Line 7 ends the procedure.

Listing 12.5 shows a more useful example of a Do Until loop in Word.

Listing 12.5

```
1.   Sub FindNextHeading()
2.       Do Until Left(Selection.Paragraphs(1).Style, 7) = "Heading"
3.           Selection.MoveDown Unit:=wdParagraph, _
                 Count:=1, Extend:=wdMove
4.       Loop
5.   End Sub
```

Analysis

Listing 12.5 contains a simple procedure that moves the insertion point to the next heading in the active document in Word. Here's how it works:

- Line 2 starts a Do Until loop that ends with the Loop keyword in line 4. The condition for the loop is that the seven left-most characters in the name of the style for the first paragraph in the current selection—Left(Selection.Paragraphs(1).Style, 7)—match the string Heading. This will match any of the Heading styles (the built-in styles Heading 1 through 9, or any style the user has defined whose name starts with *Heading*).

- Until the condition is met, VBA executes the statement in line 3, which moves the selection down by one paragraph.

Do... Loop Until Loops

The Do... Loop Until loop is similar to the Do Until... Loop loop, except that in the former case, the actions in the loop are run at least once, whether the condition is True or False. If the condition is False, the loop continues to run until the condition becomes True. Figure 12.5 shows a Do... Loop Until loop.

FIGURE 12.5

In a Do... Loop Until *loop, the actions in the loop are run once before the condition is tested.*

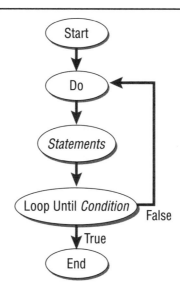

Syntax

The syntax for Do... Loop Until loops is as follows:

```
Do
    [statements]
    [Exit Do]
    [statements]
Loop Until condition
```

VBA enters the loop at the Do line and executes the *statements* in the loop. When it encounters the Loop Until line, it checks the *condition*. If it's False, VBA loops back to the Do line and again executes the *statements*; if it's True, VBA terminates the loop and continues execution at the line after the Loop Until line.

As an example, say you wanted to continue displaying an input box for adding new worksheets quickly to a workbook until the user chose the Cancel button or entered an empty string in the text box. You could use code such as that shown in Listing 12.6.

Listing 12.6

```
1.  Sub Create_Worksheets()
2.      Dim strNewSheet As String
3.      Do
4.          strNewSheet = InputBox _
                ("Enter the name for the new worksheet " _
                & "(31 characters max.):", "Add Worksheets")
5.          If strNewSheet <> "" Then
6.              ActiveWorkbook.Worksheets.Add
7.              ActiveSheet.Name = strNewSheet
8.          End If
9.      Loop Until strNewSheet = ""
10. End Sub
```

Analysis

Here's what happens in the Create_Worksheets procedure:

- Line 2 declares the String variable strNewSheet.
- Line 3 begins a Do... Loop Until loop.

- Line 4 displays an input box asking the user to enter the name for the new worksheet.
- Line 5 uses an If statement to make sure that strNewSheet is not an empty string. If it's not, line 6 adds a new worksheet to the active workbook, and line 7 assigns to the active sheet (the new sheet) the value of strNewSheet. Line 8 ends the If statement.
- Line 9 contains a Loop Until strNewSheet = "" statement that causes the procedure to loop back to the Do line until the user enters an empty string in the input box.
- Line 10 ends the procedure.

Using an *Exit Do* Statement

As with an Exit For statement in a For loop, you can use an Exit Do statement to exit a Do loop without executing the rest of the statements in it. Again, the Exit Do statement is optional, and you'll probably want to use Exit Do statements relatively seldom in your loops—at least, if the loops are properly designed.

When you do need an Exit Do statement, you'll generally use it with a condition. We could make our lottery a little more interesting by adding an If condition with an Exit Do statement to take effect if the win is less than a certain amount—say, $500, as in Listing 12.7.

Listing 12.7

```
1.  Sub Lottery_2()
2.      Dim sngWin As Single
3.      Do Until sngWin > 2000
4.          sngWin = Rnd * 2100
5.          If sngWin < 500 Then
6.              MsgBox "Tough luck. You have been disqualified.", _
                    vbOKOnly + vbCritical, "Lottery"
7.              Exit Do
8.          End If
9.          MsgBox sngWin, , "Lottery"
10.     Loop
11.  End Sub
```

Analysis

The procedure in Listing 12.7 works in the same way as the previous one, except that line 5 introduces a new If condition. If the variable sngWin is less than 500, the statements in lines 6 and 7 run. Line 6 displays a message box announcing that the player has been disqualified from the lottery, and line 7 exits the Do loop.

Exit Do: **The Sign of a Sinner?**

Some people consider using an Exit Do statement to exit a Do loop a method of last resort, or at least clumsy programming. Others disagree, and Visual Basic stays mum on the subject, patiently executing whatever valid code it's given.

Truth be told, there's no harm in using an Exit Do statement, but then again, you can often create code that avoids using an Exit Do statement but has the same effect. For example, a condition that you check in the middle of the loop to decide whether to exit the loop can often be built into the main condition of the loop by using an operator such as And, Or, or Not.

If this code is simple, you might be better off using it. But if it's a severe pain in the anatomy to create and maintain, there's no good reason to force yourself to use it when an Exit Do statement will do the trick instead.

While... Wend Loops

In addition to the For... Next loop, the For Each... Next loop, and the four flavors of Do loops that we've examined so far in this chapter, VBA also supports the While... Wend loop. While... Wend is VBA's version of the While... Wend looping structure used by earlier programming languages, such as the WordBasic programming language used with versions of Word up to and including Word 95. VBA includes While... Wend more for compatibility with those earlier versions than as a recommended tool in its own right, but you can use it if you choose to. To some extent, the Do loops supersede While... Wend, but it works fine.

The syntax of a `While...Wend` loop is as follows:

```
While condition
    [statements]
Wend
```

While the *condition* is True, VBA executes the *statements* in the loop. When it reaches the `Wend` (While End, not what you do on your way home from the bar) keyword, it returns to the `While` statement and evaluates the *condition* again. When the *condition* evaluates as `False`, the statements in the loop are no longer executed, and execution moves to the statement after the `Wend` statement.

As an absurdly simple `While...Wend` loop using Word, consider these statements:

```
While Documents.Count < 10
    Documents.Add
Wend
```

While the number of documents in the `Documents` collection (measured here by the `Count` property of the `Documents` collection) is smaller than 10, the loop runs. Each time through, the `Documents.Add` statement in the second line creates a new document based on the Normal template. After the new document is created, the `Wend` statement in the third line returns execution to the first line, where the `While` condition is evaluated again.

 WARNING   When using a `While...Wend` loop, make sure the only way for execution to enter the loop is by passing through the gate of the `While` condition. Branching into the middle of a `While...Wend` loop (for example, by using a label and a `GoTo` statement) can cause errors.

Nesting Loops

You can nest one or more loops within another loop to create the pattern of repetition you need: You can nest one `For` loop inside another `For` loop, a `For` loop inside a `Do` loop, a `Do` loop inside a `For` loop, or a `Do` loop inside a `Do` loop.

For example, if you need to create a number of folders, each of which contains a number of subfolders, you could use a variation of the `Create_Folders` procedure you looked at earlier in the chapter.

The dialog box for the procedure will need another text box to contain the number of subfolders to create within each folder. In the example here, I've named the new dialog box frmCreateFoldersAndSubFolders and the text box for the number of subfolders txtHowManySubFolders. Figure 12.6 shows the dialog box.

FIGURE 12.6

*The Create Folders And
Subfolders dialog box*

Listing 12.8 shows the code attached to the Click event on the cmdOK button of the form.

Listing 12.8

```
1.   Private Sub cmdOK_Click()
2.
3.       Dim strStartingFolder As String
4.       Dim strFolderName As String
5.       Dim strSubfolderName As String
6.       Dim intSubfolder As Integer
7.       Dim i As Integer
8.
9.       frmCreateFoldersAndSubfolders.Hide
10.      Unload frmCreateFoldersAndSubfolders
11.
12.      strStartingFolder = CurDir
13.
14.      For i = 1 To txtHowManyFolders.Value
15.          strFolderName = txtISBN.Value & "c" & Format(i, "0#")
16.          MkDir strFolderName
17.          ChDir strFolderName
18.          For intSubfolder = 1 To txtHowManySubfolders.Value
19.              strSubfolderName = "Section" & intSubfolder
20.              MkDir strSubfolderName
21.          Next intSubfolder
```

```
22.          ChDir strStartingFolder
23.      Next i
24.
25.  End Sub
```

Analysis

Here's what the code in Listing 12.8 does:

- Line 1 begins the procedure, and line 25 ends it. Line 2 is a spacer.
- Lines 3 through 5 declare three String variables, strStartingFolder, strFolder-Name, and strSubfolderName, respectively.
- Line 6 declares the Integer variable intSubfolder, and line 7 declares the Integer variable i. Line 8 is a spacer.
- Line 9 hides the user form, and line 10 unloads it. Line 11 is a spacer.
- Line 12 stores the name of the current folder in the String variable strStarting-Folder. You'll need this variable to make sure everything happens in the appropriate folder later in the procedure. Line 13 is another spacer.
- Lines 14 through 16 and line 23 are essentially the same as in the previous procedure. They build the folder name out of the Value property of the txtISBN text box, the letter *c*, a two-digit number, and the i variable, and then use the MkDir statement to create the folder.
- Line 17 uses a ChDir statement to change folders to the folder that was just created, strFolderName.
- In line 18, the nested For… Next loop starts. This loop is controlled by the loop invariant intSubfolder and will run from intSubfolder = 1 to intSubfolder = txtHowManySubFolders.Value, which is the value entered by the user in the Number Of Subfolders To Create text box in the dialog box.
- Line 19 builds the String variable strSubfolderName out of the word *Section* and the value of the intSubfolder counter variable. For this procedure, you can assume that there will be fewer than 10 sections for each of the chapters, so you can stay with single-digit numbering.
- Line 20 creates the subfolder by using a MkDir statement with the strSubfolder-Name String variable.
- Line 21 uses the Next Subfolder statement to loop back to the beginning of the nested For… Next loop. VBA reevaluates the condition and repeats the loop as necessary.

- Line 22 changes folders back to strStartingFolder for the next iteration of the outside loop. (Otherwise, the next folder would be created within the current folder, strFolderName.)

- Line 23 then loops back to the beginning of the outer loop.

 TIP When nesting For loops, make sure that you use the *counter* argument to identify the loop that's ending. Using this argument makes your procedures much easier to read and may prevent VBA from springing any unpleasant surprises on you. As you'd expect, your nested loops must end in the exact reverse order of their starting, and the counters need to match.

 NOTE You can nest up to 16 levels of loops in VBA, but you'll be hard pressed to read even half that number of levels. If you find your code becoming this complicated, consider whether you can take a less tortuous approach to solve the problem more simply.

Avoiding Infinite Loops

If you create an infinite loop in a procedure, it will happily run forever and a day, or until your computer crashes. For example, one type of loop we haven't examined yet is the Do... Loop loop. As you can see in the example in Listing 12.9, without a condition attached to it, this structure creates an infinite loop.

Listing 12.9

```
1.  Sub InfiniteLoop()
2.      Dim x
3.      x = 1
4.      Do
5.          Application.StatusBar = _
                "Your computer is stuck in an endless loop: " & x
6.          x = x + 1
7.      Loop
8.  End Sub
```

Analysis

In Listing 12.9, Line 2 declares the variable x, and line 3 assigns it the value 1. Line 4 begins the Do loop, which displays a status-bar message and increases the value of x by 1. The effect of this loop is to display an annoying if informative message and an ever-increasing number on the status bar until you press Ctrl+Break to stop the procedure or until the value overflows the variable. This is all thoroughly pointless (except perhaps as part of a procedure for burning in a new computer), and is perhaps a good reason not to use the Do... Loop structure—at least not without a condition attached to one end of it.

No matter what type of loop you use, to avoid creating an infinite loop, you need to make sure the condition that will terminate the loop will be met at some point. For example, for an editing or cleanup procedure, you'll often want to perform an action until the end of the document is reached, and then stop. Often, you'll want to include some form of counting mechanism to make sure that a Do loop doesn't exceed a certain number of iterations.

In this chapter, you've seen the formal types of loops that are available as VBA commands. These For loops and Do loops are vital weapons in your VBA arsenal, and they're versatile enough to take care of almost all your looping needs.

CHAPTER 13

Making Decisions in Your Code

I n this chapter, I'll show you the conditional expressions that VBA provides for creating decision structures to direct the flow of your procedures. By using decision structures, you can cause your procedures to branch to different sections of code depending on such things as the value of a variable or expression, or which button the user chooses in a message box or dialog box.

VBA provides assorted flavors of If statements (some of which you've met without formal introduction in the previous chapters) suitable for making simple or complex decisions, as well as the heavy-duty Select Case statement for simplifying the coding of truly involved decisions.

You'll start by looking quickly at the comparison operators and logical operators you can use when building conditional expressions and logical expressions. Then you'll get into the If statements, which will occupy you for much of the chapter. Once you've got the hang of If statements, Select Case will be a snap.

How Do You Compare Things in VBA?

To compare things in VBA, you use *comparison operators* to specify what type of comparison you want to apply: Is one variable or expression equal to another; is one greater than another; is one less than or equal to another; and so on.

VBA supports the comparison operators shown in Table 13.1.

TABLE 13.1: VBA'S COMPARISON OPERATORS

Operator	Meaning	Example
=	Equal to	`If strMyString = "Hello" Then`
<>	Not equal to	`If x <> 5 Then`
<	Less than	`If y < 100 Then`
>	Greater than	`If strMyString > "handle" Then`
<=	Less than or equal to	`If intMyCash <= 10 Then`

>=	Greater than or equal to	`If Time >= 12:00 PM Then`
		`    MsgBox "It's afternoon"`
		`Else`
		`    MsgBox "It's morning."`
		`End If`

Is	Is the same object variable as	`If object1 Is Object2 Then`

The first six comparison operators shown in Table 13.1 are straightforward, particularly if you have pleasant memories of fifth-grade math classes. Numeric expressions are evaluated as normal. Alphabetical expressions are evaluated in alphabetical order: Because *ax* comes before *handle* in alphabetical order, it's considered "less than" *handle*. Mixed expressions (numbers and letters) are evaluated in alphabetical order as well: *Word 97* is "greater than" *Word 2000* because 9 is greater than 2. (If you're familiar with how Word sorts information, this should all be familiar. You'll also remember how you used the StrComp function in Chapter 9 to compare strings a little more delicately than this.)

The seventh comparison operator, Is, is more complex and needs a longer example than the one in the table. You use Is to establish whether two object variables represent the same object—a named object, not an object such as a document or a range. For example, the following statements declare two objects—objTest1 and objTest2—and assign to each ActiveDocument.Paragraphs(1).Range, the range consisting of the first paragraph in the active document in Word. The next statement then compares the two objects to each other, returning False in the message box because the two objects are different even though their contents are the same:

```
Dim objTest1 As Object
Dim objTest2 As Object
Set objTest1 = ActiveDocument.Paragraphs(1).Range
Set objTest2 = ActiveDocument.Paragraphs(1).Range
'the next statement returns False because the objects are different
MsgBox objTest1 Is objTest2
```

However, if both the object variables refer to the same object, the Is comparison will return True, as in the following example, in which both objTest1 and objTest2 refer to the object variable objTest3:

```
Dim objTest1 As Object
Dim objTest2 As Object
Dim objTest3 As Object
Set objTest3 = ActiveDocument.Paragraphs(1).Range
Set objTest1 = objTest3
Set objTest2 = objTest3
'the next statement returns True because
'objTest1 and objTest2 refer to the same object
MsgBox objTest1 Is objTest2
```

When using Is, keep in mind that it isn't the contents of the object variables that are being compared, but what they refer to.

Testing Multiple Conditions by Using Logical Operators

Often, you'll need to test two or more conditions before taking an action: If statement X is True and statement Y is True, then do this; if statement X is True or statement Y is True, then do the other; if statement X is True and statement Y isn't True, then find something else to do; and so on.

To test multiple conditions, you use VBA's logical operators to link the conditions together. Table 13.2 lists the logical operators that VBA supports, with simple examples and comments.

TABLE 13.2: VBA'S LOGICAL OPERATORS

Operator	Meaning	Example	Comments

And	Conjunction	`If ActiveWorkbook`
		`.FullName =`
		`"c:\temp\Example.xls"`
		`And Year(Date) >=`
		`1998 Then`
			If both conditions are True, the result is True. If either condition is False, the result is False.

Not	Negation	`ActivePresentation`
		`.Saved = Not`
		`ActivePresentation`
		`.Saved`
			Not reverses the value of x (True becomes False; False becomes True). The Saved property used in this example is Boolean.

Or	Disjunction	`If ActiveWindow.View`
		`= wdPageView Or`
		`ActiveWindow.View =`
		`wdOutlineView Then`
			If either the first condition or the second is True, or if both conditions are True, the result is True.

XOr	Exclusion	`If Salary > 55000 XOr`
		`Experienced = True`
		`Then`
			Tests for different results from the conditions: Returns True if one condition is False and the other is True; returns False if both conditions are True or both conditions are False.

Eqv	Equivalence	`If blnMyVar1 Eqv` `blnMyVar2 Then`	Tests for logical equivalence between the two conditions: If both values are True, or if both values are False, Eqv returns True. If one condition is logically different from the other (that is, if one condition is True and the other is False), Eqv returns False.
Imp	Implication	`If blnMyVar1 Imp` `blnMyVar2 Then`	Tests for logical implication. Returns True if both conditions are True, both conditions are False, or the second condition is True. Returns Null if both conditions are Null or if the second condition is Null. Otherwise, returns False.

Of these six logical operators, you'll probably use the conjunction (And), disjunction (Or), and negation (Not) operators the most, with the other three thrown in on special occasions. (If the Imp logical operator doesn't make sense to you at this point, you probably don't need to use it.)

Warning: VBA Doesn't Do Short-Circuit Evaluation

Here's something to beware of when evaluating multiple conditions: VBA doesn't do short-circuit evaluation in logical expressions, unlike other programming languages such as C and C++.

Short-circuit evaluation is a somewhat forbidding term for a simple logical technique most people use several times a day when making decisions in their daily lives: If the first of two or more complementary conditions is false, you typically don't waste time evaluating any other conditions contingent upon it. For example, suppose your most attractive coworker says they'll take you to lunch if you get the product out on time *and* get a promotion. If you don't get the product out on time, you've blown your chances— it doesn't much matter if you get the promotion, because even if you do, your lunch will still be that brown bag determinedly developing its own sophisticated culture in the department fridge. There's no point in evaluating the second condition because it depends on the first, and the first condition wasn't met.

VBA doesn't think that way (nor does it have any mechanism for trying to date your coworker). It will evaluate the second condition (and any subsequent conditions) whether or not it needs to. Evaluating the conditions takes a little more time (which isn't usually an issue) and can introduce unexpected complications in your code (which can be an issue). For example, the following snippet produces an error when the selection is only one character long. The error occurs because the code ends up running the Mid function on a zero-length string (the one-character selection minus one character)— even though you wouldn't expect this condition to be evaluated when the first condition is not met (because the length of the selection is not greater than 1):

```
Dim strShort As String
strShort = Selection.Text
If Len(strShort) > 1 And _
    Mid(strShort, Len(strShort) - 1, 1) = "T" Then
    MsgBox "The second-last character is T."
End If
```

To avoid problems such as this, use nested If statements. Because the first condition isn't met (again, for a one-character selection), the second condition isn't evaluated:

```
If Len(strShort) > 1 Then
    If Mid(strShort, Len(strShort) - 1, 1) = "T" Then
        MsgBox "The second-last character is T."
    End If
End If
```

Using *Not* to Toggle Boolean Properties

Not is a handy way of turning True to False and False to True. By using Not with a Boolean property, you can toggle the state of the property without even needing to check what the current state is. For example, in either Word or AutoCAD, you could toggle the value of the Boolean property Saved (which controls whether Word or AutoCAD thinks the document in question contains unsaved changes) by using code such as this:

```
With ActiveDocument
    If .Saved = True Then
        .Saved = False
    Else
        .Saved = True
    End If
End With
```

But you can achieve the same effect much more simply by using the following code:

```
ActiveDocument.Saved = Not ActiveDocument.Saved
```

OK, so I cheated here—I took out the With statement as well. But I think you get the point.

If Statements

As in most programming languages, If statements are among the most immediately useful and versatile statements for making decisions in VBA. They're also very straightforward to use.

In this section, you'll look at the following types of If statements:

- If... Then
- If... Then... Else
- If... Then... ElseIf... Else

If... Then

If... Then statements tell VBA to make the simplest of decisions: If the condition is met, execute the following statement (or statements); if the condition isn't met, skip to the line immediately following the conditional statement.

Syntax

If... Then statements can be laid out either on one line or on multiple lines. A one-line If... Then statement looks like this:

```
If condition Then statement[s]
```

If the condition is met, VBA executes the statement or statements that follow. If the condition isn't met, VBA doesn't execute the statement or statements.

A multiple-line If... Then statement (more properly known as a *block* If statement) looks like this:

```
If condition Then
    statement
    [statements]
End If
```

Again, if the condition is met, VBA executes the statement or statements. Otherwise, VBA moves execution to the line after the End If statement.

 NOTE The single-line If... Then statement has no End If to end it, whereas the block If statement requires an End If. VBA knows that a single-line If condition will end on the same line on which it starts, whereas a block If statement needs to have its end clearly specified.

Examples

In the past chapters, you've already encountered a number of If statements—they're so necessary in VBA that it's hard to get anything done without them. In this section, you'll look at a couple more examples.

One-Line *If* Statements   Here's an example of a one-line If statement in context:

```
Dim bytAge As Byte
bytAge = InputBox("Enter your age.", "Age")
If bytAge < 21 Then MsgBox "You may not purchase alcohol.",, _
    "Underage"
```

The first line declares the Byte variable bytAge. The second line prompts the user to enter their age in an input box, which stores it in the variable. The third line checks bytAge and displays an Underage message box if bytAge is less than 21.

Nothing to it. There's just one more thing to mention about one-line If statements: They're a good candidate for including multiple statements in the same line of code by separating them with a colon. For example, if you wanted to end the procedure after displaying the Underage message box, you could include the End statement after a colon on the same line, as shown below. (Remember the use of an underscore after a space to break one logical line of code onto two or more lines.)

```
If bytAge < 21 Then MsgBox "You may not purchase alcohol.",, _
    "Underage": End
```

VBA executes this as follows:

1. First, it evaluates the condition.

2. If the condition is met, it executes the first statement after Then—in this case, it displays the Underage message box.

3. Once the user has dismissed the Underage message box (by clicking the OK button, the only button it has), VBA executes the statement after the colon: End.

If you wanted, you could add several other statements on the same logical line, separated by colons. (End would have to be the last one, because it ends the procedure.) You could even add another If statement if you felt like it:

```
If bytAge < 21 Then If bytAge > 18 Then MsgBox _
    "You may vote but you may not drink.",, "Underage": End
```

As you'll see if you're looking at the Visual Basic Editor, there are a couple of problems with this approach:

- First, you need to break long lines of code with the line-continuation character, or else they go off the edge of the Code window in the Visual Basic Editor, so that you have to scroll horizontally to read the ends of each line. You *could* hide all windows but the Code window, use a minute font size for your code, or buy a larger monitor, but you're probably still not going to have any fun working with long lines of code.

- Second, long lines of code (broken or unbroken) that involve a number of statements tend to become visually confusing. Even if everything is blindingly obvious to you when you're entering the code, you may find the code hard to read when you have to debug it a few months later. Usually it's better to use block If statements rather than complex one-line If statements. Read on.

Block *If* Statements   Block If statements work the same way as one-line If statements, except that they're laid out on multiple lines—typically with one command to each line—and they require an End If statement at their end. For example, the one-line If statement from the previous section could also be constructed as a block If:

```
If bytAge < 21 Then
    MsgBox "You may not purchase alcohol.",, "Underage"
    End
End If
```

If the condition in the first line is True, VBA executes the statements within the block If, first displaying the message box and then executing the End statement.

As you can see from this example, block If statements are much easier to read (and so easier to debug) than one-line If statements. This is especially true when you nest If statements within one another, which you'll do shortly.

To make block If statements easier to read, the convention is to indent the lines of block If statements after the first line (VBA ignores the indentation). With short If statements, like the ones shown in this section, the indentation doesn't make a great deal of difference. But with complex If statements, it can make all the difference between clarity and incomprehensibility, as you'll see in the section, "Nesting If Statements," later in this chapter.

If... Then... Else Statements

If... Then statements are all very well for taking a single action based on a condition, but often you'll need to decide between two courses of action. To do so, you use the If... Then... Else statement. By using an If... Then... Else statement, you can take one course of action if a condition is True and another course of action if it's False. For example, If... Then... Else statements are a great way to deal with two-button message boxes.

 NOTE   The If... Then... Else statement is best used with clear-cut binary conditions—those that lend themselves to a True/False analysis. (A binary condition is like a two-position switch—if it's not switched on, it must be switched off.) For more complex conditions, such as those that can have three or more positions (for example, the switch that governs the Off, Slow, Fast, and Lethal speeds on your margarita mixer), you need to use a more complex logical statement, such as If... Then... ElseIf... Else or Select Case. Note also that you need to set up the If... Then... Else statement to evaluate the conditions in the appropriate order: Each condition to be evaluated must exclude all the conditions that follow it.

Syntax

The syntax for the If... Then... Else statement is as follows:

```
If condition Then
  statements1
Else
  statements2
End If
```

If the condition is True, VBA executes *statements1*, the first group of statements. If the condition is False, VBA moves execution to the Else line and executes *statements2*, the second group of statements.

Again, you have the option of creating one-line If... Then... Else statements or block If... Then... Else statements. In almost all circumstances, it makes more sense to create block If... Then... Else statements, because they're much easier to read and debug, and because the If... Then... Else statement is inherently longer than the If... Then statement and thus more likely to produce an awkwardly long line.

Examples

As a straightforward example of an If... Then... Else statement, consider the silly and useless Electronic_Book_Critic procedure shown in Listing 13.1.

Listing 13.1

```
1.  Sub Electronic_Book_Critic()
2.
3.      Dim intBookPages As Integer
4.
5.      intBookPages = InputBox _
            ("Enter the number of pages in the last book you read.", _
            "The Electronic Book Critic")
6.      If intBookPages > 1000 Then
7.          MsgBox "Whoa! Seriously long book, dude!", vbOKOnly _
                + vbExclamation, "The Electronic Book Critic"
8.      Else
9.          MsgBox "That book wasn't so long.", vbOKOnly _
                + vbInformation, "The Electronic Book Critic"
10.     End If
11.
12. End Sub
```

Analysis

Here's what happens in Listing 13.1's frivolous example:

- Line 1 starts the procedure, and line 12 ends it. Lines 2, 4, and 11 are spacers.
- Line 3 declares the Integer variable intBookPages. Line 5 then assigns to intBookPages the result of an input box prompting the user to enter the number of pages in the last book they read.
- Line 6 checks to see if intBookPages is greater than 1000. If it is, the statement in line 7 runs, displaying a message box that delivers the Electronic Book Critic's informed opinion about the length of the book.
- If intBookPages is not greater than 1000, VBA branches to the Else statement in line 8 and executes the statement following it, which displays a message box telling the user that the book wasn't so long.
- Line 10 ends the If condition.

Listing 13.2 shows another simple example that closes the active document in AutoCAD.

Listing 13.2

```
1.  Sub Close_Document()
2.      If MsgBox("Do you want to save your changes?", _
            vbYesNo + vbQuestion, "Close Document") = vbYes Then
3.          ActiveDocument.Close SaveChanges:=True
4.      Else
5.          ActiveDocument.Close SaveChanges:=False
6.      End If
7.  End Sub
```

Analysis

Here's what happens in Listing 13.2's straightforward Close_Document procedure:

- Line 1 starts the Close_Document procedure, and line 7 ends it.
- Line 2 displays a message box asking the user whether they want to save changes to the document. (Note that the procedure hasn't checked that the document contains unsaved changes, so it's not particularly realistic.)

- The If statement (still in line 2) compares the user's response to the message box to vbYes, the constant generated by the user's choosing the Yes button in the Yes/No message box.

- If the condition is met, line 3 closes the active document and uses a True value for the Boolean SaveChanges argument to make AutoCAD save changes.

- If the condition is not met, the Else statement in line 4 kicks in, and line 5 closes the active document without saving changes (SaveChanges:=False).

- Line 6 ends the If statement.

If... Then... ElseIf... Else Statements

The last If statement you'll look at here is If... Then... ElseIf... Else, which you can use to help VBA decide between multiple courses of action. You can use any number of ElseIf lines, depending on how complex the condition is that you need to check.

Again, you can create either one-line If... Then... ElseIf... Else statements, or block If... Then... ElseIf... Else statements. In almost all cases, block If... Then... ElseIf... Else statements are easier to construct, to read, and to debug. As with the other If statements, one-line If... Then... ElseIf... Else statements don't need an End If statement, but block If... Then... ElseIf... Else statements do need one.

Syntax

The syntax for If... Then... ElseIf... Else is as follows:

```
If condition1 Then
    statements1
ElseIf condition2 Then
    statements2
[ElseIf condition3 Then
    statements3]
[Else
    statements4]
End If
```

If the condition expressed in *condition1* is True, VBA executes *statements1*, the first block of statements, and then resumes execution at the line after the End If clause. If *condition1* is False, VBA branches to the first ElseIf clause and evaluates the condition expressed in *condition2*. If this is True, VBA executes *statements2* and then moves to the line after the End If line; if it's False, VBA moves to the next ElseIf clause (if there is one) and evaluates its condition (here, *condition3*) in turn.

If all the conditions in the ElseIf statements prove False, VBA branches to the Else statement (if there is one) and executes the statements after it (here, *statements4*). The End If statement then terminates the conditional statement, and execution resumes with the line after the End If.

You can have any number of ElseIf clauses in a block If statement, each with its own condition. But if you find yourself needing to use If statements with large numbers of ElseIf clauses (say, more than five or ten), you may want to try using the Select Case statement instead, which you'll look at toward the end of the chapter.

The Else clause is optional, although in many cases it's a good idea to include it to let VBA take a different course of action if none of the conditions specified in the If and ElseIf clauses turns out to be True.

Examples

In this section, you'll look at two examples of If... Then... ElseIf... Else statements:

- A simple If... Then... ElseIf... Else statement for taking action from a three-button message box
- An If... Then... ElseIf statement without an Else clause

A Simple *If... Then... ElseIf... Else* Statement   A simple If... Then... ElseIf... Else statement, as used in Listing 13.3, is perfect for dealing with a three-button message box.

Listing 13.3

```
1.   Sub Creating_a_Document()
2.
3.       Dim lngButton As Long
4.       Dim strMessage As String
5.
6.       strMessage = "Create a new document based on the " & _
                "VP Report project?" & vbCr & vbCr & _
                "Click Yes to use the VP Report project." & vbCr & _
                "Click No to use the default project." & vbCr & _
                "Click Cancel to stop creating a new document."
7.
8.       lngButton = MsgBox _
                (strMessage, vbYesNoCancel + vbQuestion, "Create New Document")
9.
10.      If lngButton = vbYes Then
11.          PerfectScript.TemplateSelect "f:\common\Template\VP_report.wpt"
```

```
12.        ElseIf lngButton = vbNo Then
13.            PerfectScript.FileNew
14.        Else    'lngButton is vbCancel
15.            End
16.        End If
17.
18.    End Sub
```

Analysis

The Creating_a_Document procedure in Listing 13.3 displays a Yes/No/Cancel message box inviting the user to create a new document based on the VP Report project. The user can choose the Yes button to create such a document, the No button to create a plain document, or the Cancel button to cancel out of the procedure without creating a document at all.

Here's what happens:

- Line 1 starts the procedure, and line 18 ends it.

- Line 2 is a spacer, after which line 3 declares the Long variable lngButton and line 4 declares the String variable strMessage. Line 5 is another spacer.

- Line 6 assigns to the String variable strMessage a long string that contains all the text for the message box. Line 7 is another spacer.

- Line 8 displays the message box, using strMessage as the prompt, specifying the vbYesNoCancel constant to produce a Yes/No/Cancel message box, and applying a suitable title (Create New Document). It assigns the result of the message box to the Long variable lngButton. Line 9 is a spacer.

- Line 10 starts the If... Then... ElseIf... Else statement, comparing the value of lngButton to vbYes.

- If line 10 matches, line 11 uses the TemplateSelect method of the PerfectScript object to create a new document based on the VP Report project. If not, the ElseIf condition in line 12 is evaluated, comparing the value of lngButton to vbNo.

 NOTE If you run this procedure and choose the Yes button in the message box, you will need to have a project template named VP_report.wpt in the folder f:\common\Template\ for line 11 to run. If you don't have the template, you'll get an error.

- If this second comparison matches, line 13 uses the `FileNew` method of the `PerfectScript` object to create a new blank document. If not, the `Else` statement in line 14 is activated, because the user must have chosen the Cancel button in the message box. The `End` statement in line 15 ends execution of the procedure.

- Line 16 ends the `If` statement. Line 17 is a spacer.

 NOTE   This example is a little unusual in that the `Else` statement is limited by the number of possible responses from the message box—Yes, No, and Cancel. Because the `If` statement checks for the `vbYes` response and the `ElseIf` statement checks for the `vbNo` response, only the `vbCancel` response will trigger the `Else` statement. In other circumstances, the `Else` statement can serve as a catch-all for anything not caught by the `If` and `ElseIf` statements, so you need to make sure that the `If` and `ElseIf` statements cover all the contingencies you want evaluated before the `Else` statement kicks in.

An *If... Then... ElseIf* Statement without an *Else* Clause   As I mentioned in the discussion on syntax, you can use an If... Then... `ElseIf` statement without an `Else` clause if need be. Doing so is primarily useful when you don't need to take an action if none of the conditions in the `If` statement proves True. In the previous example, you looked at a situation that had three clearly defined outcomes: In the message box, the user could choose the Yes button, the No button, or the Cancel button. So you were able to use an `If` clause to test for the user's having chosen the Yes button, an `ElseIf` clause to test for the user's having chosen the No button, and an `Else` clause to take action if neither was chosen, meaning that the Cancel button was chosen. (Before you ask, clicking the close button on the title bar of this message box is the equivalent of choosing the Cancel button.)

As an example of a situation where you don't need to take action if no condition is True, consider the `If` statement in the `Checkpoint_Charlie` procedure in Listing 13.4. This snippet checks to ensure that the password a user enters to protect an item is of a suitable length.

Listing 13.4

```
1.  Sub Checkpoint_Charlie()
2.
3.      Dim strPassword As String
4.
5.  BadPassword:
```

```
6.
7.        strPassword = InputBox _
             ("Enter the password to protect this item from changes:", _
             "Enter Password")
8.
9.        If Len(strPassword) = 0 Then
10.           End
11.       ElseIf Len(strPassword) < 6 Then
12.           MsgBox "The password you chose is too short." & vbCr _
                 & vbCr & "Please choose a password between " & _
                 "6 and 15 characters in length.", _
                 vbOKOnly + vbCritical, "Unsuitable Password"
13.           GoTo BadPassword
14.       ElseIf Len(strPassword) > 15 Then
15.           MsgBox "The password you chose is too long." & vbCr _
                 & vbCr & "Please choose a password between " & _
                 "6 and  15 characters in length.", _
                 vbOKOnly + vbCritical, "Unsuitable Password"
16.           GoTo BadPassword
17.       End If
18.
19.   End Sub
```

Analysis

This procedure forces the user to enter a suitable password for the item they're supposed to protect. (The procedure doesn't actually protect the item.) Here's what happens:

- Line 1 starts the procedure, and line 19 ends it.

- Line 2 is a spacer, after which line 3 declares the String variable strPassword.

- Line 4 is a spacer. Line 5 contains a label, BadPassword, to which VBA will loop if the password the user enters proves to be unsuitable. Line 6 is another spacer.

- Line 7 displays an input box prompting the user to enter a password, which VBA stores in the variable strPassword. Line 8 is a spacer.

- Line 9 checks strPassword to see if its length is zero, which means it's an empty string. This could mean either that the user clicked the Cancel button in the input box, or that they clicked the OK button without entering any text in the text box of the input box. Either of these actions causes VBA to branch to line 10, where it executes the End statement that ends execution of the procedure.

- If the length of strPassword isn't zero (that is, the user has entered text into the text box of the input box and clicked the OK button), the If clause in line 9 is False, and VBA moves to line 10, where it checks to see if the length of strPassword is less than 6 characters.

- If the length of strPassword is zero, VBA executes the code in lines 12 and 13. Line 12 displays a message box telling the user that the password is too short and specifying the length criteria for the password. This message box contains only an OK button, so when the user clicks it to continue, VBA continues with line 13, which returns execution to the BadPassword label on line 5. From there the procedure repeats itself, redisplaying the input box so that the user can try again.

- If the length of strPassword isn't more than 15 characters, execution passes from line 11 to the second ElseIf clause in line 14, where VBA checks to see if the length of strPassword is more than 15 characters.

- If the length of strPassword is more than 15 characters, VBA executes the code in lines 15 and 16: Line 15 displays a message box (again, with only an OK button) telling the user that the password is too long, and line 16 returns execution to the BadPassword label, again displaying the input box.

There's no need for an ElseIf statement in this case, because once the user has supplied a password that doesn't trigger the If clause or either of the ElseIf clauses, execution will continue at the line after the End If statement.

Creating Loops with *If* and *GoTo*

In the previous chapter, you looked at the formal types of loop: the For loops for repeating loops a known number of times, and the Do loops for repeating loops while a condition is True or until it becomes True. If you wish, you can also create loops with If statements and the GoTo statement, as you did in the last example.

Before I get into this, I should mention that some programmers look on the use of GoTo as somewhere between a childish habit and one of the less interesting sins. But it works perfectly well, and you should certainly be aware of how to use it even if you choose not to do so yourself.

Syntax

The GoTo statement is very straightforward, and it's so useful that it's already come up a number of times in the examples you've looked at so far in this book:

```
GoTo line
```

Here, the *line* argument can be either a line number or a line label within the current procedure.

A line number is simply a number placed at the beginning of a line to identify it. For example, consider this demonstration of GoTo:

```
Sub Demo_of_GoTo()
1
    If MsgBox("Go to line 1?", vbYesNo) = vbYes Then
        GoTo 1
    End If
End Sub
```

The first line contains only the line number 1, which identifies the line. The second line displays a message box offering the choice of going back to line 1; if the user chooses the Yes button, VBA executes the GoTo 1 statement and returns to the line labeled 1, after which it displays the message box again. (If the user chooses the No button, the If statement ends.)

It's usually easier to use a line label than a line number. A line label, as you may have noticed in some of the earlier chapters, is simply a name for a line. A label starts with a letter and ends with a colon—apart from that, it can consist of any combination of characters. For example, earlier in this chapter you used the label BadPassword: to loop back to an earlier stage in a procedure when certain conditions were met. Perhaps the quintessential example of a label is the Bye: label traditionally placed at the end of a procedure for use with this GoTo statement:

```
GoTo Bye
```

GoTo is usually used with a condition—if you use it without one to go back to a line earlier in the code than the GoTo statement, you're apt to create an infinite loop. And if you were to use the GoTo Bye statement without a condition, you would guarantee that your procedure would end at this statement (that is, no statement after this line would ever be executed).

Example

As an example of a GoTo statement with a condition, you might use the GoTo Bye statement together with a message box that made sure that the user wanted to run a certain procedure:

```
Response = MsgBox("Do you want to create a daily report for " & _
    "the head office from the current document?", _
    vbYesNo + vbQuestion, "Create Daily Report 2000a")
If Response = vbNo Then GoTo Bye
```

If the user chooses the No button in the message box that the first line displays, VBA executes the `GoTo Bye` statement, branching to the `Bye:` label located at the end of the subprocedure.

Nesting *If* Statements

You can nest `If` statements as necessary to produce the logical contortions you need in your code. Each nested `If` statement needs to be complete in and of itself. For example, if you nest one block `If` statement within another block `If` statement and forget the `End If` line for the nested `If`, VBA will assume that the `End If` line for the outer `If` belongs to the nested `If`.

As I mentioned earlier, the convention is to use indentation with block `If` statements to make them easier to read. This is particularly important with nesting `If` statements, when you need to make it clear which `If` line is paired with each `End If` line. To see how this is done, check out the following nested `If` statements:

```
1.  If condition1 Then                  'start of first If
2.      If condition2 Then              'start of second If
3.          If condition3 Then          'start of third If
4.              statements1
5.          ElseIf condition4 Then      'ElseIf for third If
6.              statements2
7.          Else                        'Else for third If
8.              statements3
9.          End If                      'End If for third If
10.     Else                            'Else for second If
11.         If condition5 Then          'start of fourth If
12.             statements4
13.         End If                      'End If for fourth If
14.     End If                          'End If for second If
15. Else                               'Else for first If
16.     statements5
17. End If                             'End If for first If
```

By following the layout, you can easily trace the flow of execution. For example, if condition1 in line 1 is `False`, VBA branches to the `Else` statement in line 15 and continues execution from there. If *condition1* in line 1 is `True`, VBA evaluates *condition2* in line 2, and so on.

The indentation is for visual clarity only—it doesn't make one iota of difference to VBA—but it can be a great help to the human reader. I've tastefully annotated the previous nested `If` statement to make it clear which `Else`, `ElseIf`, and `End If` line belongs with which `If` line, although with the indentation, doing so is unnecessary.

On the other hand, check out the unindented version of this nested statement shown below. This version is murder for the human eye to follow, even when it isn't buried in a morass of other code that might confuse things further:

```
1.  If condition1 Then                'start of first If
2.  If condition2 Then                'start of second If
3.  If condition3 Then                'start of third If
4.  statements1
5.  ElseIf condition4 Then            'ElseIf for third If
6.  statements2
7.  Else                             'Else for third If
8.  statements3
9.  End If                           'End If for third If
10. Else                             'Else for second If
11. If cond2ition5 Then              'start of fourth If
12. statements4
13. End If                           'End If for fourth If
14. End If                           'End If for second If
15. Else                             'Else for first If
16. statements5
17. End If                           'End If for first If
```

There's seldom a pressing need to go to such ludicrous levels of nesting—often, you'll need only to nest a simple If... Then statement within an If... Then... Else statement or within an If... Then... ElseIf... Else statement. Listing 13.5 shows an example using Word.

Listing 13.5

```
1.  Selection.HomeKey Unit:=wdStory
2.  Selection.Find.ClearFormatting
3.  Selection.Find.Style = ActiveDocument.Styles("Heading 5")
4.  Selection.Find.Text = ""
5.  Selection.Find.Execute
6.  If Selection.Find.Found Then
7.      lngResponse = MsgBox("Make this into a special note?", _
            vbOKCancel, "Make Special Note")
8.      If lngResponse = vbOK Then
9.          Selection.Style = "Special Note"
10.     End If
11. End If
```

Analysis

The code in Listing 13.5 searches through the active document for the Heading 5 style and, if it finds the style, displays a message box offering to make it into a special note by applying the Special Note style. Here's what happens:

- Line 1 starts by returning the insertion point to the beginning of the document.
- Line 2 clears formatting from the Find command (to make sure that it isn't searching for inappropriate formatting).
- Line 3 sets Heading 5 as the style for which the Find command is searching, and Line 4 sets the search string as an empty string (" ").
- Line 5 then runs the Find operation.
- Lines 6 through 11 contain the outer If... Then loop. Line 6 checks to see if the Find operation in line 5 found a paragraph in Heading 5 style; if it did, VBA runs the code in lines 7 through 10.
- Line 7 displays a message box asking if the user wants to make the paragraph into a special note.
- Line 8 begins the nested If... Then statement and checks the user's response to the message box.
- If it's a vbOK—if they chose the OK button—VBA executes the statement in line 9, which applies the Special Note style (which I'll assume is included in the document or template) to the paragraph.
- Line 10 contains the End If statement for the nested If... Then statement, and line 11 contains the End If statement for the outer If... Then statement.

 TIP If you expected a document to contain more than one instance of the Heading 5 style, you would probably want to use a Do While... Loop loop to search for each instance.

Select Case Statements

The Select Case statement provides an effective alternative to multiple ElseIf statements, combining the same decision-making capability with tighter and more efficient code.

Use the Select Case statement when the decision you need to take in the code depends on one variable or expression that has more than three or four different values that you need to evaluate. This variable or expression is known as the *test case*.

Select Case statements are easier to read than complex If... Then statements, mostly because there's less code. This also makes them easier to change—when you need to adjust one or more of the values used, you have less code to wade through.

Syntax

The syntax for Select Case is as follows:

```
Select Case TestExpression
    Case Expression1
        Statements1
    [Case Expression2
        Statements2]
    [Case Else
        StatementsElse]
End Select
```

This syntax looks complex at first, but stay with me: Select Case starts the statement, and End Select ends it. *TestExpression* is the expression that determines which of the Case statements runs, and *Expression1*, *Expression2*, and so on are the expressions against which VBA matches TestExpression. For example, you might test to see which of a number of buttons in a user form the user chose. The *TestExpression* would be tied to a button having been chosen; if it were the first button, VBA would match that to *Expression1* and would run the statements in the lines following Case *Expression1*; if it were the second button, VBA would match that to *Expression2* and would run the statements in the lines following Case *Expression2*; and so on for the rest of the Case statements.

Case Else is similar to the Else clause in an If statement. Case Else is an optional clause that (if it's included) runs if none of the given expressions is matched.

Example

As a somewhat frivolous first example of a Select Case statement, consider Listing 13.6, which prompts the user to enter their typing speed and then displays an appropriate response.

Listing 13.6

```
1.   Sub Check_Typing_Speed()
2.
3.       Dim varTypingSpeed As Variant
4.       Dim strMsg As String
5.
6.       varTypingSpeed = InputBox _
             ("How many words can you type per minute?", _
             "Typing Speed")
7.       Select Case varTypingSpeed
8.           Case ""
9.               End
10.          Case Is < 0, 0, 1 To 50
11.              strMsg = "Please learn to type properly before " & _
                     "applying for a job."
12.          Case 50 To 60
13.              strMsg = "Your typing could do with a little " & _
                     "brushing up."
14.          Case 60 To 75
15.              strMsg = "We are satisfied with your typing speed."
16.          Case 75 To 99
17.              strMsg = "Your typing is more than adequate."
18.          Case 100 To 200
19.              strMsg = "You wear out keyboards with your blinding speed."
20.          Case Is > 200
21.              strMsg = "Liar!"
22.      End Select
23.
24.      MsgBox strMsg, vbOKOnly, "Typing Speed"
25.
26.  End Sub
```

Analysis

Here's what happens in the `Check_Typing_Speed` procedure in Listing 13.6:

- Line 1 starts the procedure, and line 26 ends it.

- Line 2 is a spacer. Line 3 declares the Variant variable `varTypingSpeed`, and line 4 the String variable `strMsg`. Line 5 is another spacer.

- Line 6 displays an input box prompting the user to enter their typing speed. It stores this value in the variable `varTypingSpeed`.

- Line 7 begins the `Select Case` statement, predicating it on the variable `varTypingSpeed`.

- Next, VBA evaluates each of the `Case` clauses in turn until it finds one that proves `True`. The first `Case` clause, in line 8, compares `varTypingSpeed` to an empty string (`""`) to see if the user chose the Cancel button in the input box or clicked the OK button without entering a value in the text box. If `Case ""` is `True`, VBA executes the `End` statement in line 9, ending the procedure.

- If `Case ""` is `False`, VBA moves execution to the next `Case` clause—line 10 in this example—where it compares `varTypingSpeed` to three items: less than 0 (`Is < 0`), 0, and the range 1 to 50 words per minute. Notice three things here:

  1. You can include multiple comparison items in the same `Case` statement by separating them from each other with commas.

  2. Using the `Is` keyword with the comparison operator (here, less than) checks the relation of two numbers to each other.

  3. The To keyword denotes the range of values.

- If `varTypingSpeed` matches one of the comparison items in line 5, VBA assigns to the String variable `strMsg` the text on line 11 and then continues execution at the line after the `End Select` statement.

- If `varTypingSpeed` isn't within this range, VBA moves to the next `Case` clause and evaluates it in turn. When VBA finds a `Case` clause that's `True`, it executes the statement following that clause (in this case, assigning a text string to the `strMsg` variable), and then continues execution at the line after the `End Select` statement.

- For any case other than that in line 8 (which ends the procedure), line 24 displays a message box containing the text stored in the statement `strMsg`.

A Select Case statement can be a good way of taking action on the user's choice in a list box or combo box, particularly if the list box or combo box contains many different items. For example, you could check the Value property of the ListBox control or ComboBox control as the test case, and take action accordingly.

In this chapter, you've seen how to make decisions in your code using simple If... Then... Else statements for binary decisions, If... Then... ElseIf statements and nested If statements for more complex decisions, and Select Case statements for decisions involving many possibilities.

In the next chapter, I'll take you back to the wide world of objects, showing you how to navigate the object models (the object hierarchies of the applications) and giving you a look into the object models of the seven applications discussed in this book.

CHAPTER 14

Object Models

I n this chapter, I'll show you how to come to grips with the object model of the
application or applications you're working with. Understanding the object model
of the application enables you more easily to reach and manipulate the objects
you need in the application.

The object model for each application is a huge enough topic in itself for a medium-
size book, so I won't get into any object model in great depth. But you'll learn how
object models are constructed, how to navigate them, and how to use the tools discussed
in Chapter 8 to get yourself from abject muddle to object model.

As you'll have guessed if you read the quick overview of this chapter's contents on
the previous page, this chapter begins with a general section on object models. You
should probably read this section no matter which application or applications you're
working with. The rest of the chapter then shows you how to dig a little way into the
object models of each of the seven applications discussed in the book, along with an
example or two of using some of the key objects involved. You'll probably want to
read only the section or sections that deal with the application or applications that
you're using. From there, proceed on your own, digging into whichever object model
interests you.

What Is an Object Model, and What Does It Do?

As you learned in Chapter 8, VBA considers each application to consist of a number of
objects—elements that VBA uses to manipulate parts of the application. The object
model is the theoretical architecture according to which the objects are organized to
form the application. By understanding the object model of the application you're working with, you can manipulate the objects from which the application is built, and work
quickly and effectively with VBA.

Because of the complexity of today's applications, most applications contain scores
or hundreds of objects, making object models dauntingly complex to the naked eye and
even worse under magnification. (Some applications, such as Microsoft MapPoint, contain very few objects.) As a result, object models are usually depicted as complex dia-
grams involving many small boxes representing objects (grouped into their respective
collection objects where appropriate) with lines between them. You'll look at one semi-
complete object model later in the chapter as we go spelunking in the object models of
the applications this book discusses. Most of the time, though, you'll look at partial object
models that make it a bit simpler to see what's going on.

Because the seven applications discussed in this book are all different, it's hard to
generalize much about them. Here's about as much as I can say:

- At the root of the object model is the Application object that represents the
application as a whole.

- The `Application` object contains all the other objects in the application. It contains the creatable objects directly, and those objects in turn contain further objects, which in *their* turn can contain further objects, and so on.

- Generally speaking, any object that contains another object has a property for that object. You use that property to return the object. For example, AutoCAD has a `Preferences` collection object that contains all the `Preference` objects, which represent the user's preferences normally accessed through the Options dialog box (Tools ➤ Options). The `Preferences` collection is contained within the `Application` object, so the `Application` object has a `Preferences` property that you use to return the `Preferences` collection. You'll notice that I started the paragraph by saying "generally speaking." Those weasel words are there because some hosts implement methods to return child collections instead of using properties. For example, Visual Intercept uses `Application.GetIncidents()` to return the `Incidents` collection.

- Because the `Application` object contains all the other objects and provides the way to access them, most applications have a number of creatable objects that you can access directly without going through the `Application` object. Having these creatable objects makes everyone's life simpler. (There's nothing wrong with going through the `Application` object when you don't absolutely need to, but I guarantee you'll find it easier to bypass it most of the times you can.)

- Other than the people who built VBA into a given application, nobody using VBA really needs to know the details of *every* object and collection, *every* property and method, or *every* function and statement that the application's VBA environment offers. That would be like trying to learn every word in the dictionary just because it was there. What you need to know is the framework—the main objects and the properties and methods that are most useful with those objects. From this basis, you can easily expand your knowledge into new areas as you need to add to your repertoire the objects and capabilities they contain.

- In any application, you'll find some objects much more widely useful than others, much as you do when working interactively in the application. For example, do you use Word? Then I bet you use documents about 500 times as often as you use the AutoCaption feature—that is, if you use the AutoCaption feature at all (most people don't). Likewise, in VBA, you're about 500 times as likely to use the `Documents` collection and its `Document` objects as you are the `AutoCaptions` collection and the `AutoCaption` objects it contains. To do anything in Word via VBA, you'll need to be able to manipulate `Document` objects, but you'll need to manipulate `AutoCaption` objects only if you need to implement automatic captioning.

- You'll usually do best to concentrate your efforts on the objects that will be most useful to you at first, then explore other objects as you need them.

- Once you understand how to work with the key objects, you can easily learn how to work with the, uh, less compelling objects as well.

The Word Object Model

The best place to start exploring the Word object model is the Microsoft Word Objects screen in the Microsoft Visual Basic Help file. To display this screen, start the Microsoft Visual Basic Help application by choosing Help ➤ Microsoft Visual Basic Help from a Visual Basic Editor session for Word. On the Answer Wizard page, enter **Microsoft Word Objects** in the What Would You Like To Do? text box and select the Search button. The Microsoft Word Objects screen should come up as the first hit.

 TIP Two notes here: First, if you have the Office Assistant turned on, you can access the Microsoft Word Objects screen by asking the Office Assistant **Microsoft Word objects** and then selecting the Microsoft Word Objects topic it retrieves. Second, you can also reach the Microsoft Word Objects screen of the Help file by clicking the Application box in the small schematic on the Application Object screen.

Figure 14.1 shows the Microsoft Word Objects screen.

FIGURE 14.1

Start your exploration of the Word object model at the Microsoft Word Objects screen in the Help file.

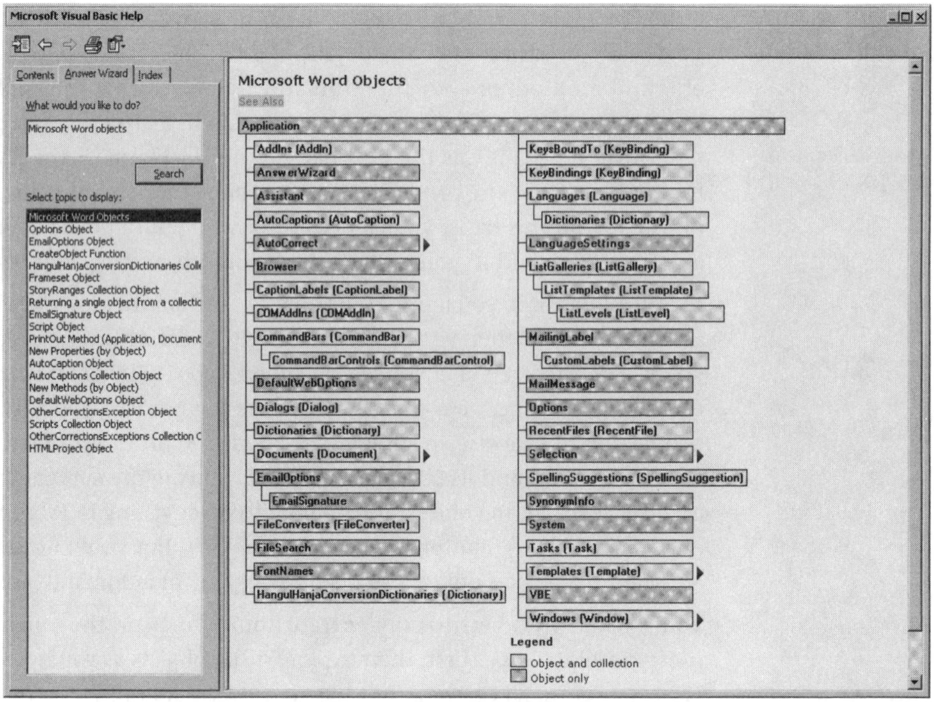

![Microsoft Visual Basic Help window showing the Microsoft Word Objects schematic with the Application object at the top branching into Addins, AnswerWizard, Assistant, AutoCaptions, AutoCorrect, Browser, CaptionLabels, COMAddins, CommandBars, DefaultWebOptions, Dialogs, Dictionaries, Documents, EmailOptions, FileConverters, FileSearch, FontNames, HangulHanjaConversionDictionaries, and on the right KeysBoundTo, KeyBindings, Languages, LanguageSettings, ListGalleries, MailingLabel, MailMessage, Options, RecentFiles, Selection, SpellingSuggestions, SynonymInfo, System, Tasks, Templates, VBE, Windows.]

The red arrows next to the AutoCorrect object, the Documents collection, the Selection object, the Templates collection, and the Windows collection indicate that further parts of the diagram are available from these objects and collections. Figure 14.2 shows the result of clicking the arrow next to the Documents collection.

FIGURE 14.2

You can drill down the schematic by clicking on one of the red arrows. Here's what you get when you click the arrow next to the Documents collection.

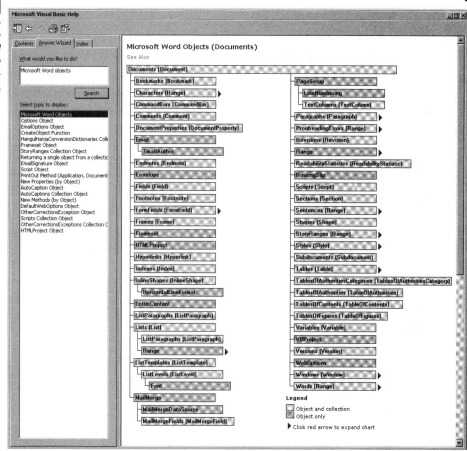

Like most VBA-enabled applications, Word has a number of creatable objects, allowing you to access the commonly used objects without having to go through the Application object. The following are typically the most useful of these creatable objects:

- The ActiveDocument object represents the active document.

- The ActiveWindow object represents the active window. When using this object, check the type of window you've gotten a hold of, because it may not be the type you imagined you'd get.

- The Documents collection contains the Document objects, each of which represents an open document.

- The Selection object represents the selection in the active document. Selection is conceptually slippery and so can be a difficult object to grasp, but it's very useful for straightforward procedures that work in the active document. Selection represents the selection (containing text or other objects) or collapsed selection (containing nothing—an insertion point) in the document. You can return all or part of the selection, as you'd expect; but you can even use the Selection object to identify objects outside the actual selection by using Selection as an entry into the object model. For example, Selection.Paragraphs(1).Range.Words(10).Text returns the tenth word in the paragraph containing a collapsed selection, no matter where that collapsed selection is in the paragraph. Figure 14.3 shows the section of the object model for the Selection object.

FIGURE 14.3

The Selection object is a powerful tool for working with the current selection in the active document.

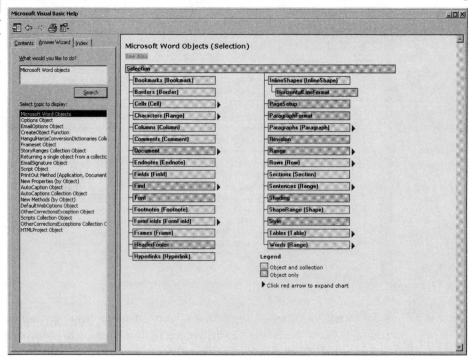

- The Windows collection contains the Window objects that represent all open windows. Again, make sure you know what type of window you're grappling with before taking any irreversible actions.

The Excel Object Model

A good starting point for exploring the Excel object model is the Microsoft Excel Objects screen in Help. To display this screen, start the Microsoft Visual Basic Help application by choosing Help ➤ Microsoft Visual Basic Help from the Visual Basic Editor. On the Answer Wizard page, enter **Microsoft Excel Objects** in the What Would You Like To Do? text box and select the Search button. The Microsoft Excel Objects screen should come up as the first hit.

 TIP Two notes here: First, if you have the Office Assistant turned on, you can access the Microsoft Excel Objects screen by asking the Office Assistant **Excel objects** and then selecting the Microsoft Excel Objects topic it retrieves. Second, you can also reach the Microsoft Excel Objects screen of the Help file by clicking the Application box in the small schematic on the Application Object screen.

Figure 14.4 shows the Microsoft Excel Objects screen.

FIGURE 14.4

The Microsoft Excel Objects screen in Help is a good place to start your exploration of the Excel object model.

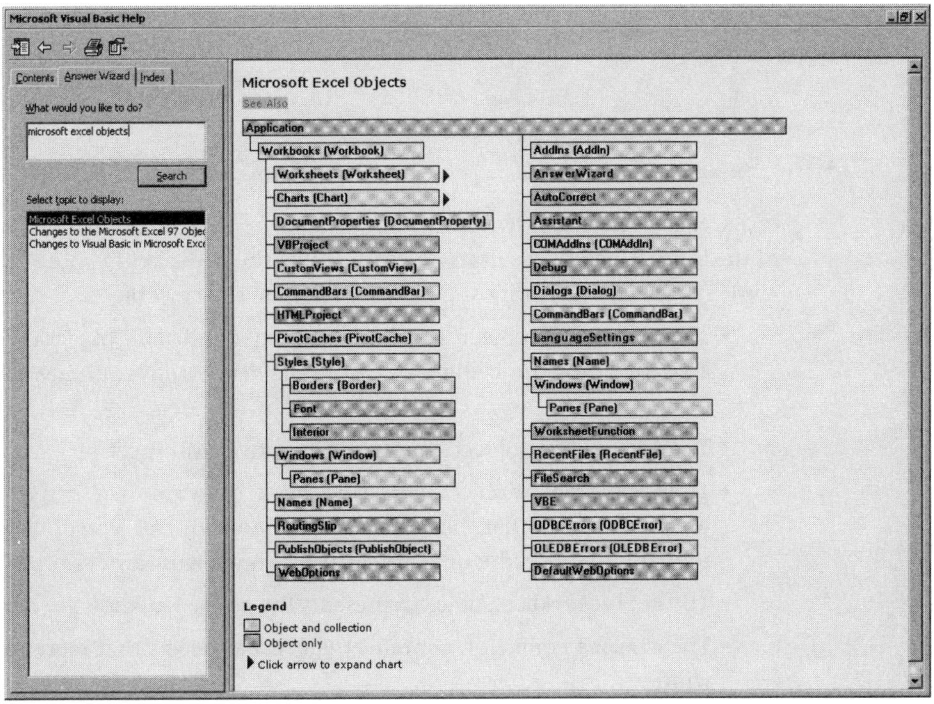

The two red arrows next to the Worksheets collection and the Charts collection indicate that further parts of the schematic are available from these two objects. Figure 14.5 shows the result of clicking the arrow next to the Worksheets collection.

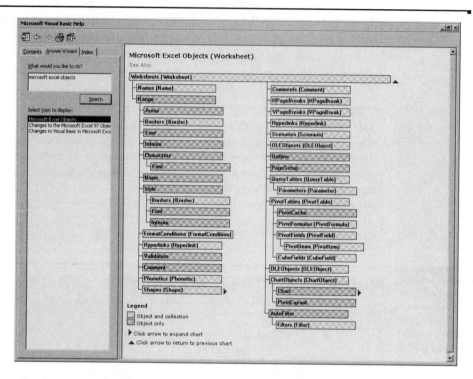

Excel exposes a handy number of creatable objects, allowing you to reach most of the interesting objects in its object model without explicitly going through the Application object. For most purposes, these are the key objects:

- The ActiveCell object represents the active cell. This object is especially valuable for simple procedures (for example, those that compute values or correct formatting) that work on a cell selected by the user.

- The ActiveSheet object represents the active worksheet.

- The ActiveWindow object represents the active window. When using this object, be sure to check that the window it represents is the type of window you want to manipulate, as the object returns whatever window currently has the focus.

- The ActiveWorkbook object represents the active workbook.

- The Windows collection contains the Window objects that represent all the open windows.

- The Workbooks collection contains the Workbook objects that represent all the open workbooks.

Within a workbook, the Worksheets collection contains the Worksheet objects that represent the worksheets. On a sheet, the Range object gives you access to ranges, which can be anything from an individual cell to a complete worksheet.

The PowerPoint Object Model

To start exploring the PowerPoint object model, start the Microsoft Visual Basic Help application and display the Microsoft PowerPoint Objects screen. Launch the Visual Basic Editor if it's not already displayed, then start the Microsoft Visual Basic Help application and reach the topic as follows:

- If you're using the Office Assistant, ask it about **Microsoft PowerPoint Objects** and choose the Microsoft PowerPoint Objects topic it offers.

- If you're not using the Office Assistant, choose Help ➢ Microsoft Visual Basic Help, display the Answer Wizard page, and search for **Microsoft PowerPoint Objects**. The Microsoft PowerPoint Objects screen should emerge on top of the list and be displayed automatically; if it's not, display it manually.

Figure 14.6 shows the Microsoft PowerPoint Objects screen.

FIGURE 14.6

The Microsoft Power-Point Objects screen in Help is a good place to start your exploration of the PowerPoint object model.

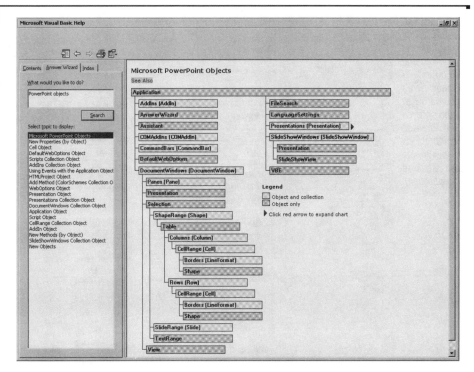

As usual, the `Application` object gives you access to everything in the PowerPoint application, from top to toe. But for many operations, you'll eschew the `Application` object and go directly through one of the creatable objects that PowerPoint exposes. The five most useful exposed creatable objects are the following:

- The `ActivePresentation` object represents the active presentation.

- The `Presentations` collection contains the `Presentation` objects, each of which represents one of the open presentations.

- The `ActiveWindow` object represents the active window in the application.

- The `CommandBars` collection contains the `CommandBar` objects, each of which represents a command bar (the toolbars, menu bar, and context menus) in the PowerPoint application. By manipulating the assorted `CommandBar` objects, you can change the PowerPoint interface programmatically.

- The `SlideShowWindows` collection contains the `SlideShowWindow` objects, each of which represents an open slide show window. This collection is useful for getting a virtual hold on a slide show that's currently displayed.

The red arrow next to the `Presentations` collection indicates that further parts of the object model diagram are available from this collection. Figure 14.7 shows the result of clicking this arrow.

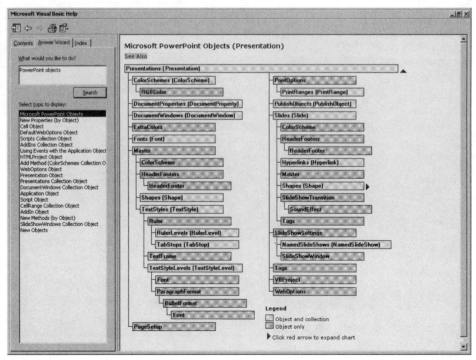

FIGURE 14.7

A red arrow indicates that you can drill down to another level of the schematic. Here's what you get when you click the only red arrow on the Microsoft PowerPoint Objects screen (next to the Presentations *collection).*

Within a presentation, you'll typically find yourself working with the Slides collection, which contains all the Slide objects that represent the slides. On a slide, most items are represented by Shape objects gathered into the Shapes collection. For example, the text in a typical placeholder is contained in the Text property of the TextRange object in the TextFrame object within a Shape object on a slide. Figure 14.8 shows the Help diagram for the section of the object model below the Shapes collection.

FIGURE 14.8

Many of the objects you create on PowerPoint slides are implemented through Shape objects in VBA.

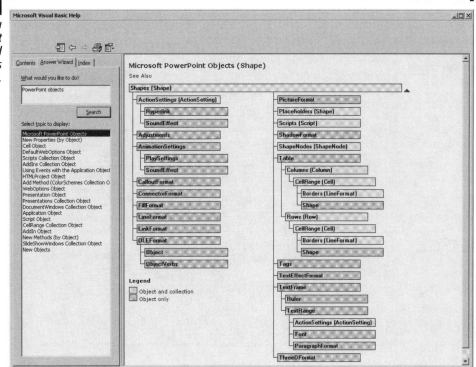

The Project Object Model

Start exploring the Microsoft Project object model by examining the Microsoft Project Objects screen in the Help file. Launch the Microsoft Visual Basic Help application from a Visual Basic Editor session hosted by Project as follows:

- If you're using the Office Assistant, ask it about **Microsoft Project Objects** and choose the Microsoft PowerPoint Objects topic it offers.

- If you're not using the Office Assistant, choose Help ➤ Microsoft Visual Basic Help, display the Answer Wizard page, and search for **Microsoft Project Objects**. The Microsoft Project Objects screen should emerge on top of the list and be displayed automatically; if it's not, display it manually.

Figure 14.9 shows the Microsoft Project Objects screen.

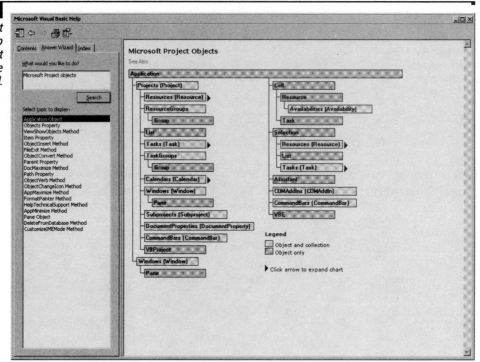

As with most object models, you can get soup-to-nuts coverage by going through the Application object, but for everyday purposes, you'll commonly bypass the Application object by using one of the creatable objects that Project exposes instead. Usually, you'll be using one of these objects:

- The ActiveCell object represents the active cell in the active project. This object too is useful for procedures that work on the user's current project and in which you need the user to indicate the cell requiring the procedure's attention.

- The `ActiveProject` object represents the active project in the application. The `ActiveProject` object is especially useful for creating simple procedures that affect only the project with which the user is currently working.

- The `Selection` object, which you return through the `ActiveSelection` property of the `Application` object (either explicitly or implicitly), represents the active selection in the active project.

- The `ActiveWindow` object represents the active window in the active project. When using this object, make sure that the window it returns contains what you were expecting it to.

- The `Projects` collection contains the `Project` objects that represent the open projects.

The WordPerfect Object Model

As I mentioned in Chapter 10, WordPerfect's object model is substantially different from the object models of the other applications discussed in this book. Instead of using a huge hierarchy of objects, WordPerfect uses only four:

- The `Application` object represents the WordPerfect application, as you'd expect.

- The `ActiveDocument` object represents the active document. You can also access the active document by using the `ThisDocument` object.

- The `GlobalMacros` object represents the global macro project, the `WordPerfect9` `.GMS` file. This project is created the first time you access the Visual Basic Editor from WordPerfect (you'll see the WordPerfect message box shown in Figure 14.10) and is automatically loaded for VBA sessions thereafter.

- The `PerfectScript` object represents the PerfectScript scripting language built within WordPerfect.

WordPerfect

The Global Macro Storage was not found. An empty Global Macro Storage will be created.

OK

There's little point in using the Application object in WordPerfect, because its Application property (Application.Application) doesn't do anything useful, and both ActiveDocument and PerfectScript are creatable objects, so you can access them without slogging through the Application object.

Most of the actions you'll take with VBA to manipulate WordPerfect documents will involve using the PerfectScript object to give VBA access to WordPerfect's built-in commands, as in the sample macro you created in Chapter 10.

The Visio Object Model

Because of the complexity of Visio drawings, the Visio object model is suitably involved. Figure 14.11 shows the most exciting parts of the Visio object model (it's not complete, because I've left off some of the more complex UI items, such as ToolbarItem objects).

The key objects you'll be working with are these objects, which are exposed and can be reached without going through the Application object:

- The ActiveDocument object represents the active document. You can also access the active document through the ThisDocument object.

- The ActivePage object represents the active page.

- The ActiveWindow object represents the active window. Before doing anything extravagant with the active window, make sure that it contains what you think it should.

- The Documents collection contains the Document objects that represent the open documents.

- The Windows collection contains the Window objects that represent the open windows.

As you can see in the figure, you'll typically start by going through a Document object to reach a Page object. Once on the page, you can manipulate the Connect objects (which represent connections between one object and another object), OLEObject objects, Layer objects, and Shape objects.

FIGURE 14.11

*The main parts of the
Visio object model*

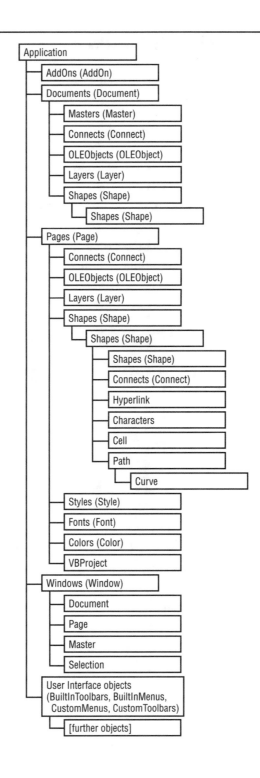

The AutoCAD Object Model

AutoCAD's object model is as complex as you'd expect—but once you take a look at it, you'll find that the number of objects you need immediately is manageable.

The best place to start investigating the AutoCAD object model is the Object Model topic in the AutoCAD ActiveX and VBA Reference Help file. To access this topic, follow these steps:

1. From a Visual Basic Editor session for AutoCAD, choose Help ➢ Microsoft Visual Basic Help to display the Help Topics: Visual Basic For Applications dialog box.

2. Type **object model** in the Type The First Few Letters Of The Word You're Looking For text box.

3. Choose the Object Model topic in the lower list box and select the Display button. You'll see the Topics Found dialog box with two suggestions, as shown in Figure 14.12.

FIGURE 14.12

To display the diagram of the AutoCAD object model, start Help, choose the Object Model topic, and then choose the Object Model (AAR– ActiveX And VBA Reference) topic.

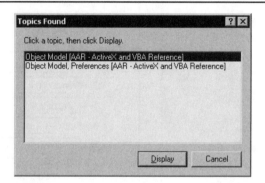

4. Choose the Object Model (AAR—ActiveX And VBA Reference) topic and click the Display button. Figure 14.13 shows the Object Model topic.

The red arrow to the right of the Preferences collection indicates that there's a separate diagram for the Preferences section of the object model. Figure 14.14 shows the Preferences diagram.

FIGURE 14.13

Start your exploration of the AutoCAD object model at the Object Model topic in the AutoCAD ActiveX and VBA Reference Help file.

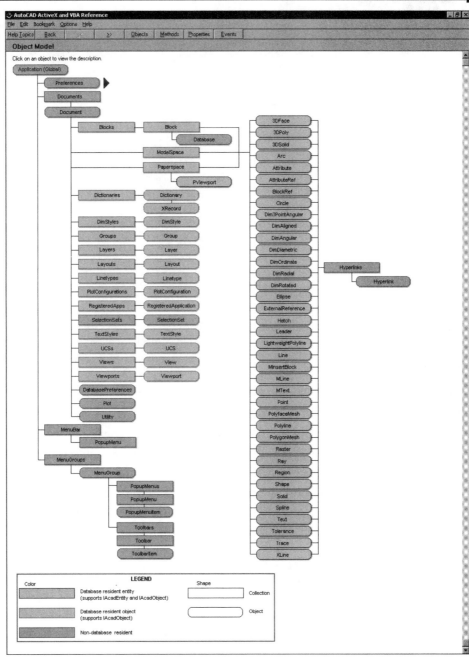

FIGURE 14.14

The Preferences section of the AutoCAD object model

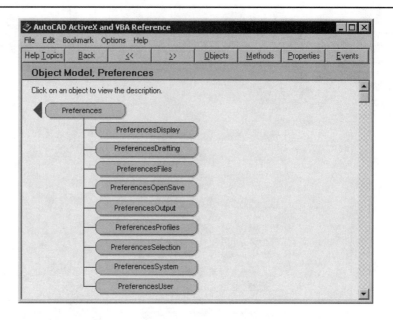

As you can see in Figure 14.13, the AutoCAD object model has four creatable collections: Documents, MenuBar, MenuGroups, and Preferences. You can access these collections, and the ActiveDocument object (which does not appear on the object model diagram), without explicitly troubling the Application object. Here's what these collections and the ActiveDocument object do:

- The ActiveDocument object represents the active document in the application. You can also access the active document by using the ThisDrawing object.

- The Documents collection contains the Document objects that represent the open drawing documents.

- The MenuBar collection (for once, a collection with a singular name) contains the PopupMenu objects that represent the currently active menus. (These Popup-Menu objects are menu-bar menus, not pop-up menus in the sense of context menus.)

- The MenuGroups collection contains a MenuGroup object that contains two collections of items that represent the menus and toolbars loaded into the current AutoCAD session. The PopupMenus collection contains a PopupMenu object containing PopupMenuItem objects, and the ToolBars collection contains a ToolBar object containing ToolBarItem objects.

- The Preferences collection contains the Preference objects that represent the options available for the user environment. These preferences are divided into nine groups, from PreferencesDisplay through PreferencesUser, that correspond to the options on the nine pages of the Options dialog box.

WARNING AutoCAD's collections are zero-based, meaning that the first element in a collection is numbered 0 (zero) rather than 1. So when working with AutoCAD collections, you need to identify the item you want by a number that is one less than its position in the collection. For example, the first Document object in the Documents collection is Document(0) rather than Document(1) (as it would be in Word or in Visio).

The collections for the menu bar, menu groups, and preferences are well and good, but you'll probably be spending most of your AutoCAD VBA time working with Document objects (active or otherwise). As you can see in Figure 14.13, the Document object gives you access not only to the blocks, groups, layers, and so on within the drawing, but also to the ModelSpace and PaperSpace collections, which represent the model space and paper space, respectively.

In this chapter, I've shown you how to start coming to grips with the object models of the seven applications this book discusses. With this basic knowledge, and with the tools discussed in Chapter 8 for finding the objects you need, you should be able to investigate in much more depth the object model of the application in which you're interested. But for now, it's time to move on. In the next chapter, you'll learn how to start adding custom dialog boxes to your procedures.

CHAPTER 15

Creating Simple Custom Dialog Boxes

I n Chapter 11, you saw how you could use VBA's built-in message boxes and input boxes to communicate with the users of your procedures, allow them to make choices about how to run the procedures, and provide necessary input for procedures. I finished the chapter by showing you a couple of instances where message boxes and input boxes proved unsuitable for providing the user with the choices the procedure needed—at least, for providing those choices in a logical and easy-to-use manner.

In this chapter, you'll start looking at the capabilities that Visual Basic for Applications provides for creating custom dialog boxes that interact with the user. Dialog boxes are one of the most powerful and complex features of VBA, and in this chapter I'll cover the more straightforward dialog box elements and how to manipulate them. In the next chapter, I'll show you how to create more complex dialog boxes, such as those that contain a number of tabbed pages and those that update themselves when the user clicks a control.

When Should You Use a Custom Dialog Box?

You'll often want to use a custom dialog box when simpler methods of interacting with the user fall short—for example, when you can't present the user with a reasonable choice using the limited selection of buttons provided in message boxes, or when you need to retrieve from the user information more involved than a straightforward input box can convey. You'll also need to use a custom dialog box when a procedure requires that the user choose non-exclusive options by selecting or clearing check boxes, when you need to present mutually exclusive choices via option buttons, or when you need to provide the user with a list box from which to make a selection. Likewise, if you need to show the user a picture or have them choose one or more items from a list box or a combo box, you'll need to use a custom dialog box.

Custom dialog boxes provide the full range of interface elements with which the user will be familiar from their experience with Windows applications. With a little effort, you can create custom dialog boxes that look professional enough to fool inexpert users into thinking that they're built-in dialog boxes.

Typically, you'll use custom dialog boxes to drive your procedures, so they usually will appear in response to an action taken by the user. For example, when the user starts a procedure, you can have the procedure display a dialog box presenting options—such as choosing the files for the procedure to manipulate—that determine what the procedure will do. You can also create dialog boxes that VBA triggers in response to events in the computer system: for example, an event that runs at a specific time or when the user takes a specific action (such as creating, opening, or closing a document).

Because creating dialog boxes is relatively complex and can be time-consuming, it's wise to consider any practical alternatives to using them. You've already looked at message boxes and input boxes, which provide a simple alternative for some of the easier tasks for which you might want to create a custom dialog box. Some applications, such as Word and Excel, even let you collar their dialog boxes and use them for your own purposes. Because the user is likely to be familiar with these dialog boxes (if they're familiar with the application, anyway), you can not only save yourself effort, but also avoid broadening the user's experience.

Creating a Custom Dialog Box

VBA uses visual objects called *user forms* to implement dialog boxes. A user form (also sometimes referred to simply—and somewhat confusingly—as a *form*) is essentially a blank sheet on which you can place controls (such as check boxes and buttons) to create a dialog box. The user form contains a code sheet that holds code attached to the controls in the form: You can attach code to any of the controls, and to the user form itself; and that code is stored in the user form's code sheet. You can display the user form's code sheet in the Code window of the Visual Basic Editor and work with it as you would any other code. You can run the user form as you would a procedure (for example, by pressing F5 with the user form selected), and the Visual Basic Editor will execute the code behind it.

Each user form becomes part of the application's user interface. In practical terms, this means that you can display a user form (a dialog box) for the user to interact with, and you can then retrieve information from the user form and manipulate it with VBA.

 NOTE You can also create user forms that aren't dialog boxes. The distinction between a dialog box and a window is one of those distinctions that people tend to argue about without reaching any firm conclusions for the rest of the world to follow. I find that the easiest distinction is that a window is resizable (you can resize it by dragging its borders or by clicking its Maximize button), while a dialog box isn't. Some dialog boxes, such as the Find And Replace dialog box in Word, have an initially hidden part that you can display (in the case of the Find And Replace dialog box, by clicking the More button). But apart from this extension, the bounds of the dialog box are fixed—you can't grab the corner of the dialog box with the mouse and drag to enlarge the dialog box.

Each user form is itself one object and contains a number of other objects that you can manipulate separately. For example, you could create a simple dialog box with two option buttons, an OK button, and a Cancel button. Each option button would be an object; the OK button would be a third object; and the Cancel button would be a fourth object. You could set properties for each object—such as the action to take when the Cancel button was clicked, or the ScreenTip to display when the user moved the mouse pointer over one of the option buttons—to make the dialog box as comprehensible, straightforward, and useful as possible.

You can set most properties for an object either at design time (when you're creating the user form) or at runtime (before or when you display the user form). For example, you can set the Value property of a check box control to True to display the check box in its selected state or to False to display the check box in its cleared state. You can set the Value property either when creating the user form (so that it will be set each time you run the user form) or when preparing to display the user form.

Now I'll go through the process of creating a custom dialog box. This is mostly theory, but bear with me. Toward the end of the chapter, I'll give you a couple of examples that step through creating a procedure and linking a dialog box to it.

Designing the Dialog Box

As you might imagine, there are several ways to design a custom dialog box:

- First, you can start from scratch and design the dialog box off-the-cuff. For straightforward dialog boxes with a half-dozen or so controls, this technique works pretty well. But for dialog boxes that need many more controls, you may find yourself wasting time on false starts before you find an arrangement of suitable controls that works both for you and the people who will use the dialog box.

- Second, you can adopt a more methodical approach and plan what you need to include in the dialog box before you start creating it: State the intended function of the dialog box and list the elements it will need in order to perform this function. Then sketch a rough diagram of the dialog box to get an approximate idea of where you'll fit in each of the elements. Unless you can sustain an uncanny imitation of the various Windows system fonts, the dialog box you end up creating will inevitably differ from your initial sketch. But by planning your design, you can make sure that you don't ruin an otherwise delightfully proportioned dialog box by having to add a couple of extra command buttons at the last minute to accommodate something vital you've forgotten.

- Third, you can draw the basic design for the custom dialog box from an existing dialog box. Study existing dialog boxes that perform a function similar to the dialog box you intend to build. Would one of them be appropriate if you were able to remove a couple of elements from it or substitute, say, a list box for a combination box? (A combination box—most widely known as a *combo box*—contains both a list box and a text box.) If so, you may be able to create a custom dialog box similar in design to the existing dialog box. Bear in mind that the major software companies have conducted thousands upon thousands of hours of usability tests for their applications, and will try to leverage this fact to your advantage. There's no point in reinventing the wheel—but if you find a particular dialog box ill-constructed or hard to use, consider how you might be able to improve on the design, and then implement those changes in dialog boxes that you create.

- Fourth, you can combine the previous three approaches into a method uniquely your own.

Inserting a User Form

Once you have a design in mind, the first step in creating a custom dialog box is to insert a user form in the appropriate template or document.

To insert a user form, select the appropriate project by clicking in the Project Explorer window. (If the Project Explorer isn't currently displayed, choose View ➢ Project Explorer or press Ctrl+R to display it.) Then insert the user form in any of the following three ways:

- Click the Insert button on the Standard toolbar in the Visual Basic Editor and choose UserForm from the drop-down list. (If the button is already displaying its Insert UserForm face, just click the button rather than bothering with the drop-down list.)
- Choose Insert ➢ UserForm.
- Right-click anywhere in the project and choose Insert ➢ UserForm from the context menu.

The Visual Basic Editor will open a new user form like that shown in Figure 15.1, which it will identify as UserForm*n*—usually UserForm1, unless the project already contains a user form named UserForm1. At the same time, the Visual Basic Editor will display the Toolbox. (If you've previously hidden the Toolbox while working on a user form, the Visual Basic Editor won't display it. Choose View ➢ Toolbox or click the Toolbox button on the Standard toolbar to display the Toolbox.)

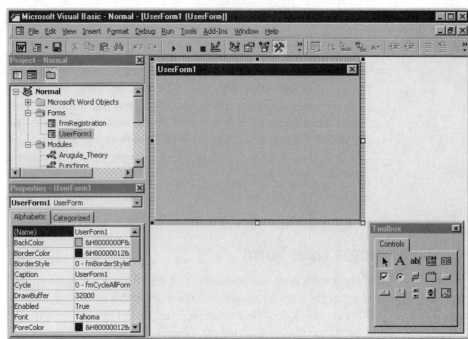

VBA will insert the user form in the Forms object (the collection of forms) for the project. If the project you chose didn't already contain a Forms object, VBA will add one to contain the new user form. You'll see the Forms object displayed in the Project Explorer.

Choosing User Form Grid Settings

The Visual Basic Editor displays a grid in each user form to help you place controls relative to the dialog box and to align controls relative to each other. To switch off the display of this grid (as in Figure 15.1) or to switch off the Visual Basic Editor's automatic alignment of controls to the grid, choose Tools ➤ Options to display the Options dialog box, select the General tab, and then clear the Show Grid check box or the Align Controls To Grid check box in the Form Grid Settings group box. You can also adjust the grid's units by specifying a different number of twips in the Width and Height text boxes. The Align Controls To Grid feature is usually a timesaver, so I suggest leaving it on.

Renaming the User Form

Once you've inserted the user form in a project, the next step is to change its default name of UserForm*n* to one that's more descriptive. (If you don't change the default name, it's surprisingly easy to get user forms confused when you start working with more than one at a time.) For advice on choosing names, refer to the sidebar "Naming Conventions in Visual Basic for Applications," a few pages ahead in this chapter, and then follow these steps:

1. If the Properties window isn't displayed, press F4 to display it. Figure 15.2 shows the two pages of the Properties window: Alphabetic and Categorized. Alphabetic contains an alphabetical listing of the properties of the currently selected object; Categorized contains a listing broken down into categories, such as Appearance, Behavior, Font, Misc., Picture, and Position. (Some controls have more categories than those listed here.) You can expand a category by clicking the plus (+) sign beside it to display the properties it contains, and collapse it by clicking the resulting minus (–) sign. If the Alphabetic tab isn't selected, click it to select it.

FIGURE 15.2

You can work on either the Alphabetic tab, or the Categorized tab of the Properties window.

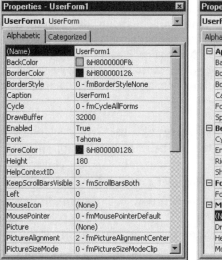 

NOTE You can enter the user form's name and caption on the Categorized tab of the Properties window if you want—you just have to look a little harder to find the right places. The `Caption` property is contained in the Appearance collection, and the `(Name)` property is contained in the Misc. collection.

2. Make sure the drop-down list is displaying the default name of the user form. If it isn't, select the user form from the drop-down list.

3. Select the user form's default name (such as `UserForm1` or `UserForm2`) in the cell to the right of the Name cell, and enter a new name for the user form. This name can be anything you want, with a few limitations:

   • It must start with a letter.

   • It can contain letters, numbers, and underscores, but no spaces or symbols.

   • It can be up to 40 characters long.

 WARNING Make sure you don't rename a user form or dialog box to a name that you've already used for a procedure: "Well, this is the `Move_Current_Paragraph` procedure, so I'll name this dialog box `Move_Current_Paragraph` so that I can remember what I called it." Because the names aren't unique, VBA will object with a message saying "Name conflicts with existing module, project, or object library." Calling the dialog box `Move_Current_Paragraph_Dialog` does create a unique name and gets around the problem. For a more elegant solution, consult the naming guidelines in the sidebar, "Naming Conventions in Visual Basic for Applications," coming up in a page or two.

4. Click the Caption cell to select the user form's default name and type the caption for the user form—that is, the text label that appears in the title bar of the dialog box. This name has no restrictions beyond the constraints imposed by the length of the title bar; you can enter a name longer than will fit in the title bar, but VBA will truncate it with an ellipsis at its maximum displayable length. As you type, you'll see the name appear in the user form title bar as well, so it's easy to see what's an appropriate length—at least, for the current size of the user form.

5. Press Enter or click elsewhere in the Properties window (or elsewhere in the Visual Basic Editor) to enter the user form's name.

 TIP Naming other objects works the same way as described here.

Naming Conventions in Visual Basic for Applications

Names for objects in VBA can be up to 40 characters long, must begin with a letter, and after that can be any combination of letters, numbers, and underscores. You can't use spaces or symbols in the names, and each name must be unique in its context—for example, each user form must have a unique name within a project, but within any user form or dialog box, an object can have the same name as an object in another dialog box.

Those are the rules; you can also use conventions to make the names of your VBA objects as consistent and easy to understand as possible. For example, by using the convention of starting a user form name with the letters frm, you can be sure that anyone else reading your code will immediately identify the name as belonging to a user form—and that you yourself will identify the name when you revisit old code you've written after a long interval. When you're writing code in a concentrated effort, you'll probably feel that the names you're using and the procedures you're putting together are crystal clear, and everything is so self-explanatory that you don't want to slow yourself down by entering comment lines about what the code does. But when you revisit the code later (perhaps to troubleshoot it), you'll have a much harder time working through what things are and what they do if you didn't document them at the time you wrote them. So it's a good idea to review quickly the code at the end of a project and enter comment lines at strategic points, or to take a moment now and then as you're creating the code to enter a quick reminder of what's what. I'll harp on this a bit more much later in the book.

Some popular naming conventions for the most-used VBA objects are shown in the following list. You'll encounter the naming conventions for other VBA objects in due course later in the book.

Object	Prefix	Example
Check box	chk	chkReturnToPreviousPosition
Command button	cmd	cmdOK
Form (user form)	frm	frmMoveParagraph
Frame	fra	fraMovement
List box	lst	lstConferenceAttendees
Combo box	cmb	cmbColor
Menu	mnu	mnuProcedures
Option button	opt	optSpecialDelivery
Label	lbl	lblUserName
Text box	txt	txtUserDescription

Continued

CONTINUED

Note that the naming convention is to begin the prefix for each object with lowercase letters and then start the rest of the object's name with a capital to make it a little easier to read. As already discussed, you can also use underscores in VBA names to separate names into more discrete chunks; you can't use spaces in any name.

Naming conventions tend to seem impossibly formal at first, and there's a strong temptation to use any name that suits you for the objects in your VBA user forms. But if you plan to distribute your VBA modules or have others work with them, it's usually worth the time, effort, and formality to follow the naming conventions.

Adding Controls to the User Form

Now that you've renamed the user form, you're ready to add controls to it from the Toolbox, shown in Figure 15.3. VBA automatically displays the Toolbox when a user form is active, but you can also display the Toolbox when no user form is active by choosing View ➤ Toolbox.

FIGURE 15.3

Use the Toolbox to add controls to the user form.

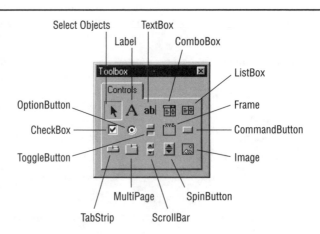

Here's what the buttons on the Toolbox do:

Button	Action
Select Objects	Restores the mouse pointer to selection mode. The mouse pointer automatically returns to selection mode once you've placed an object, so usually you'll need to click the Select Objects button only when you've selected another button and then decided not to use it, or when you've double-clicked on a control to place multiple instances of it.

Button	Action
Label	Creates a label—text used to identify a part of the dialog box or to explain information the user needs to know in order to use the dialog box effectively.
TextBox	Creates a text box (also known as an *edit box*)—a box into which the user can type text. You can also use a text box to display text to the user, or to provide text for the user to copy and paste elsewhere. A text box can contain either one line (the default) or multiple lines, and can display a horizontal scroll bar, a vertical scroll bar, or both horizontal and vertical scroll bars.
ComboBox	Creates a combo box—a control that combines a text box with a list box. The user can either choose a value from the list box or enter a new value in the text box.
ListBox	Creates a list box—a control that lists a number of values. The user can pick one value from the list, but can't enter a new value of their own. The list box is good for presenting closed sets of data.
CheckBox	Creates a check box and an accompanying label. The user can select or clear the check box to turn the associated action on or off.
OptionButton	Creates an option button (also known as a *radio button*) and an accompanying label. This button is usually a circle that contains a black dot when the option is selected. The user can select only one option button out of any group of option buttons. (The name *radio button* comes from radios with push buttons for stations, of which you can select only one button at a time.)
ToggleButton	Creates a toggle button—a button that shows whether or not an item is selected. A toggle button can be defined with any two settings, such as On/Off or Yes/No. You can add a picture to a toggle button, which provides a graphical way of letting a user choose multiple options.
Frame	Creates a frame—an area of a user form or dialog box surrounded by a thin line—and an accompanying label. Use a frame (also known as a *group box*) to group related elements in your dialog boxes. As well as cordoning off elements visually, frames can also separate them logically. For example, VBA treats a group of option buttons contained within a frame as separate from option buttons in other frames or option buttons loose in the dialog box. This separation makes it easier to use multiple sets of option buttons in a custom dialog box.

Button	Action
Command-Button	Creates a command button—a button used for taking action in a dialog box. Most dialog boxes contain command buttons such as OK and Cancel, or Open and Cancel, or Save.
TabStrip	Creates a tab strip for displaying multiple sets of data in the same set of controls. Tab strips are especially useful for presenting records in a database for review or modification: Each record in the database will have the same fields for information, so they can be displayed in the same group of controls; the tab strip provides an easy way of navigating between records.
MultiPage	Creates a multi-page control for displaying multi-page dialog boxes that have different layouts on each of their tabs. An example of a multi-page dialog box is the Options dialog box (Tools ➤ Options), which has 10 pages (often referred to incorrectly as *tabs*).
ScrollBar	Creates a stand-alone scroll bar. Stand-alone scroll bars are of relatively little use in dialog boxes unless you get particularly inventive. Combo boxes and list boxes have built-in scroll bars.
SpinButton	Creates a spin button control for attaching to another control. Spin buttons (also known as *spinners*) are typically small, rectangular buttons with one arrow pointing up and one down (or one arrow pointing left and the other pointing right). Spin buttons are useful for presenting sequential values with consistent intervals within an understood range, such as times or dates. For example, if you want the user to increment or decrement a price in a text box in 25-cent steps, you could use a spinner to adjust the price rather than letting them type directly into the text box.
Image	Creates an image control for displaying a picture within the user form. For example, you might use an image control to place a corporate logo or a picture in a dialog box.

 NOTE   The Toolbox you're looking at in this chapter contains the basic set of tools provided by VBA. As discussed in Chapter 3, you can customize the Toolbox in various ways: by adding other existing controls to it, creating additional pages for the controls, moving controls from page to page, and creating customized controls of your own making so that you can quickly place the elements you need most often.

Click in the user form to add a standard-size version of the selected control, as illustrated in Figure 15.4. VBA will place the top-left corner of the control where you click. As you place a control, it will snap to the grid on the user form (unless you've turned off the Align Controls To Grid feature as described in the earlier section, "Choosing User Form Grid Settings").

FIGURE 15.4

When you click in the user form, VBA places a standard-size control of the type you chose. If the Align Controls To Grid feature is switched on (as it is by default), VBA automatically aligns the control with the grid on the user form.

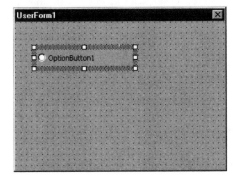

 TIP   To place multiple instances of the same control, double-click the control's button on the Toolbox. The Visual Basic Editor then doesn't revert to the selection pointer after you place the first control, but rather remains at the ready for placing more instances of that control. When you've finished with that control, click the Select Objects button to restore the mouse pointer, or click any other Toolbox button so that you can place a control of that type.

You can resize the standard-size control as necessary by selecting it and then clicking and dragging one of the selection handles (the white squares) that appear around it, as shown in Figure 15.5. When you drag a corner handle, VBA resizes the control on both sides of the corner; when you drag the handle at the midpoint of one of the control's sides, VBA resizes the control only in that dimension. In either case, VBA displays a dotted outline indicating the size that the control will be when you release the mouse button.

FIGURE 15.5

Once you've placed a control, you can resize it as necessary by dragging one of its selection handles.

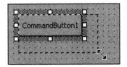

You can also create a custom-size version of the control by clicking and dragging when you place the control in the user form (as opposed to clicking to place a standard-size control and then dragging it to the size you want). Usually, however, it's easiest to place a standard-size version of the control and then resize it as necessary.

 TIP To resize the user form itself, click its title bar (or in any blank space in the form—not in a control) to select it, and then click and drag one of the selection handles that appear around it.

To delete a control, right-click it in the user form and choose Delete from the context menu. Alternatively, click it to select it and then press the Delete key or choose Edit ➤ Delete.

To delete multiple controls, select them first as follows and then delete them by using the methods described in the previous paragraph:

- To select multiple contiguous controls, select the first control and then hold down Shift and select the last control in the sequence.

- To select multiple noncontiguous controls—or to select further controls after you've selected multiple contiguous controls by using the Shift key—hold down the Ctrl key as you select each control after the first.

- To select multiple controls in the same area of the user form, click in the form outside the controls and drag the resulting selection box until it encompasses at least part of each control. When you release the mouse button, the Visual Basic Editor selects the controls.

Renaming Controls

As with user forms, VBA gives each control that you add a default name consisting of the type of control and a sequential number for the type of control. When you create the first text box in a user form, VBA will name it TextBox1; when you create another text box, VBA will name it TextBox2; and so on. Each control in a dialog box has to have a unique name so that you can refer to it in code.

Almost invariably, you'll want to change the controls' default names to names that describe their functions so you can remember what they do. For example, if TextBox2 is used for entering the user's organization name, you might want to rename it txt-OrganizationName, txtOrgName, txtO_Name, or something similar.

To rename a control:

1. Click the control in the user form to select it and display its properties in the Properties window.

   - When selecting a control, make sure the Select Objects button is selected in the Toolbox. (Unless you're performing another operation in the Toolbox—such as placing another control—the Select Objects button should be selected anyway.)

   - If the Properties window is already displayed, you can select the control from the drop-down list instead of selecting it in the user form. VBA will select the control in the user form, which helps you make sure that you've selected the control you want to affect.

   - If the Properties window isn't displayed, you can quickly display it with the properties for the appropriate control by right-clicking the control in the user form and choosing Properties from the context menu.

2. On either the Alphabetic page or the Categorized page, select the default name in the cell to the right of the Name property.

3. Enter the new name for the control. Remember that the name for a control (which is an object, like the user form) must start with a letter, can contain letters, numbers, and underscores (but no spaces or symbols), and can be up to 40 characters long.

4. Press Enter to set the control name, or click elsewhere in the Properties window or in the user form.

You can rename a control again at any point. Be aware, though, that you'll also need to change any references to it in the code that drives the user form—so you have a strong incentive to choose suitable names for your controls before you write the code.

Moving a Control

To move a control that isn't currently selected, click anywhere in it to select it, and then drag it to where you want it to appear, as shown in Figure 15.6.

FIGURE 15.6

If a control isn't currently selected, you can move it by clicking it and dragging it.

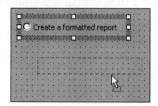

To move a selected control, move the mouse pointer over the selection border around it so that the mouse pointer turns into a four-headed arrow (as shown in Figure 15.7), and then click and drag the control to where you want it to appear.

FIGURE 15.7

If a control is selected, move the mouse pointer over its selection border, then click and drag the control.

NOTE You can use the Cut and Paste commands (either from the Standard toolbar, the Edit menu, the context menu, or the keyboard) to move a control, but it isn't a great way of proceeding: The Paste command places the control slap in the middle of the user form or container (for example, a frame), so you have to drag it to its new position anyway.

Copying and Pasting Controls

You can use the Copy and Paste commands to copy and paste controls that you've already added to a user form. You can paste them either to the same user form or to another user form. As I mentioned in the preceding note, the Paste command drops the copy of the control in the middle of the user form or container; from there you have to drag it to where you want it. The advantage of using Copy and Paste for creating new controls—versus using Cut and Paste to move existing controls—is that the new controls take on the characteristics of their progenitors, so you can save time by creating a control, setting its properties, and then cloning it. All you need to do then is move each cloned copy to a suitable location, change its name from the default name VBA has given it to something descriptive and memorable, and set any properties that differ from those of the control's siblings. For copies you paste to another user form, you don't even need to change the names of the copies you paste—they just need to be named suitably for the code with which they work.

 TIP Add customized copies of controls that you use frequently to the Toolbox. From the Toolbox, you can quickly add multiple copies of the control to a user form. You'll need to set the name for each copy of the control after the first, but all the other properties will remain as you set them for the copy of the control on the Toolbox.

If you need to set all the properties separately for each control of the same type, you'll probably find it quicker to insert a new control by using the Toolbox buttons rather than Copy and Paste.

As an alternative to using the Copy and Paste commands, you can also copy a control by holding down the Ctrl key as you click and drag the control. VBA will display a + sign attached to the mouse pointer, as shown in Figure 15.8, to indicate that you're copying the control rather than moving it. Drop the copy where you want it to appear on the user form.

FIGURE 15.8

VBA displays a + sign attached to the mouse pointer when you Ctrl+drag to copy a control.

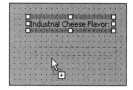

Changing the Label on a Control

For a control with a displayed label, you can change the label by working in the user form as follows:

1. Click the control to select it.

2. Click once in the label to select it. VBA will display a faint dotted border around the label, as shown in Figure 15.9. (Make sure that these two clicks are distinct enough that Windows doesn't interpret them as a double-click. A double-click will display the code sheet for the user form and will add a procedure for the Click event of the label. If this happens, press Shift+F7 or choose View ➤ Object to view the form again. Then start again with step 1.)

FIGURE 15.9

To change the label on a control, select the control, then click in the label so that it displays a faint dotted border.

3. Click in the label to position the insertion point for editing it, or drag through the label to select all of it.

4. Edit the text of the label as desired.

5. Press Enter or click elsewhere in the user form to effect the change to the label.

TIP You can also change the label by changing its Caption property in the Properties window.

When Should You Set Properties for a Control?

As I mentioned earlier in this chapter, you can set many properties for a control either at design time or at runtime. There's a time and a place for each—and a time when either is a reasonable course of action.

Generally speaking, the more static the property, the more often you'll want to set it at design time. Some properties, such as the Name property of a user form, *have* to be set at design time—you can't set such properties at runtime for a user form. You'll also usually want to name your controls at design time, though you can add controls at runtime and set their Name properties.

In most cases, you'll want to set the properties that govern the position and size of the user form itself and its controls at design time. The advantages are straightforward: You can make sure that the user form looks as you intend it to, that it's legible, and so on.

Occasionally, you may need to adjust the properties of a user form or the size or position of some of the controls on it at runtime. For example, you might need to add a couple of option buttons to the form to take care of eventualities not included in the basic design of the form. Alternatively, you might create a form that had two groups of option buttons sharing the same space—one group, in effect, positioned on top of the other. At runtime, you could establish which group of option buttons was needed, make that group visible, and hide the other group. If each group contained the same number of option buttons, you could make do with one group of option buttons, assigning the appropriate properties to each at runtime.

Given the flexibility that the many properties of controls provide, you can often design your user forms to handle several circumstances by displaying and hiding different groups of controls at runtime, rather than having to add or remove controls at runtime. Creating the complete set of controls for a user form at design time avoids most of the difficulties that can arise from adding extra controls at runtime. That said, you may sometimes need to create a user form on-the-fly to present information about the situation in which users have placed themselves.

As you'll see as you continue to work with controls, you have to set information for some controls at runtime. For example, you can't assign the list of items to a list box or combo box at design time: You have to assign the list of items at runtime. (Typically, you assign the list of items during a UserForm_Initialize procedure that runs as the user form is being initialized for display.)

Key Properties for the Toolbox Controls

In this section, I'll discuss the key properties for the controls in the default Toolbox.

First, I'll show you the common properties used to manipulate many of the controls effectively. After that, I'll go through the controls one by one, listing the properties peculiar to each control.

If you're new to VBA and find this section heavy going, skip it for the time being and return to it when you need to reference information about the properties of the controls.

Common Properties

Table 15.1 lists the properties shared by all or most controls, grouped by category.

TABLE 15.1: PROPERTIES COMMON TO MOST OR ALL CONTROLS

Property	Applies To	Explanation
Information		
BoundValue	All controls except Frame, Image, and Label	Contains the value of the control when the control receives the focus in the user form.
HelpContextID	All controls except Image and Label	Returns the context identifier of the Help file topic associated with the control.
Name	All controls	Contains the name for the control.
Object	All controls	Enables you to assign to a control a custom property or method that uses the same name as a standard property or method.

Continued ▌▶

TABLE 15.1 CONTINUED: PROPERTIES COMMON TO MOST OR ALL CONTROLS

Property	Applies To	Explanation
Information		
Parent	All controls	Returns the name of the user form that contains the control.
Tag	All controls	Used for assigning extra information to the control.
Value	CheckBox, ComboBox, CommandButton, ListBox, MultiPage, OptionButton, ScrollBar, SpinButton, TabStrip, TextBox, ToggleButton	One of the most varied properties, Value specifies the state or value of the control. A CheckBox, OptionButton, or ToggleButton can have an integer value of −1 (True), indicating that the item is selected; or a value of 0 (False), indicating that the item is cleared. A ScrollBar or SpinButton returns a Value containing the current value for the control. A ComboBox or ListBox returns the currently selected row's (or rows') BoundColumn value. A MultiPage returns an integer indicating the active page, and a TextBox returns the text in the text box. The Value of a CommandButton is False, because choosing the command button triggers a Click event. However, you can set the value of a CommandButton to True, which has the same effect as clicking it.
Size and Position		
Height	All controls	The height of the control, measured in points.
LayoutEffect	All controls except Image	Indicates whether a control was moved when the layout of the form was changed.
Left	All controls	The distance of the left border of the control in pixels from the left edge of the form or frame that contains it.
OldHeight	All controls	The previous height of the control, measured in pixels.
OldLeft	All controls	The previous position of the left border of the control, measured in pixels.
OldTop	All controls	The previous position of the top border of the control, measured in pixels.
OldWidth	All controls	The previous width of the control, measured in points.
Top	All controls	The distance of the top border of the control in pixels from the top edge of the form or frame that contains it.
Width	All controls	The width of the control, measured in points.

Continued

TABLE 15.1 CONTINUED: PROPERTIES COMMON TO MOST OR ALL CONTROLS

Property	Applies To	Explanation
	Appearance	
Alignment	CheckBox, OptionButton, ToggleButton	Specifies how the caption is aligned to the control.
AutoSize	CheckBox, ComboBox, CommandButton, Image, Label, OptionButton, TextBox, ToggleButton	A Boolean property that controls whether the object resizes itself automatically to accommodate its contents. The default setting is False, which means that the control doesn't automatically resize itself.
BackColor	All controls	The background color of the control. This property contains a number representing the color.
BackStyle	CheckBox, ComboBox, CommandButton, Frame, Image, Label, OptionButton, TextBox, ToggleButton	Specifies whether the background of the object is transparent (fmBackStyleTransparent) or opaque (fmBackStyleOpaque, the default). You can see through a transparent control—anything behind it on the form will show through. You can use transparent controls to achieve interesting effects—for example, by placing a transparent command button on top of an image or another control.
BorderColor	ComboBox, Image, Label, TextBox, ListBox	Specifies the color of the control's border. You can choose a border color from the System drop-down list or the palette, or enter BorderColor as an eight-digit integer value (such as **16711680** for mid-blue). VBA stores the BorderColor property as a hexadecimal value (for instance, 00FF0000). For BorderColor to take effect, BorderStyle must be set to fmBorderStyleSingle.
BorderStyle	ComboBox, Frame, Image, Label, ListBox, TextBox, UserForm	Specifies the style of border on the control or user form. Use BorderStyle with the BorderColor property to set the color of a border.
Caption	CheckBox, CommandButton, Label, OptionButton, ToggleButton	A text string containing the description that appears for a control—the text that appears in a label, on a command button or toggle button, or next to a check box or option button.
Font (object)	All controls except Image, SpinButton, and ScrollBar	Font—an object rather than a property—controls the font in which the label for the object is displayed. For TextBox, ComboBox, and ListBox controls, Font controls the font in which the text in the control is displayed.

Continued

TABLE 15.1 CONTINUED: PROPERTIES COMMON TO MOST OR ALL CONTROLS

Property	Applies To	Explanation
	Appearance	
ForeColor	All controls except Image	The foreground color of the control (often the text on the control). This property contains a number representing the color.
Locked	CheckBox, ComboBox, CommandButton, ListBox, OptionButton, TextBox, ToggleButton	A Boolean property that specifies whether the user can change the control. When Locked is set to True, the user can't change the control, though the control can still receive the focus (that is, be selected) and trigger events. When Locked is False (the default value), the control is open for editing.
MouseIcon	All controls except MultiPage	Specifies the image to display when the user moves the mouse pointer over the control. To use the MouseIcon property, the MousePointer property must be set to 99, fmMousePointerCustom.
MousePointer	All controls except MultiPage	Specifies the type of mouse pointer to display when the user moves the mouse pointer over the control.
Picture	CheckBox, Command-Button, Frame, Image, Label, OptionButton, Page, ToggleButton, UserForm	Specifies the picture to display on the control. By using the Picture property, you can add a picture to a normally text-based control, such as a command button.
PicturePosition	CheckBox, CommandButton, Label, OptionButton, ToggleButton	Specifies how the picture is aligned with its caption.
SpecialEffect	CheckBox, ComboBox, Frame, Image, Label, ListBox, OptionButton, TextBox, ToggleButton	Specifies the visual effect to use for the control. For a CheckBox, OptionButton, or ToggleButton, the visual effect can be flat (fmButtonEffectFlat) or sunken (fmButtonEffectSunken). For the other controls, the visual effect can be flat (fmSpecialEffectFlat), raised (fmSpecial-EffectRaised), sunken (fmSpecialEffect-Sunken),etched (fmSpecialEffectEtched), or a bump (fmSpecialEffectBump).
Visible	All controls	Indicates whether the control is visible; expressed as a Boolean value.

Continued ▶

TABLE 15.1 CONTINUED: PROPERTIES COMMON TO MOST OR ALL CONTROLS		
Property	**Applies To**	**Explanation**
Appearance		
WordWrap	CheckBox, CommandButton, Label, OptionButton, TextBox, ToggleButton	A Boolean property that specifies whether the text in or on a control wraps at the end of a line. For most controls, WordWrap is set to True by default; you'll often want to change this property to False to prevent the text from wrapping inappropriately. If the control is a TextBox and its MultiLine property is set to True, VBA ignores the WordWrap property.
Behavior		
Accelerator	CheckBox, CommandButton, Label, OptionButton, Page, Tab, ToggleButton	The accelerator key (or *access key*, or *mnemonic*) for the control—the key you press (typically in combination with Alt) to access the control (for example, to access the Cancel button, you'd press Alt+C). Note that the accelerator key for a label applies to the next control in the tab order.
ControlSource	CheckBox, ComboBox, ListBox, OptionButton, ScrollBar, SpinButton, TextBox, ToggleButton	The cell or field used to set or store the Value of the control. The default value is an empty string (" "), indicating that there is no control source for the control.
ControlTipText	All controls	The text of the ScreenTip displayed when the user holds the mouse pointer over the control. The default value of ControlTipText is a blank string, which means that no ScreenTip is displayed.
Enabled	All controls	A Boolean value that controls whether the control can be accessed (either interactively or programmatically).
TabIndex	All controls except Image	The position of the control in the tab order of the user form, expressed as an integer from 0 (the first position) through the number of controls on the user form.
TabStop	All controls except Image and Label	A Boolean value establishing whether the user can select the control by pressing the Tab key. If TabStop is set to False, the user can select the control only with the mouse. The TabStop setting doesn't change the tab order of the dialog box.

Label

The Label control is relatively simple, in that it does no more than display text on screen. It is accordingly straightforward in its use of properties: Use the positional properties to place the label and the Caption property to assign the text that you want the label to display. Use the TextAlign property as shown in Table 15.2 to align the text of the label with the borders of the label control.

TABLE 15.2: *TEXTALIGN* PROPERTY VALUES FOR THE LABEL CONTROL

fmTextAlign Constant	Value	Text Alignment
fmTextAlignLeft	1	With the left border of the control
fmTextAlignCenter	2	Centered on the control's area
fmTextAlignRight	3	With the right border of the control

TextBox

Table 15.3 lists the key properties for the TextBox control.

TABLE 15.3: KEY PROPERTIES FOR THE TEXTBOX CONTROL

Property	Description
AutoTab	A Boolean property that determines whether VBA automatically enters a tab when the user has entered the maximum number of characters in the text box or combo box.
AutoWordSelect	A Boolean property that determines whether VBA automatically selects a whole word when the user drags the mouse through text in a text box or a combo box.
DragBehavior	Enables or disables drag-and-drop for a text box or combo box: fmDragBehaviorDisabled (0) disables drag-and-drop; fmDragBehaviorEnabled (1) enables drag-and-drop.
EnterFieldBehavior	Determines whether VBA selects the contents of the edit area of the text box or combo box when the user moves the focus to the text box or combo box: fmEnterFieldBehaviorSelectAll (0) selects the contents of the text box or current row of the combo box; fmEnterFieldBehaviorRecallSelection (1) doesn't change the previous selection.

Continued ▶

TABLE 15.3 CONTINUED: KEY PROPERTIES FOR THE TEXTBOX CONTROL	
Property	**Description**
EnterKeyBehavior	A Boolean property that determines what VBA does when the user presses Enter with the focus on a text box. If EnterKeyBehavior is True, VBA creates a new line when the user presses Enter; if EnterKeyBehavior is False, VBA moves the focus to the next control on the user form. Note that if MultiLine is False, VBA ignores the EnterKeyBehavior setting.
HideSelection	A Boolean property that determines whether VBA displays any selected text in a text box or combo box. If HideSelection is True, VBA displays the text without indicating the selection when the control doesn't have the focus; if HideSelection is False, VBA indicates the selection both when the control has the focus and when it doesn't.
IMEMode	Determines the default runtime mode of the Input Method Editor (IME). This property is used only in Far-Eastern applications (for example, those using Japanese hiragana or katakana, or Korean hangul).
IntegralHeight	A Boolean property that determines whether a list box or a text box resizes itself vertically to display any rows that are too tall to fit into it at its current height (True) or not (False).
MultiLine	A Boolean property that determines whether the text box can contain multiple lines of text (True) or only one line (False). When MultiLine is True, the text box will increase the number of lines it contains to match the amount of information it contains, and will add a vertical scroll bar when the content becomes more than will fit within the current dimensions of the text box.
PasswordChar	Specifies the placeholder character to use in place of text entered in a text box. When you specify the character for PasswordChar, VBA displays one instance of that character in place of each letter in the text box. As its name implies, this property is normally used for entering passwords and other information that needs to be secured against prying eyes.
ScrollBars	Specifies which scroll bars to display on the text box. Usually, you'll do best to set the WordWrap property to True and let VBA add the vertical scroll bar to the text box as needed rather than using the ScrollBars property.
SelectionMargin	A Boolean property that determines whether the user can select a line of text in the text box or combo box by clicking in the selection bar to the left of the line.
ShowDropButtonWhen	Determines when to display the drop-down button for a combo box or a text box. fmShowDropButtonWhenNever (0) never displays the drop-down button and is the default for a text box. fmShowDropButtonWhenFocus (1) displays the drop-down button when the text box or combo box has the focus. fmShowDropButtonWhenAlways (2) always displays the drop-down button and is the default for a combo box.

Continued ▶

TABLE 15.3 CONTINUED: KEY PROPERTIES FOR THE TEXTBOX CONTROL

Property	Description
TabKeyBehavior	A Boolean property that specifies whether the user can enter tabs in the text box. If TabKeyBehavior is True and MultiLine is True, pressing Tab enters a tab in the text box. If MultiLine is False, VBA ignores a TabKeyBehavior setting of True. If TabKeyBehavior is False, pressing Tab moves the focus to the next control in the tab order.

ComboBox and ListBox

Table 15.4 shows the key properties for the ComboBox control and the ListBox control. These two controls are highly similar and share many properties.

TABLE 15.4: KEY PROPERTIES FOR THE COMBOBOX CONTROL AND LISTBOX CONTROL

Property	Description
AutoTab	See Table 15.3.
AutoWordSelect	See Table 15.3.
BoundColumn	A Variant property that determines the source of data in a combo box or a list box that has multiple columns. The default setting is 1 (the first column). To assign another column, specify the number of the column (columns are numbered from 1, the leftmost column). To assign the value of ListIndex to BoundColumn, use 0.
ColumnCount	A Long property that sets or returns the number of columns displayed in the combo box or list box. If the data source is unbound, you can specify up to 10 columns. To display all available columns in the data source, set ColumnCount to −1.
ColumnHeads	A Boolean property that determines whether the combo box or list box displays headings on the columns (True) or not (False).
ColumnWidths	A String property that sets or returns the width of each column in a multi-column combo box or list box.
ListRows	(Combo box only.) A Long property that sets or returns the number of rows displayed in the combo box. If the number of items in the list is greater than the value of ListRows, the combo box will display a scroll bar so that the user can scroll to the unseen items.

Continued ▌▶

TABLE 15.4 CONTINUED: KEY PROPERTIES FOR THE COMBOBOX CONTROL AND LISTBOX CONTROL	
Property	**Description**
ListStyle	Determines the visual effect the list uses. For both a combo box and a list box, fmListStylePlain displays a regular, unadorned list. For a combo box, fmListStyleOption displays an option button to the left of each entry, allowing the user to select one item from the list. For a list box, fmListStyleOption displays option buttons for a single-select list and check boxes for a multi-select list.
ListWidth	(Combo box only.) A Variant property that sets or returns the width of the list in a combo box. The default value is 0, which makes the list the same width as the text area of the combo box.
MatchEntry	Determines which type of matching the combo box or list box uses when the user types characters with the focus on the combo box or list box. fmMatchEntryFirstLetter (0) matches the next entry that starts with the letter or character typed: If the user types *t* twice, VBA selects the first entry beginning with *t* and then the second entry beginning with *t*. fmMatchEntryComplete (1) matches each letter the user types: If the user types *te*, VBA selects the entry that starts with *te*. fmEntryMatchNone (2) specifies no matching: The user can't select an item by typing in the list box or combo box, but must use the mouse or the arrow keys instead. The default MatchEntry setting for a combo box is fmMatchEntryComplete; the default setting for a list box is fmMatchEntryFirstLetter.
MatchRequired	(Combo box only.) A Boolean property determining whether the user must select an entry from the combo box before leaving the control (True) or not (False). This property is useful for making sure that the user doesn't type a partial entry into the text box area of the combo box but forget to complete the selection in the drop-down list area. If MatchRequired is True and the user tries to leave the combo box without making a selection, VBA will display an *Invalid Property Value* message box.
MultiSelect	(List box only.) Controls whether the user can make a single selection in the list or multiple selections. fmMultiSelectSingle (0) lets the user select only one item. fmMultiSelectMulti (1) lets the user select multiple items by clicking with the mouse or by pressing the spacebar. fmMultiSelectExtended (2) lets the user use Shift+click, Ctrl+click, and Shift with the arrow keys to extend or reduce the selection.
RowSource	A String property that specifies the source of a list for a combo box or a list box.
SelectionMargin	See Table 15.3.
ShowDropButtonWhen	See Table 15.3.

CheckBox

The CheckBox control has a relatively straightforward selection of properties, most of which you've seen already. The key property of the CheckBox that you haven't examined yet is `TripleState`, which applies to the OptionButton and ToggleButton controls as well.

`TripleState` is a Boolean property that determines whether the check box, option button, or toggle button can have a null state as well as `True` and `False` states. When the check box is in the null state, it appears with its box selected but grayed out. For example, you get this effect in the Font dialog box in Word when one of the check box–controlled properties—such as the Shadow check box in Figure 15.10—is on for part of the current selection but not for the whole selection.

FIGURE 15.10

By setting the TripleState property of a check box to True, you can display a check box in a null state. Word's Font dialog box shows check boxes in a null state (selected but grayed out) when they apply to part of the current selection but not to the whole of the current selection.

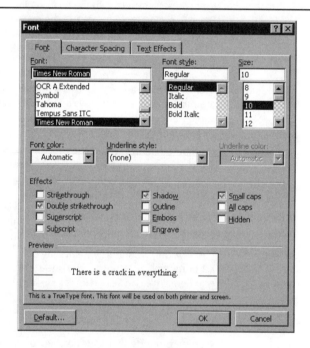

A couple of properties that I've described briefly in the context of other controls deserve more detail here:

- The `SpecialEffect` property controls the visual appearance of the check box. The default value is `fmButtonEffectSunken` (2), which displays a sunken box—the norm for 3-D Windows dialog boxes. You can also choose `fmButtonEffect-Flat` (0) to display a box with a flat effect. Figure 15.11 shows a sunken box and a flat box.

- The Value property, which indicates whether the check box is selected (True) or cleared (False), is the default property of the check box. The following three statements have the same effect:

```
If CheckBox1.Value = True Then
If CheckBox1 = True Then
If CheckBox1 Then
```

- The Accelerator property provides quick access to the check box. Be sure to assign a unique accelerator key to check boxes so that the user can swiftly toggle them on and off from the keyboard.

OptionButton

Like the CheckBox, the OptionButton control has a straightforward set of properties, almost all of which you've seen already in this chapter. In this section, I'll show you the GroupName property, which is unique to the OptionButton, and at some of the key properties for working with option buttons.

The GroupName property is a string property that assigns the option button to a group of option buttons. The default setting for GroupName is a blank string (" "), which means that an option button isn't assigned to a group until you explicitly assign it. When you enter the group name, the group is created. By using the GroupName property, you can have multiple groups of option buttons on the same form without using frames to cordon off the groups. That said, you'll need to distinguish the logical groups of option buttons from each other so that the user can immediately tell which option buttons constitute a group. In practice, a frame often provides the easiest way of segregating groups of option buttons both visually and logically—but it's useful to have the flexibility that GroupName provides when you need it.

Here are the other key properties you need to know about for the OptionButton control:

- The Value property, which indicates whether the option button is selected (True) or cleared (False), is the default property of the option button. So you can set or return the state of the option button by setting either the OptionButton object or its Value to True or False, as appropriate. Setting the Value of one OptionButton to True sets the Value of all other OptionButton controls in the same group or frame to False.

- The Accelerator property provides quick access to the option button. Be sure to assign a unique accelerator key to each option button so that the user can toggle it on and off from the keyboard.

- The SpecialEffect property controls the visual appearance of the option button. The default value of fmButtonEffectSunken (2) displays a sunken button, while fmButtonEffectFlat (0) displays a flattened button.

- The TripleState property (discussed in the previous section) lets you create an option button that has three states: selected (True), cleared (False), and null (which appears selected but grayed out). The TripleState property is disabled so that the user can't set the null state interactively, but you can set it programmatically as needed.

ToggleButton

The ToggleButton control creates a toggle button: a button that, when not selected, appears raised, but whose appearance changes so that it appears pushed in when it's selected. The key properties for the ToggleButton control are the same as those for the CheckBox and CommandButton:

- The Value property is the default property of the ToggleButton.

- The TripleState property lets you create a ToggleButton that has three states: selected (True), cleared (False), and null (which appears selected but grayed out). As with the CheckBox, but unlike the OptionButton, the user can set a triple-state ToggleButton to its null state by clicking it. In its null state, a Toggle-Button appears grayed out.

- The Accelerator property provides quick access to the toggle button.

Frame

The Frame control is relatively straightforward, but it has several properties worth mentioning; they're shown in Table 15.5. It shares a couple of these properties with the Page object.

TABLE 15.5: PROPERTIES OF THE FRAME CONTROL

Property	Description
Cycle	Determines the action taken when the user leaves the last control in the frame or on the page. fmCycleAllForms (0) moves the focus to the next control in the tab order for the user form or page, whereas fmCycleCurrentForm (2) keeps the focus within the frame or on the page until the focus is explicitly moved to a control in a different frame or on a different page. This property applies to the Page object as well.

Continued ▐▶

TABLE 15.5 CONTINUED: PROPERTIES OF THE FRAME CONTROL	
Property	**Description**
InsideHeight	A read-only property that returns the height in points of the area inside the frame, not including the height of any horizontal scroll bar displayed. This property applies to the Page object as well.
InsideWidth	A read-only property that returns the width in points of the area inside the frame, not including the width of any vertical scroll bar displayed. This property applies to the Page object as well.
KeepScrollBarsVisible	A property that determines whether the frame or page displays horizontal and vertical scroll bars when they aren't required for the user to be able to navigate the frame or the page. fmScrollBarsNone (0) displays no scroll bars unless they're required. fmScrollBarsHorizontal (1) displays a horizontal scroll bar all the time. fmScrollBarsVertical (2) displays a vertical scroll bar all the time. fmScrollBarsBoth (3) displays a horizontal scroll bar and a vertical scroll bar all the time. fmScrollBarsNone is the default for the Frame object, and fmScroll-BarsBoth is the default for the Page object. This property applies to the Page object as well.
PictureTiling	A Boolean property that determines whether a picture displayed on the control is tiled (True) so that it takes up the whole area covered by the control or not (False). To set the tiling pattern, you use the PictureAlignment and PictureSizeMode properties. This property applies to the Page object and the Image control as well.
PictureSizeMode	Determines how to display the background picture. fmPicture-SizeModeClip (0), the default setting, crops off any part of the picture too big to fit in the page, frame, or image control. Use this setting to show the picture at its original dimensions and in its original proportions. fmPictureSizeModeStretch (1) stretches the picture horizontally or vertically to fill the page, frame, or image control. This setting is good for colored backgrounds and decorative effects, but tends to be disastrous for pictures that need to be recognizable; it also overrides the PictureAlignment property setting (which I'll show you next). fmPictureSizeModeZoom (3) zooms the picture proportionately until the horizontal dimension or the vertical dimension reaches the edge of the control, but doesn't stretch the picture so that the other dimension is maximized as well. This is good for maximizing the size of a picture while retaining its proportions, but you'll need to resize the non-maximized dimension of the Image control to remove blank space. This property applies to the Page object and the Image control as well.

Continued

TABLE 15.5 CONTINUED: PROPERTIES OF THE FRAME CONTROL

Property	Description
PictureAlignment	Determines where a picture is located. fmPictureAlignmentTopLeft (0) aligns the picture with the upper-left corner of the control. fmPictureAlignmentTopRight (1) aligns the picture with the upper-right corner of the control. fmPictureAlignmentCenter (2), the default setting, centers the picture in the control (both horizontally and vertically). fmPictureAlignmentBottomLeft (3) aligns the picture with the lower-left corner of the control. fmPictureAlignmentBottomRight (4) aligns the picture with the lower-right corner of the control. This property applies to the Page object and the Image control as well.

CommandButton

The CommandButton control has three unique properties—shown in Table 15.6—that you need to know about to work with it effectively.

TABLE 15.6: UNIQUE PROPERTIES OF THE COMMANDBUTTON CONTROL

Property	Description
Cancel	A Boolean property that determines whether the command button is the Cancel button for the user form (True) or not (False). The Cancel button for a user form can bear any name; what distinguishes it is that its Cancel property is set to True. The Cancel button is activated by the user's pressing Esc (as well as by the user's clicking it or pressing Enter when the focus is on it). Only one command button on a form can be the Cancel button at any given time. Setting the Cancel property for a command button to True causes VBA to set the Cancel property to False for any button for which it was previously set to True.
Default	A Boolean property that determines whether the command button is the default button for the user form (True) or not (False). Only one command button on a form can be the default button at any given time. Setting the Default property for a command button to True causes VBA to set the Default property to False for any button for which it was previously set to True. The default button is activated by the user's pressing Enter when the focus isn't on any other command button. The default button on a form can also be the Cancel button; this is a good idea for forms that offer irreversible actions, such as deleting text or deleting a file.

Continued ▶

TABLE 15.6 CONTINUED: UNIQUE PROPERTIES OF THE COMMANDBUTTON CONTROL	
Property	**Description**
TakeFocusOnClick	A Boolean property that determines whether the command button takes the focus when the user clicks it (True) or not (False). The default setting for this property is True, but you may want to set it to False when you need the focus to remain on another control in the user form even when the user clicks the command button. However, if the user uses the Tab key or the arrow keys to move to the command button, the command button will take the focus even if the TakeFocusOnClick property is set to False.

You'll usually want to set the Accelerator property for each command button on a form other than the default command button, so that the user can quickly access it from the keyboard.

TabStrip and MultiPage

The TabStrip control has several unique properties and a number of properties that it shares with the MultiPage control. Table 15.7 lists these properties.

TABLE 15.7: PROPERTIES OF THE TABSTRIP AND MULTIPAGE CONTROLS	
Property	**Description**
ClientHeight	(Tab strip only.) A Single property that sets or returns the height of the display area of the tab strip, measured in points.
ClientLeft	(Tab strip only.) A Single property that returns the distance, measured in points, between the left border of the tab strip and the left border of the control inside it.
ClientTop	(Tab strip only.) A Single property that returns the distance, measured in points, between the top border of the tab strip and the top border of the control inside it.
ClientWidth	(Tab strip only.) A Single property that sets or returns the width of the display area of the tab strip, measured in points.
SelectedItem	Sets or returns the tab currently selected in a tab strip or the page currently selected in a MultiPage control.
TabFixedHeight	A Single property that sets or returns the fixed height of the tabs, measured in points. Set TabFixedHeight to 0 to have the tabs automatically size themselves to fit their contents.
TabFixedWidth	A Single property that sets or returns the fixed width of the tabs, measured in points. Set TabFixedWidth to 0 to have the tabs automatically size themselves to fit their contents.

Continued ▶

TABLE 15.7 CONTINUED: PROPERTIES OF THE TABSTRIP AND MULTIPAGE CONTROLS	
Property	**Description**
TabOrientation	Determines the location of the tabs in the tab strip or multipage. fmTab-OrientationTop (0), the default, displays the tabs at the top of the tab strip or multipage. fmTabOrientationBottom (1) displays the tabs at the bottom of the tab strip or multipage. fmTabOrientationLeft (2) displays the tabs at the left of the tab strip or multipage, and fmTabOrientationRight displays the tabs at the right of the tab strip or multipage.

ScrollBar and SpinButton

The ScrollBar and SpinButton share a number of properties that you haven't yet seen. Table 15.8 lists these properties.

TABLE 15.8: PROPERTIES OF THE SCROLLBAR AND SPINBUTTON CONTROLS	
Property	**Description**
Delay	A Long property that sets the delay in milliseconds between clicks registered on the control when the user clicks and holds down the mouse button. The default delay is 50 milliseconds. The control registers the first click immediately, the second click after Delay × 5 (the extra delay is to assist the user in clicking only once), and the third and subsequent clicks after Delay.
LargeChange	(Scroll bar only.) A Long property that determines how much the item is scrolled when the user clicks in the scroll bar between the thumb (the scroll box) and the scroll bar's arrow. Set the LargeChange property after setting the Max and Min properties of the scroll bar.
SmallChange	A Long property that determines how much movement occurs when the user clicks a scroll arrow in a scroll bar or spin button. SmallChange needs to be an integer value; the default value is 1.
Max	A Long property that specifies the maximum value for the Value property of the scroll bar or spin button. Max must be an integer; the default value is 1.
Min	A Long property that specifies the minimum value for the Value property of the scroll bar or spin button. Min must be an integer; the default value is 1.
ProportionalThumb	(Scroll bar only.) A Boolean property that determines whether the thumb (the scroll box) is a fixed size (False) or is proportional to the size of the scrolling region (True), giving the user an approximate idea of how much of the scrolling region is currently visible. The default setting is True.

Image

You're nearing the end of the list of basic controls and you've already looked at all the properties of the Image control. For most of the Image controls you use in your user forms, you'll want to set the following properties (in addition to the positional and size properties):

- Use the `Picture` property to assign the picture file you want to appear in the Image control. Click in the Picture row in the Properties window, and then click the ellipsis button (...) that the text box displays. In the Load Picture dialog box, select the picture and click the OK button to add it. The Image control can display `.BMP`, `.CUR` (cursor), `.GIF`, `.ICO` (icon), `.JPG`, and `.WMF` files, but not graphics files such as `.TIF` or `.PCX`.

 TIP The easiest way to display part of a Windows screen in an Image control is to capture it by using the PrintScreen key (to capture the full screen) or the Alt+PrintScreen key combination (to capture the active window). Then paste it into an application such as Paint, trim it there as necessary, and save it as a `.BMP` file.

- Use the `PictureAlignment` property to set the alignment of the picture.
- Use the `PictureSizeMode` property to set whether the picture is clipped, stretched, or zoomed to fill the Image control. Adjust the height and width of the Image control as necessary.
- Use the `PictureTiling` property if you need to tile the image to take up the full space in the control.

Page

The Page object is one of the pages contained within a MultiPage object. I've already described all its properties in the context of other controls except for the `Index` property, which it shares with the Tab object.

The `Index` property is an Integer property that determines the position of the Page object in the Pages collection in a MultiPage control or the position of a Tab object in the Tabs collection in a TabStrip. The first Page object or Tab object is numbered 0 (zero); the second Page or Tab is numbered 1; and so on. You can change the `Index` property of a tab or page to change the position in which the tab or page appears in the collection.

Tab

The Tab object is one of the tabs contained within a TabStrip object. I've already discussed all its properties in the context of other controls.

Working with Groups of Controls

By grouping two or more controls, you can work with them as a single unit to size them, format them, or delete them.

Grouping Controls

To group controls, select them by Shift+clicking, Ctrl+clicking, or dragging around them, and then right-click and choose Group from the context menu. Alternatively, select the controls, and then click the Group button on the UserForm toolbar or choose Format ➤ Group. VBA will create a new group containing the controls and will place a shaded border with handles around the whole group, as shown in Figure 15.12.

FIGURE 15.12

You can work with multiple controls simultaneously by grouping them. VBA indicates a group of controls by placing a border around it.

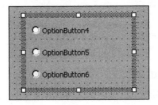

Ungrouping Controls

To ungroup controls, right-click any of the controls contained in the group and then choose Ungroup from the context menu. Alternatively, select the group of controls by clicking in any control in the group and then click the Ungroup button on the User-Form toolbar (you'll need to display this toolbar—it's not displayed by default), or choose Format ➤ Ungroup. VBA will remove the shaded border with handles from around the group and will instead display a border and handles around each individual control that was formerly in the group.

Sizing Grouped Controls

You can quickly size all controls in a group by selecting the group and then dragging the sizing handles on the surrounding border. For example, you could select the middle handle on the right side and drag it inward to shorten the controls, as shown in Figure 15.13. The controls will be resized proportionally to the change in the group outline.

FIGURE 15.13

You can resize all the controls in a group by dragging a sizing handle on the surrounding border.

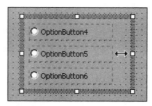

Generally speaking, this action works best when you group a number of controls of the same type, as in the illustration. For example, sizing a group that consisted of several text boxes or several option buttons would work well, whereas sizing a group that consisted of a text box, a command button, and a combo box would seldom be a good idea.

Deleting Grouped Controls

You can quickly delete a whole group of controls by right-clicking any of them and choosing Delete from the context menu, or by selecting the group and pressing the Delete key.

Working with One Control in a Group

Even after you've grouped a number of controls, you can still work with them individually if necessary. To do so, first click any control in the group to select the group, as shown on the left in Figure 15.14. Then click the control you want to work with. As shown on the right in Figure 15.14, VBA will display a darker shaded border around the group (indicating that the group still exists) and display the lighter shaded border around the individual control, indicating that that control is selected.

FIGURE 15.14

To work with one control in a group, start by selecting the group (as shown on the left) and then select the control (as shown on the right).

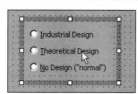 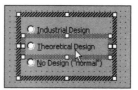

You can then work with the individual control as if it were not grouped. When you've finished working with it, click another control in the group to work with it, or click elsewhere in the user form to deselect the individual control.

Aligning Controls

For all the wonders of the Snap To Grid feature, you'll often need to align controls manually. The easiest way to align selected controls is to right-click in any one of them and choose an option from the Align submenu: Lefts, Centers, Rights, Tops, Middles, Bottoms, or To Grid. These options work as follows:

Lefts	Aligns the left borders of the controls
Centers	Aligns the horizontal midpoints of the controls
Rights	Aligns the right borders of the controls
Tops	Aligns the tops of the controls
Middles	Aligns the vertical midpoints of the controls
Bottoms	Aligns the bottoms of the controls
To Grid	Aligns the controls to the grid

VBA aligns the borders or midpoints to the current position of that border or midpoint on the dominant control—the control that has white sizing handles around it rather than black sizing handles. After selecting the controls you want to align manually, make dominant the one that is already in the correct position by clicking it so that it takes on the white sizing handles. Then choose the alignment option you want.

 WARNING Make sure the alignment option you choose makes sense for the controls you've selected. VBA will happily align controls in an inappropriate way if you tell it to. For example, if you select a number of option buttons or text boxes and choose Tops from the Align submenu, VBA will obligingly stack all the controls on top of each other, rendering them all but unusable. (You can use Undo to undo such minor mishaps.)

Placing Controls

VBA offers a number of placement commands on the Format menu. Most of these are simple and intuitive to use:

- On the Format ➤ Make Same Size submenu, use the Width, Height, and Both commands to make two or more controls the same size in one or both dimensions.

- Use the Format ➤ Size To Fit command to have VBA decide on a suitable size for an element, based on the size of its label. This works well for, say, a toggle button with a medium-length label, but VBA will shrink an OK button to a meager size that your dialog boxes will be ashamed of.

- Use the Format ➤ Size To Grid command to size a control up or down to the nearest gridpoints.

- On the Format ➤ Horizontal Spacing and Format ➤ Vertical Spacing submenus, use the Make Equal, Increase, Decrease, and Remove commands to set the horizontal spacing and vertical spacing of two or more controls. The Remove option removes extra space from between controls, which works well for, say, a vertical series of option buttons (which look good close together) but isn't a good idea for command buttons (which need a little air between them).

- On the Format ➤ Center In Form submenu, use the Horizontally and Vertically commands to center a control or a group of controls in the form. Centering controls vertically is seldom a good idea, but you'll often want to center a frame or a group of command buttons horizontally.

- On the Format ➤ Arrange Buttons submenu, use the Bottom and Right commands to quickly rearrange command buttons in a dialog box.

Adjusting the Tab Order of the Dialog Box

The *tab order* of a dialog box or a frame within a dialog box is the order in which VBA selects controls in the dialog box or frame when you move through them by pressing the Tab key (to move forward) or the Shift+Tab key combination (to move backward). Each frame in a user form has a separate tab order for the controls it contains: The frame appears in the tab order for the dialog box, and the controls within the frame appear in the tab order for the frame.

Your goal in setting the tab order for a dialog box or a frame should be to make the dialog box or frame as easy as possible to use. The general rule of thumb is to arrange the tab order from left to right and from top to bottom of the dialog box or frame, but you'll often need to vary this order for special effects.

VBA assigns the tab order to the controls in a dialog box or frame on a first-come, first-served basis as you add them. Unless you have a supremely logical mind, this order will seldom produce the optimal tab order for a dialog box, so usually you'll want to adjust the tab order—or at least check that it's right. For a frame, you're likely to place fewer controls, so you have a better chance of arranging them in a suitable order; but again, you'll want to check this before the form goes live.

To change the tab order in a dialog box or frame:

1. Right-click in open space in the user form or frame and choose Tab Order from the context menu to display the Tab Order dialog box, as shown in Figure 15.15. (Alternatively, select the user form or frame and choose View ➤ Tab Order.)

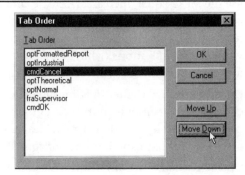

2. Rearrange the controls into the order in which you want them to appear by selecting them in the Tab Order list box and clicking the Move Up button or Move Down button as appropriate. You can Shift+click or drag to select a range of controls or Ctrl+click to select a number of noncontiguous controls.

3. Click the OK button to close the Tab Order dialog box.

Linking a Dialog Box to a Procedure

Designing a custom dialog box is only the first step in getting it to work in a procedure. The interesting part is writing the code to display the dialog box and make it perform its functions.

Typically, the code you create for a dialog box will consist of the following:

- A procedure that displays the dialog box by loading it and using the Show method. Usually, this procedure will be assigned to a menu item or a toolbar button so that the user can invoke it, but a procedure can also run automatically in response to a system event (such as running at a specified time).

- The user form that contains the dialog box and its controls.

- The code attached to the user form. This code consists of procedures for designated controls. For example, for a simple dialog box containing two option buttons and two command buttons (an OK button and a Cancel button), you'd typically create one procedure for the OK button and one for the Cancel button.

The procedure for the OK button, which would be triggered by a Click event on the OK button (either a click on the OK button or a press of the Enter key with the focus on the OK button), would ascertain which option button was selected and then take action accordingly; the procedure for the Cancel button would cancel the procedure. (You could also assign a procedure to the Click event for an option button—or to another event; more on this in the next chapter—but usually it makes more sense to trap the command buttons in a static dialog box. In a dynamic dialog box, you may often want to trap the click on an option button and display further controls as appropriate.)

 NOTE Code that runs directly in response to an event is called an *event procedure*. An event procedure can call other procedures as necessary, so multiple procedures can be run indirectly by a single event.

Once the code attached to a button has run, execution returns to the dialog box (if it's still displayed) or to the procedure that called the dialog box.

Loading and Unloading a Dialog Box

You load a dialog box by using the Load statement and unload it by using the Unload statement. The Load statement loads the dialog box into memory so that it's available to the program, but doesn't display the dialog box; for that you use the Show method, which I'll show you in the next section. The Unload statement unloads the dialog box from memory and reclaims any memory associated with that object. If the dialog box is displayed when you run the Unload statement on it, VBA removes the dialog box from the screen.

The syntax for the Load and Unload statements is straightforward:

```
Load Dialog_Box
Unload Dialog_Box
```

Here, *Dialog_Box* is the name of the user form or dialog box. For example, the following statement loads the dialog box named frmOddDialog:

```
Load frmOddDialog
```

Displaying and Hiding a Dialog Box

To display a dialog box, you use the Show method; to hide a dialog box, you use the Hide method. For example, the following statement displays the dialog box named frmMyDialog:

```
frmMyDialog.Show
```

Run a procedure containing this line, and the `frmMyDialog` dialog box will obligingly pop up on-screen, where you can enter text in its text boxes, select or clear its check boxes, use its drop-down lists, and click its buttons as you wish. When you close the dialog box (by clicking the Close button on its title bar or by clicking a command button that dismisses the dialog box), the dialog box will disappear from the screen and the procedure will continue to run. But until you retrieve settings from the dialog box and take action on them, the dialog box will have little effect beyond its graphical display.

You can display a dialog box by using the Show method without explicitly loading the dialog box with a Load command first; VBA takes care of the implied Load command for you. There's no particular advantage to including the Load command, but it makes your code easier to read and to debug. For example, the two procedures shown here have the same effect:

```
Sub Display_Dialog()
    Load frmOddDialog    'loads dialog box into memory
    frmOddDialog.Show    'displays dialog box
End Sub


Sub Display_Dialog()
    frmOddDialog.Show    'loads dialog box into memory and displays it
End Sub
```

 NOTE If you run a `Hide` method without having loaded the dialog box into memory by using the Load statement or the Show method, VBA will load the dialog box but not display it on screen.

Once you've displayed the dialog box, take a moment to check its tab order by moving through it using the Tab key. When you open the dialog box, is the focus on the appropriate control? When you move forward from that control, is the next control that is selected the next control that the user will typically need to use? Adjust the tab order as necessary, as described in, "Adjusting the Tab Order of the Dialog Box," earlier in this chapter.

Setting a Default Command Button

To set a default command button in a dialog box, set that command button's `Default` property to `True`. The button will then be selected when the dialog box is displayed, so that if the user simply presses the Enter key to dismiss the dialog box, this button will receive the keypress.

As you'd expect, only one button can be the default button at any given time. If you set the `Default` property of any button to `True`, VBA automatically changes to `False` the `Default` property of any other button previously set to `True`.

Retrieving the User's Choices from a Dialog Box

Displaying a dialog box is all very well, but to actually do anything with a dialog box, you need to retrieve the user's choices from it. In this section, I'll first show you the VBA commands for retrieving information from a dialog box. After that, I'll go through an example of retrieving the user's choices from a relatively simple dialog box, and then from a more complex one.

Returning a String from a Text Box

To *return* (retrieve) a string from a text box, you simply check its `Value` property or `Text` property after the user has dismissed the dialog box. (For a text box, the `Value` property and the `Text` property return the same information; for other VBA objects, the `Value` property and the `Text` property may return different information.) For example, if you have a text box named `txtMyText`, you could return its value and display it in a message box by using the following line:

```
MsgBox txtMyText.Value
```

VBA supports both one-line and multi-line text boxes. To create a multi-line text box, select the text box in the user form or in the drop-down list in the Properties window and set its `MultiLine` property to `True`. The user will then be able to enter multiple lines in the text box and start new lines by pressing Shift+Enter.

To add a horizontal or vertical scroll bar to a text box, set its `ScrollBars` property to `1 - fmScrollBarsHorizontal` (for a horizontal scroll bar), `2 - fmScrollBars-Vertical` (for a vertical scroll bar, which is usually more useful), or `3 - fmScrollBars-Both` (for both).

Returning a Value from an Option Button

As you saw earlier, an option button is a Boolean control, so it can have only two values: `True` and `False`. A value of `True` indicates the button is selected, and a value of `False` that it's unselected. You can check an option button's value with a simple `If... Then` condition. For example, if you have two option buttons named `optSearchForFile` and optUseThisFile, you can check their values and find out which was selected by using the following condition:

```
If optSearchForFile = True Then
    'optSearchForFile was selected; take action on this
Else        'optSearchForFile was not selected, so optUseThisFile was
    'take action for optUseThisFile
End If
```

NOTE As you saw earlier in the chapter, Value is the default property of the Option-Button control. What the previous code actually checks is the value of the default property—after all, the OptionButton has many other properties as well. The first line of code could be written out more fully and explicitly as If optSearchForFile.Value = True Then. It could also be written even more succinctly: If optSearchForFile Then.

With more than two option buttons, you'll need to use an If... Then... ElseIf condition or a Select Case statement.

Returning a Value from a Check Box

Like an option button, a check box can have only two values: True and False. Again, you can use an If... Then condition to check the value of a check box. For example, to check the value of a check box named chkDisplayProgress, you could use an If... Then condition such as this:

```
If chkDisplayProgress = True Then
    'Take actions for chkDisplayProgress
End If
```

Again, you're checking the default property of the control here—the Value property. The first line of code could also be written as If chkDisplayProgress.Value = True Then.

You could also use an ElseIf condition to take effect if the check box was cleared rather than selected. Whether you do so will depend on how the check box is used in this context:

- If the check box presents an option for a procedure that the user is about to run, you may want to take an action if the check box is selected but take no action if the check box is cleared.

- If the check box reflects the state of an option that the user may want to turn on or off, you'll need to take action if the user changes the state of the check box. If the user selects the check box when it was previously cleared, you'll turn on the option; if the user clears the check box when it was previously selected, you'll turn off the option. If the user leaves the check box in its previous state (whether selected or cleared), you won't need to take any action.

NOTE As you saw in the section, "Key Properties for the Toolbox Controls," a check box can also have a null value if its `TripleState` property is set to `True`. If you allow your check boxes to have a null state, you'll need to check for that as well in your procedures. You can't directly check for the check box's value being `Null` (for example, `If chkMyBox.Value = Null` causes an error), so use an `If` statement or `Select Case` statement to test `True` and `False` first—if the `Value` of a check box is neither `True` nor `False`, it's `Null`.

Returning a Value from a List Box

Returning a value from a list box is a little more complex than returning a value from a text box, an option button, or a check box. First, you need to tell VBA what choices you want to display in the list box.

To display items in a list box, you need to create a procedure to *initialize* (prepare) the user form and add the items to the list box before displaying it. To do this, right-click the name of the user form in the Project Explorer and choose View Code from the context menu to display in the Code window the code for the controls assigned to the dialog box. In the Object drop-down list, make sure that UserForm is selected. Then choose Initialize from the Procedure drop-down list. The Visual Basic Editor will create a new procedure named `Private Sub UserForm_Initialize` for you at the end of the procedures currently contained on the code sheet:

```
Private Sub UserForm_Initialize()

End Sub
```

VBA runs a `UserForm_Initialize` procedure every time the user form is invoked. This procedure is a good way to add items to a list box or combo box, or to set properties for other controls on the user form.

Now, to add items to the list box, use the `AddItem` method for the list box object (here, `lstMyList`) with a text string in double quotation marks to specify each item in the list box:

```
lstMyList.AddItem "Receipt of complaint"
lstMyList.AddItem "Sorry, no free samples"
lstMyList.AddItem "Bovine Emulator Information"
lstMyList.AddItem "Leatherette Goblin Information"
```

TIP By adding items when you initialize the form, you can add variable numbers of items as appropriate. For example, if you wanted the user to pick a document from a particular folder, you could create a list of the documents in that folder on-the-fly and then use them to fill the list box.

To retrieve the result from a single-select list box, return the `Value` property:

```
MsgBox "You chose this entry from the list box: " & lstMyList.Value
```

When you use the `MultiSelect` property to create a list box capable of multiple selections, you can no longer use the `Value` property to return the items selected in the list box: When `MultiSelect` is True, `Value` always returns a null value. Instead, you use the `Selected` property to determine which rows in the list box were selected, and the `List` array to return the contents of each selected row. The following statements use a `For... Next` loop to build a string named `strMsg` containing the entries selected from a multi-select list box:

```
strMsg = "You chose the following entries from the list box: " & vbCr
For i = 1 To lstMyList.ListCount
  If lstMyList.Selected(i - 1) = True Then
    strMsg = strMsg & lstMyList.List(i - 1) & vbCr
  End If
Next i
MsgBox strMsg
```

Returning a Value from a Combo Box

Returning a value from a combo box (a combination list box and text box) is refreshingly similar to retrieving one from a single-select list box: You add items to the combo box list in an `Initialize` procedure, and then check the `Value` of the combo box after the user has dismissed the dialog box. (The combo box control doesn't offer multiple-selection capabilities, so `Value` is the property to check.) For example, if your combo box is named `cmbMyCombo`, you could add items to it like this:

```
Private Sub UserForm_Initialize()
  cmbMyCombo.AddItem "Red"
  cmbMyCombo.AddItem "Blue"
  cmbMyCombo.AddItem "Yellow"
End Sub
```

To return the item the user chose in the combo box, retrieve the `Value` property of the combo box control:

```
Result = cmbMyCombo.Value
```

The item retrieved from the combo box can be either one of the items assigned in the `Initialize` procedure or one that the user has typed into the text-box portion of the combo box.

Examples of Connecting Dialog Boxes to Procedures

In this section, I'll show you two examples of how you can create a procedure and then build a dialog box into it to make it more useful and powerful. In the first example, you'll record a macro in Word (if you have Word) and link a dialog box to it. In the second example, which will work with any VBA-enabled application, you'll create a user form and its code from scratch.

Word Example: The Move-Paragraph Procedure

The first procedure, in Word, moves the current paragraph up or down within the document by one or two paragraphs.

Recording the Procedure

Start by recording a procedure in Word to move the current paragraph. In the procedure, you need to record the commands for:

- Selecting the current paragraph
- Cutting the selection and then pasting it
- Moving the insertion point up and down the document
- Inserting a bookmark, moving the insertion point to it, and then deleting the bookmark

The finished procedure will display a dialog box with option buttons for moving the current paragraph up one paragraph, up two paragraphs, down one paragraph, or down two paragraphs. The dialog box also includes a check box for returning the insertion point to its original position at the end of the procedure. Because this is presumably desirable behavior for the procedure, this check box will be selected by default; the user will be able to clear it if necessary.

First, start Word and create a scratch document, and enter three or four paragraphs of text—just about anything will do, but it'll be easier to have recognizable text so that you can make sure the procedure is moving paragraphs as it should. Then place the insertion point in one of the paragraphs you've just entered and start recording a macro as discussed in Chapter 2: Double-click the REC indicator on the status bar, or choose Tools ➤ Macro ➤ Record New Macro to display the Record Macro dialog box. Enter the name for the macro in the Macro Name box, choose a template or document if necessary in the Store Macro In drop-down list, and enter a succinct description of the macro in the Description box. Then, if you want, use the Toolbars button or Keyboard button to create a toolbar button, menu option, or keyboard shortcut for the macro.

Record the following actions in the macro:

1. Insert a bookmark at the current position of the insertion point by using the Insert ➤ Bookmark command to display the Bookmarks dialog box, entering a name for the bookmark, and clicking the Add button. I'll call my bookmark Move_Paragraph_Temp to indicate that it's a temporary bookmark used for the Move_Paragraph procedure.

2. Select the current paragraph by pressing F8 four times. The first press of F8 activates Extend mode (toggling on the EXT indicator on the status bar), the second selects the current word, the third selects the current sentence, and the fourth selects the current paragraph. Press the Escape key to turn off Extend mode once the paragraph is selected. (The EXT indicator on the status bar will toggle off again.)

3. Cut the selected paragraph by using some form of the Cut command (for example, by clicking the Cut button or pressing Ctrl+X or Shift+Delete).

4. Move the insertion point up one paragraph by pressing Ctrl+↑.

5. Paste the cut paragraph back in by using a Paste command (for example, by clicking the Paste button or pressing Shift+Insert).

6. Move the insertion point down one paragraph by pressing Ctrl+↓.

7. Move the insertion point up two paragraphs by pressing Ctrl+↑ twice. (Moving the insertion point around for no immediately apparent purpose may feel weird, but do it to record the commands in VBA that you need for the procedure.)

NOTE If you started with the insertion point at the beginning of the first paragraph in the document, you'll only be able to move the insertion point up one paragraph. This doesn't matter—press the keystroke anyway to record it. If Word beeps at you, ignore it.

8. Move the insertion point down two paragraphs by pressing Ctrl+↓ twice. (If in doing so you hit the end of the document after the first keypress, don't worry—perform the second keypress anyway to record it. Again, let Word beep if it feels so inclined.)

9. Open the Bookmarks dialog box (Insert ➢ Bookmark), select the Move_Paragraph_Temp bookmark, and click the Go To button to go to it. Then click the Delete button to delete the Move_Paragraph_Temp bookmark. Click the Close button to close the Bookmarks dialog box.

10. Stop the Macro Recorder by clicking the Stop Recording button on the Stop Recording toolbar or by double-clicking the REC indicator on the status bar.

So far, so good: You've recorded the procedure. Now open it in the Visual Basic Editor by choosing Tools ➢ Macro ➢ Macros, selecting the macro's name in the Macros dialog box, and clicking the Edit button.

You should see a macro that looks something like this:

```
1.   With ActiveDocument.Bookmarks
2.       .Add Range:=Selection.Range, Name:="Move_Paragraph_Temp"
3.       .DefaultSorting = wdSortByName
4.       .ShowHidden = False
5.   End With
6.   Selection.Extend
7.   Selection.Extend
8.   Selection.Extend
9.   Selection.Extend
10.  Selection.EscapeKey
11.  Selection.Cut
12.  Selection.MoveUp Unit:=wdParagraph, Count:=1
13.  Selection.Paste
14.  Selection.MoveDown Unit:=wdParagraph, Count:=1
15.  Selection.MoveUp Unit:=wdParagraph, Count:=2
16.  Selection.MoveDown Unit:=wdParagraph, Count:=2
17.  Selection.GoTo What:=wdGoToBookmark, _
         Name:="Move_Paragraph_Temp"
18.  ActiveDocument.Bookmarks("Move_Paragraph_Temp").Delete
19.  With ActiveDocument.Bookmarks
20.      .DefaultSorting = wdSortByName
21.      .ShowHidden = False
22.  End With
```

So far, this is pretty straightforward: Lines 1 through 5 contain a `With` statement that adds the `Move_Paragraph_Temp` bookmark. Lines 3 and 4 are unnecessary here, but the Macro Recorder records all the settings in the Bookmark dialog box, including the setting for the Sort By option button and the Hidden Bookmarks check box. Lines 6 through 10 use the Extend Selection feature to select the current paragraph. Lines 12, 14, 15, and 16 record the syntax for moving the insertion point up and down, one paragraph and two paragraphs, respectively. Line 11 records the Cut command, and Line 13 the Paste command. Finally, line 17 moves the insertion point to the `Move_Paragraph_Temp` bookmark, and line 18 removes the bookmark. Lines 19 through 22 again record the settings in the Bookmark dialog box, which you don't need here either.

You can quickly strip out the unnecessary lines (3 and 4, and 19 through 22) to give a more succinct version of the code:

```
1.    With ActiveDocument.Bookmarks
2.        .Add Range:=Selection.Range, Name:="Move_Paragraph_Temp"
3.    End With
4.    Selection.Extend
5.    Selection.Extend
6.    Selection.Extend
7.    Selection.Extend
8.    Selection.EscapeKey
9.    Selection.Cut
10.   Selection.MoveUp Unit:=wdParagraph, Count:=1
11.   Selection.Paste
12.   Selection.MoveDown Unit:=wdParagraph, Count:=1
13.   Selection.MoveUp Unit:=wdParagraph, Count:=2
14.   Selection.MoveDown Unit:=wdParagraph, Count:=2
15.   Selection.GoTo What:=wdGoToBookmark, _
            Name:=" Move_Paragraph_Temp"
16.   ActiveDocument.Bookmarks("Move_Paragraph_Temp").Delete
```

Creating the Dialog Box

Next, create the dialog box for the procedure. Take a look at Figure 15.16 to get an idea of the finished product, and then follow the steps below it.

The Move Current Paragraph dialog box you're about to create

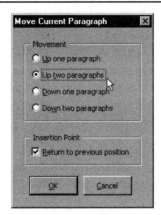

1. Start a user form by clicking the Insert button's drop-down list and choosing UserForm from the drop-down list (or just click the Insert button if it's already showing the UserForm icon) or by choosing Insert ➤ UserForm.

2. Use the Properties window for the user form to set its Name and Caption properties. Click in the cell next to the Name cell and enter the Name property there, and then click in the cell next to the Caption cell and enter the Caption property. I've named my user form frmMoveCurrentParagraph and given it the caption Move Current Paragraph, so that the name of the form is closely related to the text the user will see in the title bar of the dialog box but different from the procedure name (Move_Current_Paragraph).

3. Place two frames in the user form, as shown in Figure 15.17, to act as group boxes in the dialog box:

   • Double-click the Frame tool in the Toolbox, and then click and drag in the user form to place each frame. Click the Select Objects button to restore the selection pointer.

   • Align the frames by selecting them both and choosing Format ➤ Align ➤ Lefts.

   • With the frames still selected, verify that the frames are the same width by choosing Format ➤ Make Same Size ➤ Width. (Don't choose Format ➤ Make Same Size ➤ Height or Format ➤ Make Same Size ➤ Both here—the top frame will need to be taller than the bottom frame.)

   • Caption the top frame Movement and the bottom frame Insertion Point by selecting each in turn and then setting the Caption property in the Properties window. Then name the top frame fraMovement and the bottom frame fraInsertionPoint.

FIGURE 15.17

Start by placing two frames in the user form.

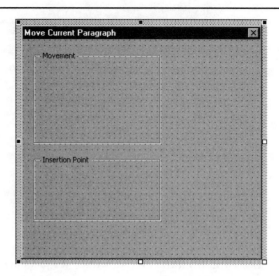

4. Place four option buttons in the Movement frame, as shown in Figure 15.18:

- Double-click the OptionButton tool in the Toolbox, and then click in the Movement frame to place each option button. This time, don't click and drag—just click to place a normal-width option button.

- When you've placed the four option buttons, click the Select Objects button in the Toolbox to restore the selection pointer. Then select the four option buttons and align them with each other by choosing Format ➤ Align ➤ Lefts Even out any disparities in spacing by choosing Format ➤ Vertical Spacing ➤ Make Equal. If necessary, use the other items on the Format ➤ Vertical Spacing submenu—Increase, Decrease, and Remove—to adjust the amount of space between the option buttons.

- Enter the caption for each option button by setting the Caption property in the Properties window. Caption them as illustrated in Figure 15.18: Up one paragraph, Up two paragraphs, Down one paragraph, and Down two paragraphs. As their names indicate, these option buttons will control the number of paragraphs the procedure moves the current paragraph.

- If you need to resize the option buttons, select them and group them by right-clicking and choosing Group from the context menu, by choosing Format ➤ Group, or by clicking the Group button on the UserForm toolbar. Then select the group and drag one of the handles to resize all the option buttons evenly. For example, if you need to lengthen all the option buttons to accommodate the text you entered, drag the handle at the right mid-point of the group outward.

- Name the option buttons `optUpOne`, `optUpTwo`, `optDownOne`, and `opt-DownTwo`, respectively, by changing the Name property of each in turn in the Properties window.

 TIP By default, all the option buttons on a user form are part of the same option group—which means only one of them can be selected at a time. If you want to provide multiple groups of option buttons on a user form, you need to specify the separate groups. The easiest way to do this is to position each group within a separate frame control, as I've done here (even though in this form there is only one group of option buttons). Alternatively, you can set the `GroupName` property for each option button.

- Next, set the first option button's `Value` property to `True` by selecting the default `False` value in the Properties window and entering `True` instead. Doing so will select the option button in the user form you're designing, and when the dialog box is displayed, that option button will be selected as the default choice for the option group. Set its accelerator key to *U* by entering **U** as its `Accelerator` property. Set the `Accelerator` property of the second option button to **t**, the third to **D**, and the fourth to **w**.

FIGURE 15.18

Place four option buttons in the Movement frame like this.

 NOTE You'll notice that I showed the values for the `Accelerator` property in the last bullet point in the case appropriate to them. So are they case sensitive? Yes—and no. If the caption for the control contains both the uppercase and lowercase versions of the same letter (for example, the caption **Industrial Disease** contains both a *d* and a *D*), you can use the case to specify the letter: An `Accelerator` property of *d* will give you **In<u>d</u>ustrial Disease**, while *D* will give you **Industrial <u>D</u>isease**. But if there's only one instance of the accelerator letter in the caption, the case doesn't matter: Either *u* or *U* will give **Ind<u>u</u>strial Disease**.

5. Place a check box in the Insertion Point frame, as shown in Figure 15.19:

- Click the CheckBox tool in the Toolbox and then click in the Insertion Point frame in the user form to place a check box of the default size.

- In the Properties window, set the name of the check box to chkReturnTo-PreviousPosition (a long name but a descriptive one). Then set its Caption property to Return to previous position. Set its accelerator key to R by entering **R** as its Accelerator property. Finally, set the check box to be selected by default by entering **True** as its Value property.

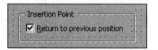

6. Next, insert the command buttons for the form (see Figure 15.20):

- Double-click the CommandButton tool on the Toolbox and click to place the first command button at the bottom of the user form. Click to place the second command button, and then click the Select Objects button to restore the selection mouse pointer.

- Size and place the command buttons by using the commands on the Format menu. (In the example, I grouped the buttons and then used the Format ➤ Center In Form ➤ Horizontally command to center the pair horizontally. Note that you need to group the buttons before doing this—if you simply select both of them, VBA will happily center one on top of the other so that only the uppermost button is visible.)

- Set properties for the command buttons as follows: For the left-hand button (which will become the OK button), set the Name property to *cmdOK*, the Caption property to *OK*, the Accelerator property to *0* (that's O as in *OK*, not a zero), and the Default property to *True*. For the right-hand button (which will become the Cancel button), set the Name property to *cmdCancel*, the Accelerator property to *A*, the Caption property to *Cancel*, and the Cancel property to *True*. Leave the Default property set to *False*.

Now you need to set the action for each command button. First, you'll set the Cancel button, because the code attached to it will be much shorter and simpler than that attached to the OK button.

7. Double-click the Cancel button to display the code associated with it. You should see something like this:

```
Private Sub cmdCancel_Click()


End Sub
```

Add an End statement between the lines:

```
Private Sub cmdCancel_Click()
    End
End Sub
```

This End statement removes the dialog box from the screen and ends the current procedure—in this case, the Move_Current_Paragraph procedure.

Now you'll set the OK button, which is where things get interesting. When the user clicks the OK button, the procedure needs to continue and do all of the following:

- Remove the dialog box from display by hiding it, or by unloading it (or, preferably, both). As discussed earlier in the chapter, the choice is yours, but using both commands is usually clearest.

- Check the Value property of the checkbox to see whether it was selected or cleared.

- Check the Value property of each option button in turn to see which of them was selected when the OK button was clicked.

8. Double-click the OK button to display the code attached to it. (If you're still working in the code attached to the Cancel button, scroll up or down from the Private Sub cmdCancel_Click() code to find the Private Sub cmdOK_Click() code.) Again, it should look something like this:

```
Private Sub cmdOK_Click()


End Sub
```

First, enter the following two lines between the Private Sub and End Sub lines:

```
frmMoveParagraph.Hide
Unload frmMoveParagraph
```

The frmMoveParagraph.Hide line activates the Hide method for the frmMove-Paragraph user form, hiding it from display on the screen. The Unload frm-MoveParagraph line unloads the dialog box from memory.

 NOTE It isn't strictly necessary to hide or unload a dialog box to continue execution of a procedure, but if you don't, you're likely to confuse your users. For example, if you click the OK button on a Print dialog box in a Windows application, you expect the dialog box to disappear and the Print command to be executed. If the dialog box didn't disappear (but it started printing the job in the background), you'd probably think it hadn't registered the click, so you'd click again and again until it went away.

---

9. Next, the procedure needs to check the Value property of the chkReturnTo-PreviousPosition check box to find out whether to insert a bookmark in the document to mark the current position of the insertion point. To do this, enter a straightforward If... Then statement:

```
If chkReturnToPreviousPosition = True Then
End If
```

If the chkReturnToPreviousPosition statement is set to True—that is, if the check box is selected—the code in the lines following the Then statement will run. The Then statement will consist of the lines for inserting a bookmark that you recorded earlier. Cut these lines from the procedure and paste them into the If... Then statement like this:

```
If chkReturnToPreviousPosition = True Then
    With ActiveDocument.Bookmarks
        .Add Range:=Selection.Range, Name:=" Move_Paragraph_Temp"
    End With
End If
```

If the check box is selected, the procedure will insert a bookmark; if the check box is cleared, the procedure will pass over these lines.

10. Next, paste in the code for selecting the current paragraph and cutting it to the Clipboard:

```
Selection.Extend
Selection.Extend
Selection.Extend
Selection.Extend
Selection.Cut
```

11. After this, you need to retrieve the Value properties from the option buttons to see which one was selected when the user chose the OK button in the dialog box. For this, you can again use an If condition—this time, an If... Then ElseIf... Else condition, with the relevant insertion-point–movement lines from the recorded procedure pasted in:

```
If optUpOne = True Then
    Selection.MoveUp Unit:=wdParagraph, Count:=1
ElseIf optUpTwo = True Then
    Selection.MoveUp Unit:=wdParagraph, Count:=2
ElseIf optDownOne = True Then
    Selection.MoveDown Unit:=wdParagraph, Count:=1
Else
    Selection.MoveDown Unit:=wdParagraph, Count:=2
End If
Selection.Paste
```

Here, optUpOne, optUpTwo, optDownOne, and optDownTwo (which piggybacks on the Else statement here and therefore isn't specified by name in the listing) are the four option buttons from the dialog box, representing the choice to move the current paragraph up one paragraph, up two paragraphs, down one paragraph, or down two paragraphs, respectively. The condition is straightforward: If optUpOne is True (that is, if the option button is selected), the first Then condition kicks in, moving the insertion point up one paragraph from its current position (after cutting the current paragraph, the insertion point will be at the beginning of the paragraph that was after the current one). If optUpOne is False, the first ElseIf condition is evaluated; if it is True, the second Then condition runs; and if it is False, the next ElseIf condition is evaluated. If that too is False, the Else code is run; in this case, the Else statement means that the optDownTwo option button was selected in the dialog box, so the Else code moves the insertion point down two paragraphs.

Wherever the insertion point ends up after the attentions of the option buttons, the next line of code (Selection.Paste) pastes in the cut paragraph from the Clipboard.

12. Finally, the procedure needs to return the insertion point to where it was originally if the chkReturnToPreviousPosition check box is selected. Again, you can test for this with a simple If... Then condition that incorporates the go-to-bookmark and delete-bookmark lines from the recorded procedure:

```
If chkReturnToPreviousPosition = True Then
    Selection.GoTo What:=wdGoToBookmark, _
        Name:=" Move_Paragraph_Temp"
    ActiveDocument.Bookmarks("Move_Paragraph_Temp").Delete
```

End If

If the chkReturnToPreviousPosition check box is selected, VBA moves the insertion point to the temporary bookmark and then deletes that bookmark.

Listing 15.1 shows the full listing for the cmdOK button.

Listing 15.1

```
1.  Private Sub cmdOK_Click()
2.      frmMoveCurrentParagraph.Hide
3.      Unload frmMoveCurrentParagraph
4.      If chkReturnToPreviousPosition = True Then
5.          With ActiveDocument.Bookmarks
6.              .Add Range:=Selection.Range, _
                    Name:=" Move_Paragraph_Temp"
7.          End With
8.      End If
9.          Selection.Extend
10.         Selection.Extend
11.         Selection.Extend
12.         Selection.Extend
13.         Selection.Cut
14.     If optUpOne = True Then
15.         Selection.MoveUp Unit:=wdParagraph, Count:=1
16.     ElseIf optUpTwo = True Then
17.         Selection.MoveUp Unit:=wdParagraph, Count:=2
18.     ElseIf optDownOne = True Then
19.         Selection.MoveDown Unit:=wdParagraph, Count:=1
20.     Else
21.         Selection.MoveDown Unit:=wdParagraph, Count:=2
22.     End If
23.     Selection.Paste
24.     If chkReturnToPreviousPosition = True Then
25.         Selection.GoTo What:=wdGoToBookmark, _
                Name:=" Move_Paragraph_Temp"
26.         ActiveDocument.Bookmarks("Move_Paragraph_Temp") _
                .Delete
27.     End If
28. End Sub
```

General Example: Opening a File from a List Box

In this example, I'll show you a user form that uses a list box to let the user select a file to open. The user form is simple, as is its code, which uses a loop and an array to gather the names of the files in the folder, and then displays the filenames in the list box. The user gets to select a file and click the Open button to open it. Figure 15.21 shows the user form in action for AutoCAD files.

You'll have noticed that the heading termed this a general example. That's because you can adapt this example to any of the applications discussed in this book by changing the file name to an appropriate type and changing a couple of the key statements. For the sake of variety, you'll create the code for AutoCAD; I'll then show you how to adapt it for the application you want to use.

FIGURE 15.21

The user form you'll build in this example contains a list box that gives the user quick access to all current files.

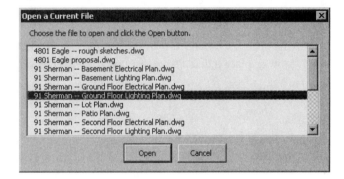

Building the User Form

Follow these steps to build the user form:

1. Start the application you want to work in.

2. Display the Visual Basic Editor by choosing Tools ➤ Macro ➤ Visual Basic Editor (in WordPerfect, choose Tools ➤ Visual Basic ➤ Visual Basic Editor) or pressing the F11 key.

3. In the Project Explorer, right-click the project to which you want to add the user form and choose Insert ➤ User Form from the context menu. The Visual Basic Editor will insert a default-size user form in the project.

4. Drag the handle at the lower-right corner of the user form to the right to make the user form a bit wider.

5. Set the name of the form to `frmOpen_a_Current_File` and its `Caption` to `Open a Current File`. Check the `Width` property: You want it to be about 350 pixels wide, though a little wider or narrower is fine too.

6. Click the Label button in the Toolbox, then click in the upper-left corner of the user form to place a default-size label there. Activate the Properties window and set the properties for the label as shown in the following list:

Property	Value
(Name)	lblInfo
AutoSize	True
Caption	Choose the file to open and click the Open button.
Left	10
Top	6
WordWrap	False

7. Click the ListBox button in the Toolbox, then click below the label in the user form to place a default-size list box there. Set its properties as follows:

Property	Value
(Name)	lstFiles
Height	100
Left	10
Top	25
Width	300

8. Double-click the CommandButton button in the Toolbox, then click twice at the bottom of the user form to place two default-size command buttons there. Set their properties as follows:

Property	First Button Value	Second Button Value
(Name)	cmdOpen	cmdCancel
Cancel	False*	True
Caption	Open	Cancel
Default	True	False
Height	21	21
Width	55	55

9. Arrange the command buttons as follows:

- Click the cmdCancel button to select it, then drag it close to the cmdOK button.
- With the cmdCancel button still selected, Ctrl+click to select the cmdOK button.
- Choose Format ➤ Group to group the buttons.
- Then choose Format ➤ Center In Form ➤ Horizontally to center the buttons horizontally in the form.
- Drag the group up or down as necessary.

Creating the Code for the User Form

Once you've gotten the user form looking more or less okay, you'll be ready to create the code that drives it. Follow these steps to create the code:

1. With the user form selected, press the F7 key to display the user form's code sheet.

2. In the declarations portion of the code sheet, enter an Option Base 1 statement to make array numbering start at 1 instead of at 0:

```
Option Base 1
```

3. Make sure that UserForm is selected in the Object drop-down list, then pull down the Procedure drop-down list and choose Initialize from it. The Visual Basic Editor will enter the stub of an Initialize procedure in the code sheet, like this:

```
Private Sub UserForm_Initialize()

End Sub
```

4. Enter the statements for the Initialize procedure shown in Listing 15.2.

5. In the Object drop-down list, select cmdCancel. The Visual Basic Editor will enter the stub of a Click procedure, as shown below. (Because Click is the default event for the CommandButton control, the Visual Basic Editor assumes that you want to create a Click procedure.)

```
Private Sub cmdCancel_Click()

End Sub
```

6. Enter the statements for the cmdCancel_Click procedure shown in Listing 15.2.

7. In the Object drop-down list, select cmdOpen. Again, the Visual Basic Editor will enter the stub of a Click procedure for you.

8. Enter the statements for the cmdOpen_Click procedure shown in Listing 15.2.

9. Customize line 9 (in the Initialize procedure) and line 32 (in the cmdOpen_Click procedure) so that the code will work with the application you're using, as shown in the following list. The procedure as shown is set up to run for AutoCAD, but you'll probably need to change the path to reflect where the target files are on your computer.

- For Word, leave the Documents.Open statement intact but specify the Filename argument instead of the Name argument:

```
If lstFiles.Value <> "" Then Documents.Open _
    Filename:=" f:\users\common\" & lstFiles.Value
```

- For Excel, use a Workbooks.Open statement and specify the Filename argument:

```
If lstFiles.Value <> "" Then Workbooks.Open _
    Filename:=" f:\users\common\" & lstFiles.Value
```

- For PowerPoint, use a Presentations.Open statement and specify the Filename argument:

```
If lstFiles.Value <> "" Then Presentations.Open _
    Filename:=" f:\users\common\" & lstFiles.Value
```

- For Project, use a FileOpen statement:

```
If lstFiles.Value <> "" Then FileOpen _
    Name:=" f:\users\common\" & lstFiles.Value
```

- For WordPerfect, use a FileOpen statement:

```
If lstFiles.Value <> "" Then FileOpen _
    " f:\users\common\" & lstFiles.Value
```

- For Visio, leave the Documents.Open statement intact and specify the FileName argument:

```
If lstFiles.Value <> "" Then Documents.Open _
    Filename:=" f:\users\common\" & lstFiles.Value
```

Listing 15.2 shows the full version of the code behind the user form.

Listing 15.2

```
1.  Option Base 1
2.
3.  Private Sub UserForm_Initialize()
4.
5.      Dim strFileArray() As String
```

```
6.        Dim strFFile As String
7.        Dim intCount As Integer
8.
9.        strFFile = Dir("f:\users\common\cad\*.dwg")
10.       intCount = 1
11.
12.       Do While strFFile <> ""
13.           If strFFile <> "." And strFFile <> ".." Then
14.               ReDim Preserve strFileArray(intCount)
15.               strFileArray(intCount) = strFFile
16.               intCount = intCount + 1
17.               strFFile = Dir()
18.           End If
19.       Loop
20.
21.       lstFiles.List() = strFileArray
22.
23.   End Sub
24.
25.   Private Sub cmdCancel_Click()
26.       Me.Hide
27.       Unload Me
28.   End Sub
29.
30.   Private Sub cmdOpen_Click()
31.       Me.Hide
32.       If lstFiles.Value <> "" Then Documents.Open _
              Name:=" f:\users\common\cad\" & lstFiles.Value
33.       Unload Me
34.   End Sub
```

Analysis

Listing 15.2 contains all the code that appears on the code sheet for the frmOpen_a_ Current_File user form: a declarations section and three event procedures. I'll show you each in turn.

The declarations section is simple but vital. Line 1 contains the `Option Base 1` statement, which makes any array used on the code sheet begin at 1 rather than at 0. Line 2 is a spacer.

Here's what happens in the `UserForm_Initialize` procedure (lines 3 to 23):

- Line 3 begins the `Initialize` procedure for the user form. Line 4 is a spacer.

- Line 5 declares the String array variable `strFileArray`. Line 6 declares the String variable `strFFile`. Line 7 declares the Integer variable `intCount`. Line 8 is a spacer.

- Line 9 assigns to `strFFile` the result of a directory operation on the designated folder (here, `f:\users\common\cad\`) for files with a `.dwg` extension.

- Line 10 sets the `intCount` counter to 1. Note that if you don't use the `Option Base 1` declaration for this procedure, you need to set Count to 0 (or the corresponding value for a different option base that you use). The first call to `Dir`, which specifies the pathname in an argument, returns the first file it finds in the folder (assuming it finds at least one file). Each subsequent call without the argument returns the next file in the folder, until `Dir` finds no more files.

- Line 11 is a spacer. Lines 12 through 19 contain a `Do While...Loop` loop that runs while `strFFile` isn't an empty string (`""`):

  - Line 13 makes sure that `strFFile` isn't a folder by comparing it to the single period and double period used to denote folders (directories, if you remember your DOS). If `strFFile` isn't a folder, line 14 uses a `ReDim Preserve` statement to increase the dimensions of the `strFileArray` array to the number in `intCount` while retaining the current information in the array, thus building the list of files in the folder.

  - Line 15 assigns to the `intCount` subscript of the `strFileArray` array the current contents of `strFFile`.

  - Line 16 then adds 1 to `intCount`, and Line 17 sets `strFFile` to the result of the `Dir` function (the first file name matching the `*.dwg` pattern in the designated folder).

  - Line 18 ends the `If` condition. Line 19 contains the `Loop` keyword that will continue the loop as long as the `Do While` statement is `True`. Line 20 is a spacer.

- When the loop ends, line 21 sets the `List` property of the `lstFiles` list box in the dialog box to the contents of `strFileArray`, which now contains a list of all the files in the folder.

- Line 22 is a spacer, line 23 ends the procedure, and line 24 is another spacer.

Here's what happens in the cmdCancel_Click procedure (lines 25 through 28):

- Line 25 starts the cmdCancel_Click procedure, and line 28 ends it.
- Line 26 hides the user form, using the Me keyword to reference it.
- Line 27 unloads the user form from memory.

Here's what happens in the cmdOpen_Click procedure (lines 30 through 34):

- Line 30 starts the cmdOpen_Click procedure, and line 35 ends it.
- Line 31 hides the user form, again by using the Me keyword.
- Line 32 checks to make sure the Value property of the lstFiles list box is not an empty string ("") and, if it is not, uses the Open method of the Documents collection to open the file selected in the list box. The statement adds to the path (f:\users\common\cad\) the Value property of the list box to produce the full file name.
- Line 33 unloads the user form from memory.

Now that you've learned the basics of customizing your dialog boxes, you can move on to the next chapter, where I'll show you how you can construct dynamic dialog boxes that change appropriately when the user chooses certain options in them.

CHAPTER 16

Creating Complex Dialog Boxes

I n this chapter, I'll pick up the discussion of dialog boxes from the previous chapter, in which I showed you how to create straightforward dialog boxes that used straightforward controls such as command buttons, check boxes, option buttons, and list boxes. These dialog boxes were static—the controls and information in them remained the same as the user worked in them. Here, you'll start by investigating how to create *dynamic* dialog boxes—ones that change and update themselves when the user clicks a control within them. Dynamic dialog boxes cost you a little more work than static dialog boxes, but they're a great way both to present information and choices, and to impress your colleagues.

From dynamic dialog boxes you'll move on to multipage dialog boxes, which you use to present more information or options to the user than the eye and mind can comfortably compass at once. You'll then look at how to create a dialog box programmatically, which you may need to do from time to time. After that, I'll show you how to adapt a dialog box on-the-fly and create modeless dialog boxes.

I'll round off the chapter by showing you how to work with the many events supported by the UserForm object and the controls you use on it. By using events, you can monitor what the user does and take action accordingly, or even prevent the user from doing something that doesn't seem like a good idea.

What Is a Complex Dialog Box?

In a nutshell, complex dialog boxes are more complicated versions of the simpler dialog boxes you learned about in the previous chapter. Even those dialog boxes varied in complexity, but they all used a single page to contain all their controls. Not only that, but the dialog boxes you saw earlier were static, in that the information in them remained the same until the user dismissed them (beyond necessary changes such as reflecting the check boxes, option buttons, or list items selected, or the text entered in a text box).

In contrast to static dialog boxes, many complex dialog boxes are dynamic, in that they change when the user clicks certain elements in them. Such changes can include the following:

- The application changes the information in the dialog box to reflect choices that the user has made. For example, if they've selected a particular check box, the application may make another check box unavailable because the option controlled by the second check box isn't available or applicable when they use the option controlled by the first check box.

- The dialog box displays a hidden section of secondary options when the user clicks a button in the primary area of the dialog box.

- The application uses the dialog box to keep track of a procedure and to guide the user to the next step by displaying appropriate instructions and by activating the relevant control. In this chapter, you'll look at a simple example of this technique.

Other complex dialog boxes include multipage dialog boxes, which provide you with the means to pack a lot of information into a single dialog box. I'll discuss these various types of complex dialog boxes in the following sections.

Creating and Working with Complex Dialog Boxes

Before taking you further into the realm of complex dialog boxes, I'll risk making an obvious point: Never go to the trouble of constructing a complex dialog box where a simple one would do the trick. By keeping dialog boxes as simple as possible, you'll make life easier for the users of your procedures—for whom you're presumably creating the dialog boxes. That said, let's start by looking at how to create complex dialog boxes.

Updating a Dialog Box to Reflect the User's Choices

You'll find it relatively easy to update a dialog box to reflect the options the user chooses in it. Your primary tool for doing this is the Click event to which most controls in a dialog box react, and to which you can add a procedure on the code sheet attached to the dialog box. Some controls have different default events than Click; you'll meet the Change event as you work with complex dialog boxes, and you'll meet the full slew of other events in the second half of the chapter.

You'll look at an example of updating a dialog box in Listing 16.1 in the next section, because it ties in neatly with revealing an extra part of a dialog box.

Revealing an Extra Part of a Dialog Box

Hiding part of a complex dialog box is a great way to simplify the user's initial interaction with the dialog box. Consider the Find And Replace dialog box in Word: When you first display it by choosing Edit ➢ Replace, you see only the part of the dialog box shown in the top picture of Figure 16.1. (If you choose Edit ➢ Find, you see an even smaller part of the dialog box.) If you need to use the more complex options than the Find And Replace dialog box offers, you can click the More button to display the bottom part of the dialog box, as shown in the lower picture of Figure 16.1.

FIGURE 16.1

Word's Find And Replace dialog box hides some of its options (above) until you click the More button to display its lower half (below).

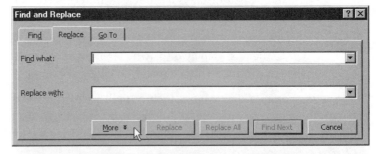

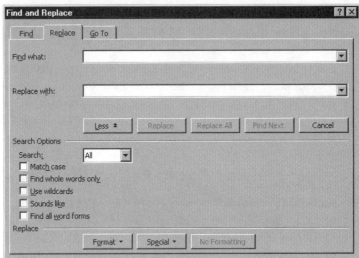

You may want to follow a similar strategy with complex dialog boxes that contain a subset of actions with which most users will be content most of the time. To do so, you can use two techniques, either separately or in tandem:

• Set the Visible property to False to hide a control that appears in a displayed part of the dialog box. Set the Visible property to True when you want to display the control.

• Increase the height or width (or both) of the dialog box to reveal an area containing further controls.

TIP With either of the above techniques, you'll typically want to set the Enabled property for hidden controls to False until you reveal them so that the user can't move to a control that they can't see.

As a simple example of the latter technique, consider the dialog box shown in Figure 16.2. When you display the dialog box, only the top part is visible; when you click the More button, the bottom half is displayed. Listing 16.1 contains the code behind the dialog box: You'll find it's surprisingly simple.

FIGURE 16.2

The top part of the Inventories 2000 dialog box (left) offers the most frequently used options. Clicking the More button reveals the rest of the dialog box (right), which contains less-used controls.

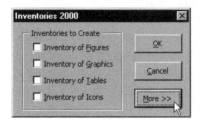
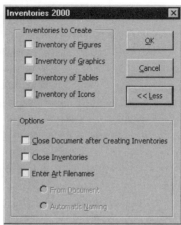

Listing 16.1

```
1.  Private Sub UserForm_Initialize()
2.      frmInventories.Height = 120
3.  End Sub
4.
5.  Private Sub cmdMore_Click()
6.      If cmdMore.Caption = "More >>" Then
7.          cmdMore.Caption = "<< Less"
8.          cmdMore.Accelerator = "L"
9.          frmInventories.Height = 240
10.         fraOptions.Enabled = True
11.     Else
12.         frmInventories.Height = 120
13.         cmdMore.Caption = "More >>"
14.         cmdMore.Accelerator = "M"
15.     End If
```

```
16.   End Sub
17.
18.   Private Sub chkArtNames_Click()
19.       If chkArtNames = True Then
20.           optFromDocument.Enabled = True
21.           optFromDocument = True
22.           optAutoNames.Enabled = True
23.       Else
24.           optFromDocument.Enabled = False
25.           optFromDocument = False
26.           optAutoNames.Enabled = False
27.           optAutoNames = False
28.       End If
29.   End Sub
30.
31.   Private Sub cmdOK_Click()
32.       frmInventories.Hide
33.       Unload frmInventories
34.       'create inventories here
35.   End Sub
36.
37.   Private Sub cmdCancel_Click()
38.       End
39.   End Sub
```

Analysis

Listing 16.1 contains five short procedures that control the behavior of the dialog box:

UserForm_Initialize   Initializes the dialog box before it's displayed

cmdMore_Click   Runs when the More button is chosen

chkArtNames_Click   Runs when the Enter Art Filenames check box is chosen

cmdOK_Click   Runs when the OK button is chosen

cmdCancel_Click   Runs when the Cancel button is chosen

Here's what happens:

The `UserForm_Initialize` procedure simply sets the `Height` property of the `frm-Inventories` user form to 120, which is enough to display only the top part of the dialog box. (To find the appropriate height for your dialog box, drag it to the depth that looks right and note the `Height` property in the Properties window.) This procedure is necessary only if the user form is set to its full height at design time: By setting the user form to a height of 120 at design time, you could avoid having to use a `UserForm_Initialize` procedure. However, for a user form that has three or more different sizes—or for a user form with two different sizes, one of which needs to be chosen at runtime depending on environmental conditions—you'll need to use a `UserForm_Initialize` procedure. The `cmdMore_Click` procedure starts by checking in line 6 if the `Caption` property of the `cmdMore` command button is `More >>`; if so, that means that only the top half of the dialog box is displayed. Line 7 then sets the `Caption` property of the `cmdMore` command button to `<< Less`, because it will be used to hide the bottom part of the dialog box again if necessary. Line 8 sets the `Accelerator` property of the `cmdMore` command button to L (to make the L in *Less* the accelerator key for the button). Line 9 sets the `Height` property of `frmInventories` to 240, which is the depth required to show all the contents of the dialog box. Line 10 enables the `fraOptions` frame (identified as Options in the dialog box and disabled in the user form, as are the `optFromDocument` option button and the `optAutoNames` option button), making it and the controls it contains available to the user.

 NOTE Checking the `Caption` property of the `cmdMore` button is an effective way of checking the current state of the dialog box, but it's not the most elegant of methods. Instead, you could maintain an internal state variable in which you stored information about whether the dialog box was displayed in its full state or its partial state. Using the internal state variable would have the added benefit of not having to be patched if the dialog box were localized (adapted for a different language locale).

If the condition in line 6 is `False`, execution shifts from line 6 to the `Else` statement in line 11. This must mean that the `Caption` property of the `cmdMore` button is already set to `<< Less`, so the dialog box is already at its expanded size; the `<< Less` button is being clicked to shrink the dialog box again. Line 12 sets the `Height` property of the user form back to 120, thus hiding the lower part of the dialog box; line 13 restores the `Caption` property of the `cmdMore` command button to `More >>`; and line 14 sets the `Accelerator` property of the `cmdMore` command button back to M. Line 16 ends the `cmdMore_Click` procedure.

The chkArtNames_Click procedure (lines 18 to 29) runs when the Enter Art Filenames check box is clicked, and enables and disables the option buttons below it as appropriate. Line 19 checks to see if the chkArtNames check box is selected. If it is, the statements in lines 20 through 22 run. Line 20 sets the Enabled property of the optFromDocument option button (identified as From Document in the dialog box) to True, thus making it available, and line 21 selects this option button as the default choice. Line 22 enables optAutoNames, the option button identified as Automatic Naming in the dialog box.

If the chkArtNames check box isn't selected, execution shifts to the Else statement in line 23, which directs execution to line 24; this line sets the Enabled property of the optFromDocument option button to False, disabling it. Line 25 then deselects this option button (whether it's selected or not). Line 26 disables the optAutoNames option button, and line 27 deselects it (again, whether it's selected or not). The End If statement in line 28 ends this If statement, and line 29 ends this procedure.

The cmdOK_Click procedure in lines 31 to 35 shows the beginning of the procedure that would run once the OK button is clicked. Line 32 hides the Inventories dialog box, and line 33 unloads it from memory. Line 34 contains a comment indicating that the instructions for creating the inventories would appear here.

The cmdCancel_Click procedure contains only an End statement to end execution of the procedure if the user chooses the Cancel button.

Tracking a Procedure in a Dialog Box

The next stage of complexity in a dialog box is using it to track the different stages of a procedure and to guide the user as to how to continue. As an example, consider the Mail Merge Helper dialog box in Word, which provides instructions that walk you through the many steps of the various mail-merge operations: merging to a letter, mailing labels, a form, or a catalog; using different merge sources, such as a Word document, an Excel worksheet, or your Outlook address book; and merging the results to a printer or to e-mail.

Figure 16.3 shows two instances of the Mail Merge Helper dialog box:

- First, at the beginning of a merge, with very little information on display and only one of the three non-Cancel command buttons available, shoe-horning the user into the right course of action

- Second, nearing the end of a merge, with all three sections filled in and not only the three primary command buttons, but also three subsidiary command buttons available

The frame at the top of the dialog box contains information on the current state of the procedure and instructs the user to choose the Merge button to complete the merge;

the Merge button is already selected so that the user can continue by simply pressing Enter. Under the 1 and 2 that denote the previous main steps of the mail merge, the Mail Merge Helper records the details of the choices the user has made: the merge type, the name of the main document, and the name of the data source. Under the Merge button, the Mail Merge Helper lists the options in effect for the merge. Even if Murphy himself were around to use this dialog box, he'd be hard-pressed to find something to do wrong with it.

FIGURE 16.3

The Mail Merge Helper dialog box keeps updating its information to give the user guidance during a mail-merge operation.

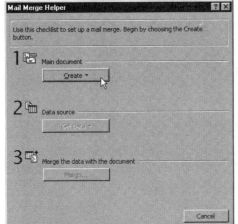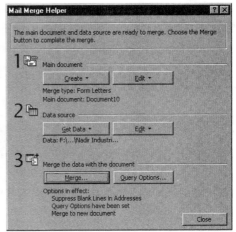

In your more complex procedures, you may want to produce a dialog box that walks the user through a procedure like this. Depending on the complexity of the procedure and the amount of time you have to cosset its users, your dialog box will probably be much less complex than this one.

 NOTE The more effort you put into making your procedures instantly understandable to their users, the better your life will be—and I don't mean karma. Rather, you'll suffer fewer demands on your time to explain for the umpteenth time what you fondly imagined was a straightforward procedure. Along with following the guidelines for creating well-behaved procedures covered in Chapter 19, providing clear information and relevant instructions in a dialog box can save you substantial amounts of grief.

Take a look at the Create New Employee Web Page dialog box shown in Figure 16.4. This dialog box guides the user through a four-stage procedure to create a Web page for a new employee. The first step is to identify the employee deserving of this honor by using either the drop-down list or the Select Other Employee command button in the Step 1 frame. The second step is to enter suitable introductory or laudatory text about the employee. The third step is to select the most (or perhaps least) flattering photo of the employee to include in the Web page. The fourth step is to save the Web page to a folder on the company's intranet.

FIGURE 16.4

The Create New Employee Web Page dialog box provides the user with instructions that it updates as they work their way through the procedure.

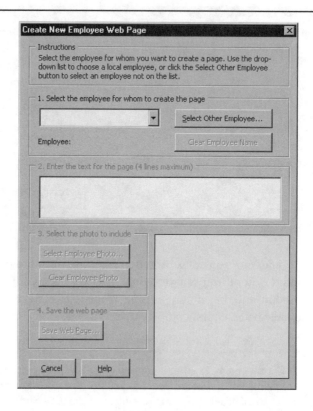

When the user first displays the Create New Employee Web Page dialog box, they will see the version of the dialog box shown in Figure 16.4, with Steps 2, 3, and 4 disabled, and instructions for Step 1 shown in the Instructions box at the top. When the user follows the instructions and selects the victim employee by using either the combo box drop-down list or the Select Other Employee command button, the code attached to the combo box drop-down list or the command button enables the Step 2 frame, making its text box available to the user as shown in Figure 16.5. Following the figure is the code for the Change event of the cmbSelectEmployee combo box; the code for the Click event of the cmdSelectOtherEmployee command button is similar, although a little more complex.

The second stage of the Create New Employee Web Page dialog box. Notice the changes from the first stage: The instructions in the Instructions frame have changed, and the use of the Step 1 combo box drop-down list has enabled the Step 2 frame.

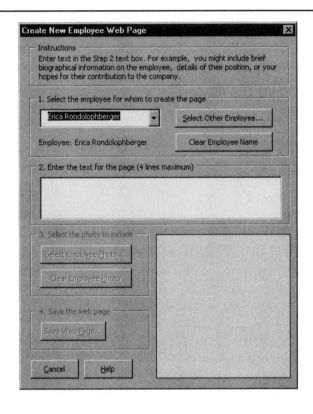

```
Private Sub cmbSelectEmployee_Change()
    lblEmployeeName = cmbSelectEmployee.Text
    fraStep2.Enabled = True
    lblInstructions = "Enter text in the Step 2 text box. " & _
        "For example, you might include brief biographical " & _
        "information on the employee, details of their position, " & _
        "or your hopes for their contribution to the company."
    cmdClearEmployeeName.Enabled = True
End Sub
```

NOTE Note in passing the ellipsis (…) on the Select Other Employee button (and the Select Employee Photo button and the Save Web Page button, although these may be hard to see in the figure). You'll recognize the ellipsis as the Windows convention for indicating that the choice (here a command button, but often a menu item) will result in a dialog box being displayed rather than an action being taken immediately. Even if you hate the convention, you might as well get as much mileage from it as you can....

These are the changes that occur when the user completes Step 1 of the dialog box:

- The text of the label in the Instructions box at the top of the dialog box is changed to contain information for Step 2 of the procedure.

- The name of the employee selected by the user is listed alongside the Employee label in the Step 1 frame.

- The frame for Step 2 is enabled (the text box it contains is enabled along with the frame).

Using Multipage Dialog Boxes and Tab Strip Controls

In addition to the controls you've learned about so far in this book, VBA provides controls that give you the capability to create multipage dialog boxes by using the MultiPage control and tab strip–driven dialog boxes by using the MultiTab control. You'll be familiar with multipage dialog boxes from your work in Windows application—for example, the Options dialog box in Word, Excel, PowerPoint, Project, Visio, and AutoCAD all contain multiple pages, and the Font Properties dialog box in Word-Perfect has a more modest number of pages. You can access any page (one at a time) by clicking the tab at the top of the page. Each page contains a different set of controls and can have a different layout appropriate to the controls.

To confuse things, most everyone refers to the pages as "tabs," either strictly or loosely. For example, in Microsoft's Help files, you'll read instructions such as "On the Tools menu, click Options, and then click the View tab." Now, clicking the View *tab* will indeed display the View *page* of the multipage, but the Help file doesn't exactly make the distinction clear between a tab and a page clear. In this section, I need to be a little clearer than most people, so I'll use the terms *tab* and *page* more strictly: The tab is the little thing that sticks out from the top of the page, not the whole page.

Multipage dialog boxes are great for packing a lot of information into a single dialog box without having it take up the whole screen and become visually bewildering.

You'll need to divide the information into discrete sets of related information to fit it onto the pages, as in the three dialog boxes mentioned earlier. Each page can (and should) have a different layout of controls that govern the behavior of discrete items; the pages can (and should) be separate in theme (to use the word loosely) except inasmuch as they can be grouped generally under the same rubric. For example, AutoCAD's Options dialog box encompasses a multitude of sins, from file locations to system printer spool alert options.

A dialog box that uses a tab strip differs from a multipage dialog box in that it contains a tab strip control containing multiple *tabs* but not multiple *pages*: The rest of the dialog box, apart from the tab strip, stays the same no matter which tab on the tab strip is selected. This means that the dialog box has only one layout, so the controls don't change. Instead, the tab strip acts as a control for accessing the set of data to display in the other controls: To change the set of data displayed in the controls in the dialog box, you select a different tab in the tab strip.

I think I'd be safe in saying that the tab strip is *not* generally seen as the best thing since self-starting mesquite barbeque briquettes or five-alarm Tabasco, but beyond that, opinion tends to be cleanly divided on how useful the tab strip is and what (if anything) you should use it for. Some people consider the tab strip a mostly failed attempt at creating the multipage control; in this scenario, Microsoft continues to include the tab strip with its other controls for reasons of backward-compatibility even though the multipage control is now here to replace it. Others see the tab strip as an ingenious control designed for a completely different purpose than the multipage control—and think their sadly misguided antagonists in the former group are misunderstanding the poor thing.

If anything, I cleave to the latter point of view—but even so, I don't find that much use for tab strips in most of my work. Your mileage will vary... but you'll probably want to restrict your use of tab strips to times when you need to display consistent sets of information, such as the records you might maintain on your company's customers. Each customer has an account number, a name (or several), an address, phone numbers, e-mail addresses, URLs, an order history, an account balance, and so on, so you can use the same set of controls (textboxes and labels, for example) to display the information and use a tab strip control to control which customer's set of information is displayed in them. Because few databases have a small and fixed number of records, you'll need to populate the tab strip on-the-fly with tabs and captions, but it works fine. You'll look at an example of using a tab strip in this way in the section "Creating and Adapting Dialog Boxes On-the-Fly" a bit later in this chapter.

Multipage Faults…Advantage: Tab Strip

The Visual Basic Editor allows you to create dialog boxes with dozens of tabs or dozens of pages; if you run out of horizontal space to display the tabs, the Visual Basic Editor adds a scroll bar to enable you to scroll through the tabs. You'll probably want to avoid creating multipage dialog boxes with more than 10 or 12 pages, as the wealth of information such a dialog box will contain is likely to overwhelm the user.

If you need more than a dozen pages to organize the information in a dialog box, you're probably trying to present the user with too much data at once. Consider an alternative way of displaying it.

Tabs are a different matter. Because you use a tab strip to move through the records in a recordset, you may need to use many tabs in a given tab strip. Unless the number of tabs is absurdly large, this shouldn't normally be a problem.

You'll look first at multipage dialog boxes, and then at dialog boxes that use tab strips.

 NOTE Table 15.7 in Chapter 15 details the properties unique to the TabStrip control and MultiPage control.

Multipage Dialog Boxes

To create a multipage dialog box, you begin by placing a MultiPage control: Click the MultiPage button in the Toolbox and then click in the user form where you want the control to appear. The Visual Basic Editor will place a MultiPage control with two pages, whose tabs will carry the labels Page 1 and Page 2. You can then move and size the control as usual. For most purposes, you'll want to create a MultiPage control that's only a little smaller than the user form it inhabits (as in most of the multipage dialog boxes you'll see in Windows applications).

Once you've created a MultiPage control, you work with a page on it by right-clicking its tab and using the resulting context menu:

- To add a page, right-click the label and choose New Page from the context menu. VBA will add a new page of the default size and will name it Page*n*, where *n* is the next number after the current number of pages (even if the other pages have names other than Page1, Page2, and so on).

- To rename a page in a MultiPage control, right-click the label and choose Rename from the context menu. VBA will display the Rename dialog box (see Figure 16.6). Enter the caption (the label text) for the page in the Caption text box, the accelerator key in the Accelerator Key text box, and any control-tip text (the tip the user sees when they move the mouse pointer over the tab for the page) in the Control Tip Text text box. Click the OK button to close the Rename dialog box.

FIGURE 16.6

Use the Rename dialog box to set the caption, accelerator key, and control-tip text for a page.

- To delete a page from a MultiPage control, right-click the label and choose Delete Page from the context menu. The Visual Basic Editor will remove the page without prompting for confirmation.

- To move a page to a different place in the MultiPage control, right-click the label and choose Move from the context menu to display the Page Order dialog box (see Figure 16.7). In the Page Order list box, select the page or pages that you want to move (Shift+click to select multiple contiguous pages, Ctrl+click to select multiple noncontiguous pages) and then use the Move Up and Move Down buttons to rearrange the page or pages as desired. When you've finished, select the OK button to close the Page Order dialog box.

FIGURE 16.7

Use the Move Up and Move Down buttons in the Page Order dialog box to change the order of pages in a MultiPage control.

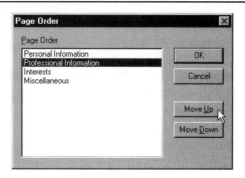

- To specify which page of a multipage dialog box to display by default, you use the `Value` property of the MultiPage control. You can set this property either at design time or at runtime. For example, you could use an initialization procedure such as the one shown here to display the third page (identified by the value 2, because the page numbering starts at 0) of a dialog box with a Multi-Page control called `MyMulti` at runtime:

```
Sub UserForm_Initialize()
  MyMulti.Value = 2
End Sub
```

Once you've created a multipage dialog box, you can populate its pages with controls the same way you would with any dialog box, as described in Chapter 15. Each control has to have a unique name within the dialog box (not just within the page on which it appears). When designing a multipage dialog box, keep the following issues in mind:

- What's the best way to divide the information or options in the dialog box? What belongs on which page? Which information or options will the user expect to find grouped together?

- Which controls should appear on each page? In most dialog boxes, you'll want to have at least a pair of command buttons such as OK and Cancel or OK and Close available from each page to allow the user to dismiss the dialog box from whichever page they happen to end up on. In rare instances, you may want to force the user to return to a particular page in order to close a dialog box. In these cases, make sure that each page that doesn't contain a command button to dismiss the dialog box gives the user an indication of where they will find such a command button.

- For settings, do you need to have an Apply button as well as an OK button to apply the changes on a particular page without closing the dialog box?

Because each control in a multipage dialog box has a unique name, when returning information from a multipage dialog box you need specify only the relevant object—you don't need to specify which page it's on.

Figure 16.8 shows an example of a multipage dialog box. The first page contains the customer's personal contact information, the second the customer's professional information, the third the associations the customer belongs to, and the fourth the certifications the customer holds.

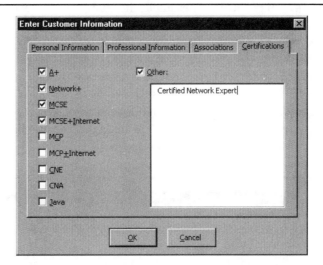

Most of the properties of the MultiPage control are straightforward, but a few deserve special mention:

- The Style property offers fmStyleTabs (the default setting, showing tabs for navigating between the pages), fmStyleButtons (which gives each page a rectangular button, with the button for the current page appearing pushed in), or fmStyleNone (which provides no means of navigating between the pages of the multipage and no indication of the borders of the multipage). fmStyleNone can be useful for creating user forms that have two or more alternate layouts of which the user will only ever need to see one at a time. By including one set of controls on one page of the multipage and another set of controls on the other page, you can present two apparently different dialog boxes by doing nothing more than changing which page of the multipage control is displayed.

- The TabOrientation property controls where the tabs (or buttons) for the pages appear on the control. Your choices are fmTabOrientationTop (the default setting, placing the tabs at the top of the control), fmTabOrientationBottom, fmTabOrientationLeft, and fmTabOrientationRight. Experiment with the effects that the bottom, left, and right orientations offer, but unless they provide significant advantages over the more normal top orientation, use them sparingly if at all—your users won't thank you for confusing the interface unnecessarily.

- The MultiRow property controls whether a MultiPage control has one row of tabs for its pages (False) or multiple rows (True). When you have MultiRow set to True, the Visual Basic Editor will add the second or subsequent rows of tabs when you run out of space on the first or current row.

As you can see in my example, the MultiPage control doesn't have to take up the whole of a dialog box—in fact, most dialog boxes keep the key command buttons outside the multipage area so that they're available to the user no matter which page the user is on. For example, AutoCAD's Options dialog box, shown in Figure 16.9, keeps its OK, Cancel, Apply, and Help buttons outside its nine-page MultiPage control, so that the user can choose one of these command buttons at any point. (Contrast this with the command buttons that appear only on particular pages of the multipage, such as the Lineweight Settings command button shown in the figure, because they apply only to those pages.)

FIGURE 16.9

Keep key command buttons outside the MultiPage control so that they're available no matter which page the user is currently viewing. AutoCAD's Options dialog box keeps its general command buttons available at all times, while other command buttons appear only on the page to which they're relevant.

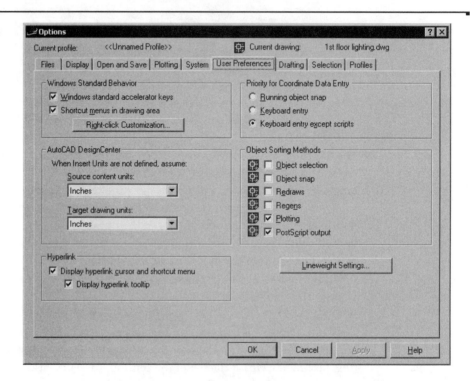

That said, it isn't usually a good idea to use a MultiPage control as a less-than-dominant part of a dialog box. In a complex and busy dialog box, a small multipage can appear to be little more than a group box, and the user may miss the tabs, particularly if they're taking only a cursory sweep of the controls presented to locate a specific option. Figure 16.10 provides an example of how a multipage can get lost in a busy dialog box. (To get around this problem, you could highlight the MultiPage control by giving it a dramatic or ugly color scheme, but to me that doesn't exactly enhance the dialog box you're presenting. Remember, the operative term is *interface*, not *in your face*.)

FIGURE 16.10

Resist the temptation to use MultiPage controls as just another element in a dialog box: Unless the multipage dominates the dialog box, you risk having the user notice only the controls on the page initially displayed to them.

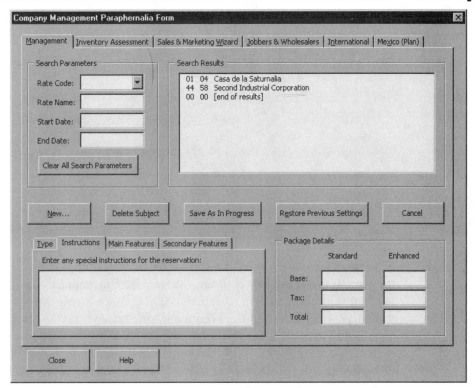

Dialog Boxes That Use Tab Strips

As I mentioned earlier, dialog boxes that use tab strips are substantially different from multipage dialog boxes: The TabStrip control is used not to arrange other controls, but to control what appears in them, as the user moves from one set of data to another.

For instance, you might use a dialog box driven by a tab strip to view and update the records in a data source such as a Word or WordPerfect table, an Excel spreadsheet, or an Access database. As I mentioned earlier, the tab strip is not exactly universally acclaimed as a good thing, so you won't be alone if you don't want to try this at home. As an example, I'll use an Excel workbook, with information stored on a number of worksheets. Figure 16.11 shows the DataSurfer 2000 dialog box, which is driven by a tab strip.

FIGURE 16.11

*Using a TabStrip
control to create a
multitab dialog box.
The tab strip is used to
control which set of
information is displayed
in the other controls in
the dialog box.*

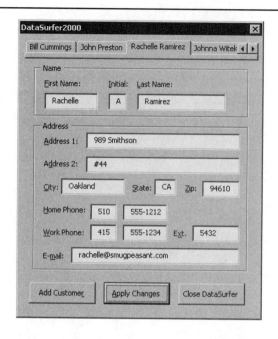

To create a multitab dialog box, you place a TabStrip control above, below, or beside the controls that it will help populate. (Above is the conventional—and default—position, but vertical and bottom tabs are showing up increasingly in Windows applications these days. As with the MultiPage control, use the TabOrientation property of the Tab-Strip control to specify whether the tab strip should appear at the top, bottom, left, or right of its control.) The tab strip can contain zero, one, or more tabs. For most purposes, there's little point in having only one tab on a tab strip, and even less in having no tab at all. But if you dynamically populate the tab strip with tabs in your procedures (as you're about to do) and create one tab for each record found, you may run into situations with only one record and so a dialog box with only one tab—or even a tab strip without any tabs at all.

Once you've placed the TabStrip control (by clicking the TabStrip button on the Toolbox and then clicking in the user form), you size it appropriately. Depending on what the rest of the dialog box looks like, you may want to make the tab strip large enough to encompass all the controls it will affect, either in one dimension (as in Figure 16.11), or in both dimensions. Bear in mind that this is only a visual connection for the user's benefit, because you establish the logical connection between the tab strip and the other controls through code. You can then add, rename, move, and delete tabs in the same way as you can pages in a MultiPage control.

If you haven't placed the other controls for the dialog box, you then do so.

Once everything's in place, you write the code that will enable the tab strip to control the contents of the other controls. Listing 16.2 shows the code for the tab strip in the DataSurfer 2000 dialog box. This tab strip is named tabSurfer, and the code works with its Change event—the event that fires when the user moves from one tab of the tab strip to another.

Listing 16.2

```
1.  Private Sub tabSurfer_Change()
2.      If blnInitializing = False Then
3.          With ActiveWorkbook.Sheets(tabSurfer.Value + 1)
4.              'load the contents of the sheet that corresponds _
                to the tab chosen
5.              .Activate
6.              txtFirstName.Text = .Cells(1, 2).Text
7.              txtInitial.Text = .Cells(2, 2).Text
8.              txtLastName.Text = .Cells(3, 2).Text
9.              txtAddress1.Text = .Cells(4, 2).Text
10.             txtAddress2.Text = .Cells(5, 2).Text
11.             txtCity.Text = .Cells(6, 2).Text
12.             txtState.Text = .Cells(7, 2)
13.             txtZip.Text = .Cells(8, 2).Text
14.             txtHomeArea.Text = .Cells(9, 2).Text
15.             txtHomePhone.Text = .Cells(10, 2).Text
16.             txtWorkArea.Text = .Cells(11, 2).Text
17.             txtWorkPhone.Text = .Cells(12, 2).Text
18.             txtWorkExtension.Text = .Cells(13, 2).Text
19.             txtEmail.Text = .Cells(14, 2).Text
20.         End With
21.     End If
22. End Sub
```

Analysis

As you can see, after some initial excitement, the code that comprises Listing 16.2 essentially repeats itself for each of the text boxes that appears in the DataSurfer 2000 dialog box. This dialog box works with a data source implemented as Excel spreadsheets in the active workbook.

Each worksheet in the workbook is one customer's record, with the name of the customer appearing on the worksheet's tab and the customer's key information (at least, the information in which this dialog box is interested) appearing in the second column: the first name in the first cell of the second column, the middle initial in the second cell, the last name in the third cell, and so on for the address, phone numbers (both home and work), and e-mail address. So to get at any piece of information, you need to know the sheet of the record in question and the appropriate cell in the second column.

Here's how the code works:

- Line 1 declares the private procedure tabSurfer_Change, which will run automatically whenever the Change event of the tabSurfer tab strip fires. The Change event will fire each time the user changes the tab displayed, so you use this event to control the information displayed in the text boxes.

- The Change event will also fire when a tab is added to (or removed from) the tab strip. Because the DataSurfer 2000 user form uses the Initialize event procedure to populate the tab strip with tabs (one per worksheet in the workbook), you need to stop the Change event procedure from running unnecessarily. So the user form declares a private Boolean variable named blnInitializing that the Initialize procedure sets to True while it's running and False just before it ends. Line 2 of the Change event procedure checks to make sure that blnInitializing is False; if it's not, the Initialize procedure has fired the event, and the Change procedure does not need to load the information into the cells—so execution continues at line 21, just before the end of the procedure. But once the Initialize procedure has finished running, blnInitializing will be set to False, and the Change event procedure will run each time the user changes tabs in the tab strip.

- Line 3 begins a With statement that works with the appropriate worksheet in the active workbook: (ActiveWorkbook.Sheets(tabSurfer.Value + 1). The Value property of the tabSurfer tab strip tells us which tab in the tab strip is selected. Because the first tab in the tab strip is numbered 0 and the first worksheet in the workbook is numbered 1, you need to add 1 to the Value of the tab strip to even the numbers.

- Line 4 is a comment. Line 5 uses the Activate method to activate the worksheet in question.

- Lines 6 through 19 then set the Text property of each text box in the user form to the contents of the corresponding cell in the second column on the worksheet. For example, line 6 sets the Text property of the txtFirstName text box (which appears under the First Name label in the dialog box) to the contents of the first cell in the second column: .Cells(1, 2).Text.

- Line 20 ends the With statement, line 21 ends the If statement, and line 22 ends the procedure.

That's all on the DataSurfer 2000 dialog box for the moment, but I'll revisit it a little later on in the chapter when I show you how you can adapt a dialog box on-the-fly before displaying it. Quite by chance, this dialog box happens to do a little of that....

Using Pictures in a Dialog Box

You can add a picture to a dialog box by using an Image control. Applied appropriately, a picture can provide a real boost to a dialog box by showing the user, for example, the effect that a setting in the dialog box will achieve or the type of document that a certain procedure will produce. You might also want to use a picture to show a company logo. For instance, if you're creating a set of procedures for a company, they might want you to include the company's logo in the dialog boxes to emphasize that the code is proprietary.

When Should You Add a Picture to a Dialog Box?

Used appropriately, a picture enhances a dialog box; used inappropriately, it can severely detract from both the aesthetics and the effectiveness of the dialog box. The basic rule of thumb goes like this: Don't add a picture to a dialog box unless the picture improves the dialog box's comprehensibility or is necessary for other reasons (such as the company logo).

One disadvantage of a picture is that it slows down the display time for the dialog box, which can look unprofessional. Test the display time for pictures in VBA dialog boxes on a slow computer to make sure the delay isn't unreasonable.

Worse, if the computer displaying the dialog box doesn't have the graphics filter for the picture type installed, the user will see an error message box. When the dialog box then displays, there will be an empty space where the picture was supposed to be. If you need to display a picture in a dialog box, make sure that the picture and the appropriate graphics filter are both available to the users of the dialog box. If the picture isn't available or the computer doesn't have the appropriate graphics filter to display it, you could display a different version of the dialog box (or the same dialog box with its dimensions reduced) to hide the missing picture, but having a picture in a dialog box is seldom worth this amount of effort.

To place an Image control in a dialog box, click the Image button in the Toolbox and then click in the user form where you want the picture to appear. Once you've placed the Image control, you can size and move the picture just like any other control.

FIGURE 16.12

To add a picture to a dialog box, select the Picture property in the Properties window and click the ellipsis (...) button that appears.

To choose the picture that will appear in the Image control, select the Picture property in the Properties window and click the ellipsis button that then appears to the right of the entry. The Visual Basic Editor will display the Load Picture dialog box. Select the picture file and choose the Open button. The Picture property in the Properties window will register the type of picture you selected (such as (Bitmap)) but not its file name, and the picture will appear in the Image control so that you can see if it's an appropriate size.

Loading a Picture into an Image Control Programmatically

When specifying the picture for an Image control programmatically, you need to use a LoadPicture statement rather than simply assigning the picture to the Picture property of the Image control. LoadPicture takes the following syntax:

```
LoadPicture filename, [WidthDesired], [HeightDesired]
```

filename is a string argument specifying the name of the picture file to be loaded into the Image control. WidthDesired is an optional Long argument specifying the width of the picture in twips, and HeightDesired is an optional Long argument specifying the height of the picture.

Continued

CONTINUED

For example, the following statement loads the picture Company Logo.jpg in f:\common\ images\:

```
LoadPicture "f:\common\images\Company Logo.jpg"
```

Once you've chosen the picture, you have various options for positioning it and formatting it:

- If necessary, set the alignment of the picture by using the PictureAlignment property. (If the picture fully fills the Image control—neither overlapping it nor leaving parts of it empty—you may not need to set alignment for it.) Table 16.1 shows the constants and values for the PictureAlignment property.

TABLE 16.1: CONSTANTS AND VALUES FOR THE *PICTUREALIGNMENT* PROPERTY

Constant	Value	Picture Alignment in Image Control
fmPictureAlignmentTopLeft	0	Top left
fmPictureAlignmentTopRight	1	Top right
fmPictureAlignmentCenter	2	Centered
fmPictureAlignmentBottomLeft	3	Bottom left
fmPictureAlignmentBottomRight	4	Bottom right

- If necessary, clip, stretch, or zoom the picture by using the PictureSizeMode property: fmPictureSizeModeClip (0) clips the picture to fit the Image control; fmPictureSizeModeStretch (1) stretches or squeezes the picture so that it fits the Image control (this option often makes for strange effects); and fmPicture-SizeModeZoom (2) enlarges or reduces the picture so that its nearest dimension exactly fits the width or height of the Image control without changing the picture's proportions (this option usually leaves an unfilled gap on the other side).
- If you need to tile the image to take up the remaining space in the control, set the PictureTiling property to True.
- If you need to adjust the position of the picture relative to its caption, set the PicturePosition property appropriately. Table 16.2 shows the constants and values for PicturePosition.

TABLE 16.2: CONSTANTS AND VALUES FOR THE *PicturePosition* PROPERTY

Constant	Value	Picture Position	Caption Alignment
fmPicturePositionLeftTop	0	Left of the caption	With top of picture
fmPicturePositionLeftCenter	1	Left of the caption	Centered on picture
fmPicturePositionLeftBottom	2	Left of the caption	With bottom of picture
fmPicturePositionRightTop	3	Right of the caption	With top of picture
fmPicturePositionRightCenter	4	Right of the caption	Centered on picture
fmPicturePositionRightBottom	5	Right of the caption	With bottom of picture
fmPicturePositionAboveLeft	6	Above the caption	With left edge of picture
fmPicturePositionAboveCenter	7	Above the caption	Centered below picture; this is the default setting.
fmPicturePositionAboveRight	8	Above the caption	With right edge of picture
fmPicturePositionBelowLeft	9	Below the caption	With left edge of picture
fmPicturePositionBelowCenter	10	Below the caption	Centered above picture
fmPicturePositionBelowRight	11	Below the caption	With right edge of picture
fmPicturePositionCenter	12	In center of control	Centered horizontally and vertically on top of picture

Once you've placed, sized, and formatted a picture, there are various possibilities for what you can do with it. One obvious option is to use a picture's Click event to trigger an action. For example, if you present the user with a choice of two formats for a document, you could have them click the appropriate picture to make their choice instead of having them select the picture and then click a command button.

Creating and Adapting Dialog Boxes On-the-Fly

You may need to create custom dialog boxes on-the-fly to present information or choices to the user. Alternatively, you can adapt a user form on-the-fly, perhaps by adding a list box, a picture, or another element to it to present a particular piece or set of information most effectively, or by populating one or more of the controls from data sources.

As you might imagine, creating a user form on-the-fly can be tricky, because you won't be able to see what you're doing. Unless you take great care, you can easily end up with a dialog box that contains confusing or overlapping controls. And even if you take extreme care, one little slip-up might result in an otherwise perfect dialog box that lacks, say, a Cancel button.

Usually, you'll do best to anticipate the possibilities for a dialog box and create controls within the user form to deal with them. You can then load information (or pictures) into the dialog box as appropriate, make visible only the controls needed, and hide everything else. As you saw earlier in the chapter, by using a MultiPage control with no tabs or buttons, you can switch a dialog box quickly from one manifestation to another.

Nonetheless, in the next section, I'll present an example of how you might create a simple dialog box on-the-fly. (Note that I said *simple*—that's the operative word in the example.) In the section after that, I'll return to the DataSurfer 2000 dialog box, which adjusts the number of tabs it contains to match the number of records in the data source used.

Creating a Dialog Box On-the-Fly

To create a user form on-the-fly, you need to automate VBA rather than the application you're working in. Start by adding a reference to the Microsoft Visual Basic for Applications Extensibility library: From the Visual Basic Editor, choose Tools ➢ References to display the References dialog box, select the check box for the Microsoft Visual Basic For Applications Extensibility item, and click the OK button. Now that you've done this, you can manipulate the objects within the Visual Basic Editor in much the same way as you can manipulate the objects within your VBA-hosting application, adding a component to the current VBProject item.

Listing 16.3 provides an example of creating a dialog box dynamically by using VBA and the Microsoft Visual Basic for Applications Extensibility library. Figure 16.13 shows the dialog box in question—a brief dialog box that notifies the user of a couple of pieces of information missing from a form.

You'll notice that, to keep this example workably brief and to avoid getting into too many topics I haven't discussed yet, I've cheated a bit: I show you how to build a dialog box on-the-fly, but I don't discuss the decisions that would go into selecting the components to include. To keep the code within a few pages, I'll trust you to imagine how these fit in.

Listing 16.3

```
1.   Sub Create_Form()
2.
3.       'declare variables to hold the user form and controls
4.       Dim FormToBuild As VBComponent
5.       Dim Label1 As Label, Label2 As Label, Label3 As Label
6.       Dim TextBox1 As TextBox, TextBox2 As TextBox
7.       Dim CommandButton1 As CommandButton, _
             CommandButton2 As CommandButton
8.
9.       'create a new user form and assign it to FormToBuild
10.      Set FormToBuild = Application.VBE.ActiveVBProject _
             .VBComponents.Add(vbext_ct_MSForm)
11.      With FormToBuild
12.          'set the properties of the user form  _
             by using the Properties collection
13.          .Properties("Name") = "frmIncompleteForm"
14.          .Properties("Caption") = "Incomplete Form"
15.          .Properties("Height") = 140
16.          .Properties("Width") = 180
17.
18.          'add three labels
19.          Set Label1 = .Designer.Controls.Add("Forms.Label.1")
20.          Set Label2 = .Designer.Controls.Add("Forms.Label.1")
21.          Set Label3 = .Designer.Controls.Add("Forms.Label.1")
22.
23.          'add two text boxes
24.          Set TextBox1 = .Designer.Controls.Add _
                 ("Forms.TextBox.1")
25.          Set TextBox2 = .Designer.Controls.Add _
                 ("Forms.TextBox.1")
26.
27.          'add two command buttons
28.          Set CommandButton1 = .Designer.Controls.Add _
                 ("Forms.CommandButton.1")
29.          Set CommandButton2 = .Designer.Controls.Add _
                 ("Forms.CommandButton.1")
30.
```

```
31.          'set the properties for the first label
32.          With Label1
33.              .Name = "lblMissing"
34.              .Left = 10
35.              .Top = 10
36.              .AutoSize = True
37.              .WordWrap = False
38.              .Caption = "The form is missing the following
                    ➥information:"
39.              .TabIndex = 0
40.          End With
41.
42.          'set the properties for the second label
43.          With Label2
44.              .Name = "lblUserName"
45.              .Left = 10
46.              .Top = 32
47.              .AutoSize = True
48.              .WordWrap = False
49.              .Caption = "User Name:"
50.              .Accelerator = "U"
51.              .TabIndex = 1
52.          End With
53.
54.          'set the properties for the third label
55.          With Label3
56.              .Name = "lblSecurityID"
57.              .Left = 10
58.              .Top = 54
59.              .AutoSize = True
60.              .WordWrap = False
61.              .Caption = "Security ID:"
62.              .Accelerator = "S"
63.              .TabIndex = 3
64.          End With
65.
66.          'set the properties for the first text box
67.          With TextBox1
68.              .Name = "txtUserName"
69.              .Left = 60
```

```
70.                  .Top = 28
71.                  .Width = 100
72.                  .TabIndex = 2
73.          End With
74.
75.          'set the properties for the second text box
76.          With TextBox2
77.                  .Name = "txtSecurityID"
78.                  .Left = 60
79.                  .Top = 48
80.                  .Width = 50
81.                  .TabIndex = 4
82.          End With
83.
84.          'set the properties for the first command button
85.          With CommandButton1
86.                  .Name = "cmdOK"
87.                  .Accelerator = "O"
88.                  .Caption = "OK"
89.                  .Left = 20
90.                  .Top = 85
91.                  .Height = 21
92.                  .Width = 55
93.                  .TabIndex = 5
94.                  .Default = True
95.          End With
96.
97.          'set the properties for the second command button
98.          With CommandButton2
99.                  .Name = "cmdCancel"
100.                 .Accelerator = "C"
101.                 .Caption = "Cancel"
102.                 .Left = 80
103.                 .Top = 85
104.                 .Height = 21
105.                 .Width = 55
106.                 .TabIndex = 6
107.                 .Cancel = True
108.         End With
109.
```

```
110.          'assign code to the OK button and Cancel button
111.          .CodeModule.AddFromString "Private Sub cmdOK_Click()" _
                  & vbCr & "    frmIncompleteForm.Hide" & vbCr & _
                  "    'add code for the OK button here." & vbCr & _
                  "End Sub" & vbCr & vbCr & _
                  "Private Sub cmdCancel_Click()" & vbCr & _
                  "    End" & vbCr & "End Sub"
112.
113.      'end With statement for the form
114.      End With
115.
116.      'display the form
117.      frmIncompleteForm.Show
118.  End Sub
```

Analysis

Here's how the code in Listing 16.3 works:

- Line 1 declares the procedure Create_Form. Line 2 is a spacer.

- Line 3 is a comment line explaining that lines 4 through 7 will declare variables to hold the user form to be created and the controls it will contain. Line 4 then declares the VBComponent variable FormToBuild, which will reference the user form; line 5 declares the three Label variables Label1, Label2, and Label3, which will reference the three label controls on the user form; line 6 declares the two TextBox variables TextBox1 and TextBox2, which will reference the two textbox controls on the user form; and line 7 declares the two CommandButton variables CommandButton1 and CommandButton2, which will represent the two CommandButton controls. Line 8 is a spacer.

- Line 9 is a comment. Line 10 then uses a Set statement to assign to the object variable FormToBuild the user form created by using the Add method with the argument vbext_ct_MSForm on the VBComponents collection of the ActiveVB-Project object.

- Line 11 begins a With statement with the FormToBuild object variable. This With statement contains most of the rest of the procedure, ending at the End With statement in line 114.

- Line 12 is a comment on lines 13 through 16, noting that they use the Properties collection of the user form to set the properties of the user form.

- Line 13 sets the `Name` property to `frmIncompleteForm`. Line 14 sets the `Caption` property to `Incomplete Form`. Line 15 sets the `Height` property to 140, and line 16 sets the `Width` property to 180. Line 17 is a spacer.

- Line 18 is a comment on lines 19 through 21, noting that they add three labels to the user form. Each uses a `Set` statement and the `Add` method with the `Controls` collection for the `Designer` object for the user form (briefly, the `Designer` object is a container object used for designing a form object—adding and removing controls, and so on).

- Line 19 assigns to the object variable `Label1` the first label; line 20 assigns to the object variable `Label2` the second label; and line 21 assigns to `Label3` the third label. Line 22 is a spacer.

- Line 23 is a comment on lines 24 and 25, noting that they add two text boxes to the user form. Like the statements assigning the label controls, these two `Set` statements use the `Add` method with the `Controls` collection for the `Designer` object of the user form.

- Line 24 assigns to the object variable `TextBox1` the first text box, and line 25 assigns to the object variable `TextBox2` the second text box. Line 26 is a spacer.

- Line 27 is a comment on lines 28 and 29, noting that they add two command buttons to the user form. Again, you'll see there are two `Set` statements using the `Add` method with the `Controls` collection for the `Designer` object of the user form.

- Line 28 assigns to the object variable `CommandButton1` the first command button, and line 29 assigns to the object variable `CommandButton2` the second command button. Line 30 is a spacer.

- Line 31 is a comment on lines 32 through 40, noting that they set the properties for the first label, `Label1`.

- Line 32 begins a `With Label1` statement that ends at the `End With` statement in line 40. Line 33 sets the `Name` property to `lblMissing`. Line 34 sets the `Left` property to 10, and line 35 sets the `Top` property to 10. These two measurements position the label appropriately as the first control in the user form, close to (but not touching) the upper-left corner of the main area of the user form (below the title bar).

- Line 36 sets the `AutoSize` property to `True`, so that the label will be only as long and as deep as the text it contains. (The default setting for `AutoSize` is `False`, which creates larger and deeper labels than you need here.) Line 37 sets the `WordWrap` property to `False` to make sure that the text in the label won't wrap onto a second line. (The default setting for `WordWrap` is `True`, allowing text to wrap.) Line 38 sets the `Caption` property to `The form is missing the following` information: Finally, line 39 sets the TabIndex property to 0, making this label the first item in the tab order. (Because this label won't be associated with a text box, the tab order doesn't much matter.)

- Line 40 ends the With statement, and line 41 is a spacer.

- Lines 42 through 52 essentially recap lines 31 through 40, working to set the properties for Label2. There are a couple of things to note here, though:

  - Line 45 sets a Left property of 10 to align the label's left edge with that of Label1. Line 46 sets a Top property of 32 to position Label2 beneath Label1 and with a suitable small gap between them.

  - Line 49 sets the Caption property to User Name: and line 50 sets the Accelerator property of the label to U. This step creates an accelerator key of *U* that appears on the label. Because a label can't receive the focus in a user form (as discussed in the previous chapter), the focus is delivered to the next control in the tab order, which will be the text box associated with the label. (The association is established visually by positioning the text box alongside the label in this case, and logically by assigning the text box the next position in the tab order, which you'll do in a moment.) So when the user presses Alt+U to access the label, VBA will move the focus to the text box next to the label.

- Line 53 is a spacer, after which lines 54 through 64 closely recap lines 31 through 40. Again, you position the new label a suitable distance (22 twips) below the previous label (giving a Top position of 54—32 + 22) and align its left edge with those of the previous two labels. You set an Accelerator property of S for the Caption of Security ID: and assign the TabIndex number 3 to the label, leaving number 2 available for the text box that will accompany the previous label. Line 65 is a spacer.

- Line 66 is a comment on lines 67 through 73, noting that they set the properties for the first text box, TextBox1.

- Line 67 begins a With TextBox1 statement that ends in line 74. Line 68 sets the Name property to txtUserName. Line 69 sets the Left property to 60, to position the text box to the right of Label2, and line 70 sets the Top property to 28, to center the text box vertically on the midline of Label2, whose Top property is set to 32. (Because a default text box control is taller than a default label control, the text box needs to be positioned higher on the user form.) Line 71 sets the Width property to 100, which should be ample for the longest of user names. Line 72 sets the TabIndex property to 2, to associate the text box with Label2 and its accelerator key. Line 73 ends the With statement, and line 74 is a spacer.

- Lines 75 through 82 closely follow lines 66 through 73 to set the properties for the second text box, TextBox2. For this text box, set a Left property of 60 to align its left edge with that of TextBox1 and a Top property of 48 to align the control's vertical midpoint around that of Label3, with which label the control's TabIndex of 4 will associate it. Line 83 is a spacer.

- Line 84 is a comment on lines 85 through 95, which set the properties for the first command button, CommandButton1.

- Line 85 begins a With CommandButton1 statement that ends in line 95. Line 86 sets the Name property to cmdOK. Line 87 sets the Accelerator property to 0, giving an accelerator key of O on the command button, and line 88 sets the Caption property to OK. Line 89 sets a Left property of 20, indented a little from the column of left-aligned labels, and line 90 sets a Top property of 85, positioning the command button below the third label. Line 91 sets a Height property of 21 and line 92 a Width property of 55, reflecting my preference for command buttons smaller than the Visual Basic Editor's default. Line 93 sets the TabIndex property to 5, making the command button the next control to receive the focus after TextBox2. Line 94 sets the Default property to True, making the command button the default button in the user form. Line 95 ends the With statement, and line 96 is a spacer.

- Lines 97 through 108 are similar to lines 84 through 95 and set the properties for the second command button, CommandButton2. Line 99 sets the Name property to cmdCancel, line 100 sets the Accelerator property to C, giving an accelerator key of C, and line 101 sets the Caption property to Cancel. Line 102 sets a Left property of 80 and line 103 a Top position of 85 to position the button a little to the right of the OK button (CommandButton1) and on a level with it. Lines 104 and 105 set the button to the dimensions I prefer. Line 106 sets the TabIndex property to 6, making CommandButton2 the next control after the OK button (and the last control in the user form) to receive the focus. Line 107 sets the Cancel property to True, so that this command button will trap a press of the Escape key while the user form is displayed. Line 108 ends the With statement, and line 109 is a spacer.

- Line 110 is a comment on lines 111 through 113, which assign code to the OK button (CommandButton1) and Cancel button (CommandButton2).

- Line 111 uses the AddFromString method of the CodeModule object within the user form to add a string containing the commands listed below to the code module for the user form. As you can see, the string contains a cmdOK_Click procedure and a cmdCancel_Click procedure. The former contains a statement to hide the user form, and a comment line indicating where further code would go. The latter contains simply an End statement to end execution of the procedure (canceling the dialog box in the process):

```
Private Sub cmdOK_Click()
    frmIncompleteForm.Hide
    'add code for the OK button here.
End Sub


Private Sub cmdCancel_Click()
    End
End Sub
```

- Line 112 is a spacer, and line 113 is a comment indicating that the End With statement in line 114 ends the With statement begun in line 11.

- Line 115 is another spacer, and line 116 is a comment noting that line 117 displays the user form, allowing you to see that it has been created properly.

- Line 118 contains the End Sub statement that ends the Create_Form procedure.

 TIP When creating a user form programmatically, take care to make sure that none of the visible controls overlap—even the smallest overlap can detract severely from both the visual effect and the usability of the resulting dialog box.

Adapting a Dialog Box On-the-Fly

As you just saw, it's quite possible to create a dialog box programmatically, provided you know exactly where you want to position each control and you take care to make sure you position each accurately. More frequently, though, you'll need to adapt a dialog box on-the-fly before displaying it. Often, you'll want to load information into a control in the dialog box: For example, you might want to display the contents of the current paragraph in a text box for editing, populate a list box with the names of drawings currently available to the user, or address the user by their first name.

Your primary tool for adapting a dialog box on-the-fly is the Initialize event of the user form in question. The Initialize event fires when the user form is loaded: If you use a Load statement to load the user form, that fires the event; if you use the Show method without a Load statement, that will fire the event instead (because Show executes Load if the user form hasn't already been loaded). If the user form contains a procedure for the event, the code is run before the user form is displayed.

The DataSurfer 2000 dialog box uses its Initialize event to add a tab to its tab strip for each customer in the table that serves as its data source. Listing 16.4 shows the code for the UserForm_Initialize procedure.

Listing 16.4

```
1.  Dim blnInitializing As Boolean
2.
3.  Private Sub UserForm_Initialize()
4.
5.      Dim i As Integer
6.
7.      blnInitializing = True
8.
9.      With ActiveWorkbook
10.
11.          'add the right number of tabs to the tab strip, _
             creating and naming one tab for each worksheet _
             in the workbook
12.          For i = 1 To .Sheets.Count
13.              tabSurfer.Tabs.Add .Sheets(i).Name
14.          Next i
15.
16.          'activate the first worksheet in the workbook
17.          .Sheets(1).Activate
18.
19.          'load the contents of the first sheet into the text boxes
20.          txtFirstName.Text = .Sheets(1).Cells(1, 2).Text
21.          txtInitial.Text = .Sheets(1).Cells(2, 2).Text
22.          txtLastName.Text = .Sheets(1).Cells(3, 2).Text
23.          txtAddress1.Text = .Sheets(1).Cells(4, 2).Text
24.          txtAddress2.Text = .Sheets(1).Cells(5, 2).Text
25.          txtCity.Text = .Sheets(1).Cells(6, 2).Text
26.          txtState.Text = .Sheets(1).Cells(7, 2).Text
27.          txtZip.Text = .Sheets(1).Cells(8, 2).Text
28.          txtHomeArea.Text = .Sheets(1).Cells(9, 2).Text
29.          txtHomePhone.Text = .Sheets(1).Cells(10, 2).Text
30.          txtWorkArea.Text = .Sheets(1).Cells(11, 2).Text
31.          txtWorkPhone.Text = .Sheets(1).Cells(12, 2).Text
32.          txtWorkExtension.Text = .Sheets(1).Cells(13, 2).Text
```

```
33.              txtEmail.Text = .Sheets(1).Cells(14, 2).Text
34.
35.        End With
36.
37.        blnInitializing = False
38.
39.  End Sub
```

Analysis

Now take a walk through the code that comprises Listing 16.4:

- Line 1 declares the private Boolean variable blnInitializing, which—as you saw earlier in this chapter—the user form uses to make sure the Change event procedure for the tab strip does not run when the Initialize event procedure is adding tabs to the tab strip. Line 2 is a spacer.

- Line 3 declares the private procedure for the Initialize event of the Data-Surfer 2000 user form. Line 4 is a spacer.

- Line 5 declares the Integer variable i, which the procedure uses as a counter variable. Line 6 is another spacer.

- Line 9 begins a With statement that works with the active workbook. Line 10 is a spacer, and line 11 is a comment introducing the For... Next loop in lines 12 through 14. This loop runs from i = 1 to i = .Sheets.Count (the number of worksheets in the workbook), with line 13 adding a tab to the tab strip for each iteration of the loop and naming the tab with the name of the corresponding worksheet (which, you'll remember, bears the customer's name). Line 15 is a spacer.

- Line 16 is a comment indicating that line 17 activates the first worksheet in the workbook—which line 17 then does. Line 18 is a spacer.

- Line 19 is a comment indicating that the next 14 statements load the contents of the first worksheet into the text boxes on the form. Each line assigns to the Text property of the text box in question the Text property of the corresponding Cell object.

- Line 34 is a spacer, line 35 ends the With statement, and line 36 is another spacer.

- Line 37 sets the Boolean variable blnInitializing to False, so that the Change event procedure for the tab strip will run when the user changes tab.

- Line 38 is a spacer, and line 39 ends the procedure.

Creating a Modeless Dialog Box

With VBA version 6, you can create a *modeless* dialog box—one that the user can leave on-screen while they continue to work in their application. You're doubtless familiar with modeless dialog boxes from working interactively, as many applications use them to allow you to continue to work in the application even while the dialog box is displayed. When you display a modeless dialog box, it takes the focus just as any modal dialog box does, and its title bar takes the color of the active title bar, but you can click in the application window to transfer the focus back to that window. When the modeless dialog box loses the focus, its title bar takes on the inactive title bar color. To restore the focus to the modeless dialog box, you click it again.

A modeless dialog box remains with the application window that has displayed it. For example, say you have two Word windows open: Document1 and Document2. If you display a modeless dialog box from Document1 and leave it on screen, you'll see it only when you have Document1 displayed. If you minimize Document1, the dialog box will disappear; it won't be displayed on Document2. When you restore Document1, the dialog box will reappear.

Creating a modeless dialog box is as simple as setting the ShowModal property of the user form to False from its default setting of True.

There are various reasons for creating a modeless dialog box rather than a modal dialog box. As a simple example, you might create a procedure and dialog box in Word-Perfect that collected information from the user for a memo or a report. By making the dialog box modeless, you could allow the user to harvest information from an open document (or open other documents and gather information from them) and paste it into the dialog box, as illustrated in Figure 16.14—saving the user from having to copy the information before invoking the dialog box and allowing them to copy multiple separate items easily. Likewise, you could create a modeless user form (perhaps shaped like a toolbar) that the user could keep on-screen and use to automatically enter text into predefined sections of three or four other documents without losing their place in the current document.

You can also use modeless dialog boxes to display complex sets of interrelated user forms in which the user needs to transfer information easily from one user form to another, or at least to access different areas of two or more displayed user forms at the same time. There are strong arguments for not presenting the user with multiple active user forms simultaneously—such a display seldom improves the user's clarity of mind or their temper—but if you absolutely need to do this, modeless user forms can help.

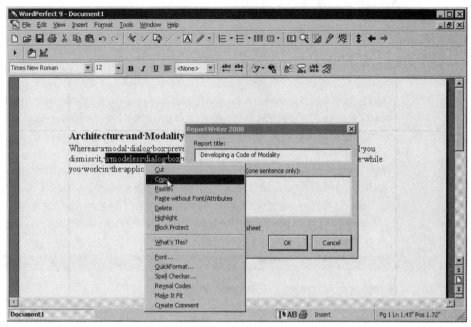

Most of the time, you'll probably want to use modal dialog boxes in your VBA procedures. With modal dialog boxes, the user must deal with the dialog box before they can continue to work in the application, and there's no risk that they'll end up with multiple dialog boxes scattered around the screen in assorted states of disuse.

Going Modal

You can use both modal and modeless user forms freely, with one restriction: You can't use both modal and modeless user forms at the same time.

You can display one modal user form from another modal user form, and you can display a modeless user form from a modeless user form. In fact, you can keep displaying one user form from another until the screen is covered with forms 10 deep if you want. But you can't mix and match modal and modeless.

Choosing the Position for the Dialog Box

By default, VBA displays a dialog box in the middle of the application window. To be more precise, it centers the dialog box on the application window as closely as possible: A dialog box larger than the application window will overlap it at the appropriate edges (without hanging off the edge of the Desktop, unless the dialog box is bigger than the Desktop). If you want, you can specify that the user form appear in a different start-up position by setting the StartUpPosition property for the user form. I'd recommend using this property only for special effects: User forms appear in the middle of the application window because this is a Windows convention that most users are by now thoroughly used to. If you start popping up user forms left and top rather than center, it will do little more than attract the user's attention in a less-than-positive way.

Still, if you decide you absolutely must specify the position for a user form, refer to Table 16.3, which lists the settings for the StartUpPosition property.

TABLE 16.3: *StartUpPosition* **PROPERTY SETTINGS**

StartUpPosition Property	Value	Effect
Manual	0	Displays the user form in the upper-left corner of the Windows Desktop.
CenterOwner	1	Centers the user form horizontally and vertically in the *owner* application—the application to which the user form belongs.
CenterScreen	2	Centers the user form horizontally and vertically on the Desktop. In a multi-monitor arrangement, this value centers the user form on the monitor containing the active window.
WindowsDefault	3	Displays the user form in the default position for Windows dialog boxes.

Using Events to Control Forms

In this section, I'll discuss how to use the events that VBA supports for user forms and for the individual controls to give yourself fine control over how your user forms look and behave. As you'll see, VBA's forms support a goodly variety of events that enable you to take action when the user does something—in fact, pretty much anything—on the user form.

So far in this chapter, you've used three of the most useful events:

- You used the Initialize event to add items to list boxes just before a form is loaded and to adjust the number of tabs on a tab strip.

- You used the Click event to take action when the user clicked a particular control in a user form. So far you've been using Click mostly for command buttons, but as you'll see, you can use it for just about any control—including the user form itself.

- You used the Change event to control what happened when the user changed the tab displayed on a tab strip.

These three events are perhaps the most useful, but you've just scratched the surface. Take a look at Table 16.4, which lists the events that VBA supports and the objects and controls with which each can be used.

TABLE 16.4: EVENTS THAT VBA SUPPORTS AND THE OBJECTS AND CONTROLS ASSOCIATED WITH THEM		
Event	**Occurs**	**Applies to These Controls and Objects**
Activate	When the user form becomes the active window	UserForm
Deactivate	When the user form ceases to be the active window	UserForm
AddControl	When a control is added at runtime	Frame, MultiPage, UserForm
AfterUpdate	After the user has changed data in a control	CheckBox, ComboBox, CommandButton, Frame, Image, Label, ListBox, MultiPage, OptionButton, ScrollBar, SpinButton, TabStrip, TextBox, ToggleButton, UserForm
BeforeDragOver	When the user is performing a drag-and-drop operation	CheckBox, ComboBox, CommandButton, Frame, Image, Label, ListBox, MultiPage, OptionButton, ScrollBar, SpinButton, TabStrip, TextBox, ToggleButton, UserForm
BeforeDropOrPaste	When the user is about to release a dragged item or about to paste an item	CheckBox, ComboBox, CommandButton, Frame, Image, Label, ListBox, MultiPage, OptionButton, ScrollBar, SpinButton, TabStrip, TextBox, ToggleButton, UserForm
BeforeUpdate	When the user has changed data in the control before the new data appears in the control	CheckBox, ComboBox, ListBox, OptionButton, ScrollBar, SpinButton, TextBox, ToggleButton

Continued ▐▶

TABLE 16.4: EVENTS THAT VBA SUPPORTS AND THE OBJECTS AND CONTROLS ASSOCIATED WITH THEM

Event	Occurs	Applies to These Controls and Objects
Change	When the Value property of a control changes	CheckBox, ComboBox, ListBox, MultiPage, OptionButton, ScrollBar, SpinButton, TabStrip, TextBox, ToggleButton
Click	When the user clicks a control or object with the primary mouse button	CheckBox, ComboBox, CommandButton, Frame, Image, Label, ListBox, MultiPage, OptionButton, TabStrip, ToggleButton, UserForm
DblClick	When the user double-clicks a control or object with the primary mouse button	CheckBox, ComboBox, CommandButton, Frame, Image, Label, ListBox, MultiPage, OptionButton, TabStrip, TextBox, ToggleButton, UserForm
DropButtonClick	When the user displays or hides a drop-down list	ComboBox, TextBox
Enter	Just before one control on a user form receives the focus from another control	CheckBox, ComboBox, CommandButton, Frame, ListBox, MultiPage, OptionButton, ScrollBar, SpinButton, TabStrip, TextBox, ToggleButton
Exit	Just before one control on a user form loses the focus to another control	CheckBox, ComboBox, CommandButton, Frame, ListBox, MultiPage, OptionButton, ScrollBar, SpinButton, TabStrip, TextBox, ToggleButton
Error	When a control or object encounters an error	CheckBox, ComboBox, CommandButton, Frame, Image, Label, ListBox, MultiPage, OptionButton, ScrollBar, SpinButton, TabStrip, TextBox, ToggleButton, UserForm
Initialize	After a user form is loaded but before it's displayed	UserForm
KeyDown	When the user presses a key on the keyboard	CheckBox, ComboBox, CommandButton, Frame, ListBox, MultiPage, OptionButton, ScrollBar, SpinButton, TabStrip, TextBox, ToggleButton, UserForm
KeyUp	When the user releases a key they've pressed on the keyboard	CheckBox, ComboBox, CommandButton, Frame, ListBox, MultiPage, OptionButton, ScrollBar, SpinButton, TabStrip, TextBox, ToggleButton, UserForm

Continued

TABLE 16.4: EVENTS THAT VBA SUPPORTS AND THE OBJECTS AND CONTROLS ASSOCIATED WITH THEM		
Event	**Occurs**	**Applies to These Controls and Objects**
KeyPress	When the user presses an ANSI key on the keyboard	CheckBox, ComboBox, CommandButton, Frame, ListBox, MultiPage, OptionButton, ScrollBar, SpinButton, TabStrip, TextBox, ToggleButton, UserForm
Layout	When the size of a frame, multipage, or user form is changed	Frame, MultiPage, UserForm
MouseDown	When the user depresses the primary mouse button	CheckBox, ComboBox, CommandButton, Frame, Image, Label, ListBox, MultiPage, OptionButton, ScrollBar, SpinButton, TabStrip, TextBox, ToggleButton, UserForm
MouseUp	When the user releases the primary mouse button (after depressing it)	CheckBox, ComboBox, CommandButton, Frame, Image, Label, ListBox, MultiPage, OptionButton, ScrollBar, SpinButton, TabStrip, TextBox, ToggleButton, UserForm
MouseMove	When the user moves the mouse	CheckBox, ComboBox, CommandButton, Frame, Image, Label, ListBox, MultiPage, OptionButton, TabStrip, TextBox, ToggleButton, UserForm
QueryClose	When a user form is about to close	UserForm
RemoveControl	When a control is deleted	Frame, MultiPage, UserForm
Resize	When a user form is resized	UserForm
Scroll	When the user moves the scroll box	Frame, MultiPage, ScrollBar, UserForm
SpinDown	When the user clicks the down button on a SpinButton control	SpinButton
SpinUp	When the user clicks the up button on a SpinButton control	SpinButton
Terminate	When a user form has been unloaded from memory	UserForm
Zoom	When the Zoom property of the control or user form is changed	Frame, MultiPage, UserForm

NOTE The `ByVal` keyword is used to pass arguments between procedures. When used with forms, it can return `ReturnBoolean`, `ReturnEffect`, `ReturnInteger`, and `Return-String` objects.

As you can see, VBA's events fall into several categories:

- Events that apply only to the `UserForm` object
- Events that apply to the `UserForm` object and other container objects (such as the Frame control and the MultiPage control)
- Events that apply to many or most of the controls, sometimes including the `UserForm` object as well.

Rather than banging through the events alphabetically, I'll divide them into these three categories and treat them category by category. Within each category, I'll present the events in approximately descending order of usefulness—the most useful events first, then the most interesting of the less useful events, and then the ones that I find least useful and most tedious.

TIP To make the maximum use of forms, you need to understand the order in which events take place. If you don't, you can confuse yourself by using events in ways that trigger each other or conflict with each other. If I seem to be harping constantly on the sequence in which related events fire, that's why.

Events That Apply Only to the *UserForm* Object

In this section, I'll discuss the events that apply only to the `UserForm` object. These are the `Initialize`, `QueryClose`, `Activate`, `Deactivate`, `Resize`, and `Terminate` events.

Initialize Event

As you saw earlier in this chapter, the `Initialize` event occurs when the user form is loaded but before it appears on screen.

VBA's syntax for the `Initialize` event is straightforward, where *userform* is a valid `UserForm` object:

```
Private Sub userform_Initialize()
```

As you've seen already in this chapter, typical uses for the `Initialize` event include retrieving information that the user form or application needs and assigning information to the controls on the user form (especially ListBox and ComboBox controls, to which you need to add the information at runtime rather than at design time). Depending on the style and complexity of your user forms, you may also want to use the Initialize event to resize the user form, resize controls on the user form, display or hide particular controls, and in general make sure the user form is as closely suited as possible to the user's needs before displaying it.

QueryClose Event

The QueryClose event applies to the UserForm object only. This event fires just before the user form closes.

The syntax for the QueryClose event is as follows:

```
Private Sub UserForm_QueryClose(Cancel As Integer, CloseMode As Integer)
```

Here, Cancel is an integer, typically 0 (zero). A nonzero value prevents the QueryClose event from firing and stops the user form (and the application) from closing.

CloseMode is a value or a constant giving the cause of the QueryClose event. Table 16.5 shows the values and constants for CloseMode.

TABLE 16.5: VALUES AND CONSTANTS FOR THE *CLOSEMODE* ARGUMENT

Constant	Value	Cause of the *QueryClose* Event
vbFormControlMenu	0	The user has closed the user form by clicking its close button or by invoking the Close command from the user form's control menu (for example, by right-clicking the title bar of the user form and choosing Close from the context menu).
vbFormCode	1	An Unload statement in code has closed the user form.
vbAppWindows	2	Windows is closing down and is closing the user form.
vbAppTaskManager	3	The Task Manager is closing the application, and thus the user form.

At first glance, QueryClose may appear to have few uses beyond double-checking that the user really wants to close a user form that they're attempting to close. For example, if you established that the user had entered a lot of data in the user form they were about to close, you might want to check that they hadn't clicked the user form's close button or Cancel button by mistake, as in the following code fragment for Word:

```
Private Sub UserForm_QueryClose(Cancel As Integer, _
    CloseMode As Integer)
    'make sure the user wants to close the user form
    'if they have entered information in it
    Select Case CloseMode
        Case 0
```

```
'user has clicked the close button or
'invoked an Unload statement
'if text box contains more than 5 characters, _
    ask to save it
If Len(txtDescription.Text) > 5 Then
    If MsgBox("The Description text box contains " & _
        "a significant amount of text." & vbCr & _
        "Do you want to save this text?", vbYesNo + _
        vbQuestion, "Close Form") <> 0 Then
        Documents.Add
        Selection.TypeText txtDescription.Text
        ActiveDocument.SaveAs _
            "c:\temp\Temporary Description.doc"
        MsgBox "The contents of the Description text " & _
            "box have been saved in " & _
            "c:\temp\Temporary Description.doc.", _
            vbOKOnly + vbInformation, _
            "Form Information Saved"
    End If
End If
```

However, QueryClose really comes into its own when the application, rather than the user form, is closing. If the user form is modeless, the user may not be aware that it's still open and that they're about to lose data from it.

Sometimes you may be able to use QueryClose to save information from a user form when the application has stopped responding and is being cut off at the knees by a general protection fault (GPF) or sandbagged somewhat more delicately by the Task Manager. Be warned that QueryClose's record isn't perfect on this—the code sometimes won't run.

To stop an application from closing, set the Cancel property of the QueryClose event to True.

Activate Event

The Activate event fires when the user form becomes the active window. Typically, this means the event fires when the user form is displayed, occurring just after the Initialize event if the user form is loaded by a Show statement rather than a Load statement. (If the user form is loaded by using a Load statement before being displayed with the Show statement, the Initialize event will fire after the Load statement. The Activate event, firing after the Show statement, will fire later.) However, the Activate event also fires when the user form is reactivated after having been deactivated. For example, if you create a modeless user form with an Activate event procedure, the code will be executed each time the user reactivates the user form after having deactivated it (for example, by working in the application window). Likewise, if you display one user form from another and then close the second user form, returning the focus to the first user form and reactivating it, the `Activate` event will fire again.

The syntax for the `Activate` event is straightforward:

```
Private Sub UserForm_Activate()
```

Bug Alert: Problems Using *Deactivate* and *Activate* in Immediate Succession

VBA manifests frustrating difficulty in executing event procedures for the `Deactivate` event of one user form and the `Activate` event of another user form in immediate succession. Sometimes things work as they should; more often, they don't. Unless you have an impeccable record of luck, you probably won't want to rely on using these two events one after the other.

For example, say you have two user forms, imaginatively named One and Two, each with an `Activate` event procedure and a `Deactivate` event procedure. If you display Two from One, the `Deactivate` event code from One should run, followed by the `Activate` event code from Two. This doesn't usually happen: Often, the `Deactivate` code of One will run, but the `Activate` code of Two won't. Run it again, and you may get the `Activate` code of Two to run but not the `Deactivate` code of One. However, if you remove or comment out the `Deactivate` event procedure from One and try again, Two's `Activate` code will run consistently each time One displays Two, indicating that the `Activate` event is firing but the `Activate` event procedure's code isn't running when the `Deactivate` event procedure is present.

Microsoft suggests placing the code for the `Deactivate` event of the first user form before the code that displays the second user form. At this writing, this "workaround" doesn't seem to make an iota of difference.

Deactivate Event

The `Deactivate` event fires when the user form loses the focus after having been the active window, but it doesn't fire when the user form is hidden or unloaded. For example, if you display a user form that contains a `Deactivate` event procedure, and then close the user form, the `Deactivate` event won't fire. However, if you display one user form from another, the `Deactivate` event for the first user form fires as the focus is transferred to the second user form. With modeless user forms, the `Deactivate` event is triggered each time you leave one user form by clicking on another.

The syntax for the Deactivate event is straightforward:

```
Private Sub UserForm_Deactivate()
```

See the sidebar for details on a bug in using the Deactivate and Activate events in immediate succession.

Resize Event

The Resize event fires when a user form is resized either manually or programmatically.
The syntax for the Resize event is straightforward:

```
Private Sub UserForm_Resize()
```

The main use for the Resize event is to move, resize, display, or hide controls to accommodate the new dimensions of the user form. For example, you might resize a text box so that it occupied most of the width of the user form it lived on (see Figure 16.15) by using code such as that shown in Listing 16.5.

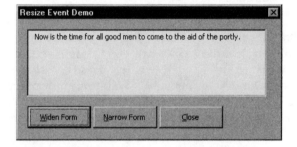

FIGURE 16.15

You can use the Resize event of a user form to resize or reposition the controls it contains.

Listing 16.5

```
1.  Private Sub cmdWidenForm_Click()
2.      With frmResize
3.          If .Width < 451 Then
4.              .Width = .Width + 50
5.              If cmdNarrowForm.Enabled = False Then _
                    cmdNarrowForm.Enabled = True
6.              If .Width > 451 Then _
                    cmdWidenForm.Enabled = False
7.          End If
8.      End With
```

```
 9.  End Sub
10.
11.  Private Sub cmdNarrowForm_Click()
12.      With frmResize
13.          If .Width > 240 Then
14.              .Width = .Width - 50
15.              If cmdWidenForm.Enabled = False Then _
                     cmdWidenForm.Enabled = True
16.              If .Width < 270 Then _
                     cmdNarrowForm.Enabled = False
17.          End If
18.      End With
19.  End Sub
20.
21.  Private Sub cmdClose_Click()
22.      Unload Me
23.  End Sub
24.
25.  Private Sub UserForm_Resize()
26.      txt1.Width = frmResize.Width - 30
27.  End Sub
```

Analysis

Listing 16.5 contains four short procedures: one for the Click event of the cmdWiden-
Form command button, one for the Click event of the cmdNarrowForm command button, one for the Click event of the cmdClose command button, and—finally, the one
you've been waiting for—a very short procedure for the Resize event of the user form.

The cmdWidenForm_Click procedure shown in lines 1 through 9 increases the width
of the user form by 50 points (1 point is $1/72$ inch) when the user clicks the Widen
Form button, as long as the Width property of the user form is less than 451 points.
Line 5 enables the cmdNarrowForm command button if it isn't already enabled. (The
cmdNarrowForm command button is disabled when the user form is displayed at its
original narrow width.) Line 6 disables the cmdWidenForm command button if the
Width property of the user form is more than 451 points.

The cmdNarrowForm_Click procedure shown in lines 11 through 19 essentially does
the reverse of the cmdWidenForm_Click procedure. It narrows the user form by 50 points

as long as the `Width` of the user form is greater than 240 (its original width), re-enabling the cmdWidenForm button if it's disabled and disabling the cmdNarrowForm button if the `Width` of the user form is less than 270.

The cmdClose_Click procedure shown in lines 21 through 23 simply unloads the user form (which it refers to by the Me keyword).

The UserForm_Resize event procedure in lines 25 though 27 sets the `Width` property of txt1, the text box in the user form, to 30 points less than the `Width` of the user form. If you step through the code for the user form, you'll notice that the `Resize` event fires when the size of the user form changes. For example, when line 4 of the cmdWidenForm_Click procedure is executed, execution branches to the `Resize` event procedure in line 25, and this procedure is executed before the code in line 5.

Terminate Event

The Terminate event fires when the user form has been unloaded (more precisely, when all references to an instance of the user form have been removed from memory or have gone out of scope).

The syntax for the Terminate event is straightforward:

```
Private Sub UserForm_Terminate()
```

I doubt that you'll find yourself using the Terminate event very frequently, but here's a quick and useless example in case you want to see it in action:

```
Private Sub UserForm_Terminate()
  MsgBox "The user form has now been terminated."
End Sub
```

Create a Terminate procedure, display the user form, and dismiss it by using a command button that unloads the user form from memory. You'll then see the message box indicating that the Terminate event has taken place.

Events That Apply to the *UserForm* Object and to Container Controls

In this section, I'll discuss the events that apply to the UserForm object and to the container controls—the MultiPage control and the Frame control. (The Scroll event applies to the ScrollBar control as well.) These events are Scroll, Zoom, Resize, Layout, AddControl, and RemoveControl. Again, these events are arranged in descending order of usefulness—at least, as I see it.

Scroll Event

The Scroll event applies to the Frame control, the MultiPage control, the ScrollBar control, and the UserForm object. This event occurs when the user moves the scroll box (the thumb) on a scroll bar on a frame, multipage, scroll bar, or user form.

The syntax for the Scroll event varies for the three controls and the UserForm object. The syntax for the Scroll event with the UserForm object is:

```
Private Sub UserForm_Scroll(ByVal ActionX As MSForms.fmScrollAction, ByVal
ActionY As MSForms.fmScrollAction, ByVal RequestDx As Single, ByVal RequestDy
As Single, ByVal ActualDx As MSForms.ReturnSingle, ByVal ActualDy As MSForms
.ReturnSingle)
```

The syntax for the Scroll event with the ScrollBar control is:

```
Private Sub scrollbar_Scroll()
```

The syntax for the Scroll event with the MultiPage control is:

```
Private Sub multipage_Scroll(index As Long, ActionX As fmScrollAction, ActionY
As fmScrollAction, ByVal RequestDx As Single, ByVal RequestDy As Single, ByVal
ActualDx As MSForms.ReturnSingle, ByVal ActualDy As MSForms.ReturnSingle)
```

The syntax for the Scroll event with the Frame control is:

```
Private Sub frame_Scroll(ActionX As fmScrollAction, ActionY As
fmScrollAction, ByVal RequestDx As Single, ByVal RequestDy As Single, ByVal
ActualDx As MSForms.ReturnSingle, ByVal ActualDy As MSForms.ReturnSingle)
```

In these last three syntax statements, *scrollbar* is a valid ScrollBar object, *multipage* is a valid MultiPage object, and *frame* is a valid Frame object.

Here are the arguments for the Scroll event:

index   A required argument specifying the page of the MultiPage with which the event procedure is to be associated.

ActionX and ActionY   Required arguments determining the user's horizontal and vertical actions (respectively), as shown in Table 16.6.

TABLE 16.6: *ActionX* AND *ActionY* CONSTANTS AND VALUES FOR THE *SCROLL* EVENT

Constant	Value	Scroll Box Movement
fmScrollActionNoChange	0	There was no change or movement.
fmScrollActionLineUp	1	The user moved the scroll box a short way upward on a vertical scroll bar (equivalent to pressing the ↑ key) or a short way to the left on a horizontal scroll bar (equivalent to pressing the ← key).

Continued ▶

TABLE 16.6 CONTINUED: *ActionX* **AND** *ActionY* **CONSTANTS AND VALUES FOR THE** *Scroll* **EVENT**

Constant	Value	Scroll Box Movement
fmScrollActionLineDown	2	The user moved the scroll box a short way downward on a vertical scroll bar (equivalent to pressing the ↓ key) or a short way to the right on a horizontal scroll bar (equivalent to pressing the → key).
fmScrollActionPageUp	3	The user moved the scroll box up one page on a vertical scroll bar (equivalent to pressing the Page Up key) or one page to the left on a horizontal scroll bar (also equivalent to pressing the Page Up key).
fmScrollActionPageDown	4	The user moved the scroll box down one page on a vertical scroll bar (equivalent to pressing the Page Down key) or one page to the right on a horizontal scroll bar (also equivalent to pressing the Page Down key).
fmScrollActionBegin	5	The user moved the scroll box to the top of a vertical scroll bar or to the left end of a horizontal scroll bar.
fmScrollActionEnd	6	The user moved the scroll box to the bottom of a vertical scroll bar or to the right end of a horizontal scroll bar.
fmScrollActionPropertyChange	8	The user moved the scroll box, changing the value of either the ScrollTop property or the ScrollLeft property.
fmScrollActionControlRequest	9	The scroll action was requested by a control in the container in question.
fmScrollActionFocusRequest	10	The user moved the focus to a different control. This movement scrolls the user form so that the selected control is fully displayed in the available area.

RequestDx The distance to move the scroll box horizontally, specified in points.

RequestDy The distance to move the scroll box vertically, specified in points.

ActualDx The distance the scroll box moved horizontally, measured in points.

ActualDy The distance the scroll box moved vertically, measured in points.

Zoom Event

The Zoom event fires when the Zoom property of the control or of the user form is changed at runtime. The Zoom property can be changed either automatically through code or by the user's manipulating a control that changes the property through code; the user can't change the Zoom property manually.

The Zoom property uses this syntax for the control and the UserForm object:

```
Private Sub object_Zoom(Percent As Integer)
```

Here, *object* is a Frame control or a UserForm object. Percent is an Integer argument used to specify the percentage (from 10 percent to 400 percent) the user form is to be zoomed to. By default, user forms and controls are displayed at 100 percent Zoom—full size.

The Zoom property uses this syntax for the MultiPage control:

```
Private Sub multipage_Zoom(ByVal Index As Long, Percent As Integer)
```

Here Index is the index (name or number) of the Page object in the MultiPage control with which the Zoom event procedure is associated.

Zooming a user form zooms all the controls that are on it. Let's look at an example of code that deals with the result of that zoom. One of the controls on frmEventsDemo, the user form in question, is a combo box named cmbZoom that offers a selection of zoom percentages. When the user selects an item in the combo box, the Change event for cmbZoom applies the combo box's Value property to the Zoom property of the user form, zooming it to the percentage selected. Zooming the user form triggers the Zoom event, whose procedure in this example sets the Width and Height of the user form to new values suited to the new zoom percentage:

```
Private Sub cmbZoom_Change()
    frmEventsDemo.Zoom = cmbZoom.Value
End Sub


Private Sub UserForm_Zoom(Percent As Integer)
    frmEventsDemo.Width = 300 * cmbZoom.Value / 100
    frmEventsDemo.Height = 350 * cmbZoom.Value / 100
End Sub
```

Layout Event

The Layout event occurs when the size of the frame, multipage, or user form is changed, either programmatically, automatically by an autosized control becoming resized, or by the user.

By default, the Layout event automatically calculates the new position for any control that has been moved, and repaints the screen accordingly. However, you can also use the Layout event for your own purposes if you need to.

The syntax for the Layout event with a Frame control or a UserForm object is as follows:

```
Private Sub object_Layout()
```

Here, *object* is a Frame control or a UserForm object.

The syntax for using the Layout event with a MultiPage control is as follows:

```
Private Sub multipage_Layout(index As Long)
```

Here, *multipage* is a MultiPage control and index is the Page object in the multipage.

 NOTE When a control is resized, VBA stores its previous height and width in the Old-Height and OldWidth properties, while the Height and Width properties take on the new height and width. To restore a control to its previous size, use the OldHeight and Old-Width properties.

AddControl Event

The AddControl event is triggered when a control is added programmatically to the frame, the multipage, or the user form at runtime; it isn't triggered when you add a control manually at design time. The event isn't triggered when the user form is initialized unless the Initialize event adds a control to the user form.

The syntax for the AddControl event varies depending on the object or control. The syntax for the UserForm object and the Frame control is as follows:

```
Private Sub object_AddControl(ByVal Control As MSForms.Control)
```

Here, *object* is a UserForm object or Frame control, and Control is the control that's being added.

The syntax for the MultiPage control is as follows:

```
Private Sub multipage_AddControl(ByVal Index As Long, ByVal Control As
MSForms.Control)
```

Here, Index is the index number or name of the Page object that will receive the control.

For example, the cmdAddControl_Click procedure shown below adds three option buttons (new1, new2, and new3, respectively) to the frame fraOptions and sets properties for the first. (A comment indicates where the code would go on to set properties for the second and third option buttons.) The fraOptions_AddControl event procedure displays a message box giving the number of controls the frame now contains. Because the cmdAddControl_Click procedure adds three controls, the AddControl event fires three times, and the fraOptions_AddControl procedure runs thrice:

```
Private Sub cmdAddControl_click()
    Set new1 = fraOptions.Controls.Add("Forms.OptionButton.1")
    Set new2 = fraOptions.Controls.Add("Forms.OptionButton.1")
    Set new3 = fraOptions.Controls.Add("Forms.OptionButton.1")
```

```
    With new1
        .Left = 10
        .Top = 10
        .Name = "optDomestic"
        .Caption = "Domestic"
        .AutoSize = True
        .Accelerator = "D"
    End With2
    'set properties for new2 and new3 here
End Sub


Private Sub fraOptions_AddControl(ByVal Control As MSForms.Control)
  MsgBox "The frame now contains " & _
    fraOptions.Controls.Count & " controls."
End Sub
```

RemoveControl **Event**

The RemoveControl event fires when a control is deleted from the frame, multipage, or user form in question, either programmatically or manually at runtime. (To remove a control manually, the user would typically use a control built into the user form for that purpose.)

The syntax for the RemoveControl event is as follows for all controls but the Multi-Page control:

```
Private Sub object_RemoveControl(ByVal Control As MSForms.Control)
```

Here, *object* is a valid object, and Control is a valid control.

The syntax for the RemoveControl event is as follows for the MultiPage control:

```
Private Sub multipage_RemoveControl(ByVal Index As Long, ByVal Control As
MSForms.Control)
```

Here, *multipage* is a valid MultiPage object. For a multipage, Index specifies the Page object in the MultiPage control that contains the control to be deleted.

Events That Apply to Many or Most Controls

In this section, I'll discuss the events that apply to many, most, or all controls. Some of these events apply to the UserForm object as well. These events are Click; Change; Enter and Exit; BeforeUpdate and AfterUpdate; KeyDown, KeyUp, and KeyPress; MouseDown, MouseUp, and MouseMove; BeforeDragOver; BeforeDropOrPaste; DblClick; and Error.

As before, I'm presenting the events in approximately descending order of usefulness.

Click Event

The Click event applies to the CheckBox, ComboBox, CommandButton, Frame, Image, Label, ListBox, MultiPage, OptionButton, TabStrip, and ToggleButton controls. It doesn't apply to the TextBox control, the ScrollBar control, or the SpinButton control, but it does apply to the UserForm object.

The Click event occurs both when the user clicks a control with the primary mouse button and when the user selects a value for a control that has more than one possible value. For most controls, this means that each time the user clicks the control, the event fires. But there are a few exceptions:

- Clicking a disabled control fires the Click event of the user form (as if the user were clicking the user form through the control).

- The Click event of an OptionButton control fires when the user clicks the option button to select it. If the option button is already selected, clicking it has no effect. (On the other hand, the Click event of a CheckBox control fires each time the user clicks the check box—either to select it or to clear it.)

- The Click event of a ListBox control or ComboBox control fires when the user clicks to select an item from the list (not when the user clicks on the drop-down arrow or in the undropped portion of the combo box). If the user clicks an already-selected item, the Click event doesn't fire again.

- The Click event of a ToggleButton control occurs whenever the toggle button is clicked and when its Value property is changed. This means that it isn't a good idea to use the Click event of the ToggleButton control to toggle its Value.

- The Click event of a selected CommandButton control fires when you press the spacebar.

- The Click event of the default command button (the button with its Default property set to True) fires when the user presses Enter with no other command button selected.

- The Click event of the command button with its Cancel property set to True fires when the user presses Esc. The Click event for a control with an accelerator key set also fires when the user presses the accelerator key.

For all controls except the TabStrip control and the MultiPage control, the Click event needs no arguments, as follows:

```
Private Sub object_Click()
```

For a TabStrip control or a MultiPage control, you react to the Index argument, a required Long argument that VBA passes to indicate the affected tab or page of the control:

```
Private Sub object_Click(ByVal Index As Long)
```

Here, *object* is a valid MultiPage control or TabStrip control.

Sequence of Events: What Happens When the User Clicks (and Clicks Again)

When the user clicks a command button, the Enter event for the button occurs before the Click event if the click transfers the focus to the command button. When the Enter event for the command button fires, it usually prevents the Click event from firing.

When the user clicks a control, the first event triggered is the MouseDown event, which fires when the user depresses the mouse button. Then the MouseUp event fires when the user releases (un-depresses?) the mouse button. The Click event occurs after the MouseUp event. If the user clicks again within the double-click timeframe set in Windows, the DblClick event fires, followed by another MouseUp event.

Change **Event**

The Change event applies to the CheckBox, ComboBox, ListBox, MultiPage, Option-Button, ScrollBar, SpinButton, TabStrip, TextBox, and ToggleButton controls. This event fires when the Value property of a control changes. This change can occur either through an action of the user's (such as selecting an option button, selecting or clearing a checkbox, clicking a toggle button, or changing the page displayed on a multipage) or through an action taken programmatically at runtime. Bear in mind that when the Change event is fired by an action of the user's, that action may also trigger a Click event. (Even when this happens, Change is regarded as a better way of determining the new Value of the control than Click—though for many purposes Click will work satisfactorily as well.)

 NOTE Changing the Value property of a control manually at design time doesn't fire a Change event.

The syntax for the Change event is straightforward:

```
Private Sub object_Change()
```

As you saw earlier in the chapter, the Change event is useful for updating other controls after the user changes a control. For example, if the user enters the name for a new report into a text box (here, txtReportName), you could use the Change event to build in another text box (here, `txtFileName`) the name of the file in which to save the report:

```
Private Sub txtReportName_Change()
    txtFileName.Text = txtReportName.Text & ".wpd"
End Sub
```

Enter and *Exit* Events

The `Enter` and `Exit` events apply to CheckBox, ComboBox, CommandButton, Frame, ListBox, MultiPage, OptionButton, ScrollBar, SpinButton, TabStrip, TextBox, and Toggle-Button controls.

The `Enter` event fires when the focus is moved from one control on a user form to another control. The event fires just before the second control receives the focus.

Like the `Enter` event, the `Exit` event fires when the focus is moved from one control on a user form to another control. However, the `Exit` event fires just before the first event loses the focus.

The syntax for the `Enter` event is straightforward:

`Private Sub object_Enter()`

The syntax for the `Exit` event is a little more complex:

`Private Sub object_Exit(ByVal Cancel As MSForms.ReturnBoolean)`

Here, `Cancel` is a required argument specifying event status. The default setting is `False`, which specifies that the control involved should handle the event and that the focus will pass to the next control; a setting of `True` specifies that the application handle the event, which keeps the focus at the current control.

By using the `Enter` and `Exit` events, you can track the user's progress through the controls on a user form.

The `Exit` event is useful for making sure that the user has made an appropriate selection in the control or has entered a suitable value. For example, you could check the user's entry in the control and, if you found it inappropriate, display a message box alerting the user to the problem, and then return the focus to the control so that the user might try again.

 NOTE Other events that you might use for checking the contents of a control after the user has visited it include `AfterUpdate` and `LostFocus`. Similarly, you might use the `BeforeUpdate` and `GotFocus` events instead of the `Enter` event. Note that a significant difference between `Enter` and `GotFocus`—and between `Exit` and `LostFocus`—is that `GotFocus` and `LostFocus` fire when the user form receives or loses the focus, respectively, but `Enter` and `Exit` don't.

BeforeUpdate Event

The BeforeUpdate event applies to the CheckBox, ComboBox, ListBox, OptionButton, ScrollBar, SpinButton, TextBox, and ToggleButton controls. This event occurs as the value of or data in the specified control is changed; you can use the event to evaluate the change and decide whether to implement it.

The syntax for the BeforeUpdate event is as follows:

```
Private Sub object_BeforeUpdate(ByVal Cancel As MSForms.ReturnBoolean)
```

Here, *object* is a valid object, and Cancel is a required argument indicating the status of the event. The default setting of False makes the control handle the event; True prevents the update from being executed and makes the application handle the event.

Here's the sequence in which events fire as you move to a control, update it, and move on:

- The Enter event for the control fires when you move the focus to the control.

- The BeforeUpdate event for the control fires after you've entered the information for the update (for example, after you've pressed a key in a text box) but before the update is executed. By setting Cancel to True, you can prevent the update from taking place. (If you don't set Cancel to True, the update occurs, and the AfterUpdate event can't prevent it from occurring.)

- The AfterUpdate event for the control fires after you've entered the information in the control and the update has been executed. If you set the Cancel argument for BeforeUpdate to True, the AfterUpdate event doesn't fire.

- The Exit event for the control fires when you move from this control to another control. (After the Exit event fires for the control you've left, the Enter event fires for the control to which you have moved the focus.)

AfterUpdate Event

The AfterUpdate event applies to the CheckBox, ComboBox, ListBox, OptionButton, ScrollBar, SpinButton, TextBox, and ToggleButton controls. This event fires after the user changes information in a control and after that update has been executed.

The syntax for the AfterUpdate event is straightforward and the same for all the controls and objects it applies to:

```
Private Sub object_AfterUpdate( )
```

KeyDown and *KeyUp* Events

The KeyDown event and KeyUp event apply to the CheckBox, ComboBox, CommandButton, Frame, ListBox, MultiPage, OptionButton, ScrollBar, SpinButton, TabStrip, TextBox, and ToggleButton controls, and to the UserForm object. (They don't apply to the Image and Label controls.) The KeyDown event fires when the user presses a key on the keyboard. The KeyUp event fires when the user lets the key up again. The KeyDown and KeyUp events also occur when a key is sent to the user form or control by using the SendKeys statement. They don't occur when the user presses Enter when the user form contains a CommandButton control with its Default property set to True, nor when the user presses Enter when the user form contains a CommandButton control with its Cancel property set to True.

When the keypress moves the focus to another control, the KeyDown event fires for the original control, while the KeyPress and KeyDown events fire for the control to which the focus is moved.

 NOTE The KeyPress event fires after the KeyDown event and before the KeyUp event. I'll tell you about KeyPress next.

The syntax for the KeyDown event is as follows:

```
Private Sub object_KeyDown(ByVal KeyCode As MSForms.ReturnInteger, ByVal
Shift As Integer)
```

The syntax for the KeyUp event is almost identical:

```
Private Sub object_KeyUp(ByVal KeyCode As MSForms.ReturnInteger, ByVal Shift
As Integer)
```

As usual, *object* is an object name, and is required. KeyCode is a required Integer argument specifying the key code of the key pressed. For example, the key code for the letter *t* is 84. The key code isn't an ANSI value—it's a special number that identifies the key on the keyboard.

Shift is a required argument specifying whether the Shift key, the Ctrl key, or the Alt key was pressed. Use the constants or values shown in Table 16.7:

TABLE 16.7: *SHIFT* CONSTANTS AND VALUES

Constant	Value	Description
fmShiftMask	1	Shift key pressed
fmCtrlMask	2	Ctrl key pressed
fmAltMask	4	Alt key pressed

KeyPress Event

The KeyPress event applies to the CheckBox, ComboBox, CommandButton, Frame, ListBox, MultiPage, OptionButton, ScrollBar, SpinButton, TabStrip, TextBox, and Toggle-Button controls. It also applies to the UserForm object. It doesn't apply to the Label control. The KeyPress event fires when the user presses an ANSI key—a printable character, Ctrl plus an alphabet character, Ctrl plus a special character, the Esc key, or the Backspace key—while the control or object in question has the focus. Pressing the Tab key, the Enter key, or an arrow key doesn't cause the KeyPress event to fire; nor does a keystroke that moves the focus to another control from the current control. The Delete key isn't an ANSI key, so pressing the Delete key to delete, say, text in a text box doesn't fire the Key-Press event; but deleting the same text in the same text box using the Backspace key does, because Backspace is an ANSI key.

NOTE   The KeyPress event fires after the KeyDown event and before the KeyUp event. It also fires when you use SendKeys to send keystrokes to a user form.

The syntax for the KeyPress event is as follows:

```
Private Sub object_KeyPress(ByVal KeyAscii As MSForms.ReturnInteger)
```

Here, *object* is a required argument specifying a valid object, and KeyAscii is a required Integer argument specifying an ANSI key code. To get the ANSI key code, use the Asc function. For example, Asc("t") returns the ANSI key code for the letter *t* (the code is 116).

By default, the KeyPress event processes the code for the key pressed—in humble terms, what you press is what you get. For example, if you press the *t* key, you get a *t*; if you press the Delete key, you get a Delete action; and so on. By using a KeyPress event procedure, you can perform checks such as filtering out all non-numeric keys when the user needs to enter a numeric value.

MouseDown Event and *MouseUp* Event

The MouseDown and MouseUp events apply to the CheckBox, ComboBox, Command-Button, Frame, Image, Label, ListBox, MultiPage, OptionButton, ScrollBar, SpinButton, TabStrip, TextBox, and ToggleButton controls, and to the UserForm object. The MouseDown event fires when the user depresses a button on the mouse, and the MouseUp event occurs when they release that button again. Not until after the MouseUp event occurs does the Click event fire.

The syntax for the MouseDown and MouseUp events is as follows for all controls except the MultiPage control and the TabStrip control:

```
Private Sub object_MouseDown(ByVal Button As Integer, ByVal Shift As
Integer, ByVal X As Single, ByVal Y As Single)
```

```
Private Sub object_MouseUp(ByVal Button As Integer, ByVal Shift As Integer,
ByVal X As Single, ByVal Y As Single)
```

The syntax for the MouseDown and MouseUp events with the MultiPage control and the TabStrip control adds an Index argument to specify the index of the page or the tab involved:

```
Private Sub object_MouseUp(ByVal Index As Long, ByVal Button As Integer,
ByVal Shift As Integer, ByVal X As Single, ByVal Y As Single)
```

```
Private Sub object_MouseDown(ByVal Index As Long, ByVal Button As Integer,
ByVal Shift As Integer, ByVal X As Single, ByVal Y As Single)
```

As usual, *object* is a valid object for the statement.

Index returns −1 if the user clicks outside the page or tab area of the control but still within the control (for example, to the right of the rightmost tab in a top-tab tab strip).

Button is a required Integer argument specifying the mouse button that perpetrated the event. Table 16.8 lists the possible values for Button.

TABLE 16.8: *Button* **VALUES AND CONSTANTS**

Constant	Value	Description
fmButtonLeft	1	Left (primary)
fmButtonRight	2	Right (non-primary)
fmButtonMiddle	4	Middle

Shift is a required argument specifying whether the Shift key, the Ctrl key, or the Alt key was pressed. Table 16.9 lists the values for Shift.

TABLE 16.9: *SHIFT* **VALUES**	
Shift **Value**	**Key or Keys Pressed**
1	Shift
2	Ctrl
3	Shift+Ctrl
4	Alt
5	Alt+Shift
6	Alt+Ctrl
7	Alt+Shift+Ctrl

You can also detect a single key by using the key masks listed in Table 16.7, earlier in the chapter.

X is a required Single argument specifying the horizontal position in points from the left edge of the user form, frame, or page. Y is a required Single argument specifying the vertical position in points from the top edge of the user form, frame, or page.

MouseMove Event

The MouseMove event applies to the CheckBox, ComboBox, CommandButton, Frame, Image, Label, ListBox, MultiPage, OptionButton, TabStrip, TextBox, and ToggleButton controls, and to the UserForm object. This event fires when the user moves the mouse over the control or object in question.

The syntax for the MouseMove event is different for the MultiPage control and the TabStrip control than for the other controls and for the UserForm object. The syntax for the other controls is:

```
Private Sub object_MouseMove(ByVal Button As Integer, ByVal Shift As
Integer, ByVal X As Single, ByVal Y As Single)
```

The syntax for the MultiPage control and the TabStrip control is:

```
Private Sub object_MouseMove(ByVal Index As Long, ByVal Button As Integer,
ByVal Shift As Integer, ByVal X As Single, ByVal Y As Single)
```

Here, *object* is a required argument specifying a valid object.

For the MultiPage control and the TabStrip control, Index is a required argument that returns the index of the Page object in the MultiPage control or the Tab object in the TabStrip control associated with the event procedure.

Button is a required Integer argument that returns which mouse button (if any) the user is pressing. Table 16.10 lists the values for Button.

TABLE 16.10: *Button* **VALUES**

Button Value	Button Pressed
0	No button
1	Left
2	Right
3	Left and right
4	Middle
5	Left and middle
6	Middle and right
7	Left, middle, and right

Shift is a required Integer argument that returns a value indicating whether the user is pressing the Shift, Alt, and/or Ctrl keys. Refer back to Table 16.9 for the list of Shift values.

X is a required Single argument that returns a value specifying the horizontal position in points from the left edge of the user form, frame, or page. Y is a required Single argument specifying the vertical position in points from the top edge of the user form, frame, or page.

As with the MouseDown and MouseUp events, you can also detect a single key by using the key masks listed in Table 16.7 (earlier in the chapter).

For a user form (in fact, for pretty much everything that happens in Windows), life is a (to the human) bewildering sequence of mouse events. MouseMove events monitor where the mouse pointer is on the screen and which control has captured it; MouseMove events fire even if you move a user form from under the mouse pointer (by using the keyboard), because the mouse pointer ends up in a different place in relation to the user form.

One use for the MouseMove event is to display appropriate text or an image for a control at which the user is pointing. For example, suppose a user form provides a list of products that are available, with the title of each product appearing in a label. When the user positioned the mouse pointer over a title in the label, you could use the MouseMove event to load a picture of the product into an Image control and a short description into another label.

 NOTE The user form traps MouseMove events when the mouse pointer isn't over any control. However, if the user moves the mouse pointer quickly from one control to another very close to it, the user form may fail to trap the movement over the short intervening space.

BeforeDragOver Event

The BeforeDragOver event applies to the UserForm object itself and to the following controls: CheckBox, ComboBox, CommandButton, Frame, Image, Label, ListBox, MultiPage, OptionButton, ScrollBar, SpinButton, TabStrip, TextBox, and Toggle-Button. The BeforeDragOver event occurs when the user is performing a drag-and-drop operation.

The syntax for the BeforeDragOver event depends on the object or control in question. The basic syntax for the UserForm and all controls except the Frame, TabStrip, and MultiPage is as follows, where *object* is a valid UserForm or control:

```
Private Sub object_BeforeDragOver(ByVal Cancel As MSForms.ReturnBoolean,
ByVal Control As MSForms.Control, ByVal Data As MSForms.DataObject, ByVal X
As Single, ByVal Y As Single, ByVal State As MSForms.fmDragState, ByVal Effect
As MSForms.ReturnEffect, ByVal Shift As Integer)
```

The syntax for the BeforeDragOver event with the Frame control is as follows, where *frame* is a valid Frame control:

```
Private Sub frame_BeforeDragOver(ByVal Cancel As MSForms.ReturnBoolean,
ByVal Control As MSForms.Control, ByVal Data As MSForms.DataObject, ByVal X
As Single, ByVal Y As Single, ByVal State As MSForms.fmDragState, ByVal
Effect As MSForms.ReturnEffect, ByVal Shift As Integer)
```

The syntax for the BeforeDragOver event with the MultiPage control is as follows, where *multipage* is a valid MultiPage control:

```
Private Sub multipage_BeforeDragOver(ByVal Index As Long, ByVal Cancel As
MSForms.ReturnBoolean, ByVal Control As MSForms.Control, ByVal Data As MSForms
.DataObject, ByVal X As Single, ByVal Y As Single, ByVal State As MSForms
.fmDragState, ByVal Effect As MSForms.ReturnEffect, ByVal Shift As Integer)
```

The syntax for the BeforeDragOver event with the TabStrip control is as follows, where tabstrip is a valid TabStrip control:

```
Private Sub tabstrip_BeforeDragOver(ByVal Index As Long, ByVal Cancel As
MSForms.ReturnBoolean, ByVal Data As MSForms.DataObject, ByVal X As Single,
ByVal Y As Single, ByVal DragState As MSForms.fmDragState, ByVal Effect As
MSForms.ReturnEffect, ByVal Shift As Integer)
```

Here are descriptions of the different parts of the statements:

- Index is the index of the Page object in a MultiPage control, or the Tab object in a TabStrip control, affected by the drag-and-drop.

- Cancel is a required argument giving the status of the BeforeDragOver event. The default setting is False, which makes the control handle the event. A setting of True makes the application handle the event.

- **Control** is a required argument specifying the control that is being dragged over.
- **Data** is a required argument specifying the data being dragged.
- **X** is a required argument specifying the horizontal distance in points from the left edge of the control. **Y** is a required argument specifying the vertical distance in points from the top of the control.
- **DragState** is a required argument specifying where the mouse pointer is in relation to a target (a location on which the data can be dropped). Table 16.11 lists the constants and values for **DragState**.

TABLE 16.11: *DragState* **CONSTANTS AND VALUES**

Constant	Value	Position of Mouse Pointer
fmDragStateEnter	0	Within range of a target
fmDragStateLeave	1	Outside the range of a target
fmDragStateOver	2	At a new position, but remains within range of the same target

- **Effect** is a required argument specifying the operations the source of the drop is to support, as listed in Table 16.12.

TABLE 16.12: *Effect* **CONSTANTS AND VALUES**

Constant	Value	Drop Effect
fmDropEffectNone	0	Doesn't copy or move the source to the target
fmDropEffectCopy	1	Copies the source to the target
fmDropEffectMove	2	Moves the source to the target
fmDropEffectCopyOrMove	3	Copies or moves the source to the target

- **Shift** is a required argument specifying whether the Shift, Ctrl, or Alt keys are held down during the drag-and-drop operation, as listed in Table 16.7 (earlier in the chapter).

You use the BeforeDragOver event to control drag-and-drop actions that the user performs. Use the DragState argument to make sure that the mouse pointer is within range of a target.

BeforeDropOrPaste Event

The BeforeDropOrPaste event applies to the CheckBox, ComboBox, CommandButton, Frame, Image, Label, ListBox, MultiPage, OptionButton, ScrollBar, SpinButton, TabStrip, TextBox, and ToggleButton controls, and to the UserForm object.

The BeforeDropOrPaste Event occurs just before the user drops or pastes data onto an object.

The syntax for the BeforeDropOrPaste event is different for the MultiPage control and the TabStrip control than for the UserForm object and for the other controls. The basic syntax is as follows:

```
Private Sub object_BeforeDropOrPaste(ByVal Cancel As MSForms.ReturnBoolean,
ByVal Control As MSForms.Control, ByVal Action As MSForms.fmAction, ByVal Data
As MSForms.DataObject, ByVal X As Single, ByVal Y As Single, ByVal Effect As
MSForms.ReturnEffect, ByVal Shift As Integer)
```

The syntax for the MultiPage control is as follows, where *multipage* is a valid MultiPage control:

```
Private Sub multipage_BeforeDropOrPaste(ByVal Index As Long, ByVal Cancel
As MSForms.ReturnBoolean, ByVal Control As MSForms.Control, ByVal Action As
MSForms.fmAction, ByVal Data As MSForms.DataObject, ByVal X As Single, ByVal
Y As Single, ByVal Effect As MSForms.ReturnEffect, ByVal Shift As Integer)
```

The syntax for the TabStrip control is as follows, where *tabstrip* is a valid TabStrip control:

```
Private Sub tabstrip_BeforeDropOrPaste(ByVal Index As Long, ByVal Cancel
As MSForms.ReturnBoolean, ByVal Action As MSForms.fmAction, ByVal Data As
MSForms.DataObject, ByVal X As Single, ByVal Y As Single, ByVal Effect
As MSForms.ReturnEffect, ByVal Shift As Integer)
```

Here's what the parts of the syntax are:

- *object* is a required object specifying a valid object.
- For the MultiPage control, Index is a required argument specifying the Page object involved.
- Cancel is a required argument giving the status of the event. The default setting of False makes the control handle the event; True makes the application handle the event.
- Control is a required argument specifying the target control.
- Action is a required argument specifying the result of the drag-and-drop operation. Table 16.13 shows the constants and values for Action.

TABLE 16.13: *ACTION* CONSTANTS AND VALUES		
Action Constant	Value	Action Taken
fmActionPaste	2	Pastes the object into the target.
fmActionDragDrop	3	The user has dragged the object from its source and dropped it on the target.

- Data is a required argument specifying the data (contained in a DataObject) being dragged and dropped.

- X is a required argument specifying the horizontal distance in points from the left edge of the control for the drop. Y is a required argument specifying the vertical distance in points from the top of the control.

- Effect is a required argument specifying whether the drag-and-drop operation copies the data or moves it, as listed in Table 16.12 (earlier in the chapter).

Shift is a required argument specifying whether the user has pressed the Shift, Ctrl, and/or Alt keys, as listed in Table 16.7 (earlier in the chapter).

The BeforeDropOrPaste event fires when a data object is transferred to a MultiPage or TabStrip, and just before the drop or paste operation occurs on other controls.

DblClick Event

The DblClick event applies to the CheckBox, ComboBox, CommandButton, Frame, Image, Label, ListBox, MultiPage, OptionButton, TabStrip, TextBox, and ToggleButton controls. It also applies to the UserForm object. As you might guess, this event occurs when the user double-clicks a control or object with the primary mouse button. The double-click needs to be fast enough to register as a double-click in Windows (this speed is controlled by the setting in the Mouse Properties dialog box), and occurs after the MouseDown event, the MouseUp event, and the Click event (for controls that support the Click event).

The DblClick event takes different syntax for the MultiPage control and the TabStrip control than for the other controls and for the user form. For the MultiPage control and the TabStrip control, the syntax is as follows:

```
Private Sub object_DblClick(ByVal Index As Long, ByVal Cancel As MSForms
.ReturnBoolean)
```

The syntax for the DblClick event for other controls is as follows:

```
Private Sub object_DblClick(ByVal Cancel As MSForms.ReturnBoolean)
```

Here, *object* is a required argument specifying a valid object. For the MultiPage control and the TabStrip control, Index is a required argument specifying the Page object within a MultiPage control or the Tab object within a TabStrip control to be associated with the event procedure.

Cancel is a required argument specifying the status of the event. The default setting of False causes the control to handle the event; True causes the application to handle the event instead, and causes the control to ignore the second click.

In controls that support both the Click event and the DblClick event, the Click event occurs before the DblClick event. If you take an interface action (such as displaying a message box) with the Click event procedure, it will block the DblClick event procedure from running. In the following example, the DblClick event procedure won't run:

```
Private Sub CommandButton1_Click()
    MsgBox "Click event"
End Sub


Private Sub CommandButton1_DblClick _
    (ByVal Cancel As MSForms.ReturnBoolean)
    MsgBox "Double-click event"
End Sub
```

However, you can execute non-interface statements in the Click event procedure without blocking the DblClick event procedure. The following example declares a Private String variable named strMess in the declarations portion of the code sheet for the user form. The Click event procedure for the CommandButton1 command button assigns text to strMess. The DblClick event procedure assigns more text to strMess, then displays a message box containing strMess so that you can see that both events have fired. Don't step into this code—run it full bore, or it won't work:

```
Private strMess As String


Private Sub CommandButton1_Click()
    strMess = "Click event" & vbCr
End Sub


Private Sub CommandButton1_DblClick _
    (ByVal Cancel As MSForms.ReturnBoolean)
    strMess = strMess & "Double-click event"
    MsgBox strMess
End Sub
```

That said, for most controls you won't want to use both a Click event procedure and a DblClick event procedure—you'll choose one or the other as appropriate to the control's needs.

Error Event

The Error event applies to the CheckBox, ComboBox, CommandButton, Frame, Image, Label, ListBox, MultiPage, OptionButton, ScrollBar, SpinButton, TabStrip, TextBox, and ToggleButton controls. It also applies to the UserForm objectThis event fires when a control encounters an error and is unable to return information about the error to the program that called the control.

The syntax for the Error event for the UserForm object and for all controls except the MultiPage control is as follows:

```
Private Sub object_Error(ByVal Number As Integer, ByVal Description As
MSForms.ReturnString, ByVal SCode As Long, ByVal Source As String, ByVal
HelpFile As String, ByVal HelpContext As Long, ByVal CancelDisplay As
MSForms.ReturnBoolean)
```

The syntax for the Error event for the MultiPage control is as follows, where *multipage* is a valid multipage:

```
Private Sub multipage_Error(ByVal Index As Long, ByVal Number As Integer,
ByVal Description As MSForms.ReturnString, ByVal SCode As Long, ByVal Source
As String, ByVal HelpFile As String, ByVal HelpContext As Long, ByVal
CancelDisplay As MSForms.ReturnBoolean)
```

These are the components of the syntax:

- *object* is the name of a valid object.
- For a MultiPage, Index is the index of the Page object in the MultiPage associated with the event.
- Number is a required argument that returns the value used by the control to identify the error.
- Description is a required String argument describing the error.
- SCode is a required argument giving the OLE status code for the error.
- Source is a required String argument containing the string identifying the control involved.
- HelpFile is a required String argument containing the full path to the Help file that contains the Description.
- HelpContext is a required Long argument containing the context ID for the description within the Help file.
- CancelDisplay is a required Boolean argument that controls whether VBA displays the error message in a message box.

Events That Apply Only to a Few Controls

In this section, I'll finish my discussion of events by dealing with the three events that apply only to one or two controls. The first of the three is the DropButtonClick event, which applies only to the ComboBox and TextBox controls; the second and third are the SpinUp and SpinDown events, which apply only to the SpinButton control.

DropButtonClick Event

The DropButtonClick event fires when the user displays or hides a drop-down list on a ComboBox by clicking the drop-down button or by pressing the F4 key. DropButtonClick also fires when the user press the F4 key with a TextBox control selected, though this manifestation of the event is arcane enough to be singularly useless. It also fires when the DropDown method is executed in VBA to display the drop-down list, and it fires again when the DropDown method is executed again to hide the drop-down list.

The syntax for the DropButtonClick event is straightforward:

```
Private Sub object_DropButtonClick( )
```

Here, *object* is a valid ComboBox or TextBox control.

One use for the DropButtonClick event is to add items to a ComboBox control rather than adding them at load time by using the Initialize event. By adding these items only on demand (I'm assuming the user might not use the ComboBox control at all, or might type information into its text box area), you can cut down on load time for the user form. You can also load the ComboBox with data relevant to the other choices the user has made in the dialog box, allowing for more targeted information than you could have provided by loading the ComboBox with the Initialize event.

SpinDown and *SpinUp* Events

The SpinDown and SpinUp events apply only to the SpinButton control. As you might guess, SpinDown and SpinUp are used to control what happens when the user clicks either the down-arrow button and up-arrow button, respectively, of a vertical SpinButton control, or the right-arrow button and left-arrow button, again respectively, of a horizontal SpinButton control. The SpinDown event fires when the user clicks the down-arrow or right-arrow button, and the SpinUp event fires when the user clicks the up-arrow or left-arrow button.

The syntax for the SpinUp event and the SpinDown event is straightforward:

```
Private Sub spinbutton_SpinDown( )
Private Sub spinbutton_SpinUp( )
```

Here, *spinbutton* is a SpinButton control.

By default, the SpinDown event decreases the Value property of the SpinButton by the SmallChange increment, and the SpinUp event increases it.

Once you've memorized the syntax for each of the events, you'll probably be ready for something a little lighter—perhaps a few cartwheels, a deep draught of your favorite beverage, or a pint of Bloated Coder ice cream. After that, you should be ready for Chapter 17, which discusses how to create modular code and which starts one page east of here.

CHAPTER 17

Building Modular Code

n this chapter, I'll go into a bit more depth about building modular code—code broken up into individual modules rather than all built together into a monolithic lump.

So far in this book, I've concentrated on getting things done in the various host applications by using VBA. The code you've constructed and examined up to now has worked well enough, but it hasn't been exactly concise or elegant.

 NOTE *Elegant* in the context of computer code means not only that the code is bug-free and impeccably put together, and that the interface is well designed, but also that the code contains nothing extra—it has been stripped down to the minimum required to achieve the desired effect.

In this chapter, you'll start learning how to be more concise (and perhaps even more elegant) in your code. You'll also start to understand how you can create reusable code that you can use in other procedures. Fortunately, all of these endeavors go together. The secret is to write modular code.

What Is Modular Code?

As you know from your work in the Visual Basic Editor, a module is a container for code. Modules are stored in projects, such as AutoCAD projects, PowerPoint presentations, Project's global project, and so on. Each project can contain no modules, one module, or multiple modules, and each module can contain any number of procedures (or none). Within a module, you can run the individual procedures separately, and you can call the individual procedures and functions separately from within the procedure.

The terminology is a little confusing, because *modular code* isn't so much code divided up into modules as I've just described, but code composed of different procedures that you can use in combination.

For example, suppose you're working in Word. You could take a monolithic approach and create a single procedure that created a document based on the user's choice of template, performed certain operations on that document (for example, inserting text and formatting it), saved it in a particular folder under a name of the user's choice, printed it to a specific printer, and then closed it.

Alternatively, you could take a modular approach and create a number of separate procedures—one for creating a document based on the user's choice of template, another for performing the text and formatting operations, another for saving the document, another for printing the document to the correct printer, and another for closing the document. You could then create a procedure that ran these procedures to achieve the same effect as the monolithic procedure. You could also create other procedures that used the individual procedures in different combinations with other procedures to achieve different effects.

Advantages of Using Modular Code

Modular code has a number of advantages over code that lumps everything together in one long listing. For one thing, it's often easier to write modular code, because you create a number of short procedures, each of which performs a specific task. You can usually debug these procedures relatively easily too, because their shorter length makes it simpler to identify, locate, and eliminate bugs. The procedures will also be more readable because they're less complex, and you can more easily follow what they do.

In addition, modular code provides a more efficient approach to programming, for four reasons:

- First, by breaking your code into procedures, you can repeat actions at different points in a sequence of procedures without needing to repeat the lines of code. This structure means less code to compile and thus greater speed.

- Second, by reusing parts of your code (whole procedures), you can greatly reduce the amount of code you have to write. And by writing less code, you give yourself less chance to write new errors into it.

- Third, if you need to change an item in the code, you can make a single change in the appropriate procedure instead of having to make changes at a number of locations in a long procedure (and perhaps missing some of them). This change will then carry through to all procedures that call the procedure.

- Fourth, you will be able to call individual procedures from other procedures without having to assimilate them into another procedure. Just think how tedious it would be if you had to create each of VBA's many functions from scratch instead of being able to invoke them at will. Got the idea? Good...

How much you worry about creating modular code will vary from project to project, and from procedure to procedure. For example, if you record a quick macro on-the-fly to perform a one-time task on a number of presentations, there's no need to worry about stripping it down into its components and formalizing them as procedures. On the other hand, when you sit down to plan a procedure that's going to revolutionize Visio life as people know it in your workplace, you can benefit greatly from planning the code as a set of procedures.

You can go about creating modular code in two main ways:

- Record (if the application you're using supports the VBA Macro Recorder) or write a procedure as usual and then examine it and break it into modules as necessary. This is a great way to start creating modular code, but it's usually less efficient: You'll end up spending a lot of time retrofitting your procedures as you break them into procedures.

- Plan the different actions that a procedure will take and create each action (or set of actions) as a separate procedure. This method requires more forethought, but usually proves more efficient in the long run.

Arranging Your Code in Modules

Once you've created a set of procedures, you can move them to a different module within the same project, or even to a different project. By grouping your procedures in modules, you can easily distribute the procedures to your colleagues without including procedures they don't need. And by grouping your modules in projects, you give yourself an even easier way of distributing the modules and procedures. In addition, you can remove from your immediate working environment any modules of code that you don't need, thus avoiding slowing your computer.

 TIP Give your modules descriptive names so that you can instantly identify them in the Organizer dialog box (in Microsoft applications) and other module-management tools. Don't get yourself stuck with fifty modules named Module*n* in various applications, because it's all too easy to get them confused.

Calling a Procedure

When a procedure needs to use another procedure, it *calls* it in the same way that you learned to call a function in Chapter 9. To call a procedure in the same project, you can simply enter the name of the procedure to be called as a statement in the calling procedure, or you can use a Call statement with the name of the procedure.

The syntax for the `Call` statement is the same for procedures as for functions:

```
[Call] name[, argumentlist]
```

Here, *name* is a required String argument giving the name of the procedure to call. Meanwhile, *argumentlist* is an optional argument providing a comma-delimited list of the variables, arrays, or expressions to pass to the procedure. As you'd imagine, you use the *argumentlist* argument only for procedures that require arguments.

For example, the following `CreateReceiptLetter` procedure calls the procedure `FormatDocument`:

```
Sub CreateReceiptLetter()
    'other actions here
    Call FormatDocument
    'other actions here
End Sub
```

You can also omit the `Call` keyword, using just the name of the procedure:

```
Sub CreateReceiptLetter()
    'other actions here
    FormatDocument
    'other actions here
End Sub
```

In the following example, the `Calling` procedure calls the `CallMe` procedure, which takes the String argument `strFeedMe`. Note that when you use `Call`, you need to enclose the argument list in parentheses:

```
Sub Calling()
    Call CallMe("Hello")
End Sub

Sub CallMe(ByVal strFeedMe As String)
    Msgbox strFeedMe
End Sub
```

Again, you can omit the `Call` keyword, as in the following example:

```
Sub Calling2()
    CallMe "Hello"
End Sub
```

As with functions, there's little reason to use the `Call` keyword unless you feel it serves to make it clearer that your code is calling a procedure. (If your code *is* unclear, a comment might serve you even better than the `Call` keyword.)

As well as calling a procedure in the same project, you can call a procedure in another open project in the same host application. Typically, the syntax used to call a procedure in another project is as follows:

```
Project.Module.Procedure
```

To call a procedure in another project, you need to add a reference to that project in the References dialog box (Tools ➤ References). For example, if you need to call the `Standardize_Format` procedure in Project's global project (whose filename is `GLOBAL.MPT` but which is referred to within Project's VBA sessions as `ProjectGlobal`) from a procedure in another project, you would add to that other project a reference to `ProjectGlobal` in the References dialog box, as shown in Figure 17.1.

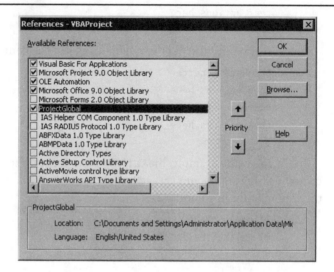

 WARNING You can't add to the current project a reference to a project that itself contains a reference to the current project. When you add the reference and close the References dialog box, the Visual Basic Editor will display a message box with the warning "Cyclic reference of projects not allowed" and won't place the reference. (It does close the References dialog box, though.)

Once this reference is in place, you can call the procedure. Figure 17.2 shows an example of using the List Properties/Methods feature to construct a call to a procedure in the `ProjectGlobal` global project in Project.

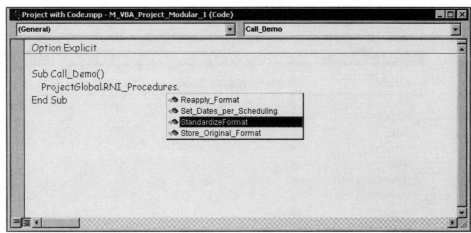

FIGURE 17.2

Once you've placed a reference to the project that contains the procedure, you can use the List Properties/ Methods feature to construct the call to the procedure.

Improving Your Code

So from now on you'll be writing modular code—but what else can you do to refine your code and make it run faster? Well, you can make at least two other types of improvements: logical improvements and visual improvements. I'll show you logical improvements first.

Logical Improvements

Breaking a procedure into procedures can improve the logic of your code by forcing you to consider each set of actions the procedure takes as modular—separate from other sets of actions (or even from other individual actions). But you can also improve the logic of your code by using explicit variable declarations, by simplifying any code you record, and by using With statements to reduce the number of object references.

Using Explicit Variable Declarations

As you learned earlier in the book, you can declare variables either implicitly or explicitly. If you declare variables explicitly, you can specify the type of each variable, which allows VBA to allocate only as much memory as that variable type needs. When you specify the data type of a variable, VBA also doesn't have to spend time checking the data type of the variable each time it encounters it. (You can also specify a data type for an implicitly declared variable by using its type-declaration character, but your code will be easier to read and to debug if you use explicit declarations.)

Table 17.1 shows the details on the amounts of memory that the different types of variables require.

TABLE 17.1: MEMORY CONSUMED BY THE DIFFERENT TYPES OF VARIABLES

Variable	Memory Needed (Bytes)
Boolean	2
Byte	1
Currency	8
Date	8
Variant/Decimal	12
Double	8
Integer	2
Long	4
Object	4
Single	4
String	Variable-length strings: 10 bytes plus the storage required for the string, which can be up to about 2 billion characters.
	Fixed-length strings: the number of bytes required to store the string, which can be from 1 to about 64,000 characters.
Variant	Variants that contain numbers: 16 bytes.
	Variants that contain characters: 22 bytes plus the storage required for the characters.

How much memory can you reasonably expect to save by specifying data types, and how much difference will carefully choosing variable types make to your procedures? Typically, the answer is, "not a lot." For example, if you dump two billion characters into a variable, the 12 bytes you save by specifying that it's a String variable rather than a Variant variable kinda pale into insignificance.... But in extreme circumstances—such as when using huge numbers of variables on a computer with limited memory—specifying the appropriate data types for your variables *might* save enough memory to enable your procedure to run where it otherwise wouldn't have been able to. The other bird you'll kill with this stone is to ensure optimal speed in your procedures, which is always a noble aim—even if the users of your code don't notice the efforts you've been making on their behalf.

A second reason for declaring your variables explicitly rather than implicitly is to make your code easier to read and to debug. In this case, you yourself will be the beneficiary of your good practice (or the good practice of whoever created the code and declared the variables explicitly).

A third reason for declaring your variables explicitly is that you can implement some runtime range checking. If you *know* something will be less than 32,768, and you declare it as being the Integer data type, you'll automatically get a helpful error when a Long creeps into it somehow at runtime.

The bottom line is that using explicit variable declarations is a good programming technique that can save you confusion and make your code easier to read. If you don't have time to do so right now, keep it in mind for future projects.

Simplifying Recorded Code

The Macro Recorder (in the Microsoft applications that support it) often provides a great way to kick-start creating code by letting you identify quickly the objects the procedure will need to work with and the methods and properties you'll need to use with them. But as you've seen, the drawback of the Macro Recorder is that it tends to record a ton of code that you don't actually need in your procedures, because it's faithfully detailing everything you might be trying to record. For example, when you record a procedure that changes one setting in a dialog box such as the Font dialog box in Word, the Macro Recorder records all the other settings on not only that page of the dialog box, but on all other pages, as well—in case you wanted them, too, I guess.

Once you've finished recording the procedure, you'll often want to open it to make minor adjustments; add loops, decisions, or UI items (message boxes, input boxes, or user forms); or even crib parts of the code wholesale for use in other procedures. At the same time, you'll do well to study the code the Macro Recorder has recorded and, where possible, strip it down to leave only the pieces that you need.

Take this Word example. Compare the Recorded_Macro_Applying_Arial_Font procedure that follows with the Stripped_Down_Procedure_Applying_Arial_Font procedure that comes after it:

```
Sub Recorded_Macro_Applying_Arial_Font()
'
' Recorded_Macro_Applying_Arial_Font
' Macro recorded 7/11/00 by Rikki Nadir
'
    With Selection.Font
        .Name = "Arial"
        .Size = 10
        .Bold = False
        .Italic = False
        .Underline = wdUnderlineNone
```

```
            .StrikeThrough = False
            .DoubleStrikeThrough = False
            .Outline = False
            .Emboss = False
            .Shadow = False
            .Hidden = False
            .SmallCaps = False
            .AllCaps = False
            .Color = wdColorAutomatic
            .Engrave = False
            .Superscript = False
            .Subscript = False
            .Spacing = 0
            .Scaling = 100
            .Position = 0
            .Kerning = 0
            .Animation = wdAnimationNone
        End With
    End Sub


    Sub Stripped_Down_Procedure_Applying_Arial_Font()
        With Selection.Font
            .Name = "Arial"
        End With
    End Sub
```

As you can see, the `Stripped_Down_Procedure_Applying_Arial_Font` code has the same effect as the recorded procedure, but it contains five lines to the recorded procedure's thirty. But because the `With` statement contains only one statement, you could make the procedure even more economical by eliminating the `With` statement:

```
    Sub Apply_Arial()
        Selection.Font.Name = "Arial"
    End Sub
```

Using *With* Statements to Simplify Your Code

You just saw how you can tighten code by eliminating a `With` statement, but this reduction tends to be the exception rather than the rule. After all, the Macro Recorder was using the `With` statement to reduce the complexity of the code it created—it just happened to record a ton of information that you didn't need.

When you're performing multiple actions with an object, you can often use `With` statements to reduce the number of object references involved, and thus simplify and speed up the code. When you need to work with multiple objects in a single object, you can either use separate `With` statements, or pick the lowest common denominator of the objects you want to work with and use a common `With` statement along with nested `With` statements.

For example, the following statements contain multiple references to the first Paragraph object—`Paragraphs(1)`—in the `ActiveDocument` object in Word:

```
ActiveDocument.Paragraphs(1).Range.Font.Bold = True
ActiveDocument.Paragraphs(1).Range.Font.Name = "Times New Roman"
ActiveDocument.Paragraphs(1).LineSpacingRule = wdLineSpaceSingle
ActiveDocument.Paragraphs(1).Borders(1).LineStyle = wdLineStyleDouble
ActiveDocument.Paragraphs(1).Borders(1).ColorIndex = wdBlue
```

Instead, however, you could use a `With` statement that referenced the `Paragraphs(1)` object in the `ActiveDocument` object to simplify the number of references involved:

```
With ActiveDocument.Paragraphs(1)
    .Range.Font.Bold = True
    .Range.Font.Name = "Times New Roman"
    .LineSpacingRule = wdLineSpaceSingle
    .Borders(1).LineStyle = wdLineStyleDouble
    .Borders(1).ColorIndex = wdBlue
End With
```

You can further reduce the number of object references here by using nested `With` statements for the Font object in the Range object and for the `Borders(1)` object:

```
With ActiveDocument.Paragraphs(1)
    With .Range.Font
        .Bold = True
        .Name = "Times New Roman"
    End With
    .LineSpacingRule = wdLineSpaceSingle
    With .Borders(1)
        .LineStyle = wdLineStyleDouble
        .ColorIndex = wdBlue
    End With
End With
```

Don't Use *With* Statements Pointlessly

With statements are great for simplifying object references and making your code easier to read, but don't use them just because you can. If you have only one statement within a With statement, as in the following absurd example (which again uses Word), you're probably wasting your time typing extra code:

```
With ActiveDocument.Sections(1).Headers(wdHeaderFooterPrimary) _
    .Range.Words(1)
    .Bold = True
End With
```

Likewise, don't nest With statements unless you need to:

```
With ActiveDocument
    With .Sections(1)
        With .Headers(wdHeaderFooterPrimary)
            With .Range
                With .Words(1)
                    With .Font
                        .Italic = True
                        .Bold = False
                        .Color = wdColorBlack
                    End With
                End With
            End With
        End With
    End With
End With
```

Again, there's no point in this code, though there's a certain appeal to the blunt arrowhead shape created by the progressive indentation. In this case, though, a With Active-Document.Sections(1).Headers(wdHeaderFooterPrimary).Range.Words(1).Font statement would be a good idea.

Optimizing Your *Select Case* Statements

Another candidate for optimization is the Select Case statement. By arranging the Case statements with the most likely ones first, you can save VBA a little work and time—it goes through the Case statements until it gets a hit, so the sooner it gets that hit, the quicker the execution of the statement.

You'll save only a little time—unless you're creating truly massive Select Case statements, or huge numbers of Select Case statements. But it might be enough to make something of a difference on a tired old computer.

Don't Check Things Pointlessly

If you need to implement a setting (especially a Boolean one) every time a particular procedure runs, there's no point in checking the current value. For example, suppose you wanted to make sure the `ObjectSnapMode` property (a Boolean property that controls whether snap mode is on or off for the document) of the `ActiveDocument` object in AutoCAD was set to `True`. You could check the current value of `ObjectSnapMode` and, if it was `False`, set it to `True` like this:

```
If ActiveDocument.ObjectSnapMode = False Then _
    ActiveDocument.ObjectSnapMode = True
```

But there's really no point in checking the current value in this case: You might as well set the property to `True` and be done with it:

```
ActiveDocument.ObjectSnapMode = True
```

That way, VBA doesn't waste time checking the current value of the property—and you've saved your fingers a little walking on the keyboard.

Removing Unused Elements from Your Code

To improve the efficiency of your code, try to remove all unused elements from it. When creating a complex project with many interrelated procedures, it's easy to end up with a number of procedures that are almost or entirely useless.

You'll find it easier to remove unwarranted and unwanted procedures wholesale if you've commented them assiduously while creating them. That way you'll know that what you're ripping out root and branch was your third, fourth, or fifth failed attempt at performing a task satisfactorily rather than the badly named but successful try that's actually running in the pre-production version of the project. If you're in doubt as to which procedure is calling which, display the Call Stack dialog box (View ➤ Call Stack, or Ctrl+L) to see what's happening. Alternatively, try one of these techniques:

- Set a breakpoint at the beginning of a suspect procedure so that you'll be alerted when it's called.

- Display message boxes at decisive junctures in your code.

- Use a `Debug.Print` statement at an appropriate point (again, perhaps the beginning of a procedure) to implement temporary logging of information in the Immediate window.

Before you remove an apparently dead procedure from your code, make sure not only that it's unused in the way the procedure is currently being run, but also that it isn't being used in ways in which the procedure *might* be run were circumstances different. If you're almost sure the procedure is dead rather than *resting*, try moving it to another project from which you can easily restore it, rather than deleting it outright. Before removing an entire module, you may want to use the File ➤ Export File command to export a copy of the module to a .BAS file in a safe storage location in case the module contains anything you'll subsequently discover to be of value.

Once you've rooted out procedures that aren't pulling their weight, take the focus down a notch (I'm tempted to suggest using a macro focus mode) and zoom in on the variables in the procedures. Even if you're furthering your aspirations to sainthood by using the Option Explicit declaration and declaring every variable explicitly (which I and this book's Technical Editor continue to urge you to do), it's easy to declare variables that you end up not using. For simple projects, you'll be able to catch most (or all) unused variables by using the Locals window to see which of them never get assigned a value. For more complex projects, you may want to try some of the assorted third-party tools that help you remove unneeded elements from your code.

If in doubt, comment out the declaration of the supposedly superfluous variable, make sure you're using Option Explicit, and run the code a few more times, exercising the different paths that it can take. If you don't get a "Variable not defined" compile error, chances are good that you've found another candidate for elimination.

Visual Improvements

The second category of improvements you can make to your code consists of visual improvements—not aesthetics, but making your code as easy to read (and modify, if necessary) as possible.

Indenting the Different Levels of Code

As you've seen in the examples so far in this book, you can make your code much easier to follow by indenting the lines of code with tabs or spaces to show their logical relation to each other. You can click the Indent and Outdent buttons on the Edit toolbar or press Tab and Shift+Tab to quickly indent or unindent a selected block of code, with the relative indentation of the lines within the block remaining the same.

 NOTE You can't indent labels. If you try to indent a label, the Visual Basic Editor will remove all spaces to the left of the label as soon as you move the insertion point off the line containing the label. This can make for an unfortunate look to your otherwise neatly indented code, but it does make labels easy to spot.

Using Line-Continuation Characters to Break Long Lines

Use the line-continuation character (an underscore after a space) to break long lines of code into a number of shorter lines. This technique not only has the advantage of making long lines of code fit within the code window on an average-size monitor at a readable point size, but also enables you to break the code into more logical segments.

Using the Concatenation Character to Break Long Strings

Because you can't use the line-continuation character to break a long string, you have to be a bit more creative and divide the string, and then use the concatenation character (&) to sew the parts back together again; you can then separate the parts of the string with the line-continuation character. For example, consider a long string such as this:

```
strBogusText = "Now is the time for all good men to come to the
➥aid of the portly."
```

It's awkward (though admittedly the restricted length of the lines of code in this book have made it appear more ugly than nature intended). Instead, you could divide the string into two, and then rejoin it like this:

```
strBogusText = "Now is the time for all good men to come " & _
    "to the aid of the portly."
```

 NOTE You can also use the addition character (+) to concatenate one string with another, but not to concatenate a string and a numeric variable—VBA will try to add them instead of concatenating them.

Using Blank Lines to Break Up Your Code

To make your code more readable, use blank lines to separates statements into logical groups. For example, you might segregate all the variable declarations in a procedure as shown in the example below so that they stand out more clearly:

```
Sub Create_Rejection_Letter

    Dim strApplicantFirst As String, strApplicantInitial As String, _
        strApplicantLast As String, strApplicantTitle As String
    Dim strJobTitle As String
    Dim dteDateApplied As Date, dteDateInterviewed As Date
    Dim blnExperience As Boolean

'next statements in the procedure
```

Using Variables to Simplify Complex Syntax

You can use variables to simplify and shorten complex syntax. For example, you could display a message box by using an awkwardly long statement such as this one:

```
If MsgBox("The document contains no text." & vbCr & vbCr _
    & "Click the Yes button to continue formatting the " & _
    "document. Click the No button to cancel the procedure.", _
    vbYesNo & vbQuestion, _
    "Error Selecting Document: Cancel Procedure?") Then
```

Alternatively, you could use one String variable for building the message, another String variable for the title, and a Long variable for the message box type:

```
Dim strMsg As String
Dim strTBar As String
Dim lngOKQ As Long
strMsg = "The document contains no text." & vbCr & vbCr
strMsg = strMsg & "Click the Yes button to continue formatting " & _
    "the document. "
strMsg = strMsg & "Click the No button to cancel the procedure."
strTBar = "Error Selecting Document: Cancel Procedure?"
lngOKQ = vbYesNo & vbQuestion
If MsgBox(strMsg, lngOKQ, strTBar) Then
```

At first sight, this code looks more complex than the straightforward message box statement, mostly because of the explicit variable declarations that increase the length of the code segment. But in the long run, this type of arrangement is much easier to read and modify.

For the record, though, I don't recommend replacing the vbOKCancel & vbQuestion part of the MsgBox statement with the variable—I just wanted to show that it's possible. Usually, you'll find it easier to read the MsgBox statement if you state the buttons in the conventional format than if you replace them with a custom designation. It's also usually easier to read the VBA constants than the values—the vbOKCancel constant rather than the value 1, the vbQuestion constant rather than the value 32, and so on—even though the values are much shorter to enter in code.

Passing Information from One Procedure to Another

Often when you call another procedure, you'll need to pass information to it from the calling procedure, and, when the procedure has run, either pass back other information, or a modified version of the same information. You can pass information either by using arguments, or by using private or public variables, though there are some powerful reasons for not doing so.

Passing Information with Arguments

Using arguments is the more formal way to pass information from one procedure to another. This is because you have to declare the arguments you're passing in the declaration line of the Sub procedure in the parentheses after the procedure's name. You can pass either a single argument (as the first of the following statements does), or multiple arguments separated by commas (as the second does):

```
Sub PassOneArgument(MyArg)
Sub PassTwoArguments(FirstArg, SecondArg)
```

To pass information with arguments from one procedure to another, you use the syntax you learned for functions in Chapter 9. I'll recap the key information here briefly.

As with functions, you can pass an argument either *by reference* or *by value*. When a procedure passes an argument to another procedure by reference, the recipient procedure gets access to the memory location where the original variable is stored and can change the original variable. By contrast, when a procedure passes an argument to another procedure by value, the recipient procedure gets only a copy of the information in the variable and can't change the information in the original variable. Passing an argument by reference is useful when you want to manipulate the variable in the recipient procedure and then return the variable to the procedure from which it originated. Passing an argument by value is useful when you want to use the information stored in the variable in the recipient procedure and at the same time make sure that the original information in the variable doesn't change.

By reference is the default way to pass an argument, but you can also use the ByRef keyword to state explicitly that you want to pass an argument by reference. Both the following statements pass the argument MyArg by reference:

```
Sub PassByReference(MyArg)
Sub PassByReference(ByRef MyArg)
```

To pass an argument by value, you must use the ByVal keyword. The following statement passes the ValArg argument by value:

```
Sub PassByValue(ByVal ValArg)
```

If necessary, you can pass some arguments for a procedure by reference and others by value. The following statement passes the MyArg argument by reference and the ValArg argument by value:

```
Sub PassBoth(ByRef MyArg, ByVal ValArg)
```

You can explicitly declare the data type of arguments you pass in order to take up less memory and ensure that your procedures are passing the type of information you intend them to. But when passing an argument by reference, you need to make sure that the data type of the argument you're passing matches the data type expected in the procedure. For example, if you declare a string and try to pass it as an argument when the receiving procedure is expecting a variant, VBA will throw an error.

To declare the data type of an argument, include a data-type declaration in the argument list. The following statement declares MyArg as a string to be passed by reference and ValArg as a variant to be passed by value:

```
Sub PassBoth(ByRef MyArg As String, ByVal ValArg As Variant)
```

You can specify an optional argument by using the Optional keyword. Place the Optional keyword before the ByRef or ByVal keyword if you need to use ByRef or ByVal:

```
Sub PassBoth(ByRef MyArg As String, ByVal ValArg As Variant, _
  Optional ByVal MyOptArg As Variant)
```

Listing 17.1 shows a stripped-down segment of a procedure that uses arguments to pass information from one procedure to another.

Listing 17.1

```
1.  Sub GetCustomerInfo()
2.      Dim strCustName As String, strCustCity As String, _
            strCustPhone As String
3.      'Get strCustName, strCustCity, strCustPhone from sources
4.      CreateCustomer strCustName, strCustCity, strCustPhone
5.  End Sub
6.
7.  Sub CreateCustomer(ByRef strCName As String, _
            ByRef strCCity As String, ByVal strCPhone As String)
8.      Dim strCustomer As String
9.      strCustomer = strCName & vbTab & strCCity _
            & vbTab & strCPhone
10.     'take action with strCustomer string here
11. End Sub
```

Analysis

Listing 17.1 contains two minimalist procedures—GetCustomerInfo and Create-Customer—intended to show how to use arguments to pass information between procedures rather than do anything that's actually useful:

- The first procedure, GetCustomerInfo, explicitly declares three String variables in line 2: strCustName, strCustCity, and strCustPhone.

- Line 3 contains a comment indicating where the procedure would assign information to the variables.

- Line 4 calls the CreateCustomer procedure and passes to it the variables str-CustName, strCustCity, and strCustPhone as arguments. Because this statement doesn't use the Call keyword, the arguments aren't enclosed in parentheses.

- Execution then switches to line 7, which starts the CreateCustomer procedure by declaring the three String arguments it uses: strCName and strCCity are to be passed by reference, and strCPhone is to be passed by value.

- Line 8 declares the String variable strCustomer. Line 9 then assigns to strCustomer the information in strCName, a tab, the information in strCCity, another tab, and the information in strCPhone.

- Line 10 contains a comment indicating where the procedure would take action with the strCustomer string (for example, dumping it into some kind of primitive database), and line 11 ends the procedure.

Passing Information with Private or Public Variables

Using private or public variables is the (much) less formal way to pass information from one procedure to another. "Less formal" is code for "most programmers consider this a grubby and unwise practice," but passing information this way is quick and effective if you can square it with your conscience, your boss, or your peers. You can use private variables if the procedures that need to share information are located in the same module; if the procedures are located in different modules, you'll need to use public variables to pass the information.

There are several disadvantages to using private or public variables to pass information among procedures. The first two disadvantages are practical:

- First, passing information this way takes up more memory than passing information with arguments. But unless you grossly abuse private or public variables, you're unlikely to notice any problems from the extra memory overhead: A few private or public variables here and there aren't going to make much difference to the performance of most computers macho enough to run VBA and its host applications at a decent clip.

- Second, and somewhat worse, it's much harder to track the flow of information from one procedure to another (to another, to another). This complexity can lead to nasty debugging situations.

The other disadvantage, and perhaps more of a deterrent, is that you risk unemployment, ostracism, or lynching at the hands of programmers who catch you perpetrating this kind of kludge.

Listing 17.2 contains an oversimplified example of how you can pass information by using private variables.

Listing 17.2

```
1.   Private strPassMe As String
2.
3.   Sub PassingInfo()
4.       strPassMe = "Hello."
5.       PassingInfoBack
6.       MsgBox strPassMe
7.   End Sub
8.
9.   Sub PassingInfoBack()
10.      strPassMe = strPassMe & " How are you?"
11.  End Sub
```

Analysis

Listing 17.2 begins by declaring the private String variable strPassMe at the beginning of the code sheet for the module. strPassMe is then available to all the procedures in the module.

The PassingInfo procedure (lines 3 to 7) simply assigns the text Hello. (with the period) to strPassMe in line 4 and then calls the PassingInfoBack procedure in line 5. Execution then shifts to line 9, which starts the PassingInfoBack procedure. Line 10 adds How are you? with a leading space to the strPassMe String variable. Line 11 ends the PassingInfoBack procedure, whereupon execution returns to the PassingInfo procedure at line 6, which displays a message box containing the strPassMe string (now *Hello. How are you?*). Line 7 ends the procedure.

In the next chapter, I'll discuss how to go about debugging your code.

CHAPTER 18

Debugging
Your Code

I n this chapter, you'll learn some of the things that can go wrong in your VBA code and what you can do about them. You'll examine the types of errors that can occur, from simple typos, to infinite loops, to errors that happen only when the moon is blue *and* it's the turn of the millennium.

I'll start by going quickly through the principles of debugging. Then you'll work with the tools that Visual Basic for Applications offers for debugging VBA code and use them to get the bugs out of a few statements. Finally, I'll discuss the various methods of handling errors and when to use each one.

Principles of Debugging

A bug, as I'm sure you know, is an error in hardware or software that causes a program to execute incorrectly. (There are various explanations of the entomology—uh, make that *etymology*—of the word *bug* in this context, ranging from apocryphal stories of moths being found in the circuit boards of malfunctioning computers to musings that the word came from the mythological *bugbear*, an unwelcome beast. But in fact, this usage of *bug* seems to come from the early days of the telegraph rather than originating in the computer age.) *Debugging* means removing the bugs from hardware or (in this case) software.

Your goals in debugging should be straightforward: You need to remove all detectable bugs from your code as quickly and efficiently as possible. Your order of business will probably go something like this:

- First, test your code to see whether it works as it should. If you're confident that it will work, you'll probably want to test it by simply running the procedure once or twice on suitable documents or appropriate data. Even if it seems to work, continue testing for a reasonable period on sample documents before unleashing the procedure on the world (or your colleagues).

- If your code doesn't work as you expected it to, you'll need to debug it. That means following the procedures in this chapter to locate the bugs and then remove them. Once you've removed all the bugs that you can identify, test the code as described in the first step.

- When testing your code, try to anticipate the unorthodox applications that users will devise for your procedure. For example, you might write a sophisticated procedure for manipulating an AutoCAD drawing on the (perfectly reasonable) assumption that the drawing will be open when the user starts the procedure running. You can test it on sample documents until you're blue in the face, and it'll work fine every time. But if a user tries to run the procedure without first opening a drawing, it'll crash every time—guaranteed.

• When you're ready to distribute your procedure, you may want to write instructions for its use. In these instructions, you may also need to document any bugs that you can't squash or circumstances under which the procedure shouldn't be run.

Debugging a procedure tends to be idiosyncratic work. There's no magic wand that you can wave over your code to banish bugs (although, as I'll discuss in a moment, the Visual Basic Editor does its best to help you eliminate certain types of errors from your code as you create it). Moreover, such simple things as forgetting to initialize a variable can wreak havoc on your code. You'll probably develop your own approach to debugging your procedures, partly because they will inevitably be written in your own style. But when debugging, it helps to focus on understanding what the code is supposed to do. You then correlate this with your observations of what the code actually does. When you reconcile the two, you'll probably have worked out how to debug the procedure.

 TIP   The more complex your code, the higher the probability that it will contain bugs. Keep your code as simple as possible by breaking it into separate procedures and modules, as discussed in the previous chapter.

The Different Types of Errors

You'll encounter four basic kinds of errors in your procedures:

• Language errors
• Compile errors
• Runtime errors
• Program logic errors

You'll look at these in turn and discuss how to prevent them. After that, you'll examine the tools VBA provides for fixing them.

Language Errors

The first type of error is a *language error* (also known as a *syntax error*). When you mistype a word in the Code window, omit a vital piece of punctuation, scramble a statement, or leave off the end of a construction, that's a language error. If you've gotten this far in the book, you've probably already made dozens of language errors as part of the learning process and through simple typos.

VBA helps you eliminate many language errors as you create them, as you'll see in the next section. Those language errors that the Visual Basic Editor doesn't catch as you create them usually show up as compile errors, so I'll show you examples of both language errors and compile errors in the next section.

Compile Errors

Compile errors occur when VBA can't compile a statement correctly—that is, when VBA can't turn into viable code a statement that you've entered. For example, if you tell VBA to use a certain property for an object that doesn't have that property, you'll cause a compile error.

The good news about language errors and compile errors is that—as you'll have noticed—the Visual Basic Editor detects many language errors and some compile errors when you move the insertion point from the offending line. For example, try typing the following statement in the Code window and pressing Enter to create a new line (or ↑ or ↓ to move to another line):

```
If X > Y
```

The Visual Basic Editor will display a "Compile Error: Expected: Then or GoTo" message box to tell you that the statement is missing a vital element: It should be If X > Y Then or If X > Y GoTo. This vigilance on the part of the Visual Basic Editor prevents you from running into this type of error deep in the execution of your code.

 NOTE   You'll notice I'm assuming that you're keeping VBA's Auto Syntax Check feature and other features switched on. Some developers choose to turn off these features because they don't want to be nagged—but working without these features can prove a worse cure than the disease.

On the other hand, you'll also make language errors that the Visual Basic Editor does *not* identify when you move the insertion point from the line in which you've inserted them. Instead, VBA will identify these errors as compile errors when it compiles the code. For example, if you enter the statement below in the code window when working with Word, the Visual Basic Editor won't detect anything wrong. But when you run the procedure, VBA will compile the code, and discover and object to the error, before running any of the statements in the procedure:

```
ActiveDocument.SaveAs FileMame:="My File.doc"
```

This error is a straightforward typo—`FileMame` instead of `FileName`—but VBA can't identify the problem until it runs the code.

The Visual Basic Editor does help you pick up some errors of this type. Say you're trying to enter a `Documents.Close` statement (in Word or AutoCAD) and mistype `Documents` as `Docments`. In this case, the Visual Basic Editor won't display the Properties/Methods list because you haven't entered a valid object (unless you've declared a collection or object named `Docments` that has a `Close` method, which would be less than brilliant). Not seeing the list should alert you that something is wrong. If you continue anyway and enter the `Docments.Close` statement (which is easy enough to do if you're typing at high speed without watching the screen), the Visual Basic Editor won't spot the mistake—it will show up as a "Run-time error 424: Object required" message (if you don't have `Option Explicit` on) when you try to run the procedure. (If you do have `Option Explicit` on, you'll get a "Variable not defined" compile error instead.)

In a similar vein, if you specify a property or method for an object to which that property or method doesn't apply, VBA will cough up a compile error. For example, say you forget the `Add` method and enter `Documents.Create` instead. VBA will highlight the offending word and will generate a compile error "Method or data member not found," which tells you there's no `Create` method for the `Documents` collection.

Runtime Errors

The third type of error you'll see is the runtime error, which occurs while code is executing. You create a runtime error when you write a statement that causes VBA to try to perform an impossible operation, such as opening a document that doesn't exist, closing a document when no document is open, or performing something mathematically impossible such as dividing by zero. An unhandled runtime error results in a crash that manifests itself as a Microsoft Visual Basic dialog box displaying a runtime error number, such as the one shown in Figure 18.1.

As an example of an impossible operation, consider the archetypal division by zero. The following statements give a "Run-time error 11: Division by zero" message:

```
Dim DZ
DZ = 1 / 0
```

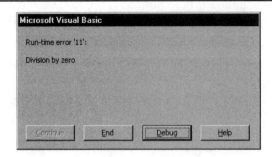

FIGURE 18.1

*An unhandled runtime
error causes VBA to
display a message box
such as this one.*

I know—you're unlikely to enter anything as witless as this demonstration line in your code; this line will inevitably produce a division-by-zero error because the divisor is zero. But it's easy to enter a valid equation, such as MonthlyPay = Salary/Months, and forget to assign a value to Months (if a numeric variable is empty, it counts as a zero value), or to produce a zero value for Months by addition or subtraction.

To avoid runtime errors, track the values of your variables by using the Watch window, which I'll discuss a little later in the chapter.

Program Logic Errors

The fourth type of error (and the grimmest) is the *program logic error*, which is an error that produces incorrect results. With program logic errors, the code has no syntactical problem, so VBA is able to compile and run it without generating any errors—but the result you get isn't the result you were expecting. Program logic errors range in scope from the relatively obvious (such as performing exquisitely accurate changes to the wrong drawing in Visio or AutoCAD because you neglected to check which window was active) to the subtle (such as extending a range to the wrong character or cell). In the first example, the graphical manipulation procedure is likely to run perfectly, but the resulting image will bear little resemblance to what you were trying to produce. In the second example, you might get a result that was almost correct—or the error might cause you to get perfect results sometimes and slightly wrong results at other times.

Program logic errors tend to be the hardest errors to catch. To nail them down, you need to trace the execution of your code and pinpoint where things start to go wrong. To do so, you need the tools that I'll introduce in the next section.

Uncatchable Bugs

The more complex your code, the more likely you are to create bugs that are truly difficult to catch. Usually, with determination and ingenuity, you can track down the bugs in a procedure; but bugs that depend on several unforeseen and improbable circumstances occurring simultaneously can be the devil's own job to isolate. For example, an error that occurs in a procedure when the user makes a certain choice in a dialog box is relatively easy to catch. But if the error occurs only when the user has made two particular choices in the dialog box, it's much harder to locate—and if the error is contingent on three specific choices the user has made in the dialog box, or if it depends on an element in the document on which the procedure is being run, you'll have a much tougher time pinpointing it.

Hacker folklore defines various kinds of bizarre bugs by assigning them quasi-jocular names derived from such disciplines as philosophy and quantum physics. For instance, a *heisenbug* is defined as "a bug that disappears or alters its behavior when one attempts to probe or isolate it." Heisenbugs are frustrating, as are Bohr bugs and mandelbugs, which I won't get into here. But the worst kind of bug is the *schroedingbug*, which is a design or implementation bug that remains quiescent until someone reads the code and notices that it shouldn't work, whereupon it stops working until the code is made logically consistent.

These bugs are, of course, ridiculous—until you start to discover bit rot at work on your code and have to explain the problem to your superiors.

VBA's Debugging Tools

VBA provides a solid assortment of debugging tools to help you remove the bugs from your procedures. The main tools for debugging are the Immediate window (which you met in Chapter 3, but which I'll touch on here), the Locals window, and the Watch window. As you'll see, you can access these tools in various ways, one of which is by using the Debug toolbar (shown in Figure 18.2). Three of the buttons—Run Sub/User-Form (Continue), Break, and Reset—are shared with the Standard toolbar; most of the others I'll introduce later in this chapter as appropriate.

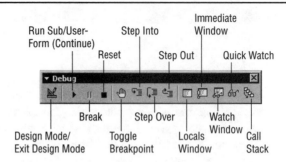

But before you dig into the debugging tools, I'll take you through a quick refresher on Break mode, which you visited briefly in Chapter 3. There, you saw how you could step through a procedure one statement at a time, and how you could check the value of a variable with the Data Tips feature by moving the mouse pointer over the name of the variable in the code. Here, you'll build on that knowledge to get results more quickly.

Break Mode

Break mode is a vital tool for debugging your procedures because it lets you watch your code execute step by step in the Code window. For example, if an If...Then...ElseIf...Else statement appears to be executing incorrectly, you can step through it in Break mode and watch exactly which statements are executing to produce the result.

Earlier in the book, I showed you the two easiest ways of entering Break mode:

- Place the insertion point in the procedure you want to run in the Code window and press the F8 key (or click the Step Into button on the Debug toolbar, or choose Debug ➤ Step Into) to start stepping through it.

- Set one or more breakpoints in the procedure to cause VBA to enter Break mode when it reaches one of the marked lines. A breakpoint allows you to stop execution of code at a particular point in a procedure. The easiest way to set a breakpoint is to click in the Margin Indicator Bar to the left of the code window beside the line you want to affect. (You can also right-click in the line and choose Toggle ➤ Breakpoint from the context menu.) You can set any number of breakpoints. They're especially useful when you need to track down a bug in a procedure, because they let you run the parts of a procedure that have no problems at full speed and then stop the procedure where you think there might be problems. From there, you can step through the statements that might be problematic and watch how they execute.

You can also enter Break mode in a couple of other ways:

- Interrupt your code by pressing Ctrl+Break and then click the Debug button in the resulting dialog box (see Figure 18.3). This isn't a particularly useful way of entering Break mode unless your code gets stuck in an endless loop (which you'll typically realize when the code appears to be doing nothing for a long time, or repeating itself when you think it shouldn't be). VBA will highlight the statement that was executing when you pressed Ctrl+Break, but (depending on your timing) it's unlikely to be the statement that's causing the problem in your code—it'll just be one of the statements in the offending loop. You'll then need to step through the loop to identify the perp.

FIGURE 18.3

You can enter Break mode by pressing Ctrl+Break and then clicking the Debug button in this dialog box.

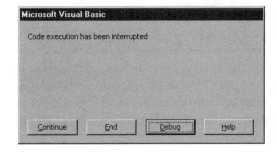

- Choose the Debug button in a runtime error dialog box such as the one shown in Figure 18.4. In the Code window, VBA will highlight the statement that caused the error. (You can also choose the Help button in the runtime error dialog box to get an explanation of the error before choosing the Debug button.)

FIGURE 18.4

Entering Break mode from a runtime error dialog box like this one takes you straight to the offending statement in your code.

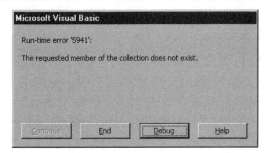

The Step Over and Step Out Commands

In Chapter 4, I showed you how to step through a procedure by using the F8 key. More formally, this command is known as Step Into, and you can also issue it by clicking the Step Into button on the Debug toolbar or choosing Debug ➢ Step Into. But you should know about three more features of Break mode: the Step Over command, the Step Out command, and the Run To Cursor command, all of which you use in Break mode to speed up stepping through your code.

 NOTE The Step Over and Step Out commands aren't available until you enter Break mode (for example, by using the Step Into command).

The Step Over command (which you can issue by clicking the Step Over button on the Debug toolbar, by pressing Shift+F8, or by choosing Debug ➢ Step Over) executes the whole of a procedure or function called from the current procedure, instead of stepping through the called procedure statement by statement, as the Step Into command would do. (It "steps over" that procedure or function.) Use the Step Over command when you're debugging a procedure that calls another procedure or function that you know to be error-free and that you don't need to test step-by-step.

The Step Out command (which you can issue by clicking the Step Out button on the Debug toolbar, by pressing Ctrl+Shift+F8, or by choosing Debug ➢ Step Out) runs the rest of the current procedure at full speed. Use the Step Out command to execute quickly the rest of the procedure once you've gotten through the part that you needed to watch step-by-step.

The Run To Cursor command (which you can issue by choosing Debug ➢ Run To Cursor or by pressing Ctrl+F8) runs the code at full speed until it hits the statement the cursor is currently in, whereupon it enters Break mode. Typically, you'll want to position the cursor thoughtfully before invoking this command.

The Locals Window

The Locals window provides a quick readout of the value and type of all expressions in the active procedure via a collapsible tree view (see Figure 18.5). The Expression column displays the name of each expression, listed under the name of the procedure in which it appears. The Value column displays the current value of the expression (including Empty if the expression is empty, or Null or Nothing as appropriate). And the Type column displays the data type of the expression, with Variants listed as

"Variant" along with their assigned data type (for example, "Variant/String" for a Variant assigned the String data type).

To display the Locals window, click the Locals Window button on the Debug toolbar or choose View ➤ Locals Window. To remove the Locals window, click its close button.

Use the Locals window to see at a glance all the expressions in the active procedure.

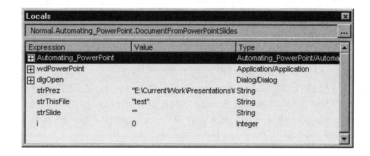

From the Locals window, you can also click the button marked with an ellipsis (...) to display the Call Stack dialog box, which I'll discuss in the "The Call Stack Dialog Box" section later in the chapter.

The Watch Window

The Watch window (identified as Watches in Figure 18.6) is a separate window that you use to track the values of variables and expressions as your code executes. To display the Watch window, click the Watch Window button on the Debug toolbar or choose View ➤ Watch Window in the Visual Basic Editor. To hide the Watch window again, click its close button (clicking the Watch Window button or choosing View ➤ Watch Window again doesn't hide it).

Use the Watch window to track the values of variables and expressions in your code.

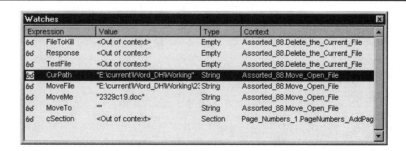

The Watch window displays *watch expressions*—expressions you set ahead of time to give you a running display of the value of a variable or an expression. This information allows you to pinpoint where an unexpected value for a variable or an expression occurs as your code executes. The Watch window lists the names of the watched expressions or variables in the Expression column, their values in the Value column, their type (Integer, Byte, String, Long, and so on) in the Type column, and their context (the module and procedure in which they're operating) in the Context column. So to track the value of a given variable, you need only look at the Watch window at any given point while in Break mode.

NOTE If a variable or expression listed in the Watch window hasn't been initialized, the Watch window will display "<Out of Context>" in the Value column, and "Empty" (for a variable other than a Variant) or "Variant/Empty" (for a Variant) in the Type column.

The Visual Basic Editor updates all watch expressions in the Watch window whenever you enter Break mode and whenever you execute a statement in the Immediate window (more on this window in the next section). So if you step through a procedure in the code window by using the F8 key (which keeps you in Break mode), you can watch the value of a variable or an expression as each statement executes. This is a great way to pinpoint where an error or an unexpected value occurs—and much easier than moving the mouse over each variable or expression in question to check its value by using the Auto Data Tips feature.

Before you can display a variable in the Watch window, you need to declare it (otherwise the Visual Basic Editor will respond with a "Variable not created in this context" error). This is another good reason for declaring variables explicitly at the beginning of a procedure rather than declaring them implicitly in mid-procedure.

Because watch expressions slow down execution of your code, the Visual Basic Editor doesn't save them with the code—you need to place them separately for each editing session. The Visual Basic Editor stores watch expressions during the current editing session, so you can move from procedure to procedure without losing your watch expressions.

Setting Watch Expressions

To set a watch expression, add it to the list in the Watch window:

1. Select the variable or expression in your code, or just position the insertion point in it. (This is an optional step, but I recommend it.)

2. Right-click in the Code window or the Watch window and choose Add Watch from the context menu, or choose Debug ➤ Add Watch, to display the Add Watch dialog box (see Figure 18.7). If you selected a variable or an expression in Step 1, it will appear in the Expression text box.

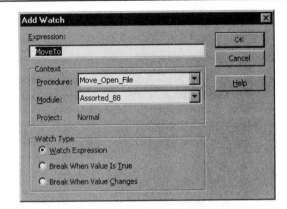

3. If necessary, change the variable or expression in the Expression text box, or enter a variable or an expression if you didn't select one in Step 1.

4. If necessary, adjust the settings in the Context group box. The Procedure drop-down list will be set to the current procedure, and the Module drop-down list will be set to the current module.

5. In the Watch Type group box, adjust the option button setting if necessary:

   • The default setting—Watch Expression—adds the variable or expression in the Expression text box to the list in the Watch window.

   • Break When Value Is True causes VBA to enter Break mode whenever the value of the variable or expression changes to True.

   • Break When Value Changes causes VBA to enter Break mode whenever the value of the watch expression changes. Use this setting when dealing either with a watch expression whose value you don't expect to change but which appears to be changing, or with a watch expression whose every change you need to observe.

TIP The Break When Value Is True option button allows you to run your code without stepping through each statement that doesn't change the value of the watch expression to True. The Break When Value Changes option button allows you to run your code and stop with each change of the value.

6. Click the OK button to add the watch expression to the Watch window.

 TIP You can also drag a variable or an expression from the Code window to the Watch window; doing so sets a default watch expression in the current context. To set Break When Value Is True or Break When Value Changes, you need to edit the watch expression after dragging it to the Watch window.

Editing Watch Expressions

To edit a watch expression, right-click it in the Watch window and choose Edit Watch from the context menu or select it in the Watch window and choose Debug ➤ Edit Watch. Either action will display the Edit Watch dialog box with the watch expression selected in the Expression box, as shown in Figure 18.8. Change the context or watch type for the watch expression by using the settings in the Context group box and the Watch Type group box, and then click the OK button to apply your changes.

FIGURE 18.8

You can edit your watch expressions in the Edit Watch dialog box.

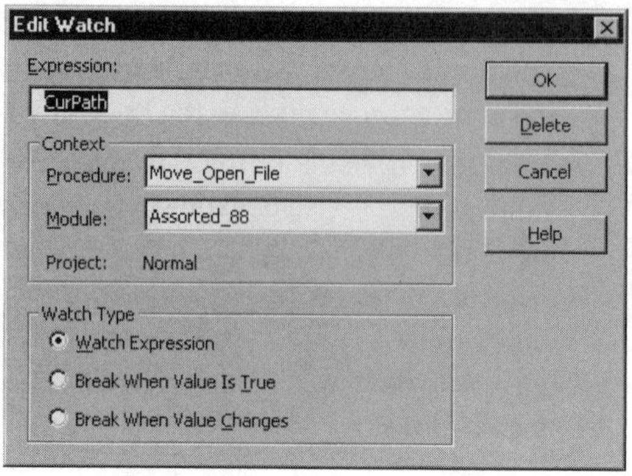

Deleting Watch Expressions

To delete a watch expression, right-click it in the Watch window and choose Delete Watch from the context menu. You can also delete the current watch expression by clicking the Delete button in the Edit Watch dialog box.

Using the Quick Watch Feature

For times when you don't want to create a watch expression for an expression or a variable, you can use the Quick Watch feature, which displays the Quick Watch dialog box (see Figure 18.9) containing the context and value of the selected expression. To use Quick Watch, select the expression or variable in the Code window and then either click the Quick Watch button on the Debug toolbar, choose Debug ➢ Quick Watch, or press Shift+F9. (If you're already working in the Quick Watch dialog box, you can click the Add button to add the expression to the Watch window.)

Use the Quick Watch dialog box to get quick information on a variable or expression for which you don't want to set a watch expression in the Watch window.

The Immediate Window

You met the Immediate window briefly in Chapter 4, where you used it to execute sample statements quickly without troubling yourself to create full procedures. You'll remember that you can use the Immediate window as a virtual scratchpad to enter lines of code that you want to test without entering them in the procedure itself, or to display information to help you check the values of variables while a procedure is executing. In the first case, you enter code in the Immediate window; in the second, you use statements entered in the Code window to display information in the Immediate window, where you can easily view it.

To display the Immediate window, click the Immediate Window button on the Debug toolbar, choose View ➢ Immediate Window, or press Ctrl+G. To hide the Immediate window again, click its close button. (Clicking the Immediate Window button, choosing View ➢ Immediate Window, or pressing Ctrl+G when the Immediate window is displayed doesn't hide the Immediate window.)

You can execute code in the Immediate window in both Break mode and Design mode.

What You Can't Do in the Immediate Window

There are a number of restrictions on the code you can use in the Immediate window:

- You can't use declarative statements (such as Dim, Private, Public, Option Explicit, Static, or Type) or control-flow statements (such as GoTo, Sub, or Function). These statements will cause VBA to throw an "Invalid in Immediate Pane" error.

- You can't use multi-line statements (such as block If statements or block For...Next statements) because there's no logical connection between statements on different lines in the Immediate window: Each line is treated in isolation. You can get around this limitation by entering block If statements on a single line, separating the statements with colons (not generally a good idea, because they become hard to read), and using the line-continuation character (the underscore) to break the resulting long lines onto two physical lines (while keeping them as one logical line). For example, the following statement works in the Immediate window as a single line, although it wouldn't work as a block If:

```
If X < Y Then : MsgBox "X is smaller than Y." : GoTo _
    End : Else : MsgBox "X is greater than Y." : End If
```

- You can't place breakpoints in the Immediate window.

Entering Code in the Immediate Window

The Immediate window supports a number of standard Windows key combinations, such as Ctrl+X (Cut), Ctrl+C (Copy), Ctrl+V (Paste), Ctrl+Home (move the insertion point to the start of the window), Ctrl+End (move the insertion point to the end of the window), Delete (delete the current selection), and Shift+F10 (display the context menu).

The Immediate window also supports the following Visual Basic Editor keystrokes and key combinations:

- F5 continues running a procedure.
- Alt+F5 runs the error-handler code for the current procedure.
- F8 single-steps through code (executing one statement at a time).
- Shift+F8 procedure-steps through code (executing one procedure at a time).
- Alt+F8 steps into the error handler for the current procedure.
- F2 displays the Object Browser.

Finally, the Immediate window has a couple of peculiar commands that you need to know:

- Pressing Enter runs the current line of code. (OK, so you knew this already.)
- Pressing Ctrl+Enter inserts a carriage return.

Printing Information to the Immediate Window

As well as entering statements in the Immediate window for quick testing, you can include in your procedures statements to print information to the Immediate window by using the `Print` method of the `Debug` object. Printing like this provides you with a way of viewing information as a procedure runs without having to be in Break mode or having to display a message box or dialog box that stops execution of the procedure.

The syntax for the `Print` method is as follows:

```
Debug.Print [outputlist]
```

outputlist is an optional argument specifying the expression or expressions to print. You'll almost always want to include *outputlist*—if you don't, the `Print` method prints a blank line, which is of little use to anyone alive. Construct your *outputlist* using the following syntax:

```
[Spc(n) | Tab(n)] expression
```

Here, `Spc(n)` inserts space characters and `Tab(n)` inserts tab characters, with *n* being the number of spaces or tabs to insert. Both are optional arguments, and for simple output, you'll seldom need to use them.

expression is an optional argument specifying the numeric expression or String expression to print:

- To specify multiple expressions, separate them with either a space or a semicolon.

- A Boolean value will print as either `True` or `False` (as appropriate).

- If *outputlist* is Empty, `Print` won't print anything. If *outputlist* is `Null`, `Print` will print `Null`.

- If *outputlist* is an error, `Print` prints it as `Error` *errorcode*, where *errorcode* is the code specifying the error.

As an example, you could log the contents of the String expressions `CustName`, `Address1`, `Address2`, `City`, `State`, and `Zip` to the Immediate window in an address format by using the following statements:

```
Debug.Print CustName
Debug.Print Address1 & ", " & Address2
Debug.Print City & ", " & State & " " & Zip
```

As another example, the following procedure prints the names and paths of all open drawings in AutoCAD to the Immediate window:

```
Sub Debug_Print_All_Doc_Names()
    Dim doc As AcadDocument
```

```
        For Each doc In Documents
            Debug.Print doc.FullName
        Next
    End Sub
```

The Call Stack Dialog Box

When working in Break mode, you can summon the Call Stack dialog box (see Figure 18.10) to display a list of the active *procedure calls*—the procedures being called by the current procedure. When you begin running a procedure, that procedure is added to the call stack list in the Call Stack dialog box. If that procedure then calls another procedure, the name of the second procedure is added to the call stack list for as long as the procedure takes to execute; it's then removed from the list. By using the Call Stack dialog box, you can find out what procedures are being called by another procedure; this can help you establish which parts of your code you need to check for errors.

FIGURE 18.10

Use the Call Stack dialog box to see a list of the procedures that are being called by the current procedure.

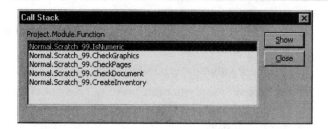

To display the Call Stack dialog box, click the Call Stack button on the Debug toolbar, press Ctrl+L, or select View ➢ Call Stack. To display one of the procedures listed in the Call Stack dialog box, select it in the Project.Module.Function list box and click the Show button. To close the Call Stack dialog box, click its Close button.

Dealing with Infinite Loops

You shouldn't find it hard to tell when a procedure gets stuck in an infinite loop: You'll notice that the procedure simply doesn't stop executing. To interrupt an infinite loop, press Ctrl+Break; this will display a "Code execution has been interrupted" dialog box.

There are several ways to guarantee getting stuck in infinite loops, such as using GoTo statements without If conditions or Do loops without While or Until constraints.

These are easy enough to avoid, but even if you do, it's still possible for infinite loops to occur in your code because of conditions you haven't been able to anticipate.

The best way to approach detecting and eliminating an infinite loop is to use breakpoints or a watch expression to pinpoint where the procedure enters the infinite loop. Once you've reached it, you can use the Step Into command to step into the procedure. Then use the Watch window or the Locals window to observe the variable and expressions in the loop, which should give you an indication of when something is going wrong and causing the loop to be endless.

If your code contains a loop that should execute only a set number of times but which you suspect is running endlessly, you can use a counter in the loop with either an Exit For statement or an Exit Do statement (whichever is appropriate) to exit the loop if it runs more than a certain number of times.

Dealing with Runtime Errors

Despite the help that VBA provides in eliminating language errors and compile errors, runtime errors remain an unpleasant fact of life. Sooner or later, you're inevitably going to get errors in your code, but you don't have to take them lying down. VBA enables you to write *error handlers*, which are pieces of code that trap errors, analyze them, and take action if they match given error codes.

When Should You Write an Error Handler?

Consider writing an error handler in the following circumstances:

- When a runtime error can cause your code to fail disastrously. For a procedure that tweaks a couple of objects on a slide in PowerPoint, you're unlikely to need an error handler; for a procedure that creates, deletes, or moves files, you'll probably want an error handler.

- When you can identify particular errors that are likely to occur and that can be trapped. For example, when the user tries to open a file, certain errors can occur—such as if the file doesn't exist; is currently in use by another computer; or is on a network drive, floppy drive, CD-ROM drive, or removable drive that isn't available at the time. You'll also run into errors if the user tries to use a printer or other remote device (say, a scanner or a digital camera) that's not present, connected, powered up, and configured correctly. Similarly, any procedure that deals with a particular object in a document (for example, a chart in Excel or a 3D solid object in AutoCAD) will run into trouble if that object is not present or not available.

NOTE In some instances, you may find it simpler to trap a resulting error from a procedure than to anticipate and try to forestall the various conditions that might lead to the generation of the error. For example, instead of checking to make sure a file existed before you tried to open it or manipulate it, you could trap any error that resulted if the file didn't exist.

Trapping an Error

Trapping an error means catching it so that you can do something about it. Usually, you'll want to prevent an error from stopping your VBA code, but you can also anticipate particular errors and use them to determine a suitable course of action to follow from the point at which they occur.

To trap an error, you use the On Error statement. The usual syntax for On Error is as follows:

```
On Error GoTo line
```

Here, `line` is a label specifying the line to which execution is to branch when a runtime error occurs. For example, to branch to the label named ErrorHandler, you could use a structure like this:

```
Sub ErrorDemo()
    On Error GoTo ErrorHandler
    'statements here
ErrorHandler:
    'error-handler statements here
End Sub
```

The label you use to identify the error handler can be named with any valid label name—you don't have to call it ErrorHandler or anything similar. Some people find that a descriptive label (perhaps one that identifies the type or types of error expected, such as HandleErrorNoFileOpen) is clearer in the long run than a generic name; others prefer to go with a generic name (such as HandleErr) for most or all of their error handlers. Your mileage *will* vary.

Usually, you'll want to place the error trap early in a procedure so that it's active and ready to trap errors for the rest of the procedure. If necessary, you can place several different error traps in a document by entering multiple On Error statements where they're needed—but only one can be enabled at a time. (*Enabled* means that an error trap has been switched on by an On Error statement. When an error occurs and execution branches to the error handler, that error handler is *active*.) Having multiple error handlers in a procedure can be useful when you're dealing with statements that require different types of action to be trapped. In the following structure, the first On Error statement directs execution to ErrorHandler1, and the second On Error statement directs execution to ErrorHandler2:

```
Sub ErrorDemo2()
    On Error GoTo ErrorHandler1
    'statements here
    On Error GoTo ErrorHandler2
    'statements here
ErrorHandler1:
    'statements for first error handler here
ErrorHandler2:
    'statements for second error handler here
End Sub
```

Each error handler is limited to the procedure in which it appears, so you can create different error handlers for different procedures and have each enabled in turn as the procedures run.

Because the error handler appears as code in the procedure, you need to make sure that it doesn't run when no error has occurred. You can do this by using either an Exit Sub statement before the error handler statement (to end execution of the procedure) or a GoTo statement that directs execution to a label beyond the error-handling code. The Exit Sub statement is better if you choose to place your error handler at the end of its procedure, which is standard practice and usually makes sense. The GoTo statement may prove easier to use if you choose to place your error handler elsewhere in the procedure.

 NOTE For a function, use an Exit Function statement; for a property, use an Exit Property statement.

The following example uses an Exit Sub statement to cause execution to end before the error handler if no error occurs:

```
Sub ErrorDemo3()
    On Error GoTo ErrorHandler
    'statements
    Exit Sub
ErrorHandler:
    'statements for error handler
End Sub
```

This next example uses a GoTo statement to skip the error handler—which is placed within the code of the procedure—unless an error occurs. When execution reaches the GoTo SkipErrorHandler statement, it branches to the SkipErrorHandler label, thus bypassing the code in the error handler:

```
Sub ErrorDemo4()
    On Error GoTo ErrorHandler
    'statements
    GoTo SkipErrorHandler
ErrorHandler:
    'statements for error handler
SkipErrorHandler:
    'statements
End Sub
```

I mentioned earlier than some people don't like GoTo statements for uses such as the second use here. Given that this GoTo statement makes the flow of the procedure a little harder to follow, you may be inclined to agree with them in this case. (The use of GoTo in the On Error statement is pretty much beyond reproach and unavoidable.)

Disabling an Error Trap

As I mentioned, an error trap works only for the procedure in which it appears, and VBA disables it when the code in the procedure has finished executing. You can also disable an error trap before the end of a procedure in which it appears by using the following statement:

```
On Error GoTo 0
```

You might want to disable an error trap while testing a procedure to enable yourself to pinpoint errors that occurred after a certain point while retaining error-trapping for the first part of the procedure.

Resuming after an Error

You use the Resume statement to resume execution of a procedure after trapping an error or handling an error with an error-handling routine. The Resume statement takes three forms: Resume, Resume Next, and Resume *line*.

Using a Resume Statement

Resume itself causes execution to resume with the line that caused the error. Use Resume with an error-handling routine that detects and fixes the problem that caused the offending statement to fail. For example, look at the error handler in Listing 18.1, which runs when VBA is unable to apply a specified style in Word.

Listing 18.1

```
1.   Sub StyleError()
2.
3.       On Error GoTo Handler
4.
5.       Selection.Style = "Executive Summary"
6.
7.       'the rest of the procedure happens here
8.
9.       'exit the procedure once execution gets this far
10.      Exit Sub
11.
12.  Handler:
13.
14.      If Err = 5834 Then
15.          ActiveDocument.Styles.Add _
                 Name:="Executive Summary", Type:=wdStyleTypeParagraph
16.          Resume
17.      End If
18.
19.  End Sub
```

Analysis

Here's how the StyleError procedure in Listing 18.1 works:

- Line 1 starts the procedure, and line 19 ends it. Lines 2, 4, 6, 8, 11, 13, and 18 are spacers.
- Line 3 uses an On Error statement to enable the imaginatively named error handler Handler, which is identified by the Handler label in line 12.
- Line 5 applies the style named Executive Summary to the current selection. If this operation succeeds, execution will continue at line 7, which in this example contains only a comment indicating that this is where the rest of the procedure would take place.
- Line 9 is a comment introducing line 10, which holds the Exit Sub statement to end execution of the procedure before the error handler.

- If the Selection.Style statement in line 5 causes an error, execution branches to the Handler label in line 12, and the error handler is activated. Line 14 compares the error value to 5834, the error that occurs if the specified style doesn't exist. If it matches, line 15 then adds the missing style to the document, and the Resume statement in line 16 causes execution to resume where the error occurred, on line 5. Because the specified style is now available, the Selection .Style statement will run without an error.

 TIP To find error numbers, either consult the "Errors" topic in the Help file or cause the error yourself and note the number and description in the resulting dialog box.

Using a *Resume Next* Statement

Resume Next causes execution to resume with the next statement after the statement that caused the error. You can use Resume Next in either of the following circumstances:

- With an error-handling routine that ignores the error and allows execution to continue without executing the offending statement
- As a straightforward On Error Resume Next statement that causes execution to continue at the next statement after the statement that caused an error, without using an error handler to fix the error

As an example of the first circumstance, if the style specified in the previous example wasn't available, you could use a Resume Next statement to skip applying it:

```
Sub StyleError2()

    On Error GoTo Handler

    Selection.Style = "Executive Summary"

    'the rest of the procedure happens here

    'exit the procedure once execution gets this far
    Exit Sub

Handler:
    Resume Next

End Sub
```

NOTE The descriptions of Resume and Resume Next apply if the error occurred in the procedure that contains the error handler. But if the error occurred in a different procedure from the procedure that contains the error handler, Resume causes execution to resume with the last statement to call out of the procedure that contains the error handler; Resume Next causes execution to resume with the statement *after* the last statement to call out of the procedure that contains the error handler.

Using a *Resume Line* Statement

Resume *line* causes execution to resume at the specified line. Use a label to indicate the line, which must be in the same procedure as the error handler.

For example, if a procedure tried to open a particular file, you could create a simple error handler that used a Resume *line* statement, as shown in Listing 18.2. This procedure works with Word, Visio, and AutoCAD.

Listing 18.2

```
1.  Sub Handle_Error_Opening_File()
2.
3.      Dim strFName As String
4.
5.  StartHere:
6.
7.      On Error GoTo ErrorHandler
8.      strFName = InputBox("Enter the name of the file to open.", _
            "Open File")
9.      If strFName = "" Then End
10.     Documents.Open strFName
11.     Exit Sub
12.
13. ErrorHandler:
14.
15.     If Err = 5174 Or _
            Err = 5121 Or _
            Err = -2032465466 Or _
            Err = -2145320924 _
            Then MsgBox _
            "The file " & strFName & " does not exist." & vbCr & _
```

```
                    "Please enter the name again.", _
                    vbOKOnly + vbCritical, "File Error"
16.         Resume StartHere
17.
18.   End Sub
```

Analysis

Here's how the Handle_Error_Opening_File procedure that comprises Listing 18.2 works:

- Line 1 starts the procedure, and line 18 ends it.

- Line 2 is a spacer. Line 3 declares the String variable strFName. Line 4 is another spacer.

- Line 5 contains the StartHere label, to which execution will return from the Resume statement in line 16. Line 6 is a spacer.

- Line 7 uses an On Error statement to enable the error handler ErrorHandler.

- Line 8 displays an input box prompting the user for the name of the file they want to open and stores the name in the variable strFName, which line 9 then tries to open. Line 10 checks strFName against an empty string and ends execution if it matches.

- If the file exists and can be opened, execution passes to line 11, where an Exit Sub statement exits the procedure, ending its execution. Otherwise, an error is generated, and execution branches to the ErrorHandler label in line 13, where the error handler becomes active.

- Line 14 is a spacer. Line 15 then compares the value of the error to 5174 (the error that occurs if VBA can't find the file), to 5121 (the error that occurs if the document name or path isn't valid in Word), to –2032465466 (the error that occurs if Visio can't open the document), and to –2145320924 (the automation error that occurs if AutoCAD can't open the document). If any of these comparisons matches, line 15 displays a message box advising the user of the error and prompting them to enter the correct file name.

- The Resume statement in line 16 then returns execution to the StartHere label in line 5. Line 17 is a spacer.

TIP   For some procedures, you may want to build in a counter mechanism to prevent the user from repeating the same error endlessly because they don't grasp what's wrong. By incrementing the counter variable each time the error handler is invoked and checking the resulting number, you can choose to take a different action after a number of unsuccessful attempts to execute a particular action.

 WARNING   You can't use a Resume statement anywhere other than in an error-handling routine (or an On Error Resume Next statement). (If you do, VBA produces an error.)

Getting the Description of an Error

To see the description of an error, return the Description property of the Err object:

```
MsgBox Err.Description
```

Error messages tend to be terse, cryptic, and of less help to the end user than to the people who built VBA and the application in question. Think twice before displaying one of these error messages to an end user. Usually, you'll get much better results by displaying a more verbose error message of your own devising that explains in more normal English what the problem is—and, preferably, what (if anything) the user can do to solve it.

Raising Your Own Errors

As part of your testing, you'll often need to cause errors so that you can see how well your error handler handles them.

To cause an error, use the Raise method of the Err object, specifying only the *number* argument. *number* is a Long argument giving the number of the error that you want to cause. For example, the following statement raises error 5121:

```
Err.Raise 5121
```

Suppressing Alerts

Many of the procedures you build will use message boxes or dialog boxes to allow the user to choose options for the procedure. In Word, Excel, and Project, you can use the DisplayAlerts property of the Application object to suppress the display of message boxes and errors while a procedure is running. In Excel and Project, `DisplayAlerts` is a read/write Boolean property that can be `True` to display alerts and `False` to suppress them. In Word, `DisplayAlerts` can be set to `wdAlertsNone` (0) to suppress alerts and message boxes, `wdAlertsMessageBox` (-2) to suppress alerts but display message boxes, or `wdAlertsAll` (-1, the default) to display all alerts and message boxes.

Unlike the `ScreenUpdating` property, which resets itself to `True` when a procedure that has set it to `False` stops running, `DisplayAlerts` is a sticky setting. You need to set `DisplayAlerts` explicitly back to one of four things: to `True` or to `wdAlertsAll` when you want to see alerts again after setting it to `False`; to `wdAlertsNone`; or to `wdAlerts-MessageBox`.

Handling User Interrupts in Word, Excel, and Project

Errors may seem quite enough of a problem, but you also need to decide what will happen if a user tries to interrupt your code by pressing Ctrl+Break while it's executing. Word, Excel, and Project offer you three options:

- You can allow a user interrupt to stop your code dead in the water. This is the easy way to proceed (and, as the default condition, needs no effort on your part), but in complex procedures, it may cause problems.

- You can prevent user interrupts by disabling user input while the procedure is running. This is simple to do, but you run the risk of creating unstoppable code if a procedure enters an endless loop.

- As a compromise between the first two options, you can allow user interrupts during certain parts of a procedure and prevent user interrupts during more critical parts of a procedure.

Disabling User Input while a Procedure Is Running

To disable user input while a procedure is executing, disable the Ctrl+Break key combination by setting the `EnableCancelKey` property of the `Application` object to `wdCancelDisabled` (in Word), `xlDisabled` (in Excel), or `pjDisabled` (in Project):

```
Application.EnableCancelKey = wdCancelDisabled
Application.EnableCancelKey = xlDisabled
Application.EnableCancelKey = pjDisabled
```

VBA will automatically enable user input again when the procedure stops executing. You can also enable user input again during a procedure by setting the `EnableCancelKey` property to wdCancelInterrupt (in Word), xlInterrupt (in Excel), or pjInterrupt (in Project):

```
Application.EnableCancelKey = wdCancelInterrupt
Application.EnableCancelKey = xlInterrupt
Application.EnableCancelKey = pjInterrupt
```

Excel and Project offer a third setting, xlErrorHandler and pjErrorHandler (respectively), that trap the Ctrl+Break keystroke as error 18. You can deal with this error as you would any other error. Here's a quick example:

```
Sub CancelKey_Example()
    Dim i As Long
    On Error GoTo Handel
    Application.EnableCancelKey = pjErrorHandler
    For i = 1 To 100000000
        Application.StatusBar = i
    Next i
Handel:
    If Err.Number = 18 Then
        If MsgBox("Do you want to stop the procedure?" _
            & vbCr & vbCr & "If not, stop pressing Ctrl+Break!", _
            vbYesNo + vbCritical, "User Interrupt Detected") = vbYes _
            Then End
    End If
End Sub
```

Disabling User Input While Part of a Procedure Is Running

You might want to temporarily disable user input while a procedure was executing a procedure that didn't bear interruption and then re-enable user input when it was safe for the user to stop the procedure again. For example, in a procedure whose actions included moving a number of files from one folder to another, you could prevent the code that executed the move operations from being interrupted so that the user couldn't stop the procedure with some files still in the source folder and some in the destination folder. Here's an example using Word:

```
'interruptible actions up to this point
Application.EnableCancelKey = wdCancelDisabled
For i = 1 to LastFile
    SourceFile = Source & "\Section" & i
```

```
            DestFile = Destination & "\Section" & i
            Name SourceFile As DestFile
    Next i
    Application.EnableCancelKey = wdCancelInterrupt
    'interruptible actions after this point
```

 WARNING Never disable user input for any code that may get stuck in an endless loop. If you do, you'll have to close down the program from the Close Program dialog box in Windows 9x (reached by pressing Ctrl+Alt+Delete) or the Task Manager in NT or Windows 2000. Doing so will cause you to lose any unsaved work in the application and might cause other applications to crash in Windows 9x. In NT or Windows 2000, other applications should be protected by the operating system.

Documenting Your Code

You can greatly simplify debugging your procedures by documenting your code. The best way to document your code is to add comments to it, either as you create the code or when you've finished creating it.

I recommend documenting your code as you create it in any procedure in which you're exploring your way and trying different methods to reach your goal. Add comments to explain what action each group of statements is trying to achieve. Once you've gotten the procedure to work, you can plow through the code and rip out abortive efforts wholesale, using the comments to identify which sections are now useless and which are still worthwhile, and leaving only the comments that are relevant to how the remaining code functions. (You might also want to leave comment lines on any methods of achieving the same goal that you decided not to use. For example, if you think that you might be able to rewrite a procedure to run a little faster when you have a few hours and some brain cells to spare, you could make a note of that. You could also note other possible applications for parts of the code in this procedure to help you locate it if you need to reuse it in another procedure.)

Likewise, add comments when you're changing an existing procedure so that you don't lose track of your changes. Once you've got the procedure working to your liking, remove any unnecessary comments and reword any verbose or unclear comments.

On the other hand, documenting your code when you've finished writing it allows you to enter only the comment lines that you want to be there permanently. This is the way to go when you're fairly sure of the direction of your code when you start writing the procedure, and the procedure needs only a few pointers to make its code clear once it's complete.

To document your code, use comments prefaced by either the apostrophe character (') or the Rem keyword (short for *remark*). You can comment out either a whole line or part of a line: Anything to the right of the apostrophe or the Rem keyword is commented out. For partial lines, the apostrophe is usually the better character to use; if you choose to use the Rem keyword, you need to add a colon before it to make it work consistently (some statements will accept a Rem without a colon at their end; others will generate a compile error):

```
Rem This is a comment line.
Documents.Add: Rem create a document based on Normal.dot
```

Generally, apostrophe-commented remarks separated by a few spaces or tabs from any statement the line contains (as in the second line below) are easier to read than comments using Rem:

```
'This is a comment line
Documents.Add     'create a document based on Normal.dot
```

If that was an eyebrow (or a finger) I saw you raising when I mentioned documenting your code, let me guess what you're thinking: You don't need to document your code because you'll be able to remember what it does. Trust me: You won't, not once you've written a good number of procedures. Coming back to a procedure six months after writing it, you'll find it as unfamiliar as if someone else had written it. And if you've advanced in your usage of VBA, you may even find it hard to think back down to the clumsy methods you were using at that time.

Most programmers have a distinct aversion to documenting their code; in some, the distaste is almost pathological. You can see why: When you're writing the code, documenting what it does slows you down and distracts you from your purpose; and when the code works, documenting it is tedious work. Besides, anyone worth their salt should be able to read the code and see what it does... shouldn't they?

Maybe so, but consider this: First, it's likely that you won't always be the person working on your code—at times, others will work on it too, and they'll appreciate all the help they can get in understanding your code. Second, the code on which you work won't always be your own—you may at times have to debug code that others have written, and in this case *you'll* be the one in need of comments.

Another way to come out smelling like roses to your colleagues is to build procedures that behave well toward their users. That's up next, whenever you can muster the enthusiasm to turn the page.

CHAPTER <u>19</u>

Building Well-Behaved Procedures

O nce you've built a procedure that works consistently, you'll probably want to distribute it to as many of your coworkers as might possibly be able to use it, or at least to those whom your imagination or industry might impress. Before you distribute it, though, you should make sure that the procedure is as civilized as possible in its interaction with the user and with the settings the user may have chosen on their computer. It's all too easy to distribute an apparently successful procedure that runs roughshod over the user's preferences, or one that fails unexpectedly under certain circumstances. In this chapter, you'll look at how to avoid such problems and how to construct your procedures so that the user will have no problem interacting with them.

Given that this book discusses seven applications, this chapter will necessarily be general in nature—more of an extended homily on the virtues (and rewards) of thoughtfulness than a slew of examples. I'll be trusting you to apply the principles I mention to the application you're working with.

What Is a Well-Behaved Procedure?

Briefly put, a well-behaved procedure is one that leaves no trace of its actions beyond those that the user expected it to perform. This means:

- Making no detectable changes to the user environment, or restoring the previous settings if the procedure needs to make changes (for example, in order to run successfully).

- Presenting the user with relevant choices for the procedure and relevant information once the procedure has finished running.

- Showing or telling the user what is happening while the procedure is running.

- Making sure (if possible) that the procedure is running on the appropriate item (before it does so).

- Anticipating or trapping errors wherever possible so that the procedure doesn't crash; or if it does crash under exceptional circumstances, doing so as gracefully as possible and minimizing damage to the user's work.

- Leaving the user in the optimal position to continue their work after the procedure finishes executing.

- Cleaning up any scratch documents, folders, or other detritus that the procedure creates in order to perform its duties.

If you stop for a moment, you can probably think of a couple of examples in which your favorite application (or should I say your most frequently used application?) doesn't exactly conform to everything on this list. For example, do you use Word? Then you'll know that if you press the Page Up key once and then the Page Down key once when working in a document, the selection (the insertion point) doesn't always return to the same exact point in the document as it should. It's hard to find this behavior impressive—or useful.

Such weaknesses in commercial applications' interfaces provoke two main reactions among developers. The first reaction is an assumption that if the user is accustomed to putting up with needless bouts with tediousness, such as having to reposition the selection or change the view when they shouldn't need to, they're unlikely to have a problem with having to perform similar actions after running a procedure—particularly a procedure that saves them a goodly chunk of time and effort. The second reaction is an impressive (if overzealous) determination to restore the user environment absolutely perfectly even if major software corporations seem incapable of producing software that itself can do so.

As you'd imagine, the first approach tends to be more economical in its code, and the second more inventive. To get your work done and retain your sanity, you'll probably want to steer a course between the two extremes.

Retaining or Restoring the User Environment

For the most part, your procedures should be able to run without unduly disturbing the user environment—but if you do need to make changes in the user environment, restore it as closely as possible to its previous state. Here are a couple of examples of such changes:

- In Word: changing the revision-marking (Track Changes) setting, so that you could change the text without the changes being marked as revisions.

- In Word, WordPerfect, or Project: changing the view to a more suitable view so that you could perform certain operations.

- In any application that lets you manipulate its Find and Replace features: using the Find and Replace features to identify and/or manipulate parts of a document, then restoring the user's last search (and replace, if necessary) so that they can perform it again seamlessly.

To store such information, you can use private variables, public variables, or custom objects as appropriate.

Leaving the User in the Best Position to Continue Work

After your procedure finishes running, the user needs to be in the best possible position to continue their work. What exactly the best possible position entails depends on the situation—and no, the best position is *never* upside down in a midden heap—but here are three simple suggestions:

- Usually, you'll want to leave the user facing the same document they were working on when they started running the procedure. There are some obvious exceptions to this, such as when the procedure creates a new document for the user and the user is expecting to work in it; but the general principle is sound.

- If the document is essentially untouched (at least from the user's point of view), the selection should probably be back where it was when the user started running the procedure. To restore the selection, you may want to define a range at the beginning of the procedure, and then move the selection back to it at the end of the procedure. In some applications, you could also use a bookmark or a named range—but if you do, be sure to remove it afterward.

- If the procedure has created a new object in the document, and the user will be expecting to work with it, you may want to have that object selected at the end of the procedure.

Keeping the User Informed during the Procedure

A key component of a successful procedure is keeping the user adequately informed throughout the process. In a simple procedure, adequate information may entail nothing beyond a lucid description in the procedure's Description field to assure the user that they're choosing the right procedure from the Macros dialog box. In a more complex procedure, adequate information will also be much more complex: You may need to display a starting message box or dialog box, show information on the status bar during the procedure, display an ending message box, or create a log file of information so that the user has a record of what took place during execution of the procedure.

The first consideration, though, is whether to disable user input during the procedure. In Word, Excel, and Project, you can disable user input to protect sensitive sections of your procedures by setting the EnableCancelKey property of the Application object to wdCancelDisabled. When you do so, you may want to indicate to the user at the beginning of the procedure that input will be disabled, and explain why.

To keep the user informed about other aspects of the procedure, you have several options, which I'll discuss in the following sections. But first, let's look at how you can *hide* information from the user (and the reasons for doing so) by disabling screen updating in Word and Excel.

Disabling Screen Updating

Word and Excel let you disable screen updating—that is, stop the redrawing of the information in the document area. (The other parts of the application window—the title bar, command bars, status bar, scroll bars, and so on—continue to update, but these items are usually relatively static compared to the document area and so don't take much updating. Still, if you change the size of the application window or the document window, you'll see that change even with screen updating disabled.)

There are two advantages to disabling screen updating:

- First, you can speed up the running of your procedures quite significantly, particularly on computers that have slow graphics cards. This speed improvement applies especially to procedures that cause a lot of changes to the on-screen display. For example, suppose a procedure in Word strips a certain type of information out of the current document, pastes it into a new document, creates a table out of it, and applies functional formatting to the table. Your computer will expend a fair amount of effort updating what's appearing on the monitor. This is wasted effort if the user isn't hanging on every operation, so you might as well turn off screen updating.

- Second, you can hide from the user any parts of the procedure that you don't want them to see. This sounds totalitarian, but it's usually more like a cross between benevolent dictatorship and public television: You shouldn't see certain things because they might upset you, and there's a lot that you don't *really* need to know about. So with VBA: If the user doesn't know about the operations that a procedure will routinely perform to achieve certain effects, they may be surprised or dismayed by what they see on-screen. For example, in a procedure that moves an open file, you might want to hide from the user the fact that the procedure closes the open file, moves it, and then reopens the file from its new location. By disabling screen updating, you can achieve this effect.

The major disadvantage to disabling screen updating is that—as you might imagine—doing so prevents the user from seeing information that might be useful to them. In the worst case, the user might assume from the lack of activity on-screen that either the procedure has entered an endless loop or the computer has hung; and so they might try to stop the procedure by pressing Ctrl+Break or shake up Windows by pressing Ctrl+Alt+Delete until they get a reaction.

To forestall the user from disrupting a procedure or an application with a two- or three-finger salute, it's a good idea to warn them in advance that a procedure will disable screen updating. For instance, you might mention the fact in a message box at the beginning of the procedure, or you might display a dialog box that allowed the user to choose whether to disable screen updating and have the procedure run faster or to leave screen updating on and have the procedure run at its normal speed with stunning visual effects.

If you don't display a message box or dialog box at the beginning of a procedure, you may want to display information on the status bar to tell the reader what's going during the procedure. (As I mentioned, Word and Excel update the status bar and the title bar of the application even if screen updating is turned off—at least, if the status bar and the title bar are visible.) To display information on the status bar, assign a suitable string to the StatusBar property of the Application object:

```
Application.StatusBar = _
    "Word is creating 38 new documents for you to edit. Please wait..."
```

Alternatively, you can disable screen updating for parts of a procedure and turn it back on, or refresh it, for other parts. Consider a procedure that creates and formats a number of documents from an existing document. If you turn off screen updating at the beginning of the procedure, and then refresh it once each document has been created and formatted, the user will see each document in turn (which conveys the progress the procedure is making) without seeing the ugly details of the formatting. What's more, the procedure will run significantly faster than if the screen were showing all of the formatting taking place.

To turn off screen updating, set the ScreenUpdating property of the Application object to False:

```
Application.ScreenUpdating = False
```

To turn screen updating back on, set ScreenUpdating to True again:

```
Application.ScreenUpdating = True
```

In Word, to refresh the screen with the current contents of the video memory buffer, use the ScreenRefresh method of the Application object:

```
Application.ScreenRefresh
```

Manipulating the Cursor

One party trick you may want to try with Word and Excel for more involved procedures is manipulating the cursor. You won't need to do this for many procedures, because VBA automatically displays the busy (hourglass) cursor while a procedure is running and then restores a normal cursor when it has finished. On special occasions, however, you may need or want to set the cursor manually.

 WARNING After using computers for even a few months, users tend to develop almost Pavlovian reactions to the cursor, with the busy cursor signifying (in ascending order) a momentary breather (or a slow computer), a chance to grab a cup of coffee or bug a colleague, or the onset of panic that the computer has hung before they've saved the last three hours of work. You usually won't want to mess with these reactions. So it's a great mistake to display an I-beam cursor or "normal" cursor when the system is in fact busy—or to display a busy cursor after the procedure has in fact finished running.

Word implements the cursor via the `System` object. To manipulate the cursor, you set the `Cursor` property. This is a read/write Long property that can be set to the following values: wdCursorIBeam (1) for an I-beam cursor; wdCursorNormal (2) for a normal cursor, wdCursorNorthWestArrow (3) for a left-angled resizing arrow (pointing up); and wdCursorWait (0) for the busy cursor. The exact appearance of the cursor will depend on the cursor scheme the user has selected.

For example, the following statement displays a busy cursor:

```
System.Cursor = wdCursorWait
```

Excel lets you manipulate the cursor through the `Cursor` property of the `Application` object. Cursor is a read/write Long property that can be set to the following values: xlDefault (-4143) for a default cursor, xlWait (2) for an hourglass cursor, xlNorthwestArrow (1) for the arrow pointing up and to the left, or xlIBeam (3) for an I-beam cursor.

For example, the following statement displays the hourglass cursor:

```
Application.Cursor = xlWait
```

 NOTE When you explicitly set the Cursor property of the Application object in Excel, remember to reset it to something appropriate before your code stops executing, because otherwise the cursor keeps its new expression just as if the wind had changed while it was pulling a face.

Displaying Information at the Beginning of a Procedure

At the beginning of many procedures, you'll probably want to display a message box or a dialog box. For this purpose, you'll typically use a Yes/No or OK/Cancel message box that tells the user what the procedure will do and gives them the chance to cancel the procedure without running it any further. A dialog box will usually present options for the procedure (for example, mutually exclusive options via option buttons or non-exclusive options via check boxes), allowing the user to enter information (via text boxes, list boxes, or combo boxes) and of course letting them cancel the procedure if they've cued it by accident. If you have time to create a Help file to accompany the procedures and user forms you create, you might add a Help button to each message box or dialog box, linking it to the relevant topic in the Help file.

 TIP As I mentioned earlier, you can also use a message box or dialog box to warn the user that the procedure is going to turn off screen updating. Likewise, if the procedure will disable user interrupts for part or all of its duration, warn the user about that, too.

Displaying Information in a Message Box or Dialog Box at the End of a Procedure

With some procedures, you'll find it useful to collect information on what the procedure is doing so that you can display that information to the user in a message box or dialog box when the procedure stops running. As you saw in Chapter 11, message boxes are easier to use but are severely limited in their capabilities for laying out text—you're limited to the effects you can achieve with spaces, tabs, carriage returns, and the occasional misformatted bullet. With dialog boxes, on the other hand, you can lay out text however you need to (by using labels or text boxes) and include images if gripped by a desire to do so.

The easiest way to collect information while running a procedure is to build one or more strings containing the information you want to display. For an example of this, look back to Listing 12.2 in Chapter 12, in which the cmdOK_Click procedure collects information while creating a series of folders and then displays a message box telling the user what it has done.

Creating a Log File

If you need to collect a lot of information during the course of running a procedure and either present it to the user once the procedure has finished, or just have it available for reference if needed, consider using a log file rather than a message box or dialog box. Log files are useful for lengthy procedures involving critical data: By writing information periodically to a log file (and by saving it frequently), you can keep a record of what the procedure achieved before any crash it suffered.

For example, say you wrote a procedure for Word that collected information from a variety of sources each day and wrote it into a report. You might want to keep a log file that tracked whether information from each source was successfully transferred, and at what time. Listing 19.1 provides an example of such a procedure. At the end of the procedure, you could leave the log file open so that the user could check whether the procedure was successful in creating the report, or leave the summary file open so that the user could read the report itself.

Listing 19.1

```
1.   Sub Create_Log_File()
2.
3.       Dim strDate As String
4.       Dim strPath As String
5.       Dim strCity(10) As String
6.       Dim strLogText As String
7.       Dim strLogName As String
8.       Dim strSummary As String
9.       Dim strFile As String
10.      Dim i As Integer
11.
12.      On Error GoTo Crash
13.
14.      strCity(1) = "Chicago"
15.      strCity(2) = "Toronto"
16.      strCity(3) = "New York"
17.      strCity(4) = "London"
18.      strCity(5) = "Lyons"
19.      strCity(6) = "Antwerp"
```

```
20.        strCity(7) = "Copenhagen"
21.        strCity(8) = "Krakow"
22.        strCity(9) = "Pinsk"
23.        strCity(10) = "Belgrade"
24.
25.        strDate = Month(Date) & "-" & Day(Date) & "-" _
               & Year(Date)
26.        strPath = "f:\Daily Data\"
27.        strLogName = strPath & "Reports\Log for " _
               & strDate & ".doc"
28.        strSummary = strPath & "Reports\Summary for " _
               & strDate & ".doc"
29.    Documents.Add
30.    ActiveDocument.SaveAs strSummary
31.
32.    For i = 1 To 10
33.        strFile = strPath & strCity(i) & " " & strDate & ".doc"
34.        If Dir(strFile) <> "" Then
35.            Documents.Open strFile
36.            Documents(strFile).Paragraphs(1).Range.Copy
37.            Documents(strFile).Close _
38.                SaveChanges:=wdDoNotSaveChanges
39.            With Documents(strSummary)
40.                Selection.EndKey Unit:=wdStory
41.                Selection.Paste
42.                .Save
43.            End With
44.            strLogText = strLogText & strCity(i) _
                   & vbTab & "OK" & vbCr
45.        Else
46.            strLogText = strLogText & strCity(i) _
                   & vbTab & "No file" & vbCr
47.        End If
48.    Next i
49.
50. Crash:
51.
52.    Documents.Add
```

```
53.        Selection.TypeText strLogText
54.        ActiveDocument.SaveAs strLogName
55.        Documents(strLogName).Close
56.        Documents(strSummary).Close
57.
58.    End Sub
```

Analysis

The procedure in Listing 19.1 creates a new document to contain a summary, opens a number of files in turn, copies the first paragraph out of each and pastes it into the summary document, and then closes the file. As it does this, it maintains a string of log information from which it creates a log file at the end of the procedure or if an error occurs during the procedure. Let's walk through the code:

- Lines 3 through 9 declare six String variables—strDate, strPath, strLogText, strLogName, strSummary, and strFile—and one String array, strCity, containing 10 items. (The procedure uses an Option Base 1 statement that doesn't appear in the listing, so strCity(10) produces 10 items in the array rather than 11.) Line 10 declares the Integer variable i, which the procedure will use as a counter.

- Line 11 is a spacer. Line 12 uses an On Error GoTo statement to start error handling and direct execution to the label Crash: in the event of an error. Line 13 is a spacer.

- Lines 14 through 23 assign the names of the putative company's 10 mythical offices to the strCity array. Line 24 is a spacer.

- Line 25 assigns to strDate a string created by concatenating the month, the day, and the year for the current date (with a hyphen between each part) by using the Month, Day, and Year functions, respectively. For example, January 21, 2000 will produce a date string of 1-21-2000. (The reason for creating a string like this is that Windows can't handle slashes in file names—slashes are reserved for indicating folders.)

- Line 26 sets strPath to the f:\Daily Data\ folder. Line 27 then builds a file name for the log file in the \Reports\ subfolder, and line 28 creates a file name for the summary file, also in the \Reports\ subfolder.

- Line 29 creates a new document based on Normal.dot, and line 30 saves this document under the name stored in the strSummary variable. Line 31 is a spacer.

- Line 32 begins a For... Next loop that runs from i = 1 to i = 10. Line 33 assigns to the String variable strFile the filename for the first of the cities stored in the strCity array: strPath & strCity(i) & " " & strDate & ".doc".

- Line 34 then begins an If statement that checks whether Dir(strFile) returns an empty string. If not, line 35 opens the document specified by strFile, line 36 copies its first paragraph, and line 37 closes it without saving changes. The procedure doesn't make any changes to the document, but if the document contains hot fields (such as date fields or links) that update themselves when the document is opened, it may have become dirty. Including the SaveChanges argument is cheap insurance against the user's getting an unexpected message box prompting them to save a document they know they haven't changed. (An alternative would be to set the Saved property of the document to True and then close it without using the SaveChanges argument.)

- Lines 39 through 43 contain a With statement that works with the Document object specified by strSummary. Line 40 uses the EndKey method with the Unit argument wdStory to move the selection to the end of the document. Line 41 pastes in the material copied from the document just opened, and line 42 saves the document. Line 43 ends the With statement.

- Line 44 adds to strLogText the contents of strCity(i), a tab, the text OK, and a carriage return, which will produce a simple tabbed list of the cities and the status of their reports.

- If the condition posed in line 34 isn't met, execution branches to the Else statement in line 45, and line 46 adds to strLogText the contents of strCity(i), a tab, No file, and a carriage return. Line 47 ends the If statement, and line 48 ends the For... Next loop, returning execution to line 32.

- Line 49 is a spacer. Line 50 contains the Crash: label and marks the start of the error handler. Unlike in many procedures, you don't want to stop execution before entering the error handler—as it happens, you want to execute these statements (to create the log file) even if an error occurs. Line 51 is a spacer.

- Line 52 creates a new document based on the default template, into which line 53 types the contents of strLogText and which line 54 saves under the name strLogName. Line 55 closes this new document (alternatively, you could leave the document open so that the user could view it). Line 56 closes the summary document (which has remained open since it was created; again, you might want to leave this open so that the user might view it, or offer the user the option of keeping it open). Line 57 is a spacer, and line 58 ends the procedure.

Making Sure the Procedure Is Running under Suitable Conditions

Another important element of creating a well-behaved procedure is to check that it's running under suitable conditions. This ideal is nearly impossible to achieve under all circumstances, but you should take some basic steps, such as the following:

- Make sure that a document is open in a procedure that needs a document to be open—otherwise, you'll get an error every time. For example, you might check the Count property of the Documents collection to make sure that at least one document is open:

```
If Documents.Count = 0 Then _
    MsgBox "This procedure will not run without a " _
    & "document open.", vbOKOnly + vbExclamation, _
    "No Document Is Open"
```

- Check that the procedure is running on an appropriate item, if the procedure has definable requirements. For example, in an Excel procedure that applies intricate formatting to a chart the user has selected, make sure that the user's victim is a chart. If it's any other object, you can bet VBA will get unhappy shortly.

- Make sure the document contains the element required by the procedure. (If it doesn't, you'll get an error.) Alternatively, trap the error that will result from the item's not being present.

Cleaning Up after a Procedure

It goes without saying that your procedures, like your children or housemates, should learn to clean up after themselves. This process involves the following:

- Undoing any changes that the procedure had to make to enable itself to run
- Closing any documents that no longer need to be open
- Removing any scratch files or folders that the procedure has created to achieve its effects

Undoing Changes the Procedure Has Made

In some (usually rare) cases, you'll need to make changes to a document in order to run a procedure successfully. Here are a couple of examples:

- In Word, you might need to apply some formatting to half of a table but not to the rest of it. In this case, it may be easier to split the table into two tables so that you can select columns in the relevant part and format or change them without affecting the columns in the other half of the original table. If you perform a procedure like this, you'll want to join the tables together again afterwards by removing the break you've inserted between the original table's two halves. The easiest way to do this is to bookmark the break that you insert; you can then go back to the bookmark and delete it and the break at the same time. Alternatively, you could use a Set statement to define a range for the break, and then return to the range and remove the break.

- In Excel, you may need to define named ranges in a workbook so that you can easily reference them from the code. (Usually, you'll do better to use ranges via VBA, which won't leave unwanted named ranges in the workbook.) Get rid of these named ranges when you're finished with them.

- In WordPerfect, you might need to add bookmarks to identify parts of the document for manipulation. Again, you should get rid of these bookmarks before the procedure stops.

- In Visio or AutoCAD, you may need to rearrange the layers of a drawing to enable the user to make interactive decisions while the procedure is running on items that would otherwise be hidden or obscured. Again, be good and put things back the way you found them.

Removing Scratch Files and Folders

During a complex procedure, you may need to create scratch files in which to temporarily store or manipulate information, or scratch folders in which to store files. For example, if you need to perform complex formatting on a few paragraphs of a long document, you may find it easier to copy and paste those paragraphs into a new blank document and manipulate them there than to continue working in the same document and risk unintentionally affecting other paragraphs as well. Likewise, in a drawing application, you might need to create a scratch drawing that you could use for temporary or backup storage of intricate objects.

Creating scratch files, while often necessary for the safe and successful operation of a procedure, is antisocial toward the user of the computer: You're cluttering up their drive with information that's probably of no use to them. Creating scratch folders in which to save the scratch files is even worse. Always go the extra distance to clean up any mess that you've made on the drive, and remove both scratch files and scratch folders that you've created. Before you ask—no, commercial applications don't always do this; and no, that doesn't let you off the hook.

If your procedure is going to remove any scratch files it creates, you may be tempted to conceal from the user their creation and subsequent deletion. This usually isn't a good idea—in most cases, the best thing is to warn the user that the procedure will create scratch files. You might even let the user specify or create a suitable folder for the scratch files, or present the user with a list that logs the files created and whether they were successfully deleted. Doing so will allow the user to safely remove any scratch files left on their computer if a procedure goes wrong or is interrupted during execution.

Another possibility is to use the API (application programming interface) commands `GetTempDir` and `GetTempFileName` to return the computer's temporary directory and a temporary filename that you can use. API calls aren't something I cover in this book (if you're interested, you might try *Visual Basic Developer's Guide to the Win32 API*, also from Sybex), but since I seem to have the pulpit, I can't resist the temptation to moralize a moment more. Just because you can identify the temporary directory, you're not licensed to fill it with files. If you can live by this rather obvious concept, you'll be ahead of a distressing number of commercial software developers....

Building a Scratch Folder

You can use a `MkDir` statement to create a folder. For example, the following statement creates a folder named `Scratch Folder` on the `C:` drive:

```
MkDir "c:\Scratch Folder"
```

Before creating a folder, check to see that the name isn't already in use; if a folder with that name already exists, VBA will throw an error. To check if a folder exists, use a `Dir` statement.

 TIP For temporary storage, you may want to build a folder name based on the date and time to lessen the chance that a folder with that name already exists. You might also use the `Rnd` function to generate a random number to use as part of the folder name.

Deleting the Scratch Folder

You can use the RmDir statement to remove an empty folder. (Make sure that the folder is empty first—otherwise RmDir will fail.) For example, the following statement removes the scratch folder named Scratch Folder on the C: drive:

```
RmDir "c:\Scratch Folder"
```

In the next chapter, I'll show you how to use VBA's security features to protect yourself against vicious code and identify your own code as being on the side of the angels.

CHAPTER **20**

Using VBA's Security Features

I n this chapter, I'll discuss how to use the security tools that VBA provides for distributing and implementing macros and VBA code. VBA security falls into three parts: securing your applications against rogue VBA code; establishing that your VBA code isn't itself rogue so that it can be run; and securing your code against theft, alteration, or snooping. Briefly, here's how each type of security works.

To secure an application against rogue VBA code, you choose the level of security that you want the application to use when running VBA code so that it will run only code from a trusted source. You can specify which sources to trust, and how well to trust them. I'm mentioning this security mechanism first, but you'll see it second in the chapter because the whole process is easier to grasp that way.

The obvious corollary to securing your applications against rogue code is being able to establish that your own code is okay for the applications to trust. You do this by signing a document or template project that contains customizations or macro project items (code modules, class modules, or user forms) with a digital signature generated by a digital certificate that uniquely identifies you or your company. I'll demonstrate this technique first in the chapter, because it sets the stage for specifying the level of security I just mentioned.

To secure your code, you can lock a macro project with a password so that nobody can open the code. Doing so serves both to prevent anyone from tinkering with your code and either stopping it from working or rendering it harmful, and to protect your intellectual property: If nobody can see your code, they can't steal your ideas. I'll discuss how to do this at the end of this chapter.

 NOTE Before getting started, you need to know that not all the applications discussed in this book support VBA's security features—so this chapter may not apply to what you're doing. For example, applications that use VBA 5 (such as AutoCAD 2000 and Visio Enterprise) do not support VBA security at this writing.

Signing Your Macro Projects with Digital Signatures

VBA provides a security mechanism for securing macro projects with digital signatures. The digital signatures provide a means of establishing the provenance of the projects, which can help alleviate (or exacerbate) concerns about the code the macro projects contain. If you trust the source of the code to produce benevolent code, you can open the project and run the code. If you suspect the source or the information of being malignant (or *know* either to be so), you can either avoid opening the project or open the project with the code disabled.

As for you, so for others: You'll need to sign your projects so that other people know where they come from and who created them. Once you've signed the projects, the code will then be available to any application that has specified you as a trusted source for macro projects. (This assumes they're using a Medium or High level of security in the application; I'll show you how you set the security level later in this chapter.)

In this section, I'll discuss what digital certificates are, what they mean in practical terms, how you get hold of them, and how you use them to create digital signatures.

 NOTE VBA's security mechanism is shared across the range of VBA-enabled applications on your computer. As you'd guess, the list of certificates and trusted sources is shared as well. So if you designate a trusted source from one application, all the other applications that support VBA security will trust that source as well. For example, if you open a document that contains code in WordPerfect and choose to trust the source of the code, Quattro Pro and Excel will also gain that trust and will open projects from that source without blinking an electronic eye.

What Is a Digital Certificate?

A *digital certificate* is essentially a piece of code that uniquely identifies its holder. You use your digital certificate to create a digital signature for a project. This project can be a document project, a template project, or an add-in. The project doesn't have to contain macros, procedures, user forms, or VBA code for you to sign it, although these contents are the usual reason for signing a project.

A digital signature applies to a whole macro project—typically, a document project or a template project. You can't apply a digital signature to just part of a project—say, just to one module of code or to one user form. Each macro project item in that macro project—each module, user form, class, and reference—is covered by the digital certificate.

This being a big world, various different technologies support digital certificates. Microsoft's technology is called Authenticode; it requires Internet Explorer 4 or later to work. Competing formats include Marimba Channel Signing and Netscape Object Signing; as you'd expect, they don't work with Microsoft applications. Because VBA is a Microsoft technology, you'll be working with Authenticode in this chapter. And because

Internet Explorer 5 is making a brave attempt to take over the world, the screens I show are from Internet Explorer 5 rather than Internet Explorer 4.

Getting a Digital Certificate

There are several types of digital certificates: those you create yourself, those you get from your company or organization, and those you get from a commercial certification authority. As you might imagine, a digital certificate you create yourself is of little use to people beyond you and those who trust you, whereas a certificate from a commercial certification authority should be good enough for anyone short of the NSA. A certificate issued by your company falls in the middle: The company will have gotten the certificate from the commercial certification authority, which means the commercial certification authority has established, to its satisfaction, that the company is trustworthy. Whom the company chooses to trust with the certificate is another matter, and introduces another link of complication into the chain of trust. For example, if IBM unwisely chose to entrust one of its digital certificates to Jane Random Hacker, and you knew Jane had a rap sheet as long as your leg, you wouldn't necessarily want to trust that certificate just because you know IBM's a big, reputable company that made your ThinkPad.

In the following sections, I'll briefly examine these different ways of getting a digital certificate. After that, you'll install the certificates.

Creating a Digital Certificate of Your Own

The quickest and easiest way of getting a digital certificate is to create one yourself. Microsoft Office 2000 and Corel WordPerfect Office 2000 both ship with a tool for creating your own digital certificates. To understand how digital certificates work, you'll probably want to create several of your own and practice with them on non-mission-critical files. By specifying some of your digital certificates as trusted and leaving others untrusted, you can get a clear idea of how digital certificates work without having to use suspect code on your system.

Here's how to create a digital certificate of your own:

1. Run the `SelfCert.exe` file from the CD. In Microsoft Office 2000, you'll find it in the `\PFiles\MSOffice\Office\` folder; in Corel WordPerfect Office 2000, you'll need to dig down to the `\Corel\Config\Redist\VBA6\PFiles\MSOffice\Office\` folder. The application will display the Create Digital Certificate dialog box, shown in Figure 20.1.

FIGURE 20.1

In the Create Digital Certificate dialog box, enter the name that you want the digital certificate to bear.

FIGURE 20.1

In the Create Digital Certificate dialog box, enter the name that you want the digital certificate to bear.

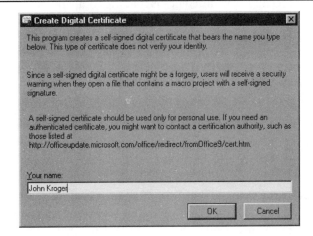

2. In the Your Name text box, enter the name that will appear on the digital certificate. As the name of the text box suggests, this might well be your own name; it might be your company's name; or—if the digital certificate is strictly for testing purposes—it might be a test name. If you want to practice with multiple certificates, you'll need a number of test names.

3. Click the OK button to create the certificate. The SelfCert application will create the certificate and display the SelfCert Success dialog box, as shown in see Figure 20.2.

FIGURE 20.2

The SelfCert Success dialog box appears, to tell you the certificate has been created.

Getting a Digital Certificate from Your Company

Your second option is to get a digital certificate from a digital certificate server that your company has. The details of this procedure will vary from company to company, so I won't try to go into it here. The key point is that the certificates the company provides via its digital certificate server are generated in the same fashion as the digital certificates distributed by the commercial certification authorities discussed in the next section. The difference is that the company distributes the certificates from a pool that it has been allocated, without needing to apply to the certification authority for each certificate as it's needed.

Getting a Digital Certificate from a Commercial Certification Authority

Your third choice is to get a digital certificate from a commercial certification authority, such as VeriSign, Equifax, or CyberTrust. To get the latest list of certificate authorities that provide certificates for use with Microsoft products, point your favorite browser at `http://www.microsoft.com/security/ca/ca.htm` and see what you find. Chances are, you'll recognize some of the names. For example, you may know (and love) Equifax as one of the Credit Report Troika that can make your credit and rental applications a joy or a misery, so you might want to see how well Equifax delivers on certificates. Then again, you may well have heard of VeriSign (`http://www.verisign.com`), which was spun off in 1995 from RSA Data Security, the company famous for the RSA public-key algorithm created by Rivest, Shamir, and Adleman. The choice is all yours, but make sure the company you select provides the type of certificate you need.

Several different types of certificate are available, depending on what you want to do. If you're creating and distributing software, you'll probably want to consider one of the certificates targeted at developers. If you want a digital certificate that identifies just you, and you're in the United States, the most dollar-efficient digital certificate is the Individual Software Publisher (Class 2) Digital ID; it will set you back a mere $20 a year. This certificate is good for distributing software electronically as an individual rather than as a commercial software publisher; you can use it to distribute freeware and shareware, or if you work for a nonprofit organization. If you're a commercial software publisher, you'll need the Commercial Software Publisher (Class 3) Digital ID, which is 20 times as expensive, at $400 a year.

 WARNING   Digital signatures are in something of a state of flux at this writing. The types of certificate available may have changed by the time you read this.

For the Individual Software Publisher Digital ID, the certification authority checks out your known information through a credit service such as Equifax or TRW. For the Commercial Software Publisher Digital ID, the certification authority checks out the company through Dun & Bradstreet Financial Services (if the company has a Dun &

Bradstreet number), the company's business license, articles of incorporation, or similar official documents.

You complete an enrollment form online (the Individual Software Publisher form is marginally less intrusive than an HMO enrollment form and a body-cavity search combined); pledge you won't sign harmful, potentially harmful, or virus-infested code; and pay up. Assuming your information is satisfactory, you then receive an e-mail (typically almost immediately) containing a URL and a PIN. You access the URL, enter the PIN, and get the digital ID, which you install on your computer. This installation means that you have the digital certificate: It's been assigned to you by the certification authority, you've downloaded it, and you've got it as a file on your computer. (You should also create a backup of your digital certificate on a floppy disk or a CD and slot it away somewhere secure, such as a bank deposit box.)

NOTE As you might imagine, the Individual Software Publisher certificate carries somewhat less weight (read: trust) than the Commercial Software Publisher certificate. For example, a corporation might choose to let its employees run code signed with a Commercial Software Publisher certificate but not code signed with an Individual Software Publisher certificate.

Installing a Digital Certificate

So—by now, one way or another, you've got a digital certificate. Now you need to install it so that the applications that will use it know where it's located.

You may find that the digital certificate is automatically stored where it needs to be on the computer on which you created or downloaded it.

NOTE The SelfCert.exe certificate-generator program automatically registers the certificates it creates on the computer on which it creates them. If you created a digital certificate for yourself, you shouldn't need to install it on the same computer. If you want to practice installing it, you'll need to use a different computer.

Here's how to install a digital certificate:

1. Start Internet Explorer. In these examples, I'm using Internet Explorer 5.

2. Choose Tools ➤ Internet Options to display the Internet Options dialog box.

3. Click the Content tab to display the Content page, shown in Figure 20.3.

FIGURE 20.3

To display the Certificate Manager dialog box, click the Certificates button on the Content page of the Internet Options dialog box in Internet Explorer 5.

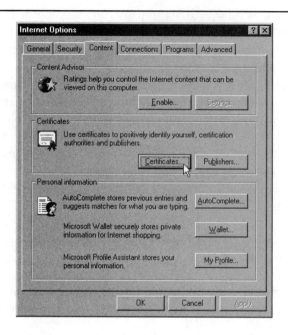

4. In the Certificates group box, click the Certificates button to display the Certificate Manager dialog box, shown in Figure 20.4.

FIGURE 20.4

Internet Explorer provides the Certificate Manager dialog box to manage digital certificates.

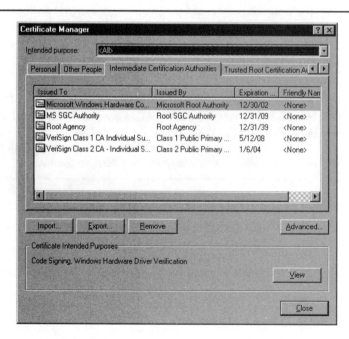

5. Click the Import button to start the Certificate Manager Import Wizard, shown in Figure 20.5.

FIGURE 20.5

The Certificate Manager Import Wizard springs into action to help you import certificates.

6. Click the Next button to display the Select File To Import stage of the Certificate Manager Import Wizard dialog box, shown in see Figure 20.6.

FIGURE 20.6

In the Select File To Import stage of the Certificate Manager Import Wizard dialog box, enter the name of the certificate file you want to import.

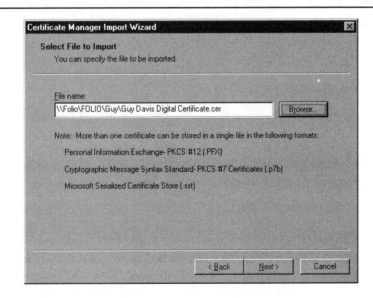

7. In the File Name text box, enter the name of the certificate file you want to import:

- Either type the name of the certificate by hand, or click the Browse button to display the Open dialog box and then locate the certificate as usual and click the Open button. Make sure the Files Of Type drop-down list in the Open dialog box is set to the appropriate type of certificate, so that the certificate's file shows up in the dialog box. In this example, because I'll be importing a .CER file, I choose the X.509 Certificate filter in the Files Of Type drop-down list so that the .CER and .CRT files are listed.

- Click the Next button to display the Select A Certificate Store stage of the Certificate Manager Import Wizard dialog box, shown in Figure 20.7.

FIGURE 20.7

On the Select A Certificate Store page of the Certificate Manager Import Wizard, choose the certificate store in which to store the certificate you're importing.

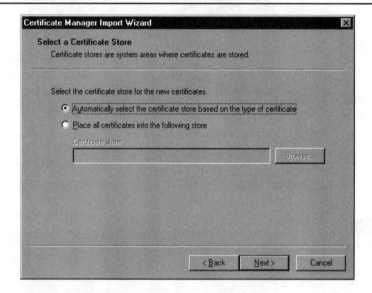

8. You can now choose to store the certificate either in a certificate store of your own choosing, or in the default certificate store for that type of certificate. By default, Internet Explorer selects the Automatically Select The Certificate Store Based On The Type Of Certificate option button. If you choose the Place All Certificates Into The Following Store option button, Internet Explorer will place the certificate in the store specified in the Certificate Store text box.

- The first time you choose this option, you'll need to specify the store by clicking the Browse button to display the Select Certificate Store dialog box, shown in Figure 20.8. Choose the certificate store (for example, Personal) and click the OK button. To specify a particular location within a certificate store, select the Show Physical Stores check box, and then click the plus (+) sign next to the store in question to display its subfolders. Select the folder you want, and then click the OK button. Internet Explorer will close the Select Certificate Store dialog box and display your selection in the Certificate Store text box in the Certificate Manager Import Wizard.

9. Click the Next button to finish setting up the import procedure. Internet Explorer will display the Completing The Certificate Manager Import Wizard dialog box, shown in Figure 20.9, to confirm the choices you've made. You'll see that the list box shows the certificate store that you or the Wizard chose, the type of content you're putting in it (a certificate, a certificate trust list, a certificate revocation list, and so on), and the name of the file from which the content is being drawn.

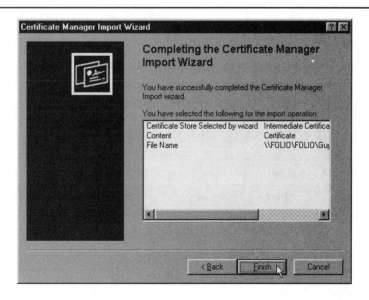

10. If you or Internet Explorer decide to import the certificate into the root certificate store rather than the personal store, the other people store, or the intermediate store, Internet Explorer will display the Root Certificate Store dialog box shown in Figure 20.10, asking you to confirm that you want to add the certificate to the Root Store. If placing this certificate in the root certificate store is correct, click the Yes button. Otherwise, click the No button. The Certificate Manager will display a Certificate Manager Import Wizard message box saying that an error has occurred. Click the OK button to dismiss this message box.

FIGURE 20.10

Internet Explorer displays the Root Certificate Store dialog box for confirmation when you're about to import a certificate into the root certificate store.

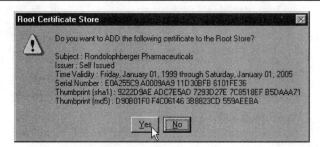

11. If you're ready to go, click the Finish button. The Certificate Manager Import Wizard will import the certificate (or whatever) and will display the message box shown in Figure 20.11 confirming that the operation was successful.

FIGURE 20.11

You've succeeded in importing a certificate.

Now that you've imported the certificate, it will show up in the Certificate Manager dialog box on the appropriate page.

Exporting a Digital Certificate

From time to time, you'll need to export a digital certificate—for example, so that you can install it on another computer. Here's how to do so:

1. Display the Certificate Manager dialog box (run Internet Explorer, choose Tools ➢ Internet Options, and then click the Certificates button on the Content tab of the Internet Options dialog box).

2. Display the tab that contains the digital certificate you want to export, and then select the certificate.

3. Click the Export button to start the Certificate Manager Export Wizard.

4. Click the Next button to display the Export Private Key With Certificate stage of the Wizard, shown in Figure 20.12. (Depending on the type of certificate you're exporting, you may not see this stage of the Wizard.)

FIGURE 20.12

In the Export Private Key With Certificate stage of the Certificate Manager Export Wizard, choose whether to export the private key with the certificate.

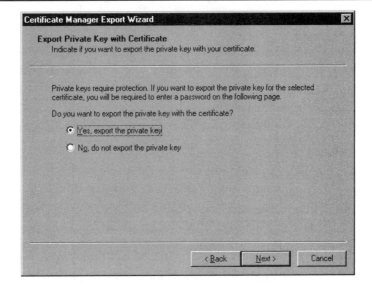

5. Choose whether to export the private key with the certificate by selecting the Yes, Export The Private Key option button or the No, Do Not Export The Private Key option button. If you export the private key, you'll need to enter a password for it.

6. Click the Next button to move to the Certificate Export File stage of the Wizard, shown in Figure 20.13.

FIGURE 20.13

In the Certificate Export File stage of the Certificate Manager Export Wizard, choose the type of file you want the exported certificate to be.

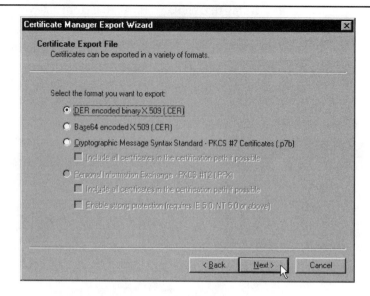

7. Choose the type of file you want to create. Your choices will depend on whether you're exporting the private key along with it:

   • If you aren't exporting the private key, the first three option buttons will be available: DER Encoded Binary X.509 (.CER), Base64 Encoded X.509 (.CER), or Cryptographic Message Syntax Standard - PKCS #7 Certificates (.p7b). With the last, you can select the Include All Certificates In The Certification Path If Possible check box to include all certificates.

   • If you're exporting the private key, the fourth option button—Personal Information Exchange - PKCS #12 (.PFX)—will be available and will be selected. For this format, you can choose the Include All Certificates In The Certification Path If Possible check box to include all certificates, and the Enable Strong Protection check box (if you have Internet Explorer 5 or Windows 2000).

8. Click the Next button. If you're exporting the private key, the Wizard will display its Password Protection For The Private Key stage. Enter the password to encrypt the private key in the Password text box, and enter it again in the Confirm Password text box.

9. Click the Next button to display the Export File Name stage of the Wizard.

10. Enter the file name for the certificate in the File Name text box, either by typing it into the text box or by clicking the Browse button and specifying a location and a file name in the Save As dialog box.

11. Click the Next button. The Wizard will display the Completing The Certificate Manager Export Wizard stage, shown in Figure 20.14.

12. Check the details in the text box—scroll if necessary—and then click the Finish button. The Certificate Manager Export Wizard will export the certificate to the file and will display a message box telling you it's done so.

Removing a Digital Certificate

Usually, digital certificates bear a distinct relation to other people's phone numbers—you just keep accumulating them in one store or another (read: one phone book or organizer or another) until you die. But sometimes you'll need to remove a digital certificate from the store—perhaps because a once-trusted associate has turned rogue, or a valued competitor has gone belly-up, or another event has occurred that removes your need for that digital certificate's services.

To remove a digital certificate from the digital certificate store in Internet Explorer:

1. Display the Certificate Manager dialog box

2. Display the tab that contains the digital certificate in question, and then select the certificate you want to remove.

3. Click the Remove button. The Certificate Manager will display a dialog box warning you of the consequences of deleting the digital certificate and asking you to confirm the deletion. Figure 20.15 shows the warning you get when removing a certification authority (above) or one of your personal certificates (below). Click the Yes button to delete the certificate; click the No button if the warning has persuaded you to relent.

FIGURE 20.15

Two of the warnings the Certificate Manager displays when you're about to remove a digital certificate

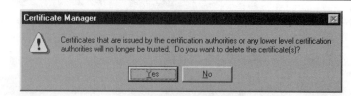

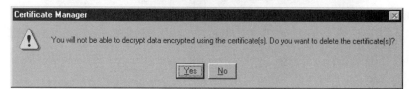

Signing a Macro Project with a Digital Signature

Once you've completed a macro project and have it ready for distribution, you sign it with a digital signature so that applications that have the level of security set to High can use it.

To sign a macro project digitally, you need to be working in the Visual Basic Editor. Here's what to do:

1. Navigate to the document or template project that contains the macro project.

2. Select the project in the Project Explorer.

3. Choose Tools ➤ Digital Signature to display a Digital Signature dialog box. The first time you display this dialog box, it will probably have no certificate listed. Figure 20.16 shows the Digital Signature dialog box with a signature entered into it.

FIGURE 20.16

Use the Digital Signature dialog box to specify the digital signature for a macro project.

4. To sign the macro project with the digital certificate shown in the Digital Signature dialog box, click the OK button. (If you haven't yet signed a macro project, the Digital Signature dialog box won't show a digital certificate yet.)

5. To select a different digital certificate than the one shown in the Digital Signature dialog box, click the Choose button to display the Select Certificate dialog box, shown in Figure 20.17.

FIGURE 20.17

In the Select Certificate dialog box, select the certificate you want to use to sign the macro project.

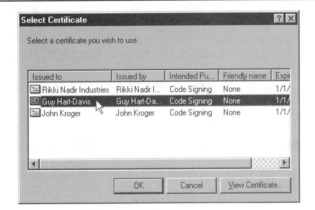

6. In the Select Certificate dialog box, choose the certificate you want to use for the macro project.

7. Click the OK button to apply the selected certificate and close the Select Certificate dialog box.

8. Click the OK button to close the Digital Signature dialog box.

Removing a Digital Signature from a Macro Project

To remove a digital signature from a macro project, choose Tools ➤ Digital Signatures to display the Digital Signature dialog box, and then click the Remove button. Both the Certificate Name readout in the The VBA Project Is Currently Signed As area and the Certificate Name in the Sign As area of the Digital Signature dialog box will display [No Certificate] to indicate that the project currently has no digital certificate assigned to it. Figure 20.18 shows the Digital Signature dialog box for a project with no digital signature assigned to it.

FIGURE 20.18

When a project has no digital signature assigned to it, the Digital Signature dialog box displays [No Certificate].

Once you've got the macro project back into shape for distribution, you can reapply the digital signature to the project as before.

Whose Certificate Is It, and What Does It Mean?

The counterpoint to signing your projects with a digital signature is, of course, that you'll probably be on the receiving end of digitally signed projects heading in the other direction. It stands to reason that you'll want to find out who has signed these projects and what grade of credibility their digital certificate carries. You probably also want to scrutinize your own digital certificate to learn what it looks like and what it tells other people about you.

Here's how to view the details of a digital certificate:

1. From the Visual Basic Editor, choose Tools ➤ Digital Signature to display the Digital Signature dialog box.

2. Click the Choose button to display the Select Certificate dialog box.

3. Select the certificate whose details you want to view.

4. Click the View Certificate button to display the Certificate dialog box, shown in Figure 20.19.

 TIP You can also view a certificate by double-clicking its entry in the Certificate Manager dialog box.

FIGURE 20.19

Use the Certificate dialog box to examine the properties of a certificate.

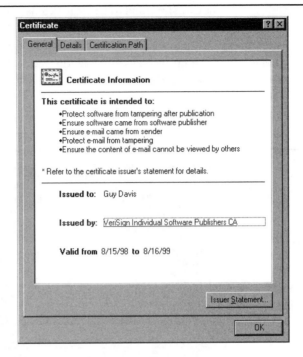

As you can see in Figure 20.19, the Certificate dialog box has three pages: General, Details, and Certification Path. I'll describe quickly what these show:

- The General page of the Certificate dialog box displays basic information about the certificate: for what the certificate is intended, to whom the certificate is issued, by whom it's issued, and the period for which it's valid. As you can see, my certificate's purposes include, "Protect software from tampering after publication" and, "Ensure software came from software publisher"—the main purposes for which I got the Individual Software Publisher category of digital certificate. The Issued By line contains a hyperlink to VeriSign, the company that issued me the certificate, and the Issuer Statement button at the bottom of the dialog box is available, indicating another hyperlink to the issuer.

- The Details page of the Certificate dialog box, shown in Figure 20.20, contains about a score of specifics on the certificate. Click one of the fields in the list box to display its value in the text box below. (In the figure, I've selected the Subject key, which, as you can see, contains far more information than the Value column in the list box can display.) To restrict the view to a subset of the fields available, select one of the following choices in the Show list box: Version 1 Fields Only (which displays the X.509 basic certificate fields), Extensions Only (the X.509 extension fields), Critical Extensions Only (fields that ensure safe operation when security is needed, such as the Key Usage Restriction field and the SpcSpAgencyInfo field), or Properties Only (the Thumbprint Algorithm field, the Thumbprint field, the Friendly Name field, and the Description field). From the Details page, you can edit some of the properties of a certificate by clicking the Edit Properties button. I'll discuss this in the next section, "Editing the Properties of a Certificate."

FIGURE 20.20

The Details page of the Certificate dialog box contains a host of details about the certificate.

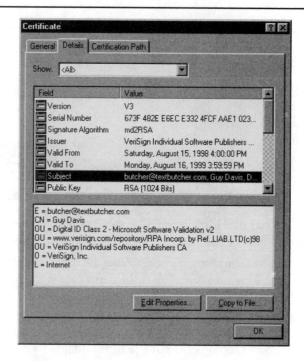

• The Certification Path page of the Certificate dialog box, shown in Figure 20.21, shows the path by which the certificate has been issued from the issuing authority to the current holder. As you can see, my certificate came directly from VeriSign, so the path is short. To check one of the links in the chain, select it in the Certification Path list box and click the View Certificate button (if it's available). The Certificate Manager will display the Certificate dialog box for the certificate in question. You can then pursue the certification path for that certificate if you choose, or click the OK button to dismiss the second (or subsequent) Certificate dialog box and return to the previous one.

FIGURE 20.21

The Certification Path page of the Certificate dialog box displays the path by which the certificate has been issued from the issuing authority to the current holder.

When you finish exploring the certificate, click the OK button to close the Certificate dialog box.

Editing the Properties of a Certificate

On the Details page of the Certificate dialog box, the Edit Properties button displays the Certificate Properties dialog box, shown in Figure 20.22. In this dialog box, you can change the "friendly name" and description for the certificate, and specify the purposes for which the certificate can be used. The friendly name is a name that humans can read easily; it shows up in the Certificate Manager dialog box in the Friendly Name column and also appears as a property on the Details page of the Certificate dialog box. The description is a text description to accompany the friendly name; it appears on the Details page of the Certificate dialog box.

FIGURE 20.22

You can edit the properties of a certificate in the Certificate Properties dialog box.

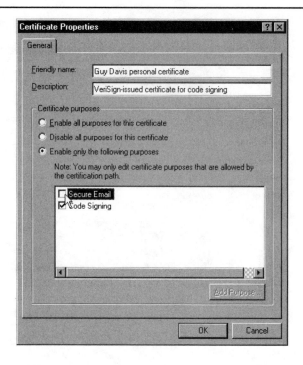

In the Certificate Purposes group box, choose the purposes for which you want to use the certificate by selecting one of the three option buttons. The default setting is the Enable All Purposes For This Certification option button, which enables all the purposes for which the certificate is valid. Conversely, you can choose the Disable All Purposes For This Certificate option button to prevent use of the certificate. In between these extremes of purpose, you can select the Enable Only The Following Purposes option button and select in the list box the check boxes for the purposes you want. Note that the list box displays only the purposes you can edit, not necessarily the full set of purposes for the certificate.

Click the OK button to close the Certificate Properties dialog box and apply your choices.

Choosing a Suitable Level of Security

As macro languages have grown in power and sophistication over the years, so has the threat they pose when misused. Using relatively simple VBA commands, you can create files, delete files, control other applications, and so on. Even code developed with the best of intentions can damage a computer when run under unsuitable circumstances; and macro viruses (discussed in the sidebar titled, "A Brief History of Macro Viruses," a little later in this section) and other malicious code can be written in VBA with distressing ease.

Word 97, which not only introduced VBA to Word but also had the arguable honor of being the most widely used word processor of its generation, bore the brunt of an explosion of macro viruses, with Excel 97 (also widely used, but less of an everyday application for all users) suffering severe collateral damage along the way. When Microsoft revved Office 97 with Service Release 1 (SR-1), the company improved its resistance to macro viruses and other malicious code. But the essential problem remained: Unless the user knew the provenance of a particular macro project (that is, the provenance of the document or template they were opening), they couldn't tell whether the code contained in the template was friendly or hostile (or dangerously incompetent, which can amount to much the same thing). When encountering a project that contained code, the Office 97 application (for example, Word or Excel) displayed the Warning dialog box shown in Figure 20.23. You could choose to disable the macros in the project, which would allow you to examine them if the project wasn't locked; to enable the macros and damn the torpedoes; or to not open the file. This protection was better than nothing, but it left a whole lot to be desired—particularly for users who had little idea what a macro was in the first place.

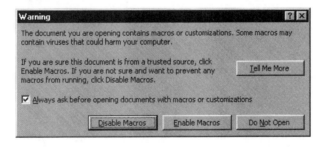

FIGURE 20.23

Word 97's way of handling the thorny problem of documents and templates that contained code—a warning rather than a solution

Opening a document or template is problematic because the action of opening it both triggers the Open event for the document or template, and causes the application to run any AutoOpen macro in the document or related project (in Word, the AutoOpen macro can be in the document, its template, any global template other than Normal.dot that's loaded, or the Normal.dot global template itself. And until the document or template is open, you can't see what's inside it, so you're stuck. Anti-virus software can tell you if a document contains macros or customizations, but it usually can't tell you whether they're benevolent or dangerous (beyond identifying some known macro viruses).

The VBA 6–enabled applications, including the Office 2000 applications and the WordPerfect Office 2000 applications, improve the security situation a great deal. You can choose different levels of security in each VBA-enabled application—in effect, specifying the degree of protection you want to use against macro viruses and hostile code, and varying it from one application to another as you deem necessary. Macro projects can be signed with digital signatures derived from digital certificates, providing a mechanism for determining with a solid to high degree of certainty the individual or company that created the macro project.

A Brief History of Macro Viruses

The last few years have seen a great deal of anxiety about macro viruses. The excitement started with the `Winword.Concept` macro virus, also known as the Prank virus. This macro, which was written in the WordBasic macro language used by versions of Word up to Word 6 and Word 95, appeared to have been built as a demonstration of the capabilities of macro viruses. Rather than harboring code that would create havoc on computer systems it infected, it contained a macro named `Payload` that contained only the comment line, "That's enough to prove my point."

`Winword.Concept` was basically harmless. It installed a new `FileSaveAs` macro that supplanted the regular Word `FileSaveAs` command and caused you to save every document as a template in the templates directory designated in your Word settings. By saving every document as a template containing the macro virus, ready to install itself on any copy of Word that opened an infected template masquerading as a document, `Winword.Concept` was able to spread rapidly—particularly because most people at that time either knew little about macro viruses, or knew about them but didn't take them seriously as a threat. At this writing, `Winword.Concept` is still widespread throughout the world of Word users. At one point, it was thought to account for up to 50 percent of all reported viruses (yes, *all* reported viruses, not just Word ones)—but that was before it had much competition.

Microsoft quickly created and distributed a fix for `Winword.Concept` called `ScanProt.dot`. (The fix is available from `http://www.microsoft.com` and from online services such as AOL and CompuServe, among other locations.) `ScanProt.dot` consists of macros that remove the virus from your installation of Word, search for infected docu-templates, and remove the virus and save each file as a plain Word document. It also replaces the File ➤ Open command with a version that checks each document you open for automatic macros.

Continued ▌▶

The Microsoft fix has a couple of minor disadvantages. First, once you've installed the fix, you can open only one file at a time from the Open dialog box, rather than using Shift+click or Ctrl+click to open two or more files. Second, if you open a file without using the Open dialog box—for example, by double-clicking it in File Manager or Windows Explorer—the scanning macro fails to kick in.

A quick way around the Winword.Concept virus (before Word 97's built-in scanning) was not to install ScanProt.dot, but to create a blank macro named Payload. When you opened a document infected with Winword.Concept, the virus macros checked for the Payload macro to see if it was already installed. If a macro named Payload was present, the Winword.Concept macros wouldn't install themselves, believing themselves already installed. This relatively elegant avoidance of the problem is limited to Winword.Concept, though, and does nothing to protect against other Word macro viruses—such as FormatC, for example, which attempts to format your C: drive and has no interest in any macro named Payload (beyond deleting it if it's on the C: drive, of course).

Needless to say, the success and resulting notoriety of Winword.Concept made many other people decide that writing a macro virus was a cool (and not too difficult) thing to do in the time they had to spare from annoying people in other ways. Some even took the trouble of creating macro-virus construction kits so that people who really don't know what they're doing can build macro viruses too. Subsequently, there has been a vast explosion of macro viruses; they now number in the thousands and infect applications ranging from other Microsoft Office applications (Excel, Access) through Lotus SmartSuite applications to Linux applications.

Much of the spread of macro viruses can be attributed to the increased number of suitable vector files (and I mean that in a quasi-medical sense—files that can carry macro viruses, such as Word documents and 1-2-3 spreadsheets—not the vector graphics file formats) being shunted from person to person via the Internet. Company networks have helped too, of course, though these have tended to be better policed, at least since macro viruses achieved their current state of infamy. Any company these days that doesn't have anti-virus software running on its e-mail server to intercept incoming viruses—and perhaps outgoing ones, too—needs its (corporate) head examined. Most companies I know of are installing anti-virus software on all computers by default—and updating that software regularly.

Affordable anti-virus software from companies such as Network Associates (*nées* McAfee and Network General), and Symantec has also helped reduce the number of systems infected with macro viruses. Most people whose computers have become infected have been smart enough to realize there's a problem ("hey, my Templates directory is getting kinda full…") and to take corrective action. And the general level of paranoia now prevailing about macro viruses means that other people have realized they need to watch out.

Continued ▐▶

CONTINUED

You'll notice I said "paranoia" a moment ago. Don't take that to mean the concern isn't justified. As the saw goes, just because you're paranoid doesn't mean they're not out to get you....

In the old days (say, 1996), many people thought e-mail security meant making sure any attachments they received with their e-mail were legitimate before opening them. Likewise with any files they downloaded. Any unknown executable has always been cause for concern, but with macro viruses, document and spreadsheet files—which in the days before macro viruses were known to be safe—can prove to be harboring contagion. Nowadays, pretty much any file you receive is suspect. A text file should be fairly safe, unless you load it into a programming environment and run it... but, of course, you can't always tell what's really a text file and what's something else pretending to be a text file.

Recently, e-mail viruses have generated much more excitement than most other macro viruses, and understandably so. After all, you can infect an Access database with a virus, but to how many people do you send databases frequently? You probably exchange more documents with your colleagues and friends in a day than you do Access databases in a year. But e-mail—why, everyone's sending it all the time. If you don't generate a good dozen messages a day, you're barely human these days... and now e-mail can contain viruses.

The threat of the notorious hoax Good Times e-mail "virus"—that reading a message (titled "Good Times") sent to you would unleash a virus that would (variously) erase the contents of your hard drive, fry your computer's memory, and cause your kids to start acting like Linda Blair in *The Exorcist*—hasn't quite come true, but it's getting close. An e-mail message can contain code in a scripting language such as Visual Basic Scripting Edition (VBScript) or JavaScript that will run automatically.

How does this work? Quite simply, particularly with an e-mail program such as Microsoft Outlook or Lotus Notes that can be set to display the current Inbox message automatically in a preview pane. Depending on the program, this display can trigger a Read event for the message or set the flag status on the message to Read (past tense). VBA, VBScript, or JavaScript can have code associated with the Read event that takes just about any action the programming language supports. So—read a message (or have the application "read" it by previewing it automatically for you), and the code runs: Pop goes your hard drive, or whatever.

Continued

CONTINUED

Bottom line? Everybody today needs to be alert for macro viruses and worse in all incoming documents, including e-mail. The sorry state of users' self-preservation instincts was illustrated several times in 1999 by viruses such as Melissa (March; major headlines worldwide); Prilissa (December; medium headlines), and MiniZip (also known as ExploreZip; December; medium headlines). Each of these viruses required the recipient to open a file (a document or a disguised executable) without virus-checking it—and a huge number of people did, to their computers' distress.

Keep your wits about you at all times; use all the security features the programs offer; and invest in quality anti-virus software, and run it consistently.

Specifying a Suitable Security Setting

The first step in choosing your security settings is to set a suitable level of security for your purposes. Start by selecting Tools ➤ Macro ➤ Security (Tools ➤ Visual Basic ➤ Security in WordPerfect) to display the Security dialog box, shown in Figure 20.24.

FIGURE 20.24

On the Security Level page of the Security dialog box, choose the level of security you want to use when running macros.

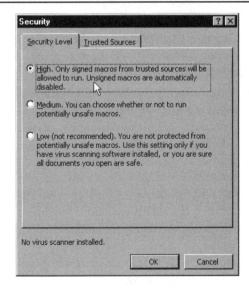

As you can see from Figure 20.24, VBA offers three levels of protection: High, Medium, and Low. Here's what those settings mean:

High security   The application will run only procedures that are signed by trusted sources (more about designating trusted sources in just a moment). High security is a good choice for most corporate environments. By specifying High security and keeping as strict control as possible over the list of trusted sources on each computer, you can provide users with known procedures (for example, those developed in-house) without encountering any problems, while at the same time preventing them from even trying to run anything inappropriate. The problem with High security is that the user has the option of electing always to trust procedures from the source of a new document, which gives an end-run around strict control of trusted sources. However, the user can't run procedures in a document from an untrusted source without choosing to trust that source.

Medium security   The application will offer the user the choice of running procedures that aren't signed by trusted sources, without trusting everything that comes from this source. Medium security is the best security choice for home use and for the VBA developer or applications support professional at work. You'll probably be using Medium security to give yourself the flexibility you need to perform your work.

Low security   The application doesn't prevent you from running—or even warn you about the dangers of—any code not signed by a trusted source. Under most circumstances, it isn't a good idea to choose the Low security setting on any computer that contains information you value, unless the computer isn't connected to a network (or the Internet) *and* you never receive documents from other people. That restricts it quite a bit, doesn't it? What's left? Well—a test computer, I suppose, but not much else.

Specifying Whom to Trust

VBA provides two ways of designating trusted sources: by trusting sources identified in templates and add-ins already installed on the computer, and by adding to them trusted sources that crop up in documents you open that contain code or customizations. I'll show you these in turn. But first, take a look to find out whom your computer trusts already.

To work with trusted sources, you first need to set the security level of the application in question to Medium or High on the computer you're using: You can't specify a trusted source when you're using the Low level of security. You also need to be running Internet Explorer 4 or Internet Explorer 5.

Whom Does the Computer Trust Already?

To find out whom the computer trusts already, choose Tools ➤ Macro ➤ Security (in WordPerfect, choose Tools ➤ Visual Basic ➤ Security) to display the Security dialog box, and then click the Trusted Sources tab to display the Trusted Sources page. Figure 20.25 shows the Trusted Sources page of the Security dialog box for Word; the Trusted Sources page for other Microsoft applications looks similar, but the page for non-Microsoft applications usually lacks the Trust All Installed Templates And Add-Ins check box.

FIGURE 20.25

The Trusted Sources page of the Security dialog box displays the computer's current list of trusted sources for code and customizations.

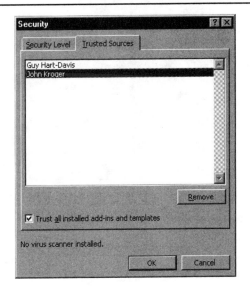

Trusting the Sources Already on the Computer

In a Microsoft Office application, you can choose to trust the sources already on the computer by selecting the Trust All Installed Add-Ins And Templates check box on the Trusted Sources page of the Security dialog box.

Doing so is handy, provided you know the provenance of what's on your computer. For example, in a corporate environment in which the administrator installs several tried-and-true templates and add-ins with each new installation of Word and Power-Point, it makes sense to select this check box and snap all the implied trusts into place. The individual user, on the other hand, needs to make sure their installation of Office won't be compromised by unquestioning acceptance of what's already on the computer.

Adding a Trusted Source

To add a trusted source, open a document or template that contains VBA code from the source you want to add. The application will detect the untrusted code and will display a Security Warning dialog box. Figure 20.26 shows an example; the protagonist is WordPerfect.

FIGURE 20.26

When you open a file (or load an add-in) that contains code from a source that isn't currently specified as trusted, the application displays the Security Warning dialog box. To add the source to your list of trusted sources, select the Always Trust Macros From This Source check box and choose the Enable Macros button.

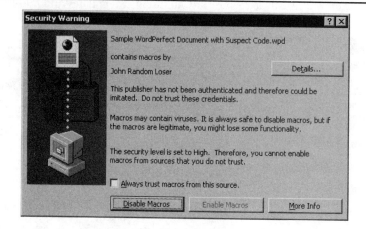

As you can see in the figure, the Security Warning dialog box tells you several things:

- The name and location of the document, template, or add-in containing the untrusted code.
- The name of the perpetrator or company that created the code.
- Whether the digital signature on the certificate is trustworthy. (In the figure, it isn't.)
- Whether you're using the High level of security, as in the figure. (If you're using the Medium level of security, the Security Warning dialog box won't mention it; and if you're using the Low level of security, you won't see the Security Warning dialog box.)

Compared to the weakness of earlier methods of identifying potentially threatening code, this abundance of useful information is great. At this point, you have essentially four choices:

- You can click the Details button to display the Certificate dialog box, and then inspect the certificate as discussed earlier in the chapter. You'll probably want to take this step first with a document, template, or add-in you're not sure about. After this, you may be better equipped to make one of the two following choices.

- You can click the Disable Macros button to open the document or template with the code disabled. Doing so will prevent it from running. As the Security Warning dialog box mentions, though, "you may lose some functionality"—that is, you'll lose *all* functionality that the code and customizations in the document or template provide. I guess that's the price of security.

- You can click the Enable Macros button to open the document or template with the procedures and customizations enabled. If you have the Medium level of security set, you can choose whether to select the Always Trust Macros From This Source check box when doing so. If you have the High level of security set, you'll need to select this check box in order to enable the Enable Macros button.

- You can click the close button (the × button) on the Security Warning dialog box to close the dialog box without opening the document or template. Doing so is useful both when you don't want to deal with the question and when you want to set a different level of security before opening the file. For example, if you have the High level of security set and you encounter the Security Warning dialog box, you might want to duck the decision so that you can set the Medium level of security instead. That setting will allow you to enable the procedures in the document or template without adding their creator to your list of trusted sources.

There is, of course, a variation on this theme that you're less likely to want to perform. You can select the Always Trust Macros From This Source check box to add the source to your list of trusted sources, but then click the Disable Macros button rather than the Enable Macros button to disable the macros in this particular document, template, or add-in. I can't think why you would want to do this, but it remains a possibility (technically, anyway).

 NOTE Once you've specified a source as trusted, any of the VBA-enabled applications will open documents containing procedures from them without raising an electronic eyebrow.

Removing a Previously Trusted Source

To remove a previously trusted source from your list of trusted sources:

1. Choose Tools ➢ Macro ➢ Security (Tools ➢ Visual Basic ➢ Security in WordPerfect) to display the Security dialog box.

2. Click the Trusted Sources tab to display the Trusted Sources page.

3. In the list box, select the trusted source that you want to remove.

4. Click the Remove button to remove the trusted source from the list.

Locking Your Code

To prevent anyone from viewing the contents of a project, you can lock it with a password. Typically, you'll want to do this before distributing a project to your colleagues. If your workplace is particularly volatile, you might want to lock projects under development on your own desktop as well. The argument against locking a project on which you're still actively working is that the lock adds an additional and tedious step to accessing the modules and forms in the project—but if you need the security, it's well worth the small amount of effort involved.

To lock a document or template project:

1. Open the document or template project in the application.

2. Display the Visual Basic Editor by pressing Alt+F11, choosing Tools ➤ Macro ➤ Visual Basic Editor (Tools ➤ Visual Basic ➤ Visual Basic Editor in WordPerfect), or clicking the Visual Basic Editor button on the Visual Basic toolbar.

3. In the Project Explorer, right-click the project that you want to lock, and choose Project Properties from the context menu to display the Project Properties dialog box. Alternatively, select the project in the Project Explorer and choose Tools ➤ Project Properties.

4. Click the Protection tab to display the Protection page shown in Figure 20.27.

5. Select the Lock Project For Viewing check box in the Lock Project group box.

6. In the Password To View Project Properties group box, enter a password in the Password text box and the same password in the Confirm Password text box. Setting a password is compulsory: You can't lock a project without specifying a password.

7. Click the OK button to apply the locking to the project. The Visual Basic Editor will close the Project Properties dialog box, but will leave the contents of the project open for you to view and work with. (After all, you just demonstrated that you know the password for the project.)

8. Switch back to the application, save the project, and close it.

Passwords: A Fine Line between Clever and Unusable

As with any password you use with computers, the longer and the more complex your locking password is, the harder it will be for anyone to crack. In practice, this means using passwords 8 to 15 characters in length; passwords longer than 15 characters tend to be difficult to remember and laborious to type in. As usual, don't use real words for passwords, even real words in other languages: Crackers (malicious hackers) can run foreign dictionary attacks just as easily as native-language ones. Concatenate words or phrases into one password, mixing in numbers and symbols (&, !, #, and so on) to make the password more complex. And memorize your passwords relentlessly.

Once you've done that, the project is locked and can't be viewed or edited without the password (unless someone breaks the password; see the sidebar titled, "How Hard Is It to Break the Password Protection on a Project?" later in the chapter). When you choose to edit a procedure in the project from the application or try to expand the project in the Project Explorer in the Visual Basic Editor, the application or the Visual Basic Editor will display the Project Password dialog box, shown in Figure 20.28. Enter the password in the Password text box and click the OK button to display the contents of the project. (If you enter the wrong password, the application or the Visual Basic Editor will display the Project Locked message box followed by the Project Password dialog box for you to try again.)

FIGURE 20.28

When you open a locked project, you need to enter the password for the project in the Project Password dialog box.

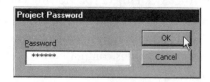

To unlock a project, open it in the Visual Basic Editor (supplying the password), display the Project Properties dialog box, clear the Lock Project For Viewing check box on the Protection page, and click the OK button.

How Hard Is It to Break the Password Protection on a Project?

I think it's safe to say that no password is unbreakable. You can create unguessable passwords by using methods such as those suggested earlier in the chapter (using enough characters, including numbers and symbols, and so on), but any password protection can eventually be broken by brute force or by decryption. If an infinite number of monkeys with an infinite number of keyboards were to hammer away at the password you set on a VBA project, chances are they'd happen upon it sooner or later.

So far as I know, nobody's yet marshaled those monkeys, but people have built any number of password-cracking programs that can try to identify a password. Most of these use brute force—they try different words as passwords until they find the one that works.

More sophisticated programs can unwrap the security of the password in question: To find the password for the VBA project in a file, they read the file and decipher the password. For instance, a company called Passware (www.lostpassword.com) produces a program named VBA Key that decrypts the VBA password for any document (in a variety of formats) or VBA module you drop onto its window. VBA Key is a great utility to have if you need to get into a project whose password you've lost or forgotten—but, of course, it also allows the user to break other people's passwords and read their VBA projects. Other products from other companies do the same thing. Given that anyone can get such a product for a fingerful of dollars, you'd do well to plan passwords as only your first line of defense (seen from the inside); to keep your secrets safe, you'll need to secure your files so that nobody gets to run password crackers on them.

Go Forth and Automate

By this point (if you've worked through the book), you should have a firm grounding in using VBA to automate the application of your choice, be it one of the seven applications I've used for examples in this book or another VBA host. You've learned how to record and edit macros; how to use constants, variables, and arrays; how to build loops and decision structures into your code; how to use message boxes and user forms to put an interface on your code; and how to streamline, debug, and secure your code.

You're ready to get some serious work done with VBA.
Go do it.

GLOSSARY

Italics indicate that a term is defined elsewhere in the Glossary.

& operator
See *concatenation operator*.

access key
Another term for *accelerator key*.

active
(Of an *error handler*.) Execution has branched to the *error handler*.

adaptive menu
A menu that changes its items to reflect the user's usage, promoting the most-used items and hiding never-used items.

ANSI
American National Standards Institute.

application-modal
(Of a message box.) Prevents the user from taking further actions in the application until the message box is dismissed.

argument
A piece of information that you pass to a *procedure* or *function*.

arithmetic operators
Operators such as + and −, used for performing mathematical calculations.

array
A *variable* that can contain a number of values that have the same *data type*. VBA supports *fixed-size arrays* and *dynamic arrays*.

array subscript
The number declaring the number of items in an *array* or the number that identifies a particular item in the array.

assignment operator
The equal sign, used to assign a value to a *property* or a *variable*.

binary comparison
A case-sensitive comparison.

binary search
An efficient means of searching a sorted *array*.

block If
A multiple-line If... Then *statement*.

Boolean
(Of a *variable*.) Has two values—True and False.

Break mode
When *code* is running, but execution is temporarily suspended. Break mode lets you step through your *code* one command or one *procedure* at a time (rather than running all the commands at once). You use it to *debug* your *code*.

bug
An error in hardware or software that causes a program to execute incorrectly.

by reference
One way of passing an *argument* (the other is *by value*). When a *procedure* passes an *argument* to another *procedure* by reference, the recipient *procedure* gets access to the memory location where the original *variable* is stored and can change the original *variable*.

by value
One way of passing an *argument* (the other is *by reference*). When a *procedure* passes an *argument* to another *procedure* by value, the recipient *procedure* gets only a copy of the information in the *variable* and can't change the information in the original *variable*.

call
To invoke a *function* or *procedure*.

character code
The numbers by which computers refer to letters. For example, the *ANSI* character code for a capital *A* is 65 and for a capital *B* is 66; a lowercase *a* is 97, and a lowercase *b* is 98.

class instance
A custom *object*.

class module
A module that contains the definition of a *class*.

clean
(Of a file.) Contains no unsaved changes. Opposite of *dirty*.

code
Instructions in a programming language.

code module
A storage *module* that may contain *subprocedures*.

collection
An *object* that contains several other *objects*, typically of the same type as each other. (For example, the Documents collection in many applications contains Document objects.)

combination box
A *control* that combines a list box and a text box.

combo box
A diminutive for *combination box*.

COM
The acronym for *Component Object Model*.

comment
A line of *code* explaining what the *code* is doing (or trying to do). Comments are not executed.

comment out
To apply a *comment* to a line of code, so that it will not be executed.

comparison operators
Operators such as < and > (less-than and greater-than, respectively) used for values.

compile error
An error than occurs when VBA can't compile a statement correctly.

Component Object Model
Microsoft's standard for defining the programming interfaces that *objects* expose so that other *objects* can communicate with them.

concatenate
To join together (literally, "chain together"). For example, if you concatenate the *strings* contra and diction, you get contradiction.

concatenation operators
The operators & and +, used for joining two *strings* together.

Constant
A named item that keeps a constant value while a program is executing. VBA uses *intrinsic constants* and *user-defined constants*.

context menu

A menu that displays items relevant to the current context. To display a context menu, you right-click an object with the mouse (click with the non-primary button).

control

An visual *object* on a *user form*.

coolswitch

To switch between applications by using the Alt+Tab keystroke.

data type

The type of data assigned to a *variable*.

data-typing

Assigning a *data type* to a *variable*.

data-typing error

An error that occurs when you assign to a strongly typed *variable* information of the wrong *data type*.

debug

To test a *procedure* and (try to) remove every *bug* from it.

Design mode

Any time you're working in the Visual Basic Editor on your *code*, except when you're running *code*.

Design time

Another term for *Design mode*.

Digital certificate

Encrypted digital information that uniquely identifies its holder. You use your digital certificate to create a digital signature for a *project*.

dirty

(Of a file.) Contains unsaved changes. Opposite of *clean*.

Double

Double-precision floating point number.

dynamic array

An *array* with a changeable number of *subscripts*.

dynamic dialog box

A dialog box that changes and updates itself when the user clicks a *control* within it.

edit box

Another term for *text box*.

elegant

(Of *code*.) Stripped down to the minimum required to achieve the desired effect.

enabled

(Of an *error handler*.) Has been switched on by an `On Error` *statement*.

error handler

A section of *code* designed to *trap* errors, analyze them, and take action if they match given error codes.

event

An occurrence that VBA recognizes as having happened. For example, the opening of a file (by the user or by a *procedure*) typically generates an event.

event procedure

Code that runs directly in response to an *event*.

expression

Keywords, operators, variables, and *constants* combined to produce a *string*, number, or *object*.

fixed-iteration loop

A *loop* that repeats a set number of times.

fixed-size array

An *array* with a fixed number of *subscripts*.

folder contents view

A view in the Project Explorer that displays the *objects* within the *projects* that contain them.

folder view

A view in the Project Explorer that shows the *objects* separated into their folders beneath the *projects* that contain them.

form

Another term for *user form*.

function

A unit of *code* that begins with the declaration `Function`, ends with the *keywords* `End Function`, and returns a result.

group box
Another term for frame.

hard-coding
Writing fixed *code* as opposed to variable *code*.

indefinite loop
A *loop* that repeats a flexible number of times.

Integer variable
A type of *variable* used for storing whole numbers (numbers without fractions).

intrinsic constant
A *constant* that is built into an application. Each intrinsic *constant* is mapped to a numeric value in the group of *constants* in which it belongs.

iteration
One cycle through a *loop*.

keyword
A word defined as part of the VBA language—for example, the name of a *statement* or of a *function*.

language error
An error caused by misuse of the programming language—for example, mistyping a word, omitting punctuation, or omitting part of a construction.

lifetime
The period during which VBA remembers the value of a *variable*. A variable's lifetime is tied to its *scope*.

linear search
A simple form of search, starting at the beginning of the *array* and continuing until the target item is found or the end of the *array* is reached.

local scope
Another name for *procedure scope*.

logical operators
Operators such as And, Not, and Or, used for building logical structures.

loop
A programming structure that repeats one or more actions.

loop determinant
Another term for *loop invariant*.

loop invariant

A numeric *expression* or a logical *expression* that controls the running of a *loop*.

macro

A type of *subprocedure*, often recorded.

method

An action that an object can perform.

mnemonic

Another term for *accelerator key*.

modal

(Of a user form.) Prevents the user from continuing work in the application while the *user form* remains on screen.

modeless

(Of a user form.) Not *modal*—allows the user to continue work in the application while the *user form* remains on screen.

modular

(Of code.) Composed of different *procedures* that you can use in combination.

module

A storage container for *code*.

object

A distinct unit of code and data, bound together. Most objects have *methods* and *properties*, and recognize *events*.

object library

A reference file containing information on a collection of *objects* available to programs.

object model

The logical hierarchy in which the *objects* in an *object-oriented* application are considered to be arranged.

Object variable

A type of *variable* used for storing references to *objects*.

object-oriented programming

Building an application out of *objects*.

operator
An item used to compare, combine, or otherwise work with values in an *expression*. VBA uses *arithmetic operators, comparison operators, concatenation operators*, and *logical operators*.

owner application
The application that has created an *object* (such as a *user form*).

page
One of the tabbed items in a multipage dialog box (for example, the Options dialog box in many applications).

procedure
A unit of *code* that performs a particular task. There are two types of *procedures*: *subprocedures* and *functions*.

procedure calls
The *procedures* being called by the current *procedure*. You can display procedure calls in the Call Stack dialog box.

procedure scope
Scope that makes a *variable* available only to the *procedure* that declares it.

procedure-level scope
Another name for *procedure scope*.

program logic error
An error that produces incorrect results, although there are no syntactical problems and the *code* compiles and runs successfully.

property
An attribute of an *object*.

radio button
Another term for option button.

read-only property
A *property* whose value you can *return* but which you cannot *set*.

read-write property
A *property* whose value you can both *return* and *set*.

redimension
To resize a *dynamic array*.

remark line

Another name for *comment*.

return

To get the current value of a *property*.

run mode

When *code* is running.

runtime

Another term for *run mode*.

scalar variable

A *variable* that isn't an *array* or an object.

scope

The area in VBA within which a *variable* or *procedure* can operate.

set

To assign a value to a *property*.

shadow

To assign to a *variable* a name that VBA already uses as the name of a *function*, a *statement*, a *method*, or another *keyword*. Not recommended.

short-circuit evaluation

A logical technique used when evaluating conditions: If the first of two or more complementary conditions is false, you do not evaluate any other conditions contingent upon it. VBA does not perform short-circuit evaluation.

Signed

(Of a number.) Carries a plus or minus designation. Opposite of *unsigned*.

Single

Single-precision floating point number.

statement

A unit of *code* that describes an action, defines an item, or gives the value of a *variable*.

static variable

A *variable* whose values you want to preserve between calls to the *procedure* in which it is declared.

step

To execute a *procedure* one command at a time (*step into*) or in groups of commands (*step over, step out*).

step into

To start to *step* into a *procedure* in *Break mode*.

step out

To execute without stepping the remaining commands in a *procedure* you've started to *step* through. When you step out of a *procedure*, VBA then reenters *Break mode* for any subsequent *procedure*.

step over

To run without stepping a *procedure* called from a *procedure* you're stepping through in *Break mode*. After running the called *procedure*, VBA reenters *Break mode* for the rest of the calling *procedure*.

String variable

A type of *variable* used for storing text characters or groups of characters.

subprocedure

A unit of code that begins with the declaration Sub and ends with the *keywords* End Sub. A subprocedure does not return a result.

subroutine

Another name for a *subprocedure*.

subscript

See *array subscript*.

syntax error

Another term for *language error*.

system modal

(Of a message box.) Prevents the user from taking further actions on their computer until the message box is dismissed.

tab

The item you click at the top of a *page* in a dialog box to display the page. Often confused with the *page* itself.

tab order

The order in which VBA selects *controls* in a *user form* or frame when you move through them by pressing the Tab key (to move forward) or the Shift+Tab key combination (to move backward).

test case

A *variable* or *expression* used to evaluate a Select Case statement.

textual comparison
A non–case-sensitive comparison.

trap
To catch an error with *code* (typically so that you can handle it with an *error handler*).

twip
A unit of measurement used for positioning *user forms* and message boxes. One twip is 1/1440 inch.

type-declaration character
A character that you add to the end of a *variable's* name in an implicit declaration to tell VBA which *data type* to use for the *variable*.

unsigned
(Of a number.) Carries no plus or minus designation. Opposite of *signed*.

user form
A custom dialog box and its associated *code*.

user-defined constant
A *constant* created by the user.

variable
A location in memory set aside for storing a piece of information that can be changed while a *procedure* is running.

Variant variable
A type of *variable* that can store any type of data. Variant is the default type of *variable*.

watch expression
An expression you designate to give you a running display of the value of a *variable* or an *expression*.

INDEX

Note to the Reader: Throughout this index **boldfaced** page numbers indicate primary discussions of a topic. *Italicized* page numbers indicate illustrations.

About the CD

The CD packaged in the natty sleeve between the previous pair of pages contains the following:

- The numbered code listings from the book
- The key user forms that appear in the book
- Video walkthroughs (as .AVI files) of recording macros, navigating the Visual Basic Editor, and creating procedures in the Visual Basic Editor

Using the Code Listings and User Forms

The numbered code listings that appear in the book are included on the CD as individual Basic module files (.BAS) named after the listing. For example, the file containing the module for Listing 10.1 is named `Listing_10_01.bas`.

The user forms included on the CD have the same names by which they're identified in the book and the extension .FRM. For example, the user form named `frmDataSurfer2000` is in the file `frmDataSurfer2000.frm`.

To use one of the code listings or user forms, import it into the appropriate project as follows:

1. Start the application (if it's not already running) and open the project file.

2. Launch or switch to the Visual Basic Editor by choosing Tools ➢ Macros ➢ Visual Basic Editor (Tools ➢ Visual Basic ➢ Visual Basic Editor in WordPerfect) or by pressing Alt+F11.

3. If the Project Explorer isn't currently displayed, choose View ➢ Project Explorer or press Ctrl+R to display it.

4. In the Project Explorer, right-click the project into which you want to import the code listing or user form and choose Import File from the context menu to display the Import File dialog box (shown below).

5. Navigate to the Listings folder (for a code listing) or the Forms folder (for a form) on the CD.

6. Select the file containing the code listing or user form that you want to import, then click the Open button to import the file. (If you have Microsoft Office 2000 Developer, you can select multiple items for import at the same time.)

7. Once the Visual Basic Editor has added the code module or user form to your project, you can use it as you would any other module or user form.